THE
CAMBRIDGE ANCIENT HISTORY

VOLUME I
PART 2

THE
CAMBRIDGE
ANCIENT HISTORY

THIRD EDITION

VOLUME I
PART 2

EARLY HISTORY OF THE
MIDDLE EAST

EDITED BY

I. E. S. EDWARDS F.B.A.
Keeper of Egyptian Antiquities, The British Museum

THE LATE C. J. GADD F.B.A.
*Professor Emeritus of Ancient Semitic Languages and Civilizations,
School of Oriental and African Studies, University of London*

N. G. L. HAMMOND F.B.A.
Professor of Greek, University of Bristol

CAMBRIDGE
AT THE UNIVERSITY PRESS
1971

Published by the Syndics of the Cambridge University Press
Bentley House, 200 Euston Road, London NW1 2DB
American Branch: 32 East 57th Street, New York, N.Y.10022

© Cambridge University Press 1971

Library of Congress Catalogue Card Number: 73–116845

ISBN: 0 521 07791 5

Printed in Great Britain
at the University Printing House, Cambridge
(Brooke Crutchley, University Printer)

CONTENTS

List of Maps   *page* xvii

List of Tables   xviii

List of Text-figures   xix

Preface   xxi

CHAPTER XI

THE EARLY DYNASTIC PERIOD
IN EGYPT

by I. E. S. EDWARDS, F.B.A.
Keeper of Egyptian Antiquities, British Museum

I   The early monarchy and the unification of Egypt   I

II   The foundation of Memphis   15

III   The cemeteries of Abydos and Saqqara   17

IV   The successors of Menes   22

V   Royalty and the State   35

VI   Foreign relations   40

VII   Religion and funerary beliefs   51

VIII Architecture, sculpture and the small arts   59

CHAPTER XII

THE LAST PREDYNASTIC PERIOD IN BABYLONIA

by the late HENRI FRANKFORT
Formerly Director of the Warburg Institute, London

Revised and Re-arranged
by LERI DAVIES

I Sources and general character of the period   *page* 71

II The earlier phase (Uruk 4)   74

III The later phase (Jamdat Naṣr)   81

CHAPTER XIII

THE CITIES OF BABYLONIA

by the late C. J. GADD, F.B.A.
Formerly Professor Emeritus of Ancient Semitic Languages and Civilizations,
School of Oriental and African Studies, University of London

I The Second and Third Early Dynastic periods; change from pre-history to history; development of writing; Sumerians as inventors of writing and application of it to history   93

II Extent and constituents of the Early Dynastic civilization; geography; population—Sumerians and Semites, Sumer and Akkad   96

III Ideas and institutions; the origin of culture and polity; gods as owners and rulers of cities; appointment of a king, and unity of the 'kingdom'   100

IV History in contemporary record and later tradition; the king-list; local rulers and their inscriptions; history of Lagash down to Urukagina   105

V Armies and warfare   121

VI Foundations of power; irrigation, agriculture, temple organization and records; evidence of private property; foreign trade; material civilization and arts   124

VII Religion; the priesthood and cult-practices; the 'royal tombs' and disposal of the dead *page* 137

VIII Society and social problems; the reforms of Urukagina 139

IX The transition to empire 143

CHAPTER XIV

THE OLD KINGDOM IN EGYPT AND THE BEGINNING OF THE FIRST INTERMEDIATE PERIOD

by the late W. STEVENSON SMITH

Formerly Curator of the Department of Egyptian Art in the Museum of Fine Arts, Boston, Mass.

I The Third Dynasty 145

II The Fourth Dynasty 160

III The Fifth Dynasty 179

IV The Sixth Dynasty 189

V The Seventh and Eighth Dynasties 197

VI Literature and art 200

CHAPTER XV

PALESTINE IN THE EARLY BRONZE AGE

by R. DE VAUX, O.P.

École Biblique et Archéologique Française de Jérusalem

I Classification of the material 208

II The fortified cities 214

III Architecture: dwellings 218

IV Sanctuaries 221

V Burials 223

VI Material conditions: industry and commerce 225

VII Foreign relations: chronology 230

VIII Outline of history 233

CHAPTER XVI

THE EARLY DYNASTIC PERIOD
IN MESOPOTAMIA

by Sir MAX E. L. MALLOWAN, F.B.A.

*Fellow of All Souls College, Oxford, and Emeritus Professor of Western Asiatic
Archaeology in the University of London*

I Babylonia: archaeological development   *page* 238

II The Diyālā valley   246

III The principal Babylonian sites   272

IV Assyria and Mesopotamia   291

CHAPTER XVII

SYRIA BEFORE 2200 B.C.

§I AND III–VI

by MARGARET S. DROWER

Reader in Ancient History in the University of London

§II

by J. BOTTÉRO

Directeur d'études à l'École pratique des Hautes Études, Paris

I The background   315

II Syria at the time of the kings of Agade   321

III Cities of the Euphrates and the Khabur   328

IV Cities of the plain and the coast   333

V Byblos and the Land of Negau   343

VI Egyptians in Sinai and Palestine   351

CONTENTS

CHAPTER XVIII

ANATOLIA

c. 4000–2300 B.C.

by J. MELLAART

*Lecturer in Anatolian Archaeology at the Institute of Archaeology
in the University of London*

I End of the Late Chalcolithic period: Cilicia;
Konya plain; west, north-west, and central
Anatolia   *page* 363

II The Early Bronze Age: introduction and chronological subdivisions; origins; economy, and
cleavage between west and central Anatolia   368

III The Early Bronze Age I period: the north-
western group; pottery   371

IV The Early Bronze Age 2 period: introduction;
architecture; burial customs; metalwork;
costume and metal vessels; pottery   383

V Chronology   403

VI The catastrophe at the end of the Early Bronze
Age 2 period   406

THE IDENTIFICATION OF TROY

by CARL W. BLEGEN

*Professor Emeritus of Classical Archaeology in the
University of Cincinnati*

VII Troy I–II   411

CHAPTER XIX

THE DYNASTY OF AGADE AND THE GUTIAN INVASION

by the late C. J. GADD

I   The reign of Sargon; his origin, and legends concerning his youth; royal names; his rise to power; campaigns; legends of his conquests, and historical criticism   *page* 417

II   Successors of Sargon: Rimush and Manishtusu   434

III   The reign of Naram-Sin; his campaigns, and legends concerning them   440

IV   State of Babylonia under the Dynasty of Agade; Sumer and Akkad; conditions in the land and agrarian changes; arts and trade; connexion with the Indus-country   446

V   Last kings of Agade and the Gutian invasion; successors of Naram-Sin; the Gutians and their supremacy; historical and archaeological evidence; reign of Gudea   454

VI   Expulsion of the Gutians; victory of Utu-khegal; a Sumerian revival   461

CHAPTER XX

THE MIDDLE KINGDOM IN EGYPT

INTERNAL HISTORY FROM THE RISE OF THE
HERACLEOPOLITANS TO THE DEATH OF AMMENEMES III

by the late WILLIAM C. HAYES
*Formerly Curator of the Department of Egyptian Art in
the Metropoltian Museum of Art, New York*

I   The Heracleopolitan Kingdom   464

II   The nomarchs of Middle Egypt   468

III   Thebes and the 'Head of the South'   472

IV   The early kings of the Eleventh Dynasty   476

v   Reunion of Egypt under Nebhepetre Mentu-
     hotpe   *page* 479

vi   Reorganization and recovery   481

vii Foreign policy: progress towards the reconquest
     of Nubia   485

viii Egypt under King Mentuhotpe III: The Heka-
     nakhte Papers   488

ix   Resumption of the Red Sea traffic and reopening
     of the Wādi Hammāmāt   491

x   The end of the Eleventh Dynasty: Mentuhotpe IV
     and the Vizier Ammenemes   492

xi   The founding of the Twelfth Dynasty: Amme-
     nemes I and the administration   495

xii Expansion under Sesostris I and his successors 499

xiii The administrative reforms and foreign cam-
     paigns of Sesostris III; The Execration Texts 505

xiv Economic measures under Ammenemes III   509

xv   Art and architecture   512

xvi Religion and funerary beliefs   518

xvii Literature   523

CHAPTER XXI

SYRIA AND PALESTINE
c. 2160–1780 B.C.

RELATIONS WITH EGYPT

by G. POSENER
*Professeur de philologie et archéologie égyptiennes
au Collège de France*

i   Syria and Palestine in the Heracleopolitan Period
     and the Eleventh Dynasty   532

ii   Syria and Palestine during the Twelfth Dynasty 537

iii Egyptian sources   550

RELATIONS WITH MESOPOTAMIA

by J. BOTTÉRO

IV Syria during the Third Dynasty of Ur *page* 559

THE ARCHAEOLOGICAL SITES

by K. M. KENYON, F.B.A.
Principal of St Hugh's College, Oxford

V Archaeological evidence from Palestine 567
VI Palestine: the sites 568
VII Syria: the sites 583

CHAPTER XXII

BABYLONIA *c.* 2120–1800 B.C.

by the late C. J. GADD

I The Third Dynasty of Ur 595
II The king and his officers 617
III Economy and wealth 620
IV Foreigners from the East 624
V The Amorite invasion 625
VI Change in art 628
VII Successors of the Ur Dynasty 631
VIII Intervention from abroad 638

CHAPTER XXIII

PERSIA *c.* 2400–1800 B.C.

by WALTHER HINZ
Professor of Iranian History in the University of Göttingen

I The Elamite kings of Awan 644
II The Elamite kings of Simashki 654
III Religion in ancient Elam 662
IV Civilization of ancient Elam 673

CHAPTER XXIV(*a*)

ANATOLIA *c.* 2300–1750 B.C.

by J. MELLAART

I   Introductory   *page* 681

II   Western Anatolia after the Luwian invasion   683

III   Central Anatolia; theories about Hittite invasions;
Cappadocian ware   685

IV   Eastern cultures; eastern Anatolia and Trans-
Caucasia   688

V   A Pontic culture; Syrian and Pontic influence on
metal work of the Caucasus   690

VI   Transition to the Middle Bronze Age, 2100–
1900 B.C.; the Kültepe *kārum*; the south-east;
Troy and grey 'Minyan' ware; theories about
east–west movement of peoples   691

TROY III–IV–V

by CARL W. BLEGEN

VII   Troy III–IV–V   704

CHAPTER XXIV(*b*)

ANATOLIA IN THE
OLD ASSYRIAN PERIOD

by the late HILDEGARD LEWY
Formerly Visiting Professor, Hebrew Union College, Cincinnati

VIII   History   707

IX   Peoples and government   715

X   The articles of trade   723

XI   Measures, weights, and time-reckoning   727

CHAPTER XXV

ASSYRIA *c.* 2600–1816 B.C.

by the late HILDEGARD LEWY

I The pre-Sargonic period *page* 729

II The Sargonic period 733

III King-list and chronology 740

IV The Old Assyrian period 752

V The religion 763

VI The calendar 769

CHAPTER XXVI(*a*)

GREECE, CRETE, AND THE AEGEAN ISLANDS
IN THE EARLY BRONZE AGE

by JOHN L. CASKEY

*Professor of Classical Archaeology and Fellow of the Graduate School
in the University of Cincinnati*

I Definition of the inquiry 771

II North-eastern Greece 773

III Central Greece; the eastern shores 777

IV The central Peloponnese and the western coasts 788

V The islands of the Aegean 793

VI Crete 799

VII Chronological summary 804

CHAPTER XXVI(*b*)

CYPRUS IN THE EARLY BRONZE AGE

by H. W. CATLING

*Senior Assistant Keeper, Department of Antiquities of the
Ashmolean Museum in the University of Oxford*

VIII The identity of the Earliest Bronze Age settlers 808

CONTENTS

CHAPTER XXVII

IMMIGRANTS FROM THE NORTH

by R. A. CROSSLAND

Professor of Greek in the University of Sheffield

I   The problem of the Indo-Europeans   *page* 824

II   The earliest known Indo-European languages   830

III   Archaeological evidence for early Indo-European
immigration   840

IV   The region of origin of early Indo-European migrations   859

V   The impact of the northerners   873

BIBLIOGRAPHIES

Abbreviations   *page* 877

Chapter XI   881

Chapter XII   892

Chapter XIII   894

Chapter XIV   902

Chapter XV   909

Chapter XVI   913

Chapter XVII   916

Chapter XVIII   924

Chapter XIX   927

Chapter XX   933

Chapter XXI   950

Chapter XXII   960

Chapter XXIII   968

Chapter XXIV (*a*)   972

Chapter XXIV (*b*)   975

Chapter XXV   977

CONTENTS

Chapter xxvi (*a*)   *page* 982

Chapter xxvi (*b*)   988

Chapter xxvii   989

Chronological Tables

A   Egypt   994

B   Western Asia   997

C   Crete, the Aegean Islands and Mainland Greece   1002

Index to Maps   1005

General Index   1013

MAPS

1   The Nile Valley, Sinai and the Oases   *page* 2

2   Lower Egypt and the Faiyūm   4

3   Middle Egypt   8

4   Upper Egypt   12

5   Nubia   48

6   Babylonia and Western Persia   *facing page* 112

7   Palestine: Principal Early Bronze Age and Middle Bronze Age sites *page* 209

8   The Lebanon, Syria and Northern Mesopotamia   316

9   Anatolia in the Early Bronze Age 1 period   373

10 Anatolia in the Early Bronze Age 2 period   385

11 Elam: Principal sites   646

12 Early Bronze Age sites in Greece and the Aegean Islands   *facing page* 773

13 Early Bronze Age sites in Crete   *page* 773

14 Neolithic sites in Cyprus   810

15 Early Bronze Age sites in Cyprus   814

16 Map to illustrate movements of northern peoples in the third to first
    millennia B.C.   *facing page* 848

TABLES

1 Chronology of Anatolian sites from the Late Chalcolithic Period to Early Bronze Age 3 *page* 404

2 Comparative numbers of Early Bronze Age 2 and Early Bronze Age 3 sites in Anatolia 406

3 Early and Middle Bronze Age levels at Anatolian sites 693

TEXT-FIGURES

1 Plan of first occupation level of Sin Temple VII at Khafājī. Early Dynastic I *page* 248

2 Plan of first occupation level of Sin Temple VIII at Khafājī. Early Dynastic II 250

3 Plan of Sin Temple IX at Khafājī. Early Dynastic II 253

4 Plan of Sin Temple X at Khafājī. Early Dynastic III 256

5 Plan of the Nintu Temple at Khafājī during Sixth Building Period of Q 45:4. Early Dynastic II 258

6 Plan of Archaic Shrine I of the Abu Temple at Tell Asmar. Early Dynastic I 261

7 Projected plan of the Square Abu Temple at Tell Asmar. Early Dynastic II 263

8 Plan of the Single-Shrine Abu Temple at Tell Asmar. Early Dynastic III 265

9 Reconstructed plan of the main level of the Shara Temple at Tell Agrab. Early Dynastic 267

10 Isometric restoration of the Early Dynastic Temple Oval of the First Building Period at Khafājī 271

11 Isometric restoration of the Early Dynastic Palace at Kish 275

12 Royal tombs and death-pits at Ur 284

13 Ishtar Temple (*c*) at Mari. Early Dynastic II, or III *a*. 293

14 Ishtar Temple (*a*) at Mari. Early Dynastic III *b*. 294

15 Stone-built 'North Temple' at Khuaira 309

16 Stone building I at Khuaira 311

17 The siege of a walled Asiatic town. Sixth Dynasty. Tomb of Inti, Dishāsha 359

18 Plan of Troy 412

19 Plan and section of an Outsize Tomb (P. 12) at Jericho 571

20 Types of pottery from an Outsize Tomb at Jericho 573

21 Plan and section of Shaft Tomb 878 at Megiddo 580

22 Pottery from a Shaft Tomb at Megiddo 582

PREFACE

In the first part of this volume the peoples discussed were classified either according to the physical or cultural stage in evolution which they had reached or according to the locality in which their material remains had first been found by archaeologists. Such terms as Neanderthal man, the Palaeolithic age, Badarians and the Tell Halaf culture are definitions with a limited application which are useful for scientific purposes, but they are nevertheless a cloak for anonymity. It was the invention of writing which enabled man to record his existence as an individual and thus to provide later generations with a means of determining his identity.

At the time when the events which are described in the opening chapters of this second part were taking place, writing had come into use in Mesopotamia and Egypt, and in Elam too, but its early script has only recently been deciphered. Elsewhere, with the possible exception of the Indus Valley, man seems to have been illiterate. Very early records, however, offer the historian but limited assistance; they generally refer to isolated incidents without giving much indication of the background. Chronicles compiled in later times supplement this sketchy information to a significant degree, but they are not always reliable. Biographical texts in narrative form do not seem to have been written before the middle of the Third Millennium B.C., the earliest known being inscriptions in the tomb of an Egyptian official named Metjen, who died in the reign of Sneferu (c. 2600 B.C.). Fortunately, both in Egypt and in Mesopotamia the value of the written document, for secular and for religious purposes, was soon recognized and long before the end of the period covered by this volume a varied, but unevenly distributed, body of literature is available to provide a framework to which the evidence of the monuments and of the very considerable quantity of uninscribed material can be attached.

Meanwhile on the islands of the Aegean Sea and on the Greek mainland Neolithic civilizations reached their maturity and attained high levels of artistic achievement. They were largely swept away by the waves of immigrants from the Near East which inaugurated the beginning of the Bronze Age in Aegean lands. As the Early Bronze Age drew towards its close, two develop-

ments began to which names may be given: on the northern
confines of the Greek peninsula the appearance of speakers of an
Indo-European language, which we label 'Greek', and in Crete
the beginning of a Palace-centred civilization, with which the
name of 'Minos' is associated.

Mention has already been made in the Preface to the first part
of this volume of the code employed in the footnotes for reference
to the bibliographies. It will be noticed that in some chapters
additions have been made to the bibliographies which were
printed in the separate fascicles. These additions, arranged in
alphabetical order, are appended to the relevant bibliographies
and the letter A is prefixed in the footnotes to the sequence
number of the book or article. The plates, to which reference is
made in the footnotes, will be published as a separate volume after
the completion of Volume II of the text.

The Editors are grateful to the Syndics of the Cambridge
University Press for allowing authors to revise their chapters and
to include information which was not available when the chapters
were first published. In two instances (Chapters xvi and xxi)
line-drawings have been introduced as illustrations to the text.
Maps and synchronistic tables, which were not included in the
fascicles, have been added in accordance with the original plan
for the bound volumes.

It is a matter of deep regret to record the deaths of no fewer
than four of the contributors: Professor H. Frankfort, Dr W. S.
Smith, Dr W. C. Hayes and Professor Hildegard Lewy. The
revision of Professor Frankfort's chapter was undertaken by Mrs
Leri Davies before it was printed as a fascicle. Dr W. S. Smith
had already revised chapter xiv before his death. Dr H. Fischer,
Curator of the Department of Egyptian Art at the Metropolitan
Museum, greatly assisted the Editors by supplying a number of
additions to chapter xx which had been written nearly ten years
ago by Dr W. C. Hayes.

Acknowledgment of assistance from several sources has already
been recorded in the Preface to the first part of this volume. In
addition to those whose names are mentioned there the Editors
owe a particular debt of gratitude to Dr E. Sollberger, Deputy
Keeper of the Department of Western Asiatic Antiquities at the
British Museum, for much editorial help in the final stages of the
preparation of this part. Professor J. L. Caskey wishes to thank
the American School of Classical Studies at Athens, the University of Cincinnati and the Institute for Advanced Study at
Princeton for their support and assistance. Professor W. Hinz

acknowledges his debt to Professor R. Borger of Göttingen for his advice on Assyriological problems in connexion with his chapter on Persia *c.* 2400–800 B.C. For the care and skill which the staff of the Cambridge University Press have devoted to the production of this book, and for their patience and helpfulness during its preparation, both the Editors and the contributors are deeply grateful.

I.E.S.E.
C.J.G.
N.G.L.H.

We must record, with sadness and a deep sense of personal loss, the death of Professor C. J. Gadd on 2 December 1969. Not only did he write the largest number of chapters by any single contributor to this History, but, as the Editor principally responsible for all the chapters relating to Western Asia, he also bore the heaviest editorial burden. This is not the place to write of his immense scholarship, but we must express our lasting feeling of gratitude for the readiness with which he always placed his wealth of knowledge and his wisdom at our disposal. At the time of his death this volume was already with the printer. In the final stages of its preparation for publication we received much assistance from Dr E. Sollberger and we wish to thank him.

I.E.S.E.
N.G.L.H.

CHAPTER XI

THE EARLY DYNASTIC PERIOD IN EGYPT

I. THE EARLY MONARCHY AND THE UNIFICATION OF EGYPT

TRADITION and a substantial body of indirect evidence suggest strongly that Egypt, in the period immediately preceding the foundation of the First Dynasty, was divided into two independent kingdoms:[1] a northern kingdom, which included the Nile Delta and extended southwards perhaps to the neighbourhood of the modern village of Atfīh (Lower Egypt) and a southern kingdom comprising the territory between Atfīh and Gebel es-Silsila (Upper Egypt).[2] The residences of the kings are believed to have been situated at Pe,[3] in the north-west Delta, and at Nekhen (Hierakonpolis), on the west bank of the river near Edfu, both of which, in historical times at least, possessed important sanctuaries of the falcon-god Horus, the patron deity of the rulers.[4] In the vicinity of Pe lay Dep, the seat of a cobra-goddess Uadjit (Edjo); the two places were together known in the New Kingdom and later under one name Per-Uadjit (House of Edjo), rendered as Buto by the Greeks.[5] Across the river from Nekhen stood Nekheb (El-Kāb), where a vulture-goddess Nekhbet had her sanctuary. Both goddesses came to be regarded at a very early date, perhaps while the separate kingdoms were in being, as royal protectresses.

Even such information about this period as was recorded in the king-lists is largely lost and what remains is difficult to interpret. The first line of the fragmentary Palermo Stone[6] consists of a series of compartments, seven only being entirely preserved, each of which contains a name and a figure of a king wearing the crown of Lower Egypt, but no historical events are mentioned. Manetho speaks of the predecessors of the kings of the First Dynasty as the 'Spirits of the Dead, the Demigods' (νέκυες οἱ ἡμίθεοι). In the Turin Canon,[7] which dates from Ramesside

---

[1] §I, 31,137–66.
[2] §I, 17, 51–5; §VII, 27, 51, n. 14.
[3] §VII, 29, 1488[b].
[4] §I, 7, 59; §I, 37, 236.
[5] G, 5, text vol. II, 187*–93*.
[6] See Plate 25.
[7] Turin Canon II, 8, 9; §I, 8. See Plate 27.

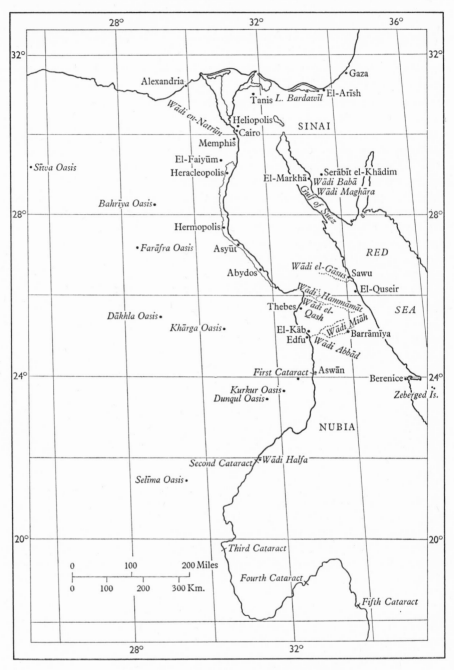

Map 1. The Nile Valley, Sinai and the Oases.

times, the last predynastic rulers are called both the 'Spirits who were Followers of Horus' (*iḫw šmsw Ḥr*) and the 'Followers of Horus' (*šmsw Ḥr*). With what appeared to be well-reasoned arguments Kurt Sethe maintained[1] that these epithets could be applied to the kings of Pe and Nekhen, in virtue of being adherents to the cult of Horus, and could also be explained as the Egyptian equivalent of Manetho's 'Spirits of the Dead, the Demigods'. As a general description of kings of the remote past the term 'Followers of Horus' does occur sporadically in Egyptian texts dating from the end of the Second Intermediate Period until Ptolemaic times,[2] and in a fragmentary papyrus of Roman date, which may well preserve an ancient tradition, two successive entries refer to the 'Souls of Pe, Followers of Horus as Kings of Lower Egypt' and the 'Souls of Nekhen, Followers of Horus as Kings of Upper Egypt'.[3] This usage of the term seems however to have been a relatively late development which resulted from a misinterpretation of the early dynastic records.[4]

At most, only two predynastic kings, both of Upper Egypt, are known from contemporary records, one bearing a name which has generally been read as Ka and the other being indicated by the hieroglyphic sign representing a scorpion. In some cases the name of Ka is written anomalously beneath the panelled door of the *serekh*—the rectangular frame surmounted by the falcon of Horus within which the official names of kings were inscribed.[5] It is, however, far from certain that Ka is the correct reading of the name; several authorities have preferred to regard the single sign with which it is written as a cursive form of a scorpion,[6] thereby identifying this king with his supposed successor, and the suggestion has also been made that the name should be read as Sekhen.[7] Scorpion is the first king of whom any historical details are known, owing to the discovery at Hierakonpolis of some fragments of a limestone mace-head decorated with scenes in relief commemorating symbolically episodes in his life.[8] The scenes are arranged in three registers: in the uppermost register there is a series of standards, each surmounted by the emblem of a particular nome. Suspended by a rope from every standard is either a bow or a lapwing (*rḫyt*), the rope being tied around the neck of

[1] §1, 30, 3–21.   [2] §1, 18, part 1 (1960), 132–6; §1, 30, 5–8.

[3] G, 6, 421–2; G, 9, pl. 9, frag. 10.   [4] See below, p. 11.

[5] G, 17, 16–17; §viii, 33, part 1, pls. 1–3.

[6] G, 32, vol. 1, 287–9; §1, 13, 134, n. 74; §1, 32, 57, n. 3.

[7] §iv, 22, 54–7.

[8] G, 2, 250–1, figs. 188–9; G, 4, 42–3, fig. 3; G, 25, part 1, pls. xxv, xxvi c; §1, 28, 25, pl. 4; §viii, 57, 113–15, fig. 30; §viii, 59, 600–2, fig. 393.

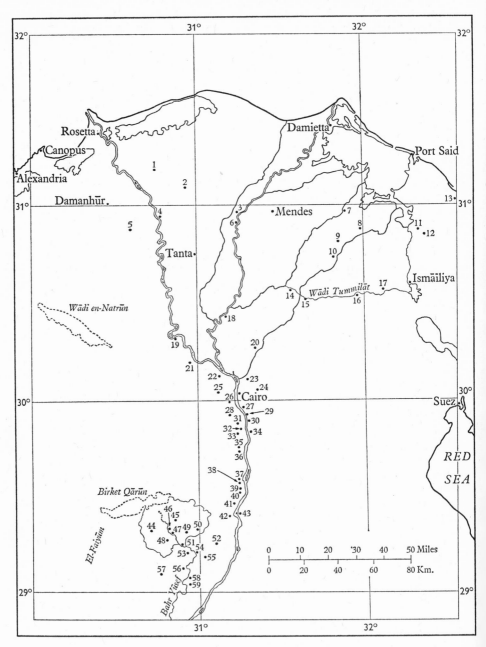

Map 2. Lower Egypt and the Faiyūm.

NUMERICAL KEY

1	Buto	22	Letopolis	41	El-Girza
2	Sakha (Xois)	23	Heliopolis (El-	42	Maidūm
3	Sebennytos		Matarīya)	43	Atfīh (Aphroditopolis)
4	Sā el-Hagar (Sais)	24	Gebel el-Ahmar	44	El-Agamīyīn
5	Naucratis	25	Abu Rawāsh	45	Biyahmu
6	Busiris	26	Giza	46	Kīmān Fāris (Croco-
7	Tanis (Zoan, Sān	27	El-Maʿādi		dilopolis)
	el-Hagar)	28	Zāwiyet el-Aryān	47	Medīnet el-Faiyūm
8	Nebesha	29	Tura	48	Abgīg
9	Qantīr	30	El-Maʿsara	49	Edwa
10	Khatāʿna	31	Abusīr	50	Seila
11	El-Qantara	32	Memphis (Mīt	51	Hawāra
12	Tell Abu Seifa (Tjel)		Rahīna)	52	Abusīr el-Malaq
13	Pelusium	33	Saqqara	53	Ghurāb
14	Bubastis	34	Helwān	54	El-Lāhūn
15	Saft el-Hinna	35	Dahshūr	55	El-Haraga
16	Tell er-Ratāba	36	Mazghūna	56	Sidmant
17	Pithom	37	El-Lisht	57	Medīnet Maʿādi
18	Athribis	38	El-Maharraqa	58	Heracleopolis Magna
19	Merimda Beni Salāma	39	Kafr Ammār		(Ihnāsiya el-Medīna)
20	Tell el-Yahūdīya	40	Tarkhān	59	Kōm el-Aqārib
21	El-Qatta				

ALPHABETICAL KEY

Abgīg 48
Abu Rawāsh 25
Abusīr 31
Abusīr el-Malaq 52
El-Agamīyīn 44
Aphroditopolis (Atfīh) 43
Atfīh (Aphroditopolis) 43
Athribis 18
Biyahmu 45
Bubastis 14
Busiris 6
Buto 1
Crocodilopolis
    (Kīmān Fāris) 46
Dahshūr 35
Edwa 49
Gebel el-Ahmar 24
Ghurāb 53
El-Girza 41
Giza 26
El-Haraga 55
Hawāra 51
Heliopolis (El-Matarīya) 23
Helwān 34
Heracleopolis Magna
    (Ihnāsiya el-Medīna) 58

Ihnāsiya el-Medīna
    (Heracleopolis Magna) 58
Kafr Ammār 39
Khatāʿna 10
Kīmān Fāris
    (Crocodilopolis) 46
Kōm el-Aqārib 59
El-Lāhūn 54
Letopolis 22
El-Lisht 37
El-Maʿādi 27
El-Maharraqa 38
Maidūm 42
El-Maʿsara 30
El-Matarīya
    (Heliopolis) 23
Mazghūna 36
Medīnet el-Faiyūm 47
Medīnet Maʿādi 57
Memphis (Mīt Rahīna) 32
Merimda Beni Salāma 19
Naucratis 5
Nebesha 8
Pelusium 13
Pithom 17

El-Qantara 11
Qantir 9
El-Qatta 21
Sā el-Hagar (Sais) 4
Saft el-Hinna 15
Sais (Sā el-Hagar) 4
Sakha (Xois) 2
Sān el-Hagar (Tanis, Zoan) 7
Saqqara 33
Sebennytos 3
Seila 50
Sidmant 56
Tanis (Zoan, Sān el-Hagar) 7
Tarkhān 40
Tell Abu Seifa (Tjel) 12
Tell er-Ratāba 16
Tell el-Yahūdīya 20
Tjel (Tell Abu Seifa) 12
Tura 29
Zāwiyet el-Aryān 28
Zoan (Tanis, Sān el-Hagar) 7
Xois (Sakha) 2

each bird. When bows—always nine in number—occur on later monuments, they symbolize the enemies of Egypt, and the lap-wing, as a hieroglyph, represents the Egyptian populace. It has therefore been surmised that the scene portrayed in this register commemorates the victory of a group of Upper Egyptian nomes, under the leadership of Scorpion, over foreigners, living in the oases and neighbouring deserts, and some Egyptians, possibly of the Lower Egyptian kingdom, dwelling either in the Delta or somewhat further south.[1] In the middle register Scorpion, wearing the crown of Upper Egypt and holding a hoe in his hands, initiates the digging of an irrigation canal; an attendant stands before him holding a basket to receive the soil removed. Possibly the artist's intention was to show the measures taken by the king to develop the land after his victory. The surviving por-tion of the lowest register shows the Nile, on the bank of which the previous ceremony had taken place, and some men engaged in agricultural work on two islands formed by its waters.

It seems evident that steps—perhaps not the first—towards the subjugation of the northern kingdom were taken by Scorpion. How far he was able to advance cannot be precisely determined. A pot found at the protodynastic cemetery of Tura was once thought to bear his name and to indicate that he had penetrated to that region, but further study has shown that this reading was incorrect.[2] Nevertheless his conquest may have reached a point as far north as the apex of the Delta. He may even have captured the eastern part of the Delta, but it is improbable that he over-came the entire northern kingdom, because the mace-head shows him wearing only the white crown of Upper Egypt; there is no parallel scene of the king with the red crown as ruler of Lower Egypt, although the suggestion has been made that a king seated under a canopy and wearing the crown of Lower Egypt who is represented on a fragment of another mace-head from Hierakon-polis is to be identified with Scorpion.[3] The distinction of com-pleting the conquest and of uniting the two kingdoms belongs, in all probability, to Narmer, who is thought to have been Scorpion's immediate successor. A remarkable record of this victory is preserved on the famous slate palette from Hierakonpolis.[4] On the obverse Narmer, followed by his sandal-bearer, is shown

[1] G, 5, text vol. I, 100*–8*; §I, 2, part I, 45; §I, 10, part I, 184–7.
[2] §I, 16, 6–9, fig. 4; A, 5, 102–3, fig. 3.
[3] G, 25, pl. xxviA; G, 26, 39–40; §I, I.
[4] G, 24, 193–4; G, 25, pl. xxix; G, 26, 41–3; §I, 27, J 25 and K 26; §I, 28, 22–3, pl. 6; §viii, 59, figs. 391–2.

smiting with a mace a captured Delta chieftain, possibly belonging to the north-western nome which had a harpoon as its ensign. Above the victim is a monogram composed of a falcon perched on a papyrus plant and a human head attached to a body deliberately flattened in order to resemble the hieroglyph of foreign land; tied to the nose is a cord, held by a hand projecting from the falcon's breast. Since the falcon was the hieroglyphic sign for the god Horus and the papyrus was the symbol of Lower Egypt, it has been conjectured that the whole group means: 'Horus brings (to the king) captives of Lower Egypt.' The sequel to this scene appears in the uppermost of three registers on the reverse, where the king is shown, accompanied by attendants, going out to inspect the slain northerners who, with their severed heads between their feet, are set out in two rows. It is unlikely that pure chance is responsible for the fact that the king wears the crown of Upper Egypt in the first scene and of Lower Egypt in the second; far more probable is it that the sculptor intended to show that this victory marked the final defeat of the northern kingdom and the assumption of its crown by Narmer.[1]

Another palette, of which only the lower portion is preserved, may well refer to a continuation of the same campaign by Narmer, but since no name is given, the identification cannot be proved.[2] One face of the palette depicts rows of cattle, asses and rams, and some trees once thought to be olives.[3] Among the trees is a hieroglyphic group reading Tjehenu-land, which is believed to have been situated in Libya, near the north-western limits of the Delta.[4] Narmer certainly conducted a campaign against this region, as is attested by an ivory cylinder from Hierakonpolis, bearing his name and that of Tjehenu-land, which shows prisoners captured in the battle.[5] On the other face of the palette there are seven rectangular outlines with crenellated sides representing walled towns. Within each rectangle is the name of a city, while above it stood originally a bird or animal, only four of which (a falcon, a lion, a scorpion and twin falcons on perches) have survived. Each of these creatures hacks with a mattock at the wall of the town which it surmounts. The identification of the individual towns presents serious difficulties, but it has been presumed that all of them lay in Tjehenu-land and that their downfall

[1] §1, 24, 17–22.
[2] G, 6, 393–4; G, 24, 105, no. 6; §1, 27, pl. G, 19–20; §1, 28, 19–21, pl. 3; §viii, 59, 590–2.   [3] §1, 26, 97–100; §1, 20 contests this identification.
[4] G, 5, text vol. i, 116*–19*; §1, 32, 57–8.
[5] G, 25, pl. xv, 7; §1, 23, 49–50, fig. 6.

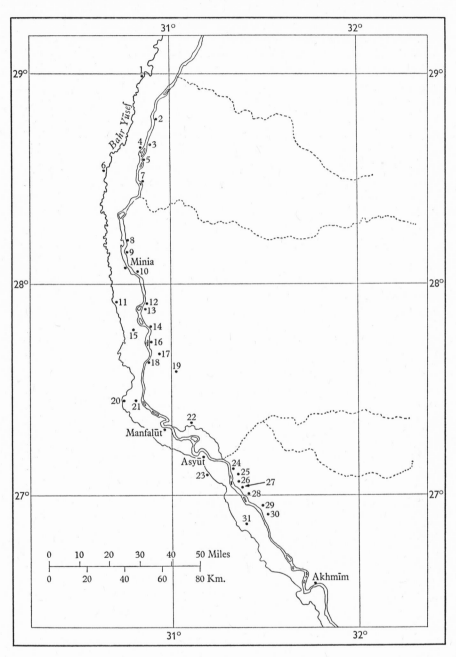

Map 3. Middle Egypt.

NUMERICAL KEY

1	Dishāsha	12	Beni Hasan	23	Deir Rīfa
2	El-Hība	13	Speos Artemidos	24	El-Matmar
3	Hipponus	14	Antinoopolis	25	Khawālid
4	Maghāgha	15	El-Ashmūnein	26	El-Mustagidda
5	Kōm el-Ahmar		(Hermopolis)	27	Deir Tāsa
	Sawāris	16	Deir el-Bersha	28	El-Badāri
6	Oxyrhynchus	17	Sheikh Sa'īd	29	El-Hammāmīya
7	Cynopolis	18	El-Amarna	30	Qāw el-Kebīr
8	Tihna	19	Het-Nub		(Antaeopolis)
9	Nazlat esh-Shurafa	20	Meir	31	Kōm Ishqāw (Aphro-
10	Zāwiyet el-Maiyitīn	21	Cusae		ditopolis)
11	Nefrusy (Balansūra)	22	Deir el-Gabrāwi		

ALPHABETICAL KEY

El-Amarna 18
Antaeopolis (Qāw el-Kebīr) 30
Antinoopolis 14
Aphroditopolis (Kōm Ishqāw) 31
El-Ashmūnein (Hermopolis) 15
El-Badari 28
Balansūra (Nefrusy) 11
Beni Hasan 12
Cusae 21
Cynopolis 7
Deir el-Bersha 16

Deir el-Gabrāwi 22
Deir Rīfa 23
Deir Tāsa 27
Dishāsha 1
El-Hammāmīya 29
Hermopolis (El-Ashmūnein) 15
Het-Nub 19
El-Hība 2
Hipponus 3
Khawālid 25
Kōm el-Ahmar Sawāris 5
Kōm Ishqāw (Aphrodito-polis) 31

Maghāgha 4
El-Matmar 24
Meir 20
El-Mustagidda 26
Nazlat-esh-Shurafa 9
Nefrusy (Balansūra) 11
Oxyrhynchus 6
Qāw el-Kebīr (Antaeopolis) 30
Sheikh Sa'īd 17
Speos Artemidos 13
Tihna 8
Zāwiyet el-Maiyitīn 10

led to the capture of the booty shown on the opposite side of the palette.[1] Equally difficult to determine is the exact significance of the various creatures attacking the walls: they have been explained as royal titles—not, however, of Narmer but of Scorpion[2]—and as symbols of either the divine or the human allies of the king whose victory the palette commemorates.[3] If they represented Scorpion himself, it might have been expected that his name would be distinguished in some way and not merely included among his titles; moreover, there is no other evidence to suggest that Scorpion ever succeeded in reaching the north-western Delta. It seems rather more likely, therefore, that deities were intended and that they symbolized the falcon-king of Hierakonpolis—supposedly Narmer—and the leaders of those nomes which assisted him in his campaign against the North.

Closely connected with the problems raised by this palette is the question of the character of the relationship between the Horus-king and the local rulers of other nomes at the time of the conquest. The most important contemporary sources of information are Scorpion's mace-head,[4] a damaged mace-head of Narmer,[5] the two palettes already mentioned and two fragments of palettes, one in the Louvre[6] and the other in the Ashmolean Museum.[7] Both the mace-heads and the Narmer palette undoubtedly display nome-standards, so integrated into the general design as to suggest that their respective nomes played an important part in the main events depicted. Even more graphically portrayed are the scenes on the two fragments: five standards which terminate in hands pulling together on a single rope are shown on the Louvre fragment; on the Ashmolean Museum fragment (which joins a larger fragment in the British Museum depicting a battlefield) two standards with projecting arms are represented leading two bound captives. In the absence of any king's name, neither of these two fragments can be precisely dated, but their style strongly suggests that they belong to the period of Scorpion and Narmer. Prominent among the various

---

1 §1, 28, 21 suggests that the palette commemorates the capture of Buto by Scorpion.
2 §1, 32, 56–7.   3 §1, 33, 122–4.
4 See above , p. 3, n. 8.
5 G, 24, 194; G, 25, pls. xxv, xxviB; §1, 28, 23–4, pl. 7; §viii, 57, 115, fig. 31; §viii, 59, 602–5.
6 G, 2, 242, fig. 181; §1, 27, pl. G, 17–18; §1, 33, 128–31; §viii, 59, 592–4, figs. 389–90.
7 G, 2, 238, fig. 177; §1, 27, pls. D, 13 and E, 14; §1, 28, 18–19, pl. 2; §viii, 59, 584–7, figs. 384–5.

standards are those bearing the wolf-god Wepwawet of Asyūt,
the ibis of the Fifteenth Lower Egyptian nome and the symbol of
Min of Akhmīm and Koptos, together with those of other nomes
which are less easily identified. The purport of all these scenes is
hard to comprehend unless it be supposed that the nomes represented contributed materially to the conquest of unification. It is
possible, moreover, that they also denote that the reigning king of
Hierakonpolis was not the omnipotent despot of later times, but
rather the leader of a confederation of nomes fighting as allies
against a common enemy. Some authorities who hold this view
consider that these allies of the falcon-king or their local gods—
and not the predynastic kings of Pe and Nekhen—were the real
Followers of Horus whose true identity must, in that case, have
been forgotten in later times.[1] In favour of this explanation is
the undoubted fact that from the Old Kingdom onwards similar
standards in representations of the *Sed*-festival—itself a re-
enactment of the episodes in the conquest of unification—are
described in the accompanying texts as the 'Gods, Followers of
Horus'.[2] From the same period there is also evidence that the
Followers of Horus could mean members of the king's retinue,[3]
while at an even earlier date a biennial tour of inspection by river
made by the king and his entourage was called the 'Following of
Horus'.[4]

According to the Turin and Abydos king-lists the first king of
Egypt was Meni, who is to be identified with Men (Μîν) of
Herodotus and Menes (Μήνης), the founder of Manetho's First
Dynasty. Not without reason, however, it has been doubted
whether the name occurs in any contemporary document and, in
consequence, whether a person so named ever existed.[5] In order
to account for its appearance in later times, it has been suggested
that the name, which means 'He who endures', was coined as a
mere descriptive epithet denoting a semi-legendary hero who in
the remote past had unified the Two Lands under one crown and
whose true name had been lost. In that event 'Menes' might
conceal the personages of Ka, Scorpion and Narmer. But it is far
from proved that Menes is not mentioned in at least one inscription
dating from the beginning of the historical epoch. An ivory label
from Naqāda, now in the Cairo Museum,[6] bears the Horus name
of Aha side by side with the framework of a building, within

---

[1] §1, 19, 196 ff.; §vii, 16, 187–214.   [2] §vii, 16, 191, n, 1.
[3] §1, 3, 5; §1, 18, part 1 (1960), 131.
[4] §1, 3, 5–7; §1, 18, part 1 (1960), 131–2.   [5] G, 11, 104–6.
[6] G, 6, 405–7, fig. 14; G, 24, 118; §1, 34, 208–34.

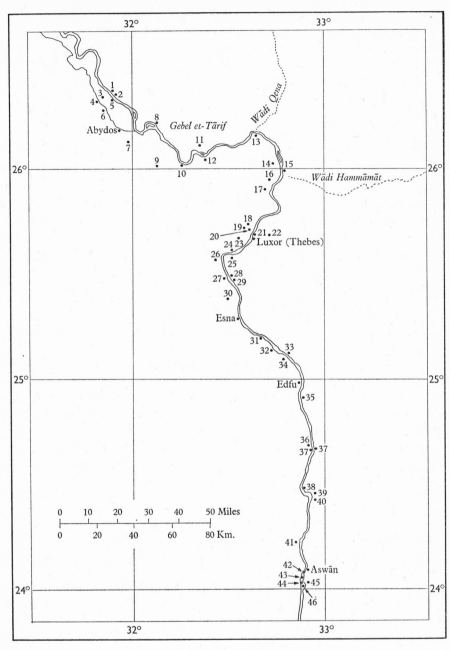

Map 4. Upper Egypt.

NUMERICAL KEY

1	Sheikh Farag	17	Naqāda (Ombos)	32	Mohamerīya
2	Naga ed-Deir	18	Dirā Abu n-Naga		(El-Maʿmarīya)
3	This	19	Deir el-Bahri	33	Elkāb (El-Kāb)
4	Beit Khallāf	20	El-Qurna (Sheikh Abd	34	Hierakonpolis
5	Girga		el-Qurna)	35	Er-Ridīsīya
6	El-Mahāsna	21	Karnak	36	Shatt er-Rigāl
7	El-Amra	22	El-Madāmūd (Mada)	37	Gebel es-Silsila
8	El-Balābīsh	23	Medīnet Habu		(East and West)
9	Gebel el-Araq	24	Armant (Hermonthis)	38	Sebīl
10	Diospolis Parva (Hū)	25	Tōd (Djeret)	39	Kōm Ombo
11	Hamra Dom	26	Er-Rizeiqāt	40	Darāw
12	Abādīya	27	Gebelein	41	El-Kūbānīya
13	Dendera	28	Ed-Dibābīya	42	Elephantine
14	El-Ballās	29	El-Miʿalla	43	Siheil
15	Koptos	30	Asfūn el-Matāʿna	44	Konosso
16	Tūkh	31	Es-Sibāʿīya	45	Esh-Shallāl
				46	Bīga

ALPHABETICAL KEY

Abādīya 12
El-Amra 7
Armant (Hermonthis) 24
Asfūn el-Matāʿna 30
El-Balābīsh 8
El-Ballās 14
Beit Khallāf 4
Bīga 46
Darāw 40
Deir el-Bahri 19
Dendera 13
Ed-Dibābīya 28
Diospolis Parva (Hū) 10
Dirā Abu n-Naga 18
Djeret (Tōd) 25
Elephantine 42
Elkāb (El-Kāb) 33
Gebelein 27
Gebel el-Araq 9

Gebel es-Silsila (East and West) 37
Girga 5
Hamra Dom 11
Hermonthis (Armant) 24
Hierakonpolis 34
Hū (Diospolis Parva) 10
El-Kāb (Elkāb) 33
Karnak 21
Kōm Ombo 39
Konosso 44
Koptos 15
El-Kūbānīya 41
Mada (El-Madāmūd) 22
El-Madāmūd (Mada) 22
El-Mahāsna 6
El-Maʿmarīya (Mohamerīya) 32
Medīnet Habu 23
El-Miʿalla 29

Mohamerīya (El-Maʿmarīya) 32
Naga ed-Deir 2
Naqāda (Ombos) 17
Ombos (Naqāda) 17
El-Qurna (Sheikh Abd el-Qurna) 20
Er-Ridīsīya 35
Er-Rizeiqāt 26
Sebīl 38
Esh-Shallāl 45
Shatt er-Rigāl 36
Sheikh Abd el-Qurna (El-Qurna) 20
Sheikh Farag 1
Es-Sibāʿīya 31
Siheil 43
This 3
Tōd (Djeret) 25
Tūkh 16

which is the royal title 'Two Ladies' (*nbty*) and a single hieroglyph
(*mn*) which most authorities have taken to represent the name
Menes. At one time it was thought that these two names belonged to the same king, Menes being the *nbty*–name of the
Horus Aha.[1] A more plausible explanation is, however, that the
label records the construction by Aha of a funerary booth (*wrmt*)
for the deceased Menes, who would thus have been his immediate
predecessor,[2] but it does not necessarily follow from this interpretation that the king in question was the Horus Narmer.
Nevertheless there are other grounds for supposing that Aha was
Narmer's successor. Indeed no further demonstration that Narmer and Menes were one and the same person would be required
if it were not also possible that the building is not a funerary
booth, but a shrine (*sh*) inscribed with its name 'The Two Ladies
Endure'.[3] A clay seal-impression from Abydos which bears the
name of Narmer alternating with the sign *mn*[4] has been considered to provide proof of the identity of Narmer and Menes,[5]
but it is hard to believe that the omission of the title 'Two Ladies'
before Men is not significant. Men, in this instance, may be the
name of an official or a prince, who was entitled to use the seal,[6]
or it may be the verb, the whole group having the meaning
'Narmer endures'.

Scribal mistakes certainly occurred in the lists of early dynastic
kings as they were recorded in later times, but in most instances
these mistakes can be explained, and it is apparent that they arose
through simple confusions or through the inability of copyists to
recognize correctly hieratic signs. Of the general soundness of
the tradition which the lists preserve there can be no doubt. No
suspicion of a misreading has been entertained by scholars in the
case of Menes. That it represents the *nbty*–name, and not the
Horus-name, may be deduced from the fact that the *nbty*–names
are given in the lists for subsequent kings of the First Dynasty.
The third king in the Abydos list, of whose name nothing except
the royal determinatives is preserved in the Turin Canon, is Iti,[7]
who is securely identified by the Cairo Annals with the Horus
Djer. Unless it be supposed, as one writer has suggested,[8] that
the second king, also called Iti in the Turin Canon but Teti in the
Abydos list, is to be equated with an ephemeral king whose

---

[1] G, 28, 41; §I, 4, 87–105; §IV, 35, 23.
[2] §I, 9, 279–82; §I, 23, 47–9, fig. 5.   [3] G, 18, 65–6; §I, 28, 113–14.
[4] G, 6, 404–5, fig. 13; §III, 11, pl. 13, 93. [5] §I, 23, 46–7, fig. 3a.
[6] §I, 11; §IV, 11, 21–2; §IV, 35, 28 and n. 3.
[7] See Plates 26 and 27.   [8] §I, 14, 9–10.

Horus-name is not known, the Horus Aha alone remains to occupy the second position, leaving the Horus Narmer to be identified with Menes. This conclusion accords well with the evidence
of his famous slate palette.[1] As the founder of the First Dynasty
tradition may well have credited him with a greater share in the
achievement of the unification of the Two Lands than was his
due, and to that extent he may be regarded as a legendary figure.

II. THE FOUNDATION OF MEMPHIS

Herodotus states that Menes, besides establishing the Egyptian
monarchy, founded the city later called Memphis and its temple
dedicated to the god Ptah.[2] In order to do so at the place chosen,
Menes was obliged to construct a dyke some hundred stades to
the south, which diverted the course of the river and protected
the city against flooding during the annual inundation. Since
Herodotus obtained this information from the priests of Ptah,
who might be suspected of a natural desire to glorify their temple
by associating its foundation with the illustrious Menes, it is
necessary to examine his account and to assess its inherent probability. There is certainly no reason to doubt that the construction of a dyke would have been required before the city could be
built. Until the introduction of modern methods of irrigation,
the whole of the Giza province owed its protection from inundation to a dyke in the neighbourhood of Wasta. Such a dyke probably existed in the time of Herodotus, but did not necessarily
date back to Menes. Diodorus, apparently quoting a Theban
tradition received from Hecataeus, ascribes the foundation of
Memphis to a Theban king Uchoreus (Οὐχορεύς),[3] whose name
may well be a corruption of Ὀχυρεύς, which would be a translation
of Menes. The two historians are therefore virtually in agreement.
Manetho does not mention the actual foundation of the city, but
says that a palace was built there by Athothis, the successor of
of Menes—a statement which need not however imply that Athothis was the first king to build a palace in Memphis. A king-list,
formerly on the wall of a Nineteenth Dynasty tomb in the Memphite cemetery of Saqqara and now preserved in the Cairo
Museum,[4] begins with the name of Anedjib, which may mean
that the priestly owner of the tomb wished to attribute the foundation of Memphis to the sixth king of the First Dynasty, but no

[1] See above, p. 7.   [2] Book II, 99. See below, pp. 52–3.
[3] Book I, 50.   [4] G, 15, pl. I; G, 27, pl. I.

other evidence supports this assumption. While tombs and funerary equipment dating from the beginning of the First Dynasty have been discovered in abundance at Saqqara, traces of an earlier occupation are absent; it must therefore be admitted that at present there is nothing to suggest that the tradition quoted by Herodotus is in any important respect unsound.

Two further questions concerning Memphis which require consideration are its original name and the motive which prompted its foundation. The name Memphis belonged in the first instance to the pyramid of the Sixth Dynasty king Phiops I (*Men-nefer*[-*Pepi*]) at South Saqqara and was only later applied to the city itself. Previously it was called the 'White Wall' or 'White Walls', sometimes abbreviated to the 'Wall' or 'Walls'.[1] White was the national colour of the Upper Egyptian kingdom and a city founded by the victorious king of the South on captured territory might have been named the 'White Wall' to emphasize the victory; equally it could be a purely descriptive name referring to the white gesso with which its walls of mud-brick were covered. The explanation offered by the early commentators of Thucydides[2] that the city was so named because it was built of white stone, whereas other cities were built of brick, is fanciful, for it is improbable that the skilled labour necessary for cutting so much stone would have been available at the beginning of the First Dynasty. With regard to the purpose of its foundation, Menes may well have intended it to serve as a bastion for the protection of Upper Egypt against possible attacks from the inhabitants of the Delta. On the other hand, being situated at the junction of the Two Lands, it stood at the most convenient point for directing the affairs of the newly-unified kingdom and may therefore have been designed from the beginning as the capital and the site of the royal residence. Some support for this view is to be found in the Palermo Stone and Cairo Annals, which show that two of the most important elements in the coronation of the early dynastic kings were the ceremonies of 'Uniting the Two Lands' and 'The Procession around the Wall', both of which undoubtedly took place at the White Wall and were intended to commemorate the two outstanding deeds of Menes, namely the unification of the monarchy and the foundation of the White Wall. If the White Wall had merely been a fortress and not the capital, it is unlikely that the commemoration of its foundation would have figured so prominently in the coronation ceremonial or that the coronation would have been performed within its

[1] §II, 5, 124–8.   [2] Book I, 104.

precincts. Manetho, however, associates the First and Second Dynasties with This, in the neighbourhood of Abydos, but his assertion may be interpreted as meaning that they were of Thinite stock and not that This was their seat of government.

III. THE CEMETERIES OF ABYDOS
AND SAQQARA

The problem of the status of Memphis in the beginning of its history is linked with the difficult question of where the early dynastic kings were buried. Archaeological discovery has shown that rulers were generally buried near their capitals, even if the capital did not coincide with their place of birth. When Amélineau, and subsequently Petrie, uncovered at Abydos several 'tombs' containing objects inscribed with the names of one queen and all the kings of the First Dynasty, and of two kings belonging to the Second Dynasty,[1] it seemed highly probable, particularly in view of the Manethonian tradition connecting these dynasties with This, that the actual sepulchres of the kings had been found. The absence of human remains in the ruined burial-chambers could easily be explained as being due to the operations of robbers. Nevertheless some misgivings concerning the purpose of these 'tombs' were expressed soon after their discovery,[2] but their title was not seriously challenged until 1938, when a large brick mastaba containing sealings with the name of Aha was excavated by W. B. Emery in the early dynastic cemetery of North Saqqara.[3] Further excavations brought to light additional mastabas which, by their contents, could be dated to later kings (and to two queens) of the First Dynasty, and, as a result, the contention of their excavator[4] that among them lie the actual tombs of six of the eight kings who comprised the First Dynasty has been accepted by several authorities.[5] Other writers have felt unwilling to go further than to admit that the weight of evidence is in favour of Saqqara[6] or have preferred to remain neutral.[7]

In almost every respect the problems set by the two cemeteries are different. At Abydos an unbroken series of 'tombs' could be

---

[1] §III, 1; §III, 11; §III, 12.   [2] §III, 9.
[3] §III, 3.   [4] §III, 2, vol. II, 1–4.
[5] §III, 8; §VIII, 23, 150–1, 162–3; §VIII, 24, 41–52, 59–62; §VIII, 48, vol. I, 56.
[6] G, 6, 410–14; §VIII, 17, vol. I, 52–5.
[7] §III, 6, 566–70; §III, 7; §VII, 26, 41, n. 73. For a reconsideration of this problem see A, 9 and 10.

ascribed each to a particular royal owner, not only by mud sealings and other inscribed objects but, in the case of Narmer, Djer, Djet, Den, Mer(it)neith, Semerkhet, Qaa and Peribsen, by stelae bearing their names which stood in pairs, one pair outside each 'tomb'.[1] Although no stelae were recovered from the 'tombs' of Aha, Anedjib and Khasekhemwy, there is no reason to doubt that they were originally provided with them. More than eight hundred subsidiary graves were constructed in trenches around the First Dynasty 'tombs' from the 'tomb' of Djer onwards,[2] and a further five hundred, which were dated to Djer, Djet and Mer(it)neith, were arranged in three hollow rectangles at a short distance to the north-east of the main cemetery.[3] The occupants of these graves, apart from a few domestic animals, were members of the royal harem and persons who had been in the service of the owner of the principal 'tomb',[4] but the discovery of an arm with four bead-bracelets of gold and semi-precious stones, which had been hidden by a robber in a hole in the north wall of the 'tomb' of Djer,[5] left little room for doubt that the burials had also included some women of high rank, perhaps queens. To sum up the problem of the royal 'tombs' at Abydos, it can be said that neither their ownership nor their sepulchral nature is open to question; what is in doubt is whether they were ever occupied or intended to be occupied by those whose names were inscribed on the stelae. If they were mere cenotaphs a further difficulty arises, because some reason must then be found to account for their construction. But first it is necessary to summarize the evidence on which the claim that the real tombs of the First Dynasty kings lie at Saqqara is based.

Near the edge of the escarpment at the north-east corner of the Saqqara necropolis excavations conducted intermittently between 1935 and 1956 revealed twelve large mud-brick mastabas of the First Dynasty, some with subsidiary graves comparable with those which surrounded the royal 'tombs' at Abydos but much less numerous.[6] Like the latter 'tombs' they had been subjected to ruthless pilferage. Structurally, however, they were better preserved and some of the burial-chambers contained human remains. There can be no doubt therefore that these mastabas were actual tombs. The whole problem in this cemetery is the determination of ownership, for none of the mastabas yielded even a

---

[1] G, 24, 78–88; §III, 16; §VIII, 11, 53–4; §VIII, 59, 724–31.
[2] See below, pp. 58–9.　　　　　[3] §III, 13; A, 9.
[4] See below, p. 58.　　　　　[5] §III, 11, 16–19, pl. I.
[6] G, 4; §III, 2; §III, 3; §III, 4.

fragment of a royal stela and only one non-royal stela was found.[1] Inscribed material included in the equipment enabled each mastaba to be dated to a particular reign, but did not provide clear evidence of the identity of the person for whom it was built. That the owners were persons of very high rank is attested both by the quantity and the quality of their funerary equipment and by the size of the mastabas, on average nearly twice as large as the royal 'tombs' at Abydos. Is it to be imagined that even the highest officials would build larger and finer tombs than the kings under whom they held office? If the answer be in the negative it seems necessary to suppose that some of the twelve mastabas at Saqqara belonged to kings and the remainder perhaps to other royal persons of importance. On the evidence of the inscribed objects among their contents two mastabas can be ascribed to queens, Mer(it)neith and Herneith, and one each to Aha, Djet and Anedjib. Since no objects were found bearing the names of either Narmer or Semerkhet, three only of the eight First Dynasty kings remain as claimants for the seven outstanding tombs: Djer, Den and Qaa. For these kings inscriptional evidence provided a choice of three mastabas for Den and two each for Djer and Qaa, the only criteria in the cases of the mastabas of Djer and Den being size and, to some extent, the relative wealth of the funerary equipment.[2] Neither criterion can be regarded as a safe guide because what has survived of the equipment is mainly the result of chance, and determination by size would entail taking into account large mastabas elsewhere, particularly at Naqāda, Tarkhān, Giza and Abu Rawāsh. It is indeed not impossible that the famous mastaba at Naqāda found by De Morgan in 1897[3] was the real tomb of Narmer, although both Queen Neithhotpe and an official whose name is written with three birds, probably ostriches, have undeniable claims to be considered as its owner. The larger of the two mastabas dated to Qaa possessed two features of great interest and perhaps suggestive of royal ownership. The first was an imposing mortuary temple reminiscent, both in its orientation on the north side of the tomb and in its plan, of the mortuary temple of the Step Pyramid of Djoser.[4] Within this temple, in a chamber partly paved with limestone, were found the lower portions of two wooden statues, approximately two-thirds life-size, certainly objects of great rarity at this period.[5] The second, rather enig-

[1] See below, p. 20. [2] §VIII, 24, 42.
[3] G, 24, 118–19; §VIII, 24, 17–22; §VIII, 59, 634–7.
[4] G, 4, 88–90, fig. 53; §III, 2, vol. III, 10, 13, pl. 2; §VIII, 24, 38–41.
[5] §III, 2, vol. III, pl. 27.

matic, feature was the single subsidiary grave situated between the mastaba and the eastern enclosure wall. This grave belonged not to a humble member of the household but to a very high official named Merka whose stela was found lying nearby.[1] So high an official, it may reasonably be supposed, would hardly have been buried in such a relatively simple grave if the owner of the principal tomb were not the king himself.

Excavations at Saqqara have not yet revealed tombs for Peribsen and Khasekhemwy, the two Second Dynasty kings represented in the Abydos cemetery. Nevertheless, a Fourth Dynasty priest named Shery, who was buried at Saqqara,[2] records in his tomb inscriptions that he was the Overseer of the Priests of Peribsen. Since it is unlikely that he would have been buried far from the scene of his official duties, it may be inferred that Shery superintended the mortuary cult of Peribsen at Saqqara and consequently that Peribsen, at least, had built a tomb there. Shery moreover mentions that he served the mortuary cult of Peribsen's predecessor Sened in the same capacity, but Sened's tomb also has not yet been found. A possible clue to the whereabouts of both these tombs may be offered by the existence of two other large tombs cut in the rock beneath the causeway and the mortuary temple of King Unas which have been ascribed, on the evidence of seal impressions, to two of the first three kings of the Second Dynasty, Reneb[3] and Nynetjer.[4] Neither of these two kings nor Sened possessed a 'tomb' at Abydos, so that even if conclusive proof were forthcoming that they were buried at Saqqara they would still fall into a different category from Peribsen. Such as it is, however, the evidence from Saqqara seems to show that the Manethonian tradition, according to which the Third Dynasty was the first dynasty associated with Memphis, need not be interpreted to imply that earlier kings were not buried in the Memphite necropolis at Saqqara.

Later Egyptian history provides several instances of the construction of more than one tomb for a king, the best known perhaps being Djoser's Step Pyramid and South Mastaba at Saqqara and Sneferu's two pyramids at Dahshūr.[5] Thus there is no inherent improbability in the assumption that the kings whose 'tombs' were situated at Abydos were also the possessors of other tombs elsewhere. Architecturally the Abydos 'tombs' display

---

[1] G, 4, 90, pl. 30 (a); §III, 2 vol. III, 13, 30–1, pls. 23, 39.
[2] G, 23, 101–2; §IV, 15, 21, n. 4.
[3] §VIII, 5, 183; §VIII, 11, 45–56; §VIII, 24, 56–9; §VIII, 27, 187–90.
[4] §VIII, 16, 521.   [5] See below, pp. 153 and 162–4

features, including the round-topped stelae, which seem to be Upper Egyptian in origin,[1] whereas the Saqqara mastabas preserve the house-tomb tradition of Lower Egypt;[2] since the dual role of the king was emphasized in so many ways in life it would not be strange if in death he were given two tombs, one as king of Upper Egypt and the other as king of Lower Egypt. The suggestion has, however, been made that the Abydos 'tombs' were constructed for the mock burials of the kings at their Sed-festivals,[3] a later parallel to which may exist in the Eleventh Dynasty 'tomb' of Nebhepetre Mentuhotpe situated within the precincts of his funerary temple and rock-tomb at Deir el-Bahri. Whether this suggestion be right or not it is remarkable how many inscribed objects referring directly or indirectly to Sed-festivals were found at Abydos, whereas very few recognizable allusions occur on objects discovered in the Saqqara mastabas;[4] a limestone relief showing two figures of a king in Heb Sed dress, obtained from the shaft of a Third Dynasty mastaba, is, however, believed to date from the First Dynasty.[5]

Neither of the theories put forward to explain the purpose of the 'tombs' at Abydos can easily be reconciled with the fact that they included one 'tomb' of a queen, but the exceptional privileges which she enjoyed in other respects render her position in the state difficult to determine. A further problem left unresolved is why Abydos should have been chosen as the location of the second tomb, especially if it were intended for the Heb Sed, a festival usually celebrated at Memphis.[6] There is certainly evidence that some of the last predynastic kings of Upper Egypt were buried (or at least built cenotaphs) at Abydos, so that its choice by the kings of the Early Dynastic Period may be explained as merely a continuance of a practice already established, prompted perhaps by a desire to possess temporary residences which they could inhabit when visiting their forbears.[7] But why were the tombs (or the cenotaphs) of these forbears at Abydos if their seat of government lay at Hierakonpolis? If the Manethonian tradition associating the early dynastic kings with This is sound the explanation may be that their immediate ancestors, who were presumably also of Thinite stock, chose to be buried in their place of origin. On the other hand it is possible that even at this

---

[1] §VII, 25.   [2] §VII, 27; §VIII, 48, vol. I, 40–2.   [3] §III, 14, 4–11.
[4] §III, 4, 35–9, pls. 17–8, 64, fig. 26; §III, 14, 13–15, nn. 9, 10, 25.
[5] §III, 2, vol. III, 84, pls. 97–8. See Plate 28 (c).
[6] §I, 7, 28, n. 1, 60; §VII, 4, 122.
[7] §VIII, 24, 50, n. 2; §VIII, 48, vol. I, 56.

early period Abydos was regarded with particular reverence. In later times, when it had become the centre of the cult of Osiris, Sesostris III, Amosis I and Sethos I built cenotaphs, and countless private persons erected stelae, on its sacred territory. It is indeed not illogical to suppose that the early kings chose Abydos as the site for the cenotaphs for the very reason which led to the transference of the dead Osiris from his home in the Delta to Abydos. What the precise reason may have been is problematical, but perhaps it was related to the special attributes of the local god Khentiamentiu, Chief-of-the-Westerners, as the guardian of the dead.

IV. THE SUCCESSORS OF MENES

Manetho declares that, after a reign of sixty-two years, Menes was killed by a hippopotamus. Diodorus, perhaps preserving a more fanciful version of the same tradition, avers that he was attacked by his own dogs when in the neighbourhood of Lake Moeris, but was saved by a crocodile which carried him across the lake to safety. Menes accordingly marked his gratitude by building on the shore of the lake a city—Crocodilopolis—and by decreeing that crocodiles should live and breed in the lake unmolested.[1] The legend, which contains obvious anachronisms, is patently devoid of historical value, an invention by priests of later times who wished to connect their cult with Menes. A scribe's palette in the Berlin Museum bears an inscription which shows that the Greek tradition crediting Menes with the construction of a temple for Ptah at Memphis dates back at least to the Nineteenth Dynasty.[2] If he is to be identified with the Horus Narmer, as seems likely, the occurrence of his name on a rock in the Wādi el-Qash, east of Thebes,[3] indicates that Menes or one of his officers conducted an expedition to the eastern desert, though for what purpose is unknown.

The final year and a half of Aha's reign,[4] which lasted according to Africanus for fifty-seven years and according to Eusebius for twenty-seven years, are probably recorded on the Palermo Stone, but only the biennial royal tour of inspection ($šms\ Hr$)[5] and the creation of a figure of the god Anubis[6] are mentioned. His

---

[1] §II, 6, part II, 207 (Book I, 89). [2] §II, I.

[3] G, 4, 47, fig. 6; §IV, 38, vol. I, 25, pl. XI, I.

[4] G, 3, 157.

[5] See *C.A.H* I³, ch, VI, sect. I; G, I, 32, n. I; G, 8, 13 n. I; §I, 3, 5–7; §I, 18, part I (1960), 131–2; §I, 19, 206. See Plate 25.

[6] G, 8, 13 n. 2; §IV, 23, part II, 19, n. 2.

name, which means the Fighter, was possibly indicative of his character and of the requirements of the time: one of the few extant records of his reign, a wooden label found at Abydos,[1] commemorates a campaign against the Nubians, which may mean that he conducted a war in the northern Sudan or that it was he who extended the southern boundary of Egypt beyond Gebel es-Silsila,[2] its probable limit in the time of Menes, to the Nubian nome terminating at Elephantine. Some other plaques bear representations of Egyptian captives, and one scene is accompanied by an inscription which reads: 'Receiving Upper and Lower Egypt';[3] his main preoccupation therefore appears to have been to consolidate the work of his predecessor in unifying the country and to establish the authority of the Double Crown over the whole length of the Nile Valley from the First Cataract to the Mediterranean coast. As an indication of his policy towards the inhabitants of the Delta, it is significant that he placed on record the foundation of a temple to Neith,[4] the goddess of Sais, which suggests that he was anxious to placate the conquered northerners. According to Manetho, Menes' successor, whom he calls Athothis, was the author of some works on anatomy, a tradition which seems to date back at least to the time of the New Kingdom, for the compiler of the Ebers medical papyrus asserts that a preparation for strengthening the hair was invented for the mother of a king named Teti,[5] who may have been Aha, though it is also possible that the founder of the Sixth Dynasty was the king in question.

In the Abydos king-list the third king of the dynasty is Iti, better known by his Horus-name Djer[6] which has sometimes been incorrectly read as Khent. Seventeen of a total of approximately fifty years occupied by his reign are recorded on the Palermo Stone and the Cairo Annals, but the events mentioned are mainly of religious rather than historical interest. One year, almost exactly in the middle of his reign, is however called 'The Year of smiting the land of Setjet'—a name which, though applied in later times to the whole of western Asia, was probably restricted in the Early Dynastic Period to Sinai;[7] it is tempting to speculate whether the turquoise of the four bracelets found in Djer's 'tomb' at Abydos[8] was not secured as a result of this campaign. Perhaps it also brought about the peaceful conditions

---

[1] §III, 11, pls. III, 2, XI, 1.
[2] §IV, 19, 24 dates this extension to the Third Dynasty.
[3] §III, 11, pl. III, 4.   [4] G, 19, 15; §III, 11, pl. IIIA, 5 and pl. x, 2.
[5] §IV, 40, LXVI, 15–16.   [6] §IV, 22, 58–64 prefers either Sekhty or Ibetj.
[7] §IV, 5.   [8] §III, 11, 16–19, pl. I; §VIII, 58, 27, pl. IIA.

necessary for obtaining the ore for some hundreds of copper objects discovered at Saqqara in the brick mastaba which contained Djer's seal-impressions,[1] but copper in considerable quantities was available nearer home in the eastern desert and the early kings may have mined only turquoise in Sinai. His name is carved on a rock at Wādi Halfa[2] accompanied by a battle scene which, in spite of its damaged condition, affords good evidence that his army reached the Second Cataract. It is possible that he also conducted a campaign against the Libyans.[3] Queen Herneith, whose mud-brick mastaba at Saqqara is dated to his reign, is thought to have been his wife.[4] At a later date which cannot be precisely fixed, his 'tomb' at Abydos was regarded as the grave of Osiris[5] and, in consequence, underwent some structural alterations in the Eighteenth Dynasty; the vast numbers of pots deposited there by pilgrims led the Arabs to call its immediate neighbourhood Umm el-Qaāb, 'The Mother of Pots', a name it has retained to the present day.

Manetho omits from his list both Djer and his successor Djet[6] and substitutes for them the names Kenkenēs and Uenephēs. Uenephēs can hardly be anything but a faulty transcription of the Egyptian *wnn-nfr*, normally rendered Ὀννῶφρις, a synonym for Osiris,[7] particularly in view of the supposed connexion of Osiris with the 'tomb' of Djer; a different kind of confusion may have led to the introduction of Kenkenēs.[8] The fourth king in the Abydos list is called Ita,[9] a name which is not far unlike Iterty, found on a label in conjunction with the Horus Djet[10] and is thought to be his *nbty*-name.[11] Historical details of his reign are exceedingly sparse, but nothing in the archaeological evidence now available suggests that any break of continuity occurred in the political and cultural development observable under his predecessors. One of his subjects, possibly the leader of an expedition, scratched the king's name on a rock in the Wādi Miāh, some fifteen miles east of Edfu along a route known to have been used in Ptolemaic times

---

[1] §III, 2, vol. I, 20–57, pls. 4–6, 8–10.

[2] G, 4, 59–60, fig. 22; §IV, 3, 27–30, fig. I, pl. 10; §VI, 1, 39–40, fig. 5; A, 15, 75, fig. 6.

[3] G, 4, 60, fig. 23; §III, 2, vol. I, 60, fig. 31.

[4] G, 4, 60; §III, 2, vol. III, 73, 94.   [5] §IV, 1.

[6] Other readings of this name are: Wadji (§IV, 20, 282–4, but see §IV, 2 and §IV, 23, part II, 7 n. 1), Edjo (G, 6, 405), Djait (Edjo) or Djaiti ([Edjot] §IV, 13), Wadj (§IV, 22, 64–6).

[7] §I, 14, 11; §IV, 25, 65.   [8] See below, p. 26.

[9] §I, 14, 9 gives Itiu.   [10] §III, 2, vol. II, 102, fig. 105, pl. 35.

[11] §IV, 12.

by caravans proceeding from the Nile Valley to the port of Berenice on the Red Sea coast.[1] Meagre though this information is, it suggests that Djet was able to despatch expeditions, of either a military or a commercial character, outside the Nile Valley.

One of the most puzzling personages of the Early Dynastic Period is Mer(it)neith. Theophorous names compounded with Neith usually belonged to women, and consequently most authorities have deduced that Mer(it)neith was female;[2] the rule, however, is not invariable.[3] None of the instances adduced for the spelling of this name with the inclusion of the feminine termination *t* is free from doubt,[4] but its omission in hieroglyphic writing at this period would not necessarily have any grammatical significance. It is at least clear that no king was intended, for the royal titles are never prefixed. If Mer(it)neith was a woman she must have attained a position seldom, if ever, equalled by a member of her sex in early dynastic times. One inscription mentions her treasury,[5] which suggests that she possessed sovereign status. Her 'tomb' at Abydos[6] differed in no material respect from the 'tombs' of the kings: like Djer and Djet she was provided with attendants, some of whom were interred within her own complex and others in the neighbouring cemetery.[7] One peculiar feature, however, was the absence of any jar-sealings bearing her name; when a name occurred it was in nearly every instance that of Djet's successor Den, but the sealings were for the most part different in design and content from those found in Den's own 'tomb'. Some examples appear more primitive than the sealings of Den and it may not be without significance that a piece of ivory inscribed with the name of Mer(it)neith was found in the tomb of Djer,[8] while at least one of her jar-sealings bore the name of Djet's vineyard.[9] From this slender evidence it may be conjectured that she was born in the time of Djer and that she died early in Den's reign; the equipment and construction of the mastaba at Saqqara,[10] which contained objects and jar-sealings inscribed with her name,[11] would seem to support this dating—a deduction which need not depend on whether Mer(it)neith was in reality the owner. As a mere hypothesis it may be suggested that she served as regent, perhaps while Den was still a minor, and

[1] §IV, 8.

[2] G, 3, 140–1; G, 6, 412; §IV, 29, 154–5; §IV, 35, 29–30.

[3] §IV, 20, 303.   [4] §IV, 29, 148–55; §IV, 35, 29, n. 6.

[5] §III, 12, pl. v, 2.   [6] §III, 12, 10–11, pls. LXI, LXIV and LXV.

[7] §III, 13, pl. XVIII.   [8] §III, 11, pl. v, 6.   [9] §III, 12, pl. XX, 20.

[10] G, 4, 66–8 fig. 30; §III, 2, vol. II, 128–70, pls. 38–56.

[11] G, 4, 65, fig. 28; §III, 2, vol. II, 169, fig. 226.

died before relinquishing the office. Such a position could only
have been occupied by a woman if she had been a queen, which
might imply that she was the wife of Djet and the mother of
Den.[1]

Two features, which subsequently became characteristic of
royalty, make their first appearance on objects dating from the
time of Den:[2] one is the so-called double crown (*shmty*, 'the two
powerful ones') and the other a title (perhaps read in this period
as *niswt-bity*, but later having the phonetic value *ni-sw-bit*, the
literal meaning of which is 'He who belongs to the sedge and the
bee'.[3] In effect, the title means 'King of Upper and Lower
Egypt', though in origin it may have referred particularly to the
towns of Heracleopolis[4] and Sais.[5] As the King of Upper and
Lower Egypt, Den's name was written with a hieroglyphic depicting hill-country repeated twice; this group possesses two
values, Khasty (*h3sty*) and Semty (*smty*), and it is not clear which
reading should be adopted in this instance. The later Egyptians
themselves experienced some difficulty with the name, but for a
different reason: when written cursively in ink the hieroglyph for
hill-country resembled two other signs, which in duplicate would
read Septy and Qenqen respectively. Hence Khasty or Semty
appears on the Abydos list as Septy, and Manetho reproduces the
same reading, but with its later value Hesepty, and transcribes it
into Greek as Usaphais. The introduction of Kenkenēs instead
of Djer into Manetho's First Dynasty may have originated with
some scribe who, when copying two possibly incomplete manuscripts, included both Qenqen of one document and Septy of the
other without realizing that they stood for the same king.[6]

Although the surviving archaeological material from the time
of Den is considerable, very few details of his personal history
are known. A recently discovered fragment naming Den has
proved that the fourteen years of a king, chronicled in the third
line of the Palermo Stone, refer to his reign[7] and are not the annals
of his successor Anedjib, as was once supposed.[8] That he was an
energetic and enterprising ruler who encouraged the arts and
crafts and developed the administrative machinery of the kingdom
is evident. Two of his officials, Hemaka and Ankhka, are men-

---

[1] §VIII, 46, 26 suggests that she was the daughter of Djet and the wife of Den.

[2] Other readings of this name are Nidjeret (§I, 28, 119, n. 1), Niudiu (§IV, 19,
21), Dwn (§IV, 22, 66–9), Udimu (§IV, 35, 39–41).

[3] G, 7, 50, n. 1, 73–4; G, 17, 44–6, 49–50.

[4] *C.A.H.* I¹, 266, n. 1.   [5] §I, 31, 66–70; §IV, 28, 68–75.

[6] §I, 14, 10–11; §IV, 29, 148–55. Cf. §IV, 22, 67–9.

[7] §I, 18, part II (1961), 45; §IV, 29; A, 2.   [8] §IV, 35, 47–8.

tioned by name on many contemporary dockets and jar-sealings.[1] In quantity, the objects recovered from the mastaba at Saqqara attributed at the time of its discovery to Hemaka represent the largest single collection of funerary equipment so far discovered in any tomb of the Early Dynastic Period.[2] An ivory docket from Abydos shows the king smiting a kneeling Asiatic with a mace— a scene which is described in the accompanying inscription as 'The First Time of smiting the East(erners)';[3] whether this docket is to be interpreted as a record of an historical event, signifying a military campaign against the inhabitants of Sinai or the nomads of the eastern desert, or merely as commemorating a ceremonial episode is a matter for conjecture. Possibly the 'Easterners' were the same people as the 'Nomads' (*iwntiw*) mentioned in the third line of the Palermo Stone as the victims of a similar fate. Two other dockets from Abydos, which also agree with an entry on the Palermo Stone, record incidents in the king's *Sed*-festival,[4] which in later times often marked the conclusion of thirty years' rule; its position on the stone certainly indicates that the festival occurred early in the second half of a reign which may have exceeded fifty-five years. In later times Den acquired a legendary reputation as the king in whose time certain spells in the Book of the Dead were found,[5] and his name also figures in connexion with medical prescriptions in the Ebers papyrus[6] and in the Berlin medical papyrus.[7]

Anedjib followed the example of Den in adopting the title 'King of Upper and Lower Egypt', but usually combined with it a new title composed of two falcons on perches.[8] This title (*nbwy*—'The Two Lords') identified the king with Horus and Seth, symbolizing Lower and Upper Egypt respectively. His personal name was Merpe (or Merpebia), which appears as Merbapen in the Saqqara list and Miebis[9] in Manetho. Such archaeological evidence as is now available seems to indicate that his reign was short, which may explain why his 'tomb' at Abydos was the poorest in construction and least productive in material remains of any king of the First Dynasty.[10] Again, the missing portion of the royal annals between the Palermo and the Cairo fragments is not believed to have contained more than fourteen

[1] §III, 4; §III, 12, pls. XXI, XXII, XXV; §IV, 20, 304–6.
[2] G, 4, 75–6; §III, 4.
[3] §IV, 29, 150, fig. 3; §IV, 37; §VIII, 13, 283, fig. 154. See Plate 28 (*b*).
[4] §III, 12, pls. XI, 5, 14, XIV, 12, XV, 16; §VIII, 57, 119, fig. 34.
[5] §IV, 6, chs. 64 and 130.   [6] §IV, 9, 119.   [7] §IV, 39, 33.
[8] G, 17, 37–8; §VII, 17, part I, 63–71.   [9] §IV, 7.
[10] G, 4, 80–1; §III, 12, 12–13, pls. 65–6; §III, 1, pl. LVIII.

year-frames; within the gap it is necessary to fit the whole of Anedjib's reign and an unkown number of years of the reign of Den.[1] A claim sometimes advanced for Anedjib that he was the first king to reside in Memphis is based solely on the unexpected occurrence of his name at the head of the Saqqara king-list, Menes and his four immediate successors being omitted.

According to the Cairo fragment of the royal annals, which preserves his reign in its entirety,[2] Semerkhet ruled for eight years and some months. His personal name underwent in the course of time vicissitudes of a kind closely analogous to those already noted in the case of Den. A hieroglyphic sign, which represented a man clothed in a long garment and holding a stick and which seems to have had the consonantal value of *iry-ntr*,[3] was mistaken for a very similar sign reading *smsw* or *smsm*; the name thus appears in the Turin Canon as Semsem and in Manetho as Semempsēs. In place of the *nbwy*-title adopted by Anedjib, Semerkhet combined the *nbty* (Two Ladies) with the 'King of Upper and Lower Egypt' title, for reasons which are now obscure. Several of the fragments of stone vases found in his 'tomb' at Abydos had originally borne the names of Mer(it)neith, Den or Anedjib, but Mer(it)neith and Anedjib were invariably erased.[4] Examples of the inclusion of vessels inscribed with the names of preceding kings are not uncommon in tombs of this period, and the erasures made in this instance suggest that Semerkhet wished to disown two of his predecessors, perhaps regarding them as usurpers; why Den should have been treated with greater respect is not evident. It is strange that Semerkhet's *Sed*-festival, which is shown on fragments of vases from Abydos,[5] appears not to be mentioned in the Cairo Annals, unless it was included in one of the two year-frames of this reign which are now illegible. Manetho's statement that a very serious calamity befell Egypt under Semerkhet is not confirmed by contemporary records.

Inscriptions of Qaa, the eighth and last king of the First Dynasty, show identical Horus and personal names; Sen, which sometimes takes the place of Qaa after the *nbty*-title, is probably not a name but is the verb 'to embrace', the meaning of the whole group being 'The Two Ladies embrace (the Horus Qaa)'.[6] The Abydos and Saqqara king-lists and also the Turin Canon give his personal name as Qebeḥ(u), which apparently owes its origin to a

[1] §I, 18, part II, 43, fig. I. [2] §IV, 17, pl. XXV.
[3] §IV, 20, 284–8. Cf. §I, 14, 9, n. *b*. [4] §III, 12, 5, 19, pls. V, 5, VI, 9–11.
[5] §III, 12, pl. VII, 5, 6.
[6] §III, 11, pl. VIII, 2, 3; §III, 12, pl. XII, 2. See, however, G, 13, 1008, n. 1615.

twofold error: in the first instance Qaa was misread as Qeb and subsequently the latter was confused with Qebeḥ(u), a mistake made possible by the fact that, in hieroglyphic writing, *qb* and *qbḥ* shared a common determinative.[1] Scarcely any information regarding his reign, apart from the bare assertion that he lived to celebrate his second *Sed*-festival,[2] can be extracted either from the numerous objects found in his 'tomb' at Abydos or from the inscribed stone vessels of his time buried under Djoser's pyramid. Some of his jar-sealings show the name of Semerkhet erased;[3] Anedjib's name, on the other hand, was allowed to stand, which suggests that Qaa regarded his predecessor with the same disfavour as Semerkhet, in his turn, had evinced towards Anedjib. A relic of Semerkhet's unpopularity may perhaps be detected in his omission from the Nineteenth Dynasty Saqqara list, which includes both Anedjib and Qaa.

Nothing is known of the circumstances in which the First Dynasty came to an end. Manetho concludes the dynasty with a king named Biēnechēs or Ubienthēs, both of which seem to represent Baunetjer of the Turin and Saqqara lists.[4] Contemporary inscriptions mention two problematical Horus-names in conjunction with sacred buildings known to have belonged to Qaa. One of these names is written with a single hieroglyph representing a bird, the true reading of which has not yet been determined;[5] the other name may be read Seneferka, Sekanefer or Neferseka.[6] If the owners of these names were independent rulers they were probably ephemeral followers of Qaa. There is certainly no clear evidence that Qaa's sovereignty was ever challenged by a rival line of dynasts or that the end of his reign was marked by untoward happenings affecting the normal course of succession. The Turin Canon enumerates the kings of the First and Second Dynasties in unbroken sequence, giving the first indication of a break in continuity at the beginning of the Third Dynasty.[7] Of the length of time occupied by the First Dynasty, widely divergent estimates have been given by modern historians using the same data.[8] Contemporary annals, mainly in the form of ivory and wooden dockets, show that regnal years were not numbered, as in later times, but were named after some important event, usually

---

[1] §I, 14, 10–11; §IV, 35, 25–7, 41.

[2] §I, 10, part II, 159, pl. I, 4; §IV, 23, part II, 24–5. *Ibid.* part I, pl. 8, no. 41.

[3] §III, 12, 26.   [4] §I, 14, 15. See below, p. 30.   [5] §IV, 23, part II, 54.

[6] §III, 2, vol. III, 11, 31, pl. 38, 1; §IV, 23, part I, 4, 15, pl. 17, no. 86. *Ibid.* part II, 40, n. 1; §VII, 14, 12–14, fig. 15; §VII, 15, 380.

[7] G, 15, 124–5.   [8] See *C.A.H.* I³, ch. VI, sect. I.

of a religious character.[1] So few dockets of this kind have however been preserved that they are useless for compiling even a
skeleton chronology of the period. The Fifth Dynasty Palermo
Stone and Cairo Annals, though invaluable, have proved to be
capable of more than one reconstruction. Manetho gives an
aggregate of 253 years for the dynasty, but the figures attributed
to the individual reigns total 263 years—a number which seems
too high to be reconciled with the annals, even after making the
maximum allowance for the lacunae.[2]

Little more than the names and order of succession of the kings
belonging to the first part of the Second Dynasty has yet been
established with any probability; of their deeds and the political
conditions of their time virtually nothing is known. An inscription
on the shoulder of a stone statuette, thought to date from the end of
the Second Dynasty,[3] in the Cairo Museum gives the Horus-names
of the first three kings, Hetepsekhemwy, Reneb and Nynetjer,
probably in their right order.[4] The apparent inversion of the names
of Hetepsekhemwy and Reneb on a stone vessel found in the pyramid temple of Mycerinus,[5] although disconcerting, has been
plausibly explained as the result of a usurpation by Reneb.[6] Hetepsekhemwy ('The Two Powers are at peace') bore the personal name
Hetep which, when written in hieratic, was misread so that it appears
as Bedjau in the Abydos list, and the hieratic writing of Bedjau
was in turn misinterpreted to give Baunetjer of the Turin Canon
and the Saqqara list.[7] Bedjau is however preserved in Manetho as
Boēthos and Bōchos. The name Bedjapu, which occurs before five
kings of the Fourth and Fifth Dynasties on a writing-board of the
Fifth Dynasty found at Giza, may also be derived from Bedjau.[8]

Reneb (Re is [my] Lord), whose tomb-stela is now in the
Metropolitan Museum,[9] provides the earliest example of a royal
name compounded with the name of the sun-god of Heliopolis,
which suggests that the cult of this deity, although not destined
to attain full power until the Old Kingdom, was already temporarily in the ascendant. Presumably Reneb is to be identified with
Kakau of the New Kingdom lists and Kaiechōs of Manetho, but
the explanation remains to be discovered. Either he or Nynetjer
bore the personal name Nubnefer.[10] Nynetjer in any case possessed a

---

[1] §IV, 27.　　　　　　　　　[2] §IV, 31. See *C.A.H.* I³, ch. VI, sect. I.
[3] §VIII, 11, 45–6, fig. 1; §VIII, 57, 15, pl. 2ᵇ.
[4] Cf. §I, 14, 12; §IV, 23, part I, 13, no. 58. *Ibid.* part II, 31, n. 3.
[5] See G. A. Reisner, *Mycerinus*, 102–3, pl. 70ᶜ.
[6] §VIII, 11, 46–7. Cf. §VIII, 55, 45, n. 2.　　　　　　[7] §I, 14, 12.
[8] §IV, 32.　　　　　　　　[9] §VIII, 11, 48–53. See Plate 28 (*a*).
[10] §I, 14, 13–14; §IV, 23, part II, 49; §VIII, 11, 45, n. 2.

personal name which was identical with his Horus-name; it is this name which the Abydos and Saqqara lists reproduce in the corrupt forms Banetjeren and Banetjeru followed by Manetho who reads Binōthris. Although nearly half of Nynetjer's reign is recorded on the Palermo Stone, the only historical fact which can be ascertained is that he ruled for about thirty-eight years; the entries on the stone, apart from enumerating the biennial censuses of the king's property, refer exclusively to the construction of buildings and the celebration of various festivals. His immediate successors, Weneg[1] and Sened, are even more obscure. Vases inscribed with the name of Weneg, and certainly dating from his time, were found under the Step Pyramid.[2] Sened, although known from a fragment of an inscribed vase discovered at Giza,[3] is better attested by inscriptions in the Fourth Dynasty tomb at Saqqara, whose owner styles himself 'Overseer of the Priests of Sened in the (Saqqara) necropolis, Shery'.[4] The names of both kings appear in the later lists, Sened (Sethenēs in Manetho) without undergoing any radical change of form, but Weneg, owing to a scribal misunderstanding, becoming Wadjnes, literally 'Green-of-Tongue', which in Coptic would be rendered Wet-las and which Manetho gives as Tlas. In view of the professed association of the second king of the dynasty with the solar cult, it is perhaps significant that Weneg should have been chosen as a royal name, because a god Weneg, who must have been venerated in early times, is described in the Pyramid Texts of the Fifth and Sixth Dynasties as the 'son of Re'.[5]

Shery, besides being a priest of Sened, served the mortuary cult of the next king of the Second Dynasty, Peribsen, in the same capacity.[6] Peribsen's name, in contemporary inscriptions, is preceded not by the traditional Horus-title, but by the Seth-title and, in one instance, by Seth-Re.[7] An interesting commentary on this new title is provided by one of his seal-impressions which reads: 'The Ombite (i.e. Seth) hath given the Two Lands to his son Peribsen'.[8] The discovery in his 'tomb' at Abydos of jar-sealings inscribed variously with the Seth Peribsen and with the Horus Sekhemib (*nłswt-błty* and *nbty* Sekhemib Perenmaat) led to the deduction, which has, however, not gained universal acceptance,

---

[1] §iv, 20, 288–92.   [2] §iv, 23, part ii, 50, 53.
[3] See U. Hölscher, *Das Grabdenkmal des Königs Chefren*, 106.
[4] §iv, 15, 21, n. 4; §iv, 20, 294. See above, p. 20.
[5] §iv, 20, 289; §vii, 31, vol. iii, 126. *Ibid.* vol. iv, 238.
[6] §iv, 20, 294. See above, p. 20.
[7] G, 17, 25, fig. 41; §iii, 11, pl. xxi, 176.   [8] §iii, 11, pl. xxii, 190.

that the two names were borne by one king who discarded his original Horus-name and title and adopted a new name with the title of Seth.[1] It is unfortunate that the evidence on this point is equivocal, for the problem has a vital bearing both on the assessment of Peribsen's claim to the throne and on the interpretation of some records of historical importance belonging to the Horus Khasekhem.[2] If Peribsen was not originally a Horus-king, he may not have been of Hierakonpolite stock, but may perhaps have been a native of some place in the province of the god Seth, whose centre was Ombos, the modern Naqāda. In that event it is conceivable that Peribsen and Khasekhem ruled concurrently, the former over the territory north of Gebelein and the latter over the region between Gebelein and the First Cataract; a state of affairs implying that the unity of the kingdom was temporarily broken would thus have existed.[3] If, on the other hand, Peribsen ascended the throne as the Horus Sekhemib, no Ombite ancestry or division of authority need be postulated, but it must be supposed that the change of name and title was governed by religious or political causes. There is, however, evidence that the early dynastic kings were always closely associated with both Horus and Seth,[4] and consequently the substitution of one deity for the other in the royal titulary need not point to changes of a revolutionary nature. Nevertheless, the innovation was certainly not without its significance, and it is at least arguable from the title Seth-Re that Peribsen was responsible for introducing the cult of Seth into Heliopolis.

The monuments of Khasekhem are chiefly characterized by their emphasis on his military achievements. One of the most graphic is a fragmentary relief which, when complete, showed the king kneeling on a prostrate Nubian, whose body, like that of the Northerner on the palette of Narmer, was depicted in the shape of the hieroglyph for foreign land;[5] beneath the scene is an inscription reading 'Excellent Sandal against foreign lands, the Horus Khasekhem'—an epithet which appears to have been no idle boast. Another reference to a campaign in the south may perhaps be detected in a scene carved on a number of commemorative vases which represent the vulture-goddess Nekhbet before the *serekh* of the king binding the symbolical plants of Upper and Lower Egypt with one claw and holding in the other a ring containing

[1] §iv, 20 295; §iv, 35, 36. Cf. G, 30, 119–24; §iv, 14, 322–33; §iv, 23, part ii, 43.
[2] See below, p. 33.   [3] §iii, 8, 162 ff.; §iv, 26, 41.
[4] §iv, 14, 318–24. See below, p. 36.
[5] G, 4, 100, fig. 64; G, 26, pl. lvii. See G. Godron, *Chron. d'Eg.* 43, no. 85 (1968), 34–5.

two hieroglyphic signs spelling the word Besh.[1] The interpretation of Besh is, however, extremely problematical; at different times it has been explained as the personal name of the king,[2] as the name of a Libyan people dwelling in the neighbourhood of El-Kāb[3] and as a more northern Libyan tribe domiciled near the Faiyūm.[4] The title of the scene, 'The Year of fighting and smiting the Northerners', favours the last interpretation, but no final proof is yet forthcoming. Khasekhem's most important campaigns were certainly conducted in the north, and it is to these wars that the reliefs and inscriptions on the bases of his two statuettes refer,[5] although the number of slain recorded—47,209 on one statuette and on the other 48,205—is certainly hyperbolical. Such campaigns within the confines of Egypt itself can only have been necessitated by a breakdown in the authority of the crown; it is difficult to believe that the circumstances which led to the adoption of the Seth-title by Peribsen were not ultimately the cause of Khasekhem's military exploits. An imaginative account of his struggle may perhaps be contained in the so-called Myth of Horus,[6] which is inscribed on a wall in the Ptolemaic temple of Edfu. According to this text, Horus, accompanied by his harpooners (*msntiw*), defeated the followers of Seth, who assumed the forms of crocodiles and hippopotami, in a series of river battles between Edfu and the sea-coast. Having completed the conquest, Horus returned southwards to quell an insurrection at Shashert in Nubia and, after accomplishing this task, he divided among his followers the territory which had previously been controlled by the adherents of Seth. While the general purport of the myth is not inconsistent with the victories recorded on the monuments of Khasekhem, the possibility that it reflects events of a later period, such as the expulsion of the Hyksos or the overthrow of the Persians, cannot be excluded. It is at least unlikely that Khasekhem's northern campaign occurred during the lifetime of Peribsen, for if Peribsen had been defeated in battle it is hard to understand how he came to have a 'tomb' at Abydos,[7] unless the 'tomb' was built and partly equipped while Peribsen was still alive and, for some reason was not dismantled after his defeat. If, however, the monuments of Khasekhem describe a struggle for the kingship which followed the death of Peribsen, the existence of the 'tomb' would not be

---

[1] G, 4, 99, fig. 63; G, 25, pls. xxxvi–xxxviii; §iv, 20, 299–300; §iv, 23, part i, 10, pl. 3, no. 18; §viii, 40, 317, pl. 66.
[2] G, 6, 418; §iv, 35, 34–5.
[3] G, 17, 25; §iv, 34, 25–7.
[4] §vi, 20, 21. See also G, 13, 1018, n. 1645.
[5] G, 25, pls. xxxix–xl.
[6] §iv, 4; §iv, 10; §iv, 26, 42–4; §vi, 33, 7–8.
[7] §iii, 11, 11–12.

surprising, because subsequent developments suggest that a policy of appeasement towards the adherents of Seth was soon introduced.

An even more perplexing question than Khasekhem's connexion with Peribsen is whether the former is to be identified with Khasekhemwy or was succeeded by him. Alone among the kings of Egypt, Khasekhemwy adopted the dual title of Horus and Seth. His *serekh* frequently contains his personal name, Nebwy Hetepimef, added to his official name, and the group thus written may be rendered 'The Horus and Seth Khasekhemwy, the Two Lords (i.e. Horus and Seth) are at peace in him'.[1] It seems clear, therefore, that a reconciliation had been effected between the followers of the two deities; whether it occurred under Khasekhem, whose name was altered to Khasekhemwy in order to signalize the event, or under a different king called Khasekhemwy from the time of his coronation, cannot be deduced with any certainty. The absence of a 'tomb' at Abydos which may be ascribed to Khasekhem, whereas the 'tomb' of Khasekhemwy in that cemetery has been found,[2] and the similarity of the two names support the conjecture that Khasekhem and Khasekhemwy represent only one person; on the other hand, it may be argued that the conditions for bringing about the reconciliation would have been more favourable under a new king.

As a consequence of the restoration of peace and order, a marked advance in technical achievements occurred under Khasekhemwy. According to the Palermo Stone, which preserves the records of the last six of the seventeen years of his reign, a copper statue of the king was made in his fifteenth regnal year,[3] showing that the figures of Phiops I and Merenre found at Hierakonpolis were by no means the first to be produced in that metal. It is also stated that two years previously he built a temple of stone named 'The Goddess Endures'—an assertion which finds support in the fact that the chamber of his Abydos 'tomb' was composed of hewn limestone. Moreover, fragments of granite door-jambs carved with inscriptions and reliefs which were found at Hierakonpolis and at El-Kāb display a thorough mastery over this stone.[4] In these and in many other respects it is evident that the reign of Khasekhemwy was culturally the forerunner of the Old Kingdom. He was closely related to Djoser, the second king of the Third Dynasty, whose mother was almost certainly the

---

[1] G, 6, 417. Cf. §IV, 14, 325–6.   [2] §III, 11, 12–14.
[3] §IV, 36. Cf. G, 8, 13, n. 2.
[4] G, 25, pl. II; §IV, 24, 44, fig. 11; §IV, 33.

'Mother of the King's Children', Nymaathap. Jar-sealings bearing her name were discovered in the Abydos 'tomb' of Khasekhemwy and consequently it has sometimes been supposed that she was Khasekhemwy's queen. In the Turin Papyrus, however, the accession of Djoser is marked as the beginning of a new dynasty,[1] which, if he was the son of Khasekhemwy, would be surprising. It seems possible, therefore, that Nymaathap was Khasekhemwy's only child and that she married a prince who was not in the direct line of succession.[2]

Contemporary records of the later kings in the Second Dynasty differ widely from the names in the New Kingdom king-lists. The Turin Canon and the Saqqara list give as the successors of Sened: Aka[3] (or Neferkare), Neferkasokar, Hudjefa and Bebty (or Beby). The Abydos list mentions only Djadja. Both Bebty and Djadja may be misreadings of a hieratic writing of Khasekhemwy,[4] while Hudjefa has been explained as being originally intended not as a name but as a scribal note meaning 'lacuna'.[5] Manetho's last four kings in the dynasty bear the names Chairēs, Nefercherēs, Sesōchris and Chenerēs. To these kings alone he ascribes reigns which in aggregate amount to 120 years. His total of 302 years for the whole dynasty, however, exceeds estimates based on other sources of evidence by about a century.[6]

V. ROYALTY AND THE STATE

The whole structure of the Egyptian constitution was founded on the general acceptance of the doctrine that its rulers were divine.[7] Throughout the Early Dynastic Period, with the exception of the reigns of Peribsen and Khasekhemwy, every king bore the title of Horus and thus signalized his claim to be the earthly embodiment of that deity; Peribsen and Khasekhemwy modified this practice only to the extent of adopting a different divine identity. At death, when a new incarnation of Horus had succeeded to the throne, the deceased king surrendered the right to his Horus-titles; for this reason the New Kingdom royal lists consistently enumerate the kings under their personal names, to which the *nbty*-title had generally been prefixed in contemporary inscriptions.[8] Perhaps the fact of deification was considered as implicit

[1] G, 15, 124–5.   [2] §IV, 21, 140. Cf. below, pp. 145–53.
[3] Turin Canon II, 25; G, 6, 416; §I, 8, 15   [4] §I, 14, 13.
[5] See below, p. 149; §I, 14, 14–15; §IV, 18.   [6] See below, pp. 147–8.
[7] §V, 1; §V, 2; §V, 9, 172–9; §V, 10.   [8] §IV, 7, 348–9; §IV, 20, 282, n. 2.

in the assumption of kingship and needed to be marked by no special ceremony either at the coronation or at the jubilee festival (*Heb Sed*), when the principal ceremonies of the coronation were re-enacted. The royal annals describe the coronation as the 'Rising of the King of Upper Egypt, Rising of the King of Lower Egypt, Union of the Two Lands and Procession around the Wall', which suggests that the ritual was mainly intended to commemorate the early division of the land into two kingdoms, the unification of these kingdoms under one crown and the foundation of Memphis by Menes. Being a deity, the king was doubtless entitled to the same degree of reverence from his subjects as other gods and he, in turn, was expected to conform with the supposed divine code of behaviour. Like the gods, he married and had children. Several of the queens of the Early Dynastic Period are known by name: Neithhotpe, Mer(it)neith, Herneith and Nymaathap are the only queens who figure in contemporary inscriptions, but the Cairo Annals record that Khenthap and Betrest (?) were the mothers of Djer and Semerkhet respectively, and it may therefore be assumed that they were the wives of Aha and Anedjib. The fact that the mothers are mentioned in this manner strongly suggests that the right of succession to the throne was, already at the beginning of Egyptian history, transmitted through the principal queen, who was variously called 'She who unites the Two Lords' (*sm3wt nbwy*),[1] 'She who sees Horus and Seth' (*m33t Ḥr Stḫ*) and 'Mother of the King's Children' (*mwt msw nїswt*). Princes and princesses are seldom mentioned by name at this period, but princesses seated on litters are occasionally included in representations of ceremonies, sometimes accompanied by their tutor (*wr ḥts*).[2] Normally the royal family lived together in the palace (*ꜥḥ*), built mainly of mud brick; no early example of such a building has yet been discovered, but it is not unlikely that the façade is reproduced in the design of the *serekh* (literally, proclaimer), within which the Horus-name of the king was written. The interior of the palace was probably divided into official and domestic quarters, the latter comprising the harem (*ỉpt*), the 'Mansion of Life' or royal dining-room (*ḥwt ꜥnḫ*),[3] wine-cellar (*ḥwt ỉrp* and *ḫnty*),[4] the slaughter-house (*nmt*), and certainly many other sections which are not specified in extant inscriptions. Courtiers, whose numbers must have been very considerable, were graded according to their position, the most

---

[1] A. Klasens (§III, 2, vol. III, 93) renders 'She who is united with the Two Lords'

[2] §v, 5, 111–20. [3] §v, 3, 83–91.

[4] §v, 7, vol. II, 64.

exalted being the 'Controller of the Two Thrones' (*ḥrp nsty*),[1] 'He who is at the head of the King' (*ḥry tp nìswt*), and possibly several bearing the title 'One concerned with Royal Affairs' (*ìry ḥt nìswt*).

In virtue of his supposedly divine nature, the king ruled as an absolute monarch with complete authority over both secular and religious affairs. He was, however, assisted by a body of officials whose titles, found on seal-impressions, fragments of stone vases and other 'documents', constitute the chief, though lamentably inadequate, source of information for reconstructing, in broad outline, the political and social organization developed by Menes and his immediate successors.[2] As in later times, the administration was centred on the capital and had its branches in the provinces. At the head of the central administration stood the 'King's House' (*pr nìswt*), which exercised jurisdiction not only over such matters as were considered to be the sole prerogative of the king, but also over all the other government departments. Perhaps the records from which the archivists of the Fifth Dynasty compiled the Palermo Stone and its congeners in the museums of Cairo and University College were kept in the 'King's House'. Usually, as its name implies, the king presided in person over this House, with the 'Master of the Secrets of the (Royal) Decrees' (*ḥry sštз n wḏt mdw*) as his principal lieutenant, a 'Companion' (*smr pr nìswt*)[3] serving as a senior official and a body of scribes to perform the clerical duties. The suggestion has been made that a hieroglyphic group *ṯt*, borne by a person who is represented in company with the king's sandal-bearer and other royal attendants on the slate palette and mace-head of Narmer, is to be explained as an early method of writing the title *ṯзty*[4] which, in the Old Kingdom and later, signified 'Vizier'. It seems more likely, however, that *ṯt* is to be connected either with *wṯt* 'beget', so that it would signify 'son', 'crown-prince'[5] or with *зṯt* 'tutor'.[6] Nevertheless the title *ṯзty* is attested by vase-inscriptions dating from before the time of Djoser,[7] all with reference to a certain Menka, but its bearer may not have occupied the same exalted position as the viziers of the Old Kingdom. Menka's two other titles 'He of the Curtain' (*ṯзyty*) and 'Judge' (*sзb*), however, show that the office was already one of great importance. Perhaps the

---

[1] §I, 10, part II, 164, 168.
[2] §III, 2, vol. III, 30–6; §IV, 23, part II, 57–72; §V, 6; §V, 11, 301–5.
[3] §III, 12, 45.
[4] G, 5, text vol. I, 19*; G, 16, vol. I, sect. 208. Cf. §V, 6, 16 and §V, 9, 179, n. 3.
[5] §VII, 31, vol. I, 11.   [6] §V, 8.
[7] See below, p. 160; P. Lacau, *Annuaire du Collège de France*, 46ᵉ année, 133; §V 6, 56, n. 8; §VIII, 59, 947, fig. 623.

3

highest administrative official was the 'Chancellor' (*sḏꜣwty*), who was in charge of the White House (*pr ḥḏ*) and the Red House (*pr dšr*), as the Treasuries of Upper and Lower Egypt were called, after the national colours of the Two Lands.[1] His staff consisted of one or more 'assistants' (*ḥry ꜥ*) and 'scribes' (*sš*). Their functions, in so far as they can be deduced, comprised not only the supervision of national revenue, which included, by the end of the Second Dynasty, the organization of the biennial 'census of gold and of fields', but also the collection and distribution of various stores, such as oils and certain other products which were levied as taxes. In such capacities they probably played a leading part in the biennial royal tour of inspection, the 'Following of Horus' (*šmsw Ḥr*)[2] recorded on the Palermo Stone. Together with the King's House, the two Treasuries received the wine from the royal vineyards, apparently situated in the neighbourhood of Memphis[3] and always supervised by a high state official. How prominently the control of provisions figured in the economic and administrative organization is shown by the many different departments which dealt with commissariat: cereals were at all times the particular care of the 'Granaries' (*šnwt*), second in importance only to the 'Treasuries'; perhaps the 'Office of the Miller' (*pr ḥry nd*)[4] was a sub-department of the 'Granaries', where the corn was ground; the distribution of supplies to the temples and to courtiers and other privileged persons was conducted from the 'House of the Master of Largess' (*pr ḥry wḏb*), a department closely linked with the 'Mansion of Life' in the palace;[5] the 'Food Office' (*is ḏfꜣw*) is often mentioned in the documents, but little is known of its activities beyond what may be deduced from the name and from the conjecture that the vineyards were under its control;[6] fats were kept in a special storehouse called the 'House of Cattle-fat' (*pr ꜥnḏ iḥ*).[7] Military affairs probably required the attention of a permanent branch in the administration; nothing is known of the constitution of the army and its terms of service are completely obscure. At the end of the Second Dynasty, under Khasekhemwy, an 'Overseer of the Foreign Country' (*imy-r ḫꜣst*)[8] is found, but it is not clear whether the title was intended to designate an official charged with foreign affairs in general or referred in a more restricted sense to some particular land beyond the frontiers of Egypt.

Numerous problems confront any inquiry into the methods of

1 §II, 5, 126–7. 2 See *C.A.H.* I³, ch. VI, sect. I. 3 §V, 4, 22.
4 §III, 11, 54. 5 §V, 3, 83–91. 6 §V, 4, 22.
7 §III, 11, 54. 8 §VIII, 2, 40, pl. IX, 9.

provincial administration adopted by the early dynastic kings. Is it, for instance, to be assumed that the nomes of Upper Egypt and of the Delta were administered in the same way? Social conditions in the Two Lands probably differed fundamentally: the pre-dynastic Upper Egyptians were mainly a nomadic folk who had settled in communities distributed at intervals along the banks of the river, whereas the inhabitants of the Delta seem to have congregated in groups at no great distance apart; a system of government, perhaps feudal in character, suited to the needs of Upper Egypt would have been impracticable in the North, where a more urban régime would seem to have been more appropriate.[1] After the unification, it is likely that a measure of uniformity in governmental control was introduced, at least in the highest posts, linking the provinces with the central administration, although special privileges may have been accorded to some of the southern nomes in recognition of their service to Menes (p. 11). How many of his successors respected the claims of these nomes to preferential treatment and in what way such events as the political upheaval which culminated in the accession of Peribsen may have affected the whole machinery of provincial government are ques-tions which cannot at present be answered. Of titles borne exclusively by provincial officials, contemporary documents pre-serve only two or possibly three: 'Keeper of Nekhen' (*iry*[?] *nḫn*), a less specific epithet usually rendered 'Administrator of a Pro-vince' (*ꜥnḏy*) and 'Hereditary Prince' (*iry pꜥt*).[2] The 'Keeper of Nekhen' (literally, He who belongs to Nekhen [?]) was probably a kind of viceroy of the southernmost nomes, whose seat at Ne-khen owed its origin to the historical association of that city with the founders of the First Dynasty. In later times the office car-ried with it the title of 'Count' (*ḥꜣty-ꜥ*), a rank ascribed to Ankhka[3] in the reign of Den, who, however, is not known to have held the post of 'Keeper of Nekhen'. The appointment of a similar dig-nitary in Lower Egypt, the 'Keeper of Pe' (*iry*[?] *P*), may not have been initiated until the Third Dynasty. Several wine-jar sealings of the First Dynasty are inscribed with the title, and often the name, of the 'Administrator' of the nome in which the vineyard was situated; there is no clear evidence that the special-ized significance of 'Customs' Official', which perhaps prevailed in the Fourth and Fifth Dynasties,[4] was attached to this title in the Early Dynastic Period. The few instances on record of an 'Heredi-

---

[1] §v, 13, 127; §viii, 48, 24.   [2] G, 5, text vol. i, 14*–19*, 108*–10*.
[3] §iii, 12, pl. xxii, 32; Cf. §iv, 20, 304–6.
[4] §v, 5, 107–11.

tary Prince' connect the office with that of the High Priest of Heliopolis. Future discoveries, not only in the Delta, but also in Upper Egypt, may well show that many of the provincial offices and institutions attested by monuments of the Third and Fourth Dynasties, such as the Council of the 'Tens of Upper Egypt' (*mdw šmʿw*), originated in early dynastic times.

VI. FOREIGN RELATIONS

It is unlikely that any close or regular connexions were maintained between Egypt and the neighbouring countries in the period immediately preceding and following the institution of the united monarchy. The evidence, admittedly sparse, points rather to brief migratory movements towards the Nile Valley, intermittent commercial dealings and isolated military expeditions by the Egyptians either in defence of their frontiers or to obtain a commodity not readily available at home. Anthropological research may some day shed much-needed light on what was perhaps the most important of the migrations by establishing the identity of the so-called 'Armenoids' or 'Dynastic Race',[1] whose presence in Egypt at the beginning of the dynastic period, although discounted by many authorities in the past, has been further attested by recent excavations.[2] Physically these people differed unmistakably from the predynastic Egyptians: whereas the latter were unusually small in stature and possessed long and narrow skulls (about 132 mm. in breadth), the newcomers were more massively built and their skulls (about 139 mm. in width) were appreciably broader than those of their predecessors.[3] The quantity and distribution of the skeletons hitherto found suggest that the 'Dynastic Race' entered Egypt in considerable numbers from the north, where the purest examples of their racial types have been discovered; this fact alone would suggest that the immigrants came from Asia, but it is doubtful whether the assertion sometimes made that they were Armenoids is anatomically justifiable.[4] Before the end of the First Dynasty they had already penetrated southwards as far as Abydos[5] and were becoming merged into the general population—a process which appears to have been intensified with the passage of time. So long as the origin of this people remains unexplained, it is difficult to determine what fresh knowledge they

---

[1] §vi, 37, 92 ff.   [2] §vi, 7; §vi, 9; §viii, 26, 68–9; §viii, 50, 249–51.
[3] §vi, 7, 84; §vi, 38, 15–36; see *C.A.H.* i³, ch. v, sect. ii.
[4] §vi, 37, 118 ff.   [5] §vi, 31.

may have brought with them to Egypt, but it is probable that a generous share of the credit for the acceleration in cultural progress observable at this time should be ascribed to their presence. Perhaps the Semitic elements in the structure and vocabulary of the Egyptian language were also introduced by them. Archaeological evidence suggests that they provided the ruling class and that they adapted their way of life to conform with the customs already prevailing in their new home; in this respect they set a precedent which was to be followed by successive invaders of the Nile Valley down to Roman times.

SOUTHERN MESOPOTAMIA

Foremost among the indications of early contacts between Egypt and southern Mesopotamia must be counted the occurrence in both countries of a small group of remarkably similar artistic designs, mostly embodying animals.[1] Fantastic monsters in the shape of serpent-necked lions, such as are carved on the Narmer and Ashmolean palettes,[2] possess striking parallels on seals and seal-impressions discovered at Uruk[3] and on a cylinder seal in the Louvre[4] which, although its provenance cannot be proved, is generally considered to be of Mesopotamian origin and to date from the Uruk-Jamdat Naṣr period. Both on the Narmer palette and on the seals, the necks of the monsters are interlaced—a well-attested motif in Mesopotamian art, to which the interlaced serpents found on three protodynastic Egyptian knife-handles may be an additional artistic parallel.[5] Equally typical of Mesopotamian products is the antithetical arrangement of these monsters and serpents. As a variation of the same motif, a central feature is sometimes introduced into the antithetical group: some slate palettes[6] and one very early First Dynasty engraved cylinder[7] are decorated with two giraffes[8] separated by a palm-tree; occasionally

[1] §vi, 16, 117–42; §vi, 35.

[2] G, 24, 193–4; G, 25, pl. 29; G, 26, 41–3; §i, 27, J 25, K 26; §i, 28, 22–3, pl. 6; §viii, 59, 595–9.

[3] §vi, 12, 109, pl. x, fig. 16; §vi, 13, 27, pl. iv; §vi, 30, 2; §vi, 35, 98, fig. 2; §vi, 36, 42 ff.   [4] §vi, 16, pl. xi, 3.

[5] G, 2, figs. 33, 37, 38; §vi, 12, fig. 41, pl. xxi; §vi, 13, 71; §viii, 59, 547, fig. 366.   [6] §viii, 53, vol. ii, 75.   [7] §viii, 50, 166, fig. 14.

[8] R. Lydekker, British Museum (Natural History) Guide to the Great Game Animals (1913), p. 39, identified the animals on the Battlefield Palette as gerenuks, but Dr M. Burton, in a private communication, has expressed the opinion that the animals are either giraffes or dibatags. A further possibility, which he mentions, is that the animals are composite, the lower portion being a giraffe and the upper portion either a dibatag or a gerenuk.

the central figure is a human figure. Without doubt the best Egyptian illustration of this latter class appears on the famous ivory knife-handle from Gebel el-Araq[1] which portrays in finely carved relief a bearded man clothed in Sumerian costume and holding apart two fierce lions; so closely does the composition of this scene resemble the so-called Gilgamesh motif, frequently represented on Mesopotamian seals, that the source of its inspiration can hardly be questioned. Also Mesopotamian in character are the ships with high and almost perpendicular prow and stern, and the lion attacking the hindquarters of a bull, which decorate other parts of the same knife-handle. Several objects, including mud seal-impressions,[2] ivory knife-handles and combs[3] and a fragment of a slate palette,[4] display a regular Mesopotamian trait in the arrangement of animals in file; a serpentine mace-head from Hierakonpolis and a shell plaque of unknown provenance[5] show a continuous file of overlapping animals, but more usually the animals are spaced in broken file and divided into registers. As a class, ceremonial mace-heads with sculptured decoration, like those of Scorpion and Narmer,[6] are reminiscent of Mesopotamian art.

In a somewhat different category from the decorative motifs must be placed two productions, one of which was also shared by certain neighbouring countries, while the other may have attained a similar form in Egypt and Mesopotamia through a parallel, but independent, process of development. These productions were the engraved cylinder[7] and a distinctive kind of brick architecture exemplified in Egypt by mastabas of the Naqāda type.[8] Outside Egypt and Mesopotamia, engraved cylinders were used at the beginning of the historical era in Elam, Anatolia, north Syria and elsewhere, but it can hardly be without significance that two of the earliest specimens found in Egypt are indistinguishable in style and decoration from some Mesopotamian cylinders of the Jamdat Naṣr period, and the most probable explanation seems to be that they were imported from that country. These cylinders were discovered in tombs of the second Naqāda period;[9] the history of two other cylinders of the same kind[10] is not ascertain-

1 §vi, 16, pl. xii; §vi, 23, 119–24.
2 §iii, 11, pl. xiv, 101–4. *Ibid.* pl. xv, 113; §vi, 3, 485–6, 498–501.
3 §vi, 2.   4 G, 2, 236, fig. 175. See above, p. 7.
5 §viii, 57, 123, fig. 41. Cf. §vi, 15, 354, n. 55.
6 See above, p. 4, n. 8, and p. 10, n. 5.
7 §vi, 13, 292 ff.   8 §vi, 15. See below, pp. 60–1.
9 §i, 2, vol. i, 47–8; §vi, 13, 293.
10 See note by A. F. Shore in the *B.M. Quart.* vol. xxiv, 35.

able, but there can be little doubt that they also came from Egypt. When, early in the First Dynasty, the Egyptians began to manufacture their own cylinders, they sometimes, as has already been shown, imitated Mesopotamian styles of decoration, which alone would suggest an association with Mesopotamia in the minds of the makers; coupled with the evidence provided by the four earlier cylinders, the indications pointing to a Mesopotamian ancestry for the Egyptian cylinder are more telling than any arguments which can be advanced in favour of other parentage. More problematical is the architectural connexion which has been claimed between the Naqāda type of brick mastaba and Mesopotamian brick temples with façades similarly composed of alternating projections and recesses. It is true that excavation in Mesopotamia has revealed the more primitive wooden constructions from which this style of architecture was no doubt derived,[1] and that the earliest Mesopotamian examples in brick are considerably older than the first mastabas of the Naqāda form found in Egypt, where they appear quite suddenly at the beginning of the First Dynasty, but it is possible to account both for the absence of any known Egyptian archetype in wood and for the discrepancy in time by assuming that brick tombs of the Naqāda pattern were a Lower Egyptian development of predynastic times, only adopted by the Upper Egyptians after the conquest of unification; if that be the case the putative antecedents of this kind of mastaba must be sought in the regions, hitherto largely unexcavated, of the Delta. In these circumstances, it seems necessary to suspend judgement, but not without recognizing that tangible evidence in support of a Mesopotamian origin is already at hand, whereas the arguments favouring independent evolution in the two countries are still hypothetical.

Although unrelated morphologically, Sumerian and Egyptian hieroglyphic scripts show certain affinities,[2] which may not be merely fortuitous, in the mechanical principles employed. Signs were not used only to denote the objects depicted, but also other words of like sound which were difficult or impossible to represent pictorially: thus, in Egyptian hieroglyphs, the sledge and the mace signified respectively both these actual objects and the verbs 'be complete' and 'be bright'. It is evident, therefore, that, at least in their developed usage, the two hieroglyphs mentioned had gained a phonographic value. By a further extension of the same principle, signs acquired a syllabic value, which in Egyptian writing specified only the consonantal composition of the syllable,

[1] §VI, 15, 332–9.   [2] §VI, 10, 62 ff.

in contrast with the Sumerian syllabic signs which defined also the vocalic content. Finally, though examples are very rare in the oldest Egyptian texts, both scripts added signs as determinatives to words (in Egyptian invariably as suffixes, but in Sumerian more often as prefixes) in order to indicate their general sense. Only in one respect, the invention of the consonantal alphabetic signs, did the Egyptians possess a graphic element unknown to the Sumerians, although the latter employed single signs as vowels. In spite, however, of the similarities, the divergences in method, when considered in combination with the purely native character of Egyptian hieroglyphs,[1] are too significant to be disregarded, and it is probably correct to assess the Sumerian contribution to the Egyptian science of writing as mainly suggestive and limited to imparting a knowledge of the underlying principles. With this assistance the Egyptians proceeded to develop one of the most characteristic and lasting features of their civilization.

While the historical fact that contacts between southern Mesopotamia and Egypt existed in protodynastic times can be demonstrated, the nature of these contacts is far from clear. Commercial intercourse, which might appear at first sight to furnish the simplest explanation, must be regarded as unlikely because of the absence of any trace of Egyptian influence on Mesopotamian productions during the Jamdat Naṣr and first Early Dynastic Periods; the movement seems to have been in one direction only— from East to West—and, unless future excavations bring to light some evidence of a corresponding movement in the reverse direction, it is necessary to conclude that the bearers of the Mesopotamian influences were Sumerians who migrated to Egypt and settled in the Nile Valley. By what route the immigrants travelled and entered the country it is difficult to decide, but two approaches were geographically possible: either by way of the Red Sea and thence by land through one of the wādis (perhaps the Wādi Hammāmāt) to the Nile Valley,[2] or by way of Syria and the isthmus of Suez to the Delta. In favour of the Red Sea route it may be argued that the foreign ships noted on the Gebel el-Araq knife-handle suggest that the immigrants were seafarers; moreover, some of the earliest traces of their presence in Egypt have come to light in the neighbourhood of the western end of the Wādi Hammāmāt. It is, however, noticeable that the period when Mesopotamian influence can most easily be detected coincides with the conquest leading to the unification of the Two

[1] §vi, 34, 70–4.

[2] §vi, 16, 136–42.

Lands, at the time when Upper Egypt might have been expected to appropriate certain productions which had formerly been confined to the North.[1] Clearly, the problem cannot be solved with any degree of finality while the early levels of the Delta remain virtually unexplored and it is by no means inconceivable that the immigrants reached Egypt by more than one route. There are good grounds for believing that the number of immigrants was not such as to constitute an invasion and that the flow could not have continued after the beginning of the First Dynasty; otherwise they must surely have exercised a deeper and more prolonged influence on Egyptian cultural and technical development. The decorative motifs in which Mesopotamian inspiration can be discerned were either integrated into an Egyptian setting or entirely adapted by the substitution of subjects familiar to the Egyptians but foreign to the Sumerians, as in the case of the antithetical group displaying so essentially African an animal as the giraffe or the dibatag;[2] furthermore the employment of these motifs, at no time common, was discontinued soon after the foundation of the united monarchy. Extant specimens of sculptured mace-heads all belong to the age of Scorpion and Narmer. Cylinder-seals, which seldom—and only at their first appearance—betray in their ornamentation the origin ascribed to them, remained in general use until the end of the Old Kingdom, when they were superseded first by the button seal and then by the scarab, but were sometimes used archaistically in later times. The Naqāda style of mastaba, if its architecture should ultimately be shown beyond doubt to have been derived from Mesopotamia and thus warrant its inclusion in this category, did not outlive the First Dynasty before being succeeded by a mastaba of a simpler and less distinctive external design. Hieroglyphic writing, alone among the possible contributions of early Mesopotamia, gained a permanent and unchallenged footing in Egypt, but the reason for its retention lies in the singular position which it immediately assumed in the religous concept of the Egyptians combined with their extreme conservatism in such matters.

SYRIA, PALESTINE AND SINAI

Excavations at Byblos have yielded conclusive proof that Egyptian products were reaching Syria from very early times. The first object which can be precisely dated is a fragment of a polished stone vase bearing the name of Khasekhemwy;[3] a figure of a

[1] §vi, 34, 64–70.   [2] See above, p. 41, n. 8.   [3] §vi, 8, vol. i, 26–7.

squatting ape, a gold bead and two gaming-pieces[1] may, however, be ascribed to the protodynastic period, while a slate palette in the form of a bird[2] is characteristic of predynastic workmanship. The fact that these objects lay beneath the pavement of a temple dating from the Middle Kingdom suggests that they had formed part of the property of an earlier sanctuary which had been rebuilt;[3] without doubt they were brought as propitiatory offerings to the local goddess, the 'Mistress of Byblos', by Egyptian traders. In later times the main purpose of such missions was to obtain timber from the Lebanon. Perhaps the commodity sought by the first traders was cedar-oil which is mentioned in an inscription dating from the time of Anedjib.[4] Moreover, various pottery vessels found in early dynastic tombs display Syrian features either in their decoration or in their shape;[5] how many of these vessels actually came from Syria, perhaps filled with oils and resins, and how many may have been made in Egypt as deliberate imitations cannot be determined, but, even if statistical analysis could prove that the ratio of imports to local manufacturers was small, the occurrence of a foreign class of ceramics in a country already well provided with established wares implies some familiarity with its place of origin, if not also with the special products with which the vessels were particularly associated.

The discovery of Egyptian objects at Byblos, a port, suggests that traffic between Egypt and Syria was conducted by sea. Passage by land would have presented serious practical difficulties in the conveyance of merchandise and would only have been feasible if the intervening territory had been either under Egyptian control or occupied by friendly peoples. Some slight evidence of sporadic intercourse between Egypt and Palestine is admittedly available,[6] perhaps from the time of Narmer,[7] but not enough to indicate a close relationship. Sinai, as in later times, was in all probability the abode of undisciplined bedawin whose presence would have rendered transport through its sandy wastes an extremely hazardous operation: Djer (p. 23) and Den (p. 27) claim to have engaged the local inhabitants in combat. The historical

---

[1] §vi, 27, vol. i, 91 (fig. 38, no. 176), 98 (no. 256), 103 (nos. 333–4). *Ibid.* vol. ii, pls. lv, lvi.

[2] §vi, 27, vol. i, 90 (fig. 37, no. 171).   [3] §vi, 14, 83–4.

[4] G, 13, 306; §viii, 33, vol. i, pl. v.

[5] §vi, 4, 35–40, pl. 27; §vi, 16, 106–11; §viii, 26, 12–13, figs. 14–15; §viii, 28, vol. 8, 162; §viii, 58, pl. 10ᵃ.

[6] §vi, 6, 72; §vi, 17, 68; §vi, 18, 72; §vi, 26, 333; §vi, 39, 198. See below, pp. 356–7.

[7] §vi, 42.

inference to be drawn from these scraps of information seems rather to be that the early dynastic kings periodically found it necessary to assert themselves against the bedawin, either in defence of the eastern Delta or for the purpose of obtaining turquoise and possibly copper, than that Sinai was included within the Egyptian realm and only became the scene of punitive action in times of revolt.

LIBYA

Of the various Libyan peoples who figure on Egyptian monuments, only the dwellers in the region called Tjehenu[1] are attested in texts of the Early Dynastic Period, unless the enigmatical Besh, mentioned on the vases of Khasekhem, is to be regarded as referring to a Libyan folk (p. 33). Painted scenes on the walls of Old Kingdom temples depict the people of Tjehenu with several typically Egyptian features:[2] their skins are dark red, a short beard projects from the chin, on the brow they have a tuft of hair suggestive of the royal uraeus, an animal's tail hangs from the back of the girdle and in front, even when the figures are of women, is suspended the phallus-sheath often worn by Egyptians when represented on slate palettes and other objects of the protodynastic and predynastic times. The people themselves are called Hatiu-a, 'Princes', probably on account of their regal-looking attire; for the same reason and also because they sometimes bear Egyptian names it is likely that they were closely akin to the Egyptians. Perhaps the separation of the two peoples resulted from the incomplete subjection of the Hatiu-a by the Upper Egyptians in the war of unification; two objects dating from that time, one inscribed with the name of Narmer, record victories in the land of Tjehenu (p. 7), but otherwise the documents of the Early Dynastic Period, apart from labels of jars denoting that their contents consisted of Tjehenu-oil (generally considered to have been olive oil),[3] contain no mention of Tjehenu-land or of its inhabitants. There can be little doubt, however, that the traditional enmity between the Egyptians and both the Libyans and the Asiatics of Sinai, which so often found expression in parallel scenes carved on the walls of later temples, originated at this time.

[1] G, 5, text vol. I, 116*–19*; §VI, 20, 12 ff.
[2] §VI, 5, vol. II, pl. I; §VI, 21, vol. II, 13–14, pl. 9.
[3] G, 13, 316; §I, 26.

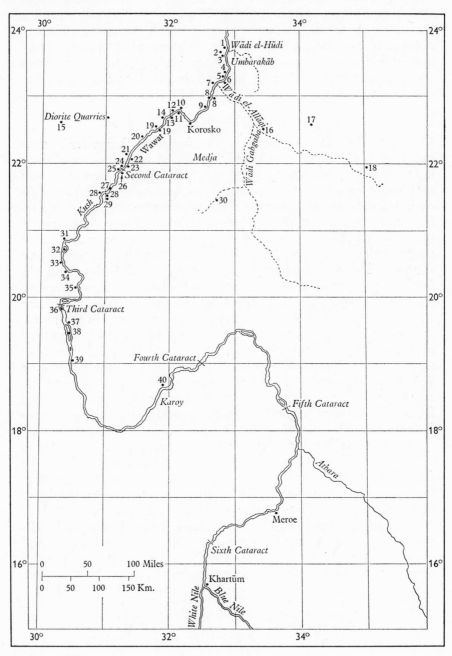

Map 5. Nubia.

NUMERICAL KEY

1	Abisko	15	Bir Nakhlai	29	Kumma
2	Beit el-Wāli	16	Umm Qareiyāt	30	Umm Nabardi
3	Kalābsha	17	Seiga	31	Amāra West
4	Gerf Husein	18	Deraheib	32	Sai
5	Ikkur	19	Tōshka	33	Sedeinga
6	Qūbān	20	Abu Simbel	34	Sulb
7	Ed-Dakka	21	Faras	35	Sesebi
8	Sayāla	22	Serra	36	Tumbos
9	Es-Sebūa	23	Wādi Halfa	37	Kerma
10	Amada	24	Buhen	38	Argo
11	Ed-Derr	25	Mirgissa	39	Kawa
12	Tomās	26	Gammai	40	Gebel Barkal (Napata)
13	Qasr Ibrīm	27	Uronarti		
14	Anība	28	Semna East and West		

ALPHABETICAL KEY

Abisko	1	Gebel Barkal (Napata)	40	Sedeinga	33
Abu Simbel	20	Gerf Husein	4	Seiga	17
Amada	10	Ikkur	5	Semna East and West	28
Amāra West	31	Kalābsha	3	Serra	22
Anība	14	Kawa	39	Sesebi	35
Argo	38	Kerma	37	Sulb	34
Beit el-Wāli	2	Kumma	29	Tomās	12
Bir Nakhlai	15	Mirgissa	25	Tōshka	19
Buhen	24	Napata (Gebel Barkal)	40	Tumbos	36
Ed-Dakka	7	Qasr Ibrīm	13	Umm Nabardi	30
Deraheib	18	Qūbān	6	Umm Qareiyāt	16
Ed-Derr	11	Sai	32	Uronarti	27
Faras	21	Sayāla	8	Wādi Halfa	23
Gammai	26	Es-Sebūa	9		

NUBIA

Ethnically the predynastic Egyptians and the main body of the so-called A-group of dwellers in Lower Nubia probably belonged to the same branch of Hamitic people;[1] whether they spoke the same language cannot be ascertained in the absence of written documents. Culturally also the inhabitants of the two countries in the Early Predynastic Period were identical; divergences are first detectable in Nubian tombs of the Middle Predynastic Period and become more marked with each succeeding age until the final disappearance of the A-group at the end of the Third Dynasty.[2] Being far removed from the influence of those forces which brought about so rapid an advancement in protodynastic Egypt, the Nubians were unable to keep pace with their more fortunate relatives in the North. Early dynastic tombs in Nubia were not only more poorly furnished than contemporaneous tombs in Egypt, but were still provided with pottery and other funerary equipment of a kind not found in Egyptian tombs after late pre-dynastic times.[3] The frontier between the two countries, when first established, probably lay somewhere in the vicinity of Gebel es-Silsila, which may explain why the Egyptians called the region southward to the First Cataract, comprising the first Upper Egyptian nome of the historical lists, the 'Nubian Land' (tꜣ sty).[4] Perhaps the wooden docket of Aha, which mentions the smiting of the 'Nubian Land' (p. 23), commemorates the annexation of this territory rather than a military expedition into Lower Nubia.[5] A mutilated battle scene carved on a rock at Wādi Halfa bears the name of Djer,[6] who may have been the actual conqueror. The Palermo Stone records that an unnamed king of the First Dynasty, who was undoubtedly Den, smote the 'Nomads' ($iwntiw$), but this designation was applied by the Egyptians to all their neighbours and it is more likely that the particular 'Nomads' overcome by Den were the inhabitants of Sinai[7] (p. 27). Kha-sekhem, in his graphic inscription discovered at Hierakonpolis,[8] leaves no room for doubt that the Nubians suffered the same severe treatment at his hands as the rebellious northern Egyptians (p. 32); the circumstances of the time were, however, exceptional and the king may have found it necessary to obviate any risk of

---

[1] §vi, 38, 15–36.   [2] §vi, 22, 2–6.   [3] §vi, 11, vol. i, 5; §vi, 32, vol. i, 319.
[4] §i, 31, 125.   [5] §vi, 33, 7.
[6] §iv, 3, 27–30; §vi, 1, 39–40, fig. 5; A, 15, 74–8, fig. 6.
[7] §vi, 40, 358–68. See below, p. 508.
[8] G, 26, pl. lviii. See above, p. 32, n 5.

attack from the rear before advancing towards Middle Egypt and the Delta. Normally relations between the two peoples were of a pacific character limited, in the main, to an exchange of merchandise. Ebony and ivory were probably among the regular commodities traded by the Nubians in return for articles such as pottery and stone vessels manufactured in Egypt.

VII. RELIGION AND FUNERARY BELIEFS

Political and social changes of so fundamental a kind as those which occurred in Egypt under the First and Second Dynasties were almost certainly accompanied by religious developments of far-reaching significance: some deities whose domain had previously been confined to one locality probably gained wider recognition, while others may have suffered a diminution in status. Few of these vicissitudes are capable of demonstration, not only because the religious history of the preceding period is largely conjectural, but also because the early dynastic records are extremely fragmentary and difficult to interpret; even in those rare instances in which sufficient evidence exists for showing that a particular deity was of importance in the First and Second Dynasties, it is generally impossible to decide whether the distinction was newly acquired or already achieved in the predynastic period. To this uncertain category it is necessary to relegate Horus, about whose early geographical connexions opinion is at present divided.[1] One fact alone stands out as fairly evident, namely that in virtue of his position as god of Nekhen, the seat of the rulers of Upper Egypt before the unification of the Two Lands, he became the patron deity of the conquerors of Lower Egypt and of their immediate successors. Nekhen was, however, only one of the centres in which Horus was worshipped in early times and the problem, which on the information now available seems to defy solution, is whether some of the other sanctuaries of the Horian cult, notably those of Pe and Behdet, were founded before or after the cult was established at Nekhen; in other words, whether Horus was in the first instance a god of Lower or of Upper Egypt. Relying mainly on later sources, some authorities take the view that his original home lay in the Delta and that the diffusion of the cult into Upper Egypt occurred in predynastic times as the result of a conquest of the South—formerly the province of Seth—by the inhabitants of the North.[2] Advocates

[1] §vii, 33, 24–30.   [2] §i, 7; §i, 17, 56–7; §i, 31, 70–133.

of the southern origin of Horus, on the other hand, deny the theory of the predynastic invasion and maintain that the advance of the cult northwards was a concomitant of the subjugation of the North by Scorpion and Narmer. Since the weight of evidence appears evenly balanced, judgement on this vital question and on a wide range of ancillary issues must be reserved. Nevertheless, the kindred problem of the position occupied by Seth in early dynastic times cannot be passed over without comment. On the mace-head of Scorpion[1] two standards bearing the Seth-animal are displayed in a setting which suggests that his worshippers, comprising the inhabitants of a group or confederation of nomes centred around his native town of Ombos (Naqāda),[2] were among the chief allies of the Horus-king in his northern conquest. A similar explanation may also account for the adoption of the titles 'Two Lords' (i.e. Horus and Seth) by Anedjib and 'She who unites the Two Lords' and 'She who sees Horus and Seth' by queens; if so, the titles designated the king as ruler of Upper Egypt only and it must be assumed that Seth was singled out from the other gods of Upper Egypt, who were also the king's allies, as a mark of particular respect, though the reason for the choice is not apparent. Later tradition in the main, however, ascribed to the two gods, when they were not depicted as adversaries, the role of representatives of Lower and Upper Egypt; the titles, if understood in this sense, would conform, except in order of geographical precedence, with the *nbty* and *nіswt-bіty* titles of the king. Whichever explanation is to be preferred and whatever view is taken of the relationship between Horus and Seth in the preceding period, it seems evident that, by early dynastic times, the adherents of the two gods were living in a state of amity, probably based on considerations of political expediency and subject to temporary interruption, as is demonstrated by the monuments of the Seth-king Peribsen and his Horian successor Khasekhem.

Among the relatively small number of deities who are actually attested in early dynastic documents, Ptah,[3] in virtue of being the principal god of Memphis, must have occupied a privileged position, and yet he is represented only twice on the extant monuments of this period.[4] Neither of the two etymologies put forward to

___

[1] See above, pp. 3–6.

[2] H. Stock (see §VII, 32) maintained that the early domain of Horus lay in Upper Egypt. Seth, he believed, belonged originally to the cosmic group of gods whose cults in predynastic times were confined to the eastern Delta. By the Second Dynasty, however, Ash, the local god of Ombos, had become identified with Seth and had surrendered to him both his peculiar animal form and his title 'the Ombite'.

[3] §VII, 24.   [4] §VIII, 39, pls. III, 1, XXXVII, 81; A, 12, 18, fig. 28.

explain his name, with the meanings 'Opener' and 'Sculptor' or 'Engraver' respectively, can be accepted without reserve on account of the late appearance of their Semitic roots in Egyptian writings;[1] nevertheless the title of his High Priest, 'Greatest of Artificers' (*wr ḥrpw ḥmt*), although not frequent in the Early Dynastic Period,[2] and the designation of another craftsman who may have been attached to this priesthood, the 'Carpenter, Sculptor and Maker (?) of Stone Vases' (*mḏḥ gnwty mḏ3ty šsw*),[3] denote that Ptah was early regarded as the patron of arts and crafts. How many of the extravagant claims attributed to Ptah in the text of King Shabako date from the Early Dynastic Period cannot be assessed, for the original text, as a whole, seems to have been a product of the ensuing age when the priests of Memphis were endeavouring to assert the supremacy of their god over the more favoured sun-god of Heliopolis.[4] Two other Memphite deities, the bull Apis and the mummified falcon Sokar, are better documented, their festivals being recorded both on inscriptions of the First Dynasty[5] and on the Palermo Stone and Cairo Annals. By the Old Kingdom, at latest, Neith also possessed a sanctuary at Memphis 'North of the Wall', so named in contrast with the sanctuary of Ptah 'South of his Wall' which tradition ascribed to Menes.[6] Primarily, however, Neith was at all times associated with the town of Sais in the western Delta, where her temple, called the 'House of the Bee' (*ḥwt bit*), was situated; the adoption of her crown by the kings to symbolize their sovereignty over Lower Egypt, the royal title 'He who belongs to the Bee' and the frequent occurrence of her name in theophorous compounds, of which Neithhotpe and Mer(it)neith are only two of the many known or suspected instances,[7] prove that the kings of the First Dynasty regarded this goddess with particular esteem and suggest that her cult held a predominant position in Lower Egypt at the end of the predynastic period. Among the deities who figure with Seth on the protodynastic mace-heads and palettes are Min of Akhmīm and Koptos, Wepwawet, the wolf-god of Asyūt, the ibis of Thoth, whose cult was associated in early times with the Fifteenth Lower Egyptian nome, and the jackal-god Anubis, all of whom seem to have been admitted as allies by Scorpion and Narmer.

---

[1] §VII, 24, 8–11. [2] A, 12, 65, fig. 108.

[3] §I, 10, part III, 165–6; §IV, 23, part II, 65–6 (where the reading *mibty* is suggested in preference to *mḏḥ*. Cf. §V, 7, vol. I, 149–50.

[4] §I, 17; §VII, 3; §VII, 8; §VII, 30.

[5] §VII, 1; §VII, 18. See W. K. Simpson, *An. Or.* 26 (1957), 139–42.

[6] §II, 5. [7] §IV, 29, 154–5.

The vulture Nekhbet of El-Kāb and the serpent Uadjit of Buto appear as protecting goddesses in connexion with the personal names of kings, first on the ivory tablet of Menes and regularly from the accession of Semerkhet. Deities whose significance at this time is more obscure include Bastet, the cat-headed goddess of Bubastis, Sopd of Saft el-Hinna in the eastern Delta, Sobk, the crocodile-god of the Faiyūm, Seshat, the goddess of writing, Khnum, the ram-god of Antinoopolis and such lesser members of the pantheon as Mafdet, a feline goddess, Kherty, a ram-god of Letopolis, Neser, a fish-god, and Ash, an anthropomorphic god with the head of the animal of Seth. No trace can be found in the early dynastic records of Osiris, whose cult was early associated with that of Andjety at Busiris.[1] Of the undoubted existence of the sun-cult at this time, the name of the king Reneb, the composite god Seth-Re[2] and the title of the Heliopolitan high-priest 'Greatest of the Seers' (*wr mȝw*)[3] constitute the sum of the written evidence hitherto recovered. Incomplete and partly fortuitous though the catalogue of deities preserved from this period must be considered, it is noteworthy both that divine iconography had, to a great extent, been finally established and that the proportion of Lower Egyptian deities is higher than might have been expected at a time when Upper Egypt was politically predominant. A legitimate inference from this latter fact seems to be that the new rulers freely recognized the deities of the conquered peoples as a means of securing their acquiescence and friendly co-operation.

Excavations carried out on early dynastic sites have so far failed to bring to light any religious texts. That such works were compiled appears likely from numerous passages in the Pyramid Texts of the Fifth and Sixth Dynasties referring to practices and conditions which were out of date at that period, and from the priestly title 'Scribe of the God's Book' (*sš mḏȝt nṯr*)[4] found on early dynastic vases. In the absence of written evidence it is necessary to turn for information to material remains, which consist of little more than tombs and their contents; the scope of possible investigation is consequently limited in the main to beliefs regarding the Next Life.

Tombs of the Early Dynastic Period were of two types: pits of varying size and interior construction surmounted by circular, oval or rectangular mounds of stones and gravel, which differed in no essential respect from the predynastic graves,[5] and secondly

---

[1] §VII, 26.   [2] §III, 11, pl. XXI, 176.

[3] G, 5, text vol. II, 267*; §IV, 23, part II, 60–2.

[4] §IV, 23, part II, 57; §VIII, 35, 4, pl. II, 16, pl. VII, 37.

[5] §VIII, 26; §VIII, 46 *passim*.

mastabas built of mud brick.[1] The objects buried in the pit tombs suggest that the needs of the after-life were thought to be similar to those of this life, but nothing definite is revealed about its nature or its surroundings. Nor can any clear inference be drawn from the orientation of the body. In the majority of cemeteries it was laid, tightly or loosely contracted and wrapped in woven reed matting or in linen, on the left side facing eastwards, but the earlier custom of placing the body on the left side facing westwards was very often maintained.[2] Only the most elaborate pit-tombs give the impression of having been designed as houses.[3] Mastabas however were probably regarded from the first as houses in which the dead would reside and enjoy their protection and amenities. This character, perhaps a legacy of Lower Egyptian practices in predynastic times,[4] is plainly illustrated in the sub-structures of some of the Second Dynasty mastabas at Saqqara, which included not only apartments believed to represent quarters for the domestic staff and possibly even stalls for cattle, but also a bathroom and a lavatory.[5] Easily distinguishable in this complex of rooms is the bedchamber where the deceased was placed, sometimes in a wooden coffin, itself in the form of a house, and sometimes lying on a bed.[6] Near the body, on pottery dishes ready for consumption, might be set a complete meal consisting of cereals, fish, meat, sweets and fruit, and a jar of wine.[7] Large quantities of similar provisions were stored elsewhere in the tomb, while further supplies of fresh food were probably brought by relatives and laid in the larger of the two niches on the east side of the superstructure. A curious custom, which seems to have been connected with alimentation, was the attaching of bulls' heads, modelled in clay and provided with real horns, to a brick bench at the base of the palace façades of some of the First Dynasty mastabas at Saqqara.[8] When, perhaps before the end of the First Dynasty, the funerary stela was introduced into the equipment of the mastaba in order to supplement by magical means the supply of provisions,[9] the bull's head was included as an item in the list of offerings, together with the heads of birds and antelopes, to serve as an abbreviation for the hieroglyph showing the entire animal, a graphic device which was retained

[1] See below, pp. 60 ff.
[2] §VII, 19, 21–4; §VIII, 20, vol. XXXVIII, 68; §VIII, 46, 11–12.
[3] §VII, 27, 53, n. 36. [4] §VII, 19, 14; §VII, 27, 20; §VIII, 48, part I, 40–1.
[5] G, 4, 129; §VII, 27, 18–9; §VIII, 42, 11–13, pls. 30–1.
[6] §VIII, 39, 23. [7] G, 4, 158, pls. 28–9; §VII, 7, 6–7.
[8] G, 4, 71, pls. 8–9; §III, 2, vol. II, 8–9, pls. I, VI, VII; §VIII, 9, 40, pl. I[a].
[9] G, 4, 169, pl. 32[a]; §VII, 25; §VIII, 59, 733–40; G, 13, 229–34.

in the offering-lists of later times. On the basis of somewhat slender evidence it has been suggested that some funerary stelae of the Second Dynasty found at Saqqara were placed near the top of the larger offering niche outside the superstructure,[1] and thus in the same position as their successors in false-doors of the Old Kingdom mastabas. Several stelae of a similar kind discovered in the Second Dynasty tombs at Helwān were, however, placed face downwards at the lower ends of shafts in the ceilings of the burial chambers,[2] apparently with the intention of enabling the deceased without moving to enjoy the benefits which they conferred by magic. Somewhat paradoxically the shafts themselves seem to have been designed to allow the spirit of the deceased more easily to leave and re-enter the tomb. How far they may have wished to travel is not revealed, but the provision of a wooden boat buried in a brick- or mud-lined pit outside some of the mastabas at Saqqara,[3] Helwān[4] and Abu Rawāsh[5] suggests that journeys of some distance, perhaps to attend festivals, were envisaged. If the royal 'tombs' at Abydos were indeed cenotaphs it must be supposed that the spirits of their owners possessed the power to transport themselves thither from Saqqara, a distance of about three hundred miles.

There is no reason to suppose that the beliefs which led to the development of mummification in the Old Kingdom were not also held in earlier times.[6] Continuity of existence depended, it was thought, on the preservation of the body or at least on the provision of a stone or wooden figure which the spirit could occupy through the powers of magic if the body were destroyed. While graves were merely shallow pits and bodies were separated from the sand by nothing more than a layer of linen or matting, physical decay was prevented by the desiccating properties of the warm, dry sand. Deeper tombs cut in the substratum of rock and covered by a superstructure of mud-brick, although giving greater protection against interference, deprived the body of the natural benefits afforded by close proximity to the sand. That the Egyptians of the Early Dynastic Period soon became aware of this consequence may be inferred from the fact that already in the Second Dynasty they had devised a method of preserving the

---

[1] §VII, 25, 351–3; §VIII, 42, 22, 35, pls. 26–8.
[2] §VII, 23; §VIII, 50, 163–4, pls. LXXIX–LXXXII; §VIII, 59, 733–5, figs. 490–1.
[3] G, 4, 131, 133, fig. 78; §III, 2, vol. I, 75, pl. 19; vol. II, 138, fig. 203, pls. 44–5; vol. III, 42, pls. 44, 66–8; §III, 3, 8, 18, fig. 9.
[4] §VIII, 50, 111, pl. 59; §VIII, 59, 678–9 (fig. 443), 817.
[5] §VIII, 20, vol. 42, 110–11, pl. XXII.　　[6] §VII, 6; §VII, 19, 20; §VIII, 9, 49.

outward form of the body by placing under the bandages, in which the various limbs and members were individually wrapped, linen pads soaked in a resinous substance and moulded to the appropriate shapes.[1] There is, however, no trace either of the removal of the most quickly decomposable organs or of the impregnation of the body with salt or natron, both of which were regular operations in the process of mummification. In general, it must be concluded that various kinds of magic, and particularly the spoken word, were invoked in order to ensure continuity of existence and, by implication, the preservation of the body. Some relics at least of the spells uttered by the mortuary priests in earlier times are to be found among the Pyramid Texts,[2] the most obvious being the spells with allusions to conditions which no longer prevailed in the pyramid tombs of the Old Kingdom, for example, 'Cast the sand from thy face' and 'The bricks are removed for thee from thy great tomb'.[3] Considerable reliance must also have been placed in the power of imitative magic. Apart from the confidence placed in it as a means of supplying the material needs of the dead, faith in its efficacy may be detected in the inclusion of wooden figures of nearly life size, no doubt to serve as substitutes for the body, in the funerary equipment. Hitherto only a very few fragments of these figures have been found[4] and the rarity of their occurrence strongly suggests that in the Early Dynastic Period their possession was a privilege confined to royalty. Even the humblest of mortals, however, might entertain the hope of physical preservation through the agency of the mound of sand and rock piled above the grave, which in origin was probably intended merely to mark the position of the grave in order to prevent accidental disturbance and to enable relatives to locate it when bringing their offerings. How early in its long history a magical significance was attached to it is unknown, but the discovery that some of the mud-brick mastabas of the early First Dynasty at Saqqara embodied within the superstructure a mound of sand overlaid with brick,[5] which had no structural purpose, shows that by that time it had become an important feature. It is not difficult to imagine that the reason for this development was the supposed resemblance of the mound to the Primeval Hill which had emerged from the waters of chaos—the so-called High Sand—and on

---

[1] G, 4, 162–4, pl. 25ᵃ; G, 14, 270; §VIII, 42, 11, 19, 28, 32.
[2] §VII, 2, 85–6; §VII, 19, 85–6.
[3] §VII, 21, vol. I, 280 (Spell 662). *Ibid.* 118 (Spell 355).
[4] G, 4, 170–2; §III, 2, vol. III, 13, pl. 27; §III, 11, 28, pl. 12, 2.
[5] See below, p. 61.

which the creator-god had manifested himself at the creation of the world.[1] By the action of imitative or symbolic magic the mound above the grave, notwithstanding its purely practical origin, would, it was believed, acquire the same vital power as the Primeval Hill and thus be able to impart life to the corpse lying beneath it.

Situated in close proximity to several of the large tombs of the First Dynasty were rows of subsidiary graves in which members of the deceased's household and certain other dependants were buried. At Abydos[2] and Abu Rawāsh[3] the graves were provided with roughly carved stelae bearing the names of the occupants, some of whom were undoubtedly women, a few apparently captives of war.[4] Among the twenty subsidiary graves surrounding the mastaba dated to the time of Mer(it)neith at Saqqara[5] were a number which belonged to artisans whose trades were indicated by the tools and other objects buried with them: model boats with perhaps a boat-builder, knives with a butcher, copper and flint tools with a stone vase carver, pots of pigment with a painter and pottery vessels with a potter.[6] Similarly at Giza, in association with the mastaba dated to Djer, one of the graves contained two palettes which suggested that the deceased was a scribe or an artist.[7] While it is evident that the occupants of subsidiary graves were intended to serve the owner of the principal tomb in the Next Life, it is very difficult to judge to what extent they were buried at the time of the funeral of their patron, either alive[8] or after receiving a lethal dose of poison.[9] In the Abydos 'tombs' of Semerkhet and Qaa only is it certain that the superstructure of the principal 'tomb' covered the subsidiary graves, and consequently there can be little doubt that all the burials in each 'tomb' were made at one and the same time. Elsewhere the subsidiary graves lay outside the principal tomb, either at intervals apart or in long trenches with brick partition walls between the graves. Both these arrangements, and particularly the detached pattern, allow of the possibility that the persons concerned were buried individually when they died a natural death, unless it can be shown that the graves in any one trench were all roofed by a single superstructure. That separate superstructures were, at least some-

---

[1] §v, 1, 151–4; §vii, 4, 42–4; §vii, 22; §viii, 48, part i, 25.
[2] §iii, 12, pls. 31–6; §iii, 11, pls. 26–30ª; G, 13, 222–6.
[3] §viii, 28, vol. vii, 22–3.   [4] G, 6, 410.
[5] G, 4, 67, fig. 30; §iii, 2, vol. ii, 133–8, 142–58, pls. 38–9, 48–51.
[6] G, 4, 66–8, 137–9.   [7] §viii, 36, 5, pl. iii.
[8] §iii, 12, 14; §iii, 13, 8; §viii, 46, 117–21.   [9] §iii, 2, vol. ii, 142.

times, built has been proved by the discovery at Saqqara of a series of sixty-two trench-graves, each with its own mastaba-form superstructure.[1] Reisner, after a re-examination of the evidence at Abydos, maintained that the number of burials which were undoubtedly made in the mass was but a fraction of the many hundreds found in the subsidiary graves surrounding the royal 'tombs'.[2] In spite of the insufficiency of the evidence to show the extent of the practice of human sacrifice during the Early Dynastic Period, the fact of its existence cannot be questioned. If the number of subsidiary graves bears any relation, as is probable, to the number of persons sacrificed, the custom reached its peak under Djer, whose two 'tomb' complexes at Abydos contained more than 590 subsidiary graves, and thereafter declined, twenty-six graves only being found in the 'tomb' of Qaa.[3] If it was continued throughout the Second Dynasty the scale was probably further reduced, but the only evidence available comes from the 'tomb' of Khasekhemwy at Abydos which Reisner estimated contained not more than ten or fifteen subsidiary burials.[4]

VIII. ARCHITECTURE, SCULPTURE AND THE SMALL ARTS

Apart from the massive brick 'fortress' enclosures with panelled faces at Abydos[5] and Hierakonpolis,[6] standing examples of early dynastic buildings are almost entirely confined to tombs. Two groups of model buildings in mud-brick associated with the mastaba dated to Aha at Saqqara provide an exception, but their purpose is uncertain; they have been compared, on the one hand, with the dummy chapels in the *Heb Sed* court of Djoser, and, on the other, with rows of objects figured at the top of the blue-tiled panels of the Step Pyramid and thought to represent granaries.[7] Traces of temples have been found both at Abydos[8] and at Hierakonpolis,[9] and a mortuary temple showing affinities with the mortuary temple of Djoser has been excavated in the enclo-

---

[1] §III, 2, vol. II, 7, pl. I.   [2] §VIII, 46, 117–21.
[3] §III, 13, 3; §VIII, 46, 105.   [4] §VIII, 46, 128.
[5] G, 4, 116; G, 24, 52–4; §VIII, 2, 1–5, pls. V–VIII; §VIII, 56, 40, pl. VI, 4, 5, 7.
[6] G, 4, 116–18; G, 24, 196–7; G, 26, 19–20, pl. 74; §VIII, 19; §VIII, 59, 526–7, figs. 354–5.
[7] G, 4, 179, fig. 101; §III, 2, vol. II, 171, pls. LVII–LXVI; §VIII, 24, 24, n. 6.
[8] G, 24, 39–40; §VIII, 33, part II, pl. 50; §VIII, 56, pl. XII, 6; §VIII, 58, 22, fig. 6.
[9] G, 24, 191–6; G, 26, pl. LXXII; §VIII, 56, pl. XII, 4; §VIII, 59, 520–1, fig. 352.

sure of a mastaba at Saqqara dating from the time of Qaa.[1] Early dynastic sacred edifices and dwellings were certainly built of soft and perishable materials, including matting of woven reeds attached to frameworks of wood, and they were probably dismantled when their purpose had been fulfilled or when replacement was considered necessary.[2] Nevertheless, it should not be supposed that because they were so constructed they were invariably simple in design and devoid of artistic character. Contemporary representations of shrines and temples on ivory and wooden tablets and cylinder seals show that these buildings embodied many distinctive architectural features, some of which were reproduced in the stone monuments of later times, notably in the Step Pyramid enclosure.

Cemeteries of the Early Dynastic Period have been found at more than forty places in Egypt between Gebel es-Silsila in the south and El-Qatta on the west side of the Delta near its apex.[3] The greater number of these cemeteries contain, however, only the graves of simple people or minor officials, which have little architectural interest except in so far as they demonstrate that the open corbel vault built of brick was employed as early as the Second Dynasty.[4] Far more instructive are the monumental tombs, and especially the group of mud-brick mastabas at Saqqara.[5] When newly built these mastabas must have presented a most colourful appearance in contrast with the monotony of their desert surroundings. A well preserved example, dated to the reign of Qaa, showed that the mud-brick walls of the superstructure were overlaid with a coat of mud-plaster covered with white lime stucco. On this surface were painted, in imitation of woven reed hangings, geometrical patterns of many kinds executed in red, white, black, blue, green and yellow.[6] Some evidence has been found to suggest that trees were planted around the superstructures, but their botanical species has not been identified.[7]

At the beginning of the First Dynasty the substructure of a mastaba usually consisted of a shallow trench cut in the rock-bed of the desert. This trench was divided by cross-walls into a series of compartments, the middle and largest compartment becoming

1 G, 4, 88–90, fig. 53; §III, 2, vol. III, 10, pls. 2, 24, 25; §VIII, 24, 38–40, fig. 12.
2 §VIII, 22, 1–16; §VIII, 48, part I, 21–38.
3 §VIII, 20, vol. XXXVIII, 59–63, fig. 17.
4 §VIII, 25, 8–9; §VIII, 46, 128–34; §VIII, 47, 12–14; §VIII, 59, 653–7.
5 See above, pp. 17–22.   6 G, 4, 189–90; §III, 2, vol. III, pls. 6–8, 16ª–17ª.
7 G, 4, 129; §III, 2, vol. I, 73.

the burial-chamber[1] while the other compartments served as store-chambers for provisions and other funerary equipment. All were roofed with wooden beams supporting a ceiling of planks, and the rock walls, coated with mud-plaster, were faced with woven reed mats. Above this trench, and extending far beyond its limits on ground level, a rectangular superstructure was built of mud-brick, its main axis running, like that of the trench, approximately north–south. The outer faces of the walls, which on the longer sides inclined inwards from the base to the top, were constructed in the form of alternating panelled recesses and projections, an architectural design known as the palace façade; the inner faces were perpendicular and plain. Within the hollow superstructure, at least in some early mastabas and possibly in all at Saqqara, a low rectangular mound of sand and rubble cased with brick was erected on ground-level directly over the burial-chamber but covering a larger area.[2] Intersecting walls were built at somewhat irregular intervals from all four inner sides of the superstructure dividing the whole of the lower part of the interior into a large number of rectangular compartments. Inside these compartments, the floors of which were raised by means of sand to the level of the top of the mound, were stored pots, stone vessels and objects of a less personal kind than those placed in the substructure. Sand and rubble were put in the space between their timber roofs and the brick roof of the mastaba. Since no large mastaba with its upper portion intact has survived, the shape of the roof is not known with certainty, but there can be little doubt that it was curved. In every probability it was bounded at each end by a flat parapet, a feature reproduced in the wooden coffins of the Second Dynasty,[3] but it is also possible that the four walls of the superstructure formed a continuous parapet of such a height that the roof was concealed from view.[4] Surrounding the building was an enclosure wall, on the north side of which lay, at least in some instances, a brick-lined boat-pit.[5] The subsidiary tombs, simple pits surmounted by plain mastabas with rounded top and one niche at the southern end of the east wall, were also constructed outside the enclosure wall in single rows set parallel to the sides of the main mastaba.[6]

[1] G, 4, 54–5; §III, 3, 17–18; §VIII, 9, 39–41; §VIII, 59, 637–40.
[2] §III, 2, vol. III, 73–7, pls. 86, 92–3; §VIII, 9, 43, fig. 3. See above, pp. 57–8.
[3] G, 4, 131, figs. 77, 79, pls. 24, 25.
[4] §VIII, 23, 154–5, pl. 19, 4; §VIII, 24, 48–51, pl. 3[b]. See Plate 29 (a).
[5] See above, p. 57.
[6] G, 4, figs. 30, 34; §III, 2, vol. II, 12–13, fig. 5, pls. I, II. Ibid. 133–8, pls. 38, 39. See above, pp. 58–9.

Until the latter part of the First Dynasty no significant change, apart from a progressive increase in size, occurred in the outward form of the monumental mastabas. Internally a gradual process of development continued throughout the period. Substructures were cut to a greater depth in the rock and were in consequence less easy of access both to the tomb-robber and to those charged with performing the burial. The large mastaba dated to Den, and once thought to be the tomb of Hemaka,[1] furnishes the earliest example of a new method of approach to the substructure by a wooden-roofed passage which sloped downwards to the burial-chamber from the floor of the open corridor outside the east wall of the superstructure.[2] Three massive slabs of limestone, set in grooves cut in the rock-walls of the passage, were lowered by means of ropes, after the fashion of portcullises, in order to block the way to the burial chamber when the body, enclosed in a wooden coffin, had been laid to rest. No doubt the mouth of the passage was filled with rubble and covered, like the rest of the open corridor, with a brick paving. Besides the portcullises and the sloping passage, part of the floor of which was cut in steps, this mastaba included as a new feature three small storerooms entirely hollowed out of the rock and connected with the burial chamber by doors. An elaboration found in a mastaba dated to the reign of Anedjib was the development of the simple brick-cased mound within the superstructure into a long mound with steps at the sides, a feature which time may show to have been the architectural ancestor of the Third Dynasty step pyramids.[3] One of the two monumental mastabas in the Saqqara group dated to the reign of Qaa provides evidence not only of the discontinuance of the practice of incorporating store rooms in the superstructure, but also of the approaching end of the palace façade, the west side of this tomb being merely panelled with a series of evenly spaced pilasters.[4] The same mastaba has preserved the latest known example of the brick bench on which were mounted model bulls' heads.[5] A most important innovation was a mud-brick temple, built on the north side of the mastaba within the inner enclosure wall,[6] one of the

[1] See above, pp. 26–7.

[2] G, 4, 75–6, fig. 38; §III, 4, 4–6, pl. 2; §VIII, 24, pl. 4; §VIII, 46, 64–5, fig. 46; §VIII, 59, 657–9, figs. 424–5.

[3] G, 4, 144–6, fig. 85; §III, 2, vol. I, 82–92, pls. 21–6, 35; §VIII, 9, 43 (fig. 4), 286–7; §VIII, 24, pl. III.

[4] G, 4, 88–90, fig. 53; §III, 2, vol. III, 5–10, pl. 2.

[5] G, 4, 71, pls. 8–9; §III, 2, vol. II, 8–9, pls. I, 6ᵇ–7ᵇ; §VIII, 9, 40, pl. Iª. See above, p. 55.

[6] §III, 2, vol. III, 10, pls. 2–3, 24–5; §VIII, 23, pl. 17, 2; §VIII, 24, 40–1, fig. 12.

rooms of which was paved with slabs of limestone.[1] Its smaller coeval, situated a short distance to the north, possessed few of the characteristics of the First Dynasty: apart from a single niche at the southern end of the east side, the exterior walls were plain and the interior of the superstructure, although divided by cross-walls into large compartments, was entirely filled with sand.[2] An unexpected discovery in the enclosure was a row of four sub-sidiary tombs, the burial-chamber of one of which was roofed with a leaning barrel-vault of brick which supported a sand-filled brick superstructure with curved roof.[3]

The subsequent architectural history of the early mastaba may be summarized as a continuation of the process of deepening and enlarging the substructure and the general adoption of the plain superstructure without interior storerooms. Sporadic examples of the palace façade, usually only partial, are known from the Second Dynasty and even later,[4] but they are not typical. As a rule the niches were reduced to two of unequal size, one at each end of the east face, the larger being at the southern end. No longer was the substructure excavated from above as a pit; it was entirely tunnelled in the rock from the lower end of the entrance stairway. In the early part of the Second Dynasty the stairway led to a large apartment which was divided by walls of brick into an entrance hall and a number of chambers, the burial-chamber being hollowed out on the west side of the entrance hall.[5] Later in the dynasty all the chambers were hewn separately on each side of a passage leading from the bottom of the stairway.[6] At the same time the mouth of the stairway, instead of lying outside the mastaba, was located under the superstructure, the rubble filling of which could therefore not have been put in place until after the funeral.

It is not difficult to deduce that the motive underlying both the deepening and the elaboration of the substructure was the hope of gaining greater security for the body and the funerary equipment; less clear is the reason for the change in the external design of the superstructure. It is however possible that the niches in the palace façade, whatever its origin,[7] had come to be regarded in the main as false-doors to the compartments in the superstructure which were used as storerooms. When the super-

---

[1] G, 4, pl. 14.   [2] §III, 2, vol. III, 98–104, pls. 114, 117.
[3] G, 4, 152, fig. 90, 185; §III, 2, vol. III, 102, 104, pls. 116, 120[d]; §VIII, 9, pl. 1[b].
[4] G, 4, 148, fig. 86; §VIII, 36, pl. 7; §VIII, 43, pl. 1; §VIII, 46, 155–7 (fig. 73), 306; §VIII, 59, 709 ff., fig. 467.   [5] G, 4, 153–7, fig. 93.
[6] G, 4, 158–61, fig. 96; §VIII, 42, 29–30, pls. 30–1.
[7] See above, p. 43.

structure was no longer used for the storage of objects, false-doors in such numbers lost their purpose and, in consequence, were reduced to two, one, the main dummy entrance to the tomb, being the place where offerings were laid and the other perhaps being considered as a subsidiary entrance.

Comparison between the monumental mastabas of Saqqara and the royal 'tombs' at Abydos is made difficult by the almost complete destruction of the superstructures in the Abydos group. Nevertheless it is clear that the substructures of the First Dynasty at Abydos, though smaller,[1] resembled both in their method of construction and in their course of development the substructures at Saqqara.[2] The initial operation in each cemetery was the excavation from above of a rectangular open pit. In the earliest 'tombs' at Abydos the entire area of the pit, apart from a lining of mud-brick around the walls, was occupied by a single chamber built of wood.[3] The three succeeding 'tombs', belonging to Djer, Djet and Mer(it)neith, were larger, and the wooden chamber, which may have been partitioned by interior walls of wood, was supported at the sides by buttresses of mud-brick,[4] the spaces between the buttresses in the 'tombs' of Djer and Djet being used for the storage of funerary equipment. Den's 'tomb' was chiefly notable for the granite floor of its burial-chamber,[5] but it also marked, as did the contemporaneous mastabas at Saqqara, the introduction of an entrance stairway, a feature which thenceforth became regular.[6] Until the time of Semerkhet, all the subsidiary burials were placed outside the main 'tomb'. Semerkhet and Qaa however used for their subsidiary graves the space between the sides of the pit and the burial-chamber, which in the 'tombs' of Den and Anedjib had been filled with thick linings of mud-brick.[7] Since the superstructures covered the entire pit and the stairways led only to the burial-chamber and some storerooms, the bodies must have been placed in the subsidiary graves before the superstructures were built. What form these superstructures, and those

---

[1] See above, p. 19.

[2] G, 4, 47–104; §III, 11, 7–15; §III, 12, 8–17; §VIII, 46, 9–16, 21–6, 57–63; §VIII, 59, 620–34, 644–7.

[3] G, 4, 53–4, fig. 14; §III, 11, 7–8, pls. 58–9; §VIII, 46, 13–16, fig. 13; §VIII, 59, 620–2, fig. 396.

[4] G, 4, 61–71, figs. 24, 31, 33; §III, 11, 8–9, pl. 60; §III, 12, 8–11, pl. 61; §VIII, 46, 22–6, figs. 18–20; §VIII, 59, 622–6, figs. 397–8.

[5] See below, p. 66.

[6] G, 4, 79–80, fig. 40; §VIII, 59, 626–7, fig. 399.

[7] G, 4, figs. 40, 42, 47, 51; §III, 11, pl. 62; §III, 12, pls. 60–1; §VIII, 46, 58–64, figs. 41–4; §VIII, 59, 626–31, figs. 398–401.

of the preceding 'tombs', were given is very uncertain. That their sides were plain, and not decorated with the palace façade, is clear from the traces of the retaining wall found above the 'tomb' of Djet,[1] and Reisner's suggestion that the earliest 'tombs' were covered with simple mud-brick mastabas[2] has not been disputed. However his theory that the superstructures of the 'tombs' of Djer and Djet rose by two and three steps respectively to a flat summit, about eight and twelve metres in height,[3] has not found favour with more recent writers, who prefer to regard their super-structures either as low flat-topped mounds of sand held together by rectangular retaining walls of brick[4] or as higher structures of the same character but with curved or slightly domed roofs.[5]

Peribsen and Khasekhemwy alone among the ten kings of the Second Dynasty built 'tombs' at Abydos. Unlike the mastabas of their period at Saqqara, these 'tombs' were constructed of mud-brick in open pits, the 'tomb' of Peribsen consisting of a burial-chamber surrounded by about a dozen storerooms and an outer corridor running between the brick lining of the pit and the back-walls of the storerooms.[6] Khasekhemwy's 'tomb', which covered a much larger area, had more than fifty compartments, chiefly storerooms but the eight nearest to the burial-chamber appear to have been reserved for subsidiary burials.[7] The most interesting feature of the 'tomb', however, was the burial-chamber itself (about 5·25 m. by 3·0 m.); the floor and walls of which were constructed of dressed limestone blocks laid in regular courses. Very different in character were two cavernous tombs at Saqqara tunnelled seven metres below ground-level and later partly covered by the Pyramid temple of King Unas.[8] On the evidence of mud-sealings found therein these tombs have been ascribed respectively to Nynetjer and to either Hetepsekhemwy or Reneb.[9]

Manetho quotes a tradition, which appears to date back at least to Ramesside times,[10] that it was Imhotep, Djoser's architect, who invented the technique of building with hewn stone. Possibly there is some truth in the tradition, for, although the Palermo

---

[1] §III, 12, pl. 62.   [2] §VIII, 46, 307–22.

[3] §VIII, 24, 44–6, fig. 13; §VIII, 46, 322–5, figs. 172–3.

[4] §VIII, 48, part II, 14–19.

[5] §VIII, 23, 156–7, pl. 20, 2, 3; §VIII, 24, 44–9, figs. 16–17.

[6] G, 4, 95–6, fig. 60; §III, 11, 11–12, pl. 61; §VIII, 46, 124–6, fig. 54; §VIII, 59, 631–2, fig. 402.

[7] G, 4, 101–2, fig. 66; §III, 11, 12–14, pls. 57 (4–6), 63; §VIII, 46, 126–8, fig. 55; §VIII, 59, 632–4, fig. 403.

[8] §VIII, 9, 46–7; §VIII, 11, 46–8, figs. 8–9; §VIII, 16; §VIII, 24, 62, pl. 6ᵃ.

[9] §VIII, 11, 46–8. See above, p. 20.   [10] §VIII, 18, 13–15.

Stone records that an unnamed king at the end of the Second Dynasty erected a stone temple (p. 34), the earliest known buildings composed entirely of stone are those in the Step Pyramid enclosure at Saqqara. Stone had, however, been employed for parts of buildings before the days of Djoser and Imhotep, the granite pavement of Den and Khasekhemwy's chamber of lime-stone blocks, in their 'tombs' at Abydos, being perhaps the two most notable examples.[1] In the mastaba of Herneith at Saqqara[2] and also in a mastaba of the early First Dynasty at Tarkhān,[3] slabs of limestone were laid above the wooden ceilings of cham-bers, while the same material was used to pave part of the temple attached to the largest of the three mastabas at Saqqara which date from the time of Qaa.[4] Large limestone slabs were also em-ployed for lining the inner walls of the First Dynasty brick mastabas at Helwān, perhaps in order to provide support for stone roofs which have disappeared.[5] Linings of a similar kind were undoubtedly used for this purpose in a brick tomb of the Early Dynastic Period at Hierakonpolis, part of the stone roof of which was preserved.[6] It is clear, from the occurrences at Tarkhān and Helwān that con-struction in stone was not confined to the tombs of royal persons; perhaps the proximity of the Tura limestone quarries was a contributory factor in the choice of material at Helwān where the pits were cut in gravel, but a similar reason cannot be given for Den's pavement, which must have been brought from the neigh-bourhood of Aswān. The skill necessary both for the cutting and for the transport of stone having once been acquired, it might have been expected that an immediate and progressive increase in its employment would have followed; that such a development did not occur may be attributed to a belief that mud-brick, which could easily be produced and handled in quantity, was sufficiently durable and also to the fact that the most essential parts of the tomb, which housed the body and funerary equipment, were in many instances already hewn out of solid rock and needed no further protection.

In sculpture and the small arts, to no less a degree than in architecture, the protodynastic and early dynastic periods were an age of progress and development;[7] artists and craftsmen were

---

1 §III, 11, 9–10, pl. 56ᴬ; *ibid.* 13–14, pl. 57.
2 §III, 2, vol. III, 77.
3 §VIII, 39, 15, pl. 16.
4 G, 4, pl. 14; §III, 2, vol. III, 10, pl. 25ᵃ.
5 §VIII, 24, 4–5, fig. 1; §VIII, 50, 163–5, pls. 61, 62, 67, 69, 70; §VIII, 51, 9–11, pl. 6.
6 G, 26, 51, pl. 68.
7 G, 2; §VIII, 57, 1–13, 110–32; §VIII, 58, 20–9.

experimenting with new technical methods and applying the materials at their disposal to fresh uses, sometimes with remarkable success and sometimes with results which betrayed their inexperience. Complete mastery was, for instance, attained in the production of stone vessels; profiting no doubt from the knowledge inherited from their ancestors, the vase-makers of the First Dynasty manufactured enormous quantities of vessels in alabaster, slate, diorite, breccia, basalt, rock crystal, granite and a variety of other stones, which were never surpassed in quality of form and workmanship. Many notable feats were also achieved by sculptors, especially when carving in relief, although their art was still in its infancy. No class of objects demonstrates the different stages of progress more impressively than the decorated slate palettes of the protodynastic period to the beginning of the First Dynasty.[1] In the examples which are considered to be the earliest, the human and animal figures are usually represented as separate units, without any overlapping, and are evenly distributed in close array over the whole surface of the palette; this method of arrangement is not displeasing to the eye, but the purport of the scene is obscured by the mass of representations, the absence of logical grouping and the uniform size of the figures. Intermediate examples display both overlapping figures and well-spaced groups. The final stage is illustrated by the palette of Narmer—a masterpiece judged by any standards—in which the scenes are divided into registers, emphasis is given to the importance of the king by magnifying his stature and some hieroglyphic captions are added. A very similar technique is to be observed on the limestone maceheads of Scorpion and Narmer,[2] which, by reason of their rounded surface, must have presented more formidable problems in carving and arrangement than the flat or almost flat slate palettes. Of subsequent works, the limestone stelae of Djet[3] and Mer(it)neith,[4] a limestone lintel with figures of recumbent lions in the mastaba of Herneith,[5] the fragmentary slate stela of Khasekhem[6] and the granite door-jamb of Khasekhemwy[7] show that the art of carving in relief was well maintained throughout the Early Dynastic Period.

Few large sculptures in the round have been discovered in a state of preservation which allows their artistic qualities to be

[1] G, 2, 226–48; §I, 21; §I, 27; §VIII, 21, pls. 2–5; §VIII, 30; §VIII, 45; §VIII, 52, pls. 2–4; §VIII, 58, 15–18, fig. 3, pls. 6 and 7.

[2] G, 2, 247–52; G, 25, pl. XXVI b, c; §VIII, 58, 16–17, fig. 4.

[3] G, 24, 82–3.

[4] G, 24, 82; §III, 12, Frontispiece.

[5] §III, 2, vol. III, 77, pl. 96; §III, 6.

[6] See above, p. 32, n. 5.

[7] See above, p. 34, n. 4.

fairly assessed, but it is difficult to believe that the earliest human figures, as exemplified by the specimens found at Hierakonpolis,[1] were not invariably heavy in appearance; nevertheless an alabaster baboon inscribed with the name of Narmer and a granite lion, both in the Berlin Museum,[2] prove that realistic likenesses of animals were sometimes achieved. Before the end of the Second Dynasty a distinct improvement in rendering the features of the human face is perceptible; the granite kneeling figure of an official, now in the Cairo Museum,[3] which bears the names of the first three kings of the dynasty and the slate and limestone statuettes of Khasekhem[4] show a striking liveliness and subtlety of facial expression. Among the small figures in stone, two in the Ashmolean Museum are perhaps the most notable, a basalt standing man[5] and a lapis lazuli standing woman,[6] the first as a vivid piece of sculpture and the second mainly on account of its material, the precise origin of which has not yet been ascertained, although both Abyssinia and Afghanistan have been suggested.[7]

Small objects composed of ivory must be reckoned among the principal works of art of this period. The knife-handles from Gebel el-Araq and elsewhere have already been mentioned (p. 42); of the many other articles, including cylinders, wands and maceheads decorated with scenes in relief,[8] perhaps the most impressive is a figure of a bound Asiatic captive carved on a gaming-piece which was found in the 'tomb' of Qaa at Abydos.[9] The incised ivory and wooden dockets are more sketchy in execution, seemingly because they were intended not for display, but merely for recording the year when the article to which they were attached was made. By reason of its softness, ivory lent itself more readily than stone to delicate modelling and to the delineation of detail; these features are especially conspicuous in the small figures carved in the round, an outstanding example being the statuette of a king clad in a woven robe which was found in the temple-deposit at Abydos and is now in the British Museum.[10] Scarcely inferior in artistic quality, but less well preserved, are a number of figurines

---

[1] G, 25, pl. II; G, 26, pl. I; §VIII, 31; §VIII, 57, 8, pl. I, *d–e*.

[2] §VIII, 14, figs. 53, 54; §VIII, 21, pl. I; §VIII, 53, part II, pl. 18; §VIII, 54, pl. II, 2.

[3] See above, p. 30, n. 2.   [4] G, 25, pls. XXXIX, XLI; §VIII, 57, pl. 2[d].

[5] §VIII, I, 27, pl. I; §VIII, 57 pl. I[b].

[6] G, 25, pl. XVIII; G, 26, 38; §VIII, 49, 84, 3.

[7] G, 14, 398–400; §VIII, 15, 124–9, 134–5.

[8] G, 25, pls. XII–XVII.

[9] G, 4, 250, fig. 148; §III, 12, pls. XII, XVII; A, 15, 72, fig. 4.

[10] §VIII, 12; §VIII, 33, part II, 24, pls. II, XIII; §VIII, 57, pl. I[a].

from Hierakonpolis,[1] while many gaming-pieces in the form of dogs and lions portray these animals in a very lifelike manner.[2]

Despite the fact that their productions were generally among the main objectives of the tomb-robber, some notable examples of clever workmanship by jewellers, metalsmiths and craftsmen of different kinds have survived. The four ornate bracelets, which were still attached to the arm of their female owner when they were discovered in the 'tomb' of Djer at Abydos,[3] consist of beads and plaques of gold, turquoise and lapis lazuli fashioned with great skill and arranged with excellent taste. No less pleasing are some necklaces of gold beads engraved with geometric patterns or shaped like snail-shells, two gold amuletic figures of a bull and an oryx, and a gold capsule in the form of a cockroach inlaid with the emblem of Neith in blue paste, all of which were buried in a middle-class grave at Naga ed-Deir.[4] Such a degree of proficiency in the fabrication of gold as is denoted by these isolated objects could have been achieved only by long practice, which presupposes that a considerable supply of this metal, obtained partly from the eastern desert, was available. The coppersmiths of the period were also most accomplished craftsmen: one First Dynasty mastaba at Saqqara alone yielded a vast quantity of well-made copper tools and instruments,[5] while smaller deposits of the same kind have been found elsewhere.[6] In the light of these discoveries the statement on the Palermo Stone that a copper statue of Khasekhemwy was made at the end of the Second Dynasty[7] does not seem incredible, although the figures of Phiops I and his son, dating from the Sixth Dynasty, are the earliest examples in copper which have hitherto been recovered. Of other types of craftsmen whose works have been preserved, the makers of inlay deserve mention, in particular, the makers of five ornamental stone disks found in the tomb formerly attributed to Hemaka, Den's chancellor.[8] The finest of these disks, which were perhaps spinning tops, is composed of black steatite inlaid with slightly raised figures in coloured stones of hounds and gazelles, one hound pursuing a fleeing gazelle and the other seizing a prostrate gazelle by the throat; both technically and artistically it is a work of consummate skill.[9]

---

[1] G, 2, 169–73, figs. 132–3; G, 25, pls. v–xi; §viii, 57, 4–7, figs. 6–7.

[2] G, 2, 178–84; §iii, 11, pl. vi; §viii, 17, vol. i, 45, fig. 35; §viii, 28, vol. viii, pls. vii, viii; §viii, 29, vol. ii, 192, figs. 698–9; §viii, 54, 11–18.

[3] See above, p. 23, n. 8.   [4] §viii, 47, pls. 5–9; §viii, 58, 27, pl. 11b.

[5] See above, p. 24, n. 1.   [6] §iii, 11, pl. ixa; §viii, 38, *passim*.   [7] §iv, 36.

[8] §iii, 4, pl. 12.   [9] See Plate 29 (*b*).

Considered as a whole, undoubtedly the most outstanding feature of early dynastic art is its contribution to the succeeding ages: forms and motifs invented during the period remained in use for generations and even, in some cases, until Roman times. The mastaba, which persisted until the end of the Middle Kingdom, is only one instance of such a survival in the field of architecture; the fluted columns of Djoser and the lotus-cluster columns of the Fifth Dynasty may have been translated into stone for architectural purposes in the Old Kingdom, but they were certainly not artistic creations of that time, for the same shapes occur in miniature on early dynastic ivories.[1] Again, the blue glazed faience tiles lining the subterranean chambers of Djoser's pyramid and mastaba at Saqqara can be paralleled by earlier specimens found at Hierakonpolis[2] and Abydos.[3] Many conventions adopted by Egyptian sculptors of all periods, such as the representation of the king as a towering figure, the placing of the left foot in advance of the right in striding statues,[4] statuettes and reliefs and the classic scene of the king smiting his kneeling enemies with a mace[5] can all be traced to the First Dynasty. It was indeed the age in which the traditional attitudes and attributes received their stereotyped forms.[6]

[1] §VIII, 10.   [2] G, 25, pl. XVIII.   [3] §VIII, 33, part II, pl. VIII.
[4] §III, 2, vol. III, 13, pl. 27.
[5] G, 4, 60, fig. 23; G, 24, 84; §VIII, 13, 283, fig. 154.
[6] G, 8, 13, n. 2.

CHAPTER XII

THE LAST PREDYNASTIC PERIOD IN BABYLONIA

I. SOURCES AND GENERAL CHARACTER OF THE PERIOD

Towards the middle of the fourth millennium B.C., civilization in the plain of the Euphrates and the Tigris was not dissimilar to that of western Asia in general, as described in the foregoing chapters. Everywhere we find farmers and stock-breeders, in possession of all the requisite crafts, obtaining a few commodities from abroad, and little given to change. Similar peasant cultures —settled, stagnant and uncentralized—existed in Neolithic times throughout Europe and Asia, and continued to exist there for centuries after the ancient Near East had evolved a more complex mode of life, and had, through the diffusion of metallurgy, brought about an improvement in the equipment of the populations of Asia and Europe. If we judge by their remains, these people do not appear inferior to the early inhabitants of the ancient Near East and of Egypt described in chapters VII–IX above. We cannot explain why the latter set out on a course which led to achievements surpassing all that had gone before. In prehistoric times the future centres of high civilization showed no signs of being exceptional. On the contrary, each of them formed part of a larger cultural province: Egypt shared its early pre-dynastic civilization with Libya, Nubia and perhaps the Sudan; northern Mesopotamia was at first indistinguishable from north Syria; southern Mesopotamia was intimately linked with Persia. It was the unprecedented development described in this and the preceding chapter which differentiated Egypt and Mesopotamia from their surroundings, as it also established their unique historical significance.

Egyptian tradition did justice to the momentous nature of the change by acknowledging a first king of a first dynasty as its central figure. The peculiar conditions of Mesopotamia—a country without natural boundaries and not, at first, ruled by kings—precluded the clear demarcation of a new beginning in its recorded history; instead of a single monarchy we find autonomous city states, each linking its present to a legendary past. But the actual remains discovered in Iraq leave no doubt as to the sweeping character of the transition from prehistory to history.

In western Asia it is the southernmost part of the Mesopotamian alluvium which is constantly indicated as the focus of the innovations. They took place in Sumer, the southern part of the country subsequently called Sumer and Akkad, the latter being, in general, the north. It is true that the social and linguistic relationship between peoples called Sumerians and Akkadians (that is, speakers of a non-Semitic and a Semitic tongue respectively) is very uncertain in the earliest times of their appearance in history, and there is increasing reason to believe that from the earliest discernible beginning they were already inextricably mixed.[1] Yet all Babylonian tradition looked back, at least, to the Sumerian language as 'original' and of superior dignity; the writing which was invented for it (or which it was the first to assume) was the ancestor of the cuneiform script, and the language of the first inscriptions which can be surely interpreted[2] is Sumerian, soon to be in possession of a literary as well as a scribal tradition.[3]

The framework for a relative chronology of the period derives from a deep sounding in the E-anna precinct at Uruk (Warka), and from the superimposed remains of successive temples found there.[4]

At Uruk, likewise, the most important known works of art of the period have been found and, furthermore, the earliest texts. But other sites, too, have contributed to our knowledge. At Ur, layers parallel in time to those at Warka have been investigated.[5] However, since they consist of rubbish and graveyards, they do not present such clear-cut divisions as a succession of building levels. The same qualification attaches to the discoveries made at Kish[6] and at Tello.[7] In addition to these sites where stratified remains of our period were found, we must name those where such remains occurred either as survivals in later layers or as more or less isolated finds: Al-'Ubaid,[8] Fārah,[9] Tell Asmar, Tell Agrab.[10] At some other sites important and coherent remains have been found: a well-preserved temple at Tell 'Uqair,[11] temples at Eridu,[12] and an insufficiently known but probably secular building at Jamdat

---

[1] See below, pp. 96 ff.; §1, 14, Descr. Cat. 1, no. 2; §1, 1, 77 f. See also R. D. Biggs, 'Semitic Names in the Fara Period', in *Or.* n.s. 36 (1967), 55 ff.

[2] §1, 4.   [3] §1, 1.

[4] *C.A.H.* 1³, ch. VIII, sect. 1 (Uruk-Warka).

[5] *Ibid.* (Ur-Al-'Ubaid and neighbourhood).   [6] §1, 8; §1, 11; §1, 15.

[7] §1, 2; §1, 12.   [8] §1, 3; §1, 6.   [9] §1, 7; §1, 13.

[10] §1, 5.   [11] §11, 8.   [12] §11, 6; §11, 7.

Naṣr,[1] the first belonging to the early, the second to the later, part of our period. Finally, we know at Khafājī a succession of temple ruins which illustrate the development of sacred architecture in our period as well as its relation (which is very close) with the succeeding Early Dynastic age.[2]

The individual character of these several remains will occupy us in the next sections; here it must be said that it is no longer sufficient, as it was at first when the discoveries were made, to describe our period in terms of the sequence at Warka, nor is a distinction of two periods named after sites—Warka and Jamdat Naṣr—wholly adequate.[3] In fact, the very significance of our period is now blurred by the terminology according to which the period is represented by two out of three prehistoric 'periods' which precede the Early Dynastic age. This terminology served its purpose when it was introduced with a view to co-ordinating, in the early thirties, a number of excavations undertaken specifically to establish a sequence of prehistoric phases in Mesopotamia. The material remains fitted well into the series of Al-'Ubaid, Uruk, Jamdat Naṣr, and Early Dynastic periods, and the reader will find these terms to be widely used. But for the historian they are awkward, since it is towards the end of the 'Uruk period' that the momentous change we have described takes place. The early part of this period is purely prehistoric in character and resembles the preceding Al-'Ubaid period, in that it is not confined to the Euphrates–Tigris valley; it extends farther towards the north. The later part of what has been called the 'Uruk period' (i.e. Uruk 5–4) is known only in southern Mesopotamia and comprises all the innovations which constitute the birth of Mesopotamian civilization. These layers, however, resemble in many respects the succeeding phase hitherto called the Jamdat Naṣr period (i.e. Uruk 3): the continuity is, in fact, so strong that these successive phases are now often comprised in the term 'Proto-literate',[4] which will sometimes be employed in this chapter.

It is difficult to determine what are the precise layers contemporaneous with the beginning of this formative phase of Mesopotamian culture. In the stratification at E-anna, the site of the Ishtar-Inanna temple at Uruk, eighteen archaic layers are distinguished. These are

[1] §1, 10; see also *C.A.H.* 1³, ch. VIII, sect. 1.

[2] §II, 2; see also *C.A.H.* 1³, ch. VIII, sect. 1.

[3] For a discussion of the names to be given to the prehistoric periods in Babylonia, see *C.A.H.* 1³, ch. VIII, sect. 1.

[4] For a critique of this term see *C.A.H.* 1³, ch. VIII, sect. 1, where 'Uruk Period' is used to cover the entire cultural development succeeding the 'Al-'Ubaid' period and the 'Jamdat Naṣr' phase is merely the end of 'Uruk'.

numbered from the top downwards and the 'Proto-literate' period ends with layer 2; layers 3, 4 and 5 certainly belong to it but it is probable that 6, and even 7, belong to it also; the latter is free of 'Ubaid ware (which survives into the prehistoric Uruk period) and contains mosaic cones, which we shall recognize as a distinctive feature of the architecture of 'Proto-literate' times. But the question precisely where, in any given sequence of remains, this period starts, will have to be decided in each case when sufficient material becomes available.[1]

The later half of this concluding period, though possessing a recognizable character, continues in almost all respects the traditions of the earlier phase. It is often difficult to decide whether an artifact should be assigned to Uruk 4 or Uruk 3 (Jamdat Naṣr phase). The polychrome pottery which counts as the most distinctive feature of the Jamdat Naṣr phase existed already in the preceding Uruk 4 phase. The indecisiveness of the situation is illustrated, for example, by the *Riemchengebäude* at Uruk. The excavators assign the structure to the Uruk 4 phase but describe the pottery found therein as typical of the Jamdat Naṣr phase. Indeed, at Warka, it is often difficult, if not impossible, to discern whether certain buildings are to be assigned to Uruk 4 or 3; the opinions of the excavators themselves seem often to reflect this uncertainty. Nevertheless, there is a difference between the earlier and later remains. In the beginning, notably in layers 5 and 4 at Uruk, we are confronted with the unheralded emergence of important inventions: Mesopotamian culture seems suddenly to crystallize. In the later layers, at Uruk, and at Jamdat Naṣr, Khafājī and other sites where similar remains are found, we observe a decreased creativity and therefore, in the field of art, a loss of quality. But we also note a consolidation of the earlier discoveries and their practical application on a wider scale than before. This phase represents a period of expansion which carried Mesopotamian influence through the length and breadth of the ancient Near East. Thus we distinguish two phases in this final period, the remains of which, respectively, we shall now describe.

II. THE EARLIER PHASE (URUK 4)

While in Egypt the monuments of Early Dynastic times celebrate the divine king, those of Mesopotamia in the like period concern

[1] See also *C.A.H.* I[3], ch. VIII, sect. I (Uruk-Warka), where there is a discussion of the limitations of the evidence obtained from this sounding.

the relations between man and the gods; the earliest monumental buildings known are, in the one case, royal tombs; in the other, temples.

At Eridu,[1] a series of eighteen temples was discovered beneath the later zikkurrat of Amar-Sin. The earliest of these (18–6) belong to the 'Ubaid period:[2] the next series, temples 1–5, may be attributed to the Uruk period. Here we have an excellent illustration of the prehistoric antecedents of the monumental architecture found in the Uruk 4 phase, the 'golden age' of Sumerian architecture. Temples 5–1, which represent the typical tripartite Sumerian plan, are said to have stood on a raised platform. The latest temple (1)[3] was raised upon a 'massive terrace' with buttresses and stepped offsets.

It was at Uruk itself, however, that the most impressive monumental layout known to us in this period was revealed. Unfortunately, the various stages of rebuilding at this complex site are often difficult to disentangle; the architectural remains sometimes appear unintelligible owing to later alterations or destruction, and it is at times impossible to attribute buildings with any degree of certainty to the Uruk 4 or Uruk 3 (Jamdat Naṣr) phase.

In the Uruk 4 b phase, at least three temple complexes existed concurrently. Temples A (on the north–south terrace) and B would appear to be typical Sumerian tripartite temples,[4] though they were only partially excavated.

Adjoining the north–south terrace was a large courtyard whose walls were decorated in places with cone-mosaic in red, white and black. At the north end of this court were two flights of steps leading up to a small platform which projected from a raised terrace. Set upon this terrace was the 'Pillar Hall', a portico consisting of a double row of four free-standing and two engaged columns, each 2·62 m. in diameter.[5] An entrance was apparently found at one end, in the axis of the portico. Part of the courtyard wall nearest to the portico on the north-east side was ornamented with a row of small, contiguous engaged columns.

The façade of the stair platform, the columns of the portico and the north-east wall of the court with its engaged columns were all decorated with cone-mosaic.[6] The portico may have led to a temple beyond but this remains a mystery as it is incompletely excavated.

[1] §ii, 6; §ii, 7.   [2] For a discussion of these, see *C.A.H.* i³, ch. viii, sect. i.
[3] §ii, 7, 106 f. For a reconstruction of this temple, see §ii, 10, pl. 30 on p. 41.
[4] §ii, 5, Taf. 1; G, 7, fig. 16.
[5] §ii, 5, Taf. 1 (Pfeilerhalle); G, 7, fig. 16 (Pillar Temple).
[6] §ii, 3, iv, Taf. 7–9.

There is no doubt, however, that the Pillar Hall must have been one of the most imposing monuments of this period.

Level 4*a* at Uruk is represented by temple C,[1] a very large (54·20 × 22·20 m.) building which would appear to be a combination of two tripartite temples set at right angles, and by temple D, of which enough remains to suggest another tripartite Sumerian plan.

The one remaining temple known to us at Uruk is the 'Stone-Cone Temple'.[2] In both its phases this temple stood in a large courtyard whose walls were decorated with stepped recesses on both sides. The inner walls of the court and the outer walls of the temple must have been covered with red, white and blue cone-mosaics, the remains of which were strewn over the site in large quantities. Again we are confronted by a tripartite plan, but this time with deviations, the most striking of which is an L-shaped room occupying the north-east side of the building. The excavator attributed this temple to the end of Uruk 4, though he admitted the possibility of an Uruk 3 date.

At Tell 'Uqair was found a series of temples, the earliest of which may have been founded in the 'Ubaid period. The most important of these was the 'Painted Temple';[3] its exact date remains uncertain but it may be described here, as there is some reason to suppose that it may be placed within the Uruk 4 phase. This temple, built of *Riemchen* bricks, was set on a platform about 5 m. high, arranged in two steps, with a buttressed façade and approached by three separate staircases. Above the niches of the façade was a horizontal band of five rows of black cone-mosaic. The temple itself also had a buttressed façade. Its plan represented the classic Sumerian tripartite temple, comparable with those at Warka and Eridu: a central cella with flanking rooms. The cella was approached through doors at the side; there may also have been an entrance at the end opposite the podium, but this was not preserved.

At the north-west end of the cella was a stepped podium 3 ft. high which projected for 12 ft. over a width of 8 ft., to which a flight of six steps gave access. Towards the other end of the cella was a smaller pedestal.

The most remarkable feature of this building was its painted decoration, traces of which survived on every square foot of the inner walls and podium. This was executed in a great variety of colours (except green and blue) on a white ground. The most

---

[1] G, 7, fig. 16.   [2] §II, 3, no. xv, Taf. 36.
[3] §II, 8; see also *C.A.H.* I[3], ch. VIII, sect. 1 (Tell 'Uqair).

usual arrangement consisted of a red wash forming a dado about 1 m. high; above, a band of geometric ornament about 30 cm. high; above this again, a band of animal and human figures. These included quadrupeds (probably bulls) and bare-footed human figures clad in knee-length kilts. Unfortunately these were preserved only to waist height, but it may reasonably be supposed that they represent men bringing cattle as offerings to the deity.

The best-preserved paintings were on the front and sides of the podium: the front bore an imitation of a buttressed façade with patterns in the recess, probably representing cone-mosaics, comparable with that found on the façade of the stair platform in the Pillar Hall at Uruk. To the side were two spotted leopards, one couchant, the other seated on its haunches.

Paintings have not been preserved at other sites but the geometric patterns found at 'Uqair recur at Uruk in E-anna, the area sacred to the goddess Inanna. As we have seen above, some of those early shrines had walls decorated on the outside with many thousands of thin cones of baked clay. These are generally 3–4 in. long and resemble headless nails; their tops are about $\frac{1}{2}$ in. or less in diameter and are often dipped in red or black paint. These cones were inserted, closely packed, into a thick mud plaster, thus covering the mud-brick walls with a weatherproof skin of baked clay cones, the coloured heads of which formed lozenges, zigzags and other geometric patterns in black and red on a buff ground.

This method of covering the walls was laborious in the extreme, and it was later restricted to the recessed panels of the brickwork. In this later form it survived at Uruk into Early Dynastic times, but elsewhere it may well have been confined to the predynastic period. The cone-mosaics must have been used in the beginning throughout southern Mesopotamia, for at many sites where traces of early settlement are found—Ur and Eridu among them—clay cones occur in greater or lesser quantity, although not in properly preserved mosaics. Mosaics were also executed in cones cut from stone and ground into shape.[1] At Eridu, gypsum cones with ends sheathed in copper were found in association with temples attributed to the Uruk period.[2]

Mosaics probably included representational as well as geometric designs, notably animal friezes such as were rendered in paint at 'Uqair. We cannot prove that these were originally produced by the use of painted cones, but that is suggested by a simplified

[1] In the *Steinstiftmosaik* temple at Warka, see §II, 3, no. xv.
[2] §II, 7, 107.

type of animal mosaic which was known at Uruk during the later part of the predynastic period: here the animals were modelled in one piece in clay, and the flat plaques so produced were surrounded by cones which covered the rest of the walls. These friezes and the paintings at 'Uqair thus form the proto-types of similar designs executed in inlay work or by means of applied copper figures at Al-'Ubaid in Early Dynastic times.[1] We observe, then, a change of technique, but continuity of usage, in the decoration of early Mesopotamian temples.

Cones of larger and coarser types were used too. Some of about a foot in length served as a border near the upper edge of the artificial temple mounds at Uruk and 'Uqair. But the most accomplished use of cone-mosaic occurs in Archaic Layer 4 at Uruk; here, as we have seen, huge columns, 9 ft. in diameter, are completely covered with small cones forming geometric designs. The same ornamentation adorns the front of the platform sup-porting the colonnade, and the walls with semi-engaged columns which flank the stairs leading up to the platform. The combina-tion of colouring and texture gives to these wall surfaces an extraordinary richness and beauty.

One of the most important monuments of the 'Proto-literate' period is an alabaster vase 3 ft. high, now in the Iraq Museum at Baghdad.[2] It was found at Uruk in a Jamdat Naṣr stratum but the style in which it is executed suggests that it belongs to the earlier Uruk 4 phase. Its outer face is covered with reliefs that, in all probability, depict a ritual which took place in the shrine where the vessel was found. The goddess Inanna appears in front of two reed posts with streamers which form her symbol. A naked figure (in Early Dynastic times priests were often naked when officiating) offers the deity a basket with fruit. Behind him are traces of a figure well known from contemporary monuments. He wears a long skirt, a beard, and long hair plaited and wound round the head to form a chignon at the back. This coiffure is worn by rulers in Early Dynastic and Akkadian times. On the vase this personage seems to offer the goddess an elaborate girdle, the tassels of which are held by a servant who follows him. Other gifts offered to the goddess are placed behind her: among them, two tall vases shaped exactly like the one we are describing; two more vases in the shape of animals—a goat, a lion—with rimmed openings on the back (and such vases have actually been found in temples of the Jamdat Naṣr phase at Khafājī),[3] two flat dishes with

[1] See below, pp. 287 f.　　　　[2] G, 6, figs. 87–90; G, 8, pls. 19–22.
[3] §II, I, 43 and notes 64–6.

fruit; two tall baskets with vegetables and fruit; and a curious object, no doubt a piece of temple furniture, which consists of the figure of a powerful ram supporting on its back a two-staged temple tower upon which stand a male and a female figure and the symbols of the goddess.

The ritual scene we have described occupies the uppermost register of the design. A lower register shows a series of naked men carrying baskets of fruit, dishes and jars. The third and the lowest bands of design show rams and sheep, date palms and ears of barley in alternation.

The vase from Uruk is not the only monument of this period which celebrates Inanna as a fertility goddess—a trough in the British Museum[1] shows rams, sheep and lambs beside a reed structure capped by the symbols of the goddess. This building is probably either an archaic type of shrine or the fold of the flock of Inanna. The design also includes an eight-petalled rosette, a stylized flower which often symbolizes the vegetable kingdom which the goddess rules. The same combination of herbivores and plants is common on contemporary seals, be it that cattle are combined with the curving ears of barley, or that the temple animals are shown being ritually fed with barley; or there are also the symbolic rosettes which we have just described.

Engravings on cylinder seals give us a more complete impression of the artistic achievements of the age than the sadly damaged wall-paintings and the rare vases with reliefs. The quality of the seal engravings is often of the highest, and the variety of their repertoire is very great. It would be pointless to enumerate their subjects here,[2] but it is important to observe (since it shows the extraordinary inventiveness of the age) that every type of design which we meet in later times was known already in the 'Proto-literate' period—with the possible exception of myths, which are commonly depicted in Akkadian times alone. We find in these earlier ages ritual scenes, and even a secular one (the 'king' on the battlefield), in other words, subjects in which the narrative is all-important. But likewise we find heraldic animals, antithetical groups, and similar subjects in which the content matters little and the decorative values count most. We find designs which are symbolical, such as ibexes flanking a pair of snakes and a rosette: in other words, a group of manifestations or attributes of the nature-deities we have discussed. But there are also seal designs consisting of files of animals, as superbly modelled as the symbolic groups, but of uncertain significance. The seals are larger than

[1] G, 8, pl. 23.   [2] General discussions will be found in §I, 1; §I, 4; §II, 4.

those of any other period; some are as much as 2 in. in diameter and more in height. Together with the stone vases they give an impression of perfection in the work of this time.

Among the secular monuments found at Uruk is a black granite stela,[1] retaining in large part the original shape of the boulder but showing on one smoothed face a bearded leader in the act of hunting lions. He uses a spear in one example, bow and arrow in the other, for he is represented twice. There is no inscription; no setting is indicated and there are no followers. The occasion of the hunt remains a mystery, and thus an innovation of great importance in the history of the stela, the free-standing stone set up merely to serve as vehicle for an inscription or design, remains problematical.

A much finer work discovered at Uruk is a female head,[2] 8 in. high, fitted originally, perhaps, to a statue of different material. It is made of gypsum and eyes and eyebrows were inlaid, as was usual in the Early Dynastic period. There is a curious contrast of treatment within the work: the face is exquisitely modelled but the hair, parted in the middle, is rendered by a succession of broad flat planes. If, as has recently been assumed, these geometric surfaces were covered with gold-foil engraved to render the hair, the contrast with the treatment of the face would disappear. In any case, the head is a work of rare beauty more in keeping with that of the earlier phase of the 'Proto-literate' period than with that of the later layers in which it was found. It is probably a survival from the earlier phase.

Beyond question the most remarkable invention (if such it was) of the earlier predynastic period was writing, not only for its own importance, but because the beginning of 'history', in however rudimentary a form, was dependent upon this resource. It is now unnecessary to describe at length[3] the form of writing which first appeared, so far as we know at present, in the period called 'Uruk 4'. This script is, however, by no means primitive in all respects, and it shows signs of development and formalizing before this first appearance. Only a minority of the signs can be recognized as pictures, and their linear descendants in the cuneiform script, where a good many of them were preserved, came to have meanings which often seem arbitrary, although they must in some way be derived from the original concepts. It is at least probable that

[1] G, 6, pl. 92; G, 8, pl. 18; see also below, p. 124. For similar scenes depicted on cylinder seals, see § 11, 9 and references therein.

[2] G, 6, fig. 105; G, 8, pls. 30 f.

[3] A full description and discussion will be found in §1, 4.

the future will reveal earlier and more elementary writings than the tablets of Uruk, but it is hardly to be expected that such will be found elsewhere than in Lower Iraq, which at present claims the glory of being the earliest nurse of man's best achievement. This geographical setting is independent of the question what language it was that the first writing preserves.[1] That in the subsequent stage (tablets of the Jamdat Naṣr period) the language is Sumerian has been sufficiently demonstrated, but if it be true that an ethnic substratum existed in the land before a (hypothetical) immigration of the Sumerians, the Uruk 4 tablets could be imagined as expressing that earlier language. At present such questions are quite beyond determination, and although future discoveries may be hopefully awaited it is hardly probable that, upon this first verge of written record, they will be decisive.

III. THE LATER PHASE (JAMDAT NAṢR)

The later phase of the 'Proto-literate' period was one of consolidation, elaboration and expansion. Its innovations were few. Its fine polychrome pottery shows black and red geometric designs on a light-coloured band round the shoulder while the rest of the vessel is covered with deep red or plum-coloured paint.[2] But the pottery was known already in the earlier phase of the period, and if it seems more characteristic for the later phase, that may be due to the fact that the remains of the latter are so much more numerous.

The building material used throughout the period consisted of small, oblong, sun-dried bricks square in section, called *Riemchen*.

Temple architecture of this phase is best represented at Uruk by the 'White Temple',[3] the latest preserved of a series of shrines whose remains are incorporated in the so-called Anu Zikkurrat—an irregular mound 40 ft. high, with an area of 420,000 sq. ft. Access to the White Temple was by three ramps. The Sanctuary itself measured 60 × 70 ft. (as at 'Uqair) and was surrounded by an open area. It was an elaborate structure, built of sun-dried bricks and whitewashed. The outer walls, and part of the inside walls, showed buttresses alternating with vertical chases or stepped recesses. In the lower part of each recess, horizontal timbers strengthened the brickwork at regular intervals and formed a visible pattern at the same time. Higher up in the recesses were

---

[1] See below, pp. 93 ff.; but the idea of an earlier substrate language is contested in *C.A.H.* i³, ch. iv, sect. iv. See also ch. viii, sect. i (Eridu).

[2] E.g. §ii, i, pls. i, 5, 6; G, 8, pl. vii.   [3] G, 7, fig. 14; G, 8, pl. 14.

small windows, triangular, if we may judge by a stone model of which fragments were recovered.

One entered the building through a door in one of the long sides; then, passing through a vestibule, one reached the cella, which occupied the centre of the temple over its whole length and was flanked by two symmetrical rows of smaller rooms; one of these served as vestibule, the others as vestries, stair-wells and storerooms. An altar stood against one of the short walls of the cella, and some distance in front of it a base of masonry may have supported a hearth; this, at least, is the rule in the temples of Early Dynastic and Akkadian times and their evidence would seem relevant since they agree with the 'Proto-literate' temples in the layout of the cella.

An important feature of the Uruk–Jamdat Naṣr period at Uruk is the *Riemchengebäude*,[1] an isolated structure measuring about 18 × 20 m., built within a pit dug into the north corner of the Stone-Cone Mosaic temple. The excavators assigned the building of the *Riemchengebäude* to the Uruk 4 phase, but many of the objects it contained were typical of the Jamdat Naṣr period.

The building consists of a series of chambers and corridors, but has no doorway in the outer walls through which it might have been entered. The innermost chamber (4 × 6·50 m.) was completely surrounded by a corridor. A blazing fire burnt here but only one wall bore traces of burning. This suggests that the flame was blown in that direction by the wind, which in turn implies that there was no roof.

A rich deposit of objects was found within the building. The plaster of the walls must have been still damp when these were placed there, as impressions of vases were found on the walls in some cases. Among the objects found were hundreds of pottery and stone vases, alabaster bowls, copper vessels, clay cones, gold leaf, and nails with heads covered in gold leaf, weapons (arrow-heads, maceheads, knives, spearheads), and animal bones. In the north-east corridor were found the remains of wooden posts, pieces of black and white stone mosaic and tubular copper sheaths once nailed to posts 1·8 m. long. The excavator considered these to be components of furniture, perhaps settles.[2] Some had been carefully set down, others were so mutilated that they must have been thrown in from above.

The evidence points to the purpose of the *Riemchengebäude* as being for the ritual dedication and burial of the furniture from a temple which was to be abandoned or superseded by a new shrine.

[1] §II, 3 no. XXI, Taf. 31 (4).   [2] §II, 3, no. XV, pls. 15 and 42.

It appears to have been built expressly for the purpose, filled with objects before the plaster was dry, and dedicated in a ritual fire-ceremony and buried while the flames still burned in the inner-most chamber. It must be stressed that no traces whatever of human remains were found in the *Riemchengebäude*. It might perhaps be regarded as simply an elaborate form of *Opferstätte*, many of which were found at Uruk and assigned to the Jamdat Naṣr phase by the excavators.[1] Some were found in the E-anna precinct, but with no trace of the buildings which might have contained them. They took the form of trenches dug at a slant and plastered on the inside. Offerings of fish, birds, animals and vegetable matter were placed in the deep end and burnt. The ashes were then swept out and the trough was replastered in preparation for the next sacrifice. In an area known as the South-east Court, a series of small rooms each contained troughs sunk into the floor. These were sometimes in the form of a shallow dish with a channel projecting at one side. *Opferstätten* seem to have been found at other sites in the Jamdat Naṣr period, though they are often described by the excavators as kilns or hearths.[2]

The civilization which had apparently evolved in a restricted area in the extreme south now flourished in a number of settle-ments further north, for instance in the region to the east of the Diyālā in the latitude of Baghdad. In that region, at Khafājī, we can follow a development in temple architecture which was signi-ficant:[3] unfortunately we cannot corroborate it with evidence from Uruk since the Inanna temple stood at this time upon a platform which is preserved while the actual shrine is lost. At Khafājī a temple dedicated, in all probability, to the moon-god Sin was founded in this phase (Jamdat Naṣr). Its plan resembles the earlier temples at Uruk: an oblong cella occupies the centre of the building, with an altar against one of the short walls. A new trend is announced, however, by an element of asymmetry: the small rooms no longer flank the cella. On the side of the entrance there are, as of old, three rooms, one of which serves as vestibule. On the opposite side there is one continuous stairway leading to the roof, with a storeroom arranged underneath the steps. This slight change in plan is the first indication of an impending development which was to change the character of the temple considerably. Hitherto, the shrine had stood unattached to other structures, a self-contained symmetrical unit. Various subsidiary buildings

[1] For a convenient summary of the evidence concerning *Opferstätten*, see §III, 23. See also *C.A.H.* I³, ch. VIII, sect. 1 (Uruk-Warka).

[2] E.g. in the second courtyard of Sin temple 4 at Khafājī.   [3] §II, 2.

such as storerooms and ovens were placed more or less haphazardly near its entrance. We notice, at Khafājī, a change from this initial situation to one in which these subsidiary structures were grouped in and around the courtyard and joined to the temple; the stairs leading to the temple roof were shifted to this courtyard and the oblong space on the far side of the cella thus became superfluous and was suppressed. This change was completed towards the end of the 'Proto-literate' period (Sin temple 4) and it changed the cella from a central room, through which one passed necessarily on many occasions, to a secluded chamber placed at the very back of an extensive building. The cella retained this character throughout later times. The temple as a whole obtained, as a result of this development, a much more complex but also a more flexible plan than the isolated symmetrical design used in the earlier phase of the 'Proto-literate' period. We do not know whether the change was correlated with one in function or significance.

At Grai Resh[1] (Jebel Sinjār), excavations yielded a building of the Uruk–Jamdat Naṣr period. It consisted of a long central room with smaller rooms opening off it and may have been a private house or a temple.

It is important to note the variations to which the early temple architecture is subject. We have already noticed that the designs executed in cone-mosaic at Uruk recur in paint at 'Uqair. Another difference consists of the variation in height of the platforms upon which the temples stand: they range from the low socles found in the E-anna precinct at Uruk or at Khafājī to the 15 ft. platform at 'Uqair, while the platform of the 'White Temple' itself rests upon a mound of accumulated débris. Yet the plans of all these temples resemble each other closely. If the opportunity offered by unlimited space is exploited, they merely show a repetition, on a larger scale, of the basic plan consisting of a long central room with suites of rooms on either side. This plan is retained for the main structure and is repeated at right angles and in such dimensions that the area corresponding with the central room becomes a long open court. This was done, for instance, in 'Temple C' at Uruk as we have seen above.

It should be mentioned here that temples built upon platforms have been considered the origin of the stepped tower or zikkurrat,[2] so characteristic a feature of later Babylonian architecture, the recollection of which is enshrined in the 'Tower of Babel'. The earliest true zikkurrats of which remains have been found are not

[1] §III, 15; see also C.A.H. I[3], ch. VIII, sect. II and fig. 12.
[2] §III, 14; §III, 19.

earlier than the Third Dynasty of Ur (2113–2006 B.C.), the best preserved being the great pile at Ur itself. The excavator of this has stated, however, that it incorporated brickwork of the Early Dynastic period,[1] which may indicate that a similar, if smaller, structure occupied the site previously. Recently it has been suggested that two Early Dynastic zikkurrats existed at Kish, but the evidence is not conclusive.[2] In the absence of ascertained remains of the buildings themselves, pictorial representations of stepped constructions are by some interpreted as showing the building of zikkurrats.[3] It does not seem likely that such a structure was part of the temple E-ninnu at Lagash, which was restored, as described by them in detail, in the reigns of Ur-Baba and Gudea.[4] The elaboration which such a construction acquired in the Middle Babylonian period has been demonstrated by the detailed examination of the zikkurrat at Dūr-Untash (Choga-Zanbil), near Susa.[5]

Outside the field of architecture too, a combination of continuity and change strikes one when one compares the two phases of the period. We have stated already that at Khafājī were found animal-shaped vases of the type depicted on the tall vase from Uruk which probably belongs to the earlier phase.[6] The low relief of that vase finds a few somewhat coarsened descendants in the vases of the later phase. Most of these, however, are decorated in a different manner. The animals' bodies are rendered in profile in relief, but the head is turned outward, and emerges from the body of the vase in the round. The parts worked in relief are not only heavier than was usual, but certain mechanical tricks replace the uniformly sensitive modelling of the earlier phase. For instance, a group of a lion sinking its claws and teeth in the hindquarters of a bull occurs on a number of vases.[7] The front paws of the lion show regularly two parallel grooves, the haunches of the bull a scalloped line; in both cases these abbreviations must serve in the place of a plastic rendering of the muscles. Yet these vases are not without merit. The more substantial relief creates a vigorous contrast between shades and highlights well in keeping with the violent struggles which form the subject of the decoration. The same tendencies are noticeable in another class of vases used in the temples. Their basic form is a cup on an ornamental base but the cup, in many cases, disappears within the elaborately carved openwork of the support.[8] The subject is, again, one of struggle,

[1] §III, 26, 7 and 99.   [2] §I, 11.
[3] G, 1, 181–6; §III, 8; §III, 14.   [4] §III, 4, 131 f.
[5] §III, 7; also *C.A.H.* II³, ch. XXIX, sect. II.   [6] See above, pp. 78 f..
[7] E.g. G, 8, pls. 26 f.   [8] G, 3, pl. 6; G, 8, pls. 24–5.

mostly between a male figure and two or four animals, either lions or bulls. The man—if it is a man—is of heroic appearance, broad-shouldered, long-haired, bearded, dressed only in a girdle. In one instance he wears the shoes with upturned toes which are used even today by the northern mountaineers. It is extraordinary that we know absolutely nothing about this figure from any text, for he plays a major part in the repertoire of the Early Dynastic seal-cutters, and is frequently found, in reliefs and on seals, down to neo-Babylonian times. There is no justification for the identification with the hero of the Gilgamesh epic which is sometimes made.

The two groups of stone vases which we discussed as typical of the later phase of the 'Proto-literate' period were made in light-coloured stones, mostly limestone or gypsum. A third class used dark stone, bituminous limestone in most cases. In this material bands and other patterns were gouged out and these were filled with inlaid geometric designs such as triangles, lozenges, concentric circles and rosettes. The materials of the inlays are coloured limestones, shell and mother-of-pearl, and the pieces were set in bitumen. The effect is, again, vigorous and rich.[1]

Other works of stone were found in the temples. It seems that the custom of placing figures of devotees before the gods—well testified for Early Dynastic times—was known already in the 'Proto-literate' period. At Khafājī a gypsum statuette of a woman was found, a muscular little person carrying her head rather forward in a strikingly natural pose.[2]

Animals too were modelled in the round; a wild boar from Ur, carved in soapstone,[3] formed part of an implement (it has a cup-like hollow in the back and was attached below); black stone figures of rams, of different sizes, were meant to be attached to a wall.[4] This is indicated by perforations for copper wire in the backs of the figures. We have met the animal frieze, not only on the alabaster vase from Uruk but also in the cone-mosaics, and we have discussed its appropriateness in a Sumerian temple. The attitude of the rams tallies with that of the animals on the first group of vases we described in this section: their bodies extended along the wall while their heads are turned outward and face the spectator. This attitude survives in the copper bulls which decorated, in a similar frieze, the Early Dynastic temple at Al-'Ubaid.[5] Other fragments of animal sculpture are more difficult to explain. Some are standing figures with stone bodies and legs of silver or

[1] G, 8, pl. vi.
[2] G, 3, pl. 9B; §iii, 6, pl. i.
[3] §iii, 25, 31 and pl. 37.
[4] Ibid. 42 and pl. 38.
[5] §i, 6, pls. xxix f.

copper; of others, rams, only the heads are known and we do not know whether they formed part of temple furniture or architectural decoration. Some of these heads are, again, modelled with great mastery. A complete figure of a ram with a copper rod fixed in the back[1] recalls the copper rushlight of Early Dynastic times from Kish where the supporting figure is a frog.[2] Such comparisons do not merely allow us to interpret with some degree of probability the monuments of the 'Proto-literate' age; they also emphasize the continuity of Mesopotamian culture.

A last characteristic category of objects consists of small figures of animals carved in stone. They are pierced and are called amulets, but we do not really know their significance. It is clear that they are in harmony with the religious preoccupation with natural forces; rams, cattle of various kinds, wild herbivores and lions are common among them, and a figure of a lioness from Tell Agrab bears the symbol of Inanna in relief on its shoulder. In quality they range from obvious mass products to splendidly finished little carvings. Sometimes they are covered with small inlays of lapis lazuli, appropriate in the case of leopards but also used in other instances. Some of these animal figures show engraved or drilled designs on the base: whether these are stamp seals remains doubtful. The religious significance of this category of charming small-scale stonework is further demonstrated by the occurrence among them of the lion-headed eagle, the embodiment of the dark clouds of the spring storms and their welcome rain. The creature is not shown with spread wings, as in Early Dynastic times, but like a crouching bird of prey. We do not know whether some of these figures belong to the early phase of the period or whether their occurrence in Early Dynastic layers marks a continuity of manufacture or merely the continued use of extant figures.

The same uncertainty attaches to some classes of cylinder seals.[3] Some of them (like some of the stone vases) merely continue older motives on a lower level of excellence. There is, on the other hand, a numerous class of cylinders which are found only in the later phase of the 'Proto-literate' period. They are tall and narrow— their height is sometimes three or four times the diameter—and they show striking combinations of various geometric designs. Even this geometric decoration disintegrates towards the end of the period, as do all the other seal designs. For instance, when the drill, a rapid tool, had been used in the early phase its traces were carefully obliterated by the subsequent engraving; in the later

[1] G, 3, pl. 4A.   [2] *Ibid.* pl. 29C.   [3] §III, 1, 3 ff.

phase the drill-marks are noticeable, and sometimes even form patterns by themselves. The general impression of late 'Proto-literate' glyptic is that of a mass product; the seals of the earlier phase are, on the other hand, individual works, all of high quality. We know, as a matter of fact, that the number of seals produced in the later phase of this period was enormous, not only because they are found in hundreds in our excavations but also because they are fairly common in Early Dynastic layers and they even turn up in deposits of much later ages, for instance in a temple of the Hammurabi period in Ishchali. It is not certain that all engraved cylinders of the late 'Proto-literate' period served as seals; of some classes impressions are not known. But in any case the call for seals must have been great during a phase which was, above all, a period of expansion, especially of trade.

The stone of the seals themselves points to trade; it had to be imported—if only from the Persian foothills. But stone was any-way remarkably abundant in this period. We have mentioned its manifold uses in the equipment of the temples. Both at Ur and Khafājī private people were buried with a greater proportion of stone vases among their grave goods than at any other age.

With the graves, we have entered on a description of secular remains. They were dug under the floors of the houses and the body was wrapped in matting and buried in a contracted position. No cylinder seals and no tools or weapons were found in these graves, in contrast with those of later times. But lead tumblers were found, as were large copper dishes, sometimes 1–2 ft. in diameter.

The houses in which the graves were found resemble those of later times and are undistinguished; they consist of a number of oblong rooms grouped within the available plot of land without any noticeable order. A building at Grai Resh may have been a private house (see p. 84).

At Jamdat Naṣr a large building was labelled 'palace'[1] but its plan has not been sufficiently elucidated for guesses regarding its function to be profitable.

Some figurative objects which may be secular are known. The so-called 'Blau Monuments' in the British Museum[2] are two tablets of green schist bearing signs and figures which show that they were made during the later phase of the 'Proto-literate' period. It has been suggested that they are the records of some transactions; they show stoneworkers drilling out vases and the bearded long-haired figure in the long skirt (who is the main actor in most

[1] §1, 10, 226; S. Langdon in *Alte Or.* xxvi (1927), Abb. 12, 70 f.; G, 7, 130–1; P. R. S. Moorey in *Iraq*, 26 (1964), 93.   [2] G, 8, pl. 15; §1, 4.

scenes of this period) holding on one monument a kid, on the other an object which might well be the tasselled girdle which is offered to the goddess on the alabaster vase from Uruk and also on a seal cylinder.[1]

Summarizing our survey, we see the later phase of the 'Proto-literate' period as a consolidation of the achievements of the earlier phase. These were now spread throughout Sumer and Akkad. Moreover, Mesopotamian influence spread throughout the Near East. The most substantial traces of this influence were found in south-west Persia. In Elam alone the Sumerian script of 'Proto-literate' times was imitated. A number of clay tablets bearing 'Proto-Elamite' inscriptions and seal impressions resemble those from the Euphrates–Tigris plain, but the signs are actually different, as is no doubt the language they render, and the seals show in both style and motives peculiarities not found in Sumer. But imported Mesopotamian seals, too, were found at Susa and spread beyond it. At Sialk, near Kāshān, in north-west Persia, Proto-Elamite tablets were found and cylinder seals which might have come from Sumer as well as from Elam, for the simplified designs of late 'Proto-literate' times were common to both. It is even possible that Mesopotamian influence reached Tepe Hisar, near the south-east corner of the Caspian Sea, to judge by the design of a cylinder seal excavated there.[2]

Another line of expansion led northwards along the Euphrates. We have not yet direct evidence of Mesopotamian expansion along the Middle Euphrates comparable with the situation prevailing in Early Dynastic times, and again under the First Dynasty of Babylon, when this valley fell entirely within the orbit of the southern centre of culture. Yet we must assume close contact to have existed in late 'Proto-literate' times in order to account for the fact that at Tell Brak,[3] on a tributary of the Khabur (which joins the Euphrates) a temple was discovered which agrees in many details of its arrangement and equipment with those of Uruk and 'Uqair. At Chagar Bazar, a bulla with Sumerian inscription was found.[4] Evidence from prehistoric Nineveh shows that a parallel development took place there, and some of the plain ceramic as well as cylinder seal impressions are similar to objects found in Babylonia.[5]

Influence from Mesopotamia reached even farther at this time.

---

[1] G, 4, pl. III; G, 8, pl. 17 (second from the top).
[2] §III, 22, 198 f.　　　[3] C.A.H. I³, ch. VIII, sect. III.
[4] §III, 18, 151 (A 391).
[5] C.A.H. I³, ch. VIII, sect. II, and below, p. 301.

In the plain of Antioch, at Tell Judaidah, and at Çatal Hüyük in Anatolia, several cylinders were found which must be either imports from Mesopotamia or local imitations of 'Proto-literate' seals. Others were bought in north Syria at a time when travel was less easy and antiquities less valuable than today, so that it is a fair presumption that they too reached north Syria soon after their manufacture in the south. Yet farther to the north, at Alişar in eastern Anatolia, and at Hisarlık, the mound of Troy, fragments of the tall seals, with geometric designs which we have described above, were found. Mention should also be made of the possibility that the idea of writing, and even some of the forms of cuneiform script in the Jamdat Naṣr period penetrated as far as modern Romania, where some remarkable discoveries have been made.[1]

The south Mesopotamian influence is noticeable in seal impressions on pottery at Byblos and in Palestine, although these may belong to a slightly later date. Only twice afterwards—under Hammurabi and under the New Assyrian empire—did Mesopotamian influence pervade the Near East in this manner. In these two periods it also reached Egypt, and the same is true for the late 'Proto-literate' period. We are not concerned here with the effects of this contact upon Egyptian civilization, then, too, in a formative phase; we want merely to recall that cylinder seals of a Mesopotamian type belonging to the Jamdat Naṣr phase have been found in Egypt, two actually in excavated graves of the Naqāda II period at Naqāda.[2] It is uncertain whether they are of Mesopotamian manufacture or Egyptian imitations of Mesopotamian prototypes. Whether contact was established on the Mediterranean coast or on that of the Red Sea also remains uncertain.[3]

It is, however, necessary to consider the significance of the period we have described within the early history of Mesopotamia. If we recall its prehistoric antecedents, the changes which it brought about gain the proper relief.

The most important single innovation is the introduction of writing. In the opinion of many scholars the whole history of writing in the West derives from this discovery since they hold (as does the present writer) that the invention of hieroglyphic writing in Egypt was stimulated by a knowledge of the principles of Sumerian writing as it existed in the last part of the 'Proto-literate' period. It has been shown above that Egypt was at that time in contact with Sumer.

[1] §III, 24; §III, 5; and see below, p. 94.   [2] *C.A.H.* I³, ch. IX (*a*), sect. II, end.
[3] For a full discussion, see above, pp. 42 f., and references therein; also *C.A.H.* I³, ch. IX (*a*), sect. II.

The signs of the early script teach us something about the early Sumerian communities. They show the preponderant importance of sheep and goats in their economy. We may assume that the wool trade, which in historical times made it possible to obtain metals and other raw materials which the alluvial plain lacked, existed already in 'Proto-literate' times, although we cannot determine its scope. The sign for 'merchant' exists already in the earliest script.[1] Cattle and donkeys were kept. We also find the sign group for 'ass of the mountains', which denotes the horse in later times, though not necessarily in the early tablets;[2] in fact there would appear to be no evidence for the use of the horse before the last quarter of the third millennium.[3] Earlier monuments do not depict it and the *equidae* which are shown drawing the Early Dynastic war chariots are probably onagers;[4] this is confirmed by actual bones found at Tell Asmar.[5]

Fishing and the chase were also of some economic importance: ibex, stag and hunting dogs occur among the signs. Most important, however, was agriculture. Barley was the commonest crop but wheat was well known. The sign for plough lacks the seed-funnel which is shown on Akkadian seal impressions, but this does not prove that it was unknown.

The four-wheeled chariot also occurs as a sign, and it is probable that the wheel was a Mesopotamian invention[6] since the sledge is known in 'Proto-literate' as well as in Early Dynastic times and the chariot appears as a sledge placed on wheels. We know that these consisted, not of rings with spokes, but of solid circular discs of planks clamped together and provided with a 'tyre' of broad-headed nails driven into the outer edge. The wheels were attached to the axle which, therefore, revolved with them through bearings fixed to the bottom of the chariot. An almost similar type of primitive cart survives in India to this day.[7] The wheel, once invented, was soon put to another use: wheelmade pottery was known earlier in Sumer than anywhere else: its traces seem to be recognizable in Archaic Level 8 at Uruk. As to other inventions, the signs include a shaft-hole axe which is common among the finds of the Early Dynastic period but very rare before that date. It indicates an advance in metallurgical technique, for it required a closed mould for its casting. Gold and silver were worked as well as copper; this we know from the texts.

---

[1] §I, 4; §III, 13.   [2] §I, 4, 53.
[3] §III, 21, 11 ff; §III, 12; §III, 27.
[4] §III, 3, an exception.   [5] §III, 9, 2 ff.
[6] §III, 2; §III, 20.   [7] §III, 16, pl. xxix, 2.

There are animal figures carved in stone, the legs of which were probably made of precious metal and added to the stone body.[1]

We may end by drawing a conclusion from the texts regarding the political organization of the early communities. The word for 'king' (*lugal*) is not found before Early Dynastic times. The words for 'elder' and 'assembly' do occur, however, on 'Proto-literate' tablets, and it seems, therefore, likely that local autonomy found expression in a system of which feeble traces are found far into historical times and which assigned ultimate authority to the assembly of all free males presided over by the elders.[2]

The development of cities is a significant feature of 'Proto-literate' times, for it suggests a form of political organization which was not only characteristic of Mesopotamia during the early phases of its history, but which reasserted itself whenever the central government collapsed. We refer to the city state, consisting of one or more cities with the land which sustained their citizens. The fact that the full development of cities like Uruk, Kish and Eshnunna seems to go back to 'Proto-literate' times elucidates the general character of that period, which consists precisely in this, that many usages and institutions which were to remain typical for Mesopotamia then made their first appearance. It is for this reason that we have described this period as the transition from prehistory to history; it saw the emergence of Mesopotamian civilization from a substratum which was neither peculiar to the Euphrates–Tigris plain nor similar to the area's civilization in historical times. The innovations of the 'Proto-literate' period established the identity which Mesopotamian civilization retained throughout its long history and the traditions of the Sumerians—like Egyptian traditions—did not reach back beyond the formative phase of their culture. Beyond this phase they saw, not the prehistoric past which excavations have revealed to us, but the superhuman origin of their society. Legend merged into myth, 'kingship descended from heaven' and was 'in Eridu' and other cities.

But neither the development of cities nor any of the other innovations of this period—the invention of writing, the introduction of metallurgy, the efflorescence of art—can by itself explain the great change from prehistory to history. It is their aggregate which creates the effect we have described and which bespeaks a prodigious quickening of the spiritual life of the times. In this sense Mesopotamian history may be said to begin in the 'Proto-literate' period even though 'historical' texts do not reach back so far.

---

[1] G, 2, vol. IV, 1992, fig. 1080.   [2] §III, 10; §III, 11; §III, 17.

CHAPTER XIII

THE CITIES OF BABYLONIA

I. THE SECOND AND THIRD EARLY
DYNASTIC PERIODS*

MATERIALLY, the changes between the first Early Dynastic period and the succeeding generations which made up the second and third were not great. The most marked was a development in the style of the cylinder-seals, which turned from patterns to a more representational set of designs and began to bear inscriptions;[1] these last are the leading characteristic of the age. For with it we enter the realm of history, of record set down by men with the conscious aim of perpetuating their acts to posterity, and very soon is added the thought of imposing upon the present by reference to the past. Writing, invented in an earlier epoch, and employed since then constantly (even if appearing sporadically) for the purpose of memorandum concerning material things, was now adopted by kings and applied to religious and political ends. Here therefore begins in Babylonia a process which was under way at about the same time in Egypt.

The earliest appearance of writing in the alluvial plain of southern Iraq belongs to a period considerably earlier than the subject of this chapter, though the distance can hardly be measured in years.[2] Owing to the scattered nature of the evidence, its development can be watched only in separate groups, and the first two of these, the tablets found at Uruk[3] and at the site called Jamdat Naṣr,[4] belong to the subject-matter of the preceding chapter. These are followed in chronological order by the archaic tablets of Ur,[5] which lay in two strata already existing when the celebrated 'royal tombs' were sunk in the ground, and since these visibly belonged to the full maturity of the Early Dynastic civilization the archaic tablets have been assigned to the beginning of this period. Somewhat later again than the tablets of Ur may be placed those of Fārah (Shuruppak) which can be proved later than the earliest reigns which have left monuments

---

* For the First Early Dynastic period see below, ch. XVI.

[1] G, 8; 17; 23; §I, 1; 10; 17; 19; see below, p. 239.
[2] §I, 5, 125 ff.　　[3] §I, 6; A, 39.　　[4] §I, 15.　　[5] §I, 2.

of their own.[1] The arrangement of the foregoing series depends upon a variety of arguments, mainly from epigraphy and archaeology, only once upon relative positions at any one site,[2] but although future discovery is sure to amplify the evidence it will hardly change the order of what is already known.

With one exception, these tablets are lists of commodities, quantities, and persons, the exception being lists which were drawn up not for administrative use but for learning; these are without numbers, and contain things of the same class, such as writing signs (or rather the pictographs out of which these developed), animals, or fish. Such non-utilitarian texts appear even in the earliest tablets from Uruk, and thenceforth continued through all the ages of Babylonian writing, being a standard method of instruction for scribes who wrote the names of things belonging to defined classes, according to their kind or material. Moreover, recent evidence has now been discovered that tablets of the Fārah period contain early examples of known Sumerian literary and lexical texts,[3] and this confirms, what is already plain for other reasons, that the Fārah tablets are the latest in the archaic series. The most important question affecting all of these earliest written records is that of the language which they attempted to reproduce. The Uruk tablets lack any visible indications of this, but those from Jamdat Naṣr have slight but sufficient clues that their language was Sumerian, and this is beyond doubt in the two later groups. An extraordinary discovery of recent years has been that of inscribed tablets at a place in Romania.[4] A leading authority upon early Sumerian writing[5] had no difficulty in recognizing the majority of these signs as closely similar to Mesopotamian signs of the Jamdat Naṣr period, and the discussion has continued.[6] The principal difficulty still seems to be that the deposits among which these tablets were found are generally held to be of much earlier date.

Whether the Sumerians were in fact, as they appear, the first inhabitants of the Babylonian territory and the inventors of its characteristic culture is a question which has been actively discussed, with arguments both archaeological and linguistic; it has come to be known as 'the Sumerian problem', though certainly

---

[1] Lugalbanda and Gilgamesh are found as divine names in the Fārah tablets; see §1, 4, *Schultexte*, no. 1, vii, 14 and rev. iii, 25. These rulers were, in various traditions, more or less contemporary with Enmebaragisi, for whose inscription see §III, 3. On the archaic tablets see further §1, 24, and A, 38.

[2] At Uruk; see §1, 6, 14 f.

[3] See A, 3 and 4.

[4] A, 40.

[5] A, 9.

[6] A, 14, 16, 17, 29, 31.

not the problem most hopeful of solution connected with that people and their language.[1] While the general debate does not belong to the present chapter, being concerned with the prehistoric period, it cannot be wholly passed over, because it implies a challenge[2] to the Sumerians' right to claim (although they never did explicitly claim[3]) this all-important achievement of writing. The linguistic side of the argument against Sumerian priority in the land has been the ingenious, and indeed effective, attempt to demonstrate that many ancient place-names and basic words for materials and professions are in fact non-Sumerian, and must be regarded as legacies of an earlier population,[4] admittedly undefinable. Whether such there was or not, it can hardly affect the invention of writing as a supreme honour of the Sumerians, for there is no reason to believe that any such elder language as may have been spoken in the land was ever reduced to writing before it was superseded by Sumerian. The tablets of Uruk belong to the archaeological period introduced by the arrival of the Sumerians (according to upholders of the immigration theory), and in themselves have at least nothing to contradict the belief that their writers were men of Sumerian speech: and this becomes demonstrable in the subsequent groups of archaic tablets. It need not be denied that there were others at about the same time capable of the same invention, for, even if Egypt is left out of account, another script is known to have been used almost in the same land as that which produced the parent of cuneiform, for numerous tablets were found at Susa inscribed with signs of an entirely different repertoire of picture-words. This system, which has been called Proto-Elamite[5] and belongs to the Jamdat Naṣr period, seems to exhibit a more developed stage of representing the pictures than the contemporary signs of what was to become cuneiform, and it would be possible to conjecture that its beginnings were even more remote. Nevertheless, it was doomed to no more than a short provincial existence, and yielded place before it had time to leave monuments which could become intelligible to a later age, thus remaining, as it is likely to continue, indecipherable. Yet its area might, at one time, have vied with its competitor's, for specimens

---

[1] §1, 23 and G, 27, 261 ff., but also §1, 18, 44 ff. See A, 24, and *C.A.H.* I³, ch. IV, pp. 147 ff. and 343 f.　　[2] §1, 3, and §1, 20, 29.

[3] A later epical text affirms that a message sent by Enmerkar was the first time that 'a word was set on clay' (see §IV, 27, line 505). This king had evidently some traditional fame in early letters, for in another place (*A.St.* v, 198 f.) he is blamed for not having written a record of his victories.

[4] See above, *C.A.H.* I³, ch. IV, pp. 148 ff.; A, 39, 162.

[5] §1, 16, introduction p. 2; §1, 6, 42 f.

have been found far to the north-east of Susa, near the border of the great Persian desert.[1] Still farther away to the east there flourished a third completely independent writing, found in the ruins of two great cities in the valley of the Indus.[2] The objects upon which this is inscribed belong, it is true, to a considerably later time than the pre-historic age in Babylonia, but future discovery may well supply an earlier history which it now lacks. While, therefore, it can remain for the present a subject of possible discussion whether the script which was to conquer the whole of Western Asia was invented by the Sumerians, it is certain that the whole of its development was the work of this people, and it was they who were now to put it into the service of history.

II. EXTENT AND CONSTITUENTS OF THE EARLY DYNASTIC CIVILIZATION

Before proceeding to relate the history thus preserved it will be necessary to survey the scene in which it was to be enacted, and to observe wherein consisted the unity which gave limits and individuality to a land for which geography has set no very definite natural boundaries. Babylonian civilization grew up on alluvial soil deposited by the Tigris and Euphrates in their lower courses. It was formerly assumed that, as Egypt was a 'gift of the Nile', so was Babylonia a creation of the Two Rivers, filling with silt the head of the Persian Gulf, which was supposed to have extended much farther to the north-west in remote antiquity. Very recent geological, and even archaeological, studies have cast much doubt upon this conception; it is now suggested that sedimentation was generally counterbalanced by subsidence, so that the southern limits of the land were perhaps not greatly different, even in pre-historic times, from what they are now. This interesting problem,[3] which still awaits conclusive evidence, is of importance here only so far as we need to know whether the whole scene of Babylonian history is open to our investigation, or whether some of it was enacted upon a stage inaccessible or unexplored; there is nothing at present to suggest this.

In Sumerian times Eridu (Abu Shahrain) was the southern limit, and was 'on the shore of the sea'. Within an arc of some 250 miles radius towards the north-west of that point stood the

[1] §1, 12, vol. 1, 65 and pls. xcii f.
[2] See, in general, §1, 25.
[3] §11, 6; 8; 9. See *C.A.H.* 1³, ch. 11, pp. 57 ff. and *C.A.H.* 1¹, pp. 357 f.

great centres of Sumerian culture and power. The geographical and climatic conditions of this territory had their inevitable influence in shaping the manner of life to be followed there,[1] but it is no exaggeration to say that a common stock of ideas and material equipment gave a definition to geography rather than the reverse. Whereas the early pre-historic cultures, which Babylonia only shared, have various but always wide extensions, the first age of history, the Early Dynastic, passes within limits which are almost narrow. Its centre was unmistakably among the great cities in the southern part of the alluvium. The names of these have been supposed to be mostly non-Sumerian,[2] and they were possibly ancient before receiving the distinctive Sumerian stamp, but if they had any importance or history before that time it is likely to remain unknown. Sumerian tradition claimed their foundation and was able to give an exact account of the means and the system of government by which they attained greatness and prosperity,[3] and Sumerian records have endowed them with a history; it is hardly conceivable that anything significant can ever be known about them which is not of Sumerian origin, or resting upon Sumerian foundations.

The leading members of this serried group are indicated by their figuring in the list of cities which were the seats of sovereignty before and after the Deluge, according to the Sumerian dynastic list which is to be described below—Eridu, Kish, Uruk, Ur, Adab, Larak, Sippar, Shuruppak, with several others of less note and sometimes uncertain location. Such famous places as Nippur and Babylon are not, for special reasons, included in this number. Certain others, of great note, have been added by modern discovery, the most remarkable being Lagash[4] and Eshnunna.[5] One more has yet to be named, Mari, because of its ancient fame and special position. In recent years, after a period of uncertainty, it has been excavated[6] and fully established as a principal centre of the Early Dynastic civilization, in accordance with the aforesaid dynastic list, which makes it the seat of a kingdom said to have once held supremacy over the whole country. This city, unlike all the rest, lies quite outside the south-Babylonian circle, being situated far away to the north-west upon the middle course of the Euphrates. Mari is to be regarded as one

---

[1] G, 9, 130 f.
[2] See, most recently, G, 27, 263, but otherwise *C.A.H.* I³, ch. IV, pp. 150 f.
[3] G, 15, 92 ff.   [4] G, 19.
[5] G, 18, 369 ff.
[6] G, 18, 495 ff., 521 ff.; see below, pp. 291 ff.; and A, 8.

of the outposts of the old Sumerian culture, although the Sumerian language may never have been used there.

A similar limit, even more distant, is found upon the Tigris, at the city of Ashur where, in one of the lowest levels to which the excavation was carried, there was a building devoted to the cult of a goddess with all the apparatus of Sumerian life, and figures of the worshippers little different in any particular from what might occur in the south.[1] Despite one or two possibly intrusive elements, the 'archaic Ishtar temple' of Ashur was Sumerian, and its users were, if not Sumerians themselves, at least a people, or possibly only a class, entirely permeated with Sumerian customs and ideas. Ashur was, it may be, a colony or a conquest, for it seems to have stood isolated not only from the Sumerian homeland but also from its own neighbours, since no traces of such exotic inhabitants were found in the deeply searched ruins of equally ancient settlements at Nineveh or the site now called Tepe Gawra. With these exceptions, however, the Early Dynastic horizon stood at the region where the great rivers now approach to each other, in the neighbourhood of Baghdad and Fallūjah. It is perhaps reserved for future discovery to find links between this boundary and the outliers of Mari and Ashur. Up to the present the only connexion upon the Tigris side is the chance occurrence of a Sumerian figure[2] at a place near Sāmarrā. Between Sippar and Mari the Euphrates has shown nothing to fill the gap of some two hundred miles. One other famous city, outside the Babylonian circle, occupied a unique place in its affairs. Susa, separated by no natural obstacle from the plain, was not a Sumerian city, but rather Elamite, and it finds no place in the dynastic list. Nevertheless it was in all ages[3] so intimately connected with the fortunes of Babylonia, either as a dependency, a trading-partner, or a rival, that the buildings and antiquities found there are as much inspired by the ideas of Babylonia as of the native Elamites; even the language of the inscriptions is frequently Sumerian or afterwards Akkadian. Susa therefore was not a stranger, and despite intermittent broils was never far out of the company of the great Babylonian cities whose civilization it had so deeply absorbed. A still wider extension of 'Sumerian' statuary has now been found at Tell Khuaira in north-east Syria.[4] It is again reported that Sumerian literary texts are among the tablets found at Gasur (Nuzi).[5]

[1] §II, 1, 53 ff.; see below, pp. 298 ff.   [2] §II, 4, 149 ff.
[3] Even from the earliest; see §II, 5, and *C.A.H.* I³, ch. VIII, pp. 427 ff.
[4] A, 25 and the publications quoted there. See also below, p. 312.
[5] A, 3, 82, n. 72.

The unifying ideas and the material equipment of this civilization are called Sumerian, and for this there is full justification but it is none the less difficult to define who the Sumerians were. Apart from the question of their ultimate origin and racial affinity, about which little or nothing can be ascertained,[1] the difficulty is to distinguish them from the other people whose influence is plainly marked from the very beginning of recorded history in the country delimited above, those who are now called Semites. It is most necessary to understand at the outset that both appellations refer exclusively to language; the basis of the statement that Semites were influential from the beginning is the occurrence of Semitic names in the earliest dynasty[2] which claimed rule over the whole land. These kings are recorded as mingled with others having Sumerian names, and this mixture characterizes the whole relation of the two. A fairly large quantity of skeletal material found in excavations has been studied with the view of establishing a racial distinction of these two peoples. While this has been generally discussed in chapter v of this volume, it may not be too bold to aver that such examination has not only failed to provide any reliable criterion of Sumerian and Semite, but it has actually raised other problems concerning the Early Dynastic representation of the human form.[3] So far as concerns the physical type there is no visible cleavage in the population and no foundation for a facile doctrine that Sumerians had short heads and Semites long.

The desired distinction has again been sought in costume and manners of treating the hair on heads and faces of figures portrayed upon the monuments; fifty years ago this seemed an acute observation. But it is now quite clear that such differences were only fashions, or more precisely styles of habiliment worn upon various occasions by the same people, due partly to lapse of time but still more to the character and occupation of the individual represented. The gods, in particular, were depicted as wearing an attire which, in most respects, had once been that of men, and was retained for these awesome shapes after it had become obsolete for their worshippers.[4] Neither, again, is the distinction of Sumerian and Semite to be found in clear traces of racial con-

---

[1] §II, 2, 53 ff.
[2] G, 26; G, 27, 245, 259, and 265; A, 4.
[3] G, 4, vol. IV, 1764, 1780, and 2326; see also *Sumer*, IV, 125 ff.
[4] §II, 7.

sciousness at this early period. It is true that an heroic poem, written down at a later date,[1] has the very ancient king Lugal-banda praying for the expulsion of the 'Amorite who knows not grain' (that is, the barbarous nomad), and this term is doubtless a near approximation in Babylonian ideas to the modern 'Semite'. But the phrase is probably anachronistic for the earliest historical period, although it reflects an abiding sentiment; enmity towards the 'Westerners' was felt through many centuries, not because they were of a different race, but because they were foreigners, intruders who neither understood nor respected the Babylonian ways of thought and life. Of war or hatred against the Semites dwelling in the land there is never any trace.[2] The most that can be adduced by way of distinction is that the northern part of the country, which in later times (and perhaps earlier than can now be traced) bore the name of Akkad was the home of those who spoke a Semitic language. The first of all Semitic names are found in the traditional dynasties of Kish, where they predominate. Yet Sumerian names too are found at Kish, and conversely Semitic names are probably not absent, although concealed, in the southern dynasties of Ur[3] and Uruk.[4] As concerns the population of Mari, already mentioned as a distant outpost deep in 'foreign' territory, there is never any doubt, for all the early inscriptions of its rulers and officials are unmistakably in the Semitic language.

III. IDEAS AND INSTITUTIONS

The early and later Babylonians alike possessed an unusually clear conception of the order of the world. Their mythology, very imperfectly as it is known to us, implies a fairly comprehensive and consistent set of notions concerning the genesis of things and the system by which the world and its multifarious workings are governed. The beginning was a watery waste which they called Apsu; this had no trace of anything which to the later generations stood for order and intelligibility in the world. In the midst of this a pair of gods came into being, shadow beings who did but increase in stature as the ages rolled on, and perhaps did not even

---

[1] §1, 20, 16; A, 18, 273.   [2] §11, 3; A, 3, 77 f.

[3] G, 10, 2 ff., and especially G, 11, 12 and 210 for the possibility that even the celebrated 'Shub-ad' of the Royal Graves at Ur bore in fact a Semitic name. The wife of another early king of Ur, upon a fragment of a dedication, calls herself DAM-su(d), and the pronoun may reveal her own speech as Semitic; now A, 37, no. 2. Some of the high-sounding styles of southern rulers seem titles rather than true names.   [4] For Uruk see G, 27, 265, note 17.

give birth to their successors 'All that is Above' and 'All that is Below'. The generations then became more distinct, and individual gods were born, most significantly the god Enki (Ea), endued with supreme wisdom and thereby minded to put an end to the reign of formlessness and chaos.[1] From this point proceeds, in most of the Babylonian creation-myths, the building-up of a world as a mould for, and yet itself moulded by, the habits of life and thought congenial to its inhabitants, that is, the universe as it was conceived by the ancient people of Lower Iraq. It is not the concern of a history to describe in more detail the Babylonian cosmologies, but only to note how they form an intelligible prelude to the rise of civilization itself in that land. Out of the primordial water a creator had either split off the heavens and then constructed the earth,[2] or he had made a separation of heaven and earth,[3] below which was the Deep; these three divisions were the realms respectively of the gods Anu, Enlil, and Enki (Ea). Various acts of creation then followed—the land, the rivers, the beasts of the field, but as yet there were no temples, and consequently no places for the gods to inhabit and enjoy the life of ease which their realms should afford them.

Their answer to this need was the creation of man, whom all the Babylonian myths regard as a mere tool for the service of his makers.[4] Most significantly, this creature must have special powers; he was formed from the blood of slain gods, sometimes noted as craftsmen-gods,[5] and Ea, the divine artificer, added to the creation other gods[6] as masters of special skills. There was a time before cities existed, but with the creation of man and his concentration these came into existence, the first to appear being named in a Sumerian poem[7] as Eridu, Bad-tibira, Larak, Sippar, and Shuruppak, to which a later text[8] adds Nippur, Uruk, and Babylon itself. All of these (and others omitted) were assigned by the supreme god to one of his divine offspring or followers,[9] who were then faced with the necessity of improving their domains. How one, at least, solved this problem and obtained the benefits of civilization is the subject of a curious Sumerian myth,[10] according to which Inanna, the divine owner of Uruk, obtained by a ruse from the jealous custody of her father Enki all the concepts

---

[1] According to the Epic of Creation; see G, 24, 61 ff.

[2] §III, 8, and §III, 5, 61 ff.   [3] G, 15, 77.

[4] §III, 4, 5 f.   [5] §III, 5, 69.   [6] *Ibid.* 65.

[7] G, 15, 177 ff. The same five cities in the ante-diluvian section of the king-list; see G, 13, 58 ff. But see now A, 11.   [8] §III, 5, 62.

[9] G, 15, 177, 179. For a Hurrian parallel see *Z.A.* 49, 223, and for a Jewish *Arch. Orient.* 18, 357.   [10] G, 15, 92 ff.

and powers which subsequently appear as ubiquitous in Sumerian ways of thinking. But this story is perhaps out of the line of logical development.

It was essential to the plan of using men for providing a life of plenty and ease to the gods that these creatures should be disciplined and directed. There must be a manager or foreman, since the gods dwelt apart, and could not condescend to be their own taskmasters. Consequently, before civilization could even begin, there must be the institution of kingship and hierarchy. All was ready for this; Anu himself was king of the gods, and a myth[1] relates that 'sceptre, crown, tiara, and (shepherd's) crook lay deposited before Anu in heaven. There being no counselling for (the earth's) people kingship descended from heaven.' It rested first at Eridu, then at the other ante-diluvian cities. With this the stage was fully set: the gods had their dominions, their slaves to toil upon them, and their representatives on earth, who were to direct the work, to secure its fruits to the divine proprietors, and protect the estates against attack.

Although they have only now been found in their native dress,[2] the well-known stories related by Berossus may take their situation here as conveying the Babylonian idea of civilization finally bestowed and grown to its maturity in the preconditions so carefully prepared—'in Babylon there was a vast multitude of men, of every tribe, those dwelling in Chaldaea. But they lived without order, like the beasts.' There follows the story of Oannes and his brethren, fabulous monsters which came up every day from the sea and 'instructed mankind in writing and various processes of the arts, the formation of cities and the founding of temples. He also taught them the use of laws, of bounds and of divisions, also the harvesting of grains and fruits, and in short all that pertains to the mollifying of life he delivered to men; and since that time nothing more has been invented by anybody.' At the time when this happened men were already in possession of the first necessity for progress, according to Sumerian ideas, for Oannes was said to have appeared under the reign of the fourth king[3] before the Deluge, he who was called Ammenon by Berossus and is now known by his native name of Enmengalanna; this at least according to one of the traditions of what Berossus wrote, but a more likely account has it that the bringer of all civilization came at the very beginning[4] of this pre-diluvian era, when men still had everything to learn. This legend in any case

[1] G, 24, 114, also §III, 12, 51.   [2] A, 6, 44 ff.
[3] §III, 10, 261.   [4] Ibid. 91, 173.

locates the first civil organization at Eridu, where the kingdom began, until the founding of which it was impossible for any progress to be made.

What the amphibians taught may perhaps be inferred from the curious Sumerian myth already mentioned,[1] which gives a detailed list of the cultural elements carried off from Eridu by a goddess who needed them to make her own city flourish. More than a hundred institutions (*me*, the word is many-sided[2]) are enumerated; they seem a strange medley, but may be described shortly as containing various notions which are abundantly found in the literature as expressive of Sumerian ways of thinking, and in that thinking assumed as the mental equipment of the civilized man. Most prominent among those which can be understood are orders of government (kingship and hierarchy), and technological terms (arts and crafts), with a strong admixture of miscellaneous social and moral conceptions. Such a list, even were it fully intelligible, cannot of course give more than a glimpse of a people's life, but if the course of man's development appeared to Sumerian minds as it has been outlined in these pages the gifts bestowed by the sea-monsters or purloined by the goddess were truly characteristic of this ancient civilization.

So far, therefore, the strictly parallel course of Sumerian ideas and institutions has been traced to the ownership of cities by individual gods, the appointment of a king to order the mass, and the dispensing of skills to make the human subjects fit to minister to the needs of the divine masters. But there could be only one king with supremacy, just as there was only one god with the 'power of Anu (or, of Enlil)', whereas there were many cities, each belonging to a god, each of whom, in turn, must have a steward to manage and make profitable his estate. The idea of overlordship is basic to the king-list, at least from the beginning of the post-diluvian period, if not before,[3] and is doubtless present, although not clearly expressed, in the narrow limits of the first surviving inscriptions. Earliest of all, Enmebaragisi[4] is already 'great man' (*lugal*), that is 'king', and despite some variations in titles borne by southern rulers[5] *lugal* remained the general designation of a 'king', and always was liable to carry the implication of an overlord. In logical subordination to the *lugal* were the governors of cities, with the title of *ensi*, which figures prominently in the early inscriptions. These two titles have a complicated history of relationship, but usage suggests that the *ensi* was so

[1] G, 15, 92 ff.   [2] A, 7.   [3] G, 13, 61 ff.
[4] §III, 3, 9 ff.   [5] G, 12, 3 ff., 10 ff., 34 ff.

called with reference mainly to his stewardship in the service of the god, and might as such be either an overlord himself or subordinate to a *lugal* in another city, while retaining his sacred charge locally.

In the earliest period it is not clear what consequences ensued from the supremacy of a *lugal* over a subject city; he is known, at least, to have had the duty of delimiting the boundaries of neighbour-gods' estates, that is, in secular terms, of settling frontier-disputes between cities.[1] This raises a question how, when one city was ousted by another, the relations of their respective gods were explained. In the last sentence of a patriot's protest over the desecration of his town by a rival governor[2] he prays that the goddess of the desecrator may cast this act upon his neck as a burden, thus implying that no god must be held responsible for the sins of his agent, which he is expected to punish, and thus preserve the harmony of the gods. But the gods were well acquainted with strife among themselves, and such a notion was probably not so offensive to the Sumerians as it seems now. Despite their formal humility of station under the gods and the king, the local governors (*ensi*) were in fact rulers, and the degree of their ascendancy was no doubt determined by the ordinary factors of opportunity and personal character. Their position was hereditary at least in practice, as both the king-list and the history of Lagash and its neighbours demonstrate; normally son succeeds father with the usual interruptions of failure and usurpation. Thus situated, the governors were moved by the normal ambitions of leaders, and aspired to extend their rule, first over their neighbours and then, as successes came, over a wider circle until the supremacy itself seemed within their grasp. The last great figure of this epoch gives a typical instance; Lugalzaggisi, beginning as governor of Umma, conquered the kingdom of Uruk, became *lugal* of the land by a successful challenge to Kish, and was finally able to undertake a career of conquest or at least a demonstration abroad, before he in his turn succumbed to a stronger.

Two questions concerning the situation of Sumerian rulers in their own domains are difficult to answer for want of evidence. First, what was the relation of the kingship with the priesthood? Some early inscriptions belong to potentates who call themselves

---

[1] This was exercised by Mesilim and by Eannatum (see G, 28, 36 (n.) ff.), and later by Ur-Nammu (see §iv, 30, 64 ff.).

[2] G, 28, 56 ff. (k). For battles of the gods depicted in art see E. D. Van Buren in *Or.* 1955, 24 ff.

en (that is, in a broad sense 'lord') of cities, but at the same time *en* is attested as meaning 'high-priest' of certain gods. The temporal and the priestly titles are not found united in one person,[1] and thus the usage of the title itself suggests a parity which might prove dangerous to one party or the other. That such a rivalry, always latent, did come into existence appears in the latter days of Sumerian history at Lagash, the only city from which we have records in that period. Under the reign of Entemena (about 2450 B.C.) a certain Dudu, high-priest of the city-god, not only dedicated objects bearing his own inscriptions,[2] but caused his name to be inserted in texts of the ruler himself; and again, in the descriptions left by Urukagina concerning his social and economic reforms (to be described in §VIII of this chapter) a cleavage of interests between the prince and the priesthood[3] is clearly marked.

Secondly, it is agreed that the ruler seems to exercise (under his god alone) absolute power in the early Sumerian cities, and that, according to Sumerian ideas, kingship was the primeval gift of civilization. But modern interest in problems of government and society has prompted diverse suggestions that the Sumerian kingship was not primitive but evolutionary, and that its action was, at least sometimes, controlled by an assembly of elders and community-heads, and even by the mass of free men.[4] From scarcity of direct information these beliefs are mainly propped upon inference, either from religious myths and epic stories, or from variously interpreted conditions of land-tenure and causes underlying the reforms of Urukagina, at the one moment when social tensions are plainly to be seen operative in a Sumerian city. The issues barely stated here have been discussed with much elaboration and ingenuity, but only a notable increase of contemporary evidence could raise the conclusions to a possibility of much affecting our conception of Sumerian government.

IV. HISTORY IN CONTEMPORARY RECORD AND LATER TRADITION

For the earliest information upon the history of the Sumerian cities we do not depend wholly or even mainly upon the sparse, brief, and formal inscriptions of contemporaries. As in Egypt the

[1] G, 7, 795 f.; G, 12, 9; A, 38, 102.   [2] G, 28, 34 (i), and cf. p. 224; §III, 9.
[3] G, 7, 800; §III, 7, 122 ff.; see also *R.A.* 49, 215.
[4] Some of the most important literature concerning these questions is named under §III, 1; 2; 6; 7; 11; 12. See also G, 15, 228 and A, 22.

order of the dynasties and the names of their members are preserved in native lists and by the fragments of a lost Hellenistic
historian, so it is also in Babylonia. Here the native evidence is
more compact, being conveyed by several copies of a single
compilation, already mentioned under the name of the 'king-
list' called by the scribes 'Kingship', from its first word. This
was given its final form, as proved by express dating, as well as
the point where it stops, at the end of the Dynasty of Isin,
1794 B.C., its authors working with a tradition preserved more or
less carefully by some half-dozen of the oldest and greatest cities.
The information supplied is regular and uniform—a city is named,
the kingship resided there, A reigned x years, B reigned y years,
if B was the son of A it is added, and so to the end of the dynasty,
followed by a summary; so many kings reigned so many years.
Occasionally a short note records some incident or detail for which
a king was celebrated, but this is the only digression. That dynasty
being concluded the formula continues '(this city) was smitten
with arms, the kingship was taken to (its successor)'. In this
fashion are enumerated twenty dynasties 'after the Flood',
counting nearly a hundred and forty kings, occupying a total of
many thousands of years.

This important document, the value of which is beyond detrac-
tion, was not composed for the benefit of modern scholars, and
from the modern standpoint it has manifest defects. It is constructed throughout upon two assumptions, that the land was an
entity made up of a number of principal cities, and that one only
of these, at one time, was supreme over the others. The two are
embodied in the statement that the kingship remained in one city
until by force of arms it was removed to its earlier seat, perhaps,
or to another. Both of these propositions have their degree of
truth. That the land was a unity is true, fully in the geographical
and in the cultural sense, but partially too in the ideal. Although
the cities fought fiercely among themselves both for the supremacy and also in territorial disputes, there was a distinct sentiment of the solidarity of 'the land', which as usual tended to
become marked at times of 'national' emergency, just as the
irreconcilable citizens of Hellas recollected, in varying shades of
consciousness, that they were all Hellenes. The second assumption, of the single rule by various cities but only one at a time, is
much more emphasized, and indeed is the principle upon which
the list is constructed, but it is so much farther from the truth
that it has vitiated the whole document as history, regarded with
the eyes of modern criticism. It has been easy to demonstrate

that the scheme of successive kingdoms falsifies[1] the perspective by concealing the fact, revealed beyond mistake from other sources, that many of these kings were reigning in their different cities at the same time, not caring or daring to challenge each other for the sovereignty. This has had the additional evil of greatly exaggerating the length of time over which this history extended, even after dismissing the legendary thousands of years ascribed to the earliest reigns. In this respect the king-list includes too much, but in another too little, for there is evidence concerning cities and rulers of the highest importance in early Sumer who yet find no mention at all in the list. Grave as these defects must be reckoned, they weigh light in comparison with the wealth of information afforded by this digest of the earliest history of their country, as it was within the knowledge of the most learned scribes of a later, but still not very remote, posterity.[2] Without entering upon the many questions to which the list gives rise we may regard it here simply as the outstanding authority for the oldest history of Babylonia, extending as it does behind even the earliest of the surviving royal monuments, for the first king who is attested both in the list and by his own inscriptions is Enmebaragisi[3] of Kish, who stands in the list as last but one in the first dynasty 'after the Flood' having before him twenty-one predecessors of fabulous reigns, the Flood itself, and beyond that the millennia of the pre-diluvian kings.

Of this legendary period, whence hoary patriarchs transmitted their names, strangely garbled, into modern texts of the late transcribers of Berossus, there remains no material trace now identifiable. Internal evidence as well as probability suggests that the list of pre-diluvian kings originated from Eridu,[4] but any attempt to place them in the archaeological context of southern Babylonia must at present be guesswork. Recent observations upon the sites of several cities, Ur, Kish, and Shuruppak, have discovered barren strata between periods of occupation, with the appearance of having been laid by water action. The most impressive was found at Ur,[5] and this is placed stratigraphically in the Al-'Ubaid period by the excavator, who has given reasons,

---

[1] It has even been suggested that past history was deliberately distorted for a political purpose by the scribes who compiled the list under the Dynasty of Isin; §IV, 29, 46.

[2] For the date of its formation see the arguments of T. Jacobsen in G, 13, 128 ff., and the, partly divergent, criticisms of F. R. Kraus in §IV, 29, 49 ff., and of M. B. Rowton in §IV, 43, 156 ff.

[3] §III, 3.   [4] G, 13, 60.

[5] §IV, 62, 15 ff.; see A, 24 and C.A.H. I³, ch. VIII, pp. 353 f.

by no means negligible, in support of his belief that the massive
layer of silt was left by the Deluge famous in Sumerian tradition.
If this could be accepted with confidence, not only would it be
proved that the Sumerians possessed the land from the earliest
antiquity (see §1 above), but the succession of post-diluvian
kingdoms could begin from that point.

Yet, although it is hazardous to speak even of historical probability in this context, it may still be affirmed that the identification is hardly acceptable, in the light of the tradition itself and of
the first inscriptional evidence. One fragment bearing the name
of (En)mebaragisi, the earliest ruler as yet represented by a
material remain, was found in a level[1] of the second Early Dynastic
period. At Ur itself the first inscriptions, those of Mesannipada[2]
(who is now known as no more than a generation removed[3]
from Enmebaragisi), were found in the strata immediately
overlying the Royal Tombs, and those, again, belong unmistakably to the third Early Dynastic period. Within the gap
between these levels and the 'Flood-deposit' lie four whole
'periods' of Mesopotamian pre-history, undefined in duration.
If the 'Flood-deposit' is the relict of the Sumerian Deluge then
the whole time between the Al-'Ubaid and the third Early
Dynastic periods is represented in tradition by the First Dynasty
of Kish, up to its last two members. It is true indeed that the
king-list itself provides more than ample accommodation for all
this in the 22,985 years which it allows to that dynasty, subtracting the two last reigns, but this hardly does more than increase
bewilderment. A more factual evaluation of the age which might
have intervened between the Al-'Ubaid period and the earliest
royal inscriptions has been sought by two modern methods.
First, a careful calculation of the rate of deposit over a site
continually in use at Khafājī has resulted in an estimate between
the forty-first and thirty-eighth centuries for the beginning of
writing,[4] which is itself considerably later than the end of the
Al-'Ubaid period. Secondly, a test by the radiological method
called carbon 14 of ashes found in the early Al-'Ubaid stratum at
the northern site of Tepe Gawra has given no more than the
average of 3400 years B.C. for the Al-'Ubaid period itself,[5]
which is lower than has been variously conjectured. It must

[1] §III, 3, 10 and 26; see *C.A.H.* I³, ch. VI, p. 225.
[2] §IV, 51, 71 ff.
[3] §IV, 15, 60 ff.
[4] §I, 5, 135.
[5] §IV, 37, 82.

remain a matter of dubious opinion whether any of these gulfs of time could reasonably be filled by a single dynasty of Kish.

If it is not possible to distinguish which age (if any) in the pre-history of Babylonia should be appropriated to the 'kings before the Flood', it is hardly more possible to relate anything of their history (again, if any). Nothing remained of it but the information given in the king-list, and a few reports of ante-diluvian founders which were current in the schools of divination and magic. The only event recorded is the Flood itself, which 'swept over' the land after 241,200 years of royal rule in five cities. The king-list places this event after the reign of Ubar-Tutu in the city of Shuruppak, but the main tradition omits Ziusudra, his son,[1] who nevertheless reappears in Berossus and is famous, through the Epic of Gilgamesh, as the man who, by the favour of one god, survived the Flood, preserved the seed of living things, and was gifted with immortality. From what reality this famous story derives it is vain to enquire; floods, endemic in Mesopotamia, are attested for early times, as already observed, by 'flood-deposits' at Kish and most significantly at Shuruppak itself. Similarly, in the reign of Ibbi-Sin, a later Sumerian king of Ur, one of his years was named[2] after a deluge 'which obliterated the bounds of heaven and earth', but the city survived it, and the disaster was not otherwise remembered.

When the kingship was restored to earth after the Deluge—which, in Sumerian ideas, was requisite to the possibility of civilized life continuing—it resided first at the city of Kish, and the prestige of this original seat may have influenced the practice of later kings in assuming the title 'king of Kish' to express an all-embracing dominion.[3] This first dynasty, counting twenty-three kings and lasting for '24,510 years, 3 months, 3 days and half a day', besides now possessing original attestation,[4] is recorded with too many significant details to be dismissed. One of these is the presence within the dynasty of a group bearing animal names, Dog, Lamb, Scorpion, Buck son of Gazelle, these names being in Semitic, whereas others are Sumerian. The first appearance of Semites in written history is that of a royal family which succeeded and passed without disturbing the course of the dynasty, or at least of the record, if they were intruders. No detail concerning these alien kinsmen is recorded by the list—they did no more than reign their hundreds of years. Only of one king in

[1] A, 11. For another tradition concerning him see G, 15, 290; see also below, p. 244.
[2] §IV, 36, 278, no. 21.   [3] G, 12, 25 f.; G, 27, 248 f; A, 34.   [4] §III, 3.

the earlier course of the dynasty is anything preserved. This was
the celebrated Etana 'a shepherd who went up to heaven, who
made fast all lands', and reigned for one and a half millennia. His
ascent to heaven upon the back of an eagle was one of the myths[1]
depicted upon cylinder seals,[2] and was probably reflected by the
story of Ganymede in classical literature[3] and art. Of his vaguely
described foreign conquests we know nothing.

More substantial are the figures of Enmebaragisi, who 'de-
spoiled the weapons of the land of Elam' during the '900 years'
of his reign, and of his son Agga, who ruled '625 years' and is
passed over by the list with only that modest achievement to his
credit. But the father's inscription was found at the somewhat
remote city of Tutub (Khafāji), and in another tradition both
father and son were known as the first builders of certain sanctuaries in Nippur, especially that called the Tummal,[4] and this
brings them into a chronological relation with other early
dynasties which has been discussed at large in a preceding
chapter.[5] More interesting is the Sumerian epical story of a war
between Agga and the famous Gilgamesh[6] of Uruk; the former
asserting his right as king of Kish, required Gilgamesh to submit
and surrender his city. But he, disregarding the opposition of a
'peace party' in the senate, and relying upon popular support,
decided to fight. The enemy began a siege, to the dismay of the
inhabitants, but after some uncertain passages between the rivals
it appears that Gilgamesh has made an accommodation with Agga
and friendship is restored. The story, apart from its political
significance, has great interest as our first glimpse of the actual
struggle for supremacy among the cities, which is the leading
motive of the king-list. Its end is perhaps to be understood as
submission by Agga,[7] for ultimate victory remained with Gilgamesh, to whose city the leadership now passed.

The four predecessors of this giant upon the throne of Uruk,
which now assumed the sovereignty, were figures no less portentous. All were partly divine and all heroes of legend; but while it
is unlikely that any of them was purely imaginary, they are too
dim to be treated as historical persons. Of the first nothing more
is known than a brief note in the list averring that 'he went into
the sea and went up to the mountain', phrases which could bear
any interpretation. His son Enmerkar, said in the list to have been

[1] G, 24, 114 ff.; §IV, 47.   [2] G, 8, 138; §IV, 6.
[3] For example the curiously faithful description in Statius, Thebais I, 548–51.
[4] A, 35.   [5] See C.A.H. I³, ch. VI.
[6] §IV, 26; §III, 6; G, 15, 28 ff.   [7] §IV, 32, 57.

the builder of Uruk, was the central character of stories[1] composed, or at least written down, much later and still only in part
recovered. These were never translated into Akkadian and therefore never attained the fame of the Gilgamesh epic. The best
preserved of them does not seem, so far as intelligible, to possess
much variety or profundity, for it relates in prolix style the course
of a negotiation with the city of Aratta, separated from Uruk by
seven mountains, over which messengers pass and repass with
obscure, perhaps riddling, exchanges between the kings, apparently concerned in sober fact with trade of the respective local
products.[2] Enmerkar makes but a slight appearance in later
generations, and yet his name survived to be written in Greek as
(S)euechoros, the grandfather of Gilgamos.

Next to sit upon the throne of Uruk were two gods, Lugalbanda and Dumuzi. The first was celebrated in stories[3] of
adventure, partly involved with those of his father; the latter is
apparently called a 'fisherman' and resisted an attack of the
Elamites.[4] Whether he was believed to be the same as the god
Dumuzi (Tammuz) there is nothing to show, for another
'Dumuzi the shepherd' is found among the kings before the
Flood. Of Gilgamesh, the next ruler of Uruk, more stories were
told than of any other name in Babylonian history. It is now clear
that the twelve tablets of his exploits which were known to the
Assyrians are not more than excerpts, mostly welded into an
effective whole, from a much larger body of legend in Sumerian,[5]
apparently diffuse and ill-connected, but so imperfectly recovered
at present that there is no following the thread of his career as it
was related in compositions written down about the eighteenth
century B.C. That Gilgamesh was a real character in very early
history was, as aforesaid, not doubted by the later native tradition
and need not be doubted now, however much may have to be subtracted from his legend. Yet the episode of his war against Agga
of Kish, which has a good claim to be considered historical, might
suggest that even the legend is not everywhere devoid of a
foundation in more sober reality.

Traditions concerning Gilgamesh are not exhausted with his
more romantic adventures, for, like all important Babylonian
kings, his name is associated with buildings. Attested by written
report only is the 'second ruin' of a sanctuary called the Tummal
in Nippur, which Gilgamesh repaired.[6] The place is still undiscovered, so no local confirmation can be had, and for the present

[1] G, 15, 15 ff., 232 ff.   [2] §IV, 27; 23; 33.   [3] G, 15, 235 ff.
[4] G, 13, 88.   [5] §IV, 15, 83 ff.   [6] *Ibid.* 61 ff.; A, 35.

the chief interest of this report is chronological; this has been discussed in a preceding chapter.[1] But it was also the boast and remaining consolation of the hero in the Epic that he had built the city wall of Uruk, and herein memory agreed with him.[2] To some extent material facts agree with him also, for this city wall of Uruk has been partly explored by the German excavators,[3] and has been found composed mainly of 'plano-convex' bricks, which are confined to the period in which Gilgamesh is presumed, on all other probabilities, to have lived.

Several kings reigned after Gilgamesh at Uruk. His son also was associated with the rebuilding of the Tummal,[4] but otherwise the successors did no more than add to the conventional thousands of years which passed under each kingdom in this distant age. With the shift of supremacy to Ur a great change comes over the record of the king-list, for both individual reigns and the total of the dynasty are suddenly reduced to human proportions. Still more reassuring is the much firmer contact which can now be made with outside and contemporary evidence, for original inscriptions of the First Dynasty of Ur[5] avouch the substantial truth of the king-list at this point, and even allow a clerical error in the list to be suspected, for the '80 years' attributed to Mesannipada probably include those of his like-named son A'annipada[6]—a typical pair of royal names taken by father and son in the fashion of this and of the Sargonic periods.[7] But in contrast with the satisfactory agreement between the list and contemporary monuments at this juncture, it must be confessed that the excavations have unearthed a serious difficulty in the splendid occupants of the 'royal cemetery', who indubitably flourished about this time and have claims to be regarded as kings, though they find no mention in the king-list. Their interest lies in the realms of art, possibly of religion,[8] rather than of history, for nothing at all is known about their acts, and their names occur nowhere in any tradition. Very little more is recorded about the two 'authentic' kings who began the First Dynasty of Ur. Their own short inscriptions relate nothing of their acts but the building of the small temple of Ninkhursag at Al-'Ubaid[9] by A'annipada, and later traditions add similar building-operations, especially at

[1] See *C.A.H.* I[3], ch. VI, pp. 201 ff.   [2] G, 28, 222 (Sin-gamil, b.).

[3] §IV, 24, no. VII, 41 ff. and no. VIII, 5 ff. See also §IV, 12 and G, 7, 807.

[4] §IV, 15, 61 and *C.A.H.* I[3], ch. VI, pp. 235 f.

[5] §IV, 51, 71 ff.   [6] G, 13, 93; §IV, 18, 29.

[7] §IV, 61, 318; G, 11, 97.

[8] §IV, 45 and 4; §II, 2; and in general below, pp. 282 ff.

[9] §IV, 20, 126 ff.; §IV, 61, 312 ff.; §IV, 11, 1 ff.

the Tummal, of which the 'first ruin' was repaired by Meskiag-nunna,[1] third(?) king of this dynasty. One more inscription, of Elulu the fourth king,[2] ends this interval of attested history, while the king-list relapses for a while into exaggeration, and rehearses many dynasties which are either quite unknown or doubtfully illuminated in their courses only by uncertain and momentary glimpses of such realities as the accident of discovery has vouchsafed.

An inscription found at Mari[3] mentions Mesannipada of Ur as the contemporary of another name(?), which the editor thinks is that of the founder of the Dynasty of Mari, the tenth after the Deluge, whereas the First Dynasty of Ur was the third. If this were so, the king-list, already known to be faulty in its assumption of successive dynasties, would have sustained another very serious assault upon its reliability. But this interpretation has not been generally accepted.[4]

Between the First Dynasty of Ur and the accession of Sargon the king-list reckons no less than eleven kingdoms and nearly 5000 years. Even subtracting a characteristically wild 3000 years for eight kings who reigned at Kish, some 1500 still remain for this interval, a length which certainly has very little relation to the truth. That these eleven dynasties, apart from possible or certain exaggerations of length, were mostly contemporary is set almost beyond question by the factual evidence which now exists,[5] and might be formally proved if the text of the king-list were not so faulty at this point. Two or three synchronisms of rulers in different dynasties have been found during this period, and others suggested; these too are plausible though the required names cannot be found in the list without a degree of speculation. The most important of these synchronisms is that of Rimush, the successor of Sargon, with 'Kaku the king of Ur' who led a revolt against Rimush and was subdued by him, as his inscriptions assert explicitly.[6] If the title of king is to be taken literally, then Kaku must have been one of a dynasty of Ur, which could only be the second,[7] though this has almost disappeared from the present copies of the list. If then it be true that Rimush fought with the Second Dynasty of Ur and doubtless brought it to an end, the six dynasties which stand in the list as between Second Ur and Agade may be dismissed chronologically as of no effect. Again,

[1] §IV, 15, 63.   [2] §IV, 46, 306; see also G, 13, 184.
[3] A, 8.   [4] See below, p. 297.   [5] See C.A.H. I³, ch. VI, pp. 200 and 220 ff.
[6] §IV, 42, 189 and 193.
[7] §IV, 61, 212, 333, 356; §IV, 5; but, to the contrary, §IV, 8, 135.

there is an inscription of Enshakushanna, king of Uruk, claiming a victory over Enbi-Ishtar of Kish,[1] and although these names cannot be placed in the list without hazardous interpretations, it is quite likely that they belonged, one to the Second Uruk and the other to the Second Kish Dynasty, thus cancelling, for the purpose of time-reckoning, a dynasty of Khamazi which is inserted between them. It is even possible that the same Enshakushanna was a son of Elili, a member of the First Ur kingdom, which would reduce three allegedly intervening dynasties to one generation.

The only reliable guide to the history, apart from the chronology, of this period is found in the affairs of a city which makes no appearance at all in the king-list, but is better known to us, by inscriptions and works of art, than any other of its compeers. The names, order, and approximate years of the rulers of Lagash are established by their own records, and they have at least one connecting link with the Second Dynasty of Uruk in the treaty made between Entemena of Lagash and Lugalkinishedudu of Uruk.[2] This epoch in the history of both cities ends with Lugalzaggisi (the 'Third Dynasty of Uruk') who was deposed by Sargon, for the list consciously begins a new era with the great conqueror, and Lagash had lost its independence to Lugalzaggisi while he yet flourished as king of Uruk. For various reasons based upon writing and archaeology the beginning of a ruling line at Lagash must be dated at about the same time as the First Dynasty of Ur, and this line was extinguished by the aggression of Lugalzaggisi. Between these points there were nine occupants of the throne at Lagash; the lengths of their reigns are mostly uncertain, but the whole probably did not much exceed a century and a half, and within this modest space there must be found room for the eleven 'dynasties' of the king-list, with their vast tale of years. If such drastic amputation seems a thankless flouting of the evidence which antiquity has preserved for us it must be answered that the evidence is of two kinds, irreconcilable between themselves, and the plain indication of contemporary facts must be given the credence over a tradition, however old, which merely attempted to register them.

A very interesting document, recently published,[3] reveals that Lagash had a king-list of its own, including some but not all of the rulers known from their own inscriptions. It must be supposed that Lagash, always an individualist, had refused its record to the scribes of Isin, who drew up the king-list which we have.

---

[1] §IV, 42, 151 ff.; G, 13, 175 f.   [2] See *C.A.H.* I³, ch. VI, p. 221 f.
[3] E. Sollberger, *J.C.S.* 21 (1967), 279 ff.

Among the multitude of unknown names which filled these eleven dynasties occur a few of whom history or material survivals have something to say. A dynasty at Adab had one king only, named Lugalannimundu, who is credited with a reign of ninety years. A long inscription has been preserved in an early copy,[1] bearing his name with an account of his victories and building. After rehearsing the king's titles it describes a revolt against him, led by thirteen princes of neighbouring lands, not the cities of Sumer. Overcoming these, he proceeded with the building of E-nam-zu, a temple of the goddess Nintu, doubtless in Adab, and the rest of the inscription is devoted to describing this work and the festival which marked the goddess's reinstatement in her house, to which eight deputy-governors of the subdued provinces brought a fitting contribution. The style of this narration is unmistakably similar to that of the Agade period, but instead of this raising a suspicion of later forgery it might be better used to demonstrate how close in time were two dynasties which the king-list separates by 450 years. At this period, and perhaps in the same line, reigned a certain Lugal-da-lu, of whom a fine statuette,[2] with the usual Sumerian dress and bearing, was found in excavating at the site of his city. A mysterious personage of this time was a queen of Kish named Ku-Baba, said to have been by origin a 'woman of wine' (such is the literal meaning of the phrase), a woman-taverner, who became the master of Kish and 'established its foundation' either before or in the course of a reign of 100 years. It is also related in a chronicle[3] that she supplanted Puzur-Nirakh, king of Akshak, in the sovereignty. Her fame, but no more of her history, survived into the tablets of divination which preserved the messages given to her by the entrails,[4] and it is possible that she was the true original of Kombabos, the eunuch-priest of Hierapolis in Syria, as well as the Anatolian goddess Kubaba, who was also worshipped in northern Mesopotamia.[5]

Finally, the dynasty of Mari, though its names have nearly disappeared from the list, has left a better memorial of itself in many statuettes of men and women portraying these rulers and their courtiers. A broken figure has long been known in the British Museum, and the recent excavations upon the site have brought to light many others of the greatest interest.[6] Chief

[1] §IV, 19, 40 ff.   [2] G, 4, vol. II, 554 f.   [3] §IV, 19, 51 and 54.
[4] §IV, 59, 229 f.; §IV, 17, 264.   [5] §IV, 38, 94; §IV, 1, 230; §IV, 7, 39.
[6] §IV, 39, pls. VI ff. and XX ff., figs. 145 ff.; §IV, 40, pls. XXI ff.; §IV, 41, vol. I, pls. XXV ff.; G, 22, 116 ff. See Plate 30 (a) and below, pp. 294 f.; also A, 38, 35 f.

among these are Lamgi-Mari and Iku-Shamagan, kings, then Ebikh-il who calls himself an overseer, Idi-Narum the 'miller', and the curiously formed and attired Ur-Nanshe 'the great singer'. The style as well as the context of all these places them unmistakably in the period when the king-list gives a brief authority to their city over the whole of Sumer. Their costume, hairdressing (or shaven heads), and their whole mien are in the full style of the Early Dynastic age when it had reached its complete development. They look 'typical' Sumerians, but they bear mostly un-Sumerian names, and thereby afford another proof, if that were necessary, how totally irrelevant is dress and appearance to the ethnic origin of its Babylonian wearers at this time.

It has been observed above that the relations of the dynasties, and especially the years allotted to them in the king-list, have to be studied in comparison with the history of a single city about which, by the chance of discovery, far more is known than about any of its possibly more important rivals. This is owing to the records left by a local dynasty in the city of Lagash, explored since the 1870s at a site known as Tello,[1] lying between the Tigris and the Euphrates, not far east of the present bed of a channel called Shaṭṭ el-Ḥayy (or el-Gharrāf) which was the medieval course of the lower Tigris.[2] At about a like distance on the west side of this stood the Sumerian city of Umma, the hostile neighbour which bulks so large in the history preserved by the monuments of Lagash. It now seems likely that the mound called Tello was only one part of a larger complex bearing the name of Lagash, the centre of which may have been at the neighbouring site of El-Hibbeh, while Tello itself was the ancient Girsu.[3] But as nearly all the monuments and records which contain the history of Lagash in Sumerian times were discovered at Tello, there is, for general narration, no need to distinguish between the two.

The oldest known king of Lagash was Enkhegal, who has left an archaic record[4] of lands bought by himself and others, but his connexion with his successors is unknown. Another ruler of the city, Lugalshagengur, is named by Mesilim,[5] who was himself a king of Kish before the local dynasty of Lagash began. The true line was instituted by Ur-Nanshe, who names his father and grandfather, but these were apparently not kings, for a tradition distinguishes Ur-Nanshe himself as the elect of a goddess. Buildings, works of art, and inscriptions attest his power and

[1] G, 19, 9 ff.   [2] G, 16, 26 f.
[3] See §IV, 21, 127 ff.; §IV, 22, 175 ff. with pl. xxviii; §VIII, 1, 12; A, 10, 17 ff.
[4] §IV, 2, no. 2; §IV, 10, 282 f.; §VI, 5, 22 ff.   [5] G, 28, 160 f.

state. These last are not, in themselves, very informative, since they deal mostly with his building of temples and shrines (but also the wall of his city), carving of statues, and digging of canals, the classic pieties of Babylonian sovereigns, destined to be reiterated by a hundred successors. In one phrase only, several times repeated, does he open a glimpse of a wider scene, when 'ships of Tilmun brought cargoes of wood from the mountains' up the Persian Gulf. For the rest he certainly reigned, or exercised authority, at Ur, where a faintly traced figure and inscription upon a stele of granite[1] are just legible enough to reveal his name, which seems to have been defaced afterwards. The most interesting monuments of his reign are small stone reliefs[2] which show the king surrounded by his family and upper servants, each with his name inscribed beside him. These and other sculptures are executed in a style which seems to evince much archaic crudeness, and this is curiously paralleled by his inscriptions which, in their arrangement of the signs and their uninflected phraseology, give the impression of inexperience in the use of writing.

Ur-Nanshe was succeeded by his son Akurgal who is seen in the family groups attending his father, but is little known[3] except in his turn as father to Eannatum the next king. With him Lagash rose to what must have been, despite the loss of its fame in later tradition, a position in the land which would have justly entitled it to claim the *nam-lugal* or supremacy over the cities of Sumer.[4] Instead of recognizing this the king-list is occupied at this point by dynasties of Kish and Akshak, whereas Eannatum boasts that he fought a victorious battle with Zuzu, a king of Akshak otherwise unknown, and pursued him with slaughter up to the walls of his own city. As for Kish, 'the goddess Inanna gave him, out of the governorship of Lagash, the kingdom of Kish'. Still wider triumphs waited upon him, for his power was extended to the limit of the Sumerian horizon by a defeat, on the one side of Mari, and upon the other of Subar, the later Subartu, a land which he couples with Elam and Urua.[5] Uncertain as the position of Subar at this time may be,[6] it came ultimately to include Assyria, and it would not be very surprising if the Sumerian inhabitants or fashions discovered in the archaic Ishtar temple at Ashur[7] were introduced there by the Lagashites.

[1] §iv, 60, vol. xii, 387; §iv, 62, 46 and pl. 39*d*; §iv, 49, urn. 40; cf. §iv, 3.
[2] G, 25, pl. 2 *bis*, 1, 2; pl. 2 *ter*, 1; G, 19, pl. v; §iv, 49, urn. 20–3.
[3] §iv, 49, 8; §iv, 32, 70 f.   [4] G, 12, 20.
[5] §iv, 42, 167.   [6] §iv, 56, 38; §iv, 16, 34; A, 32.
[7] §ii, 1, 53 ff.

It may appear strange that the inscriptions of Eannatum dwell little upon these major triumphs and reserve all their detail for his broils with the neighbouring city of Umma, a subject to which, indeed, all the historical records of Lagash are mainly devoted. The reason for this seeming disproportion is that the inscriptions were designed for local monuments, buildings, stelae, or dedications, most of them immediately connected with the struggle for territory disputed with this neighbour, and are therefore concerned chiefly with facts and claims involved in the contest. This was occasioned by boundary quarrels of long standing concerning fields asserted by the Lagashites to be the property of their god Ningirsu, but constantly usurped by their antagonists, the men of Umma, a place about thirty miles to the west now marked by the mound called Jūkhā. There had been, in days past, a famous arbitration by one Mesilim,[1] a king 'of Kish' (which possibly means no more than an acknowledged sovereign, for he is unknown among the kings of that city), who had set up a stele marking the frontier between the two litigants. This award[2] had certainly favoured Lagash, for it always happened that when the men of Umma imagined an opportunity they overthrew the boundary-marks and occupied the disputed lands. In the style of the time, this was an intolerable affront to the god Ningirsu, which the king, as the god's agent, was charged (in a dream) to avenge. Eannatum performed this task with complete success and savage fury; he utterly defeated the people of Umma in the field, slaying thousands, and pursuing the survivors into Umma itself, which he sacked. This victory was commemorated by a new stele which he erected beside the restored monument of Mesilim, and large portions of this still exist under the modern name of 'Stele of the Vultures',[3] so called from the birds of prey which are shown devouring the dead bodies. On one side it bears sculptures in relief with remarkable pictures of the king in his war-accoutrements, once on foot and once standing in his chariot, leading out his ranks of soldiers in phalanx or in marching-order before the battle. On the other side is a symbolical scene of the god Ningirsu (or perhaps the king himself) whose 'great overwhelming net' has caught the warriors of Umma in multitudes, and in these toils the conqueror smites them upon their protruding

---

[1] G, 13, 181 n. 29; G, 12, 25 f.; G, 27, 248.

[2] Cf. §IV, 30, 64 f.; the inscription of an unknown king, giving information about the boundaries of Umma (§IV, 50) is perhaps connected with a similar award.

[3] Description and bibliography in G, 19, 95 ff.; text in §IV, 49, 9 ff. A, 28.

heads. Below are the fragments of another chariot-scene which apparently showed the victory of Eannatum over Kish.

The events which led up to this crisis and its consequences are more fully described by Entemena,[1] nephew of the conqueror, who became his second successor. Going back to the beginning, he says that Ningirsu and Shara, the respective gods of the two cities, had in the first place agreed upon a boundary between their estates. But if the gods were satisfied their subjects did not long so remain, and Mesilim, as aforesaid, interposed to settle the frontier. Aggression continued and Ush (or Gish),[2] governor of Umma, is named as the first culprit. He removed the stele of Mesilim and invaded the lands of Lagash. The god Ningirsu himself commanded resistance, and as his general Eannatum fought with Ush, defeated and apparently slew him, for the terms imposed were accepted by a new leader Enakalli. Under this treaty a canal was dug up to the disputed territory from the 'princely river' (Euphrates) and the monuments were re-erected, one of Mesilim and the new one of Eannatum. Sanctuaries of the Lagashite gods were put up on the newly secured lands, and the men of Umma were compelled to pay an indemnity of grain.[3] These conditions lasted no longer than the victor's life, for when his brother Enannatum I came to the office of city-governor there was another sudden incursion under a new ruler of Umma named Urlumma, son of Enakalli,[4] who again overthrew the hated monuments and cast them in a fire, demolished the sanctuaries, crossed the canal, and invaded Lagash once more. Enannatum 'fought with Urlumma', but evidently without success, for the inscription adds hastily that his son Entemena was victorious, though it must have been in a later battle.[5] At this, Urlumma in his turn disappeared, being replaced by a certain Il, one of the same ruling family,[6] who had hitherto held a priesthood in his city. Entemena's treaty with him, confirming the supremacy of Lagash, enjoined him to restore the boundaries and the canals which marked them. These seem to have been a link in the water-communication which Entemena constructed joining the Tigris to the Euphrates, evidently a great and beneficent work, which may have coincided generally with the

[1] §IV, 49, 37 ff.; G, 28, 36 ff.; §IV, 35, 141 ff.   [2] §IV, 54, 179.
[3] §IV, 48, 161 f.   [4] §IV, 54, 177 ff.; A, 20.
[5] Another account of this war is in Urukagina, Oval Plaque, col. IV: see §IV, 49, 54; G, 28, 56 ff.; §IV, 48, 151, 156, 167; A, 20.
[6] §IV, 54, 177; §IV, 55, 90. But there seems to be a generation missing from the descent of Bara-irnun, the 'daughter' of Urlumma. See also *Sumer*, xv, 22.

present Shaṭṭ el-Ḥayy. Entemena was doubtless the greatest of his line, and his memory lived long, though it was not he whose statue was enshrined and commemorated in a year-formula, by the later Babylonian king Abieshuʻ.[1] But images of this ancient ruler were sometimes to be viewed in later ages, such as the fine life-sized figure at Ur[2] which, despite its inscription alluding only to the local lands of Lagash, may have been placed there by himself, for the rulers of Lagash, beginning with Ur-Nanshe, clearly held sway over Ur where, besides those already mentioned, an inscription of Enannatum[3] was also found. If it is true that the stele of Ur-Nanshe was defaced this might indicate a revolt of Ur, for its defeat was one of the triumphs of Eannatum.

There is but little more information of events in Lagash and in the whole of Sumer during the remainder of the Early Dynastic period, now drawing to its close. Entemena was succeeded by his son, and he by two brief rulers, Enentarzi and Lugalanda, both known as belonging, before their accession, to the priestly and official classes. A report from the martial priest of a provincial temple informed Enentarzi of the interception and slaughter of 600 Elamites returning with spoil from a sudden raid upon Lagash,[4] apart from which incident nothing is known of external events until the end of the dynasty. But a sudden increase of economic documents yields a wealth of detail concerning the internal conditions (which will be described below), and the polity, which was marked by the peculiar ascendancy of Lugalanda's wife Barnamtarra, though her prominence may be due to the origin of the economic records, which are those of the temple over which the governor's wife presided, as the counterpart of the goddess.[5] The same position was occupied by Shasha, wife to the last governor Urukagina, who violently removed his predecessor, reigned for at least eight years, accomplished the building of many temples and two canals, took the title of king, and ruled over all the territory from Lagash to the sea. His name is most honourably connected with a reform of corrupt social usages, which he carried through perhaps in the face of opposition; but this, with the end of the reformer and of his period, will be better postponed to the conclusion of this chapter.

---

[1] §IV, 57, 186, no. 198; but see *J.C.S.* v, 102.
[2] §IV, 60, vol. III, pl. XXXI; §IV, 62, 47 and pl. 40; §IV, 14, no. 1.
[3] §IV, 14, no. 2.   [4] §IV, 53.
[5] §IV, 31, 26 f.; A, 38, 33 f.

V. ARMIES AND WARFARE

The inscriptions of the third Early Dynastic period and the king-list which is the main authority for its history are all greatly preoccupied with war, and when it is added that the outstanding pictorial monuments are devoted to the same subject there can be no surprise that the age has gained an ill repute for militarism.[1] While it is probable that the inhabitants were not less pugnacious in earlier times, of which little is known, there seems to be no denying that the great increase of wealth, and particularly of technical skills, as well as the ideas which prevailed concerning the governance of the cities and their hierarchy among themselves led to the indulgence of this instinct with perhaps greater frequency, and certainly with more destructive results. The written records testify abundantly to the occasions and causes of war, but its methods also are more amply illustrated than at any other time until the Assyrian sculptures displayed the operation of an even more highly organized military instrument. The two principal monuments are the Stele of the Vultures[2] and the so-called Standard of Ur,[3] and fragments of scenes from other places, such as Kish[4] and Mari,[5] tend to prove that all the cities possessed a similar armament. These depict the Sumerian host as a well-equipped and well-ordered fighting-machine; if it lacked some of the elements introduced later into the battles of Western Asia it was far removed from the primitive and tumultuary. The numbers of men put into the field can hardly be estimated, but Entemena writes of his election by the god 'from among 3600 men' (a number which Urukagina multiplies by ten and Gudea, still later, by sixty), which figures are possibly meant to represent the population; with equal vagueness Eannatum boasts of having slain 3600 men from the host of Umma. More factually it has been reckoned[6] that one temple alone in the city of Lagash furnished 500 to 600 men from its tenants for the military levy; and Lagash was probably not one of the largest centres.

Two arms only are depicted by the monuments, the chariotry and foot. Upon the Stele of the Vultures only the *ensi* himself rides in a chariot, unaccompanied, but this impression is altered

[1] §v, 11, 413.
[2] G, 19, 95 ff. gives a description and bibliography of this; A, 36.
[3] §iv, 61, pls. 91–3.   [4] §v, 7, pls. vi and xxxvi ff.
[5] §v, 9, 7 ff. and pl. 1; G, 20, nos. 63–70. See Plate 30 (*c*).
[6] G, 5, 113.

by the Standard, which seems to give a more correct version as to
both of these details. The royal car is shown at rest, and its
master dismounted, but in the lowest register are four more
chariots going into battle with a momentum which visibly increases from the left to the right of the picture, in spite of which
artistic device[1] it is not likely that only one chariot was intended,
nor does this seem to be the king's. These vehicles are not single-
handed, for while one occupant drives the principal warrior is
free to wield his weapons, which are the spear and a curved sword,
also a leaf-shaped sword is seen in the hands of the king. Beside
the high protective front of the chariot was a quiver or 'bucket'
filled with additional spears, probably designed for throwing by
means of a sling, for spears of this kind were found in the
'Royal Tombs' at Ur fitted with a metal notch at the butt.[2] These
missiles took the place of the bow and arrow, so prominent in the
scenes of later chariot warfare, but apparently not used by either
arm of the Sumerian service, as will be noticed below. The
animals which drew these cars have predominantly the appearance
of asses, with a few inconsistent features; the species has been
debated by naturalists, but there is said to be enough evidence
from skeletal remains[3] to identify them as onagers, or wild asses,
which are now almost extinct, but were still not uncommon in
the last century, when they had the reputation of being untamable.
In the Sumerian chariots they ran four abreast,[4] guided by reins
which passed over a cleft in the high front of the chariot, through
a double rein-ring fixed to the chariot-pole, and were tied to bits
in the jaws of the animals. The chariots themselves were of a very
peculiar model which soon passed out of use. Their bodies were
wooden frames covered with hide, having low sides emphasized
by an abnormally high front with a depression for the reins and
often a pair of holes under the rail, no doubt spy-holes for the
riders when they were taking cover behind the shielding front.
Most curious of all were the wheels, four in number, and fixed to
the axles, constructed of two wooden semicircles fastened together
by clamps inside and out, with a special housing for the axles and
even sometimes with metal studs round the tyres, which reduced
wear—these can be seen used in the same way upon the much
later Assyrian chariots. Description of these primitive vehicles[5]

[1] §v, 5, 159, 198 ff.; §v, 10, 56 f.   [2] §iv, 61, pl. 149.
[3] §v, 6, 2–21; §v, 13, 44 ff. But some of the 'onagers' found at Ur prove to be
oxen, see §v, 2.   [4] §vi, 9, pls. 58 ff.
[5] G, 4, vol. i, 482; §v, 12, 117 and 156 f.; §i, 20, 59 ff.; A, 28, figs. 5, 6, 10.
For some survivals see §v, 8, vol. iii, pl. cliv, nos. 10 and 11; §v, 1; §v, 4, 70 ff.

would not be complete without special notice of the rein-rings[1] mentioned above, several of which have survived to furnish, in the little model animals which surmount them, some of the most pleasing examples of minor art. So essential was this decorative feature that it was even pointed out in the constellation which Sumerian fancy had named the Wagon. The practical efficacy in battle of these lumbering and inflexible carts might be reckoned very dubious, especially against the serried infantry now to be described.

Upon both of the principal monuments the main body of the foot-soldiers moves in a phalanx,[2] with levelled spears. The men are heavily armed, being protected in the one case by massive rectangular shields, upon which can be seen bosses of metal, and in the other by long capes garnished with similar studs. Some detached figures from a like scene of combat found at Mari seem to have exchanged this cape for a lighter shoulder-guard with broad bands hanging down the front and back of the body.[3] In advance of the phalanx the Standard shows several light-armed soldiers engaging individual enemies, whom they overcome and immediately strip of their clothes before slaying or leading them away captive. Apart from this distinction, which consists in the wearing or absence of the cape, the armament of all foot-soldiers was a protective helmet and, for attack, either the spear or the socketed and shafted axe. The helmets were of copper or bronze, flattish, and slightly ridged, with ear-protectors and chinstraps, the insides being padded with woollen material to fit the head. Such sumptuous examples as the golden helmet in form of a wig which belonged to one of the occupants of graves in the Royal Cemetery at Ur, and such as is worn by Eannatum upon the Stele of the Vultures were only rich modifications of the head-covering worn by all the troops. Spears and axes alike were used only hand-to-hand, for there is no indication that the former were thrown, except possibly from the chariots. The Sumerian armies thus seem to be almost unprovided with missile weapons and to have depended wholly upon weight, which is emphasized by the slow, unswerving chariots as much as by the phalanx. In particular, there has been found nothing to contradict the early observation that bows and arrows were not used in Sumerian warfare. That they were familiar to the people is proved both by representations upon painted pottery and seals, and by the discovery of arrow-heads in excavation, but wherever they are shown in use

[1] §iv, 61, pls. 166 f.; G, 4, vol. iv, 2096, 2210 ff.
[2] As described in the rally of the Achaeans, *Iliad* xiii, 130–1.
[3] G, 20, nos. 63–70. See Plate 30 (*c*).

it is for hunting, as best exemplified by the fine 'Stele of Warka', belonging to the Jamdat-Naṣr period,[1] upon which a man is shooting lions with a cunningly-fashioned bow and an arrow with a cutting point of triangular shape and no doubt made of flint, such as were found in the grave of Meskalamdug at Ur.[2]

While there is no extant scene of siege operations it is certain both that cities were defended with massive walls[3] and that they were captured, perhaps most often by rush at the heels of a defeated army, as when Eannatum overpowered and sacked Umma, though he more often speaks of beating his enemies and pursuing them up to the walls of their cities. Again, in its turn, Lagash was captured and looted by Lugalzaggisi and various fragments of Early Dynastic inscriptions are found upon trophies dedicated in temples from the spoil of captured cities. It may be assumed, then, that siegecraft was not unknown to the Sumerians, and that its principal resource was the piling up of a great ramp of earth at one point of the perimeter, an operation for which the military engineers of a later period were prepared with statistical calculations of the time and labour required; these may be regarded as good evidence that the device had long been studied, and it was, of course, still in full practice under the Assyrian warlords and throughout classical antiquity.[4] The effect of this operation, perhaps the only means by which an attack could be launched upon a defence of enormously thick earthwork, was to transfer the battle of shock to the height of the wall, the besiegers having the handicap that they were obliged to attack uphill, the besieged too being hampered by the want of depth in their defence. There is no evidence for the use of siege-engines so early as this, although they were certainly employed in a succeeding age.[5]

VI. FOUNDATIONS OF POWER; HUSBANDRY, TRADES, ARTS

This military power was sustained in the Sumerian cities by a wealth which manifested itself also in many splendid products of material civilization. The foundation of this wealth was the fertility

[1] §IV, 24, no. V, pls. 12 f. A cylinder-seal of the 'Uruk' period in the British Museum presents a similar but more extensive scene in miniature, with remarkable detail. See M. E. L. Mallowan in *Baghdader Mitteilungen* 3 (1964), 65 ff.

[2] §IV, 61, 160 and 381; see now A, 23.

[3] §IV, 24, no. VII, 41 ff. and no. VIII, 5 ff. See also §IV, 12 and G, 7, 807.

[4] See *Z.D.P.V.* 56, 167 ff. and Tafel 13; §V, 3, note 45—a Roman siege-ramp still existing at Masada in Palestine.   [5] §V, 14, 31 f.

of the land and that fertility depended in its turn upon irrigation. The control of the regular spring floods by an elaborate system of dams and canals must have been a slow achievement, but it was clearly recognized by the Sumerians as a supreme necessity and the resulting prosperity was so marvellous in their eyes that they were constrained to regard the completed irrigation system as the work of none less than a god. One of the most elaborate myths, not indeed written down until a later period, but doubtless formed much earlier, related[1] how the god Ninurta had fought against a demon in the mountains, named Asag, and his final victory over this monster caused the waters to rise up out of the earth and destroy by overflowing all the works of gods and men. In many vivid lines are described the baleful effects of this inundation, which was not checked until Ninurta heaped up a mighty barrier of earth and stones to control the floods and to drain the excess waters into the Tigris. In this mythological form was dramatized a human achievement which no doubt spread over several generations.

When history begins to be recorded the canals are found occupying a place of high importance in the economy of the land, and it is plain that their control and the possession of water rights were among the fruitful causes of strife between neighbours. The boundary between Lagash and Umma was marked by an important canal, which it was aggression to cross or to divert. After his defeat of the men of Umma Eannatum laid it upon them as a condition that they should not presume to cross this canal again, and he himself excavated a tank containing 3600 *gur* of water, perhaps to maintain the level of the channel.[2] Entemena in his time again had to enforce this prohibition, renew the tank, and command his nominee in Umma that he should restore and respect the boundary canal, which Entemena subsequently enlarged into a main stream uniting the Tigris probably with the Euphrates.[3] Urukagina once more excavated or renewed a great reservoir for maintenance of the level of these waterways.[4] Thereafter the digging of canals becomes a commonplace of royal self-gratulation, and ranks with building of temples, the provision of maintenance for the gods, and the waging of their wars as the chief function of the king.

[1] G, 15, 198 ff., 290 f., cf. *J.N.E.S.* 5, 146 f.
[2] G, 28, 22 f.; §iv, 48, 92 (148). This tank, renewed to the same capacity by Entemena, was hardly great enough to form the basin of a canal; its content has been reckoned as 218 cubic metres, §iv, 32, 77. See also A, 2, 113 f.
[3] G, 28, 36 f.; §iv, 48, 90 (130). The inscription is on a brick from this structure.
[4] G, 28, 46 f., cones B and c.

Upon the system of agriculture which these watercourses fostered we are amply, though perhaps one-sidedly, informed by the numerous tablets inscribed with the accountancy of a temple in the city of Lagash. The mere fact that most of the evidence is contributed by only one, and that by no means the greatest of the Sumerian cities, should warn that these tablets cannot tell the whole story, and to this must be added the further limitation that they all refer to the affairs of one temple only, that of the goddess Baba, which, as belonging to the consort of the god, was under the direction of the wife of the *ensi*—he being the manager of the god, she occupied the same place in respect to the goddess.[1] Accepting these limitations, the evidence is still impressive, and allows the suggestion that a considerable part of the city's whole territory was the property of the temples,[2] for that of Baba at Lagash was only one among several, and must have been inferior, at least, to the principal fane of the god himself. While there are no reliable means of estimating what was the extent of the whole Lagashite territory, it has been calculated that the lands of Baba amounted to more than one square mile,[3] and this estate was worked exclusively by tenants and dependants of the temple. Most of these were not slaves but feudatories, either receiving daily allowances or owing, in return for the portion of their crops which remained in their hands, not only a fixed proportion of the produce, but the duty of military service in the cause of the deity whose lands they cultivated; their different ranks regulated the extent of land which was assigned to them and the amount of maintenance which they had the right to draw from their divine employer.

In return for their service, the temple was liable for their keep all the year round, at seasons when field work was not possible, and in addition supplied them with seed-corn and the implements required for cultivation, including the plough-cattle. The principal crop was certainly barley, and this was delivered to the temple in very large quantities, part of which was used for cattle-fodder, some for brewing into beer, but most was ground in a great mill and used first as food of the god, and then for issue to the workers as rations, or wages in kind. Two other kinds of grain were raised (perhaps emmer and wheat), but in minor quantities. Nor

[1] §iv, 31, 12 f.

[2] Some discussion of the debated question of land-ownership will be found later in this section.

[3] G, 5, 79; G, 7, 791. The following account is taken mainly from these two works. See also A, 10, 41.

was grain the only crop obtained, for the tablets contain accounts of root-crops and a considerable acreage was devoted to trees producing both fruit and, what was very valuable in the bare country, timber for building and furniture. All of these kinds of produce were dependent upon irrigation, and some of the labour required for this duty of maintaining the waterways was furnished by slaves, either with their own hands or as drivers of oxen.

Still another form of industry which was pursued by the staff of the temple was cattle raising. Oxen were bred and kept not only for the plough but for their necessary products, milk and meat; sheep, goats and pigs yielded meat, fat, and especially wool and hair, which employed many hands, especially women, in its preparation, spinning and weaving. A more surprising branch of industry about which the temple-accounts contain much information is fishing;[1] there appear to have been about 100 fishermen who regularly delivered fish to the temple authorities, and these are called 'sea-fishermen' as well as 'fresh-water fishermen'. This 'state' fishery service was an institution which maintained its centralized character when much else in the economic system had altered, for under the dynasty of Larsa 'the palace' still controlled the catching and marketing of fish, employing Amorite labourers for the one operation and wholesalers for the other.[2] There is also an evident reminiscence of the sacred fisheries in a late chronicle,[3] which curiously associates the destinies of early kings with their piety as touching the supply of fish to the supreme god.

Great as were these revenues of the Sumerian temples, they were almost counterbalanced by the large expenditures necessary to maintain not only the god and his house, but to support the whole economy of the temple and the numerous persons who lived entirely for and by this institution, to whom the service of the god was not an incidental of life, as in less intensely theocratic societies, but was life itself. The needs of the god were the primary necessities of housing, feeding, and clothing. Whether the complete repair of temples was exclusively an object of royal munificence, as might be inferred from the inscriptions, or whether it was normally effected from the temples' own resources, it is beyond doubt that current maintenance of the buildings and their appurtenances was a large item of costs, and the same consideration applies to the upkeep of canals upon which revenues depended, a function also assumed with ostentation by the kings, but per-

---

[1] See R.A. 49, 210 n. 5; §vi, 2; §vi, 20, 390 f.; G, 6, iii, 68 f.
[2] §vi, 12; §vi, 10, 62.   [3] §iv, 19, 54 ff.

haps more regularly discharged by the temple economies themselves, to which, in any case, the king was indebted for a large
part of his resources. More direct expenses of the temple were
consumed in the daily or periodic necessities of the god's personal
service. Every day an ample provision had to be served to his
table, morning and evening, and not only to the principal divinity
but to a more or less numerous family and household of divine
relations and servants. All kinds of victuals appear in this provision, the flesh of sheep and goats, fish, bread and flour, butter,
fruits, honey, and beer for drink. Clothing for the divine owner
and family was another constant item of expenditure, and upon
festival days rich ornaments as well as fine robes had to be provided. That any part of these supplies of food and clothing was
taken by individuals who enjoyed the rights of priesthood is not
attested by the tablets of the temple of Baba, though it was the
practice of later ages in Babylonia, when the selling and buying of
such perquisites was one of the objects of private mercantile
transaction. Possibly the custom of Sumerian times at Lagash was
in fact different, for we shall see that the reforms of Urukagina
were directed in part to the fees which priests had been in the
habit of exacting from private persons.

Still heavier than the expenses of the god himself, his family,
and his servants of divine rank, was the cost of the multitude of
the temple staff, which embraced a whole section of the city's
population. In such a system as that traced by these temple
records the distinction between the divine and human tends to
disappear; the god is paralleled by the king or *ensi*, his family by
the *ensi*'s wife and her children, and the needs of both are supplied
by the temple organization, which is composed of managers and
workers whose services to the gods are scarcely distinguishable as
being upon the divine or the human plane. Each discharges his
function, and each receives his due return and maintenance.
There were gods, as appears by later evidence—which may
however be unhesitatingly projected back to the Early Dynastic
and doubtless to still more remote generations—who were considered to supply quite menial offices such as coachmen and goat-
herds to the lord of the city and its temple; again, the distinction
of city and temple becomes dim, for one was only an agglomeration
of the other. Thus, the temple was in fact responsible for the live-
lihood of many citizens, who in turn lived for and by the
temple. On the debit side, this arrangement naturally involved the
temple in great liabilities. What may be called the household
expenses were large and standing charges; first of these (or, at

least, first mentioned) was, rather unexpectedly, the upkeep of teams of asses, which, to judge again by what we know of the time of Gudea, were splendidly maintained animals kept to provide the carriage of the god, who proceeded on the journeys dictated by his annual occasions in such a chariot as we find upon the monuments and in the models of this time, drawn by a span of four asses. Nor is it surprising to find that such equipages were also at the service of the *ensi*, his wife and his family, and the highest officers of the temple management; again, it tends to be uncertain whether the need is upon the divine or the human plane. Next, the temple operated catering and even manufacture upon a large scale for the supply of its own needs and those of its staff, so that ample supplies were necessary every month for the kitchens, the bakery, and the brewery. With these fell to be reckoned special but regular provisions for divine and mortal heads of the administration, and the very large issues of fodder for the herds of swine, sheep and cattle.

The roll of allowances from the temple for its ordinary personnel was long and impressive, for the number of its servants and dependants has been reckoned, on the basis of the accounts, as about 1200.[1] Wages were paid exclusively in kind,[2] and the staple commodity dispensed was barley, the ordinary food of the people. In addition to this there were on special occasions distributions of bread, wheat, wool, beer, milk and fruit, apparently at festivals. Ordinary wages were drawn by male workers, both those who held fiefs from the temple with liability to military service, and those who may be reckoned as slaves. In addition to these was the large number of women employed in the temple industries connected with the main needs of food and clothing, that is, in the stores and kitchens, in the flour-mills, and spinners and weavers in the clothing factory, most of whom appear to have been slaves. Those who had children received also a small allowance for these helpers or dependants. Their employments were the preparation of the wool, its spinning and weaving; others, as said above, worked in the kitchens and flour-mills and brewhouses, a superior order of attendants waited upon the wife and children of the *ensi* as personal maids, hairdressers, nurses, or cooks, but the basic reward seems to have been alike for all, rising only according to the position and skill of the workers. Among the male workers some appear to have been slaves; they are called by a word which may mean 'blind' or a longer phrase which seems to mean 'blind and deaf', or 'witless'. How, subject to this disability,

[1] A different estimate is quoted in §iii, 1, 59.   [2] A, 13.

they could do useful service is not easy to understand, but they are found employed as gardeners and in workshops.[1] The actual raising of the large grain crops was in the hands of the temple's tenants, who farmed holdings of various extent, and were obliged by the terms of their tenure to surrender a fixed quota of their produce, and were liable, in addition, to military service. These men too are found among the recipients of wages on the temple books, and perhaps earned these additions to their emoluments by working upon the parts of the estate which were not let out but kept by the temple for its own needs. None of the wages given to any class of these workers were high, for the utmost received by any hand was about 60 litres (72 *sila*) a month, the lowest workers got no more than infants, 10 litres (12 *sila*). Consumers of this modest fare,[2] even at the highest scale, were the men who were to furnish the defenders of the god's cause in battle, and out of the whole host which the city of Lagash could put into the field, it is reckoned that the temple of Baba could supply about 500 to 600 men.

The foregoing account of society and land-holding in the early Sumerian age at Lagash is drawn, as aforesaid, from the detailed records of one temple over a rather short period. It has been widely accepted as a complete picture of the Sumerian economy, revealing almost the whole of the land as belonging to temples, and almost the whole population in various dependence upon these. But the basis for such a generalization is precariously narrow. The area of land concerned in these records is no more than about one square mile. Yet while there can be made no reliable estimate of the total extent of the city's territories, it is known (1) that they extended to 'the sea',[3] and (2) that the mound now named Zerghūl, some eighteen miles south-east of Tello, was within the city-area,[4] being the place called Nina, with the seat of a goddess Nanshe, who was an oracle to the Lagashite rulers. Within these wide if undefined limits it is reasonable to assume the presence of other temple-estates, at least one of which, belonging to the principal god himself, may be supposed even greater and richer than the domains of his consort. Making whatever deduction for these, and adding desert tracts, it still seems probable that very much land remained with owners other

---

[1] §vi, 20, 56 n. 1; §viii, 3, 174 n; *R.A.* 52, 96 f.

[2] Interesting estimates have been made concerning the dietetic sufficiency of these allowances and the standard of living among the workers: see *R.A.* 18, 129 n. 6; §vi, 16, 7; §vi, 10, 62.

[3] According to Urukagina; see §viii, 3, 174, 180.

[4] §iv, 21, 128; A, 10, 17 ff.

than temples. Nor is there wanting evidence of this, not only in the clause of Urukagina's reforms which forbade priests to gather fruits in a 'poor man's garden', but in documents of private sale, mostly of commodities such as metals, grains, animals, hides, fish, and slaves, but also land as well, comprising fields great and small. These acquisitions, at Lagash, were made by rulers or members of their family, and their possible encroachment upon the estates of temples is one subject of the impending reforms. The earliest attested purchase of land was made by Enkhegal, a predecessor of the Lagash 'dynasty', and there are later transactions by Eannatum and by Lummatur, a son of the ruling house.[1] Some of these acquisitions were large, and all were obtained by the payment not only of a main price to the principal vendors, but of sundry gifts, occasionally in silver but more often in kind, to a number of persons having collateral claims to ownership. The deal was always ratified by the ceremony of driving a peg into a wall[2] and pouring oil. From these observations it has been deduced that much land in the confines of Lagash (and hence, by analogy, in Sumer everywhere) may have belonged to family communities,[3] and could be alienated by these through the agency of the family heads, with proportionate payments to relatives sharing the property. If this is true, not only does a different picture emerge of the early Sumerian state, but certain of the decrees of Urukagina appear more intelligible, as will be seen later.

Although agriculture was, and ever must have been, the principal source of wealth in Babylonia, there is, at this period especially, abounding evidence of another form of wealth, that derived from foreign trade. A few references in the inscriptions show the official dependence upon this for building material and choice products; the most interesting are those of Ur-Nanshe, mentioned before,[4] concerning the cargoes of timber brought to him by ships of Tilmun, and the carved stone plaque dedicated by the priest Dudu, which was brought from the eastern district of Urua.[5] The semi-mythical king Enmerkar of Uruk had trading relations (as it seems) with the city of Aratta, which, however arduous the journey, was not beyond the range of a single messenger.[6] From this place he sought stone and metals in exchange for the grains of his own country. Some indications of trade

---

[1] §vi, 5; §vi, 15; §vi, 17; §iii, 1.   [2] §vi, 13, 88 f.; §vi, 19.
[3] And, at Shuruppak, to small private owners, see §vi, 5, 24 f.; §vi, 17, 441 n. 4; A, 19.
[4] G, 28, 2 f. (Tafel A), and in other inscriptions.
[5] G, 28, 34 f. (i).   [6] See above, p. 111.

beyond the boundaries of Lagash are found in the documents
of private commerce, but these again are limited to a fairly close
horizon. Places mentioned include the Sumerian cities of Nippur,
Uruk, Umma, Adab, and Dēr, but there is also a farther cast to
Elam (for silver in exchange for barley), to the unidentified Uruaz for slaves, and, farthest of all, to the familiar (but still not
surely located) Tilmun for its staple of copper.[1] But the fact
hardly needs written testimony, for the wealth of the early tombs
at Ur was displayed in a lavish employment of materials, metal
and stone, scarcely one of which is indigenous to the country,
though worked there with a mastery which evinces a long use of
handling these exotic commodities.

The origins of metals, both precious and base, used so lavishly
at Ur and in other deposits of the third Early Dynastic period,
have been investigated with much care. Most probable source of
the copper, which betrays a slight mixture of the rare and then
unisolated metal nickel, is thought for this reason to have been
Oman or possibly Sinai. The gold was alluvial and therefore
naturally alloyed with silver and other metals; the sources of this
may be sought where Gudea found it, one place probably in
Armenia, the other Meluhha, a country which, despite its
frequent appearance in the cuneiform texts, is still uncertain of
location. But at least one possibility is Nubia, which was the
general gold-mine of the ancient world and the main source of its
riches, both according to ancient testimony and in modern
surveys.[2] Stones, especially lapis-lazuli and carnelian, provide
an even more interesting pointer to a widespread commerce.
Lapis-lazuli,[3] the most prized of all, which the literature never
tires of naming as the most splendid comparison of things considered beautiful and precious, is not to be obtained nearer than
the distant Badakhshān. Carnelian is said to be found in the
lands bordering the Persian Gulf, and some of the Sumerian
supplies may have come from there. But it is still more common
in the north-west of India, especially in the form of beads with
etched or bleached patterns;[4] the most notable examples of these
were found at the celebrated site of Harappā, contemporary with
the Agade period in Babylonia, when these beads, never very
common, became better known there. There is a distinct possi-

---

[1] §vi, 15, part i.
[2] See generally upon this subject §vi, 6 and 7; also §vi, 1. But it is, in fact, very
unlikely that Meluhha, in this age, denoted Nubia or anywhere in Africa at all;
the question will be considered in chapter xix. See also A, 21.
[3] §vi, 11; G, 16, 436; A, 5.   [4] §1, 25, 59, 73 f., and 87.

bility that those found in Babylonia were of Indian manufacture and directly imported.

The indications of foreign trade in the third Early Dynastic period are therefore impressive; it followed the lines marked out by nature, to Syria and Asia Minor, down the Gulf, and over the hills and steppes of Persia and Baluchistan, but these riches were accessible only when there was strength to hold open the approaches and wealth to acquire the merchandise. The brilliant display of the tombs at Ur bespeaks a command and mastery of these foreign resources which was never again to be matched throughout the history of the land. But this phenomenon is not isolated, for about the middle of the third millennium B.C. the whole ancient world seems to have reached together the zenith of its prosperity. While in Sumer were unrolled the glories of an heroic age, the beginnings of a literature, and the rise of warlike and decorative arts, in Egypt was flourishing the Old Kingdom, age of the great pyramid-builders and of its supreme artists. It is now likely also that even Anatolia, so apt to appear a remote and 'backwoods' sector outside the great civilizations, had its full share in the wonders of this period. The treasures of Troy (II) have long been before the modern world, and a recent discovery has emphasized their significance. At Dorak,[1] south of the Propontis, were 'royal graves' replete with rich deposits not inferior to, and not unrelated with, those of Ur. The name of Sahure, second king of the Fifth Dynasty in Egypt, discloses their date, and a weapon decorated with a line of little sea-going ships tells of the overseas commerce from which all this wealth must have been derived. It is as though a sap were rising at its strongest in those years through the branches of all the ancient Near East— *ver illud erat, ver magnus agebat orbis*—nourished from what common soil we have at present no means of detecting, for in none of these places had men yet reached the capacity of expressing themselves clearly in writing. For which reason it may seem doubtful whether the future can ever explain the mystery of so manifest and simultaneous an achievement by peoples which can scarcely have heard intelligibly the report one of another. It must now be added that doubts have been expressed about the homogeneity and origin of the Dorak collection, which was seen apparently only on one occasion by one qualified observer (K. Pearson and P. Connor, *The Dorak Affair*, London, 1967).

It is for this very reason of wealth and accomplishment that

[1] See *Ill. Ldn News* 28 Nov. 1959, 754 ff.; §VI, 18, 168 f., 188; and below, pp. 390 ff.

no adequate sketch can be given of the arts which flowered so lavishly in this heyday of the early Sumerian civilization. They were not new inventions, for their origin is plainly to be discerned in the pre-historic epochs described with their products in the preceding chapter. Some of them, indeed, had already passed therein an apogee and a comparative decline. Building had attained many of the characteristic features of design and execution which it was to carry on not only into the Early Dynastic III but even into later times, and the plan of the temple was already settled in its broad lines. In materials there was now what seems a retrogression, for the odd and unexplained 'plano-convex' brick[1] had, apparently in defiance of all reason, replaced the practical rectangular brick everywhere except the outlying cities of Mari and Ashur.[2] Pottery too enters with this period an age of decline; the 'scarlet ware'[3] is found no more, and all is plain buff undecorated or at the most relieved with encrusted or incised patterns. For this there is an obvious reason and one which seems always to be operative in like conditions—the immense increase in the supply and mastery in the working of metals turned the skill of the craftsmen towards this more obviously rewarding medium, and pottery sank into an article of mere utility instead of the vehicle of high artistic achievement which it had been in ages already long past, at Susa or Arpachiyah. In turn, of course, this neglect leads to a revival, for the expensive vessels of fine metal become an inspiration to the potter, who contrives to imitate them in his own common clay, but this reaction was not witnessed during the Early Dynastic period.

In the art of engraving designs upon cylinder-seals,[4] a falling-off had occurred at the outset of this period or even earlier, and fresh progress was now noticeable. The first age is marked by long and slender cylinders with designs of continuous patterns recurring like those of modern textiles or wall-papers, which have been given the name of 'Brocade-style'. The second period is less distinctive, for its subject is almost exclusively the frieze of animals in combat interspersed with small human figures, and for the first time an inscription in a disordered arrangement appears upon a few of the seals. With the third period, although the animal frieze continues to be the favourite theme it is rendered in a more natural manner, human figures are more prominent, and the inscriptions when present begin to be organized into a formal place in the design. But there is a great increase both in the

---

[1] §vi, 3; §iv, 62, 34 f.; see below, pp. 246 f.
[2] §vi, 22, 198.   [3] §vi, 4, 60 ff.   [4] See generally G, 1; 8; 17; 21; 23.

representational quality of the pictures and in the number of
scenes depicted; the gods appear in mythological and ritual scenes,
and a favourite device is that of a banquet at which the principal
actors sometimes drink from a vessel between them through long
bent tubes, of which some highly decorated specimens have been
found in the excavations. Thus the third period uses a manner and
a repertoire which is intended to be fully pictorial, but it may be
said to fall short in this attempt as compared with the fine archaic
cylinders of Uruk. In this particular the third Early Dynastic is
an age of progress rather than of attainment, for its cylinders
lead on to the wealth in subject and beauty in execution which
was not perfected until the succeeding dynasty of Agade.

Stone sculpture both in the round and in relief is amply
represented in the Early Dynastic period. Until recently the
examples were mostly confined to the last generations and to
works executed for the rulers of Lagash, who appeared as disproportionately in the field of art as they figured in a history
where they seemed not to deserve such prominence. The discoveries of deposits of small human statues, attaining sometimes
nearly half natural size, in the excavations at Eshnunna and the
place now called Khafājī have not only carried back the examples
into the second Early Dynastic period but have introduced a fresh
local school of sculpture[1] with a tradition and technique rather
different from those of Lagash. No more than the figures formerly known can these be said to attain a very impressive degree
of mastery; the heads and faces are coarse and unsightly by
reason of the staring inlaid eyes and the black hair and beards, the
bodies are clumsy, and the legs exaggerated in thickness by the
necessity of their supporting the full weight of the figure, for this
fraternity of sculptors did not use the convention of showing the
legs only in high relief against a solid back, which in other contemporary figures has the function of taking the weight. Sculpture
in relief has also been newly illustrated by examples from the
same site. These too belong partly to the middle period of the
Early Dynastic, so that it is the more surprising that they are
decidedly superior to most of the Lagashite works in design and
execution. They are thick, roughly square, stone plaques with a
raised edge to protect the sculpture and with a wide hole in the
middle, as if to accommodate a stout peg of wood or clay fixing the
object to a wall.[2] The surface is divided into three or four registers
of figures in low relief generally depicting a banquet scene in
which a male and female person sit opposite each other drinking

[1] §vi, 8 and 9; see below, pp. 254 f.   [2] A, 15.

and attended by servants and musicians; the lower registers are usually occupied by others bringing in the materials of the feast. A significant variation in the lowest row shows a two-wheeled chariot drawn by the usual ass-like beasts, the car itself being covered with a leopard-skin. There are three men in attendance, one the owner of the equipage but standing dismounted behind it, the other two servants, one at the head of the team, one behind the driver.[1] The style of these plaques cannot be called accomplished, and the human figures especially are of archaic crudeness, but less so than the long-known 'family-reliefs' of Ur-Nanshe, which nevertheless seem to be later and for that reason are more informative since they bear inscriptions. If the significance or even the exact placing of these plaques were better known they might help to explain certain ideas which the Sumerians seem to have held about the dead, and perhaps about the effect of ceremonies performed on special occasions of burial.

Most attractive, at least to modern eyes, of the art products of this people and time are their works in metal and inlay. The representative pieces, discovered especially at Ur and Mari, are now well known, having been often illustrated and described. They have a strange mixture of accomplishment, as in the attractive little donkey on the rein-ring, and of crudity, this being sporadically displayed both in the subjects and in the workmanship, occasionally both together, as in the copper-sheeted animal figures from Al-'Ubaid. Interesting beyond all are the scenes depicted by small figures in shell or limestone inlaid upon a darker background of plain bitumen or of costly lapis-lazuli. Their purport is usually clear enough in itself, but only a part of their significance is revealed, for very seldom is it known what was the setting or the intention of such representations—the leaping goats, the animal musicians, and above all the celebrated 'standard' of Ur, are notable examples of this deficiency of context. The gold cups and vessels owe perhaps most of their fame to their ever-prized material, for it can hardly be said that their designs are remarkable; the weak and un-matching wire suspenders of the golden bowls seem especially faulty, and the elliptical fluted long-spouted pourer, with its absurd little foot, cannot be called elegant, while the golden helm of Meskalamdug is surpassing rather in craftsmanship than in taste. Among the best metal products of these early Sumerians are the ordinary bronze weapons and tools (with de-luxe versions in gold), at once well-designed, practical, strong, and of pleasing effect.

[1] §vi, 8, 43 ff.; G, 4, vol. iv, 2016 ff. See Plate 30 (b).

VII. RELIGION AND CULT-PRACTICES

It has already been observed as peculiar to this period that it had evolved a form of human government which seemed to reproduce upon earth exactly the hierarchy of heaven, so that it was some-times hardly clear whether gods or men were the acting parties. In such a society the city-governors, as deputies, should have sole access to, and authority from, the city-god, but there is evidence that priests obtained an ever-growing power in the Sumerian cities. The earlier city-governors never give themselves the style of priests,[1] and seldom mention others of that calling; the most significant personality is one who seems to be a diviner in a very obscure inscription of Ur-Nanshe.[2] From the time of Entemena priests become prominent, and Dudu the priest of the city-god Ningirsu was so important a functionary that not only was an event dated by his accession to office, but he also dedicated monuments of his own, like a ruler. Enentarzi a later governor of the city rose to his place from the priesthood and the same succession was observed in the neighbouring city of Umma, where Il, already a member of the ruling family, was at first a priest in charge of one of the sanctuaries, and was promoted to the governorship by Entemena of Lagash after deposing his uncle Urlumma. From all this and from later analogy it may be inferred that originally the *ensi* himself was the priest and that, even when the functions began to be distinguished, perhaps through delega-tion of religious duties, the priest was still the relative and sometimes the destined successor of the *ensi*. This privilege of the ruler to a close intercourse with his god derives from the ancient tradition of an age when gods were not very remote from men, when Gilgamesh or Enmerkar took counsel of gods, and divine figures still walked the earth and conversed with its denizens.

Beyond doubt the most important evidence of religious observances among the early Sumerians consists in the sensa-tional discoveries of the 'Royal Tombs' at Ur, and some other more isolated finds which may be connected with them. The manifest fact is that upon certain occasions, and in attendance upon certain exalted persons, many followers of both sexes, as well as numerous animals, with all the equipment of their services, were buried in the same tombs as their masters, visibly

[1] That is *sanga*; for the priestly (as well as royal) title *en* see G, 12, 9.
[2] See *R.A.* 45, 108 f.; A, 38, 23 and fig. 10.

as companions whose destiny it was to continue their ministra-
tions in another life. These are matters of observation, but how
they should be interpreted has long been in dispute, and is still
unsettled.[1] Contemporary written evidence is very scanty and
bears only upon a single point, the identity of the personages
concerned. There is no reliable information, even in later texts,
concerning human sacrifice, only a possible allusion in one of the
Gilgamesh stories[2] to a hero being accompanied in death by some
of his retainers. As to the personages for whom the tombs were
made, the names of Meskalamdug and Akalamdug occur several
times, and the latter bears, upon a seal, the specific title 'king of
Ur'. There were also two or three ladies bearing the title of *nin*:
one of them was the most richly attended of all, while another was
the wife of Mesannipada, first king of the First Dynasty of Ur.[3]
Thus it is reasonably well established that the tombs have a good
right to the style of 'royal', although their named occupants are
mostly unknown to the king-list; and consequently the human
sacrifice may be regarded as another striking example of a well-
known primitive but long-enduring custom,[4] although nothing is
known of such a custom in the later history of Babylonia.

Of the reasons for this seemingly isolated rite in Sumer and the
ideas which underlay it there are but few and perhaps deceptive
hints. Among the rich and varied deposits in these tombs the
only object with any purport of telling a story is the so-called
'standard', which has some pronounced similarities to the relief
plaques in stone, with a hole in the middle, found principally at
Tell Asmar,[5] and exemplified also in the 'family reliefs' of Ur-
Nanshe and certain other similar sculptures at Lagash—a
revealing fragment[6] occurred in the Royal Tombs themselves.
On most of these is depicted a scene of feasting, and sometimes
appended in the lowest register is a quadrigal chariot with sumptuous furnishings and attended by servants, but without occupants. Chariots, fully manned, appear also upon the 'standard'
as the principal arm in a victorious battle, and a scene of feasting,
on the other side, is naturally viewed as a celebration of this. Yet
it is doubtful whether there is any real connexion between these
subjects on the plaques and on the 'standard', for the mere
appearance of a two-wheeled riding chariot in the former has no
necessary relation with the picture of charging four-wheeled

---

1 See §IV above, and discussions in §IV, 45 and 4; §IV, 61, 38 ff.; §VI, 8, 43 ff.;
§VII, 1, 12; G, 4, vol. IV, 1850; G, 19, 93 f.
2 G, 24, 50 f.; §IV, 15, 67 f. 3 G, 12, 30 ff.; §IV, 51, 71 f.
4 §II, 2. 5 §VI, 8, 43 ff. 6 §IV, 61, pl. 181; A, 15.

war-waggons in the latter; and the banqueting-scene is too much of a commonplace to bear a special interpretation here. Two of the plaques of Ur–Nanshe have a different motive[1]—the king bears on his head the first symbolic basket of earth, to inaugurate the building of a temple. Another bears the statement that it was dedicated as the support of a sacred mace.[2] Again, several of those found at Lagash have only religious emblems, and lack the drinking-scene. With all this, it is quite uncertain where the plaques were placed and what was their intention. As much doubt attaches to the 'standard'; it was found in one of the greatest tombs at Ur and it seems to have been carried by an attendant who wore a peculiar headdress of beads. If rightly restored in its present form it has no visible use, and if it really was carried before a king could be nothing more than a pictorial vaunt of the royal success and prosperity, yet for this purpose it seems altogether too diminutive. No deeper significance need attach to the stone plaques, which are mostly devoted to the conventional topics of royal piety and ostentation. It is disappointing that the religious and social conceptions, unique in Sumerian history, which the 'Royal Tombs' enshrine, should remain for the present uncomprehended.

VIII. SOCIETY AND SOCIAL PROBLEMS

Disposal of the dead served to mark, in the ancient Sumerian cities as it has so constantly in all later history, the distinction of class and wealth. In one line of a story about the fabulous Gilgamesh that hero is represented[3] as drawing the most mortifying conclusion to himself from looking over the wall of Uruk, which he had just built, and beholding corpses which floated upon the river; such may indeed have been the end of the poorest citizens. A better sort could claim entombment, with grave-goods of varying richness. Burial entailed charges for the funeral, and the gradual abuse of these by the clergy as a means of extortion has helped to disclose that by the end of the Early Dynastic period public opinion had developed to the point of demanding changes in political and social conditions. The unjust exactions of religious officiants were however only one of the evils which had become burdensome enough for a prince (seeking perhaps to buttress an usurped power) to denounce and remedy.

[1] For publication and references see G, 19, 90 ff. reliefs *a* and *d*.
[2] *Ibid*. 87 f.; A, 15.   [3] G, 24, 48, ll. 25–7.

The celebrated social reforms of Urukagina, and the recording of them in his inscriptions, are striking testimony to the advanced state of civilization and political development reached at this still very early stage of recorded history. That a ruler should abrogate customs which concerned his interest or even affronted his sense of justice might not be surprising in any moderately developed society; that he should draw up a 'manifesto' exposing the abuses and instituting a new régime proves that the early Sumerians had reached a political maturity which subsequent generations, even in a world far outside the bounds of ancient Babylonia, have outgrown but little.[1]

In his second year Urukagina assumed the title of *lugal* or king, apparently in disregard of some formal supremacy of Kish, and his reforms may have been prompted at least in part by the desire to strengthen his own position and secure the support of the most effective classes among his subjects, those liable to render military service. Like most changes of this kind and, as it were, setting the tone for many a later purge, these reforms were stated to be reversions to the 'good old ways' which the city-god Ningirsu had ordained in the beginning, although some of the practices condemned were themselves of long standing. When the changes were complete Urukagina felt able to say that he had justified himself in his situation as the god's agent. So literal were the ideas of this direct relation that the new-established king proclaims in a striking phrase that he 'joined this covenant with Ningirsu that he would not deliver up the weak and the widow to the powerful man'.[2] Characteristically, too, these unique documents of social history are embedded in building-inscriptions.

A deity who appears from the inscriptions of Urukagina to have stood high in his favour may now be regarded as prompting him to his new enactments. One of his public works was the clearing of a canal which led from Lagash to a place called Nina (now Zerghūl), where stood the temple of a goddess Nanshe, consulted as an oracle by the rulers who journeyed to her shrine in boats to seek enlightenment upon the will of the gods, as described by the later governor Gudea. A hymn to this goddess[3]

[1] The measures of Urukagina have been much discussed recently, in the light of a better understanding of the texts, and a heightened interest in social questions and theories of government; the best general summary is still that of G, 5, 75. A new translation is given by §VIII, 3 and by §VII, 3: the former has been criticized in §VIII, 1, see also §VI, 21 and G, 15, ch. VI. In all of these places some different views are taken of the reformer's motives, and references are supplied to other literature.

[2] §III, 6, 160 n. 4; §VIII, 3, 182.

[3] §VIII, 2, 12 nos. 20, 21; §III, 4, 83 n. 3.

which acclaims her choice of Gudea probably dates from his reign in its present form, but it names also the ancient Ur-Nanshe as having been similarly chosen, and his devotion is witnessed by his own name. Ur-Nanshe was, even if not by direct family descent, the first in a line of Lagashite kings which ended with Urukagina. The goddess was able to interpret for Gudea the desires of the city-god Ningirsu, and could have imparted to any ruler the reasons why she had chosen Ur-Nanshe. Those reasons were moral; Nanshe is praised in the hymn as the upholder of mercy, justice, and wisdom. She protects widows and orphans, punishes oppressors, judges malefactors, maintains correct measures, and takes a special care of the temple-revenues. Urukagina does not, in the texts now extant, invoke her authority, but he listened to her counsels, and it may be that the hymn which celebrates her benign qualities and alludes so plainly to the king's expressed purposes was first composed in his reign.

The changes introduced by Urukagina, those at least which are best comprehensible, seem a genuine attempt to lighten the burdens imposed upon the general population by governors and also by priests; the latter, however, were not to be alienated by the new arrangements for, if they were deprived of certain unjust perquisites, other due enjoyments were restored to them. The classes specifically mentioned as freed from burdens and vexatious controls were boatmen, fishers, farmers and herdsmen; they were relieved of supervision and of the requirement to pay their dues in silver. These classes, together with the priests and the general population, suffered from the interference and exaction of a swollen officialdom—'in the boundaries of the god Ningirsu, right down to the sea, there were inspectors'; these were totally abolished, as the king proclaims, no doubt with some of the usual exaggeration of statecraft. The priestly class was doubly affected by the new order; on the one hand they were forbidden to oppress the subjects by illegal invasions of property and appropriation of crops, and especially were limited to less than one half of the unconscionable fees which they had extorted at funerals; making no distinction, as it seems, between two kinds of burial, richer and poorer, which the custom of the time recognized. On the other hand the priests benefited not only by the suppression of fiscal inspectors but by a more positive restitution. For many years past the city-governor had been in the habit of appropriating the gods' oxen to plough his own kitchen-gardens, and so far had his usurpation reached that he and his family had taken outright possession of the houses belonging to the god and to the divine family. But now Urukagina 'in the house of the governor and the fields of the governor (re-)installed Ningirsu as their owner'. Likewise he brought back the goddess Baba into her house which had come to be called the 'house of the Woman', that is, of the governor's wife, and the divine son into the house called hitherto 'house of the Children'. By these measures the reformer, with whatever motive, showed himself unafraid to attack unjust gains, even when they were his own.

The ordinary population of the city was given real and positive relief by the directions of Urukagina. They too shared in the benefit of losing the interference and oppression of the excisemen, but had more than this to cheer them. Priests were not to invade their property, and they were also secured from oppression by the more influential classes, who had been guilty of forcing dis-advantageous sales upon their inferiors. In future it was decreed that if a great man desired to purchase the ass or the house of a humble neighbour, the latter could require him to pay a just price in sound money, nor must the rich man spite him for his refusal— the importance of this provision in estimating the extent of private property in Lagash during this period, which seems otherwise so engrossed with the temples, has been observed above. Other measures of public benefit were the suppression of crime, and certain remissions of fees formerly exacted on the occasion of divorces, thus curbing unlawful connexions of women, who in consequence of these fines became wives of another without ceasing to be married to the former husband. Some of these pro-visions were no doubt aimed at the abolition of mere abuses, and seem to have been inspired by a genuine interest in social justice, which does honour to this earliest of all reformers whose name history preserves. What may have been the underlying tendency of these changes has been variously judged[1] and cannot be said to emerge clearly. But at least the principal loser, under this 'self-denying ordinance', seems to have been the governor himself, who restored estates to the temples and remitted taxes to the people from his own and from the priests' revenues. The clerics, to-gether with the officials, did indeed suffer some curtailment of their illicit profits, but may nevertheless be considered the chief gainers, for the main trend of Urukagina's changes was clearly in the direction of reinstating the 'original' theocracy, which could be only to their advantage.

1 See most recently §VIII, 1, 12 f.; §VII, 3.

IX. THE TRANSITION TO EMPIRE

Urukagina reigned for only eight years; his accession was by violence, his fall was effected by outside attack. Lagash was suddenly overwhelmed by the onset of a more powerful or more fortunate adversary than any of the former bad neighbours who had ruled at Umma. This was Lugalzaggisi, who afterwards became king of Uruk and figures by himself as the 'third dynasty' of that city in virtue of his defeat, not of the unrecognized king of Lagash, but of the contemporary 'sovereign' of Kish. At the time of his victory over Lagash, which thus put an end to the long and bitter struggles of these two cities, Lugalzaggisi was still *ensi* of Umma. Of the preliminaries nothing is heard, and perhaps the attack was sudden, aided by internal feuds, which there is some reason to suspect in Lagash at this time. The assault was instantly successful, the town and temples of Lagash were invaded and laid waste, blood streamed in the sanctuaries, fire and plunder raged everywhere. Of all this we are informed by an indignant protest written upon a clay tablet,[1] found in the ruins thousands of years after the catastrophe. Rehearsing the shrines desecrated by the enemy, the slaughter, arson, and pillage, it ends with a defiant challenge to the conqueror: 'the men of Umma, after Lagash had been destroyed, committed sin against Ningirsu. The hand which was laid upon him he shall cut off. Offence there was none in Urukagina, king of Girsu, but as for Lugalzaggisi, governor of Umma, may his goddess Nisaba make him carry his sin upon his neck.' How came this bold denunciation to be written under the victor's sway? It has an almost prophetic ring, and was dramatically fulfilled.

Lugalzaggisi had other hours of triumph, and has left an inscription[2] which claims for him not only the traditional sovereignty over 'the land' (which the king-list allows), but a career of conquest or at least ascendancy abroad. When the god Enlil had made him lawful king over Sumer, he then 'from the Lower Sea (by) the Tigris and Euphrates unto the Upper Sea made straight its road, from the rising sun unto the setting he made him to have no opposer'. The inscription goes on to celebrate the peace and glory which he bestowed upon each and all of the ancient cities of Sumer, and ends with a prayer to Enlil for his own military power

---

[1] G, 28, 56 (*k*).

[2] G, 28, 152 ff.; §iv, 10, 132 f.; another translation in §iii, 7, 136. See also G, 10, 1 f.

and his realm's prosperity. The king-list credits him with a reign of twenty-five years, so he was able to enjoy for a space the confidence of heaven-decreed fortune. But the curse of his forgotten victim in that Lagash which he did not condescend to include in his tale of subjects overtook him at last. A new and portentous figure had arisen from a humble state of servitude under the king of Kish, and the great Sargon of Agade, passing rapidly from demands and hostile messages to the older king, launched an attack upon Uruk, defeated and captured Lugalzaggisi, and 'brought him in a yoke to the gate of Enlil' at Nippur.

The fall of Lugalzaggisi and of his Third Dynasty of Uruk makes no more than one ordinary transition in the king-list, but the break was wider and far more significant than before. It marks a complete change of interest, and with the utmost distinctness it ends an age. The Early Dynastic period is over, and after it the face of Babylonian history changes. The cleavage is apparent in almost every aspect of civilization. For the first time another element assumed the power and imposed its language upon the official and private records. An epoch of small local states was succeeded by the creation of a wide dominion, henceforth to remain, with intermittent lapses, the pattern of political history in Western Asia until the end of the Persian empire. The style of art and even of writing underwent a marked transformation. All of this may be more obvious to us, with our heightened historical consciousness and better perspective, than it could be to any later age of native tradition, even with fuller documentation than ours. Nevertheless that tradition was in no doubt about the significance of the new kings who were to rule from the new city of Agade. If Gilgamesh was, in a sense, the typical figure of one age, Sargon and Naram-Sin were to stand for the next, and though the elder hero had retired farther into the mist of legend, his later compeers also dwelt under its shadow. To follow them in their real career and to pass with their magnified shapes into the dimmer world of national recollection will be the task of chapter xix.

CHAPTER XIV

THE OLD KINGDOM IN EGYPT AND THE BEGINNING OF THE FIRST INTERMEDIATE PERIOD

I. THE THIRD DYNASTY

EARLY in the Third Dynasty, King Djoser employed the genius of his architect Imhotep to erect the first great building of stone, the Step Pyramid at Saqqara. The name Djoser, written in a cartouche, has not been found in an inscription of the Old Kingdom. On his own monuments the king writes his Horus-name, Netjerykhet. There is no doubt that these two names refer to the same man. The wall scribblings of the Eighteenth Dynasty visitors to the Step Pyramid refer to the temple of Djoser and both names occur, together with the name of Imhotep, in the Ptolemaic inscription, on the Island of Siheil near the First Cataract.[1] The legendary character of Imhotep, who was revered centuries after his death as a demi-god, the builder of the temple of Edfu, the wise chancellor, architect and physician of Djoser,[2] has now acquired reality through the discovery of his name on a statue-base of Netjerykhet in the excavations of the Step Pyramid.[3] It is curious that modern research should, within a short space of time, have established the identity of both the wise men of whom centuries later the harper of King Inyotef sings: 'I have heard the sayings of Imhotep and Hordedef with whose words men speak so often. What are their habitations now? Their walls are destroyed, their habitations are no more, as if they had never been.'[4] The tomb of Hordedef, with the inscriptions in its chapel maliciously erased but still partly readable was found at Giza, east of the pyramid of his father Cheops, at a time when the excavation of the elaborate series of structures erected at Saqqara by Imhotep was still in progress.[5]

Netjerykhet Djoser remains the dominant figure in this period, but it can no longer be maintained confidently that he was the

---

[1] §VI, 18, 31; §I, 2, *passim*; 30, 19; 31, 11.　　　　[2] §I, 31, *passim*.
[3] §I, 8, pl. 58.　　　　[4] §VI, 6, 132; 18, 467; §I, 20, 192.
[5] G, 36, vol. III, 49.

founder of the dynasty. He is connected with Khasekhemwy, the last king of the Second Dynasty, through Queen Nymaathap who has generally been accepted as the wife of Khasekhemwy and the mother of Djoser. It must be admitted that here and in other cases later in the Old Kingdom we do not understand clearly the factors governing a change of dynasty, although we follow the division into groups of kings which is indicated in the dynastic lists of the Ptolemaic writer Manetho. It now seems likely that Netjerykhet Djoser was preceded by Sanakhte as the first king of the Third Dynasty. It has been suggested[1] that Sanakhte may have been an elder brother of Netjerykhet and that he began the flat-topped structure which was later developed into the Step Pyramid. It is also thought that Djoser may have buried Sanakhte in the most important of the galleries entered by eleven shafts which were cut in the rock on the east side of that building during an early stage of its construction. Six of these galleries were intended for the storage of equipment and two of them were completely filled with stone vessels, many of which bore inscriptions of kings of the First and Second Dynasties. None of these vessels, nor any of the stone vessel-fragments from the main part of the pyramid substructure, bore the names of Netjerykhet or Sanakhte. A mud sealing of Netjerykhet and one of Khasekhemwy were found in one of the eastern galleries, and a stone bowl with the name of Khasekhemwy came from the apartments under the southern enclosure wall. A handsome porphyry jar bore an inscription of the latter's predecessor, Khasekhem, which resembled the inscription on one of the jars which he had dedicated in the temple at Hierakonpolis.[2]

The impression of a seal of an official of Netjerykhet, possibly Imhotep, was rolled out along the plaster between the blocks of masonry lining gallery III, the proposed burial-place of Sanakhte. This evidence establishes that work was executed in these galleries by Djoser. Later tunnelling by thieves makes it impossible to be certain, however, whether gallery III could have been reached from gallery I which was the only one accessible by a supplementary sloping tunnel from outside the completed structure. All eleven shafts were blocked by the later stages of work on the pyramid. It should be remembered, also, that the only burial which has survived in the tombs I to V was that of a young boy and that the two well-preserved stone coffins and fragments of others from these galleries seem to have been intended for small

[1] §1, 18, 376; 19, 17.
[2] §1, 8, pls. 88–9; 17, vol. iii, 6, 15, 20–2, 74, pl. xix, vol. iv, pl. 3, 19.

persons, either women or children.[1] It is therefore questionable whether Sanakhte was buried here.

Sanakhte has been equated with Nebka whose name precedes that of Djoser in two of the three lists of kings (the Turin Canon and the list in the Abydos Temple of Sethos I) compiled in the Nineteenth Dynasty. The third list, inscribed on the wall of a tomb at Saqqara and now in the Cairo Museum, omits the name. Unhappily little is preserved of the Third Dynasty section of royal annals inscribed on the Palermo Stone and its related fragments. Since this list was prepared in the Fifth Dynasty, it might have provided valuable evidence from records set down at a time nearer to the period in question.[2] A recent reconstruction of the Annals attributes to Nebka the partly preserved portion of a reign in Register 5, hitherto assumed to be that of Khasekhemwy because of the mention of a copper statue of that king.[3] However, the year after the eighth biennial count, which was the last complete year of the reign, is not easy to adjust to the nineteen years[4] given to Nebka in the Turin Canon. One hesitates to accept without doubt such a long lapse of time between the death of Khasekhemwy and the accession of Djoser in view of the apparently close association between these two kings. Certainly the Turin Canon figure of twenty-seven years for Khasekhemwy cannot be made to agree with this portion of the Annals. It seems wiser in these circumstances to question this figure, as well as the nineteen years given to Nebka, and to accept the earlier theory that the Palermo Stone contains a record of the last years of Khasekhemwy and five years of a following reign which should be that of Nebka. The Cairo Stone no. 1 of the Annals, which continues (after a break) the records of the Palermo Stone, is almost entirely effaced in Register 5. No indication remains of the names of the kings or the lengths of their reigns. It is also far from certain that the reign of Sneferu occupied the whole of Register 6; nor does much survive of the records of Cheops and Redjedef which appear below this register on Cairo Stones nos. 1 and 3. The important fragments, Cairo nos. 2 and 4, deal also

---

[1] §1, 17, vol. 1, 46 ff.   [2] G, 3; 5; 9; 15; 39, passim.
[3] G, 17, 80. See Plate 25.
[4] On a fragment assigned to this reign at University College, London, the first and second count are recorded in successive years. This would appear to make the year after the eighth count fifteen but the final incomplete year must be added and allowance made for the fact that under Djer and Semerkhet no census was taken in the accession year. Thus the reign may have lasted seventeen years or even eighteen if, as in the reign which follows in Register 5, no count was made until the third regnal year. It is clear that much uncertainty is involved in making such restorations.

with the reigns of Sneferu and Cheops but they come from a slightly different version of the Annals inscribed on a thicker slab of stone. Some measure of the difficulties involved in attempting to evaluate this tantalizing evidence can be understood if it is realized that a former reconstruction[1] gave 544 years for the First and Second Dynasties, assigning the whole of Register 5 to the Second Dynasty, while the most recent study of the Annals suggests a length of only 369 years for the first three dynasties, including 295 years[2] for the First and Second Dynasties and 74 years for the Third Dynasty. The last figure, however, is derived from the Turin Canon with little substantiation from the Annals. As stated above, the part of Register 5 generally attributed to the last king of the Second Dynasty is in this case assigned to the Third Dynasty.[3]

As will be shown later, Nebka is mentioned in the second half of the Third Dynasty in the chapel of Akhetaa. An estate is named after him in the Fifth Dynasty funerary temple of King Nyuserre. However, his most important appearance is in the Westcar Papyrus where he follows Djoser. In view of various disagreements between the later King Lists it is tempting to accept the evidence of this papyrus and to place Nebka between Djoser and Sneferu.[4] Written in the form of a popular tale which dates from the Hyksos Period, this entertaining series of anecdotes is peopled with characters who are known to have lived in the Old Kingdom. It contains much which can be accepted as historical fact and it will be necessary to draw upon it repeatedly in dealing with the otherwise scantily known events of the Fourth Dynasty. Nevertheless, the recent discovery at Saqqara of a new Step Pyramid belonging to an unsuspected successor of Djoser named Sekhemkhet makes it imperative to consider again the whole problem of the succession of the kings of the Third Dynasty.

It cannot be too strongly emphasized that the Egyptians of the Old Kingdom were extremely laconic in recording historical events in their monumental inscriptions. The disappearance of the greater part of the daily records and correspondence written on papyrus leaves us largely dependent upon statements of family

---

[1] G, 3, pls. I–III.   [2] G, 17, 78–83.

[3] *C.A.H.* I[3], ch. VI, sect. I, gives 415 years for the first two dynasties and again makes the length of the Third Dynasty seventy-four years, this being the total length of the five individual reigns in the Turin Canon. The question arises whether this estimate allows a sufficient span of time for such an important formative period in Egyptian history. At least one Third Dynasty king, Nebkare, is omitted from this list.

[4] §I, 32, 518; §VI, 24, 31, note 3; §VI, 5, *passim*; 6, 36; §III, 6, 79.

relationships and the names and titles of officials and members of
the royal household. Biographical material and royal inscriptions
became more frequent as the Old Kingdom advanced. In the
Fourth Dynasty the evidence available allows of little more than
the possibility of reconstructing the intricate framework of relationships between the descendants of Sneferu. At a later stage in
the present account it will be necessary to attempt this reconstruction, as briefly as possible, in order to lend some further semblance
of life to the people whose buildings and extraordinary portraits
have survived so miraculously. Something of their daily life can
be understood from their personal belongings and from the
pictures on the walls of their tomb-chapels. In very few cases,
however, is any information given about the political events of the
time.

In the Third Dynasty there is an even greater paucity of inscriptional material. Most of the names of members of the court
are lacking; some uncertainty remains whether all the names of the
kings have been recovered and whether those known have been
correctly attached to their monuments. There is far from complete
agreement concerning the length of the dynasty. In spite of the
fact already mentioned that the lengths of the reigns preserved for
the five kings listed in the Turin Canon add up to seventy-four
years,[1] it is difficult not to believe that at least a hundred years
should be allowed for a period so important for the political and
cultural experimentation which reached its culmination in the
Fourth Dynasty. Moreover, it would seem likely that one king at
least should be added to account for the Nebkare whose name
appears, with another less easy to decipher, on the quarry-marks
in the great rock cutting for the unfinished pyramid of Zāwiyet
el-Aryān.[2] A fact which must also be borne in mind is that the
outlines of two large enclosures, which may have belonged to
kings of the Third Dynasty, can be seen under the sand and
debris to the west of Djoser's Step Pyramid at Saqqara.[3] At the
point where Nebkare's name would be expected to occur in the
Turin Canon (and where it does appear before the last king of the
Dynasty, Huni, in the Saqqara List) is a 'name' Hudjefa. It has
been argued that this 'name' and another, Sedjes, in the Abydos
list were derived from a word for 'lacuna' in an old papyrus which
was misunderstood by the compiler of the Turin Canon.[4] One
might well wonder whether a break in an early record might not
have included the name of more than one king.

[1] G, 9, 23–5. [2] §I, 3 (1912), 61, 62; cf. also 3 (1906), 266–80.
[3] §I, 13, pls. I, II; §VI, 24, 32, note 5. [4] G, 17, 14; §I, 12, 50.

If Sanakhte is really the Horus-name of Nebka, and if he was also the king who began the construction of the building later incorporated into the Step Pyramid of his younger brother Djoser, it is difficult not to doubt the figure of nineteen years given to each in the Turin Canon. The remarkable architectural achievement of Djoser and Imhotep, as well as the lasting memory which they left in the minds of later Egyptians, would seem to imply a longer reign for Djoser than for Sanakhte, at least in the present state of our knowledge of the latter's monuments which seem very scanty. Similarly, the impression is gained that Djoser's successors were not able to carry to completion the great building schemes which they began in imitation of his imposing tomb. The last king, Huni, as we shall see, is a shadowy figure, even the reading of whose name is disputed.[1] The investigation of the monuments of the other kings has either been left incomplete or else not carried out under ideal conditions. Nevertheless, until further excavation can be done, we might perhaps accept as a working hypothesis the succession of kings: Sanakhte (Nebka), Netjerykhet (Djoser), Sekhemkhet, Khaba (Layer Pyramid at Zāwiyet el-Aryān), Nebkare[2] (Unfinished Pyramid at Zāwiyet el-Aryān) and Huni.

One of these kings, or another with a Horus-name still unknown, must have had the personal name Teti. He is named after Bedjau (the first king of the Second Dynasty in the Abydos List)[3] in a list of kings which continues with Redjedef, Chephren, Sahure and Neferirkare on a writing board found in the burial chamber of a Fifth Dynasty tomb at Giza.[4] A relief from a Rames-side chapel at Saqqara shows seated figures of three kings: Djosernub, Teti and Userkaf,[5] whereas a statue of the Persian Period[6] belonged to a man who held priesthoods of the kings Netjerykhet Djoser, Djoser Teti and Teti, as well as Imhotep. The implication is that Teti should be the king following Sekhemkhet but this is far from certain.

The inscriptions on jar-sealings of the kings who bore the Horus-names Sanakhte, Netjerykhet, Sekhemkhet and Khaba resemble each other in style. Those of Sanakhte and Netjerykhet Djoser were found in Upper Egypt at Beit Khallāf, a short distance north of Abydos, in neighbouring tombs (K 1, K 2) which must belong closely together in time. Sealings of Sanakhte were

---

[1] §I, II, 18.   [2] See above, p. 148, n. 3 (Ed.).
[3] See Plate 26. Helck questioned the existence of this king, arguing that his name was derived from a scribal error. G, 17, 12.
[4] See Plate 31 (a). G, 38, 113; §VI, 23, 358.
[5] §I, 10, 41.   [6] §I, 7, 114.

also found in a pottery deposit north of the funerary temple of Djoser at the Step Pyramid.[1] The three kings Sanakhte, Netjerykhet, and Sekhemkhet carved similar monuments on the face of the rocks at the Wādi Maghāra in the Sinai Peninsula.[2] Each king is shown raising his mace above a prostrate bedawin chieftain. The cutting is rather roughly done, as in all these rock carvings, but in the case of a second figure of Sanakhte standing before a shrine (which has been removed to the Cairo Museum) better workmanship is displayed. The face presents a strong family likeness to the heads of Djoser on the carved panels of the blue-tiled galleries in the Step Pyramid complex.[3]

The relief of Sekhemkhet was until a few years ago thought to be the work of the First Dynasty king Semerkhet, due to a similarity between the hieroglyphic signs in their names. It was only with the discovery of the name on jar-sealings in his tomb at Saqqara that the work of the hitherto unrecognized Sekhemkhet could be dated correctly. The elimination of Semerkhet's name in Sinai leaves no evidence for the working of the turquoise mines in the First Dynasty. The copper which would seem more important to us today was apparently not obtained from this particular region, nor in the neighbourhood of the nearby temple-site of Serābīt el-Khādim. Ancient copper workings are known in the Sinai Peninsula but it is not certain at what date this mining was initiated, nor whether it was undertaken under Egyptian supervision.[4] However, it would now appear that Egypt began to be particularly interested in this area at the beginning of the Third Dynasty.

As we have seen, the association of the names of Netjerykhet and Khasekhemwy with that of Queen Nymaathap suggests that this queen was the mother of the first king and the wife of the second. If Sanakhte was also a son of Nymaathap we can understand that his younger brother might appear to follow closely after Khasekhemwy, although this theory hardly helps to clarify the reason for a change of dynasty. Nymaathap is called 'Mother of the King of Upper and Lower Egypt' on a mud jar-sealing found with others bearing the name of Netjerykhet in the large brick tomb of an official of this reign at Beit Khallāf (K 1). This tomb and its neighbour (K 2) which contained sealings

---

[1] For these Third Dynasty sealings, including those of Queen Nymaathap, see §1, 13, 14; 33, 73–92, 140; 9, 11, pls. IX, X, XIX; 8, 141; 17, vol. I, 5; 24, pl. 24; 27, vol. II, pl. LXX.

[2] G, 12, vol. I, pls. I, IV; 35, pls. 45–9.

[3] §VI, 23, 132.   [4] G, 12, vol. II, 5–7.

of Sanakhte were once mistakenly thought to have been built for these kings. Two smaller tombs (K 3, K 4), subsidiaries to the mastaba K 1, also had jar-sealings of Netjerykhet, as did another tomb (K 5) some distance away. In K 5 there was also a jar-sealing of a man named Nedjemankh who was probably its owner as well as being represented by two fine seated statues of hard stone in Paris and Leiden.[1] The jar-sealing of Queen Nymaathap which was found in the burial apartment of King Khasekhemwy at Abydos names her as 'Mother of the king's children'. Some generations later at Saqqara, in the reign of Sneferu, it is stipulated in the chapel of Metjen that he is to receive 100 loaves daily from the Ka-house of the 'Mother of the king's children' Queen Nymaathap.[2] The food would presumably have been transferred to Metjen's tomb after it had served its purpose in the queen's offering rites. This explanation implies that the chapel of Nymaathap was nearby and that she had been buried at Saqqara. If so, her burial near Djoser would strengthen the impression that she was his mother and possibly the mother of Sanakhte.

Queen Nymaathap may have been one of the three ladies of Djoser's family who appear on one of the precious fragments of relief from a small shrine at Heliopolis which are now preserved in the Turin Museum.[3] Her name is lost, but she appears to be called wrt ḥts, a title held only by very great ladies of the Old Kingdom. On another fragment this title is given to Hetephernebty.[4] It is not clear if the object above the hieroglyphs of the title is the bulbous end of a wand carried by the king who probably stood in front of a smaller figure of the lady. It is certainly not the piece of meat shown on an earlier copy which omitted part of the title below and led to an interpretation of the whole as 'Great Heiress'.[5] On the little relief with the three ladies, Hetephernebty sits with the Princess Intkaes beside Djoser's feet and the nameless woman clasps his ankle from her position behind it. Hetephernebty is here called 'Beholder of Horus', a title evidently related to the more familiar one 'Beholder of Horus and Seth' which was known already in the First Dynasty in the reign of Djer and Den[6] and was later given to queens in the Fourth Dynasty. Intkaes and Hetephernebty are named again on some forty conical stones shaped like offering stands, the pieces of which were re-used in the walls around the

[1] §I, 33, 180; §VI, 23, 16; 24, 37.   [2] G, 41, 4 (line 9); 3, 77.

[3] §VI, 23, 132 ff., fig. 48; cf. also §VI, 24, 35; §I, 34, 9–26.

[4] §VI, 23, 136, fig. 52.

[5] §I, 34, 11 (fragment 11); 17, vol. II, 188.   [6] §I, 24, pl. XXVII.

great court of the Djoser pyramid, as well as on about sixty fragments of round-topped stelae which were found in the court of Djoser's serdab.[1] They are thought to have been used originally as markers to delimit the area of the temple when it was being planned and would indicate that these two ladies were particularly important at the beginning of the reign. The Heliopolis shrine should also, then, have been built shortly after Djoser's accession to the throne. It has been suggested[2] that the two ladies were either daughters of Khasekhemwy or of Djoser's predecessor Sanakhte. One might speculate that the chief queen of Khasekhemwy had borne only daughters and the sons of a secondary queen Nymaathap consequently came to the throne. This might explain the kind of dynastic change which seems to occur at the end of the Third Dynasty. It would account for the titles of Nymaathap, as well as the importance of Intkaes and Hetephernebty. The latter would appear to be a queen, probably of Djoser, while the third nameless lady on the Heliopolis shrine might be either Nymaathap or the widow of Sanakhte.

The monuments of the reign of Djoser present an extraordinarily clear picture of a civilization approaching maturity which displays a freshness and vigour that is still slightly barbaric. The Step Pyramid complex, the contemporaneous tomb of Hesyre and the rare statues and reliefs which can be assigned to the period or a little later, all show boldness of conception accompanied by experimentation with materials. The contemporary visitor must have been pleasantly awe-struck by the shining white-cased surfaces of the Step Pyramid towering above the panelled limestone enclosure wall with its great dummy gates. Entering through the tall, narrow colonnade, he must have marvelled at the clever imitation in stone of structures which had hitherto been familiar to him built of wood and light materials. All the details were here even to the fences, the log roofs, the light fluted columns, the simulation of papyrus, reed and other plant forms, and wooden doors carved as though swung open on their sockets. Had he been able to penetrate into the underground galleries he would have found wall-surfaces covered with blue-green faience tiles to imitate mat-hangings or screens which framed panels of fine, low-relief carving.

The funerary priest entering the chapel of Hesyre's[3] tomb met a blaze of colour where variegated mat patterns painted on the panelled mud-brick wall replaced the blue tiles of the king's tomb but similarly framed the low carving of the wooden panels

[1] §1, 17, vol. II, 187.   [2] §1, 18, 376; 19, 17.   [3] §1, 25, *passim*.

that stood in the back of each offering niche. On the opposite wall of the long corridor, Hesyre's funerary furniture was depicted in painting with the same realistic intention which is reflected in the stone imitation of architectural details at the Step Pyramid. Weathering of the outer corridor had left only the carefully painted legs of men and cattle, with a crocodile waiting at a ford, to show that here was also one of the earliest scenes from life, such as are found again at the beginning of the Fourth Dynasty in the Maidūm chapels. It might be well to remember in looking at the wooden panels of Hesyre, as they now stand in the Cairo Museum, that their delicate low reliefs must have been somewhat obscured by the gay but garish setting in which they originally stood. In the work of the Third Dynasty one senses that the consciousness of his new-found technical facility spurred the craftsman toward attempting things which would have been more soberly discarded at a later time. One is reminded of the exuberance with which the early dynastic vase-maker played with his material as though it were clay and not stone.

The fact that the stone funerary architecture of the Fourth Dynasty did not imitate construction which had been developed in lighter materials need not mean that domestic and public buildings did not continue to employ the style of building common in the Third Dynasty and which is reflected in the Step Pyramid complex. The contrast which is usually drawn between the Chephren temple beside the Sphinx at Giza and the Djoser temple suggests a prevailing heavy monumentality in the Fourth Dynasty and stresses a lightness of spirit in the Third Dynasty. While this evaluation is generally true such a comparison exaggerates the impression that the Fourth Dynasty building presented only simple granite forms with unrelieved surfaces. It also neglects the fact that the forms of the Djoser temple are not a new development in themselves but a facsimile in stone, so to speak, of an existing architecture. It should be remembered that, with the exception of the small and perhaps incomplete temple at Maidūm and the temples of the Bent Pyramid at Dahshūr, evidence is still lacking as to the character of other buildings of the Third Dynasty and the early Fourth Dynasty. There are certain indications that the material was richer and more varied than is generally admitted. At the end of the Second Dynasty, we know that Khasekhemwy[1] had employed a large granite door-jamb sculptured with reliefs in the temple at Hierakonpolis. In the Pyramid-Temple of Cheops, at least the

[1] §vi, 23, 131.

walls of the colonnade around the court were decorated with limestone reliefs and such reliefs were probably also used in the temple of Chephren.[1] We know now, moreover, that such decoration had appeared earlier in the Valley Temple of the Bent Pyramid of Sneferu at Dahshūr.[2] Polygonal columns did not disappear with the reign of Djoser but were found in at least one Fourth Dynasty prince's chapel at Giza.[3] Unfortunately we do not know whether any of the buildings had been completed inside the large area of the enclosing wall around the newly discovered pyramid of Sekhemkhet at Saqqara. The pyramid had certainly not been finished but the excavations had to be discontinued when only a small part of the site had been explored.[4] It is not clear what state of construction had been reached in building a temple at the Layer Pyramid of Zāwiyet el-Aryān; nor was any clearance made at what appeared to be the site of its valley temple.[5] Further investigation in the area of the unfinished pyramid some distance away at this same site, as well as the exploration of the enclosures out to the west of the pyramids of Djoser and Sekhemkhet at Saqqara, may yet give us further information about the architecture of the Third Dynasty.

In the Fourth Dynasty we find a facility in the handling of stone masonry which is based on the experience gained in the preceding period. Imhotep's achievement lay both in evolving a new architectural form in the Step Pyramid and in the development of the technique of building in stone. He did not invent stone architecture which we now know had advanced considerably even in the First Dynasty. The decision to build a high structure around the original flat-topped mastaba (an Arabic term applied to tombs which resemble a mud-brick bench) inspired new methods of construction. Instead of the horizontal courses in the first building, the layers of masonry added to form the successive steps were laid in leaning courses so that the pressure was exerted inwards. Evidently this was intended to ensure stability in a structure that was rising to a height hitherto unknown and which must have seemed a daring attempt to reach up into the sky. Towards the end of the project there was a tendency to replace the small blocks with rather larger ones. Sekhemkhet clearly employed larger masonry construction in the fine stretch of panelled wall which so much resembles that of Djoser's enclosure.[6] This masonry and the fact that Sekhemkhet had to be content with a less advantageous site for his unfinished step pyramid are two

[1] §VI, 24, 54–6. [2] §II, 11, *passim*. [3] §VI, 24, 53.
[4] §I, 13, *passim*. [5] §I, 28, 56. [6] §I, 13.

of the reasons for believing that it was built after Djoser's monument. The underground galleries of Sekhemkhet resemble in
plan those of the Layer Pyramid assigned to Khaba at Zāwiyet el-
Aryān. The superstructure of the latter, like the work which had
been completed above ground for Sekhemkhet, follows the
method of construction used in Djoser's Step Pyramid.[1] The
same system of layers of tilted courses of masonry is found again
in the Maidūm Pyramid which was probably built by Huni, the
last king of the Dynasty, and in the Bent Pyramid at Dahshūr.

The name of Khaba was found on eight stone bowls in a Third
Dynasty tomb beside the Layer Pyramid at Zāwiyet el-Aryān.
The name occurs also on a seal impression from Hierakonpolis
and upon two stone bowls, one found in the provincial cemetery
of Naga ed-Deir and the other in the excavation of the Fifth
Dynasty pyramid of King Sahure.[2] Khaba is otherwise unknown,
unless he is the Teti of the Royal Lists and the Giza writing
board. His inscriptions appear to be the only royal examples of
the Third Dynasty which have survived on stone vessels. A few
with the name of Sneferu are known but inscribed stone vessels
are rare in the Old Kingdom. They increase in frequency with the
reign of Unas and in the Sixth Dynasty. We shall see that a
considerable proportion of these vessels were found abroad at
Byblos on the Syrian coast and in the Sudan at Kerma. With the
invention of the potter's wheel, the production of fine pottery
from the Second Dynasty onwards reduced the output of the
makers of stone vessels. This development is clearly to be seen in
the rougher workmanship of the examples from the magazines
of the temple of Mycerinus towards the end of the Fourth Dynasty,
and the small number of pieces found in the private tombs at
Giza.[3] The handsome vessels of the first two dynasties had
evidently been stored as part of the royal treasure and were drawn
upon by Djoser for his funerary equipment. These heirlooms
continued to be prized in the later Old Kingdom. It seems
curious, however, that no stone vessels from a Third or Fourth
Dynasty pyramid have been found inscribed with the name of
the royal owner of the tomb.

The huge limestone and granite blocks at the bottom of the
rock-cut pit of the second, unfinished pyramid at Zāwiyet el-
Aryān bore a number of rough, semi-cursive inscriptions. One
of these reads 'Lord of the Two Lands, Nebkare'.[4] Some of the

[1] §vi, 24, 31, pl. 21 (A).
[2] §i, 1, 116; 28, 54; 33, 92; §iii, 8, vol. i, 114.   [3] §ii, 39, 90 ff.
[4] §i, 3 (1912), 61, 62.

limestone blocks from the filling of the pit were also marked with a royal name in a cartouche which ends in *ka* but begins with a sign which has proved difficult to decipher. Neither Neferka nor Nebka is entirely convincing for the reading of the name in this cartouche.[1] The owner, nevertheless, would seem to be the Nebkare who precedes Huni in the Saqqara List. We can hardly accept the reading of the name as Nebka if we follow present opinion, which identifies this king with Sanakhte, the first king of the Third Dynasty. If however the name on the blocks is to be read Neferka it might possibly suggest that Neferkare replaced Nebkare in the Abydos List through some confusion in the mind of the scribe. It should be noted that King Nebkare is omitted in the Turin Canon.[2]

In our previous discussion of Sanakhte it was not mentioned that Sethe had recognized the name Nebka in a cartouche combined with the Horus-name Sanakhte on a mud jar-sealing from Beit Khallāf.[3] This identification has been questioned in recent years, largely because of doubt whether the cartouche was in use before the Fourth Dynasty. Huni, however, employed the cartouche at the end of the Third Dynasty, and on the blocks at Zāwiyet el-Aryān the name which it surrounds is unlike that known for any king who followed Sneferu. On this ground, at least, the possibility should not be dismissed that the Beit Khallāf sealing supports the suggestion that Nebka is to be identified with Sanakhte and is unrelated to Nebkare. It certainly seems unsafe to assume that the occurrence of the cartouche at Zāwiyet el-Aryān provides evidence for a later dating of the unfinished pyramid of Nebkare. The fact that Nebkare employed very large stone blocks and that the plan of his great excavation with its open sloping passage from the north resembles the cutting for the substructure on Redjedef's pyramid at Abu Rawāsh, has been taken to mean that the work at Zāwiyet el-Aryān was executed in the Fourth Dynasty.[4] On the other hand the oval coffin pit sunk in the granite floor, with a heavy lid of the same shape, is of a type otherwise unknown and suggests a transitional form that might occur towards the end of the Third Dynasty before the rectangular, monolithic hard stone coffin had been adopted for kings.

We have seen that the tendency of the time was towards the

[1] §1, 3 (1906), 257 ff.; see however, Černý, *Mitt. deutsch. Inst. Kairo*, 16 (1958), 25.
[2] The name is also omitted from the list of kings in this book (Ed.).
[3] §1, 9, 25, pl. xix.　　　　　[4] §1, 18, 368, 378.

use of larger stones. There is nothing to indicate the kind of masonry or the type of construction that was planned for the superstructure of the Zāwiyet el-Aryān tomb. Large blocks of granite had already been used for Djoser's burial chamber, which was also of an unusual type, like a sarcophagus constructed from many pieces of stone. The similar chamber under the south-ern enclosure wall seems to have been intended for the vital organs which were removed from the body and buried separately. Later in the Old Kingdom these organs were wrapped in packages and stored in the four compartments of a canopic chest which was placed in the same chamber with the coffin. The alabaster chest of Queen Hetepheres, the mother of Cheops, contained such packages. They were much shrivelled, but still lay in a small quantity of the preservative liquid which had suprisingly survived, no doubt owing to the exclusion of air from the sealed rock niche of a chamber a hundred feet below the surface of the Giza plateau.[1]

The great open excavation at Zāwiyet el-Aryān is extra-ordinarily impressive but baffling, like the chamber of Sekhem-khet with its empty alabaster coffin, the apparently unused galleries of Khaba, or the complex interior of the Bent Pyramid at Dahshūr. Nebkare's pit had been partially filled with lime-stone blocks thrown in haphazardly above the granite pavement. This fact seems to indicate that a burial had been made and measures taken to protect it, but the oval sarcophagus, even though its lid was still in place, proved to be empty. If the site was visited later in connexion with the funerary cult it might possibly account for a schist plaque with the cartouche of the Fourth Dynasty king Redjedef which was found in what were taken to be workmen's huts nearby.[2]

If we dissociate Nebka from the unfinished pyramid at Zāwiyet el-Aryān, which in the past has been attributed to him, and accept him as the first king of the Third Dynasty with the Horus-name Sanakhte, then the temple bearing his name which was served by his priest Akhetaa in the second half of the Dynasty must have been founded some fifty years earlier than the pyramid. Akhetaa built a tomb in the northern cemetery at Saqqara, the site of which has never been identified. The chapel was at least partially lined with stone. The door jambs and part of the offering niche have survived, as well as a seated statue of the owner.[3] Like the chapels in the brick mastaba of Khabausokar and his wife Hathor-neferhetepes, it seems to form a transitional step between the painted brick corridor of Djoser's official Hesyre and the stone-

[1] §II, 39, 21, pl. 44.   [2] §I, 3 (1906), 259, 261.   [3] §I, 32, 518.

lined cruciform chapels of the end of the reign of Huni and the time of Sneferu.[1]

One monument contemporaneous with King Huni has survived. This is a peculiarly shaped conical piece of red granite with an inscription on the rectangular end.[2] It was found at Elephantine and thought by Borchardt to have formed part of the early fortification of that island on the old border between Egypt and Nubia.[3] The inscription records the founding of a building, possibly this fortress, and twice gives a cartouche with the king's name, the reading of which has been much discussed.[4] The same writing of the name appears again in the designation of a piece of property in the chapel which Metjen built at Saqqara early in the Fourth Dynasty, as well as on the Palermo Stone in an endowment established for Huni by Neferirkare in the Fifth Dynasty.[5] Metjen's administration of a property of King Huni finds a parallel in his contemporary, Pehernefer, who was in charge of an estate of Queen Meresankh. This lady must be the queen whose name has been read by Černý on the Cairo Fragment no. 1 of the Palermo Stone Annals.[6] She appears there as the mother of Sneferu and therefore probably the wife of Huni, the last king of the Third Dynasty named in the Turin Canon and the Saqqara List. The Middle Kingdom Papyrus Prisse in the admonitions to an unknown vizier, Kagemni, ends with the statement that Huni died and was succeeded by Sneferu.[7] Now that it is known that the South Stone (Bent) Pyramid at Dahshūr was built by Sneferu, it seems likely that the Maidūm Pyramid was largely the work of his predecessor. We shall have to consider this question further in connexion with the problem of Sneferu's two pyramids at Dahshūr.

Chances of preservation have deprived us of the names of the princes of the Third Dynasty. Nevertheless there are certain indications that the process of centralization which resulted in a court such as that of Cheops was not yet completed. The absolute power of the king at Memphis in the Fourth Dynasty was maintained by the distribution of high offices among the members of the monarch's immediate family and the concentration of the highest administrative duties in the person of a vizier who was closely related by blood ties to the king. However, the greatest

[1] §vi, 24, 36.
[2] Cairo 41556. Knowledge of its present location is due to Labib Habachi.
[3] §i, 5, 41, n. 4.   [4] §i, 6, 12; 11, 18.
[5] G, 41, 2, 248; §i, 6, 12.   [6] §ii, 16, 118; 22, 63; 39, 6.
[7] §vi, 6, 66; 8, 71.

man of the reign of Djoser, Imhotep, was neither the son of a king
nor a vizier, although he is called 'King's Sealer', or Chancellor,
which was one of the titles later associated with that of the vizier.
He was also called 'Hereditary Prince' which, like the titles of
'Count' and 'Guardian of Nekhen' borne by Nedjemankh in the
same reign, later came to be a kind of honorary epithet of the
princes of the Fourth Dynasty. These titles, as well as others, are
thought to be vestiges of a hereditary nobility which had existed
in early times. The impression gained is that this old nobility still
retained a more prominent place at court in the time of Djoser
than it did in later times.

Although the position of the vizier assumed a new and vital
importance at the beginning of the Fourth Dynasty we have
evidently been mistaken in thinking that the office was first
established in the reign of Sneferu. A man named Menka has
the titles 'He-of-the-Curtain', 'Judge' and 'Vizier' on several
fragments of stone vessels from the great store placed in the
galleries under Djoser's Step Pyramid.[1] This official would seem
to have lived at least as early as the Second Dynasty.

It is obvious that much has yet to be learned about the administration of the country in the Third Dynasty. It does not seem
to be entirely by chance, however, that the few people whom we
know, such as Imhotep, Hesyre, Nedjemankh, Khabausokar,
Akhetaa, and the ship-builder Bedjmes, were all active, practical
men who laid particular emphasis upon their connexion with
public works and the crafts.[2] The Old Kingdom does not appear
to have known a rigid caste-system based on birth. Innate ability
and the favour of the king were the determining factors in a man's
career. Perhaps the need for able men, for example for the great
projects of the Third Dynasty, made advancement easier than in
the Fourth Dynasty when the highest favours of the king were
reserved for the members of his own family.

II. THE FOURTH DYNASTY

According to the Prisse Papyrus, Sneferu ascended to the throne
after the death of Huni. The Turin Canon assigns a length of
twenty-four years to his reign. A quarry mark on the casing of the

[1] The most complete examples of this inscription are published in A, 1, 1–3 (figs.
1–4 and pl. 1). See also *Ann. Serv.* 34 (1934), pl. III (repeated in G, 43, vol. 1, 947,
fig. 623).
[2] §1, 33, *passim*; §VI, 24, 35–8.

North Stone Pyramid at Dahshūr is dated to the sixteenth occasion (of the count), while the Maidūm Pyramid had several marks of the seventeenth.[1] It now seems fairly clear that there prevailed throughout the Old Kingdom a method of reckoning by a cattle-count taken every second year and that the figures in these dates refer to the occasion of this count.[2] The annals mentioned in the preceding section show that the record of a biennial royal tour of inspection by river called a 'Following of Horus' (*šmsw Ḥr*) was kept in the First Dynasty, although omitted for at least twelve years in the reign of Anedjib. Towards the end of the Second Dynasty a biennial count was added. This was subject to some irregularity, since the first two counts were made in successive years in the reign attributed generally to Khasekhemwy. A more troublesome example of irregularity appears in the reign of Sneferu, when cattle are first mentioned as the subject of the census. The year after a count of cattle is mentioned fairly frequently in the Fifth and Sixth Dynasties, as well as twice in the reign of Shepseskaf towards the end of the Fourth Dynasty.[3] Only statements of the year of the count have survived from the reigns of Sneferu, Cheops and Redjedef and it has been questioned whether we can depend upon a regular count having been taken every alternate year before the Fifth Dynasty, or indeed whether it was ever regularly maintained on a biennial basis.[4] However, a year after the fourth count and one after the fifth are found on three limestone ostraca which were placed in two of three adjoining graves which had been added intrusively in the old First Dynasty cemetery at Helwān. No king's name is mentioned, but another ostracon from what seemed to be the earliest grave in the group is dated to the first count of Chephren. A fourth grave, unrelated to the others, contained an ostracon with the fifth count of an unnamed king written in a very similar semi-cursive script.[5] This evidence suggests that a biennial count was kept in the reign of Chephren.

In fact the usual expression *ḥ3t sp* 'occasion' implies the existence of the ordinary cattle census in the Fourth Dynasty. In spite of some possible inconsistencies we shall certainly come nearer to the correct regnal year by doubling the figure stated than by taking it at its face value as has sometimes been done in the past. Since we cannot be certain that the first count was never

[1] §II, 28, 89. For the Maidūm and Dahshūr Pyramids, see G, 43, vol. II, 3.
[2] G, 11, 11. [3] §II, 36, 278; G, 41, 160; §II, 43, 116, fig. 4.
[4] G, 17, 53.
[5] §II, 43, 123, n. 11; cf. Zaki Saad, *Suppl. Ann. Serv., Cahier* 3 (1947), 105–7, pl. XLII, XLIII.

made in the accession year, one year will be subtracted from the
number when mentioned in the following pages to allow for this
possibility, always with the consciousness that we may be a few
years in error.   In the case of Sneferu the Annals indicate that no
census was taken in the year after the sixth count, but the seventh
and eighth came in successive years. This may mean that the
biennial count was maintained until year 13 (year after sixth
occasion) and that an annual count was then taken until the end
of the reign. The seventeenth occasion would thus be the twenty-
third year of the reign. This explanation agrees well with the
twenty-four year reign given in the Turin Canon. A maximum date
of year 32 would be reached if the count reverted to the biennial
system after the eighth year. Similarly, the sixteenth occasion
could be either the twenty-second or the thirtieth year, prefer-
ably the twenty-second. These two dates are the highest recovered
for Sneferu, the seventeenth cattle count presumably recording the
work done late in his reign in completing Huni's pyramid at
Maidūm. It may be supposed that a biennial count was made
under Huni and that if the seventeenth occasion were to refer to
his reign our estimate of its length would have to be doubled to
thirty-four (or thirty-three) years. This does not agree with the
Turin Canon which credits Huni, like Sneferu, with twenty-four
years.

The name of Sneferu, in a cartouche, has been found inside the
so-called Bent Pyramid (or South Stone Pyramid) at Dahshūr
and with his Horus-name Nebmaat amongst the marks of builders
or quarrymen on the stones of the exterior. The same Horus-name
has also been discovered with a new date of the fifteenth occasion
(of the count) on the masonry of the North Stone Pyramid at
Dahshūr.[1] Sneferu's name also appears on the walls of the valley
temple of the Bent Pyramid and on the round-topped stelae set
up in the chapel at the base of his pyramid and in front of the
subsidiary pyramid. Another pair of round-topped stelae stood
at the foot of the causeway by the valley temple.[2] No trace seems
to exist now of the valley temple of the northern of the two
pyramids, but some fifty years ago its ruins were said to be
visible and in them was found a decree of Phiops I concerned
with the two pyramids called 'Kha Sneferu'.[3] It has long been
known that in the Fifth Dynasty a certain Ankhmare prepared
a tomb for his father Duare east of the Bent Pyramid. The father

---

[1] §II, 39, I. By error §II, 43, 124 omits to mention that the king's name was at
the north-east corner, the date at the south-west corner of the pyramid.
[2] §II, 11, 515, 566, 573, pl. III.   [3] §II, 3, 1; G, 41, 209.

was overseer of the two pyramids, but his son was only overseer of the 'Southern Pyramid'. By this description he would seem to mean the Bent Pyramid, which is certainly in that geographical relationship to the North Stone Pyramid at Dahshūr. Two statues of Duare have now been found in Sneferu's valley temple.[1] The pyramid is named again on a fine round-topped stela of the time of Sneferu found in the entrance corridor of the valley temple of the Bent Pyramid. Here the pyramid is called 'Kha Sneferu khenty' instead of 'Kha Sneferu resy' as on the stela of Ankhmare. It is tempting to see in 'khenty' a parallel word for 'southern', and also to interpret the triangular sign which determines the whole as an early hieroglyph for pyramid devised at a time when the shape of the pyramid itself was in the process of development.[2]

The round-topped stela bearing the name 'Kha Sneferu khenty' imitates the form of the royal stelae at Dahshūr and the two uninscribed stones long known in the courtyard of the small temple at the base of the Maidūm Pyramid. It belonged to an important person, Prince Netjeraperef who, in addition to being priest of Sneferu's pyramid, was also 'Overseer of Inspectors' in the Fifth, Sixth and Seventh Nomes of Upper Egypt, a title also held by Metjen in this reign in connexion with the Sixth and Seventeenth Nomes of Upper Egypt.[3] The relief is cut in the same heavy bold style as that of the figures personifying Sneferu's landed properties which line the walls of this corridor. Each group is headed by the emblem of the province in which the property was situated, the whole forming an important early list of the Egyptian nomes which is unfortunately incomplete.[4] The style of these reliefs was already known from the private chapels of the period but had not previously been found in a royal monument. It is to be seen again in the fine portrait of Sneferu on the surviving stela of the pair which originally stood in front of the subsidiary pyramid. It prevails in the other representations of the king in association with various gods which adorned the square columns of the portico at the back of the court of the valley temple. Similarly carved inscriptions framed the six niches sheltered by this portico. The niches were intended for statues attached to the back wall representing Sneferu. Parts of two of these statues were recovered to complete our impression of this remarkable monument.[5]

[1] §II, 26, 189; II, 589, pl. XXIIA.   [2] §II, II, 591, pl. XXI.
[3] G, 41, 2, 3; G, 4, 77, 78; G, 18, 81, 82; §V, 3.
[4] §II, II, 577–583, pls. VIII–X.   [5] *Ibid.* 583–8, 610–23, pls. XI–XIX.

It seems very unlikely that Sneferu could have built three pyramids, but that at Maidūm, nearly thirty miles south of Dahshūr, was undoubtedly thought to belong to him by later visitors who left graffiti on the walls of its temple. The stepped structure at Maidūm, which in its final stage was cased like a true pyramid, is earlier in type than either of the two Dahshūr pyramids. If Sneferu completed a pyramid which had nearly been finished by his predecessor Huni it might provide an explanation for the association of his name with Maidūm. The quarry marks *ḥзt sp* 15 and 17, which were found on casing stones in the debris of the outer facing of the pyramid, may well belong to work which was carried out under Sneferu towards the end of his reign altering Huni's building into the shape of a true pyramid. This shape had been achieved for the first time in the North Stone Pyramid at Dahshūr. The southern pyramid there appears to have been planned as a true pyramid, but the angle was changed when the structure had reached a considerable height. This change may have been intended to lessen the superincumbent weight when an ominous fault appeared in the corbelling of the upper chamber. Certainly the interior of the northern pyramid was designed on simpler lines with no attempt at imitating the breath-taking effect of the square corbel vault of the lower apartment in the Bent Pyramid. Both the nature of the provisions made for burial in these two structures and the question which pyramid served as the tomb of Sneferu remain in doubt.

It is now evident that it is the name of the mother and not the wife of Sneferu, Queen Meresankh, which occurs with that of her son in one of the Eighteenth Dynasty graffiti in the temple.[1] A statue placed there long after the temple was built mentions the gods which are in Djed Sneferu.[2] This is the place to which Prince Hordedef was sent to fetch the magician Djedi in the tale of the Westcar Papyrus. It was probably in the neighbourhood of Maidūm and could have contributed to the association of Sneferu's name with that site. It may also be deduced that the princes buried at Maidūm belonged to the family of his predecessor since, as was long ago noted, Sneferu's family and funerary priests were buried at Dahshūr.

Sneferu married a princess named Hetepheres who bore the title of 'Daughter of the God', and it is evident that she represented the direct inheritance of the line of the blood royal. Sneferu's mother, Queen Meresankh, whose name has been found on Fragment no. 1 of the Cairo inscriptions related to the

[1] §II, 33, 40. [2] *Ibid.*

Palermo Stone, would appear to have been a minor queen of Huni, but one who was in a position of such favour that she could place her son on the throne. As Mother of the King of Upper and Lower Egypt she was certainly one of the great ladies of the time, as is attested by the number of women who continued to be named after her. If we accept the length of reigns given by the Turin Canon, it would appear that Sneferu's marriage to Hetepheres did not occur at the time of his accession to the throne but earlier, during the reign of his predecessor. This inference is to be drawn from the fact that their son Cheops must have been a man beyond his early twenties when he succeeded to the throne in order to have two middle-aged sons at the end of his twenty-three year reign. Prince Khufukhaf appears in the chapel of a tomb finished in the last year of his father's reign, both as a young man with his mother and again as a fat older man.[1] The Crown Prince Kawab, who must have died at about the same time as his father, is pictured similarly as a portly man of middle age, in the tomb of his daughter Queen Meresankh III.[2] If it be assumed that Sneferu was about eighteen years of age when his eldest son was born he could have married Hetepheres in the middle of the reign of Huni in order to establish his claim to the succession. Perhaps the occasion for this marriage was the death of the fully grown man whose body was found in the great mastaba no. 17 at Maidūm; obviously this mastaba was the first concern of the builders after the construction of the pyramid was well advanced.[3] His name is lost— only the preliminary drawings could dimly be perceived when the chapel was first excavated[4] but there is every indication that he could have been a crown prince.

Since both Huni and Sneferu appear to have occupied the throne for twenty-four years, Cheops would have been eighteen in the first decade of his father's reign. At this time he seems to have taken as wives the ladies who later became his queens and were buried at Giza. Meritites bore to him his eldest son Kawab. It may be that her position as Crown Princess during a considerable part of the reign accounts for the unusual use of a queen's title connected with Sneferu which appears on her Giza stela. Khufukhaf was the son of a minor wife, Henutsen. Both sons would have been at least forty when Cheops died at the end of his reign of twenty-three years. Cheops may have been about thirty-five at his accession and nearing sixty when he died.

[1] §vi, 23, pls. 43, 44.   [2] §vi, 24, pl. 46.
[3] §ii, 34, 4, pl. xi.   [4] §ii, 27, 72.

Meritites, who survived him into the reign of Chephren, need not have been much more than sixty-five at her death.

The legitimate heir to the throne appears to have been the eldest son of the chief queen who was of the direct line of the blood royal. We know of several 'eldest sons' of a king who were evidently children of minor queens and these men seem to have been specially favoured for their loyalty to relatives who came to the throne. Sneferu's son Kanefer became vizier, lived well into the reign of Cheops (if not longer) and was buried at Dahshūr by a son who seems to have been named after Cheops' eldest son Kawab.[1] The Vizier and Eldest Son of the King, Nefermaat, had a son, Hemiunu, who was a grown man of perhaps eighteen with important titles when his father completed the decoration of his own tomb at Maidūm. Hemiunu became vizier and was given the courtesy title of 'Prince'. Like Kawab and Khufukhaf he is represented as a fat man of advanced years in a statue of exceptional realism which must have been made when his tomb at Giza was nearing completion in the year 19 ($\underline{h}zt$ sp 10) of Cheops.[2] If he were forty at the time, it is more likely that his father, Nefermaat, was a son of Huni rather than of Sneferu. Nefermaat was granted a funerary property with a name compounded with that of Sneferu but this need mean no more than that he received it from the king he was serving as vizier.

Nefermaat would appear to have been somewhat older than Kanefer and he probably preceded him in the office of vizier, which under Sneferu formed an important new force in the centralization of the government. Kanefer could then have followed Nefermaat in the office during the latter half of the reign of Sneferu, handing it on to Nefermaat's son, Hemiunu, who served as vizier during the early part of the reign of Cheops. We know of another 'Eldest Son of the King', Ankhhaf, a vizier who probably served under Chephren but who seems to have been another child of a minor queen of Sneferu. He was the owner of the second largest mastaba at Giza and his features are portrayed in the remarkable red bust now in the Boston Museum of Fine Arts.[3] There are thus indications that Sneferu's policy, which was followed by his successors, was not only to administer the country directly through the members of his immediate family, but to maintain the loyalty of able princes, whose birth might make them aspire to the throne, by rewarding them with the vizierate.

[1] §II, 30, vol. II, 23; G, 36, vol. III, 237.
[2] G, 19, vol. I, 148–161; §I, 32, 520. See Plate 31 (*b*).
[3] §II, 39, 11; §VI, 24, 62, pl. 44 A.

The Annals of Sneferu on the Palermo Stone and Cairo Fragment no. 4 record expeditions against the Nubians and Libyans with a resulting booty of prisoners and cattle. They also mention the building of great ships of cedar and some other coniferous wood, and the bringing of forty ship-loads of cedar, some of which was used for the doors of a palace.[1] Logs of this wood were built into the upper chamber of the Bent Pyramid at Dahshūr.[2] Sea trade with Byblos, the port on the Syrian coast from which this timber was obtained, had been established early. A fragment of a stone bowl with the name of Khasekhemwy, the last king of the Second Dynasty, was found there.[3] It is not clear how far Sneferu's raid went towards subduing Nubia, but his son Cheops made use of the diorite quarries which lie in the desert to the north-west of Abu Simbel. Cheops' successor Redjedef left his name there, as did the Fifth Dynasty kings Sahure and Isesi.[4] It is from these quarries that the stone came for the well-known statues of the fourth king of the Fourth Dynasty, Chephren. The land south of Aswān must have been well controlled to enable such expeditions to be carried out across the waterless tract, a distance of some fifty miles from the river. In Wādi Maghāra on the Peninsula of Sinai, a rock-carving shows Sneferu striking down a local chieftain. Sanakhte, Djoser and Sekhemkhet in the Third Dynasty, as well as Sneferu's successor Cheops, undertook similar raids[5] to establish Egypt's authority over the turquoise mines, but it does not seem to have been necessary to repeat this show of force until the time of Sahure in the Fifth Dynasty.

There was no regular army or navy in the Old Kingdom. Men were levied and vessels commandeered as the need arose. A title which may be rendered approximately by 'General' or 'Commander' was borne by men who undertook other duties which we should term civilian. The war-like raids in the Old Kingdom were partly to protect the frontiers but were more often connected with mining operations or with exploration in connexion with foreign trade. The personnel involved was that trained in quarrying and construction operations and in the transport of stone which had developed skilled boat-crews and well-organized labour gangs. The leaders of these operations were 'charged with the king's commissions' and dealt with foreigners as 'interpreters'. The highest title in this category seems to have been the 'Chancellor of the God',[6] that is of the king. All these enterprises were

---

[1] G, 4, 66; 39, 30; 41, 236–7.
[2] §II, 11, 511.
[3] G, 7, vol. 1, 26.
[4] §IV, 17, 9; §II, 9, 65; 10, 369.
[5] G, 12, pls. I–IV.
[6] G, 18, 92 ff.; 21, 120.

probably grouped under the 'Overseer of all the King's Works', an important title held usually by the vizier himself together with his other administrative and judicial functions.

The Westcar Papyrus recounts an attractive story in which Sneferu plays a part.[1] The bored king is pictured as wandering through the palace until the magician Djadjaemankh suggests that he should seek diversion in a boat on the lake in the gardens. One of the beautiful girls, who have been dressed in nets to row the boat, loses her hair-ornament and, before the boat can continue, the magician is required to turn back the waters to reveal the ornament, a malachite fish-pendant lying on a potsherd at the bottom of the lake.

We can imagine this palace of Sneferu fitted out with furniture like the gold-cased pieces bearing his name which were placed in the tomb of his wife Hetepheres.[2] Cheops completed the burial equipment of his mother, who outlived her husband, and buried her in a tomb which was probably at Dahshūr. About the fifteenth year of his reign, Cheops learned that thieves had entered the tomb of Hetepheres. He ordered the burial to be transferred to a new secret tomb at Giza, without apparently realizing that his mother's body had been removed from the alabaster sarcophagus and destroyed. The coffin, which had been chipped by the thieves in prizing off the lid but was otherwise unharmed, was let down a hundred-foot shaft east of the Great Pyramid. With it were placed the queen's carrying-chair, her gold-cased bed and canopy, an arm-chair, gold toilet implements, pottery, linen and other objects. Only the silver bracelets, inlaid with butterflies in gaily coloured stones, survived from her plundered jewellery, and of her mortal remains nothing but the contents of the alabaster canopic chest, which was carefully sealed up in a niche in the wall. The costly materials and refinement of design of these beautiful objects give us a startling glimpse of the wealth and good taste of the time. There is the same sense of form and clean line which is embodied in the reliefs, the portrait sculpture and the funerary architecture of the period.

The literature of the Middle Kingdom sheds a most favourable light on Sneferu and the good old days of his reign. Again, the Westcar Papyrus, as Posener has pointed out,[3] displays deft touches by which the genial character of Sneferu is contrasted with the autocratic nature of Cheops. Whether this bears any relation to actual fact or not, it represents a tradition voiced by Herodotus in the fifth century B.C., who records that the Egyptians

1 §vi, 6, 38. 2 §ii, 39, *passim*. 3 §vi, 17, 10–13, 29–36.

detested Cheops and Chephren in his time. No doubt the contemporaries of Herodotus were influenced in their ideas by the
magnitude of the task of building the Giza Pyramids. However,
there may have survived some recollection of the lamentations of
the time after the collapse of the Old Kingdom when men be-
wailed the uselessness of great tombs which could not protect the
bodies of the kings buried in them.

The Horus Medjedu, Khufu, is generally known by the Greek
name used by Manetho, Cheops, as also are his successors
Chephren (Khafre) and Mycerinus (Menkaure). Several inscriptions refer to him only by his golden Horus-name which is
written with two Horus falcons above a gold collar. This famous
builder of the Great Pyramid at Giza had absolute control over
a unified country with a perfected administration which made full
use of the productivity of the land. Egypt's wealth has always
been mainly agricultural. The condition of crops, flocks and herds
depended upon irrigation which required wise planning and
vigilant control to produce the best results. Even then, the traditional seven years' famine of the time of Djoser,[1] and the starving
men and women depicted at the end of the Fifth Dynasty in the
reliefs of King Unas,[2] indicate what could happen as a result of
a series of bad Niles. Egypt suffered no outside interference
which could not have been easily dealt with by an occasional
military raid to keep order among the nomad tribes along the
border. As in the case of Cheops' predecessors we have no clear
picture of how he employed his power and wealth in public works
throughout the country. A ruined dam near Cairo[3] and a temple
on the edge of the Faiyūm[4] are in fact the only constructions of
a non-funerary character which can be attributed with any probability to the Fourth Dynasty. However, Cheops' enterprises
in the valley are reflected in the way in which the resources of the
country were brought to bear upon his grandiose plan for a city
of the dead for his family and court around the Great Pyramid.
West of the pyramid are three early family cemeteries laid out in
regular rows of tombs, at least some of which seem to have been
constructed for the older members of the Cheops family. East
of the pyramid were prepared the burial places of the king's
favourite children, in close proximity to their respective mothers
who occupied the three small queens' pyramids.[5]

[1] §I, 31, 11.　　　[2] §III, 12, 45; 30, 29; §VI, 24, 75, pl. 48 B.
[3] §II, 31, 33.　　　　　[4] §II, 13, 31; 29, 1.
[5] §II, 38, *passim* and plans of cemetery; §VI, 24, 53–59; G, 43, vol. II, 28. See
Plate 32 (a).

The titles of the men and women buried in this necropolis shed some light on the administration of the country, the temple services and the etiquette of the court. The biography of Metjen and the very full titles of Pehernefer at Saqqara[1] provide a picture of the administration of town and farm lands in the time of Sneferu, particularly in the Delta where many of the vast properties of the crown lay. At Giza not only can we see how the high administrative offices were centred in the hands of the vizier supported by other princes close to the king's person, but we can also form an idea of the duties of the less exalted officials, like a certain Nefer who served the treasury which provided storehouses for arms, grain, cloth and like products of the country.[2] These men held some ancient titles which had by then acquired an honorary significance and they performed personal service to the king, undertaking various household duties in the palace. Chief among the religious titles connected with the various gods were the High Priesthoods of Re at Heliopolis and of Ptah of Memphis. The control of funerary endowments, with the lands attached to them, looms up large in contrast with other administrative duties of a purely secular nature. The care of the great cemeteries around the pyramids presented judicial, supply and related problems similar to the government of the towns in the cultivated land.

The chief queen of Cheops appears to have been the Meritites whose name was found on a fragment of relief in the chapel of the Crown Prince Kawab. She should have been buried in the northernmost, and first constructed, of the three queens' pyramids, but no name was recovered from the destroyed chapel. The mastaba east of this pyramid belonged to Kawab; it was the earliest of the tombs of the children of Cheops to be built in the Eastern Cemetery. Unfortunately we do not know where at Giza Mariette found the now-vanished stela of a Queen Meritites who had the title *wrt ḥts* in connexion with both Sneferu and Cheops and was honoured before Chephren. There are indications, however, that the stela may have come from the mastaba of Kawab and his wife Hetepheres II, both of whom were probably children of Meritites. It seems that Meritites was the chief queen of Cheops, whatever relationship she may have borne to the other two kings.[3] She was evidently not the mother of Chephren since she did not have the title of 'Mother of the King of Upper and Lower Egypt', although Chephren is named on the Mariette stela, and she must have lived into his reign. The

[1] G, 4, 76; 41, 1; §II, 22, 63.   [2] §II, 38, 422.   [3] §II, 39, 6.

popularity of the names Meresankh, Hetepheres and Meritites among the ladies of the Fourth Dynasty is most easily explained by supposing that they were borne by three great queens, the wives respectively of Huni, Sneferu and Cheops.

Reisner concluded that the middle queen's pyramid at Giza belonged to the mother of a secondary branch of the family headed by King Redjedef. The queen's name is not preserved although her titles have survived on fragments of the reliefs in her chapel. We must give up the idea that she was of Libyan origin, an attractive theory which was based on the supposed blond hair of Hetepheres II, who was then thought to be her daughter. It is now evident that the yellow wig is part of a costume worn by other great ladies and it is probable that Hetepheres II, like her husband Kawab, was a child of the chief queen Meritites.[1]

The southernmost pyramid, like the other two, is not identified by a contemporary inscription. However, its chapel was enlarged in the Twenty-First Dynasty into a temple of Isis, Mistress of the Pyramid, somehow associated with its original owner, Queen Henutsen.[2] This lady was thought by that time to be a daughter of Cheops but was most probably his third queen and the mother of Prince Khufukhaf, in whose chapel nearby a queen is represented.[3] It is conceivable that Chephren was her son and a younger brother of Khufukhaf. Still a third son may have been Prince Minkhaf who seems to have served Chephren as vizier after Ankhhaf and before Nefermaat.[4] The last named vizier was the son of a lady named Nefertkau who was probably buried in a mastaba south of the third queen's pyramid adjoining the tombs of Nefermaat and her grandson Sneferukhaf who refer to her as the eldest daughter of Sneferu. Her mother was probably a minor queen and it is unlikely that she was herself a wife of Cheops.

In the tomb east of that of Prince Kawab was buried Prince Hordedef, the wise man of later tradition who has already been mentioned in connexion with Imhotep and Djoser. He was supposed to have discovered in the temple of Thoth at Hermopolis certain spells of the Book of the Dead written in letters of lapis lazuli. A fragment of his precepts has survived. It is characteristic that, in the practical way of the Old Kingdom, he should have advised his son to build well for the future and to provide his house in the cemetery, whereas later scribes, in praising Hordedef

---

[1] *Ibid.* 4, 7, figs. 4, 9. See Plate 32 (*b*).
[2] §II, 6, 1; G, 4, 83.   [3] §VI, 23, pl. 44 *b*.
[4] §II, 39, 7, 8, 11; cf. Reisner, Z.Ä.S. 64 (1929), 97.

and Imhotep, say that writing endures and that a book is more useful than strong buildings, a funerary chapel or a monument.[1] In the Westcar Papyrus, Hordedef appears as the sponsor for the magician Djedi. After Djedi had exhibited his magical tricks and prophesied to Cheops that there would be no change of dynasty until his son and his son's son had succeeded him upon the throne, the king commanded that the magician be taken to the household of Hordedef.[2]

It is to be noted that this prophecy of the Westcar Papyrus takes into account only the main line of kings: Cheops, Chephren and Mycerinus. It disregards Redjedef, Shepseskaf and two unknown names in the breaks of the list in the Turin Canon. Manetho seems to supply names to fill these gaps: Bicheris and Thamphthis. However, a rock inscription in the Wādi Hammāmāt, plausibly assigned to a Middle Kingdom date, now adds to our perplexity. In a row of cartouches appear the names of Cheops, Redjedef, Chephren, Hordedef and Baufre.[3] The last is certainly the Baufre, a son of Cheops and brother of Hordedef, mentioned in the Westcar Papyrus. It has seemed reasonable to assign to him the mastaba (7320) of a prince whose name is lost which adjoins that of Hordedef on the east at Giza. Neither of these men is known as a king and such a royal status for Hordedef seems impossible. He is mentioned twice at Giza towards the end of the Old Kingdom without the titles of a king, although a cult was established for him as in the case of the Vizier Kagemni at Saqqara. A man in the Western Cemetery calls himself 'Honoured before Hordedef' and another who built his small tomb in the street beside the wise man's mastaba is represented on his stela with his hands raised in prayer and with the phrase above: 'Adoring Hordedef.'[4]

The inscriptions of Cheops' grand-daughter, Queen Meresankh III,[5] suggest that dissension split the royal family when the builder of the Great Pyramid died. Work ceased on the mastabas of several of the princes at Giza and someone maliciously erased the decorations of Hordedef's chapel, although his name and titles can still be read with difficulty. Meresankh's father, the Crown Prince Kawab, died and her mother, Hetepheres II, became the wife of Redjedef who ascended the throne. Redjedef has long been viewed as a usurper. It would indeed seem that Hordedef, or one of the other princes in the northern line of great

---

[1] §vi, 3, 8.   [2] §vi, 6, 40.   [3] §ii, 8, 41.
[4] §ii, 14, 35; G, 19, vol. iii, 26; §ii, 39, 8.
[5] §ii, 37, 64.

twin-mastabas, had, as probable sons of the chief queen Meritites, a better right to succeed to the throne. However, the evidence is so scanty that we can only speculate as to the course of events at the end of the reign of Cheops. We do know now that Redjedef must have carried out the funeral ceremonies of Cheops as would have been expected of a son and successor. His name appears on one of the roofing blocks of the rock-cut excavation for the wooden funerary barque recently discovered south of the Great Pyramid. The date of the eleventh occasion (year 21) on one of these great stones would presumably mean that it had either been quarried or prepared for its place a year or two before the death of Cheops since the year would be improbably high for Redjedef.

The Turin Canon records a reign of eight years for Redjedef whose Horus-name was Kheper. He turned to Abu Rawāsh, a few miles north of Giza, and there began to build a pyramid on a high promontory of the desert edge.[1] Little is left of this construction except a huge excavation for the burial apartments within an outcrop of stone left by the quarrymen as a beginning of the superstructure. There are indications that the pyramid was to have been encased with granite. Traces of a brick temple were found on the east face and a fragment of a granite column inscribed with the king's name. Other granite columns seem to have been carried off and used in the Coptic convent of Nāhiya to the north of Abu Rawāsh. It would appear from the description that these round granite shafts imply that something like the palm columns used in the temples of the Fifth Dynasty was anticipated at Abu Rawāsh. An excavation for a sun-boat was made south of the temple and the establishment of a royal funerary cult is indicated by the smashed fragments of royal statues found scattered everywhere in this area. The name of the chief queen of Redjedef, Khentetenka, was recovered from these fragments.

Parts of the statues of three princes and two princesses were found in one of the mud-brick rooms. From the fact that the three princes are all called 'eldest son of the King' it would appear that Redjedef had other wives besides Khentetenka and Hetepheres II. One prince was named Baka and it has been suggested that he might have become the Bakare whose brief reign has been tentatively inserted between Chephren and Mycerinus, but this name is known only in the form of Bicheris as given by Manetho. The princess Neferhetepes has been plausibly identified with a queen mentioned early in the Fifth Dynasty and the suggestion made that she became the mother of King Userkaf.[2]

[1] §II, 5, 53–7; G, 43, vol. II, 86.   [2] §II, 15, 53, 64.

The condition of the pyramid at Abu Rawāsh and the wanton damage inflicted upon Redjedef's statues would accord with the conclusion that the reign was short and came to an abrupt end. The opposing party, which was supported by the two surviving princes Ankhhaf and Minkhaf, as well as Nefermaat, the son of Sneferu's daughter, the princess Nefertkau, brought Chephren to the throne. Other members of the family of Cheops outlived the reign of Redjedef. Queen Meritites, the chief queen of Cheops, may have been in disgrace. She omits the name of Redjedef from her stela. Hetepheres II, now the widow of both the Crown Prince Kawab and King Redjedef, made her peace with Chephren, to whom she married her daughter Meresankh III. The direct descent of the blood royal would have come down to Meresankh through her grandmother Meritites and her mother Hetepheres II whom Redjedef probably married for this reason. Perhaps no son was born of this union and the sons of Khentetenka or other wives of Redjedef seem to have fared badly if they survived his reign. Hetepheres II lived on into the last reign of the dynasty.

The Horus Userib, Khafre (Chephren), constructed a funerary monument only a little smaller than the pyramid of Cheops.[1] The mortuary temple at its eastern base was connected by a covered causeway with a valley temple at the edge of the cultivation. The granite hall of the valley temple with its great simple square columns is wonderfully impressive, as is the severe granite façade marked by deep entrance embrasures flanked by inscriptions. The diorite statues from this temple and those from the Third Pyramid at Giza built by his successor Mycerinus form the basis of our knowledge of the royal sculpture of the Old Kingdom. The most spectacular achievement of Chephren's craftsmen was, however, the Great Sphinx which is carved from an outcrop of rock beside the causeway leading up to the pyramid temple.

The length of Chephren's reign cannot be exactly determined, but it appears to have been about twenty-five years. Two mastabas, which seem certainly to be of this reign in the cemetery east of the Cheops Pyramid, give the years 25 (ḥ3t sp 13), 23 (ḥ3t sp 12) and 13 (ḥ3t sp 7).[2] It is not certain whether his son Nekaure made his will, which is dated year 23 (ḥ3t sp 12), in the reign of his father or his brother Mycerinus.[3]

Chephren made no attempt to lay out such a family cemetery as that of Cheops. His queens and their children were buried in rock-cut tombs in the sloping ground to the east of his pyramid,

[1] G, 43, vol. II, 45.   [2] §II, 43, 127, 128.
[3] G, 4, 89; 41, 16.

to the south of its causeway. Some members of the court utilized
the unfinished cores of mastabas in the Western Cemetery of
Cheops, and others, like Hetepheres II and a certain Akhethotep,
constructed new tombs in the Eastern Cemetery which continued
the lines of tombs laid out in the reign of Cheops. Meresankh III
was buried early in the reign of Shepseskaf in a beautifully
sculptured and painted rock-cut tomb which her mother,
Hetepheres II, had prepared under her own unused mastaba.[1]
Chephren's chief queen, Khamerernebty I, excavated a large
tomb for herself in the quarry east of her husband's pyramid.
Inscriptions in this tomb mention her daughter, Khamerernebty II,
who became the chief wife of Mycerinus.[2] Two other queens of
Chephren, Hedjhekenu and Per(senti?) are represented in the
rock-cut tombs of their sons Prince Sekhemkare and Prince
Nekaure. Near them were buried Nebemakhet, the son of
Meresankh III, Chephren's daughter Queen Rekhetre, a Princess
Hemetre and a number of other princes.[3]

The present arrangement of the fragments of the Turin Canon
allows space for two kings of the Fourth Dynasty whose names
do not appear upon the monuments. They may have been
Manetho's kings Bicheris and Thamphthis, who, Reisner
suggested, might represent otherwise unrecorded Egyptian royal
names: Bakare and Dedefptah. If it is accepted that by Ratoisis
Manetho meant Redjedef and that Sebekheres stands for
Shepseskaf, this suggestion would give an agreement between
Manetho and the Turin Canon for eight kings of the Fourth
Dynasty. The Saqqara List appears to have had nine kings. The
Turin, Saqqara and Abydos Lists accept Redjedef as a king of
the main family line but the Abydos table omits the other two
kings named by Manetho while Saqqara evidently placed them
with another nameless king at the end of the list. The Turin
Canon apparently lists Bicheris as no. 5 and Thamphthis as no. 8,
as Reisner observed when he placed Bakare after Chephren
because he was unwilling to believe that Shepseskaf could have
ruled eighteen years, which he would prefer to assign to Mycerinus.[4] It now appears that twenty-eight is a more probable
figure in the Turin Canon for Mycerinus. It can be reconciled
with the lives of various people which overlap several reigns in
the Fourth Dynasty and early Fifth Dynasty. It would however

---

[1] See Plate 32 (b).
[2] §II, 7, 41; 36, 247 ff.; 38, 152, 236; §VI, 23, 41.
[3] G, 16, vol. IV (1932–3), 103, 125; vol. VI (1934–5), 1, 43; vol. VII (1935–6)
passim. [4] §II, 36, 246.

be necessary to extend the life span of Meresankh III to sixty-one years, beyond the fifty to fifty-five years that Douglas Derry suggested after examining her skeleton.

If we accept the interpolation of a king, represented by Manetho's Bicheris, between Chephren and Mycerinus, we need not allow much intervening time for this reign, perhaps only a few months. No evidence from the monuments suggests a break in the line of the dynasty: Mycerinus appears to succeed Chephren. Chephren's eldest daughter, Khamerernebty II, became the chief queen of Mycerinus and is represented with him in the beautiful Boston slate pair-statue from his valley temple.[1] She is also shown in the tomb of their son Prince Khunere, who stands beside her, pictured as a small, naked boy holding a bird. Khunere also appears as a grown man on an adjoining wall, and in a yellow limestone statuette in Boston which shows him as a seated scribe.[2] He seems however to have died before the end of his father's reign, since, as the eldest son of the chief queen, he ought otherwise to have succeeded to the throne.

Chephren's son, Sekhemkare, records that he was honoured by Chephren, Mycerinus, Shepseskaf, Userkaf and Sahure, omitting the possible usurpers Bicheris and Thamphthis.[3] Meresankh III continued at court into the reign of Shepseskaf. An official named Netjerpunesut remained in favour under Redjedef, Chephren, Mycerinus, Shepseskaf, Userkaf and Sahure.[4] Another official named Ptahshepses, who lived into the reign of Nyuserre and became High Priest of Ptah, was brought up in the households of Mycerinus and Shepseskaf and married Maatkha, the eldest daughter of the latter king.[5] Nothing in his biographical inscription suggests a period of protracted strife resulting from the usurpation of Thamphthis or that the land was disturbed by the change of dynasty which must have occurred between the end of the reign of Shepseskaf and the accession of Userkaf. Nor is there any indication of the part that Queen Khentkaues played in this change of dynasty, although she seems to have formed the connexion between the royal house of the Fourth Dynasty and the succeeding dynasty.

Mycerinus (Menkaure, with the Horus-name Kaykhet) built a pyramid which was much smaller than the two great monuments of his predecessors,[6] but he had begun to case it in costly granite

---

[1] §vi, 24, pl. 44 *b*.
[2] §vi, 23, pl. 10 *c*, 300, fig. 253 (cf. *Bull.M.F.A.* 32 (1934), 11, fig. 10).
[3] G, 16, vol. iv (1932–3), 119.   [4] §ii, 12, 178.
[5] G, 4, 115; 41, 51.   [6] G, 43, vol. ii, 62.

from Aswān. The work of casing the walls of the mortuary temple with hard stone was not finished when the king died. His successor, Shepseskaf, who was probably his son although he does not appear to have been a child of the chief queen Kha-merernebty II, added finishing details in mud-brick and constructed a valley temple completely in this material. In the year after the first cattle count, that is the second or third year of his reign, Shepseskaf set up a decree in the portico of the pyramid temple dedicating the building as a monument which he had made for Mycerinus.[1]

King Shepseskaf had the Horus-name Shepsesykhet. The Turin Canon allows him four years. In this time he would have had to complete his father's funerary temples and construct for himself the so-called Mastabat Fara'ūn, half-way between Saqqara and Dahshūr.[2] The form of this tomb differs from the pyramids of the other kings of the Fourth Dynasty. It was a rectangular mastaba construction with a rounded top and verti-cal end-pieces which gave it the form of the usual stone sarco-phagus. Inside, the burial apartments were lined with granite. The heavy masonry and sound workmanship betoken work in the best Fourth Dynasty traditions. Nearly all the masonry of the temple has been plundered. The niched outer court and vaulted causeway were hastily finished in brick, probably after the death of the king. The monument was identified by a statue fragment bearing a broken cartouche. A stela dating from later in the Old Kingdom, which was found in the neighbourhood, indicated that a funerary cult of Shepseskaf existed there. Very few people are known who were connected with this funerary cult but an occa-sional private name is compounded with that of Shepseskaf.

One important person who undertook the funerary service of Shepseskaf was the Queen Bunefer buried in a rock-cut tomb at Giza beside the much discussed monument of Queen Khentkaues, which lies to the north of the causeway of Mycerinus, not far from his valley temple. Although it is more usual for a princess to serve the funerary cult of her father than it is for a queen to assume similar responsibilities towards her dead husband, the inscriptions in Bunefer's tomb seem to imply that she was the wife of Shepseskaf.[3] There is no better indication that the family of the Fourth Dynasty had come to the end of its power than that the son of Bunefer, an unimportant judge, did not bear the title of 'Prince'.

---

[1] §II, 36, 278. [2] G, 43, vol. II; 89; §VI, 2, 142.
[3] G, 16, vol. III (1931–2), 176.

The evidence for the relationships of the various royal personages at the end of the dynasty and at the beginning of the Fifth
Dynasty is obscure, but it is possible that Userkaf, the first king
of the Fifth Dynasty, was the son of Neferhetepes, the daughter
of King Redjedef whose statue was found in his temple at Abu
Rawāsh.[1] She would then be the same person as Queen Neferhetepes mentioned in the tomb of a certain Persen who was buried
a short distance to the south of the Pyramid of Userkaf at Saqqara.
It was confirmed in the time of Userkaf's successor, Sahure, that
certain offerings endowed by Neferhetepes in the temple of Ptah
at Memphis should be brought to supply the funerary needs of
Persen. It has been argued that these offerings would probably be
brought first to the tomb of the queen herself and then transferred
for the needs of a secondary beneficiary to a tomb which should lie
nearby. The suggestion, then, seems plausible that Neferhetepes
was the mother of Userkaf and buried in the small pyramid south
of that king's tomb. The identification with the daughter of Redjedef is strengthened by the fact that Persen possessed an estate
of Redjedef which he might well have received from the queen.

Userkaf, then, can have been a descendant of the secondary
branch of the Cheops family. It seems possible that, in founding
a new dynasty, he strengthened his position by marrying Khentkaues who was descended from the main branch of the old family
and was probably a daughter of Mycerinus. Ever since the so-
called 'Unfinished Pyramid' at Giza was identified as the tomb
of this lady it has been evident that she formed a connecting link
between the Fourth and Fifth Dynasties. The building is now
recognized to be not a pyramid but a sarcophagus-shaped construction, something like that of Shepseskaf, set upon a base of
natural rock which was smoothed down and faced with limestone.
The queen's chief title was interpreted to mean that she was
called 'King of Upper and Lower Egypt' as well as 'Mother of
the King of Upper and Lower Egypt'. However, the other
proposed reading: 'Mother of two Kings of Upper and Lower
Egypt' would appear the more probable one.[2] In addition, her
other titles resemble those borne by Queen Nymaathap and
Hetepheres I, indicating that she, like those other two great
ladies, played an important role in the change of dynasty.

The name of Queen Khentkaues was found at Abusīr in connexion with the pyramid of Neferirkare. That she was his mother
is indicated by a fragment of one of the Abusīr Papyri which
contain accounts of the temple evidently prepared later in the

[1] §II, 15, 53, 64.   [2] G, 16, vol. IV (1932–3), 1; §II, 4, 209; 23, 139.

Fifth Dynasty.[1] It has however been suspected rightly that there were two queens named Khentkaues connected with Neferirkare. An unpublished block at Saqqara, which seems to have been brought anciently from his Abusīr funerary temple, confirms this deduction. It shows the titles of a queen 'Beholder of Horus [and Seth], *wrt ḥts*, Great of favour, King's Wife'. These were evidently over a figure of the lady who, like the 'eldest [king's son] Renefer' standing above her, followed the partly preserved figure of King Neferirkare. The wife of the king, then, had the same name as his mother. The two followers of Userkaf appear to have been brothers both from the manner in which Neferirkare is shown in Sahure's temple reliefs and from the fact that Sahure's chief queen was named Neferthanebty and therefore could not have been the mother of Neferirkare.[2]

It would seem that the elder Khentkaues was the wife of Userkaf and the mother of the two kings Sahure and Neferirkare. Her funerary monument could have been completed at Giza in the reign of Neferirkare (although it might have been commenced much earlier), at a time when the inscriptions would name her as the mother of two kings. No explanation of the position of Khentkaues can be made to fit exactly with the tale in the Westcar Papyrus, which makes the wife of a simple priest of Re the mother of the first three kings of the Fifth Dynasty: Userkaf, Sahure and Neferirkare.[3] Nevertheless the story evidently reflects elements of the true facts. The tomb of Khentkaues at Giza may have stimulated the growth of another legend which made a beautiful woman, Nitocris according to Manetho and Rhodopis in the version of Herodotus, the builder of the Third Pyramid. The tradition, imperfectly handed down, of a queen's tomb of unusual form could easily have been associated in Greek times with one of the three famous pyramids at Giza.

III. THE FIFTH DYNASTY

The Westcar Papyrus legend, which makes the first three kings of the Fifth Dynasty the offspring of the god Re, evidently clothes in the magical embellishments of a folk story the actual fact of the predominance of a state cult of the Heliopolitan sun god in the Fifth Dynasty. Chephren in the preceding dynasty had already adopted the title 'Son of Re' but the epithet becomes a regular

[1] §II, 16, 116; §III, 10, 43; A, 2, pl. 46.
[2] §III, 8, vol. II, 90, pl. 17, 116, pl. 48.   [3] §VI, 6, 43–5.

part of the titulary of kings only in the Fifth Dynasty. The records of temple building and endowments on the Palermo Stone show a special preference for the cults of Re and Hathor. Above all, Userkaf introduced a special sun-temple in the western necropolis with a masonry obelisk on a platform, evidently in imitation of the Benben stone which was the central element of the structure of the temple of Re at Heliopolis. Although the names of such sun-temples are known for at least six kings of the Fifth Dynasty, only two have actually been discovered. That of Userkaf was identified by a preliminary survey which has been followed recently by more thorough investigation. The sun temple of Nyuserre was completely excavated.[1]

Userkaf had the Horus-name Irmaat. His pyramid lies close to the north-east corner of the Step Pyramid at Saqqara. On the east side of the pyramid stood only a small chapel for the food offerings supplied to the dead king, while to the south of the pyramid was a large building which seems to correspond with the portion of the funerary temple which ordinarily lay outside the enclosure wall and which contained the king's statues and served for the worship of the deified king. The plan is closer to that of Cheops and Mycerinus than it is to the Pyramid Temple of Chephren.[2] The court was surrounded by square granite columns, which also stood in the portico of the central sanctuary on the south, now walled off from the court and separated from the pyramid. Reliefs covered the walls of the court behind the colonnade. Like the magnificent head of a colossal statue found in the temple and a smaller head wearing the red crown recovered from the sun temple,[3] they belong to the finest tradition of Fourth Dynasty sculpture.

Little is known about Userkaf's reign, which lasted for seven years according to the Turin Canon. One of the rare signs of royal activity in the Theban district in the Old Kingdom is evinced by a square granite column bearing his name which was laid in the floor of the later temple at Tōd, a short distance south of Luxor.[4] A marble cup inscribed with the name of the sun temple of Userkaf was found on the island of Cythera off the tip of the Peloponnesus.[5] How this small object could have travelled so far poses a problem. Vercoutter has shown that it is unlikely that the Aegean or its inhabitants were meant by the term

[1] §III, 20, 104; 8, vol. I, 149; 2; 3; 4, passim; G, 43, vol. II, 582.
[2] G, 43, vol. II, 94; §VI, 24, 67.   [3] §VI, 14, 87, pl. VII.
[4] §III, 5, 61.
[5] §III, 13, 349; 27, 55. Athens National Museum, No. 4578.

'Haunebut' in the Pyramid Texts or in inscriptions of the time
of Cheops and Sahure. He also questions contacts with Crete
which have been claimed for the Old Kingdom.[1] On the other
hand, the expansion of royal trade by land and sea which we begin
to see more clearly in the Fifth Dynasty would suggest that the
period from Sneferu to Phiops II would have been a more propi-
tious time for Egypt to become aware of the Aegean world than
the impoverished days of political discontent in the First Intermediate Period which Vercoutter suggests. We should, at any
rate, take into account this small piece of evidence from the reign
of Userkaf in considering the growing number of instances of
Egypt's contacts abroad. Userkaf's name has not been found at
the Syrian port of Byblos. It is probably due purely to accidents
of survival that after Khasekhemwy only the names of Cheops and
Mycerinus are attested from the insriptions on broken stone
vessels. However, the name of Chephren is found on a cylinder
seal. Khufu (Cheops) was not usually written like his Horus-
name, Medjedu, in a frame, but it certainly exists on a stone
vessel fragment at Byblos. This would seem to make less doubtful
the peculiar use of Kakai (partially preserved on another) as the
Horus-name of Neferirkare. In the Fifth Dynasty it is not until
the reigns of Nyuserre and Isesi that we can be certain of the
occurrence of royal names which continue with Unas, Teti,
Phiops I and Phiops II, omitting Merenre. Since Cheops had the
same Golden Horus-name as Sahure we are again doubtful of the
ownership of an axe-blade found at the mouth of the river Adonis.[2]

A Nykaankh, who appears as a court official on one of the
unpublished reliefs of the temple of Userkaf, may be the same
person as Nykaankh whose tomb is known at Tihna in Middle
Egypt, near the modern town of El-Minya. Whether or not
this identification is correct, the Tihna inscription shows that
Userkaf continued to favour those who had served faithfully
under the preceding dynasty. He confirmed for the family of
Nykaankh both a service in the priesthood of Hathor of Tihna
and the related endowment which had been granted to a certain
Khenuka by Mycerinus.[3] Khenuka appears to have been the
father of Nykaankh. His own rock-cut tomb, which bears a

---

[1] G, 45; 46; *passim*. See, however, the titulary of Sahure on gold sheet panels
reported from Dorak near the Sea of Marmora (*Ill. Ldn News*, 28 November
1959, p. 754).
[2] G, 7, vol. i, 162, 169, 343, 200, 322, 329, 280; G, 33, 20; §vi, 25, 25; cf
A. Rowe, *A Catalogue of Egyptian Scarabs* (Cairo, 1936), 283.
[3] §iii, 16, 67; G, 41, 24; G, 4, 99.

striking resemblance to the tombs of Chephren's family at Giza, is larger and better decorated than any of the other tombs at Tihna. This family's fortunes appear to have dwindled as the Fifth Dynasty advanced; the cemetery at Zāwiyet el-Maiyitīn contains the tombs of the later notables of the Sixteenth Nome.[1] However, at Tihna, as well as at Sheikh Sa'īd and El-Hammāmīya, we begin to see the growing importance of the provincial families which was to increase greatly in the Sixth Dynasty.[2]

Sahure succeeded Userkaf on the throne and is stated by the Turin Canon to have reigned twelve years. However, since the Palermo Stone gives a year after his seventh cattle-count it would appear that he reigned at least fourteen years. His Horus-name was Nebkhau.

Sahure began the royal cemetery at Abusīr, a short distance to the north of Saqqara, where his successors Neferirkare, Neferefre and Nyuserre followed him in building their pyramids.[3] Although the pyramids from this reign onwards did not embody the same solid construction with heavy materials as had been employed, to some extent, even to the time of Userkaf, the temple had reached a developed form which was to be continued with little variation until the end of the Old Kingdom. The inner temple, with its offering chamber and false-door at the base of the pyramid, served for the cult of the food-offerings for the dead king. It, together with a small ritual pyramid, lay within the enclosure wall of the pyramid, while the great court and outer corridors of the temple formed the more public portion of the complex. A covered causeway connected the mortuary temple with a small valley temple which formed an entrance portico and was provided with a landing stage. The great court was surrounded with a row of granite columns with palm (Sahure) or papyrus-bud (Nyuserre) capitals. Although badly smashed, the wall decorations of these temples have preserved a wide range of scenes which show the public life of the king and his association with various gods.

On the south wall of Sahure's court was pictured Seshat, the Goddess of Writing, recording the numbers of sheep, goats and cattle captured in a raid on the Libyan tribes of the Western Desert. The wife and children of the enemy ruler were shown with their names written above them. Originally there was also a large figure of the king in the act of brandishing his mace above the kneeling Libyan whom he grasped by the hair.[4] A new variation with the king dominating a group of foreign enemies

---

[1] §vi, 23, 215, 218.   [2] §iii, 11; 23, *passim*.
[3] G, 8, 178 ff.; G, 43, vol. ii, 101.   [4] §iii, 8, vol. ii, pl. i.

(not as in the Sinai rock-carvings which employ only a single bedawin chieftain) appeared also in a parallel scene on the north wall with reference to Egypt's Asiatic neighbours in the north-east. A fragment of relief with several tethered bears from the Syrian mountains and tall-necked jars each with one handle,[1] such as were found in the tomb of Queen Hetepheres and other Fourth Dynasty tombs at Giza, suggests that the booty in this case was the result of state-manipulated foreign trade rather than actual con-quest. That this scene is a characteristic piece of Egyptian ex-aggeration is supported by the sea-going vessels shown manned by Egyptians on the east wall of the corridor behind the court.[2] They contain bearded foreigners who are in this case not bound prisoners but visitors who raise their arms in praise of the king. Evidently we have here the return of one of the trading expeditions which, as we know, were continually being made to Byblos for the much-prized cedar wood. The Palermo Stone mentions in this reign produce brought from the 'Turquoise Land' in Sinai and from Punt on the Somali Coast.[3] At the Wādi Maghāra in Sinai, Sahure has left the memorial of an expedition to pacify the local nomads.[4] A stela with his name was also found at the old Fourth Dynasty diorite quarries[5] in the desert west of Abu Simbel.

We have already anticipated the fact that Sahure was succeeded by his brother Kakai (Neferirkare)[6] who bore the Horus-name Userkhau. This king did not live to complete his pyramid temples which were finished by his successors Neferefre and Nyuserre. The latter appropriated whatever had been completed of the valley temple and built it into his own structure.[7] The length of the reign of Neferirkare is missing in the Turin Canon, but we have the year after his fifth cattle-count on the Palermo Stone, which would indicate that he remained on the throne at least ten years.

Little evidence has survived concerning the political events of this reign but, just as the wall-reliefs of the funerary temples of Userkaf and Sahure have shown an expansion of pictorial record

[1] See Plate 33 (b).
[2] Ibid. pls. 2, 3, 11–13; §II, 39, 64, fig. 61, 95, pl. 46d, 52b, c, 53c,f.
[3] G, 3, 70.   [4] G, 12, pl. v.
[5] §IV, 17, 9.
[6] The kings of the Fifth Dynasty from Neferirkare to Isesi and most of the kings of the Sixth Dynasty bear, in addition to the personal name, a second throne name in a cartouche which will be given in parenthesis. This is in addition to the Horus-name. G, 26, 202–3; §III, 8, vol. II, 90 contra G, 13, 114; cf. Z.Ä.S. 50 (1912), 1–6.
[7] §III, 7, 5, 49–58; 6, 34–50.

which is reflected in the chapels of the people of the court, as the Fifth Dynasty advanced there is a considerable increase in written documentation. The Royal Annals of the Palermo Stone and its related fragments were inscribed in this reign, or at least soon afterwards. Important fragmentary papyri, although prepared towards the end of the dynasty, deal with accounts connected with the administration of the funerary temple of Neferirkare.[1] Symptomatic of this tendency towards fuller record are the almost encyclopaedic lists of the names of animals, birds and plants in the remarkable representation of the activities of the different seasons of the year which appear a few years after Neferirkare's death in the sun temple of Nyuserre.[2] These lists may themselves derive from an earlier version.

In the funerary chapels of the period, small biographical details light up the daily life of the court with an occasional revealing flash. Rewer in his Giza tomb tells us how he was accompanying Neferirkare in his capacity as Sem-priest in the course of a cere-mony, when the king struck him accidentally upon the leg with his staff. The king hastened to assure him that he must not regard this action as a blow but as an honour.[3]

In another case it is not exactly clear what kind of mishap occurred to the Vizier Washptah, who seems to have been conducting Neferirkare through a new building. The court physician was called and writings consulted but in the end the vizier died.[4] The tactful apology of the king and his concern for the stricken vizier lighten the impression of stiff court ceremonial produced by the lines of bowing courtiers in the temple-reliefs or by a statement of the High Priest of Memphis, Ptahshepses. This official, who was the son-in-law of Shepseskaf, records that as a special favour he was allowed to kiss the king's foot rather than prostrate himself upon the ground.[5]

The two immediate successors of Neferirkare have made little impression upon history. The name of Shepseskare is known from the Saqqara List, but he appears to have left no monuments. However, it has been fairly well established that he also used the cartouche name Isi which occurs in the names of a number of persons and funerary estates, and that his Horus-name was Sekhemkhau.[6] The Turin Canon apparently credits him with a reign of seven years. He was followed by Neferefre (Nefer-

1 §II, 4, 210; §III, 9, 8; 10, 43; A, 2.
2 §III, 4, 319; 15, 129; 21, 33; §VI, 24, 69, 73.
3 G, 16, vol. I (1929–30), 18.   4 G, 4, 111; 41, 40.
5 G, 4, 118; 41, 51.   6 G, 14, 181.

khare) who had the Horus-name Neferkhau. This king built
a sun-temple and may have begun the pyramid which lies unfinished beside that of Neferirkare at Abusīr.[1] A break in the
Turin Canon has deprived us of both his name and the length of
his reign. He was succeeded by the important ruler Nyuserre
who built the third pyramid at Abusīr which has preserved interesting, but damaged, vestiges of its temples and reliefs. The
name of the chief queen of Nyuserre was Reputneb.[2] Three
daughters and a son-in-law are buried near his pyramid.[3] As in
the case of Sahure, a large number of the names of this king's
courtiers are preserved in the temple-reliefs.[4] The best known of
these is a man named Ti whose fine tomb has long been familiar to
every visitor to Saqqara.

It has generally been assumed that the Horus Isetibtowy, Ini
(Nyuserre)[5] had a long reign of over thirty years. No dated
monument approaches this figure and the damaged Turin Canon
indicates only that the number of years was higher than ten. In
the absence of contrary evidence a long reign can be accepted,
but reliance should not be placed upon the celebration of the
Sed-festival which Nyuserre has extensively represented in his
sun-temple.[6] This feast has been interpreted as occurring at thirty
year intervals to mark the jubilee of the king's accession to the
throne, but there are indications that kings with reigns shorter
than thirty years celebrated Sed-festivals in the Old Kingdom.
It is clear that we still lack evidence for the factors which governed
the recurrence of the Heb Sed.

Scenes of the ceremonial sacrifices of foreign chieftains now
become a regular part of the decoration of the king's funerary
temple. Nyuserre, like Sahure, is represented sometimes as
a griffon, sometimes as a sphinx, trampling upon his enemies.[7]
A statue of a bound prisoner, resembling those in the later temples
of Isesi and Phiops II, was found in his mortuary temple.[8] The
king left a rock-carving recording his visit to the Wādi Maghāra
in Sinai which, as in the case of Sahure and earlier kings, shows
him triumphantly striking down a local chieftain.[9]

Menkauhor (Akauhor), who succeeded Nyuserre, has left
little record except for a rock-inscription at Sinai.[10] His Horus-

---

[1] G, 13, 120–2; §III, 20, 105–6; 8, vol. I, 145.
[2] §III, 6, 109, fig. 88.   [3] §III, 6, 126; G, 36, vol. III, 79.
[4] G, 37, 393, 394.   [5] G, 13, 129.
[6] §III, 2, 3, passim.   [7] §III, 6, 46 ff.; 8, vol. II, pl. 8.
[8] Ibid. 42, fig. 24; §IV, 9, vol. III, pls. 47, 48.
[9] G, 12, pl. VI.   [10] Ibid. pl. VII; G, 41, 54; 14, 182.

name was Menkhau. The Turin Canon assigns him an eight-year reign. The names of his pyramid and sun-temple are known, although neither has been discovered. Since there is a reference to his pyramid in the Dahshūr decree of Phiops I,[1] it has been thought that it was in the neighbourhood of the pyramids of Sneferu. A small alabaster seated figure of the king in Cairo was found at Memphis and shows him wearing the cloak usually associated with the Sed-festival.[2]

Menkauhor was succeeded by Isesi (Djedkare) who seems to have had an even longer reign than the twenty-eight years allotted to him in the Turin Canon. His Horus-name was Djedkhau. It has been established that the account books of the temple of Neferirkare (that is, the Abusīr papyri) belong to this reign,[3] although their entries may continue into the early years of his successor. These papyrus fragments, which have recently been published, give the fourteenth, fifteenth, sixteenth and twenty-first cattle-counts of Isesi, which would indicate a reign of at least forty years for this king. An alabaster vase in the Louvre records the celebration of his first *Heb Sed*.[4] There are records of expeditions in Isesi's reign at the Wādi Maghāra, one dated in the year after his third cattle-count and a second in the ninth (year 17).[5] A letter to Isesi's Vizier Senedjemib Inti is dated probably in the year 31 (*ḥзt sp* 16?).[6]

Inti was thus serving as vizier towards the end of the reign of Isesi. His son, Mehy, completed his father's tomb, very probably in the reign of Unas the next king. He served as vizier to Unas and carried on his father's duties as Overseer of all the King's Works, acting probably with his brother, Khnumenty, who continued under Teti, the first king of the Sixth Dynasty. Nekhebu, who was probably the son of Mehy, mentions in his biographical inscription[7] that he served a considerable apprenticeship under his brother whose name has not been preserved. These two men, therefore, succeeded their father Mehy in the Office of Public Works, although not in the vizierate.[8] Nekhebu, under his second name Meryremerptahankh, appears as leader of an expedition to the Wādi Hammāmāt stone quarries in the thirty-sixth year of Phiops I.[9] He is accompanied by a grown-up son of

---

[1] §II, 3, 1 ff.; G, 1, 212.   [2] G, 43, vol. III, 31, pl. VI, 3.
[3] §II, 4, 210; §III, 9, 8; 10, 43; A, 2.   [4] G, 41, 57.
[5] G, 4, 120; 41, 55, 56; 12, pls. VII, VIII.   [6] G, 41, 63.
[7] G, 41, 215, 219 (cf. Dunham, *J.E.A.* 24 (1938), 1 ff.).
[8] §III, 28, 56.
[9] G, 4, 137; 41, 93. See below, p. 191.

the same name whose intact burial chamber was found at Giza. The son's other name was Impy and he is evidently the Overseer of all the King's Works, Impy, who appears in the temple reliefs of Phiops II.[1] We can thus follow the careers of several generations of master builders in the inscriptions of their family tomb at Giza. The grandfather, Inti, mentions various structures which he planned for the court and reproduces two letters in which King Isesi expressed his pleasure in the work. Nekhebu undertook the construction of canals and devoted six years to a monument at Heliopolis for Phiops I. Mehy describes and pictures the bringing of a limestone sarcophagus for his father from the Tura quarries. This scene provides a parallel to the reliefs in the causeway of Unas' pyramid which show the transport of granite from Aswān for that king's temple. Similarly, the offering lists painted for the first time on the walls of Inti's burial chamber probably reflect the use of the much more elaborate and exclusively royal texts on the walls of the burial apartments of Unas. Pyramid Texts were not yet employed by that king's predecessor Isesi.

Several viziers, in addition to Inti, are known from the reign of Isesi. One, Shepsesre, records a letter from the king in his tomb.[2] He has been singled out as perhaps the earliest holder of the office of Governor of Upper Egypt which was created for the better control of the southern provinces and seems to have been the step in an official's career before attaining the vizierate. It has been noted that none of the viziers of the Fifth Dynasty was a prince and that this fact, coupled with the growing concern to strengthen the government's position in the south, indicates a certain weakening of centralized control which in the Fourth Dynasty had been tightly in the hands of the king's immediate family.

Isesi made use of the diorite quarries in the desert west of Lower Nubia and his name has been found, probably in connexion with one of these expeditions, on the rocks at Tomās in the river valley more than half-way between Aswān and Wādi Halfa.[3] His Chancellor Baurdjeded brought back a dancing dwarf from Punt,[4] and at Byblos part of an alabaster vase inscribed with the king's name (Djedkare) was found.[5]

A number of people connected with the reign of Isesi built their tombs along the north side of the enclosure wall of the Step Pyramid at Saqqara. These people include the Vizier Shepsesre,

[1] §IV, 9, vol. II, pl. 48.   [2] G, 41, 179.   [3] §IV, 17, 9–10.
[4] G, 4, 161.   [5] §IV, 14, 20.

two princes, Isesiankh and Kaemtjenent, and a Queen Meresankh who was probably the mother of these two princes and the wife of Isesi.[1] The king's pyramid has been identified as the first monument of a group, a short distance south of Saqqara, which later included the pyramids of Phiops I and Merenre of the Sixth Dynasty. The excavated material has not yet been published. Although the temple was badly destroyed, it seems to have resembled those of Unas and the kings of the Sixth Dynasty. There were excellent but very fragmentary reliefs and some very remarkable pieces of sculpture in white limestone including figures of bound prisoners, a sphinx, recumbent calves and a lion which formed some sort of a support. Although only the name Djedkare was found in this temple, the name of the pyramid is compounded with that of Djedkare and Isesi interchangeably, and there need be no doubt that they both apply to this king.[2]

Isesi was succeeded by the Horus Wadjtowy, Unas, the last king of the Fifth Dynasty, who had a long reign of thirty years according to the Turin Canon. The chambers and passages inside his pyramid at Saqqara are covered for the first time with long columns of blue incised inscriptions intended to aid the king in the other world. These are known as the Pyramid Texts and they became a regular feature of the tombs of the Sixth Dynasty kings. The complex, with its covered causeway and terraced valley entrance-portico, resembles the temples of the Fifth Dynasty, although the mortuary temple has assumed a more symmetrical and compact plan which was to be followed in the Sixth Dynasty.[3]

The chief queen of Unas was named Nebet. She was buried in a mastaba to the east of the pyramid, adjoining that of another queen called Khenut. Nebet's son, Unasankh, was buried nearby, as was the Vizier Iynefert. A second vizier, Seshatseshemnefer, represented in an, as yet, unpublished relief from the pyramid causeway, is probably the official whose tomb Mariette found long ago in the northern cemetery at Saqqara (no. E 11).[4]

Unas carved a monument on the Island of Elephantine which seems to imply that he visited the southern border, perhaps to receive the Nubian chieftains as was later done by Merenre.[5] In his reliefs, the king pictures ships coming from the quarries at Aswān loaded with the granite columns for his temple.[6] A rare southern animal, the giraffe,[7] is shown on a block which is pos-

---

[1] G, 37, 407.   [2] G, 13, 133.   [3] G, 43, vol. II, 121.
[4] §III, 25, 675; G, 37, 411; §VI, 23, 205; G, 25, 405 (E 11).
[5] G, 41, 69.   [6] §III, 17, 519; 18, 182.
[7] §III, 19; Pl. XIII.

sibly part of a precious series of scenes appearing on other fragments which represent the seasons of the year, like those in Berlin from the sun temple of Nyuserre.

Bearded Asiatics are shown in large ships,[1] perhaps returning from a trading expedition as in the Sahure reliefs. This scene reminds us that stone vase-fragments with the name of Unas were found at Byblos.[2] For the first time a battle scene appears. Egyptians armed with bows and daggers attack bearded foreigners in hand to hand combat.[3] Later, in the Sixth Dynasty, a rock-cut tomb at Dishāsha, south of the entrance to the Faiyūm, shows the confusion around a bearded chief who sits within his fortified enclosure awaiting its fall to the attacking Egyptians. This event seems to have occurred on the north-east of Egypt's frontier. Another Sixth Dynasty scene in a Saqqara tomb represents a similar attack with a scaling ladder upon a stronghold into which the inhabitants have herded their cattle.[4]

The Unas reliefs contrast an emaciated group of men and women in a time of famine[5] with men bartering produce in the market place, craftsmen at work on rich metal objects[6] and the long lines of people bearing food offerings who personify the estates endowed for the king's eternal nourishment. The variety of subject matter displayed in these reliefs typifies the prodigality with which the craftsmen of the Fifth Dynasty have portrayed the life of their time. Although the simple chapels of princes even at the beginning of the Fourth Dynasty give delightful glimpses of daily life, as in the scenes of children playing with animals, and bird-trappers with the famous geese at Maidūm,[7] these informal touches were enormously increased as the Old Kingdom advanced. Just as the inscriptions become more communicative by the insertion of brief biographical texts among the lists of titles, so the wall decorations of the private tombs show men at work in the shops and fields, the life of the river and the swamps, and the pastimes of the upper classes.

IV. THE SIXTH DYNASTY

As in the case of preceding dynastic changes we cannot understand clearly what were the events which brought King Teti to the throne. His Horus-name is Seheteptowy and no second

---

[1] §III, 19, 139; 18, 182.   [2] G, 7, vol. I, 267, 278, 280; 28, 69.
[3] §III, 17, 520, pl. xcv.   [4] §VI, 23, 182, 207, figs. 85, 86.
[5] §III, 12, 45; 30, 29; §VI, 24, 175, pl. 48B.
[6] §III, 17, 520, pl. xcvI; 19, pl. XIII.   [7] §VI, 24, 45.

throne name in a cartouche is known for him. The titles of his wife, Queen Iput, who was also the mother of Phiops I indicate that, like certain other great ladies, she carried the blood royal over into the new dynasty.[1] Whether she was the daughter of Unas is not certain, although it would seem probable. The transition to a new reign does not seem to have left any particular mark. Two of the men who appear in unpublished portions of the Causeway leading to the Unas Pyramid seem to be the same as two persons whom we find associated with Teti. Isesikha appears on a fragment of relief from Teti's temple as High Priest of Heliopolis,[2] while Neferseshemptah built a fine tomb to the north of Teti's pyramid and adopted a second name which incorporated that of the new king.[3] The Vizier Kagemni, a child in the reign of Isesi, became an official under Unas and came into high favour at court in Teti's reign.[4]

The new king built his pyramid some distance to the northeast of that of Userkaf on the edge of the desert plateau at Saqqara.[5] Nearby he constructed pyramids for his chief queen, Iput, and a second queen Khuit. A third queen, Seshseshet, appears on a small piece of the king's very fragmentary temple reliefs.[6] She seems to have belonged to an older generation since the wives of a number of court officials were named after her. Unfortunately it is not possible to identify the person represented by the plaster death-mask found in the Teti temple.[7]

Teti's name occurs on stone vase fragments found at Byblos.[8] An alabaster jar of this king shows a female personification of Punt. It comes from Reisner's excavation of a provincial tomb at Naga ed-Deir and is in the collection of the University of California at Berkeley; the lid is inscribed with the titulary of Unas.[9] A record of one of Teti's missions to the south seems to appear among the names of the officials at Tomās in Nubia.[10] Teti set up a decree in the temple of Abydos establishing certain exemptions in regard to the temple lands.[11]

The year after the sixth cattle-count of Teti, recorded in a rock-inscription at the Het-nub alabaster quarries, would suggest that he reigned for at least twelve years.[12] He was followed, according to the Abydos List, by a king named Userkare whose identi-

---

[1] G, 41, 214; 36, vol. III, 84.   [2] §IV, 15, 19, pl. LIV; G, 37, 395.
[3] G, 36, vol. III, 133.   [4] G, 41, 194.   [5] G, 43, vol. II, 128.
[6] §IV, 15, 19, pl. LIV; §VI, 25, 202, pl. 54a.
[7] §IV, 15, pl. LV.   [8] G, 7, 258; 33, 20.
[9] Mitt. deutsch. Inst. Kairo, 20 (1965), 35, fig. 86.
[10] §IV, 17, 10.   [11] G, 41, 207.   [12] G, 2, pl. 9.

fication with the king Iti who left an inscription in the Wādi Hammāmāt rests on too slender grounds to be acceptable.[1] The monuments indicate that the real successor of Teti was Phiops I, the son of queen Iput, whom Phiops mentions in a decree concerning her ka-chapel in the temple of Koptos.[2] Userkare seems to have had an ephemeral reign. If Phiops were a child when his father died, it may have been that Userkare briefly occupied the throne while Iput was acting as regent for her son.

At the beginning of his reign Phiops I called himself Nefersahor, but later changed this to Meryre. His Horus-name was Merytowy. He had a long reign which is documented by a number of records from his later years. An inscription in the Het-nub quarries was cut in the time of his twenty-fifth cattle-count (year 49)[3] and he may have dated his reign from the death of his father, Teti, ignoring Userkare. One of his early expeditions left three inscriptions with his name Nefersahor on the rocks at Tomās in Nubia[4] and at the Wādi Maghāra Phiops is shown vanquishing the Asiatics of Sinai in the year after the eighteenth cattle-count (year 36). In the same year a descendant of the Giza Senedjemib family who has already been mentioned (p. 186), Meryremerptahankh, left a record at the Hammāmāt quarries[5] in which he is represented with a grown son of the same name. Both inscriptions mention the king's first Sed-festival. We have already mentioned the Dahshūr decree in the year 41 (h3t sp 21) in which Phiops I was concerned with protecting the endowments of the two pyramids of Sneferu.[6] In the Delta, at Bubastis, a badly damaged temple of the king has been cleared.[7] Phiops I constructed his pyramid near that of Isesi, a short distance south of Saqqara.[8] The temple has not been excavated, as in the case of his successor Merenre whose tomb is close by, although both pyramids have been opened and their texts copied.

A stela found at Abydos represents two queens of Phiops I who, most confusingly, bear the same name: Meryreankhnes.[9] The inscription tells us that one of these women was the mother of Phiops' successor, Merenre, and the other the mother of Phiops II. They are shown with their brother Djau who became vizier. The ladies are mentioned again with Djau in a decree concerning their statues which was set up in the temple of Abydos by Phiops II. Here they are called the mothers of Merenre and Phiops II again and with the names of the two kings' pyramids

---

[1] G, 41, 148. [2] Ibid. 214. [3] Ibid. 95.
[4] Ibid. 208. [5] Ibid. 91, 93. [6] Ibid. 209. [7] §iv, 8.
[8] G, 43, vol. ii, 132. [9] §iv, 7, 95; 3, pl. 24; G, 41, 117.

combined with their cartouches.[1] The titles of the father and
mother of Djau and his sisters indicate that they were not of
royal birth but belonged to the provincial nobility of the Thinite
Nome. Merenre appointed one of the family, a certain Ibi who
was perhaps the son of Djau, as Governor of the Province of the
Cerastes Mountain (the Twelfth Nome of Upper Egypt). There
in the cliffs of Deir el-Gabrāwi the family cut their tombs during
the following reigns.[2] Evidently Phiops I made a political marriage which secured the allegiance of a powerful provincial family.

Uni, on his monument at Abydos,[3] recounts that as a youth he
served in minor offices under Teti. He became a judge under
Phiops I and was firmly established at court. He was particularly
proud of having been summoned by the king to conduct alone
an inquiry against a queen who is not named but is referred to by
her title *wrt ḥts*. Naturally one suspects that this putting aside of
the chief queen was immediately connected with the marriage
to the mother of Merenre. In view of the extreme youth of
Phiops II at his accession, Phiops I probably married the second
sister very late in his reign. The name Meryreankhnes was
presumably given to each wife at the time of her marriage.

Uni also organized an expedition against the nomads of the
north-east. He recruited an army from all parts of Egypt and
from the Nubian tribes in the south. It is evidently Nubian
mercenaries of this kind who are the subject of clauses in the
Dahshūr decree of Phiops I which restrict their privileges. In
spite of Uni's hymn of victory upon the return of the army, an
uprising necessitated a second raid on the 'sand dwellers'. This
was followed by a campaign into southern Palestine which involved the transport of troops by ship to a place called Antelope
Nose which is thought to be the promontory of Mount Carmel.[4]

There are two indications that towards the end of his reign
Phiops I may have associated with himself as co-regent his son
Merenre (who was also called Antyemsaf, with the Horus-name
Ankhkhau). One is a gold skirt-pendant in Cairo which bears the
names and titles of the two kings.[5] The other is the Hieraconpolis
copper statue-group which shows Phiops I with a smaller figure
beside him that probably represents Merenre.[6] There are two
dated inscriptions known from the reign of Merenre, one at the
Het-nub alabaster quarries, which is damaged but appears to be
dated in the year after his fifth cattle-count (year 10),[7] and the

[1] G, 41, 278.   [2] §iv, 5; G, 4, 169.
[3] G, 4, 134, 140, 146; 41, 98.   [4] §vi, 18, 227–8.
[5] §iv, 6, 55.   [6] §vi, 24, 80.   [7] G, 41, 256.

other at the First Cataract in the year of his fifth count (year 9). The latter inscription of the year 9 records the occasion when the king received the Nubian chieftains on the southern border.[1] If Merenre had been serving as co-regent with his father it is unlikely that he would have dated such a monument until after his accession to the throne, although he might well have begun counting the years of his reign from the time when he became co-regent. A state visit to inspect the southern border soon after his father's death would seem a reasonable action to take upon becoming sole ruler. Merenre may thus have become co-regent in the fortieth year of his father's reign and the fourteen years usually restored in the Turin Canon for his own reign would include this co-regency and the five years that he reigned alone. It seems absurd to suggest a co-regency with the infant Phiops II at the end of the reign of his brother Merenre but a cylinder seal of an official with both their names enclosed in a double Horus-frame is difficult to explain in any other way.[2]

It has been stated that Merenre was only a youth when he died. The sarcophagus in his pyramid contained a well-preserved body of a young man of medium height still wearing the adolescent side-lock of hair. Elliot Smith was convinced that this mummy was prepared in the fashion of the Eighteenth Dynasty and could not be earlier, concluding that it was an intrusive burial.[3] The wrappings had been torn from the body. Since pieces of the linen bandages and parts of the bodies of Unas, Teti and Phiops I still survived when their pyramids were opened[4] perhaps the evidence with regard to the body from Merenre's pyramid should be re-examined.

The government's interest in the south, symbolized by the occasion when the Nubian chiefs assembled to kiss the ground before Merenre, is evidenced in other ways. Uni continued in service under Merenre and made two expeditions to the First Cataract to fetch a sarcophagus and bring stone for the king's pyramid. During the first of these trips he spent a year cutting five canals and building transport ships while the granite was being quarried. We also find Harkhuf established as Governor of Elephantine[5] and commencing the trading expeditions in the south which he describes in his rock-cut tomb in the cliffs opposite Aswān. These long trips were made partly by river and partly by donkey caravan to bring back incense, ivory, ebony, oil and

[1] G, 4, 145; 41, 110.   [2] §IV, 4, 40.   [3] §IV, 18, 204.
[4] See references to these early reports G, 36, vol. III, 84, 89, 90.
[5] G, 4, 150, 159; 41, 120.

panther skins, all products much prized in Egypt. It has been noted that gold is not yet mentioned and it is probable that it could still be mined in sufficient quantity in the desert east of Koptos. Although it has been questioned whether these expeditions could have reached so far into the south,[1] broken alabaster vases with the names of Phiops I, Merenre and Phiops II have been found at Kerma in the Sudan, and Reisner believed that an Egyptian trading post was already established there in the Sixth Dynasty.[2]

Merenre's name does not occur in Sinai or at Byblos, although numerous broken stone vessels with the names of Phiops I and Phiops II have been found at the Syrian port.[3] One of the expedition leaders at Aswān, whose tomb cannot be dated precisely to a reign in the Sixth Dynasty, refers in such a way to voyages to Byblos and Punt[4] as to suggest that they occurred regularly in the Sixth Dynasty.

Uni, the trusted official of Phiops I, Djau, the brother of his two queens, and Harkhuf, the Nomarch of Elephantine, seem to have been the chief supporters of the throne during the reign of Merenre. Uni, as Governor of Upper Egypt, was given special powers over all twenty-two Upper Egyptian nomes. This title was held by nomarchs whose jurisdiction does not seem to have extended beyond their provinces. Uni's unusual position was repeated in the case of Shemay in the Eighth Dynasty who, before becoming vizier, is mentioned as controlling the twenty-two Upper Egyptian nomes when he was Governor of Upper Egypt.[5] An additional curb seems to have been placed on certain local families who had come to consider the position of nomarch as an hereditary right. Qar was sent to Edfu under Merenre as nomarch and Governor of Upper Egypt,[6] while the control of the Seventh (Thinite) Nome was extended to the Twelfth when Ibi, a relative and probably the son of the Vizier Djau, was made governor of both provinces. Ibi and his son and grandson held the title of Governor of Upper Egypt, as did Harkhuf at Aswān.[7] In spite of the signs of growing wealth and power at such provincial centres as Cusae (Meir), it was upon the men who conducted its foreign trade, the nomarchs of Elephantine, that the government chiefly relied until the end of the Sixth Dynasty.

Phiops II (Neferkare; Horus-name Netjerkhau) seems to have been the child of his father's old age. Manetho tells us that he

---

[1] §iv, 17, 36, 106.   [2] §iv, 16.

[3] G, 7, vol. i, pls. xxxvi–xxxix; 28, 68–75, pls. xxxix–xli; 33, 20–1.

[4] G, 41, 140.   [5] §v, 4, 3.

[6] G, 41, 252.   [7] *Ibid.* 120, 142, 145.

came to the throne at the age of six and lived to be one hundred. The king's well-known letter to Harkhuf shows the delighted pleasure of a child in the gift of a dancing dwarf which was being brought to him by the caravan leader,[1] a marvel which had not been seen since the time of his ancestor Isesi. Manetho's reign of ninety-four years for Phiops II has been generally accepted and we know of another centenarian of the time in Pepiankh of Meir.[2] The fiftieth cattle-count (year 99) was formerly believed to be inscribed on a badly weathered decree set up by Phiops in the temple of Mycerinus but upon re-examination it would appear that the thirty-first count is the more probable reading (year 61).[3] The highest dates are the somewhat doubtful year 65 (ḥȝt sp 33?) of a decree in the chapel of Queen Udjebten,[4] and the year after the thirty-first count (year 62) at the Het-nub quarries.[5] The king certainly had a very long reign and celebrated a second Sed-festival. The Turin Canon gives a broken figure of at least ninety years to support Manetho's statement.

The magnificent funerary monument of Phiops II, which is comparable in size, quality of decoration, and display of the power of the royal house with that of the Fifth Dynasty king, Sahure, gives no indication of the collapse which was to come.[6] Nevertheless the long reign spelled the end of the Old Kingdom. The growth of the provincial nobility in Upper Egypt coincided with a gradual equalization of wealth. What had once been crown-lands were broken into smaller and smaller units through a widening circle of inheritance. The immense constructions undertaken at royal expense and the innumerable funerary endowments exempt from taxation had exhausted the king's resources. The diminished power of the royal family makes itself sharply felt at the close of the reign.

Phiops II continued the foreign trade of his predecessors, the expeditions to the Sinai mines and the quarrying operations. There are perhaps some indications of increased restlessness abroad. Hekayeb[7] had to be sent out from Aswān to put down the Nubians in the south where an inter-tribal disturbance had nearly interfered with Harkhuf's third expedition. Sabni[8] tells us in his tomb at Aswān that he hurried forth to recover the body of his father who had been killed on a caravan trip. Hekayeb made a similar trip to the Red Sea to bring back the body of an officer

---

[1] G, 4, 161.   [2] §IV, 2, vol. IV, 24.

[3] Further study makes this reading virtually certain as against the thirty-fifth count §II, 43, 113, fig. 1; see Plate 33 (a).

[4] G, 41, 274.   [5] G, 2, pl. XII.

[6] §IV, 9.   [7] G, 4, 162.   [8] Ibid. 166.

whose party had been attacked by nomads while building ships for an expedition to Punt.

A long succession of some eight or ten men followed Djau in the vizierate, two of whom,[1] at about the middle of the reign, are shown leading processions of courtiers in a room of the funerary temple. Three queens, Neith, Iput and Udjebten, were buried in pyramids beside that of the king. From a decree set up in the chapel of Queen Neith[2] in the accession year of an unknown successor of Phiops II, and from the other inscriptions in her chapel, we learn that Neith was the eldest daughter of Phiops I and Meryreankhnes, the mother of Merenre. A fourth queen of Phiops II was named Pepiankhnes. Her coffin, which had originally been prepared for some other purpose in the reign of Phiops I, has been found together with fragments of a false door which indicate that she was the mother of a king Neferkare[3] who is now thought to have been the first king of the Seventh Dynasty. The name of his pyramid differs from that of Phiops II who, as we have seen, was also called Neferkare. Phiops II is followed in the Abydos List by a Merenre who was also called Antyemsaf and must not be confused with the earlier and more important Merenre. The name is broken off in the Turin Canon, where the length of reign is given as one year. This Merenre is evidently the eldest surviving son of Phiops II, Antyemsaf, who is mentioned on a stela found near the chapel of Queen Neith.[4] His name can now be read on the badly worn decree of Phiops II in Boston which is concerned with the pyramid town of Mycerinus at Giza.[5]

With Merenre Antyemsaf II we have evidently reached the troubled time known as the First Intermediate Period but two kings who follow in the Abydos List have also been assigned to Dynasty VI.[6] The name of Netjerykare may have occupied the next broken space in the Turin Canon which continues with a Nitocris who is thought to be the Menkare of the Abydos List. The suggestion that this identity can be supported by a royal cartouche[7] in an inscription in Queen Neith's chapel is not borne out by close examination on the spot. The hieroglyphs were damaged but probably formed the name of Neferkare (Phiops II). A vertical sign not apparent in the published photographs seems to be *nfr* and precludes reading Menkare. There is thus not sufficient evidence to associate Neith with that Nitocris to whom we have seen later legend ascribed the building

---

1 §IV, 9, vol. II, pls. 48, 57; 12, 39.   2 §IV, 10, 5.   3 *Ibid.* 50.
4 *Ibid.* 55.   5 See Plate 33 (a).
6 See *C.A.H.* I³, ch. VI, sect. I.   7 §V, 9, 51; §IV, 10, pls. IV, V.

of the Third Pyramid at Giza.[1] It is a pity, for it seemed a happy idea to bring the name Nitocris of the Turin Canon and Manetho's account of an Old Kingdom queen into conjunction with the wife of the last great king of the time. Around her chapel have survived the few vestiges of contemporaneous record that exist at present for the end of the Sixth Dynasty.

V. THE SEVENTH AND EIGHTH DYNASTIES

Manetho's statement that the Seventh Dynasty consisted of seventy kings who ruled for seventy days has usually been interpreted as representing a brief period of strife which left no record for later times. The Turin Canon has only preserved the length of reign and no name for any king of the Sixth Dynasty, except the last ruler Nitocris. A new placing of the fragment containing the names of Nitocris and three followers, the last of which is Ibi of the Eighth Dynasty, now allows for two blank spaces between Ibi and the summary of kings who ruled after Menes at the beginning of the First Dynasty. W. C. Hayes has equated these kings with five of the Abydos List (nos. 51–5). With the addition of Abydos no. 56, he suggests that they formed six rulers of the Eighth Dynasty. The Turin Canon omits no. 56 and nine kings of the Abydos List (nos. 42–50) which Hayes would assign to the Seventh Dynasty. His chronological table allows twenty-one years for the time between the end of the Sixth Dynasty and the beginning of the Ninth Dynasty, eight years for the Seventh Dynasty and thirteen years for the Eighth Dynasty. In the past, some forty or fifty years have been assigned to the Eighth Dynasty and the Seventh Dynasty has been disregarded as ephemeral. It must be remembered that most of these kings are known only from the Abydos List; it is one of the darkest periods of Egyptian history, when contemporaneous records are at an absolute minimum.

We have seen that the name of the first king of the Seventh Dynasty (according to this new arrangement), Neferkare II, was recovered from the fragments of a stela found in one of the rooms of the chapel of Queen Iput, which adjoined the pyramid of Queen Neith beside the tomb of their husband Phiops II.[2] King Kakare Ibi of the Eighth Dynasty is also known from a monument in the Memphite region. He built a small pyramid not far from that of Phiops II. This pyramid contained the usual Pyramid Texts in the burial chamber, thus continuing the tradi-

[1] See above, p. 179.   [2] §IV, 10, 53.

8

tion established at the end of the Fifth Dynasty. However, the pyramid had not been cased with stone and was not provided with a mortuary chapel. The unfinished character of the structure, which is the only building known at present from this period, again testifies to the unstable character of the royal house.[1]

In Upper Egypt a series of decrees found in the Temple of Koptos were long thought to provide evidence for a local dynasty at that place. It now seems clear that these decrees were issued by the last kings of the Eighth Dynasty at Memphis[2] to two powerful men at Koptos, Shemay and his son Idi, who in turn held successively the offices of Nomarch of Koptos, Governor of Upper Egypt and Vizier. Shemay married the eldest daughter of Neferkauhor, the fifth and penultimate king of the Eighth Dynasty. This family at Koptos would thus have formed the chief support of the weak kings at Memphis, and it was under the last of these, the Horus Demedjibtowy, that Heracleopolis revolted successfully and brought the Old Kingdom to an end. As in the case of a dynasty of Koptos there is insufficient evidence to support the proposal that an Upper Egyptian dynasty centred at Abydos is indicated by the names of kings given only in the Abydos List.[3] In connexion with the cemetery of Abydos, where the monuments of the family of the Vizier Djau and his two sisters were set up in the Sixth Dynasty and where the temple of Khentiamentiu–Osiris had contained the decrees of the Memphite rulers of the later Old Kingdom, we must remember that there was another important cemetery in the Thinite nome. This was at Naga ed-Deir downstream from Abydos and Beit Khallāf and on the east bank of the Nile across the river from Girga, near which was probably the site of the old city of This, the capital of the province. In the Sixth Dynasty, from the time of Merenre into the first part of the reign of Phiops II, this province had been governed from Deir el-Gabrāwi in the Twelfth Nome by Ibi and his two sons whom Merenre had put in control of both the Seventh and Twelfth Nomes. It has been pointed out that this was made easier by the fact that Uni was controlling the south as Governor of Upper Egypt from This which served as his base. In the Fifth Dynasty and again in the Sixth Dynasty, after the régime of Ibi's successors, officials are now known who were nomarchs of This but who lived at court and were buried in the Memphite cemeteries.[4]

In contrast to this earlier situation two governors of the Thinite

[1] §v, 5.   [2] §v, 4, 3.   [3] §v, 15, *passim*; G, 6, 235–7.
[4] See Fischer, *J.A.O.S.* 74 (1954), 26–34.

nome, Tjamerery and Hagy,[1] are known at the end of the Old Kingdom, probably in the Seventh or the Eighth Dynasty, who were buried in the old Thinite Cemetery at Naga ed-Deir. This cemetery had been in use since predynastic times and a rich set of gold jewellery was found in a tomb of the First Dynasty there.[2] Other officials of the end of the Old Kingdom, who are known from the paintings and inscriptions in their rock-cut tombs at Naga ed-Deir and the characteristic rectangular stelae set up in simpler chapels, were priests of Onuris whose cult had been established from early times in his temple at This.[3] It has been observed that the titles of several of these men, including the two nomarchs, show them to have been loyal supporters of the crown, although rather vaguely connected with affairs at court. This is a situation that would be understandable in the Seventh and Eighth Dynasties with the king at Memphis, whereas the whole relationship of Naga ed-Deir with Abydos would seem impossible if we postulated a local dynasty ruling at This. In this connexion the interesting speculation has been put forward that it may well have been the cemetery of This at Naga ed-Deir and not that at Abydos which was pillaged during the struggles between Heracleopolis and Thebes that occurred soon afterwards.[4]

The Thinite nome, its cemetery at Abydos long revered for its association with the kings of the First Dynasty and now at the end of the Old Kingdom a place of pilgrimage to the shrine of Osiris who had been assimilated with the ancient local god of the dead Khentiamentiu, was undoubtedly of more importance politically than some of the other sites in Upper Egypt where cemeteries of the local notables are known from the First Intermediate Period. This is true even of Dendera where, as at Naga ed-Deir, enough material has been excavated to suggest a sequence of known persons extending from the Sixth Dynasty through the difficult period of the collapse of central authority at Memphis and the setting up of petty local government in the different provinces.[5] Thebes, which was soon to assume such importance, was still a backward village in the later Old Kingdom. The few monuments of its important men may be briefly noted. The earliest is a fragment of relief from the tomb of a Governor of Upper Egypt named Unasankh.[6] A small painted rock-cut chapel of Ihy and his wife[7] is now known to adjoin a somewhat

[1] §vi, 23, 89, 222, 226. Tomb nos. 248, 89.   [2] §vi, 24, 27.
[3] §v, 2, *passim*.   [4] §v, 10, 133 and *passim*.   [5] §v, 3, *passim*.   [6] §v, 18, 1.
[7] §v, 8, 97; G, 36, vol. I, 152 (no. 186; no. 185, Seniiker is only listed in A. Weigall, *A Topographical Catalogue of Private Tombs at Thebes* (1913), 32).

larger tomb belonging to an official named Khenti.[1] Ihy and Khenti were both Overlords of Thebes but do not mention the name of the province in their inscriptions. A tomb nearby (no. 185) had an inscribed pillar with the figure of a 'Chancellor of the God' or expedition leader called Seniiker.

More interesting information can be derived from three tombs in the region between Thebes and Aswān. The only one of these which seems to belong properly to this period is that of Setka discovered in recent years at Aswān in a fine position high up in the western promontory overlooking the island of Elephantine where the important people of the Sixth Dynasty had hewn their rock tombs. Setka was a priest of the Pyramid of Phiops II and must at least have begun his career in the Eighth Dynasty.[2] Another of these tombs was made for Iti at Gebelein south of Thebes[3] and Armant on the west bank of the Nile, while the third belonged to Ankhtify at El-Mi'alla, across the river and a little further south. The paintings in these three chapels bear remarkably close stylistic similarities to one another. This has suggested that no great length of time separated Setka from the other two men. However, with Iti and Ankhtify we have reached a time at the end of the Ninth Dynasty just before the rise of Thebes under the Inyotef family when the royal house of Heracleopolis was established in the north. Setka is our last connexion in the south with the old Memphite Royal House. It is fitting that the paintings in his tomb should anticipate a new style to be developed in the Ninth Dynasty while at the same time forming a link with the end of the Old Kingdom.

VI. LITERATURE AND ART

The collapse of the Old Kingdom is mirrored in a pessimistic literature which would have been foreign to the spirit and thought of the times that had gone before. Nothing could be further from the earlier idea of material success gained by the shrewd employment of a man's abilities in a well-ordered society than the lamentations and prophecies of Ipuwer.[4] This work seems to be nearer to the troubled times which it describes than similar compositions which belong more properly to the literature of the Middle Kingdom. Ipuwer bewails the break-down of law and order and represents a people who were the prey of violence, even the dead

---

[1] Information communicated by H. G. Fischer who discovered this tomb.
[2] §VI, 24, 84.   [3] *Ibid.*   [4] §VI, 6, 92; 18, 441.

in their tombs being subject to vicious pillage. High-born ladies are clothed in rags, the official is insulted and the peasant tills his field with a shield to defend himself from the marauder. Foreigners have strayed into the Delta. Servant girls and slaves flaunt the possession of valuables of which they cannot comprehend the use. Ships no longer sail to Byblos and, in the absence of foreign trade, one is delighted even to see people from the Oases with paltry things to barter.

The precepts of the society which we see here in ruins are embodied in two compositions which, although in their present form of a later date, seem to have their origin in the Old Kingdom. These are the 'Admonitions to the Vizier Kagemni'[1] which were ascribed to the time of King Huni at the end of the Third Dynasty, and the 'Instruction of Ptahhotpe'[2] who is called a vizier of King Isesi of the Fifth Dynasty. Both consist of practical advice on how to get on in the world, and particularly on how to behave in the presence of equals or those who are superiors or inferiors. They lay emphasis upon good manners and upon truth and justice. The 'Instruction of Ptahhotpe' points out the advantage that the gift of eloquence can bring to a man. Nowhere is there a suspicion of doubt as to the permanence of the stable world in which these precepts are to be applied.

Literary documents which are actually contemporaneous with the Old Kingdom are limited in number and are restricted almost entirely to brief biographical inscriptions, and the great body of religious literature known as the Pyramid Texts.[3] Of actual writing upon papyrus there is little more than the accounts of the temple of Neferirkare which were probably largely prepared in the reign of Isesi,[4] and some fragmentary papyri which consist of family archives of the Sixth Dynasty nomarchs of Elephantine. One of the letters from these Elephantine archives has been translated.[5] There is also a letter, probably of the reign of Phiops II, which was written by an indignant officer in charge of gangs of workmen in the Tura quarries objecting to the waste of time involved in bringing his men to Memphis for an issue of new clothing.[6] In the preceding pages have been mentioned several letters from a king which the owner of a tomb has proudly caused to be copied on the stone wall of his chapel. Similarly, certain royal decrees have survived which were inscribed on stelae set up in temples. These inscriptions have also been listed under the reigns to which they belong.

[1] §vi, 6, 66; 8, 71; 11. [2] §vi, 6, 54; 11; 18, 412. [3] §vi, 20.
[4] §ii, 4, 209; §iii, 9, 8; 10, 43; A, 2. [5] §vi, 28, 16. [6] §vi, 7, 75.

The great series of utterances which were inscribed for the first time on the walls of the burial apartments of Unas, the last king of the Fifth Dynasty, continued to be so used throughout the rest of the Old Kingdom[1] and formed the basis for the Coffin Texts of the Middle Kingdom and the later Book of the Dead. They incorporate elements of ancient kingly ritual as well as the early religious beliefs from both Upper Egypt and the Delta which had been assembled to form the doctrine of the Heliopolitan priesthood of the creator sun-god Atum-Re. Juxtaposed with these are the beliefs which eventually were to promise even the ordinary man resurrection through Osiris. This god, as one of the forces of nature, personified the growth of plant life through the stimulus of the life-giving water of the Nile. He was also identified with Andjeti the local royal hero of Busiris in the Delta and therefore embodied kingship. Finally he was assimilated with the protecting deity of the necropolis of Abydos, Khentiamentiu, who in his jackal form was related to the old god of the dead, Anubis.

The chief purpose of the magical spells of the Pyramid Texts was to make it possible for the dead king to take his place among the gods and to become one with Re, their leader. Primarily this was imagined as coming to pass in the sky but glimpses may also be caught of a different view of the afterlife due to that aspect of Osiris which was to make him the ruler of a gloomy underworld in which the dead must dwell. To this would be transferred the pleasant fields and thickets of reeds which at first were thought of as being in the heavens. Although the texts are difficult to understand one cannot fail to be stirred by the breadth and sweep of the early conception of a bright celestial afterworld in which the dead become the indestructible stars. The spells exhaust every possible means by which can be assured the king's ascent to the sky. Through an earlier imagery this was formed by the outstretched wings and bright plumed body of the falcon Horus whose eyes were the sun and the moon. Various winged forms of ascent are evoked as well as steps and ramps. To this conception, one would think, is related the daring creation of soaring structures in pyramidal form for the royal tombs of the Old Kingdom. The king's reception by the gods is pictured, as well as the moment when he takes his place in the sun-barque of Re. Nothing must be allowed to stand in his way and the savage ruthlessness of purpose reaches its ultimate conclusion in a famous cannibalistic text in which the king is portrayed as devouring the gods that he may become possessed of their most potent powers.

[1] §vi, 20; cf. R. O. Faulkner, *The Ancient Egyptian Pyramid Texts*, Oxford, 1969.

The literary form of this extraordinary assemblage of material betrays the Egyptian's partiality for expressing himself by repetitive and balanced statement.[1] The reiteration may have been thought to add potency to the spell and need not always have been a literary device. This parallelism receives varied treatment but presents most frequently a second line repeating the same idea with slightly altered wording. A form in which the same phrase is repeated in every alternate line is frequently found and is used in the hymn of victory which appears in the Sixth Dynasty biography of Uni.[2] The Pyramid Texts exhibit another dominant Egyptian trait, the tendency to assemble an accumulated mass of material without synthesis. Contradictions are not resolved but presented side by side. A deeply ingrained sense of tradition prevented the Egyptian from discarding material which to us may appear discordant. Old beliefs that went back to the earliest religious impulses of the country were incorporated into the Heliopolitan solar doctrine and these again were overlaid with the newer Osirian beliefs. The language employed is archaic. Sethe placed the compilation of the texts in prehistoric times, but present opinion supports Kees who argues in favour of a time between the Third and Fifth Dynasties.[3] The private tombs about the middle of the Fifth Dynasty begin to reflect the popular effect of the Osirian beliefs, while the Heliopolitan doctrine of Re reached its ascendancy as a state cult somewhat earlier. Thus both were in evidence before the first known copies of the Pyramid Texts begin to appear.

The compilation of religious lore in the Pyramid Texts is a characteristic Egyptian expression of what was perhaps the greatest achievement of the Old Kingdom. This was the establishment of a system of very detailed and enduring records which, as a result of the close relationship between writing and representation, are as much pictorial as they are literary. The beautifully drawn and attractively conceived hieroglyphs, which represent the sound values of the speech of the time and determine the sense of the words, are minor masterpieces in themselves. We tend to overlook this in our interest in the ideas expressed and in our frequent irritation at the laconic nature of such expression which is in some part due to our ignorance of the subtleties of meaning as well as to the fragmentary nature of the material as it has come down to us. It is fairly easy to grasp the significance of the huge architectural monuments and the remarkable portrayal of the people of the period in sculptural representation, or to be charmed

[1] §vi, 9, 5.   [2] §vi, 18, 228.   [3] G, 22, 214–70.

by the glimpses of daily life that appear in the multitude of wall-reliefs in the funerary chapels. We have been slower in sensing the ingenuity of the development which lies behind the great cycles of scenes which covered the walls of the funerary temples of Userkaf and Sahure, largely owing to the lamentable state of preservation of these first surviving examples. But we must realize that the same mental vigour and sense of organization as the ancient Egyptians applied to the construction of the Great Pyramid entered into this presentation of the vital aspects of the king's worldly life and his association with the gods.

In discussing the reign of Neferirkare attention was called to the apparent increase in the production of detailed records in the Fifth Dynasty. The royal annals, the account books of the Temple of Neferirkare and the more specific nature of the information supplied by biographical texts were cited, together with the elaborate picturing of the renewal of kingship in the *Heb Sed* scenes and the activities of the seasons of the year in the sun-temple of Nyuserre. The seasons of the year were portrayed in the so-called 'Weltkammer', a long narrow room which formed the last section of the corridor which bounded the court of this sun-temple and led to the ramp inside the base of the obelisk, the focal point of the monument. The recent publication[1] of several key pieces of this fragmentary composition, which has intrigued scholars for half a century, makes it possible to suggest something more specific concerning its general arrangement. Evidently the whole scheme was repeated in more or less exact duplicate on the long east and west walls. It consisted of large figures in human form personifying two of the three periods into which the year was divided, Akhet and Shemu, each preceded by registers of figures representing the provinces of Upper and Lower Egypt.[2] At the top of the wall, above the nomes of Upper Egypt, appeared processions of similar personifications of such entities as the Nile, the Sea, Grain and Nourishment. All brought their offerings to Re. Behind each figure of the season, a larger space, divided into horizontal sections of varying height by strips of water, was devoted to portraying the activities of the appro-

[1] §III, 4, 319; 21, 33.

[2] §III, 15, 129. Hermann Kees kindly allowed H. G. Fischer and myself to study a number of small, but important pieces, which still remain unpublished. Steffen Wenig's new work on the original stones in Berlin suggests that only two of the three seasons, Akhet and Shemu, were shown. See also E. Edel's studies, *Nachr. Göttingen*, No. 8 (1961), 209–55; Nos. 4–5, (1963), 89–217; tentative reconstruction in W. S. Smith, *Interconnections in the Ancient Near East*, New Haven, 1965, pp. 141 ff., figs. 176–83.

priate time of year. Akhet was shown as a woman, corresponding with the feminine ending of the name. Shemu was a male figure bearing on his head a sheaf of the ripened grain of his harvest time. Akhet is distinguished by a pool of lotus signifying the inundation. The three seasons, without their attributes, are shown as seated figures on a board which Mereruka is painting on a kind of easel in a relief in his chapel at Saqqara.[1]

In the sections devoted to the activities of the seasons much space is allotted to animals, occasionally interspersed with small figures of huntsmen, in a habitat which is treated naturalistically like the fishing and other swamp pursuits. Such representations and the peculiar, formally arranged, groups of birds and plants with their names attached are of too general a nature to assign to a particular time of year. The capture of song birds in an orchard appeared again in the court of the temple of Userkaf, in the temple of Sahure, in several private tomb chapels, and in the picturing of the Seasons in the causeway of Unas and in the Valley Temple of Nyuserre.[2] This subject could probably be attributed to a specific time of year, as could the propagation of animals, nesting birds, bee-keeping and agricultural activities. However, connecting these various fragmentary parts with others which actually join with a portion of one of the personifications of a season may prove a puzzle that defies satisfactory solution, in view of the duplication of so many of the elements. Nevertheless it is clear, as it has been since these reliefs were first discovered, that we have here one of man's most interesting early attempts to put into orderly sequence the various elements of his environment. In its peculiar combination of the specific and the general, the naturalistic and the formal, this production is characteristic of Egyptian method in the Old Kingdom. Like the Giza writing board[3] with its lists of kings, gods, place-names (more correctly, estates) and hieroglyphs of birds and fish,[4] the 'seasons' are in a sense related to the Onomastica of the later Egyptian scribes.

Frequent mention has been made in the preceding pages of the architecture, sculpture, painting and minor arts of the Old Kingdom because the relation which art bore to the funerary beliefs of the ancient Egyptian makes his tomb-monuments the basis of much of our historical evidence. Although the Third Dynasty

[1] §vi, 23, 355, fig. 231.
[2] §vi, 24, 46, 68; 23, 178; §iii, 6, 38, fig. 17; 8, vol. ii, pl. 15.
[3] §G, 38, 113; §vi, 23, 358; a less elaborate example giving only place-names exists in the Boston Museum of Fine Arts, no. 13–4–301.
[4] See Plate 31 (a).

was still a period of experimentation it is clear from the architecture, reliefs and statue-fragments of Djoser and the carved wooden panels and wall paintings of Hesyre, that a great measure of technical proficiency had been attained.[1] The sculptor in the Fourth Dynasty reached the goal towards which he was striving. The statues of Redjedef, Chephren and Mycerinus present an ideal of kingly majesty which still retains human individuality. Everything superficial has been eliminated. The modelling is superb but simplified. The sculptor is completely master of his material. The same simplification of natural forms is consummately expressed in the Cairo statues of Rehotpe and Nefert, the Boston Ankhhaf bust, the Hildesheim seated statue of Hemiunu and the portrait heads of white limestone from the Giza burial chambers.[2]

We need expect no more from the painter's skill than is to be found in the Maidūm wall-paintings of the reign of Sneferu.[3] Although the fragility of the medium makes it difficult to follow out a series of examples from the few traces that remain, the same excellence was maintained in the best work as late as the painted reliefs of Phiops II. The large-scale simplicity of the Maidūm paintings is reflected in the bold stone reliefs of the reign of Sneferu,[4] a style which, with some modifications, continues into the Fourth Dynasty and recurs again in the Sixth Dynasty as best exemplified by the reliefs of the chapel of Mereruka and the temple of Phiops II.[5] A delicate low relief of superlative quality, which seems to have its origin in the time of Djoser, is found side by side with the higher relief style in a few Giza chapels of the reign of Cheops and Chephren and in the royal reliefs of the Fourth Dynasty and early Fifth Dynasty.[6]

After the early part of the Fifth Dynasty, the large scale of the preceding period diminished, both in the making of statues and in architecture. On the other hand, every branch of the crafts felt the effects of the large body of skilled workmen trained in the great projects of the Fourth Dynasty pyramid builders. Just as high administrative posts were then opened to a wider group of persons than the members of the king's immediate family, so a vastly increased number of people were able to command the services of a good craftsman to construct a well-built tomb and to provide it with statues and reliefs.

Accidents of preservation have undoubtedly blurred the picture. The large copper statue-group of Phiops I[7] and his son from

---

[1] §vi, 24, 30–8.   [2] Ibid. 47, 60–3. See Plate 31 (b).   [3] Ibid. 44–7.
[4] Ibid. 41.   [5] Ibid. 76, 78.   [6] Ibid. 54, 61, 68–76.
[7] §vi, 24, 80.

Hierakonpolis warns us, as do the limestone calves recently found in the temple of Djedkare Isesi, the fragments of a basalt ram with the name of Cheops in Berlin,[1] the small sphinx with yellow painted skin from Redjedef's temple at Abu Rawāsh,[2] and the squatting naked alabaster statuette of Phiops II,[3] that there was a wider range of form and material than we are accustomed to think. The gold hawk's head from Hierakonpolis reminds us of the figures of precious metals which were undoubtedly placed in temple shrines, such as the statue of Ihi,[4] the son of the goddess Hathor, which the Palermo Stone tells us Neferirkare ordered for a sanctuary of Sneferu. Attention has been called to the appearance of polygonal limestone columns at Giza and the possibility that there were round granite columns in Redjedef's pyramid temple at Abu Rawāsh. We should therefore be careful not to draw too sharp a contrast between the light forms of the Third Dynasty temple of Djoser, the plant forms of the granite columns at Abusīr and Saqqara in the Fifth Dynasty and the severe forms of the Fourth Dynasty as exemplified in the Valley Temple of Chephren.

[1] *Ibid.* 66.   [2] §II, 21, vol. I, pl. 9.
[3] §IV, 9, vol. III, pl. 49; G, 43, vol. III, 39.   [4] G, 39, 39–40.

CHAPTER XV

PALESTINE IN THE EARLY BRONZE AGE

I. CLASSIFICATION OF THE MATERIAL

ALTHOUGH the first scientific excavations in Palestine had yielded traces of the Early Bronze Age, its chronological limits remained vague and its internal development was completely obscure. A much more exact knowledge has been acquired since 1930 by the excavation of several large well-stratified sites and by the application of the comparative method to better classified material, particularly pottery.

In 1932 seven archaic stages were distinguished on the slopes of the *tell* at Megiddo, the most recent of which, stages I–IV, belonged to the Early Bronze Age.[1] On the *tell* itself levels XVIII–XVI, which were explored in 1937–8, represent almost the same period,[2] but the stratigraphy is confused.[3] The only two tombs of the Early Bronze Age which were found belong to the very beginning of this period.[4]

In 1933, at Beth-shan, a wide *sondage* was made down to virgin soil which revealed, above the Chalcolithic levels, several levels (XV–XI) of the Early Bronze Age.[5]

Excavations at Jericho reached Early Bronze Age deposits (tombs A and 24) in the seasons 1930–2 and more especially in 1935–6 when work was concentrated on the deepest sections of the *tell*: above the Neolithic and Chalcolithic were found five levels, III–VII (with tomb 351) belonging to the Early Bronze Age.[6] Other excavations on the site in 1952–8 clarified the history of the successive ramparts; in the later seasons habitations were also explored[7] and nine tombs of the true Early Bronze Age were brought to light.[8]

The site of Et-Tell ('Ai) which was excavated in 1933–5 revealed a rampart, a palace, some houses and a sanctuary which had been rebuilt three times; some tombs yielded a large quantity of pottery.[9] A check excavation was carried out in 1964–6.[10]

---

[1] §1, 6.   [2] §1, 18; 27.   [3] §1, 16.
[4] §1, 12, tombs 52 and 1128.   [5] §1, 7; 8.   [6] §1, 9 ff.
[7] §1, 15.   [8] §1, 17, 5 ff.   [9] §1, 23.   [10] A, 4.

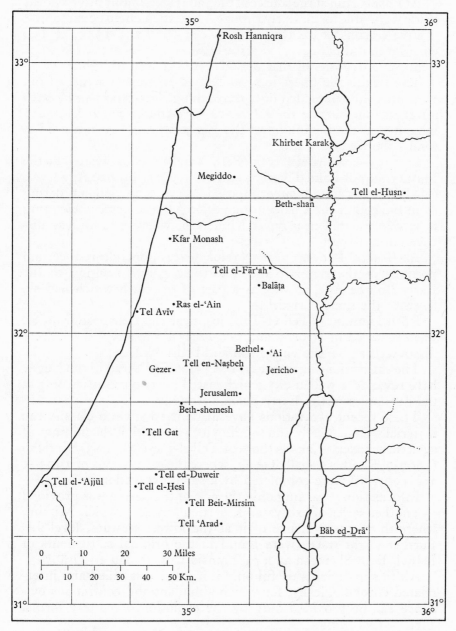

Map 7. Palestine: Principal Early Bronze Age and Middle Bronze Age sites.

At Ras el-'Ain, at the source of the Jaffa river, public utility works made it possible for an Early Bronze Age settlement to be explored.[1]

Five seasons of excavation, between 1926 and 1935, at Tell en-Naṣbeh did not reveal any Early Bronze Age levels, but some tombs and deposits of that period were brought to light.[2]

The large-scale operations at Tell ed-Duweir (Lachish) from 1932 to 1938 succeeded only in reaching the deepest strata with a trench, but outside the *tell* caves were found which had been inhabited at the beginning of the Early Bronze Age and used as tombs shortly afterwards.[3]

In 1944–6 Khirbet Karak (Beth Yeraḥ) was excavated, at the southern tip of Lake Tiberias, and three Early Bronze Age levels (II–IV) were found superimposed above a settlement dating from the end of the Chalcolithic period;[4] the cemetery belonging to it was situated nearby, at Kinnereth, where a tomb was discovered in 1940.[5]

At Tell el-Fār'ah, near Nablus, excavators cleared certain portions of the rampart and a fortified gate belonging to the Early Bronze Age, as well as a part of the town which had six levels of the same period.[6]

Rōsh Hanniqra (Tell et-Taba'iq), near the Lebanese frontier, was excavated in 1951–2 and two Early Bronze Age levels were discovered above the virgin soil and bed-rock.[7]

The excavations in progress (1963–) at Tell 'Arad in the Negev have revealed a walled city which lasted for two centuries only at the beginning of the Early Bronze Age.[8]

These recent excavations have made it possible to classify the material systematically and to bring into line with it the findings of such earlier excavations as those of Tell el-Ḥesi (1890–3),[9] Jericho (1907–9)[10] and especially Gezer, where the excavations of 1903–5 and 1907–9[11] were completed by a small excavation in 1934.[12]

Information regarding only the end of the period was provided by another series of excavations, particularly at Tell Beit Mirsim, where there was evidence of it at the lowest stratum, level J.[13] Further slight traces were found in the original settlements of Bethel, Beth Shemesh and, in Transjordan, at Bāb ed-Drā'.[14]

All this material is useful only if it can be classified and inter-related chronologically, for which abundant and continuous evidence can be provided only by the evolution of pottery forms.

[1] §1, 13, 24.   [2] §1, 20, 32.   [3] §1, 30.   [4] §1, 21.

[5] §1, 22.   [6] §1, 31.   [7] §1, 29.   [8] A, 1 and 2.

[9] §1, 5.   [10] §1, 26.   [11] §1, 19.   [12] §1, 25.

[13] §1, 1–3.   [14] §1, 4.

Although the very distinct characteristics of Early Bronze Age pottery soon made it possible to set apart material belonging to the period in general, the fundamental unity of the culture long made it difficult to formulate subdivisions. As a result of more detailed knowledge of pottery and of studies in comparison, the period has now been divided into four phases,[1] an arrangement which may be retained for the sake of convenience, subject to a certain flexibility. A process of development can be detected between the different phases when regarded as a whole, but there is no abrupt transition from one to another and the boundaries separating them must be kept fluid.

PHASE Ia

This lack of precision is apparent at the very beginning of the period. In spite of the conventional names which are used to denote the two epochs, the passing of the Chalcolithic period is characterized much less by the widespread use of metal, only sparsely attested by excavation, than by other technical developments, particularly in building and pot-making. The division between the two cultures is demonstrated clearly enough in the individual evolution of each site: the Early Bronze Age begins with level XV at Beth-shan, with level II at Khirbet Karak, with level VII at Jericho, with the first Early Bronze Age level at Tell el-Fār‘ah; the position is less clear at Megiddo, where the transition from the Chalcolithic to the Early Bronze Age appears to have occurred at stages V–IV and level XVIII. If the successions at the different sites are compared, however, there are obvious inconsistencies: stage IV at Megiddo is later than Jericho VII, which is itself contemporary with the first settlements at Ophel (tomb 3) and with the cemetery of ‘Ai. It thus seems likely that the Chalcolithic civilization in North Palestine (Tell el-Fār‘ah, Beth-shan, Khirbet Karak, Megiddo) continued to exist over the period when, in the centre, the Early Bronze Age civilization was coming into being on the ancient sites (Jericho, Gezer) or on new sites (‘Ai, Jerusalem, Tell en-Naṣbeh). The overlapping in time of the two cultures, already suggested by their blending in the tombs of ‘Ai, Tell en-Naṣbeh, Tell el-Fār‘ah,[2] was confirmed by the discoveries at Jericho,[3] where, moreover, the two levels of tomb A 13 seem to indicate that the Early Bronze Age I*a* did not begin until the Later Chalcolithic period was already well advanced.[4] But this Chalco-

---

[1] §1, 33.
[3] §1, 17, 4 ff.

[2] §1, 31, 55 (548), 56 (137–8).
[4] §1, 17, 6 f., 49 ff.

lithic civilization of the north itself coincided with the end of the Ghassūl-Beersheba civilization, and the three civilizations represented one and the same stage of human progress: that of village settlements of 'farmers, potters and metal-workers'; for this reason they have been grouped together under that heading in an earlier chapter.[1] However, the designation of Early Bronze Age I*a* for the new culture which was appearing in the central region is justified by the fact that it was the forerunner of the Early Bronze Age civilization which was about to be established over the whole country and was to continue for nearly a millennium.

PHASE I*b*

It remains true that the Early Bronze Age did not assume a definite form until phase I*b*. Apart from some survivals from Chalcolithic tradition, new techniques and new forms were established everywhere. The following sites belong to phase I*b*: Megiddo stage IV and level XVIII; Beth-shan XV (partly) and XIV; Khirbet Karak II; Tell el-Fār'ah level AB I; Rōsh Hanniqra II; Jericho V and tombs 24 (perhaps a little later) and A 108; part of the archaic deposits of Gezer; probably the original sanctuary and the town buildings of 'Ai. Typical of this phase are the large jars either without a neck (hole-mouth) or squat-necked, horizontal indented handles, dishes or bowls with incurving rims. Smaller pieces have usually a red burnish. In the central areas pottery-painting flourished with parallel red lines on the natural clay-coloured background, red bands or streaks on a white slip; this treatment made only a modest appearance in the north, which, for the painting of large jars, continued to use the 'band slip' or 'grain wash' introduced towards the end of the Chalcolithic period.

PHASE II

Whatever may have been asserted,[2] the beginning of phase II was not marked by any sudden change, and its pottery continued to preserve the same traditions, with only slight modifications in shape and some improvements in the firing and finishing of larger pieces. Certain conventions, however, like the 'band slip' in the north, were soon to disappear. On the other hand, there were innovations—in technique, such as the wares which were highly fired and resonant to a stroke, the so-called 'metallic ware'; in decoration, such as irregular or chequered combing;

[1] *C.A.H.* I[3], ch. IX. sect. VII.   [2] §I, 33, 69.

in shape, such as large, flat-bottomed dishes, slender-necked amphoras, juglets with stump-bases, or with flat or (occasionally) pointed bases, graceful jugs with a flat loop-handle attached to the lip, in addition to which there were sometimes two small vertical handles on the belly. This phase is illustrated, more or less precisely, by Megiddo stages III–II and levels XVIII–XVII(?), Beth-shan XIII, Khirbet Karak III and the tomb at Kinnereth, Tell el-Fār'ah AB II, Rōsh Hanniqra I, Jericho IV and tombs A 127, D 12 (partly), F 5, the intermediate sanctuary and the corresponding level at 'Ai, the whole of the lowest stratum at Ras el-'Ain, and most of the archaic strata at Tell 'Arad.

PHASE III

This is characterized by a class of pottery named 'Khirbet Karak ware' after the site where it was first found. This type of pottery was rather lightly fired, and is consequently fragile, but very attractive.[1] There are wide-mouthed vessels with a single loop handle, bowls, keeled or otherwise, large basins, pitchers, stands for vessels, and lids. These were shaped by hand and have a burnished slip, either red all over or red on the inside and black on at least a part of the outside. The black hue was produced by exposing the vessels to a smoky flame, and differences of tone probably resulted not so much from accidents in firing or from subsequent use over the fire[2] as from the deliberate intention to achieve an artistic effect. As well as burnish, some vessels have a fluted or incised geometric design. This beautiful pottery would be of greater value for purposes of classification if it were not for its comparative scarcity. It has been discovered in any quantity only at Beth-shan, where it comes to light in the course of level XII and continues as far as the beginning of level XI, at Khirbet Karak, where it demarcates level IV, and in the tombs of 'Affūleh; but there are traces of it on almost all the sites of the plain of Esdraelon and further north. South of the plain of Esdraelon it is rare: sherds have been found at Ras el-'Ain and at Gezer and as far as Tell el-Ḥesi and Tell ed-Duweir,[3] sherds and complete vessels at Jericho (level III and tombs A, D 12, F 2 and 4). The remaining material from the same tombs at Jericho suggests that a number of other forms may have belonged to this phase: jugs with thick stump-bases, small pear-shaped jugs pointed at the bottom and with a flat handle, bowls with disc bases, squat jars with vertical handles or horizontal handles with pushed-up

[1] §1, 28; §vii, 1, 90 ff.   [2] §1, 28.   [3] §1, 30, 44; §vii, 1, 95.

notches. Some of these types were found at Beth-shan XII–XI and Megiddo XVII–XVI and they are also characteristic of tombs A 114 and F 2 at Jericho, and of the final stage of the sanctuary and the palace at 'Ai.

<h3 align="center">PHASE IV (?)</h3>

The lower limit of phase III cannot be precisely determined, and what follows is still more uncertain, for no site has yielded a clear and continuous stratification. At 'Ai there was a break in settled occupation at the end of phase III and for a long time afterwards; at Tell el-Fār'ah, Ras el-'Ain and Rōsh Hanniqra it had ceased even earlier. The two final stages at Megiddo, II–I, can scarcely be distinguished from the preceding stage; the upper part of level XI at Beth-shan contains belated survivals inter-mingled with other types providing evidence of a settlement distinctly later; level II at Jericho is poorly represented and level I does not belong to the Early Bronze Age.

In order to distinguish a phase IV of the Early Bronze Age,[1] it is necessary to examine other sites which were beginning to be settled at that time, but without having anywhere buildings which can be related to these deposits: level J at Beit Mirsim, level VI at Beth Shemesh, the lowest level at Bethel and, in Transjordan, Bāb ed-Drā' and Ader. Other non-stratified groups can be added: tomb 351 at Jericho, which in fact appears to be a little later than tomb A of the same site, tomb 6 and the lower tombs 1101–1102 at Megiddo, which however foreshadow the Middle Bronze Age. This phase IV is therefore only a transition stage; nevertheless, and precisely on account of its poverty, it provides historical evidence which will be turned to account later.

It follows therefore that these distinctions which have been established within the Early Bronze Age are only approximate. In any case they are of secondary importance to the basic unity shown by this civilization. In order to define its main features, it is necessary to take a general view of the period as a whole.

<h2 align="center">II. THE FORTIFIED CITIES</h2>

It must be emphasized that there is one particular feature which is predominantly characteristic of this period. The Chalcolithic period was still the age of villages:[2] there were villages of huts or pit-dwellings, there were also villages of properly constructed

---

[1] §I, 33, 78 ff.   [2] C.A.H. I³, ch. IX, sects. V–VII.

houses, but neither type was surrounded by an enclosure-wall; they might cover quite a large area, but the dwellings were scattered; they were established in the valleys and plains without looking for natural defences. In striking contrast the settlements of the Early Bronze Age were cities: on sites where occupation was continuous the dwellings were concentrated and built closer together (Jericho, Tell el-Fār'ah) and for new settlements rocky citadels were chosen ('Ai, Ophel). In both cases the houses were soon to be grouped compactly within a rampart.

Parts of these ramparts have been recovered by various excavations. They are all of impressive bulk, but of varying construction. From phase I*b* onwards Tell el-Fār'ah had a rampart of crude brick blocking the west front, 2·60–2·80 m. wide and mounted on a base of three courses of stone; its defences were strengthened by towers or projecting bastions and supplemented a little later by an outer wall. In phase II a wall of stones was added, 3 m. wide and likewise set behind an outer wall; a glacis, up to 10 m. wide, was finally heaped up against the rampart.[1] Also in phase II, the northern line of fortifications was slightly moved back towards the south and a new rampart was constructed, this time in stone, 8·50 m. thick and earthed up with a glacis.[2] There is evidence of a similar rampart in crude brick and with bastions and a glacis at Tell esh-Sheikh el-'Areini (Tel Gat) belonging to phase I*b*.[3] Tell 'Arad has recently provided another example of a rampart (phases I–II) with semi-circular towers, in this case constructed of stone. Fortifications of this type can be found in representations of Palestinian cities: the Narmer palette[4] for phase I*b*, the Dishāsha relief[5] for phase III.

The rampart of Khirbet Karak belonging to phase I*b* or II was constructed of crude brick with three components: a vertical wall which was buttressed by two walls sloping on the outside, in all 8 m. wide.[6] The first rampart at Megiddo, at level XVIII, may have been a wall of ashlars 4·50 m. wide, subsequently enlarged to 8 m.[7] However, since contemporary houses were built against the outside of this 'rampart' it was most probably a wall designed to support the great embankment on which level XVII was established.[8]

The fortifications of 'Ai were cleared over a considerable length: the line followed the rocky edge of the hill and assumed the same

[1] §I, 31, 69 (212–21).
[2] §I, 31, 55 (553 f.), 62 (573 f.).
[3] §VIII, 9, 201.
[4] §VIII, 6, pl. XXIX; cf. §I, 31, 69 (215).
[5] §VIII, 5, pl. IV.
[6] §I, 21, 172 and pl. 9.
[7] §I, 18, 66 ff.
[8] §I, 16, 52 f.

shape by means of a series of angles. Both the structure and the history of this rampart are complicated, especially on the south face and at the south-west corner, and what is stated here may perhaps have to be modified as a result of excavations which are at present in progress. It appears that there was, from phase I *b* onwards, a wall 6·50 m. wide, doubled by a second wall 2·50 m. wide which was separated from the first by a passage of 2·50 m., heaped with earth and rubble. In phase III the whole lay-out was further protected, or even over some of its length superseded, by an outer wall earthed up with a glacis.[1] A little earlier the foundations of a citadel 40 × 10 m. had been constructed on either side of the rampart, which had been partially destroyed at the south-west corner.[2]

At Jericho the Early Bronze Age rampart was reached by several trenches, which provide evidence of an eventful history: on the west it had been repaired or reconstructed seventeen times, sometimes on a slightly different line. It was built of brick on a foundation of stone. The first construction belonged to phase I *b*, and the destruction of the final rampart marked the end of phase III. Between these two limits it is difficult to determine exactly the dates of the various operations. Two projecting towers were attached to the first rampart, one semi-circular and the other rectangular, and as the trenches were narrow it may be these towers were not the only ones; the plan would thus have been similar to that of Tell el-Fār'ah. In phase III, at least, the wall stood behind a ramp and a ditch;[3] an oblong tower on the east face probably belonged to the same phase.

Only one city-gate is known with certainty, that of Tell el-Fār'ah, which belongs to the same period as the first construction of the rampart, phase I *b*. Between two rectangular projecting towers there was a passage 4 m. wide, contracting to 2 m. where it went through the rampart. This opening constituted the gate properly called, which was roofed, whereas the passage between the towers was not. The gate was closed by means of two wooden leaves pivoting on sockets and it appears to have been bolted by two beams which were set crosswise against the leaves on the inside. In phase II the sill of the gate was raised to bring it up to the level of occupation which had risen inside the city and an earth staircase with steps supported by wooden beams descended across the passage towards the outside. The gate was later blocked, then subsequently put back into use towards the end of

---

[1] §1, 23, 9 f., 21 f., 31 f. [2] §1, 23, 16 f.
[3] §1, 15, 84 (64–70); 85 (88–90); 86 (55 f.); 92 (103 f.).

phase II, after which time Tell el-Fār'ah was abandoned until the Middle Bronze Age.[1]

Other sites have yielded only scant evidence. A gate belonging to phase II with its entrance staggered, the foundations of which were discovered at Rōsh Hanniqra, remains hypothetical, since it has not been possible to determine how it was joined to the rampart.[2] At 'Ai, in phase I*b*, a narrow postern went through the rampart by the side of a projecting semi-circular tower; in phase II this postern may have been replaced by a wide gate, but it is difficult to understand the lay-out.[3] At Jericho there was probably one gate close to the rectangular tower[4] and another near the oblong tower.[5]

Dwellings were huddled together within the shelter of the ramparts, but excavations have generally been too limited in scope for it to be possible to make a study of the urban life of this period. The best example still remains Tell el-Fār'ah. From phase I*b* onwards, and more precisely in phase II, groups of houses were separated by straight streets, 2 m. wide, leading to a way left clear at the foot of the rampart.[6] At Jericho[7] and at 'Ai,[8] however, houses were built against the rampart. Khirbet Karak, in phase II, had paved highways, 2·50 m. wide.[9] At Tell el-Fār'ah a system of drainage was effected by means of a channel running down the middle of some of the streets and by a sewer passing under the rampart.[10] Level XIV at Beth-shan contains a drain constructed and roofed with slabs;[11] a similar drain was found in level XVII at Megiddo.[12]

These Early Bronze Age cities are distributed unevenly over the country. They are to be found, for the most part, in the north and in the centre. In the south the site of Tell 'Arad, at the southern limit of the Judaean hills, provides the only exception up to date: excavations at present in progress (1963–) have revealed the remains of a settlement belonging to phases I and II, with a rampart fortified with semi-circular towers, which appears to have followed a settlement of pit-dwellings; the course of development here appears to have been contemporary with that of the important sites of the north.[13] Apart from this advance-post, the southernmost site representing phase I is Tell esh-Sheikh el-'Areini

[1] §I, 31, 69 (221–35). See Plate 34 (*a*).
[2] §I, 29, 73 ff. [3] §I, 23, 32.
[4] §I, 15, 92 (104). [5] §I, 9, 15 and pl. IX.
[6] §I, 31, 55, pl. IX; 68, pls. XXXIII–XXXIV. See Plate 34 (*b*).
[7] §I, 10, pl. XXIII. [8] §I, 23, pl. *c*.
[9] §I, 21, 226 and fig. 3. [10] §I, 31, 68, pls. XXXIV, XLV; 69 (252).
[11] §I, 7, 128. [12] §I, 18, fig. 392. [13] A, 1 and 2.

(Tel Gat), near Beit Jibrīn. Further south, near Hebron, Tell ed-Duweir and Tell el-Ḥesi were not settled until the beginning of phase II. South of Hebron, Tell Beit Mirsim did not begin to be occupied until the very end of the period (phase 'IV'). Finally, south of Gaza, Tell el-'Ajjūl is not found settled before the Intermediate Early Bronze–Middle Bronze period, Tell el-Fār'ah only after the beginning of the Middle Bronze Age. In the Negeb surface explorations have produced no evidence of the Early Bronze Age, a fact which has to be borne in mind in determining the character and the origin of this civilization.

III. ARCHITECTURE: DWELLINGS

The building material employed most generally—in fact almost exclusively at the beginning of the period—was brick. It continued to be very widely used for a long time afterwards, despite the fact that good stone is plentiful in Palestine, apart from the Jordan valley, where indeed the use of brick was the most persistent. This apparent paradox can be partly explained by the greater ease with which the local clay could be worked in an age when metal tools were still primitive. Such an explanation seems inadequate, however, for the beginning of the Early Bronze Age, when this method of construction appears to have been imported into Palestine (at least into the mountainous regions) by a people more accustomed to working in brick than in stone.[1] Brick remained unbaked, but, in contrast with the preceding periods, was now moulded in various dimensions; bricks were bonded with a mortar of fresh clay. Stout walls, such as ramparts, were sometimes reinforced by a framework of longitudinal and transverse tie-beams (Jericho).[2] In order to counter the danger of these structures being affected by damp, they were raised from the ground by a footing of stones; this was sometimes only a bed of pebbles, but often it was a pedestal of two or more courses of rough-hewn blocks. Rapid progress was made in working with stone: the pedestal became thicker and more expertly dressed and its height was increased until it formed an actual wall (Palace of 'Ai, phase III).[3] It is significant that at Tell el-Fār'ah stone was used to replace brick for the doubling of the western rampart and for the construction of the new northern rampart of phase II.[4]

Walls have nowhere been preserved at a sufficient height for it

[1] §11, 2.
[2] §1, 15, 87 (114).
[3] §1, 23, 14 f.
[4] §1, 31, 68 (592), 69 (215 ff.).

to be possible to determine whether there were windows and, if so, of what kind; they must in any case have been set quite high, at the top of the walls near the ceiling. Traces of doorways are often visible. Those doors which opened on to the outside had a sill of flat stones or square brick tiles; where the socket has been preserved, it is not hollowed out of one of the paving-slabs of the sill, but consists of a stone added to the sill. In the inside passages, which had no means of closing, the earth-floor of the adjacent rooms was simply continued. This floor was normally of beaten earth, and paving was rare or confined to the hearth-place. Ovens were installed in the courtyards.[1] There were also silos, which were hollowed out of the ground and which had walls of brick at Jericho[2] and at Beth-shan,[3] of limestone slabs at 'Ai[4] and at Tell el-Fār'ah.[5] Corn supplies were also stored, as were water and oil, in large jars which could be buried up to the neck in the ground.

There is no instance of the roofing of houses having been preserved; most probably it consisted of a flat terrace and was no longer the ridged roof which sometimes occurred in the Chalcolithic period.[6] Long timbers are rare in Palestine and, as soon as the rooms began to be made wider, supports were added to reduce the length of the beams. These supports were wooden posts, which could be simply driven into the ground: a room at Beth-shan, belonging to phase II, had six of these posts set in two rows.[7] Greater stability was secured by mounting the posts on a paving slab or on a small pile of stones. At Tell el-Fār'ah[8] and at 'Ai,[9] which provide numerous examples of such supports, the foot of the wooden posts was found still in position on the paving-slab. In square rooms a central paving-slab was often sufficient, but if the room were long or wide the supports were more numerous. They were arranged along the axis of the room in a line of two, three or four paving-slabs, sometimes in two rows, but they were also set along the walls or in the corners. At Byblos, where these various arrangements occur, it has been supposed that they correspond with differing superstructures and are typical of successive periods.[10] The evidence is less conclusive in Palestine; at Tell el-Fār'ah the same levels belonging to the beginning of the Early Bronze Age have yielded evidence of supports both in the axis of the room and against the walls or in the corners.[11]

Since the superstructures have been destroyed, it is not possible

[1] §1, 21, 227.   [2] §1, 15, 88 (77).   [3] §1, 7, 129.
[4] §1, 23, pl. xxxiv.   [5] §1, 31, 62 (564).   [6] C.A.H. 1³, ch. ix, sect. vii.
[7] §1, 7, 129.   [8] §1, 31, 55 (551).   [9] §1, 23, 14.
[10] §iii, 1.   [11] §1, 31, 62, figs. 6–8.

to determine the height of buildings; however, the thickness of some of the walls (2·10 m. in the palace at 'Ai)[1] or the height at which they have remained standing (as at Jericho)[2] makes it possible to infer the use of an upper storey: huddled inside its ramparts, the city grew upwards. On the other hand some idea of their ground-plan is given by the ruined walls of dwelling-houses which have survived. There is no certain evidence of round houses, such as existed in the Neolithic period, and those constructions at the lowest level of the Early Bronze Age at Jericho which have been called 'round houses'[3] were more probably large silos. There are, however, either at the beginning of the period or later, curved walls or rounded corners, and these forms can be explained by the necessity for adaptation to the available space, or even by greater ease in construction. In some cases they occur in accordance with a definite plan, that of the apsed house: one or two rectangular rooms extended by a semi-circular recess. This type, which appeared sporadically during the Chalcolithic period,[4] is found at the beginning of the Early Bronze Age, at Megiddo stage IV[5] and at the lowest level of 'Ai.[6] Very soon, however, there was a return to the rectangular plan, to the exclusion of others.

Often the whole dwelling consisted of a single room. It is sometimes hard to distinguish between these individual cells, built close together in city blocks, and dwellings which contained several rooms, just as it is difficult, when only the ground-plan has been preserved, to determine which are open courtyards and which the roofed-in areas. Moreover, very few plans have been published which are sufficiently detailed to be intelligible. The most complete are those of 'Ai[7] and of Tell el-Fār'ah[8] and it appears that there the lay-out of buildings rapidly became more compact; rooms were added in accordance with the needs of the inhabitants, thus taking up the space which had been left clear between the houses within the ramparts.

Some more elaborate plans are those of the houses of rich persons or of public buildings, though it is not usually possible to distinguish between them. The finest construction, at Beth-shan phase II, consisted of three rooms which may perhaps have formed part of a larger whole.[9] At Tell el-Fār'ah[10] a building

1 §I, 23, 14.
2 §I, 10, 152.
3 §I, 10, 153 and pl. LI.
4 C.A.H. I³, ch. IX, sect. VII.
5 §I, 6, fig. 2.
6 §I, 23, 21.
7 §I, 23, pl. C.
8 §I, 31, 68, pls. XXXIII–XXXIV.
9 §I, 7, 129.
10 §I, 31, 55 (550 f.).

which had been rebuilt three times was composed, in its most complete state, at the end of phase I, of five rooms arranged in two parallel lines between two streets; some of the rooms were quite large and one of them was connected with a vestibule by a double bay. The finest example, however, is the 'palace' at 'Ai.[1] It was probably built in phase III and consisted of a hall, 20 × 6·50 m., divided by a row of four columns. The door, which was in the middle of one of the longer sides, opened on to a courtyard facing east. On the three remaining sides this great hall was surrounded by a corridor which led into it and also gave access to the courtyard. The building must have had an upper storey.

IV. SANCTUARIES

An ancient city must necessarily have had one or more temples, and if excavation has not revealed them in all the Early Bronze Age cities of Palestine it is because only limited areas have been cleared. In fact, few sanctuaries of this period are known. The palace at 'Ai has sometimes been called a 'temple', but the arguments adduced seem inconclusive. On the other hand, there is a building quite close to the palace which was certainly a sanctuary. It was constructed against the rampart and rebuilt at least twice;[2] excavations now in progress suggest that a further stage should be added to the three previously described. The first stage was contemporaneous with the primitive rampart (phase I) and included, at the far end of the cult chamber, a table made of flat stones and bricks which was probably an altar. The second stage belonged to the same period as the bastion-citadel erected on the spot, which provided its rear wall (phase II or III); it then consisted only of a large room with a floor of beaten earth on which lay the remains of ritual vessels. The third stage (phase III) is the best known. The sanctuary was composed of three chambers: first, a hall 8·50 × 6 m. with a bench set along two sides; this was reached by a ramp of rammed earth. On this bench the offering-vessels were laid, great jars were sunk into the ground and two rectangular incense-burners were placed in the middle of the chamber. Near to these last lay a tree-trunk, very roughly squared, which, it has been suggested, may have been the remains of a sacred pole, an 'ashērāh, but it was more probably a roof-timber or a prop supporting the roof. A recess set in a corner was used for the ritual preparation of offerings. A door, preceded by a step,

[1] §1, 23, 14 ff. See Plate 35 (a).   [2] §1, 23, 16 ff., 29 ff. See Plate 35 (b).

led from this large room into a second chamber, containing a dais, on which cups had been set, and several irregular recesses into which the refuse from offerings and sacrifices was thrown. In a corner of this room a little raised chamber had been constructed containing an altar 1·70 m. long, 0·70 m. high, so placed that it could not be seen from the next room: it was the most sacred place of all, the *cella*. Above the altar was a niche of flat stones painted red; no divine symbol was discovered, but fine pottery vases, alabaster cups, a pink granite dish of Egyptian workmanship, and half of a small votive bed of terra cotta were laid on the altar or near to it. Up to the height at which they had been preserved, the walls were entirely of stone and were covered with plaster. Nothing is known of the superstructure, or even whether all the rooms were roofed.

Another undoubted example is a little sanctuary at Tell el-Fār'ah.[1] Originally, in phase I, it was composed of two parts: a cult-chamber, open on the east side and containing an altar and perhaps an offering-table, and a *cella* on the west side, entered through a narrow door and having a bench along three of its sides. The bench and the floor of the *cella* had been carefully plastered. This sanctuary was completely destroyed and replaced by a building of different plan and of a less obviously sacred character.

A building at Jericho, level VII (phase I*a*),[2] may also be regarded as a sanctuary. It is a room measuring about 5·25 × 2·50 m. on the inside. The walls are flanked by a bench which, at the north-western end, broadens into a dais about 1·50 m. deep; the door is at the opposite end on the long north side. Walls and floor had been carefully plastered and unusually strong walls separated this room from the neighbouring houses. The care applied to the building and its singular plan suggest that it was probably a chapel: useful analogies of the 'Breithaus' type could be found in Mesopotamia and in north Syria. Unfortunately, this view of its sacred function has not been supported by any discovery; there is no certainty that it was the provenance of a stone oval in section 0·60 m. long with a polished surface which was found nearby and which has been regarded as a cult symbol, a *maṣṣēbāh*.

At Megiddo, level XVII, or perhaps only at level XVI (phase III),[3] a pile of stones was found forming a rough ellipse (10 × 8·70 × 1·40 m. high), which could be ascended by a staircase. It was narrowly enclosed in a rectangular precinct.[4] Numerous

[1] §1, 31, 68 (577, 579, 584).
[3] §1, 18, 73, 76; cf. §1, 16, 54*.

[2] §1, 11, 73 f.
[4] See Plate 36 (*a*).

bones of animals and broken vases in its vicinity showed that it was a place for offerings and sacrifices, an altar. It constituted, with its enclosure wall, a sanctuary, the first example of the *bāmāh*, the 'high place', which was to have a long history in the land of Canaan and was to be mentioned frequently in the Bible.

V. BURIALS

Cities also had to provide for the disposal of the dead. Throughout the whole of the Early Bronze Age burials normally took place outside the ramparts, in caves which might or might not have been artificially enlarged and in chambers dug out of the rock on the hillside. The opening was approximately on the same level as the floor of the tomb, in contrast with the shaft tombs, reached by a vertical drop, which were to appear in the Intermediate period between the Early and Middle Bronze Ages.

Only a very limited number of tombs has been discovered in relation to the importance of the cities and the long duration of the period. Over a hundred tombs before the Israelite epoch have been excavated on the slopes of Megiddo,[1] but not one belongs to the main phases of the Early Bronze Age: tombs 52 and 1128 belong to the very beginning of the period, tombs 1101–1102 (*lower*) belong to the very end of the period. At Jericho tomb A 13 (*upper*) belongs to phase I*a* and the true Early Bronze Age is represented on this site by only twelve tombs, as opposed to 346 for the Intermediate Early Bronze–Middle Bronze period, which covers a much shorter time.[2] In fact these tombs at Jericho constitute the most important group and are, moreover, distributed over the whole of the Early Bronze Age: tombs 24 and A 108 belong to phase I*b*; tombs A 122 and A 127 belong to phases I–II; tomb F 5 and the first occupation of tomb D 12 belong to phase II; the whole of the large tomb D 12 belongs to phase III, which is also well represented by another large tomb, A, by tombs A 114, F 2, 3, 4 and, somewhat later, by tomb 351.

The small number of tombs belonging to the Early Bronze Age may be explained in several ways: they were scattered, sometimes quite far from the town, and have consequently not been located, or indeed, at certain sites, all trace of them has been eroded away.[3] But it can be explained first and foremost by the character of these tombs: burial-chambers were occupied by a

[1] §1, 12.   [2] §1, 17, 2, 52 ff.   [3] *Ibid.*

family or by a whole group over what might be quite a long period, a fact which is particularly evident during phase III: at Jericho there were at least 89 skeletons in tomb F 4; there were 54 in tomb F 2 and 50 in tomb F 3; according to probable estimates tomb A had housed about 300 bodies, tomb D 12 several hundred. This practice is in complete contrast with the individual tombs of the Intermediate Early Bronze–Middle Bronze period and explains the discrepancy in the numbers.

Bones and funerary deposits were displaced in order to make room for new corpses. The upheavals resulting from the repeated use of the same tombs over a long period, the re-use of the same caves at a later time, whether as tombs or for a different purpose, the frequent collapse of ceilings as well as destruction by erosion — all such vicissitudes combined to leave little chance of observing the position in which the body had been laid. It seems at least probable that bodies were buried intact and there is no evidence of a secondary burial except in one tomb at Gezer where, according to the excavator, bones already bare had been collected together in the sections of large jars halved lengthwise.[1] In two tombs at Lachish the last bodies to be buried were found laid on their sides, the knees bent and the hands in front of the face.[2] These same tombs, however, contained odd skulls and scattered bones which, when assembled, did not correspond with the number of skulls. A similar disparity has been generally found in the tombs of Jericho, where erosion and ceiling-collapse have obliterated the upper strata. It thus seems likely that when a space was being cleared for new burials, some of the bones were thrown out, but the skulls and funerary offerings were preserved.

There is evidence of partial cremation in the tomb at Kinnereth (the cemetery of Khirbet Karak) belonging to phase II.[3] The bones were either entirely or partially burnt, from which it could be inferred that fires had been lit near the bodies, as in certain burials, probably of foreigners, at Ur under the First Dynasty.[4] It may also have been a means of disposing of bones which had become a nuisance, as in similar instances of the Chalcolithic period.[5]

Excavations begun in 1965 at Bāb ed-Drā' at the edge of the Lisān of the Dead Sea[6] have discovered the largest Early Bronze cemetery in the Near East. The cemetery was intensely used for a millennium beginning towards the end of the fourth millennium

[1] §I, 19, 1, 77 f. [2] §I, 30, 297. [3] §I, 22, 3.
[4] §v, 1, 142 f. [5] *C.A.H.* I³, ch. IX, sect. VII.
[6] A, 5, 6 and 7.

B.C. and its use before and after the town occupation (phases II and III) suggests a traditional cultic burial ground. Shaft-tombs were the rule in phase I*a* but they continued through phase III. In phase I*a* a heap of disarticulated bones was placed on a mat in the centre of the chamber, adjacent to a line of several skulls and surrounded by heaps of newly-fired pots. A round funerary building of phase I*b* was a precursor of the most common burial type during phases II and III, the charnel house.[1] These were rectangular mud-brick buildings having an entrance on one of the broad sides and usually two storeys. Upper and lower floors were filled with heaps of disarticulated bones mixed with ordinary and miniature pots. A single building contained bones representing over 200 individuals and 800 pots, and the cemetery contained several hundred of these buildings. Phase IV burials were of articulated individuals under cairns—presumably of the destroyers of Early Bronze town life at Bāb ed-Drā'.

Funerary equipment consisted of the same vessels which were in use among the living: small jars, jugs, bowls or dishes either contained or symbolized the meal which was being offered to the dead, and juglets the oil or perfume which would be required, but neither large storage jars nor cooking utensils were included: the deceased did no cooking. There are a few instances of offerings other than pottery: ornaments such as beads, pendants or amulets left on the body of the dead, and occasionally copper weapons.

VI. MATERIAL CONDITIONS:
INDUSTRY AND COMMERCE

The development of urban life and increased building activity are indicative of a growth in population and a higher standard of living. Archaeological documentation gives only a very incomplete picture of the material conditions prevailing at the time. The majority of the population were occupied with agriculture and stock-raising. The donkey was the only beast of burden and the only mount. Wheat, barley and lentils were the main crops, but beans and peas (Tell ed-Duweir,[2] Jericho)[3] were also grown. It is significant that the Canaanite word for 'flour' was borrowed by the Old Kingdom Egyptians to designate a kind of bread, *qmḥw*. Almond-trees may perhaps have already been cultivated (Jericho)[4] and olives certainly were, grafted on to the wild olive stock of

[1] See Plate 36(*b*).   [2] §1, 30, 309 ff.
[3] §1, 10, 161 f.   [4] §1, 10, 162.

Palestine: olive-stones are numerous on all the sites and were found at Ghassūl, even in the preceding period. Vines, on the other hand, were not indigenous, but were first introduced at this period; grapes were eaten fresh and also dried,[1] and wine was produced in the same way as in Mesopotamia and in Egypt. The inscription of Uni mentions fig-trees and vine-stock which were cut down in the course of the campaigns by him in Palestine for Phiops I.[2] A kind of beer was also drunk: the bottoms of some jars found at Jericho were encrusted with remains of barley-grains.

Some fragments of material (? goat hair) were preserved at Jericho,[3] comprising eleven threads of warp and twelve threads of woof to the square centimetre. A bowl was found at Tell ed-Duweir which retained the imprint of a fine textile.[4] There is documentary evidence from Egypt illustrating the types of clothing worn: a carved ivory baton from the tomb of king Qaa, at the end of the First Dynasty, shows a captive Asiatic, probably a nomad from Sinai, clothed in a fringed loin-cloth, tied at the waist with a belt and reaching down almost to the knees.[5] A scene from the tomb of Inti, dating from the Fifth Dynasty, shows the capture of a Canaanite town: the combatants wear loin cloths and have their hair tied with bands; the women are dressed in long tunics.[6]

Almost all the sites have yielded items of adornment, such as shell-ornaments, amulets or pendants of bone or hard stone, beads carved out of semi-precious stone or made of blue faience. The goldsmith's art is represented by a bicone gold bead from Tell ed-Duweir (phase not certain),[7] and by two gold beads and a gold disc worked in *repoussé* from the tomb at Kinnereth (phase II).[8]

There is little evidence of glyptic. The bone cylinders with linear decoration found at Gezer (phase I a),[9] at Jericho (phase I b)[10] and at Megiddo (phase III)[11] must be regarded as cylinder seals rather than beads. More interesting are the cylinder impressions appearing on fragments of jars found at Megiddo,[12] at Jericho[13] and elsewhere.[14] They can be dated to phase I and are analogous to impressions belonging to the beginning of the Early

[1] §I, 10, 161; §I, 30, 310.
[2] §VIII, 1, sect. 313, ll. 24 f.
[3] §I, 10, 161.
[4] §I, 30, 72.
[5] §VI, 7, 23, pl. XII, 13; pl. XVII, 30.
[6] §VIII, 5, pl. IV.
[7] §I, 30, 73.
[8] §I, 22, pl. II.
[9] §I, 19, pl. XXVIII, 21.
[10] §I, 17, fig. 27, 4.
[11] §I, 18, pl. 160, 1.
[12] §I, 6, 31 ff.; §VI, 4.
[13] §I, 26, 97, fig. 66.
[14] §VI, 8, 9.

Bronze Age at Byblos; they are comparable in style with the cylinders of Jamdat Naṣr and of the Early Dynasties in Meso-potamia. At Byblos flat seals were used in the Chalcolithic period;[1] in Palestine they appear only in the Early Bronze Age on two fragments at 'Ai[2] and, more important, on a jar at Tell el-Fār'ah (phase II) which bears the impression, several times repeated, of two square seals, one representing a serpent and the other a wild goat and a scorpion(?).[3]

Among the industries the best known is pottery, and it has been noted how far its products have assisted the chronological classification of the period. The principal types of domestic utensils have already been mentioned in this connexion. In addi-tion to the introduction of new forms, a great advance in the potter's art is apparent at the outset of the Early Bronze Age: the clay was better prepared and was mixed with a bonding of lime or crushed quartz; supplies of these materials mark the potters' workshops at Tell el-Fār'ah.[4] The use of the potter's wheel became general for small objects and for the necks of jars and spouts of jugs; stone turntables were found at Megiddo (stage IV and levels XVIII–XVII),[5] at Khirbet Karak[6] and at Tell el-Fār'ah (phase I b).[7] These technical improvements made it possible to turn the pottery more symmetrically. Moreover, the closed kiln came into use at this time and produced higher temperatures and more even firing. The earliest closed kiln in Palestine was found at Tell el-Fār'ah (end of phase I); it was com-posed of two chambers, set one above the other and separated by a sleeper pierced with flues.[8] There is evidence of this type of kiln in the fourth millennium in Iran, first at Sialk and then at Susa, and it was to reappear later in Greece and, in Roman Palestine, at Khirbet Qumrān. These 'industrial' processes, how-ever, tended to diminish the imaginative and aesthetic qualities which had distinguished the best products of the Chalcolithic period. Nevertheless, there were some remarkably successful pieces among the 'metallic ware' of phase II and the beautiful Khirbet Karak ware of phase III.

Although the use of the metal which gave its name to this period was well established, few examples of finished work have been recovered because the precious material was carefully

[1] §VI, 3, 25–8.

[2] §I, 23, 39, no. 63.

[3] §I, 31, 55 (551 f.); cf. §VI, 8.

[4] §I, 31, 55 (551), 68 (582).

[5] §I, 6, 40; §I, 18, pl. 268.

[6] §I, 21, 170.

[7] §I, 31, 54 (405).

[8] §I, 31, 62 (558 ff.). See Plate 37 (a).

retrieved and re-used. A chance find at Kfar Monash, between
Tel Aviv and Haifa,[1] produced the most important hoard: it
consisted of thirty-five pieces, including tools (axes, adzes,
chisels, knives, a saw) and weapons (daggers, lance-heads, a
mace); together with these objects some fragments of silver
leaves and some small copper plates were found, which could
have been the components of a scaled breast-plate. Analysis has
shown the metal to be copper, but its composition varies from
piece to piece; since the objects are homogeneous in type, it
must be concluded that they were made by local metalworkers
from ingots of diverse origin; some of the metal probably came
from Anatolia. With regard to the forms, the axes follow a model
prevalent at that time in Syria and Palestine, the adzes are of a
type known in Egypt at the end of the predynastic period and in
the first two dynasties, the chisels are similar to those of the great
find in the cave at Naḥal Mishmar, attributed to the Chalcolithic
period.[2] The hoard of Kfar Monash would appear to be a little later
in date and could be ascribed to phases I–II of the Early Bronze
Age. Another important group is that of Tell el-Ḥesi,[3] consisting
of half a dozen flat axes, two spearheads and a crescent-shaped
axe, similar to the one found in a Jericho tomb belonging to
phase III[4] and thus providing a date for the whole collection.
Apart from these objects, only a few others are worthy of mention:
from phase III, a triangular javelin-head at Tell el-Fār‘ah;[5] from
phase II, chisels at Gezer,[6] at Tell ed-Duweir[7] and at Megiddo,[8]
an axe at Gezer[9] and, at the very end of the period, a dagger at
Tell ed-Duweir.[10] Some at least of these objects had been manufactured on the spot; variations in the metal of the Kfar Monash
hoard have already been discussed above and the conclusion
reached there is confirmed by the discovery at Megiddo of a
pottery mould for casting an axe with a broad blade and narrow
shoulder and of a limestone mould for casting two axes of a different type.[11] The designation 'bronze' given to these objects is
conventional; analysis of the pieces from Megiddo,[12] Tell ed-
Duweir[13] and Jericho[14] shows them, like those from Kfar Monash,
to be made of copper, more or less pure.

A large proportion of tools still had to be made of stone, but

1 §vi, 5.
2 C.A.H. i[3], ch. ix, sect. vii.
3 §i, 5, figs. 69–78.
4 §vi, 6.
5 §i, 31, 55 (555).
6 §i, 19, pl. cxciii, 16.
7 §i, 30, pl. 22, 8.
8 §i, 18, pl. 184, 1.
9 §i, 19, pl. cxciii, 1.
10 §i, 30, pl. 22, 6.
11 §i, 6, fig. 13; §i, 18, pl. 269, 1.
12 §i, 6, 40.
13 §i, 30, 328.
14 §i, 10, 162.

the working of flint was much simplified.[1] Certain types belonging to earlier periods continued to be produced; there were some axes in the Taḥunian tradition and some fan-shaped scrapers, heavier than those of the Ghassūl and late Chalcolithic periods, but with a sharper edge; such tools disappeared otherwise after phase I. Graving-tools and arrows were both rare. The most numerous and also the most characteristic pieces were blades with the central ridge removed, trapezoidal in section; they were particularly fine in phase II and were often as much as 15 cm. long. Fragments of these blades, with a finely serrated edge, were used for making sickles. Bone tools were still plentiful and included needles, awls and stout piercers, and blades sharpened to a point.

Progress in agriculture and in industry led to an increase in prosperity, as was demonstrated by the development of urban life. Economic relations were necessarily established between the cities and with foreign countries, but it is possible only to guess at the nature of this domestic and foreign trade. Production of olive oil, for example, was in excess of local needs and oil was probably exported to Egypt as it was from Syria at the beginning of the Fifth Dynasty.[2] The choice of certain sites for settlement and their ensuing prosperity can be explained only by the proximity of a trade route. The position of Khirbet Karak at least is clear: it was then a great city which had been founded at the tip of Lake Tiberias in an area poorly developed but at the intersection of two important routes—one coming from Syria and going down into the Jordan valley and the other, from the direction of Damascus and Ḥaurān, proceeding towards the Mediterranean coast. The view that it was then a trading centre, a market, has perhaps been confirmed by the discovery of an enigmatic building, probably dating from phase III.[3] It was a rectangular compound, 40 × 30 m., composed of a platform 10 m. wide which surrounded a courtyard entered by a broad passage and preceded by a small covered hall. On the platform were nine paved circles slightly lower; they were from 7 to 8 m. in diameter and each contained four low projections which did not reach the centre and which must have been the bases of partitions. For lack of a better explanation it may be regarded as a storehouse for grain; each circle marked the position of a brick cupola, whose stability was secured by interior partitions; these storehouses were

---

[1] §1, 6, 78 ff.; §1, 10, 174 f.; §1, 30, 325 f.; §vi, 2.
[2] §vi, 1, pl. 3.
[3] §1, 21, 223 ff. See Plate 37 (b).

filled from the top and emptied through an opening contrived near ground level. In exactly the same way the huge granaries of ancient Egypt were built.[1]

VII. FOREIGN RELATIONS: CHRONOLOGY

The development of Palestine during this long period can be linked up with general history through its archaeological connexions with neighbouring countries.

There is no doubt that Palestine and southern Syria shared the same culture at that time and developed along the same lines. This unity was dictated by their geographical situation, but it is not possible to draw very close comparisons while the material recovered from Phoenician soil remains so sparse. The site of Byblos, which is exceptional, is somewhat distant; nevertheless, it appears to have followed a similar course of development to the Palestinian sites from its first urban settlement, which was contemporary with the foundation of the fortified cities of Canaan, down to the destruction of Byblos at the end of the Egyptian Sixth Dynasty, when the cities of 'Ai and Khirbet Karak were also destroyed. In pottery the same techniques and methods of decoration are apparent and, even though the shapes show that originality which always distinguishes Byblite products, some of them are comparable with the Palestinian types.[2] The publication of further material is expected to multiply these analogies. Objects from tomb 6 at Lebe'a, near Sidon, which is geographically nearer, are also closer in kind; it is a miscellaneous collection, but many of the vases might have been found in Palestine, where most of them would have been attributed to phase II and some to phase III.[3]

With north Syria connexions were fewer, but it is noteworthy that they extended as far as the Plain of Antioch and involved types of pottery which had evidently been introduced into Palestine from Syria. Jugs with a flat loop-handle, some burnished and some painted, which were an innovation of phase II, were found among pottery of the phase called 'Amūq G (Tell Judaidah XII).[4] Khirbet Karak ware was also typical of 'Amūq H

[1] But see A, 3.
[2] §vii, 4, pl. clxvi, 4975, 4976; pl. clxvii, 5101; pl. clxviii, 5246, 5302; pl. clxix, 5306: to be compared with Palestinian types, especially of phase II.
[3] §vii, 9, 42 ff., figs. 8–12.
[4] §vii, 3.

(Tell Judaidah XI)[1] and was plentiful at Tabara el-Akrād.[2] The corresponding Palestinian pieces are sufficiently numerous and have come from a sufficient number of sites not to be regarded as importations: they were manufactured on the spot, but provide evidence of relations with the north and probably of a new population wave. Intermediate stages are signalled at Qal'at er-Rus and at Tell Sukas in Alawite country by the presence of 'metallic ware' and by certain shapes belonging to phases II and III;[3] at Hama, level K, by sherds of Khirbet Karak ware and of burnished bowls;[4] at Ras Shamra by Khirbet Karak ware.[5] These forms probably appeared somewhat earlier in Syria, since they originated there. Further afield than north Syria, pottery and other objects show that there was contact with Anatolia,[6] which was the source of some of the copper work in Palestine.

Palestinian contact with Mesopotamia, on the other hand, was very limited throughout the whole of the Early Bronze Age. Impressions of cylinder seals on jars from the beginning of the period have been compared with Mesopotamian cylinder seals from Jamdat Naṣr and from the Early Dynastic period, but they reflect only indirect influence. It is possible to point only to a single imported object: at Jericho in a phase II level, an ivory bull's head was found which had probably adorned the elbow-rest of a throne; cavities were provided for the insertion of horns, the ears and the eyes, and for a triangular medallion on the forehead. The style is irrefutably Mesopotamian and the same points of detail occur on a bull's head from the Square Temple at Tell Asmar which was designed to serve the same purpose.[7]

Evidence of relations with Egypt is more plentiful. In the first place there are the objects which were imported into Palestine from Egypt. From phase I, a black stone palette bordered by incised lines, found at Jericho, belongs to a class manufactured in Egypt towards the end of the predynastic period and up to the First Dynasty.[8] A First-Dynasty cylinder belonging to the Clark Collection in Jerusalem, the provenance of which (Plain of Sharon) cannot be verified, must be treated with reserve.[9] The contents of the final sanctuary at 'Ai, belonging to phase III, include alabaster cups and a pink granite dish of Egyptian origin which

[1] §vii, 2, 7; §vii, 3.   [2] §vii, 10.
[3] §vii, 5.   [4] §vii, 11, pl. v.
[5] §vii, 18, 33 f.
[6] §vii, 1; §vii, 12; and even with Transcaucasia, A, 2.
[7] Cf. §i, 9, pl. xxa with §vii, 6, 24, fig. 26 and §vii, 7, 11, pl. 52, 302.
[8] Cf. §i, 11, pl. xxxvi, 26 with §vii, 15, pl. 58, types 96–7.
[9] §vii, 17, 233, pl. xxvi, 1.

cannot have beeen imported later than the Third Dynasty; an alabaster goblet with a flaring rim and several imitations of it in pottery belong to the Third or Fourth Dynasty.[1] Probably a proportion at least of these rare offerings had been preserved from the preceding stage of the sanctuary. Other Egyptian forms were copied by Palestinian potters: in the later Chalcolithic period and continuing into the Early Bronze Age there are vases with horizontally flattened lip, small horizontal flat or tubular handles and curved spout from Megiddo and from Ras el-'Ain which betray Egyptian influence.[2] Adzes from Kfar Monash are based on Egyptian models.[3]

Palestinian pottery has, on the other hand, been found in Egypt. The relations which prevailed in the Chalcolithic period were continued for part of phase I; it was during this latter period that the horizontal handle began its distinct development in both countries. In addition, a small globular amphora decorated with red lines should be noted, which was found at Abusīr el-Malaq[4] and belongs to a known type of phase I a. It appears that after this time relations between the two countries became more remote. Although objects imported or copied from Palestine at the end of the Chalcolithic period and beginning of the Early Bronze Age are scattered about in the cemeteries of ordinary people, vessels belonging to phase II have been found only in the tombs of kings or of important personages in Egypt, as though they had been offered as tribute or had contained some costly product. They are predominantly jugs, sometimes stump-based, either without handles or with a flat loop-handle at the neck and possibly two vertical handles on the belly. They are red-burnished or may be decorated with dotted triangles, in parallel rows or zig-zags, in red or black on a cream ground, and have been found in rich tombs of the First and, occasionally, the Second Dynasties.[5] Pitchers of the same shape and with the same lustre are typical of phase II at all the Palestinian sites where this phase is well represented; the pattern of dotted triangles is more uncommon, but it occurs in the tomb at Kinnereth[6] and at Dothan.[7] It is true that these types are found in Syria and therefore that the Egyptian vessels

[1] Cf. *Syria*, 16 (1935), 312, fig. 2; 333, fig. 3 and pl. LV with §VII, 16, 159 f., type 2-X; 178 f., type 3-X; 175 f., type I.

[2] Cf. §I, 6, type 23a; §I, 13, 121, no. 65 with Egyptian stone vases having tubular handles; for the spout cf. §VII, 15, pl. XVIII, F. 58.

[3] §VI, 5.   [4] §VII, 19, pl. XIII, 59.

[5] Particularly §VII, 13, pl. LIV; §VII, 14, pl. VIII; §VII, 20, pl. VIIIg (Abusīr el-Malaq, about the Second Dynasty).

[6] §I, 22.   [7] §VII, 8, 17; see above, pp. 45 ff.

could have come from there, but it must be allowed that they could also have come from Palestine, which is nearer. At all events these contacts establish that the beginning of phase II is almost contemporaneous with the First Dynasty in Egypt. With regard to phase III, no shape which is typical of the Palestinian series has yet been observed in Egypt, but 'Syrian' vessels are depicted in a relief of Sahure.[1]

These foreign contacts make it possible to formulate a relative chronology for the Early Bronze Age in Palestine. The beginning of the period is clearly earlier than the First Egyptian Dynasty. Phase II is certainly concurrent with the First and Second Egyptian Dynasties and its continuance during the Third Dynasty seems very probable. In consequence phase III must correspond with the Pyramid age. The end of the Early Bronze Age in Palestine coincides approximately with the beginning of the First Intermediate period in Egypt. Exact dating depends on the system of chronology which is adopted for Egypt and brought into line with that of Mesopotamia. It can only be said here that Palestinian archaeology is in favour of a short chronology keeping the evolution of the Early Bronze Age within the limits of a millennium, say between 3200 and 2200 B.C., if figures, which must necessarily be only approximate, are required.

VIII. OUTLINE OF HISTORY

The history of Palestine during this period cannot be written; but it is possible, through archaeological finds and from references in certain Egyptian texts, to trace the outlines of a sketch which is provisional and incomplete.

The Early Bronze Age civilization was not evolved either from the culture of Ghassūl-Beersheba in the south of Palestine which disappeared without leaving heirs, or from the culture of the red and grey burnished ware of the north, with which at the outset it lived in close proximity. It can be explained only by the influx of a new population, the first elements of which settled in the central regions of the country, which were less densely populated than the north and where the most important evidence of phase I*a* is to be found. These immigrants did not come from the south, which was reached only in slow stages by Early Bronze Age culture. The unity of culture apparent at that time with Byblos and South Syria (impressions on jars, pottery) shows that

[1] *M.D.O.G.* 37, fig. 6.

they came from the north, perhaps by way of the Jordan valley as far as Jericho, whence they penetrated into the interior of the country. Some groups intermingled with the makers of red and grey burnished ware in the large villages of the north. Their settlement was effected by peaceful infiltration and not by way of conquest. Nevertheless, these newcomers were destined to transform the country, for they brought with them new crafts, especially an established tradition of architecture and urban life. The sudden efflorescence of fortified cities in phase I*b* cannot be explained in any other way. The intensive use of brick, even in the mountainous regions, suggests that their place of origin or of previous settlement is to be sought in an area where this material is the most readily available, in valleys or alluvial plains. Upper Syria and Mesopotamia seem too far away and provide no archaeological points of contact; excavations in the Syrian–Lebanese Biqā' might perhaps disclose the elements of a solution to the problem.

If a historical name were desired for this new population of Palestine, the only one which could be suggested would be 'Canaanite'. It is true that the name appears only in the middle of the second millennium and that it denotes strictly a geographical entity which, apart from Phoenicia, extends over only a small part of Palestine. But in the Bible the name of Canaan is extended to cover the whole of Palestine, and the Canaanites are specified as the original Semitic population, distinct from the Amorites who, according to certain Biblical texts, appear to have arrived later. It is possible to place the Amorites in history: they were to appear towards the end of the third millennium. The name 'Canaanite' may therefore be retained, at least as the conventional name, for the earlier population whose Semitic origin is indicated, in the absence of native texts, by words and place-names preserved in Egyptian documents. Since there was no change of race or of culture in the course of the third millennium, the 'Canaanites' may be regarded as the founders of the Early Bronze Age; their settlement is represented archaeologically by the first phase (phase I*a* and *b*) between 3200 and 2900 approximately.

The second phase marks the apogee of the whole period: some splendid constructions date from this epoch, the working of flint was perfected and the beautiful pottery which then appeared revealed a new influence, at least in cultural matters, coming from the north. The number of occupied sites and the density of the settlements point to a numerous population, and the great fortified cities suggest that the territory was divided into small states, often at war with one another. The political situation remains obscure, however, and especially the part played by Egypt. Apart from Byblos, where Egyptian influence established itself very early, since it could be reached by sea, the Asiatic expeditions of the pharaohs of the early dynasties seem to have had as their principal objective the securing of free access to the turquoise mines against the nomads of Sinai. Vessels of Syro-Palestinian type found in First- and Second-Dynasty tombs may doubtless have been sent as tribute; they may also have been brought for trading purposes and thus, even if they originated in Palestine, provide no proof of Egyptian domination or political influence over the country. There is another fact which may lend even more weight to the argument: Egyptian Third-Dynasty vases found in the sanctuary at 'Ai could have been sent by a ruler who, while honouring the local divinity, was affirming his own power over the devotees of the cult; it would be easy to quote parallel instances. While there is nothing here to confirm the royal character of these anonymous offerings, they nevertheless show that some kind of relationship existed between the countries, and it is not impossible that, at this time, certain pharaohs were attempting to double their maritime trade with Byblos by means of a land route, which would presuppose control over part of Palestine. The Narmer palette could be adduced as evidence: the first pharaoh of the First Dynasty is there represented overthrowing two groups of enemies, some of whom are designated by the symbol of a city surrounded by a turreted rampart similar to some of the Palestinian ramparts of the time, while others are signalled by what seems to be a representation of enclosures for flocks and herds of a kind observed in Transjordan. It is possible that this palette commemorates a campaign against the cities of Palestine and against the nomads on the other side of the Jordan.[1] As further evidence, a potsherd from Tell esh-Sheikh el-'Areini bears a graffito which is interpreted as the name of Narmer; it may signify a period of domination over South Palestine at the time of the First Dynasty.[2]

In the following epoch the arrival of Khirbet Karak ware is evidence of the entry of new groups, again coming from the north. As regards Egypt, the facts are at first uncertain. Under the Fifth Dynasty, a scene in the tomb of Inti at Dishāsha represents the capture of a Canaanite city.[3] The mutilated inscription preserves two names of cities of which the first, Nd', cannot be

---

[1] §1, 31, 69 (215); §viii, 6, pl. xxix; §viii, 8—the writer there explains as a zikkurrat what I suppose to be a fortified city.

[2] §viii, 9, 10; see, however, above, p. 46.   [3] §viii, 5, pl. iv.

identified and the second, which begins '*Ain*–, merely confirms that the expedition spread out over the land of Canaan, without revealing whether it refers to Palestine or to Phoenicia. Under the Sixth Dynasty, the evidence is at last a little more explicit. In the reign of Phiops I a powerful army was led by Uni against the Asiatic 'dwellers of the sands' and five campaigns were necessary in order to break them; the same officer was then in charge of an expedition by sea against the land of the Antelope Nose, beyond a mountainous barrier to the north of the country of the 'dwellers of the sands'.[1] Wherever the 'Antelope Nose' may have been, whether it signifies Carmel or a more northern promontory, it is certain that the earlier campaigns, which were conducted by land and were distinguished by the destruction of fortresses and the cutting-down of fig-trees and vines, were directed against a civilized country with a settled population, which could only be Palestine. It is possible to discern an attempt to establish—or re-establish—Egyptian domination over this country, but it may also be interpreted as a simple defensive action against pressure coming from the north and threatening Egypt.

Such pressure did not come directly from the other great oriental power, Mesopotamia: even at the time of its greatest expansion, under Sargon of Agade, the eastern empire never reached Palestine. A movement was beginning, however, which was to disturb the whole of the Fertile Crescent. Archaeology shows that Palestine was then entering upon a troubled period. After the end of phase II, sites such as Tell el-Fār'ah near Nablus and Ras el-'Ain were deserted. Megiddo was abandoned during phase III. At the end of this phase the movement gathered force and, at dates which were nearly contemporaneous, occupation ceased at Beth-shan, Khirbet Karak, 'Ai and probably Jericho. It was not resumed until a more or less advanced stage of the Middle Bronze age at Tell el-Fār'ah, Ras el-'Ain, Megiddo, Beth-shan; until Iron Age I at 'Ai, and until the Hellenistic Period at Khirbet Karak. Almost at the same time, however, as these urban centres were being extinguished, others were beginning to be established, such as at Tell Beit Mirsim, Beth Shemesh, Bethel. There appears to have been at first only a decadent off-shoot of the Early Bronze Age civilization, which was falling to pieces. It was at this period also that the settled occupation began of a part of Transjordan and, for a while, in the Negev.

It would indeed be rash to attribute the disappearance of so

1 §VIII, I, sect. 311 ff.

many cities and the upheaval of an entire civilization to the expeditions of Uni mentioned above. The disturbance was on an entirely different scale and it is more probable that Uni's campaigns were themselves provoked by the beginning of these troubles which, in unsettling Palestine, threatened Egypt itself. The course of Egyptian history throws light on events in Palestine: under Phiops II Byblos was destroyed by fire and, perhaps in the same reign, Ipuwer complained that there were no further expeditions by sea to Byblos.[1] According to the same sage, social disorders, which marked the beginning of the first Intermediate period in Egypt, were aggravated by the infiltration of Asiatic foreigners.[2] There even came a time when these Asiatics seized power in the Delta, whence they were expelled by the penultimate king of the Tenth Dynasty, Achthoes III. This pharaoh, in the course of instructions given to his son Merykare, gave him urgent charge of the eastern frontier of Egypt, which had to be defended against the unruly barbarians who had been expelled by him, but who remained dangerous; they were represented as nomads, warriors and plunderers.[3] In similar terms a contemporary Sumerian text describes the Amorites who were threatening Mesopotamia[4] and who are first mentioned unambiguously as far back as the middle of the Agade dynasty.[5] All these facts must be considered in relation to one another: the great thrust from the desert, which struck Mesopotamia and Egypt at the same time, necessarily had its effect upon Palestine. The Amorites were responsible for the decadence which characterized the end of the Early Bronze Age; they brought about the eclipse of urban life which was typical of the Intermediate Early Bronze–Middle Bronze period.[6] But it has been argued that in Palestine the Amorites entered a country already devastated by invaders of a different race and origin.[7] The problem should remain open.

[1] §VIII, 3, sect. 3, 7.
[2] *Ibid.* sect. 3, 1; 4, 7–8. But the dating of Ipuwer is in dispute, J. van Seters in *J.E.A.* 50 (1964), 13 ff.
[3] §VIII, 4, sects. 20–4.   [4] §VIII, 2, 20.
[5] §VIII, 7, II, 133 *a*.   [6] See below, pp. 568 ff.
[7] P. Lapp, *The Dhahr Mirzbâneh Tombs*, New Haven, 1966.

CHAPTER XVI

THE EARLY DYNASTIC PERIOD IN MESOPOTAMIA

I. BABYLONIA: ARCHAEOLOGICAL DEVELOPMENT

AN earlier chapter (XIII) has described the historical development of the cities in Babylonia and their cultural background. Here we must concentrate on the archaeological evidence, for this is by far the richest source for the study of man's development in the Early Dynastic period. Indeed, when we come to discuss developments in Assyria and Mesopotamia proper, historical records are so scarce that the archaeological evidence becomes our primary source of reference.

The Early Dynastic period of Babylonia has been divided into three parts and the archaeological development has been traced through an exhaustive analysis of stratified objects. At present the most satisfactory ground for this study is the Diyālā valley, where extensive excavations have provided a detailed and continuous relationship between buildings and the small finds associated with them. The principal objects were cylinder seals, pottery, sculpture and metal. Each category was subjected to stylistic examination and compared with similar material from sites outside the Diyālā valley. In the Diyālā district itself no mound proved more rewarding than Khafājī, where the long sequence of 'Sin Temples' could be related to many other less complete sequences of religious and domestic buildings discovered there and elsewhere.

The analysis of style is, however, complicated by the fact that development did not proceed *pari passu* everywhere. Thus solid-footed clay goblets which were used in the Uruk–Jamdat Naṣr period at Warka, Ur and Nippur did not appear before Early Dynastic I on the Diyālā; the same observation applies to reserved slip ware. Archaic seals frequently occur in contexts much later than those to which they originally belonged. Moreover, when we attempt to estimate the chronology of architectural development, we are hampered by the fact that we have no precise yardstick for measuring the time span of a building. Architectural forms can survive longer at one site than at another, so that a tendency to archaism may complicate our chronological calculations. Bearing in mind these reservations, we can, however, accept certain criteria.

The cylinder-seal displays marked changes in style. The 'brocade' pattern of design, a natural development from the Jamdat Naṣr period, is particularly characteristic of Early Dynastic (E.D.) I. It has to be remembered, however, that these seals are chiefly representative of the Diyālā valley sites but comparatively rare elsewhere, and that excavation of E.D. I levels in many places outside this valley is required to complete our picture of the glyptic styles of this period.

Combat scenes between men and animals, apparently a first attempt to illustrate current mythology,[1] appear in E.D. II; the subjects include banquet scenes, boating scenes, and the Sacred Marriage (?). Subsequently, in E.D. III, similar subjects are represented, but whereas in E.D. II the style tended to be linear, it was now in decorative relief;[2] the figures became more compact and massive and were evolving toward the heraldic arrangement that may be discerned in the Agade period. Another development of E.D. III seal-cutting is the more orderly arrangement of the inscriptions, which were neatly compartmented.

The ceramic development is too complicated to follow in detail without extensive illustration, and there are no hard and fast lines of demarcation, but some types may be noted as especially characteristic. 'Scarlet ware' pottery is perhaps commonest in E.D. I, continues, but perhaps declines, in E.D. II, and is probably almost obsolete by E.D. III. A plastic ridge on the shoulder of a vase is perhaps the best criterion of E.D. II; potstands, beakers or goblets, flasks of 'pilgrim' type, big jars with nicked shoulders, vases with tab handles and tall, elegant fruitstands were common. In E.D. III new types were rare; the pottery as a whole declined in quality and thus formed a striking contrast with metal work, which then reached its apogee. Jars with upright handles, carrying incised and plastic decoration, often depicting a 'goddess', are characteristic of E.D. III both in the Diyālā valley and at Kish.[3] Vases decorated with studs correspond with types found in the Indus Valley.[4]

Metal was still comparatively rare in E.D. I, but there was a notable development in E.D. II when the lost-wax process for the making of human and animal figures and pot-stands appears to have been much exploited. The development of metal work,

[1] §1, 2. [2] §1, 5.
[3] §II, 5, 89 f. and pl. 84b. [4] Ibid. 144.

however, reached a climax in E.D. III when armourers made heavy and efficient weapons of war, axes, spears and adzes. These instruments were frequently copied in gold and in silver, either as votive deposits for the dead, or for the gods. There was a prodigious output of jewellery and sumptuary work which was often elegant in design and restrained in decoration.

The working of lapis lazuli is also an important criterion for estimating the development both of trade and of craftsmanship. The only known source is Badakhshān in Afghanistān and the use of this stone in Babylonia implies that the distant trade routes from this point of origin were open. No lapis lazuli is known to have been worked in E.D. I; it was still relatively rare in E.D. II but became abundant in E.D. III. As this stone had been worked much earlier in prehistoric Assyria, we must assume that by E.D. III Babylonia had diverted the lapis trade route to itself, a hypothesis which tallies with the cuneiform texts: it will be remembered that Enmerkar (E.D. II) was apparently engaged in a successful struggle with Aratta, a city in southern Iran, in order to obtain this and other semi-precious stones.[1]

The style of stone vessels remained more or less static throughout the period, but characteristic of E.D. I and extinct thereafter is a bowl with an exceptionally wide-ledge rim, a carry-over from the Jamdat Naṣr period.[2] These vessels appear to have remained in the Diyālā district after they had disappeared in Babylonia. In E.D. III there is a decorated stone vessel type which found its way to the Indus Valley and provides the earliest evidence of trade with India.[3] At the end of the period stone vases were being abundantly produced and must have been a valuable article of trade.

The development of stone statuary is discussed below and we may anticipate the more detailed references to it by remarking that E.D. II was the period at which representations of gods and men became common. These carvings, for the most part in soft stone, were clumsy, both in the round and in relief, and the sculptor was unskilled in the rendering of the human limbs. In the latter part of E.D. III, however, some striking advances were made towards a greater realism; details of the body such as the nipples attracted attention and human dress became pleasingly decorative. The Sumerian sculptor displayed a greater assurance in the rendering of animals, especially in the cutting of amulets, and these, in metal as well as in stone, are a perpetual delight; the standard forms were already well established in E.D. II.

The progress of architecture will also be discussed in detail

---

[1] §I, 10.   [2] §II, 5, pl. 48; §III, 36, pl. 34.   [3] References on p. 254 below.

below. The standard form of temple persisted throughout the period and had long been established,[1] but the layout became more spacious with the advance of time and reflected both the addition of divinities to the cult and a growth in the population, which required more elaborate administrative quarters. In E.D. III we find the first palaces[2]—at Eridu, Kish and Mari; it would seem that previously the king must have resided in the temple. Finally it should be noted that the plano-convex brick became the standard component for the building of walls, but this was primarily confined to Babylonia, and the Diyālā, and was used neither in Assyria nor in Syria, except at Tell Brak, which enjoyed an exceptionally close relationship with cities on the southern Euphrates.

CHRONOLOGY AND STRATIFICATION

The most instructive series of stratified buildings is that discovered at the site of Khafājī in the Diyālā valley. The ten 'Sin Temples' situated there began with Sin I in the late Uruk–Jamdat Naṣr period, and ended with Sin X shortly before 2400 B.C. There was an unbroken tradition of architectural planning, for the kernel of the original layout may still be discerned in the latest of the series. The Early Dynastic stage began with Sin VI, where plano-convex bricks appeared for the first time, and ended with Sin X.

Delougaz has made an interesting attempt[3] to estimate the span of time which elapsed during the occupation of each successive temple and strikes a mean between several possible solutions. The basis of calculation was the measurement of the depth of débris outside the entrance to Sin Temple VII. There he was able to relate the rise in ground level to sixteen successive coats of mud plaster on the walls. Since in Mesopotamia the replastering of an old wall is normally done once a year, it is probable that the observed rise in floor levels corresponded with a lapse of sixteen years. By measuring the total height of the rubbish that had accumulated in various places from the first occupation of the temple to the last, the total lifetime of Temple VII in its two phases was reckoned at 116 years. There are many complications in making an assessment for the whole series, because the vertical depth of débris varied at different points within the building—

[1] *C.A.H.* I[3], ch. VIII, sect. I.

[2] Some authorities believe that the palaces at Eridu and Kish should be ascribed to E.D. II; see E. Porada in §III, 13, 161, and *Z.A.* 58, 262.

[3] §II, 7, 135.

for example, accumulation in the courtyard was more rapid than in the sanctuary, which was kept cleaner. Nevertheless, there is a good case for awarding a span of about 100 years to Sin VII, and using the same principle of calculation we may reckon that E.D. I (Sin VI, VII) lasted for about 200 years; E.D. II (Sin VIII and the earliest phase of Sin IX) about 100 years; E.D. III (most of Sin IX, and Sin X) about 250 years—say 550 years in all. To this we must add something for the lapse of time between the abandonment or destruction of one building and the foundation of its successor—an unknown factor, for which a total of 50 years in all may not be exaggerated. Since Sin X probably ended shortly before the Agade period, c. 2300 B.C., we thus arrive at a date of c. 3000 B.C. for the beginning of E.D. I. A case could be made for the higher, or for a lower, chronology, as Delougaz has demonstrated, but this one seems to be a solution which at present accords best with the historical probabilities, and it has a strong recommendation in that archaeologically E.D. I seems likely to follow directly after the predynastic period in Egypt, perhaps a little later than Menes, for whom a mean date of c. 3100 B.C.[1] may be assigned on the basis of Egyptian chronology.

Unfortunately, this apparently satisfactory estimate for the length of the E.D. period does not agree with recent carbon-14 findings, particularly for material from Nippur lately tested, which may require a reduction of third millennium dates by as much as six or seven centuries.[2] We have to face the possibility that if the newly emerging carbon-14 pattern for the third millennium is the right one, we must jettison the whole of the previously accepted basis of Egyptian chronology upon which the Mesopotamian in large part depends. But we should be reluctant to do this without much stronger contrary evidence, for Egyptian calculations based on written evidence can be checked on astronomical grounds with but a comparatively small margin of error and, if we accept a low carbon-14 chronology for the E.D. period, we are faced with a big and unexplained hiatus between this and the neolithic, for which the same method has given unexpectedly high dates. Some authorities are therefore for the present inclined to believe

---

[1] C.A.H. I³, ch. VI, sect. 1; and above, ch. XI, sect. 1.

[2] Recent determinations for samples from the Inanna temple at Nippur average 2253 B.C. ±23 for E.D. I, 2184 B.C. ±41 for E.D. II, and 2124 B.C. ±64 for the transition from E.D. II to III. Other examples of unexpectedly late carbon-14 dates, together with references, are quoted in §III, 28, 40, with footnotes 201–4. See also carbon-14 determinations for Saqqara, Egypt, especially B.M. 230, 231, 235, where third millennium dates are consistently low by at least four or five centuries, B.M. 234 by at least seven centuries.

that at this end of the third millennium there was some physical disturbance in the solar magnetic field, which may have affected the level of the carbon-14 activity in the carbon exchange reservoir. This level may well have been higher than normal during the third millennium B.C., and this would make all the dates appear later than in fact they were. But the problem is unreal, for very recent study has made it clear that carbon-14 determinations for the third millennium in the Near East and elsewhere are erroneous, and that published dates are more than five hundred years too low.[1]

However that may be, there is a case for making an approximate accord between the 500 years or so which, on grounds of stratigraphy, we can allocate to E.D. I–III and the Early Dynastic succession in the Sumerian king-list, although we should incline to some reduction in dating since many of the monarchs written down as successive in the lists are known to have been contemporary.[2] Nevertheless, the reduction in dating need not be anything like as drastic as that of carbon-14. On balance the great depth of accumulation, the long series of formidably constructed temples, and a much greater depth of house débris must incline us to opt for a relatively long rather than a short chronology. We have, however, no method at all of judging the length of the hypothetical dynasty or dynasties that correspond with the archaeological series defined as E.D. I. Historically these monarchs would be the ones who preceded an event which left an indelible impression on Mesopotamian folk memory, namely, the Flood.

THE FLOOD AND THE END OF EARLY DYNASTIC I

Although the Flood was not the universal phenomenon that it has often been claimed to be, there is no doubt that it was exceptional among the long series of recorded Mesopotamian floods and that it overwhelmed parts of various cities in southern Babylonia. But in spite of its volume much that was on high ground or remote from the main stream escaped and, as with many other floods, most traces of it have long been swept away. Nevertheless, there are good reasons for claiming that alluvial mud deposits which have been observed at Ur and at Kish in houses, and at Fārah (Shuruppak), corresponded with the one described in the Gilgamesh epic and transmitted, perhaps through Canaanite mytho-

---

[1] H. E. Suess in *Journal of Geophysical Research*, 70 (1965), no. 23; and see now Minze Stuiver and H. E. Suess in *Radiocarbon*, 8 (1966), pp. 534 f., where it is shewn that carbon-14 determinations for the third millennium in the Near East and elsewhere are incorrect.   [2] See above, pp. 106 f.

logy, to the Old Testament record. This important landmark in the dawn of history was associated with the person of a Sumerian king named Ziusudra who was reigning at Shuruppak, precisely where a clean flood stratum has been found. He may conveniently be taken to mark the end of E.D. I, for he was succeeded by a new dynasty at Kish which is accepted as beginning E.D. II. Unfortunately, we know nothing about the predecessors of Ziusudra, but as we have already demonstrated above, there is much archaeological material, and some buildings, particularly in the Diyālā valley, which we may assign to the Early Dynastic period I, which he terminated. For this reason we shall below attempt some description of the contemporary temples in the Diyālā valley where the evidence is at present fuller than elsewhere.

EARLY DYNASTIC II–III AND THE ARCHAEOLOGICAL RECORD

Most of the kings of Kish and Uruk that can be assigned to E.D. II are shadowy figures, but a few of them may be correlated with the archaeological sequences. Thus Enmebaragisi, the penultimate king of E.D. II in Kish, must have reigned when Sin Temple VIII at Khafājī (Tutub) was flourishing, and indeed the record of his name was discovered on this site.[1] A hero of Uruk named Enmerkar has already been mentioned as the conqueror of the Iranian city of Aratta and the records name him as the builder of Uruk; some of the early dynastic buildings on that site must therefore have been founded by him.[2] A more famous successor, Gilgamesh, once a mythical character, now joins the realm of history as repairer of the Tummal at Nippur; this building has not yet been identified, but on the other hand we may relate him to the town walls of Uruk, composed of plano-convex bricks and reputedly built by him. The reign of Gilgamesh marks the beginning of E.D. III, and his successors have been discussed above.[3]

For E.D. III the archaeological record at Ur is particularly informative. The monarchs of the 'Kalam' Dynasty, Meskalamdug and Akalamdug, are associated with two royal tombs both luxuriously equipped with gold weapons and other treasure. Akalamdug, together with 'Shub-ad' (now proposed to be read as a Semitic name, Pu-Abi[4]), belongs to the earlier part of the sequence, E.D. III*a*, and must be approximately contemporary with Sin Temple IX, in which associated objects are closely

---

[1] §1, 4, 9 ff.; *C.A.H.* I³, ch. vi, sect. ii. [2] See above, pp. 110 f.
[3] See above, pp. 111 f. [4] I. J. Gelb, *Glossary of Old Akkadian*, 12 and 210.

comparable with those accompanying these rulers at Ur. Meska-lamdug, however, who was buried in one of the higher-lying and latest of these graves, may perhaps be associated with E.D. III*b*.

The successors of the 'Kalam' Dynasty were the kings of the so-called First Dynasty of Ur (E.D. III*b*), and the two most famous names are Mesannipada and A'annipada,[1] the latter best known as the builder of the temple at 'Ubaid with its typically Sumerian frieze representing the milking of cattle outside the temple gate; his temple was also endowed with large models in copper of cattle, lions, and stags and a spread eagle, partly cast by the *cire perdue* process.

The place of these two monarchs in the Royal Cemetery of Ur poses an intriguing problem, for although their names are attested, their graves have never been found. We may, however, with confidence come to two conclusions. First, that their tombs must have been nearer the surface than that of 'Shub-ad' and the deep-shaft graves, and that in consequence they were looted and destroyed. Secondly, that comparative inaccessibility probably saved the deeper ones from similar robbery, for the later monarchs must have been buried directly above the older shafts, the upper portion of which contained only rammed earth and misled the robbers into thinking that they had nothing more to gain. The overlying stratum known as SIS 1–2, which contained scattered débris, such as cylinder seals looted from tombs, represented all that was left of the plundered graves of Mesannipada and his immediate successors.[2] The discovery at Mari in a palace of E.D. III of a present from this king of Ur to a contemporary monarch on the Euphrates provides us with a notable synchronism.[3]

There can be little doubt that a part of the First Dynasty of Ur, E.D. III*b*, was nearly contemporary with the dynasty of Ur-Nanshe of Lagash, whose stone carvings and weapons, beautifully executed, are perhaps slightly more advanced in style than the corresponding ones at Ur; at all events these Lagashite treasures were fashioned by a superior school of craftsmen.[4]

A notable break in the history of Ur occurred at the end of its first dynasty which, we may suspect, was overthrown by Eanna-tum of Lagash whose inscriptions and statuary relate that he was overlord of Ur, and whose 'Stele of the Vultures' depicts him as equipped in the style associated with the early kings of Ur. Indeed

---

[1] As above, pp. 112 f. For a contrary, unorthodox opinion, see H. J. Nissen, *Zur Datierung des Königsfriedhofes von Ur*, Bonn, 1966.

[2] §III, 35, pl. 270, illustrates the position of SIS 1–2 in relation to the Royal Cemetery.   [3] See below, p. 297.   [4] But see above, p. 117. [Ed.]

with Eannatum it is tempting to associate much other archaeological evidence concerning the sacking of Babylonian and Mesopotamian cities in E.D. III—notably the violent burning of Khafājī (Tutub) at the end of Sin Temple IX, within which a mutilated statue was found of a ruler of Akshak, one of the places which Eannatum boasts of conquering. The same king also claimed Mari, and here we find many traces of a deliberate sack in the last of the early Ishtar Temples (a), where in the ashes much scattered treasure of advanced E.D. III style was found. Before that time Mari and Ur were living in amity, as we may judge from a treasure presented by Mesannipada. There are thus valid reasons to attribute to Eannatum the archaeological evidence of destruction in both of these cities, for he is known historically to have adopted a change of policy towards them. An alternative view would, however, relate these events with later monarchs.[1]

Two other famous men, Lugalzaggisi of Uruk, and Urukagina of Lagash, the reformer, reigned towards the end of E.D. III b. It is customary to style these monarchs as belonging to the 'proto-imperial' period, but we may disregard this hybrid terminology, for the remains associated with them are hardly to be distinguished from those typical of E.D. III b, and it seems simpler to terminate the period with the advent of Sargon of Agade, whose accession to the throne ushers in a new period both in archaeology and in history. It is, however, true that significant changes in artisanship were occurring before Sargon, indeed by the time of Entemena, a predecessor of Urukagina, the plano-convex brick was becoming obsolete.[2] Urukagina, one of the last of these pre-Sargonic monarchs, will long be remembered because he waged a campaign against the multiplication of officials as well as their exactions. For this lavish increase in officialdom we may see the evidence in Sin Temple X with its numerous service chambers, which had grown in number beyond all bounds when compared with the simple appurtenances of the earlier foundations.

II. THE DIYĀLĀ VALLEY

THE SIN TEMPLES AT KHAFĀJĪ

Sin Temple VI, the first of the Early Dynastic temples, was directly derived from its predecessor, Sin V, but the walls were for the first time built of plano-convex bricks instead of the older *Riemchen* which were characteristic of the Jamdat Naṣr period.

[1] See below, pp. 296 f.   [2] §II, 13, 80.

This new unit of construction beginning in E.D. I was used throughout Sin VI–X; it was probably derived from an earlier form of pudding-shaped cement brick such as had been used at Ur and Eridu rather than from stone work, as some authorities have supposed. Stone had rarely been used for building previously and there is no reason to assume that the masons of E.D. I were influenced by stone walling from abroad.

Sin VI, as we have seen, was but an enlargement, at a higher level, of an older plan. It differed from its predecessor, however, in that the entire enclosure was surrounded with a girdle wall; all the subsidiary chambers became an integral part of the temple. Only a few of the older walls could be used as a foundation and the new temple was for the most part set on a roughly levelled surface; for the first time the approach was through a gateway which consisted of stairs between flanking towers. There can be little doubt that this formidable building, more than 30 m. in length, marked a change of dynasty.

The conservatism of the cult was, however, apparent from the arrangement of the main sanctuary, an oblong room, approximately 12×4 m. in dimension, with a large mud-brick box-podium at the short end. The older arrangement of side chambers was eliminated. Access to the sanctuary was through a long hall provided with mud tables for use in the cult; this arrangement foreshadowed the eventual transformation, in Sin X, of a second ritual chamber no less important than the sanctuary itself. In Sin VI service-rooms were introduced behind the main sanctuary, which now stood at the extreme end of the building—an older long room on its far side was abolished.

The dimensions of the sanctuary are of interest—a ratio of $3:1$ for length as to breadth, in this respect conforming with that of an earlier and larger 'Eye-Temple' at Tell Brak in North Syria which measured 18×6 m.[1] A similar ratio can be discerned at Warka and at 'Uqair in the Jamdat Naṣr period. Thus we have proof that Early Dynastic architects both in Babylonia and in Syria worked to certain canons of proportion which were applied to buildings of variant size and similar plan in far distant centres. This particular canon is, however, not constant everywhere: on many sites there are variations.

The sanctuary of Sin VI was provided with a single entrance at the far end of the building remote from the courtyard, and it is thus clear that the cult was esoteric, reserved for the priesthood and the rulers, while the public was confined to the spacious courtyard where it brought and deposited offerings for the cult.

[1] §IV, 5, 61 and 62, n. 1.

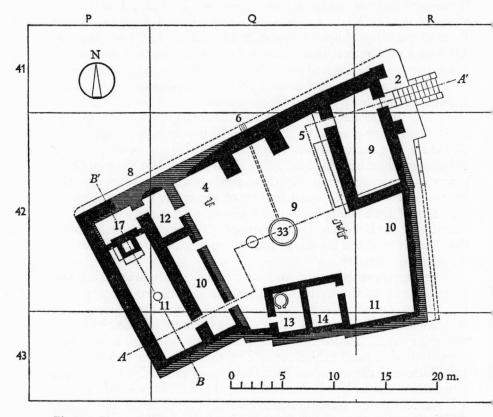

Fig. 1. Plan of first occupation level of Sin Temple VII at Khafājī. Early Dynastic I. Excavated foundations marked in solid black, reconstructed foundations by broken lines; reconstructed walls hatched. (*O.I.P.* LVIII, pl. 8. By permission of the Oriental Institute, University of Chicago.)

These offerings were cooked in spacious kitchens which formed one wing of the temple. In Sin VII hearths and lustral basins were situated in the sanctuary as well as in the court. These basic arrangements for worship survived throughout till the end of Sin X where, as we shall see, some modifications occurred, notably in the adaptations which were made so that the public might play a more intimate part in the celebration of the cult. There was but one level of occupation in this temple, which must have been kept in good order throughout its lifetime.

The plan (see Fig. 1) of the next temple in the series, Sin VII, conformed closely with that of its predecessor, except that some of the chambers in the courtyard were abolished. The walls of the new sanctuary rested directly over the old and may be assigned to the same period, E.D. I; the re-dedication was clearly marked by laying reed mats or bundles of reeds over the surface of the older ruins before the new building began.

In the courtyard of Sin VII there was a large, circular ablution pit or basin, lined with kiln-fired plano-convex bricks of a type still used in the royal tombs of the E.D. III*a* period at Ur. The entrance steps were flanked by a well-preserved and beautifully rendered step-like parapet; the stairs were waterproofed with bitumen. It was here that the excavators, by skilful technique in the uncovering of successive coats of wall plaster, succeeded in relating them to the corresponding accumulation of ground débris, and were able to make theoretical calculations for the lifetime of the temple. As we have seen, this may have lasted for 116 years in all, including two successive occupations of the same building; the later one was 30–50 cm. above the level of the earlier. These two levels, however, varied in different parts of the building; the floors of the new court were 130 cm. above the old, but the sanctuary was only 80 cm. higher. The objects associated with the temple were informative, for they included, as in Sin VI, cylinder seals in the 'brocade style' which has long been recognized as the hall mark of E.D. I.

There was one object of special significance for the history of sculpture; a limestone statuette of a squatting figure carrying a load against the back of his head, the very prototype of a Kurdish porter![1] This rudimentary carving, found in the sanctuary, is not only inferior to the skilled stone work of the preceding Uruk–Jamdat Naṣr period, but also falls far short of the development of statuary in E.D. II–III. It may be that future work in E.D. I levels will redress our estimate, but for the present it would seem that this period marked a decline in the carving of the human form, which did not claim the artists' serious attention before E.D. II.

Sin Temple VIII (see Fig. 2), which conformed with the general layout of its predecessor, none the less shared certain marked and decisive changes in structure which indicate that it must be assigned to a new period, namely E.D. II. Not only were the foundations more massive than those of any of the earlier temples, but deep trenches were dug for the first time to accommodate them. It has been suggested that when the new building was erected the ruins of the older one were no longer visible and that consequently there must have been an interval of more than

[1] §II, 10, pl. 69, no. 92.

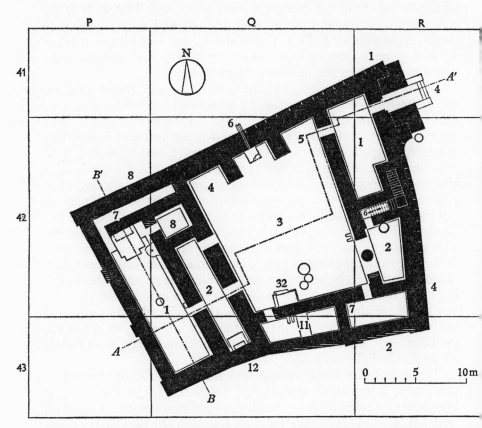

Fig. 2. Plan of first occupation level of Sin Temple VIII at Khafājī. Early Dynastic II. Foundations marked in solid black; reconstructed walls hatched. (*O.I.P.* LVIII, pl. 10. By permission of the Oriental Institute, University of Chicago.)

usual length between the two constructions.[1] However that may be, the architect of the E.D. II building must have been well aware of the older plan, as a glance at the two will show.

The whole building was lengthened—the sanctuary to approximately 15 m.—but even so, when tightly packed, it could hardly have accommodated more than about 50 persons. Perhaps, therefore, it was to meet popular pressure that for the first time an open-air altar or podium was introduced into the courtyard, in a place accessible to many. In addition, a second altar had appeared at one end of the ante-cella.

[1] §II, 7, 52 and pl. 10.

Yet another significant innovation was the introduction of a large mud column, more than a metre in diameter in the middle of an entrance separating the court from one of the large chambers on its eastern side. This, and the fact that the long eastern and northern façades of the building were pierced at intervals with small rectangular holes, brings this structure into an architectural relationship with the Early Dynastic palace at Kish,[1] which, however, is now usually assigned to the beginning of E.D. III, and indeed it seems that before E.D. III the king may have lived in the temple, for there is no evidence that any secular building was made available for him before that time.[2] However that may be, we have evidence of a close link between the two periods, both in architectural design and in material objects, as we shall see later. There was evidence in this temple of stairs leading to the roof, upon which religious ceremonies, including the ushering in of the dawn, must have taken place, as we know from late Akkadian texts.[3]

There were three main occupations of the building in all; the two later ones were approximately 30 and 60 cm. above the level of the first. As the walls were very wide and solidly built, we have every reason to believe that Sin VIII lasted as long as its predecessor—probably even longer.

The varieties of objects found in Sin VIII include some that are still in the style of the Jamdat Naṣr period, others allegedly of E.D. II, and many that are indistinguishable from products of E.D. III. On architectural grounds, however, we are justified in allocating this temple to E.D. II and the conclusion to be drawn is that the craftsmanship of E.D. II and E.D. III is often so similar as to be identical.

Cylinder seals in Sin VIII are informative. In addition to an archaic cache which had survived from the Jamdat Naṣr period we have others which are a development of the E.D. I brocade style, for example a procession of ibex in a linear style which is perhaps a good criterion of E.D. II.[4] Significant of later developments is a seal depicting a hero with a kind of cock's comb[5] as in the Royal Cemetery of Ur and in Kish A Cemetery where it was found in a grave near the Palace and may conceivably belong to the subsequent period. There is, however, one remarkable object which was certainly made for Sin VIII. This is a mobile cult-waggon, in pottery, a table on four wheels representing a house with ladder against its front and birds under the eaves of the roof

[1] See *ibid.* 59, fig. 51, and below, pp. 274 f.   [2] See above, p. 241, n. 2.
[3] §II, 18, 38 f.   [4] §II, 12, nos. 242–3.   [5] *Ibid.* no. 245.

which supported a tall pedestal vase or fruit stand. This ritual vessel, which was perhaps used for lecanomancy, cannot be dissociated from the model houses found in the Archaic Ishtar Temple G at Ashur, and the mobile terracotta waggon found in the Royal Cemetery of Ur.[1] If the Ashur models are of E.D. III*b*, as is generally supposed, they are in a direct line of descent from the object found in the E.D. II temple at Khafājī. A miniature gold bull is another object directly connected with the Royal Cemetery of Ur.[2]

No less interesting, as showing the very close relationship between E.D. II and E.D. III, is the sculpture. A copper bull's head of a rather simpler type than most of the specimens from the Royal Cemetery of Ur has been assigned to Sin VIII.[3] Among the damaged pieces of sculpture we have two figures, one behind the other in a chariot, which resemble the crude work of E.D. I,[4] and female heads[5] on which the coiffure is closely comparable with that of the gypsum maidens from Ashur Temple G.[6] Such comparisons can leave us in no doubt that E.D. II–III are in a homogeneous line of development. Even the archaic-looking schist palette in the shape of a lion-headed bird is inscribed in characters of uncertain meaning which are probably related in style to the Fārah inscriptions, but may be even earlier.

Sin IX was described by Delougaz as 'a reconstruction necessitated by normal wear and tear of Sin VIII rather than by any external causes'. Its plan (see Fig. 3) conformed closely with that of its predecessors, and its five successive occupations were not accompanied by any important change in plan. The first four of these phases were classified by Frankfort as E.D. II; only the last phase was he willing to assign to E.D. III*a*.[7] But we have to recognize that throughout Sin IX we find objects which are indistinguishable in style from those commonly associated with E.D. III, for example the Royal Cemetery of Ur, the early part of which might well, therefore, have been classified as E.D. II. Indeed, it might be better to admit the whole of E.D. II–III as a single period under the name of E.D. II, including sub-phases of minor artistic and architectural development. But rather than

---

[1] §II, 7, 57, fig. 49; §II, 4, 75 f.; §III, 35, pl. 188*a*.

[2] §II, 7, 145.

[3] Compare §II, 10, pl. 104, no. 184 with §III, 35, pls. 116–17 (PG 1332), which was more elaborate, had curls on forehead and crown, folds in the base of the ear and over the eyes, suggesting a more advanced stage of casting in detail.

[4] §II, 10, no. 91.

[5] *Ibid.* nos. 130, 133, 139, 140, 145, 147, 148.

[6] §II, 4, Taf. 46.   [7] See the chart at end of §II, 7.

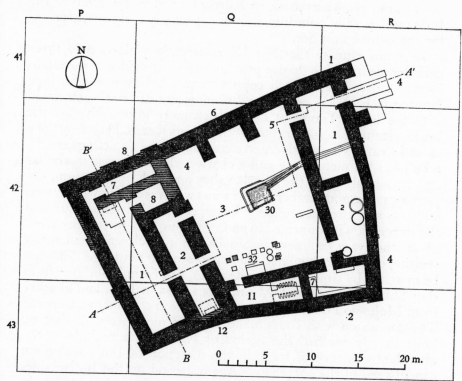

Fig. 3. Plan of Sin Temple IX at Khafājī. Early Dynastic II. Foundations marked in solid black; reconstructed walls hatched. (*O.I.P.* LVIII, pl. 11. By permission of the Oriental Institute, University of Chicao.)

interfere with a classification which has found general acceptance it seems preferable to accept the current division within which E.D. III appears to be the culmination of E.D. II.

In Sin IX we may note an interesting feature of the courtyard, namely a group of circular and square mud, or mud-brick, offering-tables which were arranged in proximity to an open-air altar. The square tables appear to have been capped with rounded tops, as in the Temple Oval.[1] We may risk the suggestion that they were used to carry garments—the garments of the gods, which later inscriptions tell us were presented to them, and doubtless dedicated in the temples at the time of the harvest or spring festivals.

Plundered though this temple had been, it contained a number of objects, some of which can be related in style to many that have

[1] §II, 6, 83, fig. 73.

been found elsewhere both in Babylonia and as far afield as the Indus valley, thus pointing to an unexpectedly early synchronism for the latter connexion.

It is unfortunate that Sin IX apparently yielded only three cylinder-seals, which do not provide sufficient evidence for establishing a date.[1] A spouted copper vessel, however, is of a type familiar in E.D. III pottery and reminiscent of vessels associated with the Royal Tombs at Ur.[2] Much more informative are the broken stone vessels decorated with various scenes. Fragments of a carved steatite vase represented a crowded scene depicting cervids, a bull-headed man, cattle and a chariot wheel. A vase in similar style, probably from the Diyālā valley and of Elamite origin, depicts a strange goddess bare to the waist with vases of flowing water, serpents and two monsters.[3] The appearance is Indianesque and the impression is confirmed in an interesting way by the discovery of another vase fragment in Sin IX, in a black stone, allegedly steatite, of a compartmental vase representing matting.[4] This can be matched by similar or cognate vases, one from Kish,[5] one from the 'Shub-ad' tomb at Ur,[6] one from Susa in Iran, and another from Mohenjo Daro; the last named piece is certainly an import.[7] The connexion with India makes it seem most probable that we have already reached the period of E.D. III, a prelude to the abundant evidence of trade in the direction of India which we can discern in the succeeding Agade period on the Indian side. Present carbon-14 determinations suggest a date relatively late in the third millennium for material connected with Babylonia.[8] Nevertheless, it would be wrong to suggest that relationships with India are altogether excluded in E.D. II and, as noted above, we have to recognize for the present the discrepancy between the results of carbon-14 and historical chronology at this period. Work on the lower levels of Mohenjo Daro may alter the tendency of present opinion.

The numerous fragments of broken statuary from Sin IX are therefore of particular importance in helping us to assess the date of the temple. Here we may say with confidence that the majority of the carved figures, male and female, show an advance over the stiff archaic statuary which the authorities ascribe to E.D. II. Frankfort reckoned that the earlier sculpture was in an abstract

---

[1] §II, 12, pl. 24, nos. 246 f.   [2] §II, 13, fig. 46.
[3] §II, 7, 69, fig. 63 illustrating cervids and bull-man, etc.; §I, 6, fig. 9 and pl. IIB.
[4] §II, 13, fig. 56 opp. p. 48.   [5] §II, 8, pl. III, 84 f.
[6] §III, 35, pl. 178a.   [7] §II, 16, 321, pl. CXLII.
[8] §II, 1; §II, 2; §II, 3; §II, 15.

style and that later carvings tended towards realism and more concentration on detail. The fact is that no rigid distinction can be drawn and that the two periods are without a break in stylistic development. Some of the statues and a statuette in Sin IX, however, do betray a greater dexterity in the rendering of the dress, and a heightened sense of its decorative values, but such developments are displayed alongside the older rigidities.[1] There has indeed been some exaggeration in assessing the merits of the unsophisticated carvings associated with E.D. II. The cult statues from the square temple of Abu at Tell Asmar are ridiculous when viewed, e.g. from the back side, which terminates in legs resembling the trunk of a tree—the best that the primitive sculptor could do after nervously freeing the arms and angular elbows from the soft, cheesy, stone matrix. Perhaps it is ungrateful to devalue these ungainly, ill-proportioned figures with their big, stark, staring eyes, which give an impression, doubtless intended, of awed reverence.[2] But there can be no question that in both E.D. II and III the sculptors were groping towards the developed assurance which they achieved with such mastery in the clear-cut forms of the succeeding Agade period. One cylindrical figure moving in this direction is an inscribed statue of Ur-kisal,[3] *sanga*-priest of the country of Akshak, the territory within which Khafājī was situated. This figure was found smashed, and partly burnt, in Sin IX and we have ventured above to ascribe the sack to Eannatum of Lagash, who comes second in succession after Ur-Nanshe. The reign of Eannatum may therefore conceivably mark the date of the end of Sin IX, a temple which must have lasted for some considerable time, and the statue itself may be brought stylistically into line with glyptic development at Lagash, which is probably slightly posterior to the First Dynasty of Ur. Other statuary leads to the same conclusion, namely that Sin IX has many examples of a primitive as well as a more advanced style, the latter well revealed in some of the lively female heads with their elaborate coiffures characteristic of the G temple at Ashur.[4] Similar considerations apply to the carvings of the numerous foundation (?) plaques which represent banquet scenes and temple festivals.[5]

[1] §II, 10, nos. 20 f.   [2] §II, 10, nos. 1–13.

[3] *Ibid.* no. 37; inscription (by T. Jacobsen) in §II, 7, 293.

[4] Compare §II, 10, no. 39, an improvement on the hideous 'dumb-bell' style portrayed by no. 22; elaborate hair-style as in §II, 10, no. 106 (statue of a female), and the vigorous, lively heads, nos. 116 f.; §II, 4, Taf. 46.

[5] §II, 10, no. 185, and one of the same period from Khafājī (§II, 10, no. 187), which is the counterpart of another from the Royal Cemetery of Ur (§III, 35, pl. 181 *b*).

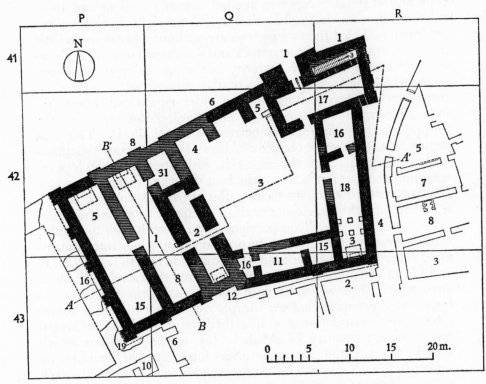

Fig. 4. Plan of Sin Temple X at Khafājī. Early Dynastic III. Foundations marked in solid black; reconstructed walls hatched. (*O.I.P.* LVIII, pl. 12. By permission of the Oriental Institute, University of Chicago.)

Sin Temple IX ended in smoke, for Khafājī at the same time suffered a severe conflagration, traces of which were found in the ashes from the west end of the temple itself, right across to the Temple Oval. It is true that most of Sin IX was spared a burning, for what reason we do not know, but its statuary was smashed and showed traces of burning at the hands of a ruthless enemy.[1]

With Sin X, which lay 8 m. above the level of the original foundation in Sin I, we come to the last of the long series at Khafājī. Traces of five successive occupations were found within the building (see Fig. 4).[2] The builders took advantage of the severe damage suffered in the sack of Sin IX to re-level the site and erect a larger building and a more elaborate temple, neverthe-less using the stumps of the old walls as foundations for the new

[1] §II, 7, 65, figs. 61, 62.   [2] §II, 7, pl. 18 and p. 132.

whenever possible. While the plan of the courtyard remained basically the same, apart from minor alterations to some of the side chambers, there was a radical change in the whole of the east wing, which was extended, owing to a shift eastwards of the house-quarters. The gate, instead of being on the east side of the building, was for the first time shifted to the north and the entrance was through two huge towers, a formidable bulwark recalling the attack to which the temple had previously succumbed. At the west end of the building the plan of the main sanctuary was unchanged except that it was lengthened by the abolition of the postern chamber; the proportions of length to breadth were now much nearer 4:1, instead of the 3:1 observed in Sin VI. Polytheism within a single building had now obviously gained ground, for not only were there two main sanctuaries and a third subsidiary one, each with an altar or podium at the west end of the building, but yet another altar was added in a long chamber at the opposite end, which also contained no less than nine round-topped offering-tables arranged in front of it.

The temple was disappointingly poor in objects, many of which had probably been looted in later times, but what had survived appears to be consistent with E.D. III and certainly pre-Agade.[1] Sin X overlapped with Oval II which was succeeded by Oval III, but only the earlier foundations of the latter building are attributed to E.D. III. Sin X therefore still falls within E.D. III and for the end of the period a terminal date of *c.* 2400 B.C. may not be far short of the mark, assuming that Sargon of Agade began to reign *c.* 2370 B.C.

THE NINTU TEMPLE AND OTHERS
IN THE DIYĀLĀ VALLEY

The examination of the Sin Temples attempted above is basic to an understanding of the Early Dynastic sequences, because of their well-stratified varieties of architectural and material evidence. But other religious buildings add much to the picture, among them a series, less completely excavated, known as the Nintu Temples from the discovery in the latest building, Nintu VII, of an inscribed stone plaque naming that divinity.[2] Since this form of nomenclature does not appear before the First Dynasty of Ur, it is clear that this temple should not be dated earlier than E.D. III *a*—possibly it should be assigned to E.D. III *b*.

The more or less complete layout of the building is known from its predecessor Nintu VI and consists of two adjacent un-

---

[1] Cylinder-seal Kh. no. 370, 1; §II, 12, pl. 24, no 248   [2] §II, 7, 82 and 290 f.

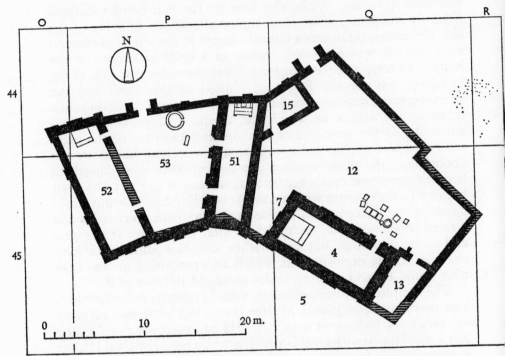

Fig. 5. Plan of the Nintu Temple at Khafājī during Sixth Building Period of Q 45:4. Early Dynastic II. Foundations marked in solid black; reconstructed walls hatched. (*O.I.P.* LVIII, pl. 16. By permission of the Oriental Institute, University of Chicago.)

connected temples built on a dog-leg plan (see Fig. 5), which is less complicated than that of the Sin Temple series and contains far fewer subsidiary chambers. These two components of Nintu VI include within them three sanctuaries of the standard type, with altar or podium at the short end and a further subsidiary chamber (room 13) with recesses between pilasters against its west wall, perhaps an accessory chamber to serve the cult.

This temple yielded a number of valuable objects including a finely carved stone statuette of a female, executed with the confidence of a well-trained sculptor in a style which we may more properly expect in E.D. III although the excavators have assigned Nintu VI to E.D. II.[1] However that may be, a copper group of two wrestlers balancing tall vases on their heads and stripped for an acrobatic act,[2] probably cast by the *cire perdue* process, is in a

[1] §II, 7, fig. 76.   [2] *Ibid.* fig. 77.

style which matches other copper figurines from Temple Oval I and is generally thought to have originated in E.D. II.

Embedded within the altar or podium of one of the sanctuaries was a beautifully carved stone statuette of a bearded cow, in the style of the famous models from the Royal Cemetery of Ur which are now classified as E.D. III*a*.[1] This object was found together with a human-headed bull and several stone maceheads and illustrates a practice common in the Diyālā valley of dedicating within the altar itself objects connected with the cult—probably as a rule those which had been used in an older foundation and though not required for the newer one were kept out of piety and reverence in the shrine's most sacred place.[2] Some of the altars had stepped tops, perhaps for the display of votive objects.

The practice of concealing objects of the cult within the altar was, moreover, often a means of preserving them in perpetuity, as may be demonstrated by another discovery within the Nintu Temple VI, for on the lower of two occupation floors, which were separated by 30 cm. of débris, fragments of headless statues of a male and a female were found. They had been deliberately burnt, for no traces of fire could be discerned except in their immediate vicinity.

Another find from the courtyard of Nintu VI was of exceptional interest: it consisted of a number of mud structures, some of which seemed to have served for persons engaged in the act of standing or kneeling—a kind of *prie-dieu* but without support. Frankfort[3] has risked the suggestion that these structures were used by the priestesses, as in the much later middle-Assyrian Ishtar temple at Ashur, where lead figures depict couples in the act of copulation, a temple cult linked with the notion of the Sacred Marriage, of which a memory survives in Herodotus' account of Babylon.

Below Nintu VI the remains of the earlier Nintu V were less extensively excavated. Here one remarkable discovery was made, in a pit anciently dug and sealed before the later sanctuary was built. Within it there was a hoard of stone statuary which had no doubt served its time after use in Nintu V. Such carvings, extravagantly praised by Frankfort, may be expressive of religious fervour, but bear all the signs of sculptural incompetence.[4] They are admittedly in a mixture of styles, earlier and later, and give rise to the suspicion that even Nintu V may overlap with E.D. III although assigned to E.D. II.

[1] §II, 7, fig. 72.   [2] *Ibid.* 89.   [3] *Ibid.* 85, n. 67.
[4] *Ibid.* 94, fig. 86; §II, 10, 21; §II, 13, 59.

Earlier sequences were revealed in the remains of the under-lying temples Nintu I–IV, which have been assigned to E.D. I, and there is evidence that by the time of Nintu III we have reached this period, for embedded within the altar there was a vase of greenish stone with exceptionally wide rim and globular belly, of a type which at Ur occurred as early as the Jamdat Naṣr period.[1] A good example of a potter's wheel was found in the same temple.

The series of seven Nintu temples which ran through a depth of about 6 m. of débris is thus seen to have spanned the greater part of the Early Dynastic period, from E.D. I to at least the end of E.D. III.[2] Once again comparisons with other sites and the mixture of styles after E.D. I lead to the conclusion that we cannot always distinguish between the styles of E.D. II and III, which merge with one another. The architectural succession of buildings indicates that these two periods correspond with a long historical sequence.

A similar span of time is indicated by nine or ten successive temples of a much more modest character, collectively known as the 'small temple in O. 43', situated in the midst of the private houses and therefore easily accessible to the townsfolk.[3] We can watch the progress of this building from a single sanctuary not more than 7·5 cm. in length, built probably in E.D. I, to a larger series of two- and three-roomed structures (including court-yard) in the later stages of E.D. They were as usual all built of plano-convex bricks.[4]

Smallest and simplest of all the sanctuaries was one known as the 'Small Single Shrine in S. 44', with an altar at one end and a circular offering-table in front of it.[5] The walls are strongly buttressed; this one-roomed box-like structure which belongs to the very end of E.D. III*b* is a characteristic survival, without any accessories, of the basic form of Mesopotamian temple.

THE ABU TEMPLE AT TELL ASMAR

Here again, not far from Khafājī, we have another informative series of Early Dynastic temples which span the entire range of the period. Successive rebuildings of the period may be correlated with the archaeological sequences as follows: Archaic Shrine, E.D. I; Square Temple, E.D. II; Single-Shrine Temple, first phase E.D. III and second phase end of E.D. III, in the period termed by Frankfort 'proto-imperial', that is to say, Entemena to

[1] §II, 7, 99, fig. 93. [2] *Ibid.* 102. [3] *Ibid.* 104 f.
[4] *Ibid.* pl. 17. [5] *Ibid.* 114, fig. 105.

Lugalzaggisi. It seems simpler to include this period within E.D. III*b*.[1]

The Archaic Shrine E.D. I is the first of the temples following the earlier Jamdat Naṣr structures to be built of plano-convex bricks. The basic plan (see Fig. 6) consists of an oblong sanctuary

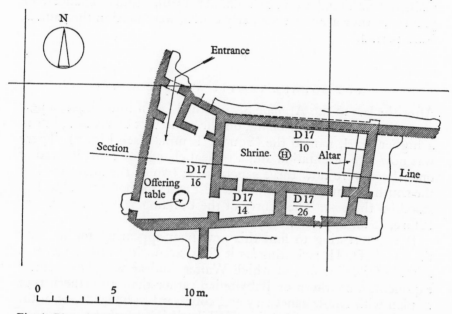

Fig. 6. Plan of Archaic Shrine I of the Abu Temple at Tell Asmar. Early Dynastic I. Broken lines indicate rebuilding at Level I B. (*O.I.P.* LVIII, pl. 19 B. By permission of the Oriental Institute, University of Chicago.)

with podium or altar at the short end, subsidiary service chambers, and, presumably, an open courtyard at the west end. That E.D. I should not be reckoned to have covered a very short space of time is suggested by the fact that 'nine distinct periods of occupation could be detected in the architectural remains of this building, each involving some change of plan'.[2] As time went on, the subsidiary chambers multiplied and there were changes in dimensions of cella and court, but the basis of the plan remained the same. Cylinder seals and an impression of the brocade style are characteristic of the period, as is a fine example of a 'scarlet ware' vase with sharp, angular neck and rim, and a design which includes sprigs on its shoulder, found in a room adjacent to Archaic

[1] §II, 7, 159, n. 7.
[2] *Ibid.* 162.

Shrine III.[1] The most remarkable discovery was made in a room D. 17/26 giving direct access to the sanctuary; here there were no less than 660 broken, solid-foot chalices, neatly laid out in rows, parallel with the walls, leaving a gangway in the middle.[2] Here we have the relics of some religious ritual which long remained traditional in Babylonia. At Uruk similar chalices, or goblets as they are more properly called, were used in the Jamdat Naṣr period.

THE SQUARE TEMPLE AT TELL ASMAR

After the last of the Archaic Shrines had fallen into disuse, a new ground plan came into being, on the same plot of ground, but at a higher level, named the 'Square Temple' (see Fig. 7). There was now a re-orientation and a radical change of plan; instead of one, there were now three sanctuaries; two of the altars were at the south end and one was at the west end; formerly the altar had stood on the east. The centre of the building was given over, as before, to an approximately square courtyard.

It is interesting to find this new plan appearing for the first time in E.D. II, reflecting as it does, according to the German school of *Bauforscher*, of which Walter Andrae was the foremost exponent, a southern or Babylonian rather than a northern type of plan with single sanctuary and courtyard to one side, as in the early Ishtar temples at Ashur. Whilst it is true that this type of squarish plan does seem to have originated in Babylonia, a secular example appears in the E.D. III Palace at Eridu[3]—it was but a convenient form of development out of the older, oblong room which had been characteristic from the beginning. The situation of the square court in the centre of a building enabled the priests and the officials to secure a greater measure of control over those concerned with deliveries and supplies and thus facilitated the co-ordination of business.

There were at least three main stages of occupation of the Square Temples (E.D. II), which, in addition to their three sanctuaries and subsidiary rooms, contained a carefully waterproofed bathroom liberally plastered over with bitumen. A priests' (?) room with rush floor contained a bread oven and fragments of stone sculpture, stone bowls, beads, and an 'Imdugud' amulet.[4]

Associated with the earliest level there was a limestone plaque

[1] §ii, 7, fig. 124. [2] *Ibid.* fig. 125.
[3] See below, p. 276. [4] §ii, 7, 180.

carved with figures in relief, As. 33:102;[1] this primitive piece
depicted two registers of bewigged male figures with beaky heads
in procession, and an amphora; the style is clearly that of E.D. II
and is comparable with another plaque of the same period from

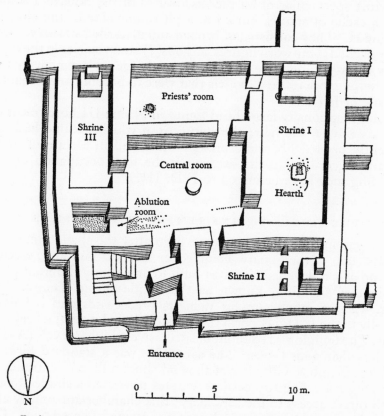

Fig. 7. Projected plan of the Square Abu Temple at Tell Asmar. Early Dynastic II.
(*O.I.P.* LVIII, fig. 133. By permission of the Oriental Institute, University of
Chicago.)

the Sin Temple IX.[2] In one of the sanctuaries cylinder seals,
beads, amulets and stamps were relics of an older period. A
bronze (?) mirror was a rarity and allows us to infer that this is
what some of the enigmatic painted figures in the more or less
contemporary 'scarlet ware' are carrying. Also associated with
one of the shrines was a stone bird-vase, of a type more familiar in
the Jamdat Naṣr period and a fiddle-shaped mother goddess

[1] §II, 7, 177 and §II, 10, no. 194.   [2] §II, 10, no. 192.

figurine.[1] Four mud pedestals, two free-standing and two engaged with the wall, were found in front of the altar, in Shrine II. Similar structures found elsewhere have been discussed above; these may simply have been offering-tables.

Most spectacular of all the discoveries of the Square Temple was a cache of statues buried in a pit to one side of the altar in Shrine II.[2] They consisted of broken and discarded statuary, carefully packed—outworn figures of gods(?)[3] and votaries in the typically clumsy, rigid style of E.D. II, ready for replacement by the less tense, more relaxed models that were to become more characteristic of E.D. III.

An exceptionally large head found in Shrine III bore traces of black paint on the hair; the statue from which it came had apparently been deliberately broken while still in a state of good repair. According to the excavators the final occupation of the building may have belonged to E.D. III.

THE SINGLE-SHRINE TEMPLE AT TELL ASMAR

Some gap in time there may have been after the abandonment or destruction of the Square Temple, for the next building, erected on top of a re-levelled site, was built to an entirely different plan. This new building, known as the Single-Shrine Temple (see Fig. 8), was much simpler than its predecessor and belonged wholly to the E.D. III period; it possibly lasted until the very end of it. The temple was re-built, in successively higher levels (A–D), no less than four times.[4] The sanctuary was a standard form of oblong chamber with altar at the end short wall, and entrance in the long side. The two earliest temples possessed a single annexe with direct access to the sanctuary; this chamber apparently also served as a kitchen, for in each case it contained a bread oven. The principal change in the last two temples was that the sanctuary was partitioned into two internal connected chambers; the main walls were more than a metre thick and there was a heavily defended, towered entrance. It seems not unlikely that the sanctuary itself carried a semicircular, vaulted roof, such as has been found in the royal tombs at Ur. There is also contemporary evidence of standing arches in the houses at Tell Asmar, and of small square windows built around a pierced terracotta grille.[5]

[1] §II, 7, 125 and figs. 143–4.   [2] Ibid. 188, fig. 149.
[3] See the discussion in §I, 20, 7 ff.
[4] §II, 7, pl. 23.
[5] Ibid. 197 and fig. 159 and §II, 11, 10 ff. for windows and arches at Tell Asmar.

Statue fragments and maceheads were found scattered throughout the building, and it is of peculiar interest that one statue had
been retained over two distinct and successive occupations, for its
feet were found in the Square Temple, E.D. II, head and trunk
in the Single-Shrine Temple, E.D. III.[1] In assessing the development of style throughout the E.D. period we must therefore
remember that antiquities were cherished and preserved by later
generations.

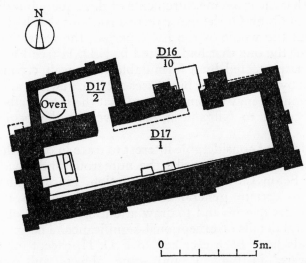

Fig. 8. Plan of the Single-Shrine Abu Temple at Tell Asmar. Early Dynastic III.
(*O.I.P.* lviii, pl. 23 A. By permission of the Oriental Institute, University of
Chicago.)

Towards the very end of this period E.D. III (in Single-
Shrine II)[2] a new fashion of bonding the mud-brick was adopted;
plano-convex bricks set on edge foreshadow the regularly made,
flat bricks of the Agade period, and indeed it is alleged that at
Lagash the use of plano-convex bricks ceases with the reign of
Entemena, at least sixty years before the accession of Sargon.[3]
A cylinder seal from the Single-Shrine Temple IV depicting the
slaughter of a seven-headed hydra, in the Agade style, proves that
the Early Dynastic period had come to an end before the final
stage in this series of temples.[4]

[1] §II, 7, 199 (As. 33.75 and As. 33. 281).   [2] *Ibid.* 201, fig. 161.
[3] *Ibid.* 200.   [4] *Ibid.* 203, fig. 164.

THE SHARA TEMPLE AT TELL AGRAB

There could be no sharper contrast with the simple plan of the Single-Shrine Temple of Tell Asmar than one discovered at the neighbouring and relatively small Diyālā site named Tell Agrab,[1] 15 miles to the east, and known as the Shara Temple from an inscription on a stone bowl of E.D. III period found within its precincts.[2] Only the western wing was excavated, but it could be deduced that the cross measurements of this square building were no less than 60 m. Of the many reconstructions that had occurred throughout the whole of the E.D. period, the clearest plan was obtained of the one that had existed in E.D. II (see Fig. 9). The temple was protected by a formidable town wall 5.50 m. thick, reinforced by semi-circular buttresses 2.20 m. in width and 2.50 m. in projection. It may be remembered that the town walls of Uruk were attributed to Gilgamesh, who lived at the beginning of E.D. III.

It would be of considerable interest to trace in detail the history of this temple and to describe the numerous finds made in the course of Seton Lloyd's skilful excavation. Here it must suffice to point to certain general conclusions which can be drawn from these discoveries and to draw attention to a few objects and architectural details of exceptional significance. The greater part of the finds have been ascribed to E.D. II, except for traces of 'scarlet ware' in E.D. I, and some objects and rebuilding manifestly appertaining to E.D. III.[3]

The better preserved western end of the building,[4] with huge external walls heavily reinforced by great buttresses, divides itself into three wings; the northern one contained at least two, possibly three sanctuaries, and a granary. The central wing contained the main shrine with big offering-table at the north end, a series of ritual tables and a screen; on one side of it there were treasuries, and on the other there was an approach through a courtyard which had contained a well lined with plano-convex bricks. This central block gave proof that the construction of its heavy defensive wall had been more than justified; for not only were sling-bolts found in various parts of the building, but in the

---

[1] §II, 7, pls. 25–7 and fig. 203 on p. 263.   [2] *Ibid.* 229.

[3] *Ibid.* 228 ('scarlet ware' found in priests' houses beyond the main mound; *ibid.* 238, cache of maceheads and eleven stone cylinder seals found in an altar; these and other Shara Temple seals which range through the Jamdat Naṣr and E.D. I–III periods are illustrated in §II, 12, pls. 72–83).

[4] *Ibid.* pl. 26.

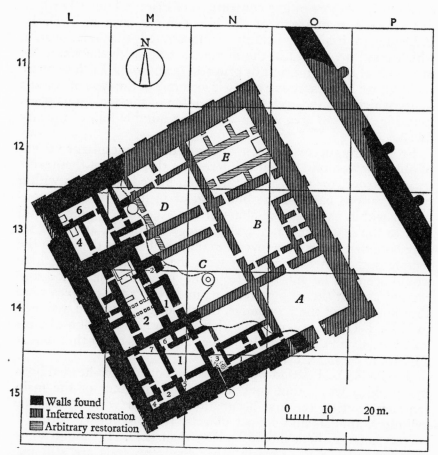

Fig. 9. Reconstructed plan of the main level of the Shara Temple at Tell Agrab. Early Dynastic. (*O.I.P.* LVIII, fig. 203. By permission of the Oriental Institute, University of Chicago.)

course of an attack sappers had by-passed the heavily defended entrance to the sanctuary and tunnelled through its eastern wall. Doubtless much treasure had been abstracted, although much remained (some of it concealed within and to the side of the altar)—both here and in the adjacent treasury and sacristy.

The southern wing of the building was quite different in character. It consisted of a central court, approached by vestibules and leading into a main hall, no doubt a reception room with subsidiary chambers; it also contained a bathroom. There can be no doubt that this was the residential wing, for its layout resembled the more or less contemporary Priest's House D which was situated at one end of the big Temple Oval in E.D. II. P. Delougaz has convincingly demonstrated this relationship, which may correspond in the Sumerian texts with the *gipar*, the residence of the high priest or priestess (*enu, entu*).[1] In this square building we have therefore a classic example of the type of priest's house which was the ecclesiastical version of the analogous plans found in the town area within which the humble folk of the city dwelt.[2]

From many successive occupations of the temple a large variety of objects was found, and it is interesting that some of them were treasure-trove, for they had either been buried, as caches within pits in various parts of the building, or in many instances concealed within the box-like altars of the sanctuaries. One should look to the seal cylinders for chronological criteria, and here we may note that there were several examples of scenes depicting the temple and its herd, executed with the cylindrical drill; these would seem to be survivors from the Jamdat Naṣr period and remind us that the earliest remains underlying the temples were Protohistoric; of the remainder, the majority should be assigned to E.D. I–II.[3] It is noticeable that we have no mention of lapis lazuli seals, and that where lapis inlay and beads occur the context appears to be E.D. III.[4]

To the E.D. II period we may assign a quadruple-headed lion-mace which was found concealed within the altar of the main sanctuary during the first occupation, together with some stone cylinders, amulets and copper objects. If the sequence dating is correct none of them should be later than E.D. II (though some may be earlier); the objects other than the seals are still unpublished in detail. Stone maceheads are abundant. A sculptured stone vase depicting 'Gilgamesh' seizing lions by the tail is probably not earlier than E.D. III.[5]

Many copper objects were found, of which the most important were small copper statuettes, probably made by the *cire perdue* process and assigned to E.D. II. Three of these awkward and ludicrous standing figures, represented in a state of ritual nudity, were found in one chamber, two male and one female, and a fourth male in another not far distant.[6] If crudeness of style be a reliable

---

[1] §II, 7, 261 ff., fig. 203; cf. *C.A.D.* 5, 83.
[2] P. Delougaz, H. D. Hill and Seton Lloyd, *Private Houses and Graves in the Diyala Region* (*O.I.P.* 88), Chicago, 1967.
[3] §II, 12, pls. 72–84.
[4] §II, 7, 239 and 256.
[5] *Ibid.* 242, fig. 189.
[6] *Ibid.* 257–8, figs. 200–1.

criterion we should have no hesitation in assigning them to E.D. I rather than to E.D. III. A little two-wheeled copper chariot drawn by four onagers and wrongly[1] described as a *quadriga* has solid wheels and is our earliest example of a simple chariot rendered in copper.[2] Other examples of copper objects have been assigned to the same period, but it is important to observe that a poker-butt type of spear found at the base of one of the altars is typical of the Royal Cemetery of Ur, and should be assigned to E.D. III.[3]

It is therefore reasonable to suggest that, in relationship to Ur, some of the Shara Temple sequences should not be placed much earlier, and this suspicion is confirmed when we reckon with the large quantities of small gold and silver objects scattered throughout the same temple. A gold toggle-pin[4] is probably indistinguishable from types known from the Ur Royal tombs, as well as many other small finds, including golden beads and amulets in the shape of animals; others in stone represent rams, birds, lions, calves and fish—all of them the very stuff of the Royal Cemetery of Ur—and we may conclude that there is probably neither a valid typological nor a chronological distinction between Shara Temple E.D. II and Ur E.D. III, that is to say, E.D. II and E.D. III*a* merge, the one into the other. Possibly this difference may be accepted: that lapis lazuli was comparatively rare in the Diyālā while copper statuettes in human form, relatively common in the Diyālā, were virtually absent from Ur.[5] There may be a case for arguing that some of the tombs such as that of 'Shub-ad' and other shaft graves where lapis lazuli was common were a little later in time, E.D. III*a*, but other arguments no less cogent could be used in support of the theory that a part at least of E.D. II in the Diyālā and E.D. III*a* as at Ur are contemporary.

It is indeed admitted by the excavators that some of the Shara Temple material is definitely E.D. III,[6] for example a remarkable limestone head of a female, in realistic style[7] comparable with gypsum heads discovered in Ishtar Temple G at Ashur.[8] The model of a human foot from a copper statuette recalls the bitumen core of a similar casting from Tell Brak in Syria,[9] but the one from the Shara Temple may be earlier, E.D. II (?). Diamond-shaped

---

[1] Note that only the inner pair of animals are fastened to the yoke.
[2] §II, 7, 257, fig. 200; §II, 9, 13, pls. 58–60.   [3] §II, 7, 256.
[4] *Ibid.* 257.
[5] §III, 35, pl. 121. A copper head of a horned deity is an exception.
[6] §II, 7, end chart.   [7] *Ibid.* 239, fig. 186.
[8] §II, 4, Taf. 46, *e–h*, and below, p. 299.
[9] §II, 7, fig. 192; §IV, 5, 184 and pl. xxxix.

beads in black and white stone could also be matched with similar types from the Royal Cemetery at Ur, E.D. III *a*.[1] An unusual cylinder seal of translucent green stone depicting animals of the chase, lion, goat and mouflon head, appears to be a good example of the E.D. II style.[2]

THE TEMPLE OVAL AT KHAFĀJĪ

The great oval *enceinte*[3] at Khafājī was a sacred perimeter surrounded by heavy double walls which enclosed an area of over 8,000 square metres of ground,[4] including a huge courtyard, workshops and magazines, sanctuary at one end, priest's house at the other. Before the original foundation an enormous cavity was dug, an excavation that involved the removal of some 64,000 cubic metres of soil, which was then replaced by the equivalent volume of clean sand. This fantastically extravagant effort shows to what lengths Early Dynastic man was prepared to go in order to prepare consecrated ground, unsullied and immaculate, as required by the god. A late Akkadian ritual[5] and the ceremonies enacted by Ur-Baba[6] and Gudea[7] of Lagash are literary evidences of this frame of mind, so well attested by archaeological discovery at an earlier period.

The Oval was rebuilt three times and the main occupations were classified as follows: Oval I, E.D. II; Oval 2, E.D. III *a*; Oval 3, E.D. III *b* and later. Once again this chronological scheme proposed by H. Frankfort seems too high for that which he also proposed for the Royal Cemetery of Ur—III *b*. We have already seen that Sin Temple IX, which is for the most part contemporary with Oval I, had much in common with E.D. III *a*. We may perhaps ascribe the burning of both temples to Eannatum of Lagash.[8]

The architectural layout of the Temple Oval (see Fig. 10) was evidently designed to congregate a vast concourse of people within a court-yard (56 × 38 m. in dimension) that stood in propinquity to the shrine, which consisted of a single chamber on an elevated platform at one end of it. On the muddy ground of the court it was still possible to trace the imprint of human feet and of the reluctant animals which had been tugged there to feast the god and

---

[1] §II, 7, 254, fig. 198.
[2] *Ibid.* 254, fig. 197, and §II, 12, pl. 76, no. 824.
[3] §II, 6, pls. III–V.   [4] *Ibid.* 16.
[5] §II, 18, 11 (sacrifice of a bull).
[6] §II, 17, 60 f.; §III, 38, vol. VI (1926), 367 f.; A. Falkenstein in *Or.* 1966, 230 f.
[7] §II, 17, 68 f. (Statue B, iv, 7–9).   [8] See above, p. 246.

his attendants. Storage magazines, kitchens, and workshops which included a sculptor's *atelier* were situated within the perimeter. The approach was through a narrow stepped entrance between towers. In one corner of the building, as we have already noticed,

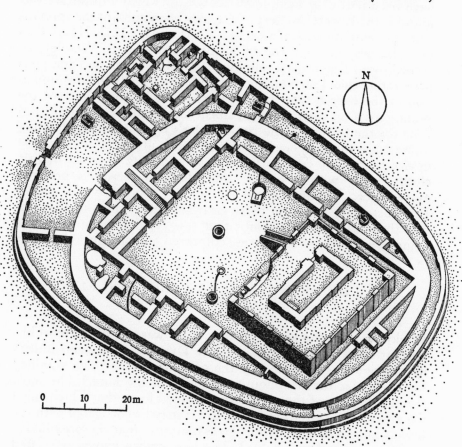

Fig. 10. Isometric restoration of the Early Dynastic Temple Oval of the First Building Period at Khafājī. (*O.I.P.* LIII, pl. v. By permission of the Oriental Institute, University of Chicago.)

there was a priest's house which in its plan bore resemblance to the Square Temple at Tell Asmar; it still contained the remains of fishermen's nets, and a hornets' nest was found in the matted roof-beams. But in spite of so many traces of public activity it is still apparent that the sacrosanct Holy of Holies was reserved for the few. Even though the temple precincts were the focus of the economic life of the city, the people can have had a full view of the gods only when they travelled in processions at the seasonal festivals.

Much sculpture and many other objects were found in the Oval. A stone foundation plaque from House D in Oval I must have been part of a Temple Palace set, of which a duplicate was found in the Royal Cemetery of Ur, another witness of the approximate contemporaneity of Khafājī E.D. II and Ur E.D. III a.[1] This plaque represents a scene of victory according to Woolley, or according to Frankfort a religious festival in which god and goddess, rather than king and queen, are celebrating their consummation of the Sacred Marriage at the Spring Festival. We see the protagonists on their thrones; musicians, cattle and offerings of wine for the feast, and the commander's chariot. Of outstanding interest are the copper ritual figures on bull-legged stands, cast in *cire perdue*; these male figures are in a state of ritual nudity, clothed only with a girdle; one of them carries a pronged excrescence, perhaps a stand for holding a bowl, on his head.[2] It is customary to assign these early copper castings to E.D. II, and there can be little doubt that this type of metal work was being developed just as early as sculptured human figures in stone.

III. THE PRINCIPAL BABYLONIAN SITES

KISH

We know from the king-lists that Kish[3] was one of the most important cities of Babylonia in Early Dynastic times, and indeed its prestige was indicated by the title *šar kiššati* which signified for its holder the paramount authority in the land.[4] The most famous dynasty of the period was deemed to be that which ruled the city directly after the Flood and it may be correlated with the period known as ED. II on the assumption that the prediluvian kings correspond with E.D. I. The best known names associated with Kish in E.D. II are Enmebaragisi, Agga and possibly Mesilim, each of whom conducted wars with neighbouring cities or settled disputes with them.[5] It is therefore unfortunate that none of

---

[1] §II, 10, 45 and pl. 107, no. 187; §III, 35, 377 and pl. 181 a.

[2] §II, 10, 41–2 and pls. 98–103; §II, 9, pl. 95.

[3] §III, 34; §III, 7. [4] See above, p. 109.

[5] See above, pp. 110 and 116 f. A. Moortgat and other German archaeologists assign him to E.D. II and even refer to a 'Mesilim period'. But as he is not in the king-list we have no good reason to assign him to E.D. II rather than to E.D. III, and indeed the celebrated macehead bearing his name could be of the E.D. III period. See §III, 33, vol. I, p. xxxv, and vol. II, p. 223; §I, 16, figs. 160A, B; §II, 17, 160 f.

them can be exactly correlated with any of the early dynastic remains which have been excavated in the extensive site of Kish.

Most of the Early Dynastic material appears to have been situated in the part of the site named Tell Ingharra, but with the exception of the great Palace A, excavated by E. Mackay, all the buildings are but fragments of a once important architecture. We know, however, that there were two big zikkurrats, built of plano-convex bricks on a great platform, the façade of which was decorated with niches and recesses characteristic of religious architecture.[1] There are grounds for thinking that these are to be numbered among the earliest true zikkurrats or staged towers known, and that they were not merely temples elevated on a platform.[2]

The domestic architecture of the period was illustrated by a succession of houses in the 'Early Houses Stratum'. Both in the streets between them and in the houses there was evidence of a series of floods at the end of E.D. I and E.D. II–III, the earliest of which may perhaps be related to Noah's, provided that we are content to identify his flood with the one mentioned in the Sumerian king-list, which occurred at the end of E.D. I, just before the kingship was transferred to Kish.[3] However that may be, an E.D. I date for the early towns is well established since brocade-style seals were found in them, and there is an extensive range of pottery which runs in this area right through to E.D. III. Associated with the houses were burials, some of which seem to have been dug beneath the house floors; the deposits included many pot types from graves that may be isolated as characteristic of E.D. I.[4]

The ceramic evidence from Kish corroborates that of other sites in demonstrating the basic continuity of the typology throughout the whole of the E.D. period, although at each stage some types were being modified and others introduced. There is, moreover, little to distinguish the stone-ware types of E.D. I–II at Kish from those found in the royal tombs of E.D. III at Ur.[5] Seal impressions may be associated with those from Fārah, generally assigned to E.D. II, and should be distinguished from the archaic texts from Fārah—perhaps E.D. III*a*. Metal work, especially copper stands for vases, is characteristic of the E.D. II period.

Much the most important of the graves at Kish, however, are the remains of chariot burials, one of which, Y 529, contained

---

[1] §III, 28, fig. I, opp. p. 19. [2] *Ibid.* 27.
[3] §III, 27. See also §III, 30, where attention is drawn to the necessity for further practical scientific investigation of the evidence on the ground.
[4] §III, 28, especially pls. VI–IX. [5] *Ibid.* pl. V.

three two-wheeled vehicles, or perhaps a waggon and chariot.[1] Associated with this one was a luxuriously made copper dagger, a long spoon, a big saw, tools, a rein-ring and copper vases. There were also two 'painted vases of a red colour', of a type not found at Ur but common in the Diyālā region in E.D. II, and rare in E.D. III *a–b*.

The Kish chariot burials, although endowed with a number of well-made articles, especially of metal, are none the less poor in comparison with the sumptuously equipped multiple burials of E.D. III at Ur, which may represent the climax and extinction of this wasteful and expensive practice, for there comes a time when the gods demand too much. Contemporary with these E.D. II burials at Kish is a modest chariot burial at Susa.[2]

It remains to consider the context of the spacious, many-roomed Palace A at Kish (see Fig. 11). This extensive building, with its fortified towered entrances, niched façades, steps and columns, has already been compared with a type of architecture which is characteristic of E.D. II in the Diyālā region and is encountered in Sin Temple VIII at Khafājī.[3] Unfortunately, the stratigraphy is insufficiently precise to enable us to decide with any confidence how it was related to other E.D. buildings at Ingharra, although Moorey has observed that if its levels have been correctly recorded it should have been situated well above the level of the Flood Stratum. On these grounds he would place it in E.D. III *a–b*. The matter must remain in doubt; but the two separate wings were probably constructed successively, and so formidable a building may well have endured for a considerable time before its final destruction by fire—there were extensive traces of burning.[4] A Fārah-type tablet, perhaps E.D. III*a*, was found incorporated within a bench in one of the rooms.[5] But it should also be recalled that associated with the Kish Palace there was a fragment of slate and limestone inlay work depicting 'the Kish hero' wearing a cap which is in a style generally attributed to E.D. II.[6]

However that may be, the Kish Palace, together with that at Eridu, may be numbered amongst the oldest of the Early Dynastic palaces.[7] There is much to commend Moorey's assumption that

---

[1] §III, 34, 30.

[2] *Mém. D.P.* 29, 122 f., fig. 89; §III, 23, 114.

[3] See above, pp. 294 ff.; §III, 24, pls. XXI, XXII and, more conveniently, the two wings juxtaposed in §I, 14, 87, fig. 94.   [4] §III, 28, 44.

[5] §III, 24, pl. XXXVI, nos. 10, 12.   [6] *Ibid.* 120 and pl. XXXV, nos. 2, 3.

[7] My attribution of the Kish Palace to E.D. II in §III, 27, table opp. p. 82, may be emended accordingly and re-assigned to E.D. III, but see the reservation concerning incrusted plaques, which may be E.D. II; see above, p. 241, n. 2.

the Kish building belongs to E.D. III *a* rather than E.D. II, and if so, we must reckon that certain architectural features which resemble those exhibited by Sin Temple VIII, E.D. II,[1] are a foreshadowing in the earlier ecclesiastical construction of devices that were later to be adopted in lay buildings.[2]

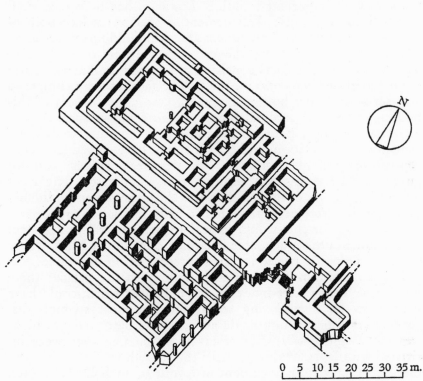

0 5 10 15 20 25 30 35 m.

Fig. 11. Isometric restoration of the Early Dynastic Palace at Kish. (M. E. L. Mallowan, *Early Mesopotamia and Iran*, fig. 94. By permission of Thames and Hudson.)

After the Kish Palace had been destroyed by fire the ruins were used as a graveyard. 'A' Cemetery, as it is called, contained many burials and votive deposits of a type known from the commoners' graves in the Royal Cemetery of Ur. The typology indicates that it begins at the end of that period, E.D. III*b*, and continues as late as the Agade dynasty.

[1] See above, pp. 249 ff,.
[2] P. R. S. Moorey, in *Iraq*, 26, 93 ff. and pl. xxi illustrates another partially excavated palace 'P' at Kish, a heavily fortified plano-convex brick residence or arsenal of E.D. III period.

ERIDU

Eridu must have been an important site in the Early Dynastic period, but the evidence concerning it at that stage of history is still defective and may have to be traced beyond the epicentre of the site. One important building, however, has been excavated by the Iraq Antiquities Department, a spacious palace built of plano-convex bricks.[1] Two almost identical buildings were found adjacent to one another; the cross dimensions of each were 65 × 45 m.; the precincts consisted of fortified double walls, and the external one was 2·60 m. thick. The façades were composed of a series of heavy buttresses and recesses; the corners of this building faced the cardinal points of the compass according to Sumerian practice. Between the inner and the outer walls there were corridors, 1·20 m. wide, which may have served as a convenient method of circulation, for storage purposes, and for guard patrols; access was through two main gates. The most interesting feature of the building was the arrangement of the big rooms, which were perhaps audience-halls, in relation to the great square court, for this would appear to be ancestral to a system well defined in the much later Palace of Zimrilim at Mari, where an Early Dynastic palace is also at present being excavated.

Few objects were found in association with the palace: there was a very heavy adze-like copper implement which could have been used for demolishing walls; but the most striking discovery was a beautifully made alabaster statuette, 16 cm. high, wearing a high *polos*—Sumerian in style. The eyes were incrusted with lapis lazuli and shell; the smooth workmanship and the use of lapis is an argument in favour of an E.D. III*a* date, and it is reasonable to suppose that the Eridu Palace may have been approximately contemporary with that at Kish; it lacks columns, but like the Kish Palace is built as two separate units.

This was the period at which the king seems first to have lived in a house of his own; indeed shortly before 2400 B.C. it was recorded in a deed of sale that 'At that time Entemena was Governor of Lagash and Enentarzi was *sanga*-priest of Ningirsu'[2]—in other words church and state were to that extent also separated. But in E.D. II we hear of Enmerkar, king of Uruk and Kullab, receiving a messenger from the distant land of Aratta in the great courtyard of the *guenna*, the 'assembly hall' of the temple.[3]

[1] §III, 32. [2] §II, 17, 224, 2*a*.
[3] G, 10, 1 and 24, line 301.

SHURUPPAK

This important Sumerian capital city, now known as Fārah, still remains to be dug *in extenso* although many soundings have been conducted there.[1] But from the evidence, both historical and archaeological, we know that it was flourishing throughout the three sub-divisions of the E.D. period. Many remains of plano-convex brick buildings have been found. We have already referred to the Sumerian canonical records which relate that the last assumed king of E.D.I, Ziusudra, was reigning there at the time of the Flood, and we are ready to accept that the fluviatile clay silt traced there by E. Schmidt may be correlated with that event,[2] for it is preceded by remains of the Jamdat Naṣr period and succeeded by Early Dynastic.

Archaeologically of considerable interest is a series of cylinder seals and impressions which are generally described as in the Fārah style and have been isolated by H. Frankfort as belonging to E.D. II.[3] They represent friezes of men and animals engaged in combat, in addition to boating scenes (the gods being ferried to their festivals), snakes, scorpions and other wild creatures.[4] Two figures, both easily identifiable, occur: one is a human being wearing a cap with two long ears, perhaps a masked magician; the other is a human being with flat cap on his head, wearing a short skirt above the knee, tucked into a girdle, and a long trailing open overmantle which leaves the skirt or kilt exposed. He is sometimes known as the 'King of Kish' because he is represented on a well-known shell plaque found on that site.[5] All these seals are in the linear style which in the Diyālā region appears to be characteristic of E.D. II.

No less important has been the discovery at Fārah of a large collection of tablets which include temple accounts, school tablets, lexicons, and incantation texts.[6] These documents never carry the Fārah seal impressions and are generally considered to be subsequent to them, belonging to E.D. III*a*; that is to say, contemporary with the earlier part of the Royal Cemetery of Ur which was dug into the ruins of houses that contained tablets of a type reckoned to be a little older than the Fārah texts.[7]

---

[1] E. Schmidt in *M.J.* 22 (1931), 193 ff.

[2] §III, 27.

[3] §I, 5, 44 ff.

[4] *Ibid.* pl. xi.

[5] §III, 24, pl. xxxv, nos. 2, 3.

[6] §III, 18; §III, 9; §III, 10; §III, 11. Much new and important information concerning the Fārah tablets has recently been disclosed in §III, 4.

[7] E.D. II; see E. Burrows in §III, 35, 313 f.

NIPPUR

This place, which lies about 45 miles south-east of Babylon, was an extensive city in the E.D. period; its ruins are spaced over an area of about 180 acres. Before 2000 B.C. it was the centre to which the princes of Sumer repaired in order to receive the crown and sceptre of kingship—the regalia which were the authentic symbols of dominion over the entire land and entitled the holder to a place in the canonical list. How early this ritual was performed we do not know, but the long series of Inanna temples situated near the zikkurrat leads us to suspect that the city was already dignified in this way in the E.D. era.

The best known of the excavated Inanna temples at present is the one built in the E.D. II period. The basis of its rather straggling plan may have originated from an earlier, prehistoric foundation and the untidy modifications which it underwent may have been conditioned by adjacent property rights. The importance of the temple may be gauged from its dimensions, for this sinuous building spreads its length over 275 ft. and is 85 ft. wide at its south-eastern end.[1] The approach to the temple's two shrines involved a long walk through three courts, two porches and several antechambers. In two of the courts there were pairs of columns of up to 3 ft. 8 in. diameter composed of segmental plano-convex mud-bricks which were encased in mud-plaster. We have already observed[2] that the column was a feature of Sin Temple VIII at Khafājī, and is thus already well attested in E.D. II; columns were erected on a more grandiose scale in the Kish Palace of E.D. III a.[3] It is strange that columned porches, which were so striking a feature towards the end of the Uruk period (Uruk IV), do not reappear till E.D. II: but the archaeological evidence is defective, and indeed there is still much to learn about E.D. I, a period that requires further investigation on the ground.

The two sanctuaries of the E.D. II Inanna temple at Nippur lay in proximity, in a secluded wing at the far end of the building. In each case the altar was set against the short wall at the end; in the first sanctuary there was a direct approach through an antechamber and in the second there was an indirect 'bent axis' approach through a side door. Temple paraphernalia included circular offering-tables and benches grouped round the altar; meals were cooked in the adjacent kitchens. The esoteric nature of the cult may be deduced from the fact that the door leading to

[1] §III, 15, fig. 1.   [2] See above, p. 251.
[3] See above, p. 274. There is a possibility that the Kish palace originated in E.D. II.

the antechamber of the first sanctuary was only 18 in. wide. At least two other E.D. temples succeeded this one before King Shulgi, 2095–2048 B.C., laid out an altogether new foundation.

A variety of objects including sculpture in the round and plaques in stone and in shell have been recovered from the débris; these appear to illustrate each successive phase of the E.D. period. One gypsum plaque may depict the goddess Inanna herself with grain sprouting from her bull-horned crown; she carries four maces and looks like an early prototype of Ishtar of battle, just as an alabaster statue of a human-headed bull foreshadows the later *lamassu*.[1] Most interesting is a series of square stone plaques, with a hole through the centre, carved with scenes which were well favoured in Sumer—a lion attacking a bull, incised, possibly E.D. I;[2] a hero dompting lions, and bulls, a banquet scene with the figures cut back in high relief giving the effect of silhouette, E.D. II; and a banquet scene in which a musician carries an eight-stringed lyre with a bull-headed sounding-box. This last named, inscribed plaque, dedicated to the goddess Ninmu, is comparable with the so-called 'Royal Standard of Ur' which came from one of the earliest graves in the Royal Cemetery at Ur.[3] The Nippur plaque was associated with Level VII B of the Inanna Temple at Nippur and provides some grounds for attributing that building to E.D. III a.[4] There is some doubt as to how these plaques were used. D. P. Hansen would, on the evidence of an obscure inscription associated with Gudea, connect them with the locks of doors to which they may have been attached by a cord fastened to a knob projecting from the hole in the centre of the plaque—if so these plaques would have been fitted to an adjacent wall.[5] None has ever been found in position, and it would seem more likely that they were originally buried, as foundation boxes, under the floor, possibly in proximity to the door. At Mari one E.D. plaque was found deposited in this way, associated with the raw materials of a smith and a lapidary—gold and semi-precious stones.

The synchronisms with other sites provided by the long succession of Inanna temples have been clearly defined. Levels XI–IX correspond with E.D. I; level VIII with E.D. II; levels VII–V with E.D. III, and many of the standard types of pottery attributed to these three main stages of the E.D. period have been found.[6] Most important of these criteria were the cuneiform

[1] §III, 15, figs. 8 and 16.   [2] §III, 17, 156 n. 54 and pl. 3.
[3] §III, 35, pls. 91–3.   [4] §III, 17, 145 and pls. I–VI.
[5] *Ibid.* 155.   [6] D. P. Hansen in §III, 13, 209.

tablets of Fārah type,[1] usually assigned to E.D. III*a*, found in level VII B, with which the inscribed banquet scene plaque, described above, was also associated.[2] This evidence corroborates the correctness of our classification of the early graves from the Royal Cemetery of Ur as E.D. III*a*, for they were dug into houses which contained tablets considered to be a little earlier than those of Fārah.[3] It is not possible, on present historical evidence, to allow the validity of recent carbon-14 determinations of material from Nippur, since these would require a reduction of six or seven centuries in the accepted dating of the E.D. period.[4]

UR

Much scattered evidence of Early Dynastic buildings was discovered at Ur, but the detailed sequences are less informative than those revealed in the Diyālā Valley. It is to be presumed that the great zikkurrat of king Ur-Nammu conceals within it the remains of a more ancient plano-convex tower which may already in the E.D. period have been a true zikkurrat rather than a temple terrace. The reason for this presumption is that extensive remains of a huge terrace not less great in extent than those of the Third Dynasty of Ur were discovered much damaged by Ur-Nammu's masons.[5]

On either side of the zikkurrat stairs, overlying a raised platform, were two big buildings of plano-convex bricks to which Woolley refers as temple kitchens, no doubt on account of the extensive traces of ash, of hearths, of bitumen-lined troughs and of careful drainage arrangements which he found associated with them. Great care was expended in the building of the terrace, within which stone had been used as well as brick.

In one of these temples a stepped altar with a bitumen-lined runnel was situated against the wall of a presumably open court which measured 12 × 6 m. Adjuncts of the temple included a number of circular brick bases, a feature which was also observed overlying some of the tombs in the Royal Cemetery of Ur, and in the north-western of the two zikkurrat temples there was a bitumen trough which contained fish offerings. Both buildings are based on a square plan and are reminiscent of domestic rather than of religious architecture. The associated offerings suggest that this may perhaps be related with the *Opferstätten* discovered

---

[1] §III, 17, 153, n. 42.
[2] *Ibid*. pl. vi; §III, 36, 376 and pl. 181 for limestone plaque from Ur.
[3] E. Burrows in §III, 35, 313 f.   [4] See above, p. 243.   [5] §III, 37, pl. 66.

at Warka and that they were primarily places of sacrifice intimately associated with the zikkurrat.

Exceptional in character are six chambers, 9 m. in length and 3 m. in width, which Woolley describes as shrines, without adequate reason. They look most like a regular row of magazines.[1] They are differentiated from any other chambers unearthed elsewhere at Ur in having very solidly laid floors not less than fourteen to fifteen courses in thickness, with bitumen mortar in the lower six or seven courses and clay in the upper ones. As the floors were raised well above the level of the court, each chamber had to be approached by stairs. It seems likely that these elaborate arrangements for waterproofing and drying were made to safeguard the storage of perishable material, and possibly they may have been magazines for grain or perishable food-stuffs required in the zikkurrat precincts. The elevation of brick pavements with mud-mortar on top of the bitumened courses must have been for purposes of insulation, in order to prevent the bitumen from melting in the summer, and indicates that these chambers were lightly roofed.

Not many small objects were found in the vicinity, but some stone carvings, seals and impressions, and hoards of beads which included lapis lazuli may be attributed to E.D. III, and a shell plaque possibly to E.D. II.[2] The plans of the two temples and the terrace belong most probably to E.D. III, but further excavation would doubtless show that they were modifications of older foundations. Traces of considerably earlier buildings were described by Woolley as Archaic I and II. Archaic II may have corresponded with E.D. I, for the walls contained a mixture of *Riemchen*-type and plano-convex bricks, as at Warka. Archaic I belonged to the Jamdat Nasr period, which was well represented by series of carved stone amulets.[3]

Enough E.D. remains have been found at Ur to indicate that the whole of the *temenos* area had already been consecrated at that period. Plano-convex brick walls, and associated objects apart from those already mentioned in the zikkurrat terrace, were found in the E-nun-mah; near the Gi-par-ku two big and well-carved stone rams which may have been the *protomai* of a throne;[4] and in the E-khursag area abundance of vertical terracotta ring-drains, far in excess of the requirements of any one building, may represent ritual arrangements for libations to the god Enki

---

[1] §III, 37, pl. 66. H. Frankfort agrees with our view; §II, 7, 302, n. 10.
[2] §III, 36, pl. 38 (U. 2826); pl. 39 (U. 18309); pl. 44 (U. 18313–14).
[3] *Ibid.* pl. 38 (U. 17832–5).   [4] *Ibid.* pl. 38 (U. 6756 A, B).

through the *apsu*; some of these drains contained deposits consisting of clay cups filled with animal bones.

Of the various examples of E.D. stone carvings we should draw attention to an alabaster statuette of a standing female figure wearing a fleecy '*kaunakes*' mantle, from a grave of the E.D. III *a* (?) period: the only complete figure of the kind recovered at Ur, and unique in that it was deposited in the grave of a soldier who was armed with a socketed axe.[1] In addition we may note three important monuments which date from the period of the Lagashite dominion over Ur; all of the period E.D. III *b*. A stone foundation plaque with hole in the centre, comparable in type with those mentioned from Nippur above, illustrates a priest in a state of ritual nudity, attended by three satellites carrying sheep while he pours a libation on an altar which stands outside the temple gate.[2] The upper register illustrates the god wearing a horned mitre, enthroned inside the temple, while the same priest, attended by the same satellites disencumbered of their offerings, pours another libation on a similar altar. The plaque is worth a detailed study because it illustrates the 'cinematographic' form of narrative which the artists of the E.D. III period had inherited from the preceding Uruk–Jamdat Nasr era.[3] A much rubbed granite stele inscribed with the name of Ur-Nanshe may perhaps have been deposited at the time of his suzerainship. The diorite statue of Entemena marks a predilection for this harder stone, which, after E.D. III had ended, was to be splendidly exploited by Gudea.[4] Entemena had inherited the overlordship of Ur from Eannatum who, as we have seen above, subdued many cities to his dynasty.

Most spectacular of all the discoveries at Ur, to which many references have already been made both in chapter XIII and in this one, was the so-called Royal Cemetery. The cemetery itself was located on the south-east side of the later *temenos* enclosure, on waste ground which overlay the ruins of houses, and was also superimposed on two strata of débris, SIS 4–5, which contained pottery and seal impressions of the Jamdat Nasr period, as well as some impressions that may perhaps be attributed to E.D. I. The latter consist of clay jar-stoppers bearing many impressions from the same cylinder, including the names of cities.[5] It is therefore certain that the earliest graves in the cemetery post-date

---

[1] §III, 37, pl. 37 (U. 19037); the axe is type A. 1, in list of contents, grave B. 36, p. 129.　　[2] *Ibid.* pl. 39*c* (U. 6831).
[3] §III, 26, and Taf. 8.　　[4] §III, 36, pls. 39*d* and 40.
[5] *U.E.* III, nos. 425, 431.

E.D. I. We have already seen that under the cemetery there were also tablets, only just pre-Fārah in date, and therefore E.D. II. It is thus certain that none of the royal graves can be earlier than E.D. II and most probably begin in E.D. III *a*, though some of their contents are indistinguishable from objects found in Sin Temples VIII and IX and in other E.D. II buildings in the Diyālā region. The late terminus or end of the richest graves in the cemetery is marked by two rubbish strata, SIS 1–2, which contain seal impressions of Mesannipada and an impression and the actual seal of his wife Ninbanda.[1] There can be little doubt that these strata contain the débris of the plundered graves of that Dynasty—the First Dynasty of Ur, E.D. III *b*, which conveniently marks a break in the sequence.[2]

More than 2,500 graves were found in the cemetery, of which a considerable number had been robbed, but some of the built tombs and death-pits were found intact, probably because they had been protected by the overlying graves of Mesannipada and his family. The robbers of these later tombs were doubtless more than satisfied with their loot and may well have thought that no more was to be found below them.

At least half a dozen of the built tombs were probably the vaults of a single family (see Fig. 12). The older ones seem to be cruder in construction than the later ones; thus 779, a big tripartite tomb with a corbel vault, stone-built, was probably earlier than 1054, a mosque-like domed tomb confronted by a courtyard, and was probably also earlier than 789/800 B, in which brick vaults were used over the stone walls. The plundered grave 779, which we believe to be the earliest, was the one that contained the so-called 'Royal Standard of Ur', decorated with scenes of peace and war which were executed in shell and lapis lazuli incrustation. It should also be recalled that grave 755, which belonged to Prince Meskalamdug, owner of the celebrated electrum wig-helmet, overlapped the shaft of 779 and was therefore subsequent to it.[3] Indeed Meskalamdug's grave is probably the latest in the series, later also than 1050, which belonged to Akalamdug, who was accompanied by forty bodies, and later than 1054 which contained the body of a princess and four men, as well as the seal of King Meskalamdug, and two daggers in a box.

The best known graves are 789 and 800 B, two vaults situated at the bottom of a deep shaft. The former is presumed to have

[1] §III, 36, 40.
[2] See above, p. 245, n. 1.
[3] §III, 35, 57 f.

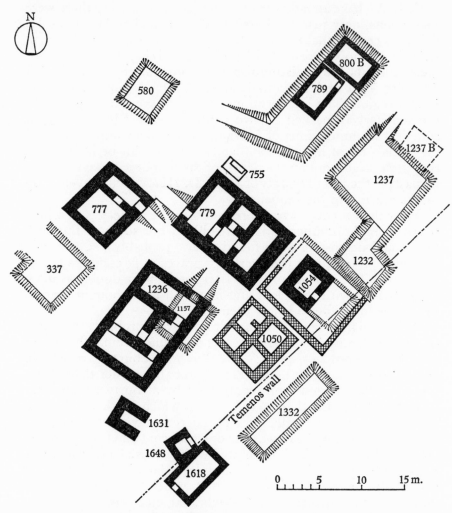

Fig. 12. Royal tombs and death-pits at Ur. (*U.E.* II, The Royal Cemetery, pl. 273. By permission of the Trustees of the British Museum.)

contained the remains of the king, whose body was never identified, because the grave had been partially plundered through the roof. Adjacent to it was the vault of a Queen 'Shub-ad' (Pu-abi) who was lying on her back, upon a bed, accompanied by female attendants. Two waggons drawn by oxen and attended by grooms had been backed down the steep *dromos*; there were fifty-nine bodies—the majority females (the males appear to have been soldiers, or attendants)—on the ground around the two tomb chambers. The treasures from these graves are beyond price, and in quantity are equalled only by the extraordinary deposits in the big shaft grave, 1237, which contained seventy-four bodies; sixty-eight of them were women, attired in full court regalia.

Woolley believed that all the persons and the animals immolated at the time of the funeral had descended into the pits alive. The animals were probably slaughtered by their attendants and the men and women took poison from little bowls which were ready for them in the shafts. To the last they may have played the funeral dirge on the gorgeous musical instruments, golden harps and bull-headed lyres, which were provided for them.

No one who was present at the time of that discovery is likely to forget the ghastly scene of human sacrifice, a crowd of skeletons so gorgeously bedecked that they seemed to be lying on a golden carpet upon which gold and silver vessels, head-dresses, jewellery and a multitude of other treasures rested undisturbed, a dream of a cave far richer than Aladdin's come to life. These things were celebrated by the lines of Robert Bridges, Poet Laureate at the time.

> Drinking vessels of beaten silver or of clean gold,
> vases of alabaster, obsidian chalices,
> cylinder seals of empire and delicat gems
> of personal adornment, ear-rings and finger-rings,
> craftsmen's tools copper and golden, and for music a harp;
> withal in silver miniatur his six-oar'd skiff,
> a model in build and trim of such as ply today
> Euphrates' flowery marshes: all his earthly toys
> gather'd to him in his grave, that he might nothing lack
> in the unknown life beyond, but find ready to hand
> his jewel'd dice and gaming board and chamber-lamp,
> his toilet-box of paints and unguents[1]

The catalogue of treasures deposited with the dead runs into many hundreds of items. In addition to those mentioned above and elsewhere[2] we may recall the many thousands of beads in gold, silver, carnelian, and a profusion of lapis lazuli the presence of which implies the existence in E.D. III of an unimpeded trade route through to Badakhshān in Afghanistān. A hilt of this material was used for the celebrated golden dagger found complete with lattice-work sheath in tomb 580.[3] The use of decorated ostrich shells probably implies trade with Arabia (the Nejd), mother-of-pearl with the Persian Gulf; silver with north-western

---

[1] Robert Bridges, *The Testament of Beauty*, book IV, lines 295 ff.
[2] See above, pp. 137 ff.
[3] §III, 35, pl. 151.

Iran (mines near Tabrīz); copper which had a nickel content, with Oman; many stones must have come from Iran. We have seen that some stone vases can be matched in India, to which we must add etched carnelian beads. A widespread trade in which many surrounding countries were involved had now reached a climax.

The gorgeous beech-leaf head-dresses, the golden and silver florally decorated combs; the wreaths composed of little amulets in the shape of bulls, rams, birds and fish, huge boat-shaped ear-rings may be accounted by the puritanically minded as in barbaric taste; but the beauty of line, the dexterity of craftsmanship, the quality of some of the golden bowls which can match the finest English silver of the Queen Anne period must command our admiration.

The problem of interpretation which these discoveries demand has been discussed in a preceding chapter.[1] Some would see here the evidence of a fertility cult, perhaps seasonal, others who follow Woolley see royal burials and they would now rely on a story concerning the death of Gilgamesh, a contemporary king who, if the tablet can be read aright, was accompanied in death by his retainers.[2]

We may call attention to a fact, often noticed, that the majority of persons found in the royal graves were women, that the evidence of kings is unexpectedly rare, and that in the great shaft 1237 there was no principal personage at all. It may be that in this case the protagonist had been buried in a plundered chamber beyond it.[3] The fact is that much of the evidence is missing and the most popular view, whether right or wrong, is likely to be that the big tombs and shafts are the remains of royal burials, both of kings and of queens, whose attendants were mostly women, therefore desirable and expendable. Barbarous practices on this scale ceased at the end of E.D. III a, for reason must have asserted that it was inconvenient to immobilize so much wealth, and that man could serve the gods better by remaining alive than by courting a premature death.

Perhaps more puzzling is the origin of the practice, which at Kish in Babylonia appears to have begun in E.D. II and persisted at Susa in E.D. III. We may well look to the precedents in Egypt where in Early Dynastic times both at Abydos and perhaps at Saqqara we find evidence of similar sacrifice.[4] But if that be the source of origin there is a missing link in Mesopotamia, for we have no evidence of the practice in E.D. I. It may be that the ground had been prepared in Babylonia itself through the increasingly large scale on which sacrifice was practised by means of the *Opferstätten*,

---

[1] See above, pp. 137 ff.   [2] §III, 22.   [3] §III, 35, 114.
[4] §III, 14, 135; see above, pp. 58f.

of which abundant traces have been found at Warka, and on a lesser scale at Ur and Eridu.[1] The classic example was the *Riemchengebäude* at Warka, where in addition to animal bones large numbers of clay and stone vases, metal objects and some incrusted canopies were deposited within mud-brick chambers and burnt.[2] No human sacrifice was made at that period, but many valuables were immobilized. Again there is a missing link in E.D. I, but perhaps the memory of this ritual at Warka, which seems to have been connected with the abandonment of an ancient temple, conditioned these much later malpractices at Ur. We need more work on an extensive E.D. I site in order to solve the problem of origins.

AL-'UBAID

The sequel to the evidence of the E.D. III a period revealed in the Royal Cemetery at Ur is best seen at the little site of al-'Ubaid[3] some 4 miles away, on the lines of an old canal. There, A'annipada, the son of Mesannipada, dedicated a temple to Nin-khursag and we have the remains of a temple plan of E.D. III b with much evidence of the contemporary art, which is closely related to that of the preceding phase, and in some cases indistinguishable from it. The building had been destroyed by fire and only the platform which supported it survived. There were heavy stone foundations, and buttresses and recesses in the façade, which was composed of baked as well as unbaked plano-convex brick. The methods of construction thus appeared more elaborate than those of the preceding E.D. III a phase. The ascent of the platform was made by means of two stone staircases; at the top there was a pair of elaborately incrusted columns, and the façade of the temple appears to have been decorated with artificial stone flowers pegged into the wall. Many fragments of cast and hammered copper reliefs survived; cattle, stags and the spread eagle were represented. Most remarkable was an inlaid frieze with limestone and shell figures depicting the temple cattle and a milking scene. This was an enlarged edition of the older, and usually much smaller, shell plaques familiar in the E.D. III a phase. After the main excavations were concluded the excavators of the Temple Oval at Khafājī rightly deduced from the plan that the *enceinte* must have been surrounded with an oval wall, and this in due course they discovered.[4]

---

[1] §III, 5, 76 ff.
[2] §I, 9, *U.V.B.* xv (1959), 8 f. and Taf. 35 ff.   [3] §III, 16.
[4] §III, 12; plan showing oval enclosure at al-'Ubaid in §II, 6, 141, fig. 124.

The remains from 'Ubaid, though somewhat rustic in character, are a remarkable example of the gradual evolution of Sumerian
art and architecture. Methods of construction are an elaboration
of E.D. III*a*, showing much experimentation: the floral cone
decoration derives ultimately from the Jamdat Naṣr period and
was applied as far north as Tell Brak in Syria;[1] the metal work is
closely allied to beginnings in E.D. II.

LAGASH

This important site, which is said to cover an area of about
4 × 3 km., lies not far from the Shaṭṭ el-Ḥayy, midway between
Tigris and Euphrates, some 10 miles from modern Shaṭrah. No
doubt in antiquity it was connected with these rivers by a system
of canals which must already have existed in E.D. times.

Much material from Tello[2] belongs to the end of the period
E.D. III*b* and is therefore closely related to finds at Ur associated
with the Dynasty of Mesannipada which we have been discussing
above.

Although abundant traces of plano-convex buildings were discovered, hardly any coherent plans of the period have survived,
because most of these early remains were dug in the nineteenth
century by de Sarzec and others, before the introduction of more
modern methods of excavation by André Parrot. But we owe to
the early pioneers large collections of late E.D. III tablets and a
remarkable series of monuments, many of them inscribed, beginning with Ur-Nanshe, a monarch who probably reigned only a
little later than A'annipada of Ur and may possibly have overlapped with him. The Lagashite carved foundation plaques, seals,
weapons and maceheads associated with Ur-Nanshe are closely
comparable with those of E.D. III*b* at Ur, but are often of
superior workmanship. The most famous monument known is
that of his second successor Eannatum, author of the famous
Stele of the Vultures which celebrated his triumph over Umma
depicting his enemies held fast in a net, and a Sumerian phalanx
of soldiers. The helmet worn by the king on that monument is
very closely related in style to that of Meskalamdug, and we may
therefore infer that the grave of that monarch at Ur cannot be
earlier than E.D. III*a* and may conceivably have belonged to the
period E.D. III*b*. No less famous is the silver vase of Entemena
finely engraved with the design of a spread eagle, emblem of the

[1] §IV, 5, pl. v and p. 95 compared with Uruk and 'Ubaid specimens.
[2] §III, 33; 6; 29.

city. The last monarch of that dynasty, Urukagina, is noted for his attempted reforms, which were inscribed in the Lagashite records; they came too late and resulted in the transfer of power to Lugal-zaggisi of Uruk, who brings the E.D. period proper to an end.

The principal building at Lagash throughout the E.D. period must have been the temple E-ninnu, 'House (of) Fifty', proper to the city's god, Ningirsu, and many of the known monuments must have once been a part of its endowment but, as we have seen, its plan was not recovered.

URUK AND OTHER SITES

Evidence concerning the E.D. period at Uruk (Warka) is defective because so much of it was destroyed by the large scale of rebuilding conducted in E-anna by Ur-Nammu and his successors. Various phases of the period are represented principally in Archaic Level I, in which the last two out of seven phases contained walls of plano-convex bricks.[1] The preceding phases contained, however, a mixture of the typical plano-convex E.D. bricks with *Riemchen*, which would indicate, contrary to Jordan's theory, that the transition from one stage to another was a gradual one.[2] R. McC. Adams was of the opinion that E.D. Uruk 'swelled in size to become the first and greatest of Sumerian cities, cultivation in the surrounding region probably being redirected largely towards fields under the close protection of its battlements'.

Early Dynastic material is widespread throughout Babylonia, at many sites, some of them still unsurveyed. In the Naṣiriyyah district alone, within which Ur is situated, Behnam Abu es-Suf has reported no less than eighteen sites hitherto virtually unknown with which E.D. sherds are associated.[3] Doubtless in all the other liwas of Iraq many more sites could be added to that list. Near Kut for example, Tariq el-Madhlum has excavated the site of Tell el-Wilayah, which contained E.D. remains as well as even more important ones of the Agade period.[4]

Two large capital cities, Umma (Tell Jūkhā), 18 miles from Lagash, and Adab (Bismaya), 16 miles north of Fārah, remain to be scientifically excavated, though the latter was partially dug, with encouraging results, by E. J. Banks at the beginning of this century.[5] Larsa may be expected to reveal remains of the period; Larak and Akshak await identification.[6]

[1] §1, 15, vol. I, 344, and §1, 9, *U.V.B.* II (1931), 16 ff., and III (1932), 5 f.
[2] §III, 36, 35.   [3] §III, 1.
[4] §III, 25; also §III, 31.   [5] §III, 2.
[6] §1, 17, 373 n. 23.

CONCLUSIONS

The size and importance of the many capital cities of Babylonia in the E.D. period are evidence of a widespread prosperity which was backed, as we know, by an elaborate and efficient administration that has been amply attested by the many economic texts discovered in Lagash and Shuruppak. But the large populations which the extent of these ruined cities implies could only have been supported by an equally elaborate and efficient system of irrigation, and we may be certain that the intricate network of canals frequently mentioned under the Third Dynasty of Ur was in existence centuries earlier.[1] Much ground work is still required to trace their limits, but the task has been begun. Already Adams has found evidence for concluding that in the Diyālā region the E.D. sites were grouped in enclaves as they had been at an earlier period. 'The network of watercourses relied upon for irrigation. . .had changed little since 'Ubaid times.'[2] In the district of Warka however it seems that the older pattern of village settlement almost disappeared.

We have already seen that we can make only an approximate estimate of the length of the whole period, but 500 years is unlikely to be an exaggeration, in spite of the incomprehensible reduction which carbon-14 computations have now given for the first quarter of the third millennium B.C.

The division of the E.D. period which claims our most urgent attention for the future is E.D. I, our knowledge of which is defective. Only in the Diyālā district can we assign any important buildings to this phase, and seals of the 'brocade style', common there, are rare beyond it. It may be that some seals now assigned to E.D. II were already in use in E.D. I, and that eventually it will be difficult to define the line of demarcation which separates this period from Jamdat Naṣr.

---

[1] §III, 3; 8; 19; 20; 21.

[2] Robert McC. Adams, *Land behind Baghdad*, 38 ff., has found evidence for concluding that in the Diyālā region E.D. sites were grouped in enclaves, as they had been at an earlier period. In the district of Warka it seems that the older pattern of village settlement almost disappeared, and cultivation was restricted under the closer protection of the capital.

IV. ASSYRIA AND MESOPOTAMIA

The history and archaeology of the upper reaches of Tigris and Euphrates during the E.D. period is much less known than that of Babylonia. At one site, Tell Brak, there was close contact with the south, in particular with Uruk during the Jamdat Naṣr period. But there and elsewhere there may have been a loosening of the ties in E.D. I–II, although it is possible that more intensive excavation in the relevant levels would show that contact was still maintained. However that may be, in E.D. III*a* and later, north and south were in close touch and the evidence reflects a high level of commercial prosperity which at that time embraced distant countries.

A complete account of the E.D. sequences in Mesopotamia and Assyria would involve the examination of much disparate material reflecting the development of native styles in many different places. Here we must chiefly concern ourselves with a brief discussion of evidence from northern sites in so far as it is related to the history and archaeology of Babylonia as described in the preceding pages.[1]

MARI

This Syrian site,[2] which was already an important city in the E.D. period, is situated $2\frac{1}{2}$ km. west of the present course of the river, on the Middle Euphrates, and was strategically placed to control its traffic. It lies 11 km. north-north-west of Abu Kamāl on the frontier between Syria and Iraq and is still a tribal centre to which the desert nomads repair; its ruins cover more than 100 acres.

The most important E.D. evidence comes from a succession of six 'Ishtar' temples (*a–f*) which spanned a total depth of about 6 m. of accumulated débris,[3] for which on comparative grounds a span of about six centuries would not seem to be excessive. Little is known about the lowest and earliest building, temple (*f*). The second in succession, temple (*e*), an important structure which covered an area of over 26 × 25 m., was built on formidable stone foundations which consisted of large gypsum blocks. To the west of it, A. Parrot exposed an expanse of gypsum, 17 × 10 m. in area, which may have been the foundations for a

---

[1] See also above, ch. XIII.

[2] §IV, 12. Successive campaigns are still being published in the same journal, e.g. §IV, 13.

[3] §IV, 14, pls. I–VIII.

tower. Hardly any objects were discovered in association with it, but the little *céramique commune* would have been equally at home in the next two temples and could conceivably be E.D. I.

The third installation, temple (*d*), includes a sanctuary on the west side and a priest's house on the east. Associated with this level was a deposit of pottery embedded in a clay podium of boat-like shape which Parrot has termed '*barcasses*'—a pronounced feature in all the succeeding sanctuaries. The pot types in these deposits appear to be North Mesopotamian rather than Babylonian in form, and are comparable with the ceramic of Chagar Bazar levels 3–4.[1] The period to which this temple should be assigned is doubtful: it is perhaps not earlier than E.D. II, and its most important feature was the presence of a number of big stone tombs constructed in pairs, composed of gypsum blocks and corbel-vaulted, therefore closely comparable with the early vaults in the Royal Cemetery of Ur which, as we have seen above, were E.D. III*a*. One tomb in temple (*d*) may have been dug down in a late stage of occupation, or possibly from the succeeding temple (*c*), with which these tombs might be contemporary. However that may be, it is fortunate that one of them, tomb 300, contained votive offerings, notably 'scarlet ware', usually attributed to the E.D. I–II periods, as well as a number of bronzes which await publication in the volume which will be entitled *Les Nécropoles*.

The fourth temple, (*c*), a building on a larger scale, represents the classic form in a steady line of development (see Fig. 13). There may have been a gap between (*d*) and (*c*), for the latter was built on a different emplacement. Temple (*c*) consists of a simple rectangular *cella* (no. 17) which measured 9.30 × 7.20 m. and was enclosed by mud-brick walls no less than 3.20 m. thick. A rectangular mud-brick podium or altar stood at one end of the room, opposite the door in the long wall giving access to a large courtyard which contained a striking architectural feature, namely a peristyle consisting of five solidly built mud-brick columns, 1.20 m. in diameter, filled with rammed earth and carefully plastered. The columnar form of architecture may be linked with Sin Temple VIII at Khafājī (E.D. II), and with the Kish Palace (E.D. II or III*a*); perhaps we may opt for the earlier synchronism. More '*barcasses*' were discovered and there was a new type of foundation-deposit which consisted of a heavy long-handled bronze implement, spade-like in shape but with a looped end through which a heavy nail was driven. Associated with the nails were two tablets, uninscribed, one in lapis lazuli; the other in limestone. Sometimes

1 §IV, 14, 59, fig. 41, and 19, fig. 12. See below, pp. 304 ff.

there was a silver tablet and a few animal bones.[1] Adjoining the
court and temple to the east side of it there was a second, large,
dog-legged courtyard which gave access to a house with at least
a dozen large rooms, doubtless accommodation for the priest. A
heavy, socketed bronze axe of a type common in the Royal Cemetery of Ur, allegedly associated with either (c) or (d) level, cannot
be earlier than E.D. II and belongs more probably to E.D. III a.[2]

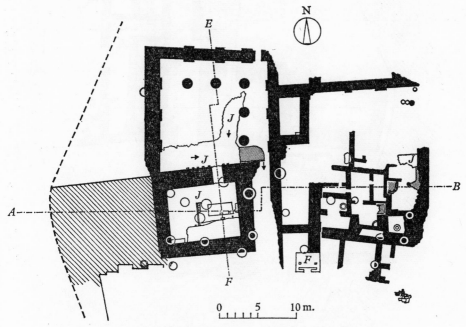

Fig. 13. Ishtar Temple (c) at Mari. Early Dynastic II, or III a.
(After A. Parrot, *Le Temple d'Ishtar*, pl. IV.)

Temple (b), the fifth in succession, was a reconstitution of (c), on
exactly the same emplacement. '*Barcasses*' continued to be deposited and there was evidence of burnt sacrifice. Lapis lazuli
amulets carved to represent bearded bulls closely match E.D. III a
types in the Royal Cemetery of Ur and from Tell Brak,[3] but
there are two Fārah-type cylinder seals, probably E.D. II: one
of them, no. 1081, depicts a figure with long ears characteristic
of that style.[4] The seals, however, may be earlier than the level with
which they are associated; two stone heads, nos. 1063, 1064,

---

[1] §IV, 14, 17, 18.   [2] *Ibid*. 184, fig. 98.
[3] *Ibid*. pl. LVIII, nos. 1018, 1072, 1079 and fig. 94 on p. 157.
[4] *Ibid*. pl. LXV, nos. 1080, 1081.

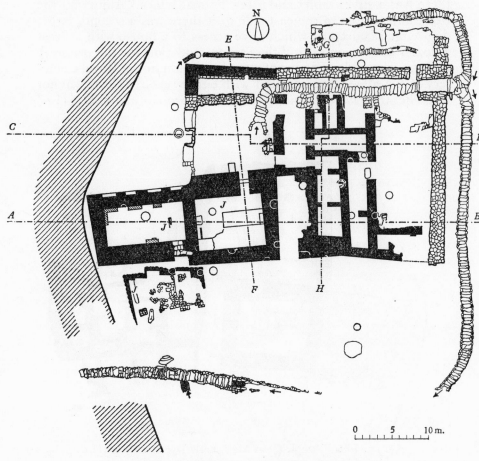

Fig. 14. Ishtar Temple (*a*) at Mari. Early Dynastic III*b*.
(After A. Parrot, *Le Temple d'Ishtar*, pl. VIII.)

rather crudely carved could be E.D. II or III,[1] probably the latter.
Fragments of bituminous vases with rows of shell incrustation
are also typical of E.D. III*a*.[2]

Temple (*a*) (see Fig. 14), the sixth and last in the series, we may
with some confidence assign to the period E.D. III*b*, that is to say,
corresponding approximately with the dynasty of Mesannipada at
Ur or about the time of the so-called 'Proto-Imperial' age. Here in
the cella was found the statue, dedicated to the goddess Ishtar,[3]

[1] §IV, 14 pl. XXXIII, nos. 1063, 1064.
[2] *Ibid.* 224 and pl. LXXI*a*.   [3] *Ibid.* 68 f. and pls. XXV, XXVI.

of a king of Mari named Lamgi-Mari, not known to the king-list but styled by the inscription great governor of the god Enlil. In the adjacent courtyard there was also found the enthroned statue of an official, Ebikh-il, seated on a basket-work throne, clad in a fleecy skirt and stripped to the waist; bearded, but otherwise clean-shaven.[1] This well-developed statuary would seem to be pre-Agade in style, more advanced and carved with more assurance than most of the statuary associated with the Diyālā sites in E.D. II–III a. The numerous pieces of shell inlay and incrustation, however, also associated with this temple (a) can be closely matched at Kish E.D. II and III a, and at Ur, E.D. III a, by the Royal Standard. They present a spirited pictorial scene which when assembled must have formed part of a continuous frieze in several panels depicting the king, his arms, his chariots, his prisoners, and his victory banquets.[2] These figures, which elsewhere are more characteristic of E.D. III a than III b, illustrate the strength of tradition in Mesopotamian art and perhaps indicate that this temple existed over a period which may have spanned more than a century. It does not seem likely on this evidence that any of the associated objects can be dated later than 2400 B.C. and many of them must be earlier. The chronology is of particular interest because within the temple precincts, close to the above-mentioned statue of Ebikh-il, were found two large stone vases related to fragmentary specimens in a dark stone that have appeared in the Indus valley and Baluchistān.[3] Many other fragments, some representing the doorways of shrines, imbrications and guilloche patterns, were also associated with this temple.[4] Perhaps some of the ivory work, though not in direct association with this temple, of which one particularly fine specimen was found, may be related to this Indian trade.[5]

The architecture of temple (a), although basically related to that of the preceding levels, was more grandiose and spacious than ever before. There were now two cellas instead of one, and a big enclosure wall embraced two courtyards and many subsidiary chambers. This, the last stage of the E.D. period, witnesses the same kind of elaboration that could be observed in Sin Temple X at Khafājī, and must imply an abundance of slave-labour, no doubt acquired by conquest. Surplus labour would have been needed for the intensive use of stone, which is one of the most remarkable features of temple (a). There was stone both in the

[1] §IV, 14, pls. XXVIII, XXIX.
[2] *Ibid.* 135 f. and pls. LV–LVIII.
[3] *Ibid.* pls. XLVIII, LI.
[4] *Ibid.* pls. XLVI–XLIX.
[5] *Ibid.* pl. LIX (representing a 'Personnage à robe kaunakès').

enceinte wall and in the floor of the court. Otherwise the amenities were much the same as before: benches for offerings in the cella, a podium or altar at the end wall of the second one, '*barcasses*', votive nails. Probably from these levels are pot types of a fine black polished ware, and grey ware, comparable with specimens from E.D. III*b* at Tell Brak and Chagar Bazar, specifically North Mesopotamian, not Babylonian in character.[1] A remarkable jar with seven spouts can be paralleled in the Diyālā Valley[2] and at Tello. Fruit-stands with high pedestals were also found.[3]

The great variety of objects associated with these levels came both from the temple precincts and from the tomb area where spacious houses with large courtyards were also found. In general the objects, which attest great material wealth, are proof of the close contact which Mari maintained both with the north, with Upper Khabur valley sites, and with the cities of Babylonia. Centrally placed to intercept traffic from both directions, it became a focus of international trade. This increase in wealth inevitably attracted covetous eyes, and temple (*a*), the richest in the entire sequence, is the first and only installation to bear the marks of a violent destruction. The entire building was consumed by fire; the fine statuary was wrecked and consigned to the ashes.

We cannot yet with certainty name the monarch responsible for this destruction, which we are inclined to attribute to Eannatum of Lagash as was first suggested by Parrot, who, however, later preferred Sargon. Both monarchs are known to have raided the district.[4] Some of the statuary was certainly stylistically related to that of Lagash. The same violent destruction encompassed the whole city, including the temples of Ishtarat, Ninkhursag, Ninnizaza and Shamash as well as the palace, where the burning must have occurred after the time of Mesannipada, as we shall see below.[5]

Not much is known, at the time of writing, about the Early Dynastic palace, except that it was a very large building of mudbrick underlying the Palace of Zimrilim at a considerable depth.[6] Excavation will eventually show whether its plan can be considered ancestral to the later palace, and if it is in any way related to that of the Eridu and Kish palaces. One remarkable discovery can, however, already be mentioned: the building was violently destroyed, and perished in the same fire that consumed

---

1 §IV, 14, 209, figs. 100–1 and 218, fig. 106, nos. 691, 692.
2 §II, 5, 43 and pl. 24*e*; §III, 6, pl. III (5481).   3 §IV, 14, 214.
4 *Ibid.* 41, n. 1 and 40, nn. 3–5. See below, p. 331.
5 *Ibid.* 40, n. 5. A. Parrot, *Les Temples d'Ishtarat et de Ninni-Zaza*. Paris, 1967.
6 §IV, 13.

the rest of the city. Lying in the ashes was a clay pot containing among other treasures a spindle-shaped lapis lazuli bead with an inscription to the effect that it had been dedicated to a temple in the city by Mesannipada, king of Ur, at a time when G[an]-su(d) was king of Mari, here written as Mera.[1] G. Dossin, who first read the inscription, has no doubt that this name may safely be identified with that of the canonical Sumerian king-list, where it is written in a variant form. There may be difficulties in equating the different readings, but on general grounds it may be accepted that a dynasty of Mari, perhaps the one named in the Sumerian lists as the tenth after the Flood, was approximately contemporary with that of the First Dynasty of Ur. We must agree with A. Parrot that both the archaeological and the historical evidence lead to the conclusion that the founder of this dynasty at Mari was contemporary with Mesannipada.[2]

It is hoped that the ashes of this palace may yet reveal further indications concerning the date of its destruction. While it is possible that Sargon himself may have been the destroyer, it may be that he found the city an easy prey after others had seized it before him. A bronze *ex voto* inscribed with the name of Naram-Sin's daughter proves that the dynasty of Agade eventually became well entrenched in the city. But long before that, the sculpture of Mari was inscribed with Akkadian, Semitic names. The art is Sumerian in origin, but ethnically the population must have been composed of Akkadian as well as of other groups. The art of Mari, like that of Tell Khuaira,[3] shows how far the influence of Sumerian culture had at the end of the E.D. period made itself felt in outlandish districts of northern Mesopotamia.

THE KIRKUK DISTRICT

It is significant, and at first sight surprising, that so far, in the Kirkuk district, midway between Assyria and Akkad, comparatively little has been found, and hardly anything has been scientifically excavated that may be attributed to the E.D. period.

At the site of Nuzi (Yorgan Tepe), 13 km. south-west of Kirkuk, for example, there would appear to be a gap in occupation between the Jamdat Nasr period and the new foundation named Gasur which can be attributed to the Agade dynasty.[4] It seems that this area, in which the resources for irrigation were comparatively defective, was not attractive to Early Dynastic enter-

---

[1] §IV, 2, 405; §IV, 15, 201.   [2] §IV, 14, 103.
[3] See below, pp. 310 ff.   [4] §IV, 19.

prise from Babylonia. Much more excavation is needed to determine the scale of occupation at the time.

On the other hand, it is important to record that the Iraq Antiquities Department has identified eleven sites in the Kirkuk Liwa which appear to have Ninevite V pottery[1] and may be attributed to the E.D. period. One site, Tell Ahmad el-Hatu near Kopri, contains much 'scarlet ware' (E.D. I–II), a northerly extension of a ceramic most at home in the Diyālā area.

Finally, it should be recalled that close to Kirkuk (ancient Arrapkha) heavy specimens of copper tools and weapons probably contemporary with Ninevite V have from time to time been accidentally unearthed, and there can be little doubt that the last named city must still contain some important Early Dynastic remains. The same observation applies to the great site of Irbil to the north of Kirkuk, now situated in the liwa contiguous to it. Here the oval shape of the city, which has probably enjoyed one of the longest unbroken occupations known to Mesopotamia, may imply a layout in Early Dynastic times, when the place may have been embraced by an oval wall, like the Early Dynastic enclosure at Khafājī in the Diyālā valley and at 'Ubaid in Babylonia.

ASHUR

This city, which was the early tribal and religious capital of ancient Assyria, was founded in the E.D. period on a high cliff overlooking the river Tigris. Our sole information concerning this stage of its history comes from the excavation of the two earliest temples, which must from the beginning have been dedicated to the goddess Ishtar—Ishtar H and G.[2] These two temples were built of mud-brick, the earlier one, H, was founded on virgin rock; only the low stumps of mutilated walls had survived; there are hardly any objects that can with certainty be attributed to it, but it is not improbable that some fragments of pottery and even a cult figurine may have belonged. We can, however, with confidence assert that Temple H must have been set up in the E.D. period, first because nothing earlier has been found on the site, and secondly because some of the G walls directly overlie H, and the basic ground plan—an oblong cella—must have been similar.

Temple G as illustrated by Andrae consisted of an oblong cella with antechamber and a niche at the far end designed perhaps to receive the cult statue. The building was approached by a street which passed through a towered gateway into an open courtyard

[1] See below, p. 302.   [2] §II, 4; §IV, 1, 72 ff. and Abb. 33–7.

where the visitor entered a door in the long western wall of the sanctuary proper. There may also have been flanking chambers in the side opposite the temple door. It must however be admitted that the precise nature of the plan is unknown to us, for the evidence was fragmentary and defective. None the less, we may be certain that the cella itself was typical of the period, an oblong room with podium at one end.

Fortunately, the evidence is sufficiently good for a reconstruction of the sanctuary itself. Mud-brick benches were set against the long walls and much of the statuary found in the débris must once have stood erect upon these podia after dedication. In the middle of the room there was once a lustral stone basin, and elsewhere were numerous models of two-storeyed houses in terracotta; open stands or pottery supports may have served as braziers, and tall pedestal vases, sometimes called fruit-vases, are related to a type of vessel more characteristic of E.D. II, which Andrae suggests may have carried incense. In general the pot forms, the use of plastic snakes, pots with bituminous markings and a few other types agree with E.D. III, probably with the latter part of that period, namely E.D. III *b*. But once again the ceramic reflects a continuous tradition, with only slight modifications from earlier and later styles; the model houses which must have been offering-tables, decorated with snakes, doves resting under the rafters and even lions, are appropriate to Ishtar and find some parallels both much earlier and much later. Perhaps they were model dovecots, but it is in any case probable that they reflect some of the grander examples of domestic architecture at this period, and it is therefore of interest that one set of façades depicts no less than three storeys with rectangular windows below, and one set of lunettes on top.[1] The triangular slit-openings are still used in many village houses at the present time.

The sharply cut gypsum statuary consists of *ex voto* male and female figures typically Sumerian in style; they are clad in fleecy sheepskin garments, are carved with assurance, and the female figures wear an elaborate coiffure; one of these is clad in an open mantle and shawl, very carefully rendered.[2] The style reveals the more detailed treatment characteristic of E.D. III *b*, though, as we have seen above[3] in discussing the female Diyālā heads, there are precedents in E.D. II.

One piece of sculpture, however, is out of keeping with the E.D. III style, a very fine head of a female wearing a fillet that cannot be earlier than the Agade period; its soft, smooth curves

[1] §II, 4, Taf. 15 *a*.   [2] *Ibid.* Taf. 37.   [3] Pp. 254 f., 269.

characteristic of alabaster, the full and sensuous mouth, are typical of this later style.[1] As it was lying in the ash, 60 cm. above a pavement in the sanctuary, and was burnt, it cannot be dissociated from the destruction of Temple G.[2] Once again, as at Mari, we find something of the Agade period apparently associated with E.D. III*b*.

To the same period we may assign a remarkable ivory figurine of a nude female, also found in the sanctuary of Temple G;[3] fragments of five other similar ones and an ivory pin surmounted by the feet of a figurine were found in the same level. They are not later than the Agade period, as we may judge from the coiffure, and provide evidence of the trade in ivory tusks which may have come from the Indian elephant, perhaps acquired in Iran from either Magan or Meluhha.[4] We therefore appear to be driven to conclude that Temple G, undoubtedly founded in E.D. III, continued to be used in the Agade period and was not sacked before that time.

The emphasis on and preoccupation with a fertility cult is clear from the model of a nude female which was made as a clay bottle, and associated with Temple G.[5] This lady is the female counterpart of an ithyphallic male figure found at Germayir, much further north, in the Khabur valley.[6]

Lastly, and perhaps most interesting of all the objects discovered in the early Ishtar temples, is the fragment of a painted gypsum model of a bedstead upon which the goddess, or her female attendant, is depicted lying on her back, upon her bed, like Queen 'Shub-ad' (Pu-Abi) or the ladies-in-waiting from the royal shafts at Ur. The Ashur lady wears a choker or dog-collar, big ear-rings and a pectoral; breasts and navel are bare, but emphasized by painted rings. Here we have the model of a lady of the Sumerian court bedecked for burial. This piece leads us to believe that Ishtar H belongs to the period E.D. III*a*, while Ishtar G is predominantly E.D. III*b* and ends with Agade.[7]

We are therefore bound to ask whether at this stage of the Early Dynastic period the Sumerians were in Ashur, and we must answer in the affirmative, so strong is the evidence of sculpture, pottery, a stone vase,[8] objects of the cult, and architecture. That is

---

[1] §II, 4, Taf. 39.
[2] *Ibid.* 68, Nr. 80.
[3] *Ibid.* 56, Abb. 43, Taf. 29.
[4] §IV, 8, 5, with references.
[5] §II, 4, 52, Abb. 32.
[6] §IV, 7, 128 and fig. 9, no. 18; photograph on front page of *Ill. Ldn News* of 27 March 1937.
[7] §II, 4, 54, Nr. 59, Taf. 27*a*, 28*b*.
[8] §II, 4, 53, Abb. 37.

to say, we believe that in the time of Temples H and G Ashur must have belonged to some Sumerian ruler by right of conquest; as we know to have been the case at a later period when Amar-Sin of Ur installed a viceroy there at a time when the Ishtar Temple E must have been flourishing.[1] But we need have no doubt that the population was predominantly of other stock—non-Sumerian, composed probably of tribal elements speaking Semitic and other tongues, as at Mari. These two temples are proof of the extent to which the leaven of Sumerian culture and civilization had spread into Assyria where, as we shall see from an examination of Nineveh, it had penetrated at an even earlier stage—in E.D. I.

NINEVITE V

At Nineveh a deep sounding through the acropolis penetrating from the top down to virgin soil provided a basis for classifying the prehistoric strata into five periods, Ninevite I–V,[2] numbered from the bottom upwards. In Ninevite IV there were many pot types characteristic of the Jamdat Naṣr period in the south, and the end of it may well have overlapped with E.D. I, which was certainly contemporary with a part of Ninevite V where many objects of a Sumerian character were found. We may note first a number of clay jar-sealings and impressions, some of them in the 'brocade style' or bearing guilloches, rosettes and other designs.[3] At least two cylinder seals and one impression were as late as E.D. III and it is indeed probable that Sumerian influence made itself felt throughout the period.

The most striking characteristic of the period, however, is a wheel-turned painted and incised pottery which appears to be native to Assyria in E.D. I–II and hardly ever appears in the south. The painted pottery consists of tall fruit-stands with high pedestal bases, high-necked vases with angular shoulders and ring or pedestal bases, carinated bowls and other types. Many of these vessels are overcrowded with designs, especially the bigger ones which depict long-necked giraffe-like goats, waterfowl, fish and many monotonous geometric patterns. Sometimes the paint is of a violet colour, strongly reminiscent of Jamdat Naṣr pottery, with which it may have been partly contemporary. But most probably the time of its *floruit* was E.D. I, a period at which the design tended to be prolonged below the shoulder as in 'scarlet ware'.

[1] §IV, I, 79. [2] §IV, 21.
[3] *Ibid.* pls. LXV, LXVI; §IV, 20, pl. LXIII, nos. 6, 10–14.

The appearance of this Ninevite V pottery presents a problem, for it has no antecedents in Assyria, least of all at Nineveh itself, where the preceding ceramic had for the most part consisted of black and grey burnished ware, and other unpainted types. It is possible to see a direct influence from Iran, which, unlike Assyria, had a strong and unbroken tradition of painting, and some examples very close to Ninevite V appear at Sialk and Hisar.[1] More probably it was a native development inspired by the fashions current on the Diyālā as well as in Iran during E.D. I. Its most southerly appearance is in the Diyālā valley, at Tell Asmar, where a fine specimen depicting panels with geometric designs and a goat was recovered from a deep shaft in the house area, in a context which included reserved-slip ware and goblets, and dated from the end of the Jamdat Naṣr period to E.D. I.[2]

No less interesting than the painted ware was the elegant and artistic wheel-made grey ware of Ninevite V, which affected much the same repertoire of shapes. The designs were incised, punctuated, *en creux* and in relief, nearly always geometric, but we find an occasional goat, sprig decoration, and there is one rather elegant drawing of a long-beaked bird with fan-tail confronting a stylized plant with a papyriform voluted top.[3] One notable example was found at Yarimjah near Mosul, a lugged vase with an all-over empanelled, compartmented design which may, like other grey ware specimens, have been based on a basketry prototype.[4] It is clear, however, that much of this pottery was a cheap imitation of metal, perhaps silver, as is indicated by scoring, feathering, and knobs or small bosses.[5] Morover, in Syria some bowls were found tightly bound with silver wire, as at Chagar Bazar.[6]

This stage of Ninevite V would, therefore, seem to correspond with a period at which metal vessels were highly prized and expensive, either a little before or during the time when silver was abundant, in E.D. III a.

Although sherds of painted and grey pottery were found at Nineveh in the same stratum of débris, it seems probable that the grey ware *floruit* is rather later in time, for this is indicated both at Tell Billa and at Chagar Bazar in Syria, where the two wares were never found in association. We may for the present assume that

[1] §IV, 9.   [2] §II, 13, 21 and fig. 20.
[3] §IV, 20, pl. LVIII, no. 16 and N. Burton Brown, *Excavations in Azarbaijan, 1948* (London, 1951), pl. III, no. 45 from Geöy Tepe.
[4] §IV, 21, pl. LXIII (B).   [5] *Ibid.* pl. LXIII, no. 7.
[6] See below, p. 305.

the painted Ninevite V may have appeared for the first time at the end of the Jamdat Naṣr period and become abundant in E.D. I, to be succeeded by the grey ware in E.D. II.

Also characteristic of the same stage of development was a series of very finely made miniature vessels with little suspension handles so finely perforated that they would seem only to have admitted a thread.[1] Chalices with heavy, pedestal bases were also common.

NINEVITE POTTERY ON OTHER SITES

The distribution of this pottery, which has been observed over a wide area of north-east Syria and Iraq, is concentrated in the district round Nineveh, which must have been one of its main centres of production. No less than forty-six sites in the Mosul Liwa have been noted by the Iraq Antiquities Department.[2] The better known ones are: Tell Billa, near Tepe Gawra, and Shenshi in the same district. It also occurs at many sites along the banks of the Khosr, a tributary of the Tigris, for example at ʿAbbasiyah. Westward it is known in the Jebel Sinjār, for example at Tulūl eth-Thalāthat,[3] and eastward in the Rania plain of Kurdistān. Perhaps it might be traced along both the Zab rivers through to Iran. Another area of concentration where the ware occurs in abundance is along the chain of prehistoric settlements which run from Irbil to Kirkuk, many of them cut by the modern railway.[4]

There is some doubt about the extent to which the ware occurred in Gawra VIII A and VII.[5] But the evidence from the neighbouring site of Tell Billa was important because here the painted and the incised grey ware occurred in succession in levels 7 and 6 respectively.[6] Here the stratigraphy suggests that the painted may have been E.D. I and the grey ware E.D. II.

We may conclude that the distribution of the characteristic Ninevite V pottery is a striking phenomenon of the Early Dynastic period, both in the heart of prehistoric Assyria and in eastern Syria, from which it has, as we shall see, a pronounced western extension. This would seem to correspond with a gradually in-

[1] §IV, 20, pl. LVIII.
[2] §III, 1, 109, and Abu es-Suf in *Iraq*, 30, 74 ff.
[3] A painted vase in the Iraq Antiquities Department, depicting long-necked goats and birds (4 Th. v, 137).
[4] References to each of the sites above mentioned are in §IV, 9, 146–9 and footnotes thereon.
[5] *Ibid.* 149 and §IV, 16, pls. XXVIII (*b*), nos. 1–2, and XXIX (*a*), no. 5.
[6] §IV, 17, 265 ff.; §IV, 18, 24 f.

creasing metallurgy, and since in Babylonia proper, where this pottery hardly occurs at all, the art of writing was beginning to develop, it is reasonable to suspect that tablets will eventually be found in the north, in association with Ninevite V. There is no need to suggest that the appearance of this pottery presupposes immigration, or the displacement of older occupants of the country, but it certainly does imply an awareness of technological changes in the south and a widespread commerce.

Moreover, developments were by no means similar on all the northern sites. There are, for instance, marked differences of development between the two neighbouring cities of Nineveh and Gawra. Whereas at Nineveh we have observed abundant evidence of connexions with the south through the seals and the pottery, at Gawra the native, rural technology remained virtually unchanged, and Ninevite V is rare. At Gawra the last stage of level VIII and level VII may have been approximately contemporaneous with E.D. I–III. A stamp seal impression in what is known as the 'dovetailing style', depicting a theriomachy, from level VIII, has been attributed to E.D. I by Edith Porada.[1] A greenish-grey ribbed bowl from the same stratum may be related to Ninevite V.[2] Some vase shapes from the same stratum can be matched at Chagar Bazar in Syria. But otherwise Gawra pursues its own line of development—it was a site in more direct touch with the hill country than Nineveh—and it is significant that the Gawran form of tripartite temple with porch persisted through this period, with some slight modifications, without diminution of ground plan.[3]

NORTHERN SYRIA: CHAGAR BAZAR

The site of Chagar Bazar,[4] a small township in the eastern district of the Khabur-Jaghjagha valley on the Wādi Dara, lies about 25 miles south-west of Kamichlie, near the present frontier of Turkey and Syria. It was in antiquity one of a chain of ancient settlements stretching across to the upper Tigris valley, and must frequently have been in touch with Nineveh, which was doubtless connected with it by caravan routes which ran through the Jebel Sinjār.

The sequences in this high and extensive mound have been classified into fifteen levels, no. 1 being the latest. The Early

---

[1] E. Porada, 'The Relative Chronology of Mesopotamia, Part I, Seals and Trade (6000–1600 B.C.)', in §III, 13, 160.

[2] §IV, 16, 42, pl. LXIII, no. 34, and Catalogue.   [3] *Ibid.* pl. IX.

[4] §IV, 6; 7; 5.

Dynastic period is represented on a modest scale in level 3, and more extensively in levels 4–5, in which ruined mud-brick houses were found, but no coherent ground plans.

The most important E.D. remains came from graves situated in levels 4–5, for level 5 consisted of a cemetery. Here some very fine specimens of Ninevite V black and grey wares were found, one of them still lightly bound with a twist of silver wire. The bowls in several cases had rounded bases, and were grooved, probably to enable them to be suspended with wire. The grey colour simulated silver, and the punctuated and zigzag designs would have been appropriate to the silver models which they imitated.[1] One big chalice was laid in the grave with the greater part of its pedestal broken away, and had perhaps been ritually broken at the graveside.[2] Bowls and vases matched specimens from Nineveh. In one grave only, outside the main cemetery, two fine specimens of painted Ninevite V were found, in association with an unpainted chalice.[3] It was clear that the painted and incised grey wares belonged to different periods, E.D. I and II respectively. Coarser specimens of the incised pottery, simulating basketry, were also found at the neighbouring mound of Arbit,[4] where one grave contained *inter alia* fluted spherical ball beads in E.D. III style as well as a cement bead inlaid with rough chips of quartz.[5] A copper socketed adze, dagger, pins and cylinder seal in the same grave were not later than E.D. III*b*; the pottery agreed with E.D. III–Sargonic types. Metal must have been plentiful at this time.

The most interesting discovery, however, was a fragment of a dagger handle made of non-meteoric terrestrial iron, found in a grave of level 5 at Chagar Bazar.[6] It was probably the remains either of a hilt or of a blade from a dagger and proves beyond a doubt that iron-working was already established in this district of north Syria at least as early as E.D. III*b*. The ore was available further north, in the country later known as Urartu, where at a much later period iron-working was practised by Armenian smiths whose names still carry the echo of their former craft. This discovery coincided remarkably with another made by H. Frankfort, in the Akkadian Palace at Tell Asmar on the Diyālā. There, beneath the floor, two hoards of jewellery, silver filigree and onyx, including lapis lazuli and copper objects, had been found, mostly in the style of E.D. III*a*. One of these objects consisted of a

[1] §iv, 6, fig. 18 and fig. 19, 1–4.   [2] *Ibid.* 38, no. 6.
[3] §iv, 7, fig. 25, nos. 1–3.   [4] *Ibid.* fig. 25, nos. 4–5.
[5] *Ibid.* 153, pl. XVIII, no. 4.   [6] §iv, 6, 26–7.

bronze open-work knife handle with traces of a blade made of terrestrial iron.[1]

A survey of the evidence from the Khabur indicates that at this period the inhabitants enjoyed free access to the sources of metal: examples from Chagar Bazar include a copper dagger blade, toggle-pin surmounted by a pair of doves, a silver bugle-bead and other specimens.[2] Other sites such as Arbit and Germayir have yielded similar evidence, which, incidentally, suggests that the incised Ninevite V grey ware probably outlasted E.D. II and continued to be used in E.D. III.

One more important discovery, from the débris in Chagar Bazar level 2, needs recording. It is a black sun-dried clay bulla, or docket, displaying the impression of a cylinder-seal. The impressions in two registers, are separated by a band containing a lozenge design with dot centres; the upper register depicts musicians playing the lyre and the bottom one a banquet scene with offering-tables and seated figures imbibing wine through straws.[3] The scene is identical with that so frequently depicted on cylinders from the Royal Cemetery of Ur, E.D. III*a*, and in addition we have on the Chagar Bazar bulla an inscription in Sumerian which perhaps refers to emmer(?).[4] A number of fragments of similar impressions were found in levels 2 and 3. Although the style of the impression is E.D., the writing seems Sargonic.

The conclusion to be drawn from these and other discoveries is that E.D. I–III was a prosperous period throughout the whole of the Khabur district of north-east Syria, that native styles in ceramic predominated, but with a strong intrusion of E.D. III Babylonian pot types at the end of the period—vases with metalliform lug-handles for example[5]—as well as an abundance of metal types familiar in the south. The impact of Sumer had made itself decisively felt and must imply intercourse on an ever-increasing scale throughout the Tigris–Euphrates valley in the E.D. period.

NORTHERN SYRIA: TELL BRAK

This site, one of the largest of the many hundreds of mounds which stud the steppe of north-east Syria, lies about 20 miles south-south-east of Chagar Bazar, and has direct access to the Jebel Sinjār, through which it must have been in contact with

[1] §II, 11, 61.
[2] §IV, 6, 27, 28 and fig. 8, nos. 1, 2, 17.
[3] §IV, 7, 96 and 151, pl. XIIIB (A. 391).
[4] §IV, 3, 178 (A. 391 and A. 393).
[5] §IV, 6, fig. 19, no. 1

Nineveh and other important centres in Assyria.[1] This once great city, which extended over an area of about 100 acres, would, if excavated further, yield an abundance of Early Dynastic remains. It was no doubt prosperous throughout the whole of that period, but although comparatively little has been dug in the levels which could illustrate it, the information available supplements in an interesting way that obtained from Chagar Bazar.

It seems that at Brak there was no interruption in ceramic continuity between the Early Dynastic and the Agade levels, where large numbers of black and grey wares were found in profusion. Tall vases with high necks and rounded bases, as well as bowls, well made, on the wheel, were especially characteristic and can be closely matched by vessels discovered in E.D. levels at Tell Khuaira in the steppe west of the Khabur valley.[2] It seems that this ceramic fashion was one that could be matched on Elburz sites in northern Iran.

The metal work, of which many good specimens were recovered, belongs mostly to the Agade period, but is clearly a carry-over from E.D., and a treasure—gold, silver, and jewellery, carnelian, lapis lazuli and agate beads and amulets found buried in pots under the floors of Agade period houses—betrays the influence of E.D. III *a–b*, as do many tools and weapons.[3] Many seal impressions are in E.D. style, and one shell cylinder seal depicting bound prisoners brought before an enthroned god is of E.D. III, but others are of the later Agade date.[4]

There is, however, one important piece of evidence which suggests that in E.D. III southern influence was very strong, for one corner of a building situated above the level of the last of the Brak 'Eye-Temples', overlying the much earlier Jamdat Naṣr series, was found, including a stone door socket and traces of a plano-convex mud-brick pavement; the bricks characteristically carry one indentation on the surface, a shallow, circular cavity.[5] It is remarkable that so far these are the only plano-convex bricks which have been discovered outside Sumer and Akkad proper, for they were not even used in the E.D. city of Mari, and the inference must be that southern brick-layers were working at Brak. Apparently associated with these E.D. remains was a white

---

[1] §IV, 5. [2] See below, pp. 313 f.

[3] §IV, 5, pls. XXXI–XXXVI.

[4] *Ibid.* pl. XXI, nos. 9–10; compare in style with §1, 5, pl. x *b*, and §IV, 22, pl. XXVIIA, a seal from Ḥammām, north Syria; Briggs Buchanan, *Catalogue of Ancient Near Eastern Seals in the Ashmolean Museum*, vol. 1, 137 ff., and M. E. L. Mallowan in *Antiq.* 42 (1967), 203 f.

[5] *Ibid.* pl. XLVIII, nos. 3 and 6.

limestone foundation-box divided into compartments which doubtless once contained the foundation-tablets—perhaps inscribed.

Since we know from discoveries in later levels that Naram-Sin,
the king of Agade, built a great palace at Brak, it seems not un-
reasonable to infer that some Early Dynastic monarch from the
south had, probably late in the E.D. III period, established himself at Brak by right of conquest, perhaps one of those who
flourished in E.D. III*b*, Eannatum, Lugalzaggisi or the like—
the problem remains a challenge for some future digger. But the
conquest of the north by southerners at this period has also been
indicated by discoveries further west.

NORTHERN SYRIA: TELL KHUAIRA[1]

This important site is the only one at present to have been excavated in the steppe between Ras el-'Ain (near Tell Halaf) and
Tell Abyaḍ, in country which contained townships at rather far
distant intervals. It lies between the Khabur and Balīkh rivers,
60 km. west of Ras el-'Ain; the main mound has maximum cross-
dimensions of about 1,000 m.

The remains so far excavated are predominantly of the Agade
period, but in the deeper levels there is evidence of considerable
occupation in Early Dynastic times, particularly in E.D. III*b*.
Much of the art and architecture of the Agade period appears
here, as it does elsewhere, to be the lineal descendant of the
earlier E.D. stage, and the basic plans of the buildings which have
been recovered in the early and late Agade levels no doubt derive
directly from E.D. forms.

Public buildings and religious establishments were frequently
constructed of undressed stone, which often consisted of heavy
dry masonry, usually surmounted by mud-brick. Some of the
temples and the houses were of mud-brick. Whitewash and gypsum were liberally used on the surfaces of walls and floors.

It is remarkable, and perhaps surprising, that the houses with
their private chapels contained a square courtyard, centrally
placed, on the Babylonian model, and represented the classical
type of Babylonian plan. Niches in the chapel walls and niched
mud-brick podia or altars were also characteristic features.

On the other hand, the basic ground plan of the temples and
smaller shrines was of the northern type. Both in stone and in
mud-brick we find oblong buildings consisting of a cella with

---

[1] The spelling *Shuaira* used in *C.A.H.* I² is incorrect. See W. J. van Liere and
J. Lauffray in *A.A.S.* 4–5, 132, n. 3. [Ed.]

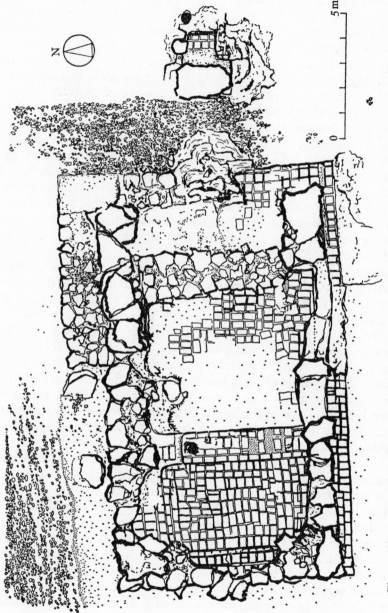

N

5 m.

0

Fig. 15. Stone-built 'North Temple' at Khuaira. (After A. Moortgat, *Dritte Grabungskampagne* 1960, Plan II.)

altar at the far, short end, approached by a porch. One of the most elaborate of these buildings (measuring 15×9 m.) is one known as the stone-built 'North temple', which is subdivided into three parts, an innermost cult chamber, an anteroom or court probably covered, approached by a porch with steps leading up to it (see Fig. 15). Outside the temple entrance there was a big vase probably intended for ablutions and set up in a manner which recalls the scene represented on the obelisk of Ashurnasirpal I, more than a thousand years later.[1]

Less elaborate and smaller *Anten* temples were also built of mud-brick; they were simplified, rustic forms of the elaborate porch-temples at Gawra, and Moortgat attributes them to a Hurrian or proto-Hurrian people indigenous to the north. The podia, benches, altars, ablution and drainage arrangements associated with these temples find parallels throughout the Tigris–Euphrates valley and reflect a general standardization of the rather simple arrangements devised throughout the country for ministering to the gods' needs.

But there is one aspect of the cult which appears to be uniquely illustrated at Khuaira, though no doubt it could be discovered elsewhere in the north. It seems that an elaborate ritual was enacted for the commemoration of the dead. This was best illustrated in a square mud-brick chamber which was separated by a gangway from a stone building (Steinbau I) and contained many deposits, mostly pottery, in honour of the cult (see Fig. 16). The brick chamber (V) had been walled up after use and contained the remains of approximately six dismantled skeletons, which had been half burnt or inefficiently cremated before being deposited. Bronze and flint daggers or knives, and a bronze spear, accompanied the dead.

The adjacent stone building with its elaborate podia and altars contained much pottery and *inter alia* a big bronze vase, as well as a big pottery pedestal vase partly decorated in relief and partly incised. Rosettes, lions and the lion-headed spread-eagle depicted on the vase recall the god elsewhere represented by the copper statuary of E.D. III*b* at 'Ubaid;[2] other motifs on the same vase include snakes, a scorpion, a bird and a male figure suspending a pair of quadrupeds by the hind legs. This and another pedestal vase found elsewhere at Khuaira representing a shepherd and his flock are Sumerian in style and are typical of E.D. III–Agade ceramic.[3]

---

[1] §IV, 11 (dritte Grabungskampagne 1960), Abb. 10.
[2] See *Ibid*. Abb. 21–6 and above, p. 287.
[3] *Ibid*. (vierte Grabungskampagne 1963), Abb. 7–11.

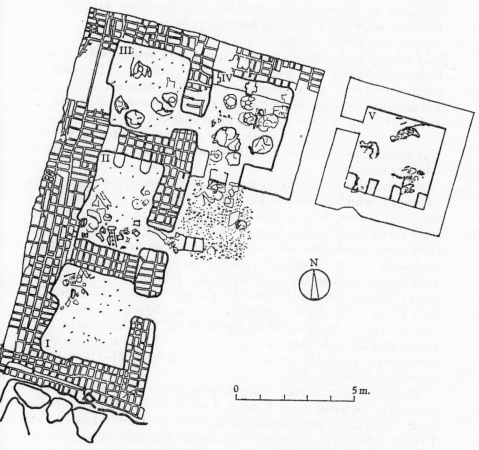

Fig. 16. Stone building I at Khuaira. (After A. Moortgat,
Dritte Grabungskampagne 1960, Plan v.)

Whatever the exact date of the stone building and its adjoining
mortuary chamber may be, it seems that at the turn of the E.D.–
Agade period we find in this North Syrian town evidence of a
funerary ritual comparable with the much later evidence of Hittite
practices connected with the death of a king, as recorded in the
texts. The Hittite ritual of the fourteenth and thirteenth centuries
B.C. involved cremation, and a gathering together of the bones in
the é-na$_4$, or 'stonehouse', where the bones and a bed were deposited.[1] The giving of offerings and lamentations continued for
seven days. The evidence in the stone-built rooms near the death

---

[1] §IV, II (dritte Kampagne 1960), 40, 41, with references to the ritual texts.

chamber at Khuaira also accorded with the later Hittite texts. For here were many traces of libation vessels, of troughs to receive liquids, and tables for solid food, all in profusion. At Khuaira we may thus be seeing traces of ancient funerary practices which were intimately linked with those adopted in Anatolia. The place enjoyed easy access to the north as well as to the south, and indeed a distinctive type of painted reserved-slip ware found in the late E.D. III levels is known to have been as much at home in Harran as it was in Tell Brak.[1] The peculiar interest of Khuaira is that it was equally in touch with Asia Minor and the remote south of Mesopotamia.

Another unique discovery was a street or processional way 70 m. in length, which appears to have been lined by high, rough-hewn, standing stones, like *menhirs*. It is possible that some of them bore carvings of human beings and Moortgat has suggested that they were commemorative—set up by some victorious foe from the south. There is perhaps a parallel in a tall double-sided basalt stele found by von Oppenheim in the Jebelet el-Beidha, a wild tract of hill country in the desert to the south-east of Khuaira. This stele is carved in high relief with a human figure carrying a club and wearing a fleecy sheepskin coat in the Sumerian style. On a much smaller scale there is a file of prisoners below him, and this monument, probably set up in the period E.D. II–III, must be symbolic of victory.[2]

Perhaps the most surprising discovery was a series of alabaster statues of bearded male figures, typical of the E.D. Sumerian style of carving, comparable with sculpture from Mari and the Diyālā, though not very elegant in form.[3] The hair styles generally conformed with Sumerian coiffure, although there was one notable deviation. The eyes had been incrusted, doubtless with shell and lapis lazuli. These statues probably represented distinguished persons who had once set up their effigies in the temple under the protection of the god, in the manner which we have observed in so many other religious buildings elsewhere. They need not have been Sumerians; they need not even have had any Semitic affinities. It may be assumed that they were wealthy natives who, like many before them and like many after, had adopted the garb and the manners of the alien peoples dominant in their world at the time.

The catalogue of objects found at this rewarding site is a long one, and it is not always easy to say whether they belong to the

---

[1] §IV, 11 (vierte Grabungskampagne 1963), Abb. 35, p. 50.
[2] *Ibid.* Abb. 36 a–b.
[3] *Ibid.* Abb. 12–28; (fünfte Kampagne 1964), Abb. 11–15.

E.D. III or to the Agade period. But several seal impressions, one of them found in the débris of Steinbau I, have been ascribed to the 'Mesilim' period by their discoverer.[1] They need not be any earlier than E.D. III *a* (for the animal designs upon them are in rather closely packed double registers), and may even be a little later, for we have to allow for a stylistic time-lag in the provinces; for example there is one shell cylinder seal, with concave sides, which in Babylonia would be a hallmark of the Agade style, but this one bears an E.D. III design,[2] which makes it less certain that other shell cylinders with E.D. designs are necessarily early.[3]

The site was very rich in metal, for it was in close touch with the metalliferous regions of eastern Asia Minor, and there are two beautiful specimens of a socketed adze, and a poker-butt spear,[4] as well as treasure trove—a vase containing gold and silver trinkets closely comparable with a discovery at Tell Brak.[5] Pins with bent heads and flattened shanks were also familiar at Ur in E.D. III *a*.[6] These discoveries prove that Khuaira kept abreast of the metallurgical developments common to the Euphrates valley at the turn of E.D. III and the Agade period.

In one of the cult-rooms of Steinbau I a collection of shell objects, a cowrie and a mother-of-pearl cut in the shape of an animal's head attest a trade as far afield as the Persian Gulf.[7] These collections include a set of shell carvings cut to represent rampant stags, goats, and gazelles, originally backed on a wooden board, together with shell rings; they recall a familiar kind of incrustation work which was popular in the cities of Mari, Kish and Ur in E.D. II–III.[8]

The varieties of pottery corresponded very closely in type with the ceramics familiar in the Khabur valley—at Brak, Chagar Bazar, Mozan and Germayir. The black and grey wares, sometimes matt, sometimes lustrous, are products of northern Mesopotamia; they were common in the Agade period and probably originated in E.D. Some of the plain pottery with metalliform tubular handles reflects development throughout Mesopotamia. One alabastron or bottle, made of a dark clay and with a deeply grooved or ridged surface throughout, is remarkable because it

[1] §iv, 11 (vierte Kampagne, 1963), Abb. 1 *a* and 29 *b*.
[2] *Ibid.* (Grabung 1958), Abb. 31.
[3] *Ibid.* (zweite Kampagne, 1959), Abb. 14–15.
[4] *Ibid.* Abb. 7–8.   [5] *Ibid.* Abb. 11–12.
[6] *Ibid.* (vierte Kampagne, 1963), Abb. 30.
[7] *Ibid.* (zweite Kampagne, 1959), Abb. 34.   [8] *Ibid.* Abb. 40.

represents a ceramic technique of which only a few examples appeared in the royal tombs of Ur—for instance in that of 'Shub-ad' (Pu-Abi), E.D. III *a*, where they were certainly imports.[1] The Khuaira specimen is said to be of the Agade period. Some specimens of Ninevite V incised pottery were found and cannot be later than E.D. III. The characteristic examples recovered from Tell Ailun, not far away, near Derbisīye on the Syrian frontier with Turkey, are, however, rather crudely executed by comparison with those from the metropolis of Nineveh itself.[2]

It is indeed most probable that excavations in the deeper levels of this rich mound will eventually reveal extensive traces of E.D. I, for a clay jar sealing found in Steinbau I is characteristic of that period.[3]

The discoveries at Khuaira have therefore extended the known zone of direct Sumerian influence in the E.D. era far into the central Syrian steppe, which appears to have been affected by Sumerian technology, and probably indeed by conquest, no less than the Khabur region of Upper Mesopotamia. But, as always, the basic, native styles, both of architecture and of pottery, remained endemic. The innovations consisted principally of statuary and of metal which bore the hallmarks of Sumerian civilization.

---

[1] §iv, 11 (zweite Kampagne, 1959), Abb. 6, p. 5, compared with §iii, 35, pl. 257 (types from Houses I at Khafājī ascribed to E.D. III in §ii, 5, pl. 164 (B. 666.540*b*) where a comparison is made with a type from Kish 'A' Cemetery).

[2] §iv, 10, Abb. 11–12.   [3] §iv, 11 (fünfte Kampagne, 1964), Abb. 29–30.

CHAPTER XVII

SYRIA BEFORE 2200 B.C.

I. THE BACKGROUND

It is necessary at the beginning of this chapter to define what we mean by the geographical term 'Syria', which includes in a single area regions which were seldom in ancient times united under one rule, and were already inhabited, it seems, during the third millennium B.C. by peoples of greatly differing ways of life, of different racial affinities and separate tongues. Yet in spite of the diversity of its peoples through the ages and the varied climatic zones into which it can be divided, the region known today as Syria and the Lebanon may be said to form a geographical entity with natural boundaries.[1] On the north and north-west it is hedged about by the Amanus and Antitaurus mountains of Anatolia and by the Upper Euphrates bend; on the west it is bounded by the Mediterranean, and on the east by the Syrian desert, the northward extension of the great Nefūd, the arid desert of Arabia. To the south it merges with Palestine, and the natural boundary of both is the Wilderness of Sin, the desert stretch which separates Egypt from Palestine, Africa from Asia. We shall see that there were close cultural links between Syria and Palestine, though the archaeology of the latter is somewhat apart and has been treated for this period in an earlier chapter.[2]

In the simplest analysis, the land of Syria falls into three distinct zones: the coastal fringe, later called Phoenicia, with its temperate climate, fertile soil and heavy winter rains; the steppe-land, separated from the coast by a high, double mountain chain which cleaves it from north to south, and experiencing a wide seasonal variation of temperature and consequently a specialized vegetation to which the name Irano-Turanian has been given.[3] The third region is that of the desert fringe with its scant rainfall and exaggerated extremes of temperature. Here the bedawin follow their flocks from well to well and in summer must haunt the borders of regions of greater cultivation. The southern part of this desert, the *hammada*, is altogether arid and waterless, but as one crosses the Jazīrah, the north-eastern extension of Syria, the

---

[1] G, 9, 34; §1, 24, 186; G, 15, 77; §1, 11, 2.
[2] See above, ch. xv.
[3] G, 9, 72 and fig. 16.

316

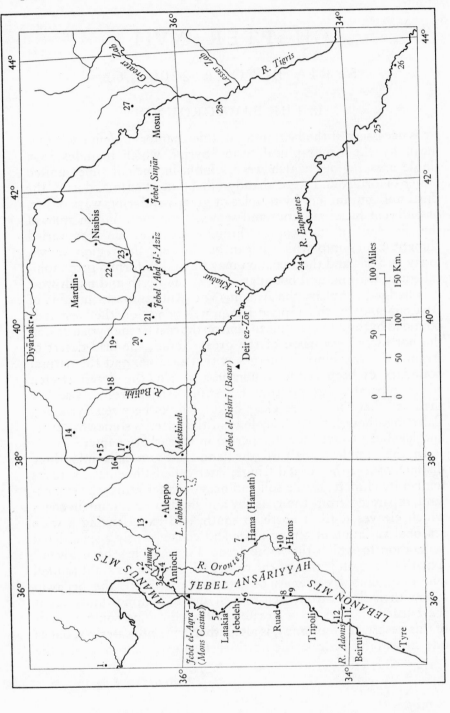

Map 8. The Lebanon, Syria and Northern Mesopotamia.

NUMERICAL KEY

1	Tarsus	8	Tabbat el-Hammām	15	Kara Hassan
2	Tell Judaidah	9	Tell Simiriyān	16	Jerablūs (Carchemish)
3	Açana (Alalakh)	10	Mishrifeh (Qatna)	17	Tell Ahmar (Til Barsib)
4	Tabara el-Akrād	11	Afqa	18	Harrān
5	Ras Shamra (Ugarit)	12	Byblos (Jubeil)	19	Tell Halaf
6	Qal'at er-Rus	13	Tell Rifa'at (Arpad)	20	Tell Khuaira
7	Tell Maṣin	14	Urshu	21	Jebelet el-Beidha

22	Chagar Bazar		
23	Tell Brak		
24	Mari (Tell Harīrī)		
25	Tuttul		
26	Rapiqum		
27	Tepe Gawra		
28	Ashur		

ALPHABETICAL KEY

Açana (Alalakh) 3	Jebelet el-Beidha 21	Ras Shamra (Ugarit) 5	Tell Khuaira 20
Afqa 11	Jerablūs (Carchemish) 16	Tabara el-Akrād 4	Tell Maṣin 7
Alalakh (Açana) 3	Jubeil (Byblos) 12	Tabbat el-Hammām 8	Tell Rifa'at (Arpad) 13
Arpad (Tell Rifa'at) 13	Kara Hassan 15	Tarsus 1	Tell Simiriyān 9
Ashur 28	Mari (Tell Harīrī) 24	Tell Ahmar (Til Barsib) 17	Tepe Gawra 27
Byblos (Jubeil) 12	Mishrifeh (Qatna) 10	Tell Brak 23	Til Barsib (Tell Ahmar) 17
Carchemish (Jerablūs) 16	Qal'at er-Rus 6	Tell Halaf 19	Tuttul 25
Chagar Bazar 22	Qatna (Mishrifeh) 10	Tell Harīrī (Mari) 24	Ugarit (Ras Shamra) 5
Harrān 18	Rapiqum 26	Tell Judaidah 2	Urshu 14

'island' between Euphrates and Tigris, the infertile gypsum gives place to a zone where cultivation is possible; the upper valleys of the Khabur and the Balīkh, tributaries of the Euphrates on its left bank, once supported an ample population.[1] From this potentially fertile plain, the Jebel 'Abd el-'Azīz and the Jebel Sinjār rise as great limestone lumps.[2]

The question has often been asked whether the climate of Syria has undergone any radical change since antiquity. The presence of large numbers of *tells*, those flat-topped mounds which testify to the ruin of ancient towns many times rebuilt and at last abandoned, and the long lines of mounds which betray the course of ancient canal systems, point to the desiccation of once fertile and well-watered lands, and the great forests of cypress, cedar and pine which once supplied timber for the shipwrights of Egypt and the architects of Assyria and Babylonia, have almost entirely vanished.[3] That panthers, lions and a species of wild horse once roamed the north Mesopotamian steppe is proved by animal remains from the excavations at Tell Brak and elsewhere,[4] and elephant and aurochs were hunted in Syria in the second millennium B.C.;[5] the presence of such large animals implies plentiful water and a far richer vegetation than the sparse undergrowth and almost treeless condition of the area today. The consensus of modern opinion appears to discount the theory that there has been any appreciable decrease in rainfall during historic times—that is to say, during the last six thousand years; the fall in the water table resulting in the drying up of wells, where this has occurred, may have been due in some cases to the lowering of the bed of an adjacent river, but more often to over-cultivation and deforestation, to the reckless destruction by man with his flocks of the vegetation around him, for timber, fuel and food.[6]

The diversity of natural conditions within the region of Syria has to a large extent determined its history. Separated from each other by mountain ranges and deep valleys, by barren plains and impassable waterways, the inhabitants of ancient Syria tended to disunity and individualism.[7] Political unity was only rarely and ephemerally imposed from outside, and commercial rivalry led to bitter warfare between neighbours. Nomads cast covetous eyes

[1] §I, 18, 5 f.; §III, 6, 10 f.; §III, 7, 12 and 39; §IV, 20; §IV, 26, 137 ff; §I, 4, 36 f.
[2] §III, 2, 123 ff.   [3] §I, 16, 136 ff.; §III, 6, 15; §IV, 29, 20; §I, 22, I, 67 ff.
[4] §III, 6, 12 ff.; G, 13, 67 and 75; §I, 12, 67 and 75 ff.
[5] G, 10, 151 f., pl. 145; G, 13, 14 and 507 f.; §I, 12, 89; *C.A.H.* II³, ch. x, sect. III.
[6] §III, 6, 13 ff.; §I, 16, 136 ff.; G, 14, 133 f.; G, 4, 18; A, 11, 263.
[7] §I, 1, 7 ff.; G, 15, 77.

on the easier life of their neighbours, the cultivators and town-dwellers.[1] Moreover, to the great powers of the Near East, Syria was no-man's-land; on either side, the armies of the flourishing riverine civilizations of Egypt and Mesopotamia stood ready to march, to use Syria as a bridge and a battleground and to exploit her resources for their own ends. To these Syria owed not only a grudge but also a debt. Along the trade routes, in the wake of the marching armies, came ideas and new techniques, raw materials and manufactured goods. The devastation of conquest, soon repaired, was mitigated by the benefits obtained through the spread of civilization and the opening up of new channels of communication.

The resultant mixture of ethnic elements and cultural influences is reflected in the material remains left by the ancient inhabitants of Syria. The archaeological evidence for the earliest periods of Syrian history is unfortunately scanty at present. On comparatively few sites have the excavators penetrated to levels below, and consequently earlier than, those of the second millennium B.C., and where they have done so, their soundings have for the most part been narrow and deep, so that, where evidence of buildings of the Early Bronze Age was found, it was not possible to excavate them entirely. With the exception of Mari and Brak to the east, and Byblos to the south-west, little notion can yet be obtained of the architecture and town-planning of the town-dwellers or villagers of Syria at this early period and only a partial picture can be drawn of their life and material surroundings. For here, in contrast with the already richly documented civilizations of Egypt and Lower Mesopotamia, we are unaided by written records.[2] No evidence of an early knowledge of writing has yet been found on any Syrian site with the exception, in the east, of Mari, where cuneiform was in use, and Brak, where Akkadian conquerors of the Khabur region imposed their sway, and, in the west, of Byblos, where the rulers of Negau enjoyed a special relationship with the kings of Egypt and were familiar with the hieroglyphic script.[3] The conclusion need not necessarily be drawn that the peoples of north Syria and the coast were otherwise illiterate during the Early Bronze Age. Our material evidence is too scanty to warrant such a hypothesis, and it is possible, indeed likely, that experiments were already being made of writing upon some perishable medium such as parchment or wood. Cylinder-seals are found on north Syrian

---

[1] G, 15, 78 f.; §1, 13, 142 f.; §11, 16, xii ff. and 260 ff.; G. 4, 14 ff.
[2] §1, 5, 90 f.; G, 2, 14.   [3] See below, pp. 345 ff.

sites in some quantity,[1] and it is improbable that they were made primarily as amulets; the practice of impressing seals upon the wet clay of pots before firing, like the maker's marks or owner's marks on the wares of Byblos and Teleilat Ghassūl in Palestine, must have pointed the way to the further extension of writing as a method of communication as well as as a means of identification.

Have we then any means of knowing who were the inhabitants of Syria in the Early Bronze Age and what language, or languages, they spoke? Most of our evidence must be drawn from a later age. The so-called 'Execration Texts' of the early second millennium,[2] for instance, contain a large number of personal names which are indisputably Semitic, and show that the inhabitants of Palestine and Syria, at the time of the Twelfth Egyptian Dynasty, were predominantly Semites.[3] The study of ancient place-names points to a somewhat different conclusion: while many of the cities of the south, Jericho for instance, and Tyre and Sidon[4] bear Semitic names, there are others such as Lachish whose early names were almost certainly not Semitic,[5] and farther to the north, the proportion of Semitic names grows smaller.[6] Most Bronze Age settlements in north Syria appear to have names which are non-Semitic in form,[7] and some still preserve their ancient endings in -az, -din and so forth.[8] Of some three hundred names of towns and villages found in the cuneiform tablets of Açana, the ancient Alalakh, near the mouth of the River Orontes, only four were identified as Semitic, and only a few as possibly Hurrian; the rest were 'of unknown linguistic affiliation'.[9] It must be remembered that whereas the name of a place can be changed and an early, non-Semitic, settlement could have been given a new name by its later inhabitants, the survival of place-names which cannot be ascribed to any of the languages known to have been spoken later in Syria should indicate that these places received their names from an earlier stratum of the population.[10] The inescapable conclusion must in this case be drawn that when these towns in north Syria were first settled, the founders spoke some tongue as yet unidentified. In the tablets of Ugarit, on the coast, the proportion of Semitic place-names is

[1] §IV, 1, 57 ff.; A, 7.
[2] See below, pp. 540 f., 548 f.
[3] §I, 9, 38 f; G, 3, 333; G, 15, 82 and 85; §I, 18, 119 f.; §VI, 1, 249.
[4] G, 15, 81; G, 1, 178 f.; §VI, 2, 208; §I, 18, 35 ff.
[5] §I, 18, 37.   [6] Ibid. 39 f.; I, 9, 39 f.
[7] Ibid. 40 f.; §I, 21, 25 n. 48.   [8] §I, 15, 151 ff.; §I, 1, 10 f.
[9] §I, 9, 40 f.   [10] G, 1, 178 ff.; G, 3, 332 ff.

higher[1] but the name of Ugarit itself is not thought to be of Semitic origin.[2]

Nevertheless, the presence of Semites in north Syria from at least the middle of the third millennium B.C. must be assumed. At this time, the rulers of Mari bore Semitic names and worshipped, besides the gods of Sumer, the Semitic god Dagan.[3] Moreover, the Sumerians themselves were conscious that to the west of their land, in the region they called Martu, they had neighbours whose way of life was different from their own, uncouth nomads who lived in tents, ate their meat uncooked, dug for truffles in the desert, and neglected to bury their dead.[4] Though they regarded these westerners with fear and distaste, they permitted individual tribesmen to settle amongst them, and the names of these Amorites, together with the deities with which they were associated, Dagan, Hadad and Yerakh the moon-god, make it clear that they were of west Semitic speech.[5] Clearly the population of Syria, even at this early epoch, was composed of peoples of differing racial origins, of heterogeneous speech and widely divergent social customs ranging from primitive nomadism to a complex urbanism.

In the course of the second half of the third millennium, cuneiform sources begin to be abundant in Mesopotamia, and these provide a certain amount of information about the physical and political geography of Syria, as seen through the eyes of the conquerors who marched north and west on their expeditions to the 'Upper Sea', the Mediterranean.

II. SYRIA AT THE TIME OF THE KINGS OF AGADE

We shall see later[6] that, following perhaps in the steps of his predecessor at Uruk, Lugalzaggisi,[7] but with more far-reaching and more permanent results, Sargon of Agade, once he had united the whole of Mesopotamia under his sway, turned towards the west and marched out to conquer it,[8] a procedure which two at least of his successors, Naram-Sin and Shar-kali-sharri, were to imitate.[9]

---

[1] §1, 9, 40 f. [2] §1, 18, 34; otherwise G, 1, 352 n. 9.
[3] §III, 12, 8; §II, 18, 68.
[4] §1, 7, 30 ff.; §1, 2, 219 and 236 ff.; G, 15, 52 ff.; §1, 3, 99 ff.; §1, 10, 220 ff.
[5] §1, 19, 18 ff.; §1, 13, 140; §1, 9, 41 ff.; §1, 20, 65 ff.; see below, pp. 564 f.
[6] See below, pp. 417 ff. [7] §II, 2, 98 f., cols. I, 14—II, 11.
[8] See below, pp. 421 ff. [9] See below, pp. 440 ff.

It is clear that it was not military glory, in the first instance, which drew them so far from their homes, but a real combination of political and, above all, economic necessities. They needed to have access to the 'Upper Sea', the Mediterranean, just as they had access to the 'Lower Sea', the Persian Gulf.[1] To be more precise, they needed to secure for themselves on better terms (and none are cheaper and more secure than the right of conquest) the riches of the west, which had always been indispensable to their country, where they were not produced—wood, stone and metals. It was not without good cause that, in one of his inscriptions, Sargon thus himself indicated the limits and, as it were, the real objective of his conquests in the west: 'as far as the Forest of Cedars and the Mountains of Silver'.[2] In this way, he and his successors were only following, as soldiers, the old route opened up by the traders of prehistoric times.[3]

In searching the accounts which have come down to us for what the conquerors saw and remembered in Syria, we can base ourselves with confidence only upon the authentic documents, namely the inscriptions of the founder of the Agade dynasty himself and those of his successors. Most of these have been preserved only in copies, later by several centuries, but scholars are agreed in considering their general tenor as being reliable enough.[4] The remaining sources,[5] themselves later, sometimes much later, would either give us no precise information,[6] or mislead us by adding imperceptibly to the original facts details which throw light on the period when they were elaborated rather than the period about which they ostensibly serve as evidence.[7]

The progressive movement from the south-east to the north-west and the principal stages in the journey from Mesopotamia are indicated in the brief authentic account of Sargon's conquest. 'At Tuttul he worshipped the god Dagan, who gave him from that time onwards the Upper Country, Mari, Iarmuti and Ibla, as far as the Forest of Cedars and the Mountain of Silver'.[8] Tuttul, which has for long been known as modern Hīt, on the Euphrates, ninety-five miles to the west of Baghdad, marks the beginning (going upstream) of the middle section of the river.

---

[1] §II, 2, 104 f., col. III, 7 ff.; §II, 13, 36.
[2] §II, 2, 108 f., col. V, 26 ff.; §II, 13, 38.
[3] See above, sect. I.
[4] See §II, 9, 6 ff.
[5] *Ibid.*
[6] For example, §II, 24.
[7] Such as §II, 28.
[8] §II, 2, 108 f., col. VI, 16 ff.; §II, 13, 38.

Half a millennium later, in the Code of Hammurabi (col. ɪv a, 30 f.), it is named along with Mari, but after that town, and as one of its dependencies; here it is named first, and all alone. Tuttul may therefore have been regarded as the 'capital' at that period of an independent territory forming the gateway, although not actually belonging, to the 'Upper Country'. This name was given to the north and north-west parts of ancient Mesopotamia, especially the region lying between the Khabur and the Mediterranean; in Agadean times, at least, this seems to have adjoined, and perhaps partly embraced, the region beginning farther to the east, then called Subartum.[1] One of the links attaching Tuttul to the 'Upper Country' was the worship of the god Dagan,[2] for this western divinity had one of his principal seats in Tuttul, and the inscription represents him as delivering over the charge of his estate to Sargon.

Like Tuttul, Mari, Iarmuti and Ibla could also have been the principal towns of as many 'kingdoms', or of confederations, making up the geographical unit here called the Upper Country. This is certain, at least for Mari, 125 miles to the north-west of Tuttul, and also on the Euphrates. In the Sumerian king-list this town is given as the capital of a dynasty of six kings, covering 136 years of reign, coming just before the Third Dynasty of Kish, towards the middle of the third millennium.[3] Futhermore, a certain number of votive inscriptions, dug up at Mari itself, and assigned with probability to the period immediately before Sargon, acquaint us with several more indigenous kings of that time: Iku-Shamash,[4] Lamgi-Mari,[5] Iku-Shamagan and Iblul-il,[6] along with a number of persons belonging to their family or court.[7] It seems likely, moreover, that the victorious visit of Sargon[8] is testified on the site itself by the state of savage destruction in which the pre-Sargonic sanctuaries have been rediscovered,[9] just as, somewhat later, annexation by the Agadean monarch left unequivocal traces.[10] The Mari seized by Sargon, therefore, was the administrative centre of a kingdom already old, and it is certainly as such that it appears in the victory inscription. How far its territory extended we do not know, but if the hypothesis put forward above holds, one would suppose

[1] For the 'Upper Country', see §ɪɪ, 3, vol. 4, 113 b; for Subartum, §ɪɪ, 8, 35 and 93 f.
[2] §ɪɪ, 16, 69 f.; §ɪɪ, 18, 55.
[3] §ɪɪ, 14, 102 f. Only the first (doubtful) name is preserved.
[4] §ɪɪ, 4, part v, pl. 2, no. 12146, 1.
[5] §ɪɪ, 27, 140 f.
[6] §ɪɪ, 19, 208.
[7] §ɪɪ, 27, 142 f.; §ɪɪ, 19, 219 f.
[8] Or of Lugalzaggisi? see §ɪɪ, 19, 219 f.
[9] *Ibid.*
[10] §ɪɪ, 20, 153 f.; §ɪɪ, 21, 195 and 199 ff.

that its frontiers made contact with those of Tuttul in the south, and those of Iarmuti and perhaps Ibla in the north.

The identification of these last two geographical names is neither easy nor certain. Ibla, however, seems to have been in the valley of the Balīkh, not far from Urshu,[1] about which we shall have more to say later.[2] The position of Iarmuti is not so clearly fixed. This place-name was at first identified with Iarim(m)uta,[3] which in the Amarna letters[4] refers to a town at a site probably to the south of Byblos, the centre of a considerable trade in cereals.[5] Then, in preference to this, the two names were dissociated and Iarmuti was sought to the north-west of Mari, but not necessarily on a direct line between Mari and Ibla.[6] This dissociation is based on the fact that, in Sargon's inscription, Iarmuti is before Ibla, and must therefore have been closer to Mari; and, above all, it was supposed unthinkable that Sargon should have carried his conquest of the west as far as to the south of Byblos. It is asserted, in fact, that since the 'Forest of Cedars' can hardly mean anything but the Amanus, and the 'Mountains of Silver' the Taurus, Sargon's advance was directed decidedly northwards.

If we consider the inscription in question, not as an itinerary, which it is not bound to be, but as the summing-up of the king's campaigns, the two territories of Iarmuti and Ibla may have been situated, not one after the other along the route of Sargon's march, but in such a way that they formed its twofold goal: the one to the south, Iarmuti; the other to the north, Ibla. As the most distant part reached by Sargon or falling under his sway, the land of Iarmuti would have included the 'Forest of Cedars', by which we should perhaps understand the Lebanon[7] rather than the Amanus, which latter Naram-Sin, a little later, was to call the 'Mountain of Cedars'.[8] In the other direction the land of Ibla would have extended westwards as far as the Taurus foothills, the 'Mountains of Silver', among which the legend placed —probably as the extreme limit of the conqueror's advance—the locality of Purushkhanda.[9]

---

[1] §ii, 17, 85 f; §ii, 6, 31. Tell el-Biya', formerly proposed (§ii, 1, 28) as the site of Urshu, is probably that of Tuttul on the Balīkh, according to M. Dossin; for this place see below, p. 334, n. 9, and p. 559.

[2] *C.A.H.* ii³, ch. i, sect. iv.   [3] §ii, 22, 225.

[4] §ii, 15, 1756 f.   [5] §ii, 17, 85, and note 1.   [6] *Ibid.* 86.

[7] The 'Cedar Forest' of the Gilgamesh Epic was perhaps located in the Lebanon —see especially the fragment published in *J.N.E.S.* 16 (1957), 254 ff., esp. 260 (rev. 13).   [8] See below, p. 326.

[9] §ii, 29, 62 f., §ii, 12, 86 f. and 91. For the 'colonies' of merchants in Cappadocia and for Purushkhanda, see below, pp. 708 ff and pp. 426 ff.

There is no real objection to this way of looking at things: by what tokens should anyone deem it impossible for Sargon, if not to have reached Iarimuta/Iarmuti, at least to have made a thrust in the direction of the most important trading centre which, we know from other sources, the region of Byblos had long been?[1] One of his successors, at any rate, made a detour southwards, because he boasts of having vanquished his enemies in the vicinity of Jebel el-Bishrī.[2]

The Syrian territory to the west of the kingdom of Mari would therefore have included, during this period, at least two large political units or confederations, of which an important centre, if not the capital, could be for the southern part the Mediterranean town of Iarmuti, and for the northern part the town of Ibla, in the region of the Balīkh. The territory of Iarmuti must have comprised the Lebanon, at least, and because of this must have constituted for Mesopotamia an important source of timber and resin imports. The territory of Ibla extended at least as far as the eastern slopes of the Taurus, which would provide Sargon's subjects chiefly with metal and stone. This is about all that we can reasonably extract from this king's extremely concise inscription.

We shall obtain some supplementary notes from the inscriptions of his third successor, Naram-Sin.[3] They tell us nothing more about Tuttul and Mari,[4] but they contain further information about the Upper Country proper. This is what we read in one commemorative inscription, of which only a copy, of the Old Babylonian period, was discovered at Ur:[5]

In all time, (since) the creation of men, no king among kings had ravaged the land of Armanum and Ibla. Henceforth(?) the god Nergal, having opened the way for the valiant Naram-Sin, has delivered Armanum and Ibla into his hands and made him a grant also of the Amanus, Mountain of Cedars, and of the upper sea. So it is that, by the arm of Dagan, who has made his royalty prevail, the valiant Naram-Sin conquered Armanum and Ibla: from the bank of the Euphrates as far as Ulisum, he having subdued the peoples of whom Dagan had lately made him a grant, they have become liable to do service to his god Aba, and he has conquered Amanus, Mountain of Cedars.

---

[1] See below, pp. 343 ff.   [2] See below, p. 327.   [3] See below, pp. 440 ff.

[4] The name of the king of Mari at that time, Migir-Dagan (see §11, 2, 140, no. 9, rev. 17; §11, 13, 25, no. 3), though not established for certain, is in itself quite credible; the text in which he appears is deeply imbued with legend, see §11, 9, 202, sub 4a.

[5] §11, 7, no. 275, cols. I–III; §11, 9, 199; §11, 13, 73 ff. The content of the text is confirmed, in its essentials, by an inscription belonging to that period; see §11, 11; §11, 9, 198.

When Dagan, having decided in favour of the valiant Naram-Sin, delivered Rish-Adad,[1] king of Arman into his hands, and he had bound him to the uprights of the entrance gate, he made himself a statue of dolerite and dedicated it to Sin in these terms: 'Thus (says) the valiant Naram-Sin, king of the four regions. When, Dagan having delivered Armanum and Ibla into my hands, I had bound up Rish-Adad, the king of Armanum, it was then that I made my image (which is here)...'

The campaign here commemorated seems to have taken place only in what we have called the northern part of Sargon's conquests. There is no question in it of Iarmuti and the 'Forest of Cedars', by which we have understood the Lebanon,[2] but only of Ibla and the 'Mountain of Cedars', which is formally identified as Amanus. The king was therefore making for Cappadocia, and in later years the heroic march of Naram-Sin, in Sargon's footsteps, as far as Purushkhanda, was likewise celebrated in epic poems.[3] If the first words of the text are not put down to bombast or vanity, it would seem that in this geographical area, Naram-Sin's conquest was more complete or more lasting in its effects:[4] it is perhaps with this in mind that, naming Arman along with Ibla, he lays emphasis on the rigorous treatment to which he has subjected the king of that town, which does not appear in the inscriptions of Sargon.

His account is not perspicuous, and widely differing geographical and historical conclusions can be drawn from it. Should one see in the first paragraph, in particular, the narration of two successive periods of the same campaign, or, as appears to be more likely, a twofold, parallel exposition of the same conquest? In this case it would have been aimed at an area which began at Armanum-Ibla, otherwise called the 'bank of the Euphrates', and went as far as the Amanus and the Mediterranean—in other words, as far as the boundaries of Ulisum. Whatever the precise location of Armanum,[5] it is clear[6] that this town and the country of which it was then the capital, were more or less neighbours and allies of Ibla in the region around the Balīkh and the Upper Euphrates.

An interesting note is provided by the end of the account, which gives to the leading personage of the town, Rish-Adad, the

[1] Not Rid-Adad: see §II, 8, 103.
[2] See above, p. 324, and n. 7.   [3] §II, 12, p. 69 ff., and see above, p. 324, n. 9.
[4] He emphasizes that he has made the peoples subdued 'liable to do the service of his own god'.
[5] See recently §II, 28, 12 f. In later legends Rish-Adad appears as king of Apishal, §II, 10, 71.
[6] Contrary to the opinion of §II, 8, 103.

title of 'king'. The town in question, like others which appear similarly in Agadean inscriptions, must therefore have been the administrative capital of a more or less extensive territory, or even of a more or less considerable confederation of small city states. There were no doubt a number of such 'capitals' at the time—not to mention towns of smaller importance—and the political geography of Syria was certainly more complicated than one would imagine from reading Sargon alone and taking him literally.[1] Iarmuti and Ibla, the only places he mentions, are in fact joined on the one hand by Armanum and on the other by Ulisum. The last of these, which seems to mark the extreme limit of Naram-Sin's conquests, could be identified with the Ullaza of the Amarna letters,[2] on the Mediterranean coast, at the level of Qadesh.[3] In that case it would have been the principal town of a kingdom, or confederation of these, stretching northwards along the coast, about as far as the Amanus. Naram-Sin, we observe, does not say he conquered the whole of this territory, and it is scarcely likely—leaving aside the southern part of the country and Palestine— that even north Syria came under the sway of the kings of Agade. Naram-Sin's campaign, coming after Sargon's and itself followed by the expedition of Shar-kali-sharri (to mention only those of which our texts have preserved the memory), shows clearly that each time there remained something to do, or to do again, in order to hold on to the country and the more or less important and more or less numerous political groups of which it was composed.

Consequently, we find Naram-Sin's successor, Shar-kali-sharri,[4] again in the vicinity. In one of the years of his reign—the exact chronology of which we do not know—he boasts that he has defeated Amurru at Basar.[5] The second of these place-names refers to a group of mountains in the Syrian–Arabian desert, to the south-west of the mouth of the Balīkh, in the direction of the Lebanon: it is the modern Jebel el-Bishrī.[6] We shall return to Amurru later on.[7] For the moment it is enough to take note of this term, in the present context designating either a 'kingdom' which included in its territory the Basar mountains or a population of related or confederated clans which infested the mountainous region.

---

[1] For an example of Mesopotamian influence, if not rule, in Syrian cities not mentioned in the texts see §II, 5, 122 f. [2] §II, 15, 1141s.
[3] §II, 6, 80; §II, 24, 78. [4] See below, pp. 454 ff.
[5] §II 23, vol. 2, 133a: date b. See also §II, 9, 102, no. 254a; §II, 16, 149, n. 3.
[6] §I, 10, 73; §II, 16, 136, 149, n. 3. [7] See below, pp. 559 ff.

III. CITIES OF THE EUPHRATES
AND THE KHABUR

It has been shown in an earlier chapter[1] that Mari was the seat of one of the dynasties listed by the compilers of the Sumerian king-lists as having held sway over the whole of south Mesopotamia for a time. The site of Mari, Tell el-Ḥarīrī, a short distance north of the border between Iraq and Syria, was situated in a strategic position of great importance, on the right bank of the Euphrates downstream of its junction with the Khabur.[2] Not many days' journey from the cities of Sumer, it had access to the well-populated valley of the Khabur and commanded the main trade route to the west, up the Euphrates to Carchemish and so across to the mouth of the Orontes and to the Beilān pass, for the timber of Amanus and Lebanon and the mines of Anatolia. The earliest levels explored at Mari revealed a prosperous city of the Early Dynastic Period. No less than six temples[3] of this age, several times renewed and rebuilt, have been laid bare; five of these lay close together in what must have been the central quarter of the town, surrounded by houses. In one of them, the temple which the excavators assume to have been dedicated, like its successor of the second millennium, to Dagan the Amorite god, tablets in Sumerian were found which contained the names of a number of deities to whom specified food offerings were due. As well as Dagan, ten other deities appear in the records of early Mari, and all are members of the Sumerian pantheon.[4] The statues and statuettes found in these temples are Sumerian in almost every respect; they wear the so-called *kaunakes*, the sheep-skin cloak familiar from a thousand Sumerian representations, and are depicted in the attitude of worship equally well known from early Sumerian times.[5] Among the objects found in the temple of Ishtar, on the edge of the mound, were hundreds of fragments of shell inlay, not unlike those of the celebrated 'standard' of Ur,[6] showing themes both warlike and ritual, the

[1] See above, p. 115.
[2] §I, 4, 104 f.; §III, 10, 495 ff. See above, pp. 291 f.
[3] §III, 11, 164; §III, 12, 7 f.
[4] §III, 12, 8. A tablet containing a list of more than thirty Sumerian deities, in the Early Dynastic palace of Mari, has been published by G. Dossin in *R.A.* 61, 97 ff.
[5] §III, 13, 64 ff. See Plate. 30 (*a*)
[6] G, 10, pls. 36 f.; §III, 17, 132 f.; see Plate 30 (*c*) and P. Calmeyer in *C.-R. Rencontr. Assyriol. Internat.* 15 (1966), 161 ff.

conduct of prisoners by dignitaries and soldiers,[1] and men and women carrying conical goblets.[2] Here the influence of Sumer was paramount, yet the kings of Mari have Semitic names inscribed on their shoulders, and some features in the architecture of the temples have no parallel in the south.[3] In particular, the presence in the courtyard of the temple of Ninni-zaza of a stone *baetyl*[4] points the way to the west, to the standing stones of Gezer and Byblos, the *maṣṣēbōt* of Canaan. Clearly the inhabitants of Mari, while adopting the dress and the deities of the Sumerian south, yet spoke an alien tongue and worshipped those deities with an alien ritual. There appear to have been at least two successive palaces below the great eighteenth-century palace of Zimrilim.[5] The massive walls are preserved to a considerable height and enough has already been found to indicate the complexity and importance of the buildings. Charred beams from the upper of the two palaces have been identified as cedar,[6] presumably brought from the forested slopes of the Amanus or the Lebanon.[7]

Away to the north-east, too, in the Khabur valley, Sumerian influence was paramount, at least in material things. Here, in the space of no more than seventy-five square miles, there are more than five hundred *tells*;[8] the area must in ancient times have supported a large population. One of the largest of the mounds is Tell Brak, on the river Jaghjagha, a tributary of the Khabur in its upper reaches, forty-six miles south of the town of Nisibis. As yet nameless,[9] it was certainly a place of great importance from the beginning of the third millennium and probably even earlier. One of the chief reasons for its prosperity may have been the reputation enjoyed by its local deity, for in a temple of the Jamdat Naṣr period (about 3000 B.C.) rebuilt at least three times, thousands of small stone images were found, carved in the shape of a human torso surmounted, in lieu of a face, with an enormous pair of eyes.[10] Double idols with two pairs of eyes, and a larger and smaller pair together, may have represented man and wife or parent and child; one or two are topped by what appears to be a high conical headdress, perhaps a mark of rank. 'Spectacle idols' of somewhat similar form are found occasionally on sites of the

---

[1] §III, 14, 136 ff. and pl. LVI; §III, 17, 138 f.; A, 11, 199 ff.; A, 9, 21 f., pl. IV.
[2] §III, 11, 164 ff., fig. 11.
[3] E.g. §III, 14, 58 ff., figs. 41–5.
[4] §II, 20, 156 f., pl. XIV; A, 11, pl. VII. See Plate 38 (*a*).
[5] A, 10, 9, 26.   [6] A, 8, 20; A, 10, 9.   [7] See above, p. 328.
[8] §III, 4, 3 ff.; §III, 7, 12; §III, 6, 10 f.; §1, 4, 36 f.
[9] §III, 1, 25; §III, 7, 24. See above, pp. 306 ff.
[10] §III, 6, 33 ff., 150 ff., pls. XXV, XXVI, LI, figs. 1–6.

Uruk period in Babylonia and Susa, but this is the largest known concentration of them[1] and it has been plausibly suggested that they may have been votive offerings to some anonymous healing deity, perhaps a goddess, who had more than a local reputation among those suffering from blindness or one of the prevalent diseases of the eye, and that Brak may have been a place of pilgrimage, a kind of ancient Lourdes.[2] Amulets and seals in the form of animals, in a style typical of the best products of the Jamdat Naṣr age,[3] and hundreds of thousands of small beads of crystal and glazed steatite, perhaps offerings of their personal adornment dedicated by worshippers at the shrine, were also neglected by the ancient plunderers; that their quest was for gold is suggested by the discovery of small strips of gold foil remaining from the mural decoration of the temple.[4] Built on a high mud-brick platform, and adorned with cone mosaic, the temple must have presented an imposing appearance. Access to the interior was by a ramp or stairway.[5] At the further end of the long narrow sanctuary stood an altar of whitewashed clay, its front decorated with panels of gold and carved stone, blue, white and green.[6] Rosettes of white marble and black shale decorated the walls.[7] There is a striking similarity between the Eye Temple at Brak and those of the Jamdat Naṣr period in Mesopotamia, especially the temple of Sin at Khafājī and the painted temple at ʿUqair.[8] But the curiously carved alabaster heads with grooved backs, perhaps intended for mounting on poles or attaching to wooden bodies, are unlike anything found in the valley of the Lower Euphrates, and seem to reflect a separate racial type and a different artistic tradition.[9]

The characteristic hassock-shaped 'plano-convex' bricks which were used in the latest of the Eye Temples, together with pottery of typical Early Dynastic shapes and copper objects of Sumerian type, indicate that Tell Brak continued to prosper in the early part of the third millennium B.C.[10] and that Mesopotamian influence still predominated. At Chagar Bazar, probably to be identified with the ancient Ashnakkum,[11] about twenty miles to the north-west of Brak, buildings of the Early Dynastic

---

[1] §III, 7, 27; §III, 6, 151 ff.   [2] *Ibid.* 205 ff.; §III, 7, 25.

[3] §III, 6, 40 ff., 97 ff., 210 ff., pls. VII–XVI, XLV–XLVII, LII.

[4] §III, 6, 32, 93 f., pl. III.   [5] §*Ibid.* pl. LVII.

[6] *Ibid.* 93 ff., 162 ff., pls. II, IV, XXX.

[7] *Ibid* 59 f., 95 ff., pls. V. XXX.   [8] *Ibid.* 38 f., 60 ff.

[9] §III, 7, 31; §III, 6, 53, 91 ff., pls. I, II; G, 10, 134 f., pl. 136.

[10] §III, 7, 31 f.; §III, 4, 10; §III, 5, 94 f.; §III, 6, 54 f.

[11] §IV, 10, 74 f. See above pp. 304 ff.

Period had been largely swept away when the city was rebuilt in the second millennium, though the thickness of the mud-brick walling that remained was enough to tell the excavators that these had been the walls of public buildings of some considerable importance, rather than private houses.[1] Two rich graves found in a trial sounding in the large mound of Tell Arbit, fifteen kilometres east of Chagar Bazar, contained metal objects of Sumerian type[2] together with grey and black burnished pottery which appears to have affinities with wares found to the east, in the Elburz region of northern Iran, rather than with the south.[3] It is not surprising that the area of the Upper Khabur should show such connexions, since merchant caravans, skirting the waterless desert, must at all times have used it in their journeys between east and west; Ashnakkum is mentioned in Babylonian itineraries as a stopping-place.[4]

A layer of ashes lies over the Early Dynastic temples of Mari; they were rebuilt, but destroyed again not long afterwards.[5] The first destruction may be due to Lugalzaggisi, who claims in his inscriptions to have marched to the Upper Sea,[6] and the second to Sargon of Agade, who also passed that way on his march to the west.[7] Either he or his successors must have rebuilt the city and a 'cache' of bronzes found in the debris overlying the temple of Dagan included objects dedicated by two of Naram-Sin's daughters, who were probably priestesses there—a custom associated particularly with the temple of the moon-god at Ur.[8] During the Agade period the Khabur Valley, together with part of northern and north-eastern Syria, must have come under the sway of the kings of Agade.[9] The most striking monument of this occupation is a remarkable brick structure with a frontage over a hundred yards long; its bricks were stamped with the name of the builder, Naram-Sin.[10] Four spacious courtyards surrounded by long narrow magazines and enclosed in an encircling wall of formidable thickness proclaimed its function as a stronghold and a repository rather than a royal residence; the palace had been looted and burnt and yielded, therefore, comparatively few objects, but enough was recovered to show that considerable wealth much have been stored within its walls, and carbonized

[1] §III, 5, 115.   [2] §III, 5, 117, 133, figs. 12, 13.
[3] Similar pottery was found at Chagar Bazar and at nearby Germayir, §III, 7, 32. See above, pp. 304 ff.
[4] §IV, 10, 74 f., 82 f.   [5] §III, 11, 170; see above, p. 323.
[6] See above, p. 143 and below, p. 421.   [7] See above, p. 296 and below, pp. 424 ff.
[8] §II, 21, 195, 199 ff., pl. XVII.   [9] See above, p. 322 ff.
[10] §III, 6, 26 ff., 63 ff., pls. LIX, LX; §III, 7, 32 ff.

grains of wheat and barley found in the storerooms indicated that not only manufactured objects but also the agricultural produce of the region was collected here, perhaps to be despatched to Agade.[1] In one of the rooms a fragment of an alabaster vase inscribed with the name of 'Rimush, King of All, Smiter of Elam and Barakhshe', a predecessor of Naram-Sin, was found.[2] A scant hoard of cuneiform tablets bearing lists of men, provisions and domestic animals shows that here, as elsewhere, Akkadian scribes were going about their orderly business of cataloguing and recording.[3]

Attention will later be drawn[4] to the rock stele near Diyārbakr which commemorates, it would seem, the farthest point of Naram-Sin's progress northwards. To the west of Brak, Akkadian control has left no tangible mark save evidence of trade in material objects. The oval city wall at Tell Jidleh,[5] 350 metres long and never less than three metres thick, was dated by the excavators to the period of Sargon and Naram-Sin. Control of the Balīkh valley was no less vital to the Akkadian conquerors than that of the Khabur, and the fortification of townships along the piedmont route leading from the Tigris to north Syria and the metal-bearing regions of the far west was, it would seem, an essential part of the imperial plan. Two small temples of about the same date as the Naram-Sin palace at Brak have been found further to the west at Tell Khuaira,[6] sixty kilometres west of Ras el-'Ain between the Khabur and the Balīkh. In front of the North Temple was a large oblong slab of stone, with cavities alongside it, perhaps to catch the blood of a slaughtered animal: a parallel has been drawn with the scene pictured on an obelisk of Ashurnasirpal I, showing the sacrifice of an ox before the façade of a temple. Cult objects of Akkadian type in a stone building to the south of the *tell*, together with a line of monolithic standing pillars,[7] proclaimed this building also to have had some religious purpose and emphasize both the links with Mesopotamia and the essentially northern, non-Sumerian character of the cult. However, the remarkable burial rites practised in the stone building (Steinbau I) appear to be unique at this period, though they have been compared with later, Hittite funerary customs.[8]

At Jebelet el-Beidha, fifty miles to the west of Tell Halaf, two

[1] §iii, 6, 63 f.
[3] §iii, 1, 60 f.
[5] §iii, 3, 117 f., figs. 4(*b*), 5.
[7] §iii, 8, 9 ff., pls. 5–9.
[8] A, 6, 40 f.; see above, pp.310 ff.

[2] *Ibid.* 27, 66, 197; pl. L, no. 4.
[4] See below, p. 443.
[6] §iii, 8; §iii, 9.

stelae of black basalt, one nearly twelve ft. high, and a rough stone statue were found.[1] The figures carved on the stelae in crude imitation of Sumerian sculpture wear the fringed garments of the Early Dynastic warrior, and the monuments may perhaps have been erected by the citizens of this unknown town to commemorate the triumphal passage of some Mesopotamian conqueror.[2] The name of Lugalzaggisi suggests itself, but we know nothing of his march to the Mediterranean[3] or what territorial conquests that march implied.[4] It is, however, more likely to have commemorated some local chieftain, since the discovery of a number of alabaster statues of votaries wearing the style of hair and beard and the sheepskin skirt of Mesopotamia[5] indicates that over a very wide area, fashion in dress transcended national boundaries.

IV. CITIES OF THE PLAIN AND THE COAST

Armies and merchants in ancient times habitually travelled along well-defined routes punctuated by towns and caravanserais at which halts could be made for a night or more. One of these routes followed the Euphrates, by water and by land, past Rapiqu and Mari as far as Emar, near the modern Meskeneh,[6] where the river was abandoned for the intermittently watered stretch, a hundred miles westward through Aleppo to the coast, or by way of Qatna to the ports of Lebanon or to Hazor and the highway leading to Egypt.[7] The Tigris route[8] left Assyria considerably north of Ashur, and skirting the Jebel Sinjār, followed the piedmont route through the upper reaches of the Khabur basin and the valley of the Balīkh.[9] The Euphrates was then crossed at one of several points according to the ultimate destination of the travellers: at one time or another, Abattum, Til Barsib and Carchemish were all places where the crossing could be made.[10] The site of Abattum is not so far known, but both Til Barsib, the modern Tell Aḥmar, and Carchemish, today called Jerāblus, were occupied during the third millennium. In both sites, so excavation has shown, the inhabitants at first buried

[1] §III, 16, 226 ff., pls. LXII, LXIII; G, 10, 135 f., fig. 59.
[2] G, 10, 59.   [3] See above, p. 331, n. 6.
[4] See above, pp. 323 f.   [5] A, 5, figs. 12–28; A, 6, figs. 11–15.
[6] §IV, 10, 81, 86; §IV, 11, 115 f.; §IV, 14, 108 f.
[7] §IV, 10, 86; §I, 4, 182 f. with maps in figs. 17 and 18.
[8] §IV, 10, 71, 87; §IV, 15, 265 ff.   [9] G, 11, 40 ff.
[10] §IV, 10, 80; §IV, 11, 119; §I, 6, 80.

their dead in pots under the floors of their houses, and later in rectangular cist graves lined with slabs of stone,[1] with an armoury of weapons and a liberal store of pottery vessels to supply them in the next world. In several instances, at Carchemish, pot burials and cist burials were found in the same room, a fact which suggested to the excavator that the older, indigenous population continued to practise their ancient funerary rites, as a conquered people, alongside their conquerors.[2]

The large hypogeum at Til Barsib has been variously dated.[3] Some of the remarkably large number of pots found in this tomb —over a thousand—may have been deposited there later, at some time in the first quarter of the second millennium B.C., but the majority are almost certainly older, probably contemporary with the latest phase of the Early Dynastic period in Mesopotamia. If this is so, a plausible explanation may be that the tomb was one of a chieftain or local hero whose cult was maintained for some centuries after his death by depositing offerings.[4] The skeletons of the two adults buried in the tomb had been disturbed. The earliest objects found in the burial included a rein-ring and weapons which are dated by analogy with material from other sites to the pre-Sargonic period.[5] Among the pots were a number of high-stemmed goblets or 'champagne-cups', found also in some numbers in the cist graves of Carchemish;[6] similar pots and weapons were found at Kara Hassan farther north.[7] During the latter part of the Early Bronze Age Carchemish was already a fortified city with strong defences: ring walls surrounded it on the landward sides, and towards the river there was a quay with a brick-lined watergate flanked by mud-brick walls built on stone foundations.[8] Til Barsib, whose early name is not known,[9] was probably of equal importance, judging by the size of the mound and the richness of the burials.[10]

No excavation has yet been possible on the site of Aleppo, another of the great cities of the second millennium B.C., and we can only suspect, from its possibly non-Semitic name Khalpu or Khalap, that the city was an early foundation.[11] Trial soundings at Tell

[1] §IV, 28, vol. III, 23, 218 ff. pls. 56–61; §IV, 25, 96 ff., figs. 28–38.
[2] §IV, 30, 88 ff.   [3] §IV, 17, 338 f.; G, 18, 81 ff.
[4] §IV, 17, 339.   [5] §IV, 17, 338 f.
[6] §IV, 30, 88 f., pl. xixa; §IV, 28, vol. III, 218 ff., pls. 50–59.
[7] §IV, 30, 89; G, 18, 80 ff.
[8] §IV, 28, vol. II, 38 ff., 58 ff., pls. 3–17
[9] §IV, 10, 79; §IV, 11, 119 suggests that it may have been Tuttul.
[10] §IV, 17, 338 f.
[11] §I, 15, 156; but see §I, 14, 265.

Rifa'at, which is probably the site of the city Arpad, later the capital of the Aramaean state Bīt Agusi, have not so far penetrated to levels of the Early Bronze Age, though a few graves which have been unearthed in the vicinity suggest that at that time the mound was already inhabited;[1] the early name of the town is unknown. A preliminary survey undertaken in the once thickly-populated region south of Aleppo[2] has shown that there, too, there were settlements of the Early Bronze Age. They include the large mounds Tell Tuqān and Tell Afis; the latter is thought to be the site of the Aramaean city Khazrek (Hatarikka in Assyrian texts).[3] The earliest level so far encountered at Tell Mardikh[4] appears not to be earlier thant he end of the third millennium B.C., and is therefore outside the scope of this chapter.

The way to Anatolia led through the 'Amūq, the plain of Antioch, north of the point where the Orontes river, bursting the barrier of the mountains, abruptly changes its course and flows westwards to the Mediterranean. This plain, the later kingdom of Unqi or Khattina,[5] was an area of great strategic importance, for whoever held it possessed the key which opened the passes through the Taurus to the rich mineral region beyond and commanded access also to the forest-clad slopes of the Amanus, the 'Mountain of Cedars' sought by the Akkadians and their successors through the ages.[6] Ancient mounds strewn plentifully over the surface of the plain bear witness to its prosperity and fertility in ancient times.[7] North of the modern road from Aleppo to Antioch, excavations have been conducted on several of these mounds and their history elucidated in terms of stratified remains. None of the group of five proved to have been a town of any great size and all were probably villages, without imposing buildings, so that no adequate idea could be gained by the excavators of the attainments of the Early Bronze Age plain-dwellers in terms of architecture and town-planning; moreover none of the sites was more than partially explored and few whole house-plans could be elucidated.[8] Four phases of occupation were distinguished, representing nearly a thousand years of gradual development, for time moved slowly in the third millennium B.C.; each phase was distinguished by certain general features, though they were separated by no clear evidence of disaster such as the layers of

[1] §IV, 23, 87.
[2] A, 4.
[3] G, 6, 237 f.
[4] A, I.
[5] G, 6, 425.
[6] §I, 6, 23; see above, p. 326.
[7] §IV, 29, 20; §I, 6, 22.
[8] §IV, 4; G, 8, 36 ff.; §IV, 16.

ash and burnt brick which on some Syrian sites mark the passage of the destroyer.[1]

In the earliest of the Bronze Age levels, numbered phase G by the excavators,[2] copper working was already advanced and a little bronze is found. The potter's wheel was in almost universal use. Stamp seals with linear designs continued a tradition going back to the earlier, Neolithic, occupation of the site,[3] but cylinder seals, introduced from Mesopotamia, made their first appearance;[4] this and other links with the Khabur and southern Mesopotamia dated phase G to the 'protoliterate' or Jamdat Nasr period, that is to say a little before 3100 B.C., at which early time there must already have been intercourse between traders and travellers along the Euphrates route linking the 'Amūq plain with the cities of Sumer.[5] Contacts with Egypt, whether direct or indirect, are to be inferred from the presence of beads of glass and of deep blue faience;[6] glazed objects were already being manufactured in the Nile valley from the Predynastic Period onwards.[7] The characteristic tall jugs known as 'Syrian bottles', with handles and narrow necks, and sometimes decorated with a simple incised pattern of triangles filled with dots, have been found on many other sites also and were imported into Egypt; their prevalence in north Syria may mean that they were of local manufacture.[8] They will be noticed again later in this chapter.

The next level in the 'Amūq plain, phase H, is represented by a fairly large excavated area at Tell Judaidah and Tell Ta'yīnāt and lesser soundings elsewhere. It is characterized by more advanced techniques and the elaboration of domestic architecture; houses were larger and more complex in plan and furnished with better accessories in the shape of clay benches, silo pits, ovens and hearths.[9] A particular kind of portable hearth or andiron of earthenware[10] was associated with the sudden introduction of a new and striking type of pottery. The predominant colours are orange, black and tan, and the surface of the pots is highly burnished and had plastic decoration, usually in parallel ridges with a chevron border, done with a modelling tool when the clay was

---

[1] E.g. §iv, 22, iv, chart 3; in G, 18, 534 ff. M. Schaeffer attributes these signs of disaster to earthquake. [2] §iv, 4, 259 ff., 516 ff.

[3] Ibid. 329 ff., fig. 253.   [4] Ibid. 331 ff., fig. 254; 516.

[5] Ibid. 517. According to Tadmor (A, 14) phase G should be subdivided into two, the first phase contemporary with E.B. I and the second with E.B. II in Palestine.   [6] §iv, 4, 341 f.

[7] §v, 14, 157, 179 f.; §v, 22, 43.

[8] §iv, 4, 270, fig. 211 nos. 11–15, pl. 28, nos. 12, 17.

[9] Ibid. 345 ff.   [10] Ibid. 373, figs. 290 f.

still soft.[1] This pottery, known as 'Khirbet Karak ware' from the site in Palestine where it was first encountered, has been much discussed. It has been found at Tabara el-Akrād near Açana, towards the coast,[2] at Ras Shamra,[3] and farther south on the coastal plain in the regions of Jebeleh and Mantar,[4] though not farther south at Byblos; in the Orontes valley it is found at Hama,[5] and in the south it occurs on Palestinian sites, notably at Khirbet Karak itself and at Megiddo, Beth-shan and 'Affūleh.[6] It is not found on or east of the Euphrates.[7] It was once thought that the introduction of this distinctive ceramic, which is not made on the potter's wheel (though that labour-saving device had long been in use), was a witness to the invasion of Syria and Palestine by a barbarian people;[8] that they came from Turkey was inferred from the close affinities seen between the pottery of Khirbet Karak and wares from the Anatolian plateau and the southern Caucasus.[9] At Ras Shamra and at Qal'at er-Rūs near Jebeleh its introduction seems to have been immediately preceded by a conflagration, and the level at which it was found was poor in metal and other artifacts in comparison with the levels that preceded and followed it,[10] but on other sites there was no sign of destruction,[11] many objects continued in use unaltered from the earlier period, and the wares themselves were imitated in local clay. Perhaps this spectacular and attractive pottery arrived in the hands of a few traders or immigrants, either by sea or through the Beilān pass, and was distributed through the plain of Antioch by way of the valley of the Biqā' to northern Palestine, where it enjoyed a considerable vogue.[12] Associated with this pottery were copper pins of various shapes and other metal objects which suggest a date early in the third millennium, perhaps about 2700 B.C.; the cylinder seals were like those of the Jamdat Naṣr period but metal objects such as 'poker-butted spears', found also at Carchemish, show affinities with a late phase of the Early Dynastic Period in Mesopotamia.[13] Most of the pottery wares characteristic of this period continued to be made in the next

---

[1] §IV, 4, 358 ff., 518 f., figs. 281–5; see above, pp. 213 f.
[2] §IV, 12, 115 ff.; §IV, 29, 31 ff.   [3] §IV, 22, iv, 204 ff.
[4] §IV, 8, 119 ff.; §IV, 5, 214 ff.
[5] §IV, 9, 37; §IV, 13, 19 f., pl. v(4), (6).
[6] G, 1, 76 f.; G, 14, 124 ff., fig. 20; §IV, 2, 93 f., fig. 2; G, 18, 211, 213; G, 2, 13.   [7] §IV, 4, 519; §IV, 20, 25 f.
[8] §IV, 12, 118, n. 2; §IV, 29, 32 f.; §IV, 3, 356 ff.; §IV, 2, 101 ff.
[9] §IV, 22, vol. IV, xxxv f.; §IV, 16, 190; §IV, 3, 361; G, 18, 34, n. 1, and 345.
[10] G, 18, 40 ff.; §IV, 22, vol. IV, xxvi.   [11] §IV, 4, 517 ff.; §IV, 12, 122.
[12] §IV, 3, 360 f.   [13] §IV, 4, 519; §IV, 16, 190.

phase (I) when the art of the potter reached a higher level of technical skill; a similar repertory of wares and shapes is found in all
the Early Bronze Age sites in North Syria.[1] Khirbet Karak ware
had disappeared by the succeeding, latest E.B. phase (J) which
contained a rich assemblage of metal objects and probably
corresponded with the Sargonic period at Mari, Brak and
elsewhere.[2]

The Nahr el-'Āṣi, the River Orontes of the classical geographers, has its rise in the Biqā', the rift valley which separates
Lebanon from Antilebanon; it flows northwards through the
deep gorge of the Ghāb, before rushing through a canyon and
out into the calmer reaches of the 'Amūq plain on its westward
course towards the sea.[3] Two great sites in the Orontes valley
whose origins archaeology can trace back into the third millennium and beyond, may be identified with cities which played a
leading part in the history of the second millennium and after.
Mishrifeh (Mesherfa), which is almost certainly the ancient
Qaṭna,[4] stands on an affluent of the Orontes a little north of the
modern city of Homs. Pottery and metalwork of the early
level here, and in a large well-furnished tomb, have parallels in
sites of North Syria of the later third millennium.[5] On the high
mound in Hama which marks the citadel of the ancient city
Hamath, nearly forty kilometres to the north,[6] deep soundings
were made below the level of the first and second millennium
occupation.[7] The lowest level here reached was Neolithic, and
the two succeeding were identified as being contemporary with
the Jamdat Naṣr and Early Dynastic levels elsewhere, while level
J, in its earlier phases, was dated by related objects to a date
between 2400 and 2200 B.C. Hama is not mentioned in the Mari
letters[8] but is probably to be identified among the names of
Egypt's potential enemies in the so-called Execration Texts of
the early second millennium;[9] though the excavators removed
only a small portion of the mound in their probings, enough
was found to show that in the Early Bronze Age it was already
a prosperous town with narrow streets and closely packed houses.[10]

At several levels of the mound, a layer of burnt debris was
observed which appeared to indicate sudden disaster. The thickest

[1] §IV, 4, 396 ff., 520 f.   [2] Ibid. 429 ff., 521 ff.
[3] §I, 24, 208 and fig. 31.
[4] §IV, 6; G, 18, 116 ff.; §V, 8, 307; §I, 6, 121.
[5] §IV, 6, 111 f., 144 ff., pls. XLIII–XLVIII.
[6] §I, 6, 114.   [7] §IV, 9; §IV, 13.
[8] §I, 23, 93.   [9] See below, pp. 541 and 548 f.
[10] §IV, 9, 14 ff., figs. 10, 19, 56.

and most marked of these destruction levels was between levels J 4 and J 5, somewhat before 2200 B.C.,[1] after which, it appears, the orderly plan of the former city was abandoned, and houses, set in disorder, were less well built and of more modest plan than formerly; a period of stagnation was observed in the crafts and the arts.[2] At Tell Maṣin, sixteen kilometres from Hama, a similar layer of burning was observed in the latest Early Bronze level.[3] To whom can such wholesale destruction be attributed? It is tempting to suggest that it may have been Naram-Sin, if his route took him south-west on his march to the sea, past Hama and through the gap formed by the valley of the Nahr el-Kebīr between the Lebanon and its northern extension, the Jebel Anṣāriyyah, to Iarimuta on the coast.[4] But this is pure speculation and it is perhaps wiser to regard the destruction of Hama at this time as an unchronicled episode in the never-ending drama of warfare between neighbours that was characteristic of Syria's early history.

South of the embouchure of the Orontes, and a little to the south of Mons Casius, or Jebel Aqra', the high promontory which acts as a landmark to sailors and can be seen on a clear day from Cyprus, lies the low hill which marks the site of Ugarit. The remarkable excavations begun at Ras Shamra in 1929 and still every year enriching our knowledge of the past of Phoenicia have revealed a civilization unfolding continuously since Neolithic times. The excavators recognize five major phases in the history of their site:[5] after the Neolithic, or fifth, level, the next is dated to the Chalcolithic age, in the first half of the fourth millennium B.C.; the third, a deep stratum representing a millennium and a half of human occupation of the site, is assigned to the Late Chalcolithic Age (Levels III C and B) and the Early Bronze Age (III A), also called 'Ugarit Ancien 3'.[6] These early levels have been reached only in a number of deep *sondages* in various parts of the mound[7] and no considerable area has been laid bare. The story told by the remains in these early levels is somewhat different from that of the settlements on the inland plain: here on the coast the people of the Early Bronze Age were less advanced than their forerunners, whose fine Chalcolithic painted pottery gave way to coarser unpainted wares; finds are sparse, the techniques of flintwork are poorer, and there is very

---

[1] §IV. 9, 80 ff., 278.   [2] *Ibid.* 272 ff.

[3] §IV, 7, 124 ff.   [4] §I, 6, 16 f.; §I, 14, 262. See, however, above, p. 324.

[5] §IV, 22, vol. IV, xxx; G, 18, 8 ff., pls. v–XIII; §IV, 21, 241 f.

[6] §IV, 22, vol. IV, xxix ff., 151 ff. For the 'Chalcolithic' levels see *C.A.H.* I³, ch. VIII, sect. III.   [7] §IV, 22, vol. IV, xxi ff., 415 ff.

little metal.[1] Disaster must have overtaken these people, for above their remains, and above and after a level of burning and destruction, came the Khirbet Karak wares and with them large piriform jars with a distinctive combed decoration which are found elsewhere down the coast where trial excavations were carried out, at El-Ḥammām and Tell Simiriyan,[2] though they are not found in Anatolia or inland in Syria. They may have been used for the storage or transport of oil, for several were found by the side of a large oil press found in a *sondage* south of the 'Library of the High Priest';[3] the vats were estimated to have a capacity of 800 litres or more. In the uppermost layers of Level III A, and under the level of destruction preceding or heralding the arrival of the '*porteurs de torques*'[4] are the remains of a people who, to judge by their weapons and pottery, had been in touch with the people of Level J in the 'Amūq and Levels J and K at Hama; on the latter site, as at Ras Shamra, there are round silos dug in the ground in the courtyards or by the side of houses.[5]

It is not yet possible in the absence of texts, or until more information can be furnished by archaeology, to obtain more than a very incomplete picture of material civilization in Syria in the early Bronze Age. It was an age of urban development, with all that this implies in terms of social organization within a closely knit community. Weapons imply armies, and temples, priesthoods. We must imagine Syria to have been divided then, as it was later, into a number of small kingdoms each centred around some city or group of cities. Houses appear to have been well furnished with ovens and hearth, benches and storage bins, and the larger ones had a courtyard and a number of rooms; at Mari there was a well-designed drainage system.[6] Usually the houses were rectangular, though they may have had beehive roofs as they do in the area today;[7] a clay model of a round house was found in the pre-Sargonic level at Mari.[8] Of the movable furniture all that has survived is the crockery; a wide variety of pots and dishes, some large and coarse for storage and cookery, others fine and well baked, indicating the use of the slow wheel and of a proper kiln with a separate combustion chamber. Elaborate

1 §IV, 22, vol. IV, 200 ff.; §IV, 21, 229 ff.
2 §IV, 22, vol. IV, xxvii; § IV, 5, 214 ff.; G, 6, 118.
3 §IV, 22, vol. IV, xxviii, 420 ff., figs 6–13, 42.
4 §IV, 22, vol. II, 49 ff.; see below, p. 585.
5 §IV, 22, vol. IV, 229 ff.; §IV, 9, 38 f., figs. 51–2.
6 §III, 14, 48 f. and pl. IX.   7 §IV, 20, 19 and pl. I(3).
8 §II, 21, 192, pl. xv, cf. §III, 14, 39 f., figs. 51–2; A, 11, 293 ff. and figs. 311–13.

shapes like the 'champagne goblet' could be turned out in mass production, showing a specialization of trades within the community;[1] well-made jugs of thin, burnished 'metallic ware' were exported far afield to Palestine and Egypt, perhaps containing some such commodity as olive oil or wine.[2]

The coppersmiths of the third millennium, too, traded their wares and it may be that itinerant smiths travelled from town to town, judging by the close similarity of such objects as toggle-pins,[3] spear-heads with the tang bent to secure it within the wooden shaft,[4] and shaft-hole axes.[5] Considerable developments in metallurgical technique took place during the period; a deliberate admixture of tin with copper ores resulted in the first bronze objects, perhaps about 2700 B.C.,[6] and a fragment of iron found in a grave of Early Dynastic date at Tell Chagar Bazar, when analysed, proved not to be meteoric.[7] Iron objects, though rare, are found in Anatolia in a third-millennium context;[8] the metal did not, however, come into general use for more than a thousand years thereafter. Bronze objects were cast in open moulds and also by the more complicated *cire perdue* process.[9] It is probable that these and other advanced techniques of metallurgy came from Mesopotamia. Decorated bone handles, presumably for hafting to metal tools, were associated with Khirbet Karak wares on some sites.[10] Barley and wheat were cultivated, and cattle, sheep, goats, asses, dogs and perhaps the pig were domesticated.[11] Much of the prosperity of North Syria must have come from the manufacture of wine and olive oil, and the large size of the Ras Shamra oil-press indicates that it was intended for more than merely domestic production.[12] Murex shells found at Tell Judaidah hint that, somewhere along the north Phoenician coast, the purple dye industry already flourished.[13]

Six little bronze figurines found together in a *cache* in the first

[1] §IV, 4, 259, 264.   [2] See below, p. 350.

[3] §IV, 4, 351, 376, fig. 292, pl. 53; §IV, 22, vol. IV, 226 f.; §III, 6, 166 ff., pl. XXXI.

[4] §IV, 4, 376 and fig. 293; §IV, 22, vol. IV, 234 ff., 335 ff., fig., fig. 29.

[5] §IV, 4, 376 and fig. 293; §IV, 19, 90 ff.; §III, 17, 148.

[6] §IV, 16, 189 f.; §IV, 4, 302, 315.

[7] §III, 4, 26 f.; §VI, 15, 247. See above, p. 305.

[8] §III, 17, pls. 144–5.

[9] §IV, 16, 190; §IV, 4, 300 ff.

[10] G, 18, 40 ff., 245, pl. xv(4); §IV, 8, 123 f. and fig. 3; §IV, 22, vol. IV, 206, fig. 18.

[11] §III, 6, 40 ff.; §IV, 4, 504 ff.

[12] §IV, 22, vol. IV, 420 ff., figs. 6–13, 42; §IV, 21, 234; §I, 16, 136 ff.

[13] §IV, 4, 344 f.

Early Bronze village at Tell Judaidah in the 'Amūq plain[1] give precious information about the panoply of the warriors and the feminine fashions of the day. They stand virtually naked, in an attitude which in Sumer would be interpreted as of adoration before a deity, and were almost certainly votive figures set in some shrine.[2] The male figures wear broad belts and a torque or collar around the throat; they are armed with spear and mace, one in either hand, and have conical helmets with a small spike at the apex. The women have their hair elaborately dressed, with a fillet or plait around the crown of the head and a chignon hanging behind, covering the nape of the neck; three or four ringlets hang down on either side of the head and the coiffure is crowned by a crescent-shaped cap. Traces of silver at the neck indicate that two of the figures may have worn a necklace or collar, in one case perhaps a double collar.[3] Elaborate styles of hairdressing are seen on other clay figures from the same area, found unstratified but of similar date; one of the figures wears a high collar of flattened clay pellets perhaps representing a bead gorget.[4] The high felt hat or *polos* worn by the wives of high officials at Mari[5] is not found further west.

The physiognomy of the little bronze figures is striking: they have large straight noses and jutting chins, but these characteristics and the slant of the disproportionately large eyes may be due to over-emphasis by the modeller. The men wear a short fringe-beard. The figures show too that circumcision was practised in north Syria in the third millennium B.C., as it was in ancient Egypt, though not in Mesopotamia with the exception of Tepe Gawra in the north, where a Syrian (west Semitic) element in the population is suggested.[6] The beaky nose and high cheekbones are seen in part of a clay 'face vase' from the latest Early Bronze Age level at Judaidah[7] but perhaps we should again not insist on the degree of accuracy of the portraiture. The carved heads from Tell Brak[8] and a stone head from Hama[9] have a cruder appearance: while certain features of the carving have been compared with Sumerian glyptic, there are distinctive features which mark them as Syrian.[10] Bronze toggle-pins must have been the usual fastening for garments such as cloaks; model boots, with

---

[1] §IV, 4, 300 ff., figs. 240–245 and pls. 56–64; G, 10, 134 and pl. 135. See Plate 38 (*b*).   [2] §IV, 16, 190; §IV, 4, 517.

[3] §IV, 4, 305 ff.   [4] *Ibid*. 466, fig. 368.

[5] § III, 14, 84 ff. pls. 36–37; §III, 11, 164; A, 11, 97, fig. 134.

[6] §III, 15, 99, pl. XLVI B; G, 7, 1, 445 f.; A, 13.

[7] §IV, 4, 453, fig. 350(5).   [8] See above, p. 330.

[9] §IV, 13, 25 f., pl. VII(1).   [10] G, 10, 135, pl. 136.

lace markings, rolled-down tops and slightly upturned toes show that, in north Syria, footwear has changed little during the last five thousand years.[1]

The north Syrian soldier appears to have been armed in much the same manner as his Sumerian neighbour; spears, javelins and daggers, maces with pear-shaped heads and battle-axes with sockets for the shaft are the usual weapons. Clay models of chariots with two or four solid wheels are not uncommon[2] and chariots appear as a recurrent motif on Syrian cylinder seals of Early Dynastic date.[3] Judging by Mesopotamian parallels, the chariot of the age, so heavy and solid that it was usually drawn by four onagers or asses, was an essential weapon of war as well as a means of transport.[4] Camels of the single-humped variety were probably domesticated early by the desert nomads, though there is no evidence for their use by travellers along the main highways of commerce until much later.[5] Boats with three oarsmen apiece are depicted on an impression of a cylinder seal found at Hama.[6]

V. BYBLOS AND THE LAND OF NEGAU

The Phoenicians of Roman times had a tradition that Byblos was the most ancient of cities, and that it had been founded by the god Ba'al-Kronos.[7] It occupied a site well favoured by nature, on a low rocky promontory surrounded by a fertile plain and backed by an amphitheatre of thickly forested mountains; a natural spring provided a focal point for settlement, and just to the north of the promontory was a sheltered beach where the little ships of antiquity could be drawn up to safety during the westerly gales of winter.[8] Archaeological investigation at Jubeil, the site of Byblos, has shown that the city had indeed a very long history and may claim to be one of the longest continually inhabited cities in the Near East. A Neolithic settlement, dating at least as far back as the fifth millennium B.C., was succeeded by a larger, Chalcolithic village in which small circular huts and rectangular apsidal cottages show slow development through the fourth millennium, in the later phases being sometimes grouped together in islands,

[1] §III, 6, 99 f., pl. VIII, no. 6, pl. LII, no. 19.
[2] §IV, 13, 37 ff., 60, figs. 12–14; §III, 9, Abb. 44(a); §III, 6, 215 f.
[3] §IV, 1, 78 ff., figs. 23–6, pl. 6(5).
[4] §III, 17, 37 ff., pls. 128–133. See above, pp. 122 f.
[5] §IV, 27, 520 f.; §I, 9, 27 and n. 2; §II, 16, x; §IV, 14, 3.
[6] §IV, 13, pl. XIV(1).   [7] G, 6, 63 ff.; G, 16, 67.
[8] G, 16, 68, fig. 4; §V, 4, 1, pl. CCXII.

the beginnings of town planning.[1] One of the rectangular houses
had a jar beneath its floor in which a child had been buried, and
skeletons in pots are found over a wide area of the site. Some of
the jars bore the impression of a stamp seal, either as a mark of
ownership, or to identify the maker.[2] The simple geometrical
and animal designs on these sealings recall those of the Uruk
period in Mesopotamia and point to a date in the fourth millennium for the Chalcolithic period at Byblos.[3] Unfortunately it has
not been possible to relate the artifacts found in these early levels
to the evolution of architectural techniques. This difficulty
results from the method adopted by the excavators, namely to
remove the soil, square by square, in rigidly horizontal layers of
uniform thickness until the whole surface is exposed to bed-rock.[4]
Although by this method of 'total excavation'[5] no object is
missed, the uneven surface of the rock and the varying thickness
of occupation-layers in different parts of the site have led to considerable difficulty in reconstructing the history of early Byblos.[6]

In the levels of the fourth millennium there is no sign of the
Egyptian influence which was later to become paramount in
Byblos. Associated with the stamp seals in jar burials were pear-
shaped mace-heads and other objects which point to ultimate
contact with Mesopotamia[7] and it may have been from the east
that the Chalcolithic inhabitants of Byblos acquired their knowledge of the working of copper. This new technique, a vital and
revolutionary step in human evolution, made rapid strides in the
west, and it seems likely that the Byblites were among the earliest
people to work in bronze.[8] In the Kesrwan district of Lebanon,
in the mountains behind Byblos, tin and copper ores are, by a
rare chance, found together, and an accidental mixture of alluvial
ores in gravel near the mouths of the rivers Fedar (Phaedrus) and
Ibrāhīm (Adonis), both of which flow through the metal-bearing
district and debouch a little to the south of Byblos, could have
been found to produce a metal harder and more durable than
copper.[9] The city was a centre of bronze-working in the time of
the Egyptian Middle Kingdom, judging by the great hoard of
bronzes found in the 'Syrian Temple' (Building II).[10] The earliest
well-dated objects of bronze, however, come from sites in north

[1] §v, 5, 72 f.; §v, 3, 5 ff.   [2] §v, 3, 56.
[3] Ibid. 46.   [4] G, 18, 50 ff.
[5] §v, 4, 11, 6. See further below, pp. 587 ff.
[6] G, 18, 50 ff., pls. xvi–xviii, figs. 57–74.
[7] §v, 4, 1, fig. 281; §v, 3, 46 f.; §iv, 34, 4 f. See C.A.H. I³, ch. viii, sect. iii.
[8] §v, 33, 31 f.; §v, 27, 92 ff.
[9] §v, 33, 30 ff., fig. 1.   [10] §v, 17, 111 ff., pls. lxvi–lxx; G, 18, 53 f.

Syria,[1] and pending further evidence priority in this respect must be withheld from the metal-workers of Byblos.

During the epoch corresponding with the Jamdat Naṣr period in Mesopotamia,[2] Byblos was already a town. The slow potter's wheel was in use, copper was in greater supply, houses were rectangular and had several rooms, with wooden pillars on stone bases supporting, no doubt, an axial ridge-pole and a gabled roof.[3] Pebbled streets with a central drain were wide enough for wheeled vehicles. The first temples appear, simple buildings enough, but built with the care that befitted houses of the gods, with foundations of well-dressed sandstone.[4] The stamp seals now gave way to cylinder seals, usually with a frieze of animals, so clearly cut that it has been suggested they may have been of wood rather than stone.[5] Here again the influence was from Sumer, but during the early centuries of the third millennium objects of Egyptian manufacture make their appearance and become ever more frequent.[6] The earliest closely dated object is a fragment of a stone vase bearing the name of the Second Dynasty king Khasekhemwy;[7] fragments with the names of Cheops and Mycerinus of the Fourth Dynasty,[8] of Unas, and of most of the Sixth Dynasty kings, proclaim the pharaohs' interest,[9] and so do certain other objects uninscribed but manifestly made in Egypt and dated by their style to the Third to Sixth Dynasties: polished axes, flint knives, cylindrical beads of alabaster, statuettes resembling those found at Hierakonpolis, and fragments of stone objects in stones such as alabaster and schist which can only have come from the Nile valley.[10] Most of the objects bearing royal cartouches are vases of alabaster or limestone, but during the reigns of Phiops I and II, small stone containers in the form of squatting apes nursing their young were also sent; perhaps these were designed for the sacred oils used in some ceremony or cult.[11] Moreover, several of the Sixth Dynasty vases are inscribed in honour of the jubilee or *Sed*-festival of these two kings, and may therefore have been royal gifts sent on the occasion of a local celebration of this important

[1] See above, p. 336. [2] G, 1, 71; §v, 3, 68 f.

[3] §v, 5, 72 f. [4] §v, 4, 1, 297 ff; §v, 5, 73.

[5] §v, 3, 61 ff., figs. 21–25; §1, 8, 230.

[6] §v, 18, 83 ff.; §v, 8, 26, n. 64; §v, 16, 17 ff.; §v, 20; §v, 23, 390 f.; §v, 34, 5 ff. [7] §v, 18, 84, fig. 1; §v, 17, 271.

[8] §v, 18, 85, fig. 3; §v, 17, pl. 125; 75, fig. 53 no. 64, pl. 39.

[9] §v, 18, 84 ff.; §v, 17, 271 ff.; §v, 9, 21 ff.; §v, 20, pl. 3; §v, 16.

[10] §v, 18, 85 ff.; §v, 34, 22 ff.

[11] §v, 8, 26, n. 64.

event.[1] Important, that is, to the Egyptians themselves, but what interest had the Byblites in such ceremonies? To suppose that they were intended for the ritual needs of a few Egyptian immigrants resident in Byblos is to underestimate the closeness of the links which bound Egypt and Byblos throughout their history, from the Early Dynastic period and even earlier, to the latest classical times.

To the Egyptians, Byblos was the key to 'God's Land',[2] the Lebanon on whose steep slopes grew the timber trees they coveted. Their own country produced no tall trees except the coarse-grained palms whose trunks were suitable only for roofing and rough constructional work.[3] Small planks of moderately fine grain, suitable for cabinet-making, could be obtained from the tamarisk, the sidder, and the sycomore-fig, but but for architectural purposes, for the long beams which spanned floors and roofs, as well as for columns and the spars of ships, conifers such as as pine, fir or cedar were needed and even in predynastic graves traces of coniferous wood are found which can only have come from the north.[5] The funerary furniture of Meryib, found at Giza, well illustrates both the value and the scarcity of this foreign timber, for the fine carpentry of the inner coffin, of long well-cut deal planks, contrasts with the clumsy workmanship of the outer, of crooked pieces sawn from a bent piece of sycomore.[6] The long flagstaves which stood at the entrance to temples and the wooden pillars of the temples of the early period must have been of coniferous wood. Deal was used for the doors of Sneferu's palace[7] and for the roofing of his pyramid chamber;[8] the Palermo Stone records that he brought forty shiploads of timber and built with it forty-four boats, some of them 100 cubits, that is, more than 170 ft. long.[9] The wood was of two different varieties, *ꜥš* and *mrw*; both these kinds of timber were regularly used in ship-building.[10] *Mrw* wood was red and was probably cedar, while the yellowish *ꜥš* has been identified not only with cedar (*cedrus Libani*)[11] but also with various other of the coniferous trees which today grow in the mountains of Syria: the cypress (*cupressus*

[1] §v, 8, 21; §v, 17, 271, pls. 45–7.
[2] §v, 30, 373; §v, 8, 277; §v, 29, 373.   [3] §v, 14, ch. 14; §v, 31, 685 ff.
[4] §v 14, 79; §vi, 11, 182.
[5] §v, 2, 62; §v, 14, 429 f.   [6] §v,11, 143 f., pl. 24; A, 14.
[7] §v, 29, part iv, 237 l. 3; G, 17, 227.   [8] G, 12, 69.
[9] §v, 29, part iv, 236 l. 6 ff.; G, 4, 1 par. 146.
[10] §v, 29, 236, 11, 8 f., 12; §vi, 35, 11, pls. 10(2), 11(2).
[11] §v, 1 *passim*; §v, 14, 432; G, 17, 227; §vi, 18, 78; §v, 25, 33.

sempervirens),[1] pine (*pinus halepensis*),[2] fir (*abies cilicica*)[3] and maple:[4] all but the last have been identified in the analysis of objects of Old Kingdom date in Egypt.[5] It is probable that the ancient Egyptians applied the name *c͞s* indiscriminately to several species of conifer which, being familiar to them rather in the shape of logs of timber than as growing trees, they did not clearly distinguish.[6] A third foreign wood mentioned less frequently in the Old Kingdom, *w'n*, whose berries are mentioned in a later prescription for a medicament, was probably juniper.[7] Hornbeam, which today grows in Europe and Asia Minor, was the material for one of the oars of Cheops' funerary boat;[8] timbers of the boat's hull were identified by analysis as juniper and 'cedar of Lebanon or an allied species'.[9] Some of the logs used must have been of enormous size, for several of the planking beams are nearly sixty feet long.[10] We are reminded that Sennefer, sent by Tuthmosis III to fetch timber from Lebanon, brought back 'the choicest trees, sixty cubits tall, more pointed than ears of corn',[11] surely a description of the Aleppo pine.

Resin, a by-product of cedar, fir or pine, was early in demand for mummification; it was imported in jars, in small round lumps. Little is known of the materials and methods used by the Old Kingdom embalmers, but the pessimist of the Ipuwer text[12] bemoans the loss of Byblos as a source of supply. 'Finest cedar unguent', probably made from the resin of conifers, appears frequently in the offering-lists of the Old Kingdom.[13]

The Egyptians called Byblos by its most ancient name *Kpn*, perhaps Kupna, whence derives the later Phoenician Gebal, 'the mountain city' and the modern diminutive Jubeil.[14] The country in which the city was situated was called by them the land of Negau,[15] and its inhabitants Fenkhu, a word which probably means 'woodcutters'.[16] After felling and trimming in the mountains, the logs must have been brought down to the port of Byblos, perhaps by way of the Adonis river. A copper axe found in the bed of the river, engraved in Egyptian hieroglyphs with

[1] §v, 8, 30.
[2] §vi, 31, 182 ff.
[3] §v, 13, 45 ff.; §v, 8, 30.
[4] §ii, 25, 44.
[5] §v, 14, 489 ff.
[6] §v, 8, 30.
[7] §v, 14, 430, 437; §v, 8, 397.
[8] §vi, 29, 45 f.
[9] *Ibid.* 46.
[10] See Plate 38 (c).
[11] §v, 30, vol. ii, 535; G, 17, 243.
[12] See beow, pp. 532–3.
[13] §vi, 26, 139; §v, 13, 39.
[14] §vi, 3, 12; G, 6, 63 ff. and n. 5; G, 16, 67; §v, 28, 7 ff.; §vi, 1, 235; §i, 18, 33.
[15] §vi, 31, 184 ff.
[16] §v, 8, 22, 277 f.; but see *C.A.H.* ii³, ch. xxxiii, sect. ii.

the name of the gang of woodcutters to whom it had belonged,[1] indicates that the felling may have been done by Egyptian lumbermen, or perhaps by mixed gangs of Egyptians and Syrians under the supervision of Egyptian foremen. Some of the timber may have been used then and there on the seashore to build 'Byblos-boats', *kbnwt*, the usual Egyptian word for ocean-going vessels.[2] These long, many-oared craft, with a tension cable or 'hogging truss' from stem to stern,[3] were much larger and of different build from the boats which plied on the Nile. They were used in the Mediterranean and on voyages down the Red Sea to Punt.[4] It is not certain whether the word *kbnt* first denoted a ship built in Byblos, a ship built of Byblos timber, or merely a sea-going vessel used on the Byblos run.[5] Timbers fashioned ready for building may in some cases have been brought by sea to Egyptian shipyards; the planks of the Cheops boat were numbered for easy assembly.[6] Large logs for shipbuilding and other purposes were probably towed behind the transports, and smaller pieces piled on the deck, like the Tyrian tribute of a later age.[7]

The legend of the death of Osiris, as preserved in its most complete form by Plutarch in *De Iside et Osiride*,[8] contains a memory of the age-old link between Egypt and Byblos. After the murder of Osiris, according to this legend, his body, enclosed in a wooden coffin, floated over the sea to Byblos, where it came to rest on the shore by the side of a cedar-tree which grew up and enclosed it. The king of Byblos had the tree cut down and made into a pillar for his palace, but Isis, coming to Syria in search of Osiris, recognized it and by magical means obtained the body and brought it back to Egypt.[9] The character of the Osiris myth, involving the death and resurrection of a deity intimately connected with vegetation, has many associations with that of the young god Adonis, who was killed by a wild boar and mourned by Astarte. Lucian indeed specifically states that the mysteries of Adonis used to be celebrated in honour of Osiris.[10] The Adonis river, only five miles from Byblos, was said to run red with the blood of the slain god,[11] and farther up the valley at Afqa, where

---

[1] §v, 24, 283 ff., pl. 36. A hoard of copper adzes and axes found at Kfar Monash near the Tel Aviv–Haifa road may have belonged to a similar wood-cutting gang, according to A, 2. Yeivin (A, 15) argues that they are not tools but weapons.

[2] §v, 25, 47 ff.; §v, 28, 10 f.; §vi, 7, 462; §v, 34, 44 n. 1; §iv, 27, 620.

[3] §vi, 7, 474 ff.; §v, 25, 57.   [4] §v, 25, 4; §vi, 7, 134 f.

[5] §vi, 18, 36; §vi, 7, 461 ff.; §v, 8, 21; §vi, 30, 19 ff., 35; §v, 25, 12, n. 4; 48.

[6] §vi, 29, 8.   [7] §v, 21, 273, fig. 108; A, 3, 70, 73 ff.

[8] §v, 10, 227 f.; §v, 12, 195 ff.   [9] §v, 28, 12 ff; §vi, 31, 190 f.

[10] §v, 15, 47 f. and n. 18.   [11] G, 16, 70.

the river gushes from a cave in an amphitheatre of sheer mountain cliffs, Astarte's rites were celebrated.[1] The story in an earlier form is embodied in the Ramesside romance of the Two Brothers,[2] in which tale Bata, whose fate resembles that of Osiris in many respects, hid his heart in the middle of a tree in the Valley of Pines, and died when the tree was cut down, but was sought and brought back to life by his brother. That the sacred pillar (*djd*) of Osiris was originally a lopped conifer has been doubted,[3] but there are many similarities between the deities Osiris, Adonis and Tammuz-Marduk in his most ancient form[4] and it may be that the worship of Osiris was linked with a Syrian tree-cult from very early, perhaps prehistoric, times.[5] As a source of the materials used in mummification and for coffins,[6] 'God's Land' would have held a special and sacred significance for the Egyptians.

Astarte herself does not appear to have been known to the Egyptians at the time of their first contacts with Byblos, though she was later to occupy an important place in the pantheon;[7] in the Old Kingdom it was the anonymous mistress of Byblos who commanded their homage. Egyptian women of the time of the Middle Kingdom were sometimes called after her and objects were dedicated to her at Byblos; in Egypt she was given the cow-horned guise of the goddess Hathor.[8] It is possible that Hathor is mentioned by name on the cylinder seal of a ruler of Byblos, in the company of two male deities, Re of the Foreign Land and Khaitaw, elsewhere described as 'he who is in Negau', the particular deity of the tree-felling district of Lebanon.[9] If this very tentative interpretation of the crudely drawn hieroglyphs is correct[10] it affords precious evidence of an early Byblite triad, perhaps no later than the Fifth Dynasty.[11]

The building from which many Old Kingdom objects were recovered is considered by some to be an Egyptian temple,[12] but this too is problematical and it may rather be that at Byblos the jubilee of the Egyptian king was solemnized in a local shrine, as an event closely touching the prosperity of Negau, for, at a time

---

[1] §1, 6, 159 ff.; G, 16, 71 f., fig. 27.　　[2] §v, 6, 197 ff.

[3] §v, 26, 425.　　[4] §v, 32, 123 ff.; §v, 8, 22.

[5] §v, 28, 12 ff.; §vi, 10, 74 ff. See §v, 9 for a different appraisal.

[6] v, 14, 309, 319 ff., 432 ff.; §vi, 16, 83.　　[7] *C.A.H.* ii³, ch. x, sect. v.

[8] §v, 7; §v, 8, 21; §v, 9, 54; §v, 17, 36, 40, 43 f., 267, 275, 280.

[9] §v, 17, 62 ff., pl. xxxix; §v, 8, 21 f.; §vi, 31, 185 ff; §vi, 21, 2 ff.

[10] §vi, 21, 1 ff.; otherwise §v, 8, 22; §vi, 30, 25; §v, 1, 44 ff.

[11] §vi, 21, 2 f.

[12] §v, 17, 129 ff.; §v, 19, 83 ff.; §v, 34, 24 n. 5.

when, as seems beyond doubt, trade between states was a monopoly of rulers, upon the well-being of those rulers depended the
continuance of prosperity.

In exchange for the timber and resin of Byblos, and perhaps
also for a little copper (though not for tin, since bronze did not
come into regular use in Egypt until the New Kingdom),[1] Egyptian
sailors brought with them manufactured articles for barter, such
as metalwork and jewellery, stone vases filled with ointment;
other commodities that suggest themselves are corn, linen,
papyrus, ivory and gold. It may have been through Byblos that
the Egyptians obtained their supplies of the prized blue stone,
lapis lazuli, passed from hand to hand along the route from the
mines of distant Badakhshān.[2]

Pottery vessels of Asiatic type are frequently found in Egypt,[3]
in particular the tall one- or two-handled jugs known to archaeologists as 'Syrian bottles', which have a wide distribution in
Syria and Palestine.[4] Such jars are depicted, along with tethered
bears, in a fragment of relief from the mortuary temple of King
Sahure at Abusīr.[5] They may have contained wine or honey, or
perhaps the moringa oil which is frequently mentioned as an
Asiatic commodity[6], or they may have been wine-jars re-used for
the resin of Negau.[7] The clay is so uniform and so distinctive,
whether found in Egypt, in Megiddo, in Byblos or in the plain
of Antioch, that it is likely that the amphorae were made in one
particular place.[8] The bears are of particular interest since this is
the earliest evidence of a familiar practice: the monarchs of the
ancient Near East, in the second millennium and later, kept
exotic animals and birds caught in the course of their campaigns,
or sent them as presents from fellow rulers, in a kind of zoological
park in or near their palaces.[9]

The arrival by boat of men, women and children, perhaps a
delegation from Byblos,[10] is also depicted in this temple, and a
relief from the causeway of Unas' pyramid presents a somewhat

---

[1] §v, 33, 31; §v, 31, 589; §v, 14, 253.

[2] §v, 14, 399; §v, 8, 28; §iv, 14, 34; see now J. C. Payne in *Iraq* 30, 58 ff.

[3] §vi, 25, 200 f.; §vi, 17, 105 ff.; §v, 8, 31 ff.

[4] G, 14, 127 f.; §iv, 4, 370 f., 516; §v, 8, 35 ff. 41, n. 27; §v, 17, 107 f.,
fig. 10; G, 8, 9; §vi, 17, 106 ff.

[5] §vi, 6, pl. 3. See above, p. 183. See Plate 33 (*b*).

[6] §v, 8, 31, 41, n. 40; §v, 3, 8.   [7] §v, 17, 108; §v, 34, 53 f.

[8] §vi, 6, vol. ii, pls. 11–13; G, 14, 127 ff. and fig. 19.

[9] G, 17, 281, 297; §vi, 25, 85; §iii, 7, 49.

[10] §v, 8, 16 and 24, n. 35. In v, 19, 191 ff. it was suggested that the scene may
represent the arrival of a Byblite princess destined to be the Egyptian king's bride.

similar scene;[1] here the heavy seagoing vessels are in marked contrast with the Nile barges which bring granite columns from Aswān. The discovery of fragile furniture of Sahure in a tomb at Dorak in north-west Turkey has thrown fresh light on the range and seaworthiness of byblos-boats.[2]

A thick layer of destruction and burning lies above the level at which objects of the Sixth Dynasty were found at Byblos;[3] the identity of the destroyers will be discussed elsewhere.[4] In the level above, nothing Egyptian was found and it was clear from the relative poverty of the finds that the first golden age of Byblos had ended. The story of the revival of the fruitful commercial partnership between Byblos and Egypt is told in another chapter.[5]

VI. EGYPTIANS IN SINAI AND PALESTINE

The farmers of the Nile valley and the cattle-raising Delta dwellers had as their neighbours the nomads of the eastern desert, of the peninsula of Sinai, and of the Negeb. Whether all these people were of the same race and tongue we have no means of telling. The Egyptians themselves appear to have called them by several different names, sometimes indiscriminately; in general they called them 'Those who live on Sand' or Sand-dwellers, perhaps best translated as 'bedawin'. There are early references to the 'Easterners' and to the *iwntiw*, a word of uncertain origin perhaps meaning originally 'pillar-folk', in reference to their standing stones, or the *'alāmāt* used by bedawin to this day to mark their paths.[6] Yet another designation was Mentjiu, meaning perhaps 'wild ones';[7] the appellations Setjetiu and Amu, which come into use in the Old Kingdom, may possibly denote the Bowmen and the Throwstick-people respectively.[8]

On the borders of the Delta, from time immemorial, small groups of these bedawin came to pasture their flocks,[9] tempted by the proximity of better grazing-grounds and possible loot. From

---

[1] §vi, 23, 138, fig. 2; §vi, 24, pl. xiv.
[2] See above, p. 181, n.1 and pp. 390 ff.
[3] §v, 5, 73; G, 18, 63.　　　　　　　　　　　[4] See below, pp. 587 ff.
[5] See below, pp. 545 ff. The mention of an *ensi* of Byblos in one of the economic texts from Drehem (§iv, 24) is proof of commercial contact between Sumer and the Lebanese coast, but need not imply that Byblos was then included in the 'empire' of the Third Dynasty of Ur.
[6] §v, 8, 13, 23, n. 12. See above, pp. 46–7.　　[7] §v, 8, 14.
[8] §vi, 30, 15 f.; §vi, 20, vol. ii, 3, n. *a*; §v, 8, 15.
[9] §vi, 22, 968.

time to time, when they became too numerous or too trouble-some, the Egyptians would chase them out. The expulsion of Moses and the Israelites from the Land of Goshen was a single episode in a constantly recurring drama. One of the type-images of the Egyptian king was a heroic figure smiting an Asiatic:[1] grasping a bearded, crouching figure by the topknot, the king strides forward, brandishing above his head the mace with which he is about to crush the head of his victim. This heraldic group appears on an ivory plaque of the First Dynasty king Den,[2] and recurs constantly thereafter as an ideographic group de-noting 'the King of Egypt victorious over his enemies'. On the pylons of New Kingdom temples the single prisoner is often multiplied to a plurality of supplicating wretches, identified by their features and attributes as Nubians, Libyans and Asiatics, and all grasped by the hair together in one improbable bunch.[3]

There was further and hardly less cogent reason for punitive campaigns east of the Delta, namely to ensure the safe conduct of caravans en route to the mines of Sinai. The peninsula of Sinai, an inverted triangle wedged between Africa and Asia, has never been able to support more than a sparse population, eking out a precarious existence. A wide coastal plain of barren sand dunes rises to a hilly central plateau of gravel, intersected by water-courses that lead down to the Wādi el-'Arīsh on the north, the River of Egypt,[4] debouching on the Mediterranean at El-'Arīsh, the ancient Raphia.[5] The plateau is for the most part arid and barren, though when rain falls, as it does occasionally in winter, the flood, fed from a thousand trickles from the hills, pours in spate down the wadis, and when the bed dries, the bedawin plough the yellow silt and grow a catch-crop of barley or wheat. For the most part, however, the plateau is and always has been a desolate spot, the home of poor nomads whose herds feed on the scrub bushes and shelter from the noonday sun under an oc-casional tamarisk or stunted palm.

The plateau rises towards the south, and it was among the towering mountains in the south-west of the peninsula that the ancient Egyptians found ores of copper, malachite, turquoise, chrysocolla and azurite.[6] Leaving the Nile valley north of Helio-

---

[1] §vi, 20, vol. ii, 27.
[2] §iii, 17, 125. See above, p. 27 and Plate 28 (b).
[3] §iii, 17, 204, 233, 350; §vi, 37, 182.
[4] G, 16, 44; G, 17, 292.
[5] §vi, 18, 342; §vi, 19, 115; §vi, 4, 3 f., fig. 2.
[6] §vi, 20, vol. ii, 4 f.; §vi, 15, 55 f.; §vi, 32, vol. i, 223 ff.

polis[1] the donkey trains, laden with provisions and perhaps also charcoal for smelting, must have traversed the Wādi Tummīlāt and entered Sinai near the present town of Suez; travelling southwards along the sandy plain bordering the Red Sea, they would supplement their meagre water-supply from an occasional spring of brackish water; then, turning inland through a gorge, perhaps through Wādi esh-Shallāl, the expedition entered a wilderness of granite and red sandstone, finally descending into the Wādi Maghāra, the 'Valley of Caves', as it is called today, because the hillsides are honeycombed with the mouths of ancient workings.[2] Here they set up their windbreaks and built rough stone houses to shelter them from the sudden cold of night and from prowling hyenas, lions and wolves. A wall built across the floor of the valley protected them from the danger of sudden flooding.[3]

Carved in the sandstone cliff above the mines, large figures of the king of Egypt smiting the nomads protected the miner from danger by magical means, and perhaps also recorded the forcible recruitment of local labour. The earliest of these inscriptions is that of Djoser of the Third Dynasty, who is shown brandishing his mace above a bearded prisoner whom he grasps by the top-knot.[4] Nearby were two stelae of King Sanakhte,[5] one of which, over the entrance to a mine, appears to mention 'Hathor, Mistress of the Turquoise', who was later regarded as the patron goddess of the region.[6] The relief left by Sekhemkhet's expedition depicts the ruler three times, as king of Upper Egypt with the white crown, as king of Lower Egypt with the red crown, and again with the white crown in the conventional attitude of smiting the local bedawin shaikh. The unnamed leader of the expedition caused himself to be depicted nearby.[7] Early Fourth Dynasty kings are commemorated in the Wādi Maghāra; both Sneferu, who was later regarded as the patron of the region, and Cheops left inscriptions;[8] the latter is shown clubbing a prisoner in the presence of Thoth, who is elsewhere described as 'Lord of Foreign Lands', and was therefore appropriately invoked here.[9] Activity in Sinai appears to have increased under the Fifth

[1] §vi, 8, viii f. and map 1.
[2] §vi, 34, 48 ff., figs. 39, 42, map 2; §vi, 39, 22 ff. and map 3, p. 25, 144 ff.
[3] §vi, 34, 38 ff.; fig. 41.   [4] §vi, 20, vol. i, pl. i, no. 2. See above, 145–6 and 151.
[5] §vi, 20, vol. i, pls. i, iv, nos. 3 and 4; §vi, 34, pls. 48–49.
[6] §vi, 20, vol. ii, 29.
[7] §vi, 34, pls. 45–47; §vi, 20, vol. i, pl. i, no. 1; see above, p. 151. Yeivin (A, 15) has recently reopened the argument for a First Dynasty date for this relief.
[8] §vi, 20, vol. i, nos. 5, 6 and 7, pls. ii–iv; §vi, 34, pls. 50, 51.
[9] §vi, 20, vol. i, no. 10, pl. vi; vol. ii, 28 f.

and Sixth Dynasty kings; the best-cut of all the stelae is that of Sahure who is shown 'smiting the Mentjiu and crushing all foreign countries'.[1] The opening of a well in the area is perhaps symbolized by the tall vase carved on the tablet of Nyuserre Ini, the largest in the wadi, which bears the superscription 'May Thoth, Lord of Foreign Lands, give cool draughts of water.'[2]

In the Fifth Dynasty it became the regular custom for the leader of the expedition, no longer anonymous, to append his name to that of the king. Expeditions begin to be dated and the inscriptions, no longer symbolic, become records of actual events. Now it is not copper but *mfka't*, turquoise, that is mentioned as the object of expeditions;[3] the region was known as 'the Terraces of Turquoise'[4] and as already stated, Hathor, the patron goddess of the region, was 'Mistress of the Turquoise'.[5] This beautiful stone, beloved of the Egyptians at all periods and successfully imitated in glass when it was in short supply[6], is still mined in Sinai; it occurs in nodules in a vein of purplish sandstone immediately below a metalliferous stratum. Mining methods were simple: galleries were driven into the soft sandstone, pillars of rock being left to support the roof at intervals. The marks of metal chisels are still visible on the walls and dolerite hammers which were used to crush the stone and extract the turquoise nodules still lie about.[7] Beads of turquoise have been found in predynastic tombs,[8] and the four bracelets from the tomb of King Djer at Abydos are partly composed of beads and amulets of this stone.[9] In one of the inscriptions set up by order of Djedkare Isesi in the Fifth Dynasty, it is said that the god (Thoth) 'caused the costly stone to be discovered in the secret mine, by means of the writing of the god himself'.[10] Turquoises tend to lose their colour with age, and the frequency of the search for 'new turquoise' was prompted by the desire to obtain gems of the finest colour for royal jewellery and the trappings of the gods. Expeditions of such importance were led by high officials, frequently the Treasurer of the God[11] and the treasury staff, often listed in the inscriptions; the leaders and their retinue may often have gone part of the way by sea, as the presence of naval personnel such as

[1] §vi, 20, vol. i, no. 8. pl. v.
[2] §vi, 20, vol. i, no. 10, pl. vi.; vol. ii, 60.
[3] §vi, 20, vol. ii, 3 ff.   [4] §vi, 9; §vi, 20, vol. ii, 1 f.
[5] § vi, 20, vol ii, 41 f.
[6] §v, 14, 212, 460 f.; §vi, 20, vol. ii, 9.
[7] §vi, 34, 49 f.   [8] §v, 14, 404; §v, 2, 27, 41, 56.
[9] §vi, 35, vol. ii, 16 ff. and pl. 1; §vi, 11, 229 and fig. 133.
[10] §vi, 20, vol. i, no. 13, pl. x.   [11] §vi, 20, vol. ii, 64.

a ship's captain, a pilot and an overseer of ships' crews suggests;[1] probably they crossed the desert to some port on the Red Sea coast, perhaps El-Quseir, as expeditions to Punt were accustomed to do;[2] the discovery of a small Egyptian port, apparently of New Kingdom date, at El-Markhā' on the coast of Sinai south of Abu Zenīma suggests a possible point of disembarkation.[3]

Whether or no the ancient Egyptians at this early time mined copper in Sinai is a matter still under dispute.[4] This metal was already in great demand in the Early Dynastic Period—the great tombs of the First Dynasty at Saqqara contained large quantities of copper objects, and ingots were probably intended to furnish the dead with a continuous supply of fresh arms and tools in the afterlife.[5] There are deposits of copper in the eastern deserts of Egypt and in Nubia,[6] and 'Asiatic copper', imported on a large scale from Syria in the New Kingdom,[7] may have found its way to Egypt through Byblos or some other port as yet undiscovered. Sinai itself is rich in copper ores, though the valleys of Maghāra and Serābīt el-Khādim, the scene of Middle Kingdom turquoise mining,[8] do not themselves show signs of having contained large deposits. Yet in and around the huts of the miners in the Wādi Maghāra, among pottery of the Old and Middle Kingdoms, were found large amounts of copper slag, chips of ore, crucibles and part of a mould for an ingot;[9] and huge slag heaps in the Wādi Naṣb and the Wādi Bābā, where there is water and a little vegetation, suggest that at some ancient time the ores must have been taken there for smelting, where fuel was more easily obtainable.[10] Only once in a Middle Kingdom inscription is reference made to 'turquoise and copper' as the dual objects of an expedition to Sinai,[11] yet the presence of a 'controller of copper' on the staff of Isesi's expedition[12] suggests that though turquoise was the main aim of these expeditions, and the only commodity worthy of so distinguished a mission, copper also was worked, perhaps by slave labour locally recruited.[13]

A little of the copper must have been brought back to Egypt

---

[1] §vi, 20, vol. ii, 11 f., 14, 63 f.
[2] §v, 25, 11 f.; §vi, 26, 121 ff.; §vi, 20, vol. ii, 12 f.
[3] §vi, 20, vol. ii, 13, n. e.   [4] §v, 8, 15; §vi, 20, vol. ii, 3 ff.
[5] §vi, 12, vol. i, 20–57; §vi, 40, 81 f.
[6] §vi, 26, 136; §v, 14, 55; §vi, 15, 10 f.
[7] C.A.H. ii[3], ch. x, sect. v.   [8] §vi, 20, vol. ii, 5 ff.
[9] §vi, 34, 51 ff.; §vi, 15, 56 ff.
[10] Ibid. 18, 27 f.; §vi, 20, vol. ii, 5; §vi, 4, 13; §vi, 5, 580 f.
[11] §vi, 20, vol. ii, 66, no. 23.   [12] Ibid. 15, 61, no. 13.
[13] §v, 8, 15; §v, 31, 564.

for other purposes: the ores malachite, chrysocolla and azurite were used as a colouring medium for glazes and glass,[1] and malachite, in spite of its rich green colour only very rarely used for beads and amulets,[2] is found commonly in ancient Egyptian graves from the Predynastic Period onwards, ground into powder for use as an eyepaint.[3]

There is no evidence that the mines at Serābīt el-Khādim to the north-east of Wādi Maghāra were worked during the Old Kingdom, save the life-size figure of a hawk in grey marble inscribed with the name of Sneferu.[4] This king was later regarded as the patron of a region he may have been the first to open up; alternatively, the figure may have been brought from elsewhere when, in the Middle Kingdom, Serābīt el-Khādim began to replace the Wādi Maghāra as the main scene of Egyptian mining enterprise.[5]

Beyond the Sinai desert lay Palestine, where already in the Early Bronze Age there were prosperous settlements that deserve the name of towns,[6] surrounded by fields and vineyards; cattle were pastured and fruit trees and olives cultivated.[7] The road thither, called by the Egyptians 'The Ways of Horus', started at the frontier fortress of Sile, the modern Tell Abu Seifa near El-Qantara, and crossed the waterless stretch of desert, following the line of the salt lagoons, to El-'Arīsh (Rhinocolura) and thence to Gaza.[8] The journey was arduous and full of dangers, yet travellers made it from very early times. Commercial relations between Egypt and Palestine during the Early Dynastic Period have been discussed in an earlier chapter.[9] Handled pitchers of red-burnished pottery with a stump base, known to some archaeologists as the Abydos vase from its prevalence in First Dynasty tombs, have been found on Palestinian sites of the second Early Bronze period, when they appear to have been objects of frequent commercial interchange.[10] An archaic cylinder seal found in the plain of Sharon[11] and a crude attempt at writing the name of King Narmer on a sherd from Tell Gath found with pots of Egyptian shape[12] are further evidence of contact. Trade must have continued during the Old Kingdom. At 'Ai, in the southern part of

---

[1] §v, 14, 160 f., 188 f.
[2] *Ibid.* 400.
[3] *Ibid.* 80, 210; §v, 2, 41; § v, 22, 43.
[4] §vi, 20, vol. ii, 24, 82 f.
[5] *Ibid.* 83; see below, pp. 539–40.
[6] G, 14, 102 ff.; G, 1, 74 ff.; see below, pp. 568 ff.
[7] See above, pp. 225 ff.
[8] §v, 8, 323 ff.; §vi, 19, 114 f., pl. xiii; §vi, 26, 190 f.; §v, 34, 46.
[9] See above, pp. 45–7.
[10] §iv, 3, 353 f.; §vi, 25, 195 G, 1, 74.
[11] §v, 24, 233, pl. xxvi, no. S 1.
[12] §vi, 42, 193 ff.; §v, 34, 11 ff. See above p. 235.

the Jordan valley, alabaster and stone bowls of Egyptian work-manship were found in the temple sanctuary together with local imitations.[1] What, if anything, they had contained can only be surmised. In the other direction, however, evidence for trade is easier to find: pottery of Palestinian origin has been found in great quantity and variety on Egyptian sites of Early Dynastic and Old Kingdom date;[2] some of the vessels may have contained oil, or else wine or honey, all of which commodities were im-ported in considerable amounts at a later date.[3] It is possible that manufactured goods of a perishable nature such as linen and ivory were exported from Egypt in exchange.

The population of southern Palestine must also from early times have furnished the Egyptians with slaves. Reference in the Palermo Stone to the 'Smiting of Asia' in the reign of Djer,[4] the figure of a bound Asiatic (Setjety) in a fragment from the tomb of Qaa at Abydos,[5] together with Peribsen's epithet 'He who carries off Asia',[6] may refer to royal raids into Palestine which had as their main object the capture of livestock both animal and human. Some scholars would go further and credit the kings of the Egyptian First Dynasty with full-scale cam-paigns among the bedawin of Hither Asia,[7] but the evidence is as yet insufficient to warrant such a conclusion, and it must be remembered that in the Middle Kingdom, if not earlier, the peninsula of Sinai appears to have been included in the general term 'Setjet', the geographical designation of Asia in Egyptian texts.[8]

Evidence for military activity on the part of the kings of the Fourth Dynasty is lacking, but from the early Fifth Dynasty onwards it becomes clear that Egyptian armies were not con-fining their operations to defensive encounters with bedawin on the eastern frontier or to guarding the route to the mines of Sinai, but were raiding northward into the plain of Sharon and perhaps even further afield, in the northern half of the country where the most prosperous cities of the Early Bronze Age lay.[9] In the mortuary temple of Sahure, mentioned above[10] fettered prisoners

---

[1] G, 14, 116 ff.; §vi, 28, 19 and fig. 2; §iv, 3, 334. See above, p. 235.
[2] §v, 8, 31 ff.; §vi, 25, 195 f.; §v, 34, 6 ff.
[3] §v, 8, 414 f.; §vi, 25, 194, 201.
[4] See above, pp. 23–4. [5] §vi, 35, vol. i, pl. 17, no. 30.
[6] §vi, 35, vol. ii, pl. 22, no. 181. See now P. Kaplony, *Inschriften der ägyptischen Frühzeit* (Wiesbaden, 1963), ii, 764; J. Černý in *Ann. Serv.* 44 (1944), 295 ff. derived Stt 'Asia' from the name of a town in the eastern Delta.
[7] §vi, 41, 1 ff.; §vi, 42, 195 f.; §iii, 17, pl. 124; A, 2; A, 15. See above, pp. 45–7.
[8] §vi, 20, vol. ii, 2 f. [9] G, 14, 120 f. [10] See p. 35.

13

of Asiatic appearance, with long hair and pointed beards, wearing only short tunics and with a fillet bound around their forehead, are led by the gods in triumph. Their demeanour contrasts with the joyful appearance of the men, women and children in the neighbouring relief depicting the arrival of a seagoing boat, which we have suggested may represent a delegation from Byblos; these latter cannot be captives, since they are not bound.[1] Whether or not such scenes in the mortuary temples may be taken as historical is a matter of debate; some have thought that their purpose is rather to symbolize than to record actual events. Yet they are likely at this time to have had a background of historical fact, and the titles of officials of the later Old Kingdom confirm this assumption. An official of the early Fifth Dynasty named Kai-Aper is described in his tomb inscription as military scribe of the king in the Turquoise Terraces (i.e. Sinai), in Wenet, in Sefrer, in Tep'a and in Ida. Each place-name is written with the battlemented surround which designates a fortified stronghold.[2] He was therefore sent not only to Sinai, but also to fortresses one of which is mentioned as early as the Third Dynasty by a 'recruiter of desert guides to Wenet and all foreign countries'. Since it takes pride of place, Wenet may have been the first foreign stronghold that an expedition making for Palestine along the coastal road of the Ways of Horus would encounter; possibly therefore it is Raphia.[3] Later on, in the Sixth Dynasty, the word *wn.t* ceased to denote a particular place and became a general designation for the walled settlements of the Asiatics.[4] These settlements or towns are twice represented pictorially in tombs of the early Sixth Dynasty, that of Inti at Dishāsha[5] and that of Kaiemhesit at Saqqara.[6] Both are depicted as under siege by Egyptian troops. The incident may even have been the same, seen through the eyes of different artists, but a number of significant dissimilarities in detail would suggest that this is not so. The Dishāsha relief (Fig. 17), which is unfortunately much damaged, shows the fortress or walled town in ground plan as an oval, with rounded bastions at intervals.[7] Within the walls, a number of events are recorded in horizontal zones: the wounded are tended by their womenfolk, who support them as they fall fainting and pull out the arrows that pierce them; a

1 §v, 19, 194; §vi, 10, 174.   2 §vi, 14, 262; §v, 8, 24, n. 41.
3 §vi, 14, 263; §v, 8, 17.   4 §v, 29, part ii, 103, *l.* 12; §v, 8, 25 n. 42.
5 §vi, 33, pl. 4; §vi, 37, 182, 207, figs. 85–6; §iii, 17, 54 ff., 146. See. Fig. 12.
6 §vi, 36, frontispiece; §iii, 17, 55, 147. See, however, below, p. 536, n. 5 [Ed.].
7 §vi, 16, 81 n. 3.

bowman is breaking his bow, perhaps in token of surrender, in the presence of a woman and child; in one of the upper registers a seated Asiatic, who appears to be the headman, tugs at his forelock in grief while his wife and daughter, an old man and a child mourn with him. In a corner at the bottom of the scene, a

Fig. 17. The siege of a walled Asiatic town. Sixth Dynasty.
Tomb of Inti, Dishāsha.

man crouches listening to the sound of mining, but it is too late: the Egyptian sappers outside have all but succeeded in breaching the wall with their crowbars. Other Egyptians have erected a scaling ladder against the ramparts and are preparing the final assault. Beyond the walls, phases of a hand-to-hand combat are depicted. The enemy, transfixed with arrows, are in every case overcome by their Egyptian adversaries, and break their bows in submission; in the lowest register an Egyptian soldier drives before him a line of roped prisoners, at the same time carrying, slung over his shoulder, a young girl he has captured. The Asiatics are again distinguished from the Egyptians by their longer hair, falling to the shoulder and bound with a fillet, and their short pointed beards. The inscription accompanying the scene is unfortunately fragmentary; the name of the fortress appears to be one of several enumerated, perhaps Nedia, which is otherwise unknown.[1]

The siege scene in the Saqqara tomb is of a similar date but is painted. Here the wall around the village is drawn as a single line, without buttresses; in two places earth appears to be heaped against it on the inside to form a shelter, and behind one of them bulls, goats and perhaps donkeys are being driven, while fleeing men and women take refuge in the other, perhaps the entrance to a dugout or cave. A similar scene of confusion reigns among the townsfolk, who appear to be unarmed, and the listening figure is there again: he hears the blows of the attackers' axes as they stand on the rungs of a scaling ladder propelled apparently on wheels. The scene, somewhat damaged, was not photographed and the facsimile copy made at the time of discovery is open to doubt in some details,[2] but it seems certain that the defenders do not, as in the Dishāsha relief, wear beards; the suggestion has been made that Libyans and not Asiatics are depicted,[3] but the figures lack the characteristic sidelock and dress of that people.

In the years to come the Egyptians were to gain much experience of siege warfare in Palestine and Syria. The motive for their expeditions must largely have been greed for plunder, and especially for captives who would be brought back to slavery. The sight of Egyptian soldiery pillaging and laying waste their land must have become familiar to the Canaanites. In the causeway of the mortuary temple of Unas, Egyptians are shown in battle with the [Sha]su, a name later given to the bedawin of Palestine,[4] but the adversaries against whom Uni led his great expedition are called 'the Asiatics, Sand-dwellers';[5] the word Amu, which became the usual word for Asiatic in the Middle Kingdom and thereafter[6] and was applied by the Egyptians of the New Kingdom to the hated Hyksos, is here used for the first time. This was a full-scale invasion, if we are to believe Uni's account,[7] for it included levies from every district of Egypt and from the Nubian and Libyan auxiliaries as well, 'an army of many tens of thousands'. The army set out 'from the northern islands, from the gate of Imhotep and from the precinct of Horus Neb-ma'at';[8] none of these places can be located but it may be surmised that they lay on or near the eastern frontier and the

[1] §vi, 3, 9; §v, 8, 20.
[2] §vi, 37, 327.
[3] See below, p. 536, n. 5.
[4] §vi, 23, 38; §vi, 24, 180.
[5] §vi, 18, 96; §v, 29, part ii, 101, l. 9.
[6] See above, p. 351.
[7] G, 17, 228, n. 6; G, 4, i, para. 312 ff.
[8] §vi, 10, 207 f.; §v, 8, 18.

special connexion of Horus Neb-ma'at Sneferu with Sinai has already been noted.[1] It is clear, however, from what follows that the expedition was not bound for Sinai and that more was involved than a mere raid against desert tribes, for the victory hymn with which the account continues gloats over the fortresses (*wnwt*) of the Asiatics which were destroyed, the figs and vines cut down by the victorious army and the dwellings they set on fire.

> This army returned in safety,
> After it had killed troops in it by many ten-thousands.
> This army returned in safety,
> After it had taken troops in it, a great multitude as living captives.[2]

Besides the prisoners, the army may have brought back (though these are not mentioned) herds of the prized Palestinian cattle which figure in later accounts. Five times Uni went by land to quell 'rebellions' of the Sand-dwellers, and the sixth time his expedition went by sea. Landing to the north of the enemy, 'behind the heights of the mountain range', at a place called the Antelope Nose, he successfully cut their forces in half and annihilated them.[3] The location of this battle is in dispute: the most obvious promontory with which to identify the scene of his landing is the ridge of Mount Carmel.[4] There seems no reason to doubt, as some have done, that a campaign could have been conducted successfully so far from base.[5]

Uni's mission in Palestine was accomplished at the command of King Phiops I; it is the last of which we have information during the Old Kingdom. During the long reign of Phiops II the records are silent, though it would be reasonable to suppose that forays into Asia continued to bring their rewards, and the extent of the king's interest in Byblos is shown by the large number of objects bearing his name which have been found there.

The extent to which Byblos came under Egyptian influence during the Old Kingdom contrasts with the extremely small effect that Egyptian incursions into Palestine appear to have had upon material civilization of the population. Almost nothing Egyptian of late Old Kingdom date has been found on Palestinian sites. The reason is not far to seek. The Lebanon, the land of Negau,

---

[1] See above, p. 356.   [2] G, 17, 228; §v, 29, part II, 101 ff.

[3] §v, 29, part II, 104, 10 ff.; G, 17, 228, n. 10.

[4] §vi, 18, 96; G, 17, 228, n. 11; see above, pp. 192 and 236.

[5] §v, 9, 18 would prefer a location nearer home, Mons Casius not far from Pelusium, perhaps the sandy hill today known as Ras el-Qastrūn, near Lake Bardawīl. See §vi, 19, pl. XIII.

was a source of fruitful commercial partnership, a land whence they could obtain what they most desired, so long as they maintained peaceful relationship with the Byblite king and paid for his timber and resin. Palestine they plundered, bringing nothing with them and carrying off without mercy. The Egyptianization of Palestine began much later, when the country was exploited for other reasons, but the tradition of 'smiting the Asiatic' persisted not merely as a recurrent theme in art and literature[1] but as a political reality and a military necessity.

[1] Cf. below, ch. xxi, sect. i.

CHAPTER XVIII

ANATOLIA, *c.* 4000–2300 B.C.

IN a previous chapter[1] we have witnessed the development of native Anatolian neolithic and chalcolithic cultures and their subsequent destruction at the hand of barbarians with inferior culture-traditions in the west, whereas some measure of continuity of painted pottery traditions was observed in the south. We must now continue our narrative of the development of the Late Chalcolithic cultures in their later phases during the first half of the fourth millennium.

I. END OF THE LATE CHALCOLITHIC PERIOD

CILICIA

With the burning of Mersin XVI, that intrusive culture from the Konya plain—rich in pottery, architecture and metalwork—was, if not completely eliminated, at least greatly weakened. The badly documented second half of the Late Chalcolithic period (Mersin XV–XII)[2] is characterized by ever increasing eastern influences from North Iraq gaining at the expense of what survived of the Mersin XVI and local Halaf traditions. Mersin was refortified[3] in level XV *a* and these defences lasted through the next two levels (XIV, XIII) furnishing eloquent evidence for unsettled conditions. The stratigraphical record is almost certainly incomplete and lacunae are expected after the successive destructions of Mersin XIV and XIII.[4] Side by side with painted wares of local 'Ubaid type, grey burnished bowls occur, having red and black counterparts in Mersin XIV–XIII, at Tarsus and a number of other Cilician sites, as well as at Sakcagözü across the Amanus, at Tell esh-Shaikh in the 'Amūq and at Tepe Gawra in northern Mesopotamia.[5] These grey bowls are fashioned in imitation of stone vessels found in the same levels and the term 'Uruk' which is often applied to them, is not only erroneous, but would seem to be misleading, in so far as their context not only in Cilicia, but

---

[1] *C.A.H.* i[3], ch. VII.   [2] §1, 3, 155–91.
[3] §1, 3, figs. 95 *a*, 100, and §1, 12, 80 f., 86 ff.   [4] §1, 3, 175.
[5] §1, 3, 166, fig. 123: 14, 15, 17, 19, and §1, 12, 81.

also at Tepe Gawra is unmistakably 'Ubaid.[1] There is no reason
to think that they are not a local Cilician ware. This is further
suggested by the stratigraphical contexts in which they occur,
for in Mersin XIII and XII in 'post-grey-ware' deposits there
were found 'scratched or scraped' bowls together with late
local 'Ubaid wares.[2] These are also familiar from Tarsus, Tell
esh-Shaikh, 'Amūq E and from Tell 'Uqair and Grai Resh in
Mesopotamia, where in every case their stratigraphical position
corresponds with the late 'Ubaid period.[3] At Tarsus we find a
post-'Ubaid painted ware (locally called 'Late Chalcolithic')[4]
with striped and chevron-painted bowls, based not on 'Ubaid, but
on lingering Halaf influence. Associated with it are 'wheel-finished
plain slipped bowls', a ware common in Cilicia, the 'Amūq (F),
Grai Resh and Gawra IX and XI*a*, which thus appears to be the
real western equivalent to the Uruk period in Mesopotamia.[5]
This final chalcolithic painted pottery, which immediately preceded the introduction of the Early Bronze Age at Tarsus, is not
represented at Mersin.

There we find once again (in level XII) an intrusive element in
the form of a black burnished ware with new shapes, ornamented
with white-painted designs, occurring side by side with a persistent late 'Ubaid painted pottery.[6] The white-painted ware has
been found at no other site in the Cilician plain, but occurs at
Silifke and Maltepe in the Calycadnus valley,[7] which would
probably be regarded as the route by which this culture reached
Cilicia from the Konya plain, where, as we shall see below, most
probably is to be found its area of origin. Both the Mersin XII
and the 'Final Chalcolithic' culture of Tarsus were soon to be
submerged by a further wave of immigrants from the same area,[8]
who introduced the Cilician Early Bronze Age at a date which
would seem to correspond with the end of the Uruk or the beginning
of the so-called proto-literate period in southern Mesopotamia.

The 'prehistory' of the Cilician plain can then be summarized
on the basis of the evidence available as follows: populated in
early neolithic times by a people which had close links with the
southern plateau (Konya plain), this bond continued during the
following period, the Early Chalcolithic. Not only were imports
from the plateau found at Mersin, but perhaps some plateau-
influence was responsible for the development there. At the

---

[1] §I, 12, 81 and note 35.   [2] §I, 3, 174, fig. 113 and §I, 12, 81.
[3] §I, 12, 86 ff.   [4] §I, 12, 84 f.
[5] §I, 12, 87.   [6] §I, 3, 182 ff., fig. 118.
[7] §I, 7, 195 ff., fig. 164.   [8] §I, 12, 345 f.

beginning of 'Middle Chalcolithic', Halaf imports show trade with eastern neighbours and there may be some influx of easterners among the old population. Some trade with the Konya plain continued, as sporadic Halaf sherds found there show. Local Halaf tendencies seemed to outlast 'Ubaid influence in eastern Cilicia. This eastern influence is first notable on Mersin XVI*a*, with an intrusive culture from the Karaman area confined to western Cilicia. The 'Ubaid influence does not seem to have been direct, but was probably transmitted through the plain of Antioch, nor is there any reason to associate it with a new element in the population. Besides lingering local Halaf and 'Ubaid traditions, new wares appear spontaneously throughout Cilicia in the later phases of the Chalcolithic, and once more Mersin receives a northern culture in level XII. Finally a wave of migration from the same source overruns the whole of the Cilician plain and imposes an Early Bronze Age of southern Plateau type.

KONYA PLAIN

The Late Chalcolithic of the Konya plain, that large and fertile basin which periodically sent its overflow down the Calycadnus into western Cilicia, can be pieced together only from surface finds. We have already quoted the evidence for a culture alike and akin to that of Mersin XVI. It is not known when it was succeeded by another—abundantly represented by black burnished wares with white painted decoration, like Mersin XII—especially prominent in the western half of the plain.[1] The same shapes as occur at Mersin are found together with numerous others and the repertoire of patterns is likewise much richer. It is interesting to note that the flowing interlaced patterns of Mersin XII can be traced back in the Konya plain to the red on cream wares of Early Chalcolithic Çatal Hüyük West. Some red on cream wares lingered on into the Late Chalcolithic here, but there is no trace of any Halaf or 'Ubaid influence, nor of any grey bowls like those of Cilicia. At the eastern end of the plain there occur however some painted sherds that show affinity to the final chalcolithic striped ware of Tarsus, and the poorly executed white and red stripes on the earliest Early Bronze Age 1 ware, found both here and in Cilicia, may be a late reflexion. On the basis of an archaeological survey[2] it would appear that the area between Karaman and the Cilician Gates was the home of Cilician Early Bronze Age 1 before its diffusion into Cilicia, where it arrived fully

[1] §1, 7, 203 (map), 194 f.   [2] §1, 9, 32.

developed. The reason for these migrations is obscure, but the very large number (over one hundred) and especially the great size of Early Bronze Age (1–2) mounds in the Konya plain might conceivably suggest the possibility of overpopulation.

WEST, NORTH-WEST, AND CENTRAL ANATOLIA

Further west, the Late Chalcolithic of Beycesultan gradually developed without serious interruption. Phase 3 is marked by the disappearance of features matched in the Konya plain, such as had distinguished the previous phase, and by the first apparition of carinated bowls with concave sides,[1] which become the hallmark of the fourth and last phase of the period.[2] The latter are paralleled not only in the contemporary north-west, but also in various cultures of the southern Balkan Peninsula (Gumelniţa, Salcuţa, Vinča, Larisa), thus for the first time establishing firm chronological contacts with eastern Europe.[3] The earlier tradition of white-painted pottery is now—in marked contrast with neighbouring areas—distinctly on the wane in the south-west. In the north-west there is a definite increase in this commodity and the idea may well be responsible for the rise of 'graphite paint' in the Gumelniţa and Salcuţa culture of Thrace (even though the patterns employed there are very much their own). Phases 3 and 4 of Beycesultan may be considered as roughly contemporary with Kumtepe I a and b and Poliochni I, where white paint replaces pattern burnish. These cultures are now known to extend over the greater part of north-western Anatolia.[4] Of the architecture of the period very little has yet been learnt; rectangular houses in mud-brick without stone foundations, including the first example of hall-and-porch or *megaron* type are found at Beycesultan, which are surrounded by an enclosure wall after level XXI.[5] At Poliochni (I) in Lemnos[6] and at Emporio in Chios partly curvilinear huts were found. Burial customs are also badly documented; extra-mural burial would seem to have been the rule, and only in Kumtepe (I a and b) were some burials, other than those of children, found within the settlement.[7] Children were often buried in pots below the floors of houses or courtyards, but funeral gifts were few or non-existent.

Further east at Pazaryeri, west of Bozüyük, bowls show

[1] §I, 10, 47, fig. 4: 9, 10.
[2] §I, 8, 122 ff., fig. 4: 4, 7, 8, 9, 11.
[3] §I, 11, fig. 2.
[4] §I, 2.
[5] §I, 10, 41, fig. 2.
[6] §I, 1, 662, fig. 1.
[7] §I, 6, 49, fig. 24: 25.

affinities with Beycesultan's final Late Chalcolithic phase and at Yazır, east of Sivrihisar within the bend of the Sangarius river white-painted bowls and triangular arrowheads not unlike those from the Konya plain have come to light.[1] Both cultures may immediately precede the beginning of the Early Bronze Age. Much of the so-called Late Chalcolithic of Central Anatolia is really of Early Bronze Age date, contemporary with its first or even the beginning of its second phase; only Büyük Güllücek,[2] a hamlet of three houses set on a hilltop in the forests north of Alaca, and perhaps also the earliest pottery from that site itself,[3] can be considered as Late Chalcolithic in western and southern terms. If so, there must have been a hiatus between it and the earliest local Early Bronze Age material, which is of late Early Bronze Age 2 date.

At the moment it is virtually impossible to date the Büyük Güllücek culture. Many of its shapes—in dark burnished ware—are reminiscent even of Hacılar, decorated in two registers of incised patterns. Horned handles are common as at Alaca, Yazır, Kumtepe I a–b, Ayio Gala, Tigani, and the eastern Balkan cultures of Veselinovo-Karanovo II[4] and Komotini, but also in Hacılar I. None of these parallels are specific enough, nor are any of the sites which provide parallels geographically close enough to place much reliance on such, perhaps fortuitous or ancestral, resemblances. White-painted decoration, though rare, occurs on the inside of flat rimmed bowls[5] as at Beycesultan, the Konya Plain, Yazır and at some sites near Firaktin, south-east of Kayseri, which may perhaps be regarded as an extension of the Late Chalcolithic culture of the Konya Plain.[6] At Firaktin also, two wheel-made Late Chalcolithic sherds were found with 'Ubaid-like patterns painted in matt black on buff ware.[7] Other 'Ubaid-like wares are reported from Malatya (Arslantepe) and it is for future explorers to define the western limit of such southern wares in the Antitaurus. The excavations now in progress at Kültepe may be expected to offer an interesting contribution. The chalcolithic cultures of Pontic and Eastern Anatolia have not yet come to light in spite of recent archaeological surveys.

[1] §1, 15.
[2] §1, 4, 34.
[3] §1, 5, 152, pl. xxxiv a–b.
[4] §1, 13, 93 f., figs. p. 93.
[5] §1, 4, pl. xi (and xii–xiii, both sides).
[6] §1, 14, 69, pl. xvii below (dated too low!).
[7] §1, 14, 69 f., pl. xviii.

II. THE EARLY BRONZE AGE

INTRODUCTION

The period following the Chalcolithic is here conveniently called the Early Bronze Age, irrespective of the surmise that only a few cultures had mastered the art of making bronze. Copper undoubtedly was still the most commonly used metal, but the confusion created by the term 'Copper Age' has been most harmful in the past, and for want of a better label, 'Early Bronze Age' will be used throughout this and a following chapter (xxiv). Though the absolute chronology is discussed in a later section of this chapter, the subdivision of this long period must here be briefly sketched in order to eliminate—as far as possible—the different chronological terminologies in use, and the difficulties in fitting the numerous cultures of this vast country into one comprehensive chronological scheme. The Early Bronze Age has been divided into three phases: E.B. 1, 2 and 3, corresponding with the old Troy I, II and III–V scheme. This division can be seen on the simplified chronological chart (p. 404) which shows the relative chronology of the more important cultures revealed by stratigraphical excavation during the last thirty years. Of these the most important are Troy, Thermi, Poliochni, and Emporio for the north-west, Beycesultan for the south-west; Demirci Hüyük for the Eskişehir plain, Tarsus for Cilicia; Alaca, Alişar and Kültepe for Central, Dündartepe for Pontic, and Karaz and Geoytepe for Eastern Anatolia. Numerous other sites produced evidence for one period only (Ahlatlibel) or had incomplete (Mersin, Kusura, Polatli) or unpublished (Karaoğlan, Aslantepe) culture-sequences.

This system, first devised for Cilicia and adopted in the south-west for Beycesultan, works satisfactorily for the south and west of the country and for Eastern Anatolia and it is possible to fit in the Central Anatolian sequence. However, synchronisms between the West Anatolian cultures on the one hand, and Central, Pontic or East Anatolian are so few that precise correlations are difficult; nor do the length, the dates, or even the names of these respective periods necessarily coincide with corresponding cultures in the west of Anatolia. For instance, let us consider the Central Anatolian sequence. Roughly corresponding with E.B. 3 of West Anatolia (*c.* 2300–1900 B.C.) we have a local E.B. 3 or 'Cappadocian period', the initial date for which varies with each authority: *c.* 2300 (K. Bittel) or *c.* 2200 (T. Özgüç and the present author).[1]

[1] §II, 3, 64 f.

If the latter date is correct, the local E.B. 3 would start a century later than its corresponding phase in the west. The preceding phase—variously called 'Copper Age', Alişar I*b* period, Central Anatolian E.B. *A*—including the royal tombs of Alaca Hüyük is generally considered to be contemporary with Troy II. This is certainly correct, but no Central Anatolian site seems to show more than five building levels in this period—Alişar has five (11–7) and Alaca four (8–5). Now Troy has more than ten, and this suggests that the West Anatolian E.B. 2 culture (to which Troy II belongs) lasted considerably longer. If Central Anatolian E.B. 2 starts a century later than its western equivalent as well, it becomes clear that its beginning cannot be placed much earlier than the middle of Troy II. What precedes it, the so-called Central Anatolian Late Chalcolithic or Alişar I*a* (with three building levels at Alişar 14–12), cannot be much earlier than early E.B. 2 (early Troy II) in the west. This leaves little if anything in Central Anatolia to be contemporary with western E.B. 1, except Alişar 18–15 (with four building levels against ten at Troy I). This example clearly shows the difficulties involved in dating the cultures of Central Anatolia in precise terms and the same applies to the Pontic area and the east.

ORIGINS

It should be emphasized at once that the beginning of the Early Bronze Age was not marked by a sudden break from the previous cultures. Only in the Plain of Cilicia was it introduced by newcomers, but elsewhere it can be shown to have developed out of the Late Chalcolithic. What stimulated this development is far from clear, but it is evident that the first phase of the Early Bronze Age was one in many respects more prosperous and progressive than its predecessor. One suspects that it was a period of more settled conditions generally, and judging by the metallic appearance of most of the pottery, metallurgy may have taken great bounds forward. In the absence of royal tombs of the period, this surmise lacks proof and the simple graves of commoners are not normally provided with metal objects. No royal tombs are available until the second phase of the Early Bronze Age, but the contents of those are so astounding as to give unmistakable evidence of a flourishing metallurgy in E.B. 1. There are also other signs of this; for though all cultures seem to have shared in the new prosperity, north-western and Central Anatolia now become conspicuous for the first time in Anatolian prehistory, and both are extraordinarily rich in metal deposits.[1] There is certainly no decline in the regions which until now have claimed our attention, for the Cilician plain, though devoid of mineral wealth, had some of the richest alluvial soil in the country and controlled an important trade route. At one end of this was the Konya plain, hardly less fertile but commanding the two great silver mines of Bulgar and Bereketli-maden in the Taurus.[2] At the other end were Syria and Mesopotamia, both countries without any natural resources in metal. South-west Anatolia also was amply supplied with copper, iron, silver and gold and its cultural distribution shows that it controlled the Maeander route to the Aegean, the other (Hermus) route being in the hands of inland north-western cultures. Finally, all along the metalliferous coast and on the off-shore islands we find the purely maritime Troy I culture, the first to import tin and produce good tin bronzes. By the end of the Early Bronze Age, Anatolia was the metal market from which much of the metal wealth of Assyria (and no doubt also Syria) was obtained, and the technological resemblances between metal-work at Ur and that of Alaca and Dorak suggest that this had been the case long before. It would then seem that the great prosperity of Anatolia—at least during the first two phases of this period—was based mainly on the systematic exploitation of its metal wealth and on its ability to trade it to its neighbours, not only Syria and Mesopotamia, but Egypt, Greece, the Balkans and the Pontic steppe as well. Superimposed on a primarily agricultural economy, basically the same as that of the Late Neolithic period, but no doubt greatly improved, fully urban communities arose. These were probably organized under kings in numerous states—as the great capital cities testify—with a considerable proportion of the population engaged in extracting, working and exporting their mineral wealth, both by land and sea. Recent discoveries tend to show that, even though illiterate and organized for geographical reasons on a smaller scale than its neighbours in Egypt and Sumer, Anatolia possessed a material culture, displayed at some of its royal courts, which was second to none.

Another marked feature of Bronze Age Anatolia is a cleavage in culture between the west and south and the centre and east. This is marked not only in pottery, metalwork, figurines, buildings and other remains of material civilization, but is equally notable in burial customs, extra-mural burial being the rule in the west, intra-mural that of the east.[3] This difference, partly geographical—

[1] §ii, 2, *passim* and maps fig. 38 (gold), 42 (silver), 61 (copper) and 80 (iron).
[2] §ii, 2, 191.   [3] §ii, 1, 191 f.

the dividing line runs diagonally from the Gulf of Izmit, east of Ankara, and through the Salt Lake to the Amanus—is distinctive in the Early Bronze Age archaeology. Very little contact takes place across this boundary, as far as our present evidence goes, until the E.B. 3 period after the frontiers of the western culture provinces had been broken down by Indo-European newcomers. The difference is evidently not only geographical, but probably ethnic and linguistic. The only realm where the divergence may not have been so pronounced is religion, for at least until the end of the first phase of the Early Bronze Age, the entire population seems to have been of pre-Indo-European stock or rather speech, practising a type of agricultural fertility-religion in which a goddess played a predominant part. The figurines characteristic of such a cult are well-nigh indistinguishable in different cultures, but it does not follow that the rituals and customs were equally alike.

III. THE EARLY BRONZE AGE 1 PERIOD

About a dozen cultures of this period have already been identified in Anatolia, and, as excavation continues, one might expect their number to rise. Nothing definite is known, for example, of Pontic cultures of this phase, and the East Anatolian first phase of the Early Bronze Age and the so-called Late Chalcolithic of Alişar (18–15) are still badly defined. Westwards, on the other hand, not less than ten cultures are known, the location of five being marked on the sketch-map, p. 373.

THE NORTH-WESTERN GROUP

A group of closely related cultures, variants on a common scheme, and probably all descended from one Late Chalcolithic ancestor— the Kumtepe culture—occupied north-west Anatolia and the adjacent region of Turkish Thrace.

Within the circle of hills that surround the great plain of the Maritsa and Ergene rivers, but just across the Bulgarian border, lay Mikhalits,[1] the only excavated site of a culture that might be described as Thracian Troy I. From this bridgehead in Europe the north-west Anatolian peoples were in a position to create or influence an Early Bronze Age in the eastern Balkans.[2] Further south, in Anatolia proper, we find the Troy I culture with a purely

[1] §iii, 17, 7–25 and §iii, 8, 45 ff., pls i–ii.
[2] §i, 11.

coastal and maritime distribution, extending from the Troad[1] and the Thracian Chersonese[2] to the Karaburun Peninsula west of Izmir. The same culture is found in the Caicus valley,[3] and on the offshore islands: Lemnos (Poliochni),[4] Lesbos (Thermi),[5] Chios (Emporio)[6] and no doubt Tenedos and Imbros, still unexplored, as well. Moreover, it is likely that it also extended from the Thracian Chersonese westward, at least as far as the mouth of the Maritsa. The fertile plains of Akhisar and Manisa, the centre of later Lydia, were occupied by a very similar culture, which displays both Troy I and Yortan elements derived from its western and northern neighbours.[7] The latter culture,[8] with a marked riverine (Macestus valley) distribution, had its centre in the plain of Balıkesir with offshoots south to the plain of Gelenbe (Yortan), east to Simav and Kula and north to the great plains around the Mysian Lakes, south of the Sea of Marmara. North-east of the Yortan culture there was still another in the lowlands east of that sea and in the plains of the Tavşanlı and Köprüören, high on the edge of the Anatolian plateau (Tavşanlı-Iznik culture).[9] The members of this group are more closely related to each other than any is to its neighbours, namely the Demirci Hüyük culture in the Eskişehir plain or those of the south-west.

Understanding of the Troy I culture—by far the best known —has been much hindered by the delay in the publication of the material from a sounding at Kumtepe, excavated twenty-eight years ago. Properly stratified below early Troy I deposits (level I *c*) Kumtepe I *a* and *b* produced pottery ancestral to that of Troy (and not, as is often maintained, 'neolithic' or Sesklo-like wares). Similar wares have now also been found in the seven building levels of Poliochni I and at Emporio in Chios, as well as at the bottom of the Bayraklı mound. Recent field surveys show that it covered not only the region of the Troy I culture, but that of the Yortan and Akhisar-Manisa ones as well.[10] Moreover, very similar wares are found at Paros and Naxos suggesting a very extensive distribution.[11] Characteristic shapes of the period are shallow

---

[1] §III, 4, 35 f., fig. 415 (supplemented by exploration of Professor J. M. Cook in 1959 and N. Bayne in 1960). [2] §III, 9, 7–59.
[3] §III, 10, 76–101. Map, p. 76; §I, 2, 99 f., 112 ff.
[4] §III, 6, 196 ff., note 1 (p. 216).
[5] §III, 14, fig. 1 (supplemented by Professor J. M. Cook and N. Bayne).
[6] §III, 12, 44, figs. 1–2; §III, 5, 246, fig. 2.
[7] §I, 2, 112 ff. [8] §III, 2, 1–31; §III, 1, 156–64.
[9] Discovered by the author (1955, 1960) and not yet published.
[10] §I, 2.
[11] §III, 22, 51, fig. 55; §III, 23, 140, fig. 35. Naxos material unpublished.

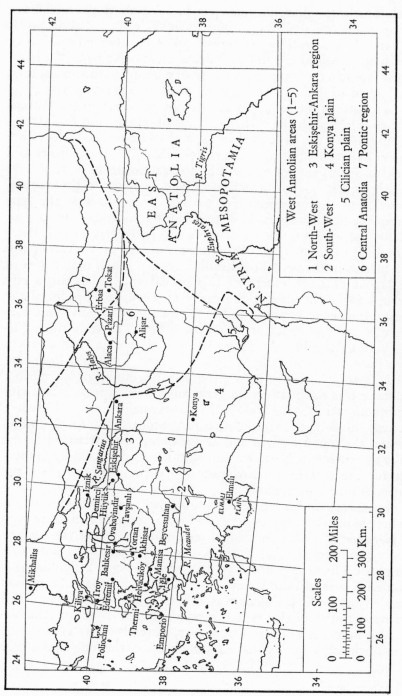

Map 9. Anatolia in the Early Bronze Age I period.

bowls on three tall cylindrical feet or on a short pedestal base, frequently adorned with openings in the side (I *a*), shallow bowls or plates with a 'roll or thickened rim' and tubular lugs (below rim) with or without a tall cylindrical stem—the so-called fruit-stands (I *b*). In the last phases the bowl with inverted rim appears, a hallmark of E.B. I. Jugs with beak and cutaway spout, so characteristic of the same period, are not yet in evidence. Pattern burnish, a link with the earlier cultures of Tigani and Beşiktepe,[1] is going out of use in Kumtepe I *a*, and white-painted decoration is rare on that site, but common at Poliochni (I).[2] Dark brown and blackish burnished wares are the rule, as during E.B. I.

Although it is Troy which has given its name to the culture, Poliochni on Lemnos may eventually take its place as the type site for the north-western E.B. I period, for, although we have an excellent stratified sequence of walls and pottery at Troy I, there is too little of either. The contemporary village of Thermi (about 100 metres in diameter) on Lesbos[3] gives a much better idea of the layout of a settlement of this period and Poliochni, a city perhaps twice the size of the castle at Troy, has produced the finest sequence of fortifications of this period. Emporio on Chios also was well fortified, but as at Troy little is known of the buildings within the walls. At Thermi only the last town (V) appears to have been surrounded by a wall, but both Troy and Poliochni were apparently fortified from the very beginning of the period. As stone was easily available great rubble walls rose, often with a pronounced batter, and perhaps originally crowned with a vertical mud-brick superstructure. Stout and solid towers flanked the narrow gates and at Poliochni slits occurred in the walls as at Mersin XVI, which could have been used by archers but for the fact that arrowheads are entirely absent from the Early Bronze Age armoury.

Houses are on the whole rectangular with the exception of the earliest house at Troy (level I *a*),[4] where a house of hall-and-porch or *megaron* type had an apsidal end, reminiscent of the oval or partly curvilinear houses of the Kumtepe period at Poliochni and Emporio. The next house (level I *b*)[5] was of normal hall-and-porch type with several raised platforms, such as may have been used for sleeping. On the floor was a hearth, and a pit served as a latrine. Houses of this type, characteristic for Western Anatolia are also found at Poliochni from level II (early Troy I) onwards. Less obviously *megaron*-shaped, but always of the long-house type

[1] §III, 24, 667 f.　　　　[2] §III, 6, 196.　　　　[3] §III, 14, plans 1, 2, 5, 6.

[4] §III, 4, fig. 425.　　　　　　　　　　　　　　[5] §III, 4, fig. 426.

and entered from the short side, are the numerous houses found in Thermi I–V. A second range of subsidiary rooms such as occurs at both Troy and Poliochni in the E.B. 2 period is not yet attested and may represent a later development.

Food was stored in large vessels or in clay-lined bins, raised or sunk in the floor. Further domestic arrangements as well as doors are often difficult to recognize in this stone architecture, which does not lend itself so well to preservation as mud-brick construction in the plains. At Thermi these houses were grouped in blocks, separated by streets and alleys. Most houses here would seem to have had a private courtyard in front, and they were lit by windows probably set rather high in the plastered mud-brick walls. Houses were one-storeyed and almost certainly had flat roofs, providing additional space for many domestic activities, such as drying of corn, grapes and other fruit, sleeping during the hot summers, etc. Pitched or gabled roofs are still almost confined to forested areas, where there was heavier rainfall and building in wood favoured such a construction.

Foundations of similar rectangular houses have recently been found in the Yortan settlement of Ovabayindir[1] and the same form of hall-and-porch house is seen in the shrine of level XVII (late Troy I) at Beycesultan in the south-western province,[2] suggesting that the architecture of Western Anatolia was much less varied than its pottery. Here we find the same arrangement with an open porch *in antis* with an open court in front. A door in the middle of the back wall of the porch led into the main room containing the altar with a raised circular kerb in front, bins for the storage of offerings in kind in the nearer corners, and with a door in the back wall leading into a further room, on the floor of which many ex-voto offerings were deposited. In the south-western province this *megaron* plan can be traced back to a level XXIV in the Late Chalcolithic period.[3] The architectural remains of all other Anatolian cultures of the E.B. 1 period are unfortunately either insufficiently known or await the spade.

Burial customs of the Yortan culture. Cemeteries of the Troy I culture, which practised extra-mural burial like all West Anatolian cultures, have not yet been discovered. The skeletons found at Hanay Tepe (B) in what is probably a Troy I stratum are often quoted as evidence for intra-mural burial.[4] It is noteworthy that all the adults, said to be brachycephalic (very unusual at this period) were found in 'earth-graves', whereas child burials—such

[1] §III, 1, fig. 24 (hearth not marked).   [2] §III, 15, 104, fig. 3.
[3] §I, 10, 41, fig. 2.   [4] §III, 24, 712 f., figs. 1540–1; §III, 20, 14, fig. 89.

as of course also occur at Troy—were put in pots or in stone or brick cists. As there is evidently a considerable stratigraphical gap between Hanay Tepe B (Troy I) and C (Troy V–VI), it is not inconceivable that the adult burials date from a period when the deserted site was used as a cemetery by another village. A site in the Balıkesir plain presents a good parallel; here Yortan graves are found in a deserted Late Chalcolithic settlement.[1] The evidence from Hanay Tepe is therefore inconclusive and does not prove the practice of intra-mural burial.

Burial customs of this period are best studied in the Yortan culture, better known from its cemeteries than its settlements, which remained undiscovered until a few years ago.[2] The only scientific excavation carried out here—at Babaköy[3]—hit a rather poor and badly plundered cemetery. Our information is therefore highly unsatisfactory as far as the arrangement of tomb gifts, chronology and social differences among the dead are concerned. Two types of graves are recorded; large clay burial vessels and stone cist-graves, but the latter are rare and may belong to the following period. The burial *pithoi* were arranged in neat rows[4] with their aperture facing east. The bodies were tightly contracted, and were laid on their left side with heads orientated east. A few pots, some articles of personal adornment, a dagger or an axe constituted the sparse funerary offerings. Sometimes, for lack of space, some pots were put outside the grave, which was closed by a vertical slab of stone the top of which projected above the ground level as a marker. The size of these cemeteries is unknown, but it is a fair estimate that some contained several hundred burials. The siting of a cemetery in relation to the settlement is not consistent, and their discovery, in each case, has been the result of chance.

The only other West Anatolian cemetery of about the same, if not a little earlier, date is that of Kusura A, again extra-mural and situated west of the site.[5] Its size is unknown, but fourteen graves were recorded. Again cist-graves are less common than *pithos*-burials (three out of fourteen). Bodies were laid in contracted position on their right sides, with heads orientated to the west. Funeral gifts are even more scanty and consisted of one or two pots only, often placed behind the head. In two cases, a pot was found outside the *pithos*, near its base.[6]

Child and infant burials, both in the Yortan area and in E.B. I

[1] Personal communication from D. H. French.
[2] Discovered by D. H. French.   [3] §III, 2, also §III, 1, pls. xxvi f.
[4] §III, 1, fig. 1, and §III, 2, fig. 3.
[5] §III, 26, 54–64, fig. 25, pl. IX.   [6] §III, 26, 57.

at Beycesultan are often touchingly provided with a feeding-bottle or juglet.[1] Most of the graves hitherto found are evidently those of the common people, but the finding in some of the graves of the Yortan culture at Ovabayindir of finely polished marble bowls, some nearly a foot in diameter, thin-walled with sophisticated profiles and tubular lugs,[2] suggests the presence of richer graves, for such objects are not to be expected in the possession of simple farmers. Evidently they were the products of a workshop of stonecarvers in some city as yet unidentified.

Metalwork. Finds of metal objects[3] are still comparatively rare for this period; bronze is known, at least in the north-west, but copper is still the more common material. Objects of silver are not frequent for the metal easily decays, and gold, rarely found except in tombs, is not likely to be brought on the market by peasant tomb-robbers. In the absence of royal tombs, it is as well not to rely too much on negative evidence, for, were one to judge E.B. 2 metalwork from the finds made in the settlement at Alaca (and not from the famous royal tombs) one could easily have come to the conclusion that metalwork, though known, had not reached an advanced stage of development. One important piece of evidence should not be overlooked, and that is the unmistakable derivation from metal prototypes of a large number of pottery shapes and decorative features. Such would not have arisen had actual metal vessels not been available and greatly admired. In the E.B. 2 period we are fortunate in having a fine set of such vessels and it is therefore not difficult to say which pottery vessels have such an origin.

The following weapons are found during this period: daggers, tanged and with a single rivet hole (Thermi I–IV, Ovabayindir,[4] at Beycesultan in the burnt shrine of level XVII*b*, Poliochni IV); daggers with three rivet holes (Thermi IV),[5] or with a strong midrib (Poliochni IV).[6] The slotted spear head appears first in Thermi IV[7] and a fine shafthole axe in Poliochni IV.[8] Curved knives (Thermi V and Kumtepe I*c*) and flat axes (Thermi, Poliochni IV and Edremit—thirteen in a hoard) also make their appearance. Among simple tools pins, including two with bird terminals (Thermi I), awls, needles, punches, drills and chisels (Thermi and Troy I) should be mentioned. A twisted tin bangle

[1] §III, 15, 122, fig. 3; §I, 12, 4.
[2] Private collection of H. Kocabaş in Istanbul.
[3] §III, 27, 84–125 (the only up-to-date study).
[4] §III, 27, fig. 1: 1–5. [5] §III, 27, fig. 2: 3. [6] §I, 1, fig. 8 (middle).
[7] §III, 14, pl. xxv, 32: 2. [8] §I, 1, fig. 10.

(Thermi IV) and copper wire bracelets from the Yortan cemetery complete the inventory of metal types. It should be noted that Thermi and Poliochni were rich in metal, obviously the result of trade, for both islands are without metal deposits.

Stone objects. Among objects made of stone, maceheads, battle axes (Troy, Thermi, Yortan, Alişar) should be mentioned, as well as marble bowls (Thermi, Troy I, Çiğle, Ovabayindir, Tepecik, Beycesultan XVII*b*), pestles in rock crystal (Beycesultan XVII*b*) and especially figurines. These are of several types; a crude flat form consisting of two more or less unequal discs,[1] sometimes incised with an owl-face, is best known from Troy, but also occurs at Thermi (where larger clay figurines are far more common)[2] and at Yortan. Next there is a flat type with long stalk-like head, represented by fourteen examples from Beycesultan XVII*b*[3] and one from Yortan, and a similar one with small disc-head and shoulders (Beycesultan XVII*b* and Thermi). A more plastically modelled form with legs, arms and head thrown back at a curious angle is known from a specimen from Thermi in the Mitylene Museum, another from Hanay Tepe, a third from Kiliya opposite Çanakkale, and by a pair found at Kozağacı in the Elmalı plain culture of central Lycia.[4]

POTTERY

The most outstanding product of this period, however, is its pottery, an intelligent study of which offers more opportunities for the definition of culture provinces and the establishment of origins, chronology, and trade-relations than any other material can provide in the absence of written records. Since all the pottery was made by hand, variants are common even within a single culture area, each site showing its own preference for types, colours and ornamentation. Unlike the Bronze Age cultures of Mesopotamia, Egypt, and Syria where pottery was degraded to a common kitchen ware, Anatolian potters tended to produce something that was not only useful but aesthetically satisfying as well. Hence the fine burnish which is essentially an Anatolian characteristic. It is ironic to observe that with the introduction of the potter's wheel in E.B. 2 the general standard in ceramic produce sharply declined and many of the finer wares continued to be hand-made.

The north-west. The five north-western cultures of E.B. 1 share a number of significant shapes. There is first of all the bowl with

---

[1] §III, 4, fig. 216.   [2] §III, 14, pls. xx–xxii.   [3] §III, 15, pl. xxviii*b*.
[4] §III, 24, 712, fig. 1551; §III, 18, fig. 125; §III, 29, pl. vii, 18 f.

inverted rim on a flat base or with a pedestal.[1] In the Troy I and Mikhalits cultures it has handles or more often tubular lugs, but in the Yortan, Akhisar-Manisa and Tavşanlı cultures tubular lugs are very rare and one or two vertically pierced knobs on the rim take their place. At Troy the tubular lugs are placed on the rim; in the Caicus valley and the Akhisar-Manisa region more often just below it. A second type of bowl, again often set on a pedestal,[2] has flaring sides and is descended from the Kumtepe I *b* predecessor with rolled rim. Now the rim is thickened and often bears incised decoration, filled with white chalk. At one point it broadens out into a rim lug, at Troy often decorated with a face.[3] Well below the rim a lug is set. In the Yortan culture this type occurs in a variant without pedestal and with pairs of rim lugs; at Mikhalits the body of the bowls also bears incised white-filled ornament. At Emporio in Chios wishbone handles take the form of rim lugs;[4] in the Tavşanlı region this type is not found, but further north it occurs again, though never decorated. A third type with incurving rim on three conical feet[5] is common in the Tavşanlı-Iznik region, but not in the Yortan area. It occurs at Troy I with or without feet and without feet at Mikhalits and Karaağaçtepe, where it has ribbed handles and is decorated with incision. These examples clearly show the individuality and versatility of the north-west Anatolian potters, each area producing its own variant of a shape common to all, but some more popular than others in each of these regions. The same applies to jugs; beak-spouted jugs[6] are common everywhere in the north-west in E.B. 1, but in the Yortan and Akhisar-Manisa culture the jug with cut-away spout[7] is just as popular, more so than at Troy. Another Yortan characteristic is the 'bird-vase', a metal type,[8] and a variant on the jug with cut-away neck. It does not appear at Troy I or Thermi, but a similar vessel was found at Emporio.[9] Funnel-necked jars[10] and tripod jars,[11] both provided with lids, are another Yortan characteristic without close parallels in the Troy I culture, but both areas share a number of pyxis shapes. A new set of these from Ovabayindir, provided with pedestals,[12] have no parallels in the Troy I culture, but are like similar vessels in the Cyclades. Lids are another common north-west Anatolian feature.

[1] §III, 4, 60 f., fig. 223*a* (A 12–13).

[2] §III, 4, 58 f., fig. 223*a* (A 6–7).   [3] §III, 4, fig. 257.

[4] §III, 5, 246, fig. 2 (top).   [5] §III, 4, 62–3, fig. 223 (A 16–17).

[6] §III, 11, pl. I, A 5, 24, 25.   [7] §III, 11, pl. I, A 11, 14, 21, 23, 31.

[8] §III, 11, pl. I, A 32.   [9] §III, 12, fig. 2.

[10] §III, 11, pl. II, 58, 60.   [11] §III, 11, pl. II, top row.

[12] Private collection of H. von Aulock in Istanbul.

Favourite decorative patterns differ as much as shapes from area to area; white-filled incised decoration is common in the Troy I culture, but more frequent at Emporio than at Troy or Thermi. It is extremely common at Mikhalits, where the designs are often impressed with rope, a technique not found in Anatolia proper. In the Tavşanlı-Iznik area the white filling is usually omitted and in the Yortan culture we find pottery both with and without it. Grooving and ribbing is less common at Troy than at Thermi and it has now been found in the Yortan area. White-painted ornament is most highly developed in the Yortan and Akhisar-Manisa cultures, and in the Troy I culture it is rare at Troy, not very frequent at Thermi, but common at Emporio. It has not been reported from Turkish Thrace, but occurs in the Tavşanlı-Iznik area. All over the north-west the pottery of this period is normally dark-coloured: black, dark-grey, brown and olive green predominate, whereas reds and buffs are rare. A cooking pot on three feet in coarse ware is a further link between them.

The south-west. The south-western pottery of this period is quite different and has a different Late Chalcolithic ancestry. Technically it is superior to the northern wares and large vessels, up to a foot high, have walls of not more than 0·3 cm. in thickness. All the pottery is highly burnished, except a class of coarse ware descended from the previous period. The predominant colours are jet-black, yellow-grey, orange, bright red and crimson, and mottled wares are very common. Lugs are almost absent—the north-western tubular lug is unknown—and broad strap handles are a characteristic feature. Decoration consists of horizontal, vertical or diagonal fluting or ribbing, the latter on small juglets only. Globular jars with short everted necks, tall-necked jugs with flat or faintly oblique rims, hesitant beak-spouted jugs (in contrast with the north-west) and cups with oblique rims are most typical. Among bowls shallowness is a characteristic and although a bowl with inverted rim occurs, as in the north-west, the rim is short and only faintly inverted. Horizontally placed handles are the only ones that occur. Metallic prototypes are particularly notable in this pottery.[1] Very characteristic are two-handled jugs decorated with reserve-slip areas filled with barbotine or fish-scale patterns. A quadruple cup on four feet is white-painted and certain jugs have parallels in the Yortan culture, its western neighbour. Different from the E.B. I of Beycesultan and the greater part of the south-western province just described is another group in the Elmalı plain, as yet known only from surface finds.[2] The fluting

[1] §III, 16, 121–2; fig. 3, pl. xxvii.   [2] §I, 7, 205–7, figs. 434–55.

so common further north is rare here, and most characteristic are shallow hemispherical bowls in pink, red, buff and grey colours like those of Beycesultan, but decorated with white-painted patterns. Multiple chevrons (as in the north-west) parallel hanging loops (like Hacılar I), and interlacing patterns (like Mersin XII and Early Chalcolithic Çatal Hüyük) are the most common decorations. Obliquely-placed handles, sharp beak-spouted jugs (often white-painted), collar-necked jars and tubular north-west Anatolian lugs occur here, strongly suggesting some contact with the north-west, perhaps by sea. This is further suggested by the figurines from Kozağacı, which have parallels only there.

The south (*Konya and Cilician plains*). The pottery of Southern Anatolia in this period is strikingly different. All over Western Anatolia the white-painted tradition survived from the Late Chalcolithic, but not so in the Konya plain and Cilicia. On the other hand, the red-on-cream Early Chalcolithic tradition appears to have weathered the Late Chalcolithic storms and continues in the Konya plain until the very end of E.B. 2. In Cilicia, however, it disappears during the first phase of the Early Bronze Age. Two distinct classes of pottery can be distinguished in these southern areas: a fine slipped and burnished ware descended from the Late Chalcolithic, and a new gritty stone-ware,[1] fired to a point where the grains of clay vitrified; the latter has no such ancestry. This pottery, called 'red gritty ware' in Cilicia and 'metallic ware' in the Konya plain,[2] is highly distinctive and often decorated with red and white stripes of paint during E.B. 1. Shapes are few and consist of globular-bodied jugs having long-necked beak-spouts with an oval orifice, globular jars with collar neck and two small lugs on the neck, and a variety of simple bowls. All three shapes often have omphalos bases. The upper part of jug-handles is frequently incised with dots and dashes. A coarse version of the same ware, intentionally scored or corrugated, the so-called scored ware,[3] is already found in the Late Chalcolithic of the Konya plain. In the E.B. 1 period it was exported to the west coast where it occurs at Heraion, Bayraklı(?), Helvacıköy-Hüyücek, Köylüce (Edremit) and Troy I. At the last site it is accompanied by an incised handle of 'metallic ware' and some painted sherds of the same fabric,[4] thus giving a glimpse of maritime trade along the Anatolian coast between the Troy I culture and the Cilician plain or Calycadnus valley.

The burnished ware,[5] plum-red, grey or black in colour, is

[1] §I, 12, 92–5; §III, 25, 130–1. [2] §I, 7; 191–4, figs. 95–147.
[3] §I, 7, 196; §II, 3, 82–3.   [4] §II, 3, 83.
[5] §I, 12, 95–6; §I, 7, 194, figs. 148–51.

again easily distinguishable from its western counterparts by its shade, the persistent crackled slip, and its own set of shapes, many of which betray the existence of metal prototypes. Flat-based bowls with flaring sides, deeper beakers, and shallow hemispherical bowls predominate. The latter are often very delicate and have black interiors with red, brown, or buff exteriors. Handles are placed both horizontally and vertically. Incision appears to be rare in the Konya plain, but is not infrequent in Cilicia. Disc and omphalos bases are common, but pedestals are rare. In Cilicia, eastern influence from the 'Amūq plain led to the introduction of wheel-made plain bowls,[1] which do not seem to have reached the plateau. In both areas the E.B. 1 developed without any significant break into E.B. 2.[2]

The Sangarius basin. Extremely little information is available for the beginning of the Demirci Hüyük culture[3] which extended throughout the plain of Eskişehir and the drainage basin of the Sangarius river in the north-western corner of the plateau.[4] The earliest pottery is mainly brown and black in colour and small cups and bowls predominate, usually rather shallow, as in the south-west and the south, with particoloured slips and much mottling. Small handles rising above the rim are characteristic for this area. Further east, in the Polatlı and Ankara regions, no remains of this period have yet come to light.

Central Anatolia. Only the 'Late Chalcolithic' of Alişar 18–15[5] and Alaca can be regarded as belonging to this period. A few sherds from Alişar, where the deposit was 20 ft. thick, were illustrated in the excavation report, and the finds from Alaca are still unpublished, so that little can be said here. Greyish buff, black, and some red-slipped or plain ware is accompanied by smoothed plain ware. Mottling, black interiors and rims, are frequent as in the south and in the Demirci Hüyük culture. A single sherd from Alişar 17 bore a sophisticated pattern of lozenges between parallel lines in faded grey paint on a cream surface. White-painted decoration is not found, and the most common form of ornamentation is red or white-filled incision or excision, a technique derived from woodcarving. This is most commonly found on the pedestals of fruit-stands, which sometimes bore a series of cut out triangular 'windows'. This is by far the most distinctive shape of the region, but bowls of simple shape, tall jars on pedestal bases, and jugs with horizontal mouths (never

[1] §1, 12, 97 (105–6).
[2] §1, 12, 346.
[3] §III, 3, 28.
[4] §III, 7, 181 (map), 184–5.
[5] §III, 19, 34–40, 52–75, 76.

beak-spouts) also occur. All these continue without a break into the next period. Fruitstands are also common in the Pontic region (Horoztepe, Tepecik, Kayapinar)[1] round Tokat and Erbaa in the valley of the Yeşilirmak, but their date cannot yet be firmly established. Others come from Pazarlı[2] and Alaca,[3] but they are not yet known from the Black Sea coast. The westernmost specimen was found at Halkavun north of Ankara, again in an undatable context. The relation between these fruitstands and those of the north-west in the preceding period needs clarification. For what it is worth one must record here the impression—open to correction by future discoveries—that the area within the Halys bend was somewhat behind the west and south of Anatolia in cultural achievement during the E.B. 1 period.

IV. THE EARLY BRONZE AGE 2 PERIOD

INTRODUCTION

The transition from the first to the second phase of the Early Bronze Age seems, on the whole, to have been a peaceful one without any drastic changes. Nevertheless, there are traces of violent upheaval in the north- and south-west of the country, where the Troy I culture was destroyed[4] and a north-western culture now spread over the former south-western province,[5] after the burning of Beycesultan XVII a. These two events are undoubtedly connected and it is tempting to link them with the introduction of local Early Bronze Age cultures in Thessaly and Greece, neither of which can possibly be regarded as local developments from the previous Late 'Neolithic' cultures. The establishment of the Macedonian Early Bronze Age, a Trojan offshoot, can be dated at the latest to this period, if it did not actually occur during E.B. 1. What caused this movement is still unknown, but the successive destructions of Troy I and II a, followed by a gradual change in culture both here and at Poliochni (at the end of level IV), the burning of Emporio, the desertion of Thermi, Bayraklı, Helvacıköy-Hüyücek, Bozköy-Hüyücek, and every other Troy I site on the Aegean coast between Edremit and the Karaburun peninsula, in the Caicus valley and the islands, suggests a catastrophe of some magnitude. In most cases these

---

[1] §III, 21, 60–1, figs. 72–7, 79–84, pl. xvi, 5 (Tepecik unpublished); §III, 28, fig. 14 b, and others in the British Institute of Archaeology at Ankara.

[2] §III, 13, pl. x.   [3] §I, 5, pl. xxxiii c (middle).

[4] §IV, 24, 29–30.   [5] §IV, 22, 114–15.

Troy I sites were not re-occupied until the end of the Early Bronze Age (Troy V) or the beginning of the Middle Bronze Age (Troy VI). Arguments for supposing that perhaps the Troy I culture continued at Troy longer than at the other type sites without a change or development are most unconvincing, especially as the number of building levels does not lend support to such an assumption. One can only suggest that the Troy I population fled, either inland or into the mountains or across the sea to other countries. The fortification of the last settlement at Thermi may be taken as evidence of some impending threat and the fact that the islands were as much affected as the coast suggests that the enemy, whoever he was, must have been seafaring. This immediately narrows down one's choice of enemy, and the most likely guess is that he came from the Thracian coast. Had Troy itself been unaffected one might have suggested that the Trojans were responsible for the upheaval, but two successive burnings at Troy make this very unlikely. It is interesting that Troy II pottery occurs only in the Troad, the plain of Edremit,[1] at Karaağaçtepe across the straits and at Poliochni (V).[2] The wealth of the two main sites of this culture (Troy and Poliochni) shows clearly that the Trojan kingdom alone survived the catastrophe which resulted in the disappearance of the Troy I culture. Events in Turkish Thrace are obscure and in the hinterland of north-western Anatolia the Yortan culture would seem to have been unaffected. Changes do, however, occur in the Akhisar-Manisa region, where a flourishing E.B. 2 culture has some (E.B. 1) coastal admixtures in its pottery shapes, suggesting the presence of refugees. Further east, Beycesultan XVII a went up in flames and though a number of features, such as the continuity of the sacred site of the shrine, immediately rebuilt in level XVI, and the persistence of a number of pottery shapes, clearly shows that the old population was not exterminated, the whole character of the south-west Anatolian E.B. 2 culture is different. North-western elements prevail now, and nearly every pottery shape has forerunners in the north-western province of the previous period. There can be no doubt whatsoever that the newcomers came from this area, and it is exactly in the Akhisar-Manisa region that the largest number of parallels can be found. From here a natural route leads up the Hermus valley (through its Cogamus branch) to the basin of Denizli, from which two passes lead to the south-western plateau. It should also be noted that the south-western province now encroaches on the previous

---

[1] Evidence collected in 1960 by N. Bayne.   [2] §IV, 3, 152, pls. XV–XVII.

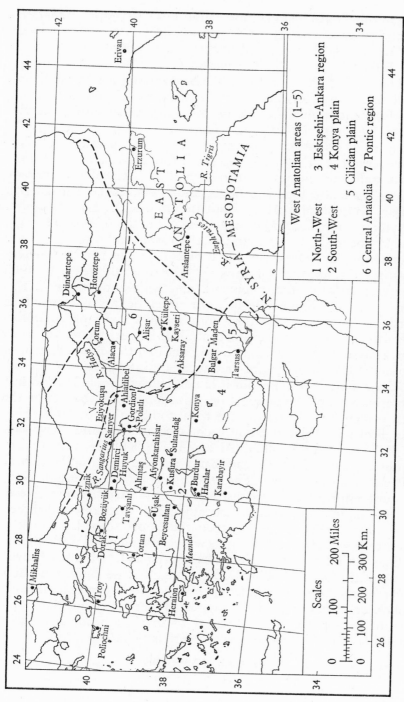

Map 10. Anatolia in the Early Bronze Age 2 period.

area of the Konya plain culture round Lake Beyşehir. A tentative identification of new ethnic elements involved in these migrations will be discussed at the end of this chapter together with those which terminated the E.B. 2 period.

The second phase of the Early Bronze Age marks the height of civilization at this period in Anatolia, the climax of the long development which started in the Late Chalcolithic. Architecturally the period is represented by the fortress of Troy II, the town of Poliochni V, the series of shrines (or rather temples) in Beycesultan XVI–XIV, the small fort of Ahlatlibel, and the town wall and houses of Tarsus E.B. 2. Remains of private houses were also found at Beycesultan XIV–XIII, Kusura (B), Alişar, Kültepe and Alaca (both unpublished). Even Demirci Hüyük was fortified. The 'treasures' left in the ruins of Troy II *g* and Poliochni V, those found in the royal tombs at Dorak and Alaca Hüyük, the less spectacular finds from the Yortan cemetery Ovabayindir, and the cist graves of Ahlatlibel all present a much clearer picture of the metalwork and wide-flung trade of this period, than it is possible to form either before or after. It is particularly noteworthy that both main schools of Anatolian metalwork (north-western and central, or Pontic, Anatolian) are of purely local origin, probably owing nothing to Mesopotamian or Syrian, still less to Cypriot or Caucasian, influences.

Texts are still absent, but it is nevertheless possible to form a tentative idea of the political organization of the country on the rich evidence presented by the royal tombs, the royal fortresses like Troy and Ahlatlibel, and such large and important city-sites as Poliochni, Beycesultan, Alaca, Alişar, Kültepe and Tarsus. From these it would appear that a number of kingdoms, both large and small, existed. The wealth and power of certain kings is most impressively demonstrated by the quantity and size of objects in such exotic materials as lapis-lazuli, turquoise and amber, which accompanied them in their tombs or escaped the sack of their towns. Rich burials of queens suggest an equal position, but it does not follow that society was matriarchal. At Alaca Hüyük some of the persons richly buried are said to be brachycephalic,[1] whereas the normal population of Anatolia was predominantly dolichocephalic. It has been suggested that the ruling class there was of foreign stock, but even if so they were not necessarily speakers of Indo-European, as recently suggested.

[1] §III, 20, 127, note 364.

ARCHITECTURE

Elsewhere the present writer recently attempted to give a coherent account of the architecture of Troy II[1] and a few remarks about the town of Poliochni V must here suffice.[2] This city, twice the size of Troy II, shows in this period evidence of organized town-planning; a main street, about two-hundred metres long, runs in a north-south direction through the settlement, linking a number of squares, each provided with a fine stone-lined well. Houses are grouped in blocks or *insulae* on either side of the road, some blocks consisting of a single large house or several smaller houses. A fair-sized dwelling consists of a hall and porch with a court-yard in front and a row of subsidiary chambers along one of the long sides. Really large houses have several rows of such rooms with subsidiary courtyard and a gatehouse and other rooms grouped around the main courtyard as well. A large and free-standing *megaron* in the main square evidently was used for public functions and it invites comparison with the large *megaron* (A) in Troy II, which probably served a similar purpose. Other public buildings of Poliochni V include an enormous granary, and a 'theatre' or rather assembly-hall with a series of steps occupying the full length of its longer side. Although it is nowhere expressly stated, one assumes that the city was still fortified.

The relation between royal castle and main town of the hypothetical Trojan kingdom would seem to be reflected in the Ankara region by Ahlatlibel and Karaoğlan. Ahlatlibel[3] is a fortress dominating the road which passes over the windswept ridge separating the plains of Ankara and Gölbaşı; Karaoğlan lies in fertile land east of the Gölbaşı lake. Even if the pattern is the same, the scale is different. Troy II measures *c.* 125 metres in diameter, Ahlatlibel not more than forty; Poliochni V has a diameter of *c.* 250 metres, Karaoğlan not more than 150. As only the foundations of Ahlatlibel have survived, the absence of doorways on the plan makes an interpretation somewhat subjective, if not impossible. Many small chambers suggest storage and one wonders—on analogy with the fort of Hacılar I—whether what one sees now is not just the basement of a building with at least two floors. Again the walls would seem to be too thick for the small rooms they enclose and the absence of doorways is also compatible with this view. In a number of these chambers cist

---

[1] §IV, 25, 131–62.
[2] §IV, 25, 154, figs. 11–13; §IV, 4, 198–203; §IV, 3, 146–51.
[3] §IV, 14, 6–12.

and *pithos* graves[1] were found with comparatively rich burial gifts, among which weapons (swords, daggers, and battle axes) predominate. This habit of intra-mural burial is in marked contrast with the lack of burials in the Karaoğlan settlement. Does this imply Central Anatolian rulers? Not necessarily so, for the Alaca Hüyük cemetery was probably extra-mural like its successor and counterpart at Horoztepe.[2] Culturally the Ankara region can still be regarded as a part of Western Anatolia, even though it lies on its eastern border. At Polatlı also, a few intra-mural burials were found, over one of which, in level 6, fragments of a round building were found in level 8, itself replaced by a stone circle in level 9.[3] Enigmatic round buildings of uncertain use were also found at Etiyokuşu, but apparently not associated with burials.[4] Houses in this region, as well as in Central Anatolia, consist of several small rectangular rooms, but grouped without any formal pattern such as is observed in the north-west, south-west and Cilicia. At Beycesultan the few houses recovered consist either of suites of rectangular rooms (level XIII), as in Kusura B,[5] or of buildings of the already traditional hall-and-porch type (level XVI). Not enough of these was excavated to enable one to say whether they stood by themselves as at Troy II (except IIg) or had the familiar row of subsidiary rooms (Poliochni V, Troy IIg), possibly represented in Beycesultan XIV. By far the most important contribution of Beycesultan to E.B. 2 architecture lies in its unique series of shrines or temples.[6]

The twin temples of Beycesultan XVI–XIV, varying in length from 15–17·5 metres, are of hall-and-porch plan, modified by the addition of a back room. Built up against the north enclosure wall they faced south into the settlement and into courtyards provided with ovens and storage bins or clay-lined rectangular pits (XV and XIV). In the earliest shrines of the period (level XVI) provisions were made for ovens inside the temples, presumably a somewhat inconvenient arrangement which was subsequently abandoned. Each of these temples was equipped with an 'altar' consisting of two stelae with a raised block of mud-brick behind (solid in XVI, box-like in XV, and containing storage jars in XIV). One of these was meant for the storage of liquids and provided with an overflow channel, whereas the other, used for solids, was provided with a stone lid. In front of the two stelae

[1] §IV, 14, 88–100, pls. VIII–XII. [2] §III, 21, 53.
[3] §IV, 21, 25–7, fig. 2. [4] §IV, 11, 30, figs. 39, 41.
[5] §IV, 19, 220–8, figs. 2–4.
[6] §IV, 22, 104–6, figs. 3–5, pls. XIXb–XXII.

stood a pair of horns of consecration, axially placed and standing at the back of a raised circular kerb, which can be either single or double in the 'male' temples. A post stood in line with this on the opposite end of the outer circle. The temples were built of mud-brick, carefully plastered over, and finally covered with a slaty blue paint. Directly behind the altar a screen, probably of mats or textile hangings strung between a series of wooden posts, sheltered the inner sanctum from the profane gaze of worshippers. The 'female' shrine is always provided with a 'blood-altar' for slaughter and a bench in the north-west corner (except in the earliest shrine in XVI). Wheat, barley, lentils, bitter vetch, and grape pips were found in these temples, especially in the 'female' ones. Some were found *in situ* in vessels, others in great clay storage bins. Woven mats and felt covered the floor. Clerestory lighting is suggested for the 'female' temple of level XV.

These are the only temples of the Early Bronze Age excavated in Anatolia, and as such they are of unique importance. As each of these was burned and a ritual taboo evidently forbade the removal of offertory deposits (except perhaps metal objects?) a rich collection of pottery was found in each. Continuity of cult between the E.B. 1 and 2 periods is most marked at Beycesultan, and the later temples find their prototype in the E.B. 1 shrine of level XVII.

At Tarsus the excavation of a quarter of the fortified E.B. 2 town gives one a vivid glimpse of contemporary building in Cilicia.[1] A fine series of private houses and the remains of two successive town walls with gate are sufficiently different from their north-west Anatolian counterparts to deserve special attention. The E.B. 2 houses of Tarsus are oblong in shape and entered directly from the street. A doorway normally leads into the main room with a built-up hearth, sometimes screened from the doorway. There may be a bench or seat near the hearth and at the back of the room one or more doors lead into a second room, sometimes subdivided into two chambers. Variations occur on this arrangement and one of these houses (no. 115) is provided with a portico, main room, and a back room with a bench running along three sides. From the contents the excavators believe that it was a tavern.[2] These houses probably were two-storeyed.

The hall-and-porch or so-called *megaron* type of house does not appear at Tarsus until the E.B. 3 period, when there is abundant evidence for an intrusive culture from the north-west. The first city wall of E.B. 2 Tarsus was thrown up in a hurry and consisted

[1] §1, 12, 12–32, plans 4–9. [2] §1, 12, 18.

of short stretches of mud-brick walling going diagonally through a series of earlier and condemned houses. As a result of this rather careless alignment both outer and inner faces are marked by a series of offsets and it is interesting that the second town wall was constructed in the same way, though this time without any apparent justification for its irregularity. The gate in this second town wall was L-shaped (that is, making full turn to the right) and approached by a long ramp leading up the side of the mound. Wooden beams were used as a foundation. The use of beams forming a framework for the mud-brick superstructure is a feature first recognized in Troy II and occurs sporadically at Beycesultan in this period, but becomes increasingly more popular in the following periods.

As no Early Bronze Age site in the Konya plain has yet been excavated little more can be said about the E.B. 2 phase there. But numerous large towns often with raised citadels appear to have been fortified, and it can be assumed that by now this was the rule all over the country.

BURIAL CUSTOMS

No change in burial customs is observed and new finds from the cemetery of Ovabayindir show conclusively that the Yortan culture continued during this period.[1] The discovery of two royal tombs of this culture at Dorak above Lake Apolyont[2] and that of thirteen at Alaca Hüyük[3] illustrate not only the differences in royal funeral customs, but also the completely different character of north-western and Central Anatolian cultures in general. A comparison is therefore most instructive. Whereas the Dorak tombs are stone cists measuring 1·8 × 0·83, and 3·10 × 2 metres, the Alaca tombs are dug into the soil and only occasionally lined with stone. Some are as much as 6 or even 8 metres long and 3·5 metres wide. The former were covered with several stone slabs, the latter with beams on which there were ranged rows of ox heads and feet, the remains of a funerary meal. The Dorak tombs, situated on a mountain spur, had no superstructure, but the Alaca tombs, placed in a crowded cemetery on the edge of the mound must have had markers. In the western tombs the dead lay either extended on their back (tomb I) or crouched on their right side with heads oriented to the east (the normal Yortan practice). In the Alaca tombs the dead were placed in a contracted position in the north-western corner of the grave, on their left side with heads to the

---

[1] §III, 27, 98–9, fig. 1: 13–14; cf. IV, 26, figs. 17, 19.
[2] §IV, 26.   [3] §IV, 1, 15, and 16.

west.[1] The Dorak skeletons faced north towards the lake, those at Alaca looked south. No traces of textiles, mats, etc. have survived in the damp tombs of Alaca, but at Dorak the king in tomb I lay on a decayed woollen *kilim*, and the king and queen in tomb II lay on rush matting. A number of casings in gold and silver at Alaca are usually interpreted as belonging to the poles of a baldaquin[2] and copper legs in the form of 'human boots' or the so-called 'lituus-end'[3] may be interpreted as legs of tables. The vast open spaces of the Alaca tombs suggest that a greater number of perishable objects, such as wooden furniture, textiles and bedding, may have been deposited, no trace of which now remains. Some decayed wooden furniture (tables or trays?) was found in tomb II at Dorak, but the most remarkable find is that of the fragments of a wooden Egyptian chair the gold casing of which bore in Egyptian hieroglyphs the name and titulature of Sahure, the second king of the Fifth Dynasty of Egypt (*c.* 2494–2345 B.C.), found in tomb I.[4] Characteristic for the Alaca (as well as the later Horoztepe) tombs is the constant interment of ritual paraphernalia with the dead; statues of bull and stag,[5] standards with animal statues[6] or geometric ornamentation,[7] such as is quite foreign to north-western Anatolia. In the Dorak tombs no ritual objects were found at all; instead only articles of toilet and personal adornment accompanied the queen and weapons the kings. These same classes of objects are of course also found at Alaca, but queens' burials often have figurines. Pottery was found in both groups of tombs, but stone vessels such as occur at Dorak and at Ovabayindir are not found at Alaca or Horoztepe. Metal vessels were even more common at Alaca than at Dorak and are of larger size, and both kings and queens at either site were buried with sceptres, as an emblem of authority.[8] Dorak is chiefly remarkable for the number and quality of its weapons: swords, daggers, battle axes and spears, the same armoury as at Alaca, but of different types. Both sites produced a number of ceremonial weapons: a macehead of gold at Alaca, of amber and turquoise at Dorak; two iron daggers at Alaca,[9] one iron sword and one dagger at Dorak,[10] etc. It is significant that at Alaca the metal-

[1] §IV, 16, pls. VII–IX, CXCI.   [2] §IV, 16, pl. CLXXXI.

[3] §IV, 16, pl. CLXXX.   [4] §IV, 26, fig. I.

[5] E.g. §IV, I, pls. CCII–CCV; §IV, 16, pls. CXXX, CL, CLXII, CLXXIII, CXCII. See Plate 39.

[6] E.g. §IV, I, pls. CXCVI, CXCIX, §IV, 16, pls. CLI, CLII, CLXXIV, CXCIII. See Plate 39.

[7] E.g. §IV, I, pls. CXCII, CXCV; §IV, 16, pls. CLXIV, CXCIV. See Plate 39.

[8] §IV, 26, fig. 12; §IV, 16, pl. CLXXXII, I, 3.

[9] §IV, 15, pl. CII; §IV, 16, pl. CLXXXII, 4.   [10] §IV, 26, figs. 20, 21.

worker's greatest skill is displayed in objects of a religious nature, whereas at Dorak his interests are profane, that is, in weapons and jewellery.

METALWORK

At Alaca several standards were cast by means of the *cire-perdue* process, and the techniques of hammering, casting in closed moulds, *repoussé* work, raising and sinking metal vessels were fully understood in both regions. Patterns were chased with a chisel (not engraved), metal inlay was practised, and sweating and soldering were familiar to both schools of metallurgy. At Troy and Dorak we find further goldsmith's techniques extensively used, that of granulation, filigree and *cloisonné* in granulation. Whereas rivets are common on weapons they are never used on metal vessels, where soldering or sweating takes its place.

The following metals were freely used at both sites and at Troy; copper (or bronze?), bronze (Troy), iron (not at Troy, probably by accident), gold, silver, electrum, and lead (Troy). All these metals are native to Anatolia, but tin had to be imported. Among various stones rock crystal, carnelian, jasper, nephrite, obsidian and meerschaum (Dorak) are native products and faience was also locally made. But ivory and amber, lapis-lazuli (Dorak and Troy), and turquoise (Dorak) must have been imported, the first probably from Egypt, the second from the Baltic (obtainable in the Usatova culture near Odessa),[1] the third from Badakhshān in eastern Afghanistān and the last either from Nīshāpūr in Khurāsān (East Persia) or from Sinai. These last four materials have not been found in the Alaca tombs, but that does not of course mean that they were unknown there. Possibly Alaca, an inland site, had less contact with foreign parts than the maritime cultures of Troy II and Dorak, which evidently—note the ships and the dolphins[2]—were much engaged in the exploration of the Black Sea as well as the Eastern Mediterranean. This, probably more than anything else, laid the foundations of their wealth, and contact with the northern barbarians in the Pontic steppe may have acted as a stimulus to the foreign invasions which put a catastrophic end to these cultures at the end of the E.B. 2 period.

It has recently been suggested that the objects from the Alaca tombs were not of local but of Pontic manufacture[3] and it is suspected that the foreign dynasty of Alaca may have been

---

[1] §IV, 7, 145, for dating see §I, 11. [2] §IV, 26, figs. 2, 18*b* and *e*.
[3] §III, 21, 59.

natives of that region. Attractive as that theory is, more proof is needed and the discovery of earlier graves at Horoztepe is therefore eagerly awaited. In the case of the Dorak tombs nothing suggests the presence of foreigners, and the bodies found there were dolichocephalic like those of their subjects.

The warlike character of the E.B. 2 cultures is emphasized by the material from lesser tombs; swords and daggers were found at Ahlatlibel together with battle-axes and at Tekkeköy on the Black Sea a cemetery with extended burials (like the king in tomb I at Dorak) was well equipped with daggers.[1] Others, to the number of at least a dozen were found in graves at Ovabayindir.[2] These were all of the Dorak type and one was plated with lead. From the same cemetery comes a crescent axe of southern provenance or inspiration.[3] Other daggers of this period come from Polatlı, Yazilikaya, Yelten and Karabayir, the last two being sites in south-western Anatolia.[4] One of the largest caches of weapons comes from the burnt fortress of Troy IIg[5] (augmented by scattered earlier deposits from II e and f). Battle-axes, including the ceremonial ones from treasure N,[6] rock crystal pommels (six for swords and forty-two for daggers) from the same deposit,[7] lion-head pommels of the same material[8] either for swords or daggers, and numerous dagger blades and spearheads, including ceremonial examples in silver[9] are closely matched in the even richer and perhaps somewhat earlier Dorak material. The absence of sword blades at Troy is probably a coincidence. What is particularly important is the early development, both in the north-western and central Anatolian provinces, of the sword from the dagger, a development which now appears to have preceded that of the spear. It is not until the end of the period that the latter seems to have caught up, and it goes through a further period of development during the E.B. 3 phase. The total absence of arrowheads remains noticeable. The development of sword (and spear) presupposes the existence of shields and helmets, which were probably made of perishable materials. Otherwise they would probably have survived in these intact tombs, for it is *a priori* unlikely that a king armed with swords should not also be provided with shield and helmet. A figure of a warrior,

[1] §IV, 12, 387, pl. IV, 7.   [2] See above, p. 390, n. 1.

[3] §III, 27, 124, fig. 14, 2.   [4] §III, 27, 96–8, map 1.

[5] §IV, 30, figs. 805, 811–14, etc.; §IV, 31, nos. 5842–56, 6146, 6153–6 etc.

[6] §IV, 31, nos. 6055–8. Cf. §IV, 26, fig. 11.

[7] §IV, 31, nos. 6059–64 and 6065–106; cf. §IV, 26, figs. 15–16.

[8] §IV, 30, fig. 547; §III, 3, fig. 359: 26 (14); cf. §IV, 26, figs. 18c, 19.

[9] §IV, 30, fig. 901.

scratched on a sherd from Troy II, seems to wear a helmet and wears a sword or dagger slung on a bandolier.[1]

COSTUME AND METAL VESSELS

About the dress of the period little can be deduced. Pins and brooches (at Alaca)[2] evidently fastened garments, for buttons are unknown. At Alaca figurines are shown wearing boots with upturned toes,[3] which are still so widespread in the Anatolian countryside that we may assume them to have been in general use. Numerous figurines show a goddess wearing a garment held by two long straps crossing across the breast,[4] but this may be a conventionalized rendering of the bodice found as early as Hacılar II. A lead figurine from Troy II*g*[5] and a mould for two similar figures found near Akhisar[6] show a goddess with long tresses, and the latter shows her wearing what looks like a flounced robe. Silver appliqué from the queen's tomb at Dorak shows that belts and aprons were worn, probably over a skirt, as on the 'Dorak' figurines.[7] The evidence of these figurines should be used with caution, for their date and provenance, though not (in the opinion of the writer) their authenticity, are open to question. Feminine jewellery of this period is best displayed by Alaca, Troy II*g*, Poliochni V and Dorak. Bracelets, anklets, necklaces and colliers of variegated stones, pins, finger-rings, earrings, diadems and elaborate Trojan earrings or breast-pieces predominate. The latter two are absent at Alaca, where the form and quality of feminine articles of jewellery are again quite different. Combs and stone toilet vessels were found at Alaca and Dorak. Lesser folk wore copper bracelets (Kusura) and in Beycesultan XV a pot handle was ornamented with the impression of two finely worked bracelets, probably made in precious metal.

The metal vessels of Alaca, made in bronze or copper, gold and silver, bear, on the whole, no relationship to the shapes of local contemporary pottery.[8] By contrast, those of Dorak and Troy are closely matched, even if not in the immediate area in which the sites lie. This is hardly surprising, for metal vessels are easily traded because of their intrinsic value, and the value attached to exotic products from foreign workshops would be far greater than that of local *ateliers*. The Chinese pottery used exclusively by

---

1 §III, 4, fig. 371: 33 (352).   2 §IV, 16, pl. cxcviii, top.
3 §IV, 16, pl. cxcv.   4 §IV, 14, 82–3.
5 §IV, 31, no. 6446.   6 §IV, 28, fig. 209 (usually dated later).
7 §IV, 26, figs. 3–8.   8 See Plate 40(*a*).

the early Ottoman court provides a good parallel for such fastidious taste. Our comparatively limited knowledge of contemporary pottery in the regions around Alaca Hüyük makes an analysis there as yet impossible, but a number of silver beak-spouted vessels,[1] ornamented with *repoussé* 'pseudo-spirals', crosses and swastikas, would look more at home in Western Anatolia. Trade between the west and Alaca is documented by a Dorak-type dagger found at Alaca. At Dorak we find besides such local Yortan shapes as bird-vessels,[2] cups with high handles such as are common around Tavşanlı and the plains east of the Sea of Marmara. A jug with cut-away spout might have been made at Beycesultan and a silver juglet with exaggerated neck is characteristic of the Isparta plain.[3] A small gold cup has affinities with the Gumelniţa culture of eastern Bulgaria and finally there is a group of Troy II vessels, including an electrum beaker like those found at Troy,[4] and two *depas*-cups, the silver one[5] like those found at Bozüyük,[6] the gold one[7] not unlike those from Maltepe and Karacaahmet near Afyon. Both, like the shape in general, are probably of Troadic origin. Hitherto only one other *depas*, a silver example in the British Museum from the Troad, was known, but one would hesitate to date it as early as Troy II.

We must now return to the evidence provided by E.B. 2 pottery, which is both abundant and varied. It should be noted first of all that the typical Troy II pottery with its wheel-made wares, introduced in phase II*b*, stands almost alone in Anatolia. With the exception of Cilicia, whence the knowledge of the potter's wheel was probably obtained,[8] the rest of Anatolia continued to make hand-made pottery. Characteristic new shapes of the Troy II pottery are wheel-made plates, the *depas amphikypellon* (a two-handled drinking-goblet) and a number of tall-necked storage-jars, to which must be added in late Troy II a group of bowls which become more common in the E.B. 3 period. Just before the end of Troy II the so-called face-urns and face-lids occur, and gain popularity in Troy III. Outside the Troad the latter are virtually unknown and not even a single piece is reported from the island town of Poliochni, but they have parallels in the less

[1] E.g. §IV, 16, pls. CXXXII, CLXXVI, CLXXIX.
[2] §IV, 26, fig. 9 (bottom).
[3] §IV, 26, fig. 10.
[4] §IV, 31; nos. 5864-5.
[5] §IV, 26, fig. 9.
[6] §IV, 13, 23, pl. I, 7; §III, 3, 4.
[7] §IV, 26, fig. 14.
[8] §I, 12, 97, 105-6; for trade see §II, 3, 82.

grotesque faces on jar rims in the E.B. 2 pottery of the Konya plain. Apart from the introduction of the wheel the pottery development in the Troy II culture proceeds along local lines. *Depas*-cups, probably to be assigned to this period, have been found with pottery of Mikhalits type at Badere near Svilengrad, suggesting that no great changes took place in Turkish Thrace.[1] In Macedonia also, the local 'Troy I' wares continued to be made and here too a *depas* was found at Stibos near Lake Langadas.[2] As signs of Trojan contact with the west the *depas* is valuable, even though the time-range of this type is very long (Troy II c–V).

The drastic changes seen in this north-western province were not shared by any of its neighbours. The pottery from the Dorak tombs is in the old tradition, and the Akhisar-Manisa group or Heraeum I in Samos now produced wares very close to those of Beycesultan E.B. 2, in what is essentially a continuation of the north-west Anatolian tradition, broken only in the Troy II group. A general feature of the E.B. 2 period was, however, a greater preponderance of red burnished wares at the expense of the black, typical of the previous period. In the south-west the change to a north-western culture has already been referred to, and it is marked not only in the pottery,[3] but also in the little metalwork we have.[4] The earliest shapes of the period can all be paralleled in the north-western E.B. 1 province and such typical features appear as white-painted pedestalled bowls with inverted rims, tubular lugs at or below the rim, but in late and somewhat degenerate forms, also jugs with beak or cut-away spout and often supported on three conical feet. Incised white-filled ornamentation is still found on black wares, but grooved ornament, often in combination with plastic ribs, bars and crescents, and the addition of horns and twisted vertical handles are new and very common. Grooved decoration had been in use in the north-west in E.B. 1, but never to such an extent as is now displayed in its south-western E.B. 2 descendant, not only in the immediate surrounding of Beycesultan itself but also in the other four groups which together constitute the south-western E.B. 2 province. The north-western influence is particularly notable (with its white-painted wares and inverted-rim bowls) in the western parts, which is only to be expected. Further south and east (Kusura B) it is less marked, but nowhere does the E.B. 1 culture survive. At Beycesultan the development of this culture is particularly well documented by the numerous vessels from the burnt

---

[1] §III, 17, 22, fig. 12.
[2] §IV, 29, col. 1411.
[3] §IV, 22, 119–21, fig. 2.
[4] §III, 27, 96 ff.

temples. Interesting is the appearance in levels XV and XIV of black burnished vessels of Yortan type, and in level XIII*a* a first contact is made with the red washed and wheel-made wares of the Troy II culture, immediately before a great catastrophe overwhelms the south-west.

Konya and Cilician plains. In the south continuity from the previous period is evident in the pottery. Wheel-made plain wares are now common in Cilicia, but the old red and black burnished wares and the 'red gritty ware' now often coated with purplish paint, are still the more numerous and characteristic.[1] Typical for the beginning of the period are fine black incised wares, bowls and cups, also found in the Konya plain,[2] and elegant pedestalled jars with 'cross-stitch' incision, also found across the Amanus mountains at Zincirli in the Karasu valley.[3] These are found as imports in 'Amūq I,[4] where at this time (phases H, I) an East Anatolian, the so-called Khirbet Karak, pottery prevails. None of this distinctive ware has been found in Cilicia. The red-gritty, but not the scored ware, would appear to be declining in Cilicia, whereas both rise to their climax of popularity in the Konya plain, especially in its eastern half. From here it was exported to the Aksaray region,[5] where it was found at Çokyatan and Öresun Hüyüks. It is not yet known what sort of culture prevailed at this time in the Niğde area. In this 'metallic-ware' the most common shapes are now rather squat jugs with a broad channel spout and lug below it, decorated in vitrified purplish paint with bands and tree-patterns, and large collared jugs similarly ornamented. Small vessels are occasionally coated all over in purple paint. One such jug was found at the silver mines of Bulgar Maden, which were evidently in the course of exploitation. Red, brown, grey and black burnished wares were equally common, and some bore white-filled incised decoration as in Cilicia. Scored ware too is extremely frequent and a fourth class (a cream or buff straw-faced ware decorated with designs in red paint) is much in evidence, but has no parallels in Cilicia. Towards the western edge of the plain south-western features such as certain types of lugs appear, showing contact with the west. Pottery from Sizma shows the blend of Konya plain and south-western elements best.[6]

Eskişehir-Ankara region. The later levels of Demirci Hüyük, apparently abandoned at the end of the period, show a change

[1] §I, 12, 104–13.   [2] §I, 12, figs. 257–8.
[3] §I, 12, fig. 255; §IV, 22, pl. 15.   [4] §IV, 2, fig. 310: 17–19.
[5] Survey of J. G. Macqueen in 1956, still unpublished.
[6] In the Konya Museum.

towards lighter coloured wares, especially red, but few changes in shape can be observed. Cog-wheel handles on shallow bowls are an innovation,[1] but their distribution goes well beyond that of this culture; on jugs they are common both at Beycesultan and at Ahlatlibel. Although the shallow bowls with one handle rising above the rim are very typical in this and the Ankara-Polatlı region, they are not exclusive to these parts as was once thought. They occur frequently in E.B. 2 deposits in the south-west, the Tavşanlı-İznik area, where their presence need not be explained by a migration from the plateau, and they already occur in E.B. 1 layers at Emporio and Bayraklı. To regard them as a Central Anatolian characteristic is quite erroneous.

What is new in the Demirci Hüyük culture in E.B. 2 is the spouted bowl,[2] also found at Bozüyük and Polatlı.[3] Here the basket-handled form occurs with horizontal fluting, reminiscent of Kusura bowls.[4] Other West Anatolian influences must be invoked for the jugs with cut-away spout and those with spouts bent backwards, found at Uluköy, Hirkaköy and Sariyer (north of Gordium).[5] Their nearest parallels come from Eskişehir, Bozüyük,[6] Ovabayindir and Troy. Other north-western vessels found at Bozüyük include a Yortan bird-vase[7] and depas-forms horizontally ribbed. All this suggests that the northern trade route from the north-west to the Anatolian plateau, which it reaches at Bozüyük, was in frequent use during this period.

At Ahlatlibel and Karaoğlan in the Ankara region the pottery is far more western in type than one would expect from their location. The Ahlatlibel jugs[8] bear close resemblances to the Beycesultan and Kusura 'cups', and the feeding-bottles are again very western. White-paint also occurs, though rarely, at Ahlatlibel and grooved ornament is far more frequent than incision. The Karaoğlan juglets are closest to those from Beycesultan. Swooping lines of interlaced chevrons at Ahlatlibel[9] still continue a pattern known at Çatal Hüyük West, Mersin XII and Elmalı plain, E.B. 1. Some contact with Central Anatolia is evident: a few Ahlatlibel shapes at Alaca are considered as actual importations.[10] Feeding bottles have similar shapes there, and a biconical potstand

[1] §III, 3, 28, pl. 8: 5; and §IV, 13, pl. III, 26.
[2] §III, 3, pl. 6, 12, pl. 7, 4–9.
[3] §IV, 13, pl. II, 16; §IV, 21, figs. 11, 1–3, and pl. vc, f.
[4] §IV, 19, pl. LXXXIII, 6, 7.   [5] §IV, 32, 343–7; figs. 1–3.
[6] §IV, 13, pl. II, 3, 4 and 6 (from Sariyer).
[7] §IV, 13, pl. II, 5.
[8] §IV, 14, 49 (and on colour plate, Ab 28 and 71).
[9] §IV, 14, 23, below.   [10] Unpublished.

has remote parallels at Büyük Güllücek and in the Khirbet-Karak wares of the 'Amūq and Palestine. Black exteriors and red interiors are another feature foreign to the west, but characteristic of Central and Eastern Anatolia. As excavation proceeds more evidence for east-west relations will undoubtedly accumulate.

The first phase of the Central Anatolian E.B. 2 culture (Alişar I a) marks the culmination of the previous culture (so-called 'Late Chalcolithic'). At Alişar (levels 14–12) red wares now steadily increase side-by-side with a black ware of high quality often incised with very fine lines; this is also found at Alaca.[1] Shapes of this period include, first of all, tall and slender fruit-stands of various profiles, tall metallic vases on cup-bases, fine carinated beakers, with or without handles, and a variety of jars, some on small pedestals.[2] White-painted decoration is found for the first time, but excision (plain or red/white-filled, mainly on fruit-stand pedestals) is still the most common form of ornament. Some pedestals are horizontally or diagonally fluted, and it would seem that metal and woodwork traditions mingle here.

The pottery of the next phase, Alişar I b, is somewhat more re-strained in shapes and red burnished wares predominate. Two different cultures can be recognized in Central Anatolia; one in the western part represented by Alaca, the other in the eastern part of the Halys, the region of Kayseri and the volcanic country between the Halys and Salt Lake, where Alişar and Kültepe are the main excavated sites.

At Alaca red burnished fruit-stands in much modified forms survive amidst much red-slipped pottery decorated with finger impressions on the unslipped parts.[3] At Alişar the fruit-stands have gone and simple bowls, jugs and cups predominate, but the beak-spouted jug is rare, though present at Alaca and Kültepe.[4] The new pottery from Kültepe is richer in form and decoration and includes ribbed and fluted cups, rare at Alişar and absent at Alaca.

The last phase of this period overlaps with West Anatolian E.B. 3 and will be described in chapter xxiv. Painted pottery with simple patterns in red on cream slip occurs in the Alişar I b culture[5] and was most common in the Kültepe region, but it even occurs at Alaca. Its main area of distribution seems to lie within the southernmost curve of the Halys; south of that it has not yet been reported.

Pontic. The stratigraphy of this region is not yet sufficiently

---

[1] §iii, 19, fig. 67, and §i, 5, pl. xxxiii, c, no. Al. j. 211.
[2] §i, 5, pl. xxxiii; §iii, 26, pl. vii, fig. 62.   [3] §iv, 16, pls. xcvii, c, cii.
[4] §iii, 19, pl. viii, fig. 166.   [5] §iii, 19, 154–64, figs. 162–3.

well known and Dündartepe near Samsun is the only site from which a fair amount of pottery has been published.[1] The distribution of this culture includes the Black Sea coast from Sinope to the mouth of the Yeşilirmak, the Amasya-Merzifon region and the Yeşilirmak and lower Kelkit valley. Suşehri marks its eastern, Imrentepe near Devrekani (north of Kastamonu) its western limits. The archaeological potential of this undoubtedly important culture-province is best illustrated by the princely tombs of Horoztepe and Mahmutlar, belonging to the E.B. 3 period and described in chapter xxiv. Dündartepe is peculiar in that the mound was occupied simultaneously by two different peoples; the summit by people of the Pontic culture and the slopes by Central Anatolians.

The Pontic people lived in houses of timber, brushwood and daub, materials native to the country, and consumed great quantities of meat and shellfish. The Central Anatolian element built in mud-brick as on the plateau. The Central Anatolian pottery, also found at Kaledoroğu, is decorated with incised kerbs and fingerprints, like the ware from Alaca and Kalecik (Çorum), but the characteristic Pontic pottery is uniformly black or grey, of fine quality, and often decorated with incision or fine white paint. Lugs, knobs and handles are more reminiscent of Western than of Central Anatolia and sharply inverted rim bowls, pedestalled bowls, and tubular lugs again suggest western influence. Extramural burial practised here is again different from Central Anatolian habits. Metal is common and the metal resources of this region are abundant.

A steatopygous incised clay figurine from Dündartepe[2] is closer to Tripolye A figurines in the Ukraine[3] than to anything found in Anatolia and may be considered as an import at this coastal site. Flat stone figures of animals, perforated for suspension, found commonly in layers of Alişar I b[4] show the closest resemblance to bone figures from the Mariupol cemetery on the Sea of Azov,[5] which is of approximately the same age. The presence of several large Pontic sites on the Black Sea coast, among them Dündartepe, suggests that seafaring and trade in the Black Sea were common at this period, and the establishment of Central Anatolians at Dündartepe and along the road leading to the coast may have been for a commercial purpose.

---

[1] §iv, 12, 369–78, pls. lxiii–lxviii; §iii, 7, 181–4, figs. 1–38; §iv, 27, pls. v–vii (Dündartepe), ix (Tekkeköy), x (Kaledoroğu).

[2] §iv, 27, pl. lxvi, 6.   [3] §iv, 9, pl. 19a (3–4).

[4] §iii, 19, 180, fig. 184.   [5] §iv, 9, 49, fig. 22b, c.

East Anatolian cultures. Research in Eastern Anatolia has lagged far behind that in the rest of the country. Excavations have been carried out at only three sites: Arslantepe near Malatya (unpublished) and Karaz[1] and Pulur in the plain of Erzurum. The origins of the East Anatolian E.B. 1 culture are nebulous but it is hoped that the excavations now in progress at Pulur will clarify the situation. An import in the 'Late Chalcolithic' of Alaca (our E.B. 1) shows that its beginning is at least as early as our E.B. 1 period.

The geographical distribution of this culture is staggering.[2] It reaches from Kangal and Malatya, west of the Euphrates, to Colchis, Trialeti and Tiflis and Nahcevan in Transcaucasia and Lake Urmia in north-west Iran, a distance of some five hundred miles. The extraordinary uniformity of this culture—always judging by surface finds—suggests a different pattern of economy from that current in Western or Central Anatolia. Sites are few and scattered or concentrated in the few areas where agriculture was practicable. The distances which separate these are much greater than anywhere further west and most of the population of these barren uplands must have been engaged in the only occupation suitable to the area—pastoralism. In the course of their seasonal migrations they may have been the agents who transmitted new inventions and ensured a homogeneous development throughout this vast area. Future excavations may, on the other hand, show that the apparent homogeneity is but an illusion. Very little is known about the dwellings in which these people lived: rectangular houses of mud-brick on stone foundations were found at Karaz,[3] but round houses of brick or *pisé* on stone foundations are reported from Eilar and Shengavit in the Erivan area of the middle Araxes valley.[4] At Tazehkand west of Tabrīz a late Early Bronze Age settlement again shows round houses,[5] but the derivative Khirbet-Karak culture in the 'Amūq and Palestine[6] has rectangular houses with numerous architectural features like later Tazehkand. Burial habits may have been as varied: no graves were found at Karaz[7] and extra-mural burial is suspected. At Bestasheni in Trialeti and at Erçis on Lake Vān (E.B. 2) the dead were buried intra-murally in stone cists,[8] but at Ozni in the same district burials were found in earth graves,

---

[1] §IV, 17, 349–84, illustrations 385–413.
[2] §IV, 6, 172, map 1.   [3] §IV, 17, plan 2.
[4] §IV, 8, 82.   [5] Personal communication from Charles Burney.
[6] §IV, 2, 345–50, figs, 263, 266.   [7] §IV, 17, 358.
[8] §IV, 6, 179.

near round houses (E.B. 1 or 3?).[1] Metal is rare at Karaz and apparently almost unknown in Transcaucasia.[2] A special feature of this culture is the care bestowed on the elaboration and decoration of hearths, such as one could expect in this bitterly cold country where the snow often lies for six months on end. Some are potstands or small hearths of horseshoe type often decorated with human faces,[3] which have parallels in many other Anatolian cultures (e.g. Khirbet Karak and Konya plain, E.B. 2). Others are most elaborate and consist of great rings with three projections, ornamented with spiraliform design (Karaz).[4]

The pottery[5] can be divided into three successive phases, here assigned to E.B. 1, 2, and 3. The E.B. 1 pottery is a heavy hand-made burnished ware, with black and brown, rarely red, exterior and a red or buff interior. Biconical bodies with everted rims are characteristic for jars of all sizes and for bowls. Handles consist of small loops, almost lugs. Circular and occasionally square lids have a loop handle. Grooved and incised ornamentation is common on lids and on the smaller jars. A decoration of alternating 'groove and dimple' is very common, but by far the most striking form of ornament is plastic (fine or bold), with elaborate geometric patterns in pothook spirals, bold double spirals and meanders, and what might be described as 'telephone' patterns. Animals occur, but remain rare. The use of spirals and meanders is unique in Anatolia and is paralleled only in the Khirbet Karak ware, which should be considered as an East Anatolian offshoot.[6] Woodwork may be responsible for some of these patterns. This E.B. 1 pottery is on the whole very attractive, partly for its fine shapes, partly for its pleasing design which is invariably applied in good taste and to a certain part of the vessel only.

The pottery of the second phase (E.B. 2) of Eastern Anatolia is much less easy to analyse and it would appear that the uniformity of the previous phase has given way to many variants. The plastic design has lost greatly in popularity, even if it has not completely disappeared. 'Nahcevan lugs', almost globular blobs of clay horizontally perforated, make their first appearance on jugs and

[1] §IV, 18, fig. 13, pl. XXVII.

[2] Where the period is called 'eneolithic'.

[3] §IV, 17, 396; §IV, 20, figs. 3, 5; for their appearance in the Khirbet Karak culture in the plain of Antioch ('Amūq) see §IV, 2, figs. 290, 291 b, fig. 307, 21–22; §IV, 10, pl. XI, A, B and fig. 29.

[4] §IV, 17, 397, cf. 398 and §IV, 20, pls. 1, 2.

[5] §IV, 6, 164–72, 178–205 and §IV, 20, figs. 2–4.

[6] §IV, 2, 358–68 (figs. 281–5), 'Amūq H; 398–403 (figs. 304–7), 'Amūq I; and figs. 358–9; §IV, 10, 132–40, and figs. 7 (12–21), 8 (17–19), and plate XII.

lids. They would seem to be far more common in the eastern half of the province and already rare at Karaz near Erzurum. Further west they are unknown. In the Malatya-Elâziğ region a finer ware occurs of which the characteristic forms are jars with globular bodies and 'rail-rims', also carinated cups and bowls, often with horizon-grooving. Around Lake Vān, on the other hand, a very austere variant of E.B. 2 is best known from a great cist grave near Erçis on the northern shore. Decoration is virtually absent here, except for some groove-and-dimple pattern and the ubiquitous Nahcevan lug. The Iğdir region, with grooved ornament, spirals and tendrils, again shows local peculiarities. The chronology of this culture is almost entirely a matter of guesswork but a recent radiocarbon date gives c. 2450 B.C. for the end of E.B. 1 at Geoy Tepe (K 1 period) in Persian Azarbāyjān.[1]

V. CHRONOLOGY

Now that the carbon-14 process provides a new method of dating archaeological remains—often with unexpected if not startling results—it would be unwise to be dogmatic about the conventional dates that have been in use over the last twenty years. Provided that relative chronology and stratigraphy be not flagrantly contradicted by radiocarbon dating, there is no reason why, for example, a radiocarbon date of c. 3500 B.C. should be rejected in favour of a conventional assumption of c. 3000 or 2750 B.C. for the beginning of Troy I and E.B. 1 in general. No radiocarbon dates are yet available for dating the Early Bronze Age of Anatolia, but a number of archaeological arguments can be raised against the conventional dates. These are:

(a) The E.B. 1 period of Cilicia follows immediately upon the 'Late Chalcolithic' of Tarsus, contemporary with the Uruk period (above, p. 364). This suggests an initial date for E.B. 1 in Cilicia in late Uruk or 'protoliterate' times of Mesopotamia, well before the end of the fourth millennium.

(b) Recent radiocarbon dates for the end of the Vinča culture give an average of c. 3500/3400 B.C. for the beginning of the next period, that of the Macedonian Early Bronze Age, itself an offshoot of the Troy I culture. This suggests that Troy I started c. 3500 B.C.[2]

(c) The great length of both Troy I and II periods has only recently been realized. It is unlikely that the ten building periods

[1] §IV, 5, 35-52.   [2] §I, 11.

	MARITIME NORTH-WEST	BALIKESIR PLAIN	SOUTH-WEST	KONYA PLAIN	CILICIA	ESKIŞEHIR-ANKARA	CENTRAL ANATOLIA	PONTIC	EAST ANATOLIA
E.B. 3 / 2300				E.B. 3 (a)				2200	E.B. 2
			LUWIAN (?) INVASION c. 2300 B.C.						2450
E.B. 2	Troy II	Y o r t a n → D o r a k	South-west Anatolian E.B. 2	Konya plain E.B. 2	Cilician E.B. 2 (+ local wares)	Demirci Hüyük I–III Ahlatlıbel Karaoğlan	Alişar I b Alaca royal tombs	Pontic culture	E.B. 1
	Destruction of Troy I		Change of culture	↑	↑	←	Alişar I A (14–12)		?
							---?---	?	
E.B. 1	Troy I	Y o r t a n	South-west Anatolian E.B. 1 (Beycesultan XIX–XVIIa) and Elmalı plain culture	Konya plain E.B. 1 ↑	Cilician E.B. 1 (intrusive) ↑	Demirci Hüyük IV	Central Anatolian Late Chalcolithic (Alişar 18–15)		
LATE CHALCOLITHIC / 4000	Kumtepe I B Poliochni I --- Kumtepe I A Beşiktepe	Kumtepe	Beycesultan Late Chalcolithic 4 --- Late Chalcolithic 3	Sarlak phase (white paint) Late Chalcolithic	Mersin XII 'Late Chalcolithic' Tarsus scraped bowls --- Mersin XIII–XIV (grey ware) Mersin XV	Yazır (white-painted pottery)	Büyük Güllücek		

of the first and the twelve of the other can be accommodated within the relatively short spans assigned to them by the conventional chronology:[1] Troy I *c.* 2750–2500 and Troy II, *c.* 2500–2300 B.C. (But C. W. Blegen has already put forward higher dates of *c.* 3000–2600 and 2600–2300 B.C.)

(*d*) Raising these dates does not in any way clash with the few synchronisms that can be established with other countries; these are as follows: (1) Cilician E.B. 2 jugs were found at Giza, one in a Fourth Dynasty tomb after the fifteenth year of Cheops, *c.* 2575 B.C. This type of jug was not in use at the very beginning of the E.B. 2 period.[2] (2) The names of Sahure (*c.* 2487–2473 B.C.) and Neferirkare (*c.* 2473–2463 B.C.) were found in the Dorak tombs, which date to the second half of Troy II (*c–g*).[3] (3) At Tarsus there occurs a button-seal (no. 25) of a type found in Egypt in the Sixth Dynasty (*c.* 2345–2181 B.C.) and the following First Intermediate Period (*c.* 2181–2040 B.C.).[4] An ivory seal in similar style was found in the destruction-layer of Poliochni V, roughly contemporary with that of Troy II.[5] The Tarsus seal is of E.B. 3 and both finds therefore date on either side of the transition of E.B. 2 to 3, or *c.* 2300 B.C. in conventional terms.

None of these synchronisms therefore necessitates Anatolian adjustments and it should not be forgotten that the Egyptian chronology here adopted is not universally accepted, higher dates being preferred by some scholars. For the purpose of this work then we may broadly define as limits for the E.B. 1, 2, and 3 periods the following dates:

Beginning of E.B. 1 possibly *c.* 3500 B.C. (conventional date 3000 or 2750 B.C.)
Beginning of E.B. 2 possibly *c.* 2800 B.C. (conventional date 2600/2500 B.C.)
Beginning of E.B. 3 {in Western Anatolia *c.* 2300 B.C. (same as conventional dates) in Central Anatolia *c.* 2200 B.C. tional dates)

Needless to say this later date may need modification as radiocarbon tests become available, but it is near enough to historical times to inspire more confidence than earlier possibilities. To attempt to date the East Anatolian Bronze Age phases closer than has been done above is somewhat premature.

[1] §IV, 25, 162.
[2] §I, 12, 60.
[3] §IV, 26, fig. 1.
[4] §I, 12, 234, 238, and figs. 393, 399.
[5] §IV, 4, 206; figs. 1, 25.

VI. THE CATASTROPHE AT THE END OF THE EARLY BRONZE AGE 2 PERIOD

The end of the E.B. 2 period is marked in Western and Southern Anatolia by a catastrophe of such magnitude as to remain unparalleled until the very end of the Bronze Age. This is perhaps most clearly illustrated in the accompanying table, though it must be borne in mind that the results are provisional.[1]

	Number of sites	
Area	E.B. 2	E.B. 3
Turkish Thrace	4(?)	—
Troad, Lemnos	5	1 (Troy)
Balıkesir-Manisa	25	13
Eskişehir region	30	5 (possibly more)
Polatlı-Ankara region	12 (possibly more)	3 (possibly more)
South-west Anatolia	225 (probably more)	55 (probably more)
Konya plain	88 (possibly c. 100)	5 (possibly c. 20)[2]
Cilician plain	27 (possibly 43)	11 (possibly more)
(Tavşanlı-Iznik)	15	15
Total recorded	421 (probably c. 450)	108 (probably c. 125)

Table 2. *Comparative numbers of E.B. 2 and E.B. 3 sites in Anatolia.*

This simple table shows a number of important facts:

(*a*) As a result of events which took place in Western and Southern Anatolia at the end of the E.B. 2 period, the number of settlements of the following period is reduced to a quarter of the number in the previous period.

(*b*) Certain areas are more affected than others; the south-west, Konya plain and Cilician plain are the most stricken regions. On the other hand the areas south-east of the Sea of Marmara and the plain of Tavşanlı remain fully settled, but not without a complete change of culture. The evidence from the Eskişehir-Ankara region is less reliable than that of other regions.

(*c*) The culture that spread all over this area in the E.B. 3 period is that of the Troy II province with its wheel-made wares. This shows that the movement was from north-west Anatolia south and eastwards and not the other way round.

(*d*) It should be noted that on most of these sites where both E.B. 2 and 3 cultures occur, the latter occupies a smaller area, amounting on a number of sites to no more than intermittent

---

[1] Mainly based on the author's own research; unpublished material.

[2] §VI, 3, 32.

squatting. For the purposes of classification no distinction has been made between E.B. 3 *a* and *b*, the latter being included. The decrease in sites is certainly not due to enforced synoecismus.

(*e*) That this decline in settlement was due to a disaster is made clear by the burning of Troy II, Poliochni V, Beycesultan XIII*a*, Kusura B, Tarsus, Ahlatlibel, Polatlı I, the desertion of Demirci Hüyük and a few hundred other sites. In the Konya plain every town site of the E.B. 2 period shows signs of conflagration, mostly followed by desertion which is neatly dated by E.B. 2 pottery on each site. Nearly every village was deserted and never again occupied. Both the Konya plain and most of the south-western province south of the line Burdur-Denizli were burnt and deserted at the same period. The lack of reoccupation strongly suggests that these regions henceforth became the grazing grounds of nomads.

Who were the people who caused this awe-inspiring wave of destruction? A comparison with similar events at the end of the E.B. 1 period in the area of the Troy I culture and with the so-called 'Aegean' (should it not be called Thracian?) invasion at the end of the Late Bronze Age is rewarding. Both were followed by almost complete blanks in the archaeological record, but the present movement was not so, at least not everywhere. Instead it introduced a north-west Anatolian culture wherever it went. Now the miserable remains of Troy III rule out the possibility of that impoverished unfortified village spreading its culture all over Western Anatolia. The north-west Anatolian culture of the invaders shows that they were either north-westerners themselves or newcomers who had adopted north-west Anatolian (maritime) culture. Now not only the Troy II, but also the Thracian sites were deserted at this period and the most likely explanation of these events is an invasion of people from the Balkan Peninsula,[1] crossing the Dardanelles. Swelled by bands of north-west Anatolians the invasion gained momentum and devastated the whole of Southern Anatolia. The introduction of the Philia phase of the Early Bronze Age in Cyprus with its affinities to Konya plain pottery may have been a side effect of this migration.

No cultural break interrupts the continuous development from E.B. 3 to the Late Bronze Age anywhere in south-western or southern Anatolia, where the Hittite records show that an Indo-European language—Luwian—was spoken as early as the Hittite Old Kingdom. No better moment can therefore be found for bringing the Luwians into their respective new homes than the

[1] §I, 11.

disastrous break between E.B. 2 and 3, *c.* 2300 B.C. This theory does not create any philological impossibilities. On the contrary, two scraps of evidence support it. In level VI at Beycesultan (*c.* 2000–1900 B.C.) a clay seal was found in a sealed deposit, bearing a hieroglyphic inscription,[1] thus showing that the invention of the hieroglyphic script antedated the beginning of the Middle Bronze Age. Now the language for which this Anatolian script was invented is generally believed to be Luwian. Secondly, in an archaeological context of a date not later than the twenty-first century B.C. (equalling E.B. 3*b* in Western Anatolia), there was found at Byblos a small limestone obelisk with an inscription[2] in Egyptian hieroglyphs. This records that Kukun, the son of the 'Lycian' (or better 'Lukka-man'), set up this obelisk for Abishemu, prince of Byblos, beloved of Herishef (Arsaphes). The Heracleopolitan epithet dates the inscription to the Tenth Dynasty, or in any case to a date prior to the Twelfth Dynasty. The name Kukun is known in fourteenth-century Western Anatolia; Kukkunnis was king of the Arzawa state of Wilusa. In the thirteenth century it is borne by Kukkuli, a king of Assuwa, and Kukkuni still occurs as a classical Lycian name. Both states lie in Luwian territory and it has recently been shown that Lycian is a kind of proto-Luwian.[3] The Byblos obelisk thus indicates that Luwians were present in Anatolia well before the beginning of the Middle Bronze Age.

If we thus equate the invaders of Western and Southern Anatolia at the beginning of the E.B. 3 period with the Luwians, who then were the invaders of the north-west at the end of E.B. 1? The situation is considerably more complicated in the north-west of the peninsula for here we have abundant evidence for not less than three movements or invasions during the Early Bronze Age, one at the end of each of the three phases into which we have divided the period. All three are best considered together, at the risk of anticipating developments in the north-west during E.B. 3, to be described more fully in chapter xxiv. The question of identifying these three groups is of more than regional importance, for it also affects Greece and the Balkans.

In 1958 the present writer suggested[4] that the first group of invaders at the end of E.B. 1 were Luwians who destroyed the maritime Troy I culture and settled in coastal north-western Anatolia without leaving any distinctive archaeological remains of

---

[1] §IV, 22, 97, pl. XXVI. Identified as hieroglyphs by Professor S. Alp, Dr R. D. Barnett and Professor H. Bossert (*Festschrift J. Friedrich*, Heidelberg, 1959, p. 80).
[2] §VI, 1, 33–4.   [3] §VI, 2, 160.   [4] §IV, 24, 32.

their own. This might suggest a less settled form of occupation, with prevalent nomadism or pastoralism, which is perhaps in keeping with early Indo-Europeans and is reflected in the archaeological evidence from the west coast. At the end of E.B. 2 the great invasion took place which we have just described. Probably originating from the Pontic steppe it left a trail of destruction from the lower Danube to the frontiers of Syria. It was this invasion which took the Luwians into their new homes in the south-west and south. Bringing an advanced form of Troy II culture with them, they—or at least a fair proportion of them—must have been settled culture-bearers. If they were the people who had settled in the maritime province of north-western Anatolia at the end of E.B. 1 they would have had the whole Troy II period to become Anatolianized. From the record of destruction both in Anatolia and the Balkans[1] it is clear that in this invasion large numbers of people were involved and elements fresh from Europe were evidently present. It was their descent on north-western Anatolia which set in motion this great stream of immigrants and it is of course perfectly possible that the newcomers also spoke Luwian. The present writer imagines that events may have taken place in a way for which the Seljūq invasion of Anatolia presents a close parallel. After a sojourn of several generations in Iran, the main body of the Seljūq Turks brought with them many elements of Iranian culture which were not shared by their numerous Turkoman followers, who, fresh from the steppe, were attracted merely by the prospects of acquiring land, loot and plunder, but had no wish to alter their existence or to rule others. Once established in Anatolia the Seljūqs founded a sultanate, but their followers, used as a buffer against possible Byzantine aggression, remained untouched by the new civilization and continued their old ways of pastoral and nomadic life on the marches. If we substitute the Anatolianized Luwians for the Seljūqs and the newcomers from the steppe for their Turkoman followers we get a movement, in the reverse direction, which would seem to fit the archaeological facts. The infrequency of E.B. 3 settlements in southern Pisidia, central Lycia and the Konya plain may reflect the importance of the uncivilized nomadic element. Perhaps a like explanation can be found for the earlier events at the end of E.B. 1 with the Troy II culture representing the settled, and the empty coast and Caicus valley the nomadic, regions after the previous invasion.

There is, however, one other point to be considered. Not many

[1] §1, 7.

migrations involve only the members of a single linguistic group. During the E.B. 3 period there develops in the regions south and east of the Sea of Marmara (in the Tavşanlı-Iznik region) a culture with the distinguishing feature of the so-called grey 'Minyan' pottery. Not until the very end of the Early Bronze Age, and as a result of further disturbances in the east, can a movement be traced which brings this pottery to the west coast and Troy (at the beginning of Troy VI), from where it would appear to have reached Greece by sea in the wake of the Middle Helladic invaders.[1] If one considers these people to have been a sort of Luwians,[2] who introduced the -*ssos*, -*nthos* and -*wa* elements into Greece (among others), then no further ethnic complications need to be introduced into north-west Anatolia.

However, most Greek scholars still maintain that the Middle Helladic invaders represent the first Greeks. If one accepts this theory (it is no more than that) then the archaeological corollary compels one to regard certain regions in north-west Anatolia as having spoken Greek during E.B. 3 and Greeks would have entered Anatolia perhaps in the wake of Luwians at the end of the E.B. 2 period. In view of their geographical position south and east of the Sea of Marmara—nearest to Europe—this is not impossible. The absence of any place-names of Greek origin in those regions is not a very strong argument against this theory, for this is exactly the area which was swamped by the Thracian invasion at the end of the thirteenth century B.C. As far as the present evidence goes, not a single Bronze Age place-name appears to have survived in this region into classical times, and the little that survived is said to be almost entirely of a Thracian character. Nor should it be forgotten that nothing historical is known about this region of north-western Anatolia in the second millennium. It is conceivable that as a result of the disturbances at the end of the E.B. 3 period *c.* 1900 B.C. the area was repopulated by Luwian elements from the plateau. For reasons which lack of space forbids developing here the present writer is inclined to locate in this region during the Late Bronze Age the powerful kingdom of Ahhiyawa together with some of the Lukka lands; and it is known that the latter spoke a form of Luwian.

The time has not yet come to make a definite choice between the two theories outlined above and we can only hope that excavations in this vital but hitherto neglected area will produce evidence bearing upon the problem.

[1] See below, chapter xxiv and §iv, 24, 9–11 and plate 1, map 1.
[2] §vi, 4, 86–100.

VII. TROY I–II

THROUGHOUT the Bronze Age a powerful stronghold dominated the north-western corner of Asia Minor. Established in a strategic position, on a low ridge somewhat less than four miles distant from the Aegean Sea to the west and from the Dardanelles to the north, it ensured its occupants control over traffic up and down the straits as well as mastery of an important land route that led from the western Anatolian coast to a crossing of the narrows. The ruins known by their Turkish name as Hisarlık[1] had already in 1822 been identified as those of Troy by Charles Maclaren, but it is to Heinrich Schliemann that full credit must be awarded for their recognition as the remains of Troy. Since the site itself has provided no inscribed evidence to fix its preclassical name, the question of identification has in the past been much disputed; but the problem is really a simple one of easy solution. If there ever was a Troy in the region where Homer and Greek tradition say there was, it can only have stood on the site of Hisarlık. Widespread searching explorations of the whole district have revealed many small settlements, where the greater part of the agricultural population doubtless lived; but there is no place other than Hisarlık that can show the characteristic features of a royal fortress. No other key site has been found in the northern Troad. There is no alternative. Consequently—whatever discrepancies may be noted in comparison with Homer's description—unless one is prepared to deny altogether the reality of Troy and to explain it as the free creation of a poet's fancy, one must agree that the site has been correctly identified.

The mound has been subjected to intensive investigation. Between 1870 and 1890 Schliemann himself conducted seven major campaigns of excavation, and after his death his colleague, Wilhelm Dörpfeld, continued digging in 1893 and 1894. More recently a fresh and independent examination was carried out through seven seasons from 1932 to 1938 by an expedition representing the University of Cincinnati.

The accumulation of debris that covered the hill to a depth of fifty feet and more was found to lie in nine principal layers, indicating as many major periods of occupation. These were recognized by Schliemann and Dörpfeld and were numbered from I to IX, beginning from the bottom. The latest excavations

[1] See Plate 40(c).

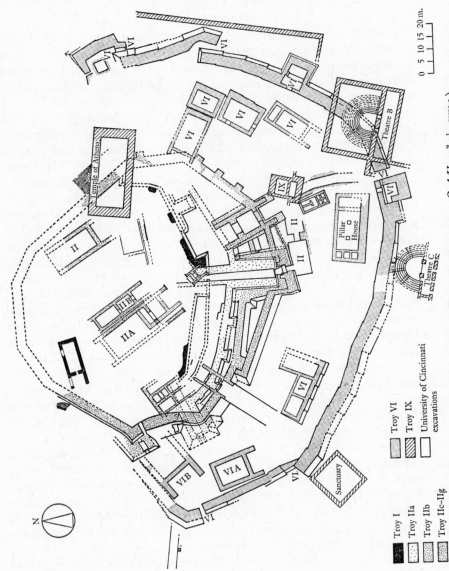

N

Troy I
Troy IIa
Troy IIb
Troy IIc–IIg

Troy VI
Troy IX
University of Cincinnati
excavations

0 5 10 15 20 m.

Temple of Athena

Pillar
House

Theatre B

Theatre C

Sanctuary

Fig. 28. Plan of Troy. (For buildings of Troy VII, see *C.A.H.* II³, ch. xxi*a*.)

revealed that each of the main layers consisted of several superposed strata which in most instances clearly represent phases. Altogether some forty-six such strata have been observed. Thirty of them, which constitute layers I to V, may be ascribed to a culture that maintained itself without a break through the Early Bronze Age. Troy VI is contemporary with the Middle and part of the Late Bronze Age in the Aegean area. Troy VII, in its two stages *a* and *b*, corresponds with the end of the Aegean Late Bronze Age.

TROY I

The site of Hisarlık was first occupied at the beginning of the Early Bronze Age when the working of copper was already known. An antecedent stage of the same culture, which seems to have had no knowledge of metals, has been found represented at Kum Tepe, a small mound beside the Menderes Su (Scamander) a short distance from its outlet into the Dardanelles: these are the only remains in the northern Troad that can yet safely be attributed to the Neolithic Period.

The First Settlement of Troy was a small fortress, hardly more than three hundred feet across, surrounded by a massive stone wall with entrances flanked by towers.[1] (See Fig. 18.) Three successive lines of fortification indicate a long era of growth and expansion, during which the settlement was often destroyed and rebuilt. It came to its end in a catastrophic fire. The debris that gradually accumulated has a depth of fifteen feet and more in which at least ten strata, or phases, all but one differentiated by architectural remains, can be recognized. Within the citadel in each phase stood a small number of relatively large free-standing houses, obviously the homes of a ruler and his entourage. They were built with stone foundations and superstructure of crude brick. One of these buildings, long and narrow, with a portico and entrance at one end and a hearth in the principal room, has the unmistakable plan of a *megaron*.

Remains of copper implements came to light in each stratum; stone was also freely used for tools and weapons. An outstanding monument is a *stele* of limestone bearing on one side, cut in low relief, a somewhat stylized representation of a human face.[2] Awls and pins and other artifacts of bone are fairly numerous; terracotta was likewise employed for figurines and especially for whorls and buttons. The potter's wheel was not known, but

[1] See Plate 40(*b*).   [2] See Plate 41(*a*).

pottery was made in abundance: for the most part it is a mono-chrome black, brownish, greyish, or greenish black ware, with highly polished surface; beaked jugs, jugs with lugs, and open cups or bowls are characteristic. Some examples in lighter colours, even approaching red, occur. Painted decoration, usually in white on a dark ground, is rare. Progress and change in the pottery can be observed through the three sub-periods marked off by the successive fortification walls.

The culture characteristic of Troy I has left its stamp on many smaller sites scattered about the Troad and also across the Dardanelles on the Gallipoli peninsula. In a wider arc it is well represented in Settlements I to V at Thermi in Mytilene, and it has a close kinship with Poliochni in Lemnos, where fortification walls, pottery, and other objects show striking resemblances to what has been found in Hisarlık I.

The Early Sub-period has revealed little evidence of foreign contacts. In the Middle Sub-period some fragments of imported pottery of Early Cycladic or Early Helladic affinities make their appearance, and the number of such pieces increases appreciably in the Late Sub-period. Some sherds of this imported pottery, including remnants of two or three sauce-boats, find their best analogies in the wares of the middle phases of the Early Helladic Period on the Greek mainland.

Pottery and other objects discovered in Macedonia have often been cited as indicating links with Troy I. An underlying cultural connexion is almost certainly to be recognized; although chrono-logical problems are by no means settled, it seems likely that the movement, such as it was, proceeded from east to west. Less in-tensive or less obvious connexions may perhaps be suspected with areas much farther to the south beyond Mytilene, in Chios, and in Samos, if not in the remoter Aegean islands. But relatively little specific evidence is yet available. Concerning relations with central Anatolia and the east not much can yet be said. A certain general kinship seems to be unmistakable, but specific points of connexion are not yet clearly recognizable.

The chronology of Troy I is thus almost wholly dependent on comparisons with the Early Bronze Age in the Cyclades and in Greece. Until further excavation in these areas has made possible a more nearly accurate dating, no precise figure can be given for the First Settlement at Troy. Provisionally it may be assigned to the first half of the third millennium, with a leeway of a century or more at each end.

TROY II

Over the burned debris of Troy I, with no sign of an appreciable interval, but with an unmistakable continuity of culture, a new citadel was laid out on a more ambitious scale. Like the First, the Second Settlement had a long history during which, the architectural evidence shows, there were at least seven phases. Here too, successive reconstructions of the fortification walls testify to progressive growth and enlargement as the diameter of the stronghold increased to some four hundred feet (Fig. 18). Schliemann and Dörpfeld distinguished only three strata, but the recent excavations have demonstrated that the settlement passed through four subsequent phases before it was utterly destroyed in a great conflagration. In the first, second, and third phases, when three monumental fortification walls and several imposing gateways were built, the interior of the citadel was occupied by large palatial buildings, chief among them the well-known palace or *megaron*. Though the latter and some of the other great structures evidently survived to the end, the late phases saw an encroachment of smaller dwellings in the areas that had previously been reserved for the élite.

Every house of the seventh and final phase that was exposed in the recent excavations gave evidence of having been deserted in haste as the fire swept through the settlement. Without exception the floors were covered with household gear that had been left where it fell as the inhabitants fled to safety. On almost every floor were found objects of gold that had been abandoned in the frantic flight. It can hardly be doubted that nearly all the 'treasures' recovered by Schliemann must have lain in this same stratum and should therefore be assigned to the end of Troy II.

The great quantity of gold ornaments and jewellery, vessels of gold, copper and bronze, and bronze weapons that constituted Schliemann's famous 'treasures' give ample proof that the Second Settlement had reached a high stage of prosperity and wealth. The source of all this gold has not yet been determined, but perhaps much of it was derived from tolls levied on all those who passed the Trojan crossroads.

In the arts and crafts a great advance was made over Troy I. The many objects made of gold and other metals speak for themselves. Four beautifully carved battle-axes and two lions' heads in crystal evince a like mastery in the working of stone. Bone continued to be utilized for pins, other implements and idols.

Terracotta whorls and loom-weights show that spinning and weaving were regular household occupations. Pottery too is affected by change and development. Black and Grey Polished Wares, following the tradition inherited from Troy I, are characteristic in the earlier phases, but in the later they give ground before a growing proportion in lighter colours, brown, tan, and red. The introduction of the potter's wheel in the second phase of the period brought about a gradual evolution also in the shapes of the vessels made. Curving profiles become more common than angular. Shallow plates and flaring bowls are made in great quantities; other characteristic pots are tall slender cups with two vertical handles (Schliemann's *depas amphikypellon*), large goblets, and jars with collar necks that are decorated with human features modelled in relief, or have lids so ornamented.

In its external relations the Second Settlement maintained connexions with the Aegean world. Early Cycladic and Early Helladic pottery and other objects were imported in increasing quantities, and one may postulate not a little seaborne traffic with the west. It is likely that there were also contacts with Central Anatolia, although actual imports from that region are not surely recognizable or datable at Troy, and possible Trojan objects or copies thereof found on the plateau are likewise involved in stratigraphic and other uncertainties that preclude exact synchronisms. The character of the terrain would not have been encouraging to much overland traffic between the Troad and the central Anatolian plateau, but relations may have been served by the sea-route along the coast to Cilicia and Syria.

So far as actual dating is concerned Troy II like Troy I is dependent on analogies and correlations with the Aegean area, but the synchronisms that can be established are far from precise, especially in the lack of a sure chronology for the Cycladic and the Helladic periods. Pending further clarification of that series and of the new evidence from Egyptian contacts with Anatolia the era of the Second Settlement may tentatively be regarded as overlapping the third quarter of the third millennium.[1]

[1] For Bibliography to sect. VII, see ch. XXIV, §VII.

CHAPTER XIX

THE DYNASTY OF AGADE AND THE GUTIAN INVASION

I. THE REIGN OF SARGON

WITH the appearance of this imposing figure, vast but dim to later generations of Babylonians hardly less than to us, the historical memory of the people was enriched with its most abiding treasure. Yet the written tradition, so far as it is at present available to us, does scant justice to a king who could not only achieve greatness but could record it for posterity more clearly than any before and most after him. The inscriptions of Sargon[1] must have been numerous and their remains show that they were informative and detailed as to his warlike and religious, possibly even his civil, transactions. With a different language something of a new spirit came into the records, and seemed for a time to overcome the historical reticence which is so disappointingly manifest in other not inglorious periods of the nation's experience. The inscriptions are mostly lost or not yet recovered, though a few remain in copies made by scribes who perused the statues and trophies laid up in the great central shrine at Nippur. The Sumerian king-list[2] spares but two or three remarks upon the founder himself and relapses into its customary tale of names and numbers for the rest of the Dynasty of Agade; and all else is anecdote preserved and perhaps adapted for special ends.

A miraculous or a mysterious origin is essential to superhuman characters, and Sargon was the first to show that the taste of the ancient eastern peoples was to be for the latter. Like several notable successors he had, and did not disguise, an obscure birth and a humble beginning. The account of this is not only explicit but conveyed in a form which purports to be his own words. Only the first few lines are preserved of Assyrian tablets which begin, 'I (am) Sargon, the mighty king, king of Agade', and go on to relate the birth and earliest years of the speaker, name in broken

---

[1] A full list of the inscriptions of Sargon and the succeeding kings of Agade, as well as of other texts relating to their reigns, is published in G, 17, 193 ff. and A, 25.

[2] G, 18.

lines some of his subsequent conquests, and then break off.[1] It is
not, indeed, likely that the words are an authentic utterance of the
great king; the class of composition to which this text belongs
was regularly cast in the form of personal record as though taken
from an inscription, but there is much to suggest that they were
the productions of a later age, having a didactic bent and perhaps
a certain philosophy of history.[2] One such recorded inscription
even purported to recount, in the god's own words, the life and
beneficent achievements of 'the god Marduk, the great lord'.[3]
Despite this element of forgery, these accounts were certainly
based upon authentic tradition, and there is nothing incredible in
the statements attributed by this 'legend' to Sargon. According
to this, therefore, his mother was a priestess, his father an unknown wanderer. He was born in secret at an obscure village on
the Euphrates called Azupiranu, perhaps 'Saffron Town', from
a local product which has kept its name almost unaltered.[4] His
mother, to rid herself of the child, enclosed him in a basket which
she covered and made fast with pitch, and launched it upon the
river. Miraculously preserved from drowning, he was carried
downstream, and fished out by one Aqqi, a labourer in a palm-
garden, who noticed the basket as his bucket dipped in the water.
Aqqi took the child and reared him as his own, making him to
follow the same profession.

At this point the tradition is taken up by two corroborative
texts; one is the king-list itself which says that Sargon was a
gardener, the other a Sumerian story of his life which repeated
the details about his place of origin, and about his mother and
father.[5] The next incident of this miraculous career was that the
goddess Ishtar bestowed her favour upon the youth, and owing
to this he was soon found in the service of Ur-Zababa, known
from the king-list as a king of the Fourth Dynasty of Kish.[6] This
potentate lived in great state, for one of the texts named above
calls him 'the shepherd (who) rose like the sun in the temple of
Kish' and he had the curious distinction of giving his name to a
musical instrument.[7] But he came to offend the god Marduk, and
this in a matter where Sargon was concerned. The latter had
attained the intimate degree of cupbearer to Ur-Zababa, who

---

[1] G, 33, 119.
[2] §1, 20, erster Teil, 62 ff.; G, 13, 28 f.; A, 25, 6, no. 4.
[3] §1, 20, erster Teil, 79 ff.; §1, 14, 70, cf. 72.
[4] §1, 40, 160 f.; G, 35, 82 and 375; G, 36, 93; A, 25, 7, no. 7.
[5] §1, 35, 175 ff.; §1, 20, erster Teil, 37.   [6] G, 18, 106 f.
[7] Z.A. 42, 147; A, 22, 115.

at this time commanded him to 'change the drink-offering of E-sagila'. Sargon, evading this impiety, and redoubling his own service to the god, weaned the divine favour from his master, and Marduk made the servant lord of the land (and, it is added, the world) in place of Ur-Zababa. But as it may be observed that the Dynasty of Kish continued for another five reigns after this successful defection, Sargon was at first no more than a rival, not a destroyer. The earlier years of his rule may have been devoted to providing himself with a capital city, for all the sources describe how he built this in a new place. But in doing so he too committed some act which the jealous god took as an impiety, for he is said to have dug out earth from Babylon for the purpose of building a city 'next to Agade', and to have called this city 'Babylon'. The incident is related in two chronicles[1] and an omen,[2] but its purport is hardly clear—it means perhaps that Sargon is accused by these late recorders of ambitiously attempting to make for himself a capital which should have the prestige enjoyed by Babylon in subsequent ages, and regarded by them as immemorial.

Such was the earlier history of the hero, with an appropriate dash of legend, but with little that need be untrue. There is much to bespeak his alien origin, and to indicate the upper Euphrates for his birthplace, although, if the story of his solitary journey be true, he cannot be considered the leader of an inferred invasion of 'Akkadians' taken to be the first 'historical' migration of Westerners into Babylonia. But his native tongue, which he was to graft upon the old Sumerian script, qualified him to enter service in the court of Kish, where kings with Semitic names had been among the earliest rulers. The rest is no more than the achievement of many an unknown youth marked out for fame— for such a man of destiny the especial favour of a deity might be taken for granted. The foundation of his new city is placed by our authorities after other chief events of his reign, but might be thought to occur more naturally after his revolt from Ur-Zababa, for he did not become master of any other existing city, and his new era could best be inaugurated from a new capital. This was signalized also by the adoption of a new name, for the obscure boy was assuredly not called at birth 'True King'. His career justified the name and gave it a magic for generations after. It was proudly borne by two Assyrian kings, the second and greater of whom disdained for it the family style of a father who had himself, upon attaining the throne, assumed the traditional glory

[1] G, 20, vol. II, 8; §1, 20, erster Teil, 54 f.
[2] §1, 30, 20, no. 73.

of the name Tiglath-pileser.[1] A just confidence in his own powers dictated his choice to Sargon of Agade, in an age to which the name adopted as an inspiration and an omen was not unfamiliar. In the reign of Naram-Sin one of his opponents, who led the revolt of Kish, adopted the defiant name 'He rallied Kish',[2] under which he has been commemorated. Even the water-man Aqqi who rescued the infant Sargon bore a name which may have proclaimed his occupation.[3] A more ancient custom was honoured when the Akkadian dynasty was established in authority, and a pair of names, 'King of all Kings' and 'Son of all Kings', which translated the old Sumerian royal convention,[4] was found among the offspring of Naram-Sin.

Upon the chronology of Sargon's reign and the order of its events we are hardly at all informed, and can be guided only by what seems the natural progression. The next dynasty in the king-list after that in which Ur-Zababa ruled at Kish was the third of Uruk, and its only member was Lugalzaggisi, who is credited with a reign of twenty-five years. The main outlines of this king's career can be traced from his own inscriptions and from other allusions. As *ensi* of Umma he took up again the inveterate war against his neighbours at Lagash, and avenged the many defeats of his predecessors by a savage destruction of the rival city.[5] Some time after this he gained possession of Uruk, and his reign of twenty-five years is doubtless reckoned from that event. During these years he added the successes claimed in his only long inscription, found upon vases dedicated at Nippur.[6] Under various titles, priestly as well as civil, he was the ruler and benefactor of Umma, Uruk, Ur, Larsa, Nippur, and two other religious centres, and specifically he asserted that the supreme god had appointed him 'king of the land', thus assuming in the most formal terms the ancient title of sovereignty among the cities of Sumer. He nowhere claims the rulership of Kish, and it is not known how or by whom the defeat of that city, posited by the king-list, was effected,[7] nor whether the victim was Ur-Zababa or one of his five successors. But a wider prospect than local domination is opened for the first time with Lugalzaggisi; in a striking passage of unmistakable import, if slightly obscure

[1] §1, 44.   [2] §1, 20, erster Teil, 78; see below, p. 441.
[3] §1, 20, erster Teil, 63, n. 1; G, 35, 82.
[4] G, 42, 318; see below, p. 454.
[5] G, 39, 56 ff.; G, 3, 86 ff.; see above, pp. 143 f.
[6] G, 39, 152 ff.; G, 3, 96 ff.
[7] A Sumerian poem (G, 22, 268; A, 14) seems to ascribe the ruin of Kish to the rise of Sargon, but in any case he afterwards 'restored its place' (G, 3, 106 f.; A, 25, 36).

wording,[1] he proclaimed that not only had the god given him the kingship over 'the land' (*kalam*, i.e. Sumer), and 'directed the eye of the land upon him', but also that he 'had rendered the foreign lands (*kur-kur*) subject at his foot, and from the rising sun to the setting he had bowed the neck (of all) to him'. When this state had been achieved Enlil in addition 'from the Lower Sea (by) the Tigris and Euphrates unto the Upper Sea made straight its road, from the rising sun unto the setting he made him to have no opposer'. If by no more than a vigorous sortie, Lugalzaggisi had broken out from those limits beyond which the Sumerian chroniclers had not looked, and had shown the way to a new world for his successor to conquer.

With its usual formula the king-list records the end of this prosperous reign, and the transfer of supremacy to Agade. That Lugalzaggisi was defeated, and also captured, by Sargon we have not only this tradition, but the explicit statement of the victor, who relates in one of his inscriptions the course of his campaign.[2] A later narrator already quoted had an account of the preliminaries to this contest, but the condition of the text and its obscure phrases show little more than that messages were exchanged between Sargon and Lugalzaggisi, the latter at length refusing to listen to the overweening demands of the challenger, but being compelled finally to admit his messenger. Appeal to arms soon followed, and Sargon was first in the field. He marched swiftly to Uruk, and seems to have carried the city by a surprise attack, for he 'smote the city of Uruk and destroyed its wall' before 'he battled with the man of Uruk and defeated him', although, as another inscription adds, this commander was aided by the forces of fifty town-governors.[3] Only after these two disasters did Lugalzaggisi himself reach the field of battle, where he shared the same fate; Sargon 'captured him and brought him in a yoke to the gate of Enlil' at Nippur as a trophy to the national god, whose choice for the kingship he was shown by the issue to have forfeited, and Sargon to have inherited.

His next task was to complete the subjugation of the rest of Sumer, and his first objective the city of Ur. Whoever was the general of its forces (its Second Dynasty was probably ended by Rimush) he was defeated in the field and Sargon 'smote his city and destroyed its wall'. Next he turned against the territory of Lagash, now as often in close alliance with Ur, but having put

---

[1] Besides the earlier translations see recently §1, 21, 135 ff. and §1, 39, 251 n. 76.

[2] A, 25, 34 f.; G, 32, 173; G, 25, 211; G, 3, 100 ff.; A, 31.

[3] A, 25, 39; G, 32, 180; G, 3, 110 ff.

aside for the nonce its ancient feud with its neighbour Umma. E-Ninmar was the first of the cities within the domain of Lagash to be attacked and destroyed, 'and its territory from Lagash to the sea he smote (and) his weapons he washed in the sea'.[1] Of this South Babylonian alliance only one stronghold now remained, and Sargon turned back to deal with Umma. The result was no different—'with the man of Umma he did battle and defeated him and smote his city and destroyed its wall'. Hereby he was master of all the old Sumerian homeland, and his principal opponents were probably all his captives. Lugalzaggisi was taken and led in triumph, the *ensi* of Umma[2] was shown beside him upon a monument which has perished but its epigraphs have come down in a later copy, and perhaps the celebrated Urukagina of Lagash was also captured at E-Ninmar, for a person of that name,[3] whose father was formerly *ensi* of Lagash, is mentioned upon a monument of Manishtusu. Another inscription of Sargon adds to this tale of victories over the old Sumerian cities a kind of summary; it reckons that he won altogether thirty-four battles, as the result of which a real advantage was gained, for 'the ships of Meluhha, the ships of Magan, the ships of Tilmun he moored at the quay in front of Agade'. That is, the Persian Gulf was now in his power, and he was able to receive the products of the lands upon its shores or accessible only by its trade routes. Ur-Nanshe, at the beginning of the last Early Dynastic age, had been the first to proclaim that he obtained timber from Tilmun, and it was this trade which now passed into the hands of Sargon. These oversea lands of the south are reckoned to his empire both in the legend of his birth,[4] and in a late geographical list of his conquests.

The chronology of events in the reign of Sargon being uncertain, because not fixed by extant date-formulae, it will be convenient to see what other sources of information have to tell about this early stage of his career, before tracing his conquests abroad.[5] Much of what is known about these portentous figures of the Agade dynasty has been preserved in a very curious medium, the lore of those who studied the interpretations of omens derived from the examination of the entrails of victims slain for sacrifice, in pursuance of an absurd but widely accepted belief that the gods would, in answer to prayer and ceremony, indicate in this strange way their decision as to the issue of an enterprise. Ability to read what the god was deemed to write upon the liver and other organs

[1] A, 15, 27 f.   [2] G, 32, 177; A, 25, 37.
[3] §1, 21, 137 n. 107; see below, p. 449.   [4] A, 25, 7, no. 7; G, 33, 119.
[5] §1, 48.

of sheep was, indeed, the most highly esteemed of all accomplishments, and was the privilege of a closed corporation of 'seers' who
professed to trace their origin from the age before the Flood, and
admitted none but those qualified by birth and personal endowment to the freedom of their mystery, which was even then to be
attained only by arduous study of their technique and scriptures.[1]
These latter were the tablets of omens so largely represented in
the literature which has survived to our own day, particularly in
the remains of the Assyrian royal library at Nineveh.

The prognostications of these are for the most part general,
foretelling success or discomfiture in battle or sometimes in
policy, but almost exclusively with regard to military affairs. A
few, however, differ by coupling the marks observed upon the
entrails with the mention of historical characters,[2] and relating
that the marks in question were formerly present when these
personages were about to accomplish the feats for which they were
celebrated in tradition. A fairly large number of the great figures
of the Babylonian past are included among this company, but
whereas most of them fall to be mentioned only once or twice
Sargon and Naram-Sin are the heroes of many episodes recollected
from notable oracles given to the diviners. Such was their
importance that not only do they occur rather frequently in the
usual form of brief allusion, but a special collection of observations, with historical notes of unparalleled form and length, was
devoted to their augural experiences.[3] How totally this differed
from the usual contents of the seers' tablets is demonstrated by the
survival of almost the same matter under quite a different guise
in a chronicle of the late Babylonian period.

The omens do not fail to mark the dramatic rise of Sargon in
his youth. Among the oldest remains of the haruspical superstition are some clay models of the liver found at Mari;[4] one of these
models shows and describes in technical terms some signs around
the gall of the liver which were 'the omen of Kish, of Sargon';
presumably they foreshadowed the fall of Kish before the former
cupbearer of its king, and his occupying the throne. From the
special collection described above comes another sign, whereby
Ishtar manifested her choice of him and her will to accomplish
all his desires. This favour of the goddess was enough; there soon
occurred to him an omen which preluded his supremacy, 'he had
no rival'. More explicit is the message of a peculiar clay model

[1] See for a general account of this G, 9, especially ch. vi.
[2] §1, nos. 17, 30 and 47.   [3] G, 20, vol. II, 25 ff.
[4] §1, 34, 41 ff.; A, 25, 7 ff.

which shows a fantastic face made up of the convolutions of an unbroken line, representing the freakish appearance of a sheep's intestines. This repulsive apparition was thought to depict the 'face of Humbaba',[1] an outlandish giant who had been slain by the comrades Gilgamesh and Enkidu. Such a portent had been found in one of his sacrifices by Sargon: 'omen of Sargon who became master of the land'. One other tradition may concern his foundation of a new residence: '(he) let the sons of his palace dwell for five leagues on every side',[2] to which a second version of the same event adds 'five districts on every side having been cut off, he enlarged his palace, and the (head)men stood by him and said to him "Where shall we go?"'[3] In these few words is sketched a re-allocation of landed possessions in favour of adherents, similar to that which may be registered by the obelisk of Manishtusu, to be described later—it was dispossessed owners who thus demanded angrily where they were to go. As well as omens concerned with campaigns of the conqueror in the northwest and in the east there are a few also which were given to him at unspecified times; one describes some occasion, perhaps upon a campaign in the east, when a great storm fell upon his army, but at length it emerged from its distress: 'omen of Sargon to whom the light returned after going through the darkness'.[4] Finally there comes the suggestion that the tempest occurred on the eve of a battle or in the midst of it: 'omen of Sargon whose soldiers a downpour enveloped and they exchanged their weapons among themselves'.[5]

Two of Sargon's inscriptions place after the account of his victories in southern Babylonia a summary description of distant triumphs in a march up the Euphrates and widespread conquests in Syria. The original inscriptions (or rather the copies of them which have been preserved) devote only a few lines to these events, but find room for some interesting details. The first stage of his march ended at the place called Tuttul, now the town of Hit, some ninety miles west of Baghdad. Here he 'knelt to the god Dagan...and he gave him the upper land, Mari, Iarmuti, Ibla, up to the cedar forest and the silver mountains'. A curious note is added upon his numbers—'5400 men ate bread daily before him'. Beside this original and authentic account the omens and chronicle have also something to relate of this western expedition; the chronicle says[6] that 'in the eleventh year the land of the west

1 §1, 37, 107 ff.; §1, 42; §1, 12.   2 G, 20, vol. II, 5.
3 *Ibid.* vol. II, 32; §1, 30, 17, no. 67.   4 §1, 30, 17, no. 62.
5 *Ibid.* 9, no. 20; G, 5, vol. IV, 334b; *J.A.O.S.* 80, 200.
6 G, 20, vol. II, 4.

to its limit his hand reached, he made its word (as) one, he set up
his images in the west, their booty he brought over (sea) on rafts'.[1]
The version in the omens[2] does not differ greatly except in naming
the third instead of the eleventh year, and this receives a certain
support from a reference to a 'third year' in the story called *King
of the Battle* to be described later. This congruent account is
nevertheless preceded in the chronicle and the omens by sentences
of completely opposite import, the chronicle averring that Sargon
crossed the 'sea in the east', whereas the omens call it the 'sea of
the west'. It seems likely that the chronicle is here in error, since
the following lines in both documents agree in relating to the
west, and include the curious detail that the conqueror 'set up his
images in the west'. Similar claims to conquest, and even to the
establishment of memorials in the Lebanon, were registered by
other early kings, Iakhdunlim of Mari[3] and his supplanter
Shamshi-Adad I,[4] but it was the much later Sargon II of Assyria
who erected his monument[5] in a unique situation far to the west of
all others, in Cyprus, possibly in emulation of his pattern. The
omens have also three other references to a conquest of the country
of Amurru, that is the west; the first two[6] relate generally that
he 'went to the land of Amurru, defeated it, and his hand reached
over the four regions (of the world)', but the third omen[7] states
that he 'went to the land of Amurru...smote it for the second
time (and) his warriors...brought him forth from the midst'—
the last phrase remains enigmatic owing to damage of the text.
Possibly the 'second time' was the 'eleventh year' of the chronicle.

Later tradition[8] thus agrees with Sargon's own testimony that
he marched up the Euphrates and became master of Syria, with its
various resources. Upon this point the only details are given by
the king's own inscription which, in addition to Hīt, mentions
three places and two districts. The latter are not difficult to locate;
the 'cedar forest' is generally agreed to be the Amanus mountains,
for their name is coupled with this description by Naram-Sin and
by Gudea. The 'silver mountains' are rather less definite, but it

[1] Chronicle *ina amāti ušebira*: omens *ina ⟨a⟩māti tāmta ušebira*; see G, 5,
vol. I, part II, 85 and G, 36, 45 *b*.
[2] G, 20, vol. II, 31 f.; §1, 30, 16, no. 61.
[3] §1, 8, 13; A, 31.
[4] §1, 9, 24 f.
[5] Upon this monument Sargon II declares that none of his predecessors had ever
heard of the island (§1, 27, vol. II, nos. 186 ff.).
[6] §1, 30, 19 f., nos. 72, 74.
[7] *Ibid.* no. 75.
[8] A, 20.

seems necessary to take 'silver' no less literally than 'cedar', assuming that Sargon was interested chiefly in the valuable products of his conquests. The Taurus range, therefore, with its many deposits of lead and silver must be indicated.[1] Mari is no longer in doubt; it was the site now called Tell el-Ḥarīrī, on the Euphrates, near Abu Kamāl, as proved by recent excavation, and a later ruler[2] couples it in his kingdom with Tuttul or Hīt, just as it was the next stage in Sargon's march. Iarmuti was a place and a port upon the coast of the Mediterranean, and the evidence of the Amarna letters seems to place it somewhere south of Byblos,[3] though a location rather nearer to the other districts mentioned might be preferred. Ibla was conquered again by Naram-Sin who couples its name with Armanum which may be Aleppo itself,[4] but the more significant reference is furnished by Gudea, in a generation not far distant, who relates that he fetched three different kinds of timber from 'the city Ursu, of the mountain of Ibla'. The situation of Urs(h)u,[5] which figures also in the Mari letters and in a picturesque episode of early Hittite history, has been the matter of much argument in recent years, but it is now regarded as most likely that it was a place upon or near the Euphrates, not far to the north of Carchemish.

While therefore it is beyond doubt that Sargon carried his arms to the limits of north Syria, later tradition avers much more. One source of this is a composition[6] which bore the name *King of the Battle*. Most of this story is preserved upon a tablet in a very imperfect condition which was found in Egypt with the Amarna letters, and there are furthermore evident allusions to its subject in a broken text accompanying the celebrated 'Babylonian Map of the World' in the British Museum.[7] After some very uncertain preliminaries it appears that Sargon hears of the complaints of merchants from the city of Purushkhanda (the Hittite Parshu-khanda), but it is not clear what their grievances were, nor to whom these were due; but they appealed to Sargon to champion their cause and offered him rich inducements. Only from the sequel can it be inferred that the alleged oppressor was a certain Nur-daggal, who was probably ruler of their city, and this must be, presumably, Purushkhanda. Despite the hesitation of his

---

[1] §1, 13, 502 f.; A, 31. [2] §1, 43, 49.
[3] G, 35, 375 ff.; §1, 24, 235; A, 20, 5 f. See above, p. 324.
[4] G, 14, 80; §1, 25, 369 ff.; §1, 18, 70; §1, 3, 30.
[5] The most recent discussions are §1, 15, 55 f.; §1, 22, 253; §1, 11, 31; §1, 38, 42; §1, 25, 371.
[6] §1, 46; §1, 20, erster Teil, 86 ff. and zweiter Teil, 45 ff.
[7] *C.T.* part 22, 48; §1, 46, 86 ff.

followers Sargon resolved to undertake this expedition and relieve the aggrieved merchants. He enquired of the road to Purush-khanda, and was told of its incredible difficulty; one stage was encumbered with blocks of lapis-lazuli and gold, another with forest trees, others with thorny thickets. At length, overcoming all these, Sargon reached the enemy's city, to the consternation of Nur-daggal who had boasted that he could never accomplish a march through the floods and forests. His appearance in these circumstances was enough, for it appears that Nur-daggal made instant submission, and presumably agreed to redress the wrongs of the merchants, who had convenanted with Sargon the price of his aid. After this the army grew apprehensive, and murmured that it was time to return home, which was done, and Sargon resumed a peaceful rule in his own city.

The central interest of this story lies in the introduction of the city called Purushkhanda, for this place, if not exactly located, is at least proved, by evidence from two different periods, to lie in the neighbourhood of Caesarea (Kayseri) in Cappadocia.[1] It figures not only in the Hittite records, but more prominently in the affairs of the early Assyrian merchants whose business documents[2] have been found in greatest number at a site called Kültepe, about fifteen miles from Kayseri; and from Kültepe (the ancient Kanesh) there were only four caravan stages to Purushkhaddum, as it is called in those tablets. It is generally concluded to have lain to the south or south-west of the great Salt Lake of central Anatolia.[3] If the *King of the Battle* has any historical foundation, Sargon did not stop short at the mountain barrier, but extended his sway deep into Asia Minor.

There are suspicious features in this narration, and these, coupled with its incomplete state and consequent want of clarity, have raised doubts whether any authentic history can be drawn from it or whether the whole incident must be dismissed as a later flourish upon a legendary figure.[4] It is hardly reassuring that the story seems to originate in Syria rather than from Babylonia itself, and that it is somehow involved in the description of strange and far regions which was inscribed upon the 'Map of the World'. Despite this it cannot be overlooked that genuine historical elements are present, especially the merchants in a district where

[1] See W. M. Calder and G. E. Bean, *A Classical Map of Asia Minor* (Supplement to *A.St.* 7, 1957), square Je; E. Forrer in *R.L.A.* II, 82.

[2] See below, ch. XXIV, sects. VII to X; A, 17.

[3] §I, 15, 64; §I, 5, 20 f.; A, 17, 123; A, 20.

[4] G, 35, 83 ff. and 375; §I, 1; §I, 6.

copious evidence exists of their activity in a later generation. It is true that some four hundred years intervened, and it might be thought that conditions of a later age were reflected back to Sargon's days. The tablet from Amarna, the application of this title 'King of the Battle' to the Egyptian overlord by another writer in the Amarna letters, and the fragment of a Hittite version,[1] are all of the fourteenth century, and consequently still farther removed from the time of the Cappadocian merchants than these were from Sargon.

The tradition of this north-western campaign no longer stands unsupported, but it is hard to decide whether the story gains in credibility from the remains of similar legends which have appeared more recently. The most relevant of these is found upon a tablet which has at least the warrant of an earlier, though still far from contemporary, date.[2] Its contents can be understood only in a small part, for not merely is it mutilated by damage, but even the more legible passages are of very obscure meaning. Yet a situation of some general similarity seems to be described; Sargon is setting out upon an expedition to the 'land of Uta-rapashtum',[3] after a dramatic colloquy with his officers in a strain of mutual exhortation. But suddenly, without transition, a city is found to be under attack and is in flames—it is utterly destroyed, and its district far about on all sides so laid waste that not even a bird could find a lodging there. This last detail recalls what is related in the chronicle and omens[4] about Sargon's victory over the city of Kazallu. But in that case there is nothing to indicate the direction of his march, for Kazallu, though still unlocated, is likely to have lain not very far from Agade and from Babylon itself.[5] In subsequent, but still less intelligible, passages of this same tablet are found (or can be restored) the names of other places conquered by Sargon, and the narrative ended with words encouraging his successors to emulate his achievements, in the same style as the lines which conclude his 'legend'.[6]

It is interesting to observe that very similar stories were current concerning Naram-Sin, the famous grandson of Sargon, whose relations with the north-west will be related in their place

[1] §I, 20, zweiter Teil, 45 ff.; cf. A, 20.

[2] §I, 31.

[3] The enemy's name is not free from doubt, but if correct it may show a connexion with 'Nur-daggal' in the *King of the Battle*. To obtain even this tenuous relation of half a name it has to be assumed that *-daggal* is the same as the Sumerian *dagal*, which is *rapšu* in Akkadian. See A, 25, 7, no. 8.

[4] G, 20, vol. I, 41 f.   [5] §IV, 11, 60 ff.; A, 27.

[6] G, 33, 119.

below. For the present purpose, the most significant feature in these is the recurrence of Purushkhanda(r) in a later text[1] which purports to tell, with many mythical accompaniments, how the empire of Naram-Sin was invaded by a demoniac horde which made that town the first conquest, as though it had been the most distant bound of the Akkadian possessions. Recently too there has come to light a fragment[2] concerning an expedition of Naram-Sin which appears to have borne a curious likeness in matter and phraseology to the *King of the Battle*, for a speaker is found urging, on behalf of himself and others, that the hero should undertake a long march through mountains and deserts. This he does, under favourable signs, and is at length met by a messenger who craves mercy for the land of Apishal. Now this campaign against Apishal is well attested as one of the triumphs of Naram-Sin, and the narration of it in a style so clearly similar to the *King of the Battle* may well suggest that Sargon's exploit was no less authentic, both stories applying the same romantic colour to facts which might seem exciting enough in themselves.

A possible foray into a west still farther than Asia Minor is doubtfully attested by another document[3] of the later Assyrian period, which is of still more uncertain authority. This is a compilation of geographical names, coupled with many figures of distances between localities, or distances of these from an unspecified centre, and in each section appears the name of Sargon as a conqueror. It is hardly possible to doubt that by this name is intended the ancient king of Agade, and that the whole document, in spite of the obscurity of its purpose (for most of it is illegible), must be regarded as at least involving a statistical survey of Sargon's empire, as that was believed by later tradition to have been constituted. This list has more importance for its bearing upon Sargon's conquests in the north and east than in the direction of Syria and farther west. But in a general view of Sargon's kingdoms at the end it names as 'lands beyond the Upper Sea' (i.e. the Mediterranean) two places called Anaku and Kaptara. The former may be interpreted as the 'Tin (Country)', the latter is doubtless the same as Kaphtor of the Old Testament, both indicating Crete, as now usually accepted. Of Kaptara or Kapturu there is definite information in the letters discovered at

[1] §III, 3.

[2] §III, 4, 46 ff. Perhaps in the same tradition is the poetical account of a conversation between Shalmaneser III and his officers at the outset of a campaign: see W. G. Lambert in *A.St.* 11 (1961), 143 ff.

[3] §1, 48.

Mari,[1] which had some trade in the products of that distant island. Sargon is said, in the omens, to have crossed the sea in the west; that he sailed farther than any subsequent Mesopotamian ruler has at least thus much testimony.

The 'Tin (Country)' is altogether incapable of giving any firm indication; the name, strangely written, perhaps does not represent a country at all, and even granted this it has not been settled whether the metal usually written as the Sumerian *an—na, nagga* was tin or lead—the evidence is now positively claimed to indicate tin.[2] If tin, the ancient sources of this are very far from clear, the Caucasus region being perhaps the most likely, with some possibility of Spain, but in either case the metal must have come in to Babylonia by long-distance trade, and from no definable place to which Sargon can be pictured as directing his arms. If lead, its origins are not very much clearer. Suggestions have ranged as far as the south of Spain,[3] but there are nearer possibilities not so hard to imagine. One is the famous lead-mine of Laurium,[4] source of the wealth of Athens in a later age, but after all the most likely location would be in the south-east of Asia Minor, and to include this among the 'lands beyond the sea' need mean no more than that the approach was across the Gulf of Issus. The Anatolian peninsula is and always has been famous for great deposits of galena, and a recent authority[5] has drawn up a list of no less than twenty-six, among which those of Bulgar Maden, of Ak Dağ, and of Ala Dağ might all come in question as attainable by Sargon. If any of these gave its name to the 'Tin (or Lead) Country', an expedition thither might coincide with the subject of the *King of the Battle*: an adventure designed to secure the double profit of a soldier-of-fortune's fee from the relieved merchants, and a load of precious metal to take home from the distant land.

In the remains of Sargon's own inscriptions there is no detail, nor indeed mention, of his conquests in the north. But the chronicle and omens[6] relate a successful war with Subartu; the aggression came from one or the other (the reports differ) and in the event Sargon 'defeated them, cast them in heaps, and overthrew their widespread host', carrying off their possessions to his city of Agade. The land of Subartu was also included in the

---

[1] §1, 7, 111 ff. For the voyage from the north Syrian coast to Crete see J. Nougayrol in *C.-R. Ac. Inscr. B.-L.*, 1960, 166.

[2] §1, 23; §1, 26, 50 ff.; §1, 45; A, 29. [3] §111, 2, 240. [4] §1, 2, 237.

[5] G, 12, 190 ff.

[6] G, 20, vol. 11, 7; G, 35, 70 ff.; G, 15, 34 ff.

catalogue of Sargon's provinces supplied by the geographical list already noticed. Near the beginning the limits of this land were defined: 'from...to Anzanzan (is) Subartu', and in a later section the 'space' of Subartu is given as 120 *bēru*, that measure being the distance covered on a march of two hours, which has been reckoned in modern equivalent as nearly seven miles.[1] It is, however, very uncertain what is meant by the 'space' of the countries here defined,[2] and since the north-western limit of Subartu is lost from the list, the south-east being perhaps Anzan (Anshan), a country which certainly lay in the nearer vicinity of Susa,[3] it is not easy to decide what territory was included in this conquest of Sargon. It was at least one of the most extensive, its 120 *bēru* being exceeded only by Akkad with 180, and its people being already described as 'widespread'. But if Subartu were taken as extending to Syria the dimension for it must in any case greatly exceed that of Akkad. Despite this difficulty it is impossible to ignore the phrase of Naram-Sin, 'ruler of Subartum up to the cedar-forest', or to evade its implication unless an improbable land of cedars was to be found somewhere in the hills east of the Tigris.[4] But in fact Sargon's own inscription leaves no room for doubt; it was by Hīt and the Euphrates that he made his way to the 'cedar-forest', and it was this region which Naram-Sin boasted of ruling over as Subartum.

The most notable part of this conquest was the district which later was known as Assyria. There is now a variety of evidence that its great cities, Nineveh and Ashur, were in the dominion of Sargon's successors, and their conquest may reasonably be ascribed to himself. At Nineveh was found an inscription of the early Assyrian king Shamshi-Adad I which records the former building of a temple there by Manishtusu, who left at Ashur an inscription of his own, as Naram-Sin left one at Nineveh.[5] The city of Ashur is named upon the tablets of Akkadian date excavated at the place then called Gasur,[6] and later Nuzi, not far from the modern Kirkuk, and there is known to have been a large proportion of Akkadian names among the inhabitants of Ashur at this time.[7] Some of the stone figures found in the lowest levels of the Ishtar temple there belong, not to the Early

---

[1] §1, 41, 133.   [2] §1, 48, 20, regards it as distance by roads. See A, 34, 16.
[3] For its location see below p. 438, n. 4.
[4] Evidence for this, however, is not altogether wanting; see G, 15, 36 n. 34; §1, 22, 83.
[5] References to all of these in G, 15, 36 n. 100.
[6] G, 40, 148 n. 7.   [7] §1, 10, 714; §1, 32, 259 f.

Dynastic period, but to the Dynasty of Agade or even later. If in the former time they were the products of Sumerian cultural influence rather than of conquest from the south, in the latter they are more probably the memorials of a ruling class established by the kings of Agade. Finally there is an impressive bronze head discovered at Nineveh which by its style and mastery alike seems to claim a place in this age of high achievement,[1] and if rightly so dated may represent one of the Sargonic kings.

The next sector, in a geographical sense, of the conquests of Sargon was in the hill country to the east and north-east of Babylonia, and upon these campaigns we are best informed, both by his own inscriptions, and by other evidence, partly contemporary, but mostly of later date. To begin with the first: a general expression in the copied inscriptions of Sargon claims that 'the man of Mari and of Elam stood before Sargon', but this is made more explicit in other passages, containing lists of the rulers and places from which the conqueror took tribute.[2] The districts were Elam, B(W)arakhshe, Awan, and some places of lesser note, and the principal characters were Sanam-simut, called *ensi* of Elam, and Lukh-ishshan, called son of Khishep-rashir, king of Elam. Here for the first time occurs a contact with the native records of Elam, for a king named Khishep-ratep was the ninth member of a dynasty ruling in the district of Awan, and this name was, according to the native king-list,[3] borne by the son of Lukh-ishshan.[4] Over all these lands and rulers Sargon's triumph was complete, and his inscriptions close with the tribute or plunder of Awan itself and of Susa, where the sole surviving monument of the great king has been discovered.[5] A passing allusion to the eastern campaigns is made by a date-formula[6] which commemorates the 'year (when) Sharrumkin went to Simurum', probably the neighbourhood of the present Altın-Köprü, on the Lower Zab, between Kirkuk and Irbil.[7] This slight information obtained from contemporary records is but little augmented by later tradition. Three omens[8] survived to mark Sargon's victorious advance into Elam, to Barakhshe or Markhashe, in the course of which he perhaps encountered a great storm, for

---

[1] §1, 28; G, 31, figs. 206, 208.

[2] A, 25, 47, 51 f.; G, 3, 114 ff. See also below, pp. 647 f.

[3] §1, 36, 1 ff.; *Mém. D.P.* 23, iv.

[4] G, 6, 27 ff. Probably both the father and the son of Lukh-ishshan had the name Khishep-ratep, but see §1, 36, 4. On the variation in the name Khishep-ratep (-rashir) see G, 6, 28 n. 22.   [5] See Plate 52 (*a*).

[6] §1, 33, no. 151; G, 30, 5, no. 10.

[7] §1, 19, 120 and 123.   [8] A, 25, 8; §1, 30, nos. 47, 54, 71.

one omen tells how the goddess Ishtar delivered him safely out of the darkness, and another states baldly that 'having marched to the land of Elam he slew the Elamites' and brought a calamity upon them. In its turn, the 'geographical survey' already described above[1] includes in Sargon's dominions the lands of Arrapkha, Lullubi, Armanum, Gutium, Parashi, Tukrish, Anshan, and Elam, which, taken as a whole, might be regarded as comprising almost the entire mountainous region in south-western Persia.

Sargon's conquests, whatever the order in which they were made, had now come full circle with his triumph over the princes of Elam. One result of them was naturally a great inflow of wealth, and there are preserved from a later age parts of a long poetical composition[2] which celebrated the rise and the fall of Agade, particularly under Naram-Sin. At its beginning this poem refers to the days of Sargon—his defeat of Kish and Uruk, and his choice by the supreme god Enlil, who granted him 'the priesthood and the kingdom from the lower to the upper (land)'. At this time Inanna made Agade into her residence and dwelt in the temple there, giving prosperity to her citizens; their food and drink were of the finest, their festivals were continual and splendid, they were enriched and diverted by an influx of useful or exotic animals, their treasuries were full, the people danced to music in the streets, and unceasingly ships were bringing to the quays the products of distant lands.

But a reversal of all this glory had not, it seems, to await the days of Naram-Sin, for there is a strong tradition that the reign of Sargon himself was clouded at the end by difficulties both external and internal. This account is preserved only in the late chronicle and omens,[3] but is not likely to be merely a lesson upon the instability of fortune. Accordingly, in his old age (such is the more probable version) 'all the lands revolted against him', and so serious was his peril that 'they beset him in Agade'. But the old warrior was still himself, for 'Sargon went forth to battle, defeated them, cast them in heaps, and overthrew their widespread host': the omens add a picturesque conclusion, 'their chattels he bound upon them and cried "(they are) thine, O Ishtar"'—thus dedicating his spoils of war. Other lines in the chronicles and omens refer obscurely to a sacrilege which he was deemed to have committed in the building of his new city of Agade;[4] it was too near, or too like, the holy city of Babylon, and attracted the wrath

---

[1] §1, 48, 4 ff.
[2] G, 22, 268 ff.; A, 14, 64 ff.
[3] G, 20, vol. I, 6, 34 f.; §1, 30, no. 68; G, 38. [4] G, 20, vol. II, 8 f.

of the god Marduk, who caused his subjects to rebel against him 'from the rising to the setting of the sun, and gave him no rest'. What was actually the state of Sargon's empire at his death may be partly inferred from the action which was forced upon his son after his accession.

II. THE SUCCESSORS OF SARGON

The next two kings of Agade and successors to the empire of Sargon were his two sons, Rimush and Manishtusu, who reigned, according to the king-list, in reverse order of age, for that authority assigns nine years to Rimush, and afterwards fifteen to Manishtusu, who is said to have been the elder brother of his predecessor; but it must be added that there are variants of the lengths of reigns.[1] Both kings seem to have begun with campaigns against rebels, involving expeditions into the lands east of the Tigris and into Elam, but it is Manishtusu who, in one of his monuments,[2] refers to 'all the lands...which my father Sargon left' as having 'in enmity revolted against me', thus implying that he was in fact the immediate successor of Sargon, as might be expected from his primogeniture. There seems no evidence at present capable of settling this, and therefore the order of the king-list may provisionally be kept.

Rimush, in any case, was clearly faced upon his succession with a general revolt. The chronology of his military measures is as little ascertainable as those of his father, but in one place[3] he tells how in the third year after the god Enlil had given him the kingdom he carried out a victorious invasion of Elam, and relates the numbers of prisoners and slain. His first years were doubtless occupied with the other campaign described in his inscriptions, one that would necessarily precede the re-subjugation of the more distant provinces in the east. The south country of Babylonia proper, the ancient 'land' and the great Sumerian cities, had taken the opportunity of Sargon's death to throw off the domination of the interlopers who, however much they had come to resemble and to imitate culturally the Sumerians, must have been regarded by these with some of the same feelings as they afterwards were to cherish against the Gutians or the Amorites—indeed, the Akkadians were in this as in other respects forerunners of the Amorites.[4] It has been observed that we find no trace of hostility

---

[1] G, 18, 111 f.   [2] §11, 7; A, 25, 14, no. 2.
[3] G, 3, 122ff.   [4] §11, 3, 29 f.

in the records between Sumerians and Semites: thus stated it is true, for there was no ethnic distinction involving these terms,[1] but the opposition comes out clearly in the campaign of Rimush which may have taken place in his first year. He states explicitly that his opponents were 'the cities of Sumer', and that he treated them with exemplary severity, for after their defeat he brought forth 5700 of their soldiers and (apparently) put them into prisons. The leader of this revolt was the king of Ur; he is called 'king' by his conqueror, and evidently occupied, by some sort of general recognition, the sovereignty over the 'land' which was the distinction recorded in the king-list. This is, in fact, duly recorded by that authority, for it is possible to insert the name of this Kaku as last of the Second Dynasty of Ur, otherwise broken out of the documents as we have them. Herewith is obtained (if the restoration be correct) synchronism between rulers named in the king-list, and also one more example of the characteristic weakness of that compilation, for in it the dynasties of Ur II and Agade are divided by no less than six other dynasties and twenty-two kings. Kaku, the leader of the Sumerian revolt, was captured together with his city, which was rendered defenceless by having its wall dismantled. The calamity which fell upon Ur at this moment is perhaps reflected, however obscurely, in the lament[2] ascribed to Enkheduanna, the first holder (known to history) of the celebrated office of high-priestess to the Moon-god in that city, which became traditionally the prerogative of sisters and daughters of the reigning monarch, and so continued until the very last years of Babylonian record. Enkheduanna has left a monument of her own, and her name upon some cylinder-seals belonging to her servants.[3] The lamentation represents her as the victim of a disaster which had afflicted Ur—the Moon-god, being angry, had ceased his care for his people, and had suffered his priestess to be driven into exile, powerless, as it seems, to appease the wrath of her own brother against the rebellious city.[4] But there was more than one centre of the revolt, for Rimush gathered his prisoners from other 'cities of Sumer', and the inscriptions reveal the names of those who, as good subjects of the national 'king' and as patriots, took part in the battle against the alien dynast. Two of these were the neighbours Lagash and Umma, ancient rivals but always likely to be under the same control as they were under the same necessities. On this occasion they were led by

---

[1] §11, 5; G, 38. [2] §11, 2; A, 25, 9, n. 76; A, 33, 127. [3] §11, 20, 49 f.
[4] Yet despite this presumed severity Rimush made a number of dedications in temples of the city; §11, 20, 51. See A, 26, 12 f.

their respective *ensi;* the name of Umma's chief is missing, that of Lagash is written with characters of uncertain reading. The ruler of Umma was probably the superior of these two, for he is described as accompanied by his 'forerunner', while other local chiefs have their 'messenger' or vizier. Notable allies, destined alike to be trophies of the victorious Akkadian, were Meskigala,[1] *ensi* of Adab, and Lugalushumgal, *ensi* of Zabalam.[2] From all of these places the inscriptions of Rimush reckon long tales of slain and prisoners.

Being as a result of this campaign secure in his rear, the king was now able to address himself to reconquest of the east. His inscriptions do not distinguish clearly between wars in Sumer and in Elam, but they have at least a tendency to relate the events in the two regions apart, and it may be assumed that the operations were spread over two campaigns in different directions.[3] The preliminaries of the Elamite campaign were prepared at the end of his subdual of the Sumerian cities, for in one place he states distinctly that, after his victory over Kaku and the southern allies, 'on his return' he smote Kazallu, took prisoner its *ensi* Asharid, and inflicted upon the rebel city an enormous loss of slain and captives. Elsewhere in the inscriptions Dēr is associated with Umma in a common disaster, and it is not likely that Umma was able to face Rimush again in a second year.

Whenever it was, the expedition against Elam, which is described in a group of texts copied at Nippur, was to prove the greatest triumph of Sargon's successor. Though Elam is named generally, the scene of his principal victory was the district of Barakhshe, where his father before him had fought one of his most glorious wars. According to the inscriptions of Rimush the armies of Elam and of a land called Zakhara had united against him. Their leader was Abalgamash, king of Barakhshe, who had with him Sidgau, called 'governor' of Barakhshe. In command of the host of Zakhara was the 'governor' of that land. Sidgau, at least, was an old opponent of Sargon, and his restoration was doubtless an act of defiance. The battle took place 'between Awan and Susa', apparently upon a river named in an obscure phrase[4] which seems to tell of 'pouring' it over them(?). However

---

[1] He was already ruling in the reign of Lugalzaggisi; see *C.A.H.* 1[3], ch. VI, sect. II.

[2] Now said to be located at Ibzeikh; see plan in *Sumer* 11, 127 ff.; §II, 6, 177.

[3] They occupied his reign up to the third year, when he summarized the slain and prisoners, G, 3, 124 f.; A, 25, 63.

[4] §II, 15, 40; A, 15, 67; R. Borger, *J.C.S.* 18 (1964), 54 f.; E. Sollberger, *R.A.* 63 (1969), 40, n. 1.

achieved, the victory was complete, and the king counted over 16,000 defeated, perhaps slain, and over 4000 prisoners, as well as a great weight of gold and copper some of which he dedicated to the god Enlil in Nippur. The result of this victory was not only the complete recovery of Barakhshe from the control of the Elamites but the destruction of some Elamite cities and the establishment of at least a tributary sovereignty over Elam itself: 'Rimush, king of Kish, was lord over Elam.' The king ends with a strong affirmation that his kingdom was now unchallenged, Enlil had revealed (?) it, and 'by the gods Shamash and Aba[1] I swear it; no lies, but truly!'

Rimush was now equal to his father and declares that 'he held for Enlil the upper and the lower sea and the mountains, all of them'. His boast has been substantiated by the widespread finding of trophies dedicated by him throughout his empire, especially fragments of alabaster vases inscribed with his triumph over Elam and Barakhshe, being themselves part of the countless spoils brought back from there. In the extreme north of Mesopotamia one of these fragments has been found at the great but still unnamed site of Tell Brak,[2] and even so far, to the headwaters of the Khabur, did the sway of Rimush extend. Concerning the remainder of his rule, nine years in all, there is no information; presumably he enjoyed his power and revenues peacefully. But his reign and life were ended by a palace conspiracy, in which he was assassinated by certain of his courtiers 'with their seals', or 'sealed tablets', as certain omens relate,[3] whatever weapons are indicated by this. Another omen[4] announces the 'presage of Agade, of Rimush and Manishtusu': what happened upon this occasion is not recorded, but it might possibly be taken to mean that Manishtusu had some hand in the murder of his brother, whom, innocent or guilty, he succeeded.

His first years may have been peaceful, for there is a stone figure of the king,[5] found at Susa, upon which Eshpum the *ensi* of that city inscribed a dedication to a local goddess for the benefit of his master. But, later or sooner, the revolt was renewed and the battles of Sargon, perhaps of his successor, had to be fought again. Yet Manishtusu, when he writes that 'all the lands... which my father Sargon left had in enmity revolted against me

[1] For this god, written A.MAL, see E. Porada in *Iraq*, 22, 119 f.
[2] §II, 12, 27.
[3] §I, 30, 13, no. 42; §I, 17, 256; A, 25, 13, B. 2.
[4] §I, 30, 23, no. 87.
[5] G, 17, 198; see below, p. 650.

and not one stood fast', seems to ignore the reign of his brother, if in fact this had preceded.

His tasks against the rebels were those which had confronted his forbears; he had to subdue both south and east. In one place occurs an interesting detail about this operation—he divided his army into two parts,[1] but he does not relate what these two divisions had as objectives. One of them, at least, met the forces of two different but allied, and presumably adjacent, lands Anshan and Sherikhum, which were defeated and their king (for both seem to have been under one ruler) carried off in triumph and led into the temple of the Sun-god in Sippar, accompanied with rich gifts for the god out of the booty captured. The other division was perhaps the force which waged a war 'on the other side of the sea' against thirty-two kings of cities who had assembled for battle.[2] These were defeated, their cities subdued, their leaders slain, and their country occupied 'up to the silver-mine'. Manishtusu took the opportunity of shipping stone from this region to the quays of Agade, and made a statue of himself to stand before the god Enlil at Nippur. He also transported timber for his temple-building at Sippar.

The scanty accounts of this campaign (no more than a few phrases divided between two inscriptions)[3] afford only a momentary and baffling glimpse, but it is of a wider world. Anshan, a name celebrated until the last days of Babylonian history, was one of the foremost Elamite provinces, generally coupled with Susa, of which it takes precedence in the titles of Elamite kings. Despite this frequent appearance in many different ages and contexts there is very poor evidence of its geographical position, and modern authorities have been in doubt[4] whether to place it north or south of Susa. Its sister-realm of Sherikhum is, on the contrary, mentioned only once by Sargon and in this inscription, which does no more than indicate a likelihood of its being a

---

[1] §II, 7. The inscription upon the curious object called the 'cruciform monument' is shown by internal evidence not to be contemporary with the kings of Agade, but its slight reference to history can be accepted for a detail which there was no need to invent; see G, 17, 8, and references there; E. Sollberger, *J.E.O.L.* 20 (1968), 50 ff.

[2] G, 3, 130 f. and 136 f.

[3] For the original inscriptions of Manishtusu, and the 'cruciform monument' see A, 25, 14 f. and 69; and above, n. 1.

[4] Recent discussions in G, 32, 234; G, 6, 31; §II, 8; §II, 9, 21; §I, 19, 117; see also below, ch. XXIII. In view of the south-eastern direction of Manishtusu's march it might be well to reconsider a proposal (quoted in §II, 8, 111 f.) to find the name of Anshan preserved in 'Ashshan, stated to be the Arabic name of Rāmhurmuz ('three days' march east of Ahwāz', G, 26, 243).

coastal region beyond Anshan. This maritime location is supported by a remarkable variant[1] to the text of the 'cruciform monument'; instead of 'Anshan and Sherikhum' (with the simple determinative of 'place') the variant substitutes 'Anshan and the city of Meluhha'. The last name has long provided one of the enigmas of ancient geography,[2] for, very briefly, later texts undoubtedly apply it to the distant African lands of Nubia or Ethiopia, whereas in earlier contexts (and some later as well) it is almost as clearly applied to a country not only less remote, but lying in the east rather than the west. The normal route to Meluhha was by sea, and there are many references, beginning from the Agade period onwards, to sea-borne imports of timber, gold, semi-precious stones, and ivory from Meluhha. Moreover, its name was regularly associated with that of Magan, a land which can now with some confidence be located on the shores of the Gulf of Oman,[3] and may even correspond in part with the medieval and modern Makrān. Since Meluhha is always implied to be more distant than Magan, its appearance in place of Sherikhum, while furnishing yet another argument in favour of the 'eastern' Meluhha, is surprising in its suggestion of nearness, for Sherikhum, whatever its true location, was not beyond the reach of a military expedition from southern Iraq, whereas Meluhha has been thought, with some plausibility, to have at least included the flourishing upstream cities of the Indus, now famous but unknown until their recent discovery, with perhaps also undiscovered ports at the delta of the great river.[4] There is unassailable material evidence of relations between the two civilizations of Mesopotamia and of Sind, in the forms both of natural products and of artefacts, and it was in the Agade period that such relations seem to have been at their height. Yet it is difficult to imagine how an army of Manishtusu can have penetrated to any country even within the radius of Mohenjo Daro, or how any such extent of territory can

---

[1] E. Sollberger in *J.E.O.L.* 20, 55 and 63.

[2] A summary of the ample but strangely inconclusive evidence concerning Meluhha is given in §1, 48, 6 ff.; recent (and diverging) opinions have been expressed in §11, 13, 16 and §11, 6, 184; A, 30.

[3] This rests upon the convincing identification of the celebrated '*mes*-wood of Magan' with the *Dalbergia sissoo* Roxb., and the native habitat of that tree (§11, 4); for the possible identity of the name with Makrān see W. Eilers in §11, 11, 29.

[4] But against this see §11, 14, 143 f. Concerning naval sites and activities of the Harappā people see §11, 1, especially the references to Lothal on p. 92. See also A, 7. What might be meant by the 'city' of Meluhha is beyond allowable conjecture. It is curious that Gudea (Statue B, vi, 64) applies the same style of 'city' to Anshan, the other member of this pair.

have been in the hand of a single ruler, 'king of Anshan and Sherikhum (or, Meluhha)', as the inscriptions variously call him. A further difficulty would be raised if the following passage in the text went on to relate that the king crossed the Lower Sea in ships to deal with the other body of his enemies. But although there is unmistakable reference to ships and to the thirty-two hostile kings assembled 'on the other side of the sea', the actual phrase[1] supposed to describe the crossing is of doubtful meaning, and it is hardly necessary to imagine an invasion of the desert coast of Arabia.[2]

III. THE REIGN OF NARAM-SIN

Manishtusu, according to an omen, was murdered in a palace conspiracy,[3] and was succeeded by his son, Naram-Sin, destined to become the second of a pair whom later history ever regarded as the greatest figures in its annals. Because of this likeness Naram-Sin was known afterwards as the son of Sargon; if the word is pressed it is incorrect for the king-list rightly calls him son of Manishtusu. His reign was long and, until its closing years, glorious. But our information upon it is of varying authenticity, depending for the greatest part upon much later tradition. Of his own inscriptions, which were certainly many and informative, and of the sculptures which illustrated his campaigns and triumphs, very little has survived. By chance he has fared scantily even in the copies of these monuments at Nippur which are comparatively informative about the wars of his grandfather.

Both the original inscriptions of Naram-Sin and their copies are marked by two significant changes in the royal styles; first, he used himself, and permitted to be used in the addresses of his subjects, the divine determinative before his name. This is not invariable in his own titulary, and may have been assumed later in his reign, but the language of obsequious servants who dedicated their seals to him was unrestrained in the attribution of divinity, for they often address him not only as divine in his nature but do not hesitate to call him 'the god of Agade'.[4] He

---

[1] In all the current dictionaries this is *locus conclamatus*; G, 5, vol. IV, 13; G, 36, 182*b*; G, 16, 14.

[2] Yet there is a recent report of the so-called 'Kulli culture' found on the western side of the Oman Peninsula (*Archaeology*, 13 (1960), 280). The 'silver-mine' which marked the limit of Manishtusu's advance is rather more likely to have lain upon the Persian than upon the Arabian side; see §I, 13, 499 and 501.

[3] §I, 17, 257.

[4] §III, 5, 59; A, 25, 23.

was perhaps the first to bear this title, which marks a monstrous usurpation according to the ideas of the older Sumerian rulers who took pride in being simply the city-god's executant. It is not impossible that some of the stories of downfall and disaster which later tradition attached to his memory were motivated in part by the belief that such presumption could not go unpunished by the offended gods. At least, he had not many imitators in later history. A second vain-glorious, but less blasphemous, title[1] was one which again appears for the first time with Naram-Sin, 'king of the four regions', a claim to universal dominion over the earth which was revived by Shulgi and his successors at Ur, when they also seemed for a time to enjoy a boundless empire.

It is not possible to write a consecutive nor even a factual account of Naram-Sin's reign. There is no chronology[2] for its thirty-seven years,[3] and no criterion for the truth of what is related, since nearly all of this is in the form of later compilations and legends, from which emerges nothing but a blurred picture of triumph and disaster; only from the course of subsequent events is it permissible to believe that disaster predominated in the end. Like his predecessors Naram-Sin probably began his reign amid a revolt of his subjects. Several of the ancient cities were prominent in this uprising, and one account[4] ascribes its leadership to Kish, which is bitterly reproached as thankless and mansworn to the house of Sargon. In this text more than twenty conspirators are named, in another[5] there are seventeen, whose realms extended from Anatolia in the extreme north-west to Magan, on the shores of the Persian Gulf, in the south-east. The issue of this vast struggle is hardly indicated by a dubious line as victory for Naram-Sin, although this may be assumed. If so, success was surely not achieved in one year or in one campaign—the extent of the rebellious lands over the whole stretch of ancient western Asia guarantees that the king had to wage a series of hard and distant wars, which doubtless exhausted his resources and left his successors enfeebled. Mari might be the first stage of his march to the west, and the second was achieved by the conquest of Armanum and Ibla, claimed in a copy of his own inscription.[6] The former of these, perhaps both, were ruled by Rish-Adad, who

---

[1] §III, 5, 49 ff.; A, 36.
[2] Several year-dates survive but give little information; listed in G, 17, 201, add J.C.S. 15 (1961), 80, n. 236. See A, 25, 22.
[3] G, 18, 112.   [4] Last translated in §II, 15, 23 f.
[5] A Hittite fragment, see §I, 20, zweiter Teil, 68 ff. Original inscriptions (G, 3, 138 f. and 142 f.; A, 25, 17 f.) claim victory in nine battles and the capture of three kings in one year.   [6] G, 14, no. 275; A, 25, 74.

was captured alive by the victor, and was represented in captivity by a sculpture dedicated to the Moon-god. Ibla had been formerly occupied by Sargon, though his grandson claims first capture of it, and the 'cedar mountain' which Sargon also possessed is defined by Naram-Sin as the Amanus. All of the places named in this inscription lay between the great bend of the Euphrates and the north Syrian coast; Armanum was probably Aleppo[1] and Ulisum a place upon the sea-shore not far from Tyre.[2] Other celebrated incidents marked the same campaign in Syria, which earned for the victor his title as 'lord of Tidnum'. Nothing is known of the other western and even Anatolian 'kings' who appear in one list of the seventeen rebels. But a siege and capture of Apishal was famous in tradition, being remembered especially by the soothsayers for its ominous accompaniments; Naram-Sin marched thither, battered breaches in its walls and took prisoner its 'king' Rish-Adad,[3] whose name cannot but recall Rish-Adad, the ruler of Armanum, though there is no likelihood that he was the same. Where Apishal lay is uncertain[4] but it must have been secluded, for the approach to it was described by a legend[5] in terms of difficulty which (as already noticed) recall the obstacles and fatigues of Sargon's expedition to Purush-khanda. Even that extreme limit was probably reached by Naram-Sin also. The copied inscription concerning his western wars contains a mention of Talkhatum,[6] a place (it says) which no king before him had ever reached, but Naram-Sin went there, and the goddess Inanna gave him no rival, and the city-governors of Subartum and the lords of the highlands supplied him with provisions. This town of Talkhatum is known again in a later age as a place where the business of the Cappadocian merchants passed sometimes, as it did also to Purushkhanda, and the two were certainly on the same route. In seeming agreement with this, one of the later stories[7] about Naram-Sin begins the invasion of his empire with demoniac hordes destroying the town of Purushkhanda(r), as though it was the utmost bound of his dominion. It will hardly be too much, therefore, to believe that

---

1 See above, p. 426, n. 4.

2 The name being perhaps the same as Ullaza; see §III, 12, 26 f. Another possibility is the better-known Urs(h)u on the upper Euphrates; see above, p. 426, n. 5.

3 G, 20, vol. II, 8 ff. and 36 ff; §I, 30, nos. 5, 76, 90.

4 Doubtless in north Syria, see §III, 15, 106 f.

5 §III, 4, 46 ff.

6 §I, 11, 29; §III, 10, 370; A, 17, 95, n. 11.

7 §III, 3, 100 f.

Naram-Sin exercised some authority, however incomplete, over districts in the south-east of Asia Minor, where his grandfather before him had accomplished the same phenomenal march which Naram-Sin or his flatterers heralded as a pioneer effort.

Towards the north there is material proof of the extent of his dominion. Farthest of all is the site now called Tell Brak, of which the ancient name is still unknown. Here has been found, upon a most imposing mound, the seat of a flourishing population and cult in ages long before the Dynasty of Agade, and the ruin of a great palace[1] built by Naram-Sin with bricks bearing his name. Such a building testifies to the order which was established in a remote district under this king's reign, for therein were collected and stored the tributes of the surrounding country, at that time fertile and prosperous. Not far away to the east has been found a stele[2] with a figure of the king and an obliterated inscription, at a village near the town of Diyārbakr. Of his presence and supremacy in the cites of Assyria there is direct and inferential evidence, which has been noticed before.[3]

Whereas it may be assumed that the supremacy of Naram-Sin in the west and north was maintained without serious contest[4] he had some hard struggles upon his eastern frontiers against the various hill peoples who enviously overlooked the Babylonian plain, and were at length to overthrow the kingdom which he left to his sons. The rock-relief[5] chiselled upon the steep side of a gorge called Darband-i Gawr in the district of Kara-Dağ south of Sulaimaniyyah is a monument reproducing *in situ* the famous scene upon the Naram-Sin stele[6] discovered at Susa which, according to its own inscription, pictures the triumph of Naram-Sin over Satuni the king of Lullubi.[7] This location, coupled with evidence from the topography of Assyrian campaigns against the Lullu, makes it appear that the centre of Lullubu was the valley of Shahrazūr; a similar conclusion may be drawn from the geographical list of Sargon's empire[8] which places Lullubi immediately after Arrapkha (Kirkuk). From this centre Lullu raiders sometimes marched out, and one of their penetrations

---

[1] §II, 12, 26 ff., 63 ff.; see above, p. 308.　　　　[2] §III, 11.

[3] See above, p. 431.

[4] For an indication of the ethnic elements among his opponents in that quarter see G, 38, 99 f.

[5] G, 35, 96 ff.; §III, 13, 8 and map; G, 11, 360 and map facing p. 440; A, 12, pl. xlv *b*; G, 35, 97.

[6] *Mém. D.P.* 1, pl. x; 2, pl. 11; often reproduced. See Plate 42(*a*).

[7] Variously written in cuneiform as Lullu, Lullubu, Lullumu; see §III, 9, 325; §III, 8, 15 and 19 n. 24; A, 28, 279.　　　　[8] §I, 48, 12.

reached the district of the modern Zuhab, near Sar-i Pul, for there has been found a well-known rock-relief with figures and the inscription of Annubanini,[1] king of Lullubi, who writes in Agadean style a description of his monument and a long imprecation against any violator. The danger from this enemy is vividly recalled in a later and confused tradition,[2] where he appears as father of a band of seven fearful ogres, with gruesome names invented to strike terror, who swept across the dominions of Naram-Sin leading a countless horde of monsters, laid waste Gutium and Elam, and were halted only at the shore of the Persian Gulf. Not far away from his monument is another rock-relief[3] with the name of Tar...dunni, doubtless another king of the Lullu.

The Gutians are not so easy to fix upon the map;[4] they were close neighbours, hardly to be distinguished from the Lullu, but no territorial monuments mark their abodes. Their descendants, called Qutu, can be found dubiously mentioned in the Mari letters,[5] but appear most prominently much later in the campaigns of Assyrian kings towards the end of the second millennium and subsequently. In those times they were a great and powerful, if loose-knit, people; their epithet was 'wide-spread' and their land seems to have been in the mountains south of the Lesser Zab,[6] to the north of Sulaimaniyyah and of the legendary Mount Niṣir, where the ark of the Babylonian Noah rested after the Deluge. The homes of these mountaineers, Guti as well as Lullu, are represented by parts of the territories occupied by the modern Kurds and Lurs, who have perhaps preserved the ancient names with some of the same turbulence.

It has been seen above (p. 432) that there was ruling over Elam in the days of Sargon a native dynasty seated in the city of Awan. The eighth and ninth members of this had been conquered by Sargon; no name of their successors appears among the coalition of rebels against Naram-Sin upon his succession, where the Elamite power is represented rather by the states of Markhashe[7] and Mardaman. Probably contemporary of Naram-Sin in this dynasty was the eleventh king named Khita, and it is most likely he who figures in a treaty written in the Elamite language and made with Naram-Sin.[8] In Susa, always the most amenable to

---

[1] §III, 6, Tafel II; §III, 7, 228; G, 39, 172; G, 3, 150.

[2] §III, 3, 100 f.; see above, p. 429.   [3] G, 6, 41; G, 39, 172.

[4] G, 6, 41 f.; §I, 19, 118; §III, 8, 14; A, 28, 279; A, 14, 46, n. 12; A, 35; A, 34, 16.   [5] §III, 1, 132; §I, 22, 95.

[6] §III, 2, 268; §III, 13, 19; §III, 8, 18.   [7] Or B(W)arakhshe.

[8] See, for details of this, below, p. 651 ; A, 24.

Babylonian influence, the ascendancy of Naram-Sin was almost complete. There he raised buildings constructed with his own inscribed bricks, set up his statues, and dedicated his trophies from Magan. In charge of this dependency he appointed a city-governor named Epir-mupi.[1] At this time so complete was the submergence of the native influences that even the documents of law and administration were written in the Akkadian, not the Elamite language; contracts, letters, lists, and even literary works are found in the all-conquering Akkadian. These tablets reveal that there was an active commerce carried on with Babylonia, for cities in the old land of Sumer, especially Shuruppak, Awal, and Umma are often named. This condition of affairs lasted as long as the office of Epir-mupi, who in later life was promoted to the status of governor-general over the whole of Elam. His successor was Puzur (Kutik)-In-Shushinak, whose reign is described in a subsequent chapter (xxiii).

To seal his mastery of the 'four regions' Naram-Sin celebrated a triumph in the south over Manium, king of Magan. This is attested by the unimpeachable consent of his own inscriptions, of later omens and chronicles, and of existing alabaster vases inscribed[2] with his name and the words 'booty of Magan'. These vases, combined with the names of Magan and Manium, have given a singular interest to this episode, for Magan was a name undoubtedly applied to Egypt in a later period of Babylonian history,[3] and the vases have a distinct likeness to Egyptian alabaster vases, which more commonly bear inscriptions in the late Fifth and in the Sixth Dynasties,[4] the dates of which accord well enough with that of Naram-Sin. It was natural, therefore, that the name of Manium, or Mannu,[5] should recall Menes, traditionally the first king of United Egypt.[6] But a synchronism is out of the question, for the beginning of the First Dynasty can by no means be reduced to the date of Naram-Sin, and the resemblance of the alabaster vases must be ascribed to no more than artistic influence and products emanating from Fifth Dynasty Egypt over trade routes to the east as they did to the north.[7] There is no sufficient reason to believe that Naram-Sin can have been a foreign invader who helped to end the Sixth Dynasty in Egypt and to bring in its First Intermediate Period.

[1] G, 16, 57 prefers this form of the name; §iii, 5, 66, but see now A, 5.
[2] G, 3, 138 f.   [3] See above, p. 439.   [4] See above, p. 156.
[5] §ii, 15, 42; A, 25, 17, n. 182.   [6] §iii, 14.
[7] See above, p. 391. Even in Old Babylonian times there is no appearance of direct communications between Babylonian and Egypt; §ii, 11, 36 f.

IV. THE STATE OF BABYLONIA UNDER THE DYNASTY OF AGADE

From the reign of Naram-Sin, as from the culmination of a brilliant epoch, it will be convenient to look back over the changes as well as the constancies of life in Babylonia under the greatest of her kings, as we may agree with all tradition in thinking them to be. It is certain, at the outset, that they brought a division into the land not present, or at least not felt, before. The belief once held that early Babylonia was the scene of a long-drawn conflict between Sumerians and Semites was founded upon distinctions now known to be unconcerned with race or nationality.[1] Semitic-speaking elements had been present and influential in the land from the earliest times, and there is no evidence of conflict between the two language-groups. No inscription proclaims victory over the hated Semite or the despised Sumerian; such a language would in fact have been unintelligible. But it was another thing as touching the external neighbours of the land. If the line in an epic poem which ascribes to Lugalbanda a prayer against the 'Amorite who knows not grain'[2] is not a complete anachronism it shows one of the first dynasties of Sumer already at grips with the foe from the north-west. And even if the name be admitted as adapted to later conditions, as the name of Akkad in the same passage doubtless is, the underlying cause of hostility is the same, whether the western invaders are called Akkadians, Amorites, or Aramaeans—they were all needy strangers attracted by the wealth and refinement of the ancient cities of the south, and against these barbarians the contempt and hatred of the citizens was unvarying. Doubtless this movement had always been afoot, and the degree of ethnic (or at least linguistic) mixture prevailing in Sumer from the beginning had been introduced by former immigrants from the same quarter. But if so the amalgamation had been fully effected and the sons or grandsons of the newcomers were now accustomed to look up the Euphrates with the same apprehension as their older-established neighbours; the vigorous Sumerian culture had soon absorbed all alien influences into its own engrossing interests and characteristic mode of life. The founding of the dynasty of Agade thus marks not only the first historically visible domination of the land by western immigrants (unless the group of Semitic-named kings in the First Dynasty of

---

1 See above, pp. 99 f.; §1, 39, 242, 260 f.
2 S. N. Kramer, *From the Tablets of Sumer*, 235 f.; A, 6, 92.

Kish be a forerunner otherwise indistinguishable), but the setting up of a distinction which divided the country permanently, made an immediate and lasting impression upon its culture, and, for all its temporary brilliance, perhaps contributed to the decline which set in after its collapse, for the Early Dynastic and its successor the Akkadian periods were the true 'golden age' of Babylonia.

That there was a large influx of Syrian people about the time when Sargon made himself king is not to be doubted.[1] It cannot have been merely a slow infiltration of families bent upon making a living in a happier land, however much this may seem to be suggested by the story of the hero's own birth and employment. He was no ordinary *ensi* of a city, ready to engage his neighbour cities in a contest for supremacy. He built instead a new seat, and this housed his own warriors and their families, not a mixed multitude from Kish.[2] It became the centre of a northern division of the country which thenceforth was to be known as Sumer and Akkad. Such a development can have been effected only by a new population conscious of its difference and even of hostility to the old. This distinction springs at once into view (p. 435 above) with the first successor of Sargon who names his revolted opponents explicitly 'the cities of Sumer' and adds that he treated them with great severity. The ancient solidarity of the land, strong through all its internal broils, is thus rudely denounced. From the other side the indications are the more striking as they are recorded by the enemy. Sargon was the conqueror of Lugalzaggisi but not of him alone; others of the most powerful Sumerian cities were allies of Uruk in a cause which they evidently perceived to be more important than the time-honoured rivalry for the 'kingship' of Sumer. All were subdued and compelled to bear what they felt as a foreign yoke, to be cast away passionately whenever occasion offered. 'All the lands' which revolted against Sargon in his old age certainly included the Sumerian cities. Thenceforward a constant feature was to mark the accession of all the three who followed him upon the throne, a bitter revolt of Sumer, suppressed each time with hard fighting and cruelty. Under this it is impossible not to feel a burning zeal of patriotic sentiment, kindled as it was to be later against the vile Gutian oppressors. The kings of Agade in their flourishing days could never make themselves and their armies accepted as of the family.[3]

Indeed the outlook of these kings was altogether different from that of the old Sumerian dynasts. It is true that we are poorly

[1] §II, 3, 27 ff. Yet see A, 2.   [2] G, 17, 12.
[3] A, 14, 49.

informed about the exploits abroad of the older kings, but we may judge from the range of Eannatum's expeditions that even the most warlike of them did not travel much beyond the outer bounds of country covered by the Sumerian institutions and ideas, that is from Mari in the west to Elam in the east. Lugalzaggisi, the predecessor of Sargon, did march to the Mediterranean, if his phrase is so to be interpreted, and perhaps was the first to do so. But Sargon established the first 'world empire'; he must already have possessed great influence in Syria, and had little difficulty in subduing the whole of it. He crossed the Taurus, if legend may be believed, he held in sway the whole of north Mesopotamia and in check the mountainous borderlands to the north and east. Doubtless he controlled the shipping of the Persian Gulf, but it was reserved for his son Manishtusu to embark upon these waters with an army, and for his grandson Naram-Sin to extend his conquests to the country of Magan in the south, and thus logically to acquire the proud title 'king of the four regions', the uttermost parts of the earth. To so wide a view as this the affairs of Sumer seemed parochial, and to the self-centred Sumerians this neglect was intolerable. Centuries of change and experience were not enough to alter this resentment. The hatred with which the later Babylonians encountered Assyrian conquerors manifested their intolerance of becoming a mere province in an empire. Impatience was shown even when the 'world power' was held by one of their own kings, Nebuchadrezzar or Nabonidus, and they were still a rebellious people under the Persians.

The rule of the Akkadian kings need not be supposed especially oppressive, although there was evidently a good deal of displacement of population, landowners and workers, to accommodate Akkadian dependants of the king. This treatment is applied to the territories of four Babylonian cities, Dūr-Sin, Kish, Marad, and another[1] in the celebrated Obelisk[2] of Manishtusu. The extent of compensation paid by the king for the estates which he acquired was wide, including all those who had any claim upon the lands, and he undertook to provide maintenance for officials and workers displaced by his new arrangements. All the fields were bought upon the computation of a yield of $3\frac{1}{3}$ gur of grain for each iku of land,[3] the price was fixed at the rate of one shekel of silver for one gur

---

[1] Written ŠID.TAB.KI, of uncertain reading; §IV, 12, but also §IV, 11, 74; its location discussed in both.

[2] Mém. D.P. tome 1, pl. IX; tome 2, 1 ff., pls. I ff. See G, 21, 206 ff.; §IV, 2, 26 ff.; A, 25, 14, no. 3.

[3] G, 28, vol. I, 355, 362.

of grain, with various presents distributed to interested parties, a whole multitude being thus concerned in the transactions.[1] These prices remained fairly stable through the succeeding period of the Third Dynasty of Ur,[2] but tended to rise thereafter, and by the time of the First Dynasty of Babylon the rate for grain had gone up by about forty per cent. The price paid by Manishtusu for his lands is fully equal to that found in other accounts of his day, and should be considered quite fair; his purchases may have been compulsory but were not confiscatory.

It is not clear from the inscription who were the recipients of the ground thus acquired, apart from the king himself who bought it. Each face of the obelisk records details of the estate purchased in each of the four townships, and concludes with a repeated list of the same forty-nine persons who are described as 'witnesses[3] of the field'—these are headed by a nephew of the king, are all 'sons of Agade', and include many officers of the state and temple administrations. It is perhaps right to assume (although it is nowhere stated) that these were the elect vavasours of the lands thus acquired, and that the obelisk is a monument to the process of dispossessing former owners in favour of the adherents or 'veterans' of a conqueror, a process which earned as much unpopularity for Sargon[4] and Manishtusu as for many later governments. Whatever the relations of the old and the new possessors, there is no mark of discrimination on ethnic lines, although the names of nearly all are either plainly Semitic or written (as all the Agade inscriptions) with a large admixture of 'ideograms' nearly always to be read in their Semitic values.[5] But the 'new men' include some surprising elements, if the obelisk is to be regarded as a monument of dispossession, for there are found among them two sons of an *ensi* of Umma and a certain Urukagina, son of Engilsa, *ensi* of Lagash, who could possibly, if not very probably, be the celebrated reformer of that name,[6] the victim of Lugalzaggisi. Such individuals as these cannot have been immigrants, and we must rather suppose that the new lessees were simply supporters of the king, rewarded without consideration of their antecedents. Nevertheless, that such operations were in some sense aimed against, or fell severely upon, the older-established population is sufficiently proclaimed by the fact

---

[1] *R.A.* 44, 101. [2] §iv, 3, 11, 12; §iv, 8, 30.
[3] §iv, 7, 187.
[4] See above, p. 424. [5] G, 17, 12.
[6] See above, pp. 140 ff; §1, 21, 137 n. 107; but otherwise G, 21, 209 f.

already noticed that every reign of the Agadean kings was ushered in by a stubborn revolt of the older cities.

Concerning the economy and conditions of life under the kings of Agade there is some information in the business and administrative documents, which have survived in fair numbers, and come from several places in north and south Babylonia, and from at least two others, Susa and Gasur, which are outside the homeland.[1] None of these provides evidence of the temple-estate economy characteristic of the old Sumerian cities, and it is probable that a change towards a more secular order of society and land-tenure had come in with the new Akkadian rulers, even if it be allowed that the temple-economy in the Sumerian cities was not so all-inclusive as most of the evidence suggests. The business tablets of the Agade period are mostly of a formal kind, lists and receipts, but legal documents are also present, depositions of witnesses, sales of fields, slaves, animals, and commodities, records of traffic, of lands and farmers, and of trade between cities. There exist also letters, characterized in this period by a peculiar exordium;[2] they deal principally with the administration of estates and the assignment of leases, having only very occasionally references to matters of wider interest.

Externally, the tablets of this period[3] are a remarkable exemplification of the profound change which came over all the arts together. The tablets of the Early Dynastic age are of a rounded contour with but slightly marked corners; their writing is not unclear, but not well spaced and arranged on the tablet, nor always well executed, and the general appearance is untidy. With the Agade period comes in a great change; the tablets mostly take on a rectangular form and the clay is finely prepared. The lines are strictly ordered and ruled, and above all the signs are written with a care and beauty which were not matched again until the Assyrian calligraphers were set to work upon the library tablets of Ashurbanipal; they tend to great elaboration, multiplying the number of wedges in serried groups, the whole presenting a highly characteristic appearance of formal arrangement, such that it is nearly always possible to recognize an Agade tablet at a single glance.

The language written in this beautiful script is that Semitic dialect which is called Old Akkadian. Its philological peculiarities have been acutely analysed elsewhere,[4] but here it may be observed as a historical fact of high importance that this was the first time

---

[1] G, 17, 7; §iv, 7, 174 ff.; G, 21, 236 ff.
[2] G, 16, 47; A, 38, 3; A, 32, 3.
[3] See Plate 41 (*b*), (*c*).   [4] Most recently in G, 17.

a Semitic language had ever been written. The instrument used was the cuneiform script invented or at least developed for the writing of the peculiar Sumerian language. From this first beginning, the cuneiform script displayed its virtuosity in rendering alien tongues, of which it had currently written half a dozen, entirely disparate, before its extinction, having become the common medium of written expression in the whole of western Asia, and being professionally studied and employed even in Egypt. The scribes of Agade made a skilful start with the use of this alien instrument. They gave the writing of Semitic in cuneiform the character it was to bear ever afterwards, that is, mixed usage of phonetic writing and 'ideograms' or sense-signs, the (Sumerian) sign for a thing or an idea being written, but read in its Semitic equivalent with complements where necessary to indicate that reading or to add Semitic affixes. In the inscriptions of Sargon a good deal of clumsiness appears in the excessive use of ideograms: in the longer inscriptions of Naram-Sin, after about a century of practice, there is a noticeable decrease in this stiffness of expression, and the writing is on its way to the full phonetic freedom of the classical period. But it is worth remarking that later ages found it convenient to revert largely to the earlier manner, and to admit for the sake of brevity or the abuse of mystification a varying admixture of ideograms.

The craftsmanship and the mastery of composition which are exemplified in the Akkadian tablets and writing have left as clear a mark upon other notable works of art produced at this period. Nothing is better illustrative of this than the cylinder-seals;[1] these either depict groups of figures, human and animal, in effective poses and strict arrangement, in which the inscription often enters as a focus, or else they venture (as no subsequent age ever ventured again) upon compressing into this minute space some comprehensively illustrated incident in a mythological story, involving several figures. That we cannot understand most of these incidents is due to our deficient knowledge of the stories, not to the manner of representing them, which is usually admirable in its statement and detail. It is composition, above all, which gives its quality to the famous Stele of Victory,[2] one of the best works of ancient art—the triangular effect of the monument itself is caught up in the cone at the mountain summit, and the two intersecting triangles adumbrated by the royal victor, his victim with the slope of his body and the crossing line of the fatal arrow, the whole

[1] See Plate 43 (a); §IV, 4, pll. XVI ff.
[2] See above, p. 443, n.6.

completed on the right by the suppliant figure. All of these are in a landscape rendered with just enough features to set the scene without distracting the mind from the martial triumph.

Wide as were the conquests of the kings of Agade, and active as the civil pursuits and arts upon which they relied for their strength, it can hardly be said that the wealth of this period is so apparent as in the preceding age of the early Sumerian dynasties. It is difficult to make comparisons, especially when there is on the one side the splendour of the 'royal cemetery' at Ur, to which no comparable discovery has been made for the Agade period—it is necessary to be on guard against building overmuch upon accidents of discovery. But there are one or two absences from the resources of the Agade kings which argue a disability as compared with their predecessors. There seems to be a falling-off in the supply of lapis-lazuli,[1] which was all ultimately derived from the mines of Badakhshān on the upper Oxus, far to the east of the Caspian Sea. It still appears in jewellery under the Agade kings, but almost vanishes as a material for inlay and ornament and especially for cylinder-seals, so much favoured before. But this change may be due to other ideas or other fashions, the popular stones for seals (which were also amulets, obtaining some of their supposed magical effect from their material) varying in most of the successive Babylonian ages. Allowing for this, it is possible to believe that communication with Badakhshān became more difficult than before. A more surprising deficit, both because of its greater utility and because it is better attested, is that of tin or other media for alloying copper so as to make bronze. It has been shown by analysis of ancient implements found in well-observed strata that in the Agade period they are sometimes of lower alloy content, more nearly pure copper, than in the preceding Early Dynastic period.[2] If this indicates, as might be supposed, that the supply of tin was partially interrupted, it is not easy to account for this. At a rather later time tin seems to have come partly from the Caucasus by way of Ashur, and in this direction the power of Agade extended far. Perhaps military conquest was a less effective purveyor than the traffic which it disrupted.

But if a few roads were blocked and some supplies curtailed, the Agadean kings may have obtained wealth by trade or even by tribute over another route which, unmentioned or at least

---

[1] G, 42, 372 ff. A like deficiency has been noticed in the ancient cities of the Indus, §II, 19, 88. But see now A, 23, 49 f. and 54; A, 3.

[2] G, 42, 30 and 285 ff.; G, 12, 251.

unidentified in the records of ancient business, has come into great prominence through modern discovery. Material evidence derived from regular excavations in Babylonia places it beyond doubt that commercial and personal contact was maintained with a region of high civilization centred in the basin of the Indus, some 1500 miles to the east across inhospitable country. At half a dozen places have been found antiquities clearly derived from or influenced by this distant culture, which has been fully revealed only within the last forty years. Especially clear is this in certain seals,[1] found mostly on the sites of Ur and Eshnunna, which are engraved with pictures of animals belonging unmistakably to the repertoire of the Indian seals, and the connexion is made certain by the presence of the beautifully formed and still undeciphered writing of the Indus people. Among the seals found in Babylonia the proportion of cylinders is much higher than at the Indian sites, where these are exceedingly rare, as though these seals had been made specially for the Babylonian trade. Careful observation of the finds in Babylonia has placed most of them in the Agade period, and although indications such as the etched cornelian beads may suggest that the connexion was older, it certainly flourished then as never before or after. The reasons for this it would be vain at present to conjecture, particularly as the major Indian sites, Harappā and Mohenjo Daro, have but an ill-defined internal chronology and none in comparative historical terms except the Akkadian synchronism.

Although possible land-routes may not yet be sufficiently explored there is much to suggest that connexion between the two regions was mostly by sea, along the Persian Gulf and the shores of Makrān and of Baluchistān.[2] Imports by shipping from Tilmun are attested even in the preceding age, and references to Magan and Meluhha, always in a maritime connexion, become relatively frequent during the Agade period. Uncertainty still persists upon the location of all these lands, but it becomes more and more likely that they were stages (in the west–east direction) along this part of a sea-trade route which possibly even then had something of the vastly wider extension which it attained in the middle ages.[3]

[1] §IV, 5; §II, 19, 85 f.; §II, 14, 207 f. and 105 ff.; A, 14, line 65 (elephants at Agade); see Plate 42 (c).

[2] See above, p. 439; A, 7.

[3] §IV, 14, 57 ff.; §IV, 10; §IV, 1; §IV, 10; A, 30.

V. THE LAST KINGS OF AGADE AND THE
GUTIAN SUPREMACY

There remained in the memory of later ages a confused tradition that the reign of Naram-Sin ended in eclipse. Most explicitly, a late chronicle[1] declares that the god Marduk twice raised up against him the horde of Gutians, who harried his people and received his kingdom as the god's gift. A less definite story, which has been noticed above (pp. 442 ff.), tells of the descent upon Sumer and Akkad of a foreign enemy called by the name given to various barbarous peoples, Umman Manda, which appears to have begun its career from the north-west, for the course of its devastation is a great sweep from its first victim the city of Purushkhandar (?), seemingly the town in Asia Minor to which Sargon made his epic march, and continuing south-eastwards until it swept over Gutium itself, over Elam, and did not end before it had overrun also the lands beyond the Persian Gulf, Tilmun, Magan, and Meluhha. Nothing indicates whether the invasion herein related took place at the outset rather than at the end of his reign. As for the chronicle, its ascription to Naram-Sin of the disaster ultimately inflicted by the Gutians is in conformity with a theory of its compiler, that all the great figures of the past had successively been unregardful of the cult of Marduk and therefore rejected by that supreme god. This, no doubt, if the text were better preserved, would be a prelude to the establishment of the only true kingdom, temple, and cult at Babylon itself.

But if Naram-Sin ended his life with a realm not much impaired, there were already signs of decay, and ample presages of the troubles which were to burst upon his son. Elam under Kutik-In-Shushinak was growing independent and almost defiant, and the wild men of the Zagros were poised to swoop upon the wealthy land which they saw protected only by a weakening arm. The old king died at length after a reign of thirty-seven years, and left this menacing situation to his son Shar-kali-sharri. Whether he was the eldest is not known, but another son of Naram-Sin bore the significant name of Bin-kali-sharri, the two brothers thus standing in a relation which among the old Sumerian dynasts would have marked a king and his son destined to reign after him. But Shar-kali-sharri was to have no successor, at least not from the old family of Sargon. No more than for the other kings of Agade is there an internal chronology of his reign, but

[1] §1, 20, erster Teil, 53 ff.; see also A, 14, 48 f.

beyond doubt his troubles began early. For almost the first time in this dynasty we have the advantage of several year-names or dating formulae[1] referring to warlike achievements. Naturally these happenings are reported under the colour of victories, but the list of enemies, short as it is, gives eloquent testimony of the precarious hold which he kept upon his nearer dominions, and of the loss of his more distant provinces.

First in the list are Elam and Zakhara, the latter a small border state which had joined in the resistance to Rimush; these allies now had the temerity to launch an invasion of Babylonia itself, where they attacked the ancient city of Akshak. Here they were met and (as he claims) defeated by Shar-kali-sharri; at least they retired to their own countries, where Kutik-In-Shushinak was so far from discredited that he proclaimed himself 'mighty king of Awan' and possessor of the 'four regions', in the very style assumed hitherto by the Agadean overlords. From this eastern battlefield Shar-kali-sharri was called away far to the north-west to face another foe. A second year-date proclaims that 'he overcame the Amorite in Basar'. A new wave of Semitic invaders, like that which had borne in the Akkadians themselves, was in motion towards the wealthy cities of the south, and the possessor was hemmed in between two converging attacks. In this posture the fate of Shar-kali-sharri was closely similar to that of Ibbi-Sin in the next age of Babylonian history, forced to turn desperately from one flank to the other, holding off with failing blows the pressure which was at length to crush in his kingdom. This battle to ward off the Amorite invasion took place at Basar,[2] which has been probably identified with the range of hills still called Jebel el-Bishrī. These hills which extend towards the right bank of the Euphrates below Raqqah were sometimes passed by Assyrian armies on the march in later ages; they are about 350 miles from Shar-kali-sharri's other battlefield at Akshak—so wide a space had the hard-pressed king to defend.

But whatever calls there were upon him in the west it was from the other side that danger came, as the year-dates imperfectly reveal. One of these records vaguely that 'a campaign was launched against Gutium', while another claims a brilliant success—'he made prisoner Sharlak, king of Gutium'. Again we are reminded of Ibbi-Sin who claimed, no doubt with truth, successes, even triumphs, against his enemies both west and east. But in both

[1] G, 17, 204; G, 41, 133; G, 30, 5 f.
[2] §1, 22, 149 f.; §11, 3, 29 f.; A, 6, 236 f.; the scene long afterwards (A.D. 692–3) of a tribal battle celebrated in Arabian history.

cases it was a battle being slowly lost. Shar-kali-sharri is recorded to have reigned twenty-five years, Ibbi-Sin about the same, and in neither case do we know how the collapse finally came. But the resemblance ends here for whereas the Dynasty of Ur disappeared, that of Agade, although it passed through a short period of convulsion with four ephemeral occupants of the throne, survived into a new lease when two kings followed each other regularly with normal lengths of rule. Very little more, however, is heard about the great dynasty of Agade, and there can be no doubt that it was practically overthrown by the mountaineers, and that their main attack ended or followed directly upon the reign of Shar-kali-sharri.

The confusion is reflected in a contemporary letter[1] from a man who was striving to rehabilitate his farm after the devastation, and in a striking poetical account,[2] written in Sumerian, which purports to describe the glories and the downfall of Agade. In the pride of dominion and wealth Naram-Sin (for to his reign is the disaster assigned in this account) had committed a sacrilegious assault upon the holy city of Nippur and its temple, leaving everything in ruins. No reason is given for this outrage, but its effect was to enrage not only the supreme god Enlil, who visited Sumer with foreign invasion of the Gutians and with famine, but other gods as well, who cursed the guilty city of Agade and vowed its desolation and the ruin of all its inhabitants. This doom was dramatically fulfilled, and life came almost to an end in the tyrant's capital. To mark this catastrophe even the king-list halts for a moment its jog-trot of names and numbers to ask rhetorically 'who was king, who was not king?' before it names four shadow-figures who claimed the throne within three years. This phrase itself came to denote the occasion, for an item[3] in the collection of the haruspices marked the occurrence of a certain sign as 'the omen of "who was king, who was not king?"' and went on to observe that this fateful occasion was marked also by the prodigy of an ox eating the flesh of an ox at the moment when the king himself was offering the sacrifice which was to read him the decree of fate. Indeed, the downfall of this monarchy provided many memories for those who could trace significant incidents accompanying the march of events, for there is a collection[4] formed by a later student of 'forty-seven strange signs which went to (announce) the fall of Akkad', and another omen inscribed upon a model of the sheep's liver[5] shows in actual representation what

---

[1] §v, 9; A, 32, no. 2. See Plate 41 (b).
[2] G, 22, 267 ff.; G, 4, 760 f.; A, 14.
[3] §1, 30, no. 56.
[4] G, 19, vol. 11, 965 ff.; §v, 14; §v, 14.
[5] §1, 34, no. 4; §1, 30, no. 86.

it was that portended the ruin of Agade. Still one more omen is worth quoting for an apparent hint of the fatal event when the Gutians overthrew the kingdom; such and such marks[1] were 'the omen of Shar-kali-sharri...ruin of Akkad; the enemy will fall upon thy peace'. It might seem from this that the vigilance of the kingdom was deceived by a sudden and overwhelming rush of the wild tribes. As for the doomed king himself, another omen[2] declares that he met the same mysterious death as Rimush, by the 'seals' of his servants.

Of the four factionary kings who could not maintain themselves even against one another hardly anything is known, as would be expected, although there has survived a short inscription[3] perhaps belonging to Elulu, one of them. These were followed by two who ended the dynasty with reigns of considerable length, probably when the first force of the Gutian invasion was spent, for a few inscriptions reveal that the rule of the last king, named Shu-Durul,[4] was of some importance and extended to Eshnunna. It is not possible to discover how this partial supremacy fitted in to the general but undoubtedly loose sovereignty of the Gutians. These are allowed in the list twenty or twenty-one kings and a total of 125 years of supremacy. At the time of the invasion either they had not a king at all, as one version runs, that is, they were typical barbarians, or their king was one whose name was not preserved, a reading which has better authority, though less point. The Gutian kings have left, in any case, very little mark upon Babylonian history, and very few monuments of their feeble and sporadic rule. Their names, outlandish at first, show a tendency towards the end to take on a Babylonian colour, for no doubt the superior culture of the plains gradually permeated the rude tribesmen. A few monuments, dedications inscribed with their names,[5] attest the decent observance of these alien rulers towards the impressive cults which they were ill able to comprehend. But for the most part they were doubtless mere destroyers and harpies of the wealth of the country. Their passage over Assyria from which we have no written evidence (as indeed there is hardly any from anywhere in this time of decadence) is marked by the condition of the ruins at the city of Ashur, where upon the site of the great and flourishing temple of Ishtar,[6] which had been filled with works of art until the end of the Agadean dynasty, there was

---

[1] §1, 30, no. 21.
[2] §1, 17, 258 f.; A, 25, p. 30.
[3] §v, 6.
[4] G, 17, 205; G, 25, 31.
[5] G, 3, 170 f. and 300 f.: G, 38, 98 ff.; A, 14, line 70.
[6] G, 1, 95 f.; G, 2, 78 f.

found nothing in the succeeding level except the remains of hovels covering the sacred site; if these were not the huts of the mountaineers themselves, they had reduced the remnant of the inhabitants to this miserable pass. Nothing was recalled concerning this period, ever afterwards held in humiliating memory by the Babylonians, except its end, a glorious deliverance hailed no less fervently and followed by no less vigorous a reaction, than the expulsion of the Hyksos from Egypt.

Although the king-list, in its usual schematic manner, would have the Gutians to reign on unrivalled until their overthrow, there is much to suggest that their ascendancy, always partial and impermanent, had shrunk before their banishment to a sporadic domination, for it is evident that other dynasties, both in the king-list and omitted from it, were ruling other parts of the land before the Gutians finally decamped. The dynasty of Agade itself, after a period of convulsion, rallied with the advent of two kings, who maintained themselves in some state for reigns of normal length. After Agade the list arranges, not yet the Gutians, but a group of five obscure kings, almost unknown otherwise, who ruled for thirty years as the Fourth Dynasty of Uruk,[1] and were doubtless contemporary with some of the Gutians, perhaps with the last kings of Agade. It happens too that Lagash is again pre-eminent in the revival of Sumerian traditions after the long Akkadian rule and the barbarian interlude, just as the same city had been in the Early Dynastic period, without in either age gaining admission to the list of sovereigns. In the latter years of Naram-Sin and the earlier of Shar-kali-sharri a certain Lugal-ushumgal was *ensi* of the city,[2] and there were several others very little known, who lived like him as vassals of Agade. But after the fall of Shar-kali-sharri, the style and dating of the business documents alter, for the years are named not with the official formulae prescribed from Agade but after religious celebrations by the local rulers.

The emergence of Lagash to a period of high prosperity is marked by the reign of Ur-Baba, who attained enough independence and wealth to undertake rebuilding of temples and irrigation works about his city, and to patronize a remarkable school of sculptors in hard stone, who were to produce, in the next two generations, the most finished masterpieces of Babylonian statuary. The small inscribed statue of himself,[3] in dolerite, and now lacking its head, gives promise but not as yet fulfilment, for

---

[1] G, 18, 114 ff.; A, 37, no. 15; A, 16, 110.   [2] §v, 10, 30 f.
[3] §v, 8, pls. 7 f.; G, 39, 60 f.; § v. 7, 144.

it is squat and lifeless. Unlike his successor Gudea this governor makes no boast of having sent abroad for the stone to make his statues, but he was not a merely local magnate, for a daughter of his was priestess of the Moon-god at Ur and dedicated an inscribed vase there.[1] Herein again is shown that close connexion between Lagash and Ur which had existed in the Early Dynastic period since the time of Ur-Nanshe. Another daughter was wife to a subsequent ruler named Ur-gar, but a better-known member of his family was Nammakhni, another son-in-law, who was also the grandson of one Kaku, but neither the count of generations nor the style of a tablet,[2] which names the accession year of Kaku, suggests that he can have been the king of the Second Dynasty of Ur, defeated by Rimush.

Nammakhni did some building in Lagash, and a few other monuments bear his name, but like certain others his reign is best known from its end, for he was the victim of another conqueror Ur-Nammu, founder of the Third Dynasty of Ur, who boasts of this victory in the prologue to his laws.[3] The synchronism, interesting in itself, gives rise to a difficult historical problem, for if Nammakhni was a predecessor of Gudea, as supposed, it would be necessary to regard Gudea himself as ruling during the time and under the sway of Ur-Nammu and the sovereignty of Ur; but the degree of independence which the inscriptions of Gudea display, the complete absence from these of the slightest allusion to Ur and to any overlord, and their actual presence at Ur itself[4] make such a dependence hardly conceivable. Yet there seems to be no room for his reign, apparently of some length, in the years between Ur-Baba and the rise of Ur-Nammu.

In the balance of contemporary power Gudea was doubtless no more than one of the local princes who were strong enough to sustain themselves in their own cities and palaces but not to meddle much with their neighbours. He maintained the connexion Ur-Baba had with Ur, and he informs us, in one of his long inscriptions, that he sent a military expedition against the districts of Anshan and Elam,[5] smote them and dedicated their spoils to his god Ningirsu. The great event of his reign was the rebuilding of this god's house, called E-ninnu. With this enterprise all of his inscriptions are connected either as foundation deposits and bricks or as objects (statues, vases, mace-heads) to furnish the interior. From the inscriptions so liberally spread

---

[1] G, 14, no. 25; §v, 10, 23.   [2] G, 39, 226 (7); A, 15, 5 f.
[3] §v, 3, 45; §v, 12, 172.
[4] G, 14, nos. 26–8; A 15, 11 ff.; A, 39, 53 ff.   [5] §v, 4, 60 f.

over these we learn many interesting details of religious observance in his time, and obtain an unrivalled picture of the life of
gods and men in the Sumerian cities, where these two orders of
beings lived in such perpetual contact and with such parallel
institutions that the universal service owed to the principal god
seemed to put all other creatures on the same level, and to make
it almost indistinguishable whether the servant, from the steward
to the ass-herd, was god or man. Upon the construction of
E-ninnu Gudea expended all his wealth and influence, and one of
his most interesting passages,[1] in describing these efforts, gives a
remarkable picture of the resources of his day and of the external
conditions in the land. Only once did the temple receive a
foreign booty, but an immense area was laid under contribution
for fine building materials—timbers of various kinds both from
the east and from the west, ornamental stones from different
parts of Syria, gold dust from Armenia, and bitumen from the
neighbourhood of Kirkuk. No doubt all of these materials were
obtained by caravan trade, and since this passes, even under the
most oppressive governments, subject to the payment of tolls,
it would not be necessary to suppose that Gudea's far-brought
conveyance implied the removal of central authority—in this case
of the Gutians. But his independent warlike foray against Elam
would not have been tolerated by an effective overlord, and it
seems to have been the case that the last king of the Gutians had
brought about a cessation of traffic, for a striking phrase in the
inscription which relates his overthrow says 'he had made long
grass to grow upon the highways of the land'.[2] Moreover, Gudea
himself represents his freedom to trade as a benefit granted by the
god himself, who 'opened the road from the upper sea unto the
lower'. There is reason then to believe that part of Gudea's reign
fell in the period after the final defeat of the Gutians.

The glory of this otherwise petty kingdom is the artistic
triumphs with which some happy circumstances endowed it.
Among the ruins of Lagash have been found, at various times in
the last seventy years, the famous statues[3] of Gudea and of his son
Ur-Ningirsu which represent to us the highest achievements of
Sumerian sculpture. They are, indeed, of different merit, some
having an unpleasing squat proportion which gives them a grotesque effect, accentuated by the formal posture of the hands, and
the accidental loss of the heads. These heads, when preserved,

---

[1] Cylinder A, col. xv; §v, 1, 152 f.; §v, 2, 86 f.
[2] §vi, 5 and 6; A, 39, 53.
[3] §v, 7, 160 ff.; §v, 11, 63 ff.; See Plate 42 (*b*).

have finely marked features, and they gain greatly, in modern estimation, by having the eyes carved, and not inlaid with other materials, a practice which gave to so many Sumerian figures a repulsive, staring look; though it is beyond doubt that the eyes of the Gudea figures also were originally painted, and may well have looked just as crude as the inlay. In the best examples the robe too, and the bare shoulder and arm are most delicately modelled. These masterpieces arouse regret for the disappearance of much more which Gudea tells us he made for the furnishings of Ningirsu's temple. But in this information he has left us another kind of masterpiece, for his inscriptions, despite their uniformity of purport, give the Sumerian language in its most developed form, divorced alike from primitive awkwardness and from late artificiality; they are, in fact, the Sumerian classic, just as the Code of Hammurabi is the Akkadian. Literary ability was native at Lagash, for it seems no accident that the same city should have produced the best descriptive (if it cannot be called historical) writing both in the Early Dynastic age and at the end of the Gutian oppression.

VI. THE EXPULSION OF THE GUTIANS

That oppression, as suggested above, came to a decisive end probably in the lifetime of Gudea himself, by the act of a national hero. This was Utu-khegal, king of Uruk, who in the king-list represents alone the Fifth Dynasty of that city, and, in accordance with its usual scheme, is proclaimed sovereign of the land in virtue of his victory over the Gutians. Apart from a few inscriptions of his own,[1] from his place in the king-list, and from some ominous recollections of his rival's fate, Utu-khegal appears in two other documents. One is a late chronicle,[2] which knew the one memorable fact about him, but quite subordinates this to a pietistic anecdote about his being a fisherman who was impiously stopped by the Gutians from offering his catch to the god Marduk, and in his turn offended the same deity and was drowned. The other is of quite unusual interest, for it is a copy of the hero's own account of his victory, which may have been carved originally upon a sculptured monument.[3]

Its language is strong and vivid. Without any preamble it

---

[1] G, 3, 360 f.; §vi, 1; §vi 4, nos. 18–20; cf. R.A. 51, 44.
[2] §1, 20, erster Teil, 55.
[3] §vi, 5 and 6; now said (A, 14, 48) not to be original.

plunges into a denunciation of 'Gutium, the stinging serpent of the hills, who was the enemy of the gods, who had carried off the kingship of Sumer to the mountains and filled Sumer with evil', robbing wives and children and committing all wickedness in the land. The god Enlil, it continues, resolved to 'destroy its name' and for his instrument chose Utu-khegal, king of Uruk. The story moves swiftly—the king prayed to his city-goddess Inanna, exposing the oppression of the Gutians, and the goddess 'chose' him by a divine sign. Marching out of Uruk with its citizen-soldiers he harangued them at a place called 'Temple of Ishkur'; assured of support by two great and two minor gods[1] he purposed to destroy Gutium. The levies of Uruk and Kullab answered with a shout and pressed behind him. On the fourth day's march he reached a canal, on the fifth a place called 'Shrine of Ili-tabba', where he met two 'lieutenants' (with good Babylonian names) sent by the king of Gutium perhaps to demand his surrender. The sixth day's march brought him to Ennigi where he besought the aid of the Weather God to whom that place belonged. Here the battle was joined, the enemy host being commanded by the two lieutenants under the king Tirigan himself, who had but newly come to the throne, for the king-list gives him a reign of only forty days. The issue was a Sumerian triumph; Tirigan 'fled away alone', and sought to take refuge in a town called Dubrum, which, however, hearing the result of the battle, rejected the fugitive, and handed him over prisoner with his wife and son to the victor, who 'set his foot upon his neck, and restored the kingship of Sumer into its own hand'. This famous victory, like so many other historical incidents, was remembered in the diviners' books —the presence of six small vessels upon the liver was an 'omen of the king Tirigan who fled in the midst of his host'.[2] Still more menacing was an eclipse of the moon with certain attendant phenomena on the fourteenth of the month of Tammuz: 'a decision will be given to the king of the Gutians, there will be a downfall of the Gutians in battle, the land will be left naked'.[3] The omen has more than a superstitious interest, for the day of the eclipse and its attendant circumstances offer to modern chronologers a possibility of fixing the date of this battle and the end of the Gutian dynasty. It may be added that another omen[4] seems to corroborate the story that Utu-khegal's life ended by drowning, while he supervised the building of a river-dam.

[1] §I, 21, 138 n. 109; A, 35.   [2] §I, 17, 259; §I, 47, 234 f.; §I, 30, no. 25.
[3] G, 19, vol. II, 554; §VI, 8, 86 f.; §VI, 3, 90.
[4] §I, 30, no. 48.

The last words of his inscription are pregnant with a sense of what this victory meant. Once again, it was not the mere supplanting of one city by another, when both were dimly conscious of an underlying unity. Two centuries of subjection, first to the alien Akkadians and then, worse still, to the execrable Gutians, had kindled the national sentiment into a flame. At the beginning of each reign the revolt had been fiercer, the repression more severe. When deliverance came at last it released a flood of Sumerian patriotism and a burst of energy which, however, had to constrain itself within narrower bounds than Sargon had set. As to the sentiment it is a probable opinion that the king-list itself, with its fundamental ideas of the nationality and unity of a common kingship, was a product of the days of Utu-khegal,[1] when the past and present experiences of the people might seem most apt to have engendered that faith. As to the energy, this was expressed in the foreign victories and the domestic state which were to be achieved by the Third Dynasty of Ur.

[1] G, 18, 128 ff. and 140 f.; criticized in §vi, 2, 49 ff.

CHAPTER XX

THE MIDDLE KINGDOM IN EGYPT: INTERNAL HISTORY FROM THE RISE OF THE HERACLEOPOLITANS TO THE DEATH OF AMMENEMES III

I. THE HERACLEOPOLITAN KINGDOM

ABOUT 2160 B.C., after several decades of nominal occupancy by the weak rulers of the end of the Sixth Dynasty and the Memphite kinglets of the Seventh and Eighth Dynasties, the throne of Egypt was claimed by Achthoes, the governor of the Twentieth Nome of Upper Egypt, whose city, called by the Egyptians *Heneneswe* and by the Greeks *Heracleopolis*, occupied the site of present-day Ihnāsya el-Medīna, on the west side of the Nile, just south of the entrance to the Faiyūm. Assuming the throne-name Meryibre, Achthoes evidently set about imposing his rule upon his fellow nomarchs with such vigour that he has been described by Manetho as 'behaving more cruelly than his predecessors' and doing 'evil to the people of all Egypt'. Though his control of the eastern Delta and its mixed Egyptian and Asiatic population is open to question, he was apparently recognized as king throughout the rest of Egypt as far south as Aswān, where his name has been noted in a rock inscription at the First Cataract.[1] It is by no means certain, as was once thought, that his adherents failed to take over This[2] and the sovereignty of his second successor, Neferkare, seems to have been acknowledged in the three southernmost nomes of Upper Egypt.[3] Elsewhere the names of Achthoes I occur on an openwork bronze vessel from Asyūt, a stronghold of the new regime in the Thirteenth Nome of Upper Egypt, on an ebony staff from Meir in the Fourteenth Nome, and on a fragment of an ivory coffer from El-Lisht, eighteen miles south of Memphis.[4] As the founder of the 'House of Achthoes' he is referred to several times in the well-known Instruction addressed to his descendant, King Merykare (see

---

[1] §1, 18, 333.   [2] §1, 17, 170; §1, 3, 644.   [3] See below, pp. 465 and 474.
[4] §1, 15, 131–2, fig. 85; §1, 11, 185–6; §1, 10, 143, fig. 86.

below), and is there cited as the author of a similar collection of precepts.[1]

Meryibre Achthoes I and the seventeen Heracleopolitan kings of the Ninth and Tenth Dynasties, who succeeded him, ruled together for an estimated 120 years, from about 2160 to about 2040 B.C. Their names are listed in whole or in part in the fragmentary fourth and fifth columns of the Turin Canon. The fact that two of these kings adopted the praenomen Neferkare suggests that the Heracleopolitans, like the Memphites whom they replaced, regarded themselves as legitimate successors of King Phiops II of the Old Kingdom.

The earlier Heracleopolitan Neferkare, the third ruler of the Ninth Dynasty,[2] is probably the King 'Kaneferre' referred to at El-Mi'alla in the tomb of the nomarch Ankhtify, who, presumably out of loyalty to his Heracleopolitan overlord, led the nomes of Hierakonpolis and Edfu against the people of Thebes when the latter, with the assistance of Koptos, first attempted to gain control of the Theban nome itself[3] (see below, pp. 473–5). Though initially successful, Ankhtify and his followers evidently soon came to terms with their foes, their capitulation, as will be seen, marking the first step toward the eventual overthrow of the pharaohs of Heracleopolis by the warlike princes of Thebes.

Achthoes II, the fourth ruler in the succession, is perhaps to be identified with King Nebkaure Achthoes, who is named on a weight found at Tell er-Ratāba near the Wādi Tummilāt[4] and is mentioned in the Tale of the Eloquent Peasant, a popular story of the time, preserved in four papyri of the late Middle Kingdom.[5] This tale concerns a peasant of the Wādi en-Natrūn who, having been robbed of his belongings by a wealthy landowner, addressed his complaints to the king's high steward at Heracleopolis with such extraordinary eloquence that the pharaoh made him present his case again and again purely for the pleasure which he derived from hearing the peasant talk. The story and the weight are interesting as indicating that at this time the Heracleopolitan sphere of influence included both the west and east sides of the Delta. The Ninth Dynasty, however, seems to have survived for

[1] P. Ermitage 1116A recto, 109.   [2] Turin Canon IV, 20.
[3] §1, 20, 185–206 (Inscriptions 5–7), 263 (Inscription 16 [18]). Cf. §1, 12, 86–97. Neither the style of the inscriptions nor the events described in them would suggest that this was the King Neferkare who was a contemporary of the early kings of the Eleventh Dynasty (Turin Canon V, 6; cf. §1, 20, 35 ff.).
[4] §1, 14, 32, pl. 33, 4; §1, 13, 123.
[5] §1, 22; §1, 21; §1, 6.

only a decade or two longer, coming to an end about 2130 B.C., probably as a result of the Theban revolution of 2133 B.C.

With the Tenth Dynasty, for which the Turin Canon apparently lists five kings (v, 5–9), we are on somewhat firmer ground. The founder of the dynasty, King Meryhathor(?), is known only from a damaged inscription in the alabaster quarries at Het-nub[1] and his successor, another Neferkare, is only a name in the Turin Canon;[2] but the third and fourth rulers of the dynasty are reasonably historical personages.

Wahkare Achthoes III was the alleged author of the justly famous 'Instruction for King Merykare', his son and heir, a statement of policy composed apparently under Merykare himself, but containing some of the finest passages in Egyptian didactic literature and much valuable information on the history of the Heracleopolitan period.[3] From this work it is clear that, with Wahkare's support, the nomarchs of the Delta succeeded in dealing with the Asiatics who had infiltrated its eastern provinces, but maintained in large part their own independence and collected their own taxes in addition to those which they levied on behalf of their complacent overlord. New colonies of Egyptians appear to have been settled in the north-east to help in reclaiming the land and strengthening the border defences. With the re-opening of the Delta harbours trade was resumed with the Syrian coast and fine coniferous woods were again imported into Egypt. Though the kings evidently resided at Heracleopolis itself,[4] Memphis seems to have remained, as before, the centre of the administration and the site of the royal cemetery.

In the South, meanwhile, matters had taken a less favourable turn. The Thebans had overcome the resistance to their regime in the first three nomes and, as the result of a long and still continuing struggle,[5] had apparently extended their power northward to the important administrative and religious centres of This and Abydos in the Eighth Nome. Impelled to action by this growing threat Wahkare and his ally and kinsman(?), the nomarch Tefibi of Asyūt,[6] fell upon the nome of This and captured it 'like a cloudburst', but unwisely permitted their troops to 'hack up' the hallowed area and plunder the tombs of the honoured dead. This, as Wahkare himself ruefully admits in his Instruction

---

[1] §1, 1, 14 n. 1, pl. 7, inscr. IX.   [2] Turin Canon v, 6.
[3] §1, 8, 1–4, pls. 9–14; §1, 23, 414–18; §1, 19.
[4] §1, 22, pls. 1–2 (R 37, 82); §1, 9, pl. 13 (Tomb IV, col. 16).
[5] See below, p. 475, n. 2.
[6] §1, 9, pls. 11, 12; §1, 2, 17–26, 40–51; §1, 16, 155–6.

to his son, was a mistake which brought its own retribution. Wahankh Inyotef, the Theban, counter-attacking with the outraged fury of the Southland now solidly behind him, succeeded in the course of his long reign in driving the Heracleopolitans out of 'the whole of the Thinite Nome' and pressed on to 'its northern boundary, as far as the nome of Aphroditopolis',[1] or Tenth Nome, which adjoins the district of This on the west side of the Nile.

It was perhaps at this stage that the Heracleopolitan rulers, despairing of ultimate victory, adopted the policy of 'peaceful coexistence' with the southern kingdom which Wahkare urged upon his successor in an oft-cited passage in the Instruction for Merykare.[2] Peace, in any case, seems to have prevailed for several decades. During this interval old King Wahkare died after a reign of approximately half a century[3] and his middle-aged son, Merykare, ruled at Heracleopolis in his place. At Asyūt the installation of a new nomarch, Achthoes II, was attended by the pharaoh and his court who journeyed upstream for the occasion in a great fleet of ships.[4] It must have been at this period, too, that the Heracleopolitans, probably through an arrangement with Thebes, were once again able to obtain blocks of red granite from the quarries at Aswān.[5]

The truce seems to have been kept by both sides until the fourteenth year of the Horus Sankhibtowy (King Mentuhotpe II) of Thebes when what a Theban text describes as 'the rebellion of This'[6] set the war machine of the southern kingdom once more in motion. This time it was not to be stopped. Before long Asyūt fell and the fighting moved northward into the Fifteenth, or Hermopolite, Nome, which found itself overrun by the undisciplined armies of the contending dynasts, including, according to Kay, son of the nomarch Neheri, troops of Nubians and 'Asiatic' bedawin. 'I rescued my city on the day of plundering from the grievous terrors of the Royal House', says Kay,[7] and it is probable that he was referring, not to the royal house of Thebes, but to the royal house of Heracleopolis.[8]

Merykare, by that time an elderly man, died before the Thebans reached Heracleopolis and was buried near Memphis in a pyramid somewhat optimistically named 'Flourishing-are-the-Abodes-

---

[1] §1, 4, sect. 16, col. 3.
[2] P. Ermitage 1116a recto, 71–8 (§1, 8, pl. 11; §1, 23, 416; etc.).
[3] §1, 19, 54. [4] §1, 16, 158–9.
[5] P. Ermitage 1116a recto, 77–8 (see above, p. 466, n. 3).
[6] §1, 4, sect. 23, cols. 15–16. [7] §1, 1, 54–5, gr. 24 (7–8).
[8] Cf. §1, 5. See, however, below, p. 471, n. 1. [Ed.]

of-Merykare'.[1] It was, however, only a few months later that the reign of his unknown successor, the last of the Heracleopolitan pharaohs,[2] was cut short by a complete victory for Thebes and a new union of the 'Two Lands' under King Nebhepetre Mentuhotpe II of the Eleventh Dynasty.

II. THE NOMARCHS OF MIDDLE EGYPT

Information on conditions in Egypt during the Heracleopolitan Period stems neither from the scanty ruins of Heracleopolis itself nor from the few remnants of a historical nature recovered at Memphis, but from the tombs and other inscribed monuments of the provincial governors of Upper Egypt, especially the rulers of the so-called 'Middle Nomes', from Akhmīm in the south to Beni Hasan in the north.

The picture which emerges corresponds with what was seen taking shape during the latter part of the Old Kingdom. The nomes, once administrative districts of a strong central government, had returned to their original status as small, independent states. Each was governed by a dynasty of local princes, whose right to power had become hereditary and who now dated events to the years of their own tenures of office, levied and maintained their own armies, built and manned their own fleets of ships, quarried stone for their own monuments, and frequently allocated to themselves privileges and titles of royal type. At death the nomarch was buried in a great tomb, rock-cut in the cliffs near his local capital and surrounded by the tombs of his own courtiers and officials.

Personal ties or the promptings of expediency at times led the nomarchs of Middle Egypt to take an active part in national affairs and to ally themselves with the cause of their sovereigns; but, for the most part, their interests were centred in their own provinces. These, they tell us, they ruled with benevolence and solicitude, suppressing lawlessness and injustice, improving the irrigation systems, restocking herds, storing up food for use in times of famine, and, as Overseers of Priests, maintaining in a state of repair the temples of the local gods.

At Asyūt the nomarch Achthoes, during the peaceful years preceding the outbreak of hostilities with Thebes, repaired and augmented the irrigation canals in his nome and made arable land which had previously been desert. In a year when the Nile was low and famine was rife in the neighbouring provinces he closed

<hr>

[1] §1, 24, 23 n. 3.   [2] Turin Canon v, 9.

his borders to outsiders and distributed grain to his own people from his well-stocked granaries. He speaks of his prowess as a warrior, states with evident pride that he was 'greatly feared by his neighbours', and tells of organizing troops of militia for the policing and defence of his nome.[1] His successor, Tefibi, boasts of the absence of lawlessness in his time: 'When night fell, he who slept by the way praised me because he was like a man in his own house. Dread of my soldiers was his protection when the beasts of the field lay beside him.'[2] During the interval of peace preceding the final Theban drive (see above) Tefibi's son, Achthoes II, set about restoring the temple at Asyūt, that his name might 'be forever in the temple of Wepwawet' and his 'good remembrance in the columned hall'.[3]

Two painted wooden tomb models of this time from Asyūt show the types of soldier which these self-styled 'Great Chiefs of Upper Egypt' placed in the field against their Theban adversaries.[4] Marching four abreast in companies of forty are native Egyptian spearmen, with shields of bull's hide and copper-tipped lances about five feet in length, and Nubian archers, each carrying a bow and a handful of arrows. Short loincloths were the soldiers' only clothing and thick shocks of hair served as protection for their heads. The Nubians, clearly distinguished by their dark skin and polychrome garments, were probably Medjay or men of Wawat, like those mentioned by Kay, son of the nomarch Neheri of Hermopolis.[5]

The marked devotion and faithful service accorded the royal house of Heracleopolis by the nomarchs of Asyūt is almost certainly to be attributed to the existence of strong ties of friendship, perhaps even of blood relationship, between the two families. As a boy the elder Achthoes was brought up with the pharaoh's children and was sponsored as nomarch by the king himself, who also seems to have joined in the general mourning which attended the death of Achthoes' grandfather.[6] It has already been stated that King Merykare and his court made the long journey upstream to be present at the installation of the nomarch Achthoes II.[7] The bond, thus attested for three generations, persisted to the end, and the house of Achthoes finally went down fighting for a pharaoh who was powerless to command the loyalty voluntarily

[1] §I, 2, 11 ff., 64 ff.; §I, 16, 160.   [2] §I, 2, 17, 43–4 (col. 10).
[3] §I, 2, 27–8, 55 (cols. 20–4).   [4] §II, 10 (4), 265. See Plate 43 (b).
[5] §I, 1, 36–7 (gr. 16, 6).
[6] §I, 2, 67 (cols. 22 ff.), 68 (cols. 36 ff.). See also §II, 1, sects. 413–14.
[7] See above, p. 467, n. 4.

bestowed upon him. When, in the Twelfth Dynasty, the history of Asyūt can again be traced a new line of nomarchs has replaced the old champions of the Heracleopolitan kingdom.

More typical of the times was the policy followed by the Hereditary Princes of the Hare Nome, whose capital city, Khmunu (modern El-Ashmūnein), later became the Greek Hermopolis and whose local divinity was the great god Thoth. In the tombs at Sheikh Sa'īd[1] and El-Bersha[2] and, even more clearly, in a series of inscriptions in the alabaster quarries at Het-nub[3] we can trace the fortunes of this ancient family from the late Old Kingdom to the middle of the Twelfth Dynasty. Following two princes named Iha and a third named Thutnakhte, who appear to have been contemporaries of the Eighth and Ninth Dynasties, we arrive, with Thutnakhte II, at the beginning of the Tenth Dynasty and find the name of King Meryhathor(?) in an inscription of this nomarch at Het-nub.[4] Then come Thutnakhte III, Ahanakhte, and Thutnakhte IV, who seem to have held office during the long reign of King Wahkare and the first years of King Merykare and who were therefore contemporary with the nomarchs Tefibi and Achthoes II of Asyūt.[5]

It was in the time of Thutnakhte's son, the great nomarch and vizier, Neheri, that the army of Nebhepetre, the Theban, passed through the Hare Nome on its victorious march toward Heracleopolis. Neheri, who had been made chief of staff by his king and placed in command of one of the two divisions of the Heracleopolitan army,[6] appears to have devoted his energies less to checking the Theban advance than to rescuing the people of his nome from violence at the hands of both armies.[7] In a graffito at Het-nub, dated to Year 5 of his nomarchy, his son Kay says: 'I prepared my troops of young men and went to fight in company with my city. It was I who formed its [rearguard?] in Shedyetsha. There were no men with me except my (own) followers when Medjayu and men of Wawat, Nubians and Asiatics, Upper Egypt and Lower Egypt were united against me. I returned successfully, my whole city with me, without loss. I was one, moreover, who rescued the weak from the strong. I made my house a gateway for all who came frightened on the day of

[1] §II, 3.   [2] §II, 9.   [3] §I, 1.
[4] *Ibid.* 14 n. 1, pl. 7 (inscr. IX).   [5] *Ibid.* 114.
[6] *Ibid.* 94 (gr. 20 [4–6], gr. 25 [6–7]).
[7] It is difficult to accept Faulkner's elaborate theory that the Hare Nome rebelled against the Heracleopolitans shortly before the Theban advance and then joined with them to oppose it (§I, 5).

tumult.'[1] Kay also recalls how he organized the youth of his city to protect the people, who had fled to the swamps, and how the older men withdrew into their houses and 'did not take the field on the day of fear of the Royal House'.[2] Another son, Prince Thutnakhte (V), says that he attacked the 'troops of the king' and, although 'free from rashness when it was hot on the day of battle', was a sheltering shade over the whole land on the long-remembered 'Day of Shedyetsha'.[3]

The danger past, Neheri seems immediately to have ingratiated himself with the victorious Thebans and to have remained in power until his death, when the nomarchy passed to his son, Thutnakhte V, and, after him, to succeeding generations of the same family until the reign of King Sesostris III of the Twelfth Dynasty—almost two centuries after the fall of Heracleopolis.[4]

North of Hermopolis the Great Chiefs of the Oryx Nome seem also to have adopted a conciliatory attitude toward the Theban conquerors since their series of rock-tombs at Beni Hasan reach back with no apparent interruption from the mid-twelfth Dynasty into Heracleopolitan times.[5] No accounts or direct references to the war between Heracleopolis and Thebes are preserved there; but in the tomb of the nomarch Baqet III, who was probably a contemporary of Nebhepetre Mentuhotpe, Egyptian soldiers, aided by Nubian archers and Libyan(?) slingers, are shown attacking a fortress, the defenders of which appear also to be Egyptians.[6] The scene is repeated, with some variations, in the tomb of Baqet's son, the nomarch Achthoes, who lived during the latter years of the Eleventh Dynasty and rejoiced in the titles, 'Administrator of the Eastern Desert' and 'Commander of Soldiers in every difficult place'.[7]

Elsewhere throughout Middle Egypt we catch glimpses of the provincial governors and their followers. In the tombs at Akhmīm are preserved the names and titles of five 'Great Chief(s) of the Panopolite Nome', who lived between the late Old Kingdom and the first quarter of the Twelfth Dynasty.[8] At Deir el-Gabrāwi the tombs of four nomarchs of the Twelfth Nome belong to the same general period, but only the small and sparsely inscribed tombs of Isi called Hemre (no. 46) and his son(?), Henqu called Kheteti

[1] §1, 1, 45–8 (gr. 16 [4–9]); §11, 5, vol. 1, 77*. W. Schenkel (A, 8, 89–94) considers that Kay's statement refers to events which occurred at the time of the death of Ammenemes I. He thinks that Kay supported Sesostris I against a revolt. [Ed.]

[2] §1, 1, 54–6 (gr. 24 [6–7]).   [3] Ibid. 59–62 (gr. 26 [5–6]).
[4] Ibid. 99–100, 114.   [5] §11, 8 (see part 11, 5–7).
[6] Op. cit. 2, pl. 5.   [7] Ibid. pl. 15.
[8] §11, 7, 108, 114–19 (Tombs 12, 24–7); §11, 2, 54–6.

(no. 39), can be assigned to Heracleopolitan times.[1] Both men call themselves Great Chief(s) of the Cerastes-Mountain Nome, and Henqu, like many of his fellow nomarchs, assigns to himself the rank of Overseer of Upper Egypt. At Qāw el-Kebīr, at Deir Rīfa, and at Meir, respectively, were buried the nomarchs of the Tenth, Eleventh, and Fourteenth Nomes, but, again, the surviving tombs are almost without exception of the late Old Kingdom or of the Middle Kingdom. North of Beni Hasan the picture is even more obscure, the nomes of Cynopolis, Hipponus, Oxyrhynchus, and Heracleopolis having produced no historical monuments of the period with which we are dealing.

That conditions similar to those in the south existed also in Lower Egypt is suggested by the words attributed to King Merykare's royal father: 'Behold, [the region] which they injured is made into nomes and large cities. The sovereignty of one man (the king) has entered into the hands of ten men who exercise the functions of princes.'[2]

III. THEBES AND THE 'HEAD OF THE SOUTH'

At the end of the Old Kingdom the city which came to be known as Wāset, or Wēse, by the Egyptians and Thebes or Diospolis by the Greeks of a much later period consisted of one or more small settlements in the neighbourhood of modern Luxor, on the east bank of the Nile, twenty-three miles south of Koptos.[3] By Heracleopolitan times the town had become the metropolis of the Fourth Nome of Upper Egypt, the Nome of the Sceptre (𓌙), and one of the seats of the local falcon-god Mont, who was worshipped also in the old nome-capital at Hermonthis (modern Armant) and in the villages of Madu (El-Madāmūd) and Djeret (Tōd).[4] Another divinity, Amun, newly imported from Hermopolis and closely related in one of his forms to the great god Min of Akhmīm and Koptos,[5] had a small temple at Karnak, a mile and a half north of Luxor; but did not achieve the status of a state-god until the Twelfth Dynasty. The cemetery of Thebes lay across the river in the area now occupied by the sprawling modern village of El-Qurna. A hill, called El-Khōkha, in the centre

---

[1] §II, 4, part II, 31–3, pls. 21, 27–8.
[2] P. Ermitage 1116A recto, 85–6. See also §II, 6, 596.
[3] §III, 14; §II, 5, vol. II, 24*–26* (A 335–6).
[4] §III, 16, 5, 82–92; §III, 15, 340–6, 363–6.
[5] §III, 25; §III, 15, 106, 348 f.; §III, 31, 147, 161.

of this village has yielded several rock-tombs of the late Sixth
Dynasty, including that of the nomarch Ihy;[1] but the cemetery of
the Heracleopolitan Period is to be found in a plain three-
quarters of a mile to the north-east, below the slopes of the Dirā
Abu'n-Naga and opposite the temples of Mont and Amun at
Karnak.[2]

Here were buried the nomarchs of the vigorous line which
governed Thebes between the Sixth and the Tenth Dynasties and
their successors, the early kings of the Eleventh Dynasty. A
Theban tomb inscription, now in Cairo, reveals that, within this
period, seven nomarchs succeeded one another in office during the
active career of a single district scribe.[3] Among these nomarchs
may be counted the Sole Companion and Overseer of Prophets,
Rehuy, who 'supplied the House of Amun with food (during)
the difficult years', and, in the period immediately preceding the
rise of the Eleventh Dynasty, the Great Chief of the Sceptre
Nome and Great Chief of Upper Egypt, Inyotef.[4] The latter
nomarch is probably to be identified with the Hereditary Prince
and Count, Inyotef, son of Ikui, whom the Theban rulers of the
Middle Kingdom regarded as one of the founders of their line. As
such, he is invoked on a stela of the Eleventh Dynasty in New York,
had a statue dedicated to him by King Sesostris I of the Twelfth
Dynasty, and is named, without a cartouche or royal titles, in the
Eighteenth Dynasty table of kings from the temple at Karnak.[5]

From the inscriptions of these provincial governors and their
contemporaries it is possible to follow the gradual expansion of
Theban control throughout the 'Head of the South', or what we
should call southern Upper Egypt, a geographic entity which at
this period seems to have comprised the first eight nomes of
Upper Egypt, from Elephantine to This.[6] Not long after the rise
of the Heracleopolitans in the north Thebes apparently formed an
alliance with Koptos, which, as the principal Upper Egyptian
stronghold of the recently displaced Eighth Dynasty of Memphis,[7]
must have been antagonistic to the Heracleopolitan regime from
the outset. The first goal which the allies set themselves was the

[1] §I, 24, 3.

[2] *Ibid.* 6–7, 11, 17, 21, pl. 33; §III, 32; §III, 27, 18 ff.; §III, 21, 33–5.

[3] §I, 4, sect. 1; §III, 19, 67 (sect. 85, 6).

[4] §I, 4, sects. 7, 11–13; §III, 19, 66–7; §III, 29, 109; §III, 24, 488–9, no. 1773;
§III, 2, 185–6.

[5] §I, 4, sect. 14; §I, 10, part I, 153, fig. 91; §III, 22, pl. I (left, 2nd register,
no. 12).

[6] §III, 13, 11; §III, 9; §III, 12, 138 n. 488.

[7] §III, 11, 19–23.

conquest of the southern portion of the nome of Thebes itself, including the ancient capital at Hermonthis. In this endeavour, as we have seen, they were immediately and vigorously opposed by the neighbouring nomarch, Ankhtify of Hierakonpolis, an adherent of the Heracleopolitan pharaoh Neferkare, who relates in his tomb at El-Mi'alla how, after having subjected the nome of Edfu to his rule, he went to the rescue of Hermonthis and invaded the Theban Nome on both the west and east sides of the Nile.[1] It may have been Ankhtify who was responsible for the destruction of the village of Yushenshen, a few miles north of Thebes, an event referred to on the tomb stela of a henchman of the Koptite nomarch Djefi.[2] His resistance, however, must have been short-lived, for the nomarchs of Thebes soon extended their control southward to the First Cataract and beyond it, into northern Nubia. One of their generals, Djemi of Gebelein, claims, indeed, that he 'made Lower Nubia (Wawat) tributary to every chief who arose in this(?) nome',[3] and the nomarch Inyotef calls himself a 'Confidant of the King in the narrow southern doorway (at Elephantine)'.[4]

Northward the Theban expansion seems to have encountered more determined opposition, especially in the powerful and important nome of This. Of the governors of Koptos who assisted Thebes in this expansion not only Djefi, his father Dagi, and his son Achthoes, but also a certain User are known; possibly User was identical with the man whose armed henchman, Fegu, says on his stela from Naqāda that he was sent by the Overseer of Prophets, User, 'on every mission' and (always) 'returned satisfied'.[5] At Dendera in the Sixth Nome at least two local nomarchs, Merer and Inoqer, held office between the end of the Eighth Dynasty and the annexation of the province by the nomarch Inyotef of Thebes, whose title, Great Chief of Upper Egypt, appears with his name on a monument found at Dendera itself.[6] Conditions in the Seventh (Diospolite) Nome at this time are wholly obscure; but at Naga ed-Deir, opposite This, at nearby Sheikh Farag, and at Deir el-Gabrāwi we find the tombs and other monuments of a series of Great Chiefs of the Thinite Nome

---

[1] §I, 20, 42, 163–6 (inscr. 2), 198–206 (inscrs. 6 and 7).

[2] §III, 9; §II, 5, vol. II, 27* (338A). According to H. G. Fischer (A, 4, 50) the stela of Fegu and the stelae mentioning Djefi are all from Naqāda.

[3] §III, 1; §III, 19, 67–8; §III, 23, 45 f. The stela of Djemi appears to be from Gebelein (§III, 10, 291; A, 2, 79–80.   [4] §I, 4, sect. 13.

[5] §I, 4, sects. 8–10; §III, 19, 66–7; §III, 26, no. 14. See above, n. 2.

[6] §III, 2, 185–6; §III, 5, revised edition, 177–8; §III, 18, 18, 65, p. 12.

dating from the Sixth to the Eleventh Dynasty.[1] The protracted struggle for the control of this nome is reflected in the words of a resident of Dendera, apparently a subject of the Theban king, Wahankh Inyotef, who, looking back on his past life, speaks of giving corn to his city 'for fifty-six years . . .when there was war with the nome of This'.[2]

As in Middle Egypt, famine, the inevitable companion of political disunity, repeatedly stalked the Head of the South during the early years of the Theban climb to supremacy. Besides the inscription just quoted, half a dozen autobiographical texts of this period mention disastrous and widespread famines and describe the steps taken by the authors of the respective texts to provide food for their own and neighbouring communities.[3] Ankhtify of El-Mi'alla, who—probably more picturesquely than truthfully—represents the starving people of Upper Egypt as driven to the point of eating their children, states that he not only fed his own district during one such crisis, but also supported towns in the First and Second Nomes and sent his 'Upper Egyptian corn' as far south as Nubia and as far north as This.[4] Some years later, under similar circumstances, the Treasurer Iti of Gebelein relates how he gave corn to Hermonthis and to Ankhtify's home town of Hefat (El-Mi'alla) 'after Gebelein had been sustained, at a time when Thebes went downstream and upstream' (in search of food);[5] and the Sole Companion, Hekayeb, of Gebelein speaks of providing his city with Upper Egyptian barley 'for many years', of 'making a loan of' corn to 'Upper Egypt', and of giving oil to the nome of Hierakonpolis, where Ankhtify once held sway.[6]

Despite their great and ever-growing power in Upper Egypt the nomarchs of Thebes do not seem to have actually broken with the pharaohs of Heracleopolis until the very end of this period, Inyotef, the last of the line, calling himself 'Confidant of the King' and 'Great Pillar (of) He-who-makes-the-Two-Lands-to-live'.[7]

---

[1] §III, 4, 29–33; §III, 17, 41, 122, 127; §II, 4, part I, 8–9; part II, 1–3. I am grateful to Dr Caroline Peck for having provided me with a list of these nomarchs and references to their extant monuments.

[2] Cairo Stela JE 46048. See §III, 8, xxxiv (top); §I, 17, 170. I am indebted to Professor Anthes, formerly of the University Museum in Philadelphia, for a photograph of this stela and to J. J. Clère for a hand-copy of the pertinent portion of the text. For further indications of military activity in the Thinite Nome see §III, 3, nos. 39, 40, 56, 78, 85; §I, 10, part I, 139.

[3] §III, 29, 9–12, 105–11.　　　[4] §I, 20, 220–31 (inscr. 10).

[5] §III, 30. See also §III, 6.　　　[6] §III, 20.　　　[7] §I, 4, sect. 13.

IV. THE EARLY KINGS OF THE
ELEVENTH DYNASTY

It was Mentuhotpe, the son(?) and successor of the nomarch Inyotef, who was traditionally regarded as the founder of the Eleventh Dynasty and who came to be known to his descendants as the Horus Tepya ('the Ancestor'), the father of the 'Gods', (King) Mentuhotpe (I), with his name written in a cartouche both in the Karnak list and on a statue which his younger son, King Inyotef II, dedicated to him at Elephantine.[1] Though Mentuhotpe may not have assumed the royal titulary during his own lifetime it was undoubtedly he who, in 2133 B.C., openly repudiated the overlordship of Heracleopolis and sired Egypt's first dynasty of Theban kings.

The 'Ancestor', or 'Original', Mentuhotpe was succeeded by his elder son, the Horus Sehertowy ('Pacifier-of-the-Two-Lands'), the Son of Re, Inyotef I, whose names follow those of his father in the Karnak list and who appears on a door-jamb from the temple at Tōd in company with his three successors, Inyotef II and III and Mentuhotpe II.[2] We know nothing of the reign of this first self-styled Theban king, but there is some probability that he was the owner of a great courtyard tomb north-east of the Dirā Abu'n-Naga, in that portion of the Theban necropolis which has come to be known as 'the Intef Cemetery'.[3] The façade of the tomb, a rock-cut portico, pierced by a dozen doorways leading to the subterranean burial complex, occupies the rear, or western end of the courtyard, and was in all probability surmounted by a small pyramid of mud brick.[4] At his death in 2118 B.C. Sehertowy and his father before him had ruled Thebes and apparently most of the Head of the South for sixteen years. There is no evidence that either of these two rulers was associated, as has been thought,[5] with the Treasurer Iti of Gebelein (see above, p. 475), who makes no mention of a change in his master's status (from nomarch to king), but says simply that he always gave satisfaction whether he served 'a great lord' or 'a little lord'.[6]

The Horus Wahaṇkh, King Inyotef II, seems to have been Mentuhotpe I's younger son,[7] born to him by a woman named

---

[1] §IV, 4, 176–84.   [2] §IV, 10.
[3] §III, 32, 13–24; §I, 24, 11, pls. 3, 33; §III, 21, 33–5.
[4] See however, *Mitt. Deutsch Inst. Kairo*, 23 (1968), 26–37. [Ed.]
[5] So §III, 30, 141–2; §I, 20, 40.
[6] §III, 8, sect. 217 (2nd ex.); §III, 6, 69–72.   [7] §IV, 4, 179–81.

Neferu, whose importance is attested by the frequency with which she is mentioned in her son's inscriptions.[1] The new king, evidently a young man at the time of his accession, reigned for almost fifty years[2] and during these years, as we have seen, fought with notable success against the pharaohs of Heracleopolis. A great stela from his courtyard tomb, just south of that of Sehertowy, describes his capture of the Thinite Nome and his expansion of the Theban kingdom northward to the nome of Aphroditopolis;[3] and at Dendera the Steward Erdiwy-Khnum, a contemporary of either Inyotef II or III,[4] speaks of his mistress, the King's Daughter and King's Wife, Neferukayet, as 'Head of the people from Elephantine to Aphroditopolis'.[5] The Overseer of Interpreters, Djari, relates that he received a citation from the Horus Wahankh after he 'had fought with the House of Achthoes on the west of This', and he, too, defines the southern kingdom as extending 'in its entirety southward to Elephantine and northward to Aphroditopolis'.[6] On the other hand, the Chancellor Tjetji, who survived the death of the king, says that he served the Horus Wahankh for 'a long period of years... when this land was under his authority upstream to Elephantine and (downstream) as far as This of the Thinite Nome'.[7] The apparent discrepancy here is probably one of expression rather than of fact, for it will be recalled that on the west side of the river the Thinite and Aphroditopolite Nomes share a common boundary. The peaceful interlude which followed the king's defeat of the Heracleopolitans (§1) permitted trade relations to be resumed with the North, and Tjetji speaks of 'every good thing that was being brought to the Majesty of (my) lord from Upper Egypt and from Lower Egypt'. At Thebes Wahankh relates that he filled the temple (of Mont?) with 'noble vases for pouring libations' and of the other gods he says, 'I built their temples, erected their stairways, made solid their gates, and established their offering-foundations...'.[8] His names are inscribed on a

---

[1] §iv, 8, 119; §i, 17, 169–70; §iii, 19, sect. 71.

[2] Dying apparently in his fiftieth year on the throne (§1, 4, sect. 16, col. 6) after a reign which the Turin Canon (v, 14) records as '49 years'.

[3] §1, 4, sect. 16, col. 3.

[4] On an unpublished stela, found at Dendera by the University of Pennsylvania's expedition, Erdiwy-Khnum is associated with a 'King Inyotef, whose mother is Neferu'—hence, either Inyotef II or Inyotef III (see §iv, 8, 119). A hand-copy of, and commentary on, this most interesting monument was provided by Dr Henry G. Fischer.

[5] §iii, 18, 52, pl. 15; §ii, 6, 105; §i, 17, 169–70.

[6] §1, 4, sect. 18. [7] Ibid. sect. 20, lines 3–4; §iv, 1, 56, 58. See Plate 44.

[8] §1, 4, sect. 16, cols. 1, 2.

boulder on the island of Elephantine,[1] and here also, in the temple of the deified governor, Hekayeb, he dedicated two statues of himself and one of his father, Mentuhotpe I.[2]

The Horus Nakhtnebtepnefer, Inyotef III, must himself have been well advanced in age at the time of his predecessor's death and it is not surprising to find that, according to the Turin Canon (v, 15), he ruled for only eight years. The brevity of his reign is further attested by the fact that two of his father's courtiers—Ka's son, Inyotef, and Henuni—survived to the days of his son Mentuhotpe II.[3] At Elephantine he carried out restorations in the temple of Hekayeb, which he describes as being in a ruinous state, and contributed a sandstone doorway to the temple of the local goddess, Satis.[4] Among the private monuments of his reign one of the more interesting is the stela of the Henchman Megegi, whose formal name, Ammenemes ('Amun-is-foremost'), wascompounded with that of the still relatively obscure local god of Thebes.[5] Under Inyotef III Abydos remained in the possession of the Thebans, but was exposed to some sort of hardship, probably a famine. Speaking of 'the day of misery', Prince Ideni of Abydos says 'the Horus Nakhtnebtepnefer, the King of Upper and Lower Egypt, the Son of Re, Inyotef the Great', approved his plan for supporting his city in the crisis and commended him for his efficiency in carrying out the royal orders.[6] Since his mother as well as his grandmother was named Neferu it is possible that Inyotef III, rather than his father, is the 'King Inyotef, whose mother is Neferu', mentioned on a fragmentary stela of the Steward Erdiwy-Khnum from Dendera.[7] He appears with his queen, Yah, and their son, King Nebhepetre Mentuhotpe II, in a relief carved during the latter's reign on the rock wall of the Shatt er-Rigāl, a ravine near Gebel es-Silsila through which a caravan track from the south-west reached the Nile Valley.[8] Another child born to the royal couple was Queen Neferu (III), the sister and apparently one of the principal wives of Mentuhotpe II.[9]

At his death Inyotef III was probably buried in western Thebes in a vast, but unfinished, courtyard tomb south of those of his father and grandfather.[10]

[1] §IV, 7, 115 (no. 1).   [2] See above, p. 476, nn. 1, 7.
[3] §I, 4, sects. 23, 24.   [4] See §IV, 3, 13; §IV, 5, 8.   [5] §I, 4, sect. 22.
[6] Cairo 20502 (§IV, 6, vol. II, 93). See also §III, 29, 11, 112.
[7] See above, p. 477, n. 4.
[8] §I, 24, 58 ff., pls. 9–12, 36. See also §IV, 2, 45–6; §I, 3, 648; §IV, 11, 41–3.
[9] §I, 24, 27; §IV, 8, 120.
[10] Incorrectly assigned by Winlock (§I, 24, 21–2, pl. 33) to Sankhibtowy Mentuhotpe. See above, p. 476, n. 4. [Ed.]

The deeds of an unidentified ruler of the early Eleventh Dynasty are glowingly described in a private tomb inscription of the period, now in Turin.[1] The king in question is said to have coped successfully with a famine, performed services for Mont, Amun, Re, and Hathor, 'seized the Two Lands with his victory', 'established the orders of eternity', and 'punished his enemies'.

V. REUNION OF EGYPT UNDER NEBHEPETRE MENTUHOTPE

When Mentuhotpe II ascended the throne in 2060 B.C. he assumed the Horus name Sankhibtowy ('Making-the-Heart-of-the-Two-Lands-to-live') and retained it until at least the fourteenth year of his reign.[2] In this year what was evidently an attempt on the part of the supporters of the Heracleopolitan pharaoh to recover the key city of This led, as has been stated, to the resumption of hostilities between Thebes and Heracleopolis and to the inauguration of a great Theban offensive which, under the vigorous leadership of the new king, was sustained until, about 2040 B.C., Heracleopolis itself fell and Egypt was once again united under a single royal house. Desultory fighting may have continued in the north for some years, but the power of the Heracleopolitans was broken and the Middle Kingdom truly launched. In a temple inscription of the Nineteenth Dynasty the names of King Menes of Dynasty I, King Nebhepetre of Dynasty XI, and King Amosis of Dynasty XVIII are listed together, obviously as the founders of the Old, the Middle, and the New Kingdoms.[3]

As his victories mounted and his rulership of all Egypt began to loom as an imminent reality Mentuhotpe II adopted a more elaborate titulary than the rulers of the Eleventh Dynasty had hitherto used, calling himself 'the Horus Netjeryhedjet, He-of-the-Two-Goddesses Netjeryhedjet, the King of Upper and Lower Egypt, Nebhepetre, the Son of Re, Mentuhotpe'.[4] Sometime between his overthrow of Heracleopolis and the carving of the Shatt er-Rigāl reliefs in the thirty-ninth year of his reign the king again revised and elaborated his titulary, so that it now read,

---

[1] Turin 1310. Vandier (§IV, 12) is inclined to identify the king referred to as Inyotef I.

[2] §I, 4, sect. 23 (see lines 3 and 15–16).

[3] §V, 12, part III, pl. 163. See also §I, 10, part I, 181, fig. 111; §V, 4, 42–3.

[4] §I, 3, 647–8; §V, 5; §V, 23, 77–81.

in its final form, 'the Horus Smatowy ("Uniter-of-the-Two-Lands"), He-of-the-Two-Goddesses Smatowy, Horus of Gold Qashuty ("High-of-Plumes"), the King of Upper and Lower Egypt, Nebhepetre...'—the throne-name now being regularly written with the *ḥpt*-oar, rather than with the angular *ḥpt*-sign, previously used.[1]

Besides crushing the hostile elements among his own people Nebhepetre appears also to have consolidated his borders and protected his quarries, mines, and trade routes by military actions directed against the peoples of Lower Nubia, the Libyan tribes of the western desert, and the bedawin of the north and east. As the Horus Netjeryhedjet he claims mastery over the traditional foreign enemies of Egypt, called collectively the 'Nine Peoples of the Bow', or, more simply, the 'Nine Bows';[2] and in the inscriptions of a chapel at Dendera he is described as 'clubbing the eastern lands, striking down the hill-countries, trampling the deserts, enslaving the Nubians,...Medjay and Wawat, the Libyans, and the [Asiatics]'.[3]

Inscriptions of the reign occur at the First Cataract,[4] at Abisko, seventeen miles further south,[5] in the quarries of the Wādi Hammāmāt[6] and at Het-nub,[7] and on the precipitous south wall of the Shatt er-Rigāl, where they were carved by the Chancellor Achthoes and other officials of Nebhepetre during their journeys to and from the lands to the south.[8]

The king's building activities appear to have been confined largely to Upper Egypt. In a sandstone chamber which he contributed to the temple of Satis at Elephantine he appeared before the goddess in the guise of the god Amun.[9] Blocks bearing his names have been discovered in the foundations of the temple of the goddess Nekhbet at El-Kāb.[10] At Gebelein, seventeen miles south of Thebes, he erected a chapel and a great door in an

---

[1] §v, 23, 77–81; §iv, 2, 48–9.

[2] §v, 1, pl. 33A. See also §i, 24, 24 n. 10; §v, 24, 39–40; §iii, 23, 54 n. 4.

[3] §v, 7; see also §i, 24, 28 n. 17.

[4] §v, 17, pl. 8, nos. 213, 243; §iv, 7, 37 (no. 151), 71 (no. 31), 73 (no. 44); §v, 12, part ii, pls. 149*b*, 150*b, c*.

[5] §v, 21, 103–11, pls. 45–7, 50, 106–8; §iii, 23, 58–60; §v, 19.

[6] §v, 6, no. 112.

[7] §i, 1, 32–67 (gr. 14–31). Though the name of the king does not appear in their inscriptions there can be little doubt that the nomarch Neheri and his sons were contemporaries of Mentuhotpe II. See, however, above, p. 471, n. 1. [Ed.]

[8] §i, 24, 58–76, pls. 9–12; §ii, 10, vol. v, 206–7; §v, 24, 41 ff.; §v, 2.

[9] Six fragmentary blocks from this chamber, now in the Aswan Museum, were discovered by Dr Labib Habachi in 1946–7. See A, 6.

[10] §v, 10, pl. 30.

ancient temple of Hathor,[1] and at Tōd he rebuilt the temple of Mont.[2] A limestone door-lintel, inscribed with his throne-name and personal name, is said to have come from the temple of Mont at Hermonthis.[3] North of Thebes he has left parts of a sculptured shrine at El-Ballās,[4] a chapel at Dendera, dedicated to Hathor, Horus, Harakhte, and Min,[5] and additions to the Old Kingdom temple of Osiris at Abydos.[6]

At Thebes Nebhepetre's most notable building was his tomb-temple, erected in an imposing bay of the western cliffs, a mile to the west of the tombs of his predecessors, in a locality later occupied by early Christian monks and called in Arabic *Deir el-Baḥri*, 'the Northern Monastery' (see below, p. 515). Sandstone statues of the king, which flanked the avenue of approach to the temple, wear the short, close-fitting garment associated with the *Heb Sed*, or royal jubilee festival,[7] and may date from the first celebration of this festival, held, presumably, in the king's thirtieth regnal year (2031 B.C.). Chief among the royal women buried in the temple precinct were Queen Tem (Atum?), mother of Sankhkare Mentuhotpe III,[8] and Queen Neferu, Nebhepetre's own full sister, whose tomb, much visited in the New Kingdom, was evidently regarded as a national shrine.[9] In the precipitous cliff to the north of Deir el-Bahri and in the lower hills to the south are the tombs of the great officials of the reign: the Viziers Dagi and Ipi, the Chancellor Achthoes, the Treasurers Horhotpe and Meru, and the Chief Steward Henenu.[10] An uninscribed tomb above the temple yielded the bodies of sixty of Nebhepetre's soldiers, slain while attacking a fortress or walled town, probably in Nubia.[11]

VI. REORGANIZATION AND RECOVERY

The steps taken by Mentuhotpe II in the consolidation of his victory and the reorganization of his country are summarized in a chapel relief from Gebelein which probably dates from the period just before the fall of Heracleopolis.[12] Here we see 'the Son of Re,

---

[1] See above, p. 480, n. 2.   [2] §v, 3, i, 10, 14, 25, 62–79, pls. 18–21.

[3] §v, 16, 362, pl. 1 (2). Cf. §v, 14, 166.

[4] §v, 13, 6, nos. 62–6, pls. 32–4; §III, 23, 60–1; §III, 19, 10, 14, 15, 19, 21.

[5] See above, p. 480, n. 3. See also §III, 18, pl. 12 (bottom).

[6] §v, 18, 14, 33, 43, pls. 24, 54.

[7] §v, 15, vol. I, 26, 60 (see pl. 25 B); §I, 10, part I, 157, fig. 93. Cf. §v, 8, pls. 12, 13.   [8] §I, 24, 43 n. 60, 48.

[9] *Ibid.* 27 n. 14; §I, 10, part I, 158–60, figs. 95–6; §v, 20; §v, 9.

[10] §I, 24, 44–7; §v, 11.   [11] §v, 25. See also §v, 22, 86.

[12] See above, p. 480, n. 2.

Mentuhotpe', striking to the ground a fellow Egyptian, clad in the goffered *shendyet*-kilt of a king or noble and accompanied in his misfortune by three foreigners, a Nubian, an Asiatic, and a Libyan—representing perhaps the foreign auxiliaries who formed an important part of the Heracleopolitan armies.[1] The accompanying inscription describes the king as 'the subduer at the head of the Two Lands who established order in Upper Egypt and the Delta, ...the Two Banks, ...and the Two Cities'—a reference, presumably, to his stamping out of the leaders of the Heracleopolitan faction and his subordination of the hereditary nomarchs of Middle and Lower Egypt to the new central government at Thebes. In a relief from the pharaoh's temple at Deir el-Bahri two of these nomarchs, labelled 'Counts of the North-[land]', are shown bowing before the king with their hands crossed over their breasts in an attitude of submission.[2] A somewhat obscure account of a journey downstream through 'all the...nomes of the entire land' and of fighting in the vicinity of the Faiyūm and in 'the North' against(?) a 'King of Lower Egypt and this, his army' is given by a Nubian soldier who served under Nebhepetre,[3] and may refer to 'mopping up' operations in the Delta, which would naturally have been the last refuge of the supporters of the old regime. It was probably also in the reign of Mentuhotpe II that (political?) 'fugitives', who had fled to the Oasis of Dakhla(?), were captured by a certain Kay, leader of the western desert patrol, and brought back to Egypt for punishment.[4] The stela on which Kay describes these missions is of special interest in showing that the western oases, although under Egyptian surveillance,[5] were not yet part of the territory actually governed by the pharaoh and were therefore logical havens for escaped criminals and enemies of the state.

At Thebes and in the provinces adjoining it on the north and south the hereditary nomarchies had long since been abolished; but in the middle nomes suppression of the feudal nobility was at this time neither practicable nor wholly desirable, and the methods employed by the king in assuring the loyalty and co-operation of the provincial governors in this area were not drastic. The nomarchs of Asyūt evidently proved irreconcilable and had to be forcibly removed from office. On the other hand, at Hermopolis

---

[1] See above, pp. 467–70.   [2] §v, 15, vol. I, pl. 14B; §1, 4, sect. 28E.
[3] See above, p. 480, n. 5. Posener (§v, 19, 165) is inclined to see in Tjehemau's 'King of Lower Egypt', not a Heracleopolitan, but a later ruler of the House of Itj-towy (see below, pp. 494–510).
[4] §vi, 1.   [5] See §v, 11, 46, pl. 4 (line 4).

in the Hare Nome and at Beni Hasan in the Oryx Nome the ruling families were unmolested and only a mild restraint seems to have been placed on their ancient liberties. In the tombs at Naga ed-Deir, Akhmīm, and Deir el-Gabrāwi there are no evidences of breaks in the succession of the nomarchs occasioned by the rise to supremacy of the Theban kings (see above, pp. 471-2).

Control of national affairs, however, was effectively centred at Thebes by the simple expedient of appointing a Theban to every key position in the government. Under Nebhepetre three Thebans in succession—Dagi, Bebi, and Ipi—held the office of Vizier and with it, as in the late Old Kingdom, the post of Overseer of the Pyramid, or Residence, City.[1] The recently established and extremely important office of Chancellor was awarded successively to four other fellow-townsmen of the king, outstanding among whom was Achthoes, son of Sitre, who was 'Chancellor throughout the land to its utmost boundaries'.[2] Another Theban, Henenu, functioned as Nebhepetre's Chief Steward and served with distinction under his successor, Sankhkare Mentuhotpe.[3] A Familiar of the King, named Itju, was appointed to the newly created post of Governor of Lower Egypt, which, since the capital was now in the south, carried with it the same responsibilities as had the office of Governor of Upper Egypt under the Memphite pharaohs of the Old Kingdom.[4] Another Familiar of the King, Mery-Teti, known from an inscription at Aswān, dated to Year 41 of Nebhepetre, served far to the north, as Controller of the Thirteenth Nome of Lower Egypt.[5] From his Theban tomb-stela we learn that a certain Inyotef, who bore the title Overseer of the Prison of the Great Doorway, was assigned by Mentuhotpe II to the nome of Heracleopolis itself.[6] Besides holding his principal office, the Chancellor Meru was Governor of the Eastern Deserts.[7] The great Chancellor, Achthoes, concerned himself chiefly with the exploitation of Lower Nubia and the lands to the south.[8] The steward Henenu states that he 'curbed the south, north, east, and west' and that in the king's name he taxed the nomes of This and Aphroditopolis and administered the [products(?) of] the Oasis.[9] The King's Herald Mahesa speaks of

[1] §I, 24, 34, 44, 45; §I, 4, sect. 28.
[2] §I, 24, 34, 44, 45, 68, 69; §I, 4, sect. 28. See also §III, 13, 77-9.
[3] §V, 11. See also §III, 13, 92 n. 3; and below, pp. 491-2.
[4] §I, 24, 68; §II, 6, part II, 596-7.
[5] §V, 17, pl. 8, no. 243. See also §I, 24, 34 n. 18.
[6] §VI, 2, 248.
[7] §I, 24, 68G.
[8] §III, 23, 57-8.
[9] §V, 11.

'the God (Mentuhotpe II) whose name is heard by the North and the South'.[1] Among Nebhepetre's 'true servants' were two men who seem to have previously served under the Heracleopolitan pharaohs. The expedition-leader Achthoes, who worked the mines and quarries on the peninsula of Sinai and travelled into neighbouring lands on behalf of his sovereign, refers to the time when he 'was in the House of the Northerner', and the Chief Sculptor Inyotefnakhte lets it be known that he 'spent years in the House of Achthoes when it was(?) the King's House'.[2] Like most of their colleagues, however, both of these men made their tombs at Thebes near that of the pharaoh whom they now served and both evidently regarded themselves and were regarded by their contemporaries as Thebans. Thus, from Wawat in Lower Nubia to Sinai beyond the north-east border of the Delta the land was under the constant supervision of representatives of the central government, all native-born or naturalized citizens of Thebes and most of them members of the inner circle of the king's associates.

In spite of the as yet unbroken power of the provincial governors there resulted from this Theban overlordship a national unity and a co-ordination of national effort which was immediately reflected in the culture and the material prosperity of the country. Art, flourishing again under royal patronage, abandoned the styleless crudities of the Heracleopolitan Period and began to return to standards of excellence suited to the tastes of a wealthy and discriminating clientele. Building was resumed on a monumental scale throughout Upper Egypt, and to supply the ever increasing needs of the royal architects and sculptors cut stone was extracted in quantity from the quarries at Aswān, Wādi Hammāmāt, Het-nub, and probably Gebel es-Silsila,[3] as well as from numerous limestone quarries up and down the river. Caravans again reached Egypt from the lands to the south and cargo ships could proceed unmolested from the First Cataract to the Mediterranean ports. Gold was almost certainly imported from Nubia and timber from the Lebanon.[4] There is no direct evidence that the mines of Sinai were worked in the time of Nebhepetre Mentuhotpe, but the inscriptions in the tomb of the expedition-leader Achthoes indi-

[1] §i, 24, 68 e.
[2] §vi, 3; §i, 4, sect. 44. See also §vi, 5; §vi, 2, 249.
[3] See above, p. 480, nn. 4, 6, 7. Though no inscriptions of Nebhepetre's time have been recorded at Gebel es-Silsila (§ii, 10, vol. v, 208–18) most of the king's buildings are of sandstone which may be presumed to have come from this convenient and much-used quarry or its vicinity.
[4] §iii, 23, 86 ff. (see, however, 55–6); §v, 11, 46, 49 (notes j and k).

cate that they were.[1] So also does the appearance of the king in a group-statue dedicated in the early Twelfth Dynasty in the temple of Hathor at Serābīt el-Khādim.[2] In his time, too, the first steps appear to have been taken to reopen the road from Koptos to the Red Sea ports, whence ships could again sail southwards to the incense-land of Punt.[3]

For several generations the martial spirit survived in the land, and noble and peasant alike prided themselves on their skill with arms and were often buried with their bows and other weapons beside them.[4] Thanks, however, to the strength, intelligence, and ability of the new king and his successors Egypt again entered a long period of internal peace and political security and reached a new high point in her history as brilliant in many respects as that which she had achieved under the Old Kingdom.

VII. FOREIGN POLICY: PROGRESS TOWARDS THE RECONQUEST OF NUBIA

There can be no doubt that throughout the Heracleopolitan Period the desert tribes on both sides of the Nile Valley, the bedawin of Sinai and south-western Asia, and the peoples of Lower Nubia had taken frequent advantage of the disrupted and weakened condition of the land to raid its borders and harass its inhabitants.

The campaigns of Mentuhotpe II against the Libyans of the west and the Asiatic nomads of Sinai and the eastern desert were probably little more than counter-raids or, at the most, punitive expeditions, designed only to protect the boundaries of Egypt from future depredations at the hands of the tribesmen, to reopen the desert routes to Egyptian caravans, and to make the oases, the mines of Sinai, and the outlying quarries safe for Egyptian patrols and working parties. In the north and east the king's troops, including Libyan and Nubian auxiliaries, attacked and routed the Asiatic Amu and Setjetiu, the Mentjiu of Sinai, and, apparently, the Retenu of Syria;[5] and west of the Nile harried both the Tjemehu and Tjehenu Libyans and slew one of the latter's chiefs, Prince Hedj-wawesh.[6] None of these expeditions seems to have been as extensive as those previously carried out under the Sixth

---

[1] §vi, 3, 35–8.
[2] §vi, 6, 123–4, fig. 128; §vi, 4, part i, 11, pl. 22, no. 70; part ii, 86.
[3] §v, 11, 46, 48 (note g).   [4] §1, 24, 47.
[5] See above, p. 480, nn. 3, 5; §v, 15, vol. i, 5, pls. 14, 15; vol. iii, 23, pl. 13; §1, 4, sect. 28A.   [6] §v, 1, 33, pl. 33A, b.

Dynasty, and none suggests that the Egyptians had as yet any real extra-territorial designs on Asia.

In Nubia, however, efforts were initiated to regain the control exercised by the kings of the Sixth Dynasty—a control which was essential to the exploitation of the rich mineral resources of the land, the levying of tribute, both in men and materials, and the resumption of the immensely valuable river and overland traffic with the countries to the south. Despite the activities of the nomarchs of Thebes and the early rulers of the Eleventh Dynasty[1] Nubia at the time of Nebhepetre's accession was apparently an independent nation with its own dynasty of kings, descended perhaps from a renegade Egyptian official of the late Old Kingdom or Heracleopolitan Period.

Our knowledge of these kings derives from a series of crude hieroglyphic inscriptions which two of them have left on the Nile cliffs between Umbarakāb and Abu Simbel in Lower Nubia and which contain royal names and titles similar to those of more or less contemporaneous kings of Egypt.[2] The Horus Senefertowyef, King Qakare In(yotef), for example, bears a throne-name which is identical with that of a Memphite pharaoh of the Eighth Dynasty and a personal name which is the same as that of a Theban nomarch and three Theban rulers of the early Eleventh Dynasty. Goregtowyef, the Horus name of King Iyebkhentre, the second Nubian king, finds an echo in the epithet, Goreg Shema To-mehu, applied at Gebelein to Mentuhotpe II and, like that of Qakare In(yotef), is similar in form to the Horus name, Sankhtowyef, borne by Mentuhotpe III. In many instances the royal Nubian graffiti are accompanied by others containing common Egyptian titles and names, such as Achthoes, Inyotef, Mentuhotpe, Kay, Khnumhotpe, and Sesostris, all of which are characteristic of the Heracleopolitan Period and the early Middle Kingdom.

An interesting but, unfortunately, fragmentary inscription found near El-Ballās, evidently from the time of Nebhepetre Mentuhotpe, describes in picturesque and often obscure terms the king's achievements in Nubia and the adjoining deserts.[3] In the

---

[1] §III, 23, 43–7, 54. See also §VII, 4, 308.

[2] §III, 23, 47–50; §VII, 1, 243; §I, 3, 657.

[3] §V, 13, no. 66, pl. 34; §III, 23, 60–1; §III, 19, 14, 15, 19, 21; §VII, 1, 243; §VII, 3, 53. A second and much smaller fragment of the same inscription, not published by Lutz, appears in Hearst Expedition negative no. 1531, a print of which was generously provided by Mr Dows Dunham of the Museum of Fine Arts in Boston. Both these fragments are now published in A, 4, 112–18, pl. XXXVII. [Ed.]

fifth and sixth lines of this text the pharaoh, speaking apparently of 'Wawat' (Lower Nubia) and the neighbouring 'Oasis' (of Kurkur?), says that he defeated 'the enemies in them' and 'attached them to Upper Egypt', adding, somewhat inaccurately, that 'there was no king to whom they had (previously) been tributary'. The tribesmen of the desert to the east of Nubia seem also to have come to him in submission, 'touching the forehead to the ground, as far as the shores of the (Red) Sea'. The victorious ruler then 'fared downstream' until he reached Elephantine, where he contributed in some way to the well-being of the city and received the homage of its citizens. He concludes by saying, 'I did this when I was king (after) I had "fetched the helm(?)" for Thebes and caused the Two Lands to come to her in', presumably, an attitude of submission and respect. In the last line he refers again to 'Wawat and the Oasis' and again claims to have 'annexed them to Upper Egypt'.

From a series of graffiti, left on the rocks near Abisko by one of Nebhepetre's Nubian mercenaries named Tjehemau, it is known that the king in person sailed south as far as a place named Ben[1]—perhaps on a recruiting expedition—and that for some years thereafter Tjehemau and his son accompanied the pharaoh up and down the river and helped to subdue the 'Asiatic' inhabitants of the otherwise unknown land of Djati and the 'sand-dwellers' of the adjoining deserts.[2] Interesting is Tjehemau's low opinion of the courage of his Theban companions-in-arms as evidenced in the engagement against the people of Djati and on the occasion of a visit which the proud and ferocious Nubian made to Thebes itself.[3]

In Mentuhotpe's thirty-ninth year, his Chancellor, Achthoes, returned from the expedition previously mentioned to the south by way of the Shatt er-Rigāl;[4] according to an inscription at Aswān, two years later, the same Achthoes, accompanied perhaps by Count Mery-Teti,[5] was once again making the return trip from Nubia, this time with(?) 'ships of Wawat'.[6] These frequent journeys by the head of Egypt's exchequer suggest either trading activities on a large scale or, more likely, the periodic collection of tribute, chiefly, it may be supposed, in the form of gold.

Though the control of Nubia regained under Mentuhotpe II does not appear to have extended as yet to a military occupation

[1] Possibly Buhen, at the northern end of the Second Cataract. See §III, 23, 59 n. 1; §VII, 3, 53.
[2] See above, p. 480, n. 5.   [3] §v, 19, 163 ff.
[4] See above, p. 480, n. 8.   [5] §v, 17, pl. 8, no. 243.
[6] *Ibid.* pl. 8, no. 213.

of the area,[1] it did almost certainly include, as we have seen, the levying of tribute on the local rulers and the maintenance of a safe right of way for Egyptian trading parties. Geographically this control did not reach beyond the Second Cataract of the Nile, embracing only the land of Wawat, or Lower Nubia,[2] and, in a looser sense, the desert areas on either side of it. In the latter areas, as Posener has shown,[3] dwelt the nomadic and warlike Medjay peoples over whom Mentuhotpe II claims a victory in his chapel at Dendera[4] and who for some years before his day and for many centuries after it served in Egypt's armed forces as soldiers, scouts, and police. Besides the Nubian auxiliary troops in Nebhepetre's armies there is evidence of the presence of both Nubian and negro women in the royal household at Thebes.[5] The king's capture of an oasis—probably Kurkur—to the west or south-west of Wawat would indicate that the Egyptians had again opened the old caravan road to the Sudan; it is probable that the gold mines of Nubia were once again being operated under Egyptian supervision.

Regardless of details, it is clear that Egypt's foreign policy, as re-established by Mentuhotpe II, followed the Old Kingdom precedent and consisted of a purely defensive attitude towards the peoples of the north and a wholehearted concentration on economic and, eventually, territorial expansion in the African lands to the south. We shall see presently how brilliantly this programme was developed under the pharaohs of the Twelfth Dynasty.

VIII. EGYPT UNDER KING MENTUHOTPE III: THE HEKANAKHTE PAPERS

When in 2009 B.C. Nebhepetre died after a reign of fifty-one years, he was succeeded by his eldest surviving son, a man already past middle age, who, as the Horus Sankhtowyef, King Sankhkare Mentuhotpe, ascended the throne of Egypt and ruled for twelve peaceful and prosperous years.[6] Although in his youth he was represented as a warrior in the reliefs of his father's mortuary temple,[7] the new king appears to have devoted his own reign almost entirely to building, and in various temples from Ele-

---

[1] §III, 23, 61.   [2] §VII, 3, 53–4.   [3] §VII, 2.

[4] See above, p. 480, n. 3. See also lines 8–9 of the Ballas inscription cited above, in this section (p. 486, n. 3).

[5] §I, 10, part I, 219–20; §VII, 3, 53 n. 122.

[6] Turin Canon v, 17 (§I, 7, pl. 2).   [7] §V, 15, vol. I, 7, pl. 12B.

phantine to Abydos has left us reliefs of a delicacy rarely surpassed in the annals of Egyptian art.[1] His name has been found as far north as Khatā'na in the eastern Delta where he was invoked as a god on a private group-statuette of the late Eleventh or Twelfth Dynasty.[2] On the top of one of the highest peaks in western Thebes he caused to be constructed a brick and limestone chapel which has been variously identified as a temple of Thoth, a *Sed*-festival chapel, and a cenotaph.[3] Curiously enough, Sankhkare's tomb and mortuary temple, founded in a magnificent bay of the western cliffs half a mile south-west of the temple of his father, never progressed beyond the cutting and grading of the temple-platform and sections of the causeway, and the partial excavation of the king's burial passage.[4]

Outstanding among the officials of the reign were the Chief Steward Henenu and the Chancellor Meketre, both of whom had previously served under Mentuhotpe II (above, p. 483). It was in Meketre's great tomb, overlooking the temple of Sankhkare, that the expedition of the Metropolitan Museum found an exceptionally interesting set of funerary models—painted wooden replicas of the chancellor's house and garden, the shops on his estate, his fleet of ships, his herds of cattle, and his servants bringing offerings to his tomb—all executed in miniature, but with the utmost accuracy and attention to detail.[5] Of Henenu and his exploits more will be said presently (below, dp. 491–2).

A rich fund of information on conditions in Egypt in the late Eleventh Dynasty and on the daily life of its people is provided by the letters and other papers of a petulant and garrulous old man named Hekanakhte who, during the reign of Sankhkare Mentuhotpe, served as a mortuary priest in the tomb of the Vizier Ipi at Thebes.[6] In the late spring or early summer of Mentuhotpe III's eighth regnal year (2002 B.C.) Hekanakhte was called south on business and in his absence his eldest son(?), Merisu, was left in charge of the tomb and of Hekanakhte's farm and extensive household at Nebsoyet, on the west side of the Nile some ten miles upstream from the capital city. Before leaving the old man turned over to Merisu two papyri with detailed inventories of grain and other farm produce drawn up in Year 8 itself and on the

---

[1] §VIII, 1; §V, 3, 62, 79, figs. 32–57, pls. 21–8; §V, 14, 2, 22–3, 166–8, pls. 88, 94–7; §V, 18, 12, 15, 33, 43, pls. 23, 25, 55. See also §I, 24, 49–50.
[2] §VIII, 4, part II, 45, pl. 42. See also §VI, 4, no. 70.
[3] §VIII, 5; §IV, 9, 4, pls. 4–8; §VIII, 2, 4–5; §I, 24, 49–50.
[4] §III, 32, 29–35, figs. 6–9; §VIII, 6, 31–4, 47, pl. 23.
[5] §VIII, 7.   [6] §VIII, 3.

occasion of an earlier trip away from home in Year 5, and during the summer of Year 8 he wrote two long and fussy letters to his family at Nebsoyet and a third letter, couched in more polite and formal language, to an influential local official regarding the collection of certain quantities of grain by members of his household. These with three other documents, including a brief letter from a woman named Sitnebsekhtu to her mother, were found in a scrap heap in a dependency of the tomb of Ipi, where Merisu had evidently thrown them after reading and noting their contents.

Most interesting are the two letters addressed to Hekanakhte's household at Nebsoyet and filled with detailed instructions on the running of the farm and the allowances and treatment to be accorded various members of the family. In the first of these letters Merisu is vigorously warned against allowing any of 'our land' in the process of cultivation to be flooded by the waters of the rising Nile. Additional land is to be rented at nearby Perhaa and the rental is to be paid in linen cloth or with some emmer already in Perhaa. Hekanakhte is annoyed over having been sent 'old, dry barley' while Merisu and the rest of the family are eating 'good, new barley'. Special care is to be taken of the boys Anupu and Sneferu, Hekanakhte's youngest sons, and the latter, obviously a spoiled brat, is to be allowed to do or have anything he wants. A maidservant who has been making trouble for Hekanakhte's concubine, Iutemheb, is to be turned out of the house and Merisu himself is questioned sharply and sarcastically about his treatment of the girl. The first letter ends with the characteristic injunctions 'and send an account of what is being collected.... Take great care! Don't be neglectful.'

In the first letter shortage of food in southern Upper Egypt is suggested by the words, 'See! This is not the year for a man to be lazy...'; and in the second letter Hekanakhte tries to impress his family with the seriousness of the situation by writing—like Ankhtify of El-Mi'alla a century and a half earlier[1]—'See! They are beginning to eat men here'. The remark follows a list of rations drawn up by Hekanakhte for his household and is followed by the reminder, 'See! there are no people to whom these rations are given anywhere'.

[1] See above, p. 475, n. 4.

IX. RESUMPTION OF THE RED SEA TRAFFIC AND REOPENING OF THE WĀDI HAMMĀMĀT

In Year 8 of Sankhkare Mentuhotpe—the year of Hekanakhte's trip south—an expedition of three thousand men, recruited from most of the nomes of Upper Egypt and led by the Chief Steward Henenu, left the Nile Valley near Koptos and headed east across the desert toward the Red Sea, ninety miles away. Their orders were to re-establish commerce by sea with the fabulously rich land of Punt on the Somali coast, unvisited by Egyptians since the days of the Sixth Dynasty.[1] Armed scouting parties went ahead to dispose of hostile bands of desert nomads and fifteen wells were dug along the route to ensure a supply of water to this and future expeditions. Each man was equipped with a staff and a leather canteen, and the pack train of donkeys carried spare sandals to replace those worn out along the way. Supplies had been carefully planned in advance and, as a result, each member of the expedition received two jars of water and twenty biscuits every day.

Upon reaching the sea coast, probably in the neighbourhood of the Wādi el-Gāsūs, Henenu caused to be built a fleet of sea-going ships of the type used in the Syrian coastal trade and called, therefore, 'Byblites' or 'Byblos-farers'. These he dispatched to Punt, laden with goods for barter, and, upon their return, transferred their cargoes—including the highly prized gum of the myrrh tree—to donkey-back for the journey over land to the Nile Valley.

On his way home the Chief Steward—now known also as the 'Confidant of the King in the Southern Doorway'—paused in the newly reopened graywacke quarries of the Wādi Hammāmāt long enough to extract 'noble blocks for statues belonging to the temples', and to carve the long and interesting inscription from which the foregoing account is drawn.[2] For Henenu this was his second expedition into the territory of the eastern 'sand-dwellers', his initial venture in the direction of the Red Sea having been made, as we have seen, under Nebhepetre Mentuhotpe II (above, p. 485, n. 3).

Although the Koptos road had been used as a trade route to the Red Sea since predynastic times, it is probable that during the Old Kingdom most of the expeditions sent out from Memphis had crossed over far to the north, in the vicinity of Suez—

[1] See §IX, 6, 8 ff.   [2] §v, 6, 81–4, no. 114, pl. 31; §v, 11, 43 n. 1.

perhaps by canal.[1] In Henenu's time we may be sure that no such canal existed, for, in spite of its proximity to Thebes and the steps taken to facilitate its use, the overland route was long and difficult and the necessity of trans-shipping cargoes at the seaward end must have been exceedingly inconvenient. Nevertheless, it remained in use throughout the Middle and New Kingdoms and well down into Graeco-Roman times, and is employed to this day by motor traffic between the Nile Valley and the Red Sea ports.

An event of equal interest to students of Egyptian history was the revival of activity in the quarries of the Wādi Hammāmāt, which now began to be worked on a scale far surpassing any that they had previously known. Following Nebhepetre and Sankhkare Mentuhotpe, more than fifty kings of Egypt from the Middle Kingdom to the Thirtieth Dynasty have left their inscriptions on the rock walls of these quarries;[2] and the hard, greenish-grey stone, characteristic of the region, appears with ever increasing frequency as the material of the finer works of Egyptian art.[3]

X. THE END OF THE ELEVENTH DYNASTY: MENTUHOTPE IV AND THE VIZIER AMMENEMES

In the Turin Canon Sankhkare Mentuhotpe is listed as the last of the six kings of the Eleventh Dynasty; but in the summary following his name there was apparently a note of a lacuna in the Canon's source-document involving a period of seven years before the beginning of the Twelfth Dynasty.[4] During this interval (1997–1991 B.C.) the throne appears to have been occupied for at least two years by the Horus Nebtowy, King Nebtowyre Mentuhotpe IV, whose mother, Imi, may have been a non-royal inmate of the harim of Mentuhotpe III.[5] There is no evidence that the new ruler was a usurper, the omission of his name from the Turin Canon and other Ramesside lists of kings being attributable, as has already been stated, to a gap in the document used as a source by the compilers of these lists.[6] In the Karnak Table of Ancestors the cartouche and figure which follow those of Nebhepetre and 'Sneferkare' (= Sankhkare) in the lowest register of the table

---

[1] §ix, 5, 264 f.   [2] §v, 6; §ix, 2; §ix, 3; §ix, 7.

[3] §ix, 4, 477–9; §ix, 2, 1–9; §ix, 1, 343 ff.

[4] Turin Canon v, 18. See §1, 7, 16, pl. 2; §x, 16, 118 n. 2; and cf. §x, 8, 14–15; §x, 6.

[5] Hammāmāt no. 191, 1 (§v, 6, 97, pl. 36).

[6] See §x, 8, 85.

are almost certainly his.[1] His brief reign forms a transition between the Eleventh and Twelfth Dynasties, and of the few objects bearing his name, which have survived to the present day, two were found near the pyramid of the founder of the Twelfth Dynasty at El-Lisht.[2] One of these objects is part of a slate bowl, inscribed on the outside with the names of 'the Horus [Neb]towy, [the Son of Re], Mentuhotpe', and on the inside with the Horus name of Ammenemes I, in both cases 'beloved of [Hathor], Mistress of Dendera'.[3]

The first and second regnal years of Mentuhotpe IV are recorded in a group of graffiti near the amethyst mines of the Wādi el-Hūdi, seventeen miles south-east of Aswān;[4] but the king is known chiefly from a series of intensely interesting inscriptions in the Wādi Hammāmāt, left there by an expedition sent out in 'Year 2' to quarry the blocks for the royal sarcophagus and its ponderous lid.[5] Encouraged by a number of wonderful omens, including the discovery of an ancient well, the expedition appears to have accomplished its work in the quarry in less than a month and on the twenty-seventh day the lid-block was turned over to a gang of three thousand seamen from the nomes of Lower Egypt for the long haul overland to the Nile Valley and the journey upstream to Thebes. Meanwhile, bodies of troops and settlers, led by the Commander of Soldiers, Sankh, were dispatched to establish a series of watering stations in the eastern desert and to found a small harbour-town on the Red Sea coast near the mouth of the Wādi el-Gāsūs.[6]

Composed, all told, of ten thousand men, recruited from both Upper Egypt and the Delta, the expedition was under the leadership of the Vizier and Governor of All Upper Egypt, Ammenemes, a man who claims—probably accurately—to have been 'overseer of everything in this entire land'.[7] There can be little doubt that it was this powerful and energetic official who, within half a decade after his return from Hammāmāt, usurped the throne of his royal master and, as King Sehetepibre Ammenemes I, founded the vigorous new line of kings which we call the Twelfth Dynasty.[8]

[1] §III, 22, pl. I (left central section, no. 24). See also §x, 14, 609 (IV, 8).
[2] §I, 10, part I, 167, 176.   [3] §x, 16, 116–19.
[4] §x, 4, 19–23, figs. 14–19, pls. 6–8.
[5] §v, 6, nos. 1, 40, 55, 105, 110A–B, 113, 191, 192, 241; §IX, 2, nos. 52–60 (pp. 76–81, pls. 18–20, 32).
[6] §v, 12, part II, pl. 149g; §II, 1, sects. 454–6.
[7] Hammāmāt nos. 110B (line 10), 113, 192 (§v, 6, 78, 80, 99, pls. 28, 29, 37).
[8] §x, 11, 51; §I, 3, 649; §x, 15, 16; §x, 17, 155.

The 'Prophecy' of the Lector-Priest Neferty of Bubastis[1] was composed by a Lower Egyptian partisan of Ammenemes I with the evident intent of winning much-needed support for the new king by the timeworn device of casting discredit upon his predecessors.[2] It presents a dismal picture of conditions in the eastern Delta during what have been thought to be the last years of the Eleventh Dynasty.[3] Representing himself as a contemporary of the revered Old Kingdom pharaoh, Sneferu, Neferty 'foretells' how in the period before the coming of King 'Ameny'[4] his part of the country is to be raided and infiltrated by Asiatics, oppressed and impoverished by a multiplicity of local rulers, and subjected to anarchy, violence, and general misery until salvation at last arrives in the messiah-like person of the founder of the Twelfth Dynasty. During the brief and apparently none-too-vigorous reign of Nebtowyre Mentuhotpe it is probable that the entry of bedawin tribesmen into north-eastern Egypt was not controlled as rigidly as it should have been and that the nomarchs of the Delta provinces were allowed to get somewhat out of hand; but the majority of the woes conjured up by Neferty's facile pen are of too unspecific a nature and too obviously inspired by earlier works of Egyptian 'pessimistic literature'[5] to be attributable exclusively to the final decade of the Eleventh Dynasty.

The usurpation of royal power by the founder of the new ruling house seems to have been vigorously opposed by adherents of the old regime and the change of dynasty was evidently accompanied by widespread disorder and civil strife.[6] At the same time, we cannot discount entirely the many expressions of loyalty and affection with which Ammenemes refers to his king in the Hammāmāt inscriptions nor can we overlook the fact that he permitted himself to be associated with Nebtowyre even after he had moved his residence to the neighbourhood of El-Lisht. Other kings of the

---

[1] P. Ermitage 1116B recto (§1, 8, 6–8, pls. 23–5; §x, 5; §x, 11, 17, 21–60, 145–57.

[2] Compare the highly partisan remarks contained in P. Harris 1, 75, 1–5 (§x, 2, 91) on the subject of conditions at the end of the Nineteenth Dynasty. See also §x, 4, 44.

[3] See §x, 11, 44 n. 2.

[4] A common short form of the name Amenemhet, or Ammenemes (§x, 13, vol. 11, 144, 234). On the identification of the Ameny referred to by Neferty with Ammenemes I see §x, 11, 22 ff.

[5] E.g. the Admonitions of Ipuwer and the Dispute of a Life-weary Man with his Soul (§x, 3, 86–108; §1, 23, 405–7, 441–4). See also §x, 11, 40 ff.

[6] §x, 11, 44–5. The Execration Texts, or Proscription Lists, cited by Stock (§v, 23, 89–90), belong, not in this period, but to the later Middle Kingdom (§x, 10, 31, 34; §x, 1, 223 n. 2).

Twelfth Dynasty not infrequently represent themselves as legitimate successors, if not linear descendants, of Nebhepetre Mentuhotpe II and Sankhkare Mentuhotpe III,[1] and in the 'prophet' Neferty's own town of Bubastis in the eastern Delta the latter was invoked at this period as a divinity.[2] An inscription from El-Lisht indicates that a high-ranking official of Sesostris I had served not only under Ammenemes I, but also under his two or three immediate predecessors.[3] In short, our picture of the *coup d'état* which ushered in the Twelfth Dynasty is at the moment neither complete nor consistent in all its details.

XI. THE FOUNDING OF THE TWELFTH DYNASTY: AMMENEMES I AND THE ADMINISTRATION

'A king will arise in the South, called Ameny, ...the son of a woman of To-Sety, ...a child of Khen-Nekhen.'[4] These words of the propagandist and pseudo-prophet Neferty emphasize the fact that the mother of Ammenemes I, whose name appears to have been Nefert,[5] was a native of the nome of Elephantine and that he himself was born in southern Upper Egypt. His coming could, then, be assumed to be a fulfilment of the 'prophecy of the Residence' concerning the Southland, referred to in the Instruction for King Merykare.[6] His father, a commoner named Sesostris, was evidently regarded by succeeding generations as the ancestor of the dynasty, the title and name of 'the God's Father, Sesostris', following those of Nebhepetre and Sankhkare Mentuhotpe in the subscription of an offering list of the early Eighteenth Dynasty at Karnak.[7] Unlike that of the God's Father, Mentuhotpe, at the beginning of the Eleventh Dynasty, the name of Sesostris is unaccompanied by any type of royal attribute, and it is clear that he himself never exercised the function of a ruler. His son, the ex-vizier Ammenemes, freely acknowledging his lack of royal ancestry, adopted as the first three names in his new kingly titulary the epithet, Wehem-Meswet, 'Repeater-of-Births', thereby consciously identifying himself as the inaugurator of a renaissance, or new era in his country's history.

---

[1] See §x, 10, 2–3.   [2] See above, p. 489, n. 2.
[3] §x, 9, 26, fig. 38.
[4] P. Ermitage 1116B recto, 57–9. See §x, 11, 47–51, 156–7.
[5] §xi, 17, 12, fig. 11.   [6] See above, pp. 464–6; §x, 11, 28, 48–9.
[7] §iv, 4, 185–9, pl. 4. See also §x, 11, 50; §i, 3, 649; §iv, 2, 46.

An Upper Egyptian by birth, Ammenemes I was also a staunch devotee of the god Amun of Thebes, whom he honoured in his own name and whom, as king, he elevated to the first rank among the deities of Egypt.[1] He saw, however, the difficulties involved in trying to rule the land from the Thebaid and at the time of his accession or, perhaps, shortly before it, he moved his residence to a place eighteen miles south of Memphis, where, on the boundary line between Upper and Lower Egypt, he built the fortified city of Itj-towy, 'Seizer-of-the-Two-Lands'. Nearby, west of the modern villages of El-Lisht and El-Maharraqa, he and his successor, Sesostris I, later erected their pyramids, surrounded by the mastabas and pit-tombs of their adherents, in conformity with the practice established centuries earlier by the Memphite pharaohs of the Old Kingdom.[2]

In his successful bid for the kingship Ammenemes had evidently relied heavily upon the support of Egypt's local governors, and it is clear that, far from attempting to abolish the hereditary nomarchies, the founder of the Twelfth Dynasty restored to the rulers of the nomes many of their ancient dignities and privileges. Everywhere we find revived the title 'Great Chief of the... Nome'. At Beni Hasan the Counts of Menat-Khufu were confirmed in their rulership of the Oryx Nome by the King himself[3] and at Elephantine, Asyūt, Cusae, and elsewhere new families of governors were installed to replace those suppressed by the Theban rulers of the Eleventh Dynasty.[4] To prevent rivalry among the nomarchs and dangerous territorial expansion by any one governor, however, the boundaries of the nomes were rigorously established and regulations were enacted covering each district's share in the supply of Nile water available for purposes of irrigation.[5] Furthermore, the nomes were evidently required, upon demand, to furnish supplies, fleets of ships, and levies of militia for the royal enterprises both at home and abroad, such levies often being led by the nomarchs themselves and forming at this time the greater part of the country's armed forces.[6]

Early in his reign Ammenemes I, accompanied by the nomarch Khnumhotpe (I) of Beni Hasan with a fleet of twenty ships, cruised the Upper Egyptian Nile as far as Elephantine wiping out the remaining pockets of resistance to his regime in this

---

[1] §III, 25, 11; §III, 31, 147–9; §XI, 9, 103–4.
[2] See §II, 10, vol. IV, 81–3; §XI, 29, 167–78. See also below, p. 516.
[3] §XI, 26, 26–8.
[4] *Ibid.* 1–7 (see 7, no. 7); §XI, 21, 104; §XI, 28; §II, 10, vol. IV, 249–54, 259–62, 264; §II, 6, 119.   [5] §XI, 26, 27.   [6] §XI, 10, 36 ff.

troubled area and perhaps conducting a warning foray against the peoples of Lower Nubia.[1] In the north his tour of inspection took him into the Delta, on the eastern frontier of which he seems to have driven off raiding parties of Asiatic nomads and provided an effective hindrance to their future inroads by constructing towards the eastern end of the Wādi Tummilāt a fortified post called in his honour 'Walls of the Ruler'.[2] The impression is given that the first two decades of the reign were taken up chiefly with an organized effort to consolidate Ammenemes I's position and that of his government. In this effort every stratagem at the wily old politician's disposal seems to have been put to use, including, as we have seen, the pens of such literary lights as the lector-priest Neferty.

In the twentieth year of his reign (1972 B.C.) the ageing king, foreseeing the dangers which at his death might beset both the dynasty and the nation, made his eldest son, Sesostris, his co-regent on the throne and turned over to the younger man the more active duties of the pharaonic office.[3] For a decade the two kings ruled Egypt together and dated events to the years of their respective reigns, 'Year 10' of Sesostris corresponding, for example, with 'Year 30' of his father.[4] The practice—an extremely sound one—was followed by Ammenemes I's successors, and throughout most of the dynasty we find the succession assured by a series of co-regencies between fathers and sons of the royal line.

It was during the co-regency of Ammenemes I and Sesostris I, and under the latter's leadership in the field, that the military occupation of Lower Nubia seems to have been inaugurated.[5] By Year 29 the conquest of the area had been extended as far as Korosko, more than half-way between the First and Second Cataracts,[6] and perhaps much further, for Ammenemes I has been thought to be the founder of a border fort at Semna near the Second Cataract[7] and of a fortified trading post at Kerma in the northern Sudan.[8] The king's name is found between Aswān and Philae (Year 23),[9] near Gerf Husein,[10] and in the ancient diorite quarries far out in the Nubian desert north-west of Tōshka.[11] On a stela dated to Regnal Year [2]4 the Commander of Soldiers,

[1] §xi, 26, 12. Cf. §iii, 23, 64.
[2] P. Ermitage 1116b recto, 66–8. See §x, 11, 55–7.
[3] See §xi, 27; §iii, 22, 67; §x, 11, 80; §xi, 22, 63–9; §xi, 12.
[4] Stela Cairo 20516 (§iv, 6, vol. ii, 108).   [5] §iii, 23, 64–6.
[6] *Ibid.* 16, 65 n. 1.   [7] §xi, 25, 66.
[8] §xi, 24, part vi, 511 f., 542 f. Cf. §iii, 23, 65, 114–15.
[9] §iii, 23, 65 n. 3.   [10] *Ibid.* 65 n. 2.
[11] §xi, 8, 70 (3).

Nesumont, boasts of victories over the bedawin peoples of the eastern desert and the peninsula of Sinai,[1] and we know of at least one expedition which Sesostris I on behalf of his father led against the Tjemehu Libyans in the vicinity of the Wādi en-Natrūn (see below). Diplomatic relations apparently existed between the pharaoh and the princes of Syria.[2]

The fine, hard stone of the Wādi Hammāmāt was quarried for Ammenemes I[3] and his name is found near the turquoise mines of Serābīt el-Khādim in Sinai.[4] In Egypt building activities were carried on in the temples of the gods from Khatā'na and Bubastis in the Delta to Thebes in the south.[5] At Memphis the king provided the temple of Ptah with a red granite altar[6] and with a statue of himself also in red granite, usurped and transported to Tanis by his successors of a much later period.[7] He adorned the temple of Hathor at Dendera with a granite doorway and the temple of Min at Koptos with fine reliefs,[8] and dedicated a granite altar to Osiris at Abydos.[9] At Karnak the temple of the new state god, Amon-Re, was honoured by Ammenemes I with a group of statues and with a granite altar and shrine,[10] and the adjacent temple of the goddess Mut, Amun's wife, was perhaps founded in his reign.[11]

The founder of the Twelfth Dynasty met his end on the seventh day of the third month of Akhet in the thirtieth year of his reign,[12] or, according to our calendar, on 15 February 1962 B.C. There seems to be little doubt that he was assassinated, conspirators within the palace taking advantage of the absence of his son on a campaign in Libya to dispose of the old man in a treacherous assault, launched in the dead of night.[13] The attack is described in the Instruction of Ammenemes I, a pseudo-autobiographical work with strong political overtones, evidently composed at the behest of Sesostris I by a talented scribe named Achthoes and purporting to be the words addressed by the dead king to his eldest

---

[1] Louvre Stela C 1. See §xi, 7; §x, 11, 54 n. 8; §xi, 27, 215, 218. See below, pp. 537–8   [2] §x, 11, 110 ff.   [3] §v, 6, no. 199.

[4] §vi, 4, nos. 63, 70, 71 c; see also no. 80.

[5] §1, 15, 152–3, 155–6; §xi, 13, 257–60; §xi, 14, 43–53; §xi, 16, 445, 448–59; §xi, 1, 305–6. See also §x, 11, 81.

[6] §xi, 18, 10, pl. 34 f.

[7] §viii, 4, part 1, 4–5, pls. 1 (3), 13 (1); §xi, 14, 50–2.

[8] §xi, 23, 110; §ii, 10, vol. v, 125.   [9] §xi, 20, 511, no. 1338.

[10] §xi, 19, 41–2, pl. 8 d, e; §xi, 14, 53; §v, 8, vol. ii, 95.

[11] §1, 15, 156; §xi, 2, 132–3, 295–6.

[12] The date is given at the beginning of the Story of Sinuhe. See below, p. 499, n. 2.

[13] §xi, 5; §xi, 6.

son and chosen successor.[1] The triple purpose of this justly famous and much-copied text was clearly to exalt the accomplishments of Ammenemes I, confound his adversaries and those of his son, and affirm the latter's position on the throne.

Another account of the king's death and its aftermath is given in one of the masterpieces of Middle Kingdom literature, the 'Story of Sinuhe'.[2] Sinuhe, an official of the royal household from whose tomb inscriptions the story was probably derived, was returning with Sesostris from Libya when messengers from Itj-towy arrived with the startling news. In his own words he describes how the young king, 'without letting his army know it', 'flew' with his bodyguard to the capital—presumably to deal with the conspirators and to crush immediately any attempt to deprive him of the crown. Sinuhe, overhearing the rival claimant to the throne in treasonous conversation with a messenger and fearing a civil war of uncertain outcome, deserted the army in a panic and passed many adventurous years in Syria before being pardoned by Sesostris and allowed to return in honour to Egypt.

XII. EXPANSION UNDER SESOSTRIS I AND HIS SUCCESSORS

Meanwhile, Sesostris I had dealt in masterly fashion with the dynastic crisis responsible for the death of his father and by skilful propaganda and other means had gone far towards restoring to the pharaonic office much of its ancient dignity and prestige.[3] Secure upon his throne, he was able to devote his great energy, ability, and breadth of vision to a programme for the enrichment and expansion of Egypt more grandiose than any heretofore undertaken.

A vigorous and ruthless campaign of Regnal Year 18 served to complete the conquest and military occupation of Lower Nubia, which was now garrisoned with Egyptian troops stationed in fortresses at Qūbān and other strategic points along the Nubian Nile as far south as Buhen, at the Second Cataract.[4] Control of a sort seems to have been extended into the area lying between the Second and Third Cataracts, including the land of Kush, now mentioned for the first time in Egyptian records, and, farther to

[1] See §x, 11, 61–86, and the references cited there.
[2] §xi, 3, 1–41; §xi, 4, 35–40; §xi, 11; §x, 11, 87–115; §i, 23, 18–22; §xi, 15.
[3] §x, 11, 69, 75, 85, 95 ff., 131–40, 143–4.
[4] §xii, 37, 81, 82, 129–31; §iii, 23, 69, 70, 88, 92, 98; §xii, 17; §xii, 18. See also §xii, 53; §xii, 15, vol. i, 132 (R.I.S. 9).

the south, the large and strategically important island of Sai.[1]
Though statues of the nomarch Djefaihapi of Asyūt and his wife,
found at Kerma, above the Third Cataract, may have been transported thither at a later period it is probable that a fortified
trading settlement was maintained there under Sesostris I, whose
name has been found even further south, on the island of Argo.[2]
The gold and copper mines of the Wādi el-Allāqi, in the desert east
of Qūbān,[3] were undoubtedly exploited by the king's engineers,
and the ancient diorite quarries of Cheops to the north-west of
Tōshka apparently swarmed with Egyptian working parties.[4]
'Amethysts of the land of Nubia' were dragged on sledges from
the mines of the Wādi el-Hūdi,[5] and blocks of red granite were
extracted from the quarries at the First Cataract, the domain of
the pharaoh's loyal appointee, the nomarch Sirenpowet (I) of
Elephantine.[6]

Gold was brought also from mines east of Koptos[7] and hard
stone from the nearby Wādi Hammāmāt, where, in Sesostris I's
thirty-eighth year, an expedition of more than seventeen thousand
men quarried the blocks for sixty sphinxes and one hundred and
fifty statues.[8] Alabaster was quarried as before, as witnessed by
inscriptions of Years 22 and 31 in the ancient quarries at Het-nub.[9]

On the west, the king's activities seem to have been confined
to punitive expeditions, or police actions, against the Tjemehu
and Tjehenu Libyans[10] and the maintenance of communications
with the oases, whither the royal messengers travelled over the
caravan route between Abydos and the Great Oasis of El-
Khārga.[11]

Though Sinuhe's statement on the subject is somewhat obscure,[12] it appears to have been true that Sesostris I had no designs
on the countries north of Egypt, other than the protection of his

---

[1] §III, 23, 70, 71; §VII, 3 (see especially pp. 45, 59–60); §VII, 2, 39–40; §XI, 26, 14 (14–15).

[2] §XII, 37, 180; §III, 23, 72, 73, 114, 115; A, 7.

[3] §III, 32, 70, 82, 85, 87. Cf. §XII, 13; §XII, 37, 318.

[4] §XII, 37, 274; §III, 23, 72 n. 1.   [5] §XII, 37, 319; §XII, 41.

[6] §III, 23, 67–9, 72; §II, 10, vol. V, 229, 238 (no. 36), 242–4, 246–8; §IV, 4, 188 f.; §XII, 24, 67, fig. 4, no. 6.

[7] §XII, 55, 16–17; §IX, 4, 257–61; §III, 23, 86; §XII, 8, 181–2; §XII, 29, 65–6; §XI, 26, 15 (8). Cf. §XII, 19, vol. II, 238 (1: New Kingdom).

[8] §IX, 2, nos. 61, 64–7; §V, 6, nos. 87, 117, 123; §IX, 7, 28–32.

[9] §XII, 22, 143–6; §I, 1, 76–8, gr. 49, pl. 31; §XII, 48.

[10] §XI, 3, 4–6; §XI, 4, 35; §I, 3, 658; §X, 11, 53, 104 (see n. 3).

[11] §XII, 44.

[12] Sinuhe B 72 (R 96): §XI, 3, 22 (1–2). See also §XI, 11, 38–9, 170; §I, 23, 19; §XII, 10; §III, 23, 67 n. 3.

own boundary, the maintenance of diplomatic relations with the tribal chieftains of Palestine and Syria, and the continuation of the lively trade in lumber and other commodities which western Asia had to offer. Garrisons were maintained at 'Walls-of-the-Ruler' and other border fortresses[1] and working parties, assisted by the inhabitants of the region, toiled in the turquoise mines at Serābīt el-Khādim on the Sinai peninsula.[2] Settlements of Egyptians were apparently to be found throughout Palestine and Syria and merchants and royal couriers passed freely north and south from Itj-towy to Byblos and other points both on the Mediterranean coast and in the adjoining hill country.[3] Among the many Egyptian objects of this period found in Syria is a collar from Ugarit (Ras Shamra) bearing the cartouche of Sesostris I.[4]

In Egypt itself at least thirty-five sites, from Alexandria on the Mediterranean coast to Aswān on the First Cataract, have yielded buildings or other monuments of King Sesostris I, and there was hardly a temple of any importance in Upper or Lower Egypt that was not enlarged or embellished by this great pharaoh.[5]

The ancient temple of Re-Atum at Heliopolis was extensively rebuilt in 'Regnal Year 3',[6] the king himself witnessing the 'stretching of the cord' and the 'driving of the stake' at the foundation ceremony.[7] Twenty-seven years later, on the first occasion of the *Heb Sed*, or jubilee festival, he erected a pair of towering granite obelisks before the pylon of this temple, and one still stands at Heliopolis.[8] A gigantic pillar, set up at Abgīg in the Faiyūm,[9] indicates a growing interest in this fertile region, soon to be developed on a grand scale by the pharaoh's successors (see below). At Karnak, the home of the great god Amon-Re, there are many remains of structures erected or decorated by Sesostris I,[10] the most interesting being a small free-standing,

---

[1] §x, 11, 56; see also 24–5.

[2] §vi, 4, part i, nos. 64–71, 81 (?), 138(?); part ii, 36, 38, 55; §xii, 12, 384 ff.; §x, 11, 108.

[3] §x, 11, 106–14.   [4] §xii, 43, 20.

[5] See §i, 15, 161 ff.; §v, 3, 6–16, 106–13, pl. 2; §xii, 21; §xii, 54, 47; §xii, 3.

[6] 1970 B.C. or 1960 B.C., depending on whether we count the date from Sesostris I's appointment as co-regent or, with Gardiner (§xi, 12), from the beginning of his sole reign. See §x, 11, 136; §xi, 27, 216 n. 8.

[7] The inscription in which the temple was dedicated is largely preserved in a hieratic copy of the mid-Eighteenth Dynasty in Berlin (no. P 3029). See §xii, 50, pls. 1, 2; §xii, 9; §x, 11, 136–9; §xii, 39, 119, 126–8.

[8] §ii, 10, vol. iv, 60.   [9] *Ibid.* 99.

[10] *Op. cit.* vol. ii, 19, 34–5, 41, 50, 53, 97; §xii, 14, vol. xxxix, 565–6, pl. 105; vol. xlix, 258, fig. 3.

peripteral chapel of limestone, dedicated to Amun on the occasion of the king's first *Sed*-festival and adorned throughout with reliefs and monumental inscriptions of extraordinary delicacy and fineness.[1]

Like his father before him, Sesostris I built his pyramid near El-Lisht, selecting as its site a broad spur of the desert plateau one mile south of that chosen by Ammenemes I.[2] In size and magnificence the new funerary complex surpassed by far the relatively modest tomb of the founder of the dynasty, and its plan and style show a more wholehearted return to the ancient Memphite tradition, as exemplified in the nearby royal tombs of the Old Kingdom.[3] An inscription of the Treasurer, Mery, tells us of the construction of the king's 'seat of eternity'—presumably his mortuary temple—in the ninth year of his reign (1964 B.C.);[4] but transport inscriptions on blocks in the foundations of the pyramid show that work was not actually begun until late in the tenth year, some seven months after the death of Ammenemes I.[5]

The inscription on a little limestone statuette of a private person found at El-Lisht, indicates that even in the Twelfth Dynasty Sesostris I was regarded and invoked as a god.[6] The perseverance of his cult for centuries after his death is attested by sealings from offerings sent to his pyramid temple by kings of the Thirteenth Dynasty[7] and by a number of stelae of the New Kingdom on which are mentioned persons who served as priests of the deified pharaoh.[8] The name of the king in its Greek form, 'Sesostris', is preserved in a legend of the Hellenistic Period, recounting the fabulous deeds of a pharaoh, whose heroic figure seems to have been inspired, not only by Sesostris I and III of the Twelfth Dynasty, but also, in part, by Ramesses II of the Nineteenth Dynasty.[9]

When Sesostris I died in the forty-fifth year of his reign, his son, Nubkaure Ammenemes II, had shared the throne with him for at least two years.[10] Previously, as young 'Prince Ameny', he

---

[1] §xii, 31; §xii, 30. See Plate 45 (*b*).

[2] §ii, 10, vol. iv, 81–5; §xii, 34; §xii, 16, 220–5, fig. 44; §i, 10, part i, 182–95; §xi, 29, vol. ii, 171–8.

[3] In both its plan and decoration the pyramid temple of Sesostris I is strikingly like that of King Phiops II of the late Sixth Dynasty (see §xii, 27, vols. ii and iii).

[4] Stela Louvre C 3, lines 5 ff. (§xii, 20, pl. 4).   [5] §x, 9, 6, fig. 4.

[6] Metropolitan Museum of Art, acc. no. 24.1.72 (§xii, 33, 35, fig. 1). See also §xii, 53, 65; §xii, 42, 51 n. 1.

[7] §x, 9, 21–2; §i, 10, part i, 191, 342; §xii, 25, 34.

[8] §i, 10, part i, 195; part ii, 51 (fig. 24), 168.

[9] §xii, 46; §xii, 32; §x, 11, 141–3.

[10] Leiden Stela V 4 (§xii, 6, vol. ii, 3 (no. 5), pl. 4).

had been sent by his father on an expedition into Nubia, accompanied by his namesake, the Governor of the Oryx Nome.[1] This expedition was evidently of a peaceful nature, and neither the new king nor his successor, Sesostris II, seems to have conducted military operations abroad; they were content to occupy themselves with agricultural and economic improvements at home, to continue the exploitation of the mines and quarries,[2] to dedicate small temples to the gods of Egypt,[3] and to maintain active, but, on the whole, pacific relations with neighbouring lands. In Nubia gold was 'washed' by local chieftains under Egyptian supervision and Nubian turquoise was mined and transported to Egypt.[4] 'The fortresses of Wawat' were inspected by an official of Ammenemes II[5] and the fortress of Anība appears to have been enlarged under Sesostris II, whose name has been found also in the fort at Qūbān, at the mouth of the Wādi el-Allāqi, and perhaps at Kumma, at the Second Cataract.[6]

The reigns of Ammenemes II and Sesostris II have produced abundant evidence of the increasingly important role played by the Egyptians of the Twelfth Dynasty in the culture, commerce, and politics of western Asia. In the foundations of the temple of Mont at Tōd in Upper Egypt were found four bronze caskets, inscribed with the name of Ammenemes II and containing a treasure of small objects sent either as a gift or as tribute to the king of Egypt by the ruler of some important Syrian principality.[7] Besides ingots of gold and silver there were vessels of silver, one, at least, of characteristic Aegean type,[8] Babylonian cylinder-seals, and amulets of lapis lazuli which must have come originally from Mesopotamia. The site of Ras Shamra in Syria has yielded the statuette of a daughter of Ammenemes II and part of a figure of the Vizier Senwosretankh,[9] while at Mishrifé was found a sphinx with the name of another daughter of the same king,[10] and at Megiddo four fragmentary statuettes of Thuthotpe, the well-known nomarch of Hermopolis.[11] In the time of Sesostris II the

---

[1] §xi, 26, 15 (3).

[2] §vi, 4, nos. 47–9, 71–80, 410(?), pp. 34, 36, 48; §v, 6, no. 104; §xi, 8, 71–2; §x, 4, 35, no. 15, pl. 13 b; §i, 1, 78, gr. 50, pl. 32.

[3] §xii, 2, 27–34; §xii, 40, 40, 41, 167, 295; §ii, 10, vol. iv, 119.

[4] British Museum Stela no. 143 [569] (§xii, 26, part ii, 8, pl. 19). The existence of the Nubian turquoise is disputed in *J.N.E.S.* 16 (1957), 228.

[5] §iii, 23, 74 (n. 3); §ii, 1, sect. 616.

[6] §xii, 49, vol. ii, 11, pl. 2 b; §xii, 15, 130, 169 (R.I.K. 129); §xii, 37, 82. See also §iii, 23, 74, 84, 88, 132.   [7] §xii, 4; §xii, 5; §xii, 51; §xii, 47.

[8] §xii, 28, 19–20, 32.   [9] §xii, 37, 394.

[10] *Ibid.* 392.   [11] *Ibid.* 381; §xii, 56. See however, p. 546, n. 7. [Ed.]

nomarch Khnumhotpe of Beni Hasan received as his guest the
'Hyksos', or bedawin chieftain, Abisha, and his colourful retinue.[1]
Throughout the Twelfth and Thirteenth Dynasties Asiatic men
and women were imported into Egypt in large numbers as
household servants and the like.[2]

It was during the Twelfth Dynasty that an Egyptian nurse,
named Sit-Sneferu, travelled to Adana in south-eastern Asia Minor,
taking with her from Egypt her diorite tomb statuette,[3] and that a
fellow Egyptian left a statuette of himself at Kürigen Kaleh, some
thirty miles east of Ankara.[4] Byblos (Gebal), which had remained
in close contact with Egypt since early historic times, was governed at this period by a dynasty of native rulers, who used the
Egyptian title, 'Count' (*ḥȝty-ꜥ*), wrote their names in hieroglyphic characters, and surrounded themselves with jewellery
and other objects of Egyptian type and, frequently, of Egyptian
manufacture.[5] We hear more and more in Egyptian texts of the
Hau-nebu, recently identified as the populations of the remote
Asiatic littorals.[6] Egyptian objects of the Middle Kingdom occur
with some frequency on the island of Crete[7] and Minoan pottery
of the type called Kamares Ware has been found in Twelfth
Dynasty town sites at El-Lāhūn and El-Haraga and in a tomb of
the Twelfth Dynasty at Abydos.[8]

Word of trading expeditions to the east African incense-land
of Punt is preserved on two stelae from the Wādi el-Gāsūs on the
Red Sea coast at the eastern end of the Koptos Road. In the
twenty-eighth year of Ammenemes II the Captain of the Gate,
Khentekhtay-wer, returned from Punt, 'his expedition with him,
safe and sound, his fleet at rest at Sawu (Wādi el-Gāsūs)'.[9] Eight
years later, in 'Year 1' of Sesostris II, the same port was visited
by the Treasurer, Khnumhotpe, who 'executed his monument in
God's Land' and showed his king receiving 'life' from the god
Sopd, the divinity of the eastern deserts.[10]

The pyramid of Ammenemes II, on the edge of the desert east
of the ancient tombs of Sneferu at Dahshūr, was built and cased
with limestone, the construction resembling closely that of the
pyramid of Sesostris I at El-Lisht.[11]

---

[1] §II, 10, vol. IV, 145–6.   [2] §XII, 38; §III, 12, 87–99, 133–4, 148–9.
[3] §XII, 37, 398; §XII, 11; §I, 10, part I, 215, fig. 132.
[4] §XII, 1, 294–6 (see also 293, figs. 11–13).
[5] §XII, 37, 386 ff. See also §I, 3, 659; §XII, 35.   [6] §XII, 52, 15–32.
[7] §XII, 36, nos. 1–3, 5, 7, 8, 14, 16, 18, 29, 52–4, 56, 297.
[8] §XII, 28, 18–19.   [9] §XII, 37, 338; §II, 1, sects. 604–5.
[10] §XII, 37, 338–9; §II, 1, sects. 617–18.
[11] §XIII, 12, 234–7; §XII, 16, 225; §XI, 29, vol. II, 179–84.

It was Sesostris II who appears to have inaugurated the great project of land reclamation and control of the Nile flood waters in the Faiyūm basin, an undertaking carried out with energy by his successors, especially by his grandson, King Ammenemes III (see below, p. 510). El-Lāhūn overlooks the mouth of the channel leading from the Nile Valley into the Faiyūm, and here, in keeping with his interest in the region, Sesostris II founded his pyramid and, nearby, the town of Hetep-Sesostris, laid out on a rectangular plan and containing quarters for the artisans and larger houses for the officials charged with the work.[1] The town boasted a small temple, the ruined archives of which have yielded hundreds of documents, written on papyrus and containing data of the utmost importance to our knowledge of conditions in Egypt during the late Middle Kingdom.[2]

XIII. THE ADMINISTRATIVE REFORMS AND FOREIGN CAMPAIGNS OF SESOSTRIS III; THE EXECRATION TEXTS

Everything considered, the pharaoh who contributed most to the enduring glory of the Twelfth Dynasty was Khakaure Sesostris III, the principal prototype of the fabulous 'King Sesostris' of later legend.[3] His reign was distinguished by two achievements of major importance, not only to his own time, but also to the future history of his country.

Under Ammenemes I and his successors the nomarchs of Upper and Middle Egypt—especially those of the Hare and Oryx Nomes—had regained much of the power and independence enjoyed by the 'feudal lords' of Heracleopolitan times and had once more begun to vie with the kings in wealth and display. The great rock-tombs of Beni Hasan[4] and the alabaster colossus which Thuthotpe of Hermopolis caused to be quarried for himself at Het-nub[5] are fair examples of the new flair for magnificence exhibited by the provincial governors.

The situation evidently proved intolerable to the autocratic nature of the third Sesostris, and some time during the latter half of his reign he appears to have shorn the provincial nobles of their traditional rights and privileges and reduced them to the status of

[1] §II, 10, vol. IV, 107–12; §XII, 16, 225–7; §XI, 29, vol. II, 184–7.
[2] §XII, 23; §XII, 7; §XII, 45.
[3] §XII, 32. See also above, p. 502, n. 9. See Plate 45 (a).
[4] §II, 10, vol. IV, 140–60.   [5] §II, 9, part I, 17, pls. 12–15.

political nonentities. How this was achieved is not known; but in the reign of Sesostris III the series of great provincial tombs came to an end, and no more is heard of the 'Great Chiefs' of the nomes and their local courts.[1] Instead, the provinces of Lower Egypt, Middle Egypt, and Upper Egypt were administered from the Residence city by three departments (*wâret*) of the central government, known, respectively, as the Northern *Wâret*, the *Wâret* of the South, and the *Wâret* of the Head of the South.[2] Each of these departments was headed by an official called a Reporter who numbered among his assistants a Second Reporter, a Council or Court (*djadjat*), *wârtu*-officers, and staffs of scribes. Like the departments of justice, agriculture, labour, and the treasury, those charged with the administration of the three main geographical divisions of the country were under the over-all direction of the office of the vizier.[3]

The suppression of the landed nobility was accompanied by the emergence of the Egyptian middle class, composed of craftsmen, tradesmen, small farmers, and the like, the rise in whose fortunes and importance in the structure of the nation can be traced in the numerous private statuettes of the period and in the countless stelae and other ex-votos dedicated by these people near the sanctuary of Osiris at Abydos.[4]

Sesostris III is remembered by posterity chiefly for his consolidation of Egypt's hold on Nubia. During the unwarlike reigns of his two predecessors Sudanese tribesmen, displaced from their homeland, had apparently pushed northward and were beginning to threaten the security of the area between the First and Second Cataracts.[5] In dealing with this threat the king's first concern was to link Lower Nubia and Upper Egypt by means of a navigable waterway through the Aswān rapids. Early in his reign, therefore, he caused a channel, called 'Good-are-the-Ways-of-Khakaure', to be opened in the Cataract, probably in the vicinity of Esh-Shallāl.[6] Wide enough and deep enough to accommodate the largest Egyptian warship or merchant vessel, this channel, less than two hundred and sixty feet in length, was probably a re-excavated section or an extension of the old system of canals made under King Merenre I of the Sixth Dynasty. In Year 8 the new canal

---

[1] At Antaeopolis (Qāw el-Kebīr) the nomarch Wahka II remained in office into the reign of Ammenemes III (§11, 10, vol. v, 11–14; §xi, 29, vol. ii, 344–5; §x, 15, 18) and at El-Kāb at a later date the nomarchy was momentarily revived (§vii, 1, 302, 307).

[2] §xii, 25, 31–3. Cf. §xiii, 10, 76–91; §iii, 13, 241–3.

[3] §iii, 12, 134–44.   [4] §x, 15, 27 ff. See also §xiii, 23.

[5] §iii, 23, 74–5.   [6] §ii, 10, vol. v, 250; §xiii, 18, 85, no. 24*a* and *b*.

was dredged in preparation for the king's first Nubian campaign, and in this year Sesostris III sailed through it on his way upstream 'to overthrow the wretched Kush'.

The expedition of the eighth year was followed by at least three others,[1] led by the king in person and calculated to enforce upon the tribesmen of Kush and the nomads of the adjoining desert a wholesome and lasting respect for Egyptian authority. With characteristic thoroughness Sesostris smashed an insurrection of the 'Iuntiu of Nubia' in the sixteenth year of his reign and ruthlessly wiped out their settlements, carrying away the women, fouling the wells, and setting fire to the grain fields.[2] In Year 19 the pharaoh had his ships dragged upstream through the Second Cataract, carrying the fighting into the Sudan itself and not returning northward until forced to do so by low water in the river rapids.[3]

The southern boundary of the new province was formally established in the king's eighth year and again in his sixteenth year, the line passing through Semna, on the river narrows thirty-seven miles above Wādi Halfa.[4] To safeguard the frontier, provide posts for trading, and blockade effectively the river against unauthorized traffic from the south a chain of eight brick forts was completed between Semna South, half a mile above the border, and the ancient Buhen (opposite Wādi Halfa) at the northern end of the Second Cataract.[5] Of the eight structures, all of which are listed by name in a papyrus of the late Middle Kingdom,[6] those at Semna West, Semna East (Kumma), and Uronarti are known to have been founded or extensively rebuilt by Sesostris III, and it is probable that several of the others were also established in his reign. Study of the existing ruins of these buildings has shown them to have been clever examples of military architecture, admirably adapted to the terrain and to the purposes for which they were intended;[7] and an interesting series of dispatches exchanged between their commanders early in the reign of Ammenemes III has thrown abundant light on the personnel and activities of their garrisons.[8]

[1] In Years 10, 16, and 19. See also §III, 23, 76–8.
[2] §XII, 37, 143, 151; §XIII, 18, 83 f.; §XIII, 8; §XIII, 11 (lines 15–16); §VII, 2, 41. On the expression 'Iuntiu' see §VII, 3, 48; §X, 10, 25, 36, 62.
[3] §XII, 37, 144 ('Quay'); §III, 23, 78.
[4] Berlin no. 14753 (§XIII, 1, 255 f.; §XIII, 18, 84). See also §X, 11, 134–6; §XIII, 7; and the references cited above, nn. 1 and 2.
[5] §XII, 37, 129, 142–56; §III, 23, 80–1, 89–98; §XII, 15; §XIII, 7.
[6] §XIII, 6; §II, 5, vol. I, 9–11, pl. 2.
[7] See §III, 23, 95 ff.; §XIII, 4; §XIII, 3; §XIII, 16; §XI, 25; §XIII, 24; §XII, 17; §XII, 18; §XIII, 21, 98–9, fig. 43, pl. 63.
[8] §XIII, 22; §VII, 2, 40–1. See also §XII, 18, 251, figs. 9, 10.

Hardly comparable with his campaigns in Nubia was an expedition led by Sesostris III against the 'Mentju' of Palestine, in the course of which he penetrated that, on the whole, friendly country as far as a place called Sekmem, probably the biblical Shechem.[1] The trip north was evidently uneventful, but on the return march the rear-guard of the king's army, commanded by an officer named Khusobk, appears to have been set upon by a band of Asiatics, including men of Sekmem and Retenu. The distinction achieved by Khusobk for his slaughter of a single Asiatic suggests that the operation, though interesting as a rare example of Middle Kingdom military activity in western Asia, was small in scale and relatively unimportant.

On the other hand, the detailed knowledge possessed by the Egyptians of the late Twelfth Dynasty on the principalities of Palestine and Syria is strikingly attested by the so-called Execration Texts, the two most important series of which date from the time of Sesostris III and from the decades following his reign.[2] These texts, written in hieratic on small pottery bowls and mud figures of bound captives, which were broken and buried near the tombs of the dead at Thebes and Saqqara, consist of lists of persons and things regarded as actually or potentially dangerous to the tomb-owner and his king; and include, besides a variety of general evils, the names of deceased Egyptians, whose malevolent spirits might be expected to cause trouble, and the names of numerous foreign princes and peoples who, unless brought under control, might constitute a threat to the safety and prosperity of Egypt.

It is probable that the names of the foreign rulers and nations were derived from official records available in the government archives. The Nubian lists, comprising some thirty peoples, including the Kushites, Medjay and Wawatis, as well as such general expressions as 'Nehesyu' and 'Iuntiu of Nubia', are, as might be expected, consistent throughout the texts, both as to composition and order of arrangement. An understandable vagueness on the part of the Egyptian scribes regarding the complicated geography of Palestine and Syria produced many variations in the Asiatic lists, which are, however, remarkable for the num-

---

[1] §XIII, 11; §X, 12, 230; §X, 10, 68 (E 6); §XIII, 2. See below, p. 543.

[2] §XIII, 19; §X, 10; §VII, 3, 42–4, 66. See also §XIII, 5, 492 n. 44; §X, 1, 223. Earlier examples of the same type of text are datable, respectively, to the late Old Kingdom or early First Intermediate Period (§XIII, 9, 30–8, pls. 6 b, 7; §XIII, 15) and to the first half of the Twelfth Dynasty (§XIII, 13; §XIII, 14, 42 ff.; §VII, 3, 43, 66; §X, 9, 23–4, fig. 32; §I, 10, part I, 329–30, fig. 217).

ber of personal and place names which they contain. Among the latter may be recognized the well-known towns of Byblos, Jerusalem, Shechem, and Askalon. In most of the extant lists the peoples of Libya are lumped together under the general designations, Tjehenu and Tjemehu. Also proscribed are all Egyptians, men and women, commoners and nobles, 'who might rebel, weave intrigues, make war, plan to make war, or plan to rebel, and every rebel who plans to rebel, in this entire land'.[1]

As a builder one of Sesostris III's most ambitious projects was his elaborate and handsomely decorated temple to Mont at El-Madāmūd, near Karnak.[2] In selecting the site for his tomb the great king returned to Dahshūr and a mile north of the tomb of Ammenemes II built a pyramid of mud brick, cased with limestone and surrounded, as usual, by the mastabas of the royal family and court.[3]

XIV. ECONOMIC MEASURES UNDER AMMENEMES III

The growth of national prosperity under the pharaohs of the Twelfth Dynasty reached its peak during the long and peaceful reign of Sesostris III's son, King Nymare Ammenemes III (1842–1797 B.C.).[4] With Nubia completely under control, Egyptian suzerainty acknowledged by many of the princes of Western Asia, and the provincial nobles no longer a threat to the power of the central government, the king now turned his attention wholeheartedly to the economic expansion of his country and concentrated his energies on increasing the production of the mines and quarries, studying and improving the irrigation system, and carrying forward the plans of his predecessors for the development of the Faiyūm.

Under Ammenemes III the turquoise (and copper?) mines of Sinai were worked as never before, forty-nine inscriptions at

---

[1] §XIII, 19, 73 d.

[2] §II, 10, vol. V, 137, 143–5, 147–9; §XI, 29, vol. II, 628–34; §XIII, 17. See also below, p. 517.

[3] §XIII, 12, 228–33; §XI, 29, vol. II, 187–90; §XII, 16, 227–8; §XIII, 20.

[4] A long co-regency between Sesostris III and Ammenemes III, proposed by Goyon (§IX, 2, 22) on the basis of four inscriptions in the Wādi Hammāmāt (§IX, 2, nos. 68, 69 [and 70]; §V, 6, nos. 81, 96), is not supported by the divergent systems of dating used in the inscriptions themselves and is inconsistent with the other data which we possess on the reigns of the two kings. See also the considerations raised by Simpson (§IX, 7, 32–3).

Serābīt el-Khādim and ten more in the Wādis Maghāra and Nasb testifying to the almost ceaseless activity of the king's mining expeditions.[1] The inscriptions range in date from Year 2 to Year 45 of the reign and include the names of the foremen in charge of the individual mine-shafts and the treasury officials who came periodically to inspect the mines and see that their output was being kept up to the required level. The former camp sites were transformed into more or less permanent stations, with houses for the officials in charge, huts for the workmen, fortifications against bedawin raids, wells, cisterns, and even tombs for those members of the expeditions who ended their days amid the sun-scorched rocks of the peninsula.[2] An extraordinary temple at Serābīt, dedicated to Hathor, Mistress of Turquoise, the patron divinity of the region, was probably founded in the early Old Kingdom, but received its first major enlargement in the reign of Ammenemes III.[3] A pectoral from Dahshūr, on which the king is shown smiting the bedawin of Sinai and southern Palestine,[4] suggests that the royal working parties still had to defend themselves occasionally against the wild tribes of the neighbouring deserts. Records of quarrying expeditions sent out by Ammenemes III have been found at Tura,[5] Hammāmāt,[6] and Aswān,[7] and in the ancient diorite quarries in the Nubian desert west of Tōshka.[8]

The project fostered by the kings of the Twelfth Dynasty in the Faiyūm seems to have been primarily one of land reclamation.[9] At the beginning of the second millennium B.C. this fertile basin, on the west of the Nile Valley some forty miles south of Memphis, was largely taken up by the waters of a great lake, called by the Egyptians 'ta-henet-en-Merwer' and by the Greeks of later times 'the Lake of Moeris',[10] the much reduced remnant of which may be recognized in the present-day Birket-Qārūn.[11] Well below the level of the adjacent Nile flood plain, the lake was fed by an arm of the river, known today as the Bahr Yūsef, which enters the Faiyūm from the south-east through the Hawāra

1 §vi, 4, nos. 23–31, 46, 50–6, 83–117, 124b, 131(?), 132(?), 138(?), [143], 405, 406, 409, pp. 15, 16, 19, 24, 28–30, 33–7, 39, 49, 144. See also §x, 11, 131–2.
2 §xii, 8, 190; §xiv, 3.   3 §xii, 37, 346 ff.; §vi, 4, part ii, 36.
4 §xiv, 15, vol. i, 64 (1), pls. 20, 21.   5 §ii, 10, vol. iv, 74 (1).
6 §v, 6, nos. 17, 19, 42, 43, 48, 81, 96, 108; §ix, 2, no. 70.
7 §ii, 10, vol. v, 246–7.   8 §xi, 8, 72–4; §xii, 37, 274–5.
9 §xiv, 4, 69 ff.; §xiv, 13, sect. 293; §vii, 1, 254. Cf. §xiv, 1, 199–210; §xiv, 2, 51–2.
10 §xiv, 7; §ii, 5, vol. ii, 115*–116* (A 392).
11 §xiv, 4, 61–104; §xiv, 1, 178–302, pl. 9; §xiv, 5, 1–17, pl. 108; §xiv, 16, 68, 69, 72, 73, folding map.

Channel, a narrow defile in the desert hills immediately north of Gebel Sidmant. Deposition of silt at the inner, or northern, end of this channel had thrown out a delta-like triangle of fertile land in the midst of the waters of the lake; and here, near the site of modern Medînet el-Faiyūm, had been built the town of Shedet (Greek Arsinoe-Crocodilopolis), already known under the Old Kingdom as a cult centre of the crocodile god, Sobk.[1] To enlarge the existing land area all that was necessary was to reduce by artificial means the flow of water into the Faiyūm basin, allowing the naturally rapid evaporation of the lake surface to do its work, and to protect the ground, so reclaimed, from re-flooding by a system of dykes and drainage canals. It was probably Sesostris II who first regulated the inflow of water by a barrage, constructed across the mouth of the Hawāra Channel in the neighbourhood of El-Lāhūn.[2] To Ammenemes III, however, belongs the credit for having carried the project to a successful conclusion, reclaiming more than 17,000 acres of arable land north and west of Medînet el-Faiyūm and enclosing this valuable tract within a vast semi-circular embankment, extending from Edwa, on the east, through Biyahmu to El-Agamīyīn.[3]

Just outside the embankment, north of Biyahmu, are the bases of two colossal quartzite statues of the king, which, at the time of Herodotus, were still surrounded by the waters of the lake.[4] A few miles to the south, at Kīmān Fāris, lie the ruins of the great temple of Sobk of Shedet and his 'guest', Horus the Elder, to which Ammenemes III contributed a broad hall with columns of red granite and other splendid monuments.[5] A well-preserved shrine to Sobk's consort, the goddess Renenutet, was founded by the same pharaoh at Medînet el-Ma'ādi in the south-west corner of the Faiyūm.[6] At Hawāra, overlooking the northern end of the channel into the Faiyūm, the king built one of his two pyramids, a structure of mud brick, cased with limestone and containing an amazing monolithic burial chamber of quartzite.[7] South of the pyramid are traces of a great architectural complex, much admired by travellers of the Graeco-Roman period and variously described

---

[1] §II, 5, vol. II, 116*–117* (A 392B); §XIV, 6, vol. II, 43 f.; §XIV, 8, vol. V, 150. See *Pyr.* 416c, 1564b (§XIV, 17; §XIV, 18, vol. II, 178; §XIV, 12, vol. II, 193; vol. III, 756); §III, 15, 14 ff.

[2] §VII, 1, 254; §XIV, 13, sect. 293; §I, 3, 653 (line 17: read 'Sénousret II' ?).

[3] §XIV, 4, 72 ff., pls. 20, 21.

[4] Herodotus II, 149. See §II, 10, vol. IV, 98; §XIV, 4, 76–7, pls. 22–4; §XIV, 10.

[5] §XIV, 9; §II, 10, vol. IV, 98–9.

[6] §XI, 29, vol. II, 619–20.

[7] §II, 10, vol. IV, 100; §XI, 29, vol. II, 192–3; §XII, 16, 232–5.

by ancient and modern writers as a labyrinth, a palace, a (mortuary) temple, and an administrative centre.[1] It is not improbable that it included all the latter elements in its vast plan and was, in fact, a walled town, similar to the one built by Sesostris II near his pyramid at El-Lāhūn.[2] Beside the northern pyramid of Ammenemes III, at Dahshūr, was found the tomb of a King Awibre Hor,[3] once believed to have been his son and co-regent, but now known to have been a near contemporary of King Khutowyre Ugaf of the Thirteenth Dynasty.[4]

Before his death in 1797 B.C. King Ammenemes III had not only raised Egypt to new heights of wealth and power but had seen his name honoured on monuments from Byblos on the Syrian coast[5] to Kerma above the Third Cataract of the Nile[6]—a scope of influence achieved by few of his predecessors and not many of his successors. He was, however, the last great ruler of the Middle Kingdom and his reign was followed by a decline which opened the way to an Asiatic overlordship of Egypt and the dark days of the Hyksos Period.

XV. ART AND ARCHITECTURE

The First Intermediate Period was an era of cultural as well as political decentralization. With the collapse of the Old Kingdom and the decline of Memphis as the artistic fountainhead of all Egypt, the tomb-owner and the patron of the arts came to depend on more or less self-trained local craftsmen to supply their needs. The result was the growth of provincial schools of sculpture and painting, scattered up and down the Nile, none entirely divorced from the old Memphite traditions, but each with its own local peculiarities which with time became increasingly marked, especially in those districts geographically remote from the ancient capital. In addition to reliefs or paintings in tombs of the Heracleopolitan Period at Beni Hasan, Deir el-Bersha, Asyūt, Akhmīm, Naga ed-Deir, Gebelein, El-Mi'alla, and other localities in Middle and Upper Egypt,[7] the work of the local ateliers is represented in numerous tomb stelae from Naga ed-Deir, Dendera,

---

1 §II, 10, vol. IV, 100–1; §XI, 29, vol. II, 193–4. See §XIV, 13, sect. 293; §VII, 1, 254, 268, 271.
2 §II, 10, vol. IV, 111; §XI, 29, vol. II, 980–4.
3 §XIII, 12, 238.   4 §XIV, 14, 138; §XIV, 11, 167.
5 §XII, 37, 386–7.   6 *Ibid.* 176, 178.
7 §II, 10, vol. IV, 181–3, 263–4; vol. V, 18, 19, 28, 170; §III, 17; §XV, 10; §XV, 9, pls. 18–21; §I, 20; §XV, 20, 223–7; §XIII, 21, 83–6.

and Thebes,[1] in the painted decoration of rectangular wooden coffins,[2] and in small wooden tomb statuettes and funerary models from many different sites.[3] Few royal monuments of any importance have survived from this period, and almost no large examples of figure sculpture in the round. Often technically inept, the sculpture and painting of the provincial schools of this time—especially those of Thebes and the other districts of southern Upper Egypt—display the simplicity and directness of approach, the freshness and spontaneity, the crude vigour and tenseness of spirit, the interest in realistic details and accessories, the taste for lively minor incident, and the natural and unaffected charm characteristic of popular art the world over and diametrically opposed to the aristocratic traditions of the now decadent Memphite school.

Many of these traits are still apparent in the work of the royal Theban ateliers of the Eleventh Dynasty and are to a large extent responsible for the distinctive character of Middle Kingdom art as compared with that of the other great epochs of Egyptian history. The remarkable advances in technical skill achieved by the court artists of Thebes under Nebhepetre Mentuhotpe appear in the fine painted reliefs from the king's mortuary temple at Deir el-Bahri,[4] in the paintings and reliefs in the adjacent rock tombs of his great officials,[5] and in the sculptured decoration of shrines at Abydos, Dendera, El-Ballās, Armant, Tōd, and Gebelein.[6] The massive sandstone statues of the pharaoh from the Deir el-Bahri temple and its approaches[7] are testimonials to the rugged individuality of the Theban sculptors and are likely prototypes of the powerful royal portrait statues of the Twelfth Dynasty. Less vigorous than that of his predecessor, the temple sculpture of Sankhkare Mentuhotpe at Abydos, Armant, Tōd, and elsewhere, is characterized by superb draughtsmanship, great subtlety in the modelling of the delicate low relief, and a somewhat excessive attention to minute detail.[8]

---

[1] §vi, 7, 33–5; §ii, 10, vol. v, 26–7, 112–15; §iii, 4; §iii, 5, *passim*; §i, 4; §xv, 20, 227–8.　　　　[2] §xv, 20, 228–31.

[3] *Ibid.* 102–4; §xiii, 21, 86; §xi, 29, vol. iii, 147–62, pls. 49–55; §xv, 1, 20–1, 34, pls. 3–5; §xv, 5, *passim*.

[4] §vi, 7, 129–33; §xv, 20, 235–6; §xiii, 21, 90–1; §xv, 1, 21–2, 37–8, pls. 14, 15.

[5] §iii, 21, 133 (no. 103), 169–73 (nos. 311, 314, 315, 319); §xiii, 21, 91–2; pls. 58, 60; §xv, 20, 234–7; §i, 10, part i, 158–66, figs. 95, 96, 99–101.

[6] §ii, 10, vol. v, 41, 117, 160, 163, 167; §xi, 23, 106; §xv, 20, 235.

[7] §v, 8, pls. 12, 13; §xi, 29, vol. iii, 163–5, pl. 56; §i, 10, part i, 157, fig. 93; §xv, 1, 36, pls. 10, 11.

[8] §ii, 10, vol. v, 41, 157, 160, 167–8, 229; §xv, 20, 236; §xiii, 21, 92; §i, 24, 49–50.

Transferred to the region of Memphis by Ammenemes I, the Theban artists profited by their contact with the masterpieces of Old Kingdom sculpture and painting, and during the Twelfth Dynasty produced a series of monuments of extraordinary liveliness, sensitivity, and elegance. Foremost among their achievements are the incomparable portrait statues of the kings, wherein we see the dignity, power, and technical dexterity of the old Memphite school combined with the taste for realism developed in Upper Egypt during the troubled years of the Heracleopolitan Period.[1] Especially searching are the portraits of Sesostris III, whose grim, disdainful face, deeply lined with fatigue and disillusionment, is preserved to us on a score of statues from Karnak, Deir el-Bahri, El-Madāmūd, and elsewhere.[2] The numerous portraits of Ammenemes III include a group of statues and sphinxes from Tanis and the Faiyūm, which, from their curiously brutal style and strange accessories, were once thought to be monuments of the Hyksos kings.[3] A revival of the Memphite style appears more clearly in ten limestone statues of Sesostris I from El-Lisht —beautifully executed, but dull and expressionless in comparison with the works just discussed.[4] The private sculpture of the period is characterized by the production of multitudes of small, somewhat stereotyped tomb and votive statuettes[5] and by the development of the so-called 'block'-statue, in which the figure, enveloped in a long cloak, is represented as seated on the ground with the knees drawn up before the chest.[6]

Painted reliefs from the pyramid temple of Ammenemes I[7] are transitional in style between the delicate low relief of the late Eleventh Dynasty and the bolder, more plastic type, developed in the reign of Sesostris I and standard for royal temple sculpture throughout the Twelfth Dynasty. The cold, almost metallic perfection of the new style, enriched here and there by fine detail, is admirably illustrated in the festival pavilion of Sesostris I at Karnak[8] and on numerous blocks of Sesostris III from the temple

---

[1] §v, 8, pls. 15–133 *passim*; §xiii, 21, 100–3; §xv, 24, 315–34, figs. 249–73; §xv, 1, 23–8, pls. 25–78 *passim*.

[2] §v, 8, pls. 77–92; §xi, 29, vol. iii, 184–95. See Plate 45 (*a*).

[3] §v, 8, sects. 700 ff., pls. 119–30. See also §xi, 29, vol. iii, 204–13; §xv, 8.

[4] §xv, 13, 30–8, pls. 9–13; §v, 8, pls. 26–30; §xi, 29, vol. iii, 173–4 ('École de Fayoum').

[5] §xi, 29, vol. iii, 224–88, pls. 75–94.

[6] §xv, 4; §xv, 19; §xi, 29, vol. iii, 235–7, pls. 79–80; §xv, 24, 342–5, figs. 281–2.   [7] §ii, 10, vol. iv, 77–9; §i, 10, part i, 173, fig. 103.

[8] §xii, 31, plates; §xv, 1, pls. 21, 22; §i, 10, part i, 174, fig. 104; §vi, 7, 19, 41, 53. See Plate 45 (*b*).

of Mont at El-Madāmūd.[1] The sanctuary reliefs in the pyramid temple of Sesostris I, on the other hand, are modelled on those of Phiops II of the Sixth Dynasty at south Saqqara,[2] and the revived Memphite style is also well represented in the provincial tombs of northern Upper Egypt, notably at Meir.[3] Among the hundreds of private stelae dedicated in the sanctuary of Osiris at Abydos and elsewhere a number compare favourably in style and quality with contemporaneous royal monuments.[4]

Painting and painted ornament are best studied in the tombs of Beni Hasan and the tombs and coffins of Deir el-Bersha.[5] Among the minor arts that of the jeweller reached in the Twelfth Dynasty a level of excellence never to be surpassed in Egyptian history, the jewels and other personal possessions of the royal ladies buried at Dahshūr and El-Lāhūn showing throughout the beauty of design, the technical perfection, and the impeccable taste which we associate only with the high classic moments of world civilization.[6]

Our present knowledge of the monumental architecture of the early Middle Kingdom is derived chiefly from the so-called *saff* ('row') tombs of the first kings of the Eleventh Dynasty in north-western Thebes[7] and from the ruins of the tomb-temple of Nebhepetre Mentuhotpe at Deir el-Bahri.[8] In each case the tomb ensemble comprises a great rectangular courtyard, leading to a square-piered portico, above and to the rear of which rises a small pyramid. In the *saff* tombs the portico is rock-hewn and the courtyard is cut away in front of it. In the Deir el-Bahri temple the court, enclosed within masonry walls and approached by a walled avenue, is flush with the surrounding ground surface, and the portico forms the front of a masonry terrace, on which the pyramid stands, surrounded by a double colonnade of square piers and a triple ambulatory of octagonal columns. A peristyle court behind the pyramid contains the mouth of the long, sloping passage to the king's subterranean burial chamber and opens into a

---

[1] §II, 10, vol. V, 145; §XV, 3.

[2] §I, 10, part I, 187 ff., fig. 114; §XIII, 21, 100, pl. 64A; §II, 10, vol. IV, 82.

[3] §II, 10, vol. IV, 248–53; §XIII, 21, 106–7; §XV, 20, 240–1.

[4] §XI, 29, vol. II, 483–98; §IV, 6; §II, 10, vol. V, 44–6; §XV, 16; §XV, 17.

[5] §II, 10, vol. IV, 141–50, 177 ff.; §XV, 20, 238 ff.; §XIII, 21, 104, 107–10; §XV, 21; §XV, 7; A, 10.

[6] §XV, 22, nos. 52001–3, 52019–65, 52233–60, 52641, 52663, 52669, 52689, 52702, 52712, 52811–53178; §XIV, 15, vol. I, 21, 60–70, 112–13, pls. 15–24; vol. II, 51–4, 58–68, pls. 5–13; §XV, 6; §XV, 23.

[7] §III, 32, 19–24, figs. 3, 4; §I, 24, 11, 17, 21–2, pl. 33, See above, p. 476, n. 4.

[8] §V, 15; §VI, 7, 129–35; §VIII, 6, *passim*; §XI, 29, vol. II, 158–64.

columned hall and a screen-walled sanctuary, partially cut back
into the cliffs. Six small shrines for the royal princesses, lined up
in a row behind the pyramid, were elaborately adorned with
carved and painted false doors and bold, coloured reliefs. The
temple grove of sycomore-fig trees and tamarisk shrubs was carefully laid out in the forecourt of the temple on either side of the
axial ramp leading up to the terrace. Much of the effectiveness
of this remarkable building is due to the skilful manner in which
it was adapted to its imposing natural setting.

The pyramids of the kings of the Twelfth Dynasty at El-Lisht,
Dahshūr, El-Lāhūn, and Hawāra followed the Old Kingdom
type, but were smaller and of inferior construction.[1] All were
cased with limestone, but only the pyramid of Ammenemes I was
built throughout of stone,[2] the others being either of rubble-
filled cellular construction or of mud brick. The grey granite cap-
stone from the pyramid of Ammenemes III at Dahshūr is adorned
with solar emblems, a pair of *wedjat*-eyes, and a series of appropriate inscriptions.[3] The best preserved of the pyramid temples,
that of Sesostris I, was a close replica of the temple of Phiops II
at south Saqqara.[4] The inner of the two massive enclosure walls
surrounding the pyramid of Sesostris I was of limestone, elaborately carved with colossal panels bearing the names of the king
and surmounted by figures of the royal falcon in high relief.[5] In
the area between the walls ten small, sharp-angled pyramids were
provided for the members of the king's family. Elsewhere, the
royal wives, sons and daughters were buried beneath mastabas of
brick or limestone. Round about each royal enclosure lay an extensive cemetery of mastabas and pit-tombs for the officials of the
reign and their families, in conformity with the Old Kingdom
practice.

In the rock-cut tomb chapels of the nomarchs at Beni Hasan,
Deir el-Bersha, Deir Rīfa, and Aswān a portico with two or more
columns gives access to a columned hall and, beyond, to a smaller
room or niche with a statue of the deceased owner.[6] Rectangular
piers or polygonal columns of the type called by Champollion

---

[1] §xiii, 12, 229–39; §ii, 10, vol. iv, 77–85, 100, 101, 107–11; §xi, 29, vol. ii,
167–94; §xv, 11; §xii, 16, 218–36.

[2] §xv, 14, 184 ff., fig. 3; §xi, 17, 11, figs. 9, 10; §xi, 29, vol. ii, 169; §i, 10,
part i, 172–3.

[3] §xv, 15.

[4] §ii, 10, vol. iv, 82; §i, 10, part i, 183; §xii, 16, 220–5, fig. 44. Cf. §xii, 27,
vols. ii, iii. See also above, p. 515, n. 2.

[5] §ii, 10, vol. iv, 83; §i, 10, part i, 183, 185, fig. 112.

[6] §ii, 10, vol. iv, 141–51, 177–81; vol. v, 233, 238–9; §ii, 2; §xi, 21.

'proto-Doric' appear in both the porticos and the halls and in the latter we also find brightly painted plant columns of the well-known 'clustered', or 'bundled', type. In the tombs at Qāw el-Kebīr the courts, porticos, and rock-cut halls and shrines are arranged in terraces, connected by flights of steps.[1]

The shrine of Renenutet at Medīnet el-Ma'ādi, built by Ammenemes III and IV, comprises a triple sanctuary and shallow vestibule, preceded by a porch with two clustered papyrus columns and perhaps at one time by an open courtyard.[2] The well-preserved little structure, which measures less than twelve yards from front to back, is covered with reliefs and inscriptions of characteristic Twelfth Dynasty style, but somewhat coarse in their execution and proportions. Remains of the foundations of the temple of Mont at Tōd, as rebuilt by Sesostris I, show a free-standing sanctuary or repository for the image of the god surrounded by a vestibule with nine small chambers and approached through a transverse hall with four rectangular piers.[3] An elaboration of this plan appeared in the larger temple to Mont at El-Madāmūd, erected by Sesostris III over a primitive Osireion of Old Kingdom date.[4] Behind the sanctuary in the temple at El-Madāmūd was an open court, flanked by porticos with Osiride pillars, and to the south and west of the temple proper were store-rooms, granaries, and priests' quarters—the whole contained in a great walled enclosure. Among numerous architectural elements with the name of Sesostris III, recovered at El-Madāmūd, are the parts of a small porch-like building of limestone with reliefs and inscriptions pertaining to the celebration of the *Heb Sed*, or royal jubilee festival.[5] The peripteral kiosk of Sesostris I at Karnak is decorated and inscribed in similar fashion, but is mounted on a high podium, provided at either end with a sloping ramp.[6] It, too, was evidently designed for use in connexion with the king's *Sed*-festival. Recovered piecemeal from the foundations of the third pylon of the Amun temple, the structure consists of a roofed peristyle of twelve rectangular piers originally enclosing a throne surrounded by four inner piers. It is built throughout of fine white limestone. Massive papyrus columns of red granite at Kīmān Fāris in the Faiyūm are from a monumental hall erected in the temple of Sobk by Ammenemes III.[7] The granite obelisk

---

[1] §II, 10, vol. v, 9–14; §XI, 29, vol. II, 340–5. [2] §XI, 29, vol. II, 619–20.

[3] §II, 10, vol. v, 167–9; §XI, 29, vol. II, 635–40.

[4] §II, 10, vol. v, 137, 145; §XI, 29, vol. II, 579–81, 628–34; §XV, 18.

[5] §II, 10, vol. v, 145. [6] §XII, 31. See Plate 45 (*b*).

[7] §XIV, 9; §II, 10, vol. IV, 98–9.

of Sesostris I near Matarīya was one of a pair which stood before the pylon, or towered gateway, of the temple of Re at Heliopolis.[1] This building, completely destroyed, but well known from documents of later times, was evidently a prototype of the great processional temples of the New Kingdom.

The civil and domestic architecture of the Middle Kingdom is represented by the ruins of the town which Sesostris II laid out and constructed near his pyramid at El-Lāhūn.[2] Here we find not only the simple, four-roomed dwellings of the king's workmen, but also the luxurious residences of his officials, with their courts, halls, and suites of chambers, numbering in some cases as many as seventy compartments. The appearance of the walled garden and front verandah of a great country house of the late Eleventh Dynasty is preserved in two painted wooden funerary models from the tomb of the Chancellor Meketre at Thebes.[3]

Military architecture may be studied in the harbour fortifications of Elephantine,[4] in the numerous brick-and-timber forts of Lower Nubia and the Second Cataract region,[5] and in two massive brick structures at Kerma, one of which—the so-called 'Eastern Defūfa'—was built under Ammenemes I or II and extensively enlarged under Ammenemes III.[6]

XVI. RELIGION AND FUNERARY BELIEFS

During the First Intermediate Period the formal religion of Egypt reverted to a stage of development generally similar to that of prehistoric times. With the collapse of the Memphite power the state religion, fostered by the pharaohs of the Old Kingdom and the priesthood of Heliopolis, ceased temporarily to exist as a unifying influence throughout the land, and men everywhere turned again to their local divinities and restored to them much of their primeval powers and significance.[7]

Among the more obscure local deities of Heracleopolitan times were the gods Mont of Hermonthis and Amun of Thebes, destined in the ensuing centuries to succeed one another as the

---

[1] §II, 10, vol. IV, 60; §XII, 39, 119–33; §XV, 2, 195–8.

[2] §II, 10, vol. IV, 111; §XI, 29, vol. II, 980–4. See also §XV, 2, 73–5.

[3] §VIII, 7, 17–19, pls. 9–12, 56–7.

[4] §VII, 1, 273 (4B); §XIII, 4, 157. See also §XIII, 6, 191–2.

[5] §XII, 37, 81, 82, 126, 128, 129, 142–56; §III, 23, 80–98; §XIII, 4; §XIII, 6; §XIII, 3; §XII, 15; §XII, 17; §XII, 18.

[6] §XII, 37, 175–6; §III, 23, 65, 75, 103–9, 114–15.

[7] §III, 15, 300 ff.; §III, 31, 147.

leaders of a new state religion, established by the Kings of the Eleventh and Twelfth Dynasties.

Mont, a falcon god probably of southern origin, is mentioned occasionally in the Pyramid Texts of the late Old Kingdom and is represented among the divinities of Upper Egypt in the funerary temple of King Phiops II of the Sixth Dynasty.[1] His principal cult centre was the town of Iuny, ancient capital of the Theban Nome, later, through association with Iunu, or On (Heliopolis), called the 'On-of-Mont', whence the Greek name, 'Hermonthis', and the modern place name, 'Armant'.[2] Mont was worshipped also at Djeret (Tōd), Madu (El-Madāmūd), and Karnak;[3] at Armant, Tōd, and El-Madāmūd he was associated with a local bull god, later known as Buchis, whose cult was also centred in the town of Hermonthis.[4] In reliefs of the early Middle Kingdom he appears with the disk and plumes of a solar deity and was evidently regarded as the Upper Egyptian counterpart of the great god Re of Heliopolis, with whom, by a process of syncretism, he was merged to produce the deity Mont-Re.[5] As the patron, or family god, of the Mentuhotpe kings of Thebes he was elevated during the Eleventh Dynasty to the first rank among the deities of Egypt and probably at this time began also to assume his special function as a god of war and a bringer of victory.

Mont's supremacy, however, was short-lived, for, with the accession of Ammenemes I, the founder of the Twelfth Dynasty, there was established a new state god, whose leadership of the Egyptian pantheon was to continue unchallenged as long as men of Theban origin or affiliations remained in power, and for many centuries thereafter. This was Amun ('the Hidden One'), originally a god of the air and a member of the ogdoad of Hermopolis, whose installation at Thebes took place early in the First Intermediate Period under circumstances which are still obscure.[6] The close resemblance of the form of Amun worshipped at Luxor to the neighbouring divinity, Min of Koptos, suggests that the transfer was accomplished by way of Koptos.[7] Like Min, Amun of Luxor was represented in human form, as an ithyphallic male figure, wearing a head-dress with two tall plumes and having the

[1] §xvi, 4, 475–9; §iii, 15, 340, 362–3; §xvi, 30, sects. 46, 224; §iii, 31, 26, 161; §xvi, 22; §xvi, 3.
[2] §ii, 5, vol. ii, 22* (A 332); §xiv, 8, vol. i, 54–5.
[3] §xvi, 3, 6–16; §xvi, 22, 75–85; §xi, 29, vol. ii, 917 ff.
[4] §xvi, 24, vol. ii, 45 ff.; §iii, 15, 343; §xvi, 26, 40 ff.; §xvi, 22, 87 ff.
[5] §iii, 15, 341, pl. 7 a.
[6] §iii, 24; §xvi, 4, 31–7; §iii, 15, 344 ff.
[7] §iii, 31, 147–8; §xvi, 4, 31–2; §iii, 15, 348. See also §iii, 25, sects. 24–7, 111.

so-called 'flail' crossed over his upraised right arm. To assure the legitimacy of Amun's position as the official god of the kingdom his royal devotees of the Twelfth Dynasty arbitrarily associated him with the ancient solar divinity of Heliopolis and created the composite deity, Amen-Re, later known far and wide as the 'King of the Gods'.[1] The principal shrine of Amun, at Karnak, was called 'the Most Select of Places', and here there were assigned to him as wife and child the vulture goddess, Mut of Ishru, and the falcon-headed lunar god, Khons.[2]

No survey of the religion of the Middle Kingdom, however brief, can fail to take cognizance of the importance achieved under the rulers of the Twelfth and Thirteenth Dynasties by the crocodile god, Sobk, or Suchos, primarily a divinity of the water and of vegetation resident in the Faiyūm, but with cult places scattered up and down the Nile from the Delta to the First Cataract.[3] At Shedet (Crocodilopolis) and Dja (Medīnet el-Maʿādi) in the Faiyūm and at Ombos in Upper Egypt the god was worshipped in company with his consort, the cobra goddess, Renenutet, and his 'guest', a form of the elder Horus.[4] Sobk, Lord of Sumenu (Rizeiqāt), a few miles south of Thebes, is mentioned with ever increasing frequency as the patron of the kings of the Twelfth Dynasty, as are also Sobk of Hes, Henet, Seya, and Busiris in the Delta, and numerous other local forms of the deity.[5] The crocodile god was not only affiliated in the minds of his worshippers with the great divinity of vegetation and resurrection, Osiris,[6] but also, like Mont, Amun, and Khnum, was drawn into the ancient solar cycle and given the name Sobk-Re.[7]

With the fall of the Old Kingdom the funerary rites and rituals, formerly reserved for the pharaoh, were taken over first by the great provincial nobles and then, gradually, by all Egyptians sufficiently well-to-do to provide themselves with the necessary equipment and texts.[8] In this 'democratization of the Hereafter' the solar version of the life to come, ruled over by the sun god

---

[1] §xvi, 4, 34; §iii, 15, 345.

[2] §iii, 25, sects. 41–61; §iii, 15, 352–5; §xvi, 4, 140–4, 491–4. On the name of the Amun temple at Karnak see §iii, 25, sects. 15 ff.; §xiv, 8, vol. i, 68.

[3] §iii, 15, 14–19, 117, 134; §xvi, 17; §xvi, 27; §xvi, 21; §xvi, 4, 755–9.

[4] §iii, 15, 16, 56, 152, cf. 430; §xvi, 33, 545 f.; §xvi, 11; §i, 10, part i, 181.

[5] §xvi, 21, 123–57, 169–71; §i, 10, part i, 201, 246, 261, 341–4; §xvi, 14, 5 nn. 1–4; §xvi, 15; §xvi, 18; §xvi, 34.

[6] §iii, 15, 18, 134, 285, 403; §xvi, 20, 147; §xvi, 4, 756; §iii, 31, 59 n. 1.
§xvi, 4, 757; §iii, 31, 21, 160; §xvi, 21, 119–20.
§xvi, 20, 160 ff.; §iii, 31, 86 ff.; §xvi, 5, 257 ff.; §xvi, 25; §xiv, 17, vol. i, vii–viii.

Horus or Re, evidently remained in favour under the Heracleopolitan rulers and dominates the texts inscribed in the earlier
coffins of the period.[1] At the end of the Heracleopolitan Period,
however, the grandiose theories of the theologians of Heliopolis
began to give way to the more appealing and more understandable
doctrines embodied in the legends of the hero-god, Osiris; and
the ascendancy of Osiris over Re as the principal god of the dead
and ruler of the Hereafter is clearly reflected in the funerary texts
and monuments of the Middle Kingdom. It is no longer to
Heliopolis that the deceased Egyptian makes his pilgrimage by
ship, but to the sanctuary of Osiris at Abydos, the legendary site
of the tomb of the god.[2] 'To be in the following of the Great God,
Lord of Abydos', was now the wish of every Egyptian; but, since
few could actually be buried beside the tomb of the god and even
a cenotaph was beyond the reach of all save the very wealthy, it
became the habit for each pilgrim to erect a funerary stela in the
sacred enclosure at Abydos and so associate himself permanently
with his divine prototype in immortality.[3] The chief occasions for
the pilgrimages to Abydos were the yearly festivals held there in
honour of Osiris, during which were re-enacted his death, his
burial, and his triumphant resurrection.[4] Added impetus to the
growth of Abydos as a great national shrine was undoubtedly provided by the Theban kings of the early Eleventh Dynasty, who
saw the advantages of associating themselves, not only with the
traditional home of the first pharaohs of united Egypt, but also
with a god whose rapidly increasing popularity was already over-
shadowing the solar cult of their rivals, the kings of Heracleopolis.[5] When, in the Twelfth Dynasty, the capital was moved
back to the region of Memphis there was a natural tendency on
the part of the kings and courtiers to return to the burial customs
of the Old Kingdom and revive the ancient solar formulae preserved in the Pyramid Texts.[6] This, however, was a political and, one
feels, a superficial gesture and in no way diminished the almost
universal belief in an Osirian immortality and the wholehearted
support of the cult of the god at Abydos, Busiris, and elsewhere.

It is in the reign of Nebhepetre Mentuhotpe of the Eleventh
Dynasty that we first find the Osirian epithet, 'justified' (literally,

[1] §xvi, 20, 226 ff. Cf. §xvi, 5, 274 ff.
[2] §xvi, 20, 230–6; §iii, 15, 333, 336 ff.; §xvi, 5, 275–90; §xiii, 23, 397 ff.
[3] §xvi, 5, 285 ff.; §xvi, 20, 231; §iii, 31, 95–6. See also above, p. 515, n. 4.
[4] §xvi, 20, 236 ff.; §xvi, 5, 287 ff.; §xvi, 29.
[5] §xvi, 20, 230; §iii, 31, 93–4; §i, 24, 15.
[6] §xvi, 20, 259–86; §iii, 31, 98–100. See also above, p. 520, n. 8 and nn. 1–3 above.

'true of voice'), appended to the name of the deceased Egyptian to indicate that, like the god with whom he is identified, the dead person has established his moral fitness and his right to a blessed immortality.[1] Henceforth it is used with such regularity in all funerary inscriptions that it comes to mean little more than 'deceased'. Equally common is the custom of referring to the dead man or woman as 'the Osiris, so-and-so', or as 'this Osiris', a practice derived from the Pyramid Texts where the title was originally applied only to the king.[2]

The Eleventh Dynasty also witnessed a significant change in the ancient formula whereby offerings were called forth for the dead. Instead of accompanying a god (Osiris or Anubis) in the presentation of the funerary offerings, the king is now said to make his offering to the god, that the latter may in turn shower blessings upon the deceased.[3] The altered formula undoubtedly reflects the common practice of re-distributing to private tomb-chapels the excess of the offerings presented by royal command to the temples of the gods.

Our knowledge of the funerary literature of ancient Egypt between the end of the Sixth Dynasty and the end of the Twelfth Dynasty is based to a very great extent on texts written in cursive hieroglyphic script on the interior surfaces of the rectangular wooden coffins characteristic of the period.[4] Here, in addition to excerpts from the Pyramid Texts, we find a new series of magical spells and incantations, composed on behalf of persons of non-royal rank and designed to protect them from dangers and discomforts in the Afterworld and to endow them with a wide variety of special powers and privileges. These spells, which we call the Coffin Texts, are peculiar to the Heracleopolitan Period and the Middle Kingdom and do not occur again in Egyptian funerary literature until Saïte times, when some of them were revived.[5] In the same coffins is preserved a group of similar texts which constitute an early version of the so-called Book of the Dead, a collection of funerary writings best known from papyri of the New Kingdom and later periods.[6] In a few coffins from Deir

---

[1] §VII, 1, 122–4; §III, 31, 97; §XVI, 5, 33–4, 147, 175, 256. See also Maspero, *Bibl. égyptol.* I, 93–114. See, however, §I, 20, 256, n. *b*. [Ed.].

[2] §XVI, 5, 256; §XVI, 20, 151, 227; §XVI, 10, 55, 119.

[3] §XVI, 10, 79–93; §III, 9, 170–3 (Excursus B); §III, 31, 97.

[4] §XVI, 8; §XVI, 32. See also §XVI, 20, 160–229; §III, 31, 86–91, 127–8; §XVI, 5, 272–94 *passim*; §XVI, 6, 149–68; §XVI, 31, 10–14.

[5] §XVI, 31, 20 n. 1; §III, 9, sect. 13 (p. 19).

[6] §XVI, 8, *passim*; §XVI, 9; §XVI, 1, 110–49; §XVI, 2, 177; §XVI, 23; §XVI, 19, 77 ff.; §XVI, 16, 66; in §XVI, 7, 39–47.

el-Bersha there occurs a map of the Afterworld, accompanied by an appropriate text for the guidance of the deceased, which together have been named the Book of the Two Ways.[1]

XVII. LITERATURE

However the Ninth to Twelfth Dynasties as a whole may have been evaluated by succeeding generations, there can be no doubt that they were generally—and deservedly—recognized as having sponsored the golden age of Egyptian secular literature.[2] The preservation of the many fine stories, didactic treatises, and pseudo-prophetic works of this time is due to the fact that for centuries they were used as model compositions in the schools of ancient Egypt and were copied again and again on papyri, writing boards, and ostraca by student-scribes of the Twelfth to Seventeenth Dynasties and the New Kingdom.[3] Middle Egyptian, the 'concise and elegant' language employed in these compositions, remained the classical idiom of Egypt well into the New Kingdom and in its later form it survived for some monumental and literary purposes right down to Graeco-Roman times.[4]

Since many of the works in question were based on actual events and conditions, they contain historical material of the utmost value, not only on the Heracleopolitan Period and the Middle Kingdom themselves, but also on the Old Kingdom and on the meagrely documented interval which followed the collapse of the Sixth Dynasty. We have, therefore, already had occasion to cite the subject-matter and the historical, political, or social background of such famous compositions as the *Tales of King Cheops and the Magicians*, the *Instruction for Kagemni*, the *Maxims of Djedefhor* and *of Ptahhotpe*, the *Story of King Neferkare and General Sisenet*, the *Admonitions of an Egyptian Sage*,[5] the *Tale of the Eloquent Peasant* (p. 465 above), the *Instruction for King Merykare* (p. 466 above), the *Prophecy of Neferty* (pp. 494 and 495 above), the *Instruction of King Ammenemes I* (p. 498 above), and the *Story of Sinuhe* (p. 499 above).

To these may be added other well-known works, each representative of one of the several categories of Heracleopolitan and

---

[1] §xvi, 28; §xvi, 13; §iii, 31, 91–3, 107; §xvi, 20, 287–9, fig. 7.
[2] See, for example, §x, 3, xxiv–xxv; §xvi, 7, 15–16; §x, 17, 166.
[3] §xvii, 66; §xvii, 46; §xvii, 31.
[4] §iii, 8, sects. 2, 4; §x, 17, 166; §xvii, 57, 12–51 *passim*.
[5] See above, ch. xiv, sects. i, iii, vi

Middle Kingdom literature. The *Story of the Shipwrecked Sailor* is a Sinbad-like romance, related by an Egyptian seaman to his master as an object lesson in self-control and confidence under adversity.[1] During a trading voyage on the Red Sea the ship of the sailor founders and he is cast ashore on an island,[2] inhabited by a monstrous, but kindly serpent, who eventually sends him home laden with gifts and good advice. The need for conscientious trained personnel in the newly re-established national administration evidently inspired the composition, in the reign of King Ammenemes I, of the so-called Book of *Kemyt* ('the Sum')[3] and, shortly thereafter, of the Instruction of the Scribe Achthoes, son of Duauf, better known as the *Satire on the Trades*.[4] The former is largely an anthology of conventional formulae of address and other samples of good prose composition, but ends with a few words of advice, including a favourable comment on employment as a scribe in the offices of the royal Residence. The latter, addressed to its author's son on his way to school, concerns itself chiefly with the merits of a formal education and the advantages of the scribe's profession over all others. Its major interest lies in its amusingly derogatory descriptions of the occupations of the uneducated. The remarkable *Dispute of a Man, Weary of Life*, with his own soul, a partially metrical composition of surprising philosophical and psychological profundity, is clearly a product of the interval of social and spiritual unrest attendant upon the fall of the Old Kingdom.[5] Here, following a prolonged verbal conflict between the reasonable and emotional elements in the unhappy man's make-up, suicide is contemplated, with the soul, however, holding out against this course of action to the end. To the same fashionably pessimistic group of writings belongs the later *Collection of Words of the Wēʿb-Priest Khakheperre-sonbe*, in the surviving introduction to which the author yearns for new phrases to describe the misery which he pretends to see about him.[6] Fragments of or references to at least eighteen other literary works of Dynasties IX to XII cover a variety of subjects, from the elevation of the common man to the pleasures of hunting

[1] §x, 3, 29–35; §xi, 3, 41–8; §vii, 1, 275 (6); §xvi, 7, 123–4; §xvii, 46, 35; §xvii, 61, 275–87; §xvii, 64; §xvii, 53.

[2] Identified by Wainwright (§xvii, 65) as Zeberged, or St John's Island, off the African coast of the Red Sea near Cape Benās. See also §xvii, 38.

[3] §x, 11, 4–7, and the references cited there.

[4] *Ibid.* See, especially, §xvii, 6. See also §x, 3, 67–72; §i, 23, 432–4; §xvi, 7, 103–4; §x, 11, 4–5; §xvii, 46, 36–7.

[5] §xvii, 16; §xvi, 7, 113–14, 127; §xvii, 59; §vii, 1, 275 (9).

[6] §xvii, 17, 95–110; §xvii, 19, 40 n. 8; §x, 3, 108–10; §xvii, 46, 37 (no. 25).

and fishing, and serve to round out our picture of this most articulate and prolific era.[1]

Long mythological epics, of which portions are preserved in later copies (for example, the *Destruction of Mankind*,[2] the *Outwitting of Re by Isis*,[3] the *Contendings of Horus and Seth*[4]), undoubtedly existed during the Middle Kingdom;[5] but the narrative form best known to us from this period is the short story. Among the stories the *Tales of King Cheops and the Magicians*[6] and the adventures of the Shipwrecked Sailor[7] are characterized by the simple objectivity of the content and the unadorned directness of the narrative style. The same is true of the *Tale of the Eloquent Peasant*[8] until we reach the point where the peasant begins to exhibit his eloquence in a welter of elaborate and, to us, far-fetched metaphors. Much of the charm, naïveté, and humour of the popular narratives is present in the classic of Middle Kingdom literature, the *Story of Sinuhe*.[9] Here, however, both the structure and style are more formal and artificial, and throughout there is a self-conscious striving after effect—often highly successful, but none the less obviously studied. The main theme of this adventure-filled autobiography[10] is the Egyptian abroad and its most unusual feature is the manner in which the character of Sinuhe is revealed through his clearly established attitudes and reactions to the various situations in which he finds himself.

Though such tales were contrived by their writers to beguile and amuse their audiences there is scarcely one which does not contain a motive over and above that of pure entertainment. Three of the stories related to King Cheops by his sons are simple tales of magic, but the fourth, and by far the longest, establishes in great detail the divine origin of the founders of the Fifth Dynasty.[11] Both the Shipwrecked Sailor and his friend, the serpent, tell tales which are patently intended to point a moral and bolster the spirits, not only of their fictional listeners, but of all who imagine themselves in desperate straits. The *Story of the Peasant* was obviously a device whereby its author might at one and the same time

---

[1] §XVII, 46, 33–40 (nos. 9, 12, 16, 18–21, 26–35); §XVII, 20; §XVII, 2; §XVII, 7, 1–39, pls. 1–16.

[2] §XVII, 37, 53–73; §XVII, 45, 26–37, 142–3; §X, 3, 47–9; §1, 23, 10–11.

[3] §1, 23, 12–14; §XVII, 43, 18–22.

[4] §XVII, 18; §XVII, 54. See also §XVI, 7, 128–9; §XVII, 43, 22–5; §1, 23, 14–17.

[5] §XVII, 43, 18 ff.   [6] §XVII, 13; §XVII, 14; §X, 3, 36–47.

[7] See above, p. 524, n. 1.

[8] §1, 22; §1, 21; §1, 23, 407–10; §XVII, 32.   [9] See above, p. 499, n. 2.

[10] Derived, perhaps, from an inscription in Sinuhe's tomb at El-Lisht (§X, 11, 91).

[11] See above, pp. 148, 168, 179

display his own wit and eloquence, attribute unexpected wisdom
and elegance of speech to a person of humble station, and bring a
bold indictment against the corruption and social injustice of his
time.[1] The glorification of King Sesostris I is a theme which runs
all through the *Story of Sinuhe*; and in two places the narrative is
interrupted while Sinuhe in one case recites a hymn in honour of
his sovereign and in the other quotes a decree indicative of the
king's magnanimity and kindness.[2] A text recounting Sesostris I's
dedication of the temple of Atum at Heliopolis provides an early
example of the historical, or royal, novel (*Königsnovelle*), wherein
the pharaoh's excellent plans to serve a deity (or win a victory)
are presented by him before a sometimes sceptical council of
royal officials, whose response is then followed by the successful
execution of the project in hand.[3]

The tendency of the writers of the Old and Middle Kingdoms
to moralize and become didactic was given free play in a much
admired literary form, called the *shōyet*, or 'instruction'.[4] This is
normally a collection of proverbs, maxims, rules of conduct, rules
of ethics, and items of sound, wordly advice with which a father
prepares his son to meet the problems of life and the requirements
of his station or office. One of the earliest 'instructions', attributed to the Vizier Ptahhotpe of the reign of King Isesi of the
Fifth Dynasty, concerns itself chiefly with good manners, dealings
with superiors and inferiors, and relations with friends and family,
and prides itself on its elegant literary style.[5] The witty and much
beloved *Satire on the Trades* was written by the scribe Achthoes of
Sebennytos, an accomplished author who lived under and served
the first two rulers of the Twelfth Dynasty.[6] Its principal theme is
summarized in the words, 'There is no calling which is free of
direction except that of the scribe; it is he who does the directing'.
Though the *Instruction for King Merykare* and the *Instruction of
King Ammenemes I* are now recognized as having been composed
under the rulers to whom they are addressed for the purpose of
strengthening the dynastic succession,[7] both are works of great

---

[1] See §xvi, 7, 127–8; §i, 23, 407–10; §xvii, 32; §xvii, 31, 79–93.

[2] See §x, 11, 94–101.

[3] *Ibid.* 17, 30, 136–9; §xii, 9; §xvii, 30; §xvi, 7, 143 ff.

[4] §xvii, 1; §xvii, 3; §xvi, 7, 90–110; §iii, 8, sect. 15 (pp. 24a–b).

[5] See §i, 23, 412–14, and the references cited there. See also §xvii, 69; §xvii, 15; §xvii, 7, 52–3, pls. 28–30; §xvi, 7, 96–100.

[6] See above, p. 524, n. 4. On the author of the Satire see especially §x, 11, 4–7, 67 ff.

[7] See above, p. 466, n. 3, and p. 499, n. 1. Among the numerous discussions of these two works see especially §xvii, 63; §x, 11, 61–86.

literary merit and both have enjoyed an enduring and well-deserved popularity. Drawing upon his own experiences and freely admitting his own mistakes Merykare's royal father is made to advise his son on what policies he should pursue in the government of his kingdom, what behaviour is to be expected of him both as a king and as a man, and what his attitude should be toward a deity who is consistently referred to as 'God'.[1] Despite the fact that the *Instruction of King Ammenemes I* appears to have been composed by the scribe Achthoes[2] after the assassination of its alleged author, there is a vigour and sincerity in its bitter narrative and cynical teaching which make it seem as if the dead king were indeed speaking from his tomb to point out his own achievements and benevolence and castigate the treacherous and ungrateful aspirants to the throne who were responsible for his death. Among the so-called 'loyalist teachings' the *Instruction* formerly ascribed to the treasurer Sehetepibre of the late Twelfth Dynasty commends obedience to the king as a means to success from the point of view of a high-ranking official,[3] while the *Instruction of a Man to his Son* endorses the same policy, but is addressed to a larger and less distinguished audience and embodies the notion of the elevation of the little man through his submission to the will of the pharaoh.[4]

The deep note of pessimism which pervades the contemplative and quasi-prophetic literature of Dynasties IX to XII had its origin undoubtedly in the years of ruin and disaster which attended and followed the fall of the Old Kingdom. The prophet Ipuwer, whose seemingly endless lamentations in prose and verse portray a state of national chaos, may actually have witnessed some of the conditions which he describes with evident gusto and considerable exaggeration;[5] and it is probable, as we have already noted, that the ideas incorporated in the *Life-weary Man's Dispute with his Soul* were direct products of a troubled period in Egyptian history.[6] On the other hand, unless he is describing a brief interval of disorder at the end of the Eleventh Dynasty, the wails of the prophet Neferty would appear to be as artificial as his prophecy, for it is clear that he lived during the reign of King

---

[1] See above, p. 466, n. 3. See also §XVI, 7, 100–2; §XVII, 55, 33, 45–7; §XVII, 10, 153.

[2] The author of the *Satire on the Trades* (see §X, 11, 4–5, 67; §XVI, 7, 102–3).

[3] §X, 11, 117–24; §XVII, 34; §XVII, 27, 21 ff.; §XVII, 35, 269 ff.

[4] §X, 11, 124–7.

[5] §XVII, 17; §I, 23, 441–4; §XVII, 67, 106–21 *passim*; §XVII, 55, 8–24, 41–5, 52–5.

[6] See above, p. 524, n. 5. See also §XVII, 55, 48–58.

Ammenemes I, the messiah whose coming, he 'predicts', will put an end to the ills which he bemoans.[1] The same would apply to the complaints of Khakheperre-sonbe,[2] whose name links him with King Sesostris II and, therefore, with a period when Egypt, far from being in dire straits, was nearing a peak of prosperity and well-being.

In addition to the metrical compositions already mentioned, the secular poetry of the Middle Kingdom is represented by a fine hymn to King Sesostris III, preserved in a papyrus from El-Lāhūn,[3] and by half a dozen short songs of a funerary or ceremonial nature, sung by harpers and recorded on tomb-stelae and in tomb-reliefs.[4] These lyrics are composed in short lines of approximately equal length, frequently grouped together in stanzas. The exact nature of the metrical structure of the lines cannot as yet be determined, but it is probably a free rhythm rather than a rigid metre. The repetition of the same word or group of words at the beginning of each line or each stanza is a common device in Egyptian poetry, as is also the juxtaposition of two parallel expressions with approximately the same meaning. Paronomasia and alliteration, although not confined to compositions in verse, are natural to and frequently employed in this class of writing.[5]

Though there seems to be no cogent evidence for the existence in dynastic Egypt of a popular theatre, in which plays were presented by troupes of professional actors for the entertainment of the general public,[6] sacramental dramas, performed within the precincts of temples at seasonal religious festivals and on other special occasions, had by the Middle Kingdom reached an advanced state of development. Portions of the scripts for two such plays, the *Memphite Drama* and the *Coronation Drama*, are preserved, respectively, in a late copy inscribed on the so-called Shabako Stone in the British Museum,[7] and in an illustrated papyrus of the late Twelfth or early Thirteenth Dynasty found in a tomb beneath the Ramesseum at Thebes.[8] The text for the

---

[1] See above, p. 494 ,nn. 1–5, and p. 495, n. 4.   [2] See above, p. 524, n. 6.

[3] §xii, 23, 1–3, pls. 1–3. See §x, 11, 128–30.

[4] §xvii, 36, 187–91; §xvii, 56; §xvii, 22.

[5] §x, 3, xxx–xxxiv; §xvii, 43, 55–69; §xvi, 7, 26–9, 158 ff.; §xvii, 26; §xvii, 27; §xvii, 23.

[6] For conflicting interpretations of the evidence see §xvii, 11, 231 ff., and §xvii, 62.

[7] §xvii, 52, 1–80; §xvii, 48; §xvii, 4; §xvii, 33; §i, 23, 4–6; §xvii, 21, 61–2, 382, 407–11.

[8] §xvii, 52, 81–258, pls. 1–22; §xvii, 49; §xvii, 21, 52–4, 382–403. Cf. §xvii, 11, 226–30.

Memphite Drama, composed apparently in the Fifth Dynasty[1] and concerned chiefly with the magnification of the god Ptah, consists of a series of dialogues preceded and linked by a continuous narrative and accompanied by appropriate stage directions. The Ramesseum text, adapted for use in connexion with the coronation of King Sesostris I, but undoubtedly of more ancient origin, provides us with the dialogue spoken by the characters in the play, a running description of the ritual acts performed by them, and interpretations of these acts in terms of the Osirian myths on which the drama is based. On a well-known stela in Berlin Ikhernofret, an official of the reign of Sesostris III, describes with gusto how he played the part of the god Horus in the passion play, or 'mystery', of Osiris at Abydos.[2]

Mention should also be made of a number of extremely interesting technical works—medical and mathematical treatises—compiled during or before the Middle Kingdom, but preserved chiefly in manuscript copies of later date.[3] The earliest of these works is a collection of surgical cases, mainly injuries, listed in order from the head downwards through the whole body and designated as belonging to one or another of three classes: curable, doubtful, and incurable. Diagnoses and instructions for treatment accompany the curable and doubtful cases, while the incurable injuries or conditions are described and diagnosed purely for their theoretical interest. The Edwin Smith Surgical Papyrus, wherein a portion of this remarkable work is preserved, dates from the Hyksos Period, but the original treatise appears to have been composed in the early years of the Old Kingdom.[4] Similarly, three well-known medical manuscripts of the early New Kingdom—the Ebers Papyrus,[5] the Hearst Papyrus,[6] and Berlin Papyrus 3038[7]—are clearly compilations of earlier material, dating back to the Middle Kingdom or to the centuries immediately following the Middle Kingdom. These works, intended for use by physicians, consist of collections of recipes to be administered for a great variety of ailments, which are briefly identified according to their salient symptoms and are occasionally diagnosed.

[1] §xvii, 48; §xvii, 33, 6–16.
[2] §xvi, 29, 20–33 (lines 17–24); §1, 23, 329–30; §xvii, 21, 41–2.
[3] On Egyptian medicine and medical texts in general see §xvii, 29; and on Egyptian mathematics, §xvii, 41, 108–12, 301–80, 413–51; §xvii, 39; §xvii, 40; §xvii, 51; §xvii, 24; §xvi, 7, 176–81.
[4] §xvii, 5; §xvii, 29, vol. ii, 88–9.
[5] §xvii, 12; §xvii, 29, vol. ii, 90–2; §xvii, 28.
[6] §xvii, 47; §xvii, 29, vol. ii, 92–3.
[7] §xvii, 68; §xvii, 29, vol. ii, 93–4.

Though tinged with magic and folklore and based more on observation and experience than on true scientific knowledge, they reflect, on the whole, a sober and sensible approach to the study and practice of medicine. Of the same general type are portions of a treatise on diseases of women and fragments of a veterinary manual occurring among the late Middle Kingdom papyri from El-Lāhūn.[1] A tomb of approximately the same date beneath the Ramesseum in western Thebes yielded the fragments of two magico-medical texts and a medical treatise 'dealing with muscular complaints, rheumatic troubles and stiffness in general'.[2]

The El-Lāhūn papyri include also some mathematical fragments,[3] but the principal source of information on ancient Egyptian mathematics is the Rhind Papyrus in the British Museum, a document copied in the reign of the Hyksos king, Apophis I, from an older manuscript compiled under Ammenemes III of the Twelfth Dynasty.[4] Numerous sample problems in arithmetic, worked out and explained in this papyrus, show that the Egyptian of the Middle Kingdom was well acquainted with the four arithmetical operations—addition, subtraction, multiplication, and division—could handle fractions, and possessed a well-defined system of decimal notation. Problems in practical geometry include finding the areas or volumes of various geometric figures—the rectangle, the triangle, the circle, the cylinder—and indicate a rudimentary understanding of the relationships between the angles and sides of a right triangle. The Rhind Papyrus was found in western Thebes and with it was found a leather roll on which had been copied in duplicate twenty-six sums in addition of fractions.[5] A somewhat earlier work, the Moscow Mathematical Papyrus, contains, among other problems, a very interesting calculation of the volume of a truncated pyramid.[6] On two writing boards in the Cairo Museum a mathematician of the Twelfth Dynasty has worked out expressions of various fractions of the bushel (ḥekat) in terms of the standard divisions of the measure.[7] An algebraic problem involving the solution of two-term quadratic equations is preserved on the scraps of a mathematical papyrus of the Middle Kingdom in Berlin.[8]

[1] §xii, 23, 5–14, pls. 5–7.
[2] §xvii, 20, 9, pls. 7–17; §xvii, 2, 15–34, pls. 10–23.
[3] §xii, 23, 15–18, pl. 8.   [4] §xvii, 8; §xvii, 42.
[5] §xvii, 25.   [6] §xvii, 58; §xvii, 44; §xvii, 60.
[7] §xvii, 9.   [8] §xvii, 50.

In addition to the medical and mathematical works just mentioned the great finds of Middle Kingdom papyri at El-Lāhūn include a large number of interesting legal and business documents, pages from official and temple journals, original letters and model letters, scraps of two stories, and the hymn to King Sesostris III referred to above.[1] The Brooklyn Museum possesses a fragmentary papyrus with part of a prison register drawn up in the reign of King Ammenemes III, to which were subsequently appended copies of an administrative letter and two royal decrees, a long list of Egyptian and Asiatic servants, and a deed covering the transfer of property from a man to his wife.[2]

Among the Ramesseum papyri of the late Middle Kingdom are fragments of the earliest Egyptian onomasticon now known.[3] This catalogue of physical entities, classified and grouped according to their kinds, comprises lists of towns and fortresses, terms used by butchers in describing the anatomy of an ox, and the names of many different plants, liquids, fish, animals, cakes, confections, cereals, condiments, and fruits.

[1] §xii, 23, 1–4, 19–20, pls. 1–4, 9–37; §xii, 7; §xii, 45.
[2] §iii, 12.   [3] §ii, 5, vol. i, 6–23, pls. 1–6.

CHAPTER XXI

SYRIA AND PALESTINE
c. 2160–1780 B.C.

I. SYRIA AND PALESTINE IN THE HERACLEOPOLITAN PERIOD AND THE ELEVENTH DYNASTY

WITH the end of the Old Kingdom (*c.* 2181 B.C.), Egypt entered upon a period of decadence, the First Intermediate Period, comprising the Seventh to the Tenth Dynasties and lasting about 140 years.[1] Egyptian activity in Asia, which until then had been considerable, suffered from the effects of the instability prevailing in the Nile Valley. Describing the beginning of the troubled period in his 'Admonitions', Ipuwer says sadly that his compatriots are no longer going to Byblos to obtain the conifer wood and resin needed for mummies.[2] It was to be a long time before economic and diplomatic relations were to become active again. Archaeological evidence of Egyptian influence in Syrian ports between the Sixth and Twelfth Dynasties is scarce and of doubtful value.[3] At Byblos, and in Syria and Palestine as a whole, no Egyptian king is mentioned in the hieroglyphic inscriptions between Phiops II and Sesostris I.[4] A similar absence of royal names can also be observed (from Phiops II[5] to Mentuhotpe II[6]) in the mines of Sinai. This silence shows how slight and irregular connexions must have been at that time.

Internal weakness, after the end of the Old Kingdom, left the Egyptian frontiers without adequate protection. The Asiatics took advantage of this state of affairs to make their way in force into the Eastern Delta and to wander through its pastures with their

---

[1] See above, ch. XIV, sect. V and ch. XX, sects. I–IV.

[2] P. Leiden 344 *recto*, 3, 6–8; §I, 17, 32–3; §I, 12, 96; §I, 58, 441; §I, 54, 43–4; A, 6, 54. A, 13, 103–20 disputes the date ascribed to this text.

[3] §I, 1; §I, 56, 25–6.

[4] §I, 39, vol. VII, 369–96. The Byblite cylinder, which bears the name of Sehetepibre (§I, 38), is usually ascribed to the second king of this name who belonged to the Thirteenth Dynasty and not to the father of Sesostris I. See *C.A.H.* II³, ch. II, sect. II.   [5] §I, 21, part I, pl. 9, no. 17. *Ibid.* part II, 64.

[6] §I, 21, part I, pl. 22, no. 70. *Ibid.* part II, 38–9, 86; §I, 19.

flocks. Some of these invaders settled there, while others conducted raids on the territory or used it for the seasonal movements
of flocks, all of which added to the prevailing condition of anarchy
in the country and contributed to its ruin.[1] In Ipuwer's words,
'the foreigners are (now) skilled in the crafts of the Marshlands'.[2]
Bedawin were also to be found in Middle Egypt, serving probably
as mercenaries in the internal struggles which were rending the
country.[3] Perhaps the introduction of copper-headed arrows into
Egypt should be attributed to the Asiatics.[4] It is not easy to
establish a connexion between the presence of these nomads and
the so-called button-seals. These objects are characteristic of the
First Intermediate Period and they are not Egyptian in origin,
but they did appear in Egypt as early as the Sixth Dynasty, before
the intrusion of the bedawin.[5] The hypothesis, built up around
the button-seals, according to which some Asiatic conquerors
ruled over the Lower Nile Valley after the Old Kingdom,[6] is
disproved by the texts and must be discarded.[7]

The situation improved during the Tenth Dynasty (c. 2130–
2040 B.C.), with a king Achthoes,[8] who helped the nomarchs of the
Delta to free the eastern province of invaders and strengthened
the frontier defences. The importation into Egypt of conifers
began once more, but by the indirect route through the ports of
the Western Delta, which did not suffer from the Asiatics and
were not threatened by their incursions. All these details are
supplied by the Instruction of Achthoes to his son and heir
Merykare.[9] This important document is also the only source of
the Heracleopolitan Period which gives information about the

[1] P. Leiden 344 *recto*, 14, 11–15, 1; see 1, 9; 3, 1; 4, 5–8; §1, 17, 90–1;
see 20–1, 30–1, 37–8; §1, 12, 107; see 94, 96, 97–8; §1, 58, 443–4; see 441–2.
P. Ermitage 1116A *verso*, 83–107; §1, 23, pls. 12–13; §1, 55, 42–58; §1, 18, 29–32;
§1, 12, 80–1; §1, 47, 19–21, 28–38; §1, 58, 416–17. P. Ermitage 1116B *verso*,
18–19, 30–7; §1, 23, pls. 23–4; §1, 18, 103–4; §1, 12, 112–13; §1, 58, 444–5.
On this last text, the Prophecy of Neferty, see below, p. 537.

[2] P. Leiden 344 *recto*, 4, 8; §1, 17, 37–8; §1, 12, 98; §1, 58, 442.

[3] §1, 2, no. 16, 6; no. 25, 14; §1, 48, 84–95, suggests a later date for these
graffiti and would place them after the death of Ammenemes I; see below, p. 541,
n. 10. Cf. above, ch. xx, sects. I–II.

[4] P. Ermitage 1116B *verso*, 40; §1, 23, pl. 24; §1, 18, 104; §1, 12, 114; §1, 58,
445; §1, 16, 91, n. 3; §1, 41, 43.

[5] §1, 16, 88–95; §1, 46; §1, 28, 10.

[6] §1, 37, 3; §1, 36, 119–25; §1, 57, vol. 1, 256–60; §1, 16; §1, 55, 92, n. 1.

[7] §1, 47, 39, n. 2; §1, 52, 20–1. Contrary to common belief all the royal names
of the period are Egyptian, including *Trrw*. Better arguments than those adduced
by Ungnad (§1, 53) must be forthcoming before it can be accepted that Naram-Sin
came to Egypt.   [8] See above, ch. xx, sect. I.

[9] P. Ermitage 1116A *verso*, 82–107; see above, n. 1.

customs of the nomads and their Asiatic homeland. The passage which concerns them deserves to be quoted :[1]

'The wretched Asiatic, bad is the country where he lives, inconvenient in respect of water, impracticable because of many trees, its roads are bad on account of the mountains. He does not settle in one single place, for (lack of) food makes his legs take flight.[2] Since the time of Horus he has been at war ;[3] he does not conquer, nor yet can he be conquered. He does not announce the day of fighting. . . .' The author goes on to describe the military operations which have the effect of giving 'the Asiatic a distaste for Egypt' and he adds : 'Do not trouble thyself concerning him. The Asiatic is a crocodile on his bank ; he leads towards an isolated way, he bears not towards the port of a populous city.'[4]

This text does not give a picture of living conditions in Syria and Palestine as a whole. The description is concerned only with the Asiatics who came to trouble the life of the Delta ; the author's preoccupation is solely with them. He refers to them by the name Amu, an ethnic term attested from the Sixth Dynasty[5] for which both Egyptian and Semitic etymologies have been sought.[6] It usually has a wide meaning ; it is applied to the peoples of Asia, whether nomadic or settled.[7] The Amu of whom Achthoes speaks live in a mountainous, wooded region, which we must probably look for in Palestine.[8] They are famished, bellicose nomads, living in a continual state of war, characteristics which are by no means uncommon,[9] although the historicity of the passage is not for that reason suspect. Never conquerors, never conquered, the Asiatics must have operated in small mobile groups, acting without any co-ordination and aiming at limited objectives, all of which made a decision one way or the other an impossibility. They did not practise the custom, attested in Egypt

---

[1] P. Ermitage 1116 A *verso*, 91–8.   [2] §1, 40, 176–8.

[3] I.e. since primordial times when the god Horus ruled over the land.

[4] The author seems to mean that it is no use pursuing the Asiatic to his own country. Different translations have been suggested for this difficult phrase ; thus §1, 55, 50 : 'He may be able to commit robbery on a lonely road, but he cannot steal on the territory of a populous town.' See §1, 47, 33 (68).

[5] §1, 13, vol. I, 167 (19)–168 (2) ; §1, 22, vol. I, 133–5 ; vol. IV, 211 ; §1, 26, 92, n. 347.

[6] §1, 32, 123 ; §1, 24, 37 ; §1, 11, 311 ; §1, 50, 27 ; §1, 29, 15–16 ; §1, 60, 163–4.

[7] The '*ʒmw* are also found in the desert between the Red Sea and Egypt. They are mentioned in an inscription located some twenty-two miles south-east of Aswān. §1, 14, 46, no. 31 ; pl. 19, B.

[8] §1, 12, 80, n. 8. Sinai has also been suggested, §1, 10 ; §1, 47, 31 (53) ; §1, 16, 97, n. 2.

[9] For a similar description of the customs of the Libyan nomads, see §1, 40, 178.

for internal struggles[1] and among many other peoples,[2] of giving the enemy warning of the day of combat. Achthoes, who had made war against them, was in a good position to know their tactics, in which, it can be seen, the effect of surprise played an important part, as it did with the Hebrews and Arabs. This text has its counterpart in cuneiform literature.[3] The people in question there are Amorites, but although it is tempting to offer as a hypothesis that it was with them that Achthoes had had to deal, no positive assertion to that effect can be made.

With Mentuhotpe II of the Eleventh Dynasty, Egypt found unity again and a strong central power (c. 2060–2010 B.C.).[4] Asiatic policy took a more active turn. From the reign of Mentuhotpe we have some indications of military operations against the peoples of the east;[5] the only precise fact is that there was a campaign against the Amu of the land of Djaty (D_3ty)[6] of which nothing else is known. Until more information is available, it seems doubtful whether these expeditions went beyond the desert and the mountains of Sinai.[7] The mines of the peninsula were worked again,[8] and it seems clear that the king's envoys went to the Lebanon in search of timber.[9] About twenty years after Mentuhotpe II's death, in the eventful early years of the Twelfth Dynasty, Ammenemes I used a flotilla of twenty ships made of Asiatic wood on the Nile to fight his enemies.[10] Since it is doubtful whether this usurper had had time to obtain the materials and build the ships, it is probable that the importation dates back to the Eleventh Dynasty. A representation recently discovered in a Theban tomb dated from the time of Mentuhotpe II shows the Egyptian army storming a stronghold held by Asiatic people.[11]

Asiatics are several times depicted on the monuments of Mentuhotpe II. A block from the chapel of Gebelein preserves a scene of the royal triumph over the four races which made up humanity,[12] but the person on his knees, who is identified by the legend as an Asiatic, does not have the usual characteristic features. Of greater interest are some fragmentary reliefs from

[1] §1, 20; §1, 15, 62–3; §1, 30, 231.
[2] §1, 9, 267–8 and Appendix L, 431–6.
[3] See below, pp. 563–4.   [4] See above, ch. xx, sect. v.
[5] See above, ch. xx, sect. vii.
[6] §1, 44, vol. I, 104–5; vol. II, pl. 107, no. 1; §1, 45, 58–9.
[7] See above, ch. xx, sect. vii.   [8] See above, p. 532, n. 6.
[9] §1, 25, 46 and 49.   [10] §1, 51, 12, 3; §1, 6, §463–5.
[11] A, 4, 50–1 and fig. 2.
[12] §1, 3, vol. I, pl. 33A, a; §1, 59, 184A, 6; §1, 6, §423H.

the funerary temple of Deir el-Bahri. These reliefs have not retained any legends giving a clear indication of the ethnic group to which the different types of foreigner represented belong,[1] but two of the mutilated inscriptions, which must have stood above such scenes, mention Asiatics;[2] we thus have confirmation that they were depicted on the walls of the monument. It is generally agreed that they are to be recognized in the persons with the following features: hooked nose, sometimes large; narrow and fairly long goatee beard, the point of which curves inwards towards the neck; abundant hair reaching to shoulder-level and held by a narrow, light headband knotted behind the head, the ends of which fall to the nape of the neck; their only garment is a loin-cloth, the length of which cannot be determined because in none of the representations is the base of the garment preserved.[3] One of the fragments, now in the British Museum, shows the original colours: yellow skin and yellow eye-pupil, hair and beard red, loin-cloth red.[4] It is many-coloured and short in the newly discovered battle scene (p. 535).

Representations of Asiatics on monuments of the Fifth and Sixth Dynasties[5] show similar hair-styles with headband, while under the Twelfth Dynasty the Asiatics are always depicted without headband, their hair shorter and their clothes sometimes longer.[6] Thus there was no change between the twenty-sixth and the twenty-first centuries, but a certain modification is observable between the twenty-first and the twentieth–nineteenth centuries. The evidence of the monuments would have been of considerable interest for tracing the history of the inhabitants of the countries east of Egypt if the changes had been more radical.

About fifteen years after Mentuhotpe II's death, the Eleventh

---

[1] The meaning of the legend is obscure in §1, 33, vol. I, pl. 15, E–F; §1, 8, 38 ζ, η.

[2] §1, 33, vol. I, 5, fig. 1; §1, 8, 37.

[3] §1, 33, vol. I, pl. 15, F, 1; vol. II, pl. 9, C; see vol. III, pl. 13, 1. No account is taken of representations of foreign soldiers in tombs nos. 15 and 17 at Beni Hasan, which are usually dated to the Eleventh Dynasty, §1, 34, vol. II, pls. 5 and 15; §1, 59, 9–10; not only is it difficult to determine the racial type of these soldiers, but according to §1, 48, 78–84 the tombs are later than the Eleventh Dynasty.

[4] §1, 7, part VI, pl. 24, no. 109. I am indebted to M. Malinine for details of the colours.

[5] §1, 5, vol. II, pls. 3, 5–7, 12–13; §1, 4, pl. 12; §1, 35, pl. 4; see §1, 60, 159–60; §1, 59, pls. 4–5; §1, 42, figs. 1 and 41–2; §1, 31, 22–3; pls. 2, 3 and 5. See also §1, 27, vol. II, pls. 36 and 38; vol. III, pls. 12–14; §1, 49, 139, fig. 2. Contrary to what has been supposed, it is improbable that Asiatics figure in a scene carved on the walls of a mastaba at Saqqara (§1, 43, 25 and frontispiece) which shows an attack on a fortress as in the well-known scene at Dishāsha, §1, 35, pl. 4. See above, p. 359, Fig. 17.

[6] See below, p. 551.

Dynasty, which he had adorned, disintegrated and for a short time Egypt relapsed into disorder. The nomads took advantage of the situation to return in force into the Eastern Delta. We know of their misdeeds through the Prophecy of Neferty, which combines in one sinister picture these recent memories with older memories of the depredations of the Asiatics during the First Intermediate Period.[1]

II. SYRIA AND PALESTINE DURING THE TWELFTH DYNASTY

The founder of the Twelfth Dynasty, Ammenemes I, had barely come to the throne when he expelled the bedawin[2] and, in order to prevent further incursions, built a fortress in the eastern part of Wādi Tummilāt.[3] Access to the eastern marches was, however, not entirely forbidden to the Asiatic herdsmen; they could be authorized to go there 'as a favour[4] in order to water their flocks'.[5] This is the first reference to a practice which was continued during the New Kingdom[6] and brings to mind biblical memories.[7]

Ammenemes I did not confine himself to defensive measures. With his reign a new era began in Egypt's relations with Syria and Palestine, relations which in a short time were to assume the form of expansion in these countries by the pharaohs. In this connexion the word 'empire' has been used.[8] Is it appropriate? The question has direct bearing on the history of Syria and Palestine, and thus merits careful scrutiny.[9]

First of all, the wars: evidence is extremely scarce and in this respect our information is probably incomplete. From the time of the coregency of Ammenemes I and Sesostris I we have the stela of the General Nesumont, which records a victorious cam-

---

[1] See above, p. 533, n. 1 and ch. xx, sect. x.

[2] P. Ermitage 1116b verso, 63; §1, 23, pl. 25; §1, 58, 446; §11, 33, 104; perhaps also §1, 51, 12, 5–6; see §1, 41, 52–5.

[3] P. Ermitage 1116b verso, 66–7; Sinuhe B 17; §11, 15, 11–12; §1, 58, 19; §11, 33, 7; §1, 41, 24–7, 55–7.   [4] Variant: 'in the usual way'.

[5] P. Ermitage 1116b verso, 67–8. P. Butler 527 verso, 11 indicates the presence of 'foreign shepherds' in Egypt, but without being more precise, §11, 24, pl. 3 and transcription.

[6] P. Anastasi vi, 51–61; §1, 58, 259; see §11, 61, 2085.

[7] Genesis, xii. 10; xlvi ff.   [8] See below, p. 547.

[9] The sources of information are very numerous. The essential facts are given in chronological sequence above, ch. xx, sects. xii–xiv and in C.A.H. ii³, ch. ii, sect. 1. Here the evidence will be grouped according to its nature and content, in order to give a comprehensive picture.

paign against the Asiatics (whose fortresses have been destroyed) but omits to say where these operations took place.[1] Khusobk, in his biographical inscription,[2] is a little more explicit about an expedition made by Sesostris III. The king, known for his Nubian conquests,[3] reached as far as Shechem (*Skmm*), in the mountains west of the Jordan, where he turned back; his rear-guard, commanded by Khusobk, engaged the Amu in combat. The reasons for these two campaigns, their importance and their outcome are not known.

Apart from this concrete but too laconic evidence, we have only more or less conventional clichés, the historical value of which is questionable. Thus, in the Story of Sinuhe, it is mentioned that Sesostris I 'was created in order to smite the bedawin and to crush the Sandfarers';[4] of the same pharaoh it is said on a stela that he is 'the one who severs the neck of those who are among the Asiatics'.[5] His vizier, Mentuhotpe, describes himself in his own eulogy as 'one who pacifies the Sand-dwellers',[6] another way of designating the inhabitants of Asia. The treasurer and general of Sesostris III, Mentuemhat, claims on his stela that he was 'appreciated by the king more than his (other) officials for mastering the insurgents of Asia, the rebels of the northern territories'.[7] This general may have taken part in the expedition against Shechem. The legend on a pectoral of Ammenemes III from Dahshūr, which accompanies the traditional scene of royal triumph over the enemy, reads: 'Smiting the Asiatic.'[8] Scenes of the same type figure on blocks from the funerary temple of Sesostris I at El-Lisht, and show also livestock taken as booty from the vanquished foreigners, we know not where, as well as files of 'prisoners of war', including a Syrian.[9] It is difficult to know how far these scenes, inspired by themes from the Old Kingdom, conform with reality. The Story of Sinuhe, which covers the greater part of Sesostris I's reign and has Asia as its main setting, makes no reference to military operations by the Egyptians in Syria and Palestine; indeed it presents relations with the inhabitants of these countries in a favourable light. This testimony is important, because it reflects the feelings of the pharaoh's government.[10]

[1] §II, 60, 81–2; §I, 6, §§469–71; §I, 39, vol. VII, 382.
[2] §II, 49; §II, 60, 82–3; §I, 6, §§676–87; §I, 58, 230; §I, 39, vol. V, 66.
[3] See above, ch. XX, sect. XIII.
[4] Sinuhe B 72–3; §II, 15, 22; §I, 58, 19; §II, 33, 11.
[5] §II, 56, 189, l. 2.   [6] §II, 32, no. 20539, I, l. 10; §I, 6, §532.
[7] See Janssen, *Arch. Or.* 20, 442–5.
[8] §II, 43, pl. 20, 2; 21; §II, 70, vol. II, pl. 2.
[9] §II, 25, part I, 188–90.   [10] §I, 41, 106–7.

It appears to be certain that peaceful relations existed with Sinai, where the Egyptians went to exploit the deposits of turquoise and, occasionally, deposits of copper.[1] In addition to continuing operations at the mines of Wādi Maghāra, which had been worked since the Early Dynastic Period, and some secondary sites, mining was begun in the Serābīt el-Khādim district during the Twelfth Dynasty; a small temple and a chapel were built there in honour of Hathor in association with Sopd and other deities.[2] The largest expedition, numerically, of which we know consisted of 735 persons;[3] it dates from the reign of Ammenemes III, who developed these mines to a high degree of activity. Moreover, all the kings of the Twelfth Dynasty are represented there by monuments, the total number of which—over 200—exceeds that of all the other dynasties put together. At no other time did the Egyptians frequent Sinai to such an extent, and working conditions there, at that time, are particularly well documented.

The pharaohs of the Twelfth Dynasty are never represented in Sinai in the act of smiting an Asiatic enemy, as was customary in the mining area in the Old Kingdom.[4] It is true that a text glorifying the king, engraved at Serābīt el-Khādim and belonging to the Middle Kingdom, speaks in vague terms of conquered foes and, in connexion with the Retenu, mentions the 'vigilance' of the Egyptian troops.[5] But the mining expeditions in the peninsula, during the Twelfth Dynasty, did not include detachments of police or soldiers.[6] Asiatics, singly or in groups of six, ten and twenty men, came to join the mining parties.[7] They were not enemies who had been conquered and reduced to forced labour: among them was the brother of a prince of the Retenu, Ḥbdd(m), who arrived with his own escort.[8] We may therefore only hesitate between friendly co-operation and an obligation to serve stemming from ties of vassalage. However this may be, the access routes and the region itself were secure; relations between

---

[1] §1, 21, part II, 1–21.

[2] *Ibid.* 32–51.

[3] §1, 21, part I, pl. 10, no. 23; part II, 66–7.

[4] §1, 21, part II, 25–6. On the somewhat restricted incidence in Syria and Palestine of this theme of smiting an enemy, see §II, 44.

[5] §1, 21, part I, pl. 49, no. 136, W. face; part II, 136.

[6] §1, 21, part II, 16–17.

[7] *Ibid.* 19. It is reasonable to attribute the proto-Sinaitic inscriptions to these Asiatics; see Gardiner, *J.E.A.* 48, 45–8. But see A, 3, 12.

[8] See §1, 21, part II, 19. Also to be noted is a small obelisk (§1, 21, part I, pl. 51, no. 163; part II, 147) set up by three local soldiers who are represented bearing arms; they cannot be hostages. See §II, 17.

Egyptians and the local inhabitants seem to bear the stamp of mutual confidence.

If there is rarely any question of actual hostilities in the relations of the Twelfth Dynasty with Asia, as we know them, diplomatic activity and exploration were, on the other hand, intense. An official of the treasury has left an inscription in Sinai in which he describes himself as 'reaching the boundaries of the foreign lands with his feet, exploring the inaccessible valleys, reaching the limits of the unknown'.[1] The text expresses the spirit of the time. On a stela dating from the reign of Sesostris I, we read that 'his numerous emissaries are in every land, the couriers do what he has willed'.[2] From the time of Ammenemes I or of Sesostris I dates the Satire of the Trades, which names among the more common of the callings that of the courier, and speaks of the danger he runs from the Amu,[3] thus revealing which direction the messengers normally took. The story of Sinuhe refers to the coming and going of Sesostris I's messengers in southern Syria.[4] A silver cup from the Tōd treasure, which dates from the reign of Ammenemes II and is of Asiatic provenance,[5] mentions a messenger.[6] One is reminded of the diplomatic activity revealed by the archives of Mari[7] and El-Amarna.

The story of Sinuhe informs us, moreover, that it was to the advantage of the Syrian princes to maintain loyal relations with the pharaoh by correspondence,[8] that the latter was able to make them come to his court[9] and was in the habit of sending them costly presents:[10] these are the diplomatic practices made familiar by the archives of Mari and El-Amarna.[11] The story of Sinuhe also contains interesting and reliable information about southern Syria;[12] it testifies to the interest Asia aroused among Egyptians of the Twelfth Dynasty, an interest which can be surmised from other literary texts.[13] For the second half of the Middle Kingdom,

---

[1] §1, 21, part 1, pl. 18, no. 54; part 11, 80. This inscription is dated to Ammenemes III, year 45.

[2] §11, 56, 189, l. 8.

[3] §11, 16, 155–6, see 23, 39–40; §1, 58, 433; §1, 32, 1–2.

[4] Sinuhe B 94–5; §11, 15, 24; §1, 58, 20; §11, 33, 12.

[5] On this treasure, see below, pp. 543–4.

[6] §11, 10, 116–17.   [7] §11, 45, 99–108; §11, 38, 13–16.

[8] Sinuhe B 73–5.   [9] Sinuhe B 219–21.

[10] Sinuhe B 174–6; see §1, 41, 109–12. From the same period there is evidence of the practice of sending precious gifts to foreign deities who were well disposed towards Egypt, see Shipwrecked Sailor, P. Ermitage 1115, 146–8; §1, 23, pl. 6; §11, 15, 46; §1, 12, 33; §11, 33, 37–8.

[11] §11, 45, 96–9.   [12] See below, pp. 553–5.

[13] §11, 52, 46 (30); §11, 63.

the Execration Texts provide long lists of Asiatic countries and their princes ;[1] the older series, which can be assigned to the reign of Sesostris III, mentions twenty countries and thirty princes ;[2] the second series, of slightly later date, gives more than sixty princes and countries.[3] The area covered by these enumerations extends as far as the Eleutheros Valley in Phoenicia, in the north, and inland as far as Gilead and the region of Damascus.[4] These documents show that the pharaoh's chancellery had an extensive knowledge of these areas, kept abreast of the least changes of petty princes and recorded them in its archives. It was not done better at El-Amarna.

The close and continuous relations which are revealed in these texts, and the regular movement between Egypt and Syria and Palestine have left many traces. In the first place there is the well-known presence of various Asiatic people in Egypt. In the story of Sinuhe we read that a bedawin sheikh from the Sinai desert had once been to Egypt ;[5] judging from the chronology of the story, this visit took place in the reign of Ammenemes I. A well-known scene in tomb no. 3 at Beni Hasan depicts the arrival of an Asiatic prince and his followers, men, women, children and asses, in year 6 of Sesostris II ; they are bringing the nomarch eye-paint (*kohl*).[6] It has been thought that these Amu were coming to seek hospitality in Egypt,[7] but the texts accompanying the scene say no such thing. The newcomers have none of the appearance of poverty-stricken nomads ; they are travelling without herds. It is rather a question of an official visit, not unconnected with trade.[8]

In the tombs of Beni Hasan which date from the reigns of Ammenemes I and Sesostris I, scenes of military life show some oriental warriors among the Egyptians ;[9] there is no inscription explaining the presence of these men, whom one would be tempted to take as mercenaries.[10] The great majority of Asiatics

[1] See above, ch. xx, sect. xiii. See also below, pp. 548-9, 554-5.
[2] §i, 50, 43-58. The new series discovered at Mirgissa is much shorter; A, 11, 284-7.   [3] §ii, 51, 62-96.
[4] §ii, 3, 33; §ii, 37, 66-7.   [5] Sinuhe B 26.
[6] §i, 34, part i, 69 and 72; pls. 28, 30, 31, 38 (2); §i, 59, 6; §ii, 19, vol. i, pls. 10-11; §i, 39, vol. iv, 145-6 (7)-(11).
[7] E.g. §ii, 39, §289.
[8] §i, 32, 36-7; §i, 6, 281, n.d.
[9] Tomb no. 14: §i, 34, part i, pl. 47; §i, 59, 8; §i, 39, vol. iv, 151 (6)-(8). Tomb no. 2: §i, 34, part i, pl. 16; §i, 59, 7; §i, 39, vol. iv, 143 (15).
[10] See above, p. 533. The mercenaries (Amu) mentioned in the Het-nub graffiti, according to §i, 48, 84-95, date from the beginning of the Twelfth Dynasty; if so they would be contemporaneous with the warriors represented at Beni Hasan.

who settled in Egypt during the Middle Kingdom were humble, peaceful people. They are to be seen in large numbers employed on domestic tasks in private houses, and they are also encountered in the service of temples. The earliest dated instance belongs to the reign of Sesostris II; the most important group, of about fifty, dates from the middle of the Thirteenth Dynasty.[1] There is no text giving any information about the circumstances in which they came. The biblical story of Joseph brings to mind the slave-trade;[2] voluntary recruitment is, however, attested, during the Middle Kingdom, for nomads of Nubia.[3] If an analogy may be drawn from the New Kingdom, it would suggest most strongly captures made during wars and levies raised in territory under Egyptian domination. Such an interpretation finds support in the captives who are represented in the funerary temple of Sesostris I. In any case, it is more than probable, taking into account the extent to which Egypt was state-controlled, that the government regulated the inflow of labour. Moreover, it is known that there existed during the Middle Kingdom, not far from the royal residence, camps of Asiatics under the direction of Egyptian officials.[4]

During the Twelfth Dynasty, Egypt also obtained livestock from Asia. A tomb at Meir, dating from the reign of Ammenemes II, includes a scene representing a herd with the accompanying legend: 'Oxen of the Asiatics brought from (or as). . . .'[5] In the tomb of Thuthotpe at Deir el-Bersha dating from the time of Sesostris III, the caption above a file of cattle[6] contains the words read by Blackman[7] as 'cattle from Retenu'. The presence in this text of this name for Syria and Palestine is not, however, established beyond doubt.[8] But in what follows it goes on to say, addressing the cattle: 'You have wandered across the sand, (now) you walk on herbage . . .', which would be appropriate for a herd brought from Asia. Furthermore, Thuthotpe had Asiatic connexions, having resided at Megiddo.[9] Blackman's translation may well be accurate, particularly in view of the indisputable evidence at Meir. How did all these cattle reach Egypt? It has been mentioned that herds captured from the enemy were shown in the funerary temple of Sesostris I. For the reign of Sesostris III,

[1] §1, 26, 92–9; §11, 53; §11, 30, 15–18.
[2] Genesis, xxxvii, 28, 36; §1, 26, 99.
[3] §11, 67, 9 and pls. 5–5a, 8–9.   [4] §11, 23, 264; §11, 53, 151–2.
[5] §11, 13, part III, 13 and pl. 4; see part II, 18, n. 1.
[6] §11, 46, part I, pl. 18; §1, 51, 51, 13–52, 4.
[7] §11, 14.   [8] §11, 73, 134, n. 13.
[9] See below, pp. 543–546.

to judge from the methods used by the Egyptians in Nubia at that time, both war and trade must be borne in mind.[1] We know of this same king's campaign against Shechem; it is possible that the expedition brought back booty which included herds. Khusobk does not mention them in his account, but that is of no consequence, because the author was interested only in his own story.[2] Another possibility which cannot be excluded is that the cattle represent requisitions in subject territories. The Megiddo excavations have brought to light the seal of a 'steward, accountant of cattle'.[3] If this is taken in conjunction with the statue of Thuthotpe found on the same site and with the scene in his tomb, we cannot escape the impression that the government of the pharaohs exploited the resources of the plain of Jezreel, which was rich in cattle.[4]

The importation of Asiatic products during the Twelfth Dynasty is as well documented as the importation of men and livestock. We have already referred to the intensive working of the mines of Sinai. The extensive use of bronze and lapis lazuli, which are Asiatic in origin, begins in Egypt during the Middle Kingdom.[5] The still unpublished dedicatory inscription of the temple of Sesostris I at Tōd[6] describes the presentation to this temple of offering-tables made of precious materials 'twice as beautiful and twice as numerous as all one was accustomed to see in this country before, and representing what foreigners and explorers, who travel across the lands, had delivered'.[7] Certain materials named in the text, such as silver, lapis lazuli and turquoise, were imported from Asia. The treasure discovered in the foundations of the same temple in four caskets inscribed with the name of Ammenemes II serves as an illustration to the inscription quoted above. This treasure[8] includes gold, silver and lapis lazuli; each of these materials is present in its crude state (ten ingots of gold and thirteen of silver, pieces of lapis) and as objects which

[1] Boundary stelae dated to the years 8 and 16; §1, 39, vol. VII, 143 and 151; §1, 45, 76–7.

[2] Khusobk mentions only weapons which he has received as a reward, no doubt taken from the enemy whom he has vanquished; §11, 49, 5 and pl. 2, l. 5; above, p. 508.

[3] §11, 34, pl. 149, no. 32.

[4] The booty taken at Megiddo by Tuthmosis III comprised some 2000 head of cattle, §11, 61, 664, 12.

[5] §11, 35, 253, 455–6, 530.   [6] §11, 10, 10–11.

[7] Sesostris I made a similar gift to the temple of Abydos, §11, 32, no. 20539, 11, 1. 8; §1, 6, §534. The provenance of the materials is not mentioned.

[8] §11, 10, 113–21 and pls. 15–17; §11, 11; §11, 12; §11, 69; §11, 62; §11, 42, 91–6.

have been worked (for instance, more than 150 metal cups and twenty-five metal chains, amulets, beads and more than fifty stone cylinders). Most of the cups have been bent and flattened by hammering; the majority of the cylinders are broken. It is probable that the broken items, and perhaps those which are intact as well, were there only for the weight of the material of which they were made. The cylinders, some of which bear cuneiform inscriptions, are clearly oriental in origin;[1] the cups and a silver pendant are of Cretan provenance, or else Asiatic imitations of Cretan models.[2] This treasure gives an idea of the material which the pharaohs of the Twelfth Dynasty received from Syria, the hub of a vast system of exchanges which had developed in those days throughout the Near East and the Eastern Mediterranean.[3]

In the temple of El-Madāmūd a mutilated inscription tells of deliveries of goods from Asiatic countries to the palace of Sesostris III.[4] During the same reign, precious materials from the same regions were used to embellish the temple of Osiris at Abydos.[5]

Movement in the other direction, from Egypt into Asia, is amply attested by objects found in Syria and Palestine as well as by texts. Reference has already been made to wars, diplomatic missions and mining expeditions beyond the Isthmus of Suez. It was not only official enterprises which took Egyptians into Asia. On the death of Ammenemes I, Sinuhe fled the country for political reasons, taking refuge in Syria whence he did not return until very nearly the end of his life.[6] On arriving at a Syrian prince's court he found fellow-countrymen in his entourage, but he does not say how they came to be there.[7] It has been asserted that tombs and a house found at Gezer date back to the Middle Kingdom and that they belonged to private Egyptian citizens, but this claim is at least open to question.[8] It amounts to very

[1] §ii, 12, 15–20 and 34, n. 7; §ii, 31, 119. For other cylinders of the Middle Kingdom found in Egypt see §ii, 64; §ii, 2, 217–18; §ii, 65, 13–14.

[2] §ii, 12, 21–35; §ii, 29, 19–20.

[3] §ii, 66, 113–19.

[4] §ii, 9, 67.

[5] Stela of Ikhernofret, Berlin 1204, ll. 11–12 and 15; §ii, 60, 70–1; §i, 6, §667–8; §i, 39, vol. v, 97.

[6] §ii, 15, 1–41; §i, 58, 18–22; §ii, 33, 1–25.

[7] Sinuhe B 31–4.

[8] §i, 16, 97, n. 1; §ii, 48, 98. This claim is based on the statements of §ii, 36, vol. ii, 307–8, and not on an examination of the material found which does not allow of such a deduction, see §ii, 36, vol. i, 303–4, 389–92; vol. ii, 307–8; vol. iii, pls. 121–2.

little, all told; emigration was never part of the Egyptian way of life. Moreover, since external trade was a royal monopoly, Egyptians rarely left their country on private business. Those encountered abroad are nearly always there on official duty. This evidence will be taken into account when we look into the reasons for certain Egyptian objects being in Syria and Palestine.

The amount of Egyptian material belonging to the Middle Kingdom which has been found in Palestine and Syria is considerable. Byblos, with which traditionally Egypt maintained a connexion dating back to the Early Dynastic Period, has supplied some remarkable pieces,[1] notably a pectoral of Ammenemes III, made of gold and precious stones.[2] The tomb of a prince, no. 1, contained an obsidian vase inlaid with gold bearing the same king's name,[3] as well as other precious objects either of Egyptian workmanship or inspired by Egyptian models. Another prince's tomb, no. 2, which was contemporaneous with Ammenemes IV, provided an obsidian and gold casket inscribed with the pharaoh's name,[4] and many other objects of high quality, Egyptian or in the Egyptian style. Either they were presents given to the princes of Byblos by the pharaohs, which no doubt served as compensation or as encouragement for the despatching of wood to Egypt, or they were local products bearing witness to the profound influence which Egypt exercised over Byblos.[5] The local rulers had Semitic names, which they wrote in hieroglyphs; they used this script on their monuments and gave themselves the Egyptian title of 'governor',[6] which was used in the pharaoh's government service by the heads of administrative districts. At the same time, they did not hesitate to have their names inscribed in cartouches after the manner of the kings of Egypt.[7] Formally they were, at one and the same time, sovereigns and Egyptian officials.

The monarchs of the Twelfth Dynasty sent sphinxes to Syria. The site of Ras Shamra has yielded fragments of a pair of sphinxes of large dimensions found at the entrance to the temple of Ba'al; the best preserved of these retains the cartouche of Ammenemes

---

[1] §II, 40; §II, 21, *passim*; §I, 39, vol. VII, 386–92. The first king of the Twelfth Dynasty certainly attested at Byblos is Sesostris I, §II, 21, vol. II, 196–7 and pl. 188, no. 8503. See above, p. 532, n. 4.

[2] §II, 18, 7–8 and pl. I, no. 1; §I, 39, vol. VII, 387.

[3] §II, 40, 155–7 and pls. 88–9.

[4] *Ibid.* 157–9 and pls. 88, 90.

[5] §II, 66, 113.

[6] E.g. §II, 40, 174–7 and pls. 99–100; 196 and pl. 117. See A, 10.

[7] E.g. *ibid.* 165, 212, 277 and pl. 97.

III.[1] Aleppo Museum has a sphinx of the same pharaoh.[2] A sphinx of Ammenemes IV obtained at Beirut can be seen at the British Museum, as well as a pectoral bearing the same king's name, perhaps from the same town.[3] A broken sphinx of Ammenemes II's daughter was discovered at Qatna (Mishrifé).[4] A fragment of the sphinx of a princess of the Twelfth Dynasty was found at Byblos.[5] Another princess is known to us through the lower part of a statuette which was dug up at Ras Shamra.[6]

If all these royal objects were found in Syria, the two statues of high Egyptian officials found in western Asia are shared between Syria and Palestine. The incomplete statuette of Thuthotpe discovered at Megiddo has already been mentioned;[7] a nomarch of the Hermopolite nome, he lived from the reign of Ammenemes II until that of Sesostris III. Neither the inscriptions in his well-known tomb at Deir el-Bersha,[8] nor those on his statuette explain what he was doing abroad. The Ras Shamra excavations have brought to light a small broken group representing the Vizier Sesostrisankh with his wife and daughter; the style of the sculpture suggests a date in the second half of the Twelfth Dynasty. The texts which survive on the monument do not help us to understand why he was in Phoenicia.[9] Other Egyptian statuettes of the Middle Kingdom have been found at Ras Shamra,[10] Megiddo,[11] Tell el-'Ajjūl (near Gaza),[12] Gezer,[13] Byblos,[14] Qatna[15] and as far away as Turkey;[16] they are either without inscription or else bear the names of men and women generally of modest station.

Small objects and fragments of the Middle Kingdom discovered in Syria and Palestine are too numerous to describe individually. We must therefore confine ourselves to mentioning

---

[1] §1, 39, vol. VII, 393; A, 12, 212–20.
[2] Ibid. 395.
[3] Ibid. 384–5; §II, 59, 44 and pl. 10.8.
[4] §1, 39, vol. VII, 392.
[5] §II, 21, vol. II, 66 and pl. 159, no. 7099.
[6] §1, 39, vol. VII, 394; A, 12, 212–20.
[7] See above, p. 543; §II, 34, pl. 265; §II, 72. There is one statue only, not four statues as stated in §1, 39, vol. VII, 381; §II, 26, 2.
[8] §1, 39, vol. IV, 179–81.
[9] §1, 39, vol. VII, 394.
[10] Ibid. 393; §II, 58, 19–20.
[11] §1, 39, vol. VII, 381. See also A, 7.
[12] Ibid. 370–1.
[13] Ibid. 374.
[14] Ibid. 388. Vol. II of §II, 21, which appeared after §1, 39, vol. VII, had been published, contains twelve statuettes or groups, intact or broken, which date from the Middle Kingdom. See Atlas, pl. 95 (no. 15378), 156 (nos. 7049, 11057, 13762, 14151, 15606), 157 (nos. 11595, 12437), 158 (nos. 7105, 11398, 12420), 188 (no. 8664).
[15] §1, 39, vol. VII, 392.
[16] Ibid. 398–9.

some seals, not those adorned with royal names of the Twelfth Dynasty,[1] but a selection bearing the names and titles of soldiers and officials. From Tell el-'Ajjūl we have the scarab of an 'archer',[2] the scarab of the Chief Treasurer Senbi,[3] a person of importance, of whom we have other scarabs and several inscriptions,[4] as well as the scarab of a Great Scribe of the Chief Treasurer;[5] Jericho has produced impressions of the seal of a Scribe of the Vizier.[6] Reference has already been made to the seal of a Steward, Accountant of Cattle found at Megiddo.[7] The scarab of a Scribe of the Troops was found at Byblos.[8] Some of these objects are slightly later than the Twelfth Dynasty and date from a period when Egyptian power was on the decline; the evidence they provide gives only a sketchy idea of the state of affairs during the great period of the Middle Kingdom.

In concluding this rapid review of discoveries, it must be emphasized that, apart from the sites already mentioned, objects of the Middle Kingdom have also been found at Tell Jemma,[9] Tell ed-Duweir (Lachish),[10] Balāta (Shechem),[11] Beth-shan (Beisān),[12] Açana (Alalakh).[13]

These, then, are the most striking facts. Widely differing conclusions have been drawn from them regarding the reasons for the presence of Egyptians and Egyptian objects in Syria and Palestine during the Twelfth Dynasty. Some scholars have inferred that there was political domination,[14] while others prefer to talk in terms of diplomatic and commercial relations.[15] These divergences of opinion stem from the lack of explicit texts; the royal inscriptions of the Twelfth Dynasty have almost totally

[1] See §I, 56, 38–9; the author has endeavoured, as far as possible, to place these objects outside the Twelfth Dynasty. See, however, A, 8.

[2] §II, 50, part III, 4 and pl. 3, no. 33.

[3] §II, 50, part I, 7 and pl. 13, no. 23.   [4] §II, 68, 169, nos. 56–7.

[5] §II, 50, part I, 7 and pl. 13, no. 26. Petrie notes another scarab which belonged to him. Perhaps this scribe was Senbi's subordinate.

[6] §II, 55, 235 and pl. 26 (S. 5); §I, 39, vol. VII, 373.

[7] See above, p. 543.

[8] §II, 21, vol. I, 246 and pl. 129, no. 3594. No account is taken of the scarab §II, 55, 4 and pl. I, no. 15, the provenance of which is unknown and the reading debatable, §I, 56, 43. For some other scarabs of the Middle Kingdom found in the Near East and bearing titles see *ibid*. 42–3 and 130.

[9] §I, 39, vol. VII, 370.

[10] *Ibid*. 372.   [11] *Ibid*. 375.

[12] *Ibid*. 379.   [13] *Ibid*. 395.

[14] E.g. §II, 1; §II, 65, 14–15 and 29; §II, 37, 34; §II, 72, 236; later J. A. Wilson changed his opinion, §II, 73, 134.

[15] E.g. §II, 26, 1–2; §I, 56; A, 5, 103–4, 106–8.

disappeared. The sources at our disposal are evasive, and do not permit us to settle the question. We do not know precisely how to interpret the sending of sphinxes and statues by the pharaohs and princesses to Syria. To regard them as gifts,[1] as it is customary to do, does not answer the basic question, because it is not known whether these gifts were addressed to friendly or to vassal powers.

The position is no clearer with regard to the Execration Texts. The rites for which these documents were used are attested from the Old Kingdom, at least, down to the Graeco-Roman period;[2] their object was to forestall every hostile act, every event which might harm the pharaoh and, for his benefit, to keep the whole of humanity in submission to him. If there is any reference in the formulae to foreigners 'who would conspire', 'who would think of rebelling' against the king of Egypt, this does not mean that they were all in fact his subjects. In using these expressions, the text is not referring to historical reality, but to the dogmatic belief in universal domination by the pharaohs, according to which every human being, wherever he might be, must submit to him and owed him obedience. We cannot therefore base our ideas on these lists in determining the extent of the empire belonging to the Twelfth Dynasty pharaohs, nor in determining which part of it was causing disquiet as to its loyalty. The testimony that this rite was practised at a given point in history is not proof that the internal and international situation at that time was troubled, and that the Egyptian government had recourse to magic, being unable to reply with force. The wealth of evidence suggests, in fact, that this practice was a routine matter and not an exceptional measure imposed by circumstances. This being so, the use of these documents as a source for political history is very hazardous indeed.

There are, however, omissions in the Execration Texts which may be significant. The people of the region of Byblos are named among potential enemies,[3] while the princes of Byblos, whose close relations with the pharaohs are known to us, are not mentioned.[4] Megiddo, Ugarit (that is, Ras Shamra) and Qatna do not appear at all: they are precisely the towns in which, as we have seen, the presence of Egyptians made itself especially strongly felt. Are we to think that these princes and these towns

[1] See above, p. 540 with n. 10.
[2] §II, 28, 30–8; §II, 54; see §II, 47.
[3] §I, 50, 55 (f2).
[4] These texts thus make a distinction between the government of the coastal city and the inhabitants of the hinterland, §II, 6, 30; §II, 7, 32–3.

were not included in the lists because, unlike those which are named, they had an unbreakable friendship with Egypt and gave no cause for anxiety ?[1] This conclusion is far from being certain, and even if it is accepted, one cannot say for certain that these princes and countries recognized the domination by the pharaohs completely. The one certain fact which these texts provide has already been pointed out: the Egyptian government had an astounding knowledge of the situation in Syria and Palestine. It was certainly not, in this case, gratuitous curiosity.

With the group statuette of the Vizier Sesostrisankh and with the statuette of the nomarch Thuthotpe, we shall go a step further. Instead of seeing another Sinuhe in the latter[2] one must compare both him and the vizier with the high Egyptian officials who left traces at Kerma, south of the Third Cataract, dignitaries like the nomarch Djefaihapi, whose statue was found at this remote Egyptian trading-post.[3] In the Sudan, Egypt maintained a permanent, official establishment, situated far beyond the frontiers, and we must assume that the functionaries were sent out to be in residence there in order to represent their government and to supervise commercial transactions. Arguing by analogy, Sesostrisankh at Ras Shamra, and Thuthotpe at Megiddo, probably occupied somewhat similar positions, which would mean that Egypt maintained more or less permanent missions in the two towns.

Reference has already been made to the exploitation of the Megiddo region by the Egyptian authorities.[4] What chance discoveries indicate there gives an idea of what happened in many other areas. Seals bearing titles show that officials of the pharaohs were present and functioning at the place where the objects were found. Egyptians were well established in Sinai; they occupied a high position at Byblos. Cattle and slaves came from Asia into Egypt. From these facts there emerges the impression of domination by the pharaohs, uneven and interrupted, no doubt, but on the whole vigorous.[5] Its precise nature still eludes us; fifty years ago it was barely suspected. In view of this progressive increase in our knowledge, we shall err less if we exaggerate than if we

[1] In this respect see §i, 50, 55; §ii, 22, 218; §ii, 41, 22; §ii, 5, 40-1; §ii, 71, 206; §ii, 6, 29-30.

[2] §i, 56, 40-1.

[3] §i, 45, 103-16.

[4] See above, p. 543.

[5] The Egyptian texts of the Twelfth Dynasty compare the Asiatics with dogs, a figurative expression for submission and obeisance, P. Millingen, 3, 3; Sinuhe B, 222-3; §i, 58, 21 and 419; §i, 41, 113.

minimize the hold the Twelfth Dynasty had over Syria and Palestine.

For the first time in history, these countries experienced the effects of a considerable expansion on the part of Egypt and were likewise subjected to her cultural influence.[1] This influence, which at Byblos is of ancient date, made itself felt there particularly strongly;[2] it has also left traces which cannot be regarded as negligible at other sites. The Megiddo excavations produced a magical wand of ivory dating from the Middle Kingdom, with a hieroglyphic formula bearing the name of a Palestinian woman.[3] Three stelae from Ras Shamra, which have been assigned to the opening centuries of the second millennium, show local deities with attributes borrowed from the Egyptian pantheon.[4] It was the period when Egyptian iconographic themes and symbols, like the sphinx, the winged disk and the sign of life, were being propagated in Syria; from the north of Syria some of them were to pass into Mesopotamia and Anatolia.[5] A seal impression found at Alalakh even bears the image of a god which has all the characteristics of an Egyptian god; it was worshipped by a member of the royal family of Iamkhad (Aleppo).[6] Thus language, writing, religion, magic and decorative motifs had found their way from the banks of the Nile into the Levant.

III. EGYPTIAN SOURCES

On Egyptian monuments of the Twelfth Dynasty there are a number of representations of Asiatics. The sources are the tombs of Beni Hasan, no. 14 (dating from Ammenemes I),[7] no. 2 (Sesostris I)[8] and, above all, no. 3 (Sesostris II),[9] some engravings

[1] §II, 73, 134.   [2] See above, p. 545.

[3] §II, 34, pl. 203; for the personal name see §II, 4, 231.

[4] §II, 57, 89–95 and pl. 22.

[5] §II, 20, 24–34; §II, 8, 37–8; see §II, 74, pl. 60, no. 9=pl. 67, no. 150; pl. 60, no. 12A; A, 9, nos. 190 and 369.

[6] §II, 65, 13; §II, 74, pl. 60, no. 12B. §II, 8, 38 supposes that Egyptian cults were transferred to North Syria.

[7] §I, 34, part I, pl. 47, first register; §I, 59, 8; §I, 39, vol. IV, 151 (6)–(8).

[8] §I, 34, part I, pl. 16, fifth register; part IV, pl. 23, 3; §I, 59, 7; §I, 39, vol. IV, 143 (15).

[9] §I, 34, part I, pl. 28, 30, third register, and 31; §I, 59, 6; §II, 19, vol. I, pls. 10–11; §I, 39, vol. IV, 145–6 (7)–(11). It seems wiser to ignore the foreign soldiers represented in tombs nos. 15 and 17, §I, 39, vol. IV, 153 and 156–7 (8)–(14); the racial connexions of these warriors are uncertain, although in some respects they appear similar to Asiatics.

from the mines in Sinai (Ammenemes III),[1] an unpublished relief from the funerary temple of Sesostris I at El-Lisht,[2] and, lastly, a pectoral from Dahshūr bearing the name of Ammenemes III.[3]

Leaving aside elements which are not indicative[4] and taking into account only those features which are characteristic, Asiatics, in these representations, have hooked and prominent noses,[5] a fair, yellow[6] or brownish-yellow[7] skin, black[8] and sometimes red[9] hair. The abundant hair of the men, not held in place by any headband, hangs over the forehead and ends, usually, at the nape of the neck;[10] their beards, extending around the chin, are short and pointed.[11] The women have a lighter skin than the men;[12] their hair reaches down to the breast and back; they have a band around their heads.[13] Clothes are of many colours; in the cases where they are white or not coloured it may be surmised either that the painter did not want to paint them in detail,[14] or that the colours have disappeared.[15] Blue and red predominate in horizontal stripes, either straight and broad,[16] or narrow and undulating.[17] Vertical stripes also occur;[18] in the finest examples there are geometrical designs arranged in lines from top to bottom.[19] The men are dressed in a straight loin-cloth which may reach down to below the knee;[20] their ceremonial cloak is of the same length, without sleeves and attached at one shoulder.[21] The women wear a garment of the same style as the cloak of the men, but fitting close to the waist and slightly longer.[22] The men wear sandals[23] and the women shoes which reach above the ankle.[24]

[1] §1, 21, part I, pl. 37, no. 112; W. face; pl. 44, no. 103, W. face; pl. 85, no. 405, S.-E. face; pl. 39, no. 115, W. face; pl. 51, no. 163; see §II, 17.

[2] See §II, 25, part I, 188; W. C. Hayes kindly sent me a sketch of this representation of an Asiatic. §II, 43, 116–17, figs. 270, 274.

[3] §II, 43, pl. 20, 2 and 21; §II, 70, vol. II, pl. 2.

[4] Thus in the Sinai reliefs the Asiatics have heads which in no way differ from those of the Egyptians, except in no. 163.

[5] Beni Hasan, no. 3, affords the best example.

[6] Sinai, no. 405; pectoral from Dahshūr.   [7] Beni Hasan, nos. 2 and 3.

[8] Beni Hasan, no. 3; Sinai, no. 405; pectoral from Dahshūr (blue for black).

[9] Beni Hasan, no. 2; see above, p. 536, the Asiatic of the Eleventh Dynasty at Deir el-Bahri.

[10] Beni Hasan, no. 3 and the pectoral from Dahshūr are the most typical in this respect.

[11] The same examples are the best.   [12] Beni Hasan, no. 3.

[13] *Loc. cit.*   [14] See §1, 59, 6, commentary.

[15] See §II, 17, 387.   [16] Sinai, no. 405.

[17] Beni Hasan, nos. 2 and 14.   [18] Pectoral from Dahshūr.

[19] Beni Hasan, nos. 3 and 14.   [20] Beni Hasan, no. 3.

[21] *Loc. cit.*   [22] *Loc. cit.*

[23] *Loc. cit.*   [24] *Loc. cit.*

Scenes depicting Asiatics also provide information about their weapons. There are lances with points in the shape of a laurel-leaf; sometimes the shaft is rather short.[1] Axes, on the contrary, have fairly long handles with a forward curve in the direction of the blade.[2] The blade itself may be semicircular, and in that case invariably has two apertures;[3] excavations in Syria and Palestine have provided similar specimens in large numbers.[4] Another type of blade, which never has any aperture, is narrow and is either pointed[5] or tongue-shaped;[6] this kind is also known from actual specimens.[7] Daggers, of which many examples exist, have triangular blades and rounded pommels.[8] Wooden throw-sticks and curved staves are well represented; they vary both in curve and in thickness.[9] Bows are either simple in line and apparently reinforced,[10] or have a double curve, in which case they would be of composite construction;[11] the arrows are carried in a quiver, the Egyptian name of which is derived from the Sumerian.[12] Also included in the armoury of the Asiatics was a small shield, rectangular in shape and rather narrow.[13] Describing his single combat with a Syrian champion, Sinuhe mentions a bow and arrows, dagger, axe, shield and an armful of javelins.[14]

Asiatics used the ass not only as a beast of burden,[15] but as a mount, even for princes.[16] Surprised and amused by this use of

[1] Beni Hasan, nos. 2 and 3; Sinai, no. 405 and possibly no. 112.

[2] Handle very curved: Beni Hasan, no. 14 and possibly no. 3 (last man); opposite end slightly curved: Beni Hasan, no. 2; general shape curved: Sinai, no. 163, 115 and 405. See §III, 11, 38.

[3] Beni Hasan, nos. 2 and 14; see §III, 40, 34.

[4] §III, 11, 30–4; §III, 28, 117–19; §II, 25, part I, 283 and fig. 185. See, among others, the magnificent specimens in gold and silver found at Byblos, §II, 21, vol. II, *Atlas*, pls. 119, 120, 127, 133–5.   [5] Sinai, no. 163.

[6] Sinai, nos. 115, 163, 405; possibly Beni Hasan, no. 3 (last man).

[7] Compare §III, 11, 34–7.

[8] Beni Hasan, no. 14; pectoral from Dahshūr; possibly Sinai, no. 112; see §III, 40, 43; §II, 25, part I, 283–4 and fig. 186.

[9] Beni Hasan, nos. 2, 3 (3rd and 4th men), 14; pectoral from Dahshūr; see §III, 11, 108–11; §II, 25, part I, 284 and fig. 181.

[10] Beni Hasan, no. 14. See §III, 11, 134.

[11] Beni Hasan, no. 3. See §III, 40, 56.

[12] Beni Hasan, no. 3 (last man); §III, 11, 175–6; §III, 40, 51.

[13] Sinai, no. 163; see §III, 11, 190–1; compare §I, 34, part II, pl. 15 (sixth register).

[14] Sinuhe B 127–8, 134–40; §II, 15, 27–8; §I, 58, 20; §II, 33, 13–14.

[15] Beni Hasan, no. 3.

[16] Cf. *A.R.M.* VI, 76, 22–5 (reference supplied by D. A. Kennedy); Judges v. 10; x. 4. See at Byblos §II, 21, vol. II, 696–8 and pls. 114, 5, 117 and 118; for the date of this object, note that it formed part of the same cache as a small bronze sphinx attributable to the beginning of the Twelfth Dynasty, §II, 21, vol. II, 702 and pl. 116, no. 14499.

the ass, which was not normal on the banks of the Nile, the Egyptians on several occasions in the mines of Sinai depicted a Palestinian noble riding an ass, the animal being led by a servant holding a rope or halter fixed by a ring to its nose.[1] Tools, instruments and utensils of the Asiatics are rarely represented during the Middle Kingdom : notable exceptions are a heart-shaped vase with flared orifice and two large round handles,[2] and particularly a kind of zither, which an Asiatic is playing in a well-known scene at Beni Hasan.[3]

The story of Sinuhe[4] gives some idea of the nature and conditions of life in Upper Retenu, where he settled as a fugitive, somewhere in the interior of southern Syria.[5] The country produces crops of barley and spelt and has extensive vineyards, numerous olive-groves, various kinds of orchards, as well as fig trees ; honey is produced in abundance, herds (of every kind) are innumerable and there is hunting. The food includes meat, poultry, game, wine, pastries and dairy-produce.[6] The position occupied by agriculture in this idealized description would suggest a population which was for the most part settled. But when he makes a brief enumeration of his own possessions, Sinuhe speaks only of his herds and fruit trees.[7] The words 'town' and 'village' do not occur in the part of the narrative which deals with Retenu, but only 'encampments';[8] the 'tent' is mentioned twice,[9] compared with one reference to the 'house'.[10] Armed conflicts, which were frequent, had as their aim chasing the enemy from his pastures and watering-places, plundering his goods and seizing his herds, his subjects and his foodstuffs;[11] there is never any question of laying waste places or destroying crops. All this is in conformity with bedawin customs. However, Sinuhe did receive from the prince who was protecting him a clearly defined district on the frontiers of the territory of another principality,[12] which shows that a certain stability had been reached. In order to account for all the facts, it may be supposed that the

---

[1] Sinai, nos. 103, 112, 115, 405.
[2] Sinai, no. 112. The type appears not to have been in use in Palestine during the Middle Kingdom. See at Ras Shamra, §II, 58, 250, fig. 106A ; 259, fig. 110, no. 25.
[3] Beni Hasan, no. 3.
[4] Sinuhe B 30–241 ; see §III, 9.
[5] §III, 18, vol. I, 142*. Alt, §III, 9, 25–32, still maintains that it was located in the south of Palestine, §III, 7, which seems hardly likely.
[6] Sinuhe B 79–92 ; §III, 10, recto 37–9.   [7] Sinuhe B 240–1.
[8] Sinuhe B 115, 146, 201.   [9] Sinuhe B 110, 145.
[10] Sinuhe B 155.   [11] Sinuhe B 101–6, 112, 143–6.
[12] Sinuhe B 79–81.

inhabitants were nomads or semi-nomads in the process of settling in a region already partly cultivated.

This conclusion accords with what is known concerning the social and political organization of the time. The Execration Texts,[1] one or two centuries later in date than the Story of Sinuhe, confirm in a general way his testimony on this point. The prince entrusts to Sinuhe both a district and a 'tribe (*whyt*), the best in his country'.[2] As they appear in the story, district and tribe seem to be independent of each other; the tribes belonged to a larger framework, that of the 'country' (*ḫꜣst*, literally, 'foreign country'). This relationship between 'tribes' and 'countries' is confirmed by the Execration Texts, which mention the 'tribes' of various countries, as unlike one another as Byblos[3] (meaning not the town but the mountainous hinterland)[4] and *Kwšw*,[5] which corresponds with Midian.[6] Sinuhe becomes 'ruler (*ḥḳꜣ*) of a tribe',[7] but, according to the story, a tribe is normally led by a champion (*nḫt*, literally 'mighty, victorious man').[8] As a general rule, the title of 'ruler' is reserved for princes governing a 'country'; this use of the term is customary during the Middle Kingdom for designating heads of small foreign powers. The 'ruler' who protected Sinuhe had authority over the tribes living in his 'country';[9] he had an army[10] and he had Egyptians at his court.[11] The Sinai inscriptions speak of a 'brother of a ruler', a person of some importance who travels mounted on an ass with a small escort.[12] It is the first mention in an Egyptian text of a class of nobleman which is well attested during the New Kingdom[13] and in cuneiform texts.[14] As an exception, the governors of a country are called 'great ones' (*wrw*),[15] a title which in the New Kingdom was to supplant *ḥḳꜣ* as the

---

[1] See above, pp. 541 and 548–9 .

[2] Sinuhe B 78–81, 86–7; §III, 9, 49.   [3] §II, 51, 94 (E 63).

[4] See above, p. 548, n. 4. See also 'the tribes of '*ꜣḳti*', §II, 51, 93 (E 61), similarly in Phoenicia, §II, 37, 60.

[5] §II, 51, 88–9 (E 50–1).

[6] §II, 3, 34, n. 8; §II, 37, 37–8 and 59.   [7] Sinuhe B 86.

[8] Sinuhe B 92–4, 109, 113. See §I, 50, 41.   [9] Sinuhe B 86–7.

[10] Sinuhe B 100–1.   [11] Sinuhe B 31–4.

[12] §I, 21, part I, pl. 23, no. 85, N. edge; pl. 24, no. 87, W. face; pl. 27, no. 92, S. edge; pl. 37, no. 112, W. face and S. edge; see above, pp. 539 and 553.

[13] E.g. in Syria: §II, 61, 690, 2; 1308, 19; Hittites: §III, 22, 263, no. 152; 375, no. 23; Libyans: §III, 33, pls. 25–6; §III, 27, 66, l. 10; §III, 39, 2, l.7. In Egypt during the Middle Kingdom the expression 'brother of the governor' occurs, §III, 41, 24.

[14] E.g. §III, 6, 17–18; §III, 26, 220–3, 228.

[15] §II, 51, 93 (E 62).

ordinary designation for foreign kings. During the Middle Kingdom the two terms seem to refer to different forms of power. The
country *Kwšw* had at its head 'great men of the tribes',[1] which
is perhaps a sign of a nomadic type of organization. A passage
in Sinuhe seems to hint at the existence of military coalitions;[2]
a prince of Byblos styles himself 'ruler of rulers';[3] Sesostris III's
campaign against Shechem[4] suggests that this town, which was
the centre of a principality,[5] played the role of leader in its
region.[6] Although the indications are slight, it is reasonable to
think of the small states grouping themselves into confederations
led by the more powerful members, an arrangement for which
there is evidence in the archives of Mari[7] and during the New
Kingdom.

Palestine and southern Syria were divided politically into many
units, as the Execration Texts show. The red vases at Berlin
name twenty different countries,[8] while the Saqqara figurines
enumerate sixty-two,[9] and this figure obviously does not exhaust
all the territorial units. Frequently they are referred to by the
name of a town, as for instance Askelon, Achshaph, Hazor,
Byblos, Ullaza, etc.[10] It is in these texts that we find, for the first
time in history, mention of Jerusalem.[11] Among the localities
which have been identified there are relatively few names of
regions; they include Damascus and its environs (*Api*), Midian
(*Kwšw*), probably Biqā' and Antilebanon (Sirion). The older
catalogue, that of the vases, names several rulers for most of the
localities, two, for instance, for Jerusalem, and for some places
three or even four.[12] Here again the enumeration no doubt gives
only an incomplete idea of the fragmentation which existed. This
multiplication of princes under the same heading suggests a tribal
type of organization, as it is known among nomads.[13] In certain
cases it seems possible to detect evidence of the break-up of small
city states, which had existed previously, into still smaller political

[1] §II, 51, 88–9 (E 50–1).
[2] Sinuhe B 97–9; on this difficult passage see §III, 10, 10–11.
[3] §II, 40, *Text*, 196, 203; *Atlas*, pl. 117, no. 787.
[4] See above, p. 538.   [5] §II, 51, 68 (E 6).
[6] §III, 20, 4–5.   [7] §II, 45, 74–84.
[8] §I, 50, 55–8.   [9] §II, 51, 62–96.
[10] For the identification of the place-names in the Execration Texts, the following,
in addition to §I, 50; §II, 51, should particularly be consulted: §II, 1; §III, 3;
§II, 3; §II, 5; §II, 6; §II, 22; §III, 15; §II, 37; §II, 71; §I, 60, 155–9; §III, 42;
§III, 13; §III, 17, 90; §III, 25; §III, 23, 83–95.
[11] §I, 50, 53 (e 27–8), 58 (f 18); §II, 51, 86 (E 45).
[12] §I, 50, 45–55. See also A, 11, 285–6.   [13] §II, 1, 253; §II, 2, 218–19.

units.[1] The Saqqara figurines, which are slightly later in date, name only one ruler for most of the countries.[2] This change may reflect an historical development, either the reconstitution of the old principalities or the merging of related groups.[3] A short passage at the end of the repertory of princes on the figurines bears witness to an earlier state of the text.[4] For two of the countries, it mentions only 'tribes'; for another country this version gives 'all the rulers', while the catalogue which precedes names only a single ruler. Finally, for one country we find 'the great ones', whereas the catalogue gives it a ruler. These comparisons give an idea of the confusion produced by the arrival of nomads, or semi-nomads, and of the fairly rapid return to a certain degree of stability. A parallel has been drawn between the evidence of the Egyptian sources and the facts as they are known from excavation: at about this time a noticeable decline occurs in the material civilization and in the urban life; it was followed by a speedy renaissance.[5]

In contrast with what can be observed in Mesopotamia, the movements of people which took place in the Fertile Crescent at the turn of the second millennium have left no trace in Egyptian vocabulary or in written documents during the period of the Middle Kingdom. The earliest known mention of Amor[6] is much later, and dates from about 1300 B.C.[7] The occurrence of the term Khurri[8] has not been established for certain earlier than the 15th century B.C.[9] No doubt the changes which took place were slow in being noticed in Egypt and by the time they reached the frontiers were toned down; such changes as occurred are less easy to perceive in Egypt than elsewhere and, in any case, the

[1] §II, 6, 37–9; §III, 9, 41–2; §II, 71, 208.

[2] §II, 51, 64–93.   [3] See above, n. 1.

[4] §II, 51, 25 and 93–4 (E 61–4).

[5] §II, 2, 218–19; §III, 5, 80–3.   [6] See below, pp. 562–5.

[7] §III, 18, vol. I, 187*–90*. The attempt to discover Amurru in the Execration Texts, see §II, 22, 221–3; §II, 41, 25, with regard to §I, 50, 47 (e7) and 56 (f6), has been abandoned, see §II, 1, 239; §III, 8. Moreover, the presence of the god Amurru in the list of theophorous names of these texts, see §II, 22, 227 with regard to §I, 50, 50 (e15) has not been confirmed, see §III, 19, 31.

[8] See below, pp. 565–6.

[9] §III, 18, vol. I, 180*–7*. It was thought that an example of Khor in the Twelfth Dynasty had been found, §III, 12, but this is actually an Egyptian word, §III, 30; §III, 31, used in a title for officials; for parallels see §III, 16, 174–5, where this example has been omitted. P. Berlin 3056 (Twenty-Second Dynasty) attributes to the Twelfth Dynasty a text (*verso* 8, 4–9, 8) which contains a mention of Khor (*verso* 8, 11; §III, 29, pl. 33); too much reliance should not be placed on this document.

Egyptian civilization was less receptive of change than that of its neighbours. Egypt of the Twelfth Dynasty, in fact, limited itself, so far as Asiatics were concerned, to the traditional vocabulary going back to the Old Kingdom; the ethnic term which is most recent in date, '*ʒmw*, had been in use since the Sixth Dynasty.[1] Only in place-names are any innovations to be observed. Retenu (*Rtnw*)[2] makes its first certain appearance in the story of Sinuhe (dating from the end of the reign of Sesostris I).[3] It is possible that very early, if not from the outset, this name had a wide meaning[4] and included Palestine and Syria, as it did during the New Kingdom.[5] Attempts have been made to connect Retenu with Lōtān,[6] Lydda[7] and even Resaina on the Khabur;[8] there are, however, serious objections to each of these identifications. Without knowing the etymology of Retenu for certain,[9] we cannot take it into account in studying the population of Syria and Palestine.

In this connexion, some positive facts are provided by the texts of the Middle Kingdom, especially by the Execration Texts.[10] From the formation of the names of persons mentioned in the texts much can be learnt about the language and the beliefs prevailing among the ruling classes of the population, the names being nearly always the names of princes. The first point to note is that there is no certain example of a personal name which is not

[1] See above, p. 534.

[2] Thus, in preference to *Rtnw*: the place-name is, in fact, written in Sinuhe B with determinatives from the root *ṯni* which, in the Middle Kingdom, was pronounced *ṯni* and was used with such a value for transcribing from the Semitic, §II, 51, 66–7. Different forms of the place-name, perhaps earlier: *Tnw* (Sinuhe B), '*Itinw* (? §I, 21, part I, pl. 39, no. 115, W. Face); the last example is not quite certain.

[3] Very debatable example under Mentuhotpe II, §I, 33, vol. I, pl. 15 F; §I, 8, 38.

[4] It appears, in fact, from Sinuhe B 130–1 that Retenu encompassed various 'countries'. The title 'ruler of Retenu' attested by the story of Sinuhe B 30–1, 99–100, and the inscriptions of Sinai, see above, p. 554, n. 12, has suggested a limited area of this country. Actually this title is not exclusive in character; the Execration Texts show, as we have seen, that there could be several princes of the same country.

[5] §III, 18, vol. I, 142*–9*.

[6] §III, 24 following many others.

[7] §III, 7.

[8] §III, 21, 100–3.

[9] See several suggestions, §I, 32, 147; §III, 1, 9, n. 23; §II, 37, 39.

[10] Other sources: inscriptions of Sinai, §II, 17; Byblos, §II, 40, *Texte*, 165, 174, 212; §II, 21, vol. I, *Texte*, 197–8; vol. II, *Texte*, 130, 174–5, 878; §II, 41, 90–3; §II, 42, 96; §I, 1; §III, 4; §III, 34, 109; §III, 35, 54; there are some unpublished documents from Byblos. See also the name of the prince in the story of Sinuhe, §III, 14; §III, 10, *recto*, 20; the name of the prince in §I, 34, part I, pl. 28; §III, 38, 45 and pl. 9, l. 3; A, 10; A, 2.

Semitic.[1] Secondly, a high degree of homogeneity prevails; the names, as far as it has been possible to explain them,[2] belong to the north-west Semitic dialects; they are of the same type as the names found in the cuneiform texts of Mesopotamia and northern Syria at about this period. Egyptian texts therefore indicate how far the Amorite movement had advanced westwards and they confirm its basic unity throughout the Fertile Crescent. Among the characteristic features in the formation of the names may be noted the frequency of terms of kinship referring to some deity and establishing a close link between it and the bearer of the name. This feature is reminiscent of nomadic traditions.[3]

Theophorous names make mention of a dozen deities. Hadad, the god of storm, occupies first place, taking precedence even over the generic term 'El. Next in order of frequency is the god Anu, male counterpart of Anat, and the sun-god Shamash. Then come the mountain-god Har, made familiar by Hyksos names, and the Palestinian god Haurān, who was to become popular in the Egypt of the Eighteenth Dynasty.[4] In addition may be noted the god Star (that is, morning star), the craftsman-god Kushar, who plays a far from negligible role in the mythology of Ugarit, the god Lim, made familiar by the names of the kings of Alalakh and Mari, etc. Ba'al appears only once, and it seems that 'the Master' was still a divine epithet and not an independent god.[5] Since all the persons whose names have been studied are men, the absence of the names of goddesses is not surprising. The only feminine name in the texts is a component of Ba'alat,[6] whose worship is well attested by the proto-Sinaitic inscriptions about the end of the Twelfth Dynasty.[7] A list of slaves, the majority of them women, from the middle of the Thirteenth Dynasty, contains, however, both a theophorous name compounded with the name of this goddess and two others compounded with the name of Anat.[8]

---

[1] A possible instance: §II, 51, 87 (E 48); see §III, 36, 27; §I, 60, 164; at Byblos, §I, 1.

[2] Principal studies: §II, 1; §II, 22; §III, 15; §III, 36, 20–32; §III, 19; §III, 32.

[3] §III, 2, 185–6.   [4] §III, 37.

[5] §II, 4, 231   [6] Ibid.

[7] See above, p. 539, n. 7.   [8] §I, 26, 92–9; §II, 4.

IV. SYRIA DURING THE THIRD DYNASTY
OF UR

For lack of documentary evidence we do not know what became of the Mesopotamian conquests in Syria after the end of the Agade Dynasty and during the Gutian period. That the country remained under the cultural influence of Sumer and Akkad is *a priori* highly probable, and in the absence of texts certain archaeological finds show this fairly well. But the rare written testimonies which have survived make specific note only of commercial relations; we shall see that they add something to our knowledge of Syrian geography at this epoch.

So it is that we find again the 'Mountain of Cedars', Amanus, as the origin of the 'cedar trunks, 50 and 60 cubits in length' and the 'boxwood trunks, 25 cubits in length', which Gudea, governor of Lagash, obtained to build the temple of Ningirsu in his city.[1] There is a similar note concerning stone imported by the same prince from the region of Basar, written Basallu, and named along with Tidan/Ditan[2]—both of these are called by Gudea 'Mountains of Amurru'.[3] This is apparently the same region as that which he calls elsewhere the 'Upper Country',[4] as it was already known in the days of Sargon.[5] In the same group of inscriptions we have Ibla, and with it, named for the first time, Ursu (Urshu), in a mountainous district from which wood-resins were procured.[6] Other localities named by Gudea in proximity to these must also have been in Syria, such as the country of Khahhum, from which came gold,[7] and that mysterious mountain 'Uringiriaz of the Upper Sea'.[8] Possibly in Cilicia was 'Umanu, a mountain of Menua'.[9]

When Mesopotamia was reunited once more as an empire during the 'neo-Sumerian' period of the Third Dynasty of Ur, documents which have any bearing upon the extent of its authority in the west and north-west are still too rare and say too little. There is a date-formula of Ur-Nammu, first king of this dynasty,

---

[1] See above, p. 460; §IV, 54, 68 f. and 104 f.

[2] For orthographic variants of this name see §IV, 24, 232; §IV, 5, vol. III, 164 f.; §IV, 44, 68 f., n. 5; §IV, 39, 156 f.

[3] §IV, 54, 70 f., col. VI, 5 and 13.   [4] *Ibid.* 102 f., col. XII, 5.

[5] See above, pp. 420 f.

[6] §IV, 54, 70 f., col. V, 53. For Urshu see §IV, 38 and §IV, 21, 31. In §IV, 32, 103 *b Amurru* and (*lú*) *Uršu* are found as equivalents.

[7] §IV, 54, 70 f., col. VI, 33; §IV, 23, 75 ff.; §IV, 21, 10.

[8] §IV, 54, 144 f. *e*, II, 2.   [9] *Ibid.* 70 f., col. VI, 3 f.

which states barely that 'he went the road from down below to up above',[1] an expression which might be understood of an expedition into the Upper Country, perhaps as far as the Upper Sea, which would suggest that the new power at least attempted to lay hands upon the Syrian heritage of the old kings of Agade. But the formula is too concise to found anything upon. The neo-Sumerian kings of Ur again took the title 'King of the Four Regions', inaugurated perhaps by Sargon,[2] and this could be understood of an empire stretching to the four cardinal points,[3] thus including the west and north-west. But this again indicates nothing precise about the real extent of the sway of the Third Dynasty, and the place which Syria might have occupied in it.

In this absence of explicit facts the only evidence is the presence in various towns of representatives of the kings of Ur —governors (*šakkana*) and lieutenants (*ensi*). Thus at Mari have been found the names and traces of a whole line of these delegates, the *šakkana*-officers Apil-kîn,[4] Idi-ilum, Ilum-ishar, Ishme-Dagan, Ishtup-ilum, Izi-Dagan, Niwar-Mēr, Puzur-Ish-tar, and Tura-Dagan.[5] Perhaps it was the Tuttul downstream from Mari where ruled an *ensi* named Iashilim, mentioned in a tablet from Drehem.[6] Much farther to the west, possibly in Cappadocia itself, was Abarnium, the seat of another governor.[7] Again in the north, but apparently in the Khabur district, we hear of another *ensi* at Apishal.[8] Finally, on the Mediterranean coast, Byblos appears on another tablet from Drehem; its *ensi*, Ibdati, was also in relation with the kings of Ur.[9]

Along with these Syrian and even Cappadocian towns, thus known to have been in touch with the Mesopotamian empire, the mass of administrative documents contains allusions to others which may be assigned to the same region, whether their location is known or not—a second Tuttul,[10] apparently in the area of the Balīkh; the Khahhum already mentioned by Gudea, which must have been an important mercantile centre at this time;[11] likewise

---

[1] §IV, 16, vol. II, 140 *a*, no. 18.
[2] §IV, 7, 11, no. 4, 1–5; but this is only a late allusion.
[3] §IV, 42, 218 ff.
[4] For this reading of the name see §IV, 14.
[5] §IV, 12.
[6] §IV, 52, 120, rev. 18.
[7] §IV, 23, 66.   [8] *Ibid.* 71.
[9] §IV, 52. Fragment of Sumerian vocabulary from Byblos dated to this period, §IV, 15, tome II, atlas pl. CXLV, no. 14023; see also *Bull. A.S.O.R.* 163 (1961), 45.
[10] §IV, 23, 74; §IV, 31, 121.
[11] §IV, 23, 75.

Urshu,[1] and in the same area Armanum,[2] Ibla,[3] and Mukish,[4] also Terqa, farther down the Euphrates, about twenty miles upstream from Mari.[5] In Zidanum[6] it has been proposed to recognize the Phoenician city of Sidon, but it would be more reasonable to look for this elsewhere, on the Balīkh, for example, not far from Raqqah, where is found Tell Zaydān, which must cover some very ancient city.[7]

Several of these places and others as well figure also in the archives of Assyrian traders, small 'colonies' dwelling in Cappadocia at least in the closing years of the Third Dynasty of Ur, but no doubt already at an even earlier period.[8] The existence of these Mesopotamian 'colonies' in the heart of Anatolia is ample proof of the strong cultural influence of Sumer and Akkad even there—much more in Syria, whether there was political dependence or not. The following are the towns frequented by these Cappadocian merchants : Abarna/Abarnium ;[9] Khahhum ;[10] Ibla ;[11] Urshu,[12] these being known to us already, while the following are as yet not mentioned in our Syrian records : Abum/Apum ;[13] Elakhut (with various spellings) ;[14] Khaburrata ;[15] Harran ;[16] Nakhur ;[17] Nikhriia ;[18] Razama ;[19] Tadmor, which is Palmyra ;[20] Talkhatum ;[21] and Zalpa (Zalpakh).[22]

Perhaps it will be a surprise not to see figuring either in the neo-Sumerian lists or in those of the Agade period (which are rarer) one or other of those great and ancient Syrian cities such as Carchemish, Aleppo, or Damascus, which we have every reason to suppose already existed, and had probably existed long before. If they are not concealed by some of the names listed above—a fragile hypothesis, which may nevertheless be ventured—it should be remembered that our records, not necessarily complete even

---

[1] §IV, 23, 84.
[2] §IV, 29, no. 50, 4.
[3] §IV, 23, 77.
[4] Ibid. 81 f.
[5] Ibid. 83 f.
[6] §IV, 25, 104.
[7] According to information from M. G. Dossin.
[8] See below, pp. 707 ff.
[9] §IV, 3, 32.
[10] Ibid. 33.
[11] Ibid. 33.
[12] Ibid. 37.
[13] Ibid. 32 ; §IV, 30, 67 ; §IV, 21, 2 ; §IV, 1, 34 f.
[14] §IV, 3, 33 f.; §IV, 30, 67 ; §IV, 21, 8 f.
[15] §IV, 3, 23 ; §IV, 30, 66 f.; §IV, 21, 7 (sub Buralum).
[16] §IV, 3, 33 (sub Harrana).
[17] Ibid. 34 ; §IV, 21, 20 ; §IV, 39, 8, n. 2.
[18] §IV, 3, 34 ; §IV, 30, 61 f.; §IV, 21, 20 f.
[19] §IV, 3, 35 ; §IV, 30, 64 and 66 f.; §IV, 21, 23 f.
[20] §IV, 3, 36.
[21] Ibid. and §IV, 30, 67 ff.; §IV, 21, 29.
[22] §IV, 3, 36 ; §IV, 30, 69, n. 35 ; §IV, 21, 33 f.

in their own day, have come down to us only as minute scraps; each new find may amplify them and add to our knowledge of the physical and political geography of ancient Syria.

Even when these sources have been exhausted so far as concerns geography they still provide one more fact which may illustrate the ethnography and demography of Syria in this period. Less than a century after the beginning of the Third Dynasty of Ur the Mesopotamian kings, far from going like their predecessors to war in the north and north-west, had to withstand attacks from these directions, for it is recorded that in the third year of his reign Shu-Sin 'built a rampart against Amurru (called) Fender of Tidnum'[1]—the stronghold in question was later called 'town of Amurru'.[2] Another inscription of the same king adds 'and he chased the armed force of Amurru out of his country'.[3] These attacks, or at least this state of war, doubtless went back earlier. Revolts of already conquered peoples against the older kings of Agade would perhaps explain their repeated campaigns in that direction. Again, under Shulgi[4] and Amar-Sin,[5] the two predecessors of Shu-Sin, there are allusions to 'prisoners of war from Amurru'.

We have already encountered Tidnum, or Dit(a)num,[6] which Gudea names side by side with Basallu (Basar),[7] the mountain where Shar-kali-sharri had defeated Amurru on its own ground.[8] Whatever the original meaning of these two names, it is clear that for Shu-Sin they were almost equivalent, both referring to the invaders he had to resist. Comparison with the older evidence leaves no doubt as to the origin of these opponents—they came from the Syrian region, from the Upper Country, as the next king Ibbi-Sin[9] and his enemy Ishbi-Erra[10] were each independently to confirm.

We are therefore in presence of an ethnic group called *martu* in Sumerian and *amurrū* in Akkadian,[11] which occupied a part

---

[1] §IV, 16, II, 114 f., no. 80. Variants in §IV, 39, 157, n. 1, and §IV, 24, 232; see also §IV, 3, 30. See below, pp. 609 f.

[2] §IV, 39, 160 f., but cf. also *ibid.* 165, n. 1.

[3] §IV, 8, 16, no. 20, 24 ff.; §IV, 55, 180 f. For a slightly later date, §IV, 36, 39 and §IV, 39, 157.   [4] §IV, 47, no. 9, 5.

[5] §IV, 6, 17, no. 32, 5 f.   [6] See above, p. 559, n. 2.

[7] See above, p. 559.

[8] Ditnu is identified with Amurru by a vocabulary, §IV, 41, 114, line 209.

[9] §IV, 19, 62.

[10] §IV, 36, 39.

[11] §IV, 39, 149 and n. 1. The geographical meaning of 'western' is attested from the Agade period, §IV, 27, 30 a and n. 12.

of the Syrian territory, at least during the second half of the third and the beginning of the second millennium. Before defining them more clearly it should be noticed that these Amurru were not making their first appearance in Mesopotamia at the time of the Third Ur dynasty. In the archaic tablets of Fārah (Shuruppak) mention is made twice of individuals called *martu*,[1] and under the Dynasty of Agade such persons appear more frequently, both singly[2] and in groups,[3] their names being written not only in the Sumerian[4] but also the Akkadian[5] form. In some cases perhaps these immigrants were bodies of men recruited for some official service, civil or military, for a stela of that period found at Lagash mentions one of their 'officers' (*nu-banda martu-ne*), named Uṣi-Malik, among the receivers of an allocation of land, which must have been as a reward for services to the crown.[6] 'Amorites' also figure along with Gutians in a document from the end of the Agade period.[7] Finally, they are found more and more often (and thus appear to have been more and more numerous) in documents of the neo-Sumerian period.[8] This process suggests a continuous immigration, for the most part peaceful, extending back very far in time, perhaps even before the beginning of the third millennium. After the end of that millennium came intermittent massive thrusts, such as are attested under Shu-Sin and Ibbi-Sin. These must have been more than revolts against Mesopotamian authority—real attempts, if not at invasion, at local conquests or raids.

The cuneiform documents allow us to build up a fairly clear picture of these 'Westerners'. First, we see that the majority, at least, of these people were nomads or semi-nomads.[9] Ibbi-Sin speaks of them as 'vagabonds who have never known what a town was',[10] and Sumerian literary texts emphasize this still more by describing the *martu* as barbarians 'knowing neither cereals nor house, feeding themselves on wild truffles and undressed meat, possessing no fixed abode in all the course of their life nor a tomb

---

[1] §IV, 10, 61, no. 78, rev. 10; §IV, 37, no. 648, obv. II, 4. The supposed mention of Ditnu in an inscription of Eannatum is doubted by §IV, 35, 131, n. 90 (cf. §IV, 20, 281, n. 5), but admitted by §IV, 17, 249 f.

[2] §IV, 46, 78, no. 180, 9.

[3] §IV, 34, I, no. 1475 (ten); §IV, 50, 77, no. 18 (twenty-one, in Elam). Other references in §IV, 39, 150 ff.

[4] See the two preceding notes.

[5] §IV, 39, 167, n. 1.

[6] §IV, 54, 170 f. *b*, III, 9 f.

[7] §IV, 22, no. 43, rev. 6.

[8] §IV, 39, 151, n. 3, also 152 f. and 167, n. 1.

[9] *Ibid.* introd. x.

[10] §IV, 16, II, 146 *a*, no. 98; §IV, 53, 43.

after their death'.[1] Even if the poets were exaggerating so as to
blacken their enemies' character[2] it remains that, in the eyes of
the Mesopotamians, these Amurru must have seemed a turbulent
and unstable people. They infested the country round about
settlements, and especially the fringes of the desert, where they
practised a little cattle-raising and the meagre harvesting possible
in those arid lands, but were always ready for a sudden attack
upon the peasants and city-dwellers. Texts of slightly later date
help, however, to correct this rather too unfavourable view, for at
Mari there is some mention of 'Amurru kings'.[3] Some at least
of the Westerners were thus settled and grouped into 'kingdoms',
centred no doubt on some of the Syrian cities named in the
inscriptions of the Agade kings, of Gudea, and of the Third
Dynasty of Ur.[4]

The documents give evidence also that these Amurru were
Semites; this appears from their names which are often supplied
by the scribes. These names occasionally have a Sumerian or
Akkadian stamp,[5] for some of the immigrants, after an extended
sojourn in their adopted country, had assumed names like those
of their fellow-citizens, whose language and mode of thought they
must have adopted. But others, when they were recorded in the
tablets, still kept their original names, and a review of these leaves
no doubt of their Semitic character.

We can be still more precise, for among the elements of these
personal names occur typically 'western' deities like Dagan,[6]
Adad, Lim, and Mēr or Wēr.[7] The presence too of the suffix
-anum,[8] and the verbal prefix of the third person singular in ia-[9]
(whereas in Eastern Semitic it is i-) obliges us to assign the
language of Amurru to the western branch, more specifically to
North-western Semitic, sometimes called Canaanite.[10] This dia-

---

[1] §iv, 18, 31 f., texts quoted d–g.   [2] §iv, 39, 160.

[3] §iv, 13, 37. The word 'king' is applied to rulers of realms centred upon an
urban administration.

[4] Especially that part of Syria about the middle Orontes, later called 'land of
Amurru', §iv, 39, 178 f.

[5] §iv, 39, 153 f.

[6] Ili-Dagan of Ibla, §iv, 11, 56 and 59; see §iv, 23, 77; Izin-Dagan of Ibla,
§iv, 32, 105; Dagan-abu of Tuttul, §iv, 32, 120. Also many Dagan-names at
Mari, e.g. above, p. 560.

[7] Rish-Adad of Apishal, Iashilim of Tuttul, Niwar-Mēr of Mari, see above,
p. 560.

[8] Thus Elanum, §iv, 43, no. 295, 15; §iv, 39, 154; §iv, 18, 40.

[9] Ianbi-ilum, §iv, 28, pl. xxi, no. 5508, col. i, 11; Iashilim of Tuttul, above,
p. 560, n. 6. See also §iv, 39, 155 and §iv, 18, 41.

[10] §iv, 39, 239 f.

lect is quite distinct from Akkadian, and very close to that spoken by the Western Semites, who had come to Mesopotamia in such numbers before the beginning of the First Dynasty of Babylon. Of these the Amurru, it seems clear, were none other than the ancestors in the exact sense of the word.[1] Thus, then, we are led to place in Syria, during the second half of the third millennium at the latest, a West Semitic population, partly nomadic or semi-nomadic, but partly settled and grouped into kingdoms.

Were these Western Semites the only people to be found in Syrian territory at that time? Undoubtedly not, for among the names of individuals coming then from Amurru are some which clearly cannot be assigned to any of the great linguistic branches flourishing in the Near East in those days; they are neither Sumerian nor Semitic, eastern or western. Thus there is Gababa from Mukish[2] and Memeshura from Ibla,[3] to give only these examples.[4] On the other hand, these names are not Hurrian. During the Third Dynasty of Ur it seems clear that the Hurrian invasion had not yet touched the extreme north and north-east of Mesopotamia. Certain districts of Upper Syria were occupied, such as the town of Urkish,[5] where reigned Tisari, author of one of the oldest Hurrian inscriptions, which may go back to the end of the Agade period.[6] But there is nothing to prove—quite the contrary—that the Hurrians had in those days already advanced both to the south and in the direction of the Mediterranean, as they were to do by the time of the First Dynasty of Babylon.

It would seem therefore, from written evidence of this period, that Syria was far from being one political and ethnic unit; it was divided into principalities and 'kingdoms', more or less small, more or less confederated, each centred upon an important town —a division which was certainly fluid and variable according to the times and the hazards of wars and supremacies. These towns and their territories were occupied by a population largely consti-tuted by Semites of the western branch. There were also uniden-tified peoples, not assignable, with our present knowledge, to any definite group, and it is not clear whether they formed any kind of ethnic or linguistic unit among themselves. Nor can the numerical proportion of this element be estimated: compared

---

[1] §IV, 39, 155 f. and 240 f.   [2] §IV, 4, no. 203, 8 f.

[3] §IV, 9, no. 27, 3.

[4] See also §IV, 25, 100 ff. and §IV, 26, *passim*.

[5] §IV, 33, 27 f. According to information from M. Dossin this tablet was found at 'Amuda, twelve miles west of Nisibis, which may thus be Urkish.

[6] §IV, 26; §IV, 51, 180, n. 2.

with the great extent of time and space for which they provide evidence the personal names are too few to form the basis of statistics. It is barely possible to hazard a conjecture about the population in a particular city, according to the greater or lesser proportion of Semitic and other names. At Mari, for example, the Semites are in a great majority,[1] but elsewhere the list that we possess is far too meagre to judge, and chance has played too great a part in its make-up.

Nevertheless we can regard it as almost certain that among the whole population of ancient Syria the Semites were the latest comers. It has long been observed that most of the old place-names in the country cannot be explained as Semitic, but belong to one or several unknown linguistic complexes.[2] The Semites were thus preceded by various peoples of different race, to whom the non-Semitic elements in the names must be attributed. On top of these ethnic strata a final layer began to add itself towards the end of the third millennium—the Hurrians, coming no doubt from the north or east. But at the period now being described we have as yet no authority for making them descend any great distance into Syrian territory.[3]

Leaving the Hurrians aside, part of the Syrian population, and particularly of the Semites, was still composed, in a proportion as yet undefinable, of semi-nomads. Wandering about the fringes of the desert in unstable groups, a constant threat to the peace and possessions of the settled, they were nevertheless attracted by peasant and especially urban life, and numbers of them, little by little, allowed themselves to be absorbed by the towns. For this process of settlement, which seems to embrace the whole ancient history of the Semites, there is abundant evidence in Mesopotamia, for there it is clear that all the immigrants from the west quickly lost their instability, joining the population of cultivators and townspeople and losing their old identity.[4] For others, who remained in Syria, it is likely that a similar change took place locally.

The documents in cuneiform writing permit us to reconstruct only an outline, still blurred and imprecise, of Syria in archaic times. But it fits well enough into the more exact and detailed picture which much richer records allow us to draw in the second millennium and onwards.

[1] §IV, 27, 34 f.   [2] Ibid. 40 b.
[3] Ibid. 38 f.   [4] §IV, 39, Introd. xiii ff.

V. ARCHAEOLOGICAL EVIDENCE
FROM PALESTINE

At the end of the Early Bronze Age there was a complete and absolute break in Palestinian civilization. The town dwellers of the earlier period were succeeded by semi-nomadic pastoralists who had no interest in walled towns. They seem to have destroyed the towns of their predecessors, and with the exception of Megiddo, which is a special case, their contribution to the history of towns is negligible.

It is for this reason that this stage in the history of Palestine has received only tardy recognition. Nearly all the evidence concerning the newcomers of this period comes from tombs, and earlier excavators did not realize the implications of the lack of association between the types of tombs and the successive layers on the town sites. The first to recognize that in tombs of this period he was dealing with a distinct period was Petrie in 1932,[1] who gave to them the designation of Copper Age, since they were rich in weapons that appeared to be copper rather than bronze. The first to place the phase in a sequence of periods on a site was Albright, in his reports on Tell Beit Mirsim published in 1932 and 1933.[2] In a sequence of levels starting at an Early Bronze Age level J, the period in question was represented by I–H, to which Albright gave the designation Middle Bronze I, for he recognized that it contained material distinct from the Early Bronze Age and from that of the classical Middle Bronze Age.

As knowledge of the period has increased, it has appeared that this designation was unfortunate, for it is a stage just as distinct from the Middle Bronze Age as it is from the Early Bronze Age.[3] This was recognized by J. H. Iliffe in his arrangement of the exhibits in the Palestine Archaeological Museum. He gave to it the name Intermediate Early Bronze–Middle Bronze period, and this, with the abbreviation E.B.–M.B., seems the best name to use.

The reasons for insisting on the break at the beginning and end of this period will emerge from the description of the evidence from the different sites, but it will be convenient to summarize them in advance. There is in the first place a complete stratigraphic break at all the sites for which there is evidence. Secondly, there is no evidence at all for any walled towns of this period, whereas this was the characteristic form of settlement in the Early

[1] §v, 3.   [2] § v, 1.   [3] §v, 2, 135 ff.

Bronze Age, and became so again in the Middle Bronze Age. The contrast in domestic architecture is equally great, for there is in the period no evidence of the solidly built houses of the preceding and succeeding periods. Thirdly, the Early Bronze Age burials are in large tombs with multiple burials. At all sites in the E.B.–M.B. period, with the exception of Megiddo, burials were essentially those of single individuals. In the Middle Bronze Age, burials are once more usually multiple in tombs, though sometimes single in graves. Fourthly, the material equipment is completely different. The pottery forms are absolutely distinct from those of the Middle Bronze Age. They are rather closer to those of the Early Bronze Age, but the technique is so different, with the complete disappearance of red slip and burnishing, with the characteristic thin, gritty texture of the ware, and with the practice of making the body of the vessel by hand and the rim on a fast wheel, that there is seldom any difficulty in distinguishing vessels or even sherds of the two periods. The second great contrast is in weapons. Metal weapons are rare in the Early Bronze Age, and not very common in the Middle Bronze Age. In the E.B.–M.B. period they are very common, with an especially large number of daggers, of form quite distinct from the few Early Bronze specimens known and from the well-established forms of the Middle Bronze Age. Other weapons, javelins and axes, are equally distinctive. It is also probable that the E.B.–M.B. weapons are of copper and that bronze first appears in the Middle Bronze Age,[1] though more analyses on this subject would be valuable.

VI. PALESTINE: THE SITES

It is at Jericho that the clearest evidence of the differentiation of this period from the preceding and succeeding ones has emerged, and also of the character of the occupation, so it will be convenient to begin with that site.

The Early Bronze Age levels at Jericho provide evidence of a series of occupation levels and a series of reconstructions of the walls. In the most complete section through the town walls,[2] seventeen stages of building and reconstruction were identified. The seventeenth stage was violently destroyed by fire, and it was succeeded by an occupation of an entirely different character. In the ditches belonging to the final stage of the defences appeared E.B.–M.B. pottery. It was only when the silt in the ditches had

[1] §vi, 4, 160 ff.   [2] §vi, 10.

accumulated to a depth of at least 2·25 metres that structures (of a new character) appeared.[1] The inference is that there was a period of occupation that left no structural evidence, that is to say a camping period. At the end of this period, the buildings that appear are strikingly different from the buildings of the preceding (and succeeding) periods. They are built of brick of a distinctive greenish colour, and the walls are only one brick thick. The evidence for the plan of the buildings is limited, but it suggests that they were irregular in layout.

Most of the structures found were clearly dwelling houses. One building only may have been other than domestic. In this[2] on either side of a partition wall were massive brick blocks that could have been tables, but seem more likely to have been altars. Adjacent to one was a large clay bin, which again could have served domestic purposes, but could have been a receptacle for offerings. Beneath one of the walls of the building was an infant burial, presumably a foundation sacrifice; again this could be found in connexion with a domestic building, but is not found elsewhere at Jericho at this stage, so may again have ceremonial implications. The combination of these features suggests that the building may have been a shrine. However, even if this is accepted, too little of the plan could be recovered to provide clear evidence of the religious practices of the period.

The non-urban character of the occupation is emphasized by the absence of any town walls. Jericho was a nucleus of population rather than an urban centre. Indeed, it would appear that part of the town site was unoccupied, while on the other hand there were dwellings on the surrounding hill slopes. In two areas on the eastern side of the *tell*, excavated by the 1952–8 expedition, squares E III–IV and squares H II–III,[3] there was no evidence at all of E.B.–M.B. houses; in the case of the latter area the Middle Bronze levels directly succeeded those of the Early Bronze Age, while in squares E III–IV the ruins of the Early Bronze Age houses showed no sign of destruction or disturbance in the E.B.–M.B. period, but no overlying Middle Bronze levels survived here. These areas contrast with those excavated in the centre of the west side of the *tell* and at the north and south ends, in all of which characteristic E.B.–M.B. structures were found.

The evidence for contemporary occupation beyond the limits of the *tell* comes from the hill slopes to the north and north-west,

[1] §vi, 8, 12 ff.　　　　[2] §vi, 8, 14 and pl. xiii, 1.
[3] §vi, 6, fig. 3.

which was one of the main cemetery areas. In several places there were traces of occupation levels,[1] and in one area slight wall foundations survived. Moreover, in a number of instances there were sherds of E.B.–M.B. pottery in the filling of the tomb shafts, of forms found in the houses but not in the tombs. In none of the areas in which dwellings were traced was there evidence of prolonged occupation. In some cases, rebuildings and modifications to the plans could be traced, but the evidence is clear that the period during which houses of this type were used was not very long.

The evidence from the tomb area is very different. Of the total of 507 tombs excavated in the 1952–8 expedition, 346 belong to the E.B.–M.B. period.[2] As will be seen, this number is enormously inflated in comparison to preceding and succeeding periods by the practice of individual burial in tombs, but nevertheless, with a proportion in the northern cemetery of 356 estimated individuals to 722 of the Middle Bronze Age, the importance and character of the period is clear.

The evidence from the *tell* thus suggests a destruction of the pre-existing Early Bronze Age town, followed by a camping period in which there were no solid structures on the site; subsequently there were buildings, slight in character and entirely different from the buildings of the Early Bronze Age. The evidence from the tombs suggests that there was a numerous and virile population, of which the burial practices were entirely different from those of the Early Bronze Age occupation of Jericho.

The Early Bronze Age tombs at Jericho contained multiple burials in large chamber tombs.[3] The E.B.–M.B. burials are in tombs that may be similar in size, but the burials are characteristically of a single individual, with at most two bodies in a single tomb.[4] There is here therefore a very different approach in burial practices.

In the E.B.–M.B. burials the emphasis is on individual tombs, but the Jericho finds show that there was a variety in the method of tomb excavation and burial that is significant for the interpretation of the evidence. Seven types of tomb could be identified, all of them consisting of rock-cut chambers approached by a vertical shaft. In the first type,[5] described as the Dagger type, there was an individual burial of a complete skeleton in each tomb and the

[1] §vi, 6, 192.   [2] §vi, 7, vol. ii, 1.
[3] §vi, 7, vol. i, 52 ff.   [4] §vi, 7, vol. i, 180 ff., vol. ii, 33 ff.
[5] §vi, 7, vol. i, 186 ff., vol. ii, 50 ff.

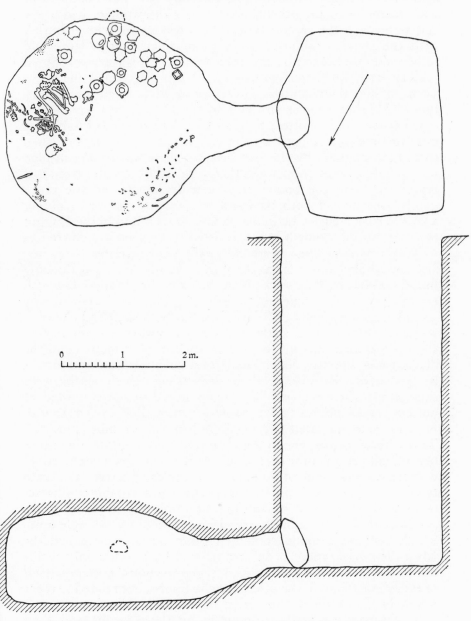

Fig. 19. Plan and section of an Outsize Tomb (P. 12) at Jericho.

tomb was of modest dimensions, carefully cut; most bodies had with them a dagger, others, presumably the women, had a pin and beads. In the second type,[1] there was an individual burial, with the skeleton almost always disarticulated, in a large and rather roughly cut tomb; the grave goods in this type were small pottery jars, and there was usually a lamp placed in a niche cut in the wall of the chamber. These tombs were called the Pottery type. There were never any pots in the Dagger type tombs, nor any weapons in the Pottery type tombs. A third type of tomb was intermediate in size between the first two, but was distinguished from both of them by the fact that the shaft was square in plan instead of round; they were therefore called the Square-shaft type.[2] In them the bodies were usually intact, and the grave goods consisted of both pots and weapons, the latter including a javelin with a curled tang, which was never found in the Dagger type tombs. The fourth type consisted of very poorly cut tombs with relatively shallow shafts and very poor offerings with disarticulated skeletons; since the only type of offering commonly found was beads, they were given the name Bead type.[3] The fifth type was the most remarkable (Fig. 19). They still contained only a single or occasionally two skeletons, but both shaft and chamber were enormous. The shaft was almost always rectangular in shape, in dimensions up to 3·90 metres by 4·45 metres and the deepest was 7 metres deep. The largest chamber was 5·90 metres by 4 metres. Because of their dimensions, these tombs were called the Outsize type.[4] The main grave goods consisted of pottery vessels, some of the types found in the Pottery type tombs, but also many spouted jars not found in those tombs (Fig. 20). There were no weapons in these tombs, but a considerable number of copper or bronze fittings which had been attached to wooden objects, some of them certainly poles or staves. The sixth type was called the Composite type,[5] since it combined characteristics of shape and dimensions of tomb and types of grave goods of all the preceding types. Finally, there was a single tomb which because it alone contained three burials was called the Multiple-burial type.[6] It differed from the others not only in this but in the fact that it contained, besides weapons, pottery vessels of types not found in the other Jericho tombs, but related to types found in the tombs of the period in southern Palestine.

The features shared in common by these tombs and their

[1] §vi, 7, vol. i, 199 ff., vol. ii, 57 ff.   [2] §vi, 7, vol. ii, 87 ff.
[3] §vi, 7, vol. ii, 81 ff.   [4] §vi, 7, vol. ii, 92 ff.
[5] §vi, 7, vol. ii, 143 ff.   [6] §vi, 7, vol. ii, 157 ff.

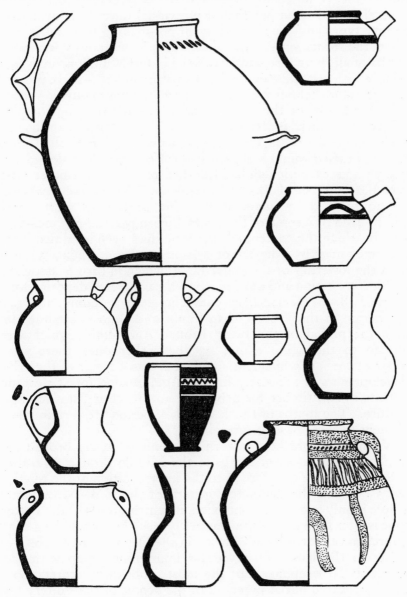

Fig. 20. Types of pottery from an Outsize Tomb at Jericho.

contents leave no room for doubt that they belong to the same general period—the practice of individual burial, the overlap in pottery types and the similarities in pot-making techniques even when the forms varied, the similarities in weapon-types. Some tombs of all these forms were re-used in the Middle Bronze Age, usually with very clear evidence of an original E.B.–M.B. use, and they therefore belong to the earlier period. They are distinguished from the tombs of the Early Bronze Age not only by complete difference in burial practices but also by the evidence of an absolute environmental break. The rock in which all the Early Bronze Age and earlier tombs were cut had suffered so much denudation that without exception all had lost their roofs. On the other hand, very nearly all the E.B.–M.B. tombs still have intact roofs and are approached by intact shafts. The contrast is most clearly emphasized by a tomb of the Proto-Urban period,[1] c. 3300–3000 B.C., in which the contents of the tomb had been solidified into a concreted mass by a deposit of gypsum, a phenomenon associated with the lowering of the water-table, which in turn is associated with deforestation and erosion. Into the concreted deposit a tomb of the E.B.–M.B. had been cut. Therefore, certainly later than the period of the Proto-Urban tombs and almost certainly later than the period of the Early Bronze Age tombs, which were eroded to the same extent as the earlier ones, there was a phase of erosion, which it is suggested[2] was a result of the urban developments of the Early Bronze Age, causing forest clearance both to obtain timber for urban use and to clear fields for agriculture. The tombs of the E.B.–M.B. period are certainly subsequent to this phase of erosion.

Within this bracket between the denuded Early Bronze Age tombs and the re-use of tombs in the Middle Bronze Age, there is less conclusive evidence as to the interpretation of the relationships between the distinctive groups of the E.B.–M.B. tombs. There is only one direct connexion, in which a tomb of the Pottery type is later than one of the Dagger type.[3] There could be a slight impression that the people buried in the Dagger type tombs were closer to the habits of a warrior immigrant group with their emphasis on weapons. But the most probable interpretation of the remarkable burial practices of the people of the Pottery type tombs is that they also were close to a nomadic way of life. The practice of burying desiccated, dismembered and incomplete skeletons in elaborate tombs must surely be derived from the practices of a period in which the group followed a seasonal

[1] §vi, 7, vol. i, 3, vol. ii, 3 ff.   [2] §vi, 7, vol. i, 3.   [3] §vi, 7, vol. i, 23.

routine of movement, with a periodic return to an ancestral burial ground. Though after the entry into Palestine the groups presumably ceased to be truly nomadic, they may have remained basically pastoralist; Jericho as an early *point d'appui* may have remained their centre, but for much of the year the groups would have pastured their flocks in the hill-country, and only brought their dead back to Jericho in the winter months. The people of the Dagger type tombs and the Pottery type tombs therefore seem both to be close to nomadic origins, and can be best interpreted as separate immigrant groups. The people of the Bead type tombs could possibly be poor relations of those of the Pottery type tombs. Those of the Square-shaft type and the Outsize type tombs have certain connexions with the others, but the other features that they exhibit are so distinctive that they are probably not derivative though they may have some ancestral relation. Only the Composite type tombs may provide evidence of interconnexions and cross-fertilization after settlement had taken place. The single Multiple-burial type tomb, unique in its connexions with occupation of the period in other parts of Palestine, may provide evidence of the transitory appearance of groups *en route* elsewhere, or a backwash from these other settlements.

The very clear evidence of the Jericho tombs is therefore of the presence in the neighbourhood of a number of loosely connected groups. The newcomers were tribal groups, joining in a general movement, a movement that resulted in the submergence of the pre-existing civilizations, but one which did not impose a truly unified culture on the occupied area, except in the general sense that it was one that was semi-nomadic and pastoral rather than urban and agricultural.

This evidence from Jericho for the arrival in Palestine of a number of separate groups is confirmed when one studies the evidence from other sites. On some sites, for instance Tell el-Fār'ah, near Nablus, Tell en-Naṣbeh and 'Ai, there is, on present evidence, a complete gap for this period. On many others there is an occupation that is comparable with that at Jericho but has distinctive features.

As already mentioned, the first site at which the existence of the period was recognized was Tell el-'Ajjūl, where Petrie ascribed two groups of tombs to the Copper Age.[1] His instinct, as so often, was correct, in that he isolated these tombs from others found, but his description of them as 'Copper Age', though based on the visual appearance of the implements as

---

[1] §v, 3.

copper rather than bronze, was confusing technologically in that
the period which is called (probably incorrectly as far as Palestine
is concerned) the Early Bronze Age precedes this stage.

Petrie located at Tell el-'Ajjūl two separate cemeteries, the
100–200 cemetery and the 1500 cemetery. It can be shown that
these cemeteries are almost as distinct as the different types of
tombs at Jericho,[1] though like the Jericho tombs they both
contained only single burials. In the 100–200 cemetery, the
great majority of the burials are of disarticulated skeletons in
tombs of which the shafts were ordinarily round in plan. In the
1500 cemetery, the burials were of intact crouched bodies, and
the shafts were rectangular in plan. Both pottery vessels and
weapons were found in each cemetery, but the characteristic
shapes in one cemetery differ from those in the other; as regards
weapons, daggers are common in the 1500 cemetery and very
rare in the 100–200 cemetery, where, however, two javelins with
curled tangs occur.

At 'Ajjūl, then, it is again reasonable to deduce the presence of
two separate but related groups. Neither used burial practices
identical with those of the Jericho groups, but the tomb offerings
are related. The daggers are similar but not identical.[2] The only
Jericho tomb that contained closely similar vessels was the single
Multiple-burial tomb, but the peculiar pot-making technique,
with the body of the vessel hand-made and the rim added on a
fast wheel, is the same. The appearance of the groups at 'Ajjūl
has another feature in common with the Jericho groups in that
they left no evidence of settled occupation on the *tell*.

The general type of jar found in the 'Ajjūl tombs, flat-based,
with somewhat ovoid body and high, flaring rim, is found on
other south Palestinian sites, notably Tell ed-Duweir and Tell Beit
Mirsim, but each site has its local variations in these and the
other vessels.

The lower levels at Duweir have hardly been excavated. The
few soundings into them show no trace at all of occupation of the
E.B.–M.B. period. It would seem that the site of the considerable town of Early Bronze III was abandoned, or perhaps, like
Jericho, occupied only in parts. The only evidence of occupation
came from a ridge about 500 metres away. Here, a number of
caves had been occupied in the Chalcolithic period and especially
in the Early Bronze Age.[3] In three of them there was also
E.B.–M.B. occupation,[4] and some wall foundations in the area

[1] §vi, 11.   [2] §vi, 7, vol. ii, 46 ff.
[3] §vi, 14, 253 ff.   [4] §vi, 14, 259 ff., caves 1518, 1527, 1529.

were ascribed to the same period, but there was no sound evidence for this. The pottery from the occupation level was, as at Jericho, considerably different from that from the tombs. Some of the shapes were like those from occupation sites at Jericho and Beit Mirsim, and there was the same type of decoration with wavy and straight combing, but some shapes were peculiar to Duweir.

The main evidence from Duweir came, as at the other sites, from tombs, which were located in an area *c.* 900 metres north of the *tell*.[1] The tombs were of moderate size and could be classified in five categories as to shape, but the shapes did not seem to be associated with any significant differences in contents. The skeletal remains were ill-preserved, but since no intact skeletons are recorded, it is probable that most bodies were disarticulated. The pottery forms include vessels of both the categories in the 'Ajjūl cemeteries. The vast majority, however, are of the categories found in the 'Ajjūl 100–200 cemetery, and, of the 103 tombs of which details are given, only nine have forms characteristic of the 'Ajjūl 1500 cemetery, and eleven others have a mixture. Other finds support this emphasis. There are only two daggers, which are similarly rare in the 100–200 cemetery, and common in the 1500, and four javelins, which are also found in the 100–200. Though the pottery forms do fall into the same categories, there are nevertheless differences; the flat-based ovoid jars with flaring rims, for instance, tend to be taller for their width and sometimes have lug handles at the neck, while bowls and cups are more common and have greater varieties of shape.

The third well-known site with pottery similar to that of 'Ajjūl is Beit Mirsim. There, above a first occupation of the site late in the Early Bronze Age, two strata, I and H, are assigned to the period.[2] The evidence concerning I is not very satisfactory, and the published finds are mixed. In H, some remains of houses suggest that there was occupation on the *tell*, but there was no trace of a town wall. Most of the pottery was found in a cave, apparently used for occupation. The forms are very similar to those from Duweir, particularly in the use of wavy combed decoration, but there are again variations, such as the predominance of knob handles on the large ovoid jars.

The evidence from these three Palestinian sites gives the same general picture as that provided by Jericho. By far the greatest amount of evidence comes from tombs, which attest the existence of a numerous population. The people which buried its dead in the tombs had little interest in the town sites of the preceding era,

---

[1] §VI, 14, 277 ff.   [2] §V, 1, 1, 8 ff.; 1A, 8 ff.

either ignoring them or occupying them incompletely, with a spread out over the surrounding countryside, and in no case building town walls. Between the people living at these three places there was, on the pottery evidence, a close connexion, but not identity. The two cemeteries at 'Ajjūl could well indicate tribal groups; the less pronounced differences at the other two sites may suggest some amalgamation and interconnexions after groups had settled down.

The distinctions between these groups and those burying in the Jericho tombs is much greater. Only the single tomb of the Multiple-burial type had comparable finds. On the other hand, the pottery from the *tell* at Jericho much more closely resembles that from the southern sites.[1] The significance of this is not yet clear, partly because work on the finds from the site has not at present been completed. But since the stratigraphical evidence suggests that there was an interval between the destruction of the Early Bronze Age town and the earliest E.B.–M.B. buildings, it may be that the pottery found on the *tell* represents a later stage belonging either to a later influx or to a stage when nomadic, tribal, separatism was breaking down, and a more unified culture growing up. This would mean that all the tombs except one discovered belonged to the earlier tribal stage, and the cemetery used later must lie elsewhere.

The two main sites in the north for which there is evidence for the E.B.–M.B. period are Megiddo and Beth-shan, both very important places with a long history from the Neolithic and Chalcolithic periods onwards and both probably walled towns in the Early Bronze Age. The evidence concerning Megiddo is considerably the fuller.

There, the excavation of one section of the *tell* was carried down to bedrock. By a period probably relatively late in the Early Bronze Age[2] the area was covered with buildings laid out on a series of terraces; on the upper one an imposing altar represents the first stage of a sacred area that was to last to the end of the second millennium B.C. The next stage of this sacred area was the construction of a pair of temples with square cellas and porches the full width of the cella in front. Neither the stratification of the successive stages nor their chronology is easy to interpret, but it would appear that these two temples were succeeded by a third, and in the fourth stage this was modified.[3] This final stage is certainly E.B.–M.B., for incorporated in the rebuild was a fenestrated axe

---

[1] §vi, 6, fig. 9.   [2] §vi, 12, 55*.
[3] §vi, 12, 55* ff.

typical of the period.[1] The inadequate stratigraphic record makes it impossible to date the earlier stages by associated objects, but it seems most probable that this type of temple arrived at the site with the newcomers who destroyed the Early Bronze Age civilization. With the successive temples are probably to be associated buildings on the terrace below.

If the attribution of these monumental structures to the E.B.–M.B. period is correct, the occupation at Megiddo at this stage is different in character from that so far identified elsewhere in Palestine. The tombs of the period could, however, be interpreted as confirming a variation in the more widespread type of culture. On the one hand, they agree in suggesting the arrival of immigrant groups with differing equipment and practices, for there are two entirely different types of tombs. The pottery is of the same general character and technique of manufacture as that of the other sites of the period, though most of the forms are quite distinct, differing especially from those of the southern group of sites. Further, the practice of burying disarticulated skeletons is found in both kinds of tombs. There is no doubt that the tombs provide evidence at Megiddo of yet further tribal groups arriving in Palestine.

The first type of tomb, consisting of the burials in Tombs 1101 B–1102 Lower, differs from those already described by containing multiple burials in linked natural caves. It must be pointed out that they do not provide evidence of a development from the Early Bronze Age; the confusion has arisen because the E.B.–M.B. burials were made above occupation levels of the Early Bronze Age, and the two groups, really entirely distinct, have been published as one.[2] An important find was a swollen-headed toggle pin[3] of the type so common at the period in Syria.[4]

It is the second type of tomb at Megiddo that is the more important, both in perhaps providing a background for the structural evidence in the settlement and in furnishing clear evidence of the connexion of the group with inland Syria. These tombs, known as the Shaft Tombs (Fig. 21),[5] have an obvious architectural character. The plan is stereotyped, and its elements are remarkably rectilinear and rectangular. A vertical shaft, rectangular in plan, has opening off its base a central chamber with other chambers on the remaining three sides, all rectangular in plan, flat-roofed and vertical-sided. This tomb structure suggests a degree of sophistication unknown in the tombs of any of the

---

[1] §VI, 12, 58*; §VI, 13, pl. 182.
[2] §VI, 4, 24 ff.
[3] §VI, 4, pl. 86, 2.
[4] See below, pp. 585 f. and Plate 46(a).
[5] §VI, 4, 135 ff.

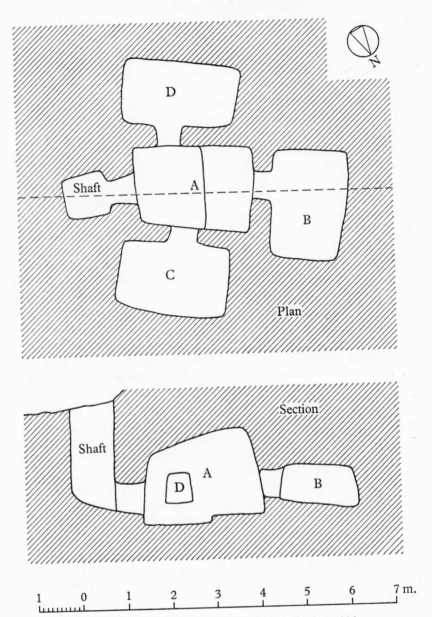

Fig. 21. Plan and section of Shaft Tomb 878 at Megiddo.

other contemporary groups. There was much re-use of these tombs at later periods, but enough survived intact to indicate the character of the original burials. The bodies consisted of disarticulated bones.[1] The pottery (Fig. 22) includes vessels similar to, but not identical with, those in the other type of tomb at Megiddo, and related to those found at Beth-shan and in the Outsize type tombs at Jericho. More important still, there are a number of vessels with clear links with inland Syria, small teapot-like vessels, often with a dark slip and zigzag decoration, that can be paralleled, for instance, at Qatna and Tell 'As.[2] Also, there were some pins, a type with a flattened head of which the tip is curled over and toggle pins with a mushroom-shaped head, both very common in the rich metal industry of the period in Syria.[3] Swollen-headed toggle pins (see above) were also found.[4] These links with Syria are important both chronologically and also as an indication of the direction from which these groups arrived. It would also seem reasonable to suggest that they represent groups that had already been in touch with a settled civilization, and were thus already introduced to architecture, whereas the groups farther south had come more directly from the desert.

Megiddo is the site from which the evidence of these groups is best known and most fully published. But there is sufficient evidence to suggest that in fact they dominated the northern part of Palestine. They are certainly to be found at Beth-shan, the great site that balances Megiddo at the eastern end of the plain of Esdraelon. The publication of the excavations at this site is unfortunately far from complete. In the published pottery from levels XI and XII, mixed, through inadequate stratigraphic evidence, with pottery of Early Bronze III, there are a number of vessels certainly belonging to this period and group.[5] In the unpublished material from tombs,[6] there are many more vessels identical with those from the Megiddo Shaft Tombs,[7] and the plans of at least three tombs are very closely similar to these same tombs.[8] Unfortunately, it is not possible to say, from the limited area of the lower levels excavated and the incompleteness of the

---

[1] §VI, 7, vol. II, 184.   [2] See below, p. 586.

[3] See *ibid.* and Plate 46(*b*).

[4] §VI, 4, pl. 118, 4, in a re-used shaft tomb, and certainly belonging to the E.B.–M.B. period and not to the subsequent Middle Bronze use.

[5] §VI, 1, pl. x, i, 10, 11, 15.

[6] Kindly made available by the University Museum, Philadelphia, and communicated by Mrs Garner James.

[7] From Beth-shan tombs 26, 203, 296, 89, 262, 74, 89, 67, 74, 108, 219.

[8] Tombs 227, 231, 228.

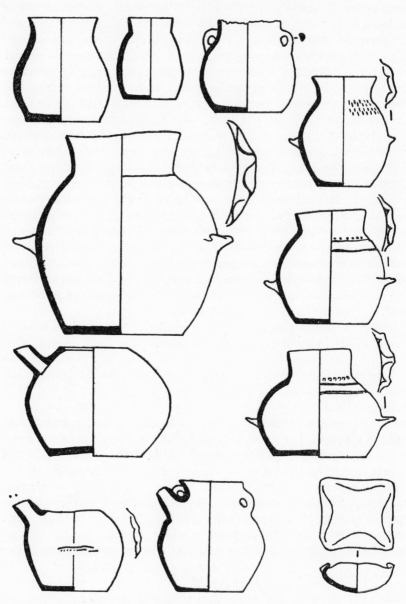

Fig. 22. Pottery from a Shaft Tombs at Megiddo.

publication, whether on the town site there are any buildings of the period.

The same group also established itself east of the Jordan, for at Tell el-Ḥuṣn, near the modern village of El-Ḥuṣn, a tomb was found, of a cave-like character, containing a long range of pottery of which part can be closely paralleled in the Shaft Graves at Megiddo, and including also the same group of pins with Syrian connexions.[1]

The Palestinian picture must be completed by reference to the fringe areas, the semi-desert area of the Negeb to the south and in Transjordan to the east. The surface surveys of Nelson Glueck in those areas have shown that much pottery of the period is to be picked up.[2] These finds indicate a wide distribution, though it is very definitely to be doubted whether Glueck's conclusion that there was a widespread *civilization* in the Negeb[3] is to be accepted. Rather, there was a non-nucleated occupation that left abundant evidence which has remained accessible to surface surveys since the areas were never occupied by a settled population and never could be. Moreover, it is very probable that these nomadic pastoralists remained in occupation for long, perhaps centuries, after a settled occupation was introduced into lands more suitable to an agricultural economy.

VII. SYRIA: THE SITES

The archaeological evidence from Palestine has been dealt with before that from Syria, for it is more clear-cut than that from the area to the north. This may partly be due to the quality of the archaeological evidence, and partly to the more complex history of the richer and less constricted northern area, more directly in contact with Mesopotamia to the east, and, by sea, with Egypt. But, in spite of complexities, the general picture is similar, that of a major interruption in urban development at the end of the third millennium B.C., which accords well with the textual evidence from Mesopotamia and Egyptian sources described in the preceding sections of this chapter.

The evidence for a break that terminated an urban civilization which had lasted for most of the third millennium B.C. can be seen most clearly at Ras Shamra-Ugarit. Here, the vast mound that represents the town of the second millennium has in its centre a higher mound, called by the excavator in his earlier reports the

---

[1] §VI, 5.   [2] §VI, 2 and 3.   [3] §VI, 3.

acropolis, and subsequently the upper town. An analysis of the stratification and finds as so far published makes it clear that this higher mound represents the Early Bronze Age town of the third millennium. The schematic section published[1] shows that above a level containing typical Early Bronze pottery, including Khirbet Karak ware, which on Palestinian evidence should be contemporary with the Fourth Dynasty of Egypt (*c.* 2613–2494 B.C.),[2] was a layer of decayed mud-brick. This need represent no more than the collapse of the buildings of the preceding level, and therefore no appreciable passage of time; indeed, if there were no successive layers of buildings within it, it can presumably be so interpreted, for the collapse of a single town layer of mud-brick structures would take place in a very few years if the site were abandoned, more rapidly still if there were an initial destruction.

Into this layer of decayed mud-brick was dug a number of graves, containing objects completely different from those of the preceding and succeeding periods. To this stage Schaeffer gives the designation Ugarit Moyen 1. In so doing, he is following the lead of the Palestinian archaeologists who designated the first period following the Early Bronze Age Middle Bronze I. But at Ras Shamra, as in Palestine, the finds of U.M. 1 are entirely distinct from those of U.M. 2. The resemblance of this stage at Ras Shamra to the E.B.–M.B. stage in Palestine goes much further. The finds on the original town site seem to come only from graves, and no buildings are recorded. Not only are graves found on the town site, but they spread over the area at the foot of the mound. It would appear that wherever excavations were carried down to rock or undisturbed soil in the area that was included within the walls of the greatly extended Middle Bronze Age Town (U.M. 2), graves of this same sort were encountered.[3] The period is thus one of an abundant population that was not town-dwelling. The newcomers occupied the site of Ras Shamra, but used the town and its neighbourhood as a place for burying their dead and not for building houses.

Further links with Palestine are provided by the actual finds. In a grave on the *tell* was a vessel[4] decorated with the characteristic combination of straight and wavy combed lines of the Palestinian E.B.–M.B. pottery.[5] Among the most frequent finds are pins with swollen heads,[6] of which an example is found at

---

[1] §VII, 9, pl. XIII.   [2] §V, 2, 116 f.
[3] §VII, 9, pl. V, pl. VIII.
[4] §VII, 9, pl. XIII; §VII, 11, fig. 101, 35.
[5] E.g. §V, 1, 1A, pl. 3, 3, 5.   [6] §VII, 11, fig. 22.

Megiddo,[1] and fenestrated axes[2] found at Megiddo[3] and Jericho.[4] It is also possible that there are at Ras Shamra different groups characterized by different classes of offerings, for apparently pottery vessels were found only in one tomb (or at least in a restricted group) and were absent from others. But since the finds have not so far for the most part been published in groups, the evidence cannot be analysed.

Schaeffer recognizes very clearly the implications of the appearance of the newcomers at Ras Shamra. In his article 'Porteurs de Torques',[5] he selects as an especially characteristic ornament in the graves of the period a bronze torc with curled-back terminals.[6] Also included in the objects in the tombs were mushroomheaded pins,[7] swollen-headed pins,[8] daggers with triangular hilts and three rivets,[9] socketed spears[10] and fenestrated axes,[11] watchspring spirals[12] and biconical beads.[13] It is quite clear that among the newcomers was an important element well-versed in metal working. With this may be compared the group burying in the E.B.–M.B. Dagger type tombs at Jericho and the group in the 1500 tombs at 'Ajjūl, though the types of weapons are different and in the tombs at Jericho and 'Ajjūl the other bronze objects are missing. Schaeffer makes out a strong case for the northern connexions of the characteristic bronze objects from the Ras Shamra burials.[14] He also has assembled remarkable parallels for, especially, the torcs and pins, extending into Europe as far as Bohemia and Alsace. The influence of groups from Anatolia and the Caucasus on Syria at this time must be accepted, and it is tempting to believe that there was a corresponding spread to the north from these regions, but more evidence is required. Ras Shamra thus produces the evidence for the arrival in Syria of nomadic groups with northern connexions.

There is similar evidence from almost all western Syrian sites that have been examined, most of it assembled by Schaeffer.[15] A site of considerable importance is Qatna, some 18 kilometres north-east of Homs. It is important not only from the scale of the site, but also as showing that the history of the inland Syrian plain is similar to that of coastal Ras Shamra. The history of the

[1] §vi, 4, pl. 86, 2.
[2] §vii, 11, fig. 19, 13–14.
[3] §vi, 13, pl. 182, 3.
[4] §vii, 12, 117 ff.
[5] §vii, 11, 49 ff.
[6] E.g. §vii, 11, pl. xvi, 45.
[7] E.g. §vii, 11, fig. 27, F.
[8] E.g. §vii, 11, pl. xiii, fig. 19, 6–8.
[9] E.g. §vii, 11, fig. 18, 23–5, 30–1.
[10] E.g. §vii, 11, fig. 19, 1–2.
[11] E.g. §vii, 11, fig. 19, 13–14.
[12] E.g. §vii, 11, fig. 21, 52.
[13] E.g. §vii, 11, pl. xiii.
[14] §vii, 11, 106 ff. See Plate 46(c).
[15] §vii, 9, chs. iii–iv.

site[1] would seem to resemble that of Ras Shamra, with a mound representing the original third millennium site of the Early Bronze Age standing in the middle of a greatly enlarged area enclosed by ramparts of the Middle Bronze Age. Beneath the temple that was established on the original mound, probably in the twentieth century B.C., was pottery that would link with the Palestinian E.B.–M.B. pottery and there were tombs of the period on the flanks of the original mound and elsewhere in the area covered by the subsequent town. The most important is Tomb IV.[2] This contained a considerable number of swollen-headed, mushroom-headed and curled-headed pins like those found at Ras Shamra, and, as will be seen, at Byblos, and also similar daggers. With them was a considerable quantity of pottery, all of types similar to the E.B.–M.B. forms of Palestine, and some, for instance the spouted vessels, close to the forms found in the Outsize type tombs of Jericho, providing a hint as to the direction from which the group burying in these tombs came.

Other sites in the same general area as Qatna were sounded by Du Mesnil du Buisson.[3] The soundings were insufficient to produce a clear picture of the history of the sites, but they gave clear evidence of tombs of the same period. Three tombs at Tell 'As are particularly important.[4] With the same range of types of pins as at Qatna, there was a large collection of pots of the same general types and a number that are excellent parallels for pots in the Jericho tombs, both in the Outsize type and in the Pottery type.

Farther east still, the same range of pins appears at Tell Brak,[5] dated by Mallowan to 2200 B.C. Here, however, the pottery is that of the Mesopotamian region, and as this is a different cultural area it is not dealt with here. The evidence that groups similar to those found on the Syrian coast and central plain also penetrated here is important.

The links between coastal and inland Syria are plain. But the differences are significant. In the coastal area, at Ras Shamra and, as will be seen, at Byblos, the chief evidence of the newcomers is their metal work. At Ras Shamra, very few, perhaps only one, of the burials contained pottery. In the inland sites, most of the tombs have much pottery, while in the metal work only pins are common and there are very few weapons. It would seem that, as in Palestine, there was a number of groups, clearly contemporary,

---

[1] §VII, 6; §VII, 7, 39.   [2] §VII, 6, tom. XI, pls. XXXI–XXXIV; §VII, 9, fig. 99.
[3] §VII, 6, tom. XI, 160 ff.   [4] §VII, 6, tom. XI, 162; §VII, 9, figs. 104 f.
[5] §VII, 5, pl. XXXI.

but each with their own customs, especially as regards burials. At Ras Shamra, as in Palestine, the evidence is clear that they were not town dwellers; on the other sites, excavation has not been complete enough to provide full evidence, but such as there is suggests a similar conclusion.

The site of Byblos stands by itself. The settlement of the Early Bronze Age was a well-developed town beside the excellent port, defended by massive walls. Its relations with Egypt were exceptionally close, for it was the port from which the products of the hinterland, notably timber and minerals, were traded to the Nile Valley.

These contacts existed from early dynastic times onwards.[1] Objects, probably mainly gifts to the temple of the local deity, bore the names of pharaohs from the Second Dynasty onwards.[2] All the dynasties are represented down to the Sixth. There are many alabasters of Phiops II of this Dynasty (c. 2269–2175), and his name is the last of the series.[3] The level in which objects with the name of this pharaoh occur was covered with a thick layer of ashes, and some of the alabasters bearing his name are calcined. It was at the end of his reign that the disasters that brought about the disintegration of the Old Kingdom of Egypt began. These disturbances would be enough to account for the cessation of Egyptian voyages to Byblos, but the layer of ashes would seem to be proof that Byblos itself suffered a similar disaster.

The evidence of the succeeding period is not easy to interpret. Byblos was excavated in a series of rigidly horizontal spits (levées) of 20 centimetres. The true stratification was neither published nor observed, and the objects are published[4] purely by spit and location, with no regard for the admittedly irregular contours of the site. Though a laborious analysis of find-spots might produce a general picture of the architecture and finds of the successive phases, the absence of observed stratification makes it impossible to recognize intrusions and accidental irregularities. The finds can thus be discussed only in the light of evidence from elsewhere.

The promised architectural analysis has not yet appeared. But in an article[5] M. Dunand recognizes that there was an important change in domestic architecture towards the end of the third millennium. The houses of the types that had developed from the time of the Second Dynasty onwards had a number of rooms, were solidly built and regularly orientated and arranged. Their successors were single-roomed and scattered irregularly about the

[1] §VII, I, 90. See above, pp. 45 ff.   [2] §VII, 8, 271.
[3] §VII, 3 (2), 181 f.   [4] §VII, 2, vols. I and II.   [5] §VII, 4.

area of the town. With the change in architecture is said to go a change in pottery. The evidence concerning this change is difficult to assess.[1] It is stated that the new type of buildings begins to appear before the fire that produced the level of ashes. But as there are no published sections, and as the sherds and general household pottery related to the different buildings have not been published, the significance of the new developments cannot be checked. The excavator's interpretation of a new phase must be accepted as deduced from field observations, which, as reported, must mean that an infiltration of newcomers with new customs was succeeded by a destruction of the old civilization and its replacement by the culture of the newcomers, whom M. Dunand identifies as the Amorites.[2] Following this occupation of the Amorites, M. Dunand would see a rapid evolution from a semi-nomadic way of life to a sedentary one, with the revival of the town of Byblos and the reconstruction of its temple on the site of that of the period of the Old Kingdom.

It is the evidence for the period following the fire that is the most difficult to interpret from what is published. From at least three sacred areas, the Temple of the Ba'alat,[3] the 'Champs des Offrandes'[4] and the Temple of the Obelisks[5] came a remarkable series of offering deposits. Most of the deposits were contained in jars, many of which, of an elongated barrel shape, were probably specially made for the purpose; others would appear to be in the Early Bronze Age tradition. The enormous majority of the objects contained in the jars was of bronze, and it cannot be doubted that a group skilled in bronze working had suddenly arrived in Byblos; the unfinished state of many of the objects makes it quite clear that they were not imports. It is also quite certain that the newcomers are related to those who appear at Ras Shamra in U.M. 1. The characteristic swollen-headed pins, torcs with curled ends, watch-spring spirals, fenestrated axes, short daggers with triangular butts, socketed spearheads, all appear, some of them in great numbers.[6] In addition, there are enormous numbers of little bronze figurines of men, some naked except for a pointed cap, some wearing a kilt,[7] and of horned animals. These are not found at Ras Shamra, but they are linked with the Ras Shamra finds by the fact that some of the little men carry fenestrated axes.

The evidence of Byblos thus agrees with that of Ras Shamra, Qatna, Tell 'As and elsewhere in indicating the arrival of new-

[1] §vii, 4, 86.　　[2] §vii, 4, 88 f.　　[3] §vii, 2, vol. i, 79 ff.
[4] §vii, 2, vol. ii, 393.　　[5] §vii, 2, vol. ii, 272.
[6] See Plate 47.　　[7] See Plate 48.

comers in Syria at the end of the third millennium, and the evidence of most of the sites is that they were nomadic or semi-nomadic with a tribal organization. The chief difficulty in inter-preting the Byblos evidence is to assess the culture of the newcomers at this site. M. Dunand claims that the foundation deposits were associated with a rebuilding of the sacred sites that he believes took place within a generation or so of the destruction of the buildings in use in the period of the Old Kingdom of Egypt,[1] that is to say, around about the end of the reign of Phiops II (c. 2175 B.C.). In the case of those associated with the Temple of the Ba'alat,[2] the deposits were in a fill of imported earth beneath a fragmentarily surviving pavement of the temple. In the case of the 'Champ des Offrandes'[3] there was a massive concentration of twenty-two deposits in an area of very much destroyed structures, but no stratigraphic evidence of their rela-tionship was published. Also unclear is the stratigraphic relation-ship of the deposits in the area of the Temple of the Obelisks (one of these obelisks bore the name of a king of Byblos probably contemporary with Ammenemes III).[4] It is therefore impossible to say whether all the offerings are contemporary, or inserted successively into the sacred area, and whether they are contemporary with the observed architectural remains or belong to a destroyed earlier structure.

Though it is necessary to make these reservations, it must for the time being be taken that fairly soon after the nomadic new-comers arrived at Byblos they established their headquarters there and became settled to the extent of building or rebuilding sacred structures. What is lacking is the evidence, either stratigraphical or in artefacts, to connect the deposits with the new type of architecture referred to above.

In assessing the evidence, a number of factors has to be considered. In the first place, the grouping of the deposits makes it clear that there were several areas, even if stratigraphical evi-dence is lacking that they were associated with any extant remains. The great majority of the deposits contain objects that are both new in comparison with the Early Bronze Age contemporary with the Old Kingdom, and are not found in association with levels or deposits of the time of the Middle Kingdom. The clearest evidence of this is the distinction between the finds in the foundation deposits and the objects in the tombs of the princes of Byblos which on inscriptional evidence are contemporary with

[1] §vii, 4, 88 f.   [2] §vii, 8, chs. iii–v; §vii, 2, vol. i, 79 ff.
[3] §vii, 2, vol. ii, 393 ff.   [4] §vii, 9, 62.

the Middle Kingdom pharaohs Ammenemes III and Ammenemes IV (1842–1797 and 1798–1790 B.C.).[1] The distinction is
absolute. The pottery forms of the nineteenth–eighteenth century
B.C. tombs are new, and the multitudinous metal objects of the
foundation deposits are not found in the tombs. It cannot be
doubted that the deposits are earlier than the second half of the
nineteenth century B.C. On the other hand, there are objects in
the deposits that could lead on to the finds of Middle Bronze I
in Palestine and Syria, in a way that the E.B.–M.B. finds in
Palestine certainly do not. For instance, there are the occasional
metal[2] and pottery[3] forms that would certainly seem to be ancestral to the Middle Bronze I forms of Palestine.[4] Also, though
there is no direct connexion between the E.B.–M.B. daggers of
Palestine[5] and those of the beginning of the Middle Bronze Age,[6]
the short daggers with triangular butts and pronounced midribs
of some of the Byblos deposits[7] would seem to be the obvious
predecessors of the Palestinian Middle Bronze Age forms.

The earliest of the foundation deposits, or the stock-in-trade of
temple craftsmen, is the so-called Montet Jar.[8] It contained almost
a thousand small objects for personal use or ornament, some of
them unfinished or in need of repair. There were torcs, bangles,
watch-spring spirals, swollen-headed pins, and over six hundred
beads.[9] Most of the stone beads are comparable to those of the
Old Kingdom and First Intermediate Period of Egypt, but a few
show affinities with beads of Mesopotamia, and an unusual
number of silver beads are clearly derived from that area. Pendants
and figurines in ivory, stone, copper or bronze, and glass are
closely related to Egyptian parallels of First Intermediate date,
even if they are not actual imports. Especially striking is the
collection of about a hundred scarabs, together with three cylinder
seals and some seal-amulets, which are to be distinguished from
the earlier button-seal.[10] The predominant decoration is a design
of concentric circles, usually associated with the Aegean world.

[1] §VII, 8, 143 ff.
[2] §VII, 2, vol. I, pl. VIII, 2062 ; §VII, 8, pl. LXXI, 605, 607.
[3] §VII, 2, vol. II, pl. CCVII, 10715.
[4] E.g. §VI, 4, pl. 29, 2–4 ; §V, 1, 1A, pl. 4, 5 ; §V, 2, fig. 36, 1–2, fig. 22; §VII, 2.
[5] E.g. §VI, 11, fig. 10.   [6] E.g. §VI, 4, pl. 118, 5.
[7] E.g. §VII, 2, vol. II, pl. LXVIII, 9660, 9664.
[8] §VII, 8, 111–25, pls. LXI–LXXI.
[9] See a reappraisal of the contents based on drawings of the originals by O.
Tufnell, and W. A. Ward, 'Relations between Byblos, Egypt and Mesopotamia at
the end of the third millennium B.C.' In Syria, 43 (1966), 165–241.
[10] See above, p. 533.

But here again the soundest links are to be found in simple hiero-glyphic signs and emblems well-known in Upper Egypt during the First Intermediate Period, about the Tenth Dynasty, when trade had improved after the disruption at the end of the Old Kingdom. It seems unlikely that the deposit was buried at a much later date, since there were no scarabs or beads of amethyst in the jar, and the mines producing this material near Aswan were already exploited in the late Eleventh and early Twelfth Dynasties.[1] Despite the absence of objects bearing royal names at Byblos and elsewhere in Syria–Palestine between the Old and Middle Kingdoms, it cannot be held that trade between Byblos and Egypt was completely cut off.[2] However, the scarabs of the Montet Jar predate the common use of scarab-seals beyond Egypt by some decades,[3] and apart from this important group, scarabs of purely Egyptian type have not been found in association with the torc-wearers.

The evidence of the sacred area deposits cannot be adequately associated with the contemporary developments, firstly in the absence of stratigraphical evidence, secondly because the objects published from the town in the interim report[4] comprise clearly a very small selection only. Moreover, though it may be neces-sary to revise this impression if the full pottery evidence from Byblos is published, it would appear that the pottery ascribed to the stage of the new type of domestic architecture ranges from surely Early Bronze Age forms[5] to probably Late Bronze Age forms;[6] the general impression is that the stratification is con-fused, though it may be necessary to revise this impression should full evidence become available.

There are therefore many difficulties in interpreting the Byblos evidence. But the general impression is that it is a centre in which the old urban culture of the Early Bronze Age, the greater part of the third millennium, was strong. It received the new influences of the nomadic groups which had a strong metallurgic tradition (perhaps comparable with that of the modern 'tinkers' who in the East are very similar to the gypsies), and out of this amalgam it fairly rapidly produced a new urban civilization. This civiliza-tion, fully established by the time of the tombs of the princes of Byblos contemporary with Ammenemes III and Ammenemes IV of the second half of the nineteenth to the early eighteenth

[1] §I, 14, 19 ff.   [2] See below, pp. 593 f.
[3] See above, p. 547 and below, p. 594.   [4] §VII, 4, pl. VI.
[5] E.g. §VII, 4, pl. VI, 2nd row, and bottom row left.
[6] E.g. *ibid.* 4th row, 2nd from left; bottom row, 2nd from left.

century B.C., spread northwards to Ras Shamra and southwards to Palestine.

The new culture, of which the material evidence appears both to north and south, covering a distance of at least 300 miles from north to south, demands a centre of development and expansion, and this it seems very likely that Byblos and its district provide.

The evidence derived from three sources, the archaeological remains, the textual evidence from Egypt[1] and that from Mesopotamia,[2] combines to present a very coherent picture. The interests of the successive dynastic rulers of Mesopotamia, Syria and the Mediterranean coast are patent, though it is not always possible to identify the regions named, for, from the time of Sargon (2371–2316 B.C.), more and more the Mesopotamian rulers tend to take account of the Amurru, and the accounts show that groups, some still nomadic and others clearly largely settled, are included under this description. The expansion in Mesopotamia may have had the character of peaceful infiltration in the first instance, but at least by the time of the Third Dynasty of Ur there were warlike thrusts.[3]

The Egyptian picture is similar. Ipuwer's statement that Egyptians no longer go to Byblos[4] is confirmed by the fact that no Egyptian rulers between Phiops II and Sesostris I, that is to say, between *c.* 2175 B.C. and 1971 B.C., are represented in the epigraphical finds from Syria. The penetrations of bedawin into the Nile Valley may have been halted in the time of the Eleventh Dynasty, but conditions in Syria may not have been affected. Moreover, the Twelfth Dynasty records refer continually to bedawin and dwellers in the desert, and opponents to law and order are found down to the time of Sesostris III (1878–1843 B.C.). while, when there is trade, it is in flocks and herds, therefore with a pastoral rather than an urban people. The Beni Hasan illustrations of Asiatics confirm the continuance down to this time of the E.B.–M.B. culture of Syria–Palestine, for some of the Asiatics have fenestrated axes, and many of the other weapons would fit those that appear in the Byblos deposits.[5]

Disruptive elements thus appear in Syria and Palestine in the

[1] See sects. I–III of this chapter.
[2] See sect. IV of this chapter.   [3] See above, p. 564.
[4] See above, p. 532.   [5] See above, p. 552.

last third of the third millennium b.c., just as they do in Egypt and Mesopotamia. The newcomers were strangers to the urban civilization of the coast and of the North Syrian part of the Fertile Crescent, just as they were in the great river valleys. The epigraphic evidence is clear that the majority were Semites speaking the western branch of the language,[1] and it is therefore to be presumed that they represent nomadic groups emerging from the Syrian desert to occupy the more fertile bordering areas. But there is linguistic evidence for the presence of non-Semites, as yet not identified,[2] and it seems reasonable to ascribe to them the great progress in metallurgy which is so especially evident at Byblos, and it is also reasonable to expect that their origins will be found to the north-east, where close parallels for many of the metal forms are to be found.

The archaeological picture of an abrupt destruction and disruption of the pre-existing urban civilization in Syria and Palestine is completely in accord with the literary evidence. The literary evidence suggests an evolution from the tribal, nomadic or semi-nomadic way of life to a settled way of life; for instance, in the earliest Execration Texts there are several rulers in most of the territories, and in the later ones there is only one for most territories,[3] while the account of Sinuhe, in the time of Sesostris I, suggests that the economy was one of nomads engaged in settling down.[4] The archaeological evidence concerning this transitional stage is not as complete as it almost certainly would be if more key sites in Syria had been sufficiently excavated. In Palestine the evidence is clear that the newcomers made little progress towards urban life or an agricultural economy, except perhaps at Megiddo. Everywhere, even at Megiddo, the next stage, out of which an urban civilization grew, represents a new external influence. In at least some sites in Syria a new culture would seem to appear abruptly and for most of the others the evidence is lacking. At Ras Shamra, for instance, the objects found in the tombs of U.M. 2, which provide the only published material so far available, are completely new and owe nothing to the preceding stage. Only at Byblos there would seem to be a real transition, in which objects attested in the Middle Bronze Age culture of Syria and Palestine appear together with those of the intrusive Intermediate Early Bronze–Middle Bronze culture. Byblos may be the centre of the area in which developed the Middle Bronze Age culture that spread to the north over Syria and to the south over Palestine,

[1] See above, p. 564.
[2] See above, pp. 565
[3] See above, pp. 541 and 555.
[4] See above, p. 553.

and in the evolution of this culture Amorite nomads and northern metallurgists may have played a part.

The chronology of this stage in Syria and Palestine need not correspond exactly with that of the appearance of the nomads in Egypt and Mesopotamia. The strong kingdoms of the river valleys would resist the nomadic incursions much longer than the little city states of Palestine and longer than the kingdoms, probably loosely organized, of North Syria.[1] The Palestinian evidence would seem to suggest that the Early Bronze Age civilization did not last for so very long after the Early Bronze III stage, linked with Egyptian finds of the Fourth Dynasty.[2] That is to say, the break may have come as early as the twenty-fifth–twenty-fourth century B.C. This could be in reasonable agreement with the Mesopotamian evidence that the Amurru were beginning to attract attention by the time of Sargon of Akkad (2371–2316 B.C.). On the evidence of Byblos, they did not force their way to the Syrian coast until after the time of Phiops II, early in the twenty-second century B.C., and the Mesopotamian evidence suggests that the Third Dynasty of Ur still tried to maintain control in North Syria.[3] Such a gradual spread of nomadic infiltration would be perfectly reasonable. For the chronology of the end of the period, there is the evidence of the major incursion of Amorites into Mesopotamia a little before the beginning of the First Dynasty of Babylon (*c.* 1894 B.C.), showing that they still included invading and nomadic groups at that date. In North Syria and Palestine objects indicating Egyptian connexions begin to appear on a number of sites at least by the time of Sesostris I (1971–1928 B.C.), and even if the scarabs ascribed to this king are not necessarily contemporary with his reign, the evidence for the beginning of the full Middle Bronze Age in Palestine suggests that it was gradual, brought by a few groups that settled down on sites that became the flourishing towns of Middle Bronze II. From at least the twenty-fourth to the twentieth centuries B.C. Syria and Palestine were overrun by nomads, amongst whom the Amorites predominated, with a culminating period of complete nomadic control in the two centuries *c.* 2181–1991 B.C.

---

[1] See sect. IV of this chapter.   [2] §V, 2, 130 ff. and 159.
[3] See above, p. 560.

CHAPTER XXII

BABYLONIA, *c.* 2120–1800 B.C.

I. THE THIRD DYNASTY OF UR

THE ancient kingship of Sumer, so gloriously regained by Utu-khegal with his expulsion of the Gutians, was his for a very brief space, his reign lasting for not much more than seven years,[1] coming to an abrupt end, and his city of Uruk therewith losing the sovereignty. During these years and for some three decades longer the great impulse of national sentiment and strength which had thrown off the enemy seemed to have exhausted itself in that one exertion. Of Utu-khegal himself nothing more was preserved by the historical memory of his country than his one heroic act and a story about his fate.[2] But the hazard of modern discovery has been kinder; at Ur and in its neighbourhood inscriptions have been found which show the sovereign concerning himself with the affairs of that city, and thereby they explain the origin of the Third Dynasty of Ur which was to supplant Uruk—by conquest, according to the king-list's unvarying phrase, but nothing is known of a war. In the first of these inscriptions[3] occurs the name of Ur-Nammu, not yet king but only deputy over the city for Utu-khegal, on whose behalf he undertook to restore a part of the great temple at Ur, a work of which so much remains to this day.

The Third Dynasty of Ur began therefore with the appointment of its first member by the preceding king, who doubtless selected one of his principal adherents, perhaps not a native of the place he was given to rule. Another inscription, upon modest little clay cones from unknown sites,[4] is of Utu-khegal himself. These cones are dedicated to the deities Ningirsu and Nanshe, the owners of Lagash, and relate that Utu-khegal fixed the boundary of their possessions 'to the man of Ur'. It is natural to conclude from this that a boundary dispute had arisen between Ur and Lagash, in which Ur was the aggressor, and that Utu-khegal was called upon, in his superior capacity, to decide, whereupon he drew the boundary between two cities as Mesilim had done in a former age when the disputants were Lagash and

---

[1] G, 19, 120 f.
[2] §1, 27, erster Teil, 55.
[3] G, 15, no. 30; §1, 29, 52.
[4] §1, 18; §1, 60, nos. 18–20.

Umma,[1] each then, as now, being the domain of its divine land-lord. Several of these little clay cones have been found and no doubt hundreds of them were made to fix in a low wall which, together with a canal,[2] marked the boundary. The aggressive 'man of Ur', to whom the award is clearly indicated as a rebuff, can be no other than Ur-Nammu, and it is not unlikely that the offence given by this adjudication contributed to his casting off allegiance to Uruk, and possibly provoking a contest in which the rebel was successful.

Sparsity of information about the history of the Third Dynasty of Ur, how it won, sustained, and finally lost its sway, is one of the major disappointments of Babylonian records. The geographi-cal extent of its authority, even if it should not be compared with that conquered by the kings of Agade,[3] was certainly wide, but no royal inscriptions make any mention of it, and few discoveries outside the nearer Babylonian limits shed any light upon it. Most of the information which exists is in the date-formulae appended to business documents, that is, the official 'names' given to each year by which almost every administrative or legal tablet was concluded. This cumbrous system had been in use long before, but with the Third Dynasty the formulae are, for the first time, preserved with tolerable completeness. Valuable as these are, their shortcomings as historical evidence are manifest—their extreme brevity, their arbitrary selection of one among the events of a year to give a designation to it,[4] their preoccupation with purely ceremonial occasions, and their dependence for chronological value upon our having the means to fix their order. For reasons unknown the obvious and much more satisfactory method of dating by the regnal years of kings was not brought into general use until the Kassite period.[5] In respect of the Third Dynasty we are fortunate enough not only to possess most of the formulae but to know also their official order,[6] and can therefore take full advantage of such information as they afford. This does not apply to the whole period. At the beginning the dates of Ur-Nammu are largely unknown and unfixed, and even for the first half of his successor's reign they are not well attested, and have little interest. Again, at the end, when the dynasty was sinking under converging attacks, the gallant and effective struggle of

---

[1] See above, p. 118; §I, 40, 87.

[2] G, 33, 188 (i); §I, 2, 16; §I, 30, 27, no. 28.

[3] §IV, 12, 80; §I, 57; §I, 24; A, 34, 59 ff.

[4] For the method used see G, 7, 26 ff.; G, 31, 12 ff.

[5] See *C.A.H.* I³, ch. VI, p. 197.   [6] §I, 54; §I, 57; G, 5, vol. II, 140 ff.

Ibbi-Sin is but faintly adumbrated by the mention of events which cannot be observed in a fixed order.

Ur-Nammu reigned eighteen years, counted probably from his breach with Uruk. By no means so many date-formulae can be attributed with certainty to these years.[1] One of them shows him appointing a son to the priesthood of Uruk, another marks a step to security, when 'the wall of Ur was built'. From a boast put into his mouth by a hymn[2] it appears that he still had to finish purging the land from the Gutian invaders, but the only positive military achievement which is attested (and that by himself) is a victory over Nammakhni, the ruler of Lagash, as recorded in the prologue to his laws.[3] This forcible reversal of the diplomatic defeat inflicted by Utu-khegal can hardly have been a major event in the rise of Ur to sovereignty, for even amid the general collapse left behind them by the Gutians there must have been stronger rivals than Lagash. Most interesting of the date-formulae preserved is that which proclaims that 'he made straight the road from below to above', which can be understood to mean a march from the lower sea (the Persian Gulf) to the upper sea (the Mediterranean, on the north Syrian coast), but nothing more is known about it and there is no external evidence, unless some doubtful indication of a palace-building at the site now called Tell Brak, on the Upper Khabur,[4] may be thought enough to attest the presence of Ur-Nammu in the farther northwest. But nearer home was the city of Mari, on the Middle Euphrates, which clearly owed him no allegiance, for it was then under independent governors whose names have been found in the recent excavations;[5] one of these had a daughter taken by marriage into the family of Ur-Nammu,[6] in the same way as the second king of Ur allied himself with neighbours on his northeastern borders. Moreover, tablets of this period found at Mari do not bear the date-formulae of Ur,[7] and in those formulae themselves, through the whole course of the dynasty, there is little appearance of the Euphratean lands or of Syria until, in the fourth year of Shu-Sin, the 'wall of Amurru' was built,[8] and this, so far from a measure of conquest, was a defence against invasion from that quarter. There is the same complete want of

---

[1] §1, 41, 397; §1, 57, 10 ff. [2] §1, 4, ii, 123, line 90; A, 7, 46, n. 12.
[3] See below, p. 620, and above, p. 459; §1, 39.
[4] §1, 50, 68 ff.; see above, pp. 506 ff.
[5] §1, 44, 152; A, 27, 21 f., n. 3. [6] §1, 5.
[7] §1, 9, 168; §1, 33, 185 ff.; §1, 44, 152; §1, 62, 174 f.
[8] See below, pp. 609 f.

information concerning any activity of Ur-Nammu in the districts beyond the Tigris, where his successors had to fight so many campaigns.

The fragmentary Laws of Ur-Nammu have recently received an, at least probable, addition with the publication of two parts of tablets found at Ur.[1] The laws thus preserved deal with sexual offences, with defence of women against such charges, with punishment of a slave-girl who presumes to set herself on a level with her mistress, and with wrongful acts in connection with land belonging to others. Juridical comments upon these have now been published by V. Korošec,[2] J. Klíma,[3] and J. J. Finkelstein.[4]

Perhaps in tacit acknowledgement of his limited sway he forbore to take the conquerors' title 'king of the four regions', which was assumed afterwards by his dynasty.[5] The largest attributions of power and wealth to him are made in some extant hymns of praise, one uttered by himself,[6] extravagantly celebrating the benefits he had conferred upon Ur and the glories vouchsafed to him by the grateful gods; indeed, he was hailed as a god himself in a song[7] which, amid much conventional eulogy, has a passing allusion to the 'righteousness' of the king, that is, to his laws.[8] Somewhat more explicit is another hymn about him[9] which was evidently composed to honour the king's exertions and munificence in restoring the temple of the divine ruler at Nippur. A last poem,[10] by contrast, is concerned with the death and obsequies of Ur-Nammu, his laments and the mourning of his family and city, consoled by the knowledge that rich gifts to the underworld deities have secured for him a fitting place among the shades. But the style of boast and flattery, as vague as it is vain, which swelled these courtly compositions and set the pattern for many others in the following generations, is destitute of real information upon the actual events of the reign or upon the personality of the monarch.

Inscriptions of Ur-Nammu[11] are found upon bricks, clay cones, and stone door-hinges from the numerous buildings and other works which he dedicated to the presiding gods in his capital and his subject cities. These works, of which imposing remains still survive, were undertaken principally in and about Ur, Nippur,

[1] A, 13.
[2] A, 17.
[3] A, 16.
[4] In *J.C.S.* 22 (1968–9), 66 ff.
[5] §I, 29, 52.
[6] §I, 4, ii, 118 ff.; §VII, 9, 113; §I, 55.
[7] §I, 46, 45 ff.; G, 4, part 44, pl. XIII; G, 12, 89; §I, 38, 6, n. 11.
[8] §I, 39; §I, 61; §VII, 3, 101 ff.
[9] G, 8, 87 ff.; §I, 4, ii, 106 ff.; §I, 55.
[10] §I, 4, i, 10 ff.; A, 19, II, 17.
[11] §I, 30, 24 ff.

Uruk, and Larsa. Probably in virtue of his rule at Nippur he assumed a new title 'king of Sumer and Akkad',[1] and there he built the temple of Enlil, leaving to his son as tradition required the renovation of Tummal,[2] shrine of the god's consort. At Uruk his chief operations were upon the zikkurrat or temple-tower of the goddess Inanna and the enclosure surrounding it,[3] a worthy counterpart to the greatest of all his monuments, the tower of the Moon-god at Ur. Of this the main structure still exists,[4] impressive alike by its plan, its mass, and the excellence of its construction and materials. Two or three later kings who undertook to repair this gigantic pile have left traces of what seem by comparison pygmy hands upon it. The last builder, Nabonidus, relates that it was begun by Ur-Nammu and carried on by his son,[5] but that even he did not complete the work. Substantially it was the achievement of Ur-Nammu, and the story of its building was related by him in picture and word upon a great stone monument, of which a few scenes remain.[6] Of the inscription[7] nothing is left but the mention of certain canals which the king dug out, among these being one which is the subject of a clay cone[8] found at Lagash—the canal called Nanna-gugal, of which he made 'its reservoir like a sea'. This waterway, it is added, was a boundary-mark which must have divided the territories of Lagash and of Ur, and since Ur-Nammu goes on to celebrate the 'justice' he had established we may surmise that his canal took a different line from that imposed upon Ur in the days of his subordination to Utu-khegal.

Canals indeed figure prominently in the surviving texts of Ur-Nammu, and it is likely that restoration of the country's means of communication and water-supply accounted for much of his activity in repairing the dire effects of Gutian wastage and neglect. Nor was his purpose only local, although much work no doubt accompanied his re-survey of the boundaries of city-states,[9] in which canals were a notable feature. An operation of much wider importance is attested by clay cones[10] found in an area called Diqdiqqah,[11] north-east of Ur, which relate in rather

---

[1] §1, 29, 77 ff.   [2] G, 16, 61 ff.; §1, 59, 44.
[3] The modern discoveries are summarized in G, 25, 255.
[4] §1, 64. See Plate 49 (a).   [5] §1, 45, 250 f.; §1, 64, 133.
[6] G, 35, vol. v, 397 ff.; §1, 4, i, 5 ff. (refs.). See Plate 49 (b).
[7] G, 15, no. 44; §1, 30, 27 (Ur-Nammu 29).
[8] G, 33, 188 (i); §1, 2, 16; §1, 30, 27 (no. 28).
[9] §1, 42, 64 ff.
[10] G, 15, no. 50; §1, 30, 27 (no. 26); G, 27, 14 ff.; §1, 32, 181 ff.; §1, 39, 46.
[11] G, 35, vol. v, 18 ff.; §1, 32.

obscure terms that merchant-ships from Magan were again able
to berth in a harbour at this place thanks to the operations of
Ur-Nammu who had restored its direct communication with the
open sea. This attests the resumption of an overseas trade which
had flourished under the Dynasty of Agade, but its range is now
found to be more restricted, for the remoter Meluhha[1] (wherever
that is to be sought) is never mentioned, and seems no longer to
lie within the orbit of voyages from southern Babylonia.[2]

To whatever limits confined, the reign of Ur-Nammu was
beyond doubt a time of increasing power and wealth, sufficiently
witnessed by his many great public works, although the tablets
of administration, which furnish ubiquitous evidence of thriving
activity under his successors, make but a scanty appearance in his
time. A like progress may be assumed for the earlier years of his
successor, a famous king whose name is invariably written with
the signs ŠUL (or DUN)-GI, the reading of which is uncertain,
but it is known that the name ended in *r*; for the present he can
be called Shulgi.[3] He reigned most probably forty-eight years,[4]
but of these the first twenty-one seem to have passed with little
distinction, and the events commemorated by the date-formulae
are almost entirely religious observances of a local character. The
most interesting exception gives a glimpse of foreign affairs; his
eighteenth year was that in which a daughter of his 'was raised
to the ladyship of Markhashe', the Elamite district (Barakhshe,
Warakhshe)[5] which had played so prominent a part in the history
of the Agadean kings. But there is no information how this
alliance (if such is meant) was brought about—conquest is in no
way indicated. In all of these earlier years tablets are still rare,
and nearly all of those extant were found at Lagash.[6] In the
capital itself, among more than seventeen hundred tablets of this
period published from the excavations,[7] not one is dated before
the twenty-fourth year of this reign, the same in which these
become common at other centres of the administration. It may
be concluded that new regulations were issued at this time for
strict collection and control of the revenues and outgoings, and
this is also attested by a date-formula[8] (probably of the twenty-
first year) which records that the king, by divine commandment,
set in order the registry of lands belonging to the supreme god
of Nippur and his consort. From care of this real estate the same

---

[1] See above, pp. 439 and 453.   [2] G, 27, 15.

[3] §1, 57, 14, n. 14.   [4] §1, 24; §1, 56.

[5] See above, pp. 432 and 436.   [6] G, 9, 36 f.

[7] G, 23.   [8] §1, 24, 153; §1, 57, 18.

rigour of book-keeping extended into all other branches of revenue, expenditure, and temple-business, and henceforth the accounting was so multifarious and minute that even single articles or heads of cattle and temporary lists were consigned to tablets, large or (mostly) small, of excellent quality and writing. Such 'business documents of the Third Dynasty' are now by far the most numerous in modern collections of cuneiform tablets.

While it is not possible to explain, for want of evidence, why this increased activity should have been postponed, much contrary to usage, until almost half-way through a long reign, it seems clear that the new fiscal control from the twenty-first year of Shulgi was imposed as a mobilization of resources to support a policy of expansion. The twentieth year was named as that when 'the men of Ur were sworn in as archers', and the twenty-fourth carries the record of the first foreign conquest. This campaign set the direction for all that were to follow, as moves in the never-ending struggle against the mountain-peoples of the north and east. Its objective, or at least its conquest, on this occasion was a place called Karakhar,[1] as yet unlocated, but its occurrence in company with other localities, attacked in subsequent campaigns, makes it certain that all of these are to be found in southern Kurdistān, among the troublesome neighbours or the elusive victims of later Assyrian kings. Some fixed points determine the general situation of all; Urbilum, captured in later expeditions of Shulgi and of his son, is the town called by the Assyrians Arba'ilu and now Irbil, in the plain between the two Zab rivers. Another place, Simurrum, has been sought in the neighbourhood of Altın Köprü on the Lesser Zab,[2] or to the south of this, being a neighbour to the land of Lullubum, which lay in the district of Sulaimaniyyah, as indicated by the rock-reliefs of Naram-Sin;[3] and finally the town of Shashrum, conquered by Shulgi and by his son, may with sufficient confidence be found at the place called in the following age Shusharra and now bearing the little-altered name of Shemshāra, an ancient mound 'on the right bank of the Lesser Zab, eight kilometres south-east of Rania and five kilometres west of Darband-i Ramkan (Sungasur Gorge)'.[4]

Other towns listed as destroyed in the unremitting wars of Shulgi and his son in this region are Kimash and Khumurti,[5] named with Madqa, from which Gudea had obtained asphalt,

---

[1] §IV, 2, 57; §I, 22, 118 f.; §IV, 6, 15; A, 22, 24; A, 33, no. 153.
[2] §IV, 6, 15, n. 8; §IV, 12; §I, 22, 123; §IV, 2, 114.
[3] See above, p. 443.   [4] §IV, 6, 70; A, 22, 24.
[5] §I, 22, 118; §I, 23, 105, n. 9.

and therefore likely to be near the places associated with the
present petroleum industry; and Kharshi, which seems to be
identified by a seal-inscription[1] as near Tuz Khurmatli, on the
'Adhaim river. Although the suggestion that Shashrum was an
older form of the name of Ashur itself[2] has now been superseded
by the discoveries at Shusharra (Shemshāra), noticed above, it is
evident that so much concern with the immediately neighbouring
lands of the later Assyrian kingdom implied control of the
Assyrian territory itself by the kings of Ur, and there is direct
witness of this. From Ashur itself comes a stone tablet dedicated
by Zariqum,[3] calling himself governor of Ashur, 'for the life of
Amar-Sin the mighty, king of Ur, king of the four regions',
whereby it is certain that Ashur was a vassal-city of Ur under its
next king. Hardly less clear is the testimony of certain stone
figures found in the excavations there; a headless statue and a
relief,[4] perhaps also a female figure,[5] are in a style which assigns
them to the Third Dynasty. More recently the aforesaid discovery of written documents at Shemshāra has revealed how the
rule of these neighbouring lands passed naturally to Assyria itself
when a powerful kingdom had been established there following
upon the collapse of Ur under the flood of West Semitic immigration, and how the troubles of controlling the borderlands with
their alien and unruly inhabitants were then transferred to the
new overlords.

Compared with the almost boundless conquests achieved by,
or at least attributed to, the greatest kings of Agade, these wars
of the Ur Dynasty may appear local,[6] but they were far from
being mere jars with neighbours, although perhaps waged as
much with the ultimate purpose of defence as of acquisition.[7] The
theatre of war was at a mean distance of 400 miles from Ur, by
the road up the east bank of the Tigris, rendered difficult by the
successive tributaries to be crossed and by the nature of the
ground. Reason enough for these repeated expeditions of Shulgi
and of his sons, in which the same places may be 'destroyed' as
often as 'nine times',[8] may be found in the opponents, among
whom still appear the Gutians,[9] unreconciled to banishment from
their long supremacy. But these were only one of several peoples

---

[1] G, 33, 174 f.; §IV, 2, 57; §IV, 8, 11.
[2] G, 5, vol. II, 144; §IV, 11, 148 f.
[3] §I, 10, 2 f.; §I, 28; §I, 30, 36, no. 15.   [4] G, 2, pls. 38a and 23a.
[5] G, 1, pls. 38 f.   [6] §IV, 12, 80.   [7] §I, 48, 16; §I, 34, 298.
[8] Simurrum and Lullubum (Shulgi, year 44).
[9] See above, p. 597; §I, 43, 153.

having in common the character of hardy mountaineers, difficult to encounter, and inhabiting towns and villages of simple construction, easily restored after the retirement of each punitive expedition—such troublesome neighbours have continued to pose a problem unsolved by a succession of governments in Mesopotamia even down to the present day. At this time a fresh element of unrest was making its presence felt—the people called Hurrians,[1] first discernible in the period of Agade, were now gathering strength in the north-east, and a number of individuals with names characteristic of this nation appear in the tablets of the Third Dynasty. As yet it seems that they were still mostly confined to the lands east of the Tigris, and that the spread of their population to northern Mesopotamia and Syria took place in the succeeding generations.[2] One of their homes was the oft-stricken Simurrum, and it was perhaps there that Shulgi captured a persistent enemy, Tappa-darakh, as the omens recorded;[3] it is almost the only detail preserved concerning the wars of Shulgi.

More to the south, and despite the nominal rule of an Elamite king of Simashki,[4] the ascendancy of Shulgi over the settled land of Susiana, with its appendages to the east and north, was well established, and what can be discerned of his policy there is described in the next chapter. From the north-west of Babylonia, the region of the Euphrates, there is virtually no news, and peace seems mostly to have been kept. A slight allusion to Mari and Rapiqum appears in a fragmentary letter to the king,[5] there is one mention of 'booty from Amurru' towards the end of his reign,[6] and not long beforehand two of the date-formulae appointed were 'year' [and 'year after'] 'the wall of the land was built'.[7] Nothing, however, is known of the location or purpose of this defence, but it might be at least supposed a predecessor of Shu-Sin's wall against western invaders, so that Shulgi may have found in his later years a necessity to hold this other front while his main strength was employed in the east. It is true that a very different picture of the situation in this quarter is suggested by one or two isolated tablets[8] which record the delivery of single sheep to the official cattle-park from the governors of four cities not merely of the middle and upper Euphrates (Mari, Tuttul,

[1] §IV, 2, 50; see below, pp. 624 f.
[2] §IV, 8, 18 f.; §IV, 3; §V, 3, 232 ff.; see *C.A.H.* II³, ch. I, sect. IV.
[3] §I, 21, 259 f.; §IV, 12, 75; §I, 22, 120 f.
[4] For the reading *Simashki* (instead of *Simash*), see J. R. Kupper, *Iraq* 31 (1969), 24–7.
[5] §I, 7, 12.
[6] §V, 3, 156.
[7] §I, 54, 17; A, 19, II, 18 f., no. 42.
[8] §I, 58, 120; cf. §I, 25, 18.

and Ibla) but of farthest Syria (Byblos itself). Two of these governors have the title of *ensi*, normally given to local officers appointed by the kings of Ur over their subject cities. But in the total absence of supporting evidence this is not enough to make it seem likely that the dynasty of Ur really held any effective sway in the north-west.

The very little more that tradition has to relate about a king who was nevertheless held to be one of the outstanding figures of the past may suggest that the want of historical records for this period was a real omission, not a mere accident of time. Chronicles and omens, which contribute so much to our knowledge of the Agadean kings, do not entirely omit Shulgi, but what they have to tell of him is jejune, unimportant, and not wholly trustworthy. He was remembered as a builder of the Tummal at Nippur,[1] and he appears in two passages of the chronicles; one of these, from a tablet found at Ashur,[2] relates that the god Marduk 'gave to Shulgi the son of Ur-Nammu the kingdom over the whole of the lands', but 'he did not fulfil the ordinances, he defiled its ritual, and his sin (was grievous)'. In this passage, apart from the neglect of Ur-Nammu as king, the ignoring of everything but the election by Marduk and the forfeiture because of impiety betrays not only the bigotry but perhaps also the ignorance of the compiler. His preoccupation makes it certain that the Ashur chronicle was a copy of a Babylonian original, and it was at Babylon where the other chronicle concerning Shulgi was found.[3] Its notice of the great king is no less trivial and biased—he 'cared greatly for Eridu which is on the shore of the sea, but he sought after evil, and the possessions of E-sagil and of Babylon he brought forth sacrilegiously'. The care for Eridu, as a rival seat of the god Ea, may have seemed to this partial scribe almost as criminal as the plunder of Marduk's temple, and it is possible that Shulgi did in fact despoil Babylon on behalf of his work at Eridu. A like accusation against Sargon reveals the same distortion in this writer's view of history, and his allegations are the more improbable or irrevelant as Babylon was not, in the days either of Sargon or of Shulgi, a place of much importance, though it did receive a royal appointee as governor[4] in the latter years of Shulgi. One or two quite insignificant references in omen-texts,[5] and the beginning of an alleged self-description,[6] are all that we

[1] §1, 59.   [2] §1, 27, erster Teil, 53 ff.
[3] §1, 36, vol. II, 11; G, 29, 266.   [4] §1, 63, 27; §1, 35, 15 f.
[5] G, 30, no. 5; G, 26, no. 19; §1, 21, 259; see above, p. 603.
[6] §1, 27, erster Teil, 81.

have from later generations concerning one of the greatest kings; unless indications are deceptive, not very much more was long remembered.

But at least until the succeeding age—the Old Babylonian period—Shulgi remained a conspicuous figure in the scribal schools, where two kinds of literary texts concerning him were studied and freely copied by pupils. One of these was letters, written by or to the monarch,[1] and preserved apparently more for their style as courtly addresses and elegant compositions than for the importance of their contents; for most of their lines, when addressed to the king, were occupied by reiterated salvoes of extravagant compliment. Several of such letters belonging to the reign of Shulgi have been identified.[2] The best preserved are a report from Ir-mu,[3] a royal representative abroad, and what is apparently a reply to this from the king. Ir-mu was a very important and powerful officer, probably the one who, under the name of Ir-Nanna, was able later to build a shrine at Lagash to the reigning king and dedicate it with an inscription detailing his great domains and calling himself 'high commissioner'.[4] In the days of Shulgi he was (if the same) in charge of a military force and detailed to represent his king in discussions with border chieftains. The letter of Ir-mu[5] relates to an occasion of this kind, when the opposite party was an independent or rebellious ruler, perhaps designated by his own name or by a title, but not otherwise known, and having his realm in some northern district no less vaguely called Subir (Subartu). The envoy reports that he was received by this potentate and his court without the becoming marks of respect, the ruler behaving in his presence with ostentatious freedom. He was, nevertheless, entertained honourably, which did not save him from some insults by the servants. What was the outcome of this mission does not appear. Shulgi's answer was discontented but ineffective—he complains that his representatives did not so act as to compel proper deference from the opponent, and he seems to exhort them to bear themselves more imperiously, but nothing solid can be gathered from the empty phrases which occupy most of the letter.

The other kind of literature, in which Shulgi is more prominent than any other king, is the royal hymns, where he appears saluted with almost divine honours from his court-poets, or speaking of

---

[1] §I, 12, 1 ff.; §I, 15, 73; §I, 11, 3, n. 27; A, 19, II, 18 f. (nos. 42, 43).
[2] See §I, 11; §I, 43, 153 ff.   [3] Otherwise read Arad-mu, Irda-mu.
[4] G, 33, 148 f., 202 f.; §I, 30, 38, no. 13; §I, 25, 9 f.; A, 33, no. 183.
[5] G, 22, 331 ff.; A, 5.

himself in a like strain. Some thirty of these hymns are still extant, in whole or parts ;[1] amid much verbiage of extravagant eulogy appears some light upon the personality and even upon the achievements of their hero. The blessings of his rule and the signal favour which he received from the gods are naturally common topics, but this favour was bestowed not upon a stranger, however meritorious, but upon a kinsman, a descendant himself of gods and kings ; his father (i.e. ancestor) was, he declares, the ancient demigod-king Lugalbanda, and his mother the goddess Nin-sun, mother also of Gilgamesh, whom Shulgi therefore freely called his 'brother'.[2] Going still farther, he audaciously claimed a like relation with the Sun-god himself.[3] A boast which he makes of his education and literary talent[4] might suggest that some of these fulsome effusions of his own praise were of his own composition. More factually, the king sometimes refers to his military successes in terms which clearly recall the manifold 'destruction' of places so prominent in the date-formulae.[5] The enemies inhabiting these are grouped under the name of 'Gutians', evidently as a general designation for the mountain-peoples, of sinister memory. Most informative of all, though concerning a matter more important to the king's pride than to his history, is the hymn[6] which celebrates a journey made by him at wondrous speed in the same day from Nippur to Ur and back, in defiance of a raging storm of wind and hail. This feat was made possible not only by Shulgi's own physical powers (described, of course, as superhuman), but by using the roads and relay-houses which his prudence had constructed.[7] Such were the bubbles of regal vanity and of hireling adulation, which were blown anew with the old breath in many of the succeeding reigns, until a desert orator came forward with the bare truth 'no king is powerful by himself'.[8] But upon Shulgi, at least, in a period of greater consolidation, no such verdict could have been justly pronounced.

As if literary pre-eminence were not enough, a recently published text[9] ascribes also to Shulgi the title of first royal musician, traditionally claimed by David. It reckons up no less than eight instruments upon which he was a master-performer, including the lyre of thirty strings, and the instrument so strangely named after the Sargonic king of Kish, Ur-Zababa; (see above, p. 418).

1 §I, 16, 62 f.; §I, 17, 141; §VII, 9, 113; §VII, 9.
2 §I, 16, 74 ff.; A, 34, 69.
3 §I, 16, 76.
4 §I, 13, 172; G, 22, 69.
5 §I, 17, 146 f.
6 §I, 16.
7 §I, 16, 81 f. See A, 23, 83, no. 1.
8 See *C.A.H.* II³, ch. I, sect. II.
9 A, 11, 1, no. 81; also A, 15, 261.

The half-century-long reign of Shulgi ended with his burial in a splendidly built, and doubtless richly furnished, sepulchre at Ur,[1] but not a trace of his family's remains or of their funeral pomp has survived the disaster which was to overwhelm the last of his line. Meanwhile, the succession of Amar-Sin (or Bur-Sin),[2] his son, followed without any appearance of domestic strife or revolt, in strong contrast with the experience of the Agadean kings. The legitimacy of the Third Dynasty was accepted by the people, and the splendour of Shulgi's reign continued to adorn the nine years of his son. There was little respite in the north-east, and the second year of the new reign received the name 'year (when) King Amar-Sin ravaged Urbilum', renewing the chastisement inflicted five years before by Shulgi. Likewise the sixth and seventh years were called after expeditions against Shashrum and some new names in the date-lists—Khukhnuri with two other localities perhaps to be read Bitum-rabium and Beshru, and another town called Iaprum.[3] The first of these, Khukhnuri, was afterwards described by Ibbi-Sin as the 'bolt of the land of Anshan (or, Elam)',[4] and may perhaps therefore be sought east of Eshnunna: others are unknown but not likely to be far away.

These are all of the incidents which appear in the dates, apart from religious ceremonies, and the evidence of the tablets draws no very different picture. In sundry districts and towns, even upon the eastern frontier, commanders and governors are appointed by, and hold their office in submission to, the king of Ur, often undisturbed from one reign to the next. But there are signs that the empire was consolidated, even if not extended, by Amar-Sin, for governors are found installed for the first time in Markhashe, Simanum, Khamazi, and even in the newly subdued Khukhnuri.[5] From the east and north a continual traffic of 'messengers'[6] thronged the roads into Babylonia, testifying to and perhaps securing the peaceful condition of the realm. In this happy situation Amar-Sin was able to devote much of his ample revenue to temples and public edifices; he worked extensively at Nippur, where he seems to have received some special mark of favour from the god, which he included in his titles,[7] but his principal activity was in the capital itself, where several important

---

[1] G, 35, vol. xi, 345 ff. and vol. xii, 358 f. See Plate 50(a).
[2] I.e. according as the name was read in Sumerian or Akkadian: the question is open.   [3] §viii, 3, 53; A, 33, p. 105 (no. 111).
[4] G, 15, no. 88; §1, 54, 38 (b); G, 5, vol. ii, 146; §1, 11, 2, n. 16.
[5] §1, 35, 16.   [6] §iv, 5; §1, 34, 280 ff.; A, 33, no. 1.
[7] §1, 29, 133.

buildings are named in the inscriptions, and others found in the excavations have proved to be his. Most of all, his monument was the vast temple and tower called the *apsu* in Eridu, where the remains of his great structures cover the site and have been investigated by recent excavators.[1] Here the credit belongs to him more than to his father, despite the beginning made by the latter and the 'great care' of the sacred city for which he was praised —or perhaps blamed—by the chronicler. Later tradition knew hardly anything about Amar-Sin: as though in derision of our ignorance an omen[2] mocks us with the detail that he died from the 'bite' of a shoe, presumably a poisoned foot. He had built on to the funerary dwelling of his father in Ur a smaller addition with a similar plan,[3] which also included two vaults for the principal burials.

In regular succession again he was followed on the throne by Shu-Sin (or Gimil-Sin), whom the king-list calls his son, but more direct evidence establishes that he was a brother.[4] From the date-formulae it might seem that his reign was mostly peaceful, but one of the troublesome neighbours in the north-east, Simanum, had to be punished in the third year, and similarly Zabshali in the seventh. The bare mention of these names is supplemented by the remains of some inscriptions[5] graven upon trophies and monuments which the victor dedicated in Nippur. These inscriptions were copied by scribes, and consequently something of their contents survives while the monuments have long disappeared— just as similar copies are the source of much that is known about the kings of Agade.[6] Both of the campaigns figuring in the date-formulae were represented by sculptured or cast figures. From conquered Simanum captives were carried away and were settled in a new cantonment which the king founded near Nippur, probably as a labour-camp for slaves to toil upon his public works. Of Zabshali more details are preserved from the copied inscriptions. The principal enemy was named Indasu, called governor of Zabshali (but Ziringu, and perhaps another, bear the same title). Together with him some ten more princes are named, with the places over which they ruled; the monument showed the king setting his foot upon the neck of Indasu, followed by the other captives, each marked with his own name, and the whole scene might be imagined not much unlike the celebrated sculpture of Darius at Bihistān. From Zabshali and its neighbouring lands

[1] §I, 49; §I, I, 91 f.　　　　　　　　　　　[2] §I, 21, 261.
[3] G, 35, vol. XI, 355 ff.; A, 32, p. 7, no. 33.　[4] §I, 57, 20 f.
[5] §I, II, 31.　　　　　　　　　　　　　　　[6] See above, p. 417.

was brought back a rich spoil of metals,[1] copper, tin, bronze, but also gold, out of which the king made a figure of himself[2] which he set up before the supreme god Enlil.

Despite all this, the peace in the east was uneasy, for although Shu-Sin was able to put in his officers as governors of Elamite cities (Urua[3] and Susa[4]), and to exact the homage of a temple erected to his 'divinity' in Eshnunna,[5] he found it necessary to entrust the warding of the eastern marches to a lieutenant with exceptional powers. For this responsibility he chose Ir-Nanna, governor of Lagash, who subsequently built there a shrine in honour of his master, upon the door-hinge stones of which he inscribed his titles. He was, first, 'high commissioner' (*sukkal-mah*)[6] of the king, and bore as domestic offices the governorship of Lagash and the priesthood of the god Enki. Others of his styles are governor (*ensi*) or commander (*šakkana*)[7] of a number of towns and districts on the eastward frontiers, the best-known of which are Urbilum, Khamazi, and Karakhar, all familiar from the wars of Shulgi, and also the *Su*-people[8] or Subarians, at that time living in the country east of the modern Mosul, perhaps including Assyria itself, which was certainly subject in the reign of Amar-Sin. Over this extensive lordship the exertions of Ir-Nanna, whatever they were, sufficed to keep order among or against the petty princedoms which existed in a state of semi-independence interspersed between the vassals of the king.

But no doubt the weightiest reason for this appointment of a commissioner in the east was the emergence, early in the reign of Shu-Sin, of a new danger menacing the empire of Ur as it had the Akkadian empire under Shar-kali-sharri.[9] The fourth official formula was 'year (when) the wall of Amurru was built', and a fuller version adds that the wall was called Muriq-Tidnim, 'keeping away Tidnum',[10] which was another name for the tribes of western origin and the lands from which they came. A double shadow began to fall again over Babylonia, but it could not close in until the successor of Shu-Sin was exhausted by a long and not unsuccessful defence. In what circumstances the tribes attacked is quite unknown, but it seems clear that they were defeated in battle and forced to flee by the way they came, along the Euphrates, pursued by the royal troops who advanced some

---

[1] §1, 48, 16; §1, 48, 247 f.; A, 21, 195; A, 32, 7, no. 34; A, 19, 11, 19, no. 43.
[2] §1, 11, 2, n. 36.   [3] §1, 25, 6, n. 73.   [4] See below, p. 567.
[5] §11, 7; A, 34, 66.   [6] §1, 29, 114 f.   [7] §1, 25, 8.
[8] A recent summary of the discussion concerning these in §1, 11, 16 ff.; A, 29, 16.
[9] See above, p. 455.   [10] §v, 3, 156; §v, 2, 30; see also A, 1.

distance upstream[1]—how far is not clear. The question depends largely upon the location—whether at Hīt[2] or farther north[3]—of a town Duddul or Tuttul; in view of what follows the nearer seems the more likely. How slight a confidence was inspired by this victory is shown by the decision to build a defensive line against a fresh advance of the Amorites, a measure of doubt, if not of despair, whether in Babylonia, in China, or in Britain, when the limits of power are thought to have been reached, and barbarians are to be fenced off, no longer subdued in their own haunts.

This defence for the kingdom of Shu-Sin was ominously close to its heart. A fragmentary Sumerian letter gives some curious and surprising particulars about the extent and location of the 'Fender of Tidnum'. Its writer was Sharrum-bani, probably not the same as one of that name who had been already a city-governor in the reign of Amar-Sin;[4] the receiver's name is missing; it was not the king himself but rather a minister, for Sharrum-bani introduces himself as 'expert of the committee,[5] your servant', that is, a member of the board of technicians assembled by the king to plan and execute the great work. His instructions were to take advantage of the repulse of the Amorites and to build a wall so as to bar their further access. The work would involve the breaching of the banks both of the Tigris and the Euphrates (perhaps to fill a moat), but he was to take care that the breaching did not overwhelm the fields. The earthwork began from the Apkallat canal, and certain other intermediate points marked the line, but their names are not adequately preserved for the most part. There is, however, a clear statement that the (total?) length of the wall was 26 *danna* or *bērū*, that is to say some 275 kilometres or 170 miles.

There are two principal arguments which suggest that the wall ran across the country in a region not far north-west of Baghdad.[6] The first is its beginning from the Apkallat canal—this name was already modified in a later syllabary to Aplakkat, which may be supposed the same as the Pallakottas canal cleared by Alexander in a later age, and this stream is associated with the town of Pallukat, generally sought in the modern Fallūjah.[7] Secondly, the length of the wall, about 170 miles, although much greater

1 Refs. in §1, 11, 2, n. 24; §1, 30, 38, no. 9. See Plate 49 (*c*).
2 See above, p. 424.
3 §1, 22, 121; §1, 58, 121.   4 §1, 25, 15.
5 *gal-zu ukkina*. A, 11, 11, no. 183; §1, 3, 20 f.
6 Its location recently discussed in §1, 3, 20 f.   7 §1, 3, 11 f.

than the distance between the rivers at their closest, requires that it should have been situated where they approach each other, for the wall must have rested against some natural bastions on the far sides of each river. For the western end the neighbourhood of the present Lake Habbaniyah is strongly suggested, for the eastern there is only the possibility that a 'Fortress before the Mountain'[1] (which was easily carried or outflanked by the nomads)[2] lay near a ridge of high ground between Fallūjah and 'Aqarqūf. If subsequent discovery is able to confirm this siting it will be necessary to conclude that Shu-Sin was already narrowly constricted by the twin pressures which were finally to crush his successor. As for his great wall, it proved even more ineffectual than such barriers have always been in the end. No more is heard of this vast and vain work, even if, as seems likely, it furnished a line or a foundation for similar works in later ages. Babylonia has no natural defences, and they were not to be provided by an artificial rampart so long that it could have hardly been effectually garrisoned.

The reign of Shu-Sin closed in this uneasy equilibrium, and his son Ibbi-Sin entered upon a tenure of twenty-four years,[3] destined to be illuminated by flashes of glory and heroic episodes, with which the king himself may be fairly credited, though it was to close in utter disaster. His first two years were untroubled and devoted to civil duties. Then came a routine chastisement of Simurrum, one of the troublesome north-eastern neighbours, then two or three more years of peace, during which, however, the approach of danger was signalled by the need to repair the walls of Ur and Nippur. Chronology after this is uncertain[4]—more date-formulae are preserved, with much interesting information, but no list of their order has been found. It is best, consequently, to consider in distribution the events which the formulae briefly indicate as occurring upon the two warlike fronts and at home.

To begin with the east—Ibbi-Sin in his sixth year repeated the policy of attempting to secure the fidelity of a foreign prince by a marriage-alliance, and sent his daughter Tukin-khatta-migrisha to the ensi of Zabshali, doubtless with as little permanent result as before. A later occasion upon the eastern frontier was one of triumph, for in a long formula Ibbi-Sin claims that he 'smote like a tempest Susa, Adamdun, and the land of Awan, subdued them in one day, and captured their ruler.' This prisoner may be identified as one of a local dynasty which had recently occupied

---

[1] §1, 3, 21 f.; §1, 31, 39; G, 7, 47, no. 207; §v, 4, 73; A, 19, 11, 18 f., no. 42.
[2] See below, p. 615. [3] §1, 57, 38, n. 149. [4] Ibid. 43.

the throne of a border state named Simashki.[1] His defeat was not
severe enough to bring down the state, for a successor upon the
throne of Simashki was certainly the wreaker of the great Elamite
revenge upon the city of Ur. An ally was found by the insurgents
in the land or city of Khukhnuri, the old opponent of Amar-Sin,
for over this enemy too Ibbi-Sin boasted of a resounding victory ;
he calls it 'the bolt of the land of Anshan', and says that he smote
it 'like a tempest and a deluge'. These valiant exploits staved off
calamity for a considerable time, but it is only too clear that the
successes were far from decisive. Other allies of the Elamites, at
least in the final struggle with Ur, were the *Su*-people ;[2] however
these are to be identified, they seem to have lived in more primitive communities, not such as to suffer much from a mere burning
and devastation.

Events at home were closely bound up with those on the
Euphrates front, but the defect of chronology obscures the
picture. It may be assumed that pressure on this side was
continuous, since it had first been felt before the fourth year of
Shu-Sin, but with the reign of his successor the menace became
formidable. This coincided with the emergence of a dubious
figure Ishbi-Erra, the 'man', that is governor, of Mari ; not, as
it seems, a westerner himself but a time-serving vassal who was
able to turn the western invasion to his own advantage. There is
no doubt that the invaders had easily passed the unavailing wall
of Shu-Sin, and were already in the northern parts of the homeland early in the reign of Ibbi-Sin. Two models of the ominous
sheep's liver found at Mari[3] show the fatal marks which accompanied the loss of part of his kingdom—not so much a revolt as
detachment of his territory under Amorite lordships. Ibbi-Sin
was not without his successes against these intruders, for one of
his dates celebrates a year in which 'the Amorites, a torrent force
which from of old knew not a city, made submission' to him.[4]
Cowed as a vanguard may have been by this reverse the following
hordes were but little affected and evidence of the inroads of
Ishbi-Erra soon became ubiquitous. There are tablets[5] which
contain lists of articles in gold, silver, bronze, and copper,
collected from the temple-treasuries to pay 'the price of Isin',[6]

[1] See below, pp. 635 and 657.
[2] See above, p. 609, n. 8.
[3] G, 30, 42, nos. 6 and 7 ; G, 26, nos. 89 and 93.
[4] G, 23, 278, no. 13.
[5] G, 23, 225 f., nos. 702 and 704 ; §1, 47, 124 f. ; G, 7, 46 f. ; §1, 48, 180.
[6] G, 23, no. 702.

whether as a ransom for the city or to buy supplies for the capital. It is certain that negotiations were going on between the two rulers, possibly up to the eve of the Elamite raid which obliterated Ur and led to the captivity of Ibbi-Sin. In the year of triumph over Susa, Adamdun, and Awan a tablet from Ur[1] registers the issue of a travelling allowance to three men described as 'messengers of Ishbi-Erra' and a 'man of Isin'. By this time, therefore, Ishbi-Erra was in possession of Isin, and the fear which he inspired is proved by this payment to his envoys, perhaps the bearers of other unwelcome messages.

To judge by the cessation of documents bearing the official date-formulae of Ur, the defection of various cities began early in the reign of Ibbi-Sin.[2] But Isin seems to have retained some degree of loyalty until about the twelfth year of its nominal overlord,[3] after which Ishbi-Erra began using independent formulae as a ruler in his own right. Many scraps of information about the manœuvres of this man and other wavering vassals are conveyed by a number of letters, very imperfectly preserved in later schoolcopies.[4] One of the more complete[5] is from Ishbi-Erra himself, written at the time when he was still active in the service of Ur. He had been sent, he writes, to buy supplies of grain in the cities of Isin and Kazallu, north-west of the capital,[6] and had laid out the great sum of twenty talents of silver, with which he had amassed a vast quantity of provisions. But the invaders had broken in and were spreading everywhere, and because of the general insecurity Ishbi-Erra had concentrated his stores in Isin; he now had to find transport to Ur, and his letter asked for 600 barges to be sent up for this purpose. It ended with an encouragement to the king that he should press on with his war against Elam,[7] not being deterred by fears for his own country, since (the writer assures him) there was a great surplus of provisions in hand, and all the cities, particularly Isin and Nippur, were firmly held by him (probably in usurpation). Ibbi-Sin's reply to this reveals the strait to which he had been reduced[8]—he was willing to pay double the cost of the grain, but he had not the barges to send, his agent must try to find these among the northern cities. As to Isin and Nippur, the king behoved to grant formal confirmation of the authority which Ishbi-Erra had already assumed.

---

[1] G. 23, no. 1421. [2] §1, 31, 38. [3] *Ibid.* 43; §1, 57, 44.
[4] For a list of the parts available see §1, 11, 3, n. 27.
[5] §1, 31, 39 f.; §1, 3, 21 f.
[6] For the site of Isin §1, 32, 178 and pl. xxviii; for Kazallu §1, 42, 59 ff.
[7] §1, 8, 274 f.; §1, 3, 21 f. [8] §1, 31, 41.

A similar correspondence, of which something is preserved, was going on with the governor of Kazallu, a man who seems to have borne different names at different periods in his career. He is once addressed, by the king, as Puzur-Numushda, but again as Puzur-Shulgi,[1] and in either name there is a letter from him to the king.[2] The alternation is significant, in that he probably changed his name when renouncing the allegiance of Ur, his style of Puzur-Shulgi being official and indicative of loyalty to the empire. Further, it is of interest that a Puzur-Shulgi, so named and not likely to be a different person, was one of the 'messengers' of Ishbi-Erra to whom a viaticum was paid by Ibbi-Sin, as related above. The letter of Puzur-Shulgi (or Puzur-Numushda) reports the successful usurpation of Ishbi-Erra, and his attempt to add Kazallu to the cities which had already fallen under his sway. He had sent a messenger with a summons to surrender; the message was a mixture of boasts and promises, detailing the lands which had already acknowledged his rule, along 'the banks of the Tigris and Euphrates, the Apkallat and Me-Enlil canals,[3] from the land Khamazi to the sea of Magan'. To these he announced that he would soon add Nippur and Ur itself, and would fortify his own capital Isin. All this, writes Puzur-Shulgi, he has already accomplished; he has seized Nippur, plundered Khamazi, installed his own nominees in Eshnunna, Kish, and elsewhere, and severely chastised those who sought to resist. The letter ends with a despairing appeal to a master who no longer had power to help, for Ibbi-Sin was penned closer and closer in his own territory.

A letter from him to the same vassal,[4] possibly a reply to the above, throws light upon the position in the north—reinforcements, it seems, had already been sent to Kazallu, but had not come into action, for fear of Ishbi-Erra, who had already begun his revolt, with so much success that (the king bitterly concludes) he must have been elected by the gods to rule over Sumer, despite his mean origin and alien birth. Yet Puzur-Numushda should beware—when Ishbi-Erra is master of everything he will be unmindful of those who helped him to triumph, and will not confirm them in the rule of their cities, as they expected. But the hard-pressed king had not yet abandoned hope: the god Enlil (he continues) has brought in the Amorites from their deserts, and he seems to rely also upon alliance with Elam.[5] Evidently the

---

[1] §1, 25, 18, n. 84; §1, 11, 3, n. 27; A, 5, 534.   [2] G, 22, 333 f.
[3] §1, 32, 177; §1, 3, 15.
[4] §1, 15, 60 ff.; G, 22, 334 f.   [5] G, 7, 49.

political situation was one of sudden change, with the friends of today becoming the foes of tomorrow. Especially surprising is it to find Ibbi-Sin, at some moment in his reign, looking for aid to an Amorite invasion, for it appears from other places in the letters that the beginning of disaster for Ur had been the breaching of the 'Amorite wall'. One extremity of this had been the 'Mountain' so described in the letter of Sharrum-bani,[1] and this key-point was defended by a stronghold called 'Fort before the Mountain'. In one of Ibbi-Sin's letters[2] there is a bitter complaint that the commander of this, named Puzur-Marduk,[3] had by cowardice or treachery abandoned it to the enemy, thus allowing them to turn the whole flank of the defences.

Neither the course of events nor the final agency of the conquest which led to the downfall of Ur can be accurately described. It was not, at least outwardly, a steady progress of decline, but an era of vicissitude. There was a year remembered for a natural disaster when 'a great flood by the will of the gods devastated the bounds of heaven and earth',[4] but Ibbi-Sin was still able to save his city from the wrath of nature as from the envy of man. Other years were tranquil, and once the king had even leisure to admire 'a huge ape which its country captured'[5] and sent to him. Upon the whole success predominated and at last seemed secure, with victories over the Amorites and the Elamites, and favourable signs from the gods in heaven, when 'for Ibbi-Sin, king of Ur, the Moon-god his beloved rose brightly',[6] and even this seemed to be outshone in a 'year (when) the god Enlil yoked the splendour of Ibbi-Sin upon the lands'[7] —a plain reference to the appearance of the Yoke-Star (Jupiter) standing in a region of the sky known as the 'way of Enlil', accompanied with other circumstances interpreted as a presage of triumph. But the downfall of an empire, which was in fact portended, required a more fatal sign; an eclipse of the moon was observed with terror by the citizens on the 14th of the month Adar,[8] 'beginning in the south and ending in the north, beginning in the first watch and ending in the last'. It bore a message to the doomed emperor, 'desolation of Ur, destruction of its walls'. Even the sign of Jupiter found its true interpreta-

---

[1] See above, p. 610. [2] §1, 31, 41.

[3] A letter from this man to the king, G, 7, 47, no. 208; §1, 11, 3, n. 27, but it now appears that the letter was sent to Shulgi: A, 19, 11, 18 f., no. 42.

[4] G, 23, 278, no. 21.

[5] G, 23, 278, no. 22; G, 27, 12, n. 21.

[6] G, 23, 278, no. 11. [7] *Ibid.* no. 14.

[8] But with hope by modern chronologers, §1, 52, 50 ff.; §1, 53, 89 ff.

tion, after the event, in one of the darkest passages of the astrologers' books—'if the Yoke-Star rises with its face towards the west and looks at the face of heaven and no wind blows at all, there will be famine, the ruler will meet the fate of Ibbi-Sin, king of Ur, who went in bonds to Anshan'.[1] The gods, or the star-gazers, had cruelly paltered with the people's faith.

A reference in the correspondence of Ibbi-Sin with his lieu-tenant, described above,[2] suggests that he may have relied at one moment upon Elamite aid against Ishbi-Erra. In this fragile alliance too were the people of the land of Subartu; for the date-formulae of Ishbi-Erra (which he was certainly issuing before the fall of Ur)[3] relate once that 'he smote the man of Subartu and Elam'.[4] The wavering passions and faithless conduct of the actors in this many-sided drama are exposed by another of the liver-models found at Mari—'when the Subarians sent unto Ishbi-Erra, but then the Subarians turned elsewhere, this (liver) was thus disposed'.[5] The situation was chaotic, every party fighting the other, but rushing desperately into short-lived leagues ; Elam and Ur were equally threatened, but they had not the wisdom to combine. Meantime, the city had come into desperate straits, and famine prices were prevailing. Tablets found at Ur indicate the values of oxen, sheep, barley, dates, and oil, first in terms of each other, and then in silver, at a level of prices multiplied many times the normal for that period,[6] and still more exorbitantly above those which kings were accustomed to boast or beseech for their prosperous reigns. Despite these marks of distress the tablets detail fairly large supplies of all these commodities, and might be taken to show that Ur had not then, at least, sunk into the plight of Samaria, where 'an ass's head was sold for fourscore pieces of silver'[7] before its miraculous deliverance.

In the final catastrophe, as all the evidence agrees, it was chiefly the peoples of the east and north who turned upon Ur and sacked it with a ferocious thoroughness which was never forgotten in Babylonian tradition. The perpetrators named are the Elamites and the Subarians, to whom are added the Gutians, as the historic enemies. This national disaster was commemorated in two poetical lamentations which, amid much pathetic but prolix detail of ruin and longing for recovery, have some allusions

[1] G, 34, 236.   [2] See above, pp. 614 f.
[3] §1, 57, 43 f.; G, 7, 49 and 62; A, 28, 16 and 20.
[4] §1, 6, 9; G, 7, 49.   [5] G, 30, no. 10; G, 26, no. 43.
[6] G, 23, 247, no. 1207; cf. §1, 31, 42; §1, 51, 80; A, 34, 68.
[7] II Kings vi. 25.

to actual or believed occurrences at the time. According to these, devastation was by no means confined to Ur, but widespread over much of Sumer and Akkad. The first lament has two lists of destroyed or occupied cities,[1] the second has one,[2] very much fuller. All include many cities in the south, some in the middle of the country.[3] It may be observed that in all of them figure Isin itself and Nippur, while Kish, Kazallu, and Eshnunna also make an appearance. Since these cities were respectively the capital of Ishbi-Erra and subsequent acquisitions of his,[4] it is not possible to regard all the places named as victims of a single invasion from the east. To the authors of the laments, citizens of Ur and witnesses of the collapse of its rule together with its walls, all the cities of Sumer and Akkad were limbs of the body centred in Ur, and their disaster was one, whether inflicted by easterners or westerners—for Tidnum too is once numbered among the destroyers. But wherever else ruin descended it was in the capital that the drama centred and has left traces even until today, for the excavations have revealed abundant evidence of plunder and devastation which no later building-up was able to obliterate. Never again was Ur to play an important part in history, and Ibbi-Sin became the typical figure of an ill-starred king, remembered only for his captivity and death in a strange land.

II. THE KING AND HIS OFFICERS

The attempt made in the preceding pages to follow the fortunes of the Third Dynasty of Ur has met at every turn a tantalizing want of information due to the singular unwillingness of the age to record even the triumphs, much less the failures, of its kings. For the internal conditions of the land at this time there is, on the contrary, a wealth of documentation which is hardly less embarrassing; it is copious beyond measure, and yet is very one-sided. The 'business-documents' of this dynasty, which are ubiquitous in all collections of tablets, begin to be abundant with the expansion of conquest in the middle years of Shulgi. Visibly under the impulse of the king himself a most meticulous system of book-keeping was instituted, and since this clerking was consigned to admirably made tablets in a fine clear style of writing, we are now in possession of ample records, from five of the main centres of

[1] §1, 37; G, 7, 50 ff.
[2] §1, 14, 377 ff.; G, 8, 189 ff.; §1, 19, 59 ff.; A, 16, 171 f.
[3] G, 7, 56.   [4] See above, p. 614.

the kingdom,[1] concerning administration of temple or royal properties, ranging in contents from digests of accounts over a period of time[2] to half-a-dozen lines registering the receipt of a goat. The impression produced by this soulless industry is that of a rigid bureaucracy, a system highly congenial to the Sumerian mind and having its roots deep in their past.[3] The 'scribe' is everywhere, busily employed in the presence of almost as many overseers and checkers, without whom not the slightest affair can be transacted.

Over these again stood greater officers, such as the managers of the temple workshops[4] or the city governors or the stewards[5] of the temples who administered the whole of their estates and activities.[6] Above all of them, at the apex of the pyramid, was the king himself. It has already been observed that his was the impulse which set in motion this formidable accounting machinery, and there is evidence that Shulgi was himself the inspirer of more efficient methods of business, for he rearranged the calendar,[7] set up a bureau of standards,[8] and issued accurate weights which were preserved and imitated to the latest days of Babylonian history.[9] Far more than this, the king was the principal contributor to the wealth and offerings of the temples, the head to whom all officials owed their appointments, and he is individually acknowledged as master of all these underlings upon their seals, a few of which are engraved with the image of the king upon the seat and in the attitude of a god, making a presentation of an office and a special mark of favour to the owner of the seal, which itself bears a statement that it was conferred by the king.[10]

A superior rank among his servants was held by the governors of provinces and cities, with the titles of *šakkana* or *ensi*,[11] and it is in their position that we may best understand the assumption of divinity by the kings of the Third Dynasty. There is some reason to believe that the revival at this period of the old Sumerian ideas was strict (in reaction against the Gutian oppression), and one of the most deep-seated of these had been the representation of the city-god in earthly affairs by his agent, the *ensi*. In the older centuries of the Sumerian states interference by the *lugal*, even in such important matters as the personality of the governor,

[1] §I, 34, Introd., ix.   [2] *Ibid.* 239 ff.; §II, 9, 16 ff.
[3] §II, 13; §II, 14; §II, 15.   [4] §I, 48, 166 ff.
[5] §II, 23, 122 ff.   [6] §II, 10.
[7] §I, 57, 17 ff.   [8] G, 23, no. 179.
[9] §VI, 7, no. 118; §II, 18, 181, n. 11.
[10] G, 13, 146; G, 14, pl. 54A; §II, 19, 119 f.; §I, 30, lists of seal-inscriptions. See Plate 51 (*b*).   [11] §I, 25, 8.

seems to have been limited, he being content with formal acknowledgement and possibly some payment of tribute and service.[1] But the formation of a great empire by the kings of Agade had put an end to this easy condition, and the constant unrest of the Sumerian cities under their rule had obliged them to take care that only men well-affected towards themselves were placed in positions of control there. The king had thus openly assumed the function of a god, and a god he must become.[2] In the dynasty of Agade this need must already have been sensible, and no doubt the vast accession of power and width of sway won by such a mighty figure as Naram-Sin helped to make him appear superhuman.

In the Third Dynasty of Ur this assumption of divinity coincided similarly with the great expansion in the middle years of Shulgi.[3] Vainglory and popular superstition supported it, but it may also have been deemed a necessary measure of policy to justify the otherwise inadmissible appointment of an earthly governor by another human. There is, indeed, one example of a governor (*ensi*) who was himself deified,[4] presumably upon the sole account of his achievements, but this must be regarded as anomalous and perhaps merely a piece of flattery. These new-minted gods caused to be set aside or built for them their own temple in each city,[5] receiving the daily provision and special allowances for their images. Thus they lived among their people and upon their own estates and set their own stewards to manage their properties; in short, they fulfilled the strictest ideas of human life and divine government. As there could not well be two masters in a house, it may be supposed that they often tended to dispossess the older patron-deities of their privileges; it has been noticed above that a city governor is found to have taken the king's name to the exclusion of the old god of his city,[6] and to have been ready to lay it aside when the power of Ur was visibly doomed.

The other side to this conception of the royal office was the necessity of doing right, of 'shepherding' the people under their charge,[7] or committed to the rule of an agent with a like responsibility. At the outset of this period is found the beginning of legal regulation in Babylonia.[8] What the state of formal justice was under the old Sumerian rulers of the Early Dynastic age we have little ability to judge. But the language and proceedings of Urukagina certainly suggest that the *ensi* of that time was

[1] See above, pp. 103 f.
[2] §II, 4; §II, 5; §II, 6.   [3] §I, 29, 60 ff.   [4] §II, 20, 17 ff.
[5] §II, 7, 2; G, 15, 18 f., no. 81; §II, 24, 257 ff.; A, 34, 56 ff.
[6] See above, p. 614.   [7] §II, 8, 41 ff.   [8] See above, p. 598.

regarded as so entirely the god's representative that justice was administered by him under his 'contract' with the god, and thus depended upon his own sense of propriety and his own integrity alone,[1] so that he could, like Urukagina, quite alter custom and rule, if it seemed to him unjust, and would have the full authority of the god to do so. But now, again, the king had become in an effective measure the local god of each city and found himself thereby obliged to let his will be known in more precise terms, which would apply to an area far wider than one city. Few Sumerian laws survive which are or may be of Third Dynasty date,[2] but it is significant that, in the closely sequent period, compiling of 'codes' of law was undertaken by several kings, that of Hammurabi being not unique, but only the first known and the best preserved. This widespread activity does no more than create a supposition that the ideas of fixed law and regular justice were realized in the preceding dynasty, but there is much more positive evidence. Among the multifarious tablets of administration more than 150, mostly from Lagash, form a special class[3] concerned with proceedings and decisions of the law-courts in cases of family transactions, debts, purchases, and criminal offences. These proceedings were heard occasionally before the king himself, but more often by city-governors or members of an order of judges, many of whom, residents in Lagash, are named in the tablets.

III. ECONOMY AND WEALTH

To give any sufficient description of the economic system over which the king thus reigned supreme is hardly yet possible, in spite of the superabundant material of one kind offered by the business documents—and indeed also because of this super-abundance. For although very large numbers of these tablets have been published[4] perhaps as many more are known to be extant, and to resolve their endless details into a comprehensive picture of the whole society is a task which only the future and perhaps the application of techniques now evolving can expect to master. How these records were kept is partly revealed by clay dockets attached to the boxes or jars which contained various

---

[1] §VII, 3, 100 ff.
[2] See above, p. 598; §I, 39; §II, 16, 101 ff.; §II, 2, 11 ff.; §II, 17.
[3] §II, 3, erster Teil, 147 ff.; §II, 12.
[4] §III, 17, 215 ff.; §I, 34, Introd., viii f.

classes.[1] Upon these labels were inscribed the container to which they belonged, the kind of records which it contained, and the date-formula; from the second entry it is possible to summarize the principal orders of accounts which were kept. The simplest were the single lists or mere notes of commodities received and issued. These details were digested and summarized and a kind of balance struck in the larger tablets called 'reckonings',[2] which totalled the receipts and outlays over periods of time.[3]

The two other principal classes of documents, according to the container-tickets, and according to the surviving material, were the offering lists, detailing the food and treasures offered to the gods upon ordinary and special days;[4] these tablets yield incidentally much information about the divine 'inhabitants' of the temples, their daily life and service, the religious calendar of the months and years,[5] even the topography and furnishings of the various buildings in which the cult was performed. Most interesting of all, perhaps, are the tablets called 'inspections' which survey the stocks, personnel, output, expenses, and work in hand of the large workshops[6] which were maintained by the temples to supply their own needs and probably to furnish a quotum to the court,[7] even perhaps to sell in the market, but there is little evidence about the disposal of the produce. Wool,[8] dates,[9] and onions[10] seem also to have been distributed in part under a like system. It may be supposed that the surplus produce of the temple estates and manufactories was also put on sale in this way to private consumers.

It has already been said that the abundant evidence of business activity in this period is mostly confined to the temple economy, which covered so many undertakings that it may be considered as no inadequate index of the general economy of the land. But it has the disadvantage that no reliable notion is given of the extent and importance of private property. Just as before, in the old Sumerian period, the accident of the preponderance of one kind of record only has perhaps distorted our view of the affairs and even the polity of that time,[11] so the Third Dynasty appears in its business documents as too exclusively a world of officials[12]

---

[1] §III, 5; §III, 21; §II, 3, erster Teil, 17.
[2] §I, 34, 239 ff.; §II, 9.
[3] §III, 1, 108 ff.
[4] §III, 4.
[5] §II, 10, 527.
[6] G, 23, no. 1498; §I, 48, 166 ff.
[7] §II, 10, 529.
[8] §II, 3, zweiter Teil, 12; §I, 48, 80 and 100; §III, 1, 110.
[9] §I, 48, 102; §III, 1, 109 f.
[10] §III, 1, 124 f.; A, 12.
[11] See above, pp. 130 f.
[12] §I, 34, 291.

and serfs,[1] between whom the private citizen is scarcely visible. Yet among the endless lists there appear 'contracts',[2] using already the form and many of the clauses found in the more numerous deeds of the succeeding age, and letter-requisitions[3] (but these are probably official). A book of legal phrases, in Sumerian and Akkadian,[4] which in its extant version belongs mostly to the succeeding period, yet takes some of its formulae out of clauses already exemplified in the private deeds of the Ur dynasty. From both of these sources it may be learnt that property in slaves and houses was bought, sold, and exchanged, though most land, perhaps, belonged to temples and certainly most of the accounts concerning it, including surveys of estates, are records of its cultivation and produce for the profit of these corporations.[5] Borrowing of commodities is also a prominent article in these documents, and there is no proof that the borrowing was always from the temple stores. Among the objects of dealing in this form were cattle, birds, metals, bricks, reeds, and especially wool, an item in the life of the land hardly less important than cereals. Grain, dates, and silver were loaned at interest, the time of due repayment, often after the harvest, being specified, guarantees of payment given, penalties fixed for non-fulfilment, an oath required by the life of the king, and the deed was concluded with names of witnesses and notary and the official date. Such tablets were produced as proof in the courts of law.[6] From this description it will be clear that the general form of the Old Babylonian 'contracts' had already been moulded in the preceding age.

A factor in the economy of the Third Dynasty which cannot be overlooked because it is so prominent in the account-tablets was the raising of large and small cattle, and the great numbers of these which were maintained prove in their turn the fertility of the soil and the abundance of the grain-crops. Apart from a religious text glorifying the Moon-god of Ur,[7] which professes to reckon the number of his cows only in multiples of 36,000, there is the more factual evidence of the constant motion of flocks and herds in and out of a central cattle-park, 'The House of Puzrish-Dagan',[8] near Nippur, at the site now called Drehem.[9] Lists register, similarly, the quantities of barley and bran fed to animals upon a sheep-run near Lagash;[10] it appears that in one

---

[1] §II, 3, erster Teil, 95 f.; §III, 9. [2] §II, 3, dritter Teil, 32.
[3] §III, 15, 98; A, 33. [4] §II, 16, Einleitung, ii f.
[5] §I, 34, 272. [6] §II, 3, erster Teil, 121 ff.
[7] A, 11, 1, no. 68; §III, 22, 15 ff.; A, 19, 13, no. 7.
[8] For this name see §I, 26, 34. [9] §I, 34, 212 ff. [10] §III, 20.

month there was maintained a stock of over 22,000 sheep, nearly a thousand cows, and still more of other meat cattle; in three months fodder was provided for over 50,000 sheep and 1500 oxen, and this was but one of many such stations. If anything like a comprehensive figure could be reckoned for the whole country it would, on this proportion, be massive.[1] Another necessity which employed a great many hands was the grinding of the grain crops; this was largely a female occupation but in some places women were outnumbered by men, and always helped by children. A typical account of one mill[2] which employed about forty hands gives a register of the names of all workers, the kind of work they were doing, and their output, and it shows that their wage accounts were made up daily, these wages being in kind, consisting of the primary articles of diet, barley, beer, and oil, some of which it was permissible to forego in one kind so as to have more of another.[3]

Wool working was the other principal occupation of women and girls,[4] though again not to the exclusion of men. The kinds of wool used, the operations performed, the colouring, and the cloths manufactured and made into garments give rise to a wealth of technical terms which can hardly be interpreted in detail. The wool-workers and tailors were, in the capital at least, but one department of a great manufactory, of which we possess comprehensive surveys. One such establishment comprised no less than eight workshops;[5] apart from the clothiers there were (1) carpenters and joiners who turned out furniture[6] (tables, chairs, boxes, shrines, and cabinets) as well as constructional work, (2) carvers of wood and ivory, who decorated this furniture with inlaid work, and made small figures, (3) smiths,[7] of precious and base metals, with whose work was closely associated that of (4) the jewellers,[8] who produced all kinds of little figures and ornaments and often enriched with gold mounts the beads and other miniature products of (5) the cutters and engravers of gems and semi-precious stones. The last two shops were occupied by (6) the leather workers[9] and (7) those who used reeds[10] and bitumen for making mats[11] and baskets and for waterproofing the seams of boats.[12]

---

[1] §III, 16, 218.
[2] §III, 19.
[3] I. J. Gelb in *J.N.E.S.* 24, 230 ff.
[4] G, 23, no. 1554; §III, 2.
[5] G, 23, no. 1498; §I, 48, 166 ff.
[6] §VI, 8, 187.
[7] §III, 6; §I, 48, 170 ff.
[8] §I, 48, 140 ff.
[9] §III, nos. 7, 10, 11 and 12; §III, 14.
[10] §III, 8.
[11] §III, 13.
[12] *Ibid.*; §III, 18, 146 ff.

IV. FOREIGNERS FROM THE EAST

The foregoing sketch of the economy which reigned in southern Babylonia under the Third Dynasty of Ur gives a measure of the contrast between its wealth and the primitive condition of its neighbours. Babylonian caravans and ships had travelled near and far in search of the primary resources needed to support this complex civilization, and had brought back as associates or slaves inhabitants of the foreign lands, some of whom remained to make a career or at least a living for themselves in the empire, while others returned to inflame their ruder countrymen with tales of the riches to be plundered if ever the strong man armed grew weak. Even while guard was fully maintained the population of Babylonia was unequally affected by peaceful immigration of foreigners from the two directions, north-east and north-west, which had never ceased to pour their bolder spirits into the wealthy plain, favoured by the lack of natural boundaries to keep them out. This inflow was no doubt continuous and mostly unnoticed, producing a turmoil only when it became too violent.

In this period the accession from the eastern frontier is noticeable chiefly in the names of a people, using neither the Sumerian nor the Akkadian language, who, whatever they may have called themselves, are now most often known as Hurrians, a name certainly used by themselves afterwards in their own documents ; they were the 'Horites' of the Old Testament.[1] This people was to form, in later centuries, a distinct and powerful nation under their own kings, but for a long time after their first appearance they are found only as individuals. That first appearance may be placed under the Dynasty of Agade, when a few names more or less certainly identified with this people are borne by local rulers, some said to have been conquered by Naram-Sin.[2] The geographical position of their kingdoms (Karakhar, Markhashe, Simurrum, Tukrish, to which other names can be added subsequently— Shashrum, Simanum, Urbilum), although only a few of these have been definitely located,[3] was in most cases within that area which was the persistent enemy of the kings of Ur, bounded by the Tigris, the Diyālā, and the mountains to the east. Only Urkish, a place prominently identified with the Hurrians by their

1 §IV, 2, 51 and 69; see also *C.A.H.* II³, ch. I, §IV.
2 §IV, 2, 55; see above, p. 444.
3 See above, p. 601 ; A, 22, 24.

two most ancient surviving monuments,[1] has been sought as far west as the tributaries of the Khabur.

Continual hostilities did not prevent inhabitants of these lands beyond the Tigris from moving more and more frequently into Babylonia, so that in the tablets of the Third Dynasty is found a quotum of Hurrian names, most of them, it is true, still dwelling in their home-lands east of the Tigris, where men of this stock are mentioned as governors of cities. But in Babylonia itself there is a sprinkling of these names, some borne even by minor officials who soon showed the thoroughness of their assimilation by giving, in certain instances, Akkadian names to their sons.[2] If these foreigners cannot be said to have introduced a serious or disturbing factor into the life of Babylonia, even less noticeable was the admixture of another eastern race, the people called *Su*, the Shubaru or Subarians.[3] These tribesmen, against whom one of the campaigns of Sargon had been directed,[4] were also originally inhabitants of a district east of the Tigris, but seem to have spread themselves widely at an early period over North Mesopotamia, whither the Hurrians were to follow them in the years after the end of the Third Dynasty. Indeed, these two peoples were so alike in origin and destiny that their difference has been argued mainly upon dissimilarity of names.[5] There was little difference in the status of their immigrants, who came for the most part as menials or even slaves, occasionally made their way upwards in the society which adopted them, and in either case sank unperceived into the mass.

V. THE AMORITE INVASION

Far different was the effect of a much more weighty migration from the north-west, bringing in those forces which were to aid in subverting the kingdom of Ibbi-Sin and, after a second conflict, to expel the Elamites and set up new kingdoms with most of the old traditions in the Babylonian homeland. In the reign of Shu-Sin began an inflow of those western Semites who were called *martu* or *amurrū*, Amorites, propelled down the valley

---

[1] §IV, 10; §IV, 8; §IV, 4; A, 25.; see above, p. 565. See Plate 50(*b*), (*c*).
[2] §IV, 2, 60.   [3] *Ibid*. 108.
[4] *Ibid*. 34 f.; see above, p. 430 f.
[5] A copious discussion upon the origin, individuality, and components of Hurrians and Subarians has not produced a conclusive result: recent contributions are §IV, 9; §IV, 3; §IV, 1; §I, 11, 16 ff.

of the Euphrates by indefinable forces. Neither the name nor, essentially, the people were new; as well as the occurrence of individuals in the older tablets,[1] references to their barbarous character were put even into stories about Lugalbanda and Enmerkar, old kings of legend in the First Dynasty of Uruk,[2] but these are perhaps anachronous. Equally uncertain is a 'Khuwaruwash king of Amurri' in a Hittite version of the revolt of seventeen kings against Naram-Sin.[3] As a menace to Babylonia they first appear in the reign of Shar-kali-sharri, who defeated them at Basar,[4] when the double threat from east and west was hanging over him, as later over Ibbi-Sin. Little more is heard of this people until the reign of Shu-Sin, when they came in force upon the north-western quarter of Babylonia and not only compelled the withdrawal of the power of Ur from whatever it held in Syria but could be checked from actual invasion only by the desperate expedient of building the 'Western Wall'.

These intruders were regarded with distaste by the native Babylonians, who looked upon them as barbarians, had many scornful things to say about their manner of life, and even regarded their territorial god Amurru as a crude nomad who had not so much as a house when he came towards the civilized districts and had to be provided with a decent establishment and a wife before he could be admitted to the divine society.[5] Yet this hostility was almost more of a class than of a national feeling; these Semites were not of the same tribes nor even of the same language among themselves, and none of them were utterly alien to the society of the great southern cities, which already contained as ordinary citizens a large admixture of Semitic immigrants, who differed from the newcomers only in being assimilated to the predominantly Sumerian civilization. Infiltration from the Syrian steppe to the alluvium was, in truth, an unceasing process, which caused no alarm, and even had its advantages, when it was gradual. But when circumstances, always invisible to us, quickened this flow, as at the times of the Akkadian and afterwards the Amorite invasion, the immigrants seized power by their very weight and provoked an indignant reaction which took on the unreal appearance of a national resistance. In turn these strangers themselves were assimilated and though they modified they never

[1] §v, 3, 150.
[2] See above, p. 100; §v, 3, 159 f.; G, 7, 31 f.; A, 1, 330 ff.
[3] §1, 27, zweiter Teil, 68 f., line 12.
[4] See above, p. 455; §v, 3, 149 f.; G, 7, 35; A, 1, 236 f.
[5] §v, 4, 74 f.; G, 7, 32 f.; §11, 8, 6; see above, pp. 563 f.; A, 1, 90 f.

could have transformed the society which had striven to reject them. It was possible to speak of driving out Gutians, but after a comparatively few years who could have found the Akkadians or the Amorites, to cast these out from the land where they had ceased to be distinguishable?

The Amorite invasion evidently had all of these characteristics; there is no doubt that 'Amorites', that is, men of Syrian origin, were always entering Akkad and Sumer between the days of Shar-kali-sharri and of Shu-Sin. These are not always distinguishable in written records, for they bore (or assumed) names common to the land where they came to sojourn.[1] On entering the country they were recruited as soldiers or as a menial class of 'coolies',[2] some having been brought in as slaves, and it is these, no doubt, who are sometimes shown upon monuments wearing a peculiar short dress and occupied in lowly tasks.[3] 'Amorite' was indeed a designation signifying 'workman' (a term which in Babylonian ideas applied to both civil and military duties),[4] and their work was done in groups under their own officers,[5] with ranks such as 'general', 'chief', 'lieutenant', 'overseer', 'scribe', the functions of which are barely definable. Though all (when distinguished particularly) were called *martu* or Amorites it is possible to trace earlier and later waves of these Syrians coming into the south country. The earlier, beginning under the Third Dynasty of Ur, is marked by a set of names characterized by the ending -*ānum*;[6] a later, which followed after the rise of Ishbi-Erra, had names of a very distinctive cast, which are the earliest representatives of what is now called the West-Semitic dialect. Despite the extraordinary limitation of a material confined to a mere set of names,[7] with no other literature, it is beyond doubt that a real difference was found between the language of these newcomers and those both of the Semitic-speaking Babylonians and of previous western immigrants. The clearest indication is the verbal form of the third person which began with *ia-*, whereas Akkadian used the form beginning with *i-*.[8] In addition the West-Semitic names contain both ordinary words and special divinities which were unknown to Akkadian and peculiar to the language (that is, the names) of this people.[9]

With this criterion it is possible to discern that the forces

---

[1] §v, 3, 153 f.   [2] *Ibid.* 195; G, 7, 38.   [3] G, 32, 142; A, 1, 344 f.
[4] G, 3, vol. XVI, 54*b*; A, 1, 339 ff., 356 f.   [5] §v, 3, 185 ff.; G, 7, 37.
[6] §v, 5; §v, 3, 154 f.; G, 7, 41 f.; A, 1, 213, 224 f.
[7] §v, 1, 5 ff.; A, 14; §v, 2, 47.
[8] See above, p. 564; A, 1, 195 f., 218.   [9] §v, 1, 3 ff.; G, 7, 39 ff.

which contributed to the overthrow of Ur were somewhat in advance of the tribes with West-Semitic speech. The kings of Isin bore Akkadian names, but the founder of the kingdom at Larsa was Naplanum,[1] whose name was of the older 'Amorite' style first found under the Dynasty of Ur. West-Semitic names come into Larsa with the later kings Abisarē and Sumuel,[2] then, with the establishment of a third parallel dynasty at Babylon, about the same time as these, West-Semitic names appear at once in the royal family and become common in the documents of private business. The evidence, given its limitations, is thus fairly clear ; at a point of time before half-way through the dynasties of Isin and Larsa a new wave of Syrian invaders, with a characteristic dialect, appeared in southern Babylonia where, although unable to subvert the established if inglorious kings who nominally divided the land, they conquered several cities and finally set up, at a place almost unknown before, a third kingdom which was eventually to devour the survivor of the other two. At about the same time men of this stock were found ruling in Kish and Sippar, in the neighbouring land east of the Tigris, and up the Euphrates at least as far as Mari.

VI. CHANGE IN ART

The long-sustained infiltration, sometimes the inrush, of foreign elements and the resultant change in the population is clearly marked for us by its effect upon the representational arts of the country. The period of the Third Dynasty of Ur and of the succeeding, mainly Amorite, kingdoms is still not very well supplied with surviving artistic productions, even after the more recent discoveries both in the capital city and at certain outlying places such as Mari and Eshnunna. It is now evident that stone sculptures continued to be produced in all the principal centres at a high level of technical ability, both in relief and in the round, though our evidence suggests that the latter was the more in favour. The most important monument executed in relief was the great stele of Ur-Nammu at Ur.[3] This work appears to have been, when complete, a vividly descriptive presentation of all the episodes attending that king's building of the Moon-god's temple at Ur, of which imposing remains are still to be seen. Both the

---

[1] §v, 3, 155 f.; A, 1, 319 f.   [2] G, 7, 108 f.; A, 1, 360 f.
[3] G, 14, 51 and pl. 53; §vi, 7, 285, no. 306; §vi, 1, vol. ii, 774 ff. See Plate 49(b).

religious preliminaries and the actual operations were depicted in detail, so that the whole, had it survived, would have been the best illustration we could have of contemporary life.

The most striking difference it shows from the style of the Early Dynastic and Agade periods is in the costume of the principal figures. This dress first comes to notice in the statues of Gudea; it is a wide shawl, with fringed edges, draped round the body and thrown over the left shoulder (leaving the right arm and shoulder bare), with one of the corners tucked into the first fold of the garment and another edge of the shawl supported over the left arm. The material seems to be of smooth texture and is sharply distinguished from the shaggy fleece-like robe worn by the earlier Sumerian figures—this is now reserved for gods.[1] No longer is there, in the figures of this time, the preponderance of shaven heads which marks the style of the earlier ages. Again it is the heads of Gudea which lead the change of fashion; one, perhaps two,[2] of these are still shaven, but the rest wear a kind of turban with an exaggeratedly thick band made of some fabric which displays symmetrical tufts or curls. The same form of head-dress continues in the Ur and Amorite dynasties as a close fitting cap with a less bulky bandage; in the case of a bronze figure from Mari[3] this cap is garnished with horns to mark the 'divine' nature of the wearer.

Another difference in the sculpture is the apparent preference for harder stones. Once more the change comes in with the statues of Gudea. It was made possible by an increasing access to, or at least exploitation of, foreign supplies, such as Gudea describes.[4] Something may be due also to improved methods of stone-working, but of this there is no clear evidence. The statues themselves are undoubtedly much better rendered, and beginning from the Gudea figures the level remains generally high. Among the Gudeas there are indeed some markedly inferior, especially in the fault of a squat appearance, a lack of proportion being accentuated by shortness or even absence of the neck. Under the Amorite dynasties the costume remains much as it was under the kings of Ur, save that there is an increasing tendency to decoration; the robe is more richly ornamented, and the beards are fancifully dressed. These characteristics are particularly noticed upon examples of the more provincial art which come from Ashur,[5] Mari,[6] or Eshnunna.[7] Two beautiful little female heads

---

[1] E.g. §VI, 6, pls. 119–23, 132; A, 34, 9 f. [2] §VI, 5, 168 f., pls. XVI, XVIII.
[3] §VI, 4; §I, 9, 164 f.; §VI, 9, 74 f. [4] See above, p. 460.
[5] §VI, 9, 52 f. and 57 f. [6] §VI, 6, pls. 108 f. [7] §VI, 9, 72 ff. See Plate 51 (a).

found at Ur[1] give an indication of what the capital made and might have yielded if the Elamite sack had not been so thorough.

A still more notable change was in the style of the cylinder-seals which, in fact, underwent two alterations within the periods of Ur and of the Amorites. The first was the more complete, for it meant turning away entirely from the highly varied, closely packed, narrative themes of the Agade period and reducing the device almost to a bare uniformity of subject. This produced the familiar 'introduction scene', in which three figures only are essential, and occasionally there are less.[2] It can hardly be doubted that the centralizing effort of royal policy brought about the imposition of this style. Most of the surviving seals and impressions are those of officials in various ranks, with whom the expression of individual piety, or interest in the scene, gave place to the need for an act of homage to the king or the local governor, that is, the inscription became paramount. In a few of the Third Dynasty seals the royal prescription of the device is peculiarly apparent; these examples actually portray the king in the dress and attitude of the gods (except perhaps for the horns) seated on the throne in the god's usual place, and receiving, like him, the owner of the seal, sometimes with his advocate. The monarch tenders to his worshipper a small vial, and the inscription declares that the king 'has presented to him' (this seal), no doubt along with his office, a prerogative which, in certain cases, he seemed to have usurped from the god himself.[3]

The second change began to come into the seals under the dynasties of Isin and Larsa, but was not in full vigour until about the middle of the First Dynasty of Babylon. The 'introduction scene' continued to be the common device and the individuality to depend mainly upon the inscription, but most often now the god was standing, not seated, and there is a preponderance of western weather-gods, Amurru or Adad.[4] The escorting deity now hardly ever takes the owner by the hand, but is generally a goddess and stands beside the owner, holding up hands in prayer for him. Yet whatever the fresh elements of the population may have been able to effect in altering certain styles of art, the remarkable absorptive power of the old Sumerian civilization was still impressively demonstrated. Barbarian leaders began almost instantly to play the traditional part of kings, to adopt language,

---

[1] G, 35, vol. vi, pl. lxii; §vi, 2, 39 and pl. xxd; together in G, 32, pl. x; §vi, 12, pl. 24; §vi, 1, vol. ii, 782 ff.

[2] G, 13, 146 ff. For two later manifestations see §vi, 11, 18 and §vi, 3, 85.

[3] §ii, 19; §ii, 22; §i, 30, 39 f. See Plate 51(b).   [4] §v, 4, 12 f. and 54 f.

expression, and modes of thinking accepted from their Sumerian predecessors, while the subjects, though they introduced no small changes in the social and economic structure of the country, adopted with equal rapidity and thoroughness a city life under gods and kings, conformed with the general pattern of their physical and cultural environment, and produced articles of use, devotion, and luxury little different in their various kinds from the traditional types. It cannot be observed that any new art was invented or any old one discarded by the Amorite kingdoms, if compared with the Early Dynastic cities of Sumer. Indeed, in a few details such as the reintroduction of clay cones[1] and bronze figures[2] as bearers of foundation records, this age went back to the customs of its remoter forerunners.

VII. SUCCESSORS OF THE UR DYNASTY

After the few stirring years when Ishbi-Erra was engaged in war and intrigue against the last king of Ur, and then in a struggle with his Elamite associates[3] from whom he finally wrested the devastated city,[4] his reign, of thirty-three years in all, was devoted to the defence of his capital[5] and his territories[6] by the building of fortifications, to the discharge of his religious functions as king, and to the forming of widespread commercial relations—with cities of the Upper Euphrates, the eastern lands of Karakhar and Simurrum (old enemies of the Third Dynasty),[7] and even with overseas Tilmun.[8] He had no scruple (though he had several competitors) in assuming, while the empire of Ur yet subsisted, the divine designation[9] and also the title of universal dominion,[10] and he plainly regarded himself and his city of Isin as the legitimate successors of Ur in the old Sumerian tradition of struggle for the 'kingship'. Accordingly, it is this dynasty which concludes the Sumerian king-list, and the obvious attention given to its compilation at this time, bringing down the tale of succession from 'the Flood' to the present, evinces the ambition of Isin[11] to claim a supremacy as of right amid circumstances which were far from assenting to it.

[1] §I, 40.   [2] §VI, 10. See Plate 51 (c).
[3] §I, 6, 9 (10b, 11a); G, 7, 62.
[4] §I, 6, 14 f. (20b, 21), also p. 18(E); G, 7, 63.
[5] §I, 6, 16.   [6] §I, 6, 8 f. and 11; G, 7, 62 f.   [7] See above, p. 601.
[8] G, 7, 64.   [9] §I, 29, 63.   [10] G, 7, 60.
[11] §VII, 11, 46.

Even while Ishbi-Erra was struggling to free himself from the failing grasp of Ur, similar local potentates, former vassals of the empire or newcomers, were active in setting up 'kingdoms' for themselves in their own cities and as much of the neighbouring territories as they could control. Almost at the same time as Ishbi-Erra[1] arose a parallel founder of a dynasty at Larsa, one Naplanum, of whom nothing more is known than what can be inferred from the form of his name[2]—he was the first of the immigrant Amorites to make himself a ruler in Babylonia. East of the Tigris, and thus farther removed from the old seat of power, rulers at Eshnunna[3] and also at Dēr,[4] not far away, set themselves up as 'gods', as royal benefactors, as independent rulers, and even as conquerors.[5] In the following generations appeared yet others, including that which was finally to absorb them all—a veritable 'heptarchy' (if the number be taken no more strictly in Old Babylonian than in Old English history), more or less flourishing within limits much narrower than the recent dominions of Ur, and little exceeding the old homeland of Sumer and Akkad.

Amid this growing confusion the parallel dynasties of Isin and Larsa settled down as best they could to divide a limited realm which they ruled long but uneventfully. That they could thus subsist for about two centuries less than a hundred miles apart without more than occasional jars simply proves their weakness. Nearly all that is known of these obscure kings has to be gathered from date-formulae of their years, incompletely preserved and sometimes lacking a fixed arrangement. Their few inscriptions are limited to building-records,[6] and in later tradition there is nothing but a slight anecdote concerning the succession of a 'gardener' Enlil-bani, to his master Erra-imitti on the throne of Isin.[7] Even the date-formulae mostly concern religious occasions, thus leaving their age one of the dimmest in Babylonian history. But it is hardly probable that more evidence would have much to reveal about the unenterprising figures who occupied the twin thrones of Isin and Larsa for so many years. Each of the cities could boast one ruler of some distinction, but their achievements were different and although their reigns partly coincided, neither city challenged the other.

---

[1] §vii, 12; G, 7, 21; L. Matouš in *Arch. Or.* 20, 295.
[2] §v, 5, 237; A, 1, 371.   [3] G, 7, 66 f.
[4] *Ibid.* 68 f., with n. 327; A, 33, p. 107.
[5] *Ibid.* 73; see below, p. 661.
[6] Listed in G, 7, 187; §vii, 8.   [7] §1, 36, vol. ii, 12 and 15; G, 7, 140 f.

A recently-published Sumerian text[1] has revealed an important incident in the broils of cities during these rather uneventful years. The city of Larsa was attacked and reduced to great straits (described in very conventional language) by an uncertain enemy, perhaps the Babylonians. The inscription was set up by King Sin-iddinam, the sixth king of Larsa, to accompany a silver statue of his father Nur-Adad, which, according to the ideas of the times, was to address the Sun-god in the terms of the inscription. Nur-Adad, to whom the tablet ascribes a special election by the Sun-god, waged a victorious campaign by means of which he restored the water-supply of Larsa and overcame the enemy. Sin-idinnam claims for himself the rule over Ur, Larsa, Eridu, and Lagash.

At Larsa it was Gungunum, the fifth king, who in a reign of twenty-seven years won a certain meed of military glory. His arms were directed against the eastern boundary-lands; in the king's third year is recorded the devastation of Bashimi, a city belonging to the Elamite king, and in the fifth year an attack was pressed home into Anshan itself. The land was overrun and, though no more than the bare event is recorded in the date-formulae, some further details are perhaps to be gathered from an inscription of Anum-muttabil, governor of Dēr,[2] who claimed to have smitten the heads of Anshan, Elam, Simashki, and to have conquered Warakhshe: but it is uncertain whether these two rulers were contemporaries, and thus whether the date-formula and the inscription relate to the same campaign.[3] It is significant that about this time the long line of kings who had lorded over Elam from the city of Simashki came to an end, the last of his line being Indattu II.

After this success early in his reign Gungunum devoted himself to peaceful works until his nineteenth year, when in circumstances unknown he defeated the army of Malgium, a place on the Elamite border,[4] built relay-houses along his roads, as the great Shulgi had done before him,[5] and set in order the waterways of his realm.[6] An event of importance in his reign was the transfer of Ur into his authority from that of Isin. This is, strangely, not recorded in any date-formula, and has been revealed only by inscriptions found at Ur; why the transfer was made, and

---

[1] A, 3.
[2] G, 33, 176 f.; see, for this and the following, below, p. 661, and §viii, 3, 65.
[3] §vii, 12, 305; but also G, 7, 73, n. 350.
[4] Unlocated, but see §vii, 6, 94 f.   [5] See above, p.606 with n. 7.
[6] G, 7, 112 f.

by what process, warlike or peaceful, is unknown. An ancient and especially sacred institution at Ur was the office of high-priestess to the Moon-god,[1] which was always held by daughters or sisters of reigning monarchs. Ishme-Dagan, fourth king of Isin, had accordingly dedicated his own daughter,[2] who took the sacerdotal name of Enannatum, after a pattern prescribed by custom. In several inscriptions this lady calls herself only 'child of Ishme-Dagan, king of Sumer and Akkad', but in three she invokes blessings upon the life of 'Gungunum, mighty man, king of Ur',[3] whereby it appears not only that Gungunum had taken over the charge of Ur from the king of Isin, but that he had, out of scruple or perhaps by agreement, allowed the daughter and nominee of the former masters of the city to remain undisturbed, in return for an overt expression of her homage.[4] This transfer, unexplained and only indirectly attested, took place under Lipit-Ishtar, himself the most considerable figure of his line after its founder.

The glory of Lipit-Ishtar sprang from a work of peace notable rather for what still remains of it than for any unique quality it had in its own age. In a date-formula at the outset of his reign, and in various inscriptions,[5] he refers with pride to his having 'made righteousness' in Sumer and Akkad. The phrase employed, both Sumerian and Akkadian, became almost a hall-mark of the Old Babylonian kings from Ishme-Dagan of Isin downwards, and was often embroidered with other phrases announcing in high but vague terms the reforms and justice which the ruler had bestowed upon his land[6]—the tradition of these goes back to the beginning of the Third Dynasty and even, in the earlier period, to Urukagina.[7] There is ample evidence to prove that the immediate significance of the phrase was a cancellation of charges upon certain classes or individuals arising out of social conditions or out of specific contracts; a typical example is the clause in a later enactment (of the Babylonian king Ammiṣaduqa) decreeing that all inhabitants of certain cities and lands in the king's dominions who had been compelled by debt to sell themselves or their families into slavery should be forthwith released and restored to freedom,[8] 'since the king has made righteousness for the land'. Either in connexion with such proclamations or later in their

---

[1] See above, p. 435.   [2] §1, 57, 42; G, 7, 76, n. 372.

[3] G, 33, 206 f.; G, 15, no. 297; A, 32, no. 64.

[4] §vii, 4.   [5] G, 7, 93 f.; §vii, 9, 114.

[6] §1, 16, 78 ff.; §ii, 11, 196 ff.; G, 7, 80 ff.; A, 8.

[7] See above, pp. 140 ff.   [8] §ii, 11, 40 f. sect. 18'.

reigns[1] a number of kings issued 'codes' of laws, as best exemplified in the celebrated 'Code of Hammurabi', generally garnished with a prologue and an epilogue setting forth the king's services to the gods and to men, and embodying those rules and principles of conduct which he ordered to be observed and was prepared to enforce. These were by no means always changes, for much of each 'code' appears in the others, so far as their preservation allows of a judgement, but they aimed to demonstrate their authors' attachment to justice, as opinion at the time conceived it.

Some later material bearing upon the 'righteousness' ($m\bar{e}\check{s}$-$arum$) decreed by kings has now been obtained; there is a new edict of King Samsuiluna of Babylon and discussions by J. J. Finkelstein and J. Klíma.[2] The laws of Lipit-Ishtar have also received a probable accession.[3]

The laws of Lipit-Ishtar, so far as they are preserved,[4] are written in Sumerian; it is possible that an Akkadian version was also published. The existing provisions, all from the latter part of the document, treat a variety of civil causes—hire of boats, care of orchards, regulations concerning slaves, possession of a house, family laws concerning marriage and inheritance, nearly all of which have more or less close analogies with the better-known laws of Hammurabi, nearly a century and a half later in date. Even more markedly is this the case with the laws of Eshnunna,[5] large extracts of which have recently been recovered; it has been reckoned that the substance of about three-quarters of these reappears in the Hammurabi 'Code', and the rest are concerned with similar subjects.[6] The date of these laws, which are written in Akkadian, is not certain—the extant copies seem to be of about the time of Dadusha, a contemporary of Hammurabi himself, but their composition may go back to the age of the earlier legislator, Lipit-Ishtar.

Eshnunna was not the least among the powers contending for mastery or at least independence in these centuries of division. Like many other cities it had broken away in the last days of the Ur Dynasty and proclaimed its own kings, only to fall later under the precarious sway of Isin.[7] Emerging gradually from this, in proportion as the grasp of Isin loosened, Eshnunna was to have its years of glory under three kings, Naram-Sin, Dadusha, and Ibalpiel II, whose reigns occupied the century ending with

[1] §vii, 3, 103. [2] A, 20; A, 8; A, 16. [3] A, 2.
[4] §vii, 14; G, 22, 336 ff.; G, 7, 95, n. 463; A, 2; A, 16; A, 17.
[5] §vii, 7; G, 7, 166, notes 897, 902.
[6] §ii, 2, vol. i, 9. [7] G, 7, 66 ff.; A, 34, 90 ff.

Hammurabi. The first of these even made himself for a while
king of Assyria,[1] and all three were prominent in the affairs of
Upper Mesopotamia, the last of them being directly concerned
in putting an end to the Assyrian rule in Mari,[2] and attaining a
height of power such that he could at one moment be reckoned
the equal both of Hammurabi and of Rim-Sin.[3] But fortune
declared for Hammurabi, and in rapid succession both Larsa and
Eshnunna fell before him. Being somewhat out of the direct path
of the invaders, Eshnunna had no West-Semitic names of kings
until the end of their line; on the contrary, its faith in the old
tradition is testified by the Sumerian names Ur-Ninmar and
Ur-Ningizzida borne by two of its earlier kings.

A like resistance, however unavailing, to the all-pervasive inflow of the tribes is still better attested at Uruk, the very kernel
of Sumerian culture, which also makes its appearance in this
'heptarchy'. Not only did two of its kings similarly bear Sumerian names, Anam and Irdanene,[4] but the former, when he
repaired the city wall, recalled with patriotic pride that it was an
'ancient work of the divine Gilgamesh'.[5] The anxiety of these
kings to rescue their city and its treasured values from the
enveloping flood of tribesmen, whose aid they nevertheless did
not scruple to call in against their local enemies, is exposed by
a curiously prolix and embarrassed letter,[6] mingling explanations,
excuses, appeals, and protests, which Anam addressed to Sin-
muballiṭ of Babylon, the father of Hammurabi. Not unexpectedly
in view of the West-Semitic names among his predecessors, Sin-
muballiṭ is addressed as the acknowledged ruler of bedawin tribes
called Amnan-Iakhrur and Iamutbal, which had established themselves mainly in the neighbourhood of Sippar and in a district
east of the Middle Tigris.[7] It is in singular contrast with the
deep distrust of the nomads manifested by Anam in his letter
that Sin-kashid, the first of this line of kings at Uruk, took pride
in his title as chief of the Amnan.[8] The purpose, in fact, of this
oddly rambling screed is to justify and to maintain Anam's refusal
to admit into his city the tribal auxiliaries sent by Sin-muballiṭ as
a military reinforcement, almost certainly against Rim-Sin of
Larsa, although no enemy is named. It appears also from the
letter that ever since the early days of the dynasties at Babylon
and Uruk, when Sabium and Sin-kashid were kings, there had

[1] *Ibid.* 164; §v, 3, 8, n. 1 and 210, n. 3; see *C.A.H.* I³, ch. vi, pp. 209 f. and
C.A.H. I³, sect. iii.   [2] §v, 3, 38.   [3] See *C.A.H.* ii³, ch. i, sect. ii.
[4] §vii, 1, 35 ff.; G, 7, 118.   [5] G, 33, 222 f., 2 b.   [6] §vii, 1, 56 ff.
[7] §v, 3, 74 f.; G, 7, 106 f.   [8] J. J. Finkelstein in *J.C.S.* 20, 102.

been continual co-operation (as there was also a marriage alliance)[1] between the two kindred families. But the Babylonian branch had later, as it seems, taken over the headship of the tribes, for Anam appeals to a friendship only once interrupted in the past, and protests his loyalty in the present. Since the letter was found at Uruk it was evidently not despatched, and may perhaps be regarded as a draft for an actual missive which should be better considered and kept more to the point.

After seven kings each had reigned at Isin and Larsa in a mutual forbearance which they durst not violate, their impotence was exposed by the setting up of a third power within an even shorter distance on the other side of Isin. At Babylon, which herewith comes for the first time into history as a capital city, the Amorites founded a dynasty which established itself without effective opposition from either of the constituted kings. Absence of hostility from Larsa is partly explained by names of the two contemporary kings, Abisarē and Sumuel, which show that the Amorites had gained a footing at the same moment in that older seat of power. Isin itself, since the reign of Lipit-Ishtar, was probably no longer formidable, and the kings, both of Babylon and of Larsa, were then more preoccupied by a danger from the town of Kazallu,[2] where a turbulent character named Iakhzirel continued to give trouble for several years, notwithstanding the defeats which the armies of Babylon and of Larsa are alleged by the date-formulae to have inflicted upon him.

Thus the three major dynasties which now divided Sumer and Akkad included by no means all the independent rulers of that day. Petty kings set themselves up in cities hard by the greater seats of power and were little molested by these. At about the same time as Sumuabum possessed himself of Babylon other Amorite chiefs were ruling over Kish, only a short distance away, others were at Sippar, a related line has been noticed at Uruk, others again at Marad,[3] and elsewhere, all of them revealed by no more than a few date-formulae or by their names in oaths ratifying private contracts. As an epitome of its age may be viewed the inscription which Ashduni-arim,[4] a minor potentate otherwise unknown but calling himself king of Kish, has left written upon appropriately diminutive clay cones which sort ludicrously with the pompous language in which his achievements are set forth. The four regions of the world (no less) were at

---

[1] §vii, 1, 6 f.
[2] §v, 3, 202 f.; G, 7, 126 f.   [3] G, 7, 127 ff.; A, 1, 329.
[4] §vii, 15; G, 4, part 36, pl. 4; G, 21, 143 f.; G, 7, 130 f.

enmity with him, and he fought for eight years until his army
was reduced to three hundred men. But the gods of Kish came
to his aid; he took provisions, went out a full day's march, and
in forty days he subdued the hostile land. Then he repaired the
wall of Kish and of another place and put in order two canals.
The success was real, but only among dwarfs could so small a
figure boast himself a giant.

VIII. INTERVENTION FROM ABROAD

When the gaze is lifted to a wider horizon than Sumer and Akkad
alone still other faces are seen bearing in upon that centre. Withdrawal of the power of Ur had left in fragments the whole of the
world once under its sway, and some of these fragments had
coalesced into powers now able to exercise considerable influence
in the opposite direction. The greatest of these was certainly
Subartu, a land which had been in various conflict with Sumerian
and Akkadian rulers since the Early Dynastic period.[1] Though
its limits are always hard to define there can be no doubt that it
included, at this time, the city and land of Ashur, or that its
rulers, whatever the extent of their authority, may be identified
with the early kings of Assyria, known both by their own inscriptions[2] and from their inclusion in the royal lists of that country.[3]
One of these, Ilushuma, who lived in the generation before
Sumuabum,[4] founder of the First Dynasty of Babylon, and uses
the old title *iššak* of the god Ashur, has left two inscriptions in
which, after relating his continuance with building the temple of
Ishtar, he adds that he established the immunity of Akkad,
specifying as recipients of his benefit the cities of Ur and Nippur
in Sumer together with Awal, Kismar, and Dēr of the god
Sataran in the lands east of the Tigris. These he decreed to be in
the same status as Ashur with respect to freedom from taxation,
for this is the meaning of the term he employs.[5] If he imagined
these arrangements were likely to be long-enduring he was much
deceived. There is no record from the south which gives any hint
of this Assyrian incursion, nor of the king at whose expense it was
made. Despite the suggestion of permanence, it can have been

---

[1] See above, pp. 117 and 430 f.; A, 29, 16 ff.
[2] §I, 10.   [3] See *C.A.H.* I³, ch. VI, pp. 195 f. and 202 f.
[4] This is now generally concluded (e.g. *C.A.H.* I³, ch. VI, p. 203), although a late
chronicle (§I, 36, vol. II, 14) seems to make these two contemporary; further
discussion in G, 7, 92.   [5] §VII, 5, 120 ff.; §VIII, 5; G, 32, 179 f.; A, 3, 24 f.

no more than a raid, and the six next successors of Ilushuma, although there were powerful kings among them, did not again interfere in the affairs of Sumer and Akkad.

Nearly a hundred years after this a new dynasty was founded in Assyria by Shamshi-Adad, the greatest figure of his generation, who was to exercise upon the politics of Babylonia an influence which far outmatched any of the principalities established there. His own inscriptions[1] claim the control of 'the land between the Tigris and Euphrates', and boast the tribute of the kings of Tukrish[2] and the 'upper land', districts to the east of Assyria. Far wider conquests in the west are announced not only by himself but by much other evidence. The history of his origin and of his reign does not belong to this place,[3] but he seems to have been a freebooter chief who had in his earlier days been obliged to escape into Babylonia before a danger which threatened him, evidently from the reigning king of Assyria. After certain years of exile strength or opportunity allowed him to re-enter Assyria with forces sufficient to depose the reigning king and raise himself to a throne which he occupied for thirty-three years. That he afterwards interposed strongly in the affairs of Babylonia is not directly attested, but one who wielded decisive power in two of the neighbouring states must have largely controlled the fortunes of the south itself in the period of native decline before a limited supremacy was achieved by Hammurabi. The death of Shamshi-Adad is known to have occurred after the tenth year of Hammurabi,[4] so that his reign in Assyria had extended back over Sin-muballit's reign in Babylon. But he was not paramount in the south for all this time, as is proved by the freedom of those kingdoms to indulge in mutual strife, which they could never have done under an effective overlord. Nevertheless it is at least probable that the early years of Hammurabi himself were passed in a state of deference, if not subservience, to this formidable neighbour.

The later years of the dynasties of Isin and of Larsa coincide with the middle years of the First Dynasty of Babylon, and thus for some sixty years they were sharing a territory of only moderate extent, without more than occasional collisions. The date-formulae of all three cities exhibit sporadic conflicts, both with one another and with places farther afield. But these broils were intermittent, and not apparently of much importance, the three

[1] §I, 10, 22 f.   [2] G, 32, 200; §IV, 2, 57; A, 10, 99.
[3] G, 32, 198 ff.; see *C.A.H.* II³, ch. I, sect. I.
[4] See *C.A.H.* I³, ch. VI, p. 210, and references there.

being, in fact, too weak or too much subject to pressures from outside to indulge in a struggle to the death. This became a possibility only with a change in the ruling family at Larsa, where after the brief and violently interrupted reign of Ṣilli-Adad[1] the throne was taken by Warad-Sin, as a nominee of his father, Kudur-Mabuk.

The advent of this family, father and two sons, to power in Larsa and Ur is an event of which no specific record exists. But in several inscriptions Kudur-Mabuk alludes to enemies who had done mischief to Larsa and its Sun-temple, of which he proclaims himself the vindicator. In one place these enemies are specified as the armies of Kazallu and Mutiabal,[2] and Kudur-Mabuk boasts of having expelled these from Larsa, pursued them into Emutbal and discomfited them, and then captured Kazallu and beaten down its wall. The same victory is also commemorated in the second year-formula of Warad-Sin,[3] and must therefore have been won in the first year of his reign, preluding his occupation of the throne. The father's patronage in this appointment is repeatedly attested by the son, who includes his father in prayers for blessings to be vouchsafed in reward for his pious foundations. Throughout all his reign, and even into that of his brother Rim-Sin, who came to the throne twelve years later, the father's influence was predominant; the origin and the rise of such a commanding figure are consequently of interest.

First, his name itself is significant in the same sense as his father's, whom he often mentions, Simti[4]-Shilkhak, for there can be no doubt that these are Elamite: Kudur(Kutir)- is unmistakable, although -Mabuk, which should be a divine name, is unknown,[5] and again -Shilkhak perhaps derives from, and certainly recalls, the king Shilkhakha,[6] who reigned not much before this time, and was celebrated through a long line of Elamite dynasts. These names, consequently, leave no doubt that both father and son had passed their lives at least on the border of Elamite territory, and had probably assumed names in compliment to the Elamite court. But secondly, in seeming opposition to this stands a curious title 'father[7] of Amurru', or 'of Emutbal', double both in form and content, for as well as the geographical difference, it is also written both in Sumerian and Akkadian. The

---

[1] G, 7, 150; A, 34, 81 f.   [2] §VIII, 4, 122.   [3] G, 15, no. 266, 13.
[4] Probably the Elamite Temti- (§VIII, 3, 70, n. 7).
[5] As with the familiar 'Chedorlaomer' (Kutir-Lakamar)—see below, p. 666, n. 4.
[6] See C.A.H. II³, ch. VII, sect. I; §VIII, 3, 70; §VIII, I, 35, n. 35.
[7] See C.A.H. II³, ch. VII, sect. I; §VIII, 3, 71.

location of Emutbal is fairly well fixed[1]—it lay in the plains east of the Tigris and in front of the mountains, the district traversed by the Diyālā river. On the other hand, the name Amurru denoted for the Babylonians their north-west in general, the home of those Amorites whose invasions dominated the history of this period. The seeming contradiction must be explained by the movement, probably a generation before, of the Amorite tribe Iamutbal which, instead of following the Euphrates downstream, had crossed the steppe and settled in the east-Tigris land,[2] where their chiefs had accepted some kind of vassalage to the Eparti kings of Elam.[3] It was, therefore, from this neighbouring chieftaincy that the powerful tribal leader Kudur-Mabuk had moved into the boundaries of Larsa during a period of decline, possessed himself of the city itself, driving out an enemy in brief possession, and set up there as kings in succession his two sons who were for a while to revive its fortunes.

Warad-Sin has left a number of wordy inscriptions, chiefly upon clay cones from buildings which he repaired in Ur and Larsa, but his rule extended over Nippur and some other minor cities as well.[4] Perhaps the most interesting event of his untroubled years was the appointment of his sister to the high dignity of priestess to the Moon-god at Ur, an office customarily reserved for the closest female relatives of kings.[5] The solemn occasion was registered as one of the year-formulae, a ceremonial name Enanedu, in the form prescribed by ancient usage, was assumed by the new abbess who later in the reign of her second brother was able to restore her 'convent' at Ur with funds provided by him after his final victory over Isin. Of this work she had composed a memorial written upon clay cones in a high-flown Sumerian style; this was recovered and perused with satisfaction by Nabonidus in the last years of Babylonian independence,[6] and has lately reappeared after another twenty-five centuries.[7]

Rim-Sin, who succeeded his brother, must have been a young man at his accession, for not only was he to reign sixty years[8] but it would seem that some natural anxiety recalled Kudur-Mabuk to supervise his first steps in kingship, for the father's name occurs again in dedications by his son.[9] This tutelage cannot

---

[1] §v, 3, 177 and 216. [2] *Ibid.* 216.
[3] See *C.A.H.* II³, ch. vii, sect. 1 for the Eparti kings; §viii, 3, 71, for the title *atta*; A, 1, 335.
[4] G, 7, 174 f.; A, 32, no. 75; A, 6. [5] See above, p. 634.
[6] §viii, 2, 164 ff. [7] §vii, 4. [8] G, 7, 22.
[9] G, 33, 218 and 220; G, 15, nos. 141, 142; A, 32, no. 87.

have lasted long in Rim-Sin's reign, which began to unroll quietly enough in the company of the rival dynasties of Isin, now in its decline, and Babylon, now approaching the verge of its greatest days. These early years have nothing to record but religious buildings, care of canals, and dedications of statues representing Kudur-Mabuk, his brother Warad-Sin and, surprisingly, his predecessor Sin-iddinam.[1] The first warlike enterprise is men-tioned in the date of his fourteenth year, when 'the army of Uruk, Isin, Babylon, Sutium, and Rapiqum, and Irdanene, king of Uruk, were smitten with weapons', an event related in similar terms upon clay cones found at Ur,[2] which add the picturesque detail that he trod with his foot upon the head of the hostile king of Uruk as though he had been a serpent. This struggle was in itself no more than characteristic of the petty warfare which had been endemic since the strong control of Ur had disappeared, but it was nearly the end of the local dynasty at Uruk,[3] and it foreshadowed the contest for supremacy with Isin and Babylon, whereas the more distant alliance with Rapiqum[4] and of the Sutu nomads must have been the outcome of a temporary political grouping.

In this fourteenth year of Rim-Sin the last king, Damiq-ilishu, was on the throne of Isin, and Sin-muballit recently come to that of Babylon. The succeeding years were divided between civil undertakings and desultory warfare in which Rim-Sin captured several towns of little account and uncertain location; in his twenty-first year he claims a victory, which he used mercifully, against Uruk. At length, in his twenty-fifth year, he appears as beginning the decisive struggle with Isin, for he announced the capture of a 'city (of) Damiq-ilishu' with thousands of prisoners whom he brought captive to Larsa and 'established his victory for ever'. Despite this emphatic language and the name of Damiq-ilishu it is difficult to construe this as the capture of Isin itself, for that triumph was not expressly claimed until five years later, and it is still more curious that in the seventeenth year of Sin-muballit, a year which fell between the twenty-fifth and the thirtieth year of Rim-Sin, a capture of Isin is actually recorded by the king of Babylon.[5] The strange situation that a complete victory over Isin was related on at least two and possibly three occasions within five years, and that by two different rulers, is

---

[1] G, 5, vol. II, 161, no. 208. Possibly explained by the presence of then-existing figures, see A, 3.

[2] G, 15, nos. 138, 144.

[4] §v, 3, 38, n. 2.

[3] §vii, 1, 38; G, 7, 156.

[5] G, 7, 158 f.

not one that we can elucidate with the slight information that we have. What is certain is that Rim-Sin upon his thirtieth year published a long and almost lyrical date-formula to describe how 'with the exalted weapon of Anu, Enlil, and Enki the true shepherd Rim-Sin captured Isin, the royal city, with every one of its inhabitants, as many as there were, and then bestowed life upon its widespread people, and made his royal name famous for evermore'.

Thus ended the kingdom saved by Ishbi-Erra out of the ruins of Ur and lost by Damiq-ilishu two and a quarter centuries afterwards. Its fall left the dominion to be contested by two powers, so long its rivals, Larsa and Babylon itself. The decision was to be delayed for another thirty years, during which Rim-Sin rested so complacently upon his laurels that he suffered no other reckoning of time than 'year x (after) he captured Isin', thereby cutting off our only supply of historical information. This royal lethargy, however, was by no means typical of the times, for there is massive and ever-growing testimony that the reigns of Rim-Sin, of Hammurabi, and of his son Samsuiluna embraced the period when literature, crafts, and all kinds of learning, true and false, were cultivated and even created with an ardour and achievement never matched again. Concerning these something may be reserved for a more general survey of what is called, from its dominant figure, the age of Hammurabi.

CHAPTER XXIII

PERSIA, c. 2400–1800 B.C.

I. THE ELAMITE KINGS OF AWAN

THE history of Persia before the migration of the Medes and the Persians in about 1000 B.C. is almost entirely limited to the history of Elam. This is because Elam, south-west Iran, alone has left behind any documents worthy of mention from the pre-Persian era. Only very few remnants of Akkadian inscriptions on rock reliefs survive from the non-Elamite part of south-west Iran. From the remainder of Persia there is silence until the coming of Zoroaster, the great prophet of eastern Iran (probable dates, 630–533 B.C.).

Compared with the long duration of the Elamite Kingdom, the actual number of documents surviving is indeed pitifully few. They are partly in Akkadian, and partly in Elamite, and to an overwhelming degree come from the age-old capital of Elam, Susa, which has been under excavation by a French archaeological mission ever since 1897. A further difficulty is that Elamite, being related to no other known language, is still insufficiently understood.

The ethnological definition of the Elamites also causes great difficulties. The most reasonable assumption is that which holds the Elamites to be the Proto-Lurs, whose language became Iranian only in the Middle Ages.[1] The Elamites wrote the name of their country in cuneiform as *Ḫaltamti* or *Ḫatamti*, which they probably pronounced *altamt*. This word may mean 'God's Land', if it is composed of *hal* 'land' and *tamt* [*tämpt*] '(gracious) Lord'. For the Sumerian and Akkadian neighbours, Elam (written with the Sumerian sign (NIM) was connected with the idea of 'high-land'[2]—and rightly so, because although its frontiers fluctuated with the course of centuries, they always included not only the low plain of Susiana (with the river network of the Karkhah, the Āb-i Diz, and the Kārūn), but also the mountains and plateaux to the north and east of Susiana.

[1] G, 4, 61 ff.
[2] §1, 17, 20 ff.; G, 15, 26.

This link between the plain and the mountains, which endured for thousands of years, is one of the fundamental factors of Elamite history. It was broken only when the Medes and the Persians conquered all the mountain lands of Elam in about 600 B.C. It was this union between fertile, artificially irrigated ploughlands and the mountains, rich in wood and metallic ores, that rendered possible an Elamite civilization on a high level, with its own distinctive characteristics.

The political merging of Susians and highland Elamites probably succeeded only after bitter quarrels and fierce fighting. The way to political unity led through the federative composition of the Elamite state. The links in the federation were evidently formed by consanguinity between overlord and the principal chiefs, and these links were further strengthened by marriages between brothers and sisters. The form of succession resulting from this will be discussed in greater detail in volume II, chapter VII of this History, as this problem first becomes tangible in the Old Babylonian period. But unmistakable glimpses of it are caught as early as the third millennium B.C.

The earliest mention of Elam probably goes back as far as the seventh century of that millennium. The half-legendary king Enmebaragisi of the First Dynasty of Kish is recorded in the Sumerian king-list as having 'carried off the arms of the land of Elam as booty'.[1] Thus as early as this the historian can recognize the leitmotiv of relations between Elam and Mesopotamia, one of hereditary enmity, mitigated at the same time by equally persistent economic and cultural exchanges, for Mesopotamia needed the products of the Elamite highlands, timber, metallic ore (lead, copper, tin and silver), stone (alabaster, diorite and obsidian), semi-precious stones and also horses. The countless campaigns of the Sumerians and the Akkadians against Elam were due to the need to control these important materials. At the same time they followed the political aim of warding off and keeping in check the Elamites, who were always ready to plunder the lowlands. In this context should be mentioned the legend, historically quite credible, of the famous Sumerian king of Uruk, Gilgamesh, who, a generation after Enmebaragisi, is said to have penetrated even into the lands beyond Elam.[2]

However, Elamite attacks on Mesopotamia, attracted by the riches of its civilized cities, are equally numerous. Thus the Sumerian king-list, somewhat later, probably between 2600 and 2550, records dolefully that the kingdom of Ur 'was smitten with

[1] §I, 13, 82 ff.   [2] G, 14, 541.

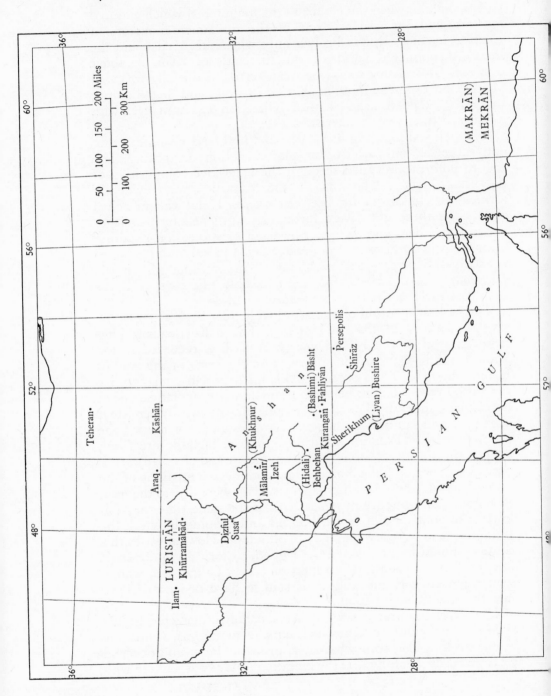

arms, its kingship taken to Awan'.[1] The name of the victorious Elamite, who founded a dynasty of three kings, is not recorded. The king-list gives only the first syllable of the third king's name; it may have been Kurishshak.[2] The site of Awan has not yet been identified with certainty; occasional notices in cuneiform texts indicate the area of the present-day Dizful on the north-east rim of Susiana. Susa, lying on the north-west rim of the depression, evidently then served as an entrepot for the lively trade between Elam and Mesopotamia.

There was thus at this early date a powerful Elamite kingdom of Awan which was able to exercise authority over Mesopotamia for some considerable time.[3] About 2550 B.C. a king of Kish, of whose name once again we possess only the first syllable, was able to shake off this overlordship. 'Awan was smitten with arms', says the Sumerian king-list, 'its kingship was taken to Kish.'[4]

After a period of presumed unrest in Elam, a new dynasty of twelve kings emerged in Awan.[5] Of the founder, Peli (the name is not absolutely certain), and of his six successors we know nothing but their names.

By the time of Sargon of Agade (about 2371–2316) we are treading on firmer historical ground. His policy of expansion enabled him not only to master the mountain tribes of the Zagros (the *Su* people) but also to banish the Elamite danger for some time to come. The more detailed of the two Sargon inscriptions which relate his campaign against Elam also gives us the first synchronism, and hence the first certain date in Elamite history; that is, about 2325 B.C. the king Lukh-ishshan was on the throne at Awan as the eighth ruler of the dynasty of Peli.[6]

In spite of the brevity of its wording, the inscription gives important indications. We learn that under Lukh-ishshan there was a viceroy of Elam named Sanam-Simut, and also a governor of Khukhnur named Zina.[7] His territory lay in the Bakhtyari mountains of western Persia (Anshan), or more accurately near the present-day Mālamīr/Izeh.[8] Khukhnur was later named the 'Key to Anshan',[9] and in fact to this day Qal'a-i Toll near Mālamīr commands the road from Susiana to Isfahān. The

[1] §I, 13, 95.
[2] §I, 19, 8 ff.
[3] §I, 18, 128.
[4] §I, 13, 96.
[5] §I, 20, 1 ff.; *Mém. D.P.* 23, iv.
[6] §I, 2, 114, J; §I, 20, 2.
[7] G, 2, 28, no. 19.
[8] Deduced from two tablets from Mālamīr (*Mém. D.P.* 23, no. 270, 1; and no. 273, 1). The name Aiapir for Mālamīr is late Elamite.
[9] §II, 21, 146 (no. 103).

inscription also gives us the name of an otherwise unknown Elamite district of Gunilakha, and its governor Khidadida[....].

From all this it is evident that the structure of the Elamite state was in the nature of a federation. 'Governors' (Elamite *halmenik*, Sumerian *ensi*, and Akkadian *iššiakkum*) ruled over the various provinces. The governors were under the control of a 'viceroy' (*šakanakkum* in Akkadian, written GÌR. NITA). The viceroy was subject to the actual king of Elam (*zunkir* in Elamite, *lugal* in Sumerian, and *šarrum* in Akkadian). Whether the kings of Awan resided in their original home (in the vicinity of Dizful), whether they reigned from Susa, or whether they had two capitals, our sources do not show; but the first is the most likely.

From what this Sargon inscription says about the conquered ruler of W(B)arakhshe, it can be recognized that this state, allied to Elam, also had a federative structure. We do not learn the name of the king of Warakhshe, but only that of his brother, Dagu, and of the 'judge' of Warakhshe, Kumduba; perhaps these two persons held the regency for the defeated ruler. It is important to note that Warakhshe also had a viceroy, a certain Ul[.....], who, evidently as a result of the Akkadian conquest, was succeeded by the viceroy Sidgau.

The second Sargon inscription may not have been composed until after a further expedition of the ruler of Agade against the stubborn East. It repeats the names of several persons mentioned in the first inscription, amongst whom is the viceroy Sidgau. Thus he must have played an important part, and was confirmed in his office as a vassal of Sargon. A new figure is the governor [.....]ru of Sherikhum,[1] the Elamite 'Sealand'. If this region between the Anshan mountains and the Persian Gulf was not subjected by Sargon until his second campaign, then it must have fallen at the end of his reign, about 2316.

The most important conclusion to be drawn from the two Sargon texts is that both Elam and its north-western neighbour Warakhshe had a definitely federal composition. We shall find this to be the case in Elam for the next 800 years.

However, it must be admitted that the persons mentioned in the inscriptions remain mere shadows to the historian. It appears as if Sargon was content to allow the conquered rulers to retain their positions, but as his vassals. The booty that he carried off to Agade was great, for these inscriptions were mainly lists of plunder, recounting the cities sacked by Sargon, amongst which we find Awan and Susa. That Sargon himself entered Susa as a victor has

[1] §1, 2, 166, N.

been deduced from a stele of the king found there;[1] but probably this stele was a plundered trophy brought to Susa by some middle-Elamite ruler. Nevertheless, there is no need to doubt Sargon's conquest; the finds show a widespread Akkadization of Susa from that time onwards, continuing into the thirteenth century.

Amid the meagre evidence of the Sargon inscriptions, a fresh fact is that Lukh-ishshan, the king of Elam, was the son of a certain Khishep-ratep.[2] But the latter was not his immediate predecessor, for according to the Elamite king-list[3] this was Kikku-siwe-temti. Judging by the Elamite system of succession in later times, it is permissible to assume that these two kings were brothers; that is, the younger Lukh-ishshan succeeded his elder brother Kikku-siwe-temti on the throne of Awan. Being of the same generation, he did not long survive his brother, for the second Sargon inscription[4] acknowledges Lukh-ishshan's son (bearing the same name as his grandfather, Khishep-ratep) as king of Elam, and the ninth of the Awan kings of the house of Peli. As he was of the next generation, we can ascribe to him a long reign. Thus it is likely that Khishep-ratep survived his overlord Sargon as a vassal in Elam for some considerable time.

When Sargon was succeeded by his son Rimush (about 2316–2307), the kings of Elam and Warakhshe, Khishep-ratep and Abalgamash, took this opportunity to make an alliance to throw off the yoke of the Sargonids. The leaders were evidently the new ruler of Warakhshe, Abalgamash, and his viceroy Sidgau. The third member of the alliance was the prince of Zakhara, with his viceroy Ungapi.[5] The district of Zakhara evidently bordered on Warakhshe towards the north-west, around the modern Ilam.

The campaign of Rimush against these eastern rebels has been related above (chapter xix). It will be enough to repeat here that, according to the victor's inscriptions, a disastrous defeat was inflicted upon the country of Warakhshe, with the slaughter of more than 17,000 men and the capture of 4000 more. Amongst the latter were the deputy-kings Sidgau and Ungapi, but the kings themselves of Warakhshe and of Zakhara presumably escaped. As for the king of Elam, he appears to have come off lightly; however, his country was severely pillaged as is evident from vases discovered in Nippur and Ur, which were dedicated to the gods by Rimush as booty from Elam 'after he had subjugated

---

[1] G, 2, 29; *Mém. D.P.* 10, 4 ff. See Plate 52 (*a*).   [2] §1, 2, 114, 116.
[3] §1, 20, 2.   [4] §1, 2, 116.
[5] §1, 2, 122 ff., I and J.

Warakhshe and Elam'.[1] From this booty the king of Agade also
dedicated to his god Enlil 'thirty pounds of gold, three thousand
six hundred pounds of copper and six slaves of both sexes'.[2]

A further document listing the rebel princes subjected by
Rimush gives the name of a certain Zinuba, the brother of a ruler
of an unnamed land, together with his 'regent' (in Sumerian
sukkal) Epir-mupi.[3] However, as the latter appears on a tablet
which describes various campaigns as governor (*ensi*) of Susa,[4]
the unnamed land is evidently Elam, and so Zinuba must have
been viceroy of Elam, and a younger brother of king Khishep-
ratep. If this followed the regular pattern of succession in Elam,
Epir-mupi, being governor of Susa, was probably the eldest
son of Khishep-ratep. Epir-mupi's son Lamgium is mentioned
in the obelisk of Rimush's successor Manishtusu.[5]

According to the Elamite king-list Khishep-ratep was succeeded
by an otherwise unknown king Khelu of Awan.[6] His viceroy was
evidently a certain Eshpum,[7] perhaps his younger brother. His
accession may well have coincided with the seizure of power in
Agade by Rimush's brother Manishtusu (about 2306–2292).
Eshpum caused a statuette of Manishtusu to be made in Susa, and
dedicated it as 'his servant' to the goddess Narundi, in whose
temple it was subsequently found.[8] By chance a seal-impression
of the oracular priest of the temple, Egigi, who was installed by
Eshpum, has also been found at Susa.[9]

During the reign of Naram-Sin (about 2291–2255), the successor of Manishtusu and the last great king of Agade, not only
Elam but the whole of western Iran advanced into the clear
light of history. However, the sources mention nothing of a war
between the king of Agade and Elam; so evidently it did not par-
ticipate in the general revolt of the highland peoples. This is
confirmed by a treaty between Naram-Sin and the king of Awan,
his vassal, which is also the first important document of Elamite
history. It is a badly damaged clay tablet inscribed in six columns
and on both sides, and was found in Susa.[10] The most astonishing
fact is that it is written in Elamite, whereas all other documents of
the Sargonic age up to Naram-Sin are in Akkadian. Although in a
very early form of the language, the Elamite of the treaty shows

[1] §1, 2, 128.   [2] §1, 2, 124.
[3] §1, 2, 122; A, 5.   [4] *Mém. D.P.* 14, 5.
[5] *Mém. D.P.* 2, pl. 1, col. 3.   [6] §1, 20, 2.
[7] *Mém. D.P.* 14, 4, read thus by §1, 6, 48 and 198.
[8] *Mém. D.P.* 10, 1.   [9] *Mém. D.P.* 14, 4.
[10] *Mém. D.P.* 11, pl. 1; §1, 14, no. 3; A, 10.

all the signs of the so-called classical Elamite of ten centuries later. Unfortunately our understanding of this most important document is limited by lacunae and breaks in the tablet, as well as by our still very limited knowledge of the Elamite vocabulary.

The main question is, with whom did Naram-Sin conclude this treaty? G. G. Cameron[1] rightly suggests that the partner would have been king Khita of Awan. However, the problem cannot be resolved with certainty. On the other hand, the fact of such a solemn treaty proves that Naram-Sin valued the alliance of the king of Elam highly, perhaps as a precaution against the danger threatening from Gutium in the north. Apparently the document was solemnly guarded in the temple of In-Shushinak, the chief god of Susa, where it remained among the débris until the present age.

The following can be interpreted of the contents of the treaty: it begins with this appeal: 'Hearken (goddess) Pinikir, and you good gods of heaven.' In all, over thirty-five divinities are listed by name in the first two columns (see sect. III below), summarized by the emphatic statement: 'Even the kings pay homage to the gods.' It continues: 'A king is the faithful servant of the god Nahhunte, a king is subject to the god In-Shushinak.' The end of the second column reads: 'A king is faithful to the goddess Siashum, to the god Napir, and to the goddess Narundi.' In the third column the Elamite king asserts: 'Naram-Sin's enemy is my enemy; Naram-Sin's friend is my friend.'

A recently undertaken closer study of this oldest document of Elamite history reveals that Agade had asked military aid from Elam.[2] Naram-Sin sent an envoy to Susa with rich gifts, and Khita complied with the request of the king of Agade by detaching troops headed by an Elamite general who was to fix the details of the treaty with Naram-Sin's prime minister. Besides, the king of Agade probably married a daughter of Khita. This is to be inferred from certain passages in the treaty purporting that the Elamite king wishes Naram-Sin's wife male offspring as a legitimate successor to the throne. Khita further agreed to place statues of Naram-Sin in the sanctuaries of Susa; he expressly mentions such a statue in the temple of In-Shushinak. Naram-Sin evidently concluded the treaty of alliance with Elam during the earlier part of his reign which began c. 2291 B.C. amid a revolt of his subjects,[3] possibly towards 2280 B.C.

The fact that Naram-Sin himself made this treaty with the king of Awan may be deduced not only from the document but also

---

[1] G, 2, 34. [2] A, 10, 95.
[3] See upon this above, pp. 444 f.

from an inscription found on a statue dedicated in Susa. It refers to Naram-Sin's minister and oracular priest Sharrish-takal, who dedicated this image in Susa on behalf of his master to an otherwise unknown divinity.[1] We may infer that this act of worship was connected with the ceremonies of the signing of the treaty between Naram-Sin and Khita. We also know of this minister Sharrish-takal through a seal found at Tello.[2]

Kutik-In-Shushinak, whose name was previously known only from Akkadian sources as Puzur-In-Shushinak, is one of the most important historical figures of ancient Elam.[3] He has left to posterity a large number of inscriptions, not only in the Akkadian language and script, but also in the so-called 'proto-Elamite' script. This linear writing, deciphered only in 1961, has revealed the name of its last user Kutik-In-Shushinak as meaning 'the protégé of the god In-Shushinak'. That he used his own native script alongside the Akkadian from the very beginning shows unmistakable national pride.

All indications go to show that Kutik-In-Shushinak was governor of Susa as a vassal of Naram-Sin during the lifetime of king Khita of Awan. This is the modest title he gives himself on an Akkadian door-post inscription, and also several Elamite stone inscriptions.[4] His father Shinpi-khish-khuk was probably a younger brother of king Khita. Some time later, probably in the reign of Naram-Sin's successor Shar-kali-sharri, about 2250, Kutik-In-Shushinak was promoted. On four inscriptions of considerable length, one of them bilingual, he bears the title 'governor of Susa, viceroy of the land of Elam'.[5] Khita would still have been ruler of Awan at that time. Although Kutik-In-Shushinak was not yet king, he was able to increase his power to the extent that he could undertake widespread campaigns. Officially these were measures taken by a loyal vassal; in fact they show the decline of his overlord, Shar-kali-sharri.

The first campaign was occasioned by a rebellion in Kimash and Khurti, and thus upon Mesopotamian soil, to be precise in the upper Diyālā region, and it is possible that the king of Agade had requested his Elamite vassal Kutik-In-Shushinak to subdue this rebellion. At the same time Khupsana (in Elam) was also subjected. An inscription on a limestone statue of Kutik-In-Shushinak tells of the warlike deeds of this 'viceroy of Elam'. To this is added a list of over seventy places which were 'thrown

---

[1] *Mém. D.P.* 6, pl. 1, no. 2; §1, 2, 142, no. 15.
[2] §1, 2, 142, no. 18.
[3] See Plate 52 (*b*).
[4] *Mém. D.P.* 6, 7; §1, 2, 156, no. 3. See A, 4.
[5] *Mém. D.P.* 6, pl. 2, 1.

beneath his feet at one blow'[1]—doubtless an exaggeration. Only a few of these are known elsewhere. One such place is Gutu, which is evidently the home of the Gutians. This would seem to mean that Kutik-In-Shushinak's first major campaign was directed against the north-west mountain country to take pressure off the king of Agade by attacking the Gutians. On the other hand, the mention of Khukhnur in this list proves that the inscription records several campaigns, for it can be demonstrated that Khukhnur lies in the Bakhtyari mountains on the eastern rim of Susiana. The inscription concludes with the proud assertion that the king of Simashki[2] himself had come of his own accord, and had 'seized the feet of Kutik-In-Shushinak', in other words, acknowledged his suzerainty. It was the princes of Simashki, in Elam, who succeeded the kings of Awan, of whom Kutik-In-Shushinak was the last. In all probability Simashki was the territory to the north of Susiana, centred upon the present-day Khurramābād in Luristān.

The rise of Kutik-In-Shushinak reached its peak when he succeeded to the throne of Awan as heir of Khita, probably about 2240. In two of his Akkadian inscriptions[3] he calls himself 'mighty (*dannum*) king of Awan', and in Elamite linear inscriptions 'king of the land, an elect, a victor'.[4] On a stele he claimed that the god In-Shushinak 'looked graciously upon him and gave him the four quarters of the earth'.[5] The last remnant of vassaldom to Agade has now vanished, when claim is laid to supremacy over the bounds of Iran and Mesopotamia.

Kutik-In-Shushinak was responsible for a great deal of building in the sacred acropolis at Susa, and presented numerous sacrificial offerings to his 'lord In-Shushinak'. In addition the cutting of a canal near Sidari is ascribed to him. In the same inscription he boasts that 'he gave just judgements in his city'.[6] If we consider that the fairly numerous inscriptions surviving can be only a small proportion of those originally written, we can appreciate that in this ruler Elam found the embodiment of its national greatness. Evidently Kutik-In-Shushinak felt himself protected and encouraged by the gods. With great feeling he claims (as far as my interpretation of the very difficult Elamite inscriptions can be considered correct) that his splendid religious services had brought him fame as a reward from the gods, 'they

[1] §1, 158, no. 6.
[2] For this reading of the place-name, see above, p. 603, n. 4.
[3] §1, 2, 158 and 160.   [4] §1, 11, 13 f.
[5] *Mém. D.P.* 10, 9; §1, 2, 158, no. 8.   [6] §1, 2, 156, no. 5.

made me victorious, they gave me the land'.[1] Or in another place 'I possess this land (Elam). As an elect of the divinity, the land was preserved for me.'[2]

But the fall of the kingdom of Awan followed unexpectedly after the greatness of Kutik-In-Shushinak's power, and the Elamite script disappeared together with the proud national ruler. Like its weakened neighbour and erstwhile overlord, the kingdom of Agade, Elam probably fell a victim to the anarchy brought in by the Gutians.

II. THE ELAMITE KINGS OF SIMASHKI

The Elamite king-list of Susa[3] shows, following after the twelve kings of Awan, a similar number of kings of Simashki—a new dynasty from the mountains of Luristān to the north of Susiana. The exact correspondence of the number twelve seems artificial, and must be regarded with caution. We shall consider only those kings of Simashki who through contact with their western neighbours emerge, albeit indistinctly, into the light of history.

Scarcely any of these kings of Simashki has left behind any record, perhaps because they lived in Simashki (Khurramābād?) and not in Susa. During the entire period of Gutian rule, which ended miserably under Tirigan, about 2120, that is for over a century, Elam is named only by inscriptions of Gudea of Lagash. On one of his statues Gudea boasts that he had conquered 'the city of Anshan in Elam with arms',[4] and on a cylinder he claims that 'Elamites came from Elam, Susians from Susa' to help him build the temple of his god Ningirsu.[5] Thus during the rule of the Gutians over northern Babylonia Elam seems to have come under the control of the princes of Lagash.

During the second century of the kings of Simashki, Elam again presents to history a picture of weakness, this time under the suzerainty of the Third Dynasty of Ur, which began in 2113 with Ur-Nammu. Whereas the lowlands of Susiana fell to the Sumerians, the highlands to the east (Anshan) remained half-independent, whilst Simashki in the north seems to have been in effect free, but also without history.

The most important ruler of this dynasty was Shulgi (about 2095–2048) who, as a result of his far-reaching policies, has left

---

[1] §1, 11, 14 ff., Inscription D.   [2] *Ibid.* Inscription H.
[3] §1, 20, 2.   [4] §11, 20, 70, iv, 64 (B); §1, 2, 184.
[5] §11, 20, 104, xv, 6 ff. (A); §1, 2, 218.

in Elam numerous traces of his long reign. In his eighteenth year he married one of his daughters to the governor of Warakhshe, and in his thirty-second year another to the governor of Anshan.[1] In this diplomatic manner the quasi-vassaldom of the mountain lands on the east and west borders of Susiana was reinforced. However, in the case of Anshan it was of little avail, for the date-formulae of Shulgi specifically mention a punitive expedition against Anshan[2] only a few years after the marriage, and another year of Shulgi was named as that in which 'Anshan was laid waste once again'.[3] Shulgi undertook no fewer than nine campaigns against the mountain peoples further to the north-west, the notorious Lullubi,[4] and this also applied to the regions on the edge of the Iraqi-Kurdish mountain territory (Simurrum/Altın Köprü, Urbillum/Irbil, Karakhar, Kharshi, Kimash, etc.).

On the other hand Susiana, after its conquest by Shulgi in the twenty-eighth year of his reign (2078), seems to have accepted Sumerian rule willingly, for shortly after we hear of a governor of the Third Dynasty in Susa who may not even have been an Elamite.[5] It is quite certain that one Zariqum, whom Shulgi's successor appointed to Susa as governor in 2043, was not an Elamite. Shulgi had appointed him governor of Ashur, a post he held for six years before his transfer to Susa, where he remained until 2035.[6] Appearances thus show that peaceful circumstances prevailed in Susa under strict Sumerian control. This calm may have been because Shulgi evidently considered it of importance to win the allegiance of the native priesthood. Excavations in Susa have revealed evidence of extensive building activity on his part in the temple of the god of the city, In-Shushinak. It appears that Shulgi founded a new temple, for he expressly states on a stone tablet that he, the mighty king of Ur, Sumer and Akkad, had built the beloved temple 'for his king, the god In-Shushinak'.[7] In addition Shulgi's votive offerings for the newly-built temple of In-Shushinak were very numerous. Several of these have been preserved, for later Elamite rulers incorporated them as dedicatory gifts into the foundations of later temples.[8] Shulgi also established a holy place in Susa to a goddess, for two of his Sumerian officials dedicated an artistically-worked mace[9] to this 'Mistress of the city' for the benefit of their king. A cornelian bead has also been found in Susa, which Shulgi dedicated to 'his

[1] §II, 20, 230.   [2] §II, 20, 231.   [3] §II, 14, 18.
[4] §II, 20, 232.   [5] G, 2, 50.   [6] §II, 8, 221.
[7] Mém. D.P. 7, pl. 11; Mém. D.P. 6, pl. 6, no. 1; §II, 20, 192 (p).
[8] Mém. D.P. 7, 61 ff.   [9] Mém. D.P. 14, 22.

mother, the goddess Ningal' (the wife of the Sumerian moon-god) 'for the salvation of his life';[1] this however may have been looted from Ur by the Elamites.

Towards the end of his forty-eight-year reign, Shulgi devised a new form of defence for the kingdom of Ur, which endured for three more generations before recoiling upon its founders. As far as can be gathered from the Sumerian economic documents, this consisted of keeping the tumultuous mountain-peoples in check by means of Elamite 'foreign legionaries', that is, by mercenaries to strengthen the Sumerian garrisons, above all in the threatened frontier-province of Lagash. These 'legionaries' came from Susa, Anshan, Simashki and other Elamite regions; someof them were prisoners of war. These Elamites were formed into groups of five to twenty-five men, and received a daily ration of barley bread and beer. They were under the command of a high dignitary in the service of the kings of Ur who bore the title of 'Grand-Regent' (*sukkal-maḫ*), and may be considered as commander of the frontier guards against Elam and the eastern mountain peoples.[2] As *sukkal-maḫ*, he gradually gained so much power that he was able to found a kind of dynasty in Lagash. His high rank made a deep impression on the neighbouring races. From this a later Elamite dynasty evidently took the proud title of *sukkal-maḫ*.[3]

Under this system of Elamite 'foreign legionaries' in the service of the kings of Ur, Elam long remained quiet. As a result Shulgi's successor, Amar-Sin (2947–2039), took little notice of his eastern neighbours. In the year 2041 he undertook a campaign against Khukhnur in Anshan, which was laid waste;[4] such an undertaking assumes complete control of Susiana. Three years earlier he had transferred the Akkadian Zariqum (mentioned above) from Ashur to Susa as governor. He was installed cere-moniously in the presence of ten highly-placed witnesses, and remained in this office for more than eight years.[5] At the same time Amar-Sin appointed a new governor of neighbouring Warakhshe called Libanugshabash. One of his governors in Elamite Awak (the site of which is unknown), Sharrum-bani, a Semite like Zariqum in Susa, actually remained undisturbed in office for eighteen years:[6] a *pax Sumerica* reigned in Elam.

Whereas Amar-Sin himself undertook no building in Susa, several inscribed tablets have been found of his successor, Shu-

[1] *Mém. D.P.* 6, 22.
[2] §II, 17, 139; §II, 12, 1 ff.; §II, 13, 294 ff.; §II, 6, *passim*.
[3] §I, 10, 128.   [4] §II, 20, 144.
[5] §II, 18, 152 ff.   [6] G, 2, 53.

Sin (2038–2030). The tone of the four identical texts[1] is no longer as reverential as those of his father Shulgi; they proclaim proudly 'the divine Shu-Sin, beloved of the god Enlil, the mighty king, king of Ur, and king of the four quarters'.[2] There is now no trace of any reverence towards In-Shushinak, and therewith to the Susians.

In the sixth year of Shu-Sin, the figure of a king of Simashki appears from the shadows of history for the first time since the fall of the kingdom of Awan two hundred years earlier; his name was Girnamme. The Susian king-list[3] names him, however, as the first of the twelve rulers of Simashki, which cannot be right. A tablet gives us a valuable synchronism, which records that an agent of king Girnamme in Ur had received several sheep for his maintenance at the court of Shu-Sin. This envoy from Simashki was present at the same time as a messenger from Libanugshabash, the governor of Warakhshe.[4]

As his father Shulgi had done, Shu-Sin married one of his daughters to the governor of Anshan. In the second year of his reign (2037) a representative of this governor, a certain Dai-Salkhupa, son of Akuta, arrived in the capital city Ur. The princess began the long journey into the Bakhtyari mountains richly equipped with many jars of oil, butter, cream, sour milk, beer,[5] etc. She could hardly have guessed that her brother Ibbi-Sin would be taking the same road thirty years later as a prisoner of the king of Elam.

In the meantime her father Shu-Sin, the ruler of Ur, attempted to maintain his position by force. During his reign of only nine years he twice undertook campaigns against rebellious mountain tribes in the Zagros, against the so-called *Su* people. The first expedition was evidently in quest of booty—lead, copper, and bronze—which was carried to the temples of the chief divinities of Nippur. From the plunder of gold Shu-Sin caused a statue of himself to be cast.[6] Ziringu, the governor of Zabshali (or in Elamite texts Zapzali) was taken to Ur a prisoner. Zabshali is probably to be placed in the mountains of Luristān to the west of Khurramābād, on the upper Karkhah. The second campaign, in which Shu-Sin apparently did not take part himself, was also mainly directed against Zabshali, where a new governor Indasu had allied himself to other highland princes. All eleven of them were taken prisoner, and carried off to Mesopotamia in the

---

[1] §1, 10, 69, n. 1, corrected by R. Borger in *Arch. f. Or.* 19 (1959–60), 163.
[2] §1, 2, 292, no. 1.   [3] §1, 20, 5.   [4] §11, 10, 7 ff.
[5] §11, 22, 384.   [6] See above, p. 609.

eleventh year of Shu-Sin (2038).[1] His building activity in the temple-quarter of Susa shows that his rule over Susiana was unimpaired.[2]

But when Shu-Sin's younger son Ibbi-Sin succeeded to the throne of Ur III in 2029, it was felt in Elam that the time for liberation was drawing near. It does not of itself mean much that the Sumerian tablets in Susa break off in the third year of Ibbi-Sin; the paucity of material could be responsible for this. But it is certain that in 2021 the king of Simashki was sure enough of his strength to attack the southern lowlands from his own mountains.

It was now of no avail to Ibbi-Sin that he had married his daughter Tukin-khatta-migrisha to the governor of Zabshali four years previously.[3] The cities of Susa, Adamdun and Awan in the north of Susiana rebelled. Ibbi-Siu, now alone, accepted the challenge. After careful religious preparations, he led a lightning campaign against Elam, retook these cities,[4] and their ruler was led prisoner to Ur. This ruler may be the one who in the Susian king-list appears as Lu...luhhan[5], a successor of King Girnamme.

Five years later, probably in 2017, despite the reduction of his power in Mesopotamia, Ibbi-Sin again marched into Elam, which had now become rebellious. This time he attacked Khukhnur.[6] The fourteenth year of his reign was entitled 'the year in which he, with a great army, marched against Khukhnur, the key of the land of Anshan, and made it obedient'.

This was the last attempt of the declining Third Dynasty of Ur to keep Susiana in subjection. The attacks of the West Semitic Amorites and the desertion of Ishbi-Erra of Mari had undermined Ibbi-Sin's power. Thus the new king of Simashki, in alliance with the prince of Zabshali and with the other *Su* peoples of the Zagros was able to overrun southern Mesopotamia at one onset. Ibbi-Sin, who had defended himself desperately in Ur, was obliged 'to leave his palace and go into the land of Elam, from Mount Sabun, the "breast" of the mountain, to the end of Anshan', as a Sumerian dirge informs us—evidently along the Kabīr-Kuh right across Susiana, and thence to the road from Mālamīr to Isfahān 'like a bird that has fled from its nest, like a stranger who (does not return) to his native country'.[7] 'The *Su*-people and the Elamites, the hostile people' reduced Ur 'to

---

[1] §II, 3, 31; §II, 20, 234.   [2] *Mém. D.P.* 10, 12; *Mém. D.P.* 25, 211.
[3] §II, 11, 37.   [4] §II, 19, 14.
[5] See Sollberger in *R.A.* 64.   [6] §II, 21, 146.   [7] §II, 5, 379 and 382.

mounds of ruin and ashes.'[1] The king of Simashki lodged an
Elamite garrison, which perhaps had been assisted by the 'foreign
legionaries', in the temple-acropolis of Ur. The statue of the
Sumerian moon-god Nanna and other divine images were carried
off to Anshan together with the captive Ibbi-Sin. There, exiled in
Elam, died the last king of Ur.[2] As the people of Mesopotamia
realized, a period of their history had come to an end.[3] These
revolutionary occurrences made a great impression on the people,
and were long remembered in dirges and omens.

Unfortunately none of our sources reveals the name of the king
of Simashki who overthrew the kingdom of Ur. The Susian king-
list is unreliable, as it cites three names between Girnamme and
Lu...luhhan, who, as can be proved, reigned in succession. After
Lu...luhhan it names a king Kindattu, whereas it is very probable that a ruler of Simashki, whom the list does not even
mention, must be inserted before him. We consider this king,
Khutran-temti, to be the conqueror of Ibbi-Sin.

This king of Simashki was preserved in the memory of Elamite
posterity; for in the twelfth century Shilkhak-In-Shushinak
places him first in his table of ancestors, before all the four kings of
Simashki who were then known.[4] To deserve such a leading position, Khutran-temti must have performed some great feat—the
overthrow of the kingdom of Ur. This agrees with a year name on
a tablet discovered in Susa: 'year in which Khutran-temti caused
his statue to be cast in bronze'.[5] It is probable that he entered
Susa triumphantly, having thrown off Sumerian rule, and as a sign
of this, dedicated his bronze statue in the temple of In-Shushinak,
about the year 2005.

However, Elam under the kings of Simashki was not permitted
to enjoy its independence from Mesopotamia for long. The inheritance of Ur was assumed by the vigorous princes Ishbi-Erra of
Isin and Naplanum of Larsa who must have been concerned to
regain Susiana at least. Thus it is not surprising, when in 1993,
only thirteen years after the fall of Ur, Ishbi-Erra 'smote Elam
with arms', notably in the same year that he married his daughter
Libur-nirum to the son of the regent (sukkal) Khubasimti.[6] The
latter, evidently an Elamite (Khuban-Shimti), may have been a
son of Khutran-temti, and thus after the Elamite custom 'governor' of Susa. The scanty evidence leaves no doubt that the heirs to
the kingdom of Ur continued the earlier policy of Mesopotamia

[1] §II, 2, 50.   [2] §II, 2, 51.   [3] G, 14, 569.
[4] §I, 12, 69, no. 48a.   [5] Mém. D.P. 24, no. 385.
[6] §II, 2, 62.

towards Elam, military pressure combined with diplomatic marriages.

After the time of Kindattu (about 1990–1970), who to us is a mere phantom, there followed once more a distinct personality as a ruler in Elam, Idattu I, king of Simashki, as he is named in the Susian king-list, whose full name was Indattu-In-Shushinak, son of Pepi and *ruḫušak* of Khutran-temti.

The Elamite expression *ruḫušak* still presents a problem. As it corresponds with *mār aḫāti* in Akkadian diplomatic language, its principal meaning ought to be 'sister's son',[1] and this is doubtless connected with the Elamite system of succession through the female branch.

An Akkadian inscription found in Susa gives Indattu-In-Shushinak, whom we must regard as a grandson or a great-nephew of Khutran-temti, the following title: 'Governor of Susa, viceroy of the land of Elam.'[2] This title was also borne by the last ruler of Awan, Kutik-In-Shushinak, before he became king. Although this implies vassaldom, it would hardly be towards the lords of Isin or Larsa, but rather towards the overlord of Elam, the king of Simashki, Kindattu, whom we assume to have been his grandfather.

Indattu-In-Shushinak must still have been 'viceroy' when he ordered this Akkadian inscription, which shows that he was an active builder in Susa. The inscription tells of the dilapidated fortifications of the city, which he repaired, of a new exterior wall and of a brick temple. The limestone basin on which the inscription stands was dedicated by him to the god In-Shushinak for the benefit of his life.

When Indattu-In-Shushinak became king of Simashki (in about 1970?) he appointed his son Tan-Rukhuratir to the governorship of Susa according to custom. He also married him to Me-kubi, the daughter of Bilalama, governor of Eshnunna. The Babylonian bride evidently brought a rich dowry to Susa, for she founded a special temple there to Inanna as goddess of the sacred acropolis.[3] Her father-in-law Indattu-In-Shushinak then bore the title of 'King of Simashki and Elam',[4] which is its first appearance. Father and son, Indattu-In-Shushinak and Tan-Rukhuratir, in loyal conjunction, erected buildings within the sacred quarter in Susa, as is shown by their brick-inscriptions. Almost a thousand years later, King Shilkhak-In-Shushinak could refer to them with praise as architects when he restored the temple of In-Shushinak.[5]

---

[1] See, concerning this, *C.A.H.* II³, ch. VII.
[2] *Mém. D.P.* 6, 16.
[3] *Mém. D.P.* 14, 24 f.
[4] *Mém. D.P.* 14, 26.
[5] *Mém. D.P.* 3, 57, no. xxxix; 56, no. xxxvi.

In about 1945 Tan-Rukhuratir succeeded his father Indattu-In-Shushinak. His marriage to the Babylonian Me-kubi produced a son, who later (about 1925?) followed his father Tan-Rukhuratir on the throne as Indattu II. Considerable building activity in Susa was also undertaken by the second Indattu whilst he was still 'governor' under his royal father. Inscriptions show that he rebuilt the surrounding walls of the temple quarter using fresh baked bricks instead of the old construction with bitumen mortar.[1]

Later Elamite kings who, as we have seen, possessed reliable information about their predecessors, ended the line of the kings of Simashki with Indattu II. In fact the last rulers of this line do seem to have lost power. Otherwise the *condottiere* Anum-muttabil, viceroy of Dēr (Badrah), a contemporary of Bilalama of Eshnunna, would never have been able to assert that he had 'smitten the head of the troops of Anshan, Elam and Simashki, and captured Warakh-she'.[2] This internal weakness of the kingdom of Simashki is confirmed by the expedition against Bashimi made by Gungunum, the fifth ruler of Larsa, about 1930; Bashimi is probably in the neighbourhood of the present-day Bāsht (between Bihbahān and Fahliyān). Two years later Gungunum boasts of a further victory in Anshan.[3] Evidently the prince of Larsa was able to win a lasting influence in Susiana; a tablet found in Susa gives the Sumerian date-formula of his sixteenth year.[4]

In the ancestral tables of the middle Elamite period, a certain Eparti follows immediately upon Indattu II. As they are silent concerning his ancestry, we may assume that he was the founder of a new Elamite dynasty.[5] The fifth king of his house was a contemporary of Hammurabi of Babylon (1792–1750). If we allot a period of seventy-five years for these five kings, the house of Simashki may be presumed to have vanished around 1860 B.C. But it remains uncertain which rulers of this dynasty occupied the previous half century (about 1910 to 1860). The Susian king-list is unreliable with regard to Simashki. It cites as eleventh king Indattu-napir, and as twelfth and last Indattu-temti.[6] History tells us nothing about them, as the Mesopotamian sources remain silent concerning Elam throughout this period. The impression is created that Susiana and the south-west Iranian highlands re-

[1] §II, 20, 182.   [2] §II, 20, 176.   [3] §II, 16, 304 f.
[4] Discovered by G. G. Cameron (G, 2, 66).
[5] *Mém. D.P.* 11, no. xcvi, line 18.
[6] §I, 20, 5. G. G. Cameron considers both names false; yet the name Indattu-napir at least existed (*Mém. D.P.* 10, no. 21, line 4).

mained left to their own devices, untouched by the struggle for
power in Mesopotamia, where political factors were leading up to
the foundation of Hammurabi's empire. The fall of the kingdom
of Simashki is thus wrapped in the same darkness as the end of the
kingdom of Awan. The following dynasty of 'kings of Anshan
and Susa' was founded by Eparti and stabilized by his son Shilkhakha. These, who for generations merely styled themselves
'grand regent' (*sukkal-mah*), will be included in a subsequent
chapter.[1]

III. RELIGION IN ANCIENT ELAM

Sparse and brief as our documents are, they nevertheless reveal
distinctly what an overpowering influence religion exercised upon
the rulers and people of ancient Elam. This religion had much in
common with that of neighbouring Mesopotamia, but a well-
defined Elamite character is always present. Typical of these
Elamite characteristics is a reverence for the female element in
magic and in powers of the underworld, together with a particular
preference for the worship of serpents. At all times Elamite
religion had a strong savour of the magical and the uncanny, which
impressed even the hard-tempered Assyrians. For Mesopotamia,
Elam was always the land of witches and demons.[2]

In the following paragraphs we shall consider the few historical
and archaeological testimonies before the Old Babylonian period,
for clarification of the ancient Elamite religion. But for the sake of
clarity we shall also consider aspects of the middle and later
Elamite periods.[3] It is certain that Elamite religion (as indeed
everything Elamite), displays an almost incomprehensible continuity throughout thousands of years.

In our earliest document, the treaty between Khita of Awan
and Naram-Sin of Agade,[4] which can be dated approximately
2280, we encounter almost all the divinities who composed the
Elamite pantheon at the time of the fall of the kingdom to Ashurbanipal, about 644. In these one and a half millennia even the
order of the gods has scarcely altered. The Elamite gods first enter
into the light of history in the twenty-third century, and they do so
in a definite order, which indicates that the pantheon was even
then very old.

[1] *C.A.H.* ii³, ch. vii.   [2] §iii, 17, 5 f.
[3] Upon Elamite religion in these periods see *C.A.H.* ii³, chap. xxix.
[4] §i, 14, no. 3; A, 10.

The Khita treaty begins with the following appeal, 'hearken goddess Pinikir (Pinenkir[1]), and you good gods of heaven'. At the head of the pantheon, and indeed standing apart from the others, is a goddess. This fact alone reveals the Elamite attitude towards the numinous. In later ages Pinikir is described as 'Commander of heaven'.[2] On many occasions she appears in theophorous personal names among the common people;[3] and a middle-Elamite princess, a daughter of the famous Shilkhak-In-Shushinak, was named after her *Utu-e-ḫiḫḫi-Pinikir* ('I have dedicated her womb(?) to Pinikir').[4] The Akkadians saw in Pinikir a type of Ishtar.[5] Everything points to the conclusion that she was the 'great mother goddess' of the Elamites.

Because of this it has been suggested that Pinikir can be identified with the Elamite goddess Kiririsha.[6] She is not in fact mentioned in the treaty, but this may be due to the fact that *Kiririsha* means 'Great Goddess', in which case it is not so much a personal name as an epithet. If this were so, Kiririsha would merely be a title of Pinikir. But the matter is not quite as simple: from our scattered sources it is clear that Kiririsha was at home in the southeast, the 'Sealand' of Elam, and that her main seat was at Liyan (Bushire) on the Persian Gulf. All the texts found there are dedicated to this goddess.[7] Hence the earliest extant Elamite document, the fragment of an inscription of an unknown ruler of Liyan, probably comes from the sanctuary of the goddess there; this prince describes himself as her 'servant'. Gradually the 'great goddess' penetrated into Susiana, and middle and late Elamite kings erected temples and chapels to Kiririsha in various places. In Susa she bears the proud title 'mother of the gods' and 'mistress of the high temple, the lady who takes care (?) of all'.[8] Kiririsha nevertheless was not simply confused with Pinikir. King Untash-napirisha,[9] for example who built a zikkurat in Chogha-Zanbil in about 1250, erected a chapel there for Pinikir, as well as one for Kiririsha.[10] On the warrior bronze of the late Elamite period now in the Louvre, both goddesses together with their temples are named in one and the same inscription.[11] This is not all, for about 710, in Aiapir (Mālamīr), a prince Khanni

---

[1] The most accurate phonetic reproduction may be *pi-ne-en-ki-ir*, in *Mém. D.P.* 23, 181, line 6.

[2] §III, 7, 287, note 13.

[3] E.g. *Mém. D.P.* 22, no. 3; *Mém. D.P.* 24, no. 338.

[4] §I, 14, no. 40, line 16.   [5] §III, 3, 327.

[6] §III, 15, 102.   [7] §III, 22, *passim*.

[8] §I, 14, no. 54, obv. I, 3; no. 47, obv. I–2.   [9] A, 9.

[10] *Mém. D.P.* 32, 58 and 63/64.   [11] *Mém. D.P.* 11, fig. 18.

appealed to both Kiririsha and to Parti, whom he described as 'good Mother of the gods'.[1]

The confusing picture presented by our sources of a double or triple 'mother goddess' is explicable by historical development; it reflects the federal structure of Elam. In early days each province evidently had its own mother goddess, Susiana its Pinikir, the 'Sealand' its Kiririsha, the Mālamīr province of Anshan its Parti. Doubtless this list will be increased when further evidence comes to light from other parts of Elam.

It seems that these 'mother goddesses' were the original rulers of the Elamite pantheon. Slowly, and unwillingly, they made way (probably in the second millennium) in favour of male divinities. But they were never removed from the group at the summit. In the hearts of the people they were sure of a favoured position. This is proved by the countless clay images of the so-called 'naked goddess', holding her breasts in both hands, representing Pinikir or Kiririsha. These idols form a constant feature throughout the archaeology of Elam.[2]

Surprisingly the Elamites do not seem to have been troubled by the duality of a 'great mother goddess'. It never fully came to an intermingling of the two, as has been suggested. It is true that Kiririsha rose in esteem throughout Elam, but the traditional local mother goddess remained in honour. As a precaution, sanctuaries were founded to both the local and the immigrant goddess. But it seems that more than two mother goddesses were never recognized in one place, and in Liyan Kiririsha remained permanently without a rival. This exceptional honour paid to the mother goddess by the Elamites has a parallel with the Lullubi, where king Annubanini had himself portrayed on his reliefs together with, and only with, Inanna (Ishtar). She reaches out to him the ring of lordship, she leads enemies captive to him. Her symbol is the eight-pointed star.

If we return to our earliest document, the Khita treaty of about 2280, we find the second place among the gods invoked taken by Khumban. Contrary to the many mother goddesses, Khumban remained the principal male divinity in all Elam throughout the whole of its history. His name is probably derived from the root ḫŭpa 'to command'. Khumban is thus the 'commander of heaven' and husband of the mother goddess, who bears a feminine version of this title. It is not for nothing that she (as Kiririsha) is also called 'Great Wife'.[3] From this marriage was

[1] §III, 9, 113. [2] Mém. D.P. 36, 67.
[3] §I, 14, no. 45, obv. I, 3.

descended the god Khutran, who takes only the fifteenth place in our list (out of thirty-seven divinities). In one inscription Khutran is described as 'beloved mother's son' (*ruḥu ḥanek*) of Kiririsha and Khumban;[1] the normal word for son (*šak*) seems to have been considered unworthy for the offspring of a divine marriage.

The leading position of Khumban in the Elamite pantheon is reflected in his titles. He is the 'keeper' (*kukki*), the 'powerful god' (*nap azzak-ri*),[2] the 'great lord',[3] the greatest of the gods, under whose (magical) protection (*kiten*) stands a king.[4] In the last-mentioned phrase (although very late) we encounter the significant Elamite word *kiten* (in Akkadian *kidinnum*),[5] which was of great importance in legitimacy from the very earliest times. The word describes the numinous ban, the mysterious tabu of the godhead. Upon this magical 'protection' the rulers of Elam based their power, they were the administrators of the *kiten* vis-à-vis their subjects. Apparently each god had his own *kiten*; but that of Khumban was the most powerful, the special numen of rulers.

The gods of the chief cities were strong competitors of Khumban for the first places in the Elamite pantheon, chief among whom was In-Shushinak. His name derives from the Sumerian *nin-shushinak* 'lord of Susa', evidently dating back to some remote period of Sumerian influence in Elam; but this foreign name for a national Elamite god is still remarkable.[6] As Susa rose to be the unquestioned capital of Elam, In-Shushinak rose with it into the neighbourhood of Khumban; yet he was listed only in sixth place in the Khita treaty. At this time a king of Awan ruled Elam, and even for the kings of Simashki who followed. In-Shushinak had a merely local importance. He first appears in a leading position during the Old Babylonian period. In the middle Elamite period he forms part of a definite triad together with Khumban and Kiririsha,[7] mostly in the order Khumban–Kiririsha–In-Shushinak, and occasionally Khumban–In-Shushinak–Kiririsha; he never attained the first place.

It seems significant that in the arrangement Khumban–In-Shushinak–Kiririsha referred to above, the goddess is specifically entitled 'great wife'. This would seem to indicate that Kiririsha was wife not only to Khumban but also to In-Shushinak.[8]

---

[1] §1, 14, no. 45; vi, 18–vii, 1 f.   [2] §1, 14, no. 45; vii, 13–14.
[3] §1, 14, no. 47, obv. 1.   [4] §iii, 9, 107.
[5] See upon this *C.A.H.* ii³, ch. vii.   [6] §iii, 2, 55.
[7] §iii, 15, 102.
[8] So also F. W. König (§iii, 15, 102).

Inevitably we are reminded of the remarkable relations between the leading members of the Elamite royal families: legitimacy descending through the female branch, when a king died his brother usually inherited the throne together with the royal widow, who may well have been the sister of both rulers. It appears that relations between the principal gods Khumban, In-Shushinak and Kiririsha reflect the state of affairs within the ruling houses of Elam.

As In-Shushinak was originally a local god, we find similar parallels in other Elamite provinces. In Khukhnur (Qal‘a-i Toll, in Anshan), the god Rukhuratir takes the equivalent place. Logically, in the Khita treaty, a Susian document, he is missing in the same way as is Kiririsha, of the 'Sealand'. Legal texts from Mālamīr denote clearly that Rukhuratir's position was parallel to that of In-Shushinak. In Susa the list of witnesses always begins with the sun-god and In-Shushinak, whereas in Mālamīr they begin with the sun-god and Rukhuratir.[1] It must be emphasized that both in Susa and in Mālamīr it was customary to swear by In-Shushinak (not by him alone, but he is always mentioned); so that In-Shushinak was the god of oaths for all Elam. This may be due to the fact that In-Shushinak was originally a god of the under-world. The sources from which this deduction is made belong to later ages, but they probably reveal the position in ancient Elam. It is noteworthy, however, that in legal texts the sun-god and In-Shushinak appear together as divine witnesses—evidently as rulers over light and darkness, over life and death.

Two goddesses, Ishme-karab and Lakamar (or Lakamal)[2] supported In-Shushinak in his position as 'judge of the dead'. Apparently neither of these is mentioned in the Khita treaty, and so caution is needed for the earlier period. But in the Old Babylonian period Ishme-karab frequently appears in theophorous names, and she also functions as a goddess of oaths in Susa together with In-Shushinak.[3] Lakamar can first be traced on Iranian soil in the middle Elamite period,[4] and if In-Shushinak can correctly be viewed as originally a god of the underworld, probably his only assistant at that time was Ishme-karab. As her name makes good sense in Akkadian ('she who has heard the prayer') it is possible that she arrived in Elam only with the Akkadians.

---

[1] *Mém. D.P.* 22–4, *passim*.   [2] §III, 25, 169.

[3] *Mém. D.P.* 22–4, *passim*.

[4] The oldest reference to her outside Iran is probably in the name of 'Chedor-laomer' (i.e. Kutir-Lakamar) in Genesis xiv. 1; he is unknown to the native inscriptions.

Returning to the list of gods in the Khita treaty we find, after Pinikir and Khumban, that a foreign god Aba takes the third place. The king of Awan had doubtless given this favourite god of Sargon of Agade[1] such a prominent position for reasons of diplomatic politeness towards his partner Naram-Sin. For the same reason several other Sumero-Akkadian gods were also mentioned in the treaty; they are Ninurta (sixteenth in the list), the goddess Nin-karrak (nineteenth in the list) and the goddess Ashkhara (thirty-first in the list); the latter is no doubt identical with the Mesopotamian Ishkhara.[2]

During the Old Babylonian period that followed, when Susa was subjected to overwhelming Mesopotamian influences, the fashion for Akkadian personal names went so far that the divine element was derived almost entirely from the Sumero-Akkadian pantheon. The gods who figure in these are Adad, Ea, Enki, Enlil, Erra, Ishum, Kabta, Martu, Nanna, Ninshubur, Sataran, Sin and Shamash, and the goddesses Ishtar, Lama, Ningal and Ninkhursag.[3] It would be wrong, nevertheless, to read anything more into these names than the fact that during the early Babylonian period everything Mesopotamian was in fashion in Elam. The actual acceptance of Sumerian or Akkadian divinities occurred only in very few cases. In early times we find Nergal, Enki (Ea), and the goddesses Ninegal (= Inanna) and Anunitum; and in the middle Elamite period Adad, Nabu, and the goddess Shala. The only figure to play a permanent part from the early Babylonian period until the end of Elam, was the goddess Ishme-karab.

The fourth place in the list of gods in the Khita treaty is occupied by an otherwise unknown figure, Zit, apparently a god of healing, as the abstract word *zitme* signifies 'health'. Next, in front of In-Shushinak, follows the sun god Nahhunte (at that time still spelt *Nahiti*).

Nahhunte has often been held to be a goddess, but his masculinity stands beyond doubt, for he is invoked as 'protecting lord' in a middle Elamite text.[4] That he was the sun god of the Elamites has long been known from an Akkadian syllabary.[5] The word *nahhunte*, besides its divine sense, simply means the sun itself, and is found in the curse-formula 'he shall make no name for himself under the sun'.[6] The word may well be derived from

---

[1] *J.A.O.S.* 59 (1939), 491, notes 16 and 17; 492, note 18; see above, p. 437, n. 1.
[2] §III, 2, 90.
[3] *Mém. D.P.* 22–4, *passim.*
[4] §I, 14, no. 54, I 5.
[5] §III, 28, 758.
[6] §III, 4, 27.

nan 'daylight',[1] and a verbal root *ḫunte*, which is still not clear, but which together may mean 'day-bringer'. Nahhunte is a frequent element in theophorous names, for example the famous king Shutruk-Nahhunte of the early twelfth century ('he whom the sun god leads aright').

Just as in the legal texts of the Old Babylonian period in Susa, Nahhunte immediately precedes In-Shushinak in the Khita treaty. Both gods are thus closely and prominently associated in legal matters. This will explain the quotation from the Khita treaty cited above (p. 651: 'a king is the faithful servant of the god Nahhunte, a king is subject to the god In-Shushinak.' Nahhunte was in fact the Elamite 'god of law'. Legal cases were heard in his temple grove in Susa.[2] His particular domain was trade. He fixed rates of interest, he standardized the weights and measures.[3] As a 'capitalist' he entered into business partnerships with human associates. A classic example of this is given by a tablet of the Old Babylonian period, found at Susa, which reads 'in city and country, for (business) with silver and gold, Nahhunte and (a certain) Arad-kubi are partners as was his father. What his father had done (in business) he had done for the sun god.'[4] Nahhunte and his partners were principally concerned with lending capital and corn (both to men and women). Annulment of debts and payment of interest usually took place in the month of the 'great goddess' (August).[5]

As well as a sun-god, there was also a moon-god in Elam throughout its history, whose name however was always written as a logogram from earliest times, so that his Elamite name cannot be identified with certainty. Most probably the moon-god was called Napir, because of his epithet *sipakir-ra* 'the luminous'.[6] Because of missing lines his name is not to be found in the list of gods of the Khita treaty, but it appears in the text itself.[7] The Elamites considered the moon-god as the 'father of orphans'.[8] In early days he is not mentioned very often, but a late Elamite text refers to the magical aura (*kiten*) of the 'luminous god Napir, the protector of the gods'.[9]

In the Khita treaty to which we have just referred, the god Napir twice appears closely connected with three goddesses,

[1] §III, 13, 221.
[2] *Mém. D.P.* 23, no. 320.   [3] *Mém. D.P.* 23, no. 185; no. 310, line 18.
[4] *Mém. D.P.* 22, no. 119.
[5] *Mém. D.P.* 22, no. 124; 23, nos. 179, 180, 273.   [6] §III, 8, 411.
[7] §I, 14, no. 3, II, 23 and IX, 8: (*d*)*na-ap-[ir]*.
[8] *Mém. D.P.* 22, no. 67, line 27.   [9] §III, 9, 110.

evidently as a group of witnesses to oaths. These goddesses are Shiashum (seventeenth in the list of gods), Narundi (in twentieth place) and Niarzina (twenty-seventh in the list). All three goddesses appear to be sisters to the 'great goddess'. Thus, for example, we find Shiashum in women's theophorous names such as Shiashum-amma 'the goddess Shiashum is a mother', or Par-Shiashum 'offspring of Shiashum'.[1] In the late Elamite period she is entitled 'keeper of the palace of the gods'.[2]

In ancient Elam the goddess Narundi enjoyed special favour. Khita's successor Kutik-In-Shushinak dedicated a temple with images and inscriptions to her. On a white limestone statue of the goddess[3] he appeals to her in Akkadian: listen (to my prayer), preserve my rights'.[4] Narundi sits bare-footed, in a pleated skirt, on a throne with arms, decorated with six heraldic lions; unfortunately her head is missing. In her right hand Narundi seems to be holding a beaker for libations, in her left hand perhaps a palm-fan.[5] The fragmentary inscription of Kutik-In-Shushinak in obscure linear script begins (assuming it has been correctly deciphered) with the affirmation, 'victory (*mete*) was granted by Narundi'.[6] It seems that in Susa at that time, about 2250, Narundi was honoured as a goddess of victory—together with In-Shushinak. This would explain why the Elamite governor under Manishtusu should have dedicated a statue of his Akkadian overlord to Narundi in Susa.[7] The ordinary people had an affection for this goddess, as seen in the Elamite woman's name Narundi-ummi ('Narundi is a mother to me').[8]

The divinities Shimut (or Simut) and Manzat also formed part of the 'leading group' of the Elamite pantheon. The god Shimut, as would be expected from his importance, occupied the seventh place in our earliest source, immediately after In-Shushinak. He was described as the 'mighty herald (*perir*) of the gods'.[9] With remarkable emphasis middle Elamite inscriptions call him 'god of the Elamites' (*nap ḫatamt-ir*).[10] In theophorous names we meet Shimut repeatedly; a striking example is in the name Shimut-khumban,[11] which confirms our translation of the divine name Khumban as 'commander'. No less important was Shimut's wife, Manzat (or Manzit), although she occupies only the eighteenth

[1] *Mém. D.P.* 22, no. 162, line 11; no. 5, line 11; no. 76, line 23.
[2] §III, 27, Bronze plaque, rev. lines 30 f.
[3] See Plate 52 (*c*).   [4] *Mém. D.P.* 14, 18.
[5] *Mém. D.P.* 14, plate IV.   [6] §I, 11, 15f.
[7] *Mém. D.P.* 10, plate I.   [8] *Mém. D.P.* 22, no. 66, line 7.
[9] §I, 14, no. 54, I, 7–8; §III, 9, 110.   [10] §I, 14, no. 53, line 24.
[11] *Mém. D.P.* 28, no. 471, 11.

place in the Khita treaty,[1] between Shiashum and the foreign god-dess Ninkarrak. A middle Elamite king calls her 'great lady': he also dedicated a wooden image to her, which he placed 'in the temple of Manzat and Shimut, the god of the Elamites'.[2] Manzat also appears frequently in personal names of the Old Babylonian period in Elam.[3]

No temple has survived from the early Elamite period, not even the foundations of one. The only idea we can form of them is from cylinder seals of the third millennium.[4] On these the ancient Elamite temples are shown as rather high, rectangular buildings, on a form of terraced foundation, their brickwork ornamented on the façade by false niches. The actual temple is recognized by the two high door frames close to each other; but only the left-hand door seems to have been used as an entrance. A reed-curtain covers the top half of the door. The right-hand frame seems to have been a false door. The roof of the temple was flat, formed of several horizontal layers (of wooden beams?). A row of small rectangular windows between door frames and roof served to ventilate and lighten the interior.

The most striking feature of the temple was three huge horns, rising out of the walls on both sides. This is a characteristic of Elamite temple architecture that has not been observed pre-viously. Middle Elamite inscriptions show that these horns (*ḫusa*) were an important component of all temples; Shilkhak-In-Shushinak boasts that he had restored twenty 'horn-temples'.[5] About 644, Ashurbanipal tells how he had caused the 'horns of cast bronze' to be removed from the zikkurat of Susa, and a sculpture from his palace in Nineveh showed the sanctuary on top of this very zikkurat with two massive pairs of horns on the front.[6]

We know virtually nothing of the interior decoration of ancient Elamite temples, but assume they contained the countless votive statues and other dedicatory gifts mentioned by Elamite documents of all periods. The statues represented both the gods and the members of the ruling families. Presumably they stood on shelves and in niches. About 2250, Kutik-In-Shushinak dedi-cated an alabaster statuette of himself to an unknown divinity; the last king of Awan wears a sacral pleated garment, his hands being folded on his breast. In the accompanying Akkadian inscription appears the remark that the statuette was made 'neither of silver,

[1] §I, 14, no. 3, I, 20: (*d*)*ma-zi-a*[*t*].
[2] §III, 7, 285 ff.   [3] §III, 26, 149 f.
[4] §III, 20, 106, fig. 19 and plate xxiv, fig. 3.
[5] §I, 14, 48, line 273.   [6] §III, 10, 35.

nor of gold, but of alabaster', so that no one else might use it.[1]
Kutik-In-Shushinak invokes the curse of the gods In-Shushinak,
Nahhunte and Narundi on any future thieves: 'Nergal shall
destroy their progeny.'[2]

At the time of the kingdoms of Awan and Agade, an acropolis[3]
with its holy precinct probably existed already at Susa, distinct
from the lower city on the river. Kutik-In-Shushinak's temple
building for his god was, according to his inscriptions, completed
with a great portal that was named 'completion of this house of
god', and was anointed with twenty measures of oil when consecrated. The foundation peg consisted of bronze-covered cedar
wood[4] to the dedication of which Kutik-In-Shushinak refers on
several monuments in both Akkadian and Elamite. The building
known as the 'high temple' (*kizzum*) probably had the form of a
richly decorated sanctuary, on which the pairs of horns mentioned
above were mounted.

Other gifts of the same king for the consecration of the temple
included silver implements, a tabu-sign of In-Shushinak of gold
and silver, a long sword, a massive four-bladed axe, and much else
besides. He also commanded musicians to sing and play every
morning and evening in the doorway of the temple of In-
Shushinak.[5] An Elamite musical instrument named after the
mountain Sabun (Kabīr-Kūh?) became well known and popular
in Babylonia, where it was known as 'sabitum'.[6]

At the consecration of his new temple Kutik-In-Shushinak
arranged for the daily sacrifice of 'a sheep at the high temple, a
sheep at the low temple'.[7] In the Old Babylonian period the
kizzum, that is the high temple of In-Shushinak, and the foreign
gods Nergal, Enki and the goddess Ninegal were all regular
recipients of sacrificial sheep. Each received a 'barley-fed' sheep
as a daily sacrifice. It is possible that such a sacrifice was also
made daily before the throne of the ruler and in front of his
statue.[8] We know only of one occasion where sacrifices were made
for a distinct material aim: when sheep were sacrificed in front of a
giant statue of a lion in Susa, probably at the city gate,[9] at the
beginning of a campaign. Not only the king, but the queen also
appeared as donor of the daily temple-offering.

---

[1] A similar phrase is found later in Mesopotamia in an inscription of Gudea of
Lagash: see R. Borger in *Bi. Or.* 18 (1961), 153.

[2] *Mém. D.P.* 2, 64.

[3] In Sumerian Uru-anna, later in Akkadian *ālum elûm* 'acropolis', §III, 23, 139 f.

[4] See below, p. 675. [5] §1, 2, 156, no. 5.

[6] §II, 5, 382. [7] §1, 2, 156.

[8] *Mém. D.P.* 10, no. 34. [9] *Mém. D.P.* 10, no. 69.

Two special occasions for ritual sacrifice of animals are noteworthy in ancient Elam. The most important was the festival of the goddess known as the 'mistress of the acropolis' who was doubtless the mother goddess Inanna (i.e. Pinikir or Kiririsha). This festival took place during the new moon at the beginning of autumn. Full-grown fattened sheep were sacrificed inside the holy grove of the goddess in a ritual manner known as *gūšum*. This day was called the 'day of the flowing sacrifice', which must refer to the blood of the victims. The accounts of the royal chamberlain's office marked the beginning of the purification (*elūl*) not only of the sacred precinct but also of the palaces of the king and queen. The requisite beasts for sacrifice were taken from the crown flocks during the month of Abum (September), and were written off in a good bureaucratic manner by the responsible secretaries.[1]

A special day was also dedicated to the god Shimut. Every year—it seems to have been on 25 Adar, that is in the middle of May—a bull was slaughtered for his festival which was named *tūga*. Once, it seems, the king Gungunum of Larsa himself presented the bull for the festival of Shimut. For this purpose he had the bull fetched from the region of Zaban, on the Lesser Zab, to Susa, where it was kept in the royal cowsheds until the day of the festival.[2]

From the very earliest days numerous priests with their servants were attached to the temple buildings in the acropolis of Susa. Apparently these performed their ceremonies naked, to judge by the Elamite seals and several small finds from stratum D at Susa onwards—that is before the time of the Akkadian empire. A bitumen carving of the period shows naked priests with a sacrificial lamb, crowned with a pair of snakes.[3] On a seal of the governor Eshpum (about 2300, in the reign of Manishtusu) priests are recognizable wearing nothing but a crown of horns, and in some cases a loin-covering in the shape of a snake.[4] The crown of horns is the visible symbol of their relations with the divine. Representations of gods in ancient Elamite sculpture regularly show this crown of horns, and the horns fastened to the temple walls confirm this symbolic relation to the supernatural world.

Scarcely anything is known about the organization of the Elamite priesthood. There was certainly an oracular priest (if not several?); the governor Eshpum had one named Egigi.[5] In what

[1] *Mém. D.P.* 10, 36, no. 24; 23, no. 5; 38, no. 27.
[2] *Mém. D.P.* 10, nos. 3 and 14.   [3] §III, 20, fig. 43, 9.
[4] *Mém. D.P.* 14, pl. III, no. 1.   [5] *Mém. D.P.* 14, 4.

way these oracular priests were consulted we cannot tell, perhaps partly through reading the omens at animal sacrifices, perhaps partly by means of a trance, as practised by shamans. The Elamite word for priest remained constant for centuries, *šaten*; we know only the Akkadian word *pašīšu rabū*[1] for high priest. Priests also administered the landed properties of the gods, which were certainly of great extent. Thus, in the Old Babylonian period, a large field in Susa belonging to the goddess Anunitum was let out by her on lease through the agency of a priest.[2] Priestesses (in Akkadian *mārāt bīti*, 'daughters of the temple') also had a place in the economy; a document relates that they had demanded and received considerable quantities of barley.[3] A priestess, together with a capitalist, sold a house; the deed of sale still preserves the imprint of her finger-nail.[4] Within the female priesthood a special group was formed by women who had dedicated themselves to the service of the great goddess (in Akkadian *ištarītu*). We know of them only through economic texts, which prove that they possessed and administered real estate.[5]

IV. CIVILIZATION OF ANCIENT ELAM

The most important work of ancient Elamite art, in point of size, is a relief cut in the rock-face at a place of worship high up on the ridge of a range of mountains in southern Anshan, to the north-west of the present-day Fahliyān on the road from Bihbahān to Persepolis. This Kūrangān relief has rightly been ascribed to the age of Gudea (about 2150) by its discoverer.[6] The main panel, led up to from the left side by flights of steps, shows a pair of gods crowned with horns, together with five worshippers. The bearded god sits on a coiled snake which he holds in his left hand, whilst pouring out the water of life from a vase held in the right hand. (On the relief he is pouring backwards and forwards, by which is meant to the five worshippers, who are supposed to be in a row together, in front of the divine couple.) No doubt the god represents Khumban, and the figure sitting near him must be the 'great goddess' whether she be called Pinikir or Kiririsha. In front of the gods stands an altar. The five worshippers, distinguished by their long robes, have their hands raised in devotion.

[1] *Mém. D.P.* 10, 28, no. 11.   [2] *Mém. D.P.* 22, no. 101.
[3] *Mém. D.P.* 28, no. 471.   [4] *Mém. D.P.* 23, no. 240.
[5] *Mém. D.P.* 23, no. 288, 2–7.
[6] §iv, 7, 78; G, 6, 5; G, 16, 27 f. See also *C.A.H.* ii³, ch. xxix, and Plate 53 (*b*), (*c*).

In the rock walls on both sides of the steps the figures of a whole procession of worshippers have been carved, to the number of about forty. To distinguish them from the five principal worshippers, who doubtless belong to the royal family, they are clad only in half-length skirts. Their leaders are distinguished by their larger dimensions. All are beardless and, with one exception (possibly the chief priest), wear their hair woven into a plait, and have their hands folded in front of their bodies.

The Kūrangān relief presents us with a probable representation of ancient Elamite worship, which evidently took place for preference on high places, either natural (as here) or artificially created (as in Susa). The upper classes of the population went to such acts of worship in long rows, and took up position on the steps or terraces in a prescribed order. One and a half millennia later the relief of an Elamite prince, Khanni, in Aiapir (Mālamīr, c. 710 B.C.) gives a similar picture of a long procession of people up to an altar table.[1]

The Kūrangān sculpture certainly displays Sumerian influence in the representation of the divine couple with crowns of horns and vase of the water of life, but the Elamite elements predominate. This rock-relief has only one parallel in Iran, on the rocks of Naqsh-i Rustam near Persepolis. There the Sassanian Bahrām II (A.D. 276–93) had his own image carved on top of an Elamite relief that has much in common with Kūrangān; but in my opinion the original relief can be ascribed only to the middle Elamite period, and is thus roughly a thousand years later than that of Kūrangān. The elements in this which are particularly Elamite consist of the procession on the steps and the use of a coiled snake as a throne for the gods. Mesopotamian art knows only representations of a serpent god, the upper part of whose body degenerates into the coils of a snake,[2] and even this motif of the serpent god, which is also found at Susa,[3] is probably of Elamite origin.

The snake is indeed a leitmotiv of Elamite culture.[4] Even the earliest pottery from Susa abounds with the serpentine form. As an apotropaic symbol they appear on lids of jugs and pots. On cylinder-seals of the Akkadian period from Susiana snakes are particularly frequent.[5] The Elamite fertility symbol of two copulating snakes even penetrated as far as Egypt.[6] The motifs of the

1 *Mém. D.P.* 3, plates 28–30.
2 §IV, 10, plate XXI, *b* and *f*.
3 *Mém. D.P.* 29, 57.
4 §IV, 23, *passim*.
5 §IV, 21, 172.
6 §IV, 1, 127.

serpent on the tree of life, and the horned snakes as door-keepers are found in Elam from the earliest times onwards.[1]

Another example of ancient Elamite art is found in the stone-relief commissioned in Susa by Kutik-In-Shushinak about 2250. It shows the god In-Shushinak on his knees, with a divine crown of horns on his head, his long beard well trimmed, holding with both his hands some object that rests on the ground. This may well be the peg of bronze and cedarwood mentioned in several inscriptions. Behind In-Shushinak stands a female figure in a long robe, her hands raised in prayer, perhaps the goddess Narundi. A giant snake coils above the couple. Near this there is an Elamite inscription in linear script, dedicated to the god In-Shushinak, which is unfortunately incomplete.[2]

Figures engraved upon seals give us a better idea of ancient Elamite art than the few surviving reliefs. Connoisseurs recognize their high quality.[3] The masters of Elamite art preferred the symbolic to the merely descriptive. They also preferred animals to men, though they often gave human attributes and activities to their animal figures. As ancient Elamite and Mesopotamian sculpture were closely related, it is difficult to determine the specifically Elamite elements. As well as the serpent motif, a definite preference for the fantastic was one of the specifically Elamite characteristics, which showed itself in ever-new composite beings and in fabulous beasts.[4] The gryphon, a mixture of eagle and lion, was an Elamite invention. The gryphon has been found in Susa at such an early date that its appearance in Egypt can be ascribed to a borrowing from Elam.[5] The deeply rooted inclination of the Elamites towards the uncanny and the fantastic is most visibly presented in glyptic figures. As one author has said, these products are 'sometimes comical, sometimes gruesome, but always convincing'.[6]

A remarkable attainment of the ancient Elamites was the development of their own script. The so-called 'proto-Elamite' script—the designation applied to the earliest pictographic stage in contrast with the later Elamite 'linear script'—is first found in Susa at the level Cb. This epoch, within the Jamdat Naṣr period, is later than Uruk level IVa, in which the Sumerian script first appears.[7] Despite differences in detail there are sufficient resemblances to show that the proto-Elamite script was developed

[1] §IV, 23, 180 and 193.
[2] §I, 11, 3 ff.; see Plate 53 (a).   [3] §III, 20, 122; A, 8, 20 ff.
[4] §IV, 17, 30 f.   [5] §IV, 1, 126.
[6] §IV, 10, 25.   [7] §IV, 9, 11.

from the Sumerian. However, with its masterly 'abstract' representations—for example the animal pictures of Susa A pottery—
Elam would certainly have been predestined to develop a pictorial
script of its own, but evidently the need arose earlier in Sumer
than in Susiana.

The proto-Elamite script can be dated back roughly to about
2900. It spread itself out over the highlands of Iran by the trade
routes, as shown by finds near the present-day Kāshān.[1] As in
Sumer, the script was originally, and remained for a long time, a
series of pictograms; animals, jugs, vases and other objects can be
recognized. On a particularly attractive tablet horses are cata-
logued. Only the heads are reproduced, with the following variations: if the mane stands upright, a stallion is meant, if the mane
hangs downwards, it represents a mare, and if there is no mane at
all, the animal in question was a foal.[2]

These tablets are exclusively economic documents, inventories,
delivery notes, or receipts. We can only guess at their contents, as
the meaning of many symbols is not yet known, and probably
never will be known with any certainty. The interrelation of the
proto-Elamite and the Sumerian scripts is particularly clear in the
numbers, which are partly identical. But it would be a mistake to
assume that this was a plain borrowing by Elam. For as well as the
sexagesimal system of the Sumerians with the figures 1, 60, 600
and 3600, a foreign decimal system was in use in Mesopotamia
for measuring corn during the Jamdat Naṣr period.[3] This was
probably the Elamite system, which according to the proto-Elamite
tablets included the figures 1, 10, 100, 300, 1000, 10,000.[4]

One of the systems of fractions in use in Mesopotamia shows
similar Elamite influence. It is based on the ancient Elamite
system of weights, a binary system, which had the following
fractions, $\frac{1}{64}$, $\frac{1}{32}$, $\frac{1}{16}$, $\frac{1}{8}$, $\frac{1}{4}$ and $\frac{1}{2}$.[5] This series of fractions in the
archaic texts from Uruk has been described as 'particularly
strange'.[6] The more closely the economic and cultural relations
between Elam and Mesopotamia are examined, the clearer it
becomes that both sides practised give-and-take at all times.

In the course of the succeeding centuries the proto-Elamite
script developed—parallel with the Sumerian—from a pictographic script with several hundreds of word-symbols to a syllabary with scattered word-signs. The Elamite 'linear' script was
probably formed by about 2500. We know it only through a

1 §IV, 11, 65 f.   2 See *Mém. D.P.* 17, 15, tablet no. 105; A, 14.
3 §IV, 8, 49.   4 List in *Mém. D.P.* 31, 40.
5 §IV, 3, 138.   6 §IV, 8, 49.

meagre dozen stone inscriptions of Kutik-In-Shushinak of about that date; they were first deciphered at any length in 1961.[1] Their syllabary in the last stage contained 65 to 70 signs, of which 44 have been identified so far (42 syllable signs or monosyllabic words, and two polysyllabic word signs).

It is not yet possible to compare the Elamite linear script with the proto-Elamite pictorial script; the material found so far is too scanty. The characters are usually written from top to bottom, but occasionally the reverse is found. Sometimes the lines begin in the left-hand corner, and sometimes in the right-hand corner; and occasionally a change of direction of 180 degrees is made within a single line, but never inside a word itself. As the symbols of the Elamite script were partly developed from the same pictograms as the Sumerian, many signs are the same in both scripts, which has led some to suppose they were pronounced alike. But this is true only of the sign *ki*; and even that is a coincidence; on the other hand the Sumerian sign *lum* represents *šu* in Elamite; *hi* becomes *ḫu*, and so on.[2]

The use of the Elamite linear inscription under the patriotic and last king of Awan, Kutik-In-Shushinak, was of short duration; it died out with him, and was finally replaced by the cuneiform script. The scribes at Susa, however, adapted the foreign script in their peculiar Elamite manner. In fact, until the fall of the kingdom, the Sumero-Akkadian cuneiform script underwent its own development in the writing schools of Elam.[3]

These differences are visible principally in the syllabary. As is shown by the oldest surviving Elamite document from the time of Agade (the famous Khita treaty), the chanceries of Susa had adapted the almost purely syllabic principles of the native linear script to the borrowed cuneiform. Apart from two 'Sumerograms' (names of gods), the document contains nothing but syllable signs, and more often open syllables (such as *ka*, *ak*) than closed syllables (such as *kap*, *šum*).[4] The Elamite scribes had thus thrown overboard the tedious ballast of logograms and other ambiguities still preserved by their Mesopotamian colleagues. In a deliberately rational manner the Elamites had exploited all inherent possibilities of cuneiform up to the threshold of an alphabetic script. This step however they never took, not even when they assisted, about 520 B.C., in moulding the Old Persian cuneiform, which was a script half syllabic and half alphabetic. And yet the Sumero-Akkadian cuneiform was basically unsuited

[1] §1, 11.   [2] *Ibid.*   [3] §1, 12, 41; A, 6.
[4] §1, 14, no. 3, *passim.*

to reproduce the Elamite language, with its nasal sounds and multiple consonants; for example, cuneiform groups *te-ip-ti* and *te-im-ti* in fact represented *tempt* 'lord'. In other respects Elamite phonetics were in no way suited to the Akkadian cuneiform. The confusion in the texts is correspondingly great.

Elamite, as yet not fully mastered, was an agglutinative (non-inflective) language, and was related to no other known language. As the bilingual and trilingual inscriptions of the Achaemenid period contain a very limited Elamite vocabulary, this must be deduced from internal evidence in the original documents.[1] This language, as one would expect from such a conservative people, altered astonishingly little over the centuries. It was rich in possibilities of expression, corresponding with the cultural and creative talents of its users. This makes it the more regrettable that so little of Elam's history and nothing at all of its literature has come to light so far.

The Elamite calendar was so overwhelmed by foreign influence during the period of Akkadian rule in Susiana that it is difficult to envisage it in its original form. Only two Elamite month-names were still in use under Babylonian rule. Two names (Adar and Abum) were borrowed from Mesopotamia, but were given to other months. The remaining eight month-names present a chaotic mixture of titles under Sumerian or Akkadian influence, and of Elamite names, which are very difficult to arrange in order.[2]

The following list[3] enumerates the month-names of the original Elamite calendar with their approximate equivalents. Numbers III and IX–XI are very uncertain; the only complete certainties are numbers I and V.

I	*Lanlupe*	October
II	*Ḫalpat*	November
III	*Kizir-zu(n)-kaliki*	December
IV	*Elamat*	January (*Alame* in the Achaemenid period, when it was also IV)
V	*Zililitum*	February (*Zillatam* in the Achaemenid period, when it was also V)
VI	*Ḫuršupi*	March
VII	*Papakum*	April
VIII	*Alalima*	May (*Alilit*? in the Achaemenid period, but then it was VI)
IX	*Kazzip*	June (Month of the smiths?)
X	*Tati*	July
XI	*La(n)ḫum*	August
XII	*Tarpit*	September (and intercalary month)

[1] For further information upon the Elamite language see §IV, 15; §IV, 4; §III, 7.

[2] Some other details concerning the Elamite calendar may be found in §IV, 5, 41, note 4; §III, 19, 45; §IV, 16, 260, note 56.   [3] §IV, 14, 12 ff.

Elamite seal-impressions of the third millennium give us a good insight into daily life. We can observe the manifold occupations and the environment of the people of Susiana.

The landscape is cut up by water channels, between the reed-strengthened banks of which fishes are seen. Buffaloes, mountain-goats, and chamois graze beneath the pines, cedars and terebinth trees. Many kinds of animals appear in the grass of the plains, or in the undergrowth, grazing peacefully or fleeing before lions.[1] In this scene the Elamite appears as a hunter, naked, or dressed only in a loin-cloth, armed with bow and arrow and a spear or pike. Followed by dogs—large short-tailed Molossians, or another breed with tail erect—he hunts the red deer, antelope, wild pig, or even the great felines.[2] Naked fishermen drag giant turtles to the shore.[3] Cattle graze in the fields, behind them peasants and milking-vessels can be seen.[4] Herdsmen drive the goats home to their pens, made of crude bricks, their gates flanked with a strong tower;[5] doubtless these belonged to the palace or the temple. Men with three-pronged hoes work in the fields; women, their skirts spreading downwards, gather fruit.[6]

In the cities thriving activity reigns. Labourers work with tools and implements, whilst a procession passes by: four men carrying a cult-statue in front of which sits a musician.[7] In the potter's shop men work on stone jugs; whilst one polishes the handles, others smooth down plates by rubbing them against each other.[8] Women, too, are employed in workshops; sitting on low wooden stools they are occupied in weaving, pottery, or baking.[9]

The people are particularly busy around the granaries; the seals show us silos made of mud-bricks with a long row of domes. The façade is decorated with false niches, above which narrow apertures beneath the flat roof serve to illuminate and ventilate the store rooms. Workmen loaded down with sacks or jugs carry their load on their heads or their shoulders up ladders or flights of steps on the outside of the building to the apertures in the domes.[10] A terrace-like foundation isolates the store from the earth; but there were other silos that were half-underground, as is proved by a mathematical text found in Susa.[11] Near the stores scribes sit cross-legged, and record on their tablets the quantity of grain

[1] §IV, 17, 16.   [2] §IV, 17, 26.
[3] §IV, 24, 16.   [4] G, 8, 93.
[5] §IV, 2, 39.   [6] Mém. D.P. 29, 23.
[7] Mém. D.P. 29, 19.   [8] Ibid.
[9] §IV, 17, 32 f.   [10] §IV, 2, 43 f.
[11] Mém. D.P. 34, 84, no. XIV.

brought to the silo. The royal cup-bearer also sits cross-legged, whilst filling his *qa* measure, or removing the bungs from his jugs.[1] From lists of witnesses we learn about professions in ancient Elam. There were peasants and labourers, fishermen and gardeners, butchers, washermen, smiths, carpenters and potters, merchants, scribes, notaries and priests.[2] Although this list is incomplete it reveals quite clearly the variety and stratification of professional and hence social classes in ancient Elam.

The dead in the third millennium were buried in earthen coffins, and later in ribbed clay coffins, which were often covered with bitumen or pitch. The dead man's skull was usually covered with a cloth to which fine leaves of gold, silver or bronze were sewn. Grave gifts consisted of clay, bitumen, alabaster and copper vessels, often decorated with fine reliefs; as well as needles, bead necklaces, silver bracelets, gold and silver ear-rings, cylinder seals, weights and clay idols.[3] All this proves that the Elamites had some conception of an after-life, in which the various burial gifts would be of use. However, we can know nothing about their ideas of life after death since we have not as yet discovered any burial texts from Elamite antiquity.

[1] §iv, 17, 32.   [2] *Mém. D.P.* 22–4, *passim*.   [3] §iv, 6, 347 f.

CHAPTER XXIV(*a*)

ANATOLIA, *c.* 2300–1750 B.C.

I. INTRODUCTORY

T H E period with which this chapter is concerned is of particular interest to the historian, for it is during these five and a half centuries or so that the greater part of Anatolia came to be dominated by newcomers from the north, speaking a variety of Indo-European languages, and having a culture, religion, economy and customs which had little in common with those of the earlier populations. During this period were laid the foundations for the historical kingdoms of the later second millennium, but their beginnings are hidden by the veil of illiteracy, lifted (but only in Central Anatolia) in the fourteenth and thirteenth centuries B.C. To visualize events during the later centuries of the third and the beginning of the second millennium—the Early Bronze Age 3 and Middle Bronze Age 1 periods of the archaeologist[1]—we are almost entirely dependent on evidence from excavation and exploration,[2] since the earliest written records—the so-called Cappadocian texts—do not appear till the very end of the period with which we are concerned. Being mainly concerned with trade and litigation, they shed only occasional light on the political conditions in Central Anatolia. Historical texts are extremely few.

We have seen, as the end of the second Early Bronze Age approached, a sequence of migratory movements culminating in a great invasion, perhaps of Indo-European newcomers, which divided the peninsula diagonally into two almost equal parts, causing immediate and unmistakable changes in the south and south-western regions.[3] Widespread destruction is followed by an overall decline in material culture. Throughout the wide cultural provinces of the previous period, the entire Konya plain and the southernmost part of the south-west Anatolian region, evidence of settled occupation becomes rare, and one may suspect a corresponding relapse into nomadic conditions. Although the Konya plain recovered by the beginning of the Middle Bronze

---

[1] See below, p. 693, Table 3.
[2] Mainly by members of the British Institute of Archaeology at Ankara.
[3] See above, ch. xviii and §1, 5, 18

Age, *c.* 2000 B.C., these conditions seem to have persisted in Pisidia and Central Lycia throughout the second millennium. The Aegean coast south of the Troad and the plain of Edremit, as well as the Caicus valley,[1] remain almost a complete blank on archaeological maps until the appearance of a Middle Bronze Age culture, datable there to *c.* 1900 B.C., whereas it is interesting by contrast to infer from recent finds that Caria emerged from obscurity several centuries earlier.[2] On the off-shore islands, Poliochni (VI) and Thermi were not reoccupied until a period corresponding with the fifth settlement at Troy, whereas the site of the Heraeum on Samos has a good representative series of buildings and pottery covering Troy III and IV, but seems to be deserted in the period Troy V.[3] From these changes along the Aegean coast something may be learned regarding Anatolian trade with the Cyclades and Greece.[4]

In the areas of Central and Pontic Anatolia, which appear to lie beyond the limits of the Indo-European migration, local and indigenous cultures persisted and no significant changes are observed until about 2200 B.C., when a new epoch is introduced by the famous 'Cappadocian' painted pottery, about which more will be said presently. By this time contact had been re-established with the Indo-European-dominated west and nearby Paphlagonia had itself obtained a western-type culture.[5] For in the western settlements that had survived the great migration distinctive new cultures had again begun to evolve, and by about 2100 B.C. a general resurgence of civilization is to be observed. At Kültepe and Boğazköy in Cappadocia a new Middle Bronze Age culture can now be recognized and its influence spreads southwards towards the Konya plain. South-eastward also, in Cilicia, new developments are evident.[6] Both here and across the Amanus range in the plain of Antioch it is an intrusive painted pottery culture which appears, perhaps associated with a south-westward expansion of the Hurrians. Elsewhere the transition from Early to Middle Bronze Age culture seems to have been a smooth domestic process, unaffected by foreign influences. At individual sites, such as Troy, new wares take the place of old; but the arrival, for instance, of the so-called grey 'Minyan' pottery, which is now known to have been in use long before in neighbouring areas, suggests rather a peaceful acquisition than a foreign intrusion.

[1] §I, 2, 95.
[2] Unpublished evidence from Yokarı Mazı, Damlıboğaz, etc.
[3] §I, 6.   [4] §I, 4, ch. VIII.
[5] §I, 1, 188 f.   [6] §I, 3, 62 and 348 f.

For the first time in the history of the place Troy III–IV would appear to have fallen into some sort of provincial isolation, which lasted until the foundation of the sixth settlement. The beginning of the Middle Bronze Age, to which the latter corresponded in time, also saw the reoccupation of the western seaboard generally after a lacuna (at present conjectural) which may in places have lasted since the end of Troy I. Here and throughout Anatolia, the Middle Bronze Age appears to have been a period of remarkable prosperity, to which the final phase of the Early Bronze Age may be regarded as a prelude. The decline which set in towards its end in the eighteenth and seventeenth centuries B.C. should perhaps be attributed less to the termination of the metal trade with Assyria, the beneficial effects of which can hardly have been felt beyond the limits of the high plateau, than to the rise of an aggressive new power in Central Anatolia, the Hittite 'Old Kingdom'.

II. WESTERN ANATOLIA AFTER THE LUWIAN INVASION

When we take a further look at the evidence upon which these broad conclusions are based and observe how cultural developments in the various provinces are reflected in the material remains available to us (pottery, architecture, and metalwork) we note first of all a breakdown of the old ceramic provinces and a new tendency towards greater uniformity in ceramic design and technology. The use of wheel-made pottery brought about a general decline of the vessels most commonly in use, for these were now usually left plain or covered with a carelessly applied red wash. Better examples were coated with red slip and burnished in the old tradition. Among distinctive shapes, the two-handled drinking cup or *depas amphikypellon* became popular along the west coast, in Cilicia, and at such island stations as the Heraeum on Samos, the elegance of the tall Trojan form contrasting favourably with clumsy local variants. Inland this vessel was less popular, but its rare appearances, for instance at Kültepe and Ališar, show an interesting preference for the wide 'beaker' type from Cilicia. Chance finds of this type have also been made along the trade route leading from the north-western province to Central Anatolia, but these have little interest owing to the uncertainty of their stratigraphical context. Bowl-shapes, by contrast, are now fairly uniform throughout western Anatolia, everted rims being a new characteristic. Beak-spouts, with which jugs are still often provided, become distinctively elongated, and where surface ornament is concerned, plain incised designs are most common. Although the general repertoire of shapes shows greater uniformity than ever before, there are obvious local variations in their respective popularity.[1] For instance, all over the north-west the wheel-made plate is common; in the south-west it is not. 'Tankards', 'face-urns' and *depas* cups, characteristic of Troy III,[2] are unknown in the south-west until the period of Troy IV, when a small variant of the *depas* form appears, standing on a foot and ornamented with horizontal grooves. This shape with the same decoration is also found at Tiryns, and at Lerna in Early Helladic III it is painted in local fashion. The *askos* or 'duck-vase', on the other hand, common in the Cyclades as well as in Samos, Calymnos and in the Izmir region, occurs in Troy IV and in a contemporary setting at Beycesultan. Troy IV jugs and cups have been found in Early Cycladic graves near Chalcis in Euboea, and Early Helladic III 'patterned ware' was imported into Troy IV. Lentoid jugs with cut-away spouts are another feature of the Troy IV phase, found simultaneously at Troy, Yortan, Beycesultan (X), Heraeum (IV), and in the Chalcis graves. Then there is the bifoil or trefoil-mouthed jug, an innovation of this period, and a forerunner of a long series in the second millennium B.C.

More notable still is the sudden appearance of strap-handles rising vertically above the rims of cups and bowls—a feature borrowed from metal prototypes. These are found simultaneously at Beycesultan (XII) and in the Akhisar–Manisa, Balıkesir, Tavşanlı and Inegöl–Iznik[3] areas, that is, in the hinterland of the Aegean and Marmara seaboards, whereas in the coastal areas themselves vertical loop handles are preferred. The 'metallic strap-handle' does not appear here until the arrival of the 'Minyan' wares of the second millennium, which again are often horizontally ribbed or grooved. In south-western Anatolia these handled cups take the place of the *depas* forms. In the inland area at this period the general standard of design shows a livelier imagination than that of the Trojan potters, who in their temporary impoverishment during the Early Bronze 3 phase seemed to lack the capacity for invention. For instance, cups with pedestals and two handles, which appear inland during the Troy III phase, are belatedly imitated in a less developed form in Troy IV;[4] 'bead-rim' bowls which first appear in Troy V have

[1] §I, 4, ch. VIII; §II, 3, 76 f.   [2] §II, 1, 26, 31 f.
[3] New evidence from recent explorations.
[4] §I, 5, 117, figs. 2, 23; §II, 1, 126 (A 37).

long been known elsewhere[1] and grey 'Minyan' ware also makes a late appearance on the coast.[2] To distinguish the early period of uniformity and decline from a subsequent renaissance when the country reverted to a regional regrouping such as had existed before the Luwian invasion the author has suggested the following subdivision of the Early Bronze 3 phase:—E.B. 3 a corresponding with Troy III and IV and E.B. 3 b with Troy V.

In the architecture of the third Early Bronze Age period, we find no great evidence of change and little distinction. E.B. 3 a houses at Troy, Heraeum (IV), and Tarsus are rectangular and sometimes of the hall-and-porch type. The best examples of these latter are found at Beycesultan (X–VIII) and in a 'palace' in the early 'Cappadocian' level at Kültepe.[3] At Beycesultan an increasing use of timber, in foundations and superstructure alike, characterizes the E.B. 3 phase and those which follow it. The *megara* have porches both in front and behind, as in Troy II, and are likewise free-standing, with a great raised circular or oval hearth, benches and obtuse-angled 'sleeping-platforms'. The Kültepe 'palace' is remarkable in that it reproduces a form of plan (already known at Poliochni V and Troy II g),[4] comprising a great hall-and-porch unit with large 'sleeping-platforms' and a range of subsidiary rooms on one side. The main hall again has benches and a huge circular raised hearth, in this case surrounded by four wooden columns, an arrangement exactly repeated in Mycenaean palaces of nearly a millennium later. The appearance of this typical west Anatolian building-form in so remote a setting as Cappadocia may serve to emphasize the contact that was maintained between Central Anatolia and the Luwian-occupied areas. Supplementary evidence of this was found among the pottery in the Kültepe 'palace', for wheel-made plates and cups of Cilician E.B. 3 manufacture were found beside early 'Cappadocian' vessels painted with patterns which are repeated as incised ornament on pottery of the E.B. 3 a period at Beycesultan.[5]

III. CENTRAL ANATOLIA

Ceramic developments in Central Anatolia may now be considered in greater detail. The third Early Bronze Age period must be taken to start a little later here than in the south and west, corres-

[1] §II, 1, 242 (A 23) and Beycesultan VIII (i.e. Troy IV).
[2] §I, 4, 17 f.   [3] §I, 4, 97 ff., fig. 2 and §II, 2, 187, fig. 4.
[4] §II 4, 154, figs. 12, 13.   [5] §II, 5, 20.

ponding in fact chronologically with the beginning of Troy IV. We are thus brought immediately into contact with the beginnings of the so-called Cappadocian ware, the origins and significance of which have in the past proved so controversial. In the eastern half of the Halys region there was at this time a sudden and general increase in the use of painted pottery. The earliest Cappadocian ware, known as 'Intermediate',[1] was really no more than an improvement on the simple painted ware of Alişar I*b*, which has a much wider distribution in the area than was believed until recently. This ware gradually developed into more sophisticated products culminating in a true polychrome pottery, the development of which can now be followed through its full sequence of phases at the site of Kültepe,[2] and its indigenous origin is no longer in doubt. This of course disposes of the theory, once commonly maintained, that the appearance of this ware symbolized the arrival of the Hittites, newcomers with an Indo-European language.[3] Its home in fact was the eastern Halys area and Kültepe in particular, from where it spread westwards to the Boğazköy–Alaca region and southwards to the Develi plain, Acigöl, Acemköy near Aksaray, and Zincirli, at the eastern end of the plain of Konya. If indeed any ethnic label should be attached to it 'Khattian' would be more suitable, denoting as it does a pre-Hittite and non-Indo-European origin. But we must also be prepared to think of the Cappadocian pottery as a comparatively late invention of the Hattic people long established in Central Anatolia. There would then be no obstacle to associating them with the destruction, in about 2200 B.C., of Alaca Hüyük by a people using this pottery, which has in the past been too easily coupled with the Hittite invasion. The identity of the dynasty buried in the Alaca royal tombs has not yet been established, but a new clue has been provided by the discovery of similar tombs at Mahmutlar and Horoztepe,[4] which fall within the Pontic province to the north. Here an identical tradition of craftsmanship in metal is found surviving throughout the twenty-second century B.C.; and it is therefore tempting to think of the Alaca-tomb régime as a temporary extension of Pontic domination in the western Halys country, brought to an end about 2200 B.C. by Khattian Cappadocians.[5] This is by no means proven, but it provides a promising alternative to the 'Hittite invasion' hypothesis.

[1] §III, 3, 236, figs. 232 ff.   [2] §III, 4, 77–80, figs. 22–6, 29, 35 ff.
[3] §III, 2, 44.
[4] §III, 2, 481 ff., pls. 35–52 and §III, 5, 53 ff. See Plate 54 (*a*).
[5] §I, 5, 66.

Rivalry between Pontus and the Halys peoples, which came to a head with the Kashka wars in later times, may have been a long-standing tradition.

More must now be said of the actual character of the Cappadocian painted pottery.[1] First, it is accompanied in smaller quantities by a red, brown or buff monochrome ware, very similar to that already in use in E.B. 2 (Ališar I*b*) times. Inverted rim bowls, with or without handles, bars or plastic crescents, all have earlier prototypes at Ališar. Cups with everted rims and rounded or carinated profiles recall western fashions, but they often have a pointed base, unknown in the west. Jugs with tall funnel-necks are an innovation. Beak-spouted jugs now appear,[2] though only in very large sizes, and a variety of two-handled jars with everted rims ranges from storage jar to pithos size.

Three phases have now been detected in the evolution of this pottery. In the first, 'intermediate ware' still predominates; vessels are decorated with simple patterns in red or purplish-brown paint on a reddish buff slip—and there are also small 'fruitstands' ornamented with vertical bands of paint. In the *middle* period dark brown to black or red paint is used on an orange or buff polished slip, and in the *last* phase bichrome painting in black and red is common on a red slip with cream-slipped panels. Patterns are exclusively geometric—groups of parallel lines, often with heavy borders, zigzags, lozenges, chequer-patterns, wavy lines and so on. Pot-hook spirals and swastikas are common, and in the latest phase complicated panel-fillings surrounded by lozenge borders sometimes strongly recall textile patterns, from which indeed many of these motifs may have been derived. At Kültepe, this attractive pottery continued in *kārum* Levels IV and III (Late Cappadocian), whereas on the city mound it was used even later, in fact into the period contemporary with Level II of the *kārum*.[3] The earlier Cappadocian phases are known only on the mound.

In the *kārum* itself useful parallels with Cilician pottery can be established. Bowls with elaborate 'cross' decoration (Late Cappadocian) found in *kārum* IV contexts have counterparts at Tarsus dating from the beginning of the Cilician Middle Bronze Age, and Cilician painted pottery of the same period is found as an import in *kārum* IV and II. Parallel with the middle Cappadocian ware are grey bottles of Syrian workmanship as well as Cilician E.B. 3 vessels. Through these synchronisms,[4] the transition from Cilician E.B. 3 to the Middle Bronze Age can be correlated with

---

[1] See above, p. 686, n. 2; and Plate 54 (*b*), (*c*).   [2] See Plate 55 (*c*).
[3] §III, 6, 25.   [4] §II, 3, 64.

that from middle to late Cappadocian (*kārum* IV) or, in terms of western Anatolia, from E.B. 3 *a* to E.B. 3 *b*, about 2100 B.C.

Turning to evidence other than ceramic, the subject of contemporary architecture has already been touched upon in reference to the 'palace' on the Kültepe mound. A further example which suggests itself is the citadel at Ališar, which was at this time fortified with a mud-brick enclosure-wall on log foundations.[1] Among the smaller objects there is a striking series of alabaster figurines found at Kültepe in the early and middle Cappadocian levels (twenty-second century B.C.). Two principal types can immediately be distinguished—one representing a seated goddess and the other, more abstract, consisting of a disc-like body from which project up to three heads with pigtails and conical headdresses. Still others are shown holding children. Occasionally more elaborate group-subjects are attempted. In one example, a male figure is holding a lion and in another, found at Zenzidere, three standing figures in short skirts are freely carved with their hands folded on their breasts.[2] The symbolism of these objects is difficult to interpret; but the predominance of a goddess figure is natural in Anatolia and compatible with pre-Indo-European religious beliefs. Comparative material from western Anatolia is unfortunately lacking and at Beycesultan the E.B. 2 shrine-complex was not rebuilt, nor did investigations penetrate below the Middle Bronze Age shrines in the second area.

IV. EASTERN CULTURES

The sudden and conspicuous appearance of painted pottery in Central Anatolia during the final phase of the Early Bronze Age, is not, as it proves, an isolated occurrence. East of the Cappadocian area and beyond the Antitaurus painted pottery related to Cappadocian has been found in the plain of Elbistan,[3] and a large province of other painted wares stretches from Malatya to Divriği and from Divriği to beyond the Euphrates.[4] In the handmade painted pottery of this area two main shapes are characteristic, a globular jar with thickened rim and a shallow bowl with inverted rim. Lugs take the place of handles, which do not occur. The pottery is painted in a brown or blackish paint on a buff to yellow slip. Designs are simple but very distinctive, consisting of horizontal bands with zigzags, triangles, or multiple chevrons, often left 'in

[1] §III, 3, 210, fig. 207.   [2] §III, 4, 71 ff., figs. 1–21.
[3] §IV, 7, 86.   [4] §IV, 1, 202 ff.

reserve'. The lowermost band usually shows a fringe reminiscent of textile designs. More will perhaps be learned about this pottery when the excavations at Arslantepe near Malatya are finally published.[1] In the Sivas district, still another painted ware was found at Maltepe[2] overlying deposits of the E.B. 2 period, but quite unlike the wares just described. The contemporary pottery of the eastern provinces is quite different and shows connexions with the areas south of the Caucasus and with Azarbāyjān. In the east generally, black burnished wares continue, mostly plain, but sometimes ornamented with fine incision as at Karaz, Tepecik near Erzurum, Trialeti above Tiflīs and Zülfübulak, north-east of Vān.[3] Peculiar knobbed handles, known as 'Nahcevan lugs' are still common and they have recently been found on black incised pottery at Nalchik north of the Caucasus.[4] The latest Early Bronze Age pottery of Tazehkant near Tabrīz[5] continues the old shapes but without the incision prevalent in the earlier (E.B. 1) ware; a change which accompanies the substitution of rectangular houses for the earlier round ones. Other links with the steppe region north of the Caucasus are suggested by the presence of several East Anatolian metal vessels in the famous royal tomb at Maikop on the Kuban,[6] which is usually dated c. 2300 B.C. or a little later. Apart from the little animal sculptures which have frequently been compared with the not dissimilar metal figures of animals from Alaca and Horoztepe, one might mention the occurrence in this tomb of meerschaum and, as its only known source is at Eskişehir in West Anatolia,[7] trade-links with that area must be inferred. Finally, at Trialeti tumuli have been found to contain black burnished pottery with shapes and incised ornament, which seem related to that of East Anatolia at this period.[8] The use of burial mounds was a practice at this time alien to Anatolia, and was probably introduced from the direction of the Pontic steppe. This first appearance of tumuli at Trialeti, on a barren upland suitable to the lives of pastoral people, could well indicate the arrival in Eastern Anatolia of Indo-European-speaking people from the north; and the termination soon afterwards of the East Anatolian Early Bronze Age might well have the same significance. A date of c. 2100 B.C. suggested for the arrival of these people at Trialeti, and about 2000–1950 B.C. for the end of the period in Eastern Anatolia,[9] could suggest the

[1] §IV, 9, 151 f.   [2] §IV, 8, 662, pls. cxxivff., figs. 28–65.
[3] §IV, 4, 406 (a117, a159); §IV, 1, 186, figs. 64 ff.
[4] §IV, 5, 18, fig. 5: 4–5.   [5] §IV, 2.   [6] §IV, 6, pl. II, 9; pl. cxxx, no. 330.
[7] §IV, 3, 22 n. 1, 23, 46 and map.   [8] §IV, 1, 176.   [9] §IV, 1, 178.

movement of Indo-European elements westward during the Kültepe II (*c.* 2000–1900 B.C.) period. The trail of burnt or deserted settlements from the eastern borders to the Kayseri region is suggestive. Whatever happened, these disturbances were serious enough to prevent the reoccupation of numerous sites during the following Middle Bronze Age, and nothing is known of events in Eastern Anatolia for the next half millennium.

V. A PONTIC CULTURE

While discussing events in Central Anatolia during the E.B. 3 period, some reference has already been made to its northern neighbour, the high culture of which is chiefly known from the contents of a number of partly robbed royal tombs. Only one of these was found intact. The beginning and end of this interesting culture are still a matter of speculation and it is possible that, as the excavator suggests, these burials may even have continued into the twenty-first century B.C.[1] In addition to Horoztepe there are similar graves at Mahmutlar and Kayapınar,[2] but as the condition of these tombs was mostly disturbed little can be said about the burial habits. It would appear that the cemeteries, like those of Alaca and Tekkeköy,[3] were extramural. Our knowledge of the Pontic E.B. 3 culture depends almost entirely upon discoveries in such graves and, since these consist almost exclusively of metal objects, it is metallurgical detail which merits attention. The Alaca tradition of metalwork is not only continued, but enriched. New types of cult-object, such as *sistra*,[4] appear; weapons also, including a new class of swords with a prominent mid-rib,[5] crescentic axes and beautiful but effective-looking socketed battle-axes.[6] There are new forms of metal vessels such as bowls, cups, fruitstands and basket-handled 'tea-pots'. Metal tables on human legs are another invention, and there are appealing but somewhat clumsy figurines, one of which represents a naked deity suckling her child.[7] This copper figure and another in silver,[8] with gold hair and cross-bands over the breast, show bolder realism in modelling than was ever attempted at Alaca. Large bull figures are now set on detachable pedestals and among the smaller figures of bulls and deer there is an example where twin animals

[1] §III, 5, 58.
[2] §V, 6, 324 ff., figs. 15, 19.
[3] §V, 3, 382 ff.
[4] §III, 5, pls. XII, XVII, 1–3.
[5] §III, 5, pl. XVIII, 15–19.
[6] §III, 5, pl. XVIII, 3–7; §III, 2, pl. 40, 3.
[7] §III, 5, pl. X. See Plate 55 (*a*).
[8] Ankara Museum (unpublished).

are mounted on a single base.[1] The crescentic axes[2] and a spear-head with a 'poker-tang'[3] suggest relations with north Syrian metalwork, which is itself based on Mesopotamian tradition. But the bulk of the finds represents the native Pontic (and Alaca) school of craftsmanship. At Horoztepe swords and spearheads of the slotted type seem to have increased in popularity since Alaca times. Both here and at Mahmutlar, the crescentic axes with their alien associations look less impressive than the fluted and finely decorated battle-axes of Pontic design.

The appearance has been mentioned above of some north Syrian influence among the products of Pontic metal-workers. The first manifestation of this influence may in fact be regarded as a more general characteristic of the E.B. 3 period in Anatolia.[4] New features such as 'poker-tangs' on spearheads, daggers with three or five rivets,[5] round-heeled daggers in Alişar III and Kültepe *kārum* IV[6] all point in this direction. But the adoption of such innovations as these did not affect the general character of Anatolian industries, nor do they seem to have reached regions so remote from Syria as the western provinces. They did, however, penetrate as far as Trialeti and the Tiflīs area[7] and it is interesting to speculate whether it was by land or by the Black Sea that contact was here established with the centre of north Syrian metal trade near distant Carchemish and Til Barsib. It is also certain that Anatolian metalwork in its turn extended its influence to Caucasia. The animals from Maikop,[8] the shaft-hole axe from Karaz,[9] the silver pins from Horoztepe[10] all point to this. Other apparently southern features such as the 'transverse' axe may however have reached the Caucasus by an alternative road from Mesopotamia.[11] The sources of the tin that was needed to produce the bronzes of Horoztepe and Alaca are still unknown.

VI. TRANSITION TO THE MIDDLE BRONZE AGE, 2100–1900 B.C

The last century of the third millennium B.C. and the first of the second saw a sort of cultural renaissance in Western Anatolia and the first budding of the Middle Bronze Age cultures in

[1] §III, 5, pl. XVII, 4a–b.   [2] §III, 5, pl. XVIII, 1–2. See Plate 55 (b).
[3] §III, 5, pl. VIII, 6.   [4] §v, 5, 90, 113 ff., map 4, fig. 9: 2, 4, 6.
[5] §v, 5, 99 f., map. 2.   [6] §v, 5, 100 f.
[7] §v, 4, 516, fig. 293 (Zages, Géorgie).
[8] §v, 2, pl. XLI; cf. pl. XLII, 6.   [9] §IV, 4, 376 and 409, a 174.
[10] Ankara Museum (unpublished).   [11] §v, 1, 115, pls. LIb and LIIa.

Central Anatolia and Cilicia. Everywhere there are manifest signs that the rate of cultural progress is rapidly increasing; new sites are founded, new wares abound, new tools and weapons appear and trade becomes brisker than it had been for a long time. It is a period of transition during which new cultures are born out of old, a period in which old and new exist side by side. There are no sharp cultural breaks between the Early Bronze Age 3 period and the following Middle Bronze Age, just as there are none between the Middle and Late Bronze Ages, except in Cilicia. This continuity of the culture development should not be obscured by a conventional terminology with its sharply defined periods. Troy V and Beycesultan VII–VI a are still called Early Bronze Age, whereas contemporary cultures in Central Anatolia and Cilicia are already labelled as Middle Bronze Age, each for a good local reason. Nothing can be gained by forcing them all into a chronological strait-jacket and the terminology depends in each case on whether one stresses this period's links with the past or with what follows. Archaeologically speaking the period from c. 23/2200–12/1100 B.C. is a cultural entity, not a succession of E.B. 3, M.B. and L.B. cultures. It is sharply defined from the periods that precede and follow it (Late Chalcolithic–Early Bronze Ages 1 and 2 and the Iron Age) by catastrophic invasions, but in itself it is indivisible. The chronological labels are kept only for the sake of convenience but they have no cultural implications. Various cultures can be chronologically linked by a useful series of synchronisms based on specific pottery shapes or features. Of these, the 'red-cross' bowl and its 'multiple-cross' variant, which have been found at no less than twenty-five sites, must be considered the most important.[1] At Tarsus in Cilicia these occur (in a peculiar shape on three voluted feet) just before the beginning of the Middle Bronze Age, in the very last building-level of the Early Bronze 3 period. At Troy also they are already present in late Troy IV, but are most characteristic of Troy V. Inland they have been found at a great many sites, of which Beycesultan (VII–VI a), Kusura ('transitional'), Polatlı (11 and 12) and Karaoğlan (IV) show their stratigraphical context. Their absence in Central Anatolia is noteworthy, but in the Late Cappadocian (kārum IV) period at Kültepe, a 'patterned cross' bowl provides the eastern variant, and this finds a Middle Bronze Age parallel in Cilicia.[2] Volute handles and feet, neatly rolled in this period, occur at Troy V (and perhaps already in IV), Poliochni (VI),

[1] §VI, 15, 321 ff.
[2] §II 3, 64; §I, 3, fig. 289 (813), 290 (811, 812).

Early →←— Middle Bronze Age

Site					
BOĞAZKÖY	8a and *kārum*	? — —	8b	8c / 8d	9
KÜLTEPE	Ia	Ib	Gap	II	Late Cappadocian: III / IV — Cappadocian: Middle / Early	E.B. 2
CILICIA	Cilician Middle Bronze Age				Cilician E.B. 3	
KONYA PLAIN	Kara-Hüyük I		II	III IV V	VI and earlier	→?
SOUTH-WEST	Beyce-Sultan V		VIa VIb	VII	VIII IX X	XI – XIIc
NORTH-WEST	Early Troy VI	Marmara Grey-ware Province	Troy V		Troy IV	Troy III
	I	b			a	
	Middle Bronze Age	Early Bronze Age 3				
DATE B.C.	c. 1750	1900	2000	2100	2200	2300

Table 3. *Early and Middle Bronze Age levels at Anatolian sites.*

Maltepe near Afyon, Beycesultan (X–VI*a*), Heraeum (IV) as well as at Mersin, Tarsus, Kabarsa and Tartalı in Cilicia[1] in late E.B. 3 contexts. A third West Anatolian feature is the imitation plastic handle or 'eyeglass',[2] used on bowls and apparently more common inland than on the coast, where it would seem to belong to the Middle Bronze Age (e.g. at Bayraklı). It is found in the south-west: occasionally at Kusura, frequently at Beycesultan (VIII–V) and is very common on E.B. 3*b* bowls from the Tavşanlı–Kütahya region and the Inegöl and Eskişehir plains. In the Konya plain it is found at Karahüyük-Konya (IV and V), Sizma and other sites; but it is apparently not known in the Ankara region or Cilicia. In Central Anatolia, it occurs in the earliest pottery of Boğazköy (Level WH 9), contemporary with *kārum* IV at Kültepe, from which site comes an unstratified stone bowl with the same motif.[3] Another was found on an Early Helladic bowl at Zygouries in the Peloponnese.[4] Features such as these therefore serve as useful links between the various E.B. 3*b* cultures of the west and Cilicia and Central Anatolia in the east and they testify to the existence of much trade and contact.

A glance at the Late Cappadocian remains (*c.* 2100–2000 B.C.) found in the *kārum* (the trading-settlement) at Kültepe, which belongs to this period, bears out the idea of increasing welfare in Central Anatolia. Not only does the Late Cappadocian pottery here reach its highest development in the bichrome painted ware, but a significant change simultaneously appears in the lay-out of the settlement itself. Near the foot of the great mound on which the old walled city stands a new suburb or lower town, two-thirds of a mile long, comes into being, possibly surrounded by an outer defensive wall. This is the area which in later times (*kārum* Level II) becomes *kārum Kaneš*, the foundations of which, in Level IV, are laid upon clean soil in a hitherto uninhabited area. Since the evidence of written texts does not become available until its third rebuilding (Level II), it is not known whether its original purpose was to accommodate the first merchants, be they local Anatolian or Assyrian, or merely to take a surplus population from the city above. In any case another notable ceramic development corresponds with its foundation. This is the appearance of a new wheel-made monochrome ware, often mis-called 'Hittite', which is considered by its excavators to have no

---

[1] §I, 4, 129, fig. 2: 10; §II, 1, fig. 251: 19, 21, 23; §I, 3, fig. 273: 448, 445 and fig. 355: 447, 445.

[2] §I, 4, 124, fig. 2: 24 and much new evidence; §VI, 15, 332 ff.

[3] §II, 1, 227.   [4] *Ibid.*

connexion with the monochrome Cappadocian ware that preceded it.[1] This ware, which awaits detailed publication, is the ancestor of the fine red, brown, and buff fabrics that are the glory of the later Middle Bronze Age levels at Kültepe. The appearance of a similar wheel-made monochrome ware at this same period has been observed at other sites in Central Anatolia (Alaca Hüyük and Boğazköy lower city, Level V), and beyond the Halys at Ahlatlibel, Etiyokuşu, Karaoğlan and Polatlı II in the Ankara region, which all suggest that it is part of a wider distribution. The 1961 excavations at Boğazköy have now shown that the earliest occupation of the site is due to people arriving with pottery that is strikingly similar to that of Beycesultan VIa in south-western Anatolia. Once again we find in this earliest burnt level (WH 9)[2] wheel-made wares accompanied by hand-made red, grey or black-washed burnished wares of a new type besides imported Cappadocian ware. At all the Central Anatolian sites mentioned, this new monochrome burnished ware is said to be foreign to the region and the parallels quoted would tend to confirm this. At Beycesultan, on the other hand, this VIa pottery itself arrives comparatively late and is mixed with earlier local wares such as the cups and beakers in wheel-made buff ware with string-cut bases which also occur at Boğazköy, Kültepe and other sites. At Beycesultan, there is evidence to suggest that this pottery comes in from the north and in the Tavşanlı-Kütahya region, surface finds have established its presence. It is perhaps in this area of north-west Anatolia that its origin should be sought. That contacts were not entirely one-sided is clear from the appearance of Central Anatolian shapes at Beycesultan, among which we may mention the Kültepe type of 'tea-pot', now occurring side by side with local versions of the same shape. Such contacts with the west seem to be prolonged throughout the later history of the *kārum*.

Although little is as yet known of the earlier occupations in the Kültepe *kārum* (Levels IV and III)—a situation now paralleled at Boğazköy in the lower city—Level II brings Kültepe and indirectly much of Central Anatolia into the light of history, owing to the arrival of literate Assyrian merchants, who made their home in this suburb by permission of the local ruler. Their records, written in cuneiform, reveal the existence of other similar trading establishments, widely distributed over Central Anatolia in the twentieth century B.C. Since the contents of these texts, their archaeological context, and the facts which they reveal about

[1] §III, 4, 77.   [2] §VI, 5, 23.

contemporary Anatolia are dealt with in a succeeding part of this chapter, it remains here only to add some supplementary conclusions, made from unpublished or less familiar archaeological evidence.

The Cappadocian and Kültepe II phases roughly coincide in their western distribution towards the Salt Lake (Tuz Gölü), the Aksaray region and the plain of Bor, which may imply control of the great silver mines of Bulgar and Bereketli Maden in the Taurus above the Cilician Gates. Certain finds in the regions of West Anatolia, the Konya plain and Cilicia suggest contact and trade with the *kārum* of Kültepe; they include, for example, Cilician Middle Bronze Age painted pottery-jugs and pedestalled cups, a Troy V knife, etc. These connexions, like the obvious links with Karahüyük-Konya,[1] might easily be attributed to the independent activities of Anatolian merchants. Luwians are attested in the Kültepe tablets and it is not impossible that the original *kārum* of Kültepe (and perhaps that of Boğazköy also) was founded for trade with the western and southern regions long before the participation of the Assyrians.

The benefits reaped by local traders, not necessarily in contact with the Assyrians themselves, but certainly with their Anatolian agents at Kültepe, are perhaps best reflected in the prosperous Middle Bronze Age culture in the Konya plain.[2] About twenty-five large mounds of city-size are scattered over the district, though of these only Karahüyük-Konya has yet been excavated. At that site vast walls with impressive double gates and bastions at regular intervals surround a town the size of Kültepe; and its contemporary cultures (Levels I and II), with roots in the Early Bronze Age, seem hardly inferior to that of the famous Cappadocian city, to which its debt, though striking, is strictly limited. In Karahüyük II there were copies of Kültepe cylinder-seals, only their cuneiform inscriptions being omitted. In Level I, side by side with seals of the Tieszkewicz type—possibly a local adaptation—there is a fine collection of impressions evidently made with metal stamp-seals, where animal shapes and other signs are enclosed in a pretentious border of spiral and guilloche ornament. These were found in a large building which may have been the local ruler's palace. In Level I also the so-called *kantharos*, a quatrefoil cup with two handles and a fine high pedestal base, is more common than at any other site in Anatolia and it is doubtless from here that it reached Middle Minoan Crete, probably by way of the Calycadnus valley.[3] It was certainly

---

[1] §VI, 1, 373 f.; §VI, 2, 30 f.   [2] §VI, 15, 311 ff.   [3] §VI, 15, 327.

through this same valley that the Middle Bronze Age inhabitants of the plain conducted their trade with Cilicia, and painted wares from this region are found along the trade route and at Karaman.[1]

This ware is distinguished by its designs in matt paint on a plain or polished white or cream surface and its preference for low pedestalled bowls and 'eye-jugs'.[2] Metope-patterns, dots, 'butterflies' and 'eyes' are among its most typical patterns. Equally notable is the comparative rarity in Cilicia of beak-spouted vessels, 'bead-rim' bowls and other characteristic 'plateau' shapes. But when these disparities have been mentioned there remains little at this period to distinguish the common run of ceramic fashions above and below the Taurus, for the cultures of Cilicia and the southern plateau seem to share a common root in the Early Bronze Age. In Cilicia indeed it is thought that the fashion for painted pottery may be derived from the plain of Antioch, where 'eye-jugs' and pedestal-bowls may antedate their appearance in Cilicia, but this is as yet by no means proven, and it is equally possible that both may actually be a local reflection of the widespread fashion for painted pottery on the southern plateau in the E.B. 3 period, but executed in an inferior technique. Certainly the priority of appearance invalidates attempts to derive it from the Khabur ware in northern Mesopotamia.

In the Ankara region the sequence of events is not yet clear. At the unpublished site of Karaoğlan, a final Early Bronze Age phase with white-painted cups and bowls, often with cross decoration,[3] is followed after a general destruction by pottery with Kültepe I *b* (?) affiliations, among which beak-spouted jugs with pointed bases and a rhyton are found.[4] Other finds include grey burnished and incised vessels, red cups with two handles and other sherds that look like Beycesultan VI *a*. This monochrome ware is also reported from Ahlatlibel and Etiyokuşu and Polatlı II and probably belongs to the very end of the Early Bronze Age. Its parallels at Boğazköy and Kültepe have already been pointed out. At Polatlı II, the last phase of western E.B. 3 *b* is again destroyed by fire and Level III produces a painted ware that might be described as a decadent local imitation of Cappadocian ware.[5] This clumsily painted pottery marks the beginning of the local Middle Bronze Age and has been found at a number of other sites between the

[1] §vi, 15, 324.
[2] §i, 3, 164, fig. 295: 860, 859, and fig. 386, top row.
[3] §vi, 4, figs. 21–4.   [4] §vi, 3, pls. LIII, LV.
[5] §vi, 10, 58, fig. 13: 1–8.

Halys and Sangarius rivers, perhaps marking a movement of refugees from further east. The destruction of Karaoğlan, Polatlı II and Gordion[1] all suggest some upheaval in the area, followed by a change of culture. Westward again, in the plain of Eskişehir, surface exploration has shown that many sites with E.B. 3 pottery were deserted after the end of the period. In the Emirdağ region there are traces of a painted late Early Bronze Age pottery which may have links with a few pieces from Polatlı II or with the painted wares of E.B. 3 period at Karahüyük-Konya. At Gordion, Tez, and Hisar the first Middle Bronze Age remains are of Central, not West, Anatolian type. West of Eskişehir, from Kütahya to the lake of Iznik, there are again traces of destruction and desertion of many sites at the end of the Early Bronze Age 3. The fortified sites of Tavşanlı, Köprüören, Üyücek went up in flames and so did Çakırca and Yeniköy on the northern shores of Lake Iznik and numerous other sites are deserted.[2] Finally, when Troy itself is reached, one finds in the sixth settlement a culture which is clearly not of native growth, and indications are that its origin should be sought in the last mentioned area directly to the east. The interpretation of these far-reaching disturbances will be discussed presently.

In the south-west at Beycesultan[3] the transition from Early to Middle Bronze Age is well documented. During the earlier E.B. 3*b* (Levels VII and VI*b*), the traditional red-washed pottery is still prevalent together with more commonplace wheel-made cups and bowls on string-cut bases, jars with plastic and volute handles, bead-rim bowls, etc. In Level VI*a*, a significant change takes place. Fine wheel-made wares now appear in a variety of colours which include black, deep red, red, orange, pink, buff, cream and—rare in these south-western parts—grey. The vessels are slipped and burnished, and incised or *pointillé* designs, white-filled or not, are frequent. Shapes include enormous beak-spouted vessels, smaller ones with squat or biconical bodies and miniatures of the same vessels. There are jugs with round mouths (already known at Troy IV and Heraeum IV), jugs with cut-away spouts, Yortan-like bird vases, and a conspicuous pattern-burnished beak spout in grey ware. Bowls with one or two handles are common and all these vessels are also copied in the local red-wash ware, which clearly demonstrates their foreign origin. That we are here dealing with northern

---

[1] §vi, 16, 51 and §i, 5, 10 and pl. i, i.
[2] §i, 5, 10 and pl. i, i, supplemented by new evidence from 1960–1 surveys by the author and D. H. French.   [3] §i, 4, 126, fig. 2; pl. xii, *d–e*.

elements is beyond doubt and proved by numerous parallels in the Tavşanlı–Kütahya and the Bursa–Iznik region, where there is a whole E.B. 3 culture complex with exactly these shapes. Other vessels again point to the north. There is a fine *depas* of classical Trojan shape, but painted, cups with high-flung handles, ribbed bowls which look like forerunners of the north-west Anatolian shapes of the Middle Bronze Age. Red-cross bowls, lids with red crosses, jars on volute feet, all have parallels in the Troy V culture of the north-west. The shapes of the intrusive northern wheel-made class are also purely West Anatolian, a point which must be borne in mind, for it is exactly this class that appears in the Ankara region, at earliest Boğazköy and in the *kārum* IV of Kültepe. The significance of this distribution cannot yet be assessed and must await the publication of the eastern material.

Of the E.B. 3*b* metalwork of the region little is known, but a knife with curling tip occurs at Denizli,[1] Troy and Kültepe I*b*,[2] where it must be regarded as an import. The imitation in pottery of basically metal forms, combined with the appearance of a fine grey ware, prevalent in the north-west but appearing in the south-west with Beycesultan VI*a* and emulating the elegant shapes peculiar to metal vessels, may well suggest a more intense exploitation of the numerous silver deposits of western Anatolia. Like the sites in the Tavşanlı region, Troy V and Beycesultan were surrounded by defensive walls, but little is known of domestic architecture other than that buildings were constructed on a rectangular plan.

It is not until the full Middle Bronze Age is reached at Beyce-sultan (Level V) that there is at last an abundance of architecture to supplement the evidence of pottery, which is essentially the same as that of the previous level, shorn of its northern mono-chrome wares. The eastern of the mound's twin summits is crowned by the ruins of an enormous palace,[3] almost eighty yards in diameter, while the broader hill top to the west is covered by a complex of other public buildings within its own enclosure wall.[4] There is also for the first time a substantially built temple[5] and the whole city is fortified with a wall that takes in much of a lower terrace near the river. The examples thus provided of contemporary forms of building in the more heavily wooded parts of Anatolia are in themselves of great interest, providing as they do a

---

[1] §vi, 17, 56, pl. xlviii, 3 (Denizli). See Plate 55 (*d*).
[2] §vi, 17, 56, fig. 62, pl. xlviii, 2.
[3] §vi, 13, 32 ff.
[4] §vi, 11, 96 f.
[5] §vi, 12, 35 ff., fig. i.

traditional basis for the native architecture of Turkey up to the present century. Walls have a substructure of undressed stone, sometimes standing on log foundations, and above this are panels of mud-brick in a framework of timber, which is tied into the roof beams above. Upper stories are more lightly built of timber and have wide, open balconies for summer use. A peculiarity is the treatment of floors which are usually left unpaved, but covered with a bedding of rushes or (presumably) woven matting. The best local craftsmen were carpenters and joiners rather than masons, for few dressed stones were ever found, in marked contrast with the well-built walls of later Troy VI. But the character and sheer size of these buildings suggest, by their unmistakable dignity, the attributes of a capital city and the state of which it was at this time the administrative centre can be identified with the kingdom of Arzawa, so frequently mentioned in the Hittite records. Its total destruction by some enemy at a date which has been estimated on archaeological grounds at about 1750 B.C., corresponds closely enough with the beginning of the Old Hittite Kingdom to suggest that the place was sacked during some Hittite raid. It is however clear that the town was evacuated before this happened and the only finds of value from the palace are a number of silver bracelets and a fine earring dropped in the courtyard. The latter has a good parallel in a gold one found at Köprüören near Kütahya.

The north-western province is the next to be considered, and it should at once be observed that here evidence for the transition from Early to Middle Bronze Age is of more than regional significance. For the arrival of the Troy VI culture with its grey 'Minyan' pottery in the Troad, the Caicus valley and the Aegean coast north of Izmir is now usually considered as related to the movement which brought Middle Helladic culture into Greece, and with it, as is generally thought, the first speakers of the Greek language.[1]

The American excavators of Troy agree that the Troy VI culture is not derived from Troy V[2] and link the appearance there of grey 'Minyan' ware with its arrival in Greece. Other scholars[3] suspect them of underestimating the element of continuity and draw attention to the persistently Anatolian character of the Troy VI culture, which they think lacking in alien elements. In fact, both views may in a sense be right, but both are based on an estimate of finds which is limited to the site of Troy itself or, at most, the Troad. If, however, one discards these parochial

---

[1] See *C.A.H.* II³, ch. xxxix, sect. iii.
[2] §II, 1, 226.
[3] §VI, 6.

limitations and views the wider background of events in Western Anatolia generally, one can see the phenomenon of the grey 'Minyan' ware in its proper context, and one finds that its own strictly Anatolian character is no less obvious than that of the red-washed, red-coated and ordinary grey wares, which were already present in Troy V. In fact, what at Troy itself appear to be innovations, prove to have been for a long time familiar features of contemporary culture, as in the Tavşanlı region or around the lake of Iznik. It is understandable, therefore, that scholars as yet unaware of recent discoveries in the interior of West Anatolia, when faced with the simultaneous appearance of grey 'Minyan' on the Greek Mainland and at Troy, should have wrongly located its common source or even suspected its arrival at Troy from Greece. This view must certainly now be corrected. Recent archaeological surveys[1] have shown that the best known criteria of the Troy VI culture have a distribution-range which, far from being limited to the Troad or the Aegean coast, extend inland to the regions of Akhisar, Manisa, Balıkesir, Biga, Bursa, Inegöl, Yenişehir, and Iznik in the hinterland of the Aegean and Marmara seaboards, and extending on to the plateau as far as Bozüyük, Tavşanlı and Köprüören. At Troy itself, it may be possible to distinguish between the ordinary grey ware of the fifth and the grey 'Minyan' of the sixth settlement, but further east such a distinction is meaningless. Here we find the same shapes in grey wares, some with the soapy quality of 'Minyan', others darker in colour and even black, but all these wares are burnished (like much of the Greek grey 'Minyan'). With them are red and buff burnished wares, often with the same shapes, red-washed and wheel-made plain wares, all familiar both in the E.B. 3 and in the early Middle Bronze Age contexts. Much of the simpler wares of the two periods is in fact indistinguishable when unstratified.

In the area east of the Sea of Marmara, pattern-burnish is extremely common on ordinary grey and red and on grey 'Minyan' wares. Common on the grey ware of Troy V, it appears but rarely on the 'Minyan' ware of Troy VI,[2] when its popularity seems to be waning. In the Marmara area, the shapes with which this pattern burnish associates itself are of the Troy V period (or earlier), and at sites further south, including Beycesultan, their stratification is dated by such features as red-cross bowls which do not survive the end of the Troy V period. At Köprüören the

---

[1] By D. H. French (1959–60, 1961) and the author (1955, 1960), unpublished. See provisionally §1, 5, 15 ff., pl. 3 and §vi, 14, 61 ff.

[2] §vi, 7, 76 ff.

cross form reappears in the actual pattern of the burnishing on the interior of soapy bowls of 'Minyan' fabric and round the lake of Iznik multiple cross patterns are a frequent ornamentation on the grey bowls. Although such patterns are features of the Troy V period not only at Troy but throughout western Anatolia, they are unknown in Troy VI, or the Middle Bronze Age. All this tends to show that in these areas up to two hundred miles east of Troy there existed in the Troy V (or broadly speaking Troy III–V) period a culture or cultures distinguished by the use of pattern-burnished grey (and red) ware and by its preference for certain shapes that may be considered ancestral to those of the grey 'Minyan' ware of Troy VI. This was evolved from local antecedents, independently of any possible influence from Troy itself. Recent evidence from the plains of Balıkesir, Akhisar and Manisa strongly suggests that these areas also partook in the early development of this pottery—developments totally absent at Troy itself or on the Aegean coast, throughout the E.B. 3 period.

This theory is based on abundant though still largely unstratified material. But if, as seems likely, it is proved to be correct, first there can be no longer any doubt about the Anatolian origin of the Troy VI grey 'Minyan' and its offshoot in Middle Helladic Greece, even if the grey wares of Early Helladic III Lerna provide an—as yet isolated—parallel to the Anatolian development.[1] Secondly, this ware will be unmistakably recognized as a late arrival in the Troad and on the Aegean coast and Caicus valley, from an original home in areas further east. It is perfectly possible that on the west coast new shapes were developed, which have no counterparts further east, but which, like the goblets, become more popular in Greece than they ever were in Anatolia.

The shift in population from the interior to the coast, indicated by the archaeological remains, would seem to be no more than one incident in a movement of peoples or groups from east to west, as noted earlier in this chapter, which culminated in the arrival of Middle Helladic people with grey 'Minyan' and other wares in mainland Greece. This subject is still controversial[2] and the view of the present writer may conflict with those expressed by others in this *History*.[3] But since an event so important as the arrival of the Hittites in East Anatolia may be related to, if not instrumental in producing this movement, a word must finally be said about the archaeological evidence from which it can be reconstructed and about its probable repercussions.

[1] §vi, 8, 299 ff.   [2] §i, 5, 1 ff.   [3] See Index.

At the conclusion of chapter XVIII we discussed the evidence for a migration into western and southern Anatolia at the end of the E.B. 3 period, and in endeavouring to identify it with the arrival of a particular people, we claimed the Luwians as the most likely candidates. The general opinion that Hittites, Luwians, Palaeans all migrated simultaneously into Anatolia at the end of the Early Bronze Age, c. 1900 B.C., a theory not disputed until 1958, is flatly contradicted by archaeological evidence. Hittitologists are now agreed that both Luwians and Hittites were already present at Kültepe II in the twentieth century B.C. With the former, who may have been merchants, we are not here concerned, but the presence of Hittites, combined with an attractive theory[1] that Kanesh (Kültepe) was transformed into Nesha by Indo-Europeans, would seem to agree with the Hittite appellation of their own language as našili, that is, 'of Nesha'. Admittedly, one previously held opinion[2] that the Hittites were responsible for the destruction of Kültepe II, has come to seem less plausible. But this need in no way impair the validity of our conclusion, supported by an accumulating volume of evidence,[3] that the indigenous culture of East Anatolia was disintegrated at this period by some convulsive movement of peoples from east to west. The burning or desertion of a line of settlements along the eastern approaches to Kanesh, probably between 2000 and 1950 B.C., has its own unmistakable significance. Nor can we ignore similar evidence found, for example, at Polatlı where painted pottery of eastern affinities suddenly appears after the destruction of a west Anatolian settlement corresponding with Troy V. When one adds to these the disturbances already recorded in the Eskişehir plain, the destruction of many sites in the Marmara area at the end of E.B. 3b, the appearance of elements from this region in the Troad and on the Aegean coast, followed by the Middle Helladic invasion of Greece, a most convincing picture is then created, not of independent disturbances, but of a single coherent chain of movements. If the arrival of the Hittites in Khattian Central Anatolia can be posited as the event which gave this movement its initial impetus, or for that matter if the one is to be in any way associated with the other, it will be a great deal easier to imagine Hittite immigration from an easterly direction than to bring them from the west, against the tide of contemporary displacements, as some scholars are disposed to do for philological reasons.

[1] §VI, 9, 46 ff.   [2] §I, 5, 10, 14, 33.   [3] §IV, 1, 178.

TROY III–IV–V

VII

FOLLOWING the destruction of Troy II, three further settlements rose one after the other on the site, all carrying on, with no discernible break, the culture that had gone before and all assignable to the closing stages of the Early Bronze Age. Since Schliemann in clearing the central part of the mound dug away, without adequate plans and records, almost all the deposit, averaging some six feet deep for each of these settlements, our only real stratigraphic information is derived from soundings by Dörpfeld and the work of the Cincinnati expedition.

The Third Settlement, which covered more ground than the Second, had a town plan with blocks of small houses separated by narrow streets. There may have been more stately buildings in the middle of the citadel, and perhaps there was a fortress wall, but no remains of these have survived. Characteristic of the architecture is the custom of building exterior house-walls entirely of stone instead of using crude brick for the superstructure. Implements of copper, stone, bone, and terracotta exhibit little change from what had preceded. Crude figures of animals in terracotta seem to be an innovation. The pottery is hardly distinguishable from that of Troy II in shapes and fabric. Face pots and face lids are common as are also tall slender two-handled cups. Flaring bowls occur in countless numbers.

Troy III endured through four chronological phases which are marked by superposed strata, some six feet deep altogether and suggesting a span of at least a century. How the town came to its end is not known, but there is no sign of a large conflagration. External relations continued to be primarily with the west, as is shown by a large quantity of imported Early Helladic pottery. Connexions undoubtedly also subsisted with Central Anatolia and Cilicia, but the evidence is still inadequate for precise synchronisms.

The Fourth Settlement was larger than the Third, but similar in its general lay-out. It certainly had a fortification wall, one section of which has been identified. What buildings stood in the central area of the citadel cannot now be determined, but there may have been a ruler's residence. Private houses seem now again to have been constructed with foundations of stone and a superstructure of crude brick. The minor objects and pottery recovered differ very little from those of Troy III, and again a clear continuity of culture is evident. Some small changes and developments may be noted, such as the gradual disappearance of flaring bowls and an innovation in the use of straw for tempering the clay in the making of coarse pottery; but there is nothing to point to any intrusion from outside.

The deposit, ranging from six to nine feet in depth, usually consists of three, in some places of five strata that seem to mark phases, and it is likely that the period lasted considerably more than a century. No traces of a great fire were observed, and it was not possible to ascertain what brought an end to the settlement. Imported Early Helladic pottery still occurs in some abundance, making it clear that relations with the Aegean continued to be maintained. Troy IV must also have kept in touch with the south Anatolian and Syrian coast, and perhaps via the same route with the central plateau.

The Fifth Settlement, like its predecessor, was undoubtedly a fortified stronghold, though little if anything of the wall itself has survived. Again we do not know what buildings occupied the middle of the citadel. In the outer fringes, however, new houses were erected, apparently of more complex plan than those of Troy IV. The walls were relatively thin and neatly built; hearths, ovens, and corner seats or benches are fairly regular features. Housekeeping had also improved, as a result of which most of the floors were found tidily swept and clean. The culture is nevertheless the same as that of the preceding settlements and there is no indication of appreciable outside influences. But in the minor objects and the pottery signs of gradual change and development are not lacking. The pottery both in fabric and shapes registers an improvement over what had gone before; well-made shallow rounded bowls bearing on the inside or the outside, or on both, a large cross painted in red bands are distinctive. Red-cross bowls of the same kind have been found at many places in central and southern Asia Minor and corresponding vessels are familiar in Early Helladic contexts on the Greek mainland.

The accumulated debris of Troy V had an average depth of five feet; it lay in some places in four clearly marked strata, and here too it is clear that we have to deal with successive phases that must have spanned a hundred years or more. The continued presence of imported Early Aegean pottery demonstrates that shipping still plied the seas to the westward; to what extent and how relations with the east were maintained is a more complicated question; but contacts were no doubt becoming more easy and frequent. The stratum representing the final phase of the settlement has yielded no evidence of a destructive fire, and the precise manner in which Troy V met its end is an unsolved problem.

Exact dates for Troy III, IV and V cannot be given, but it is likely that the three settlements together, with allowance for their twelve strata and phases, must account for some three or four centuries. The terminal date may provisionally be set some time between 1900 and 1800 B.C., but this figure depends on conjecture and analogies with the Aegean, where, however, the chronology has not yet been unshakably established.

CHAPTER XXIV(b)

ANATOLIA IN THE OLD ASSYRIAN PERIOD

VIII. HISTORY

THE oldest contact of Anatolia with the Akkadian-speaking peoples appears to go back to the time of the Dynasty of Agade. A legendary account, the so-called epic *King of the Battle*,[1] relates that a group of merchants from the Anatolian city of Purush-khanda sent a delegation to the king Sargon of Agade, urging him to undertake a campaign to their city and vividly describing the wealth of their country. Sargon is reported in the legend to have, after some hesitation, acceded to the merchants' request leading his troops to Purushkhanda.

Another historiographical text, the Legend of Naram-Sin,[2] implies that the city of Purushkhanda belonged to the realm of Sargon's grandson. Here it is related that a strange host, descending from the city of Shubat-Enlil in the country of Subartu, i.e. from northern Mesopotamia,[3] invaded Naram-Sin's kingdom, first attacking Purushkhanda and then, turning east and finally south, advanced toward the heartland of the Akkadian Empire. It is significant that Hittite versions of both of these tales have come to light at Boğazköy and that Sargon's exploits in Asia Minor are alluded to by the Hittite king Khattushilish I (c. 1650 B.C.) in an historical inscription;[4] for this tends to show that the later population of Anatolia considered the Old Akkadian period the beginning of their country's recorded history. It is further worth noting that in the *King of the Battle* one of the principal actors bore the name of Nur-daggal, which stands for Nur-Dagan. Since, in the belief of the Akkadians, the lands dominated by the god Dagan lay west and north-west of the city of Tuttul (near the mouth of the river Balīkh)[5] the name Nur-Dagan perhaps implies that the merchants of Purushkhanda were not Akkadians but western Semites who were anxious to enter into commercial relations with Akkad.

---

[1] See above, ch. XIX, sect. I, with references; also *Arch. f. Or.* 20 (1963), 161 f.
[2] See above, ch. XIX, sect. III; §VIII, 5.
[3] §VIII, 12, 331, n. 2.   [4] §VIII, 7.   [5] §VIII, 13, 15, n. 1.

The first ruler whose contacts with that part of Asia Minor which, in the Hellenistic period, was called Cappadocia, are well attested is Erishum I of Assyria (c. 1941–1902 B.C.).[1] Two copies of an original inscription of this king[2] recording his building activity in the complex of the Ashur temple in the city of Ashur were excavated in 1948 at Kültepe,[3] a site near the modern village of Karahüyük, not far from Kayseri in central Asia Minor. With this ruler began an era in the history of Asia Minor which is characterized by close political and economic ties with Assyria. The latter country, in the middle of the twentieth pre-Christian century, had initiated a policy of expansion which, to judge by two royal inscriptions of this period, served the purpose of establishing commercial relations with foreign countries. In an inscription dealing with his campaign to Babylonia, Erishum's father, King Ilushuma (c. 1962–1942) remarks: 'The freedom of movement[4] of the Akkadians and of their children I established. Copper for them I washed. From the marshy regions and the city of Ur and the city of Nippur, the city of Awal and the city of Kismar, the city of Dēr of the god Sataran up to the City [i.e Ashur] I established their freedom of movement.'[5] Accordingly, Ilushuma compelled the then overlord of Ur and Nippur, King Ishme-Dagan of Isin, and three vassal states of his, to grant the merchants of Akkad access to their cities and the right to market in these their own goods as well as merchandise which they purchased in Ashur. The phrase about 'washing copper' for them implies, on the other hand, that Ilushuma kept a state monopoly on the native copper found in countries dependent upon Assyria and processed through crushing and washing; but he obviously granted the Akkadian traders the privilege to purchase this copper from him and to sell it in their own country as well as in southern Babylonia. State monopolies of the copper trade existed in most ancient Near-Eastern countries. They were motivated by the fact that weapons of war were made of copper. By keeping the sale of the red metal in his own hands, a ruler could determine who was allowed to make, to market, and to own weapons.[6] However, Ilushuma's son, Erishum, relinquished this last state monopoly

---

[1] Dates assigned here to these Old Assyrian kings are some forty years earlier than those of the general scheme followed in *C.A.H.* Some explanation will be given in the following chapter.

[2] At this period the Assyrians used the title 'king' (*šarrum*) only for the national god Ashur. Their earthly rulers bore the titles *waklum* 'overseer', *iššiakkum* 'priest-prince' or *rubā'um* 'prince'.

[3] §VIII, 10.

[4] *adurār*; see §VIII, 20, 27, n. 57.

[5] §VIII, 25, 115, lines 49 ff.

[6] Cf. 1 Sam. xiii. 19 ff.

also, at least in so far as Assyria proper was concerned. In one of his inscriptions unearthed in Ashur he writes: 'I established the freedom of movement of silver, gold, copper, lead, wheat, wool', and two other commodities.[1]

Three sites in Asia Minor attest the eminent success of this Old Assyrian trade policy. Near the afore-mentioned village of Kültepe, the ancient city of Kanesh, thousands of inscribed clay tablets have been found, attesting the activity of Assyrian merchants who dispatched goods from their homeland to Anatolia, sold them there, and sent back to Ashur gold and silver, at least part of which was to be used for the purchase of more merchandise for export. Smaller archives of the same nature were found at Alişar, the ancient city of Ankuwa, and at Boğazköy, the site of the famous city of Khattum, or Khattusha, where, several centuries later, the Hittite kings established their residence.

In view of the commercial character of these archives, historical data are rather scanty. For the purpose of estimating the length of the period covered by the archives mention must be made of the date formulae which are found on numerous juridical documents, in particular promissory notes. In the manner practised by the Assyrians throughout their history, the years in these date-formulae were named after an eponym-official called *līmum* (*limmu*)[2] appointed annually at Ashur. Lists of these officials made it possible to ascertain their sequence, and the practice of making the king *līmum* in one of the early years of his reign served to co-ordinate the eponym-list with the king-list. However, neither of these lists has yet been found in Asia Minor.

The number of eponyms named in date-formulae on tablets from Asia Minor thus far amounts to about eighty-four.[3] Of these six occur on tablets from Boğazköy, five on texts from Alişar, and the remaining seventy-three on Kültepe tablets. There is some evidence, both archaeological and calendric, which indicates that the eighty-four years represented by these officials were not consecutive years, but that an older period of some seventy years, designated by the excavators of Kültepe as 'level II' must be distinguished from a very short later period, called by the excavators 'level I*b*'. The occurrence in the texts of some royal names combined with a prosopographic analysis of some of the prominent merchant families makes it possible to delimit the two periods. The name of King Ikunum, who appears to have

---

[1] §viii, 9, ii, no. 11, lines 20 ff.; §viii, 19, 99.   [2] See below, p. 742.
[3] §viii, 2, 79 ff.; corrections in §viii, 18, 34 ff.; additions in §viii, 21, 348 f. and in §viii, 3, 62 f.

ruled for only a few years, occurs in a promissory note from Kültepe.[1] His father, Erishum, was involved in one of the typical business operations which, however, dragged on beyond Erishum's lifetime, throughout Ikunum's reign, and into that of his son, Sharrum-kēn.[2] One of the documents recording this transaction is a letter, now preserved in the University Museum of Philadelphia,[3] which bears an impression of the seal of King Sharrum-kēn.[4] It is addressed to a merchant named Pūshu-kēn who is known from numerous letters and documents as the head of one of the prominent business houses. Mention is made in the letter of an interview which Pūshu-kēn had with Sharrum-kēn's father, Ikunum; and whereas the latter addressed the merchant as 'my son', King Sharrum-kēn respectfully called him 'my father'. Accordingly, Pūshu-kēn, while younger than Ikunum, must have been considerably older than King Sharrum-kēn. Pūshu-kēn's father, Sinea, on the other hand, who thus would have been a contemporary of Erishum I, does not appear as an acting person in the texts. It is, therefore, reasonable to conclude that the older period, represented by Kültepe level II, began during the last years of King Erishum I, which means around 1910 B.C.

Pūshu-kēn's sons and daughters are known to have carried on the business after their father's death. A grandson of his, another Pūshu-kēn, son of Buzazu, appears as a witness in an unpublished Kültepe text. The same three successive generations are traceable in the family of another outstanding member of the Assyrian business community, Enlil-bani. His father, Ashur-malik, was a contemporary of Pūshu-kēn, and, like the latter, the first acting member of the family appearing in the texts. One of Enlil-bani's sons, Nāb-Sin, is mentioned in numerous texts, either under his own name or as 'Enlil-bani's son'. The three generations, or seventy *līmum*-years, of the level II period, must accordingly have covered the years from around 1910 to 1840 B.C.

The above-mentioned letter in the Philadelphia Museum is not the only document attesting the rule of Sharrum-kēn during the period covered by the Kültepe texts. A tablet in Edinburgh[5] records a judgment by the highest court of Assyria which, as was traditional in the ancient Near East, was presided over by the

---

[1] §VIII, 15, 184; see below, p. 711.
[2] §VIII, 19, 101. [3] §VIII, 19, 99 f.
[4] On the legend of this seal see below, p. 711.
[5] §VIII, 4, no. 327. Three more impressions of Sharrum-kēn's seal are now known, §VIII, 16, plate v, fig. 4, and §VIII, 2, figs. 1–5.

king. In fact, the text begins by stating that the king (*waklum*)[1] sealed the case-tablet. The cylinder-seal which was rolled over the envelope bears this inscription: 'Sharrum-kēn, priest-prince of Ashur, son of Ikunum, priest-prince of Ashur.' A further text written under Sharrum-kēn's rule[2] lists, among various items carried by a caravan, 'five garments of Puzur-Ashur, son of the prince', obviously referring to Sharrum-kēn's son and successor, Puzur-Ashur II, as crown-prince. However, there is as yet no evidence to show that the archives covered either the reign of Puzur-Ashur II or that of his son, Naram-Sin.

The period in which the bulk of the Kültepe texts originated thus being definitely established, it is possible to interpret another group of seal impressions to which historical significance was attributed when they first became known. A case-tablet in the Louvre Museum was sealed with a cylinder bearing the following legend: 'Ibbi-Sin, the mighty king, king of Ur, king of the four quarters [of the world]; Ur-Lugalbanda, the scribe, the son of Ur-nigin-gar, is your servant'. This legend first led scholars to the belief that the tablet in question was written at the time of the last king of the Third Dynasty of Ur[3] (*c.* 2029–2006 B.C.), a conclusion which appeared all the more legitimate since the script as well as the seal impressions of the Kültepe tablets bear a considerable resemblance to those of the Ur III period. Yet a closer examination of the envelope and the enclosed tablet reveals that the seal was rolled over the case not by the scribe Ur-Lugalbanda but by an Assyrian royal scribe who, by using this seal, wished to emphasize that he was the legitimate successor of the royal scribe from Ur. An analysis of the persons involved in the text further reveals that they are all Assyrians, and that the scribe's royal lord was King Ikunum, the son of Erishum, and predecessor of Sharrum-kēn.[4] Two tablets recently excavated at Kültepe bear a seal with the legend: 'Ibbi-Sin, the mighty king, king of Ur'. In this case, the Assyrian owner of the seal had his own name, Amurru-bani, engraved on the cylinder besides the name of the king of Ur.[5] Even though the secondary use of the Ur III seals is thus proved beyond doubt, it remains an open question whether, slightly more than a century before the establishment of the Assyrians, the city of Kanesh and parts of the surrounding country had been under the domination of Ibbi-Sin of Ur. The very presence of the cylinder-seals from Ur at Kanesh

[1] See above, p. 708, n. 2.   [2] §VIII, 6, no. 58, line 24.
[3] §VIII, 24.   [4] §VIII, 15, 184.
[5] §VIII, 22, 124.

may be taken to point in this direction even though no other supporting evidence has come to light as yet.

As regards the later period of Assyrian settlement in Central Anatolia, a text acquired in the years before systematic excavations were undertaken at Kültepe is dated by the eponym Awilia.[1] This official is known by texts from Chagar-Bazar as well as from Mari[2] to have held office at the time when Iasmakh-Adad ruled over Mari, which means in the last few years of the reign of King Shamshi-Adad I (1813–1781 B.C.).[3] Since, according to the previous computation, the older period ended around 1840 B.C., or some 25 years before the accession of Shamshi-Adad I, it is obvious that the year named after Awilia belonged to the later, or 'Ib', period of Assyrian occupation. The conclusion that this later period coincided with Iasmakh-Adad's rule over Mari is compatible with its comparative shortness as evidenced by the dearth of tablets as well as by the small number of eponym-years as compared with those of the older period; for Iasmakh-Adad's rule lasted no more than nine years.[4] It was preceded by some four or five years during which Shamshi-Adad reconquered from Iakhdunlim of Khana the region of Mari and Terqa as well as the Khabur valley. Since, during these years, the newly con-quered region was not incorporated yet into the Assyrian Empire, no *līmum* dates were being used at Mari. Instead, the documents were dated by formulae in Babylonian style recording events of Shamshi-Adad's reign.[5] Even so, this conquest restored the communications between Assyria and Asia Minor which, of necessity, had been interrupted when the king of Khana expanded his realm by conquering seven neighbouring kingdoms, including Zalmaqum in northern Mesopotamia.[6] With Iasmakh-Adad's defeat and the installation on the throne of Mari of Zimrilim, hitherto king of Khana, these communications obviously were interrupted again; for Zimrilim ruled not only over the Euphrates valley down to the Babylonian border but also over the Khabur valley and northern Mesopotamia. Accordingly, the later period of Assyrian activity in Cappadocia is likely to have lasted for no more than fourteen years, i.e. as mentioned before, nine years of Iasmakh-Adad during which Assyrian *līmum* dates were used at

---

[1] §VIII, 4, no. 276; §VII, 2, 43 f.

[2] §VIII, 1, vol. VII, 170, with n. 1. That Awilia's eponym-year occurred in that part of Iasmakh-Adad's rule which fell before his father's death can be inferred from §VIII, 1, vol. VIII, no. 9.

[3] Cf. §VIII, 14, 445 ff.   [4] *Ibid.*

[5] §VIII, 23, 53, nos. 1–4; add perhaps the formula in §VII, 1, vol. VIII, no. 45.

[6] §VIII, 23, 52, no. 2. On the conquests of Iakhdunlim of Khana see §VIII, 11.

Mari and five years with names in Babylonian style preceding his accession. If the Mari texts contain altogether about eighteen different names of eponyms[1] this is due to the fact that they cover three unconnected periods of Assyrian overlordship, *viz.*, several years (including that of Ibni-Adad) before Shamshi-Adad's accession, several years of Sumu-iamam,[2] and the years of Iasmakh-Adad.

Whereas the end of the later period thus appears to be historically well established, the question remains to be answered what caused the apparent eclipse of the Assyrians between the end of the older and the beginning of the more recent epoch. In this respect attention must be called to the occurrence on tablets from Kültepe and Alişar of the names of several non-Assyrian princes who are known from Hittite sources. A promissory note excavated in 1925[3] bears this unique date formula 'When Labarsha took over the princely functions'. Regardless of whether this take-over was a legitimate accession to an ancestral throne or a seizure following a conquest, the new ruler does not appear to have interfered with the activities of the Assyrian merchants; for the text stipulates that the debt recorded in the promissory note was payable as soon as the creditor, who bore the Semitic name Idi-Ishtar, should return from Khattum. The mention of Khattum raises the question whether it was the throne of this city-state to which Labarsha acceded and whether, accordingly, this Labarsha is identical with the King Labarnash who, according to Hittite tradition, heads the list of Hittite kings of the so-called Old Kingdom.[4] Labarnash was accorded a special place in Hittite history because he allegedly enlarged his original kingdom by conquering the entire territory which separated it from the sea. If, however, it was Kanesh where Labarnash took over the throne, this date formula would represent the moment when a native replaced a Semite as prince of Kanesh.[5] For the present discussion it is important to note that the Assyrian merchants, while finding this accession an event sufficiently important to replace with this unusual formula their usual dating by month and eponym, did not discontinue or interrupt their commercial activities.

A similar conclusion can be reached with respect to the city of Zalpa; here it can be shown that, about the time of the second of

---

[1] Seventeen of these in §viii, 23, 53 f.; the eighteenth is Akhiia-aia whose eponym-year occurs in §vii, 1, vol. viii, no. 52.

[2] §viii, 11.

[3] §viii, 8, 1 no. 178, lines 2 ff.; §ix, 13, 114.

[4] See *C.A.H.* ii³, ch. vi, sect. iv.   [5] See §viii, 15, 181 ff.

the three generations of Assyrian merchants traceable in the level II period, a political change took place, Assyrian domination of the city being replaced by that of a native ruler.[1] Yet there too the Assyrians continued their business without interruption, no doubt because the native rulers found it to their own advantage to maintain the export–import trade at a high level.

The names of several local princes are mentioned in texts dealing with the affairs of the native population. The most noteworthy among these princes occur in the divorce record of a non-Assyrian couple which contains the following clause: ' In the hand of Pitkhana, the prince; Anitta [was] commander of the fortress '.[2] The Hittite inscription of a King Anitta, son of Pitkhana, found at Boğazköy, relates how this king, extending his father's conquests, took over large parts of eastern Anatolia and, after having conquered and destroyed Khattusha, the subsequent capital of the Hittite kings, assumed the title 'great king'. Proof of the identity of this King Anitta with the 'commander of the fortress' of the Kültepe tablet is furnished by one of the documents excavated at Ališar. Dealing with the release of six native prisoners, this text contains the clause: ' In the hand of Anitta, the great prince; Peruwa was commander of the fortress'. Another text from Ališar, obviously somewhat earlier, refers merely to 'Anitta, the prince'.[3] Still another text from Ališar, this one from the Assyrian settlement, refers to the ruler of the town as 'the princess' and her 'commander of the fortress', it being a priori uncertain whether this princess preceded or followed Anitta.[4] To round out the evidence concerning Anitta, it must be mentioned that a dagger bearing the inscription 'palace of Anitta, the prince', was unearthed on the mound proper of Kültepe—that is to say, not in, or near, the Assyrian settlement which was located in the plain surrounding the mound.[5]

Owing to the fact that three of the native witnesses of the divorce record mentioning Anitta's father, Pitkhana, can be traced in documents involving Assyrians, it is possible to integrate these native rulers into the three-generation scheme previously established for the Assyrians. The first of these witnesses was Khaduwa, who appears also in two documents[6] listing

---

[1] §viii, 15, 196 ff.

[2] Literally, 'chief of the stairway'; see the text §ix, 19, no. 214, studied in §viii, 17, 2, 111 ff.; and see *C.A.H.* ii³, ch. vi, sect. iii.

[3] §viii, 6, nos. 49 and 1 respectively.

[4] *Ibid.* no. 5.   [5] §viii, 2, 78.

[6] §ix, 19, no. 158; also in §ix, 3, no. 163; see §viii, 17, 2, 124 f.

bundles of cloth which were presented as gifts to various natives, among them Khaduwa and the 'chief of the weapons'. These textiles are said to have been brought up 'to the palace', whence it seems that, as in the afore-quoted divorce record, Khaduwa was an official of the local prince. Now the list of textiles also states that the *kārum* at the place where this prince resided received some of the items for the account of Shu-Ishtar, son of Ilish-tikkal, and he is attested as a contemporary of the well-known Imdi-ilum,[1] who belonged to the first generation of Assyrian merchants.

Two more of the witnesses in the first-named deed of divorce are found again in another deed of divorce[2] in the company of a certain Ennanum, son of Alabum, and this man again is attested[3] as a contemporary of Imdi-ilum.

From all this it results that Pitkhana was himself a contemporary of the first generation of Assyrian merchants, and probably a vassal of the Assyrian king, for in the second deed of divorce mentioned above[4] it is said that two of the natives concerned in the action swore an oath 'by the City' (i.e. Ashur). Furthermore, according to the afore-cited list of textiles,[5] Pitkhana's principality was the seat of a *kārum*, and it will be shown[6] that the Assyrian governing-body was called *kārum* only in those city-states where the local ruler had submitted to Assyrian supremacy.

Consequently Anitta and the conquests which prompted him to assume the title 'great prince' fell within the second generation of Assyrian merchants at Kanesh. It is therefore unlikely that his expansionist policy was the cause, or a contributing cause, of the abrupt end to the older period of Assyrian occupation at Kültepe. As will be seen below, the end of the 'level II' period is more likely to have been brought about by circumstances which made the caravan traffic between Assyria and Asia Minor unprofitable.

IX. PEOPLES AND GOVERNMENT

At the time of the Assyrian penetration into Asia Minor this region was divided into a considerable number of small city-states each of which was ruled by a native prince (*rubā'um*) or princess (*rubātum*). Establishing a pattern of domination which subsequent generations of Assyrian rulers followed throughout their country's history, the Assyrians left these rulers unmolested on

---

[1] §viii, 4, no. 298; §ix, 26, v, 41 *b*.   [2] §viii, 4, no. 6.
[3] §viii, 8, ii, no. 78.   [4] §viii, 4, no. 6.
[5] §ix, 19, no. 158.   [6] See below, p. 722 f.; §viii, 15, 189 ff.

their thrones if they were willing to submit to Assyrian supremacy. A vassalage treaty was concluded and sworn to by the two contracting parties by their respective gods, and the local prince became a 'son' of the Assyrian king who frequently sent a female member of the royal house to marry his new vassal and troops to protect his kingdom.[1]

Among the few non-commercial documents that have come to light at Kültepe there are several which allude to the oath of allegiance sworn by a native ruler to the Assyrian authorities. In one of these texts it is reported that messengers of the Assyrian governing body of the town of Durkhumid had requested an audience with the prince of Tamnia in order to make him swear the oath; however, the prince refused to have the oath administered by the envoys from Durkhumid, asking instead that 'his fathers', the authorities of Kanesh, should come and administer the oath to him.[2] In another letter, the Assyrian administration of the town of Wakhshushana reports to its superiors at Kanesh that a message arrived from the prince of the city-state of Washkhania informing the Assyrians that he had acceded to his father's throne and added: 'Make me swear the oath!'[3] In an unpublished letter, finally, the prince of the town of Khurumu-[. . .] writes to the Assyrian authorities at Kanesh: 'I am your son! I hold on to the oath.'[4]

To judge by the name Peruwa borne by the youngest member of the afore-mentioned dynasty of Kushshar, ethnically at least some of the native princes were Indo-Europeans, either Hittites or Luwians.[5] The same seems to be true of the princes Warshama and Warpa known to have ruled at Kanesh.[6] As regards the subjects of these rulers, the numerous documents dealing with the affairs of natives contain male and female personal names which can be regarded as Hittite or Luwian.[7] On the other hand, it cannot be denied that among the geographical as well as among the native personal names a considerable number are Hurrian. It is certainly not a mere coincidence that the Cappadocian city name Ullama recurs as Ulamme in the region of Nuzi, near Kirkuk, where it is found in documents from the fifteenth pre-Christian century written in Akkadian by a Hurrian population.

[1] §VIII, 1, vol. VI, no. 26; §VIII, 12, 343 f.   [2] §VIII, 2, 73 f.; §VIII, 18, 27 ff.

[3] §IX, 28, no. 14; §IX, 22, 17 ff.

[4] *anāku mērakunu mamītam ukāl*.

[5] Texts relating to the god Pirwa are written in both Hittite and Luwian, §IX, 25, 68 ff.

[6] On the former §VIII, 3; on the latter §IX, 4, no. 122, lines 15 f.

[7] §VIII, 9, 74 ff.; §IX, 10, 48 f.; §IX, 8, 133 ff.

Hurrian also are the Anatolian town-names Taishama,[1] Taia,[2] Khurrama, and possibly Mama.[3] Since, according to the Mari texts, Hurrian princes[4] ruled over parts of northern Mesopotamia, from the slopes of the Ṭūr-'Abdīn westward, in the time of Shamshi-Adad I, it might appear that the region about the headwaters of the Khabur, subsequently the heart-land of the great kingdom of Khanigalbat, had previously been the centre of a Hurrian territory extending far beyond the Euphrates into Asia Minor.

Among the Hurrian personal names occurring in the Old Assyrian tablets the most typical are Zigi ('the little one'), Irwi-sharri ('The Lord is King'), Enish(ar)ru ('God is King'), and Taia, all of which are well known from the Nuzi documents.[5] Unlike the Indo-Europeans whom the Assyrians contemptuously designated as 'barbarians' (*nu'ā'ū*), the Hurrians appear to have dealt with the Assyrians on equal terms. Enishru was one of the most influential merchants in Kanesh who controlled a considerable part of the trade in cereals and other agricultural products, buying grain futures from the Indo-European farmers and granting them loans at high rates of interest. His daughter, Khatala, married an Assyrian.[6] Another Hurrian, Irwi-sharri, was treated like one of their own men by Pūshu-kēn, the aforementioned prominent Assyrian merchant, and his associates.[7]

Among the Semitic population, a distinction can be made between the Assyrians and the Amorites. The members of the Assyrian business community who left the bulk of the Old Assyrian texts belonged to the same aristocratic families which, in the mother country, furnished the eponym officials. Usually, the senior member of the family resided in Assyria and directed from there the export–import business with Cappadocia. The younger generation, in the meantime, managed the subsidiaries of the firm in the different towns in Asia Minor, especially in Kanesh, returning to Assyria only when the head of the family died or retired from business. Frequently their wives remained in Assyria, taking care of their houses and bringing up their children. In these cases, the men concluded temporary marriages with native women in Cappadocia, with the understanding that the alliance could be dissolved at any time by either of the contracting

[1] §viii, 3,6, lines 5, 9, 19; also *Taišuḫ(we)* in the Nuzi text §ix, 2, 23, lines 5, 6, 31.
[2] §viii, 3, 35, line 11.   [3] §ix, 24, 53 ff.
[4] E.g. Shukru-Teshub of Elakhut, *C.A.H.* ii³, ch. i, sect. iv
[5] For Hurrian personal names in the Old Assyrian texts see §ix, 8, 155 ff., but also *O.L.Z.* 60 (1965), col. 148, n. 1.
[6] §viii, 8, i nos. 3, 67, 69.   [7] §ix, 19, no. 276, lines 14, 19.

parties against payment of divorce-money. Whenever the Assyrian husband was ready to return permanently to his homeland, he paid off his native wife and took, if he so desired, the children with him to Assyria.

Even the smaller communities had their own temple of Ashur, the national god, which contained the deity's statue, emblems, and cult objects. In a letter addressed to their superiors at Kanesh, the authorities of one of the provincial towns wrote that thieves entered their local temple of Ashur and stole all the gold and silver objects including a golden sun from the god's breast.[1] Golden suns as votive gifts for Ashur and other deities are repeatedly mentioned in the business letters, in one instance as much as one mina, or approximately one pound, of gold being spent for its manufacture.

In many of the aristocratic families at least one daughter was dedicated to the service of Ashur or one of the other protective deities of Assyria. In two letters, the wife of a prominent merchant writes to her husband in Kanesh: 'The little girl has grown considerably; arise, come here, and lay her in Ashur's lap and grasp your god's foot.'[2] The title of at least some of the priestesses was *gubābtum*, whereas some others served as *qadištum*. In messages to their relatives abroad these priestesses frequently promised to pray to their god or gods for the addressees. Other typically Assyrian deities figuring prominently in the religious life of the community were Sin, the Moon-god; Ishtar, the planet Venus; Ishtar-ṣād, the star Sirius; Adad, the weather god; and Shamash, the Sun-god. Besides, each family or clan had its own protective deity which was usually referred to as 'my god' or 'your god' or 'our god', frequently also as 'the god of our fathers'.[3] In tablets recording the last will of some of the prominent merchants, it is sometimes stipulated which among the testator's heirs should inherit the statues of these family gods. That these figurines belonged to the most valuable assets of a family can be gathered from the fact that, in case of a financial crisis, they could be pledged as security for a debt.

As regards the language used by the Old Assyrian merchants, it is a highly literary but archaic Akkadian dialect which, however, exhibits most of the features distinguishing the later Assyrian dialect from Babylonian.[4] To mention only a few, regressive vowel harmony is applied consistently, the shift of

---

[1] See the text partly translated in §ix, 14, 11.
[2] §ix, 26, iii, pl. 20, lines 38 ff.   [3] §ix, 18, 51 ff.; §ix, 11, 35 ff.
[4] §ix, 16, 39 f.

initial *wa* to *u* is in the state of development, the treatment of the weak verb closely parallels that of Middle Assyrian. In contradistinction to Middle Assyrian, however, mimation is used by most scribes and probably the *m* was pronounced throughout. The shift of *št* to *lt* had not yet taken place, and double consonants are rarely expressed in writing. The characteristically slanted cuneiform signs, while bearing a certain resemblance to those used under the Third Dynasty of Ur, differ radically from the Middle Assyrian forms; *d*, *t*, and *ṭ* are not distinguished in writing, nor are *g*, *k*, and *q* or *z*, *s*, and *ṣ*. The plural sign MEŠ is unknown, the plural being indicated after ideograms by the symbol ḪI.A. The use of ideograms is very limited, and determinatives before personal and geographical names are rarely employed, but word dividers are very frequent. The rows of script are usually separated from each other by straight lines drawn with a ruler. The scribe's name is not given in the text unless a scribe appears among the acting persons. Many letters and juridical documents are enclosed in clay envelopes on which the seals were impressed. Sealed single tablets are very rare and record only transactions involving natives.

The second Semitic element of the population of Anatolia at the time of the Old Assyrian texts was formed by western Semites whom the Assyrians called Amorites.[1] Whereas there is no doubt that many of these Amorites were permanent residents of Assyria who came to Asia Minor with the Assyrians, there is evidence to indicate that others had settled in Anatolia, perhaps even before the arrival of the Assyrians. To be sure, there are no written records in the Old West Semitic language spoken by the Amorites, but it is significant that the term by which the Old Assyrian tablets designate the priests of Akkadian as well as of non-Akkadian deities is *kumrum*, the Assyrianized form of the Aramaic term for priest. The passing of this word into the Old Assyrian language was obviously the concomitant of the reception into the pantheon of several West Semitic deities. Evidence to this effect comes from personal names containing theophorous elements such as Dagan,[2] Tibar (occurring in the name Shu-Tibar),[3] Laban,[4] and Ilaprat. The latter deity's name occurs not

[1] §VIII, 4, 148, note a. That these were not nomads is established in §IX, 23.

[2] For this god as ruler of western Mesopotamia and northern Syria see the inscription §IX, 12, 37 ff. ('Sargon b 2').

[3] §VIII, 8, 1, no. 96, ll. 3 f. The god Tibar belongs to Mt. Tibar in Palestine, see §IX, 7, 191 ff. and §IX, 21, 357 ff.

[4] The frequent name Shu-Laban reflects the worship of the Moon-god in the region of the Lebanon.

infrequently in solemn affirmations together with that of the Assyrian national god. Thus we find in a letter addressed by a priest to his son: 'May Ashur and Ilaprat look on [as witnesses],'[1] or, even more characteristically, 'may Ashur and Ilaprat, the god of our fathers, look on [as witnesses] !'[2] In another letter of the same correspondence, mention is made of a sun-emblem for Ilaprat made of fifteen shekels of gold.[3] By nature, he appears to have been a fertility god of much the same type as Tammuz, the Sumerian equivalent being NIN-ŠUBUR, 'The Lord Boar'. Some conclusions about the original home of the cult of Ilaprat can be derived from the Bible which defines the Hebrew equivalent of the name Ilaprat, viz., Efrath, as an old name of the city of Bethlehem.[4] In view of the widespread practice of the ancient Semites in giving towns the name of the principal deity worshipped there it might appear that Ilaprat was originally the god of the town of Efrath (Bethlehem). This conclusion is well in line with a statement in Saint Jerome to the effect that, at the time when the fertility cult of Bethlehem enjoyed the protection of the Roman overlords of Palestine, the sculptured head of a swine adorned the gate by which one left Jerusalem for Bethlehem.[5]

Another west Semitic god whose name is a theophorous element in Old Assyrian personal names is Amurrum; this deity, too, is invoked by some of the writers of Old Assyrian letters in the formula 'May Ashur and Amurrum, the god of my father, look on [as witnesses] !'[6] It is not without significance that the god Anna, who was considered by the Amorites the father of their god Amurrum,[7] was recognized by the Semitic as well as by the non-Semitic inhabitants of Kanesh as their city's patron god. Evidence to this effect is contained in two contracts in which the oath is sworn by Ashur, Anna, and the prince,[8] a formula in which (as in contemporary Babylonian documents from Sippar, Larsa, and elsewhere) the first-named deity was the god of the country and the second the numen of the city in which the contract was concluded. The fact that a west Semitic deity was the patron god of Kanesh tends to indicate that the Amorite community of this city looked back to a long and well-established

---

[1] §IX, 4, no. 15, lines 17 f.; §IX, 18, 51.

[2] §IX, 26, III, pl. 16b, lines 4 ff.   [3] §IX, 27, no. 30, lines 3 ff.

[4] As in Gen. xxxv. 19; xlviii. 7; Ruth iv. 11; Micah v. 2.

[5] Eusebi Chronicorum libri duo (ed. A. Schoene), vol. II, 169 (year 2153 of Abraham).

[6] E.g. §IX, 26, v, pl. 1a, lines 31 ff.   [7] §IX, 23, 37.

[8] §VIII, 8, 1, no. 32, lines 10 ff. An unpublished contract names in addition an official, the rabi sikkıtım.

tradition. It is well in line with this conclusion that Kanesh was, so far as can be judged by the material at present available, the only town in Anatolia where the local prince, at least at one time, was a Semite.[1]

As the Amorites were assimilated to the Assyrians to such an extent as to be almost indistinguishable from them, it seems hazardous to attribute to them a particular function in the trade between Ashur and Cappadocia. Yet it deserves mention that a town in the immediate vicinity of the city of Ashur was named Amurrum and that this town or suburb was the place where the caravans destined for Asia Minor were assembled.[2] As there can hardly be any doubt that the town of Amurrum was so named because the majority of its inhabitants were worshippers of the god Amurrum, it would thus appear that these westerners were particularly active in the shipping and transportation business.

For their governing body the Assyrians used the term *kārum* followed by the name of the respective city: *kārum Kaneš*, *kārum Purušḫaddum*, etc.[3] The actual seat of the government was the *kārum*-house which, at least in so far as Kanesh was concerned, was situated in the plain at the foot of the mound on which the *ekallum*, or residence of the prince, was located. Whereas primarily the *kārum* was an office where collectors of revenue were stationed,[4] the function of these Old Assyrian establishments in Anatolia was manifold: first, they collected tolls and taxes from the arriving caravans and had the power to enforce the payment of these duties in cases where the merchants tried to circumvent them. To judge by one tablet,[5] the *kārum Kanesh*, for this purpose, occasionally dispatched envoys to cities such as Khurrama and Timilkia where the so-called 'danger-road' (*ḫarrān sukīnim*) branched off from the main highway to Kanesh in the direction of Durkhumid, Zalpa, and Khattum.[6] Since by way of this road merchandise could be conveyed without passing through the customs offices at Kanesh, these envoys, who are known to have 'seized' some of the travelling merchants, obviously acted to enforce the payment of the import duty. Secondly, these bodies

[1] §ix, 22, 24 ff.; §viii, 15, 181 ff.

[2] §ix, 23, 48 and 62 ff.

[3] Besides these two the following are attested as seats of a *kārum*: Durkhumid, Khahhum, Khattusha (Boğazköy), Khurrama (near modern Elbistan), Nikhriia, Tawinia (in the region of modern Sungurlu, §ix, 6, 12), Urshu, Wakhshushana, and Zalpa (Alaca Hüyük, see §ix, 5, 239); see also §ix, 22, 66, n. 280.

[4] §ix, 22, 37 ff. The designation ot both seaports and riverports as *kārum* is obviously due to the collection there of import duties (*miksi kāri neberi*, §viii, 9, 1, no. 51, col. iii, 6).　　[5] §ix, 17, no. 7 *b*.　　[6] §ix, 15, 103 f.

were the superiors (fathers) of the native princes who had submitted to Assyrian supremacy.[1] Thirdly, they functioned as
courts of justice and saw to it that their decisions were carried out.
An instance of this kind may be quoted;[2] a merchant had left a
debt unpaid in the town of Shinakhūtum which belonged to the
district administered by the *kārum Puruṧḫaddum*. This latter body
ordered the merchant to return to Shinakhūtum and to pay the
debt within ten days. It dispatched one of its own officers to
accompany the delinquent debtor and to make sure that the debt
was actually paid. In another case[3] the *kārum Puruṧḫaddum* had
paid a debt for two Assyrians, and then entrusted the same
officer with the task of collecting the money in equal parts from
the two debtors. Fourthly, the *kārum* provided storage facilities
for merchandise and, lastly, acted as a financial institution, extending credit to, and maintaining accounts of, individual merchants
and groups of merchants.

The *kārum Kaneṧ* had special functions in so far as it was the
superior of all the others. Together with the 'envoy of the City
[i.e. Ashur]', it received orders from the government at home
which it transmitted to these others. In one instance, the metropolitan government requested ten minas of silver for the construction of fortifications;[4] the *kārum Kaneṧ* was advised to levy
this amount from the others under its control and forward the
money to Ashur. The *kārum Puruṧḫaddum*, too, had special
functions. To judge by the legendary traditions referred to above,
Purushkhaddum appears to have held a privileged position since
the very beginning of Anatolian history. It obviously owed this
status to the proximity of copper deposits and the ensuing concentration of trade in copper and copper products. According to
researches conducted on the site in 1958 by J. Lewy, the city is most
likely to be buried under the huge mound known today as Acem
Hüyük located some ten miles west-north-west of Aksaray. As indicated by the name Madenşehir, 'Mine City', of a district (today
completely abandoned) south of Aksaray, mines appear actually to
have existed in that region. In the Old Assyrian as well as in the
Hittite period, Purushkhaddum, obviously owing to its wealth,
was the seat of a 'great prince' (*rubā'um rabīum*). As regards the
kārum of Purushkhaddum, it appears to have controlled the
mining operations in the city's surroundings, because it was one

---

[1] See above, p. 716. [2] §vIII, 8, vol. I, no. 21.
[3] *Ibid.* no. 26.
[4] See in particular the letter §IX, 4, no. 1, translated in §IX, 8, 197, discussed in §IX, 22, 65 ff.

of the main centres of supply of raw copper. It sold large quantities of copper-ore to the Assyrian merchants who dispatched it to the smelting-furnaces, operated mainly by natives; by this process they were said either 'to make [it] long-lasting'[1] or 'to turn the copper into refined [metal]'.[2] This was then either sold or used as currency in Asia Minor.

Towns under the jurisdiction of the *kārum Kaneš* which were too small to have a *kārum* of their own were ruled by a body called 'the decade', apparently a group of ten of the town's senior citizens.[3] In those parts of Anatolia, however, where the local princes had not submitted to Assyrian rule but were nevertheless anxious to maintain trade relations with foreign merchants, the Assyrians were organized in what the Kültepe texts call *wubartum* or *ubartum*.[4] The settlements so designated were located at some distance from the native community of the same name, and they comprised not only merchants but also military personnel. As was customary in the ancient Near East, soldiers and officers were settled on farmland in the surroundings of the native towns, thus fulfilling a double function—while holding the natives in check and being ready to defend their region in case of an emergency, they were self-supporting farmers[5] who paid their taxes to the government. The Assyrian authorities thus were able to control the roads over which their merchants and military supplies travelled while, at the same time, avoiding sieges of unfriendly towns the conquest of which might have been costly in material and human lives. On the other hand, it is self-evident that friction between the native troops stationed in the citadel of the town proper and the Assyrian soldiers in the surroundings was almost unavoidable. In fact, whenever the texts allude to hostilities between the Semites and the natives, they occurred in, or near, *wubartum*-settlements.[6]

X. THE ARTICLES OF TRADE

The merchandise which the caravans transported from Ashur to Asia Minor consisted almost exclusively of commodities called *ṣubat kutānu* and *annukum*, textiles and a metal. From the rather

---

[1] *ka"unum*; §IX, 26, 1, pl. 19*b*, lines 1–5, and pl. 22*a*, lines 1 ff.

[2] *eri'am ana dammuqim tu'ārum*.   [3] §VIII, 4, 255, n. *a*.

[4] §VIII, 15, 189 ff. The following *wubartum*-settlements are found in the texts: Ankuwa (modern Ališar), Badna, Karakhna, Khanaknak, Mama, Shalatiwar, Shamukha, Tukhpia, Ullama, Washkhania, and possibly Kushshara (see §IX, 24); §IX, 22, 59, n. 251.   [5] §IX, 22, 62 ff.   [6] §VIII, 15, 195 f.

uniform size and weight of the former it can be concluded that a *ṣubat kutānu* was a piece of cloth sufficient for one garment for a grown-up person.[1] For transport, the cloths were either wrapped in other cloths or put into bags designed to preserve the merchandise from the hazards of the weather. These containers were then loaded on asses at a rate of about twenty-five parcels to each animal. In addition to the cloths packed and sealed in the containers, most shipments comprised some pieces designated as 'cloths on hand'. These were sold *en route* by the ass-drivers and other caravan personnel and thus served to defray their travel expenses. Besides cloths of Assyrian manufacture, the merchants frequently re-exported cloths which they themselves bought from foreign traders such as e.g. Babylonians.[2] The prices of the parcels of cloth varied considerably not only in accordance with the quality but also depending upon supply and demand. The sale-price in Asia Minor amounted to approximately three times the purchase price in Assyria,[3] which is not surprising if the length of the haul and the hazards of the journey are taken into consideration.

The identity of the metal *annukum* has been for many years a matter of controversy, some maintaining that it was lead whereas others believed that it was tin. At present, the evidence is overwhelmingly in favour of lead; in the first place, because this metal is found in abundance in the valley of the Greater Zab river, in the immediate vicinity of the capital city of Ashur, in territory under Assyrian control. In the second place, numerous leaden objects, pots and figurines as well as heavy sarcophagi, were discovered by the excavators both at Kültepe and at Ashur, whereas no objects of tin were found in either place. The purpose of the lead-exports to Asia Minor is not expressly stated in any of the extant texts since it was known to all concerned. Yet the unusual abundance of silver in circulation among the Assyrians in Anatolia suggests that the primary use of the lead was in the production of silver. As is well known, lead ores such as galena contain a small percentage of silver which can be recovered by the so-called cupellation process. This method, which all primitive metallurgists were able to carry out,[4] is based on the observation that lead is easily oxidized while the noble metals, silver and gold, remain unchanged. In antiquity, there probably was enough wood in the valley of the Greater Zab to generate the temperatures necessary for the de-silvering process at, or near, the place

---

[1] §x, 2, 183, n. 6.
[2] Cloths of Babylonian make were called 'cloths of the Akkadians'.
[3] §ix, 8, 289.   [4] §x, 4, 79 ff.

in Assyria proper where the lead was mined. However, large amounts of lead are also needed in de-silvering copper ores, for this requires two cupellation-processes—in the first the copper is oxidized and the non-oxidized silver is dissolved in the lead; in the second the silver is separated from the lead. Now since, at the time of the Old Assyrian texts, Asia Minor possessed a highly developed copper industry, it is likely that the de-silvering of copper ore was the primary purpose of the lead imports. In fact, the mention in several texts of the copper centre Purush-khaddum as the ultimate destination of such lead consignments and as the place of origin of the silver expected to 'come forth' in the process,[1] supports this conclusion. It also accounts for the abrupt end of the Assyrian caravan traffic to Asia Minor which, as was seen above,[2] cannot be explained on the basis of political developments. But as soon as the natives of Asia Minor dis-covered that their own country was rich in galena, the shipments of lead from Assyria became uneconomical and therefore had to be discontinued.[3]

The price of lead fluctuated less than that of textiles. The average quantity of the metal obtained at Ashur for 1 shekel of silver varied between 12 and 16 shekels, to all appearances depending upon the percentage of silver it contained or was assumed to contain. The sale-price in Anatolia averaged 1 shekel of silver for 6–8 shekels of lead.[4] The lead was carried by asses, each being loaded with a maximum charge of $2\frac{1}{2}$ talents[5] (i.e. approximately 150 pounds). The asses used for this purpose are described in the texts as 'black asses', which probably means that they belonged to the dark-haired, particularly strong breed known to-day as Damascus asses.[6] The owner in Ashur pur-chased the asses for each journey and the driver sold them upon the arrival of the caravan at its destination. As the texts never mention caravans proceeding from Anatolia to Assyria, the sale and subsequent re-purchase of the beasts of burden apparently was more economical for the owner than an empty east-bound trip would have been. The equipment which, together with the food for the asses, was likewise purchased at Ashur for each journey was also sold on arrival in Asia Minor.

Among the articles traded by the Assyrians wool is sometimes mentioned. The best wool came from Mama, a caravan station in

---

[1] E.g. §IX, 27, no. 205, line 20.   [2] See above, p. 715.

[3] According to §VIII, 2, 42 the tablets from the later level of the Assyrian settle-ment at Kültepe make no mention of caravan-traffic.

[4] §IX, 8, 280.   [5] §X, 2, 183 ff.   [6] §IX, 23, 74.

the plain of Elbistan in eastern Anatolia, whence it was shipped to both Kanesh and Ashur. Agricultural products play a certain part in the local trade between various Anatolian cities, but the major article of the intra-Anatolian commerce was copper. It was transported both on donkey-back and by waggon. Large quantities, up to 10,000 minas,[1] were sent from the producer to the processor, from there to the fabricator, and finally on to the eventual user. In the trade with natives, copper served as currency. For this purpose it was shaped into the form of small tools such as sickles, axes, or plough-shares which were weighed out to the recipient.

The silver and gold which the Assyrian merchants traded for their lead and textiles was not transported to Ashur by caravan but was carried by trustworthy, speedy messengers. These were, to all appearances, the same men who carried the mail between the capital and the distant province. So far as can be seen, they left both cities at regular intervals throughout the travelling season which extended from spring into the late autumn. During the cold and rainy season communications, both east- and west-bound, came to a standstill and it seems that at least four months elapsed before traffic was resumed. This is not surprising since, no matter by which route they travelled through northern Mesopotamia, the caravans had to pass through difficult mountainous terrain once they reached the Antitaurus chain. In fact, some of the road junctions frequently mentioned in the texts such as Khurrama, modern Elbistan,[2] lie as high as 3300 feet above sea level, while the mountains surrounding it reach a height of almost 9000 feet. It is, therefore, reasonable to assume that these roads became impassable by the end of October or early in November.[3] In Anatolia itself, particularly between Kanesh and the towns further west, communications remained open much longer. Before reaching Asia Minor other climatic problems had to be reckoned with. Nowadays the direct road leading westward from Ashur through the desert and north of the Jebel Sinjār to the Upper Khabur is passable only in spring and in the autumn, since the river Tharthar alongside which this road runs is dry during the summer months. According to the Arab geographers, however, the Tharthar was, in antiquity, a navigable stream. There is as yet no evidence whether in the Old Assyrian period the caravans were able to proceed on this road during the hot season, or whether they travelled, like the merchants in the Islamic period, from the region of Ashur and Nineveh northward

[1] §VIII, 19, 93. [2] §IX, 24, 52.
[3] For climatic conditions in Anatolia see §X, 1, 111 ff.

along the Tigris up to Jazīrah-ibn-'Umar, continuing from there westward toward Nisibis and then on to the Euphrates which they crossed, probably in the region of Malatya. From there they travelled, by way of Timilkia (Darende), Tegarama (Gürün) and thence directly westward to Kanesh; or else they could cross the Euphrates further south near Kızılin and journey from there to Kanesh via Khurrama (Elbistan).[1]

XI. MEASURES, WEIGHTS, AND TIME-RECKONING

Whereas the weights occurring in the Old Assyrian texts are those used throughout the centuries in both Assyria and Babylonia (*viz.* the talent, the mina, the shekel, and the grain, being to each other in the relation of $3600:60:1:\frac{1}{180}$), the measures of capacity differ markedly from those known from later Assyrian sources. These latter, being used mainly for grain and cereal products, were adapted to the carrying capacity of the domestic ass in such a way that 1 ass-load comprised 100 *qa*, which means 100 times the minimum daily grain ration of a primitive worker. Since, as was mentioned before, the 'black asses' which were the basic means of freight shipment of the Old Assyrian merchants were a particularly strong breed, it is not surprising that the unit of capacity reflecting the load carried by these was larger than that in the later Assyrian texts. The Old Assyrian unit was called the sack (*naruqqum*) and comprised 120 *qa*;[2] the sack was sub-divided into 4 jars (*karpatum*), each of which contained 30 *qa*. A further sub-unit not attested in other sources was the *šaršaranum*, which contained one half of the volume of a jar, or one-eighth of a sack. With regard to the measures of surface also the Old Assyrian texts do not agree with the later Assyrian. Whereas the Middle Assyrian texts use a system based on the Babylonian measure *ikū* as unit, while the Neo-Assyrians used as a unit the surface seeded with 1 ass-load of grain, the Old Assyrian texts reveal the use of a surface measure *šubtum*, i.e. 'residence'[3]. It represented a lot large enough to build one house and was sub-divided into 60 '(surface) shekels'. If, as it has been suggested,[4] the *šubtum* was equal in size to the Old Babylonian SAR, it would have measured 144 square cubits, or 324 square feet. However, since the houses excavated at Ashur as well as at Kanesh are of much larger size, this identification is open to doubt.

[1] §IX, 8, 96 ff.   [2] §X, 2, 192 ff.   [3] §X, 3.   [4] §X, 3, 221.

As mentioned above,[1] the years in the Old Assyrian texts from Asia Minor are named after the *līmum*, eponym-officials who held office at Ashur for one year. Yet the date formulae from Cappadocia exhibit an important deviation from the usual Assyrian scheme. Very frequently, one finds, instead of the well-known date formula 'month A, *līmum* B, the son of C', the following wording: 'month A, *līmum* of the hand of B, the son of C'. The fullest version of this formula reads: '*līmum* [was the one] who took over (*iṣbutu*) from the hand of B, the son of C'.[2] This fuller wording as well as the interchange of the 'hand' formula with the version '*līmum* who [was] after (*warki*) B, the son of C' makes it clear that it designates the year as that of the successor of B, the son of C. The frequent use of such 'successor' formulae suggests that it was a consequence of the long distance which separated Kanesh from the mother country. Yet under normal travelling conditions a messenger on horseback who left Ashur immediately after the name of the new eponym had been announced could have reached Kanesh about three weeks later. Instead it can be shown that in every year at least three, but frequently as many as four and sometimes even five months are dated with the successor formula. This makes it clear that in the period in question the annual change of eponym took place at the beginning of winter when the regular messenger service between Ashur and Kanesh had ceased.

A further important difference between the calendar of the texts from Asia Minor and that of the later Assyrian sources is the frequent occurrence of seasonal festivals in the date-formulae. These festivals which occur predominantly in loans of agricultural commodities are the following: of *Anna*, of *Barqa* (or *Birqa*), of *Nibas*, of *Ḥariḥari*, and of *Duḫduḫanim*. At the time when only four of these festivals were known the view was expressed that they marked the beginning of the four seasons. As by now the number has risen to five, this view can no longer be maintained. It is likely, however, that each festival marked the beginning or the end of a certain agricultural activity, so that the loan in question was expected to be paid back from the sales price which a farmer received for his crop or else in kind from the crop itself. This is all the more likely since the contracts stipulating payment of a loan at one of the five festivals interchange with others in which the loan was to be paid 'from the wage for ploughing','at the time of the threshing floor', 'at the taking of the sickle', 'at the falling of the sickle', and the like.

---

[1] See above, p. 709.   [2] §viii, 18, 20, n. 3.

CHAPTER XXV

ASSYRIA, *c.* 2600–1816 B.C.

I. THE PRE-SARGONIC PERIOD

THE north-east corner of Upper Mesopotamia, where the river Tigris runs from north-west to south-east, constitutes the region usually designated as Assyria. The narrow valley of the Tigris river and those of its tributaries are studded on both banks with ruin mounds covering major and minor Assyrian towns several of which served as royal residences. The knowledge about some of the cities buried under these mounds was never lost. That the mound of Nimrūd, on the east bank, close to the point where the Greater Zab flows into the Tigris, was the town of Kalakh mentioned in Genesis x. 11 was told by the natives to a British representative of the East India Company who explored the site in 1820.[1] They even knew that the country to which this town had once belonged was named 'al-Assur'. In much the same way, the natives of Mosul were well aware that the huge ruin mound across the river from their city covered Nineveh, the metropolis to which, according to the Book of Jonah, this prophet had been sent and where he died. Small wonder then that these sites attracted the curiosity not only of Bible scholars but of all those interested in the ancient world, and that excavations were undertaken which filled the museums of Europe's capitals with Assyrian antiquities.

Only at a much later time archaeologists turned their attention from the Neo-Assyrian to the Old and pre-Assyrian levels of the two ruin mounds which, by their size and the importance of their buildings stood out among all the others, namely that of the royal city of Ashur, today Qal'at Sherqāt, and Nineveh the most important mound of which is known today as Koyunçik, the smaller one as Nabi Yūnis. At Ashur archaeological evidence precedes by only a few centuries the period in which Mesopotamia and Assyria belonged to the Old Akkadian Empire. As was pointed out by the excavator of Ashur,[2] the extensive earth movements of later Assyrian kings who tried to create a level foundation for their buildings on the rocky slopes of the temenos may have destroyed the remains of earlier periods of the city's history. The

[1] G, 9, 3 f.   [2] G, 1, 71.

rather frequent changes of the bed of the Tigris river and its affluents may likewise account for the scarcity of pre-Sargonic remains at Ashur and some of the lesser mounds. In the region of Nineveh, on the contrary, as well as on sites such as Sāmarrā[1] and Tepe Gawra[2] a millennia-old stratification precedes the Sargonic level.

Since at least some conclusions with regard to the early population of Assyria can be derived from a comparison of this stratification with that of Babylonia and northern Mesopotamia, it is in order briefly to summarize it according to the results obtained at Nineveh[3] and Arpachiyah.[4] In the earlier levels, referred to by the excavators as Nineveh 1–3, the remains, particularly the pottery, are closely related to that of Al-'Ubaid and Tell Halaf, a ruin mound near the headwaters of the Khabur river in northern Mesopotamia. In fact, the very existence of an agricultural, undefendable village community in close proximity to Nineveh such as that of Arpachiyah is a feature most characteristic of the pre-Sumerian urban centres such as Ur, Eridu, etc. in southern Babylonia. The level Nineveh 4 corresponds to the Jamdat Naṣr period in Babylonia, which is the earliest tablet level in that country.[5] Level Nineveh 5, on the other hand, is apparently earlier than the First Dynasty of Ur.[6] The comparison suggests that the early population of Assyria was more or less identical with the pre-Sumerian population of southern Babylonia; the absence of any remains corresponding to the so-called Early Dynastic period of Babylonia makes it clear, on the other hand, that Sumerians never occupied Assyria.[7]

The evidence pointing to the identity of the pre-Semitic population of Assyria and the pre-Sumerian inhabitants of Babylonia is not limited to the superficial similarity of the pottery and other material remains. The combination of cuneiform signs with which the city name Ninua 'Nineveh' was written was used also for the name of a south Babylonian town, one of the typical rural communities in the immediate vicinity of Lagash, named Nina.[8] The close relation between the city names Ninua and Nina becomes apparent if it is remembered that they are to each other in the relation of the variants Nuzue and Nuza of the name of the well-known Hurrian city of Nuzi, south of the Lesser Zab.[9] Whereas there is no direct evidence to indicate whether the divine

---

[1] §1, 7.   [2] §1, 24.   [3] §1, 16.
[4] §1, 17.   [5] §1, 16, 141.   [6] *Ibid.* 174.   [7] §1, 27, 96.
[8] *C.A.H.* 1³, ch. III, sect. VIII; G, 16, 20 f. Feldstein A, col. III, ll. 10 and 92 f., col. IV, l. 4.   [9] §1, 26.

patroness of the pre-Semitic city of Ninua was identical with the
fish-goddess Nanshe worshipped in the Babylonian city of Nina,[1]
it is significant that the goddess Ishtar of Ninua was one of the
principal deities worshipped by the inhabitants of the Hurrian
city of Nuzi and other towns in its vicinity.[2] Other geographical
names follow a pattern similar to that of Ninua and Nina: the
name of the very old south Babylonian city of Uruk is obviously
identical with Urkish; this latter name is augmented by an ending
-*iš* found in country names such as Tukrish and Mukish. The
country of Urkish, located in northern Mesopotamia, was, in the
period immediately preceding Sargon of Akkad, the homeland
of a king Tisatal, an inscription of whom has been found.[3] This
king's inscription as well as his name are Hurrian, whence it is
apparent to which ethnic element the population which chose
these and similar geographical names belonged: their language
was that which is nowadays commonly called Hurrian, but to
which the name Subarian would be equally applicable.[4] This
conclusion is well in line with the findings of the excavator of
Ashur in the oldest stratum of the Ishtar temple at Ashur; he
describes this building as 'ein churritischer Breitraum'.[5]

Two further Assyrian geographical names must be mentioned
in this connexion. The one is the city name Baltil or Baltila which
was used by later Assyrian kings with reference to the earliest
precursor of the city of Ashur.[6] Baltila, too, is a Hurrian name,
being identical with a personal name found not infrequently
among the Hurrian population of the Nuzi region.[7] In fact, the
very feature that a personal name figures as a town name is a
characteristic of a Hurrian population; whereas the Semites were
wont to name their cities for the deity that was worshipped there,
it was customary among the Hurrians that a prominent citizen
such as for instance the scribe Apil-Si(n) gave his name to the
community which he founded and where he lived. Other town
names of this type in the Nuzi region are Ili-malik-we; Pukhi-
shenni-we; Irimadad-we, standing for Iriba-Adad-we; Wardish-
pak-we standing for Warad-Tishpak-we, etc. That the founder
of Baltila worshipped the Hurrian god Tilla, whose name is
known from theophorous personal names such as Tekhip-Tilla,
Pai-Tilla, Elkhip-Tilla, Akip-Tilla, Khishmi-Tilla and so on, can
be inferred from his own name which has the meaning 'Knowing

[1] §1, 23; see also below, p. 763.
[2] §1, 9, no. 49, l. 48; no. 140, l. 9; §1, 22, no. 491, l. 2; no. 690, l. 2; no. 799,
l. 15.   [3] §1, 21; §1, 20, 213 f.   [4] §1, 25.
[5] G, 1, 72.   [6] §1, 14, 467 ff.   [7] §1, 5, 111.

is Tilla', the verbal stem *pal-* having the meaning 'to know'.[1]
To judge by the legend of a seal impressed on an Old Babylonian
tablet from Larsa,[2] this god Tilla figured as the son of the storm
god Enlil who, throughout the ages, played a role in the pantheon
of the city of Ashur.[3] To be sure, the legend of this seal defines
Baltil and not Tilla as a 'mighty hero and son of Enlil'; but it is
likely that the owner of this seal concluded from the ancient
city name Baltil that a god of this name must have existed because, as was mentioned before, among the Semites it was customary to name a city for the god worshipped there rather than
for its human founder.

In a passage from Nabonidus's stela from Hillah dealing with
Marduk's wrath against Babylon which prompted him to take up
residence abroad, the king refers to the country in which the
tutelary god of Babylon took refuge as the land of Subir,[4] and to the
city where he established his temporary residence as Baltila.[5] As
Nabonidus, who was a descendant of the Assyrian royal family,[6]
can be trusted to have been well acquainted with Assyrian tradition, this passage suggests that, at the time when the capital city
was called Baltila, the country was named Subir, a name which
occurs also in the variant forms Subar and Subartu. That these
forms as well as Shubar and Shubartu are synonyms can be
gathered, *inter alia*, from texts which deal with the role the
Subarian deities played in the later Assyrian rituals. Whereas
some such texts speak in this connexion of 'gods of the land of
Shubari',[7] others designate the same gods as those of Subarti.[8]
In fact the variation between an unsuffixed masculine form and a
form including the Semitic feminine ending *-ti* occurs also in
names of other non-Semitic countries such as, for example, Elamu
and Elamtu.

The reason why, in contrast with the archaic city name Baltila, the country name Subartu was not used by the later Assyrians
as a designation of their country in ancient days must be sought
in the derogatory sense with which this designation was used by
non-Assyrians. An early example of this usage is provided by a
date formula from Eshnunna, in which the army of Iasmakh-
Adad, the son of King Shamshi-Adad I (1815–1783 B.C.),[9] is

---

[1] §1, 19, 322, *sub* 2.
[2] For the tablet: §1, 8, no. 192; for the seal: §1, 1, 147, *sub* A 532B.
[3] See below, pp. 766 f.   [4] §1, 10, 73 f., col. I, l. 35, col. II, l. 18.
[5] *Ibid.* col. I, ll. 17 and 24.   [6] §1, 11, 35 ff. with notes.
[7] §1, 3, 199, l. 56.   [8] §1, 2, 29, 2. Seite, linke Kol., l. 15.
[9] For this date see below, p. 751.

referred to as 'the host of Shubartu and Khana.'[1] A well-known example from a later period is offered by an inscription of the Babylonian king Marduk-apal-iddina II, the biblical Merodach-Baladan (721–710 B.C.), who designates his Assyrian adversary, King Sargon the Younger (721–705 B.C.) not as 'king of Assyria' but as the 'Subarian' and his army as 'the host of Subir'.[2] The Assyrians themselves used this terminology only when quoting astrological omina, to all appearances of Babylonian origin. Thus, an astrologer reports to the Assyrian king that '[If the moon is seen] in the month of Nisan, on the 30th day, [the land of Su]-bartum [will devour] the Akhlamū'. He adds by way of explana-tion: 'We are Subir.'[3] The origin of the derogatory sense of the names Subir, Subartu, etc., must be looked for in the custom, traceable in a considerable number of Old Babylonian texts, of importing Subarian slaves because they were highly appreciated in Babylonia. The use of Subarian slaves thus became so widespread that the term Subarum or, in Old Assyrian, Subrum, eventually became a general designation of a slave.[4] In the historic period few, if any, of the original Hurrians were left in Assyria proper. When the Akkadian-speaking Semites arrived and settled in Assyria, they obviously pushed the Subarians into the east-Tigridic foothills of the Kurdish mountains and into the mountainous regions of northern Mesopotamia where they are actually traceable at the time of Shamshi-Adad I.[5]

II. THE SARGONIC PERIOD

The Sargonic Period is well attested at Nineveh, both archaeo-logically and in inscriptions. On the site of the Ishtar temple, identified as such by numerous fragments of several duplicates of a building inscription of Shamshi-Adad I[6] and of later Assyrian rulers,[7] a solid rectangular building of unburnt brick was un-earthed in what the excavator called the sixth level.[8] It was identified as belonging to the Sargonic Period by stone cylinders the oldest of which bears an Old Akkadian inscription; this text,[9] only partially preserved, is the duplicate of a monument erected at Nippur by king Naram-Sin, the fourth king of the

---

[1] §1, 13, 448.   [2] §1, 4, 133, ll. 9 and 17; §1, 10, 60, col. 1, l. 29.
[3] G, 14, no. 62, ll. 1 f. and 4.   [4] §1, 15.
[5] See above, p. 717; §1, 12, 331, n. 2.
[6] §11, 20, 105 ff. and plates 81 ff.; G, 2, 9.   [7] §11, 20, 57 ff.
[8] *Ibid.* 58; §1, 27, 96.   [9] §11, 15; §11, 23, 280b.

Sargonic Dynasty. To be sure, the original of this monument is not known, but a copy made by an Old Babylonian scribe was found at Nippur.[1] The evidence that Naram-Sin's realm comprised Nineveh is well in line with the statement contained in Shamshi-Adad's inscription, namely that the previous builder of the Ishtar temple at Nineveh was 'Manishtishu, the son of Sargon, king of Akkad'. From Ashur, too, comes information attesting the rule of the third Old Akkadian king over Assyria. A short inscription engraved on the point of a spear dedicates that object to 'Manishtusu, king of the universe'.[2] Some further texts from the Sargonic period found at Ashur, among which is a purchasing contract engraved on a stone tablet, were never published.[3]

Important information about the city of Ashur in the Sargonic period is furnished by the Old Akkadian texts from Nuzi which repeatedly refer to Ashur (always spelled A-$šur^{KI}$),[4] implying at the same time that administrative personnel of the Akkadian kings, among others one Akhu-ṭāb and one Puzur-ekallim, were stationed in the city. That Ashur was an important administrative centre of the Akkadian Empire can be gathered also from the remains of palatial buildings belonging to this period. At least one prominent archaeologist dates the so-called Old Palace, a huge building adjoining the temple tower of Enlil, to the Sargonic period on the strength of its striking similarity with the palace built by Naram-Sin at Tell Brak.[5] A private house of almost palatial dimensions which the excavator himself dated to the period here under discussion yielded a mace-head of haematite with the inscription 'Rimush, king of the universe',[6] which recurs on a mace-head found at Ur.[7] In fact, what is perhaps the oldest Assyrian royal inscription was found in the ruins of the Ishtar temple at Ashur. It can be dated with fair certainty, because the shape of the signs, the choice of the words, and the orthography are those of the Old Akkadian period.[8] It reads: 'Ititi, the *iššiakkum* (PA), the son of Inin-labbā, dedicated (this object) to Ishtar out of the booty (made in the campaign against the city) of Gasur.' For the dating of the text it is further significant that the names Ititi and Inin-labbā occur repeatedly in the Old Akkadian texts from Nuzi, which city is either identical with, or in the immediate vicinity of, Gasur. Ititi's title *iššiakkum* is one

[1] §II, 17, no. 36; §II, 16, 209 ff. [2] §II, 24, 85; §II, 9, 109, n. 206.
[3] G, 6, 230, *sub* §6. [4] §II, 14, p. xi.
[5] §II, 13, 27 f. and 63.
[6] §II, 18, plate 22 b, item no. Ass. 20580; cf. pp. 5 f.
[7] §II, 5, no. 10. [8] §II, 1, 53 and plate 64 a; G, 11, 259.

of the well-known designations of the Old Assyrian rulers who, as will be pointed out in greater detail below, did not use the title king.

As this inscription makes it clear that the conquest of the Nuzi region which, owing to its wealth in gold and in agricultural products, was a bone of contention between Assyria and Babylonia throughout the ages, started from Assyria, the question arises whether the Akkadians did not have a more solid base of operations in Assyria than they had in Babylonia. In fact, in many respects the impression the Akkadians left in Assyria was deep and permanent. In so far as the language is concerned, Old Assyrian is the only Akkadian dialect which has preserved certain features typical of the Old Akkadian language; one of the most characteristic ones is the use instead of the usual *ina*, 'in', of the short form *in*, the *n* of which was assimilated to the following consonant. While the shape of the signs of the two dialects differs conspicuously, a common feature is the consistent use of GA for *ga*, *kà*, and *qá*. Also certain personal names are common to Old Akkadian and Old Assyrian: first, the frequent occurrence of names of the type Ititi, Buzuzu, Ṣilulu, Sulili, etc. Typical of the personal names of both dialects is further the use of forms without an ending such as Lāqīp, a name frequent in Old Akkadian as well as in Old Assyrian. The use by the Assyrians of typically Old Akkadian names is of particular significance. Even as many other Semites, the Assyrians of the Old Assyrian period used to name a child born shortly after the death of his or her grandparent for this deceased ancestor. Underlying this habit was the idea that the soul of the deceased, inseparably attached to his name, entered the body of his youngest descendant and thus lived on in his family. Therefore the use of Old Akkadian names in the Old Assyrian period can be taken to indicate that many of the prominent Old Assyrian families proudly traced their ancestors back to Old Akkadians.

The most significant impact, however, which the Akkadians left in Assyria was ideological. Whereas in Babylonia the memory of the Sargonic kings was despised[1] and their actions condemned as offensive to their national god,[2] the Assyrians throughout their history cherished their memory and tried to emulate them. Whereas in Babylonia they were remembered as foreign conquerors, the later Assyrians thought of them as their very own. Foremost among the ideas which, in the eyes of later generations, were embodied by the kings of Akkad was the creation of a uni-

[1] §II, 3, 91 f.
[2] §II, 2, 14, no. 41; G, 8, 8 f; A. Falkenstein in *Z.A.* 57 (1965), 43 ff.

versal empire, comprising what later princes used to call *kiššat mātāti*, 'the totality of the countries'.[1] Rarely was a Babylonian king interested in 'widening the bounds of his country'; with the exception of some Kassites, who were influenced by Assyrian ideas, they did not use titles such as *šar kiššati*, 'king of the universe', *šar kibrāt erbettim*, 'king of the four regions (of the world)', etc. The Assyrians, on the contrary, were expansion-minded throughout their history. As will be pointed out in greater detail below, the time of the empire builders Sargon and Naram-Sin was for the Assyrians a golden age, for the eventual return of which they hoped at periodic intervals; whenever computations revealed that the time was approaching when a new universal empire would materialize comprising all the lands 'from the Upper Sea where the sun sets to the Lower Sea where the sun rises',[2] a king of Assyria chose the throne name Sargon in the belief that *nomen est omen*. The first Assyrian ruler who adopted both the title *šarrum* 'king' and the more ambitious and programmatic 'king of the universe' was Shamshi-Adad I, who actually assembled an empire of impressive proportions under his sceptre; the last was Nabonidus, king of Babylon, who tried to emulate his illustrious ancestor, Esarhaddon.

The idea of a universal empire as that created by the Akkadian kings and aimed at by subsequent generations of Assyrian rulers had its origin in the cult of the moon which, throughout Assyrian history, played an important role in the pantheon.[3] The moon was the prototype of a universal god in contrast to the various national deities. It is visible everywhere; it was worshipped and had sanctuaries wherever Semites settled or travelled. In southern Babylonia, Sin's holy city was Ur, on the fringe of the desert whence his original worshippers came. In Mesopotamia, the centre of moon cult was Harran. In the Lebanon, the moon was worshipped as Laban, 'The White One', as attested by Old Assyrian personal names such as Shū-Laban, Laban-na'da and the like. In Palestine, one of his holy cities was Hazor, in the Arabian peninsula among others Temā[4] and Hureidha.[5] Since it was assumed that each of the national deities bestowed upon the king of his choice the region which was the centre of his worship, the moon-god evidently could convey the entire Semitic world upon the king he selected. Nabonidus, when speaking of his royal ancestors, clearly expressed this idea: 'Esarhaddon, the king of Ashur, and Ashurbanipal, his son, upon whom Sin, the

---

[1] E.g. §11, 8, plates 26 ff., col. 11, ll. 37 f.   [2] §11, 12, 23, ll. 13 f.
[3] See below, p. 768.   [4] §1, 11, 37 ff.; §11, 10, 155 f.   [5] §11, 19.

king of the gods, bestowed the totality of the countries.'[1] Sargon
the Younger, in turn, expressed the same idea in a prayer to Ningal, Sin's divine consort, by asking for 'the rule over all the
inhabited places to the end of days'.[2] That the moon cult actually
was popular under the Old Akkadian dynasty is evidenced by the
name of the fourth king, Naram-Sin, which means 'The beloved
one of Sin'.

The Assyrian rulers showed their reverence for Sargon and
Naram-Sin not only by their conquests. The Babylonians bitterly
resented it when a king built his residence in a city other than
Babylon; this resentment is traceable from the earliest times down
to the end of their empire: in the Chronicle concerning Sargon
and Naram-Sin, they blame the founder of the Akkadian dynasty
for having built, near Akkad, 'a likeness of Babylon'.[3] With the
same bitterness they blamed Nabonidus, in the so-called Verse
Account, for having built, in the far-off oasis-town of Tēmā, a
palace as his residence like the palace of Babylon.[4] In fact,
Nebuchadnezzar II prides himself on not having built for himself
a residence outside of Babylon itself, not having embellished any
holy city beyond Babylon.[5] The Assyrian practice, throughout
the ages, differed radically from this narrow-minded nationalism.
Whereas the kings of the Puzur-Ashur dynasty[6] appear to have
resided at Ashur, Shamshi-Adad I transferred his residence far
to the north, to Shubat-Enlil, in northern Mesopotamia.[7] That no
one in Assyria resented this transfer can be concluded from the
fact that Shamshi-Adad remained throughout Assyrian history
one of the most beloved figures whose name was chosen by later
princes over and over again, because it was a symbol of success
and prosperity for the country. Other equally successful rulers
built new residences such as Kar-Tukulti-Ninurta, Kalkhu,
Nineveh, Dūr-Sharrukēn, and from all that is known their
subjects were happy and satisfied with their activities. In fact,
far from being arbitrary, these changes in the royal residence
appear to have been dictated by a religious principle. It was believed that the ten deities representing the moving and the fixed
stars took turns in ruling the universe; and the earthly ruler of
the 'totality of the countries' was assumed to reside in one of the
cities dedicated to the cult of the deity whose turn it was to rule
the world and its inhabitants. When Sargon of Akkad founded his

[1] §II, 8, plates 26 ff., col. II, ll. 37 f.
[2] §II, 11, 133, no. 7, l. 7.
[3] G, 8, 8, ll. 18 f.; §II, 2, 14, *sub* no. 41.
[4] §I, 11, 59.
[5] §I, 11, 38.
[6] See below, pp. 754 ff.
[7] See *C. A. H.* II³, ch. I, sect. I; §I, 12, 331, n. 2.

empire, Ishtar, the patron goddess of the city of Akkad (Agade), was assumed to rule the universe.[1] When Shamshi-Adad established his residence at Shubat-Enlil, the rule of Enlil, which is alluded to in a birth-omen from Nineveh, was thought by him to have begun. Particularly characteristic was the belief in the dawning of the age of Ninurta or Shulmānu, the planet Saturn, whose holy cities comprised, among others, Jerusalem in the west and Kalkhu in Assyria. It was at that time that Kalkhu became the residence of the Assyrian kings and that royal names composed with theophorous elements alluding to the Black Planet became current in the dynasty, the most prominent examples being Shulmānu-ashared (Shalmaneser) I and his equally illustrious son, Tukulti-Ninurta I. When the rule was assumed to have again passed to the planet Venus, Nineveh became the royal residence, and several indications point to Harran, the moon-god's holy city, as the king's residence during the last decades of Assyrian rule when the moon-god's term was assumed to be imminent or to have begun. That here again the Assyrians perpetuated a belief common to the Semitic world but strange to the Babylonians is evidenced, *inter alia*, by the prophecy in Micah iv. 8 according to which its former domination would eventually return to Jerusalem. A personal name such as Palē-Shamash, borne in Babylonia under the Amorite dynasty, also bears witness to the common Semitic origin of this belief. It is likely that the length of each deity's rule was assumed to be 350 years, a span of time which will be discussed in greater detail below.[2] Eventually, however, the cycle was assumed to end with the moon-god's rule, which then would last for ever.

Further ways in which the Assyrian rulers showed their devotion to the principles presumed to have been laid down by Sargon of Akkad are based on the so-called *Legend of Sargon*.[3] In the second part of this composition, Sargon admonishes 'whichever king will arise after me' to repeat his exploits as the most noteworthy of which he lists an expedition to Dilmun (i.e. the island of Baḥrain in the Persian Gulf), the capture of the city of Dēr (today Badrah slightly more than one hundred miles northeast of Babylon), and the conquest of mighty mountains with the help of copper axes.[4] The first Assyrian king who emphasized in one of his inscriptions that he had heeded Sargon's advice is Ilushuma[5] who mentions not only that he established 'the free-

---

[1] G, 8, 3, l. 1.   [2] Pp. 741 ff.
[3] G, 8, 87 ff.   [4] §1, 14, 463 with note 276.
[5] More correctly Ilu-shumma; on the etymology see below, p. 767.

dom of movement of the Akkadians and of their children',[1] but also that he conquered the city of Dēr.[2] Several kings stressed their adherence to the principle of breaking through the mountains with copper axes which amounts, of course, to the creation of roads through the mountains establishing communications between various parts of the world. Evidently for an empire builder nothing is more important than communications between the various parts of his realm. Tiglath-pileser I mentions his doing so after having crossed the Tigris on his way to Armenia;[3] so does Ashur-bel-kala in his Annals.[4] Sargon the Younger, too, prides himself on having followed his older namesake's advice in his campaign against Urartu.[5] Tukulti-Ninurta I let it be known in one of his inscriptions[6] that he was familiar with Sargon's admonition.

The Old Akkadian period in Assyria ended in a catastrophe which is well attested both archaeologically and in literature. In the area of the Ishtar temple at Nineveh[7] as well as in the ruins of the same deity's shrine at Ashur[8] evidence of violent destruction following a conquest was clearly discernible. Literary evidence is contained in the *Legend of Naram-Sin*[9] which, as shown by the existence of the Old Babylonian version,[10] is obviously an early outgrowth of the Babylonians' wrath against the dynasty of Akkad. The story, in brief, tells that a strange-looking host, which was for good reasons identified with the Lullubi[11] (subsequently the eastern neighbours of the people of Nuzi), invaded Naram-Sin's realm, overrunning first Purushkhaddum in Asia Minor, penetrating then into northern Mesopotamia, a region which here, as frequently in the Old Babylonian period,[12] is called Subartu, taking the principal city, Shubat-Enlil. The invaders then conquered Gutium and Elam and finally Babylonia, where they eventually reached the Persian Gulf. That some sound historical information is contained in this tale can be gathered from the results of the excavations at Tell Brak, in the valley of the Hirmās river. They revealed, in the first place, that Naram-Sin of Akkad was in firm possession of northern Mesopotamia, having constructed an elaborate palace at the site of Tell Brak which was located on the caravan road linking Assyria with Asia

---

[1] §iv, 29, 115, ll. 49 ff.   [2] *Ibid.*

[3] G, 3, 39, col. ii, ll. 7 f. and 65, col. iv, l. 67; G, 2, 108 ff.

[4] §ii, 22, 82, ll. 33 f.   [5] §ii, 21, l. 24.

[6] §ii, 7, vol. i, no. 18, l. 7.

[7] §i, 16, 129.   [8] G, 1, 74.   [9] §ii, 6; §ii, 4.

[10] §ii, 4.   [11] §ii, 6, 95.   [12] §i, 12, 331, n. 2.

Minor. Several items discovered in the ruins of this palace were definitely imports from Asia Minor,[1] hence it is likely that the legends linking the Sargonic kings to the region of Purushkhaddum are historically well founded. The archaeological evidence at Tell Brak further reveals that Naram-Sin's palace was sacked by an invader and there is every reason to connect this sack with the invasion of the Lullubi. On their way from there to Gutium, Elam and Babylonia the barbarians naturally followed the course of the Tigris river, thus passing through Assyria and destroying both Nineveh and Ashur as they proceeded.

III. KING-LIST AND CHRONOLOGY

In many respects, Assyrian chronology is easier to reconstruct than Babylonian, because the Assyrians from the earliest periods on were deeply interested in chronology and therefore did themselves much of the work which the modern historian has to do when attempting to restore Babylonian chronology. The Assyrians' interest in history, which is traceable in their inscriptions from the Old Assyrian period down to the end of the empire, was prompted by the belief in the periodic recurrence of historical events. This belief, in turn, was based to all appearances on the assumption of an interconnexion of events on earth and the motion of the stars: since, owing to the large planetary periods, certain heavenly constellations recur at periodic intervals, events on earth were expected to repeat themselves periodically. Yet lack of precision obviously impaired the earliest astronomical observations, whence it is not surprising that round numbers which had a special magical appeal replaced the actual numbers of years of the planetary periods.

The oldest occurrence of this way of thinking is found under the Puzur-Ashur dynasty which immediately preceded the reign of Shamshi-Adad I and in Shamshi-Adad's own inscriptions. In his afore-quoted building inscription from the Ishtar temple at Nineveh,[2] Shamshi-Adad remarks that, since the end of the dynasty of Akkad, to which Manishtusu, the previous builder, had belonged, '7 *dāru*-periods' had elapsed. The length of this span which, according to Shamshi-Adad's computation, separated the dynasty of Akkad from 'the capture of Nurrugu' in the beginning of his own reign can be easily determined from the practice of later Assyrian kings to reconstruct sacred buildings after

---

[1] §II, 13, 29.   [2] See above, p. 733, with n. 6.

350 years, or a multiple of this number, had passed since the previous construction or reconstruction. A particularly pertinent example is offered by the afore-quoted Annals of Tiglath-pileser I.[1] This king reports that the Anu-Adad temple at Ashur had fallen into decay and that King Ashur-dan, Tiglath-pileser's great-grandfather, demolished the old structure but refrained from rebuilding it because only 641 years had elapsed since the previous construction. After the structure had lain in ruins for another sixty years, so the text reports, which means altogether 701 years after the previous work, Tiglath-pileser himself proceeded with the reconstruction.

Among numerous other pertinent examples, that of Ashurbanipal's report on the restoration of E-khulkhul in Harran may be quoted. This building, according to the king's account,[2] had previously been restored by Shalmaneser, the son of Ashurnaṣirpal; its walls collapsed so that its reconstruction became necessary and it was dedicated in Ashurbanipal's accession year, 669 B.C. A glance at the king-list shows that exactly 350 years separate this year from the previous builder, Shalmaneser II, who died in 1019 B.C.[3] An even later example of the reckoning in 350-year periods is preserved in an inscription of Nabonidus who, naïvely, used Assyrian tradition in trying to reconstruct Babylonian history. He states that Hammurabi, the previous builder of the Shamash temple and the temple tower at Sippar, restored it '700 years before Burnaburiash'.[4]

Applying this evidence to Shamshi-Adad's inscription from the Ishtar temple at Nineveh, he obviously believed that the shrine which Manishtusu of Akkad had built was ripe for being reconstructed in his own day because 350 years had passed since the end of Akkad. That similar calculations had been carried out by Shamshi-Adad's predecessors can be inferred from their names, Sharrum-kēn (Sargon) I, his fourth predecessor, and this king's grandson, Naram-Sin of Assyria, Shamshi-Adad's second predecessor. The omission of the names of Sargon of Akkad's two sons and successors, Rimush and Manishtusu, shows conspicuous familiarity with the tradition according to which both of these kings met a violent death. Yet not only in Assyria the expectation of a new universal empire like that of the Old Akkadian kings was current in this period. Approximately during the first decade of Shamshi-Adad's reign a king named Naram-Sin ruled over Eshnunna.

[1] See above, p. 739, n. 3.   [2] §III, 20, 170 ff. and particularly 172, l. 51.
[3] Cf. §III, 22, 127.   [4] §I, 10, 238, ll. 20 ff.

25

The data necessary for such computations were ascertained by the Assyrians with the help of two compilations, the Assyrian king-list and the *līmum* or eponym canon. By co-ordinating these two lists Assyrian scholars had developed a workable system of recording events in their actual sequence at a time when in Babylonia the compilers of the so-called Sumerian king-list uncritically added the dynastic list of one city-state to that of another, enumerating them as if they had followed each other even if they had actually overlapped or even ruled simultaneously. The eponym canon was an outgrowth of the habit of the Assyrians of naming the years from an annual official, the *līmum*,[1] a term derived from a root meaning 'to circle, to encircle',[2] and hence denoting a 'cycle'. It has been shown that, in the Neo-Assyrian epoch, the office rotated among the high officials and governors of the various provinces of the vast Assyrian empire of those days.[3] In some cases, however, the lot seems to have decided who was to become *līmum*.[4] Consequently, a man could become eponym for the second time after a comparatively short interval.[5] In the older periods it appears that, rather than provincial governors, the *līmum*-officials were hereditary princes of some of the prominent and important Assyrian cities, a conclusion which was reached on the basis of the evidence concerning the eponym Ashur-mutakkil,[6] his father, Ashur-daiiān, and his son who were the rulers of the fortress city of Qabra on the Lesser Zab[7] and belonged to the time of Eriba-Adad I[8] and Ashur-uballiṭ.[9] At least from the Middle Assyrian period on the royal house was one of the families entitled to hold the eponym office; in the Old Assyrian period, however, there is no evidence to this effect, none of the rulers being mentioned as an eponym.

The Assyrians had two ways in which they transmitted the names of the successive eponyms. Each holder of the office received a stela which was erected beside that of his predecessor; the whole row extended over a large square in the city of Ashur, near the fortification wall. Each stela was inscribed with the name and the title of the respective official.[10] The other way of preserving the knowledge of the names and the sequence of the *līmum* officials consisted in inscribing clay tablets with their names, their

---

[1] Thus in Old and Middle Assyrian; only in late Assyrian a form *limmu* was used; see G, 13, 554. [2] G, 13, 541.
[3] §iii, 6, 6 ff. [4] §iii, 16, vol. 2, 230, ll. 174 f. and 231, n. 40.
[5] §iii, 10, no. 437, l. 26. [6] §iii, 5, 23.
[7] §i, 13, 441, n. 3. [8] Or rather Irība-Adad; see below, p. 753.
[9] §iii, 12, 8 ff. and 24 f. [10] §iii, 1.

titles, and the most important event that took place during their year in office.[1] As persons such as businessmen, court officials and scribes dealt with numerous dated documents in their daily work, they obviously possessed tablets with the eponym list; the average citizen, however, who was only occasionally confronted with the necessity of ascertaining the number of years that had elapsed between two eponymies, could consult the row of stelae and simply count the number of stelae separating those of the two men in question.

The stelae excavated thus far cover only office holders in the Middle and early Neo-Assyrian periods; it is not known whether for the earlier eponyms any such monuments existed. However, the existence of clay tablets recording the names of the eponyms of the early Old Assyrian period can be inferred from a remark in the king-list according to which the names of the *līmum* officials whose tenure of office coincided with the reign of the rulers named in the pertinent section were 'eaten up'[2] (col. 1, ll. 25–6), an expression referring to the surface of a clay tablet the script of which was rubbed off. This remark makes it obvious that the practice of naming the years from eponyms preceded by far the eighty-four officials known from the texts from Asia Minor.[3]

As regards the king-list, there exist three major copies of it representing what had become, in the Neo-Assyrian period, the 'standard version'. The oldest of the three, poorly preserved, ends with the year 912 B.C.[4] The second one, which was excavated at Dūr-Sharrukēn, modern Khorsabad, is much better preserved and was written in 738 B.C. by a scribe of the Ishtar temple of Arbela who copied it from a tablet at Ashur.[5] The latest, in the best state of preservation, ends with the year 722 B.C. and belonged to a priest of the Assyrian national god.[6] Among various other related compilations one deserves special mention because of the remarkable scholarly endeavour to which it bears witness. It lists in one column '82 kings of Assyria from the time of Erishu, the son of Ilushuma, to Ashurbanipal, the son of Esarhaddon', and in the second column '98 kings of Akkad from the time of Sumulael to Kandalanu' attempting to establish synchronisms between the two lists.[7]

The first section of the 'standard version' lists seventeen men

---

[1] §III, 23 and §III, 27. Additional lists are scattered throughout Assyriological publications.   [2] §III, 15, 515 f.; G, 11, 279, n. 84.
[3] See above, p. 709.   [4] §III, 17.
[5] G, 11 and §III, 7.   [6] §III, 7.
[7] §III, 24 and 25.

who are summarized as '17 kings, tent-dwellers'. Of these seventeen men, the penultimate, Ushpia, is known as an early king of Assyria from two building inscriptions of later Assyrian kings, Shalmaneser I[1] (1272–1243 b.c.) and Esarhaddon[2] (680–669 b.c.), both of whom reconstructed the Ashur temple at Ashur. In accordance with the principles outlined before,[3] each of the two kings secured first the foundation stone of the building deposited by the previous builder in order to make sure that a full cycle of years had passed since a previous reconstruction. Both kings report that the first known builder of the principal national shrine of the Assyrians was Ushpia and that the next one was Erishum (more correctly, in this period, Irishum),[4] the son of Ilushuma; yet neither of the two subsequent builders, while taking great pains to determine as exactly as possible the intervals between Erishum, the following builder, Shamshi-Adad I, and themselves, attempts to date Ushpia of whom, however, at least one of the subsequent builders must have found a record. As regards the thirteenth of the seventeen tent-dwellers, Abazu, it has been suggested that he was the person who dedicated the afore-quoted spear point to Manishtusu, king of Akkad.[5] Upon closer examination, however, it turned out that the donor of the spear point was named Azuzu[6] and that therefore no chronological conclusions could be based upon his alleged occurrence in this section of the list. However, the name of the ninth tent-dweller, Didānu, furnishes the clue to the nature of the list of Ushpia's predecessors. In Genesis xxv.3, it is stated that a Dedan was the ancestor of the Ashurīm; by further making this Dedan a grandson of Abraham, the Jewish tradition obviously makes him the chieftain of a nomadic tribe which journeyed around with Abraham between Mesopotamia and Egypt. In fact, a second among the tent-dwellers, Khanū, who immediately follows Didānu, is definitely the tribal ancestor of the Khanians who are now well known from the Mari texts where they appear partly settled in the region of Terqa, but partly still roaming the adjoining desert as nomads. The name Kharkharu of the fifth tent-dweller admits a similar explanation. In the Neo-Assyrian period, Kharkhar was a province of Media;[7] as it is known from the Mari texts that several of the nomadic tribes passed into east-Tigridic territory and then returned to Mesopotamia, so that geographical

---

[1] §ii, 7, vol. i, no. 13, col. iii, ll. 32 ff.   [2] §iii, 4, 3, col. iii, ll. 16 ff.
[3] See above, p. 741.   [4] See below, p. 767.
[5] §ii, 24, 85.   [6] §iii, 2, 2; cf. §ii, 9, 109, n. 206.
[7] G, 10 vol. ii, 462, *s.v.*

names such as Idamaraz, Iamutbal, Karana, etc., chosen for such tribes occur both east and west of the Tigris, the name Kharkhar may well be that of another tribal ancestor whose name remained attached to the Median province. Imṣu (no. 7 in the list) is a younger variant of the Old West Semitic personal name which occurs as Iamṣum in the Mari texts.[1] Since the king-list does not claim any family relationship between the fifteen predecessors of Ushpia, it thus becomes apparent that the tent-dwellers were not successive Assyrian kings but the ancestors of the nomadic tribes which constituted the Assyrian nation. They thus closely parallel the twelve sons of Jacob who figure in Jewish tradition as the ancestors of the twelve nomadic tribes of which the Israelite nation was composed. By placing Ushpia, the first known builder of the national shrine, at the end of the section of tribal ancestors, the original compiler of this part of the king-list wanted to indicate that the construction of the Ashur temple at Ashur marked the end of the nomadic period of the Assyrian people; he probably visualized Ushpia as the actual founder of the Semitic city of Ashur. In attempting to date this period of Assyrian history it must be kept in mind (1) that it must have preceded the Sargonic period, because, as was mentioned before, the Old Akkadian texts from Nuzi attest the use of the city name Ashur and thus indirectly the worship of the god Ashur for that period; and (2) that the extant archaeological remains at Ashur attest a period of about two hundred years prior to the Sargonic period.

The second section of the king-list must have been copied from a royal inscription, for it is drawn up in the style of the Old and Middle Assyrian texts in which a king lists not only his father but several of his more distant ancestors. Typical in this respect are the inscriptions of Ashur-uballiṭ I (1362–1327 B.C.): 'Ashur-uballiṭ, priest-king of Ashur, (is) the son of Eriba-Adad; Eriba-Adad, priest-king of Ashur, (was) the son of Ashur-bel-nisheshu; Ashur-bel-nisheshu, priest-king of Ashur, (was) the son of Ashur-nirari....' In this way Ashur-uballiṭ proceeds backwards for seven generations to Puzur-Ashur III.[2] In exactly the same manner the king-list begins with an Aminu, son of Ila-kabkabu whose ancestors he traces back for nine generations until he reaches Apiashal, the son of Ushpia, which means the two men who terminated the tent-dweller section. The king-list summarizes these men with the remark: '10 kings who were their ancestors'. The question has, of course, been asked by modern scholars whose ancestors the compiler of the list had in mind. It

---

[1] §III, 9, 41.   [2] G, 4, 42 ff., nos. 4 and 5.

was suggested on the strength of the name Ila-kabkabu (the West Semitic reading of the name being well assured by brick inscriptions from Ashur),[1] that they were the ancestors of Shamshi-Adad I who was the son of an Ila-kabkabu.[2] Yet it is difficult to see why the compiler should not have inserted Shamshi-Adad's ancestors immediately before Shamshi-Adad, but should have separated two allegedly consecutive generations by at least ten other persons. Moreover, the name Ila-kabkabu is not unique, other bearers in the period of continuous West Semitic immigration into Mesopotamia being well attested. Since, on the other hand, the list continues with a section beginning with Sulili, the son of Aminu, Aminu being the last of the 'ancestors', it need not be doubted that the men listed in inverse order were the ancestors of this Sulili. The reason for this insertion is not difficult to guess: the dynasty which begins with Sulili was eventually overthrown and replaced by Shamshi-Adad I who, in turn, was succeeded by his son, Ishme-Dagan. After Ishme-Dagan's death, a lengthy struggle between competing contenders appears to have taken place and it is therefore possible that a partisan of the Sulili–Puzur-Ashur dynasty should have inserted the long line of their ancestors in order to prove that they were the legitimate successors of Ushpia.

At some place prior to the accession of this dynasty the king-list must be assumed to be incomplete, the gap spanning the period when Assyria was under the domination of the Third Dynasty of Ur. Evidence to this effect is furnished by an inscription unearthed in the ruins of the Ishtar temple at Ashur in which a Zariqum who calls himself 'governor' (*šakkanakkum*) of Ashur dedicates a chapel in the temple to the goddess Bēlat-ekallim for the life of Amar-Sin, king of Ur.[3] Since no king of this name figures in the king-list and since, moreover, the two authors of dedicatory inscriptions to kings of Akkad, Azuzu and Ititi, are not mentioned either in this compilation, it is a legitimate conclusion that the Assyrian king-list comprises only sovereigns who were responsible only to the god Ashur and not to any human being. This conclusion is in line with later sections of the 'standard version' where gaps are attributable to foreign domination.[4]

That the group of kings headed by Sulili, the son of Aminu, actually began their rule in the period of Ibbi-Sin when the power of the Third Dynasty of Ur declined rapidly is well supported by

1 §III, 13; §II, 24, 94, n. 57.   2 §II, 9, 33 ff.
3 G, 4, 2 f., no. II; §III, 8.   4 See below, p. 749.

the fact that Kikkia, the second ruler of this group, is mentioned in two building inscriptions of later kings, namely Ashur-rīm-nishēshu[1] and Shalmaneser III.[2] Whereas the former king speaks of Kikkia only as the earliest known builder of a 'wall' which he himself renewed, the latter specifies, though not in the same text in which he mentions Kikkia, that the wall was that of the city of Ashur,[3] a conclusion which is confirmed by the fact that the pertinent inscription was unearthed in the foundation of the old fortification wall, north of the temenos.[4] Numerous instances from all periods of Assyrian and Babylonian history demonstrate that the construction of a fortification wall around a capital city was the first, and perhaps partly symbolic, action of a prince who had won his independence; inversely, the destruction of the wall of a city always followed a conquest, even if it was a matter of peaceful surrender to an overlord.[5] It is therefore apparent that Kikkia was the first ruler who succeeded in throwing off the domination of the kings of Ur and in restoring Assyrian independence. Even though some setbacks appear to have occurred—Shalmaneser III lists among the early builders of the fortification wall Puzur-Ashur, the founder of the illustrious Old Assyrian dynasty, and Ikunum, his fourth successor[6]—Assyria rose rapidly to the rank of a major power once its independence was firmly established.[7] The king-list enumerates, as Kikkia's successors, four kings, including Ilushuma, and summarizes these six princes with the afore-quoted remark that the *līmum*-officials who held office under their rule were 'eaten up'.[8] That this damage to the list was of comparatively late date is shown by the fact that, at the time of Tukulti-Ninurta I (1242–1206 B.C.), the length of Ilushuma's reign was known. This ruler, in reporting about his restoration of the sanctuary of the goddess Ishtar Ashuritu, the consort of the national god, relates that since the previous restoration by Ilushuma 720 years had gone by. Since, as will be outlined presently by the example of Esarhaddon's report on the early builders of the Ashur temple at Ashur,[9] it was the practice to figure from the beginning of one builder's rule to the beginning of the next builder's rule, it is apparent that Tukulti-Ninurta comprised in his figure the number of regnal years of Ilushuma. As he himself, however, did not complete the

---

[1] G, 4, 34 ff., no. xiv.
[2] §iii, 16, 1, 391, l. 17.
[3] *Ibid.* 260, rev., l. 6.
[4] G, 4, p. 35, n. 11.
[5] §iii, 11, 267, n. 1; 280; §iii, 14, 30 with n. 4.
[6] §iii, 16, 1, 391, ll. 17 f.
[7] See below, pp. 754 ff.
[8] See above, p. 743 with n. 2.
[9] See below, pp. 748 and 750 f.

sanctuary within his accession year, it is apparent that he figured twenty-one years for Ilushuma's reign and left one year for himself to complete the project, thus allowing, as customary, two 350-year periods between the previous builder's death and his own inauguration of the new sanctuary. Hence the exact number of Ilushuma's regnal years was known to him as twenty-one.

In the following section, the 'standard version' enumerates the six princes separating Ilushuma's rule from that of Shamshi-Adad I. Beginning with Erishum I, the list specifies for each of the subsequent rulers how many years he 'exerted the kingship' (*šarrutta epuš*). In doing so, the compiler, in accordance with the general Assyrian practice, used the post-dating method, counting the year in which a ruler died and his successor acceded to the throne as the last full year of the king who died. The next king's first, accordingly, was the first full year following his accession to the throne. A certain difficulty arose, of course, in cases where a king did not survive his accession year. In these instances the king-list writes his name followed by the remark: *tuppišu šarrutta epuš*. While the exact meaning of this expression is unknown, it can be shown from several instances that the Assyrians interpreted it as meaning 'he exerted the kingship for less than a year'.

In the section beginning with Erishum I, the number of his own regnal years, namely forty, is the only one preserved in the extant copies of the list; those of the other immediate predecessors of Shamshi-Adad I are broken or rubbed off so as to be illegible. However, the two afore-quoted building inscriptions from the Ashur temple at Ashur[1] make it possible to recover at least the sum of the lost numbers. Shalmaneser I reports that from the reign of Erishum to that of the next builder, Shamshi-Adad I, 159 years had elapsed.[2] Esarhaddon, on the other hand, lists the same lapse of time as 126 years.[3] If it is taken into consideration that Shamshi-Adad, according to the king-list, ruled over Assyria for thirty-three years, it becomes apparent that the two reports agree in so far as Shalmaneser includes these thirty-three years whereas Esarhaddon's number excludes them. It results that the five successors of Erishum I ruled together for eighty-six years.

Shamshi-Adad I, as was mentioned before, was one of the most beloved and celebrated rulers who ever occupied the Assyrian throne. The 'standard version' acknowledges this special condition by describing, in a short annalistic excursus, this great

---

[1] See above, p. 744.   [2] See §II, 7, vol. I, no. 13, col. III, ll. 36–41.
[3] §III, 4, 3, col. III, l. 22.

empire-builder's career prior to his accession to the throne. It then continues to relate that 'he caused' his predecessor, Erishum II, 'to arise from the throne, and exerted the kingship for thirty-three years.' Under Shamshi-Adad's son and successor, Ishme-Dagan I, Assyria experienced a period of decline which culminated, at the end of his rule, in a catastrophe the nature of which is not known. The difficulties which Assyria encountered in these years are clearly reflected in the king-list tradition. In the 'standard version', one list gives Ishme-Dagan forty regnal years, the other fifty. With him, however, it ends the Shamshi-Adad dynasty and continues with an Ashur-dugul who is characterized as the 'son of a nobody', which means a man not of royal descent. It continues to state that, during the six years of his rule, six other 'sons of a nobody' arose, but not one of them ruled beyond his accession year. The last of these six is Adasi, whom all the subsequent Assyrian rulers regarded as the founder of their dynasty. However, the 'standard version' here leaves out rulers who are attested by at least some fragmentary king-lists from Ashur. One of these precious fragments[1] draws a line after Erishum II in order to indicate that with him the dynasty ends; it then lists Shamshi-Adad and Ishme-Dagan, followed by Mut-Ashkur who is known from the Mari texts as Ishme-Dagan's son and heir-apparent and, as the fourth member of the dynasty, Talmu-Sh[arri], 'Great is the King', a name well known from the Nuzi texts. This Hurrian name of Mut-Ashkur's son and successor is not surprising if it is remembered that, in a desperate attempt to end an extended war with King Zaziya of the Hurrian tribe of Turukku, Ishme-Dagan arranged a marriage between Zaziya's daughter and his own son, Mut-Ashkur, the future king.[2] That this Hurrian on the royal throne who was considered a foreigner and probably maintained himself only with the help of troops from his maternal homeland, Turukku, infuriated the Assyrians can be gathered from two pieces of evidence. There is, in the first place, a fragmentary inscription from Ashur in which a certain Puzur-Sin, who calls himself with the usual title 'priest-king of Ashur,' prides himself on having removed from the throne a man of 'foreign seed, of non-Assyrian flesh',[3] who is further said to have been a descendant of Shamshi-Adad. Since this same Puzur-Sin reports that he demolished this foreigner's palace and built instead a sanctuary, he must have been able to maintain himself on the throne for at least some years. The second piece of

---

[1] §III, 19, no. 14; §II, 9, 31.   [2] §III, 3, vol. II, no. 40.
[3] §II, 9, 32.

evidence is the lack in the 'standard version' of any reference to either Mut-Ashkur or Talmu-Sharri, which lack is well in line with the afore-stated principle of omitting men who were dependent upon a foreign ruler.

It thus becomes apparent that the rule of at least three kings following Ishme-Dagan I, *viz.* this latter's two descendants and Puzur-Sin, is missing in the 'standard version'. In order to ascertain the correct, or at least approximately correct, datings of the Old Assyrian kings, sources other than the 'standard version' must therefore be used; this all the more since there is some evidence to indicate that the 'standard version' is incomplete in still another period, namely when Assyria was part of the empire of the kings of Khanigalbat. With the help of building-inscriptions of various Assyrian kings who, as was stated before, were very thorough in ascertaining the interval between two successive reconstructions of a sacred building, it can be shown that, besides the 'standard version', there existed a more complete, and therefore 'longer' list of kings. In starting this analysis it must be pointed out that both Shalmaneser I and Esarhaddon in their afore-quoted inscriptions dealing with the reconstruction of the Ashur temple at Ashur used the 'standard version'. The basic information with the help of which the rule of these two kings can be dated is provided by the entry in the eponym canon that in the month of Siwan of the ninth year of king Ashur-dan III an eclipse of the sun took place. Astronomical computation furnished several possible dates of this eclipse, but by comparison with certain data contained in Ptolemy's canon of Neo-Babylonian rulers and the mention of lunar eclipses in various sources it could be determined beyond doubt that the solar eclipse mentioned in the eponym canon was that of 15 June 763 b.c. Starting from this date it is possible to determine, with the help of the 'standard version' and the eponym canon, the reigns from Ashur-uballiṭ I (1362–1327 b.c.) down to the end of Ashurbanipal's reign. Shalmaneser I reckons 580 years from the beginning of Erishum's reign to his own. Deducting from this the afore-quoted 159 years from the beginning of Erishum to the end of Shamshi-Adad I, one obtains 421 years from the end of Shamshi-Adad to the beginning of Shalmaneser I. If minor differences in the various copies of the 'standard version' are taken into consideration, one obtains 422 years for this interval,[1] whence it is apparent that Shalmaneser used a king-list almost identical with the extant ones. Esarhaddon, in turn, reckons 434 years from Shamshi-Adad

[1] G, 11, 2, 86 f.

to Shalmaneser, having probably reckoned fifty years for Ishme-Dagan I instead of the 40 years of the Khorsabad version. There are, however, building inscriptions in which the computation is based on a different king-list. One of these is the afore-mentioned inscription of Shalmaneser's son and successor, Tukulti-Ninurta I,[1] in which he gives the interval between his own reign and that of Ilushuma as 720 years, figuring, as was pointed out before, from the beginning of Ilushuma's reign to which he assigned twenty-one years.[2] Deducting from the remaining 699 years the 159 years which, according to Shal-maneser, separated the beginning of Ilushuma's successor, Erishum I, from the end of the reign of Shamshi-Adad I, one obtains 540 years for the interval from the end of Shamshi-Adad to the beginning of Tukulti-Ninurta I. Accounting, furthermore, for the thirty regnal years of Shalmaneser, Tukulti-Ninurta's reckoning yields 510 years for the interval from the end of Shamshi-Adad to the beginning of Shalmaneser for which, as was just pointed out, the latter king reckoned 421 years. Since it is obvious that Tukulti-Ninurta was well acquainted with the king-list perused by his father and the computation contained in his father's inscription, it is apparent that he made use of a king-list which contained eighty-nine years more than the 'standard version'. The reason why, among the two available king-lists, he chose the longer one is easy to grasp if the significance of the 700-year span of time is kept in mind. In terms of the Christian Era, Tukulti-Ninurta's dating indicates for the end of Shamshi-Adad's reign the year 1782 (i.e. 1242 + 540) B.C. Taking into consideration the one-year leeway which the kings themselves allowed in reckoning the interval between their own rule and that of the previous builder, the year adopted for Shamshi-Adad's death in these pages is 1783 B.C.

Exactly the same dates as those from the inscription of Tukulti-Ninurta I are obtained with the help of the chronological data contained in the afore-discussed report of Tiglath-pileser I on his restoration of the Anu-Adad temple.[3] He reckons 701 years from his own reign to that of Shamshi-Adad, the previous builder; as he ruled from 1114 to 1076 B.C., his computation and that of his great-grandfather, Ashur-dan, yield the year 1815 for the be-ginning of Shamshi-Adad's reign.

Thus the king-list perused by these rulers of the twelfth century yields the years 1815 to 1783 for the thirty-three years

[1] See above, pp. 747 f. [2] See above, p. 748.
[3] See above, p. 741, n. 1.

of Shamshi-Adad's rule. It will be noted that the complete correspondence between their date and that of Tukulti-Ninurta I makes it clear that these two rulers based their computation on the same king-list. The only difficulty resides in the naming by Tiglath-pileser of Shamshi-Adad, the son of Ishme-Dagan, as the previous builder; yet if it is assumed that his king-list was of the type of the afore-mentioned small fragment from Ashur, mentioning four members of the Shamshi-Adad dynasty instead of only two of the 'standard version', this error is easily explained, because this list does not state the kings' patronymics.

IV. THE OLD ASSYRIAN PERIOD

Unlike Babylonia, Assyria is not a naturally rich country. The narrow Tigris valley with its comparatively high mountains on both banks yielded hardly enough agricultural products to support its population. Yet being, in contrast to the sedentary Sumerians and Hurrians, the descendants of a nomadic, which means a travelling population, the Assyrians looked beyond the narrow borders of their own land in order to supplement their resources by trading with other countries. It goes without saying that, in order to carry on a profitable trade with other nations, the Assyrians had to have products of their own which they could exchange for food or other foreign merchandise. One such product was woollen textiles, in the mass production, the spinning, weaving, and dyeing of which they appear to have developed an early lead over other peoples. Sheep could easily be raised in the hilly region along the banks of the Tigris river. A certain amount of trade could also be carried on, and actually was, by buying foreign merchandise and re-selling it to others, transporting the goods over long distances. It is particularly significant and not due to a mere coincidence that the oldest private Assyrian documents were unearthed at Nuzi[1] and attest the commercial activity of the Assyrians there as well as in Arrapkha.[2] Familiar Old Assyrian names such as Puzur-Ashur and Sin-rabi leave no doubt about the nationality of the businessmen. That they, like subsequently the merchants in Asia Minor, came from the city of Ashur can be inferred from the typical reference *ina ālim*, 'in the City (*par excellence*)',[3] a manner of speaking about the city of Ashur which is familiar not only from the documents from Asia

---

[1] §II, 14, nos. 223–7.   [2] *Ibid.* no. 224, ll. 1 and 7.
[3] *Ibid*, no. 227, rev., l. 1.

Minor but also from the Shamshi-Adad correspondence excavated at Mari.[1] The persons with whom they traded were local men, as can be gathered from names such as Tishpak-bani which was borne by a person described as a resident of Arrapkha.[2] The mention of a caravan[3] referred to by the usual Old Assyrian term suggests an exchange of merchandise on a considerable scale. It is further important to note that, scanty as the available material is, it still permits us to conclude from certain linguistic features that the Old Assyrian letters from Nuzi are slightly older than the oldest texts from Asia Minor. Aside from the archaic genitive form *a-ḫa-im* to which attention was called years ago,[4] the spelling *i-ir-dá-kà*,[5] 'your servant', instead of the more conventional Assyrian *erdaka*[6] shows that the shift from *i* to *e* before *r* had not even begun at the time when the pertinent letter from Nuzi was written. This is a very characteristic feature of the archaic Assyrian language; King Erishum's scribes, for instance, spell their royal lord's name consistently with an initial *i* and not with the *e* used by the late scribes of the 'standard version' of the king-list, who probably no longer understood the name.[7] It is not without interest to note that, at least in the Middle Assyrian period, the scribes were well aware of this difference in the pronunciation between the older language and their own. The royal scribe who wanted to use an archaic spelling wrote *I-ri-ba-ᵈAd-ád* when writing the name of the father of Ashur-uballiṭ I.[8] In the latest texts from the older level of Old Assyrian tablets from Kanesh, on the other hand, the shift from *i* to *e* before *r* and *ḫ* is in its early stages.

In consideration of these linguistic features it appears therefore reasonable to place the Old Assyrian texts from Nuzi slightly before those from Asia Minor, which means either in the early years of Erishum's long reign or toward the end of that of Ilushuma. The fact that they possibly antedate the penetration of Asia Minor which, as was seen, began on a large scale in the later years of Erishum's reign[9] makes it significant that one of the two fairly well-preserved letters mentions a payment of *x* minas of silver,[10] while the other one speaks of two items of gold[11] the larger of which amounted to no less than one third mina and five shekels, which is equivalent to almost half pound of gold. Moreover,

[1] §I, 13, 444, n. 2.　　　　　　　　[2] §II, 14, no. 224, l. 2.
[3] *Ibid.* ll. 9 and 15; cf. §IV, 19, 454.
[4] §IV, 19, 459 with note 35 followed by §IV, 1, 68, n. 24.
[5] §II, 14, no. 223, l. 5.　　　　　　[6] §IV, 26, 271.
[7] For the meaning of the name see below, p. 767.
[8] §II, 8, plate 16, l. 26.　　　　　　[9] See above, pp. 708 f.
[10] §II, 14, no. 223, l. 18.　　　　　[11] *Ibid.* no. 224, ll. 6 and 9.

mention is made of several 'hundreds' of copper said to have been paid out in Arrapkha.[1] Thus these letters exhibit one of the features which are a most striking characteristic of the Old Assyrian texts from Asia Minor, namely the great wealth in precious and other metals in the possession of private individuals which bears no comparison with the corresponding amounts mentioned in contemporary Old Babylonian documents. Since the excavator of the archaic levels of Nineveh stresses the paucity of metals in the early periods of Assyrian history,[2] the question arises as to the source of this wealth. Whereas the gold is easy to trace as coming from the Nuzi region where placer gold was recovered from the river Zab and its affluents and where occasionally real estate taxes were paid in gold,[3] the question still remains as to how the Assyrian merchants got this gold and the large amount of silver into their possession. As military might never creates wealth but is rather the consequence of the accumulation of wealth in a country, one must look for a technical discovery having, as so often in history, created the wealth which, in turn, produced the political power of a nation. The texts from Asia Minor suggest the nature of this discovery: it was the production of silver first from lead ore and subsequently from copper ore. With an abundant supply of lead in their own country and thus (once the discovery that it contains silver was made) a wealth of silver in their hands, the Assyrian businessmen could penetrate every foreign market they wished.

There is actually evidence to show that the penetration of foreign markets was the guiding principle of the Assyrian rulers prior to Shamshi-Adad I. Little is known so far of Puzur-Ashur whom his three successors, Shallim-akhum, Ilushuma, and Erishum, name as their ancestor. He rebuilt the fortification wall of Ashur and thus appears to have firmly established Assyria's independence which, after Kikkia, appears to have been temporarily lost again. An inscription of his son and successor, Shallim-akhum, was discovered at Ashur in the oldest level of the courtyard of the Ashur temple.[4] It relates that the god Ashur had requested him to build a temple and that he complied with this order 'for his own life and the life of his city', a formula which recurs in all the building inscriptions of the period prior to Shamshi-Adad. It is a further characteristic of all the royal inscriptions of this period that the kings do not use the title 'king' (*šarrum*), but call themselves *iššiakkum*[5] of the city of Ashur.

---

[1] §II, 14, no. 224, ll. 7 f. [2] §I, 16, 145. [3] E.g. §IV, 11, nos. 228 and 229.
[4] G, 4, 4 ff. [5] Spelled out in §IV, 12, 224, l. 4.

This title denotes in Babylonia a city-ruler who exercises his functions in the name of an overlord bearing the title 'king'. The use in Assyria fully agrees with this basic meaning, the only difference being that the overlord in Assyria was the divine ruler, the title king being, in this period, strictly reserved for the national god, Ashur. 'Ashur is king, (the earthly ruler's name) is Ashur's *iššiakkum*' is a kind of credo which occurs on the seal of the afore-discussed[1] Assyrian prince of Kanesh[2] as well as in the inscription of Erishum to be discussed presently. Equally characteristic are several letters found in Kanesh which the king himself had addressed to some of the prominent merchants of this city; in the introductory clause of these letters, the ruler used for himself the modest title *waklum*, 'overseer'. The reluctance to use the title 'king' sharply distinguishes the Assyrians from the Babylonians, who believed that, in the beginning of all things, 'kingship descended from heaven'.[3] It is, on the other hand, a feature which the Assyrians share with the Israelites and other peoples descended from nomads; as is known from the Mari texts, the nomads called their chieftains 'fathers' so that, for instance, the heads of the various clans constituting the tribe of the Khanians were 'the fathers of Khana'.[4]

It is not without interest to note in this connexion that at least some of the linguistically Sumerianized Amorites who ruled in Babylonia between the Sargonic period and the rise of Assyria did not use for themselves the title 'king' either; Gudea of Lagash, for instance, speaks of his god as 'king' and of his goddess as 'queen', but for himself he uses the more modest title 'city-ruler'. The theme of Shallim-akhum's inscription that the god Ashur demanded a sanctuary which he, the earthly ruler, hastened to build is another trait which the Assyrians of the Old Assyrian period shared with those Amorite princes of Babylonia. The most detailed description of the manner in which the earthly ruler received such an order in a dream-vision is contained in the famous *Cylinder A* of Gudea of Lagash;[5] pictorial representations of such visions are very numerous, too,[6] one of the most famous being that of Ur-Nammu of Ur receiving from the moon-god the order to build his sanctuary at Ur.[7]

[1] See above, pp. 710 f.

[2] This is perhaps the place to state that, in so far as Old Assyrian is concerned, the name of this city was Kanish and not Kanesh as in the Hittite sources. Except for one of the latest level II tablets, the name is always written *Kà-ni-iš*, *iš* and *eš* being carefully distinguished by the Old Assyrian scribes.

[3] §iv, 9, 70, l. 1.   [4] §iv, 4, 15, l. 29.   [5] G, 16, 90 ff.

[6] Cf. below, pp. 767 f.   [7] §iv, 14, planche i.

Shallim-akhum's son and successor, Ilushuma (1962–1942 B.C.), was the first king of Assyria who had the power to take a hand in Babylonian affairs. In order to understand this development, a few data of contemporary Babylonian history must be called to mind. After the downfall of the Third Dynasty of Ur, two powers that had been allies against Ibbi-Sin, shared the spoils of their victory, namely Kazallu in northern Babylonia and Isin in the south. One of the kings of Kazallu was Sumuditana, who is known from tablets from Kish to have been the overlord of that city. Evidence to this effect comes from contracts in which the oath was sworn by Sumuditana and Numushda, the patron god of Kazallu.[1] With Sumuditana's death, however, Kish succeeded in freeing itself from the supremacy of Kazallu; for in the year named from Sumuditana's death, the oath was sworn by a Iawium and Zababa, the patron god of Kish.[2] At the same time as Iawium, Sumuabum of Babylon made himself independent of Kazallu, constructing a fortification wall around his city; this event gave its name to Sumuabum's first two regnal years as independent king of Babylon and to Iawium's second and third, the oath in these two years being sworn by Iawium and Zababa.[3] Yet after about nine years of independence,[4] Kish was conquered by a certain Manana as attested by several year names: First, the oath was sworn by both Manana and Nanna and Zababa and Iawium,[5] the year being named 'Manana seized the throne'.[6] There followed a year 'after that when Manana seized the throne',[7] and finally a year 'Manana became king',[8] the reference obviously being to his having seized the throne at Kish. That Manana was a foreign conqueror results from the fact that under his rule Iawium's real estate buyer Ṣisu-nawirat was replaced by a Shumshunu-watar, and that the oath in the contracts by Zababa and Iawium was replaced by an oath by Nanna and Manana. After Kish had fallen to Manana, Sumuabum could not maintain himself on his throne for any length of time. A date formula from Eshnunna reports that 'Sumuabum was driven away to Dēr'.[9] Since many other date formulae of Manana and his successors have come to

---

[1] §iv, 10, 101, sub K, and §iv, 13, no. 1, ll. 15 f.
[2] §iv, 25, no. 3, ll. 13 and 24.
[3] §iv, 25, no. 4; for the year name also §iv, 13, no. 11.
[4] Besides the three years just listed, §iv, 28, 193 sub nos. 7, 8 (2 years), 10, 11 and §iv, 10, 100, sub D.   [5] §iv, 10, 99; §iv, 13, no. 7, ll. 12 f.
[6] §iv, 10, 279, sub F 51; §iv, 25, no. 5, ll. 8 ff.; §iv, 13, no. 7, l. 25: traces of name Manana visible on photograph.
[7] §iv, 23, 2, 76, sub gg.   [8] §iv, 13, no. 16; §iv, 23, 2, 76, sub hh.
[9] §iv, 6, 191, sub no. 113.

light at Kish and other sites,[1] there can be no doubt that both Kish and Babylon remained subjected to the rule of this dynasty for at least one generation. In fact, a prosopographic investigation into the contemporary dated documents from Sippar, Maradda, and Dilbat reveals that Sumuabum and Sumulael, the second independent king of Babylon, who again started his rule by constructing the fortification wall, were separated from each other by at least one generation.[2]

The afore-mentioned date formula from Eshnunna suggests at the same time the place of origin of the Manana dynasty. Dēr was the capital of Iamutbal, a state which, as is well known from an inscription of Kudur-Mabuk, a later conqueror coming from Dēr, was devoted to the cult of the moon-god Nanna or Sin. It is well in line with the conclusion that Manana's dynasty originated in Iamutbal that one of his successors was named Sumu-Iamutbal.[3]

It was, to all appearances, this dynasty of Dēr in which Ilushuma saw a danger to free communications and against which, therefore, he undertook his campaign. In his brick inscription from the temple of Ishtar at Ashur,[4] in the passage quoted above,[5] he lists Dēr as one of the cities which he opened for trade to 'the Akkadians and their children'. It is likely that the 'Akkadian' king in whose favour he acted was Sumuabum. This identification suggests itself not only because the catch-line of the afore-cited Chronicle concerning Sargon and Naram-Sin[6] makes the two kings contemporaries, but also because there is at least one year name from Sippar from Sumuabum's rule which, being in Akkadian and not included in the list of his year names as king of Babylon,[7] indicates that he ruled as a vassal king of Kazallu long before he and Iawium made themselves independent. The absence from Sumuabum's as well as from Iawium's list of year names of a formula stating that either of them became king confirms the conclusion that the accession to the throne of both men preceded, possibly by a considerable number of years, their first year as independent rulers.

Ilushuma's reference to his providing the Akkadians with copper is significant in more than one respect; primarily because it shows that he had enough copper at his disposal to provide for his own needs and in addition sell some to his Akkadian friends, obviously in exchange for merchandise of which he was short.

---

[1] §IV, 22, I, p. 212; §IV, 23.   [2] §IV, 3, 102a.   [3] §IV, 21.
[4] §IV, 29.   [5] See above, p. 708.
[6] G, 8, 14, l. 14.   [7] §IV, 27, no. 1, left edge; no. 2, left edge.

It further indicates that he did not hesitate to arm the people of northern Babylonia, of whose loyalty he must have been fully certain. In fact the friendship and co-operation between the First Dynasty of Babylon and the Assyrians extended over many generations; the last testimony is Hammurabi's campaign to Ashur and Nineveh, which was directed against the king of Eshnunna and in the course of which he recovered the gods of both cities and restored them to Ishme-Dagan.[1] Was Sumuabu, whose name appears as *Su-abu* in the afore-mentioned chronicle, a descendant of the *Su-abu* who figures as no. 11 among the tribal ancestors in the first section of the Assyrian king-list? Or did the Assyrians see in these kings of Babylon the successors of the dynasty of Akkad?

The question remains as to the origin of Ilushuma's abundant supply of copper. As the evidence discussed previously indicates that Asia Minor was opened to Assyrian trade only at the time of Erishum,[2] the copper is likely to have come from the famous mine of Ergani Maden, where a very high-grade copper is said to have been mined in antiquity.[3] As it contains some tin, it could be used as bronze for making weapons without any additions. It is probably this site which the Old Assyrian merchants knew as Kharāna,[4] and to which they referred not only as the place of origin of copper but also as a station on the caravan road between Ashur and Kanesh,[5] located close to the point where the caravans crossed the Euphrates river into Asia Minor. Its possession by Ilushuma would explain not only his ample supply of copper and that of the merchants doing business at Nuzi, but it would suggest that this was the gateway through which, one generation later, the penetration of Asia Minor, both commercial and partly also military, took place.

To judge by the afore-discussed events in Babylonia, Ilushuma's attempt to keep the Manana dynasty of Iamutbal in check does not appear to have met with lasting success. It is also worth noting that his name was never chosen again by an Assyrian king, which tends to show that posterity did not consider him a successful ruler. The restoration of the temple of Ishtar of Ashur[6] is the only major construction of his that is known.

His son Erishum (1941–1902 B.C.), on the contrary, must have been an outstanding ruler. His most far-reaching decision was alluded to before; it was he who decided to leave the initiative for commercial transactions on a large scale entirely to his

---

[1] §I, 12, 350 f.   [2] See above, pp. 708 f.; also §IV, 7, 48.
[3] §IV, 2, 44.   [4] §IV, 20, 22, n. 95.
[5] *Ibid.*; §IV, 7, 118.   [6] See above, pp. 747 and 751.

individual subjects which means, in modern terms, he initiated, or at least perfected, the first experiment of free enterprise on a large scale. To be sure, there were various public institutions such as the administrations of the major temples, and that of the capital city, and the king himself, who took part in the exchange of merchandise between Assyria and Asia Minor. But the main financing was done by private bankers who, accordingly, bore the main risk of the long haul of merchandise from Ashur to the various cities in Asia Minor, but who also earned considerable profits if the transaction was successful. On principle, the business was carried out as follows: The banker entrusted a certain amount of capital, frequently two minas of gold or a multiple of this amount, to a commercial traveller or one of the merchants who set out from Ashur to settle for several years in the distant province. The recipient of the capital pledged himself to return twice the amount which was designated as his 'sack' or 'pouch', after a specified number of years, usually after four years. If any profits beyond the amount he had to pay back accrued to the salesman, they were divided between the contracting parties at a specified ratio, either 1:1 or 1:2.[1] The hired hands, such as ass drivers, messenger boys and other personnel, were also paid by being given an opportunity to take part in the business. They received, at the outset, a certain capital which was called their *be'ulātum*, a term indicating that they could use this money as they saw fit. They had to pay back the same amount at the end of the journey. The men usually invested the money in woven materials which they purchased in Ashur and sold at a profit in Asia Minor or on the road. The profit they made was the payment of their labour. In later periods, this method, under various designations, became the usual way of paying hired hands.[2] The Assyrians in the Old Assyrian period must have developed this method of payment out of the experience that there is no limit to the individual's ingenuity when he is given an opportunity to make a profit.

The ample funds which Erishum generated by levelling tolls and taxes on his businessmen were, at least in part, invested in construction activity in the capital city. He rebuilt the Ashur temple at Ashur with all its auxiliary buildings,[3] and he built a sanctuary for the god Adad on the site where subsequently a double sanctuary, dedicated to Adad and Anu, was erected by Shamshi-Adad I and rebuilt by Tiglath-pileser I.[4] Besides brick inscriptions from these sanctuaries, only a rather fragmentary

[1] §iv, 16, 308 ff.   [2] §iv, 15; §iv, 18, 188, with n. 2.
[3] G, 4, 10 ff., nos. 1–8.   [4] See above pp. 741 and 751; G, 4, 16 ff., nos. 9–11.

alabaster statue with an inscription of about twelve lines was found in the ruins of the Ashur temple;[1] but at Kanesh, a long and most interesting inscription of Erishum was excavated in a building which had served as a scribal school, the text apparently having been used as a specimen of good styling.[2] The inscription deals with the construction of the 'sacred *mušlāl*', which is what might be called in modern terms 'the supreme court building'. The structure was known from an inscription of Adadnirari I (1304–1273 B.C.), who rebuilt it but who, to all appearances, had not been able to determine the previous builder. However, the excavator of the structure which is located at the foot of a steep trail leading up to the temple tower of Ashur had found bricks inscribed with Erishum's name.[3] One of the two gates of this building, most likely that leading up to Ashur's temenos, was called 'Gate of the oath of the god of the Land', whereas the other, obviously that leading down to the abyss, was the 'Gate of the Divine Judges'. From Erishum's inscription the names of these seven divine judges are known; one of them is called 'Justice', another one 'He listens to Prayer', a third one 'His Word is true', and so on. It may be mentioned here that the 'gate of the god' is several times mentioned in legal documents from Asia Minor as the place which a person had to enter in order to swear an oath or make a solemn declaration before the judges.[4] Some texts mention legal decisions rendered by 'the City', and it is likely that it was in the *mušlāl*-building that the judges representing the City held their sessions. One such legal decision makes it clear that the ruler himself presided over the supreme court sessions. It begins with these words: 'Seal of the *waklum*; the City rendered judgment (thus).'[5] The case tablet of this decision bears the seal of Erishum's grandson, Sharrum-kēn (Sargon I of Assyria), which was discussed previously.[6] In one instance, a merchant owed a considerable amount of money to one of the eponyms. Three other men were inscribed in the promissory note as guarantors, and the court of the City then ruled that one of the guarantors had to pay the debt. In this case it is likely that the court of the City was involved in the matter because the creditor was the eponym who appears to have had the function of a finance minister.

---

[1] §III, 26, 159.
[2] §IV, 12, 10; some improved readings §IV, 8, 48, n. 243; §IV, 24, 145 f., n. 1.
[3] G, 1, plate 30 and pp. 68 and 120 f. and 121, n. 1.
[4] §IV, 5, no. 286.　　　　　　　　　　　　　　[5] *Ibid.* no. 327.
[6] See above, pp. 710 f; also below, pp. 767 f.

Under Erishum's son and successor, Ikunum, the fortification wall of the city of Ashur was rebuilt. This is known not only from the mention of Ikunum as one of the previous builders in the afore-cited building inscription of Shalmaneser III,[1] who lists Ikunum's restoration after that of Puzur-Ashur, but also from one of the texts from Kanesh[2] which deals with a message from the City to the *kārum* Kanesh informing it that their contribution to the cost of the fortification wall had been set at ten minas of silver. The prince, so it is reported, had written himself for the money and his message was to be read to each of the *kārum* organizations in Asia Minor; then the money which was collected was to be sealed and sent to Ashur as soon as possible. It would be interesting to know which other cities outside of Asia Minor had been ordered by Ikunum to send contributions. The peculiar fact is that numerous Assyrian settlements in Asia Minor and in northern Mesopotamia are mentioned many times in the Old Assyrian texts, and also Gasur-Nuzi is mentioned; but no city in Assyria proper except Ashur is referred to in any of the documents. Nor do any of the royal inscriptions of this period make mention of any building activity in any city other than Ashur. It is not known either whether the fortification wall had been destroyed or damaged in a war or whether it needed repairs because of ordinary wear only. It is known, however, that the contemporary kings of Eshnunna pursued an aggressive policy and the possibility must be reckoned with that an enemy army had advanced as far as the capital city. Ikunum's reign does not appear to have been very long; for not only did the afore-mentioned business transaction which had begun under Erishum[3] drag on until the reign of Sharrum-kēn, but, to judge by the pertinent information contained in Ashur-rīm-nisheshu's account, also the restoration of the fortification wall of the capital city was completed by Sharrum-kēn. This king's reign must have been remembered by posterity as the apogee of the Old Assyrian period representing an age of wealth and of power for the country. For reckoning in terms of the 'long' king-list, about three 350-year periods later, an ambitious young king chose the name Sargon the Younger in the hope of bringing back the golden age of his two older namesakes.

At the time of Sharrum-kēn's second successor, Naram-Sin of Assyria, events took place which threatened to upset the peace

[1] See above, p. 747 with n. 6.
[2] § v, 2, no. 1; § iv, 7, 197; § iv, 20, 65 ff.
[3] See above, p. 710; *J.A.O.S.* 78 (1958), 101.

and prosperity which seem to have characterized Sharrum-kēn's rule. The 'standard version' of the king-list tersely reports: 'At the time of Naram-Sin, Shamshi-Adad went to Babylonia.' For what purpose and under what conditions he went is not known. On the positive side, however, it is known that Ibiq-Adad II of Eshnunna had conquered Rapiqum,[1] and it is further known from previous and subsequent captures of this border town that the Assyrians considered Rapiqum in unfriendly hands a danger to their security and to their lines of communication.[2] And it can further be shown that the end of the rule of Ibiq-Adad II of Eshnunna occurred a few years before Shamshi-Adad's accession to the Assyrian throne. Dadusha's last year corresponded with Shamshi-Adad's 29th;[3] Dadusha ruled for at least eleven years;[4] his brother and predecessor, Naram-Sin of Eshnunna, ruled for at least twelve years;[5] at least two years must be reckoned for Iqish-Tishpak and his father, Ibni-Erra,[6] and besides there are at least six year names that are thus far unattributable. It becomes apparent that Naram-Sin of Assyria despatched Shamshi-Adad, at that time a subject of his, with an army to Babylonia, to drive Ibiq-Adad II away from Babylonian soil. That Shamshi-Adad was successful in this undertaking can be inferred from the appearance on the throne of Eshnunna of two men, Ibni-Erra and Iqish-Tishpak, who obviously did not belong to the dynasty of Ibiq-Adad II and separated the rule of this king from those of his two sons. They must have been placed on the throne by the victorious Assyrian army, but they could not maintain themselves once the Assyrians withdrew their troops.

Acting like many a successful army commander throughout history, Shamshi-Adad then seized, on his return from Babylonia, first Ekallatum and then, after having resided there for three years, Ashur. To judge by the Khorsabad copy of the 'standard version' of the king-list, Erishum II, the last ruler of the Puzur-Ashur dynasty, must have ruled for at least two years, because in the fragmentary line which contained the number of his regnal years the plural sign after year is preserved. Thus it is most likely that, for the final phase of his usurpation, Shamshi-Adad awaited the death of his overlord, Naram-Sin of Assyria.

---

[1] §IV, 6, 127.   [2] §I, 13, 442 ff.   [3] *Ibid.* 445.
[4] *Ibid.* 440, n. 1.   [5] §IV, 23, 1, 82.   [6] *Ibid.* 1, 78.

V. THE RELIGION

Since, aside from the few afore-mentioned texts from the school of scribes, all the documents excavated in Asia Minor come either from commercial or administrative archives, it is not surprising that texts of purely religious contents are very scarce. One such text has been known for many years,[1] some others have come to light in the excavations of the past decade. The former text is a poem describing an evil demon, a daughter of Anum, whom her heavenly father cast down to earth because of her evil scheming. Yet even the evil demon's actions worked out for the benefit of mankind—'the godless person she straightforwardly attacked', and of the lions which might have represented a major threat to the travelling merchants, she weakened the limbs. An interesting feature of the text is contained in the introductory line of the poem; it states that the demon 'is one'. This 'oneness' which appears here for the first time in Akkadian literature obviously means 'she is unique', in so far as she is 'pure' (line 1), on the one hand, and 'evil', on the other, even as her actions work out for the best although they are the result of wicked planning.

Another religious text of which so far only a summary translation has been published[2] appears to deal particularly with the problems confronting the travelling merchants. It tells of a black dog lying in wait for a caravan. This black dog demon may possibly embody thirst, because the text continues to speak of the daughters of the sweet-water god Ea and of drawing pure water from the river. This latter reference is of particular interest because, as is well known from the abundant material from Lagash, one of the daughters of Ea was intimately connected with the rivers and canals around this Babylonian city; it was Nanshe, the divine patroness of Nina whose identity with the original patroness of Nineveh was suggested above.[3] A similar relationship may well exist between another religious text from Kanesh[4] and a text from Lagash; for so far as can be judged from the few words of the Kanesh text published in translation only, both invoke reeds and reed thickets as the gods' favoured plants.[5] Religious features such as these, common to the Babylonian city of Nina and the Old Assyrian material, may well bear witness to Ninevite influence on the religion which otherwise is overwhelmingly dominated by the national god, Ashur.

[1] §IV, 24. [2] §v, 1, 20 f. [3] See above, p. 731 with n. 1.
[4] §v, 1, 21. [5] For Lagash see G, 16, 6, *sub* h.

Even though texts of a purely religious nature are rare, allusions to religious subjects are sufficiently numerous to provide information about the ideas of the Assyrians in the early centuries of their history. Their national god Ashur embodied for them more or less their homeland and their capital city. While the people of Sippar swear their oaths by Shamash and their king, those of Babylon by Marduk and their king, the Assyrians swore by 'the City and the prince' (*nīš ālim u rubā'im*)[1] or 'the City and the lord'.[2] The fact mentioned above that the supreme court building was at the foot of the Ashur temenos also suggests that it actually represented a religious court over which the king presided as Ashur's earthly representative. It is significant in this respect that, on the seal with which he legalized the judgement of the city,[3] Sharrum-kēn (Sargon I of Assyria) was called '*iššiakkum* of the god Ashur',[4] whereas in other instances the title is followed by the 'City of Ashur'[5] and again in others by 'the divine City of Ashur',[6] thus proving without any doubt the identity, in the view of this period, of the god and the city. When a man had to be absent from the city of Ashur for an extended period of time, the members of his family who remained in Assyria urged him to 'come and see the eye of Ashur',[7] or, in another instance, 'to seize Ashur's foot'. Ashur was assumed to disapprove of a person who, for the sake of earning more money, remained absent from his city for an extended period of time. Two women, after having consulted various priestesses and women-seers in the capital city, write to Imdi-ilum, one of the prominent members of the Assyrian business community at Kanesh: 'Ashur warned you over and over again. You love money, (but) neglect your soul; can you not do Ashur's will in the City! Urgent! When you hear this message come and see Ashur's eye and save your soul!'[8] In a letter written by the aforementioned Pūshu-kēn, who corresponded repeatedly with the royal house, he mentions that he 'asked the god' for a certain number of years before he set out to Asia Minor; and he obviously was afraid to incur Ashur's wrath by extending the leave of absence he had been granted. All this notwithstanding the fact that there were sanctuaries of Ashur in the major cities of Asia Minor.[9] It was probably in order to exculpate those merchants

---

[1] §IV, 5, 277, n. c.
[2] *Ibid*. II, 15, n. a; 76, n. d.; cf. the frequent personal name *Ili-ālum*, 'My God is the City'.   [3] See above, p. 760.   [4] §V, 5, pl. V, Abb. 4.
[5] G, 4, 4 ff.   [6] *Ibid*. 4, n. 3.   [7] §IV, 8, 75.
[8] §V, 2, no. 5.   [9] See above, p. 718.

whom their business compelled to spend the greater part of their lives in Asia Minor that a certain religious theory extended Ashur's rule from the homeland on the Tigris to the far-off province. Instead of being merely 'god of the land' (as he was called in the afore-discussed supreme court building) or 'king of the land', Ashur was sometimes called Sharra-mātēn, 'king of the two lands', the second land of Ashur obviously being the region around Kanesh. However, the merchants' wives who remained in Ashur do not appear to have been convinced by this solution.

The 'City' which thus appears to be virtually identical with the god Ashur was also an administrative organ. The envoy of the city, together with the *kārum* Kanesh, was the executive power in Asia Minor, and the afore-discussed letter requesting a contribution to the construction of the fortification wall by Ikunum was transmitted to the pertinent officers by 'the envoy of the City'. This same administration called 'the City' also took part in the profitable business of sending merchandise to Asia Minor for sale there; in many cases the lead shipments from Ashur are reported to have been provided with the 'seal of the City'. That here again the ruler himself presided over the city organization is suggested by a letter in which, even though the beginning is broken, the formula 'before Ashur and my god I will bless you', indicates that it was written on the king's initiative, for only he uses this formula.[1] The letter deals with the shipment of merchandise among which was a large amount of lead 'with the seal of the City'. A letter addressed by the *kārum* Kanesh to all the *kārum* organizations under its jurisdiction and to its own envoy in Tukhpia deals with a shipment of lead belonging to the City.[2] The parallelism between this letter and that dispatched by the same sender to the same addressees on behalf of the ruler when he wished to raise funds for the fortification wall makes it clear that here again the owner of the lead was the organization headed by the 'prince'.

As was intimated above when discussing the functions of the supreme court building, one of the important attributions of the god Ashur was the administration of justice. It will be recalled that one of the gates of this building was named from the 'oath of the god of the land'. Oaths invoking the 'god (or) goddess of the oath' are said to have recently come to light in the excavations at Kanesh.[3] It is also worth noting that in Kanesh, in the absence of a building such as the *mušlāl* at Ashur, testimony was given

[1] §v, 3, 1, no. 189, l. y+7.
[2] §v, 8, plate 34a, no. K. 155, now numbered K. 326.
[3] §v, 1, 20.

and judgements were rendered in the presence of 'Ashur's dagger' or 'Ashur's boomerang',[1] the idea being that the one who gave false testimony or who passed an unjust judgement would be struck down by these weapons. This idea appears, in fact, to be expressed in Erishum's *muŝlāl* inscription, but the context is too fragmentary to make out what would have happened to him who 'arose for false testimony' and to the judge who pronounced a false judgement. Honesty and dependability were, of course, vital in a business community in which, at least among the Semites, much of the business was done on credit.

By his nature, the god Ashur is the heavenly sphere referred to in the Epic of Creation by the Sumerian designation AN.ŜAR. Yet as the genuinely Sumerian pantheon does not contain a deity of this name and function—closest to it would be the Sumerian AN—it is obvious that AN.ŜAR is a comparatively late Sumerianization of the Assyrian god's name. That Ashur was originally a deity of west Semitic origin can likewise be inferred from the Epic of Creation where Ashur is said to be the son of Lakhmu and Lakhamu. The fact that these two divine names appear in the variant forms Lakhma and Lakhama, i.e. with the ending *a* of the Amorite determined state, suggests *a priori* that they belong to the west. If it is further remembered that in the western part of the Fertile Crescent city names are frequently composed of a divine name preceded by *bēth*, 'house, residence of' (e.g. Bēth 'Anath, Bēth Dagōn, Bēth Shemesh, Bēth El, Bēth Ba'al), it is apparent that 'Bethlehem' is a name of this type containing the divine element Lekhem. As west-Semitic Shemesh appears in Amorite as Samsum, Lekhem is bound to appear as Lakhmu. In other words, Ashur's father and creator is one of the deities worshipped in 'Bēth Lekhem'. This conclusion is well in line with the evidence referred to above,[2] that Ilaprat, another deity worshipped by the Assyrians of the Old Assyrian period, likewise originated in Bethlehem.

Second in importance among the gods of the city of Ashur was Enlil, who had both a temple and a temple tower. The origin of the cult of Enlil which, at first approach, seems surprising in a country where Sumerian influence was virtually non-existent, becomes manifest from a passage in an inscription of Esarhaddon[3] who connects the cult of Anu and Enlil with Baltil; accordingly, he was of the opinion that these cults actually belonged to the pre-Semitic period of the capital city. That this opinion is correct in so far as Enlil is concerned is apparent from the important

[1] §v, 6.   [2] See above, p. 720.
[3] §III, 4, 2, ll. 27 ff.

role the weather-god plays in the Hurrian pantheon.[1] When Tiglath-pileser I and others allude to the sanctuary of the 'Old Lord' (*bēlu labiru*),[2] they obviously refer likewise to the weather-god of the former Subarian population without, however, using for this Hurrian deity the Sumerian name Enlil. In fact, it may have been during the Old Akkadian period that this name was applied to the pre-Semitic weather-god of the capital city. Among the Old Assyrian merchants, the cult of this deity was not popular. Only a few men bear theophorous names composed with the element Enlil.[3]

Far more popular was the west Semitic weather-god Adad from whom almost one-tenth of the men in the Old Assyrian texts were named; it may be stated here that, at least in so far as Assyria is concerned, the pronunciation of this divine name was Adad as evidenced not only by Middle Assyrian spellings such as that already quoted[4] and by the Nuzi name *Re-ša-dá-ad-we*, but also by Old Assyrian writings such as *Ṣí-la-da-ad*.[5] Among the Assyrian rulers of this period even as among their Babylonian contemporaries names composed with the element *šumu* or, in the Amorite form used in Babylonia, *sumu*, 'the holy name', are rather frequent. *Ilu-šum-ma* has the meaning 'God is really the holy name', while Erishum (i.e. Irishum) signifies 'He who shepherds is the holy name'. Outside the royal family, however, these names were not popular. Very popular, on the contrary, was the astral Ishtar, both as the planet Venus, as which she appears under the name Ishtar *kakkubum*, 'Ishtar, the star', and as Ishtar-ṣād, the star Sirius.[6]

Some significant insight into the religious ideas of the Old Assyrian period can be derived from the scenes depicted on the seal impressions which are found on the letters and documents from Asia Minor. Taking as a typical example the finely engraved seal of Sharrum-kēn,[7] one sees to the right a deity seated on a throne; in the style of the period, the god is characterized as such by the archaic sheepskin frock and the horned crown. Before the deity's head there is a lunar crescent including a sun-emblem, characterizing the seated deity as Ashur, the god of the heavenly sphere comprising both the sun and the moon. A lower deity, likewise with a horned crown and a sheepskin frock, but walking and raising one hand toward the seated god in the attitude of adoration, introduces the king, whom he holds by the

---

[1] See above, pp. 731 f.   [2] G, 3, 87, l. 87; §1, 3, 200, ll. 20–32.
[3] §IV, 8, 32.   [4] See above, p. 753.
[5] §IV, 8, 2.   [6] §V, 4.   [7] §V, 5, plate v, Abb. 4.

hand, into the presence of the supreme god. The lower deity is characterized as the moon-god by the lunar crescent behind his head. This scene which recurs on many Old Assyrian seals with individual variations is easily explained as a dream vision which the king beheld when he retired for his sacred sleep on the summit of the temple tower. Frequently it was an order for the construction of a sanctuary which the god conveyed to the king in such an interview. However, as is known from an inscription of Sennacherib as well as from biblical passages, in the course of the interview the supreme god was also expected to bestow upon the human being that sublime wisdom which was to enable him to give authoritative orders agreeable to his divine lord.[1] It is in full agreement with this religious idea that, according to the results of the excavations at Ashur, the temple towers belong to the oldest buildings traceable in the city.

It is equally significant that the god introducing the king into Ashur's presence was the moon-god. For this shows that Sin, who was the royal family's patron god in the Neo-Assyrian period,[2] played a preponderant role in Assyria's state religion already in the Old Assyrian period. Among the Old Assyrian merchants, one-tenth of the theophorous names are composed with the divine element Sin. The percentage is even higher if names composed with Laban (the moon-god's name in the Lebanon region) or with elements such as Washib-Uri are included in the count. Several priests of the moon-god (*kumrum*) are mentioned in the texts. Incidentally, it should be stated that, in spite of various spellings, the pronunciation of the moon-god's name in Assyria throughout the centuries was Sin; this can be gathered from spellings such as *Sí-in-iš-me-a-ni*,[3] *Sí-in-rabi*,[4] *Sí-ri-me-ni*,[5] etc. The frequency of personal names composed with the divine elements Ishtar, Sin, and Shamash shows that basically the Assyrians were worshippers of the heavenly bodies. That these deities also figured as the protective gods of the various tribes and clans can be gathered from exclamations such as 'May Ashur, Amurrum, and Ishtar *kakkubum*, the gods of our fathers, look on as witnesses!'[6] The strong west-Semitic ties which the Assyrians of this period still maintained in spite of their having been sedentary for more than half a millennium are shown by the fact that the gods most frequently mentioned in these exclamations as the 'gods of my father' or of 'our fathers' are Amurrum, Ilaprat,

[1] §I, 11, 84 ff.
[2] *Ibid.* 73 ff., with n. 198.
[3] §v, 3, 1, no. 97, l. 16.
[4] §II, 14, no. 224, l. x + 8.
[5] §v, 9, no. 23, l. 2; no. 20, l. 3.
[6] §v, 7, 43 with n. 71.

and Ishtar *kakkubum*, all three of whom belong to the western part of the Fertile Crescent. In view of the preponderant role which the cult of the stars played in Assyria ever since the Semites replaced the original Subarian population, the possibility must be reckoned with that those portions of the Epic of Creation which deal with the creation of the heavenly sphere and of the stars originate in Assyria in the Old Assyrian period and not in Babylonia where they are without parallel.

VI. THE CALENDAR

The fifth tablet of the Epic of Creation begins by relating that the creator assigned to each of the great gods his position in the sky, each star or stellar constellation being the image of one of the gods.[1] He then defined the year as consisting of twelve months to each of which he allotted three constellations so that ten days corresponded to one constellation. The month thus was divided into three ten-day periods. Calendars of this type are well known to have been in use by the Egyptians and by the Arabs who, at least linguistically, divide the month into three decades of days. The Old and Middle Assyrian calendar was of this type. The following are the names of the months as used in the Old and Middle Assyrian periods: Ab sharrāni; Khubur; Ṣippum; Qarrātum; Tanmarta; Ti'inātum or Sin;[2] Kuzallu; Allanātum; Bēlti-ekallim; Narmak Ashur sha sarrātim; Narmak Ashur sha kinātim; Makhur ilī. Several of these names betray the astronomical origin of the calendar: Tanmarta, '(heliacal) rising',[3] was, at least theoretically, the month of the heliacal rising of Sirius, the brightest of all the fixed stars. As mentioned before, this star was represented in the pantheon of the Old Assyrian period by the goddess Ishtar-ṣād. Bēlti-ekallim, the name of the ninth month, was the name of a goddess represented in the sky by the large fixed star Vega (α Lyrae), the heliacal rising of which occurred in the course of the fourth month after the rising of Sirius. The name of the twelfth month, Makhur ilī, 'Meeting of the gods', refers to the conjunction of the moon and the Pleiades preceding the latter's heliacal setting.[4] The second month, Khubur, 'the nether world', was the month of the heliacal rising of the Pleiades which represented the Evil Seven, a group of seven deities hostile to mankind who were believed to

[1] §vi, 1, 136.
[3] §vi, 2, 91.
[2] §vi, 6, 36, n. 4.
[4] §ii, 10, 144 with n. 2.

reside in the nether world. Hence the early part of the second month was dedicated to the service of these evil spirits.[1]

Besides the time-unit month, the Assyrian calendar contained a time-unit called *ḫamuštum* which had originally contained five days. For the sake of convenience, however, two such periods were usually joined so as to form ten-day units, traces of which are still found in documents from the time of Ashur-uballiṭ I. These periods, even as the years, were named from officials, so that each ten-day period bore the names of two men.

The eponym year did not have the same length as the commercial year, for the annual change of eponym moved slowly backwards through the months; hence the eponym year was determined either by an astronomical phenomenon such as the heliacal rising of a certain star or by an agricultural season. The commercial year, on the other hand, appears to have comprised 365 days, the extra five days most likely having been added in the form of an intercalary month every six years. To be sure, intercalary months are mentioned neither in the Old nor in the Middle Assyrian texts. However, there is evidence that at the time of the eponym change a month was sometimes doubled in such a way that the month which ended one eponym year was repeated as the first month of the next eponym year. In this way, for instance, the month Narmak Ashur sha kinātim of eponym A was followed by the month Narmak Ashur sha kinātim of the eponym A + 1.

Even as in other countries and ages where a calendar based on a year of 365 days was being used,[2] the months of this calendar moved slowly forward through the seasons or, in other words, the seasons moved slowly backward through the months, the speed of this move amounting to one month every 120 years. An adjustment of the Assyrian calendar to its original seasons was made in the reign of Shalmaneser I (1272–1243 B.C.). However, since after this calendar reform the months continued to move slowly away from the seasons to which they belonged, the Assyrians turned increasingly toward the Babylonian luni-solar calendar. Double dates equating an Assyrian and a Babylonian date occur at the time of Tiglath-pileser I, and eventually the Assyrian dates together with the Assyrian month names became entirely obsolete.

[1] §VI, 5.   [2] §VI, 4, 4 ff.

CHAPTER XXVI(*a*)

GREECE, CRETE, AND THE AEGEAN ISLANDS IN THE EARLY BRONZE AGE

I. DEFINITION OF THE INQUIRY

THE Bronze Age in lands bordering the Aegean Sea was a period of roughly two millennia that followed the age of Neolithic cultures. The name is not perfectly accurate; men did begin to use metals more or less systematically in this time, but chief among them at the outset was natural copper, not yet deliberately alloyed with tin. None the less the phrase has useful connotations, reflecting the Greek memory of an older γένος μερόπων ἀνθρώπων χάλκειον, and it is firmly established. The terms Chalcolithic and Copper Age, logical and correct in themselves, are now best reserved for Anatolia and other areas where their meanings have won acceptance.

As a source of confusion the name of the metal is of minor consequence. More perplexing are the formidable quantities of material remains that have been gathered in three generations of archaeological research, for they beckon the student of this area to conclusions more positive than are in fact justified. Since written records are lacking in Greece during the early period with which we are here concerned, one must rely upon stratification and comparison of objects at the known sites in order to establish a relative chronology. An approach to absolute dates may be made through proven relationships with Egypt and Mesopotamia, but these are few in number and less exact than one is often led to suppose. New and promising methods of dating, including particularly the process of radiocarbon (C–14) analysis, are still in experimental stages and the results they yield must be regarded objectively. Important facts to bear in mind are that much of the excavation in the Aegean area was carried out by pioneers in the field, often without adequate means, before proper methods had been devised; that superficial exploration and the testing of stratified sites by trial trenches alone have sometimes given deceptive results; and that objects of similar appearance are not necessarily contemporary or directly related to each other.

These limitations accepted, one may turn with confidence to

the real advances in knowledge that have been made, thanks to a goodly company of philhellenic scholars from many lands.

Geographical divisions had a significant influence on events and on the development of civilization in Greece, in early as in later times. Certain general similarities of culture in the Early Bronze Age seem indeed to have existed, and these have sometimes been taken as proof of a widespread uniformity: simple village life, peaceful communication, primitive but somewhat idyllic existence before the age of the palaces in Crete and the succeeding era of Mycenaean power. But a picture of that sort is not accurate. There were fortresses and relatively great wealth in some places, poor hamlets in others; there were inland people and coastal people, farmers and seafarers. Discoveries in recent years have altered the image of amiable savages dwelling in fraternal if rather unenterprising accord, and have substituted a more realistic appreciation of the facts.

Macedonia and Thrace in the north are large and rich by Aegean standards, and had cultural relations extending into the Balkans and north-western Asia Minor. Southward, beyond mountain barriers, are the wide plains of Thessaly. The valley of the Spercheus makes a transition to east-central Greece, which embraces Phocis, Locris, Boeotia, the Euripus and Euboea. Attica, as always, had local peculiarities while maintaining contacts with northern neighbours, with the islands of the Aegean, and with the nearer parts of the Peloponnese. Corinthia and the Argolid make up a fairly unified district, which also looked toward the Cyclades and Crete. Achaea, Arcadia, and Laconia, archaeologically less well known than the eastern regions, were inhabited in this period and not isolated. The Spartan land may have had contacts with Crete from very early times onward. Messenia and Elis, beyond big mountains, were not altogether cut off from the Aegean world but naturally had another outlook, as did the north-western mainland and the Ionian Islands.

In the following account these areas will be surveyed separately, not exhaustively but with attention to some of the principal archaeological evidence, and with outlines of stratigraphical observations at a few characteristic sites. A truly historical treatment cannot be undertaken at present, but some general conclusions will be summarized. The accepted terminology is employed, the major periods being called Early, Middle, and Late (E., M., L.), while the cultural areas are designated by the words Helladic, Cycladic, and Minoan (H., C., M.); 'Macedonian' and 'Thessalian' as parallel designations are not yet

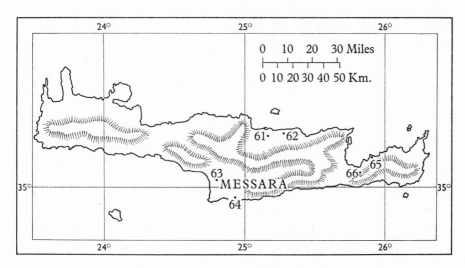

Map 13. Early Bronze Age sites in Crete.

sharply defined. Chronological divisions of the periods, often three in number, are called phases and marked with roman numerals; occasionally there are smaller subdivisions which are distinguished by letters.

II. NORTH-EASTERN GREECE

MACEDONIA AND THRACE

Sites of early settlements abound in the broad plains of Macedonia and Thrace, but archaeological investigation has not yet moved far enough to provide a clear image of the cultures that they represent. Surveying and recording of the mounds began at the close of the First World War, when various services and facilities of the French Armée d'Orient were usefully employed to this end. The report of these activities by Leon Rey is of basic importance.[1] Thereafter exploration was extended by others, especially W. A. Heurtley, who tested many of the mounds and incorporated his observations in a comprehensive handbook that appeared in 1939.[2] A few Neolithic sites have been properly excavated, but the Early Bronze Age is known chiefly from surface explorations and soundings. These show more than a score of sites around Thessalonica and northward in the valley of the Axius and the basin of Lanka-

[1] §II, 6.   [2] §II, I.

dhas, a concentration in Chalcidice, and a scattering westward in the valleys of the Tserna and Haliacmon rivers. The long coastal strip eastward from Mount Pangaeum to the Hebrus awaits exploration; remains assignable to the Early Bronze Age are known at Dikili Tash near Philippi,[1] and one cannot doubt that the whole region was inhabited in this period.

At Kritsana, the site of a small settlement in Chalcidice, six building levels were distinguished in the test pits.[2] All are assigned by Heurtley to the Early Bronze Age, though Neolithic sherds are plentiful in the first strata. Whether there was truly a chronological overlapping of the cultures, here or at other places in Macedonia where mixtures of this sort have been noted, is not yet ascertained. Pottery reminiscent of late Troy I is found in the early strata at Kritsana. This probably indicates some contact with the Troad, and the presence of similar wares and shapes (for example incurving bowls and horizontal lugs with flaring ends) in E.H. I contexts at Eutresis in Boeotia suggests a further extension of the same influences.[3] The earliest stratum at Kritsana produced a copper pin and one piece of Melian obsidian. From succeeding deposits came jugs with high spouts, cups and tankards, and handles belonging apparently to askoid vessels. These may well represent the stage of ceramic development that is seen in the middle phases of the Early Bronze Age in Greece (E.H. II) and western Asia Minor. Sauceboats, which are hallmarks of the second E.H. phase in the south, are not well attested in Macedonia.[4]

Burning is recorded in the third and fourth levels at Kritsana, but neither here nor elsewhere in this region is there clear evidence of an invasion or a sudden change of culture. Progress is gradual, reflecting neither the disaster of Troy II nor the abrupt breaks that may be seen at the end of E.C. II and E.H. II in the islands and north-eastern Peloponnese. A single sherd of E.H. III patterned ware, small but unmistakable, was found in the sixth layer at Kritsana and indicates some slight contact with the south in this period, a time when the Argolid seems also to have been in touch with Troy IV. Bored hammer axes begin to be used earlier in Macedonia and Asia Minor than in southern Greece, and small terra-cotta double hooks ('anchors') are reported in the lowest strata of the Chalcidian site, whereas they appear only in the fourth settlement at Lerna.[5] These are distinctive objects, and a proper understanding of their wide dis-

---

[1] §II, 3.   [2] §II, 1, 17–22.   [3] §II, 1, 166–7; §III, 7, 137–48.
[4] §II, 1, 190, no. 312.
[5] G, 5; G, 9; G, 26; §III, 9, vol. xxv, pl. 47; vol. xxvi, pl. 42. See Plate 60 (c).

semination may ultimately give a useful clue to interrelationships. Wheel-made pottery is reported in stratum III at Kritsana, the technique having come perhaps from north-western Anatolia where it was known from Troy II*b* onward. Horses are said to have appeared in central Macedonia in the Early Bronze Age, but exact contexts are not given and the zoological evidence needs verification;[1] *equus caballus* is not surely attested in southern Greece or north-western Asia Minor till the Middle Bronze Age.

It seems not improbable that bearers of Bronze Age culture arrived first in Chalcidice and moved steadily onward into the region of the Axius and westward, superseding the earlier population but settling occasionally on the same village sites and adopting local ways. Some Neolithic sites, on the other hand, were abandoned. Of the architecture little can be said at present; houses were apparently small and crowded, their walls built of crude brick, usually on stone socles. Further excavation could quickly provide much information. The sites are easily recognized standing conspicuous in the plains, often in the form of a high rounded eminence on a broad flat table. One which exhibits this characteristic shape is Vardarophtsa on the bank of the Axius, where tests revealed strata and objects that correspond in most respects with those seen at Kritsana.

THESSALY AND THE SPERCHEUS VALLEY

Investigation of prehistoric sites in Thessaly began effectively with the work of Tsountas in the years 1901–3[2] and was carried on and extended by Wace and Thompson in 1907–10,[3] others contributing supplementary researches. After a long interval excavations were resumed in the 1950's by the German Institute[4] and by Greek archaeologists. The results have made the Neolithic cultures relatively well known, but, as in Macedonia, major settlements of the Early Bronze Age have not been examined extensively. Here too sites abound, since the rich soil supported a large population; but deposits are deep, containing tons of disintegrated crude brick from the walls of buildings (stone was far away in the hills); hence archaeological digging is slow and costly.

The area is large and local variations are so numerous that ceramic wares and chronological phases have tended, even more than elsewhere, to be designated by the names of sites where they are best known or most typical. The painted pottery of Dhimini is

[1] §II, 1, 88.
[2] §II, 7.
[3] §II, 8.
[4] §II, 4; §II, 5.

the hallmark of Tsountas's second Thessalian period, Neolithic in character. Long recognized as probably somewhat later are the two classes called after Larissa and Rakhmani. A question remained whether these three overlapped each other in time or were successive, and whether the E.H. period of southern Greece was contemporary, at least in part, with the stages represented by them. The German excavations at Argissa and elsewhere seem now to show that the Larissa and Rakhmani classes, themselves distinct, are clearly later than that of Dhimini. Milojčić assigns them to a Copper Age. The Early Bronze Age, which he finds to be roughly contemporary in Thessaly with that known in the south, follows in sequence.[1]

Few examples of the architecture of this period have been discovered. At the sites around Larissa house walls were made almost entirely of crude bricks and clay. Sometimes wooden posts gave extra support. Stratified debris shows that the occupation, notably at Argissa, lasted a long time; slow change and development are evident in the pottery, which may be assigned to three stages. In the earliest of these one may see affinities to Troy I; the second yields bowls and other vessels that have distant parallels in E.H. II. Glazed ware (coated with *Urfirnis*) and fragments of sauceboats are reported both here and in the vicinity of Volo, but this material has not yet been published in detail. Anchor hooks of terra-cotta occur in the late strata at Argissa, where also there are evidences of widespread destruction by fire.

Soundings made in 1909 at Tsani Magula[2] in the great southwestern plain of Thessaly showed that settlements of the Early Bronze Age followed those of the Neolithic period. Glazed ware is said to have begun in the third of the eight strata that were distinguished. It is not common, being perhaps an imported product. The shapes resemble those of E.H. I and II (shallow bowls and askoi), but high-swung handles and a small bowl with everted rim may possibly be related to types that occur further south in E.H. III, and one terra-cotta 'anchor' was found.

Places in the south-eastern region, Phthiotis, were occupied also in the Early Bronze Age, among them certainly Zerelia and probably Phthiotic Thebes.[3] Some of the objects from the upper (post-Neolithic) strata at Zerelia suggest parallels of a general sort with materials of Troy II–IV and of middle and later E.H. phases in Central Greece. With these was found a small seated ithyphallic figure in terra-cotta, unlike anything known in the

---

[1] §ɪɪ, 5, 19.   [2] §ɪɪ, 8, 135–49.   [3] §ɪɪ, 8, 150–69.

south and matched only by another similar but larger figure from the region of Larissa.

In the valley of the Spercheus, the border land between Thessaly and central Greece, a large mound near Lianokladhi was tested by Wace and Thompson in 1909, giving useful and promising results.[1] Above a Neolithic layer there is a second layer, quite distinct, which contains the local version of glazed ware in shapes assignable to middle phases of the E.H. period, for example bowls and askoi. In the third principal layer, again sharply set off, remains of a house were found, its walls straight but the angles irregular. Some of the pottery is in wheel-made grey Minyan ware, ring-stemmed goblets being plentiful. Vases with linear decoration in dull paint are also abundant, and the settlement has been assigned without question to the Middle Bronze Age. It must now be noted, however, that some of the shapes and patterns seem very close to those of the fourth settlement at Lerna (E.H. III). The significance of this similarity is not altogether clear. Surely the whole thick layer represents more than a single phase of occupation, since it contains a typical M.H. cist grave above one room of the house. Possibly it represents a stage that began in the final years of the Early Bronze Age and continued into the fully developed M.H. period.

III. CENTRAL GREECE: THE EASTERN SHORES

The regions from Mount Oeta and the range of Callidromus southward to Cithaeron, comprising chiefly Phocis, Locris and Boeotia of classical times, yield abundant evidence of habitation in the E.H. period. The valleys are small but fertile and water is not lacking, the river Cephissus flowing through them into Lake Copaïs, which drains partly underground into the Euripus. Central Euboea is geographically related to this area of the mainland but is yet insular and, not surprisingly, shows numerous connexions with the Cyclades. The rich Crisean plain and western Locris should be taken with this region also, though shut off by Mount Parnassus and looking naturally across the Gulf of Corinth to the Peloponnese.[2]

Orchomenus was one of the principal centres from very early times, but the report of the excavations of 1903–5 leaves much in doubt. The same is true of the old explorations of Phocian sites. Eutresis near Leuctra, south-west of Thebes, provides the most reliable key to developments at the beginning of the Bronze Age.

[1] §II, 8, 171–92. [2] §III, 10; §III, 20.

Eutresis was occupied in the Middle and Late Neolithic periods, and then again, probably without a chronological interruption, at a time when heavy grey-brown pottery[2] of sub-Neolithic types was in use. This ceramic ware resembles some early fabrics of the Cyclades, Lemnos, Lesbos, and Troy I closely enough to indicate that it belongs to the same cultural stage and, one may infer, roughly to the same period. It may be thought to carry over traditions of the latest Stone Age, but the threshold has been passed.

Early Helladic I, with its characteristic red burnished pottery, is represented in a long series of successive buildings and habitation-levels at Eutresis. Miss Goldman observed many, beginning with cuttings in virgin soil that marked the places of round huts. At least eight levels were noted in the supplementary excavations of 1958. Early in the sequence was a round building, a precursor perhaps of the *Rundbauten* at Orchomenus but singular in having a deep well-like shaft at its centre. This was probably not a well, since water was more easily accessible at a spring nearby; one may surmise rather that it was associated with worship of chthonic powers. The succeeding structures seem to have been rectangular, and there were many pavements made of pebbles or rough cobblestones. Samples of carbonized wood taken from the lower, but not the lowest, strata yielded C–14 dates of 2670 ± 59 B.C. and 2673 ± 72 B.C.[3]

The red burnished ware of this period, which is found also in north-eastern Peloponnese, is exemplified abundantly at Eutresis in bowls and small jugs and jars.[4] Notable also are a large two-handled basin in buff ware with red bands, and numerous sherds with incised and stamped patterns which are a characteristic feature of Cycladic decoration. Trade with the islands was undoubtedly maintained. Miss Goldman assigned to the end of E.H. I a neat rectangular house that was discovered on the southern plateau at some distance from the chief mound of Eutresis.[5] It contained a store of objects, including one sauceboat, an early example of the vessels that become plentiful and typical in the succeeding phase, E.H. II.

The change from the first to the second main phase seems quite clear at this site, where, if one may judge from the small areas sampled, it occurred quickly. Buildings become larger;

---

[1] §III, 7; §III, 13. [2] See Plate 56 (a). [3] G, 17.
[4] See plate 56 (b) [5] §III, 13, 12–15.

objects of copper appear more frequently; in pottery, which is still handmade without the wheel, the biscuits are thinner and harder, often coated with glaze (*Urfirnis*), and new shapes appear: in addition to the sauceboat there are askoi, squat pyxides, and a multitude of small saucers.[1] These changes may indicate the arrival of other people with new ideas—presumably a peaceful incursion since there are no signs of violence—or an improvement in communications, or technological discoveries that affected economic conditions. Comparable developments took place elsewhere in central Greece and in parts of the Peloponnese.

Early Helladic II is represented by a series of houses, streets, and floor-levels at Eutresis. Most notable among the remains discovered is House L, a large building, rather irregular in plan, with three rooms.[2] The western, innermost, of these (Room III) had a pan-hearth, bothroi, and a stone bench. It has been suggested that the room, and perhaps the whole building, served religious purposes, a theory strengthened by the discovery that it stood beside a big funnel-shaped cavity that still existed in the ground over the much earlier tholos and shaft of E.H. I. House L was altered and repaired more than once and may be supposed to have been in use over many years altogether. C–14 analysis of charcoal from the earliest floor in room III gave a date of 2431 ± 58 B.C.[3] There is no evidence that House L was immediately superseded by any other building in E.H. II, but it is possible that strata have been lost here, or even that the area was left vacant for a time. There are no signs of a general conflagration or other major disaster at the end of this phase, a fact conspicuously in contrast with evidences of destruction at the corresponding stage in the Argolid.

Remnants of walls and floors testify to a succession of houses in E.H. III, among them an ample rectangular megaron, House H, and some very small horseshoe-shaped structures. Hearths were built beside the walls rather than in the centre of the rooms, and small basins of unbaked clay were made in the floors for domestic activities of some kind. The pottery is now distinctly different from that found in earlier strata. Sauceboats die out and the repertory of E.H. II is replaced by other shapes: the two-handled tankard, bowls with everted rims, jugs and jars of new forms. Patterns are drawn frequently in white paint on a dark ground,[4] but with this style there occur also a few examples of dark linear decoration on a light ground, like that employed at Peloponnesian sites in E.H. III.[5] New contacts with the Cyclades bring the

[1] See Plate 57 (*a*) and (*b*).   [2] §III, 13, 15–20; §III, 7, 151–7.   [3] G, 17.
[4] See Plate 59 (*a*).   [5] See Plate 59 (*b*).

characteristic jug shape, with narrow back-turned spout, that begins in the islands (for example, Paros and Melos) in E.C. III. Terra-cotta 'anchors' are reported much earlier than this at Eutresis but are wholly absent in E.H. III.

This final stage of E.H. habitation ended with a general burning of the town, the evidence being recognizable in a stratum of ashes and cinders almost everywhere. A few traces of a 'transitional' stage have been noted, but the next higher level follows directly, containing all the typical marks of a M.H. settlement.

LOCRIS, PHOCIS

The three clearly distinguishable phases of the E.H. period at Eutresis deserve close attention, since stratification of this kind has not been reported at many other sites. There is, however, no lack of Bronze Age settlements in the general area. Cirrha below Delphi was occupied in E.H. II, if not earlier, and in E.H. III.[1] Burning at the end of the Early Bronze Age is reported, but the evidence is not wholly certain. Orchomenus had a notable series of round buildings in its initial E.H. stage (probably E.H. II rather than E.H. I) and these were succeeded by other architectural complexes, which seem to have gone on without interruption throughout the Bronze Age. One *depas amphikypellon*[2] and a fragment of a second were found there, both of local manufacture, imitations of the well-known vessels of Troy II and Troy III. The late stage of the E.H. settlement at Orchomenus is characterized by apsidal houses and many bothroi. As elsewhere at this time in central Greece, there is a distinctive type of pottery bearing rectilinear decoration in white paint on a dark ground. This is known as the Ayia Marina class, after a big mound in the Phocian plain that was tested in 1910 and 1911 but never thoroughly excavated.[3] The ware appears to be a counterpart of Peloponnesian pottery with decoration in the dark-on-light style; the relationship between them needs further study.

THE EURIPUS, EUBOEA

Early Helladic settlements are found along either side of the Euripus. At the village of Dramesi, south of Aulis, sherds representing the whole Bronze Age have been picked up on a mound that may mark the site of Homeric Hyria.[4] On the Euboean

[1] §III, 10.   [2] §III, 19, pl. xxiii, 1; §v, 6, vol. i, 2, figs. 381–2.
[3] §III, 27.   [4] §III, 4.

shore just north of Chalcis a promontory called Manika[1] has remains of a considerable town that seems to have been surrounded by a wall of defence. On the landward side was a cemetery, the tombs being small chambers approached by vertical shafts in the rock. Surprisingly few E.H. burial places have been found anywhere, and the tombs at Manika have scarcely any parallels; one at Corinth, assignable to E.H. II, and another in the area of the Athenian Agora, believed to be of earlier date, may be cited.[2] Among the offerings in the Euboean tombs were pots and stone objects of E.C. types and a series of long-beaked jugs that find parallels in Anatolia. Clearly the inhabitants of Manika, like those of other towns on the eastern coasts of Greece, were seafaring people who engaged in trade across the central Aegean. That some of them came originally from the Cyclades is not unlikely, but of this one cannot be sure.

Two bowls of heavy gold and one of silver, with incised rectilinear patterns, are among the treasures of the Benaki Museum in Athens.[3] They are said to have come from Euboea, and may have been in a single tomb (this is uncertain, and even their genuineness has been questioned). If not made locally, these very fine pieces may have been imported from the Cyclades or from Asia Minor, probably in an early phase of the Early Bronze Age.

ATTICA AND AEGINA

Burnished red pottery like that of the early strata at Eutresis has been found in various places in Attica, showing that here too the land was settled in the first stage of the Early Bronze Age. The valleys and plains are smaller and agriculturally poorer than in Boeotia today. Probably there was more woodland and better earth in the third millennium B.C., but even then the inhabitants looked to the sea. Their settlements are generally near the coasts, often on little promontories,[4] and sea-food was a principal element in their diet.

These first successors to the extensive Neolithic population may well have reached Attica from the islands. The earliest settlements have not yet been thoroughly investigated. In the second E.H. phase, of which more is known, contacts with Cycladic culture are clearly marked. Graves at Ayios Kosmas,[5] the Cape Colias of classical Greek times, were stone-lined cists, often built with a small symbolical doorway that could not have been used in

---

[1] §III, 24, 1–20; §III, 31, 292–306. [2] §III, 15; §III, 26, 235.
[3] §III, 25, 11–14, 211–12. [4] See Plate 57 (c).
[5] §III, 22.

practice. Similar graves have been found at half a dozen other coastal sites, all being of types known from cemeteries in Syros and elsewhere among the islands. The burials themselves and many of the funerary offerings, pottery with incised and impressed decoration, stone vessels, and figurines of white marble, are wholly Cycladic in character, whether their connexion with the islands was immediate or remote.

Not only the burial customs, which are especially revealing, but the ways of life in general suggest affinity with the people of the central Aegean. Most conspicuous are the great quantities of obsidian from Melos that appear all along the Attic coast.[1] Obviously it was imported in a rough state, to be chipped and worked into blades and other tools, some for local use and some for trade with inland settlements.

Domestic architecture is seen best at Ayios Kosmas, where two successive strata of E.H. remains were distinguished by G. Mylonas. In plan the houses are roughly rectangular, made up usually of two rooms and a small courtyard that opens on to a narrow street. Some of the roadways were paved, and the pot-holes filled, with beach pebbles. From the arrangement of the buildings it seems almost certain that the roofs were flat, with only a slight pitch for drainage. Hearths and traces of built furniture were found in the rooms. The characteristic pottery of both phases includes sauceboats, askoi, and small saucers typical of E.H. II, and it is to this stage that the entire early settlement should be assigned.[2] At the end it was destroyed by fire, like many other establishments of this age, probably by the same wave of invaders who sacked the Argolid. Ayios Kosmas was deserted thereafter for a long time. Only a handful of stray potsherds assignable to E.H. III and the M.H. period came to light in the excavations.

Changes in the level of the coast have caused sites of this kind to be partially eaten away by the sea. It is not known whether Ayios Kosmas and certain of the other sites were fortified in E.H. times. Some undoubtedly were; among them, for example, small acropolises at Raphina and Askitario in eastern Attica,[3] inhabited in E.H. II, and a considerable town across the southern waters in the island of Aegina.[4] The site of the latter is a headland near the modern port, marked now by a lone column of a classical temple. It was partially excavated but the results have not been fully pub-

---

[1] §III, 34.
[2] *Pace* the excavator, §III, 22, 157–62; cf. *Archaeology*, XIII (1960), 81.
[3] §III, 29; §III, 30.   [4] §III, 33, 11.

lished. Segments of massive circuit walls, built in successive periods of the Bronze Age, were uncovered. Pottery of E.H. II was found here, and it appears probable that at least one of the walls belonged to the same flourishing period as is attested in Attica, in the third settlement at Lerna in the Argolid, and at Chalandriani in Syros. The settlement in Aegina continued to be occupied in E.H. III but objects assignable with certainty to that phase are notably rare on the Attic mainland.

THE NORTH-EASTERN PELOPONNESE

Corinthia and the Argolid, though broken by much barren hill country, are yet thrown together geographically by the great barrier of mountains on the west. Their centres are two rich well-watered plains, where the chief cities were to be established in classical times, but many other smaller valleys supported flourishing settlements. Rarely united, these were yet closely interrelated at all times. In the Early Bronze Age the whole region was populated; scores of sites are known and a dozen of them have been excavated in the past half century.

Neolithic villages preceded a number of these. There has been a question whether material elements of the latest Stone Age culture persisted for a time alongside the earliest Helladic, since pottery of both types was found together in intermediate layers at a few places, for example at Corinth itself and at Gonia nearby.[1] Evidence of conflict has not been observed, and one supposes that the earlier stock was indeed not wholly destroyed when the new people arrived, but it now appears probable that the cultures were distinct and successive.

The E.H. period was of long duration in this area. It may be divided for analysis into three principal phases, E.H. I, II and III, which correspond approximately with those observed elsewhere, notably at Eutresis in Boeotia. Some of the sites were inhabited in all three of these successive phases, others in only two; some may have thrived in one only. The earliest phase is not well defined as yet. Red and brown pottery, slipped and burnished to varying degrees of lustre, is found at representative settlements from the Isthmus south to Asine. Simple rounded shapes are normal at these sites, as in central Greece, and a few incised pieces in the same strata show that here also relations with the Cyclades began—or were maintained—at the beginning of the Bronze Age.

[1] §III, 3; §III, 32.

LERNA IN THE ARGOLID

A mound beside the Lernaean spring, south of Argos, was excavated in the 1950's and yielded extensive information about the second and final phases of the period.[1] The strata were remarkably well preserved at this place, and a brief description of them may be useful. Underlying the E.H. are Neolithic deposits more than three metres in depth, assignable to major periods called Lerna I and II. These go back probably to the earliest pottery-making culture and end with traces of an occupation that may be related to the 'Larissa' and 'Rakhmani' stages in Thessaly. Thereafter, during a considerable interval, the site was apparently not inhabited, since nothing assignable to E.H. I came to light in the excavations.

Lerna III was founded by new settlers and was occupied throughout the long period of E.H. II. Soon after their arrival these people levelled the site, cutting away the higher parts and filling the hollows, and then turned it into a fortified citadel, encircling it with a double wall which had interior compartments and projecting towers. Large buildings occupied the space inside this fortress. Solidly constructed, each may have stood for many years, but occasionally they were razed and replaced. In one part of the site this happened at least six times. A palace, known as the 'House of the Tiles', which replaced a similar building of earlier date, was the last and finest in the series.[2] Rectangular in plan, about 12 metres by 25 metres, it was divided into many rooms and corridors and had stairways leading to at least one upper storey. The main entrance was at the eastern end, the back door being at the west, and another door, which led directly to the upper apartments, being on the north side. The brick walls and their stone socles were coated with plaster, and the gabled roof was covered with flat rectangular terra-cotta tiles. There were wooden jambs in some of the doorways and heavy timbers must have been used in the superstructure. This palace seems to have been in the course of construction or remodelling, and the walls of the citadel to have been temporarily dismantled, when a great fire destroyed them, marking the end of the period.

The pottery of Lerna III belongs to classes already well known. It is all handmade. Some is coated wholly or partly with glaze, some has a light-coloured lustrous slip, and much is plain. The sauceboat, most striking of E.H. shapes, belongs exclusively to this period. With it occur askoi and small saucers, basins, two-

[1] §III, 9.   [2] See Plate 58 (a).

handled jars, and lentoid pyxides.[1] Painted decoration is rare on these pots. Big pithoi are encircled by raised bands, which often bear impressions of rough cylinder seals. Valuable property was stored in jars and boxes, and these were secured with clay that was stamped with small round seals.[2] Here the designs are deftly executed and display extraordinary versatility in a strictly limited field. One regrets the lack of other decorative art from this period; it may have been executed only in perishable materials.

An era ended at Lerna with the burning of the House of the Tiles, and in the whole surrounding region there are evidences of a similar catastrophe. To be sure, fires occur accidentally everywhere from time to time, and one cannot always be sure which are contemporary, but it is extremely probable that the great round building at Tiryns,[3] which had a roof of similar tiles, fell at the same time as the palace of Lerna III. There was a disaster also at nearby Asine,[4] where one of the burnt buildings had been roofed likewise with tiles. Everywhere the debris contains broken sauce-boats. A few miles further north, at Zygouries in the valley of Cleonae, houses of the same age were destroyed in a general conflagration.[5] Corinth seems to have been abandoned as a result of this wave of violence, which left its mark on Attica also. Quite clearly, a foreign invader had conquered the land. Just how far his domination extended is not yet ascertainable.

At Lerna the debris of the House of the Tiles must itself have formed a huge mound. Here a strange thing happened. People carried away a vast amount of the fallen matter, leaving only a low convex tumulus, circular and c. 19 metres in diameter, to mark the place of the great building.[6] A ring of stones was set at the border, and for some time—decades perhaps—nobody encroached upon the awesome ground within it.

New inhabitants soon occupied the area around the tumulus and built a town of different character. There were no great fortifications. The houses were relatively simple, many being apsidal in form and comprising a large rectangular hall with its central hearth, an open portico with one or two wooden columns between antae at one end, and a semicircular room at the rear. It has long been known that apsidal houses of this type were built in M.H. times, but we see now that they were introduced before that, in the fourth main period at Lerna which spans the final phase of the Early Bronze Age, E.H. III. Shorter than the

[1] See Plate 56 (d).
[2] §III, 14.
[3] §III, 21, vol. III, 80–8.
[4] §III, 11.
[5] §III, 6.
[6] §III, 9, vol. xxv, 165. See Plate 58 (b).

preceding phase, it was yet not negligible. Generation succeeded generation, and remains of no less than five substantial houses have been found in some parts of the site, one above the other in sequence.

A new array of pots and artifacts appears also in Lerna IV. There are no more sauceboats, and other old forms drop out. Instead one finds tankards and small cups, two-handled bowls with everted rims, and round-bodied jars with flaring mouths.[1] Rectilinear patterns occur often, drawn usually in dark semi-lustrous paint on light ground, occasionally in light paint on dark surfaces as in Phocis and Boeotia. Bowls are made in a thickly slipped ware, red, brown, or black, and a few of them in a light grey ware that is indistinguishable from the fabric known as Minyan. Some vases of Lerna IV, especially those in grey ware, show unmistakable marks of the potter's wheel. Imported vases are rare, the most notable being a jar of Trojan shape, probably from Troy IV. Small anchor hooks in terra-cotta occur in this period. Near the level of transition to Lerna V was found a bone object with a row of hemispherical bosses on one side, related to similar pieces from Troy, southern Italy, Sicily and Malta.[2]

The transition from the fourth to the fifth period at Lerna occurred without any violent interruption. There were certain changes in customs, as will be shown in a later chapter, and it is not improbable that another wave of new settlers arrived at this time. Lerna V was a typical M.H. town.

THE SEQUENCE OF EVENTS IN ARGOLIS AND CORINTHIA

Archaeological evidence from previous excavations in Corinthia and Argolis seemed to indicate that cultural development was gradual and peaceful throughout the Early Bronze Age, and that it ended with violence at the time of a M.H. incursion.[3] But a discrepancy between the sequences of major events at Lerna and at neighbouring settlements is highly improbable. Local differences existed of course even in small districts; here, however, it is a question of an overwhelming invasion by foreigners, and the testimony of the recent excavations cannot be ignored. Only by an heroic stretch of the imagination could one suppose that marauders took Lerna and maintained themselves there for some 150 years, supplying pottery and other goods to neighbouring communities of the older population, before a second wave of migration came to destroy the rest of the towns. A more plausible

[1] See Plate 60(a) and (b).   [2] G, 8; G, 9.   [3] G, 13; G, 31, 81-3.

interpretation of the evidence is that the foreign invaders reached the Argolid together and defeated the local population at the end of E.H. II.[1]

Chance, clearly, has played a deceiving role at some of the sites excavated earlier, particularly at Zygouries and Asine where, as a result of erosion, the strata representing E.H. III were almost entirely lacking above the burnt houses of the preceding towns. The painted ware of this period occurs sporadically at many of the sites. At Tiryns it is plentiful but in a layer not easily accessible below the Mycenaean palace. Only at Lerna has the layer been found intact.

Absolute dates derived from C–14 analyses indicate that the House of the Tiles and certain smaller buildings immediately preceding it spanned at least parts of the twenty-third and twenty-second centuries b.c.[2] The great fire may have occurred around 2100 b.c., and the new settlement, Lerna IV, may have lasted until the middle or the end of the twentieth century. There is considerable variation and latitude in the results of the several tests, however, and these dates cannot be taken as precise.

In summary, we may say that the region was inhabited from the beginning of the Bronze Age. Early Helladic I, a period about which not enough is yet known, is represented by deep deposits at some sites and may well have occupied several centuries. Early Helladic II is widely represented from the isthmus southward through the valleys of Phlius, Nemea, and Cleonae to the Argive plain itself and eastward in Epidauria and the Hermionid. Since this is the time of the sauceboat, a shape that is distinctive and often to be recognized even in small fragments, one may be led to give the period undue prominence when surveying the material evidence, but we can scarcely be wrong in seeing it as a long and prosperous era. There was trade throughout the region; it is known, for example, that big pithoi from the hand of a single, perhaps itinerant, potter were used at Zygouries, Tiryns, and Lerna.[3] Commercial relations were maintained with the Cyclades and probably also with Crete directly, as well as with central and southern Peloponnese and the mainland north of the gulf. It is important to observe that certain seals and sealings from Asine[4] that have often been adduced as evidence of synchronisms with the Aegean islands and Egypt belong not to the last phase of the Early Bronze Age but to E.H. II, a time of seafaring when

[1] The argument is presented at greater length in §III, 8.
[2] G, 17.   [3] §III, 8, 293.
[4] §III, 11, 234–9; §v, 7; §v, 10.

mariners undoubtedly coasted the eastern Mediterranean and may even have crossed straight over to Africa.

Some of the old towns and villages were reoccupied in E.H. III after the invasion; not all, and not in every case at the sites that one might think most favourable. Corinth seems to have been abandoned,[1] while certain of the smaller places in the district flourished again. Some new sites may have been settled at this time. They were presumably less numerous than those of E.H. II.

About the origin of the newcomers we can only guess. The apsidal houses that they built, derived in form, one supposes, from simple huts and tent-like structures, point to a pastoral and semi-nomadic ancestry, perhaps in the north. The connexion may be very remote, however, since architectural types are persistent in a culture over long periods, if changes of natural surroundings do not compel people to adopt other forms. The pottery of the period might be expected to offer a clue, since it exhibits distinctive shapes and decorative patterns, but nothing quite like it has been found in other regions. It is rare even in Boeotia, and scarcely known farther north. Probably the closest parallels are to be seen in the painted wares of E.C. III, for example in the later phases of the first city at Phylakopi in Melos, and this fact coupled with ties between Lerna IV and Troy IV gives reason to look for connexions in the east. Further study of the bored stone hammer-axes and other domestic tools of E.H. III may shed more light on the problem.

IV. THE CENTRAL PELOPONNESE AND THE WESTERN COASTS

ACHAEA, ARCADIA

The narrow strips of habitable land in Achaea, where steep slopes below Cyllene and Aroania come down to the Corinthian gulf, have not been thoroughly searched for early remains. Settlements probably existed there, where the soil is good and water plentiful, as also in the upland valleys of northern Arcadia. The central plateau, on the other hand, is known to have been occupied. A mound near the village of Ayioryitika (Hageorgitika) in the eastern part, where the main road from Argos enters the plain, yields evidence of habitation in E.H. times after a long Neolithic period. Another strategic area, in western Arcadia, around Heraea where routes descend to Elis, is reported to be the source

[1] §III, 8, 300.

of a rare and wonderful object, a gold sauceboat that was acquired by the Louvre in 1887, long before the date and associations of the shape were known.[1]

Asea in the south-central part of the province was excavated thoroughly in the years 1936–8.[2] The site is high on a rocky eminence that dominates one of the valleys and the main road from Tripolis to Megalopolis, presumably always a chief path of communication. There was a settlement here in Neolithic times and throughout the Bronze Age. Walls of rectangular E.H. houses were found. Some of the pottery is probably assignable to E.H. I; much belongs certainly to E.H. II, and only a little to the final phase. There had been disturbance of the ground through constant rebuilding at this site, obscuring the stratification, but the sequence seems very similar to that of the Argolid. Fragments of E.C. pottery, found chiefly in the lower strata, show that relations with the islands had also been established early, even in this remote region of the interior.

LACONIA

Laconia has been much more intensively studied, and though excavation of E.H. sites has not advanced far yet, surveys show that the whole valley was settled in this period.[3] Evidences of habitation appear at a score of places and more are being found. Since observation has been limited chiefly to surface reconnaissance it is not surprising that readily identified fragments, like those of sauceboats and in general of vessels bearing characteristic coatings of slip and glaze, should dominate the list, perhaps more heavily than statistics from excavations will ultimately support. At present one sees a heavy preponderance of the types that belong to E.H. II in the Argolid and a lack of those which are characteristic of E.H. III, for example the distinctive patterned wares and new shapes. It remains to be determined whether the sequence of events and development in Laconia was different from that in the north-eastern districts across the barrier of Mount Parnon.

Recent investigations of a site at Ayios Stephanos have revealed a series of cist graves, some of which contained pots that are typical of E.H. II.[4] As noted above, burials of that period have been unaccountably rare at the mainland settlements examined up to now, and those which have been found are almost all at

---

[1] §IV, 5. See Plate 56(c). [2] §IV, 10.
[3] §IV, 19; §IV, 20. [4] §IV, 17.

places with strong Cycladic affinities. In form these graves of southern Laconia resemble those of M.H. cemeteries.

The Laconian gulf looks southward toward Crete, and it will be surprising if evidence of relationship with E.M. culture is not forthcoming. There are stepping stones on the way. Early Helladic pottery and much obsidian are reported from a large site on the islet of Elaphonisi off Cape Malea,[1] and the soil of Cythera has produced both Helladic and Minoan objects. A veined marble jug found there is closely related to E.M. II vessels from Mochlos.[2]

Sites of a dozen or more E.H. settlements have been recorded in western Peloponnese.[3] Only one, Malthi in Messenia, has been thoroughly excavated, and even there certain questions are left unanswered. The term Helladic itself must indeed be applied with some reserve to the early period in this region, for the word is associated with a typically Aegean culture which was thinned out and altered when it first reached the west coast, coming into contact with other influences from the Adriatic sphere. These different strains and the purely local developments have yet to be analysed and defined. A systematic gathering of the evidence has begun; it is a fruitful field for research.

The settlement at Malthi[4] was on the top of a large rocky hill commanding a chief passage from the northern Messenian plain to the sea. Its surface is very uneven and the ancient deposits have suffered from erosion. Below the remains of a large fortified town of the Middle and Late Bronze Ages walls and debris of earlier habitations were found. The most ancient pottery is assigned to the Neolithic period; next come deposits and remains of straight and curving house walls that the excavator dated in the time of E.H. II and III. Three graves seem to belong also to this period. There were two architectural levels, and at least one of the apsidal houses could be shown to belong to the older of these. Precise distinctions could not be made in most cases. In the associated strata there was very little glazed ware of E.H. type; some jars have a shape that is not unknown in E.H. II, but no sauceboats or askoi could be recognized with certainty; and the few fragments of patterned wares that were called E.H. may be intrusive. The ceramic sequence is confused by constant recur-

[1] §IV, 20, part II, 146–8.   [2] §V, 30, 53; §IV, 20, part II, 148-60.
[3] §IV, 14; §IV, 16.   [4] §IV, 18.

rence, throughout all strata from Neolithic to Mycenaean, of coarse vessels with rough incisions which were classed together in the publication as 'Adriatic Ware'. In eastern Peloponnese these are closely paralleled in the earlier phases of the M.H. period but not at other times.[1]

Thus at the present stage of our knowledge it seems not improbable that Malthi, after a modest occupation in Neolithic times, was nearly or quite abandoned till the late phase of the Early Bronze Age, and that it was resettled only after the civilization of E.H. II had collapsed in the north-east. Further evidence of activity at this time is being accumulated; a remarkable tumulus with pithos burials,[2] said to be one of many in the region around Pylus, is perhaps to be dated in E.H. III rather than in the fully developed M.H. age. The exact chronology remains hypothetical, however.

THE COASTAL REGION, ELIS

Habitation in E.H. II is attested along the coast. Sauceboats and other pots in fabrics unquestionably assignable to this phase have been recorded at Ayia Analepsis near Methone and northward at various sites to Pheia, the sanctuary of Olympia, and Dyme at the mouth of the Corinthian gulf.[3] Recently a very early grave was discovered at Elis.[4] Communication with the Aegean was doubtless maintained by sea, and it is significant that marble figurines of Cycladic types appear on these western shores.[5] Obsidian is found also, but it is not yet known whether this came from Melos or across the Ionian Sea from Lipari.

THE NORTH-WEST

On the northern shore of the Corinthian Gulf, over against Patras, there were settlements at Kryoneri in the Neolithic and Middle Bronze Ages but E.H. objects have not yet been found there. Pottery of the Early Bronze Age is reported further north at Astacus and across the water in Cephallenia and the little island of Meganisi,[6] as well as at excavated sites in Ithaca and Leucas. Prehistoric sherds from Dodona[7] are difficult to classify; they are probably not older than the Middle Bronze Age and

---

[1] §IV, 18, pl. I, 1; cf. §IV, 10, fig. 106.
[2] §IV, 12, fig. 55.
[3] §IV, 13.
[4] *Ergon*, 1961, 178–9.
[5] §IV, 14; §IV, 15.
[6] §IV, 3.
[7] §IV, 8.

seem to indicate affinities with Macedonia. A site in Corfu[1] has yielded pottery of sub-Neolithic types quite unlike that of Aegean Greece but suggesting parallels with Molfetta in Apulia.

ITHACA AND LEUCAS

The settlement at Pelikata near the northern tip of Ithaca was carefully tested by W. A. Heurtley in 1930–1.[2] Little remained of the houses, which had been demolished repeatedly by the earthquakes that afflict this region; the debris was often found to consist of stones from fallen walls, packed into hollows to level the ground. This tidy practice has been observed at other E.H. sites also. In spite of the ruinous state of the architectural remnants, none the less, it is clear that Pelikata was occupied in two of the main phases that are known in eastern Greece. Certain of the areas examined produced pottery that must be assigned to E.H. II: sauceboats, askoi, saucers, basins, and jars. In two other areas these types were rare but there was material character-istic of E.H. III: patterned ware, including a bit of an imported tankard and a sherd with a frieze of opposed triangles and vertical strokes; numerous two-handled bowls with everted rims;[3] and a terra-cotta double hook. Significantly, the same two areas yielded some Minyan ware in the upper levels. The excavator rightly observed that these elements reflected a strong influence from north-eastern Peloponnese, a conclusion now reinforced by our knowledge of the fourth settlement at Lerna.

Dörpfeld's unshakable conviction that modern Leucas was ancient Ithaca, and that the house of Odysseus was to be sought there, sustained him through years of excavation with meagre returns and led ultimately to valuable discoveries, a cave at the south end of the island, occupied in Neolithic times and there-after, and cemeteries of the Early and Middle Bronze Ages in the Nidri plain on the eastern shore.[4] His interpretation and dating of the tombs were mistaken but his report of the facts is clear and sound. The earlier group comprises thirty-three round tumuli over circular stone platforms, with burials in the mounds and, occasionally, just outside. The circles range from 2·70 metres to 9·60 metres in diameter. On them the dead were burned, according to Dörpfeld, but not completely consumed, before the remains were placed in individual graves. The first of these graves were built in the platforms themselves and those which

[1] §IV, 4.
[2] §IV, 9.
[3] §IV, 9, fig. 20; cf. §III, 8, pl. 70, i, and cf. Plate 60(b).
[4] §IV, 6.

followed were set in the covering mound or near it. Pithoi contained some of the skeletons, while others were placed in cists that were constructed with large flat slabs or walls of smaller stones; still others in plain pits, which, however, may have held wooden sarcophagi.

Funeral gifts, found chiefly in the pyres, include gold and silver ornaments; bronze blades, tools and a fishhook; flint points and obsidian blades; and numerous pots. Sauceboats, askoi, squat pyxides, and certain bits of plastic decoration show unmistakably that there were direct connexions with Aegean culture of the second E.H. phase and presumably that the settlement here represented was roughly contemporary. Yet this cemetery remains unique except for resemblances in the tumuli of Messenia and elsewhere in the western Peloponnese, which are clearly later in date, and one may not assume that the Leucadians were wholly of the stock from which the E.H. peoples came.

V. THE ISLANDS OF THE AEGEAN

Obsidian, the hard black volcanic glass that splits to make sharp points and blades, provided the early people of the Aegean area with many of their cutting implements. There are beds of it in several of the islands, but by far the most important source is a high ridge, now called Dhemenagaki, near the eastern shore of Melos. Big lumps of the substance lie thick on the surface. Gathered here from remote Neolithic times onwards, it was transported not only to the other islands but virtually to all parts of Greece, the northern Aegean and western Asia Minor, if not further still.

The wide distribution of obsidian is clear testimony, if any were needed, that people moved about freely among the Cyclades in the Early Bronze Age. There are scores of islands in the archipelago, almost all having bays and harbours that offer shelter to small craft. The land is steep and rocky, poor in water, soil and vegetation. Agriculture was never very rewarding; fishing and trading were always the natural pursuits of men. Stylized representations of ships and waves and fishes appear in the decoration of their early pottery. It is not clear just how the ships were built, but we may suppose that oars and sails moved them easily from one harbour to another in fair weather, over the length and breadth of the Aegean and occasionally well beyond its limits.

Fixed settlements were plentiful in the Cycladic islands, most of them being situated on the bays and promontories, but some inland. Not many have been excavated; certain of them have been covered and largely obliterated by the towns of later ages, down to modern times, as people continued to choose the same sites for the same reasons as the earliest inhabitants, but even more have been lost by erosion. Since clay for brick-making was scarce, the walls of houses were often built all of stone and when they fell they were scattered down the hill-sides instead of remaining in heaps and gradually forming mounds. One site in Melos, at a place called Phylakopi on the north coast, was systematically investigated in the years 1896–9 and again briefly in 1910.[1] This has provided much of the stratigraphical information that we have. The rest comes principally from the fruitful researches of Chr. Tsountas who explored widely and excavated hundreds of tombs in various islands during the period 1894–8.[2] In the twentieth century excavation in the Cyclades has not been extensive. Clearly much new work is needed.

The big islands on the eastern side of the Aegean, though showing relationships with the central group, are more directly associated with Anatolia in the Early Bronze Age. Reliable testimony is provided by full reports on sites in Lesbos and Samos[3] and by preliminary reports from Chios and Lemnos.[4] Little is known of the early period in Thasos and Samothrace, where the principal connexions were presumably with the north.

PHYLAKOPI IN MELOS. EARLY CYCLADIC III

At Phylakopi the excavators distinguished three successive architectural periods. The latest is marked by remains of a palace and segments of a great defensive wall that belong obviously to the Late Bronze Age, and the preceding period is clearly assignable, on the evidence of imported pottery, to the Middle Bronze Age. Houses of the first settlement have therefore been dated logically to E.C. times. Chronological problems remain, however; for this early period in the islands spanned many centuries and its subdivisions are not easily determined.

Below the footings of the first walls at this site there were deposits of earth that contained pottery of a different kind, obviously still more ancient. It resembles the type found in a cemetery at Pelos (sc. πηλός) further inland.[5] No architectural remains could be associated with these very early deposits at Phylakopi.

---

[1] §v, 2; §v, 11.   [2] §v, 28.   [3] §v, 19; §v, 22.
[4] §v, 18; §v, 4.   [5] §v, 13.

It seems probable that there was a long interval, with very little if any substantial habitation of the site, between the time of the Pelos wares and the establishment of the so-called first city. The latter may well have been contemporary, throughout much or most of its existence, with the third E.H. period on the mainland. Certain ceramic shapes and some of the incised patterns that are typical of Phylakopi I find their closest parallels in period IV of the settlement preceding the Samian Heraeum, in Troy IV and V, in the fourth period at Lerna, and even in the first Middle Helladic phases in the Argolid and at Eutresis.[1] The first painted wares of Phylakopi ought probably to be recognized as counterparts of late E.H. patterned wares on the mainland. Rare or wholly absent at the Melian site are certain types of objects, for example frying pans and sauceboats and marble vessels, that are common in other islands—an indication that the first real town at Phylakopi was not built until their time had already passed.

THE SEQUENCE OF EARLY CYCLADIC PHASES

It is convenient to refer to initial, middle, and late phases of the Early Bronze Age in the islands as E.C. I, II and III. These terms are not yet precise; one must bear in mind that the phases are not necessarily co-terminous with those on the mainland (still less with the E.M.), and that they may not correspond exactly at all places in the islands themselves. With these reservations, however, we may say that Phylakopi I represents E.C. III in Melos. The preceding stage is to be found elsewhere.

In 1915 a limited excavation by Rubensohn in the *Phrourion* of Paroikia in Paros revealed parts of a settlement in which both straight and curving walls occurred.[2] The pottery matches that of Phylakopi I and II; nothing, or almost nothing, of earlier types was found. The site was occupied, then, in E.C. III and M.C. times. In the same island, however, other places had been investigated previously (in 1897) by Tsountas. He opened tombs at Pyrgos and cleared remains of houses among which there were rectangular and apsidal forms.[3] Apparently similar to those of the *Phrourion*, they are in fact earlier. A goblet from one of the rooms is closely related to mainland vessels of the second E.H. phase and the pottery in general belongs to a large Cycladic class that is best exemplified in Syros.

[1] §III, 13, figs. 255–6. [2] §V, 25.
[3] §V, 28, part I, 168–75.

CHALANDRIANI IN SYROS. EARLY CYCLADIC II

At Chalandriani on the north-eastern coast of that island more than five hundred tombs were cleared by Tsountas in 1898.[1] The early town (not excavated) and the cemeteries occupied a sloping terrain high above the shore. The summit of a nearby rocky hill, Kastri, which is all but isolated by deep ravines on the landward side, was fortified with a thick wall and projecting U-shaped towers. Inside the fortress there were scant remains of rooms or small buildings, once more illustrating apsidal and rectangular plans.

Chalandriani, the centre of what is often called the 'Syros culture', was an important place and its foreign relations are significant.[2] The fortifications on the acropolis are obviously similar to those of the third settlement at Lerna (E.H. II) and belong probably to the same epoch. In the debris were found part of a *depas amphikypellon* of Troy II or III, a jar with seal impressions which have been likened to designs of the First Intermediate Period in Egypt but may be even earlier, a remarkable silver diadem assignable to E.C. II, and crucibles and moulds for manufacturing copper tools. There can be little doubt that the stronghold flourished in the second phase of the E.C. period.

The cemetery must have been used over a long period but the graves are consistent in type. They were small walled chambers with corbelled slab covers of a form that is paralleled at Ayios Kosmas in Attica. Regularly there was a doorway in the side, symbolical rather than practical. Single burials were normal; in a few graves intermediate floor-slabs were inserted above one group of bones to make a resting place for the next. Offerings were plentiful: copper pins and tweezers, colouring matter in decorated bone tubes, marble figurines, stone vessels (relatively few in number), frying pans and jars in burnished ware with incised and stamped patterns, sauceboats and saucers duplicating those of the mainland, and fine pots with linear decoration in lustrous dark paint on a light ground.[3] This painted ware is of, or very near, the class that occurs in E.H. II (not E.H. III) at Peloponnesian sites. It appears in other islands also, for example in Siphnos and Naxos.[4]

Correspondences between Chalandriani and the stratigraphically certified remains of E.H. II on the mainland are sufficient, it would seem, to prove close relationships and contemporaneity.

---

[1] §v, 28, part ii.   [2] §v, 7; §v, 10.   [3] See Plate 61 (*a*).
[4] Papathanasopoulos, G. A., Κυκλαδικὰ Νάξου, I. In *Arch. Deltion*, 17 (1961/2), 104-51.

Further, it seems probable that this flourishing centre was wholly, or almost wholly, abandoned at the end of the period which we are calling E.C. II, since parallels with the third phase (for example, in Melos and Paros, and in E.H. III) are lacking. The beginning of the settlement at Chalandriani, on the other hand, is not so easily correlated with developments elsewhere. That there was an established culture in the islands still earlier, in what one may call E.C. I, is not to be doubted, but its chronological limits cannot be sharply defined as yet.

EARLY CYCLADIC I

The graves at Pelos contained pottery that must be assigned to one of the first stages of the Early Bronze Age, chiefly jars and pyxides with simple incised patterns. This is the stage of the so-called 'Pelos culture', to which objects in Amorgos, Antiparos, and other islands have been attributed, largely on typological grounds and not without disagreement among the experts. Certain pieces from Naxos, as yet inadequately published, may belong to it. Schachermeyr observes that some of the vases and figurines have an underlying Neolithic character; this is true, though the line of development to the period of Chalandriani is also clear. A steatopygous figure in marble from Naxos, if not truly Neolithic, looks back to the Stone Age, as does another (of Cycladic origin?) that was found in Athens, and there are further examples in museums.[1] Recent excavations at Kephala in Ceos have produced pottery of primitive types, including some with burnished patterns and part of a scoop-like vessel that finds a close parallel in Sesklo, possibly contemporary with the 'Dhimini period'.[2] Until further evidence is forthcoming E.C. I must be left suspended between late Neolithic times and the period when imported elements of E.H.II become recognizable in the islands. The existence of a real break or distinct change between E.C. I and E.C. II has not been demonstrated.

MARBLE OBJECTS AND POTTERY

Marble is found in many of the islands, and the people used it from earliest times as material for their splendid craftsmanship, producing vases of many shapes and a long and wonderful series of human figures.[3] The latter have been discovered throughout

[1] §v, 9; §v, 17; §v, 31.   [2] *Hesperia*, xxxi (1962), 265 and pl. 92 f.
[3] §v, 31.

the Cyclades; they occur also in Crete and on the mainland, brought perhaps by islanders who settled for a time at coastal centres to trade. The types differ. Truly steatopygous female statuettes are rare, but small flat fiddle-shaped 'idols', thought to be derived from a squatting Neolithic type, are plentiful. They vary considerably in shape; some have cursorily incised features and there is a general resemblance to Trojan types, with which they are roughly contemporary. More distinctive is the class of naturalistic but highly stylized figures, standing with arms crossed over the chest.[1] Most but not all are female. Sexual characteristics are not emphasized, and only in a few instances is the abdomen swollen slightly to suggest pregnancy. The head is elongated and tilted backward; the features sketched, sometimes painted. These figures are block-like, austere, and yet delicate; rigidly uniform as a class but displaying infinite minor variations. Although generally about 20 centimetres high, they range in fact from tiny miniatures to three-quarters life size. The largest, and many of the finest, are from Amorgos. Most attractive of all is another series depicting musicians, a standing flute-player and a seated harpist from Keros, a harpist from Naxos and two more from Thera, marvellously joyous people.[2]

Most of the figurines and statuettes were found in tombs, but some come from houses in the settlements. Hundreds of them are known. Clearly they had a special significance to the islanders, and at a time when representations of human beings were very rarely made on the mainland. Their chronology has not been determined precisely. The little flat ones may be typologically closer to an old tradition, but they overlap the naturalistic class. Both kinds appear in the E.C. I and II phases; they were much less common, if indeed they were made at all, in E.C. III.

Heavy dark-coloured burnished pottery is characteristic of the early period. Many pieces are decorated with incised or stamped patterns or both.[3] There are a few basic shapes. The name 'frying pan' is a technical term; these objects are not pans at all, for the ornament is on the flat side and was meant to be seen. They would serve as lids but surely had some further special significance, equipped as they are with strange projecting handles and marked often with a female pubic triangle. They occur at Ayios Kosmas in Attica and at Manika in Euboea, where Cycladic influences are very strong in E.H. II, but also at other mainland sites in E.H. I as well as E.H. II contexts. Stamped patterns are normal at Chalandriani but not at the more ancient island sites which go

[1] See Plate 62 (a).   [2] See Plate 62 (b) and (c).   [3] See Plate 61 (b).

back to E.C. I.[1] Another typical pattern is made up of impressed triangles (*Kerbschnitt*) so arranged as to leave a zigzag band. True and 'false' spirals joined by tangent lines are common in many variations; the basic motif is thought by some to show a derivation from northern *Bandkeramik*. These designs appear not only on frying pans but on a series of jars with rounded bodies and tapering necks, standing usually on a high foot, a shape seen also in marble (E.C. I and E.C. II). The pyxis, another common form in the islands, is often decorated with simpler hatched patterns.

From the various elements of early culture in the Cyclades that are summarized above one derives an impression of general uniformity in the first phases. Contacts with lands on the borders existed, but evidence of 'colonization' from one side of the Aegean or another has not been forthcoming. Therefore the question of origins must be left unanswered at present. As to the course of events, it is here suggested that a very long period of gradual development was brought rather suddenly to a close at the end of E.C. II, in a period when there is evidence also of sharp disturbances both in Asia Minor and in parts of the Greek mainland. The following stage, E.C. III, of which we have caught a glimpse in only a few of the islands up to now, appears to have been distinctly different from what went before and to look forward rather toward the Middle Bronze Age.

VI. CRETE

Successive phases of the Early Bronze Age in Crete were analysed by Sir Arthur Evans and designated E.M. I, II and III. His contemporaries, and most of those who carried on and extended the investigations, adopted the same terminology and in general the same basic system of relative chronology. This was outlined comprehensively and with great clarity by J. D. S. Pendlebury just before the Second World War.[2] Gaps and discrepancies were indeed recognizable already, as must soon be the case in any rigid system of archaeological and historical classification. Evans himself had not failed to observe them, though he and his followers were sure that the framework was essentially right. Since the war new excavations and studies have revealed further problems, and efforts to examine these objectively have produced a change in nomenclature, the period between the Neolithic and the beginning of the great palaces being called simply Prepalatial, without

[1] §v, 7.   [2] §vi, 13.

sharply defined subdivisions. In this there are obvious advantages, as in the altered names of the succeeding periods, M.M. and L.M. being apportioned to Early (Proto-) and Late (Neo-)Palatial and Postpalatial.[1] But Evans's terms are so firmly established in archaeological usage that they may not be wholly replaced.

Long Neolithic and M.M. sequences exist and can be observed, at Cnossus particularly but also at Phaestus. At no site yet known, however, is there any extensive series of E.M. remains in place between the Neolithic layer and that of the first Palatial period. It is assumed that the palace builders often cut away debris of the preceding age. Undoubtedly this happened, for levelling and grading are obviously necessary when major construction is undertaken; but the resulting debris had to be dumped somewhere, and one might expect to find greater masses of earth containing E.M. potsherds than have in fact been discovered near the palace sites. For this and other reasons various students of the problem have been led to conclude that E.M. never existed as a major chronological stage but was a local, provincial, phenomenon contemporary with the Early Palatial period of the great centres.[2] This theory cannot be disproved altogether at present, but although it accounts for certain inconvenient lacunae in the evidence it creates too many other contradictions to be convincing.

The habitation of Crete was not uniform. The island is nearly 160 miles long, its impressive landscape being dominated by big mountain ranges; these divide the cultivable area into relatively small plains. The western part seems scarcely to have been occupied in the Early Bronze Age.[3] Concentrations appear in the north-central region around Cnossus, in the south-central throughout the Messara before Phaestus, and in the eastern, especially around and below the Gulf of Mirabello. Connexions among them exist clearly enough, but there are differences. Cnossus, an important centre in Neolithic times, played a lesser role in the E.M. period, while vigorous and fairly rapid progress appears to have taken place first in the east and then in the south.

EARLY MINOAN I

Settlements of the first E.M. phase are generally near the shore. The people may have been seafarers, and it seems not improbable that they came from Asia Minor; hence their landfall in eastern Crete and certain resemblances between their pottery and that of Anatolian coastal lands. Incised vases of very early Cycladic type

---

[1] §VI, 14.   [2] G, 1; §VI, 10; §VI, 11.   [3] See Map 13.

(the 'Pelos group') appear here also, and there is pottery of a sub-Neolithic character, for example the tall chalices of Pyrgos, dark-faced and decorated with burnished patterns.[1] The latter may be likened, though only in a general way, to late Neolithic wares of the Greek mainland and of the Troad and Samos, if not still further east. A distinctive class of pottery with linear patterns in red-brown paint on a light ground occurs in the Messara, where it may be divided into two successive sub-phases, and in the east.[2] A scrap of copper was found in an E.M. I context in Mochlos. Crude seal-stones and figurines can be assigned to this early stage only tentatively and on stylistic grounds. Traces of rectangular structures in Mochlos may represent the first houses of the period. The dead were buried in caves and rock shelters, but also (for example, at Leben) in the first of a series of big circular tombs.[3]

EARLY MINOAN II

The second E.M. phase develops from the first without interruption but with suddenly accelerated progress. Eastern Crete continues to lead, while the south gains and the north-central region still lags. There is an elaborate complex of buildings at Vasiliki, the thick walls having stone socles that supported crude bricks and a framework of timber, all coated with fine red stucco.[4] Tombs also were now constructed with some care: rectangular houses of the dead occur in the east, larger tholoi in the Messara.[5] The latter went on being used thereafter for centuries and ultimately held hundreds of burials with their funeral gifts. The objects are of great archaeological interest, comprising a varied array of pottery, jewellery, and other items, but in most of the tombs they lay in confusion after the many successive burial ceremonies and can now be dated only by style. Stratified settlements of the E.M. period have not been found in the Messara. This is one of the facts that was taken by Åberg and others to indicate that the tholoi were not in fact earlier than the M.M. palaces, but contemporary with them, and that all so-called E.M. objects were to be ascribed to that time also. In reply Pendlebury pointed out that objects of E.M. types were not found with those of M.M. in the palaces, and he predicted that the early settlements would be discovered ultimately, perhaps under some of the modern villages which occupy the permanently

[1] §vi, 18. See Plate 63 (a).   [2] See Plate 63 (b).
[3] G, 27, 120–4.   [4] §vi, 15; §vi, 16.
[5] §vi, 19.

favourable sites. In any case, the sequence of burials observed recently in a few of the tombs makes Åberg's theory untenable.

The pottery of E.M. II includes grey ware and red-on-white patterned ware, descended from the preceding phase, and a distinctive class of red-brown mottled ware that is associated particularly with Vasiliki;[1] in some cases the mottling was deliberately controlled for its decorative quality. Tall beaked jugs of Anatolian type are characteristic, as are squat jugs with fantastically long horizontal spouts (a shape that persists later in modified form). Anthropomorphic and theriomorphic vessels begin. A splendid series of stone vases, inspired undoubtedly by Egyptian prototypes but Minoan in character, is found in Mochlos and elsewhere.[2] The materials—limestone, alabaster, variegated marble and breccia—occur locally. There are boxes carved of steatite. A famous lid with a figure of a reclining hound[3] is thought to have Syrian connexions. Copper is now relatively common: tweezers, pointed tools, a double axe-head, and dagger blades that develop from a short triangular to an elongated form. Fine gold jewellery occurs in the tombs in Mochlos.[4] The seal-stones and figurines, most of which come from big common graves, are hard to date accurately.

Sir Arthur Evans saw a parallel between Libyan tholoi and those of the Messara. The stone bowls provide further evidence of contact with Africa, probably in the most prosperous era of the Egyptian Old Kingdom, from the Fourth to the Sixth Dynasties, though objects of this sort obviously might survive over long periods and therefore they rarely furnish exact dates. Relationships with the Aegean area also were undoubtedly maintained; production of glaze-paint for pottery may have been learned from E.H. Greece, and figurines of Cycladic type were imported or copied. Anatolian influences persist in E.M. II but there is no evidence of new migrations.

EARLY MINOAN III

It is generally agreed that the third E.M. phase marks a transition from the culture of the Early Bronze Age to that of the Palatial period in Crete and that there is a certain chronological overlapping of M.M. I*a*, especially at Cnossus, with E.M. III in other parts of the island.[5] To what extent these periods coincided is not yet certainly known. Again the architectural and strati-

---

[1] See Plate 63 (*d*).
[2] §vi, 17; §vi, 21, figs. 152–75.
[3] §vi, 15, fig.5; §vi, 21, figs. 146–7.
[4] §G, 15, 55–8; §vi, 21, figs. 200, 202.
[5] §vi, 6, 137–8.

graphical evidence is meagre. Only a few poor houses were built over the ruins of the E.M. II complex at Vasiliki. Old cemeteries continued to be used in east Crete and in the Messara.

Another class of pottery becomes popular at this time, taking root firmly in the eastern and southern regions, where it persisted, but being superseded sooner through rapid development at Cnossus. In the new technique vases large and small were often coated with lustrous black slip and on this ground designs were drawn in dull white or cream-coloured paint.[1] At first geometrical patterns prevailed, but curves and spirals followed. Old shapes persisted, with gradual modifications in E.M. III, while new shapes were being introduced, for example those of the hole-mouthed jars and various small cups and jugs which were to be carried on into the M.M. period. A bridge-spouted jar that was made in Crete at the time of transition, E.M. III–M.M. I a, was found in a tomb at Lapethus in Cyprus with red polished pottery of Early Cypriote III.[2] Jewellery and metalwork in E.M. III were like their precursors, copper daggers keeping the elongated form. Stone vessels were now less colourful. Seals of steatite and ivory with carved handles and designs including human and animal figures, found in tomb deposits of the Messara, are generally thought to belong to this period.

Numerous objects of Cycladic origin make their appearance in E.M. III. Pyxides in brown ware with incised and impressed patterns, like those of E.C. III in the first city at Phylakopi, were found at Pyrgos. Marble figurines of the developed Cycladic type are plentiful, especially in the Messara, and are copied in bone in Lasithi.[3] Ships and fishes appearing in the designs on seals have been taken as prototypes of the marine motifs that became popular in later Minoan times, but they should be recognized principally as descendants of E.C. prototypes. Close synchronisms are not established by many of these objects, since the finding places allow wide margins. The figurines and the maritime designs are earlier, in origin at least, than E.M. III. Phylakopi I, however, may well be contemporary, and a correspondence with the First Intermediate Period in Egypt, suggested by similarities among the seals, would seem probable.

Looking back over the E.M. period, one sees that its first elements are bound up with a very early, sub-Neolithic, stage of primitive Aegean culture, and that its third phase extends to a time not far from 2000 B.C. The absolute date of the upper limit

[1] See Plate 63(c).   [2] §vi, 3.
[3] B.S.A. xxxvi (1935–6), 116–22.

is not known, but evidence from the Greek mainland and Asia Minor proves that the Bronze Age began near the outset of the third millennium and developed gradually. To reduce or eliminate the E.M. period as a chronological entity is therefore to regard Crete as an unaccountably slow and backward part of the Aegean world, living a primitive life until the bright civilization of the Palatial age came almost overnight into flower. Though not quite inconceivable, this course of events appears extremely improbable. Rather, Minoan history should be seen as roughly parallel with that of neighbouring lands.

VII. CHRONOLOGICAL SUMMARY

After an extensive survey of the material remains one may hope to discern at least an intelligible sketch of human life and experience in the Early Bronze Age, but no amount of diligence in counting sites and artifacts can make up for the lack of contemporary written documents, and any general picture that emerges will necessarily be somewhat tentative, containing many blank spaces.

It is clear that the people of the Aegean area were not a single race or an altogether homogeneous cultural group. Part of the human stock must have survived from Neolithic times, and new elements made their way into various districts at different junctures throughout the long period in question. When they settled and established themselves, there was inevitably a fusion of population and customs among neighbouring communities. Whence the several migrations came is not yet determined; anthropological[1] and archaeological data are still far too meagre to fix their origins and the routes they followed—if indeed these can ever be fixed. There is no reason to doubt that the chief impulses began ultimately in richer lands of the east and moved through Anatolia, or perhaps rather along its coasts, to the Aegean, but the process was not continuous. Influences directly from Egypt were slight in the early periods; those from the north seem not to have penetrated significantly into the Greek peninsula, and of those from the west only vestiges can be seen along the shores of the Ionian Sea.

Archaeological observations indicate that cultural traditions were seriously interrupted at various times in this period. Neolithic ways of life were superseded rather abruptly in most areas with the coming of other people who knew the fashioning of copper tools

[1] §III, 1.

and weapons,[1] although stone and bone continued to be used long afterwards for many purposes. Early in the third millennium a current of new influences seems to have spread from north-western Asia Minor into Macedonia and southward, sporadically and somewhat diluted, into central Greece. About the same time or perhaps a little earlier a parallel movement must have brought people to the small islands of the Aegean, where Neolithic settlements appear to have been scarce. Crete, which on the contrary had supported human communities for several thousand years already, was also affected. Logic suggests that the first E.H. occupants of southern Greece itself must likewise have come by way of the islands, but at each step along this path we find the evidence less convincing. Objects made in Samos and Chios look Anatolian and can be likened, for example, to others from Iasus, Smyrna, and Troy.[2] The forms had undergone a sea change, however, before they reached the Cyclades and Crete, and still more before their counterparts appeared in Euboea or the Argolid. These facts do not disprove the theory, nor do they prove that the movement was slow and halting. In new environments people may well have changed and adapted their ways quickly. The Hellenizing power that the land of Greece has demonstrably possessed in historical ages, quite apart from deliberate human agency, presumably was active long before any people who could be called Hellenes had come into existence.

Minor shifts in the course of development are observable in the early strata of this period at some excavated sites. Doubtless many were of local character. Then in certain regions—Boeotia, for example, as seen at Eutresis—there was a more general alteration. This is the stage which for convenience we mark as the transition from E.H. I to E.H. II. It occurred also in other places on the mainland, some sites being occupied now for the first time or after a long interval. How far it extended is not clear. In the Cyclades the dividing line eludes precise definition; in Crete a new phase of development begins obviously with Early Minoan II. If another migration accounts for these changes it must have been a singularly peaceful one, for signs of destruction and capture are not visible.

The second main phase of the Early Bronze Age has left the greatest quantity of material evidence, the most striking types of objects, and the most impressive architectural monuments. These are described at some length in the foregoing account. Examples

[1] Copper was worked at Kephala in Ceos.
[2] §v, 1; §v, 6; §v, 20.

of them have been found over a wide area from the Spercheus southward and westward and among the islands on either side of the Greek peninsula. They are not well attested in the north but perhaps still await discovery, for their presence at Troy is beyond question. This was a prosperous era, a time of enterprising men who sailed the seas; sensitive imaginative people, one must think, who brought home wealth and new ideas from their journeys. Some were rich enough to attain a measure of power in their districts and presumably to rule as princes from their palaces at centres like Tiryns and Lerna, or from forts like the one at Chalandriani in Syros, maintaining contact with their royal cousins on the Hellespont. It was a microcosm, admittedly, and no more to be compared with the great monarchies of the third millennium than the Cephissus is to be compared with the Nile, but none the less an astonishing advance over anything that had preceded it in the Aegean.

Then toward the end of the millennium there came another marked change, with sudden violence in the Argolid, perhaps more gradual in central Greece, palpable also in the Cyclades if the slender store of evidence has not deceived us. Crete seems not to have been affected immediately, and signs of the event are scarce in the north and north-west. The new phase, which we call E.H. III, appears clearly at Lerna as a stage of culture quite different from that which went before, reflecting an invasion by people of other antecedents, who came we know not whence. It was more than a local raid, since these people stayed and established themselves over a considerable area, but the full extent and nature of the occupation are as yet not known. There are puzzling gaps in the evidence; for example in Attica, where much excavation has yielded few traces of the settlements that are attested in neighbouring provinces. Some of the material may have been overlooked up to now; or we may ultimately conclude that Attica was partially abandoned in this period. Almost certainly population was reduced along the whole eastern coast of central Greece and in many of the Cycladic islands.

One wonders what happened to the survivors. Some undoubtedly were absorbed in the new communities. Others may have made their way to Crete, where conditions were relatively stable, and have joined in the final development of E.M. culture which led to the age of the palaces. A general relationship between the Early Helladic and Cycladic peoples on the one hand, and the Minoan on the other, has long been recognized. Fleeing before an invasion, a number of the former might well seek refuge in a kindred land, themselves too poor and wretched to make a conspicuous impression at the moment, but bringing with them some of their former customs and a measure of the enterprise and imagination and grace that were soon to appear so brightly on the soil of Crete.

In the Argolid—to which we keep returning not only because it was a crucially important area but also because it is archaeologically best known at present—the new towns and villages maintained themselves through a period of many generations, perhaps as long as two centuries, which makes up the final phase of the Early Bronze Age. In some ways this period marks a transition or a beginning, rather than an end, for in it are found few elements of E.H. II and relatively many that are carried on into M.H. times. However, it is not truly a part of the succeeding age, and the accepted terminology should be retained. At more than one site there were in fact distinct breaks at the close of E.H. III; elsewhere the life of the communities appears to have gone on without serious interruption, rapidly adopting the new features that were then introduced. These, and the conclusions that may be drawn from them, will be described in a later chapter. Tentatively we may place the change at the beginning of the second millennium, noting that imported pottery of M.M. I*a* style occurs for the first time in the earliest M.H. stratum at Lerna.

CHAPTER XXVI(*b*)

CYPRUS IN THE EARLY BRONZE AGE

In Cyprus, as in other regions, the course of the Bronze Age has been divided into three main stages, Early, Middle and Late. Each stage is further subdivided into three phases, I, II and III, which, in their turn may be split into subperiods, A, B, and C. By analogy with Early, Middle and Late Helladic, Minoan and Cycladic in Greece, Crete and the Islands respectively, the terms Early, Middle and Late Cypriot (abbreviated to E.C., M.C. and L.C.) are used.

The beginning of the Early Cypriot period synchronizes fairly closely with the disastrous end of the E.B. 2 period in Anatolia, *c.* 2300 B.C.; it may, indeed, prove to have been a direct outcome of this major Anatolian catastrophe. Its duration seems to have been between four and five hundred years; the transition to the Middle Cypriot stage is an ill-defined process, but may with some probability be placed in the century between 1900 and 1800 B.C., in view of synchronisms with Crete demonstrated by Minoan vases and weapons found as imports in north Cyprus.

The account that can be given of the Early Cypriot period is very imperfect, depending almost wholly as it does upon the evidence of cemeteries and their contents. Only at the very end of the period is it possible to draw on evidence provided by settlements.

VIII. THE IDENTITY OF THE EARLIEST BRONZE AGE SETTLERS

The Early Cypriot period starts with acute uncertainty, which is aggravated by serious controversy among those best qualified to describe its beginnings. To start with, it is not known with what degree of continuity the gap is to be bridged between the residual Chalcolithic communities and the bearers of the new culture. That the end of Chalcolithic I was catastrophic has already been seen to be a reasonable inference from the long tale of abandoned settlements of that period. Chalcolithic II, which occupies the 200-year interval between the end of Chalcolithic I and the start of E.C. I, is at present so ill-defined that the future may even show that *it* contains the real beginnings of the Early Bronze Age. The lack of a firm chronological landmark within this shadowy period is a great handicap to any attempt at resolving its difficulties.

The focus of Early Cypriot controversy lies in the problem of the period's beginnings.[1] On the one hand, there is a sequence of tomb groups from the *Vounous* cemetery at Bellapais on the north coast which was held by J. R. Stewart[2] to illustrate the development of material culture continuously from E.C. I down to M.C. III, though 'E.C. I at *Vounous* does not mark the very beginning of the Bronze Age'. Nevertheless, in Stewart's view, the earliest tombs at *Vounous* provide the earliest evidence of Early Cypriot culture yet identified. On the other hand, however, there is the so-called Philia culture,[3] a phase of the Early Bronze Age which takes its name from a group of sites (all but one of them cemeteries) located among the river valleys in the western half of the central plain; offshoots have been identified at Nicosia,[4] at Vasilia[5] on the north coast, at Anoyira and Sotira on the south coast.[6] Differences between the material culture of E.C. I at *Vounous* and the Philia culture can be seen in a comparison of pottery fabrics and shapes, types of copper tools and weapons and certain small objects.[7] These differences have been regarded either as of chronological significance[8] or as of regional importance only,[9] representing variations upon an original parent culture which developed in Cyprus. Stewart, indeed, visualized the Philia culture as an inbred regional phenomenon,[10] standing aside from the main course of the Early Cypriot period, with a separate identity to be traced as late as M.C. III. This explanation raises serious difficulties, particularly in view of the distribution of the Philia sites.

The main focus of Philia-culture sites lies in the Ovgos valley, near the villages of Dhenia, Philia, Kyra, Khrysiliou and Morphou. The contents of graves found in this area give a clear picture of the material culture of the Philia stage.[11] Though much of the pottery belongs to the Red Polished class, there are also painted wares (Red-on-White ware, in Dikaios' terminology) and Black Slip-and-Combed ware.[12] While Red Polished ware is also the principal fabric of the classic Early Cypriot sequence in the *Vounous* tombs, there is no counterpart in that sequence for the painted and

---

[1] G, 2, 13; §VIII, 4, 202–3; §VIII, 10, 577–80; §VIII, 11; §VIII, 15.

[2] §VIII, 15, 269–72.   [3] §VIII, 4, 190–1.

[4] §VIII, 15, 269.   [5] §VIII, 15, 216.

[6] G, 2, 14.   [7] Especially the Philia pendants.

[8] §VIII, 4, 190–1.

[9] §VIII, 15, 296.   [10] §VIII, 15, 269–70.

[11] §VIII, 4, figs. L–LII.   [12] §VIII, 4, fig. 83.

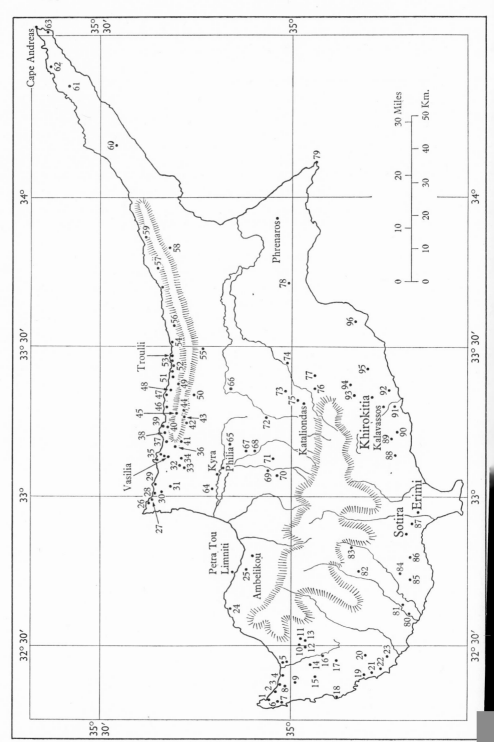

NUMERICAL KEY

#		#		#		#		#		#	
1	Nisi Tou Ayiou Yeoryiou	17	Theletra	33	Karpasha	49	Bellapais	65	Dhenia	81	Souskiou
2	Ayios Nikolaos	18	Ayios Yeoryios	34	Kambyli	50	Dhikomo	66	Nicosia	82	Kedhares
3	Loutra Tis Aphroditis	19	Kissonerga	35	Vavilas	51	Ayios Epiktitos	67	Akaki	83	Omodhos
4	Latzi	20	Mesakhorio	36	Larnaka	52	Xylomandra	68	Meniko	84	Anoyira
5	Polis	21	Khlorakas	37	Lapithos	53	Toumba	69	Kato Moni	85	Ayios Thomas
6	Ayios Yeoryios	22	Ktima	38	Karavas	54	Platymatis	70	Ayia Marina	86	Paramali
7	Ayios Konon	23	Yeroskipos	39	Platani	55	Kythrea	71	Eliophotes	87	Koufovounos
8	Neokhorio	24	Kokkina	40	Elea	56	Kharcha	72	Anayia	88	Armenochori
9	Androlikou	25	Loutros	41	Sisklipos	57	Akanthou	73	Margi	89	Pyrgos
10	Peristerona	26	Liveras	42	Krini	58	Ayios Iakovos	74	Dhali	90	Moni
11	Meladhia	27	Galales	43	Keumurju	59	Phlamoudhi	75	Analiondas	91	Mari
12	Trimitousha	28	Kornos	44	Aghirda	60	Lythrankomi	76	Mathiati	92	Maroni
13	Philousa	29	Orga	45	Karmi	61	Rizokarpaso	77	Sha	93	Skarinou
14	Terra	30	Kormakiti	46	Ayios Yeoryios	62	Aphendrika	78	Pyla	94	Kophinou
15	Inia	31	Dhiorios	47	Kyrenia	63	Apostolos Andreas	79	Cape Greco	95	Alaminos
16	Ayii Anargyri	32	Myrtou	48	Thermia	64	Khrysiliou	80	Kouklia	96	Kiti

ALPHABETICAL KEY

Aghirda	44	Karmi	45	Krini	42	Meniko	68
Akaki	67	Karpasha	33	Ktima	22	Mesakhorio	20
Akanthou	57	Kato Moni	69	Kyrenia	47	Moni	90
Alaminos	95	Kedhares	82	Kythrea	55	Myrtou	32
Analiondas	75	Keumurju	43	Lapithos	37	Neokhorio	8
Anayia	72	Kharcha	56	Larnaka	36	Nicosia	66
Androlikou	9	Khlorakas	21	Latzi	4	Nisi Tou Ayiou Yeoryiou	1
Anoyira	84	Khrysiliou	64	Liveras	26	Omodhos	83
Aphendrika	62	Kissonerga	19	Loutra Tis Aphroditis	3	Orga	29
Apostolos Andreas	63	Kiti	96	Loutros	25	Paramali	86
Armenochori	88	Kokkina	24	Lythrankomi	60	Peristerona	10
Ayia Marina	70	Kophinou	94	Margi	73	Philousa	13
Ayii Anargyri	16	Kormakiti	30	Mari	91	Phlamoudhi	59
Ayios Epiktitos	51	Kornos	28	Maroni	92	Platani	39
Ayios Iakovos	58	Koufovounos	87	Mathiati	76	Platymatis	54
Ayios Konon	7	Kouklia	80	Meladhia	11		
Ayios Nikolaos	2						
Ayios Thomas	85						
Ayios Yeoryios and	6, 18 and 46						
Bellapais	49						
Cape Greco	79						
Dhali	74						
Dhenia	65						
Dhikomo	50						
Dhiorios	31						
Elea	40						
Eliophotes	71						
Galales	27						
Inia	15						
Kambyli	34						
Karavas	38						

Polis	5
Pyla	78
Pyrgos	89
Rizokarpaso	61
Sha	77
Sisklipos	41
Skarinou	93
Souskiou	81
Terra	14
Theletra	17
Thermia	48
Toumba	53
Trimitousha	12
Vavilas	35
Xylomandra	52
Yeroskipos	23

A number applies to one or more sites in a named locality.

combed wares of Philia. Dikaios has related[1] to the contents of the Philia-stage grave-finds of pottery from a test excavation in a small settlement site at *Alonia*, in Kyra village. Black Slip-and-Combed pottery and Red Polished material from this site have close parallels in the cemeteries. Red Lustrous, Red-and-Black Lustrous and Black Lustrous Pottery look back to the Chalcolithic II material illustrated by Ambelikou. This evidence favours a very early date within the E.C. period for the Philia culture. Nevertheless, it does not imply that the transition from the Chalcolithic period to the Early Bronze Age in Cyprus took place without outside interference. This is clear enough from the many signs of novelty in material culture, including the appearance of new pottery shapes (particularly jugs with flat base, tall neck and cut-away mouth)[2] and the introduction of a considerable series of metal objects. There was also a new attitude to the disposal and care of the dead. Innovations of this kind imply that the Early Bronze Age was inaugurated by newcomers to Cyprus, who first established themselves in the Ovgos valley. In this case, then, the cultural stage at *Vounous* which has been called Early Cypriot I[3] should be regarded as a secondary phase. There are typological arguments to support this view; shapes of pottery vessels which belong to the Philia stage, particularly the beak-spouted jugs, have recognizable counterparts in the earliest *Vounous* tombs,[4] which are demonstrably more advanced. This is most easily seen in the manner in which flat bases diminish in size as the period advances. Philia-stage jugs were made with relatively[5] broad flat bases for people who must habitually have stood their vessels on level surfaces. This trivial detail deserves emphasis; the broad flat base had not been a characteristic of the Chalcolithic pottery series, and it does not appear again in Cypriot ceramics until a developed stage of the Late Bronze Age. In fact, during the Early Cypriot period the flat base degenerated first into a stump,[6] then into a nipple and finally disappeared,[7] leaving round bases almost ubiquitous, irrespective of the type of vessel. It is tempting to argue from the vessels to the appointments of the houses in which they were used, and to infer that the bearers of the Philia culture came from a considerably more sophisticated environment than that of the residual Chalcolithic culture which they encountered on arrival in Cyprus. They and their descendants coalesced with the native population, succumbing to

[1] §VIII, 4, 190.   [2] §VIII, 4, fig. 80. See Plate 64 (*b*).   [3] §VIII, 14.
[4] §VIII, 15, fig. LV.   [5] §VIII, 15, fig. LIV.
[6] §VIII, 15, fig. LXI.   [7] §VIII, 15, figs. LXVI–LXVII.

their influence sufficiently to adopt changed standards in many aspects of their lives; it was not to be the only time that such a process took place.

The end of the second phase of the Early Bronze Age in Anatolia was accompanied by widespread destruction and disaster, in which hundreds of settlements were affected;[1] the progress of an implacable invader is seen in this tale of desolation. The movement seems to have spread from the north-west towards the south-east, and to have rolled up the E.B. 2 population before its advance. However destructive its effects, there must have been survivors who managed to escape. Mellaart has pointed[2] to affinities between E.B. 2 pottery types of the Konya plain region and Philia-stage pottery in Cyprus; he suggests that the latter may have been the result of these upheavals in Anatolia. Certainly, the coincidence of massive disturbances in Asia Minor and the appearance of newcomers in Cyprus are too striking to be overlooked. If for the moment a precise archaeological horizon in Anatolia cannot be shown in which all the characterizing features of the Philia stage are present, this does not disprove the association.

The date of the Anatolian catastrophe has been fixed at c. 2300 B.C.;[3] this harmonizes satisfactorily with the date proposed for the first appearance of the Philia stage in Cyprus. The distribution of sites implies that the newcomers made their landfall in Morphou bay and their initial settlement in the Ovgos and Serakhis valleys; the Philia-stage graves in the Bronze Age cemetery at *Áyia Paraskevi*, just south of Nicosia, may belong to this first phase.[4] The next phase is full of uncertainty, and the evidence is clearly far from complete. It should include the northward expansion to the coast at Vasilia, at the west end of the Kyrenia hills[4] and perhaps the rather surprising move outwards to the south side of the island at Anoyira and Sotira.[5] The latter sites lie on the south side of the Troödos massif, nearly forty miles away from the original focus.

If the new arrivals in Cyprus had seen the river valleys of the western plain as the ideal zone of settlement, their descendants were of a different mind, for their sites have been found in greatest profusion sheltering at the mountain foot on both sides of the Kyrenia hills[6] in regions which had been quite densely occupied during Chalcolithic I. The evidence of surface survey

[1] See above, pp. 406 f.   [2] Above, p. 407.
[3] Above, p. 404.   [4] *Arch. Reports*, 1955, 41.   [5] G, 2, 14.
[6] G, 1, 138–9.

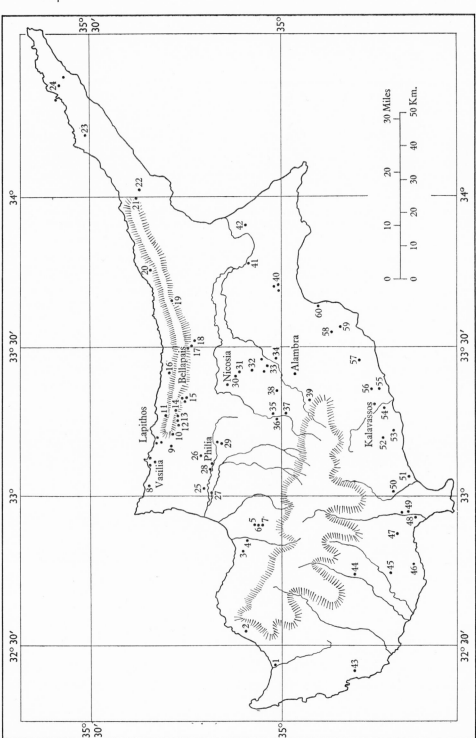

Map 15. Early Bronze Age sites in Cyprus.

NUMERICAL KEY

1	Polis	25	Khrysiliou
2	Yialia	26	Ayia Marina
3	Ambelikou	27	Morphou
4	Lefka	28	Kyra
5	Skouriotissa	29	Dhenia
6	Katydata	30	Eylenja
7	Linou	31	Athalassa
8	Kormakiti	32	Yeri
9	Larnaka	33	Ayios Sozomenos
10	Sisklipos	34	Potamia
11	Karmi	35	Pera
12	Pileri	36	Politiko
13	Krini	37	Kambia
14	Aghirda	38	Margi
15	Dhikomo	39	Lythrodondas
16	Ayios Epiktitos	40	Pyla
17	Kythrea	41	Kalopsidha
18	Bey Keuy	42	Akhyritou
19	Trypimeni	43	Kissonerga
20	Akanthou	44	Kedhares
21	Komi Kebir	45	Anoyira
22	Livadhia	46	Evdimou
23	Yialousa	47	Sotira
24	Rizokarpaso	48	Episkopi
		49	Erimi
		50	Polemidhia
		51	Limassol
		52	Pyrgos
		53	Moni
		54	Mari
		55	Maroni
		56	Psematismenos
		57	Alaminos
		58	Klavdia
		59	Arpera
		60	Larnaka

ALPHABETICAL KEY

Aghirda	14	Kissonerga	43
Akanthou	20	Klavdia	58
Akhyritou	42	Komi Kebir	21
Alaminos	57	Kormakiti	8
Ambelikou	3	Krini	13
Anoyira	45	Kyra	28
Arpera	59	Kythrea	17
Athalassa	31	Larnaka	9 and 60
Ayia Marina	26	Lefka	4
Ayios Epiktitos	16	Limassol	51
Ayios Sozomenos	33	Linou	7
Bey Keuy	18	Livadhia	22
Dhenia	29	Lythrodondas	39
Dhikomo	15	Margi	38
Episkopi	48	Mari	54
Erimi	49	Maroni	55
Evdimou	46	Moni	53
Eylenja	30	Morphou	27
Kalopsidha	41	Pera	35
Kambia	37	Pileri	12
Karmi	11	Polemidhia	50
Katydata	6	Polis	1
Kedhares	44	Politiko	36
Khrysiliou	25	Potamia	34
		Psematismenos	56
		Pyla	41
		Pyrgos	52
		Rizokarpaso	24
		Sisklipos	10
		Skouriotissa	5
		Sotira	47
		Trypimeni	19
		Yeri	32
		Yialia	2
		Yialousa	23

A number refers to one or more sites in the same locality.

suggests that Early Bronze Age settlement avoided the old Chalcolithic sites, here as elsewhere. The Philia-stage site at Vasilia
seems to be intermediary between the culture in its purest form in the
Ovgos valley and the developed E.C. I which is typified by *Vounous*;
this site and its E.C. I contemporaries may already have developed
their distinctive characteristics, while something much closer to
Philia still survived at Vasilia. Recent fieldwork has shown[1]
that the large number of sites on the seaward side of the Kyrenia
hills is equalled by those on the southern, inland side, particularly
those that are close to the Kyrenia pass in the lands of Aghirda
and Krini to the west, Dhikomo to the east. Both sides of the hills
are well furnished with springs, both sides command extensive
areas of well-drained and easily cultivable soils. Water and agricultural land determined the choice of site, and access to the sea
was evidently of comparatively minor importance.

The next stages in the Early Bronze Age settlement of Cyprus
are more difficult to follow, since the relative chronology of the
large number of sites that have been located, but remain unexcavated, is largely unknown. However, it is clear that from at
least the end of E.C. I at *Vounous* onwards there was a substantial
expansion of settlement in many parts of the island. Of several
sites in the Karpass peninsula, that at Rizokarpaso[2] was probably
the most important. In the Mesaoria there is little sign of occupation save on the south-east side, at Kalopsidha, Akhyritou and
Pyla. On the south coast, between Larnaka bay and the mouth of
the Kouris river at Episkopi, there was a considerable succession
of sites in one or other of the river valleys which form the natural
boundaries within the region. The sites at Kalavassos[3] (immediately adjoining a copper ore-body) and Episkopi[4] itself were
the principal centres. An important group of sites was established
before the end of E.C. III in the valleys of the Pediaios and
Yalias rivers, where these leave the Troödos foothills to enter the
central plain.[5] There were at least four main foci of settlement
of this type, at Politiko[6] (site of ancient Tamassus), Margi,[7]
Alambra,[8] and Ayios Sozomenos. It may be significant that these
sites are quite close to the copper-mining areas on the east and
north-east sides of the Troödos foothills, and that they command
the heart of the island's inland communications. There was very
little trace in the E.C. period of the extensive manner in which
the Paphos region had been settled in the Chalcolithic period.

---

[1] G, 1, map facing p. 144.   [2] G, 1, 153, no. 143.
[3] G, 1, 150, nos. 51–3; §1, 8.   [4] §viii, 16.   [5] G, 1, 139.
[6] §viii, 6, 5.   [7] §viii, 8, 146–52.   [8] §viii, 6, 19–27.

Because excavation has concentrated on cemeteries at the expense of occupation sites, nothing is known of E.C. architecture until virtually the end of the period. A part of a settlement which was probably founded during E.C. III *b* has been investigated at Alambra;[1] it continued to be used until M.C. I, possibly even later. Here was found a house with two-roomed plan, rectilinear in intention if not in execution. The lower courses of the walls were of masonry, the upper, it seems, of mud-brick. The type of roof was not established. Domestic installations included a large courtyard where beasts could be penned, a built oven, grinding equipment, and hearths. Two periods of occupation were separated by a destruction level.

Contemporary with the Alambra house is the well-known terracotta model of an open-air sanctuary, found in a tomb at the *Vounous* cemetery.[2] The model shows a circular sacred area enclosed by a low temenos wall, for whose type of construction no hint is offered. The shrine is entered by a single doorway with raised lintel. Within, the architectural appointments are of the simplest. To left and right of the doorway are rather irregularly planned pens in which oxen are tethered; they may well be sacrificial beasts. The cult images are set against the temenos wall almost opposite the doorway. On either side of the images are low benches on which some of the participants are seated.

Most information about the E.C. period comes from its cemeteries. These were found outside the occupation sites, but at no great distance from them. Though the slopes of a hillside provided a popular location, cemeteries were often sited on a level plateau, as at Dhenia[3] and Nicosia, *Ayia Paraskevi*. In rare cases, as at *Vrysis tou Barba*, Lapithos, they are found in low-lying flat land. Many of the cemeteries that were first opened during the Early Cypriot period continued to be used into the Middle Bronze Age, and cases occur, as at Dhenia and Nicosia, where this continuity was maintained until an advanced stage of the Late Bronze Age. The tombs of the Philia stage stand aside from the types characteristic of E.C. I at *Vounous* and elsewhere. With the exception of Vasilia, most Philia cemeteries contain simple oval pit-graves, excavated in bed-rock, or even in superficial deposits of earth.[4] At Philia, however, irregularly shaped burial chambers, preceded by a short entrance passage, were hollowed out of the edge of the rocky plateau at whose flank the cemetery is situated.[5] Naturally weathered hollows under a capping of

[1] §viii, 6, 19–27. [2] G, 3, pl. 9; §viii, 2; §viii, 3, 118–25. See Plate 64(*a*).
[3] *Op. Ath.* iv, 225. [4] §viii, 15, 216. [5] §viii, 4, 160–5.

harder rock may have stimulated the construction of this type of grave. The Philia-stage tombs of Vasilia are very much more pretentious.[1] A particularly fine example is as much as 16 m. in length from the beginning of its entrance passage to the end of the inner chamber. The chambers are usually, though not invariably, subrectangular in plan, the greatest dimension being between 3 and 4 m.; they were often reinforced by a buttress left standing in the back wall. Structural refinements include a lining of plaster on the faces of the entrance passage, niches in a chamber wall and, in one case, a small aperture connecting the tomb chamber with the world above, possibly used for making offerings in a continuing cult of the dead. So elaborate, indeed, are the tombs of Vasilia that the community to whom the cemetery belonged may have maintained a special necropolis staff, in the Egyptian manner.[2]

Dating from the beginning of E.C. I at *Vounous* a type of tomb was used which varied only in detail throughout the rest of the Early Cypriot period.[3] A cave-like chamber was quarried in the bed-rock, reached by a short entrance-passage. The doorway between passage and chamber was sealed by a large stone slab, not infrequently reinforced by a structure of small stones. Occasionally the façades were cut to resemble door-frames, and in one case at least the doorway was decorated with incised ornament.[4] It was not uncommon for more than one chamber to be opened from a single entrance passage. During E.C. I it was customary to use each chamber once only, though it was quite normal for two bodies to be buried simultaneously. Later, the practice grew of reopening burial chambers to make secondary interments. In E.C. I the dead were laid on their sides in a contracted position. As the period advanced, the bodies were extended on their backs. It was probably not until the very end of the Early Cypriot period that the custom started of sitting the dead against the walls of the tomb chamber, a habit that continued into the Middle Bronze Age. At all stages of the E.C. period, from Philia onwards, a very liberal allowance of grave offerings was given to the dead. These offerings consisted chiefly of pottery vessels of varying types, whose role in the funeral rite was to serve as containers of foodstuffs; it is quite usual to find the bones of food animals preserved inside basins or jars.[5] By analogy, jugs and pitchers can be assumed to have held liquids; cups and bowls

[1] §VIII, 15, 218–19.   [2] §VIII, 15, 294.
[3] §VIII, 3; §I, 14.   [4] §VIII, 12; §VIII, 15, 217.
[5] §VIII, 14.

were for eating and drinking. Other gifts included terracotta models of household goods, such as spindles,[1] brushes[2] and knives with their sheaths.[3] The latter might suggest that metal was too precious to be given to the dead, but in fact copper objects are relatively common. Weapons include the highly characteristic rat-tanged swords and dirks,[4] and daggers whose perishable hilts had been pinned on with metal rivets. Tools[5] are represented by flat axes, chisels and awls, while care of the person is suggested by de-pilatory tweezers and razors.[6] Plain pins and toggle pins hint at the garments in which the dead were clothed at the time of their burial. Objects of gold and silver have only rarely been recorded.[7]

Little imagination is needed to see the motive for providing the dead with the type of gifts so far enumerated; they presuppose a belief in some kind of existence after death for which food and clothing, tools and weapons were essential. Other objects found in the graves are more difficult to interpret in this role. Amongst them are the so-called plank-shaped figures of terracotta,[8] ex-tremely stylized representations of female figures, whose incised ornament suggests draped rather than nude figures. A *kouro-trophos* is a rare variant,[9] and another type appears to show a wedded pair in a bed.[10] Very occasionally, elaborate models of terracotta were given to the dead, like the shrine already mentioned and a model, also from *Vounous*,[11] depicting two ox-drawn ploughs at work in the fields, accompanied by preparations for sowing the newly cultivated ground. While the religious significance of this group escapes us, it is of extreme interest for showing a type of plough and a method of cultivation still in use in Cyprus at the present day.[12] Similar plastic work often decorates pottery vessels with figures of animals or birds,[13] not to mention such domestic scenes as bread-making and corn-grinding, and other ploughing representations,[14] all providing valuable pendants to the *genre* models themselves. Without evidence from settlements it is impossible to decide whether these elaborate vessels were only used as grave-gifts, still less whether they figured in the furnishings of such sanctuaries as the original of the *Vounous* model.

The E.C. episode in the development of Cyprus resulted from the arrival from Anatolia of bands of refugees, who had escaped

---

[1] §VIII, 3, 130. [2] §VIII, 3, 129–30. [3] §VIII, 3, 129.
[4] §VIII, 15, figs. 97–8. [5] §VIII, 15, fig. 100. [6] *Ibid.*
[7] §VIII, 15, 254–6. [8] §VIII, 15, figs. 92–4. See Plate 64 (*c*).
[9] §VIII, 1, pl. 38:106. [10] §VIII, 15, fig. 94:3.
[11] §VIII, 3, 127–9. [12] G, 4, 8–9.
[13] G, 3, pl. VI; §VIII, 3, pls. 14–17. [14] §VIII, 15, 278–80.

from the destroyers of E.B. 2 culture in that region. They appear to have mixed with, and not to have destroyed the sparse Chalcolithic II population they encountered in the area of Morphou bay, their first landfall. They introduced metallurgical skills, new types of pottery and methods of decorating it, particularly incision;[1] they were also responsible for new ways of treating the dead. All this is clear from their graves and grave-offerings; the future, when their occupation sites begin to be excavated, will no doubt show other innovations for which they were responsible. As the E.C. period developed, human society prospered considerably, spreading widely throughout Cyprus, though most successfully amid the foothills on both sides of the Kyrenia mountains and in the river valleys to the east and north-east of the Troödos massif. Yet, by the end of the E.C. phase, this pattern of settlement was already breaking up, shifting, and rearranging itself, no doubt in response to the political and economic factors which account for the changed character of occupation and culture in the Middle Bronze Age.

Self-sufficiency may be taken as the keynote of the E.C. period; very few material objects found in E.C. contexts are of foreign origin, and the evidence is even slighter for the trafficking overseas of Cypriot-made goods. Indeed, much of the evidence for the foreign relations of Cyprus during the E.C. period is confined to typological comparisons that suggest themselves between Cypriot artifacts and those of other regions;[2] the value and significance of such comparisons vary from case to case. The meagre nature of the cross-references between Cyprus and the areas adjacent to her during the Early Bronze Age is largely responsible for the extremely fluid nature of the chronological framework of the E.C. period.[3]

It was at one time seriously proposed[4] that the copper ores of Cyprus were unworked until after the end of the Bronze Age, notwithstanding the remarkable liberality with which the E.C. dead were equipped with copper objects as grave gifts. The series of metal objects is very much *sui generis*, and only the tiniest proportion can have been imported; all the rest must have been made within the island. The 'remotely conceivable alternative' that raw copper was imported from a neighbouring region can surely be dismissed; it cannot be doubted that copper was mined and smelted in Cyprus from E.C. I onwards. It should be noted

[1] §viii, 4, 168–70.   [2] §viii, 15, 274–80.
[3] G, 2; §viii, 4, 204; §viii, 11; §viii, 15, 282–5.
[4] *B.S.A.* 30, 74–85.

that most of the richest E.C. sites, in whose graves the highest proportion of metal objects has been found, were located at considerable distances from the nearest possible mining areas. A trial excavation has been made by Dikaios, but not yet reported fully, in an E.C. III settlement at Ambelikou,[1] in the heart of the copper-producing area. Finds included clay crucibles, stone and terracotta moulds for casting axes. It is doubtful whether Ambelikou was a manufacturing centre that served a wide area with finished goods, despite its position. But it, and other settlements of the same kind within the 'copper-belt', probably were responsible for mining and smelting, and for marketing raw copper to such main centres of population as *Vounous*, Lapithos, Politiko and Alambra. Each of these centres presumably supported an industrial quarter where the finished goods were manufactured. However important to the island's economy its copper deposits may have been, it is quite clear that in the E.C. period, as later in the Bronze Age, the location of the copper-belt was far from being the determining factor in forming the settlement pattern; water, agricultural land and grazing grounds were of pre-eminent importance.

Though the date at which Cyprus first caught the attention of her neighbours as a source of copper is uncertain, this may well have taken place before the end of E.C. III, by which time objects imported from abroad begin to appear with greater frequency. Earlier, the evidence of contact is slight. For the Philia stage, vessels of calcite found at Vasilia[2] may be direct Egyptian imports, though satisfactorily dated parallels have not yet been adduced. Egyptian influence has been proposed for the terracotta *genre* models[3] and the comparable plastic work on pottery vessels. Such modelling originated in Egypt during the Old Kingdom, but the idea may not have reached Cyprus until the Twelfth Dynasty. Egypt may also have been the ultimate source for the faience beads which first occur in E.C. III grave groups.[4] A plain-ware pitcher of non-Cypriot type and fabric was found in an E.C. I tomb at *Vounous*;[5] it has been attributed to the caliciform series of M.B. I, but may have come from Lebanon rather than Palestine. From a M.B. II*a* context at Ras Shamra (Ugarit) have been reported fragments[6] of bowls of Red Polished Ware,

[1] *Ill. Ldn. News*, 2.3.46, 244–5; §viii, 11, 148–9.
[2] §viii, 15, 259–60.   [3] §viii, 15, 278–80.
[4] §viii, 15, fig. 105, pp. 264, and 280.
[5] §viii, 11; §viii, 15, 276; §viii, 10, 339–40; §viii, 17.
[6] §viii, 15, 281.

decorated with incised linear patterns. These are almost certainly from Cyprus; but this particular class of decorated bowls was current for a long period, from E.C. II to M.C. I–II, so that the synchronism is less precise than could have been hoped for.

In view of the close ties which developed between Cyprus and the Aegean area during the Late Bronze Age, it is interesting that objects from Minoan Crete should constitute a high proportion of the goods that reached Cyprus[1] from abroad during the final phase of the E.C. period. These objects include two bronze daggers from graves at *Vounous*,[2] while at Lapithos has been found a painted bridge-spouted pottery jar,[3] as well as one or two daggers and a razor of bronze.[4] It is improbable that these goods came at second hand from markets in the Levant which had direct trade contacts with Crete. On however modest a scale direct trade contacts must have existed between Crete and north Cyprus. No corresponding Cypriot objects have yet been found on Minoan sites; the return trade may have included raw copper, but there is no means of proving this hypothesis.

The date of the arrival of the first Philia-stage settlers in Cyprus may be placed soon after 2300 B.C.[5] The interval between this event and the development of the *Vounous* version of E.C. I is uncertain, though it is suggested that the phase was contemporary with M.B. I in Western Asia. The end of E.C. I may fall *c.* 2000 B.C., if a nebulous synchronism with Egypt is valid.[6] E.C. II is without a chronological landmark, but the Minoan imports define the end of E.C. III with reasonable precision. The E.M. III (= M.M. I*a* at Cnossus) painted pot found in an E.C. III*b* tomb at Lapithos,[7] on the one hand, the MM. II Kamares cup from a late M.C. I group at Karmi[8] on the other, place the end of the E.C. period near the middle of the nineteenth century B.C.

Though the E.C. period can be defined both in terms of its material culture and its occupation pattern, it is virtually impossible to interpret its succession of phases in terms of history once the naturalization of the original Philia-stage settlers had reached the *Vounous* E.C. I stage of development. This must now await the investigation of settlement sites and the closer analysis of regional variations in material culture which can then be attempted. For the time being it can be no more than a suspicion based on the increasing proliferation of weapons buried with the

[1] *B.S.A.* 55, 109–27.   [2] §VIII, 3, 137–8; §VIII, 14, 330.   [3] §VIII, 7.
[4] *B.S.A.* 55, 111.   [5] §VIII, 4, 204.
[6] §VIII, 15, 282.   [7] §VIII, 7.   [8] *Op. Ath.* IV. 202–4.

dead that by E.C. III, at least, Cyprus had become divided into mutually hostile tribal federations. A further guess would equate such federations with the areas of some of the much later city kingdoms. The hostility implicit in the evidence would have resulted from the strains imposed by a steadily increasing population on the enjoyment of such basic amenities as land, water, communications and raw materials.

CHAPTER XXVII

IMMIGRANTS FROM THE NORTH

I. THE PROBLEM OF THE INDO-EUROPEANS

FOR several thousand years before the third millennium B.C. the new way of life based on agriculture, which had developed in the Near East and perhaps also in certain adjacent areas, spread out of these regions into lands which lay around them. There is no doubt that it was disseminated mainly by peoples or smaller groups who migrated out of its original centres. Then the trend was largely reversed. In the third millennium 'barbarians' moved into Mesopotamia. Semites from poorer lands to the west settled in the south in such numbers that their language super-seded that of the Sumerians, although they adopted Sumerian civilization. Gutian invaders from the highlands to the east ruled southern Iraq during the twenty-second century, but they proved less assimilable and were eventually expelled.[1] After *c.* 2000 B.C. similar intrusions had more important results. The infiltration of Semitic tribes, 'Amorites', from Syria into Meso-potamia continued,[2] but the migrations which caused the greatest changes appear to have come from further north.

In many cases the names of the incoming peoples have not been preserved in the records of older civilized states or in documents in their own languages. The earliest of them spoke languages of various types and affiliations. But most of those who came from the north and who are identified for the first time after *c.* 2000 B.C. spoke languages which belong to the 'Indo-European' family.

It is generally accepted that the languages which are classed as Indo-European were disseminated over the region in which they are first found in early historical times by actual migrations and not merely by processes of borrowing. They are so similar in basic vocabulary and grammatical inflection that the resemblances between them cannot plausibly be explained as coincidences or as the results of borrowing among prehistoric languages which were not derived from a single earlier 'ancestor'. Words for members of the family which they share include cognates of English 'father', 'brother' and 'sister': cf. Latin *pater*, Greek πατήρ,

---

[1] See above, pp. 454 ff.   [2] See above, pp. 625 ff.

Sanskrit *pitar-*; Latin *frater*, Sanskrit *bhrātar-*, Greek φράτηρ (with the secondary sense of 'member of a clan or brother-hood'); Latin *soror*, Sanskrit *svasar-*, Lithuanian *sesuõ*, Old Slavonic *sestra*. Names for common animals and objects include: Latin *ovis*, Greek ὅ(ϝ)ις, Sanskrit *avis*, Lithuanian *avis*, 'sheep', English *ewe*; Latin *equus*, Sanskrit *aśvas*, Old Irish *ech*, Gaulish *epo-*, Old English *eoh*, 'horse'; Greek (ϝ)οῖκος, Sanskrit *veśas*, 'house', Latin *vicus*, 'district'. Among words for common actions are: Latin *fero*, Greek φέρω, Sanskrit *bharāmi*, English *bear*, 'carry'; Sanskrit *vasāmi*, Greek ἄεσα (aorist), Gothic *wisan*, 'stay, pass the night'; Latin *mulgeo*, Middle Irish *bligim*, Greek ἀμέλγω, Lithuanian *melžu*, Old Slavonic *mlĭzq*, Albanian *miel*, 'milk'; Greek εἰμί, Sanskrit *asmi*, Avestan *ahmi*, Lithuanian *esmì*, Old Slavonic *jesmĭ*, Gothic *im*, 'I am'. Similarity in inflexion is obvious, for example, in the present tenses of this verb in Greek and Sanskrit: cf. Greek εἰμί, εἶ, ἐστί, ἐσμέν, ἐστέ, εἰσί (*eimí, eî, estí, esmén, esté, eisí*), Sanskrit *asmi, asi, asti, smas, stha, santi* (cf. Latin *sunt*); in those of a verb with the sense 'go': Greek εἶμι, εἶ, εἶσι, ἴμεν, ἴτε, ἴασι (*eîmi, eî, eîsi, ímen, íte, íasi*), Sanskrit *émi, ési, éti, imás, ithá, yánti*;[1] and in the imperfect tenses of the related verbs φέρω and *bharāmi* in Greek and Sanskrit: cf. ἔφερον, ἔφερες, ἔφερε, ἐφέρομεν, ἐφέρετε, ἔφερον (*épheron, épheres, éphere, ephéromen, ephérete, épheron*); *abharam, abharas, abharat, abharāma, abharata, abharan*.[1]

The language-groups and isolated languages which were classed without doubt as Indo-European at the end of the nineteenth century are the Celtic, Italic, Germanic, Baltic, Slavonic, Iranian and Indic groups, Albanian, Greek and Armenian. No contemporary document mentions a people who may be identified with the 'Indo-Europeans',[2] the original speakers of the postulated parent language. But it seems inconceivable that languages so similar as those which make up the Indo-European family would have been in use in lands extending from Ireland and Norway in the west, across Europe and the Pontic[3] area, to

[1] G, 2, 13 ff.; G, 4, 439 ff. (Tabelle); G, 7, 19 ff.; §1, 10, 378 ff.; §1, 12, 14 ff., 249 ff.

[2] Throughout this chapter *Indo-European* has a linguistic sense, indicating that a people so called spoke one of the languages classed as Indo-European, or that it is thought to have spoken an extinct language related to these. *Indo-Europeans* has the meaning explained above in the text. *Aryan* should be used only of the peoples who spoke proto-Indic or proto-Iranian languages; see pp. 837 f.

[3] I.e. the region which comprises the lands lying to the north of the Black Sea, the Caucasus and the Caspian Sea, approximately from the River Dniester in the west to western Kazakhstān in the east, and the zone of temperate steppe lands to the north of them.

Anatolia, Iran and northern India in the east at the beginning of history, unless they had been spread by extensive migrations out of some centrally situated area in late prehistoric times.

The role of Indo-European peoples in the ancient world has, however, been romanticized and perhaps exaggerated. They have been portrayed too often as the incarnation of northern virility sweeping down in massed chariots to bring new vigour to a decadent south. It is still impossible to identify with certainty the region from which their migrations started, and their historical importance has recently been questioned, and even their existence at any time as a distinct and coherent people. It is now recognized that in prehistoric times, as today, communities which used the same language may not have shared a single culture or have been homogeneous in physical type. So one may postulate the existence of a prehistoric people who spoke dialects of 'primitive Indo-European' without reviving the myth of an 'Aryan race'.

Nevertheless, the conclusion that northern peoples, mainly Indo-Europeans, caused major political changes and introduced new social traits in the Near East and the eastern Mediterranean area in the second millennium B.C. should now be re-assessed. It is justifiable to concentrate on Indo-European migrations. Among the newcomers from the north only the Hurrians[1] demonstrably spoke a non-Indo-European language, and they were in part led and ruled by men of Indo-European origin. From the standpoint of Near Eastern and Mediterranean history it is the effects of immigration from the north that are most important. But the problem of the region of origin of the Indo-European movements, the so-called 'homeland',[2] is not irrelevant. Until this 'homeland' has been identified and the original Indo-Europeans can be associated with one or more archaeologically attested cultures, our account of their historical role, and in particular of the development of their society and its impact on others, will be incomplete.

To judge by later 'Völkerwanderungen' the course of the early Indo-European movements was not simple and they probably lasted over several centuries. Movements of groups large enough to cause a change of language may well have been preceded by sporadic incursions or immigrations of scattered small groups, and Indo-European migrants may in some cases have

[1] *C.A.H.* ii³, ch. i, sect. iv.
[2] I.e. the region in which the Indo-Europeans lived immediately before their primary dispersal, and in which their language reached the stage of its development which has been reconstructed by linguistic comparison.

amalgamated with linguistically alien peoples before arriving in literate areas, or have driven alien peoples before them. The Hurrians who appear in northern Mesopotamia and Syria *c.* 1800 B.C. may have been driven south from the Caucasus in this way.

The past sixty years have brought both new languages and advances in linguistic method to the study of the Indo-European problem. The language usually called 'Tocharian' came to light in Buddhist and Hindu religious texts of the eighth century A.D. which were found in Chinese Turkestān between 1893 and 1897.[1] The German excavation of Boğazköy–Khattusha[2] in central Turkey led to the rediscovery of the three 'Anatolian' Indo-European languages of the second millennium B.C., Hittite, Luwian and Palaic.[3] The decipherment of the 'Minoan Linear B' texts from the Bronze Age sites of Epano Englianos (probably Pylus), Mycenae and Cnossus has proved that Greek was in use in the Peloponnese by *c.* 1300 B.C. at the latest.[4] Recent discoveries and research have also brought a better understanding of Indo-European languages known only from onomastic material or a small number of texts (Venetic, Illyrian, Thracian and Phrygian, to name the most important), and of their position in the Indo-European language-family; and it has been recognized that Lycian and probably also Lydian belong to the new 'Anatolian' or Hittite-Luwian subgroup. The advance in method which is most important for Indo-European studies is that of 'linguistic geography', or more precisely 'historical dialectology', which has been utilized in reconstructing the process by which the Indo-European language differentiated into the dialects from which the known historical language-groups and isolated languages evolved.[5] The second new line of study which will be valuable if it proves successful is 'glottochronology'. This deduces the date at which related languages began to diverge from the proportion of their basic vocabularies which has changed. It has yielded a likely date for the divergence of certain Indo-European language-groups, but its general validity is still doubtful.[6]

In reconsidering the question of the early Indo-European migrations it will be best to discuss first the earliest attestations of Indo-European languages in written documents; secondly,

---

[1] §v, 1; §v, 13; §v, 14.

[2] The present author considers that the transcriptions of some Hittite names in this *History* do not indicate their probable pronunciation in all respects: see *Trans. Philol. Soc.* 1951, 122 ff.; §ii, 49, 12, 25 f.

[3] See pp. 830 ff.   [4] See p. 839.

[5] See pp. 863 ff.   [6] §i, 8; §i, 13; §i, 15.

archaeological evidence for movements which might have brought the earliest known Indo-European languages into the lands in which they appear; and after that the linguistic and archaeological evidence for the location of the 'homeland' and for primary migrations out of it.

At the end of the third millennium B.C. the lands from which Indo-European languages appear to have been introduced into parts of the Near East were inhabited by peoples at a neolithic or chalcolithic cultural level. One people with such a relatively primitive culture would rarely, if ever, have adopted the language of another unless immigrants had introduced it into its territory. It is only the languages of highly civilized peoples that are borrowed by other peoples without migration and consequent ethnic admixture having occurred. If it appears that an Indo-European language replaced one of a different type in some area at the edge of the region of urban civilization *c.* 2500–1500 B.C., it may be assumed that it had been introduced there by immigrants, and archaeological evidence of their migration should be sought. On the other hand, every migration which resulted in a change of language in prehistoric or protohistoric times will not necessarily have left its mark in the archaeological record. In some cases immigrants clearly became dominant, and their language superseded that of a pre-existing population, while at the same time their arrival was followed by no noticeable change in material culture. Moreover, it is often difficult to decide whether a change in the material culture of an area was the result of immigration or just of the introduction of new artifacts, styles or methods into it by trade or imitation.

The phenomena which are usually thought to indicate extensive alien immigration are widespread destruction of settlements and the appearance of whole assemblages of new artifacts. When the two appear in conjunction it may be considered likely that immigrants have introduced a new language into an area in question. When such evidence indicates the arrival of immigrants in an area at a time shortly before that at which a particular language is first recorded in it, it will be reasonable to conclude that this language has been introduced by those immigrants. When no such evidence indicates extensive migration into an area during a period of some four or five hundred years before the time when a particular language is first attested in it, it will usually be impossible to connect the introduction of this language convincingly with any still earlier migration into the area which may be deduced from archaeological data. And, on the other hand, the earliest known language of an area may sometimes have been introduced into it only shortly before the time of the oldest records in that language, without there being any obvious archaeological indication of the movement which brought it in.

Archaeological evidence for the introduction of Indo-European languages into the areas in which they are first recorded should therefore be sought, but it may not always be forthcoming. It may prove even more difficult to obtain evidence of that kind for the location of the 'Indo-European homeland', the region from which all Indo-European peoples are thought to have dispersed. Ideally it might be possible to trace the course of one or more migrations right from an apparent region of origin to localities in which Indo-European languages are found in early historical times. But no migration has yet been traced in this way, and the chances that any will be are not good. Warlike, primitive peoples who migrated into territory inhabited by more advanced populations in prehistoric times must often have dominated them, and have adopted their culture, and then have led them on to further conquests. In such cases the continuity of their own culture will have been broken.

If the entire course of relevant migrations cannot be traced by archaeology, there are three alternative ways in which the 'homeland' may be identified. First, it may be possible to associate an archaeologically attested culture with the original Indo-Europeans (i.e. the people who spoke the postulated ancestral language before their dispersal and its differentiation). If so, the spread of the culture may indicate the initial stages of their expansion. Secondly, vocabulary shared by historical Indo-European languages may indicate the habitat of the Indo-Europeans and the level and nature of their material culture and society before their dispersal, and this may assist in associating an archaeologically attested culture with them. Thirdly, the linguistic similarities and differences between historical Indo-European language-groups may reflect the process by which the original Indo-European language differentiated into dialects and by which these dialects then dispersed and developed into the languages and groups which were current in historical times.

II. THE EARLIEST KNOWN
INDO-EUROPEAN LANGUAGES

(a) ANATOLIA

AT the end of the nineteenth century it was almost universally agreed that Vedic Sanskrit was the oldest recorded Indo-European language and that it and Homeric Greek were the least modified derivatives of the ancestral tongue. The discovery that a language with Indo-European characteristics was in use in Anatolia at least as early as 1500 B.C. was unanticipated. The earliest known native languages of the region (other than Phrygian, thought to be a late arrival) were regarded as non-Indo-European. The available evidence suggested that the civilization of the Hittites (Assyrian *Khatti*, Egyptian *Kheta*) had its centre in northern Syria and that the monuments in Hittite style found north of the Taurus Mountains reflected northward political expansion.[1] The only documents which could reasonably be attributed to the Hittites were inscriptions in a 'hieroglyphic'[2] script, which had not been deciphered, of the tenth to eighth centuries B.C. Unexpected new information came with the excavation of the extensive pre-classical site at Boğazköy (or Boğazkale), near Sungurlu, about ninety miles east of Ankara, which was undertaken by the Deutsche Orient-Gesellschaft and the Deutsches Archäologisches Institut between 1906 and 1912. Cuneiform tablets in Akkadian found at the site identified it as that of Khattusha, the capital of an earlier Anatolian Hittite state of considerable importance, of the seventeenth to thirteenth centuries. The much larger number of cuneiform documents from the site which were written in languages other than Akkadian brought a further surprise. One of these, now known as 'Hittite', the principal native idiom of the early state, had unmistakable Indo-European characteristics. For example, the word which proved to mean 'I am' was *esmi* (cf. Greek εἰμί, Sanskrit *asmi*), and that for 'water' was *wattar*. In morphology, features such as a class of verbs in -*nu*- with inflexion closely similar to that of their Greek counterparts was striking (cf., for their formation, Hittite *arnumi*, 'bring', Greek ὄρνυμι, 'urge on').[3] Historians outside Germany at first hesitated to accept that this Hittite language was Indo-European in type

---

[1] *C.A.H.* II,³ ch. VI, sect. I; §II, 22, I ff.

[2] §II, 26, 44 ff.; §II, 37, Préface, v ff., 247 ff.; §II, 49, 6; *C.A.H.* II³, ch. VI, sect. II.

[3] § II, 10, 5 ff.; § II, 19, 56 ff.; § II, 26, 37 ff.

and that Indo-European immigrants brought it into central Anatolia by the eighteenth century B.C. at the latest; but more thorough comparative study of the Hittite texts during the 1920s put the conclusions of the philologists beyond doubt.

Texts from Boğazköy provide limited but plausible information about the origin of the Anatolian Hittite state. Its founders were two kings of Kushshar, a central Anatolian city whose site has not yet been identified. They unified the surrounding regions under their rule during the seventeenth century B.C. The next king of their line, Labarnash II (Khattushilish I), captured Khattusha and made it his capital. Khatti then became the dominant state of Anatolia, a 'world power' on a par with Egypt, Babylon and Assyria, from the beginning of the fourteenth century until its obliteration at the end of the thirteenth.[1] The extant Hittite texts were almost all written during the fourteenth and thirteenth centuries, but some are certainly copies of originals of the seventeenth or sixteenth. A few fragments in Hittite are reported to have been found at Boğazköy in a level dated to the sixteenth century.[2] No text contains even any tradition or legend about the immigration which had evidently introduced one or more Indo-European languages into Anatolia before this time. In addition to Hittite[3] three other previously unknown Anatolian languages of the second millennium were identified in the Boğazköy material, those now known as Luwian, Palaic and Khattic.[4] Luwian was soon seen to be Indo-European and a close cognate of Hittite.[5] It was in use at least as early as the fifteenth century in the south-western part of Khatti proper (i.e. the territory of the Hittite state after its establishment c. 1675 B.C., approximately from the Kızıl Irmak (River Halys) and the plain of Konya in the west to the mountains in the region of Malatya in the east). In the fourteenth it was demonstrably in use in the area known to the Hittites as Kizzuwadna (Cilicia) and in Arzawa, which lay immediately to the west of Khatti proper, though its limits are uncertain. Palaic was the language of the district Palā, incorporated in Khatti, and it appears to have been no longer spoken in the fourteenth century. It is known only from ritual texts and its Indo-European character and close relationship to Hittite and Luwian were first

[1] C.A.H. II³, ch. xxi (a); C.A.H. II³, ch. xxiv, sects. i–iv.
[2] §II, 43; §II, 51, 12 f.; C.A.H. II³, ch. vi, sect. i. See also: R. Naumann, M.D.O.G. 86 (1953), 21; B. Landsberger, J.C.S. 8 (1954), 52; A. Goetze, J.C.S. 9 (1955), 22, J.C.S. 11 (1957), 70 and nn. 183, 184; Bull. A.S.O.R. 146 (1957), 26.
[3] I.e. the principal or official language of the Anatolian Hittite state c. 1700–1200 B.C.; cf. §II, 24.   [4] Cf. C.A.H. II³, ch. vi, sect. ii.
[5] §II, 9, 215 ff.; §II, 36, 8 ff., 131 ff.; §II, 42.

demonstrated in 1948.[1] Khattic is a non-Indo-European language
with no obvious extant cognate, and it must also have passed out of
vernacular use by the fourteenth century.[2] Its preservation in
Hittite rituals shows that at least one non-Indo-European idiom
remained in use in central Anatolia until the time when the Hittite
state was formed, or somewhat later. Recent research has shown
that three other ancient languages of Anatolia are closely related
to Hittite, Luwian and Palaic. These are Lycian and Lydian,
known from fifth- and fourth-century inscriptions in modified
varieties of the Greek alphabet, and the language of the 'Hittite
hieroglyphic' inscriptions, which date from the thirteenth century
to the eighth.[3] Within this new 'Anatolian' or 'Hittite-Luwian'
language-group, 'Hieroglyphic Hittite' and Lycian are specially
closely related to Luwian. A detailed comparative study of the
'Anatolian' Indo-European languages among themselves has
still to be completed. Hittite, Luwian and Palaic give the impression of having differentiated within a 'linguistic continuum'.
(A people is said to live in or to form such a continuum when its
constituent tribes or other linguistic subdivisions live near enough
to each other, or otherwise are in sufficiently close contact, for
linguistic changes to spread through them all.) No pronounced
relative archaism indicates that any one of them was introduced
into Anatolia before the others.

Anatolia cannot well have been part of the area out of which
the first Indo-European migrants dispersed. There are no signs of
Indo-European linguistic influence on languages in use to the
south of it in the third millennium, and the currency of Khattic in
the vicinity of Khattusha as late as c. 1700 B.C. is a counter-
argument. Moreover, prehistoric Anatolia enjoyed a largely
continuous cultural development, and influences stemming from
it which may imply considerable emigration are only to be observed in one sector, to the west and north-west.[4] The presence of
Indo-European languages as established local idioms in the central
Anatolian area in the fourteenth century is thus sufficient proof
that Indo-Europeans had immigrated somewhat earlier. Moreover, their arrival is put back to the beginning of the seventeenth
century by evidence from the Boğazköy material alone. The
written tradition of Khattusha clearly began in the seventeenth
century, if not earlier, and diachronic linguistic differences between the earlier and later compositions in Hittite indicate that

[1] §II, 40.   [2] §II, 33.
[3] §II, 23, 17 ff.; §II, 35; §II, 37; §II, 38; §II, 39; §II, 45; §II, 50.
[4] §IV, 14, 118 ff.; see C.A.H. I³, ch. x, above, pp. 596 ff., 774 f. and 805.

this language was in use at the city from that century onwards at
least. Further, since there is no evidence for a change of ruling
class there, or permanent conquest, between the reign of Labarnash II and the fifteenth century, it is probable that Hittite was
the language of the kings of Kushshar who created the historical
Hittite state.

Earlier onomastic evidence shows that the Indo-European
immigration had taken place by the end of the twentieth century.
During the nineteenth and eighteenth centuries Assyrian merchants maintained trading colonies at a number of native cities in
central Anatolia. The most important so far investigated was at
Kanesh, modern Kültepe, near Kayseri.[1] The cuneiform commercial documents of these stations are written in Akkadian, but
they contain many obviously native names. Certain of them have
Indo-European stems or inflexions, some of which reappear in
Hittite as it is known from the Boğazköy texts: e.g. *Takshanu-
man(-)*; the stem *taksh-*, cognate with that of Greek τέκτων and
Sanskrit *takṣan*, 'carpenter', reappears in the Hittite verb
takk(i)smi, 'join'.[2] A language of the Hittite-Luwian group was
evidently in use in central Anatolia at least as early as the end of
the twentieth century B.C.

Only the occurrence both in names in these 'Kültepe texts' and
in Hittite, as we know it from the archives of Boğazköy, of some
idiosyncratic linguistic feature, or of a considerable number of
shared stems, would prove that the language to which the names
belonged was directly ancestral to Hittite; but no feature suggests
that it was not. Most recent studies conclude that the Indo-
European ancestors of the Hittites entered Anatolia from the
north-east, but philological arguments for this view seem to have
been overvalued. Even if it can be shown that the historical
Hittite state came into existence as the result of the annexation of
city-states situated in the western part of it by others lying in the
eastern part, this will not imply that previous Indo-European
immigration into the region as a whole must also have come from
the east.[3] Nor is it likely that the Hittites learnt to use cuneiform
before they entered Anatolia and therefore in a more easterly
region.[4]

One document in Hittite, the so-called 'Anitta(sh) Text',
throws some light on conditions in central Anatolia in the cen-

[1] See above, pp. 709 ff.
[2] §II, 1, 3 ff.; §II, 2, 15 ff. See above, pp. 713 ff.
[3] §II, 46, 1 ff.; cf. author, *Bi. Or.* 10 (1953), 120 f.
[4] §II, 13.

turies immediately before the formation of the Hittite kingdom.[1] The earliest extant version dates from *c.* 1400 B.C. or a little earlier, but the text itself is in archaic Hittite and may reasonably be attributed to the seventeenth century. It purports to record the deeds of two kings of the city of Kushshar, named Pitkhana(sh) and Anitta(sh), who are now known from references in contemporary documents from Kültepe and other Cappadocian sites to have lived in the time of the Assyrian trading colonies (in the nineteenth century or the eighteenth).[2] The exploits of the two rulers were mainly the conquest of adjacent cities which are mentioned later in Hittite texts but have not yet been identified on the ground. A puzzling feature is the inclusion in the narrative of what is apparently the alleged wording of an inscription set up by Anitta. There are difficulties in assuming that the text was composed in the eighteenth century or that it was based on written records of that time. The Hittites probably did not adopt the variety of cuneiform in which the Boğazköy tablets are written until the seventeenth century, and it is doubtful whether one of their scribes could have read a cuneiform inscription which had survived from the time of the trading colonies. Such a monumental document might, however, have been written in a script less aberrant from the main line of Mesopotamian cuneiform than that used in the Kültepe tablets. The text, at all events, is unexpectedly factual in tone and probably contains accurate tradition, however transmitted. It shows us a pair of city-state dynasts still operating on a parochial scale in comparison with the kings of Khatti in the seventeenth century, and it gives no indication whether they or their people were recent arrivals in central Anatolia or, conversely, whether they were threatened by attack from outside it. The achievement recorded of Pitkhana (the father) is that he captured the city of Nesha(sh), which has been proposed as the first centre or capital of the Hittites, since they used a word *nasili* (also *nesili*, *nesumnili*) in referring to their own Indo-European language. Anitta destroyed Khattush (later Khattusha), where Khattic must still have been current in view of its continued use in religious rituals after the city had become the Hittite capital.

---

[1] §11, 41, 37 ff.; *C.A.H.* 11³, ch. VI, sect. III. See also: E. Forrer, *Die Boğhazköi-Texte in Umschrift,* 11 (Leipzig, 1926), Nr 7, 30; J. Friedrich, *Alte Or.* 24/3 (1925); B. Hrozný, *Arch. Orient.* 1 (1929), 273 ff.; H. Otten, *M.D.O.G.* 76 (1938), 43 ff.

[2] On the date of their reigns see: §11, 41. See *C.A.H.* 1³, part 1, p. 212, and above, pp. 714 ff. *C.A.H.* 11³, ch. VI, sect. III.

The names Pitkhana and Anitta are neither demonstrably Indo-European nor clearly non-Indo-European. The only possible Indo-European name in the text is that of the god of Nesha, *Siusmis*; its first syllable has been equated with the stem **dyeu*-[1] of Zeus, Juppiter and Sanskrit *Dyaus*, but there is no independent support for this etymology, since the Indo-European sequence **dy-* is not represented in any other Hittite word except the possibly related *siunas*, 'god'. A dagger bearing the name of Anitta has been found in the destruction level above Level 1 *b* of the palace at Kültepe–Kanesh, and it is tempting to link this evidence with the statement in the text that he captured Nesha, to equate the two places, and to deduce that he transferred the capital of a growing kingdom there, only to be brought down by the attack of an unidentified enemy before he could consolidate his power. But all this is uncertain. What is clear is that the events recorded in the text are not obviously to be interpreted as part of a large-scale invasion or military immigration from outside central Anatolia. On the evidence, Pitkhana and Anitta were operating as rulers of an already established city-state, in competition with rivals who ruled similar kingdoms. Nothing shows which of these was Indo-European-speaking in the eighteenth century, though one or more presumably were so, in view of the Indo-European names in the Kültepe texts; and no philological evidence indicates how long before the nineteenth century Indo-European immigrants had arrived in central Anatolia. Probably they established themselves at first only in one district, or in a few, and did not succeed in dominating the whole region until the seventeenth century. If so, they may well have been few in number and may have caused little cultural change.

The circumstances in which the Luwian language or its immediate ancestor was introduced into Anatolia are also obscure. Luwian is first directly attested in cuneiform texts of the fourteenth or thirteenth century from Boğazköy. It was evidently in use in the sixteenth in territory immediately to the west of that in which Hittite was spoken. The Hittite 'Law Code', whose earliest version appears to go back to that century, mentions revisions of rulings concerning Luwians. Other evidence shows that Luwian was spoken in the fourteenth century in Kizzuwadna (Cilicia) and over a considerable territory to the west of Khatti, Arzawa.[2] It is uncertain whether it was spoken in the north-west, the extreme west, or the south-west of Anatolia in Hittite times. The

---

[1] The asterisk denotes that a word, sound or sequence is reconstructed or not found in extant texts.　　[2] §II, 12, 21, 91 f.; §II, 19, 49; §II, 46, 17 f., 23 ff.

people known to the Hittites as Lukka(-) presumably spoke it, or at least a language almost identical with it. The Lycian language is closely related to Luwian, either by direct derivation or collaterally, and it can hardly be doubted that the Λύκιοι of Hellenic times were descendants of the Lukka people. (The location of the land of the Lukkans within western Anatolia is disputed. The statement in the Amarna Letter No. 38 that Lukkans were frequently raiding towns in Alashiya, apparently Cyprus, supports the view that their country corresponded with later Lycia.[1]) It is reasonable to assume that Luwian was in use in Anatolia at least as early as Hittite, but no unambiguous contemporary document proves that it was. Neither the name *Ihaa* (H. T. Bossert's transcription of the 'hieroglyphic Hittite' signs on the seal from Beycesultan VI *c*. 2000–1900 B.C.),[2] nor the stems *Kukun* and *Lukk(a)*, which occur in an Egyptian inscription of the twenty-first century at Byblos,[3] belong without doubt to the Indo-European vocabulary of Luwian. (The Luwian recorded at Khattusha had clearly, like Hittite, taken over many words and stems from pre-Indo-European languages.) It is also doubtful whether specifically Luwian names occur in the documents of the Assyrian trading colonies.[4] Nevertheless, the deduction that Luwian was current in most of western Anatolia from *c*. 2300 B.C. onwards is not improbable in itself.

Most recent discussions of the interrelation of the languages of the Hittite-Luwian group seem to accept that they evolved from dialects of a single primary derivative of Indo-European (often termed 'proto-Anatolian') and that they developed in contact during the centuries which preceded the period of the Boğazköy archives. By implication, no one of them represents a language or dialect which came into Anatolia much before the others. A number of features common to Hittite, Luwian and Palaic are most naturally explained as the results of the differentiation of related dialects which were still in contact. The Indo-European sound-system had certainly undergone similar simplification in the three languages; similar innovations had been made in the system of verbal inflexions in Hittite and Luwian, at least; and in all three languages sentences regularly begin with an introductory particle (*nu-* in Hittite and Palaic; *a-* or *pa-* in Luwian) followed by enclitic pronouns and modifiers, as in Hittite *nu-*

---

[1] *C.A.H.* II[3], ch. XXII(*b*), sect. IX.
[2] See S. Lloyd and J. Mellaart, *A.St.* 8 (1958), 97.
[3] See W. F. Albright, *Bull. A.S.O.R.* 155 (1959), 33 f.; see above, pp. 408 ff.
[4] §II, 32; §II, 34, 104 f.

war-at-si appa pier, 'And (I say) they gave it back to him'. The patterning of the initial complexes, which have no close parallel in other Indo-European languages, is similar in the three languages, but the elements employed differ.[1] This suggests parallel development, perhaps under the influence of the same substrate language or of a group of such languages which were related among themselves. It has been claimed that Luwian is archaic in comparison with Hittite and that it must therefore have been introduced into Anatolia earlier.[2] The supposedly significant feature is its retention of Indo-European -*t*- unchanged before -*i*-, while in Hittite it is assibilated (cf. Luwian *asti*, 'is', and Hittite *eszi*, with *z* pronounced much as in modern German). It is, however, at least as likely that the languages differ in this respect because -*t*- was assibilated before -*i*- in Hittite alone, at a time when it and the cognate dialects were already established in Anatolia. A similar reliance on retention of Indo-European -*t*- before -*i*- as a significant feature would lead to the conclusion that the West Greek dialects were the first to be introduced into Greece; they have -*t*- in δίδωτι, 'gives', etc., while the southern and eastern dialects, undoubtedly in use in Greece earlier, have δίδωσι, etc., with assibilation.

Linguistic evidence thus permits only two firm conclusions about the immigration of Indo-Europeans into Anatolia. One group, almost certainly those who became the dominant element among the historical Hittites, entered the central region in the nineteenth century B.C. at the latest. The ancestors of the Luwians and the Palaeans had probably arrived in more westerly areas by the same time, but not necessarily much earlier. The 'proto-Anatolian' language may already have begun, while still outside Anatolia, to differentiate into the dialects which developed into Hittite, Luwian and Palaic. But the differences between these languages are not so great as to imply that the peoples who spoke the dialects from which they evolved lost contact with each other for a considerable time either before or after entering Anatolia.

(*b*) NORTHERN MESOPOTAMIA AND SYRIA

In these areas the earliest appearance of an Indo-European language is again in onomastic material. Akkadian and Hurrian texts of the sixteenth to fourteenth centuries found in them contain

---

[1] §II, 11, vol. I, 63 ff., 131 ff., 147 ff.; §II, 35 (53), 161 ff.; §II, 36, 144 f.
[2] §IV, 10, 26. Cf. §II, 19, 48 ff., 61 f.; §II, 42, 91 f., 109 ff.

personal names which are clearly Indo-Iranian ('Aryan'):[1] cf. *Artatama* with Sanskrit *ṛta-dhāmā*, 'abiding in the Law'; *Birashena* with Sanskrit *Vira-sena*, 'possessing an army of heroes'.[2] Names of gods previously known from the Veda appear in the lists of deities which are invoked as guardians of the oath in Hittite treaties with a ruler of Mitanni: cf. *Mitrashshil, Uruwanashshil, Indar, Nashattiyana* in the treaties with *Mitra, Varuna, Indra,* and the *Nāsatyā* in Vedic mythology.[3] A treatise on the training of chariot-horses found at Boğazköy, written in Hittite but attributed to a certain Kikkuli(sh) of Mitanni, has several technical terms of obvious Indo-Iranian origin, e.g. *panzawartanna,* 'course of five circuits', cf. Sanskrit *pañca-,* 'five', and *-vartana-,* 'turning'.[4] The individuals who bore the Indo-Iranian names were rulers of states in northern Syria and Mesopotamia in which the dominant language in the fourteenth century (that of a ruling minority, anyway) was Hurrian. The currency of Indo-Iranian names and technical terms among them shows, at the least, that they were in cultural contact with an 'Aryan' people, or that their ancestors had been. In all probability 'Aryans' had become the rulers of Hurrian-speaking communities[5] and had led them in their conquests in Syria. The Indo-Iranian branch of the prehistoric Indo-European-speaking people, or part of it, must thus have been living in an area close to northern Mesopotamia, probably in northern Iran, in the fifteenth century at the latest. It is still not agreed whether the names and loanwords reflect the proto-Indo-Iranian language as it was before it differentiated into proto-Iranian and proto-Indic groups of dialects, or a proto-Indic idiom. They certainly show no specifically Iranian features, and one element in them, *aika-,* 'one, single', reappears in Sanskrit but not in Old Iranian.[6] Moreover, the change of *$*s$* to *h* which is characteristic of Iranian is shared by Armenian and Greek, and this suggests that the prehistoric Indo-European languages from which the three derived remained in contact relatively late. Rulers like Artatama were probably outliers of the migration which took Indo-European speech into northern India. The Iranian group of languages is first attested in the inscriptions of the Achaemenid kings in Old Persian of the sixth and fifth centuries B.C. It is doubtful whether

---

[1] See p. 825, n. 2.
[2] §III, 2; §III, 6, 12 ff.; §III, 10, 149 ff.; *C.A.H.* II³, ch. XVII, sect. II.
[3] §II, 52, 55; §III, 14.
[4] §II, 9, 180 ff.; §II, 30, 15 ff.
[5] See p. 826, n. 2.   [6] §III, 6, 36 ff.

the language of the Kassites who dominated Babylonia in the seventeenth to fourteenth centuries contained any Indo-European element.[1]

(c) GREECE

The Greek language was demonstrably in use in the Peloponnese and also at Cnossus in Crete, though there perhaps only among a minority, in the thirteenth century B.C. at the very latest.[2] Proof of this has come with the decipherment of the 'Minoan Linear B' script of the Late Bronze Age tablets of Cnossus, Epano Englianos (probably Pylus) and Mycenae by M. Ventris in 1952.[3] Certain deficiencies of the script for representing Greek, and above all the conventions of abbreviation which were evidently observed in using it, have the result that a considerable proportion of the words in the texts have not yet been identified with known or reconstructed Greek words. But there is a decisive consensus of opinion that the decipherment is correct. One strong argument for its validity is the nature of the Greek which it yields. This is archaic in certain respects even in comparison with the language of the Homeric poems. Other features classify it as either a dialect ancestral to the Arcado-Cyprian group of the classical period or one belonging to a still only slightly differentiated eastern or south-eastern dialect-group.[4] If the lowest date proposed for the Linear B tablets of Cnossus is accepted, the linguistic evidence will indicate the early part of the thirteenth century as the latest possible time for the introduction of Greek into the Peloponnese. On the more generally accepted dating it indicates the fourteenth century or the fifteenth.

(d) OTHER AREAS

In areas other than the Aegean, Anatolia and the Near East, Indo-European languages are first attested at dates which range from the sixth century B.C. onwards. In Italy, the earliest Latin inscriptions date from that century. The Celtic language-group is first represented by short inscriptions in Gaulish of the last century B.C. and by slightly earlier borrowings in Greek and

---

[1] §III, 1, 102 ff., 122, 192 ff.

[2] This *terminus post quem* is based on the low date which L. R. Palmer has proposed for the Linear B tablets from Cnossus; see now L. R. Palmer and J. Boardman, *On the Knossos Tablets* (Oxford, 1963); M. H. Popham, 'The destruction of the palace of Knossos and its pottery', in *Antiq.* 40 (1966), pp. 24–8.

[3] *C.A.H.* II³, ch. XXXIX.   [4] *Ibid.*

Latin; the Germanic by onomastic material in Greek and Roman sources of that and subsequent centuries.[1] The linguistically most archaic compositions in Indic and Iranian languages, the Veda and the oldest parts of the Avesta, certainly go back to the first centuries of the first millennium B.C. at least. The Veda may have been composed c. 1000 B.C. or even somewhat earlier.[2] But the earliest extant manuscripts of both these corpora are of the Christian era, and neither contains a historical reference which gives a precise date for the composition of its most archaic sections. The earliest contemporary documents in an Indic language are in-scriptions of King Aśoka of c. 250 B.C. The Slavonic and Baltic language-groups, Armenian, Albanian and Tocharian, are first represented in texts of the European Middle Ages or late anti-quity. A number of Indo-European languages of the Graeco-Roman period are either known only from exiguous contemporary documents or are postulated as independent idioms on the basis of onomastic material, mainly in Greek and Roman sources. Of the former, Phrygian was spoken in central Anatolia from the seventh century B.C. to the fifth A.D.; Venetic was in use in the vicinity of Venice from the sixth to the second century B.C.; Messapic, probably an Illyrian language, is known from inscriptions in south-eastern Italy of the fifth and subsequent centuries B.C. Illyrian, Thracian and Dacian were autonomous Indo-European languages, the two latter being closely related to each other and to Phrygian.[3] The evidence for the Indo-European character of the languages of the Siculi and the Ligurians seems inconclusive.[4]

III. ARCHAEOLOGICAL EVIDENCE FOR EARLY INDO-EUROPEAN IMMIGRATION

Evidence from archaeology for the arrival of Indo-European immigrants may be expected above all in Anatolia and Greece, because it is in those countries that Indo-European languages are recorded at the earliest dates. The 'Aryan' names in Syrian and Mesopotamian documents of the second millennium were evidently borne by minorities in Hurrian- and Semitic-speaking populations, and so do not imply extensive Indo-European im-migration. In both Anatolia and Greece and in the intermediate

[1] G, 7, 11 ff.; §I, 10, 57 ff.; §v, 16, 59 ff.
[2] See p. 851.
[3] G, 7, 98 ff.; §II, 8, 333 ff., 594 ff.; §v, 16, 39 ff.; §v, 17, 157 ff.
[4] G, 7, 160 ff., §v, 16, 43 ff.; §v, 17, 173 ff.

Thracian area the archaeological record is complicated and there are still troublesome gaps, although recent surveys and excavations have added much new information.

(a) ANATOLIA

Discussion of the ethnic prehistory of this region may well begin with the reconstructions recently advanced by J. Mellaart.[1] They are difficult to evaluate at present because they are largely based on his own extensive investigations, the results of which have not yet been published in detail. But it should be useful to examine how far they correlate with the conclusions which are most naturally drawn from the linguistic data.

Mellaart finds strong archaeological indications of large-scale or very disruptive movements into north-western Anatolia at two points in the Anatolian Early Bronze Age: at the end of his cultural phase 1, when Troy I was destroyed, c. 2800 B.C. according to his dating (c. 2600 B.C. in previous systems); and at the end of his phase Early Bronze 2, c. 2300 B.C., when Troy II and other settlements suffered destruction.[2] In each case the evidence which he has adduced is mainly of cultural change and catastrophe within western Anatolia itself; but in each he sees the initiating cause in invasion or immigration from Thrace or the lower Danubian region. He suggests that the first series of migrations brought the Luwian language into the Troad, and that after an interval of four or five centuries, during which the descendants of the immigrants lived in north-western Anatolia, perhaps largely as nomads, the second series, initiated by further movements out of Thrace, spread Luwian over the rest of western Anatolia. In central Anatolia the evidence is more complex. At no time between c. 2500 and c. 1800 B.C. does there appear to have been a movement as extensive and as destructive in its effects as that which occurred in the western region c. 2300. Three phenomena might seem to indicate the appearance of a new people in the central region in the last centuries of the Early Bronze Age: (1) the appearance and spread of the so-called 'Cappadocian' painted pottery c. 2200 B.C.;[3] (2) destructions dated c. 2100–2000 B.C. in a region extending from Bayburt, near Erzurum, in the east to Eskişehir in the west and southwards to Aksaray;[4] (3) the appearance of monochrome pottery of the so-called 'Hittite' type in the Ankara region, in the adjacent areas east of the River Halys

---

[1] §IV, 10; see above, pp. 371ff., 406ff., 681ff. and 691ff.   [2] See above, pp. 406ff.
[3] §II, 3, 48 ff.; see above, pp. 686 ff.   [4] See above, pp. 689 and 703.

(Kızıl Irmak) and in northern Cappadocia (e.g. in Level IV of the *kārum* at Kültepe) *c.* 2100–2000 B.C.[1] Mellaart associates the arrival of the Hittites (i.e. the immigrants who introduced the Indo-European language from which the historical Hittite language developed) with the destructions, which he dates to just before *c.* 1900 B.C. He concludes that the Hittites entered central Anatolia from the north-east, from the Caucasian region.

A conclusion that one or more of the 'Anatolian' Indo-European languages, or a language ancestral to them, was introduced into Anatolia *c.* 2300 B.C. does not conflict with comparative linguistic evidence. They are all archaic in certain respects in comparison with Greek and Sanskrit; and if Greek is thought to have been introduced into Greece *c.* 1900 B.C., it is not improbable that a language ancestral to Hittite or Luwian or both should have come into use in Anatolia some four hundred years earlier.[2] It is hardly possible to decide on linguistic grounds whether earlier invaders of *c.* 2800–2600 B.C. would have spoken an Indo-European language of proto-Anatolian type, or indeed of any other kind. Calculations about the length of time during which Indo-European existed as a unitary language and about how long it took to differentiate into the known historical language-groups are too uncertain. If immigrants do appear to have entered Anatolia from Thrace *c.* 2800–2600 B.C., it will only be justifiable to regard them as Indo-European if their culture is both highly specialized and closely similar to that of later waves which can be identified as Indo-European.

The feature of Mellaart's reconstruction which does seem to conflict with the conclusions of most philologists about the interrelation of the 'Anatolian' Indo-European languages is his deduction that (proto-)Luwian and (proto-)Hittite were introduced at opposite ends of the Anatolian peninsula and at times some four hundred years apart. Prima facie, at least, Hittite, Luwian and Palaic look like closely related languages, derived from the same dialect of Indo-European, which had remained in contact throughout the time during which they had differentiated; unless, indeed, their differentiation began only after that ancestral dialect had been introduced into Anatolia. In either case, the immigrants who came to speak these three languages presumably entered Anatolia by the same route during a relatively short period.

The archaeological evidence on which Mellaart bases his conclusions is itself not free from difficulties. The migration which appears to have taken place in western Anatolia *c.* 2300 B.C.

---

[1] See above, pp. 694 ff.   [2] See pp. 845 ff. and 866 ff.

would certainly have been of the kind which Indo-European peoples are known to have made in later times, and it might well have spread a new language southward through the region. But neither this movement nor the one postulated for $c.$ 2800 B.C. has been reliably connected with an antecedent migration in a more northerly area which might have initiated it. There appears to be much less evidence for destruction of settlements and for cultural change at appropriate times in south-eastern Europe than in Anatolia itself. The Thracian region has not yet been well explored and the chronology of relevant sites there is notoriously difficult. But it appears that at least in the early part of the Early Bronze Age cultural influences from Anatolia were meeting others from the north in the Thracian region. At all events, the archaeological evidence does not indicate a simple process of successive migrations from the north through the Thracian region into Anatolia.

To consider the problem in a broader context, no Anatolian culture of the late Early Bronze Age or the early Middle Bronze Age has been shown to be derived from an earlier culture which might be attributed to the Indo-Europeans or to one branch of them before their dispersal. The customs and the material equipment of the Hittites of the historical period have traits which are typical of some Indo-European peoples at the end of the second millennium B.C. and in the first millennium. One such trait was the practice of cremating the dead and burying the bones of individuals separately in urns. This was characteristic of the peoples of the 'urnfield' cultures which extended, in the first place, over much of central Europe from the thirteenth century onwards.[1] Texts recovered at Boğazköy in the second series of excavations show that the bodies of Hittite kings were cremated,[2] and excavation of the cemetery at Osmankayası near the Hittite capital in 1952 has proved that the rite was not reserved for royalty alone.[3] At Osmankayası the dead were buried in a grotto, not in an 'urnfield' in the strict sense, and interments of unburnt corpses as well as of ashes were made apparently throughout the period of its use. But the custom of urn-burial after cremation was certainly well established. The cemetery was in use in the seventeenth century, and possibly earlier, some three hundred years at least before urnfield cemeteries are known in Europe. The rite of cremation was virtually unknown elsewhere in Anatolia and the Near East before $c.$ 1500 B.C. Significantly, a fifteenth-century text from Nuzi in the Hurrian region mentions

[1] G, 6, 18 ff.   [2] §II, 4; §II, 44.   [3] §II, 4, 22 ff.

the cremation of a king named Parattarna, perhaps an 'Aryan' dynast.[1] Cremation had become the normal rite in northern India by early historical times and the descriptions of the funerals of Patroclus and Hector in the Iliad[2] show that it was known to Greeks of the early Iron Age, though not practised in Mycenaean communities. It seems probable that the Indo-European element in the Hittite population introduced the rite into Anatolia, but up to the present there is no evidence that it was customary in any area farther to the north before the thirteenth century. It is found only sporadically in Europe and the Pontic region before that time. Only future archaeological discoveries will solve the question whether it developed in Anatolia in the second millennium or was introduced from an area of origin elsewhere.

All early historical Indo-European communities had domesticated horses, and many used war-chariots. In Anatolia the earliest known occurrence of the bones of horses is in Troy VI. Skeletons of a powerful breed which must have been domesticated were found at Osmankayası.[3] These finds at least accord with the view that Indo-European immigration began before 1900 B.C. It is doubtful whether any Indo-Europeans knew the war-chariot before coming into close contact with peoples of the Near East, probably in the second quarter of the second millennium.[4] A Hittite text mentions the use of chariots at the siege of Urshu in the seventeenth century, but it was written some time later and may be anachronistic.[5] Certain features of Hittite monarchy and society which may be Indo-European will be discussed later.[6] In the third millennium, the splendour of the late E. B. Age tombs at Alaca Hüyük, of c. 2300–2200 B.C., points to an aristocratic society of the kind which several historical Indo-European peoples developed, but there is no other indication that Indo-Europeans had settled in the vicinity of the site by that time.[7]

The archaeological evidence which, according to Mellaart, shows that the Indo-European ancestors of the Hittites migrated into central Anatolia from the east c. 1900 B.C. also seems inconclusive. It has not been shown that the destructions which occurred in central Anatolia about that time took place in sequence from east to west, or that new cultural traits appeared after them. It now seems to be agreed that the 'Cappadocian' style of pottery

---

[1] §II, 4, 30; Bull. A.S.O.R. 93 (1944), 16.

[2] Iliad XXIII, 110 ff.; XXIV, 782 ff.

[3] §II, 4, 60 ff.; §II, 5, 113; C. W. Blegen, Troy, vol. III/1 (Princeton, 1953), 10, 397, 403.   [4] See p. 873.   [5] C.A.H. II³, ch. VI, sect. IV, 19 f.
[6] See pp. 874 ff.   [7] See above, p. 686.

was not brought in by Indo-Europeans.[1] It may have originated in Anatolia, and it certainly does not appear to have developed from any similar style known in more easterly areas. It may be that the appearance of monochrome 'Hittite' pottery *c.* 1900 B.C. reflects the arrival of the (proto-)Hittites and perhaps also of the people who spoke Palaic, further to the west.[2] If this pottery proves to have appeared first in the Tavşanlı-Kütahya area,[3] it may be deduced that the (proto-)Hittites entered Anatolia from the north-west at about the same time as the (proto-)Luwians, and remained in a north-westerly area in linguistic contact with them until the twentieth century, after which they migrated further eastwards. This conclusion fits the comparative linguistic evidence well.[4] The view that Hittite and Luwian were introduced into Anatolia from opposite directions and at a considerable interval implies that two related languages first diverged little while separated for nearly four hundred years, and then developed in closely parallel fashion after coming into contact again in Anatolia. This cannot be said to be impossible. It would, however, be an exceptional linguistic phenomenon and does not seem probable.

To summarize, while linguistic evidence may be considered to prove that Indo-Europeans migrated into Anatolia before *c.* 1900 B.C., the details of the event must still be regarded as uncertain.

(*b*) GREECE

For over thirty years the general opinion has been that the Greek language, or at least one or more dialects of it, came into use in Greece at the beginning of the Middle Helladic period, *c.* 1900 B.C.[5] At that time many settlements were destroyed in Greece, at least in the southern and central parts, and a characteristic new pottery appeared, the so-called 'Minyan' ware, usually grey or yellow.[6] An invasion is the obvious cause of these developments, and archaeology indicates no other considerable intrusion between *c.* 1900 B.C. and the fourteenth or thirteenth century, when Greek is known to have been current in the Peloponnese.[7] Recent research suggests that the assumed immigration may have taken longer than had been supposed, and that it may have had more than one phase. At Lerna the severe destruction occurred at the end of Early Helladic II, not later, and 'Minyan' pottery has

---

[1] §II, 3, 48 ff.; see above, pp. 686 ff.   [2] See above, p. 842.
[3] See above, p. 694.   [4] See above, pp. 836 ff.
[5] §IV, 6, 154.
[6] *C.A.H.* II³, ch. IV(*a*), sect. II, 4 ff.   [7] See above, p. 839.

been found there in the latest level of Early Helladic III.[1] Moreover, the significance of the appearance of 'matt-painted'
pottery alongside 'Minyan' in the Middle Helladic period is not
yet clear.[2] Nevertheless, the reasonable conclusion is that the
first considerable body of Greek-speaking immigrants moved into
central and southern Greece c. 1900 B.C.[3] The destruction of
Lerna may have been the work of an earlier wave of proto-Greeks,
or of men who belonged to a different Indo-European people, but
at present it is not useful to speculate about their identity.

The usual view has been that the people who began to produce
'Minyan' ware in Greece came in from the north. But no likely
prototype of this pottery has been reported from a more northerly
area. Published discussions do not make it clear whether the ware
or a similar one occurs in significant quantity in Macedonia and
Thrace or not.[4] In 1932 C. W. Blegen found a little similar
pottery in Troy VI.[5] Prima facie, this might have been imported
from Greece, or the ware might have been introduced both at
Troy and in central Greece by migrants from further north.
Recent discoveries in Turkey have prompted new and more
complex explanations of its appearance in Greece c. 1900 B.C.

Since 1955 J. Mellaart has reported that grey wares very
similar to Greek grey 'Minyan' were widely distributed in north-
western Anatolia at the end of the E. B. Age and the beginning of
the M. B. Age.[6] He believes that the 'Minyan' style developed in
an area about two hundred miles east of Troy in the period Troy V,
and that the ware came into use in areas further to the west,
including the Aegean sea-board, at the beginning of the M. B. Age
in the period Troy VI. He concludes that it was introduced into
Greece from these areas. He reconstructs the course of events as
follows. Proto-Greeks (tribes who spoke an Indo-European
language which developed into Greek) settled in north-western
Anatolia, probably arriving from Bulgaria, during the last centuries of the third millennium. They learnt to make grey 'Minyan' ware there and became skilful seafarers. In the twentieth
century they emigrated under pressure from peoples in the
interior, and won new homes for themselves in Greece. Their

---

[1] See above, pp. 786 ff.; *C.A.H.* II³, ch. IV(a), sect. II, 11, sect. III, 21 ff.

[2] *C.A.H.* II³, ch. IV(a), sect. II, 5 f.

[3] No archaeological evidence appears to indicate extensive migration into Greece
between c. 1900 and c. 1100 B.C.

[4] *C.A.H.* II³, ch. IV(a), sect. II, 7 f.

[5] §II, 5, 140 ff.; C. W. Blegen, *Troy* II, 1 (1951), 317; III, 1 (1953) 408; IV, 1
(1958), 319.

[6] §IV, 10, 15 ff.; see above, pp. 700 ff.

arrival in Greece is marked by the appearance of 'Minyan' pottery and they introduced the Greek language there.

L. R. Palmer has offered a different interpretation of the data.[1] He considers that 'Luwians' inhabited the north-western part of Anatolia as well as the central western part at the end of the third millennium, and that it was they who introduced 'Minyan' pottery into Greece. The first Greek-speaking immigrants would have come into Greece during the fifteenth century or perhaps late in the sixteenth.

These mutually exclusive theories may only be evaluated provisionally at present. Little information has been published about the relevant new north-western Anatolian styles of pottery. But some problems should be pointed out. In the first place, the possibility that 'Minyan' pottery was introduced both into Anatolia and into Greece from the north remains open until Macedonia and Thrace have been well surveyed and it has been established that no wares which might have been the prototype of both Anatolian and Greek 'Minyan' ceramics were in use in those regions between c. 2300 and c. 1900 B.C. Secondly, the development and the interrelation of the Anatolian types of pottery which have been classed as 'Minyan' or 'grey' wares need elucidation. One at least of the shapes which are regarded as characteristically 'Minyan', the vase with high looped handles, occurs at Beycesultan in a red ware in Level VII (c. 2100–2050 B.C.) and possible prototypes from the same site are considerably older.[2] During the middle centuries of the third millennium such 'Minyan' shapes might have been imitated widely, in areas outside Anatolia as well as within it, especially if they imitated metal vessels which were luxury articles. It is not unthinkable that a style of pottery which was brought into Anatolia from the north-west c. 2100–1900 B.C. should have had features which went back ultimately to an Anatolian prototype of an earlier period. There was considerable cultural diffusion from Anatolia into south-eastern Europe in the earlier phases of the Early Bronze Age. The relative chronology of the various north-western Anatolian wares of late E.B.A. and early M.B.A. still seems uncertain. It is not clear what evidence indicates that the earliest grey ware in the Marmara area was contemporary with Troy III.[3] The occurrence of certain features of decoration on pottery of Troy V and on the earliest 'Minyan'

---

[1] §iv, 13.

[2] §iv, 10, 18; see above, pp. 692 ff.; S. Lloyd and J. Mellaart, *A.St.* 6 (1956), 126.

[3] See above, pp. 701 ff.; §iv, 10, 18.

of the Marmara area, while they are not found on pottery of Troy VI, is not to be explained only on the assumption that the 'Minyan' type developed in the Marmara area during the Troy V period and was introduced at Troy subsequently. The Marmara area might have been conservative in its use of decoration. The 'Minyan' style, or rather one version of it in which pre-existing decorative motifs of the area continued to be used, might have developed there during the Troy VI period. Any important archaeological discovery will naturally bring with it problems of this sort which cannot be resolved immediately. But it seems premature to conclude that the appearance of 'Minyan' pottery in Greece *c.* 1900 B.C. must reflect an extensive, direct migration from north-western Anatolia, while so much is still uncertain about the history of similar pottery in Anatolia, and while the Thracian and Macedonian regions are still imperfectly known.

The linguistic data are compatible with Mellaart's reconstruction of the migrations of the proto-Greeks but do not specifically support it. Some considerations suggest that proto-Greek developed in the third millennium in an area to the north or west of that in which proto-Phrygian took shape, so that it would be surprising to find (proto-)Greek introduced into Anatolia some centuries before Phrygian.[1] Indo-European migrations may sometimes have crossed or have diverged from the main lines of movement which we deduce. Nevertheless, place-names and personal names of north-western Anatolia in the Hittite period have no characteristics which appear to have belonged to, or to have been inherited from, an early form of Greek. The present writer believes that the country whose name the Hittites wrote as *Ahhiyawa*, apparently based on Greek *'Aχαιϝός or *'Aχαιϝία, was Rhodes, or at least had its main centre there.[2] If so, Ahhiyawa will represent a name which the Hittites took over from Mycenaean Greeks, not a survival from a form of Greek which had been current in Anatolia some centuries before their time.

L. R. Palmer's reconstruction, in which the people who introduced 'Minyan' pottery into Greece were 'Luwians', is based primarily on linguistic evidence. Place-names ending in syllables which contain -*ss*-, e.g. Halicarnassus, Larissa, and others in -*nth*- or -*nd*-, are common in south-western Anatolia in classical times, and also occur in Greece and Crete.[3] Comparable names in

---

[1] G, 3, 33.
[2] See *Bi. Or.* 10 (1953), 120 f. *Contra*, p. 410 above. The name should be written *Akhkhiyawa* according to the conventions followed in this *History* in transcribing other names from Hittite texts.   [3] §IV, 6, 141 ff.

-assas (probably pronounced [-assas] or [-asas]) and in *-andas* or *-antas* appear in the Boğazköy texts. Some of the places with names in *-assas* were certainly in areas in which Luwian was spoken. It has long been thought that the distribution of names of the two types might indicate a prehistoric migration from south-western Anatolia to Greece. Palmer's new deductions are that this movement occurred after Luwian had come into use in western Anatolia; that the formant *-assas* belonged specifically to the Luwian language; and that Luwian became at least the principal language of central and southern Greece, and also of much of Crete, from the nineteenth century B.C. to the fifteenth. The theory is attractive in so far as it explains the similarities between place-names on opposite sides of the Aegean, but there are difficulties in it. One lies in the variants in -ττ-, e.g. Hymettus in Attica, which are typical of certain dialects of Greek, and in some comparable forms in classical Anatolia. A sound or sequence which was written with -ττ- in Greek does not seem a natural development from one which was represented as *-ss-* in the cunei-form of Boğazköy. At the least, the Greek forms must have been derived from a form of Luwian which was antecedent or collateral to that which was known at Khattusha.[1] Palmer's explanation of the place-name Parnassus as Anatolian in origin is attractive; cf. Hittite and Luwian *parna-*, 'house'.[2] And in Greek legend Pelops came from Lydia or Phrygia and the charioteer who helped him win his kingdom in the Peloponnese was named Myrsilus or Myrtilus;[3] cf. the Hittite name Murshilish. Perhaps individuals or small groups of people who spoke Luwian did settle in Greece during the second millennium B.C. But the natural conclusion from the linguistic evidence as a whole is that 'Lu-wians' did not migrate to Greece in large numbers.[4] No charac-teristic of the Greek language, other than the formants in certain place-names, has plausibly been explained as Luwian in origin, and it is inconceivable that the identifiable Luwian elements in Greek would have been so small if Luwian had been spoken in Greece for some centuries before Greek superseded it. The linguistic arguments for Luwian migration to Crete rest on doubtful interpretations of 'Minoan Linear A' texts.[5]

It has been suggested that an Indo-European language related

[1] §IV, 13, 88 ff.   [2] §IV, 12, 13.
[3] Diodorus Siculus, IV, 73; Pausanias, VIII, 14, 10–12.
[4] §IV, 11.
[5] See M. Pope, 'The goddess Asasara: an obituary', in *Bull. Inst. Cl. St.* 8 (1961), 29 ff.

not to the 'Anatolian' group but to Illyrian was current in Greece before Greek itself.[1] The Adriatic connections of some Bronze Age pottery in western Greece make this idea worth considering,[2] and it is based on more varied linguistic comparisons than is the theory of a Luwian substrate. But the case for it is still inconclusive. 'Illyrian' itself is a linguistic concept based on rather limited material.[3]

It still seems most satisfactory to associate the arrival of the first Greek-speaking tribes in Greece with the appearance of 'Minyan' pottery there, though it may be that their immigration began before 2000 B.C. or that a closely related people preceded those who introduced the Greek language. In the author's opinion this language was already a well-differentiated idiom before it was brought into central and southern Greece, and tribes who spoke one or more dialects of it probably remained behind in some area to the north, to appear as the 'Dorians' and as speakers of 'north-western' Greek dialects at the end of the second millennium B.C. It is still uncertain from which region Greek was introduced into the Balkan peninsula.

(c) INDIA AND IRAN

Since 'Aryan' personal names appear in northern Mesopotamia and Syria as early as the fifteenth century B.C., Iran and northern India are regions in which archaeological evidence for early Indo-European immigration might be expected. At first sight the chances of determining when this took place in India look good. There is no historical account of an 'Aryan' conquest in Indian literature, but the earlier hymns of the Rigveda portray a situation of conflict between the *Āryas*, the people for whom the poets sing, and enemies whom they call *dāsas* or *dasyus* and regard as racially different from themselves, dark-skinned men, unlovely and irreligious.[4] The dividing line between events on earth and mythology is not clearly maintained in these poems and was probably not even logically conceived. The gods of the Āryas help them in their fight against the Dāsas, who are looked upon as agents of the supernatural forces of evil and darkness. Conversely, the gods' struggle against these forces on the superhuman plane is visualized in terms of the warfare of the Āryas against their earthly enemies. However, it may be accepted that the poems do

---

[1] §IV, 3; §IV, 4; §IV, 5.
[2] See above, pp. 790 ff. See also *C.A.H.* II³, ch. IV(*a*), sect. II, 12.
[3] §IV, 9.   [4] §III, 7, 79 ff.; §III, 11, 251 ff.

reflect a historical conflict or preserve the memory of it. There is much that is realistic in the descriptions of the fighting, and one of the terms of abuse used of the Dāsas is significant. They are called *anāsas*, 'noseless', a natural description of the delicately snub-nosed physiognomy of the Dravidian Indian from the point of view of an ill-disposed northerner. The advanced Bronze Age civilization of the Indus valley declined in the second millennium B.C. and the final destruction of its two most important cities, those at Harappā and Mohenjo Daro, appears to have been caused by military action.[1] Closer dating of the events which led to their downfall is still uncertain, and it is difficult to correlate in detail the archaeological and literary evidence for invasion and war in the region in the middle and late centuries of the millennium. Few sites have been excavated in northern India and their absolute chronology is hard to establish. The Vedic literature is imaginative or primarily concerned with religious ritual. It is not demonstrably older than *c.* 1000 B.C., although it is often said to be.[2] It mentions many tribes, places and rivers which are probably historical, but for the most part they cannot be satisfactorily identified or located. The region known to the poets apparently lay north of the Thar desert, from the Punjab in the west to the vicinity of Ambala and the river Jumna in the east, while the river Ganges is mentioned only once. There are other indications besides this that the Āryas were migrating or extending their territories during the period in which the poems were composed, and that this movement or expansion was in an eastward direction. Some of the river-names in the poems are thought to survive in Afghanistān (the names Kubha, Suvastu, Krumu and Gomati being identified with those of the Kabul, the Swat, the Kurram and the Gumal) and this suggests that the Āryas entered India from that country. One river-name, Sarasvati, occurs also in Avestan (in the Vendidad) in the corresponding Iranian form Harohvaiti. But this hardly proves that the proto-Indians and the proto-Iranians were still in contact when the Rigveda and the earliest hymns of the Avesta were composed. The name may have been remembered by the Āryas from times before they lost contact with the proto-Iranians, and it may have been given later to a river in India (perhaps the Sutlej).

The latest archaeological research indicates a complex or at least protracted pattern of immigration into India from the north-west, perhaps lasting over most of the second millennium. It does not appear that the cities of the Indus valley were overwhelmed in

[1] §III, 5, 75 ff.   [2] §III, 6, 35.

one sudden onslaught or mass incursion. The first apparently intrusive culture in the region is the one known by the site name Jhukar. It was introduced by a people who drove away the inhabitants of the Harappan town at Chanhu Daro.[1] D. H. Gordon dates its appearance to shortly after *c.* 1800 B.C., and it is said to have points of similarity with the cultures of Tepe Hisar III and Sialk (Cemetery A) in Iran.[2] The cities at Mohenjo Daro and Harappā evidently survived for some time after this invasion. The former was eventually captured, sacked and abandoned. That at Harappā fell to a people of an inferior and alien culture, named Ravi I by Gordon.[3] A change in burial customs at Harappā from inhumation to pot-burial after exposure or cremation may indicate a second wave of immigrants there. At sites in the Ambala area and in the eastern Punjab there is also evidence of a new element in the population at approximately the same time, but no cultural parallels to it in an area outside India have yet been suggested.

There is even less evidence at present on which to base a reconstruction of events in northern and eastern Iran in the second millennium. Destruction levels and cultural changes which may reflect immigration are reported at Tepe Hisar, southeast of the Caspian Sea, and at Tepe Giyan, in Luristān, in each case at the beginning of the excavators' Level III, and it is natural to consider whether they mark the arrival of Indo-Europeans, perhaps proto-Indians. The dates of the two levels are controversial. Those proposed by the excavators seem too high. Those now generally accepted, *c.* 2000 to perhaps *c.* 1550 B.C., will give a date for the immigration some centuries before the earliest attestation of 'Aryan' names in the Near East.[4] But it is possible to assume that a proto-Indian population remained in northern Iran during the first centuries of the second millennium, while related tribes were already migrating further to enter northwestern India. There was apparently no radical cultural change in Iran during Tepe Hisar III or Tepe Giyan III. Gordon's date for the Jhukar culture (*c.* 1800 B.C. onwards) is consistent with its having been introduced into India by an early wave of proto-Indian immigrants. However, the first effect of Indo-European immigration into Iran may have been to drive native non-Indo-European peoples southward. In any case the Āryas of the Rigveda may represent a relatively late wave of immigrants. The high date of *c.* 1500 B.C. formerly proposed for the earlier parts of the Rigveda is not based on firm philological evidence and should not

[1] §III, 5, 79 ff.   [2] §III, 4, 51 f.   [3] §III, 5, 83 ff.   [4] §III, 4, 60.

be used as an argument for dating the migration of the Āryas so early. The Iranians would appear to have followed the proto-Indians into Iran, presumably displacing or dominating them there, in the second half of the second millennium at the earliest. Names with specifically Iranian characteristics appear first in Assyrian documents of the ninth century.[1] A linguistic argument supports the conclusion. Iranian shares at least one of the features which distinguish it from Indic, the change of *s* to *h*, with Greek and Armenian (cf. Sanskrit *sapta*, Avestan *hapta*, Greek ἑπτά, Armenian *evt'n*, 'seven'). So proto-Iranian presumably remained in contact with the dialects from which those languages developed longer than did proto-Indic, and in a region further to the north.

(d) OTHER AREAS

In areas other than Anatolia, Greece, Iran and India, direct evidence of the use of an Indo-European language or plausible tradition about its introduction is available only considerably later, at times from the sixth century B.C. onwards, and it is correspondingly more difficult to identify by means of archaeological data the movements which brought in Indo-European speech from its original area. Much secondary migration, amalgamation and differentiation of Indo-European peoples may have taken place by the end of the first millennium B.C. In central Europe, and in the Danubian region in particular, material progress in the Bronze Age was rapid and diverse. It is generally accepted that Indo-European peoples, or communities whom they had dominated, created the more advanced civilizations, notably those of the Tumulus and Urnfield cultures, which appeared in these regions between c. 1750 and c. 1300 B.C., and that migrations out of them introduced Celtic languages into France and northern Spain, and the Italic languages (at least Oscan and Umbrian) into Italy.[2] It would be inappropriate to treat the cultural history of Europe in the Bronze Age and the prehistory of its peoples at length in this chapter. But the geographical location of all Indo-European groups at the times when they can first be identified should be stated as far as it can be determined, since it must be taken into account when the question of the area of origin of primary Indo-European expansion is discussed.

[1] §III, 8; §III, 9. C. Burney informs me that there is substantial continuity in pottery at Hasanlu in northern Iran between periods V and IV, the latter beginning c. 1000 B.C., but that a new 'Triangle Ware' appears in the seventh century B.C.
[2] G, 6, 18 ff.

Onomastic evidence shows that Celts were present in Bohemia
and France in the second century B.C. and there is no doubt that
the peoples of the La Tène civilization in its Middle and Late
phases, when it extended over most of Czechoslovakia, southern
Germany and France, were Celtic-speaking. E. and J. N.
Neustupný, who have treated the question most recently, think
that Early La Tène evolved in Bohemia, southern Germany and
perhaps part of France as the result of successive changes in local
cultures between the thirteenth and the eighth centuries, changes
which suggest no influx of new population.[1] They trace the
development of the La Tène culture in Czechoslovakia back to
the Knovíz and Velatice cultures, themselves derived from the
wider Tumulus complex. This implies that a Celtic or proto-
Celtic population was settled in Bohemia as early as c. 1300 B.C.

There is no obvious archaeological evidence for migration into
Italy from the east or north-east on a large scale between c. 2000
and 500 B.C., although there are similarities between the most
important late Bronze Age civilizations of the peninsula, the
Apennine culture and that of the *terramare* (the settlements of
pile-dwellings and mounds in the central Po valley of c. 1300–
1000 B.C.), on the one hand, and slightly earlier cultures in
Hungary and northern Yugoslavia on the other. These resemblances suggest that small groups of migrants moved into
Italy from the latter areas. The Terramara culture had the custom
of cremation. In the Iron Age the Villanovans in Etruria and the
vicinity of Bologna practised cremation and burial in urnfields,
and their art shows central European features. Further south in
the same period cremation and urnfield burial occur sporadically.[2]

In general, this evidence suggests that proto-Italic languages
(represented later by Latin, Oscan and Umbrian, together with
their less well-attested cognates and perhaps Sicel) were brought
into Italy from the north-east between c. 1500 and 900 B.C., but
it is difficult to point to a precise area of origin for the Italic
group outside Italy or to correlate the spread of Latin, Oscan and
Umbrian with particular cultures or movements at the end of the
second millennium. As a language Latin appears to be more
archaic than Oscan and Umbrian and was probably introduced
into Italy ahead of them. The Veneti, at the head of the Adriatic,
were certainly later arrivals from the zone of Urnfield cultures.
Their language should be regarded as an autonomous Indo-
European idiom, though it has points of similarity to the Italic
group. They presumably moved into their historical territory

[1] §v, 15, 117 ff., 128, 145 ff.   [2] G, 6, 27.

after the Italici[1] had entered Italy, in the ninth century.[2] The Etruscans constitute a special problem in the prehistory of northern Italy. At the beginning of the historical period in the fifth century they are found over much the same territory as the Villanovan culture, but their language is not closely related to any western Indo-European group and is not to be explained as pre-Italic. Only the language of the isolated non-Hellenic stele of Lemnos, probably of the sixth century B.C., resembles it closely, but it appears to be related to Lydian and so to the Hittite-Luwian group;[3] the paucity and shortness of both the Etruscan and the Lydian texts make the question difficult to resolve. If the connexion is demonstrated, the ancient tradition[4] that the Etruscans migrated to Italy from Anatolia may be considered proved, even if there is no clear archaeological evidence of their arrival in Etruria and the central Po valley. Etruscan presumably replaced an Italic language, or perhaps one more closely related to Venetic, in the region of the Villanovan culture.

The Illyrians were recognized as a distinct people by the Greeks of the classical period, who knew them as warlike neighbours living to the north-east, in modern Albania and Yugoslavia. Their language, strictly defined, survives only in place-names and personal names. Messapic appears to be related to it, but not simply as a dialect. It shares certain features with the Indo-European languages of Europe other than Greek, particularly with those of the Germanic group. It is doubtful whether Albanian is derived from this Illyrian language or whether it contains any considerable Illyrian substratum.[5]

The culture of the historical Illyrians appears to have developed from one belonging to the Iron Age Hallstatt complex and they practised both cremation and inhumation.[6] They may therefore have migrated into Illyricum from the north or north-east as late as the first quarter of the first millennium B.C., perhaps replacing Italic peoples who moved into Italy. Some modern studies have assigned an important historical role to them. They have been identified with the people of the Lausitz (Lusatian) group of Urnfield cultures, centred in southern Poland c. 1300–900 B.C., and it has been supposed that they moved southward in

[1] I.e. the prehistoric peoples who introduced the Italic languages into Italy.
[2] G, 6, 24; G, 7, 114 ff.
[3] G, 7, 153 ff.; §II, 10, 74 ff.; §II, 23, 25 f.; *C.A.H.* IV[1], ch. XII; W. von Brandenstein, *Die tyrrhenische Stele vom Lemnos (Mitt. d. Altoriental. Gesellschaft* 8/3; Berlin, 1934). [4] Herodotus, I, 94.
[5] G, 7, 113 ff. See also N. Jokl, *Die Sprache*, 9 (1963), 48 ff.
[6] G, 6, 23.

large numbers in the thirteenth and twelfth centuries, not only to settle in Illyricum but also to displace other Indo-European peoples in south-eastern Europe, and perhaps even to initiate the migrations which disturbed the Aegean region c. 1200–1100 B.C. More recently it has been stated that there was no important expansion of the Lausitz culture,[1] and the linguistic evidence for Illyrian populations outside Dalmatia and Apulia has certainly been over-estimated.

However, it does seem that the region of the Urnfield cultures was a source of important movements of Indo-European peoples in the thirteenth century and shortly afterwards, and these may well have been the primary cause of the onslaught that destroyed the Hittite empire. They may also have started the movement of the Dorian Greeks southwards from Macedonia and have caused the mass migrations of the 'Peoples of the Sea' from the southern Aegean area, which the Egyptians halted with difficulty on their borders in 1232 and 1194 B.C.[2] Archaeology does show a great improvement in armament in the zone of the Urnfield cultures (from western Rumania to Bohemia and southern Germany) at the end of the second millennium B.C., and exceptionally rich graves indicate the development of aristocratic societies organized for war, like those of the Greeks of the Iliad, the Āryas of India, and the Celts of early historical Ireland. More information is needed about events in the extreme south-east of Europe at that time.

The obliteration of the Hittite empire in Anatolia certainly seems to have been the work of immigrants from Thrace, probably the ancestors of the Phrygians who occupied the central part of the Anatolian plateau in early classical times, or a closely related people. Khattusha itself was sacked c. 1200 B.C.; its archives broke off abruptly and it ceased to exist as a Hittite city. The next settlement on the site has been defined as Phrygian on the basis of its pottery.[3] The latest Hittite texts say nothing about the events which led to the final disaster, but they record that a chieftain with the name Mitash or Midash was giving trouble on the north-eastern frontier, in Pontus, c. 1230 B.C.[4] His name may have been identical with that of Midas, the legendary early Phrygian king who in Greek story was so ludicrously punished for his lust for gold. The Phrygians, however, need not have entered Anatolia from the north-east; a group of

---

[1] §v, 15, 111 ff., 122 ff.

[2] *C.A.H.* II[3], ch. XXIII, sects. IX and XII; ch. XXVIII, sect. III; ch. XXXIII, sect. I.

[3] §II, 3, 81 ff.; §II, 19, 186 f.; T. Beran, *M.D.O.G.* 94 (1963), 35 ff.; E.-M. Bossert, *ibid.* 53 ff.   [4] §II, 21.

them might have established itself in Pontus, which the Hittites never controlled, before their main invasion of Hittite territory was launched. So far, there is no archaeological evidence for a migration from Thrace to north-western Anatolia or from there to the central region c. 1250–1200 B.C. and no Phrygian settlement has been identified which is certainly older than the ninth century. On the other hand, the people of settlement VII B 2 at Troy, c. 1150 B.C., appear to have been immigrants from Thrace (among other indications, the 'Knobbed Ware' or 'Bückelkeramik' which they introduced has its nearest counterpart in Hungary);[1] and the Phrygian language is most closely related to Thracian.[2] The ancient tradition cited by Herodotus that the Phrygians were of Thracian origin thus appears to be true.[3]

The Armenians were first mentioned in sources of the sixth century B.C. and were at that time already settled in their historical habitat. Herodotus had heard that they were Phrygian colonists. Their language has similarities to Phrygian but is apparently not simply a later form of it.[4] No published archaeological evidence shows when they settled in Armenia.

It is doubtful whether tribes from Thrace were among the very mixed collection of homeless marauders whom the Egyptians called the 'Peoples of the Sea'. These were more probably made up of communities and groups of refugees driven out of western and southern Anatolia by the attacks of invaders from further north. Lukkans (Lycians) took part in the invasion of 1232 B.C. The identification of the other enemy peoples mentioned in the Egyptian records is less certain.

The historical Indo-European peoples of northern Europe, the Germans (i.e. all who spoke Germanic languages), the Balts and the Slavs, appear to have been descended from tribes who did not take part in the development of the advanced cultures of the central European Bronze Age. During the second millennium B.C. cultures of a more primitive kind survived and developed in the regions in which the Germanic, Baltic and Slavonic language-groups were centred later. It seems probable that these cultures, or styles and practices which became characteristic of them, had been introduced into northern Europe by Indo-European peoples who spoke the proto-Germanic, proto-Baltic and proto-Slavonic languages.[5] No non-linguistic evidence throws light on the date of the migration which brought the Tocharians to Turkestān.

[1] §II, 5, 165, 169 ff.
[2] §II, 26, 71 ff.; §II, 27; §IV, 8.
[3] Herodotus, VII, 73.
[4] *Ibid.*; §II, 8, 333 ff., 594 ff.; §II, 26, 79 ff.
[5] See pp. 870 f.

From the seventh century B.C. to the fifth A.D. the region extending from the southern Ukraine to Kazakhstān was the source of successive migrations which disturbed countries lying to the south and west of it. During that period it was occupied mainly by the peoples known to the ancient world as Scyths and Sarmatians.[1] To judge by the names of their chiefs they were Iranians. The name of the Scyths first appears in Assyrian documents of the region of Esarhaddon, 681–669 B.C., in the form *Ashguzai*, and Herodotus records that they were at war with the Medes in the last decades of the seventh century.[2] The first considerable effect of their expansion was to drive the people known to the Greeks as Κιμμέριοι (the *Gimirrai* of Assyrian sources) and also a Thracian tribe, the Treres, into invading Anatolia on several occasions between c. 710 and 645 B.C. The Cimmerian invaders ruined the Phrygian kingdom, which had shown a certain vigour and éclat in the eighth century, and sacked Sardis and more than one of the flourishing Greek cities of the Aegean seaboard. They were checked primarily by the Lydians and the Assyrians. The latter defeated them decisively in Cilicia or the Hatay district c. 650 B.C. and after this they disappeared almost at once as a distinct people.[3] They were no doubt Indo-Europeans, but it is uncertain whether their language belonged to one of the known groups or was an autonomous idiom which died out completely. The fact that one of their leaders had the name *Shandakshatru*, which may be explained as Iranian (cf. either Sanskrit *candra-*, 'shining', or Avestan *zanta-*, 'country', from earlier **žantra-*; Sanskrit *ksatra-*, 'leadership'), is not decisive. They were in close contact with the Scyths, who were Iranians, and they might have borrowed names from them. The Scyths and related northern Iranian peoples were fast-moving nomads who were a recurrent threat to the settled nations which lived to the south of them, although they were held back first by the Assyrians, then by the Persians and the succeeding civilized powers of the Near East. In the fifth century B.C. the artistic style which the Scythians of the western Pontic region developed spread into eastern Europe and had a certain influence as far west as Slovakia:[4] it was probably disseminated by small groups of conquerors rather than by whole tribes on the move.

From the sixth century B.C. onwards, if not earlier, other Iranian peoples were settled east of the Caspian Sea, at least as

---

[1] *C.A.H.* III[1], ch. IX, sect. I.
[2] Herodotus, I, 15, 103–6; IV, 1, 11–12. §II, 26, 93 f.
[3] *C.A.H.* III[1], 295, 510 f.   [4] §V, 15, 136, 144.

far as Uzbekistān (ancient Sogdiana). It is not yet clear whether they had lived in these areas from a considerably earlier period, perhaps from the time of Indo-European unity, or whether they had migrated into them from the west relatively late. They were presumably in contact with proto-Turkic peoples, but it is uncertain to what extent and how early they were influenced by them or when admixture began.

IV. THE REGION OF ORIGIN OF EARLY INDO-EUROPEAN MIGRATIONS

The evidence so far outlined gives reasonably consistent, though somewhat imprecise, indications of the date and area of origin of the earliest Indo-European movements into the Near East and adjacent regions. They appear to have begun before 2000 B.C., possibly as early as c. 2400–2300 B.C., and to have come from a zone extending from south-eastern Europe across the southern Pontic area and perhaps as far as Kazakhstān in the east. Can the location of the so-called 'Indo-European homeland' be deduced more exactly from linguistic or from other archaeological evidence?

(a) LINGUISTIC EVIDENCE

This has been used in two main ways in attempts to locate the 'homeland'. The first is in 'linguistic palaeontology', the object of which is to deduce from the vocabulary of 'common Indo-European', as reconstructed by comparison of relevant words in the historical languages, the physical environment which the Indo-Europeans knew, and the material culture and social organization which they had achieved, while they still lived within a 'linguistic continuum'. Such study has its limitations and risks of error. In any language over a given period some changes will occur without obvious reason. Moreover, the Indo-European languages were first recorded at widely different dates. Also, a language such as Greek or Hittite, which was adopted in an area that already had a dense and civilized population, is prima facie more likely to have borrowed words from a non-Indo-European language and to have lost inherited equivalents than is one, such as proto-Germanic, which appears to have been introduced into a backward and sparsely inhabited area. It is frequently difficult to decide whether a word which is shared by only a certain number of 'primary' groups or languages (e.g. by Germanic, Greek and

Tocharian) should be regarded as 'common Indo-European' or not. Conclusions will depend on how the original language is thought to have differentiated into dialects and derivatives. In most published studies it is accepted that if a word is shared by Indic or Iranian and Greek, Celtic, Italic or Germanic, it is likely to be original. This now seems questionable.[1] Recent work has added little to the results which O. Schrader and V. G. Childe felt able to accept.[2]

Shared vocabulary indicates that the Indo-Europeans knew animals of the northern temperate zone, such as the wolf, the bear and the otter, but not those confined to sub-arctic regions, or to central Asia, or to Mediterranean, Near Eastern or tropical countries. There are no common words for the camel, the lion or the tiger. It is hardly surprising that the Indo-European languages of Europe share words for trees such as the beech and the pine, and that these are lacking in Iranian and Indic. Much has been made of the occurrence in Germanic and Slavonic languages and Latin of related words for the beech (cf. English *beech*, Latin *fagus*; Greek φηγός is related but is used of a kind of oak, and Kurdish *buz* similarly of an elm). It is argued that, since the Indo-Europeans knew the beech, their 'homeland' did not lie east of a line running roughly from Königsberg (Kaliningrad) to the Crimea, the eastern limit of its modern distribution. The argument is impressive, with one qualification. In ancient times beeches may have grown somewhat further to the east. One variety grows today near the Caspian Sea.[3] Arguments from the distribution of cognates of the German word *Lachs*, 'salmon', are not convincing. The occurrence of words related to German *Lachs* and meaning 'salmon' in the Baltic, Germanic and Slavonic language-groups does not prove that the Indo-Europeans lived in a region where salmon were found, presumably in northern Europe. The word has now been identified in Tocharian, and in that language it has the generic meaning 'fish'. A common Indo-European word for 'fish', preserved with that meaning in Tocharian, might well have developed the more specialized sense of 'salmon' in the northern European groups.[4]

It may be accepted that the Indo-Europeans were at the 'chalcolithic' cultural stage: they knew one metal, either copper or bronze (cf. Latin *aes*; Gothic *aiz*; Sanskrit *ayas* with change of meaning to 'iron'). They practised a primitive form of agriculture, but apparently depended on stock-farming to a greater extent

---

[1] See p. 865.   [2] G, 2, 78 ff.; G, 3, 21 ff.   [3] G, 3, 27.
[4] G, 3, 27; G, 8, 551 ff. (17 ff.).

than did the neolithic peoples of south-eastern Europe. Words for the cow, the sheep and the pig are common to several of the early historical languages (cf. Latin *bos*, Greek βοῦς, Sanskrit *gaus*, English *cow*; English *ewe*, Latin *ovis*, Sanskrit *avis*). They knew the horse (Latin *equus*, Irish *ech*, Sanskrit *aśvas*) and they had wheeled vehicles, though not necessarily the chariot. Most terms for agricultural operations and implements are shared by European languages only (e.g. English *sow*, *seed*; Latin *semen*; Old Irish *sil*; Lithuanian *sė'ti*, Old Slavonic *sěti*). This, however, does not prove either that the 'homeland' was in Europe or that the Indo-Europeans as a whole did not practise agriculture before their dispersal. The Hittites, the Armenians, the Iranians and the Āryas all settled in countries where the native populations had a long tradition of advanced agriculture, and they no doubt borrowed words connected with it from them. Moreover, the Āryas and such Iranian peoples as the Medes and the Persians must have accomplished long migrations through inhospitable country before settling in their historical lands, and they may well have come to depend mainly on their herds in the course of them. Mobile pastoral nomadism of the kind which the Scyths and later the Turks and Mongols practised seems to have been a specialized way of living, not a primitive cultural stage which generally preceded that of simple agriculture with some stock-farming.

It is reasonable to conclude that the Indo-Europeans had a patriarchal social organization. There is a considerable common vocabulary of terms for agnatic relations, and hardly any for kindred on the mother's side. This accords with the strongly patriarchal character of society among the Romans, the Āryas and the early Celts and Germans, though allowance should be made for the effect of parallel tendencies among peoples who for some time had lived a migratory life in which wars were frequent. The Hittites, or at least their aristocracy, about which we have evidence, also had patriarchal institutions. The Decree of King Telepinush *c.* 1500 B.C. lays down patrilinear rules of succession for the royal house, and Khattushilish I in the seventeenth century is clearly concerned to choose a successor in the male line of descent.[1]

These deductions about the material culture and society of the Indo-Europeans are unfortunately of limited value as a basis for associating them with any culture or cultures defined by archaeology. All cultures of the immediate periphery of the region of urban life and advanced agriculture in the third and early second millennia B.C. were at a late neolithic, chalcolithic or early

[1] §II, 47, 2 ff., 207 ff.; §II, 48, 188 f.; *C.A.H.* II³, ch. VI, sects. IV, V.

Bronze Age stage of development, and all which can be clearly identified were based to some extent both on agriculture and on stock-farming. It has been suggested that certain features of the late neolithic cultures of central Europe, notably the large, presumably communal dwelling-houses, indicate 'matriarchal' (matricentric) societies; and that changes in the normal type of house and the size of settlements point to a change to an economy based to a greater extent on stock-farming, and with patriarchal social organization, in the chalcolithic period, c. 2200 B.C.[1] If this were accepted, one might look for the first appearance of Indo-Europeans in the region at that time. Some deductions about Indo-European religion may be made on the basis of shared vocabulary,[2] but none imply features which might be identified in excavations, such as characteristic shrines in durable materials.

Two recent theories about the cultural and social development of the Indo-Europeans should be mentioned here. The first has been advocated particularly by H. Krahe. It holds that the Indo-European peoples first known in central and western Europe, the Celts, the Italici, the Germans and the Illyrians, and perhaps also the Balts, had been in contact among themselves for longer than any one of them had been in contact with any other of the early historical groups, either because the 'homeland' was in Europe and they had stayed in or near it, or because they had remained in contact after immigrating from further east. This prolonged contact among the 'European' peoples is supposedly proved by the use in their languages of the same stems and extensions in forming river-names, and by their having common terminology for agricultural operations and features of social organization, tribal government and religion, in all of which they are thought to have developed common cultural traits.[3] The present writer finds this theory unconvincing. It is to be expected that the European languages (as defined) should have borrowed from each other and developed some common features, in view of their proximity in late prehistoric and in historical times, while those which are first known farther to the east are likely to have undergone greater changes, particularly in vocabulary, since they were separated from each other and in contact with civilized non-Indo-European peoples. Moreover, from time to time a word thought to be a significant common possession of the European languages and to be absent from the eastern groups is found to have survived vestigially in one of the latter: e.g. the Hittite word *tuzzis*,

---

[1] §v, 15, 72 ff., 84 ff.   [2] See p. 875.
[3] G, 7, 48 ff. *Contra*, G, 3, 35 f.

'army', may well contain the stem of *teutā, 'people', long thought to be confined to the European languages.

The second theory comes from L. R. Palmer.[1] He considers that the type of monarchy and the system of social classes which he reconstructs for the Mycenaean Greek states on the basis of Linear B texts from Epano Englianos (probably Pylus) have such close similarities to those found among the Hittites and the early Germans that both must be regarded as inherited from the time of Indo-European unity. The Indo-European king was supposedly either a ruler regarded as divine or one with predominantly religious functions. He was assisted by a 'war-leader', and the people were divided into commoners and a class of hereditary nobles. Where an Indo-European people had recently conquered a territory, the commons might have consisted mainly of the subjugated native inhabitants, or these might have become a class of serfs, themselves subordinate to the yeomen of the invading tribes. If this theory is correct, the Indo-Europeans must have had an evolved type of feudal society which would have needed a sedentary population as its basis, and early Indo-European settlements should be characteristic of such a society and so identifiable.[2] There are, however, objections to Palmer's conclusions. The interpretation of the relevant Linear B texts which inspired them is not undisputed;[3] among the Hittites the king was both high priest and commander-in-chief; their feudal system was paralleled in part in contemporary non-Indo-European states of the Near East; and in general some similarity of development is to be expected in aristocratic societies considerably preoccupied with war.

To sum up, linguistic palaeontology supports the general conclusion already stated about the region of origin of the first known Indo-European movements but does not delimit it more closely.

The second line of linguistic investigation which might throw light on the location of the area from which the Indo-Europeans dispersed is 'historical dialectology'. This is the reconstruction of the process by which a postulated prehistoric language differentiated into dialects, and of the development of these into the historical language-groups which represent it. In the early days of Indo-European comparative linguistics it was tacitly assumed that the initial dispersal of the Indo-Europeans took place over a short period, and that the dialects which were spoken by the

---

[1] §vi, 3.   [2] G, 6, 48 f.

[3] See M. Ventris and J. Chadwick, *Documents in Mycenaean Greek* (Cambridge, 1956), 232 ff.; Chadwick, *Minos*, 5 (1957), 117 ff. Cf. L. R. Palmer, *Interpretation of Mycenaean Greek Texts* (Oxford, 1963), 186 ff.

various groups of emigrant tribes only began to diverge considerably after they had lost contact with each other. More recent studies of the dialects of modern languages have shown that differentiation may take place in a language which is still spoken over a continuous area, and that it is a complex process. The changes in pronunciation, grammar and vocabulary which produce dialectal variation do not operate in such a way that each local dialect, as it develops, is characterized at any time by a number of idiosyncratic features none of which occurs in any other developing dialect. Each linguistic innovation makes its appearance over an area which overlaps one or more of those in which others are developing. The limit of distribution of a characteristic linguistic feature is termed an 'isogloss'; the term is also used less accurately of such a feature itself. Certain recurrent patterns of change are found in the case of languages which have differentiated within a linguistic continuum. Dialects in the central area change most rapidly; those at the periphery or in isolated areas like mountain valleys tend to be conservative, retaining archaic linguistic features. If isoglosses between the earliest known languages of the various Indo-European language-groups show this pattern, then the reasonable conclusion will be that the groups were in the same relative positions, when first attested, as the dialects from which they had evolved had been in the 'homeland'; and therefore that the initial dispersal was radial, from an area which was centrally placed in relation to the earliest known historical locations of the groups. If a language was in use at the periphery of the whole region in which Indo-European idioms were spoken at the end of the first millennium B.C. and if it has characteristics which are best explained as archaic, it may be considered probable that the dialect ancestral to it was carried out of the 'homeland' at a relatively early date. On the other hand, if a single language or group at the periphery shares characteristic features with a number which form a central group, it is likely that it was brought to its peripheral position by a late migration.

One difference between two sets of historical Indo-European language-groups was long regarded as fundamental. It is defined as the 'centum–satəm' distinction.[1] It was observed in the middle of the last century that the Germanic, Celtic, Italic and Greek languages (the 'centum' languages) have two series of dorsal consonants, velars and labio-velars[2] (or sounds or sequences

[1] G, 3, 28; G, 7, 22 f.; §1, 10, 421 ff.; satəm is the Avestan word for 'hundred'.
[2] I.e. a consonant pronounced with simultaneous closure of the lips and at the back of the mouth.

clearly derived from them); while the Baltic, Slavonic and Indo-
Iranian groups, Albanian and Armenian (the 'satəm' languages)
have simple velars (or derivatives) corresponding to the labio-
velars of the 'centum' languages, and, contrasting with these
velars, palatal consonants (e.g. like *ch* in English *church*) or
derivatives of them, which correspond to the velars of languages
of the 'centum' group (cf. Gk. κλέ(ϝ)ος, Old Irish *clu*, Latin
cluor, Sanskrit *śravas*, Old Slavonic *slovo*, with meanings 'glory',
'hear' and 'word'; Latin *linquo*, Greek λείπω with change of *k^w
to *p*, Lithuanian *liekù*, Armenian *elikh*, Sanskrit *rinákti*, 'leave').
Since the two sets of languages formed western and eastern groups,
it appeared that the first important differentiation of Indo-
European was into corresponding groups of dialects, probably
spoken by two bodies of tribes that lost contact at an early stage.
The rediscovery of Hittite and Tocharian proved hard for this
sancta simplicitas: both languages reappeared east of the Bosphorus
and both are undeniably 'centum' according to the accepted
criteria (cf. Hittite *kuis*, Latin *quis*, 'who'; Tocharian *kante*,
Latin *centum*).

The first comprehensive study of the distribution of isoglosses
over the recognized Indo-European language-groups gave the
expected result in one respect. Many clear isoglosses link groups
which are geographically adjacent: e.g. the Italic and Celtic
groups and no others have future tenses in *-bh-* (cf. Latin *amabo*,
Old Irish *leicfea*); the Germanic, Baltic and Slavonic alone have
instrumental or dative plural case-forms of nouns in *-m-* (cf.
Gothic *sunum*, Lithuanian *sunumis*, Old Slavonic *synūmi*).[1] This
suggests that the peoples who spoke the languages which were
ancestral to the main known groups reached their early historical
territories by migrations out of a region situated centrally among
these. Tocharian, however, breaks the pattern, since it has the
'centum' system of dorsal consonants although it is separated
from the other, western, 'centum' groups by the Baltic, Slavonic
and Iranian areas. At first it was supposed that Tocharian must
have been brought to Turkestān by a long, secondary migration
across this 'satəm' territory, similar to that which carried a
Celtic language across Europe to Galatia in the third century B.C.

More recent studies have led to discrepant conclusions.
W. Porzig considers that isoglosses confined to the Germanic,
Celtic, Italic and Baltic groups (or to some among these) are so
numerous as to indicate that the Indo-Europeans dispersed from
a region in central or north-western Europe, and that the first

[1] §I, 11.

large-scale migrations were a series which carried Indo-Iranian, Hittite, Armenian, Greek and Phrygian eastwards.[1]

According to a second interpretation, which the present writer finds more satisfactory, similarities in morphology between the Celtic, Italic and Hittite-Luwian groups and Tocharian imply that the dialects from which these evolved were in peripheral positions in the Indo-European continuum and were probably the first to be carried out of it.[2] The derivative languages share a feature which formerly appeared to be confined to Italic and Celtic, and so to be an innovation in them: medio-passive or passive verbal forms characterized by -r(-); cf. Latin *amatur*, Old Irish *carthir*, 'is loved'; Hittite *kittari*, 'lies' (cf. Greek κεῖται); Tocharian *yatar*, 'makes'. In this they contrast with Greek and with Indo-Iranian, Germanic and Slavonic languages, in which present or other 'primary' medio-passive (or derivative) forms mainly end in reflexes of *-ai* or, more probably, *-oi* (cf. Greek φέρεται, Sanskrit *bharate*, Gothic *bairada*). It seems significant that they share three further morphological features: third person plural forms of active perfect or past tenses in -r(-) (cf. Latin *vixere*, 'lived'; Old Irish *lotar*, 'went'; Hittite *eper*, 'took'; Tocharian *koṣtar*, 'struck'; these also occur in the Sanskrit perfect); relative pronouns in *$k^w i$- or *$k^w o$- (cf. Hittite *kuis*, Latin *quis*, Tocharian *kus*; contrast Sanskrit *yas*, Greek ὅς, Old Slavonic *i-že*); and relatively incomplete systems of special feminine grammatical forms.[3] (Hittite and Luwian do not have formally distinct masculine and feminine grammatical genders.) The peripheral distribution of these features within the early historical region of Indo-European speech strongly suggests they are archaic. If this is accepted, several features which have generally been regarded as primitive because they are common to Greek and Sanskrit (e.g. the special feminine forms of the participles) will more reasonably be explained as innovations, which developed in a number of dialects which remained in the original continuum and in contact until a late stage, while other dialects, which were at the periphery or had already been carried outside the continuum, were unaffected and preserved the characteristics of an early phase of Indo-European.

This interpretation gives some support to the view that the 'homeland' was centrally situated relative to the areas in which the

[1] §I, 14, 213 ff. Cf. G, 3, 32 ff.
[2] G, 3, 30 f.; §I, 9. The question will be discussed in the author's forthcoming books, *The Indo-Europeans* and *The Anatolian Languages*.
[3] §II, 11, vol. I, 76 ff., 135 ff., 167 f.; §II, 49, 82, 115, 141, 145 ff.

Celtic and Italic languages, Hittite, and Tocharian are first attested. It suggests that the first Indo-European movements into Anatolia were among the earliest of all, and that proto-Celtic, proto-Italic and proto-Tocharian were in use in peripheral parts of the Indo-European-speaking region early in the second millennium B.C. The peripheral position of the Indic languages in the first millennium B.C. may appear discrepant, but proto-Indic may not have been introduced into northern India until the last quarter of the second millennium.[1] From the standpoint of linguistic method the decisive question in these studies is whether a large number of isoglosses of various kinds between languages is the more reliable indication of close or prolonged prehistoric contact between them, or similarities which lie mainly in morphology and basic syntax; that is, whether it is thought that changes in these latter aspects are less likely to spread from one language to another than are individual words or idioms. The similarities between the 'European' Indo-European languages are largely in vocabulary and may well result from borrowing in comparatively late times. Those between the Celtic and Italic languages, Hittite, and Tocharian seem more likely to have been inherited from the time of Indo-European unity. If these languages are considered archaic, it is natural to regard the 'centum' system of dorsal consonants as that of Indo-European at an early stage of its development and to explain the 'satəm' system as the result of secondary changes which took place only in certain dialects within a residual group. This implies that the peoples who spoke the dialects from which Greek and the Germanic, Baltic, Slavonic and Indo-Iranian groups evolved remained in contact within the original continuum until relatively late. A number of isoglosses indicate specially close or late contact between the dialects which were ancestral to Greek, Armenian, Phrygian and Iranian.[2]

One further linguistic problem should be mentioned: the question whether Indo-European was either genetically related to, or in contact with, any other prehistoric 'proto-language' from which a recognized historical language-group evolved. There are a few impressive similarities in vocabulary between individual Indo-European languages and some of those which make up the Uralic family (of which the Finno-Ugric is the best known branch).[3] Most of these isoglosses are between Uralic languages and Iranian only, but some of them may well go back to a time when Indo-European was still in use in its original continuum, although already somewhat differentiated into dialects. They

[1] See pp. 851 ff.   [2] G, 3, 37.   [3] §I, 2, 125 ff.; §I, 4; §I, 7; §III, 6, 37 f.

certainly suggest that the Indo-European and proto-Uralic languages were in contact in late prehistoric times, even if they had not evolved from the same still earlier 'ancestor'. If it is shown that they were in contact while Indo-European was still substantially homogeneous, this will support the view that the Indo-European 'homeland' lay in the Pontic region. The Finno-Ugrians appear to have lived in the vicinity of the River Oka in the Russian Soviet Socialist Republic before they migrated northward in the latter part of the first millennium B.C. and in the following centuries.[1]

Theories that Indo-European was derived from a language which was also ancestral to the Hamito-Semitic family or to a postulated Caucasic group seem premature. 'Proto-Semitic' has not yet been reconstructed even as precisely as Indo-European, and it is still not clear whether the languages of the Caucasus are a genetically related group. No-one has yet demonstrated systematic correspondence in grammatical or phonetic structure between the Indo-European languages and either the Semitic group as a whole or any considerable group of Caucasian languages. Such similarities in vocabulary as there are between early Indo-European languages and Semitic may well be the result of borrowing in the course of trade.[2]

(b) ARCHAEOLOGICAL EVIDENCE

The linguistic evidence which has just been reviewed locates the Indo-European 'homeland' only within wide limits. It restricts it to a zone which lies between the Alps and the sub-arctic regions, from central Europe in the west to the Urals in the east. Closer identifications depend on particular theories about the pre-historic differentiation of Indo-European or on the conclusion that it was in close contact with proto-Uralic.

Recent attempts to correlate archaeological and linguistic evidence about its position have also resulted in several different conclusions. One view is that the initial expansion took place between c. 4000 and 2750 B.C. and that Indo-European peoples already occupied a considerable territory in eastern and south-eastern Europe by c. 2500 B.C. at the latest.[3] The migrations which are thought to have introduced Indo-European languages into eastern Mediterranean and Near Eastern countries are regarded

---

[1] G, 2, 178; §v, 4, 35 ff.; §v, 8, 177 ff.

[2] G, 3, 36; G, 4, 33 f., 37 ff.; §1, 3. See also E. Polomé in W. Winter, *Evidence for Laryngeals* (2nd ed., The Hague, 1965), 11 f.

[3] G, 1, 138 ff.; G, 4, 76 ff., 341 ff.

as secondary movements out of it. A second view puts the 'homeland' in the northern part of central Europe. P. Thieme identifies it with the upper valleys of the rivers Vistula, Oder, Elbe and Weser. He argues that it must have been small because the Indo-Europeans were not specialized nomads who would have ranged over an extensive territory.[1] A third view regards the Pontic region as the area of origin. The first theory allows ample time for the linguistic differentiation which had already taken place in Hittite and Greek by the middle of the second millennium. The serious objection to it is that the neolithic and early chalco-lithic cultures of south-eastern and central Europe and the Ukraine imply societies and ways of life very different from those which we find among the earliest known historical Indo-European peoples. All those cultures (the Vinča, Starčevo and 'Linear Pottery'/ 'Bandkeramik' groups in the fourth millennium; the Cucuţeni, Tripolye, Lengyel and others in the third) are typical of peasant communities, living by agriculture rather than stock-raising, occupying the same sites for long periods and migrating only sporadically and slowly as they needed new lands to cultivate. Their settlements were mainly unfortified and nothing suggests that they were ruled by warlike aristocracies of the kind which the Iliad and the Vedic Hymns show us. There is no obvious evidence of large-scale migrations out of the region in question in the second half of the third millennium. If Indo-Europeans were settled in it during its long period of apparently peaceful de-velopment, then radical social changes must have occurred among them c. 2500 B.C. to produce the kind of tribal organization which would have been effective in migrations and wars of conquest. The farmers of the Lengyel culture in Czechoslovakia are thought to have developed cattle-breeding to a greater extent than their predecessors.[2] But nothing indicates a serious climatic change or general exhaustion of the land in a relevant area c. 3000–2500 B.C.

It is generally agreed that the people who developed the earliest agricultural civilizations of the south-east (the Vinča and the Starčevo) were immigrants from Anatolia. If so, it is most unlikely that they spoke Indo-European languages. Anatolia can hardly have been an original centre of Indo-European speech.[3] If Indo-European was the language of any Danubian or adjacent region in the third millennium it must presumably have been derived from that of some mesolithic population with which immigrants from the south-east had amalgamated. Thieme's theory of a northern

[1] G, 8, 562 ff. (28 ff.).   [2] §v, 15, 53 ff.   [3] See pp. 832, 843.

29

'homeland' is based on linguistic suppositions which the present author finds unconvincing: the deductions that Indo-European first differentiated into 'western' and 'eastern' groups of dialects and that the Indo-Europeans used for the salmon the word from which the German *Lachs* is derived.[1] No archaeological evidence indicates extensive movement southward from the Weser-Oder-Vistula region *c.* 2000 B.C.

From the linguistic standpoint there is much to be said for equating the 'homeland' with the Pontic area or with part of the zone of steppe lands which lies to the north-west, north and north-east of it. Such an area is a likely point of departure for the migrations which brought Indo-European languages to Greece, Anatolia and Iran, and a natural centre for the radial dispersion which, in the author's opinion, best explains the similarities and differences between the historical Indo-European language-groups. The identification has also been advocated on archaeological grounds. There was undoubtedly widespread disturbance of older cultures in the Danubian area and central Europe at the beginning of the second millennium, and some evidence points to warlike movements within the Pontic region and from it into the Danubian region *c.* 2400–1800 B.C.[2] It is suggested that the course of these migrations is marked by the following complex of cultural features: burial of the dead in particular contracted positions, often painted with red ochre, individually or in pairs or in small groups in pits, usually under a small barrow (*kurgan* in Russian); remains of domesticated horses; 'battle-axes', i.e. shaft-hole axes of particular types in stone but imitating metal prototypes; also, according to some interpretations, pottery of types classed as 'Corded Ware' (wares decorated mainly with impressions of plaited cords) or supposed prototypes of them. These features, all or in part, are traced back to the so-called 'Pit Grave', 'Ochre Grave' and 'Kurgan' cultures of the Pontic region and its eastward extension.

M. Y. Merpert concludes in a recent discussion that the characteristic 'pit grave' cultural pattern took shape in the Lower Volga region early in the third millennium and that in the first place it spread from there into the Crimea and the valleys of the Dnieper, Don, Donetz and middle Volga.[3] M. Gimbutas has suggested that the sequence of events which disseminated Indo-European languages began in the steppe lands which lie between the lower Volga and Uzbekistān. Semi-nomadic tribes of this region, the 'Kurgan' people in her terminology, supposedly

[1] See pp. 860 f.   [2] G, 5; §v, 2; §v, 12.   [3] §v, 3, 176 ff., 193 ff.

migrated into the Pontic lands *c.* 2500–2400 B.C. They dominated the people of the Mariupol ('North Pontic') culture in the eastern Ukraine, and in the northern Caucasus came under the influence of the civilized inhabitants of Transcaucasia (the upper valleys of the rivers Araxes-Aras and Murat and the Lake Van area), from whom they learnt metallurgy, including the design of the 'battle-axe', and possibly also the use of wheeled vehicles, which they certainly possessed *c.* 2300 B.C. With these, together with horses and a superior armament, they would have been well equipped for further migrations and conquests.[1]

This hypothesis of a rapid dispersal of Indo-European peoples from the Pontic region is attractive, but it has weaknesses. Merpert's reconstruction would seem to explain the linguistic phenomena more satisfactorily. If the Indo-Europeans are identified with the people of his Lower Volga group of 'pit grave' cultures, his chronology allows time for the incipient differentiation of their language into dialects, which the historical pattern of isoglosses suggests, before extensive emigration began. If Indo-European was first introduced into the eastern Pontic area and then was spread across the whole of central and northern Europe and into Anatolia and Greece by small groups of migrants during a period of some five hundred years at the most, it seems unlikely that a pattern of 'peripheral' and 'central' peculiarities in the historical languages would have resulted. The archaeological evidence offers more serious problems. The relevant finds in the Danubian region, which may be considered true assemblages of 'kurgan' features, do indicate migration from the Pontic region *c.* 2300–1900 B.C.; and, prima facie, the simultaneous appearance of 'battle-axes' and 'Corded Ware' in north-western Europe and the Baltic lands points to a similar infiltration by related warlike tribes or bands. It certainly appears to reflect some immigration of a new element from the south or south-east.[2] The 'battle-axe' cannot well be a diagnostic of immigration from the north into Anatolia. It is ultimately of Near Eastern origin and may have been diffused into Anatolia and from there into south-eastern Europe by the north-western route across the Bosphorus, as well as across the Caucasus, even before Indo-Europeans could have adopted it north of the Black Sea. The objections to regarding the 'battle-axe' movements into northern and north-western Europe as part of a primary Indo-European dispersal lie in their date and in the question of the origin of the 'Corded Ware' which they apparently introduced; and more generally in the wider

[1] §v, 7.　　　　　　[2] §v, 18, 98 ff.; §v, 19, 20 ff.

problem of the definition and relative chronology of all the cultures classed as 'Corded Ware', 'Globular Amphora', 'Pit Grave', 'Ochre Grave' and 'Kurgan'. Carbon 14 dates for the appearance of 'battle-axe' groups in Denmark and the Netherlands lie around c. 2400 B.C.[1] This is hardly compatible with Gimbutas's date of c. 2400–2300 B.C. for the arrival of 'proto-Kurgan' immigrants in the eastern Pontic region, if that is precise. Merpert's longer chronology makes a rather rapid expansion from the Ukraine to north-western Europe conceivable, if his second Pontic phase may be dated c. 2750–2500 B.C.

The problem of the origin of 'Corded Wares' is still more troublesome. Both Gimbutas and Merpert consider that their characteristic style of decoration evolved from that of the ovoid pottery of the 'Pit Grave' cultures in the Middle Dnieper area, and regard this region as the point of origin of important Indo-European movements, perhaps those which introduced proto-Germanic, proto-Baltic and proto-Slavonic languages into north-western and northern central Europe.[2] However, it is still uncertain whether the characteristic decorative technique and motifs of European 'Corded Wares' are to be derived from those of 'pit grave' pottery, or whether all wares which have been classed as 'corded' belong to the same tradition. L. Kilian has shown that at two sites in the western Ukraine, Jankoviči and Jackowica, which have been thought to show a transition from 'pit grave' to 'corded' pottery, the types which occur belong to late phases of the two traditions, which implies that both the 'Corded Ware' and the 'Pit Grave' cultures had had some centuries of independent development by the time in question.[3] Pottery belonging to earlier phases of the two cultures has not been reported from one and the same site. If, as Kilian believes, the type of 'Corded Ware' found at Jackowica had evolved in central Germany, and if the 'battle-axe' invaders of northern Europe were Indo-European groups ultimately of Pontic origin, then the course of Indo-European migration into Europe was complex. Indo-European immigrants from the east must have amalgamated with native peoples in one or more areas in central or northern Europe, which then became points of departure for further migrations. 'Reflux' movements to the south and southeast would then have carried developed 'corded' pottery to the Ukraine, into areas where 'pit grave' traditions survived. The main argument against regarding northern or central Europe as

---

[1] §v, 19, 25.   [2] G, 5, 820 ff.; §v, 3, 180 ff.; §v, 7.
[3] §v, 9, 163 ff.; §v, 11, 53 ff.

the 'homeland' is that no archaeological evidence indicates an extensive migration out of it to the south-east, or any movement out of it which occurred early enough to introduce proto-Hittite or proto-Luwian into Anatolia even by c. 2000 B.C.

The 'Indo-European homeland' must therefore be considered still unidentified. It is possible that the Indo-Europeans were a people who ranged over a wide section of the steppe belt, from which groups of their tribes migrated both into northern Europe and into the Pontic region at the beginning of the third millennium. It seems probable, however, that the Pontic region was an important area of origin of Indo-European movements c. 2500–2000 B.C. even if the continuum over which the Indo-European language had developed previously was more extensive. Steppe or plain country, rather than the forests and swamps of northern Europe, seems the more natural environment for the development of a migratory way of life utilizing the horse and primitive waggons. A more definite identification of the region from which the Indo-European peoples originally dispersed will not be possible until a clear account can be given of the evolution of neolithic, chalcolithic and Bronze Age cultures over the whole of the region which extends from western Europe to Central Asia.

V. THE IMPACT OF THE NORTHERNERS

The prehistoric Indo-European movements which linguistic comparison implies are still proving difficult to identify and reconstruct. It does not appear that Indo-European peoples brought any important practical innovation into Mediterranean and Near Eastern countries except the use of the horse. Did their arrival have any lasting effect beyond causing change of language? They were evidently able to establish themselves as rulers even where they were not numerous enough to affect the ethnic characteristics of the pre-existing population or its basic culture. What made them successful conquerors or acceptable leaders? It now seems unlikely that they already had an effective war-chariot. Carts with solid wheels were in use in parts of the Pontic and Danubian regions by c. 2250 B.C. but not fast vehicles with spoked wheels,[1] according to present evidence. These could hardly have been made without good bronze tools. The war-chariot was probably developed early in the second millennium in an area which knew the horse and was at least at the edge of the contemporary region

[1] §v, 19, 76 ff.

of advanced Bronze Age civilization, perhaps in north-eastern Syria or northern Mesopotamia (Hurrian areas) or Iran.[1] However, possession of well-trained horses may itself have given the northern peoples a sufficient military advantage. Even if they could not fight effectively on horseback, they may have used their horses for raiding and riding into battle. It has been assumed too readily that Bronze Age peoples would not have developed the chariot if they had previously been accustomed to riding. The chariot was probably devised as a better means of using the breeds of horse which were available in flat country. It was superseded in the first millennium B.C. partly because many communities could no longer afford the cost of chariotry, partly because stronger breeds of horse and better harness and bits had made cavalry more effective. At the end of the third millennium the horse was still a novelty. Even rather inefficient horsemen on small mounts would have spread terror by their raids and attacks, and they would have been able to migrate rapidly and defeat and dominate settled peoples much more numerous than themselves.

The Indo-Europeans also appear to have developed a kind of tribal society which made for effective leadership in war. Deductions about their social organization should be cautious. They are based on what is known of Indo-European communities living a thousand years or more after the presumed primary movements, and the migrations themselves would have promoted parallel development of institutions which made for success in minor wars. However, the same general pattern of monarchy is found among the Hittites of the sixteenth century B.C., in classical Greek communities of a conservative kind, and again among the early Romans, the Macedonians in the fifth century B.C., and the Germans five hundred years later.[2] The king appears to have been chosen for his ability as a leader in war. This is indicated by the formal acceptance which the earliest Macedonian kings received from their nobles, even though the succession had become essentially hereditary. All the peoples mentioned had a council of elders or nobles, or, as in the case of the Germans, an assembly of all free men of the tribe, or both. Where both existed, the 'council' advised the king, and the 'assembly' approved or rejected what he proposed. Classical Sparta had its *gerousia* ('council of elders') and an *apella* which all male citizens over thirty could attend. Rome had its *senatus* and *comitia*. Hittite texts of the Old Kingdom mention two councils: the *pankuš* (apparently meaning 'the

---

[1] §II, 30, 8 ff.; §VI, 1, 68–71, 77; §VI, 5; §VI, 6.
[2] G, 3, 24 f.; §VI, 3; see also p. 863.

whole'; cf. Sanskrit *bahus*, 'great') and the *tuliyaš*. Khattushilish I commends his chosen successor to the *pankuš* in his 'Testament'. Telepinush, *c.* 1500 B.C., calls on the *pankuš* to put a prince and perhaps even a king on trial before the *tuliyaš* for his 'head' if he has murdered a relative.[1] These passages suggest that the *pankuš* at least still had important powers in the Old Kingdom period and formally approved the king's successor. But in both cases the circumstances are exceptional. Khattushilish had previously disinherited his son. Telepinush was attempting to end dissension and dynastic murder in the royal family and may have tried to give new powers to the *pankuš* and the *tuliyaš*. The custom of having both a hereditary, priestly king and an elected war-leader does not necessarily go back to Indo-European times. The Hittite king was both high priest and commander-in-chief. It is also doubtful whether the threefold social division into classes of nobles, free, land-owning yeomen, and serfs or non-citizens, which is found among the Hittites and the Germans and in some early Greek communities, was inherited. It would have developed naturally in any society in which invaders had dominated an alien population.

Indo-European migrants do not appear to have disseminated any important body of religious practices or myths. Their chief deity was evidently a god of the sky and the storm: Zeus in the Greek pantheon, Juppiter ('father Dyeus')[2] among the Romans, Dyaus in India. The Greeks and the Indic peoples also worshipped similar 'heavenly twins', the Dioskouroi and the Vedic Nāsatyā and Aśvinau. Indic and Iranian languages share some ancient religious and social vocabulary with the Celtic and Italic, e.g. a word for some kind of priest, Latin *flamen*, Sanskrit *brahman*.[3]

In general Indo-European peoples who moved into civilized lands adopted the culture and beliefs of the peoples whom they conquered, or assimilated their own to them. Their contribution lay in introducing or stimulating more effective political organization. In Anatolia Indo-European immigration was followed within a few centuries by the formation of what was almost certainly the first large, coherent state north of the Taurus, the kingdom of Khatti. 'Aryans' became the leaders of Hurrian migrants and conquerors in Syria. The Medes and Persians were the first peoples of Iran to impose their rule on Mesopotamians without becoming culturally assimilated themselves, and the Persians far surpassed the Babylonians and the Assyrians as organizers of an

---

[1] §II, 47, 29 f., 207 ff.; §II, 48, 190 f.; §VI, 2; *C.A.H.* II³, ch. VI, sect. v; *C.A.H.* II³, ch. XXIV, sect. v.   [2] Derived from earlier *Dyeus-pater.

[3] G, 2, 80 ff.; §I, 10, 399 ff.; §I, 16.

empire. The strong fortifications of Mycenaean cities and the extent of Mycenaean trade and colonization speak for enterprise and organizing ability which went well beyond what the Minoans had shown. Moreover, in two areas, central Anatolia and Greece, Indo-European conquest notably accelerated cultural borrowing from highly civilized countries in the second millennium B.C. To judge by the rich offerings in Mycenaean, Scythian and Celtic 'royal graves', the warrior aristocrats of early Indo-European peoples had a well-developed taste for 'conspicuous consumption'. This led them to trade with the wealthier peoples of the south when they could not conquer them, and the borrowing of more advanced techniques and artistic styles and even of systems of writing followed naturally. The Indo-European migrations at the beginning of the second millennium caused the frontiers of urban civilization to advance, even if those of c. 1300–1000 B.C. temporarily pushed them back.

Speculation about an Indo-European or northern 'spiritual' contribution to the thought and society of the Mediterranean world is now suspect. However, peoples who had for some centuries lived a semi-nomadic existence in steppe lands would certainly have differed in outlook and society from the long-established peasant and urban communities of the south, and it would be surprising if the northerners did not cause some change in attitudes and customs in the lands in which they settled. At least, rulers and aristocrats of northern origin were perhaps less bound by religious conservatism than their native predecessors. Throughout the Near East in the second millennium the role of the king as military leader was emphasized at the expense of his functions as priest. The relatively equalitarian character which may be deduced for Indo-European tribal monarchy may also have had some effect. Although Hittite monarchy and religion conform closely to Mesopotamian patterns by the fourteenth century, non-Mesopotamian traits may be seen in the exceptionally strong anthropomorphic conception of the gods which allowed a Hittite king to address them as beings who might be brought to reason like a liberal human ruler,[1] and perhaps also in certain relatively humane tendencies in law and the treatment of enemies. Iranians produced in Zoroastrianism one of the first religions based on ethical principles rather than on the conception of gods as capricious forces of nature. In Greece, it may well have been the Indo-European pattern of tribal kingship which provided the basis from which city-state democracy developed, when the Greeks for the second time reached an urban level of civilization.

[1] §III, 12, 394 ff.

BIBLIOGRAPHY

ABBREVIATIONS

A.A.S.   *Annales archéologiques de Syrie*

Abh. Berlin (München, etc.).   *Abhandlungen der Preussischen (Bayerischen, etc.) Akademie der Wissenschaften, Phil.-hist. Klasse*

Abh. D.O.G.   *Abhandlungen der Deutschen Orient-Gesellschaft*

Abh. Mainz.   *Abhandlungen der Preussischen Akademie der Wissenschaften, Math.-naturwiss. Klasse*

Acta Or.   *Acta Orientalia*

Äg. Abh.   *Ägyptologische Abhandlung*

Ägyptol. Forsch.   *Ägyptologische Forschungen*

A.J.   *Antiquaries Journal*

A.J.A.   *American Journal of Archaeology*

A.J.S.L.   *American Journal of Semitic Languages and Literatures*

Alte Or.   *Der Alte Orient*

An. Aeg.   *Analecta Aegyptiaca*

An. Biblica.   *Analecta Biblica*

An. Or.   *Analecta Orientalia*

Anc. Egypt.   *Ancient Egypt* (continued as *Ancient Egypt and the East*)

A.N.E.T.   *Ancient Near Eastern Texts relating to the Old Testament*

Ann. Arch. Anthr.   *Annals of Archaeology and Anthropology* (Liverpool)

Ann. Arch. de Syrie.   *Annales Archéologiques de Syrie*

Ann. A.S.O.R.   *Annual of the American Schools of Oriental Research*

Ann. D.A.J.   *Annual of the Department of Antiquities of Jordan*

Ann. Inst. phil. hist. or.   *Annuaire de l'Institut de philologie et d'histoire orientales* (later *Annuaire...orientales et slaves*)

Ann. Mus. Guimet.   *Annales du Musée Guimet*

Ann. P.E.F.   *Annual of the Palestine Exploration Fund*

Ann. Serv.   *Annales du Service des Antiquités de l'Égypte*

Antiq.   *Antiquity*

A.O.S.   *American Oriental Series; American Oriental Society*

Arch. Anz.   *Archäologischer Anzeiger.* Beiblatt zum *Jahrbuch des deutschen Archäologischen Instituts*

Arch. Delt.   Ἀρχαιολογικὸν Δελτίον

Arch. Eph.   (Ἀρχ. Ἐφ.) Ἀρχαιολογικὴ Ἐφημερίς

Arch. f. äg. Arch.   *Archiv für ägyptische Archäologie*

Arch. f. Or.   *Archiv für Orientforschung*

Arch. hist. dr. or.   *Archives d'histoire du droit oriental*

Arch. Orient.   *Archiv Orientální*

Arch. Reports.   *Archaeological Reports of the Society for Hellenic Studies*

A.R.M.   *Archives royales de Mari*

A.R.M.T.   *Archives royales de Mari* (translation vols.)

Art. A.   *Artibus Asiae*

A. St.   *Anatolian Studies*

Ath. Mitt.   *Athenische Mitteilungen, Mitteilungen des deutschen archäologischen Instituts, Athenische Abteilung*

[877]

B.C.H.   *Bulletin de Correspondance hellénique*

Berichte Leipzig   *Berichte über die Verhandlungen der Sächsischen Akademie der Wissenschaften zu Leipzig. Phil.-hist. Klasse*

Bibl. Aeg.   *Bibliotheca Aegyptiaca*

B.I.N.   *Babylonian inscriptions in the collection of J. B. Nies, Yale University*

Bi. Or.   *Bibliotheca Orientalis*

B.M. Quart.   *British Museum Quarterly*

Bo. Stu.   *Boghazköi-Studien*

Boll. d'Arte.   *Bollettino d'Arte*

B.S.A.   *Annual of the British School of Archaeology at Athens*

B.S.A. Egypt.   *British School of Archaeology, Egypt*

Bull. A.S.O.R.   *Bulletin of the American Schools of Oriental Research*

Bull. I.E.S.   *Bulletin of the Israel Exploration Society*

Bull. Inst. Cl. St.   *Bulletin of the Institute of Classical Studies*

Bull. Inst. d'Ég.   *Bulletin de l'Institut d'Égypte*

Bull. Inst. fr. Caire.   *Bulletin de l'Institut français d'archéologie orientale, Le Caire*

Bull. M.B.   *Bulletin du Musée de Beyrouth*

Bull. M.F.A.   *Bulletin of the Museum of Fine Arts* (Boston)

Bull. M.M.A.   *Bulletin of the Metropolitan Museum of Art* (New York)

Bull. Ryl. Libr.   *Bulletin of the John Rylands Library* (Manchester)

Bull. S.O.A.S.   *Bulletin of the School of Oriental and African Studies* (London)

Bull. Soc. fr. égyptol.   *Bulletin de la Société française d'Égyptologie*

C.A.D.   *The Assyrian Dictionary of the Oriental Institute of the University of Chicago*

C.A.H.   *Cambridge Ancient History*

Cah. H.M.   *Cahiers d'histoire mondiale*

C.C.G.   *Cairo Museum, Catalogue général des Antiquités Égyptiennes*

Chron. d'Ég.   *Chronique d'Égypte*

C.-R. Ac. Inscr. B.-L.   *Comptes-Rendus de l'Académie des Inscriptions et Belles-Lettres*

C.-R. Rencontr. Assyriol. Internat.   *Compte-Rendu de la* 1re (2e, 3e...) *Rencontre assyriologique Internationale*

C.T.   *Cuneiform Texts from Babylonian Tablets in the British Museum*

Denkschr. Wien.   *Denkschriften des kaiserlichen Akademie der Wissenschaften in Wien*

E.E.F.   *Egypt Exploration Fund*

E.E.S.   *Egypt Exploration Society*

E.R.A.   *Egyptian Research Account*

Flles Inst. Fr. Caire.   *Fouilles de l'Institut français du Caire*

G.G.A.   *Göttingische gelehrte Anzeigen*

G.J.   *Geographical Journal*

Harv. Stud. Class. Phil.   *Harvard Studies in Classical Philology*

Harv. Theol. Rev.   *Harvard Theological Review*

H.U.C.A.   *Hebrew Union College Annual*

I.E.J.   *Israel Exploration Journal*

Ill. Ldn News.   *Illustrated London News*

Jahrb. des d. arch. Inst.   *Jahrbuch des deutschen archäologischen Instituts*

J. Bibl. Lit.   *Journal of Biblical Literature and Exegesis*

J.A.O.S.   *Journal of the American Oriental Society*

J.C.S.   *Journal of Cuneiform Studies*

J.E.A.   *Journal of Egyptian Archaeology*

J.E.O.L.   *Jaarbericht van het Vooraziatisch-Egyptisch Genootschap 'Ex Oriente Lux'*

J.E.S.H.O. *Journal of the Economic and Social History of the Orient*
J.H.S. *Journal of Hellenic Studies*
J.N.E.S. *Journal of Near Eastern Studies*
J.P.O.S. *Journal of the Palestine Oriental Society*
J.R.A.S. *Journal of the Royal Asiatic Society*
J.S.O.R. *Journal of the Society of Oriental Research*
J.W.H. *Journal of World History*
K.F. *Kleinasiatische Forschungen*
Kgl. Dan. Vid. Selsk., hist.-fil. Medd. *Konglige Danske videnskaplige Selskap, historisk-filosofiska Meddelninger*
L.S.S. *Leipziger semitistische Studien*
M.A.D.G. *Mitteilungen der Altorientalischen Gesellschaft*
M.C.S. *Manchester Cuneiform Studies*
M.D.O.G. *Mitteilungen der Deutschen Orient-Gesellschaft*
Mél. Dussaud. *Mélanges Syriens offerts à M. R. Dussaud*
Mél. Maspero. *Mélanges Maspero (Mém. Inst. fr. 66–8)*
Mél. Polotsky. *Studies in Egyptology and Linguistics in honour of H. J. Polotsky*
Mém. Ac. Inscr. B.-L. *Mémoires de l'Académie des Inscriptions et Belles-Lettres*
Mém. D. Iran. *Mémoires de la Délégation en Iran*
Mém. D.P. *Mémoires de la Délégation en Perse*
Mém. Inst. fr. Caire. *Mémoires publiés par les membres de l'Institut français d'archéologie orientale du Caire*
Mém. Miss. fr. Caire. *Mémoires publiés par les membres de la Mission archéologique française au Caire*
Metr. Mus. Studies. *Metropolitan Museum Studies*
Mitt. des d. arch. Inst. *Mitteilungen des deutschen archäologischen Instituts*
Mitt. deutsch. Inst. Kairo. *Mitteilungen des deutschen Instituts für ägyptische Altertumskunde in Kairo*
M.J. *Museum Journal, University of Pennsylvania*
Mon. Piot. *Fondation Eugène Piot. (Académie des Inscriptions et Belles-Lettres.) Monuments et mémoires*
M.S.L. *Materialien zum Sumerischen Lexikon*
M.V.A[e].G. *Mitteilungen der vorderasiatisch-ägyptischen Gesellschaft*
Nachr. Göttingen. *Nachrichten von der Gesellschaft der Wissenschaften zu Göttingen, Phil.-hist. Klasse*
O.E.C.T. *Oxford Editions of Cuneiform Texts*
O.I.C. *Oriental Institute Communications*
O.I.P. *Oriental Institute Publications*
O.L.Z. *Orientalistische Literaturzeitung*
Op. Ath. *Opuscula Atheniensia. Acta Instituti Atheniensis Regni Sueciae*
Or. *Orientalia*
Or. antiq. *Oriens antiquus*
Or. Suecana. *Orientalia Suecana*
Öster. Akad. Wiss., Phil.-hist. Klasse. *Sitzungsberichte der Österreichischen Akademie der Wissenschaften, Phil.-hist. Klasse*
P.B.S. *University of Pennsylvania. The University Museum. Publications of the Babylonian Section*
P.E.F.Q.S. *Palestine Exploration Fund, Quarterly Statement*
P.E.Q. *Palestine Exploration Quarterly*
P.J.B. *Palästina Jahrbuch*
P.P.S. *Proceedings of the Prehistoric Society*
Praktika Arch. Et. Πρακτικὰ τῆς ἐν Ἀθήναις Ἀρχαιολογικῆς Ἑταιρείας

Proc. Amer. Philosoph. Soc.   *Proceedings of the American Philosophical Society*

Proc. Brit. Acad.   *Proceedings of the British Academy*

Proc. Linn. Soc.   *Proceedings of the Linnean Society of London*

P.S.B.A.   *Proceedings of the Society of Biblical Archaeology*

Pub. M.M.A.E.E.   *Publications of the Metropolitan Museum of Art, Egyptian Expedition*

P.W.   Pauly–Wissowa–Kroll–Mittelhaus, *Real-encyclopädie der classischen Altertumswissenschaft*

Q.D.A.P.   *Quarterly of the Department of Antiquities of Palestine*

R.A.   *Revue d'Assyriologie et d'Archéologie orientale*

R.D.A.C.   *Report of the Department of Antiquities, Cyprus*

Rec. Champ.   *Recueil d'études égyptologiques dédiées à la mémoire de Jean-François Champollion*

Rec. trav.   *Recueil de travaux relatifs à la philologie et à l'archéologie égyptiennes et assyriennes*

R.E.G.   *Revue des études grecques*

Rev. arch.   *Revue archéologique*

Rev. bibl.   *Revue biblique*

Rev. d'égyptol.   *Revue d'égyptologie*

Rev. ét. anc.   *Revue des études anciennes*

Rev. hist.   *Revue historique*

Rev. hist. rel.   *Revue de l'histoire des religions*

R.H.A.   *Revue hittite et asianique*

Riv. stud. or.   *Rivista degli studi orientali*

R.L.A.   *Reallexikon der Assyriologie*

S.A.O.C.   *Oriental Institute of the University of Chicago, Studies in Ancient Oriental Civilization*

Sitzungsb. Berlin (*München*, etc.)   *Sitzungsberichte der Preussischen* (*Bayerischen* etc.) *Akademie der Wissenschaften*

Sov. Arkh.   *Sovetskaya Arkhitektura*

T.C.L.   *Musée du Louvre, Départment des Antiquités orientales. Textes cunéiformes*

Top. Bibl.   B. Porter and R. L. B. Moss, *Topographical Bibliography of Ancient Egyptian Hieroglyphic Texts, Reliefs and Paintings*

Trans. Philol. Soc.   *Transactions of the Philological Society*

Trans. Phil. Soc.   *Transactions of the Philosophical Society*

T.T.A.E.D.   *Türk Tarih, Arkeologya ve Etnografya Dergisi.* (After vol. 6: *Türk Arkeoloji Dergisi*)

T. u. M.   *Texte und Materialien der Hilprecht Sammlung, Jena*

U.E.   *Ur Excavations*

U.E.T.   *Ur Excavations: Texts*

Unters.   *Untersuchungen zur Geschichte und Altertumskunde Ägyptens* (ed. K. Sethe, later H. Kees)

Urk.   *Urkunden des ägyptischen Altertums*

U.V.B.   *Uruk: vorläufiger Bericht*

V.A.B.   *Vorderasiatische Bibliothek*

V.A.S.   *Vorderasiatische Schriftdenkmäler*

We. Or.   *Die Welt des Orients*

W.O.   Wilcken, *Griechische Ostraka aus Aegypten und Nubien*

W.V.D.O.G.   *Wissenschaftliche Veröffentlichungen der Deutschen Orient-Gesellschaft*

W.Z.K.M.   *Wiener Zeitschrift für die Kunde des Morgenlandes*

Y.O.S.   *Yale Oriental Studies*

Z.A. Zeitschrift für Assyriologie und vorderasiatische Archäologie
Z.Ä.S. Zeitschrift für ägyptische Sprache und Altertumskunde
Z.A.W. Zeitschrift für alttestamentliche Wissenschaft
Z.D.M.G. Zeitschrift der Deutschen Morgenländischen Gesellschaft
Z.D.P.V. Zeitschrift des Deutschen Palästina-Vereins
Z.f. vergleich. Sprachforschung. Zeitschrift für vergleichende Sprachforschung
Z.M.R.W. Zeitschrift für Missionskunde und Religions-Wissenschaft

BIBLIOGRAPHY

CHAPTER XI

G. GENERAL

1. Borchardt, L. *Die Annalen und die zeitliche Festlegung des Alten Reiches der ägyptischen Geschichte.* Berlin, 1917.
2. Capart, J. *Primitive Art in Egypt.* London, 1905.
3. Drioton, É. and Vandier, J. *L'Égypte* ('Clio': *Introduction aux études historiques. Les peuples de l'orient méditerranéen,* 2). Ed. 3. Paris, 1952.
4. Emery, W. B. *Archaic Egypt* (Penguin Books). Harmondsworth, Middlesex, 1961.
5. Gardiner, A. H. *Ancient Egyptian Onomastica.* 3 vols. Oxford, 1947.
6. Gardiner, A. H. *Egypt of the Pharaohs.* Oxford, 1961.
7. Gardiner, A. H. *Egyptian Grammar, being an Introduction to the Study of Hieroglyphs.* Ed. 3. London, 1957.
8. Gardiner, A. H. 'Regnal Years and Civil Calendar in Pharaonic Egypt.' In *J.E.A.* 31 (1945), 11–28.
9. Griffith, F. Ll. and Petrie, W. M. F. *Two Hieroglyphic Papyri from Tanis* (E.E.F. Extra Memoir). London, 1889.
10. Griffiths, J. G. 'Remarks on the Horian Elements in the Royal Titulary.' In *Ann. Serv.* 56 (1959), 63–86.
11. Hall, H. R. *The Ancient History of the Near East.* Ed. 9. London, 1936.
12. Hölscher, W. Review of S. Passarge, *Die Urlandschaft Ägyptens und die Lokalisierung der Wiege der altägyptischen Kultur.* In *Arch. f. Or.* 14 (1941–4), 359–61.
13. Kaplony, P. *Die Inschriften der ägyptischen Frühzeit (Ägyptologische Abhandlungen herausgegeben von W. Helck und E. Otto,* Band 8). 3 vols. Wiesbaden, 1963.
14. Lucas, A. *Ancient Egyptian Materials and Industries.* Ed. 4 (revised by J. R. Harris). London, 1962.
15. Meyer, E. *Aegyptische Chronologie (Abh. Berlin,* 1904). Berlin, 1904.
16. Meyer, E. *Geschichte des Altertums,* vols. I and II. Ed. 5. Stuttgart and Berlin, 1926.
17. Müller, H. *Die formale Entwicklung der Titulatur der ägyptischen Könige* (*Ägyptol. Forsch.* 7). Glückstadt–Hamburg–New York, 1938.
18. Naville, E. 'Deux rois de la période thinite.' In *Z.Ä.S.* 47 (1910), 65–7.
19. Newberry, P. E. 'Egypt as a Field for Anthropological Research.' (Presidential Address to the Anthropological Section of the British Association, 1923.)
20. Otto, E. 'Ein Beitrag zur Deutung der ägyptischen Vor- und Frühgeschichte.' In *We. Or.* 1 (1952), 431–53.

21. Passarge, S. *Die Urlandschaft Ägyptens und die Lokalisierung der Wiege der altägyptischen Kultur.* Nova Acta Leopoldina, Neue Folge, Bd. 9, Nr. 58. Halle, 1940.
22. Petrie, W. M. F. *The Making of Egypt.* London, 1939.
23. Porter, B. and Moss, R. L. B. *Memphis* (Top. Bibl. 3). Oxford, 1931.
24. Porter, B. and Moss, R. L. B. *Upper Egypt: Sites* (Top. Bibl. 5). Oxford, 1937.
25. Quibell, J. E. *Hierakonpolis,* Part 1 (E.R.A. 4th Memoir). London, 1900.
26. Quibell, J. E. and Green, F. W. *Hierakonpolis,* Part 2 (E.R.A. 5th Memoir). London, 1902.
27. de Rougé, E. *Recherches sur les monuments qu'on peut attribuer aux six premières dynasties de Manéthon* (*Mém. Ac. Inscr. B.-L.* 25). Paris, 1866.
28. Scharff, A. und Moortgat, A. *Ägypten und Vorderasien im Altertum* (*Weltgeschichte in Einzeldarstellungen*). Munich, 1950.
29. Vikentiev, V. 'Études d'épigraphie protodynastique: II—Deux tablettes en ivoire (I dyn.) et les linteaux de Medamud (XII–XIIIe dyn.).' In *Ann. Serv.* 56 (1959), 1–30.
30. Weill, R. *La IIe et la IIIe Dynasties.* Paris, 1908.
31. Weill, R. 'Notes sur les monuments de la période thinite.' In *Rec. trav.* 29 (1907), 26–53.
32. Weill, R. *Recherches sur la Ire dynastie et les temps prépharaoniques* (*Inst. fr. Caire, Bibliothèque d'Étude,* 38). 2 vols. Cairo, 1961.
33. Yoyotte, J. 'Égypte ancienne.' In *Histoire universelle,* 1: *Des origines à l'Islam* (*Encyclopédie de la Pléiade*). Paris, 1956.

I. THE EARLY MONARCHY AND THE UNIFICATION OF EGYPT

1. Arkell, A. J. 'Was King Scorpion Menes?' In *Antiq.* 37 (1963), 31–5.
2. Baumgartel, E. J. *The Cultures of Prehistoric Egypt.* 2 vols. Oxford, 1947, 1960.
3. von Beckerath, J. '*Šmsj-Ḥrw* in der ägyptischen Vor- und Frühzeit.' In *Mitt. deutsch. Inst. Kairo,* 14 (1956) (*Festschrift zum 70. Geburtstag von Hermann Kees,* 1–10).
4. Borchardt, L. 'Das Grab des Menes.' In *Z.Ä.S.* 36 (1898), 87–105.
5. Borchardt, L. 'Ein neuer Königsname der ersten Dynastie.' In *Sitzungsb. Berlin,* 48 (1897), 1054–8.
6. Fischer, H. G. 'A Fragment of a Late Predynastic Egyptian Relief from the Eastern Delta.' In *Art. A.* 21 (1958), 64–88.
7. Gardiner, A. H. 'Horus the Beḥdetite.' In *J.E.A.* 30 (1944), 23–60.
8. Gardiner, A. H. *The Royal Canon of Turin.* Oxford, 1959.
9. Grdseloff, B. 'Notes d'épigraphie archaïque: 1. La tablette de Naqâda et le roi Ménès.' In *Ann. Serv.* 44 (1945), 279–82.
10. Gunn, B. 'Inscriptions from the Step Pyramid Site: 1. An Inscribed Statue of King Zoser.' In *Ann. Serv.* 26 (1926), 177–96; III. 'Fragments of Inscribed Vessels.' *Ibid.* 28 (1928), 153–74.
11. Helck, W. 'Gab es einen König "Menes"?' In *Z.D.M.G.* 103 (=N.F. 28, 1953), 354–9.
12. Helck, W. 'Herkunft und Deutung einiger Züge des frühägyptischen Königsbildes.' In *Anthropos,* 49 (1954), 961–91.
13. Helck, W. 'Das Horusgeleit.' In *Arch. Orient,* 18, no. 3 (1950), 120–42.
14. Helck, W. *Untersuchungen zu Manetho und den ägyptischen Königslisten* (*Unters.* 18). Berlin, 1956.
15. Helck, W. *Zur Vorstellung von der Grenze in der ägyptischen Frühgeschichte* (*Vorträge der orientalistischen Tagung in Marburg*). Hildesheim, 1951.

16. Junker, H. *Bericht über die Grabungen der kaiserlichen Akademie der Wissenschaften in Wien auf dem Friedhof in Turah, Winter 1909–1910* (*Denkschriften. Akademie der Wissenschaften in Wien. Phil.-Hist. Kl.* LVI, 1912). Vienna, 1912.

17. Junker, H. *Die politische Lehre von Memphis* (*Abh. Berlin*, 1941, Nr. 6). Berlin, 1941.

18. Kaiser, W. 'Einige Bemerkungen zur ägyptischen Frühzeit'—Part I, 'Zu den *šmsw Ḥr*'. In *Z.A.S.* 84 (1959), 119–132; *ibid.* 85 (1960), 118–37; Part II, 'Zur Frage einer über Menes hinausreichenden ägyptischen Geschichtsüberlieferung', *ibid.* 86 (1961), 39–61.

19. Kees, H. 'Zum Ursprung der sog. Horusdiener.' In *Nachr. Göttingen*, 1927, 196–207.

20. Keimer, L. 'A propos d'une palette protohistorique en schiste conservée au musée du Caire.' In *Bull. Inst. fr. Caire*, 31 (1931), 121–34.

21. Legge, F. 'The Carved Slates from Hieraconpolis and Elsewhere.' In *P.S.B.A.* 22 (1900), 125–39.

22. Newberry, P. E. 'The Horus-title of the Kings of Egypt.' In *P.S.B.A.* 1904, 295–9.

23. Newberry, P. E. 'Menes: The Founder of the Egyptian Monarchy.' In Brunton, W. and others, *Great Ones of Ancient Egypt*. London, 1929. Pp. 35–53.

24. Newberry, P. E. 'The Petty-Kingdom of the Harpoon and Egypt's Earliest Mediterranean Port.' In *Ann. Arch. Anthr.* 1 (1908), 17–22.

25. Newberry, P. E. 'Some African Species of the Genus Olea and the Original Home of the Cultivated Olive-Tree.' In *Proc. Linn. Soc.* 1937–8, 1, 3–16.

26. Newberry, P. E. 'Ta Teḥenu—"Olive Land".' In *Anc. Egypt*, 1915, pp. 97–100.

27. Petrie, W. M. F. *Ceremonial Slate Palettes* (B.S.A. Egypt, vol. 66 A). London, 1953.

28. Schott, S. *Hieroglyphen, Untersuchungen zum Ursprung der Schrift* (*Abh. Mainz*, 1950, Nr. 24). Mainz, 1951.

29. Schott, S. 'Kulturprobleme der Frühzeit Ägyptens.' In *M.D.O.G.* (Berlin), 84 (1952), 1–37.

30. Sethe, K. 'Die Horusdiener.' In *Beiträge zur ältesten Geschichte Ägyptens* (*Unters.* 3, 1). Leipzig, 1905. Pp. 3–21.

31. Sethe, K. *Urgeschichte und älteste Religion der Ägypter* (*Abh. für die Kunde des Morgenlandes*, 18, 4). Leipzig, 1930.

32. Sethe, K. 'Zur Erklärung einiger Denkmäler aus der Frühzeit der ägyptischen Kultur.' In *Z.Ä.S.* 52 (1914), 55–60.

33. Steindorff, G. 'Eine neue Art ägyptischer Kunst.' In *Aegyptiaca* (*Festschrift für Georg Ebers zum 1. März 1897*), 122–141.

34. Vikentiev, V. 'Les monuments archaïques: I. La tablette en ivoire de Naqâda.' In *Ann. Serv.* 33 (1933), 208–34.

35. Vikentiev, V. 'Les monuments archaïques: III. A propos du soi-disant nom de Ménès dans la tablette de Naqâda.' In *Ann. Serv.* 48 (1948), 665–85.

36. Waddell, W. G. *Manetho, with an English Translation* (The Loeb Classical Library). London and Cambridge (Mass.), 1940.

37. Wilson, J. A. 'Buto and Hierakonpolis in the Geography of Egypt.' In *J.N.E.S.* 14 (1955), 209–36.

II. THE FOUNDATION OF MEMPHIS

1. Erman, A. 'Historische Nachlese: 1. König Menes.' In *Z.Ä.S.* 30 (1892), 43–6.
2. Godley, A. D. *Herodotus*, with an English Translation. 4 vols. (The Loeb Classical Library). London, 1931.
3. Kees, H. *Ancient Egypt, a Cultural Topography*. London, 1961.
4. Kees, H. 'Memphis.' In *P.W.*, neue Bearbeitung begonnen von G. Wissowa: Halbband 29, cols. 660–88. Stuttgart, 1931.
5. Sethe, K. 'Menes und die Gründung von Memphis.' In *Beiträge zur ältesten Geschichte Ägyptens* (*Unters.* 3, 6). Leipzig, 1905. Pp. 121–41.
6. Waddell, W. G. 'An Account of Egypt by Diodorus the Sicilian, being the First Book of his Universal History translated into English.' In *The University of Egypt: Bulletin of the Faculty of Arts*, 1, part 1 (May, 1933), 1–47; part 2 (December, 1933), 161–218.

III. THE CEMETERIES OF ABYDOS AND SAQQARA

1. Amélineau, E. *Les nouvelles fouilles d'Abydos* (1895–98). 3 vols. Paris, 1899–1905.
2. Emery, W. B. *Great Tombs of the First Dynasty*. 3 vols. Cairo and London, 1949–58.
3. Emery, W. B. *Ḥor-Aḥa* (*Service des Antiquités de l'Égypte*: Excavations at Saqqara, 1937–8). Cairo, 1939.
4. Emery, W. B. *The Tomb of Hemaka* (*Service des Antiquités*: Excavations at Saqqara, 1935–6). Cairo, 1938.
5. Helck, W. 'Die Herkunft des abydenischen Osirisrituals.' In *Arch. Orient.* 20, nos. 1–2 (1952), 72–85.
6. Kees, H. 'Neues vom archaischen Friedhof von Sakkara.' In *O.L.Z.* 54 (1959), 565–70.
7. Kees, H. 'Zur Problematik des archaischen Friedhofes bei Sakkara.' In *O.L.Z.* 52, no. 1/2 (1957), 12–20.
8. Lauer, J.-P. 'Sur le dualisme de la monarchie égyptienne et son expression architecturale sous les premières dynasties.' In *Bull. Inst. fr. Caire*, 55 (1955), 153–171.
9. Naville, E. 'Les plus anciens monuments égyptiens.' In *Rec. trav.* 24 (1902), 109–20, and 25 (1903), 199–225.
10. Petrie, W. M. F. 'Les plus anciens rois de l'Égypte.' In *Rec. trav.* 24 (1902), 214–16.
11. Petrie, W. M. F. *The Royal Tombs of the Earliest Dynasties*, 1901, Part II. (E.E.F. 21st Memoir) and vol. of extra plates. London, 1901.
12. Petrie, W. M. F. *The Royal Tombs of the First Dynasty*, 1900. Part I (E.E.F. 18th Memoir). London, 1900.
13. Petrie, W. M. F. *Tombs of the Courtiers and Oxyrhynkhos* (B.S.A. Egypt, and E.R.A. 28th year, 1922). London, 1925.
14. Postowskaja, N. M. *Sind die Königsgräber der 1. Dynastie von Abydos Kenotaphe?* (*Zur Charakteristik der Geschichtsurkunden dieser Epoche*). (XXV. internationaler Orientalisten-Kongress, Vorträge der Delegation der Ud SSR.) Moscow, 1960.
15. Ranke, H. 'The Origin of the Egyptian Tomb Statue.' In *Harv. Theol. Rev.*, vol. 28, no. 1 (1935), 45–53.
16. Shoukry, M. A. 'The So-called Stelae of Abydos.' In *Mitt. deutsch. Inst. Kairo*, 16 (1958), 292–7.

IV. THE SUCCESSORS OF MENES

1. Amélineau, E. *Le tombeau d'Osiris*. Paris, 1899.
2. Anthes, R. 'König "Schlange", dt- Schlange und Schlangengöttin Uto.' In *Z.Ä.S.* 83 (1958), 79–82.
3. Arkell, A. J. 'Varia Sudanica.' In *J.E.A.* 36 (1950), 24–40.
4. Blackman, A. M. and Fairman, H. W. 'The Myth of Horus at Edfu II.' In *J.E.A.* 30 (1944), 5–22.
5. Borchardt, L. 'Königs Athothis asiatischer Feldzug.' In *Orientalistische Studien Fritz Hommel zum sechzigsten Geburtstag (M.V.A.G.* Jahrg. 22), 342–5.
6. Budge, E. A. W. *The Book of the Dead: The Chapters of Coming forth by Day.* 3 vols. London, 1898.
7. Černý, J. 'King "Adiebis".' (Philological and Etymological Notes II, 5.) In *Ann. Serv.* 42 (1943), 348–50.
8. Clère, J. J. 'Un graffito du roi Djet dans le désert arabique.' In *Ann. Serv.* 38 (1938), 85–93.
9. Ebbell, B. *The Papyrus Ebers, The Greatest Egyptian Medical Document.* Copenhagen, 1937.
10. Fairman, H. W. 'The Myth of Horus at Edfu I.' In *J.E.A.* 21 (1935), 26–36.
11. Fischer, H. G. 'A First Dynasty Bowl inscribed with the Group *Ḥt*.' In *Chron. d'Ég.* 36, no. 71 (1961), 19–22.
12. Gardiner, A. H. 'The Personal Name of King Serpent.' In *J.E.A.* 44 (1958), 38–9.
13. Garnot, J. S. F. 'Sur le nom de "l'Horus cobra".' In *Mitt. deutsch. Inst. Kairo*, 16 (1958), 138–46.
14. Garnot, J. S. F. 'Sur quelques noms royaux des seconde et troisième dynasties égyptiennes.' In *Bull. Inst. d'Ég.* 37 (1954–5), 317–28.
15. Gauthier, H. *Le livre des rois d'Égypte*, I. *Des origines à la fin de la XIIe Dynastie (Mém. Inst. fr. Caire*, 17). Cairo, 1907.
16. Gauthier, H. 'Quatre fragments nouveaux de la pierre de Palerme au Musée du Caire.' In *C.-R. Ac. Inscr. B.-L.* 1914, 489–96.
17. Gauthier, H. 'Quatre nouveaux fragments de la pierre de Palerme.' In *Le Musée Égyptien*, III (Cairo, 1915), 29–53.
18. Goedicke, H. 'King *Ḥwḏfꜣ?*' In *J.E.A.* 42 (1956), 50–3.
19. Goedicke, H. 'The Pharaoh *Ny-Swtḥ*.' In *Z.Ä.S.* 81 (1956), 18–24.
20. Grdseloff, B. 'Notes d'épigraphie archaïque II-VII.' In *Ann. Serv.* 44 (1945), 282–306.
21. Junker, H. 'Die Grabungen der Universität Kairo auf dem Pyramidenfeld von Giza.' In *Mitt. deutsch. Inst. Kairo*, 3 (1932), 123–49.
22. Kaplony, P. 'Sechs Königsnamen der 1. Dynastie in neuer Deutung.' In *Or. Suecana*, 7 (1958), 54–69.
23. Lacau, P. et Lauer, J.-Ph. *La pyramide à degrés*, tome IV, *Inscriptions gravées sur les vases (Inst. fr. Caire)*. 2 parts, 1959, 1961.
24. Lansing, A. 'The Egyptian Expedition: The Museum's Excavations at Hierakonpolis.' In *Bull. M.M.A.* 30 (1935), November, sect. 2, 37–45.
25. Maspero, G. 'Notes sur différents points de grammaire et d'histoire.' In *Rec. trav.* 17 (1895), 56–78.
26. Newberry, P. E. 'The Set Rebellion in the IInd Dynasty.' In *Anc. Egypt*, 1922, 40–6.
27. Newberry, P. E. 'The Wooden and Ivory Labels of the First Dynasty.' In *P.S.B.A.* 34 (1912), 279–89.

28. Newberry, P. E. 'To what Race did the Founders of Sais belong?' In *P.S.B.A.* 1906, 68–75.
29. Newberry, P. E. and Wainwright, G. A. 'King Udy-mu (Den) and the Palermo Stone.' In *Anc. Egypt*, 1914, 148–55.
30. Otto, E. 'Der Gebrauch des Königstitels *bjtj*.' In *Z.Ä.S.* 85 (1960), 143–52.
31. Petrie, W. M. F. 'New Portions of the Annals.' In *Anc. Egypt*, 1916, 114–20.
32. Reisner, G. A. 'A Scribe's Tablet found by the Hearst Expedition at Giza.' In *Z.Ä.S.* 48 (1910), 113–14.
33. Sayce, A. H. and Clarke, Somers. 'Report on Certain Excavations made at El-Kab during the Years 1901, 1902, 1903, 1904.' In *Ann. Serv.* 6 (1905), 239–72.
34. Scharff, A. 'Vorgeschichtliches zur Libyerfrage.' In *Z.Ä.S.* 61 (1926), 16–30.
35. Sethe, K. 'Die auf den Denkmälern der ältesten geschichtlichen Dynastieen vorkommenden Könige.' In *Beiträge zur ältesten Geschichte Ägyptens* (*Unters.* 3). Leipzig, 1905. Pp. 22–41.
36. Sethe, K. 'Hitherto Unnoticed Evidence Regarding Copper Works of Art of the Oldest Period of Egyptian History.' In *J.E.A.* 1 (1914), 233–6.
37. Spiegelberg, W. 'Ein neuer Denkmal aus der Frühzeit der ägyptischen Kunst.' In *Z.Ä.S.* 35 (1897), 7–11.
38. Winkler, H. A. *Rock-Drawings of Southern Upper Egypt* (E.E.S. *Archaeological Survey of Egypt*). 2 vols. London, 1938–9.
39. Wreszinski, W. *Der grosse medizinische Papyrus des Berliner Museums* (3038). Leipzig, 1909.
40. Wreszinski, W. *Der Papyrus Ebers: Umschrift, Übersetzung und Kommentar.* Leipzig, 1913.

V. ROYALTY AND THE STATE

1. Frankfort, H. *Kingship and the Gods.* Chicago, 1948.
2. Gadd, C. J. *Ideas of Divine Rule in the Ancient East* (*The Schweich Lectures of the British Academy*, 1945). London, 1948.
3. Gardiner, A. H. 'The Mansion of Life and the Master of the King's Largess.' In *J.E.A.* 24 (1938), 83–91.
4. Garstang, J. *Mahâsna and Bêt Khallâf* (E.R.A., 7th year, 1901). London, 1902.
5. Grdseloff, B. 'Notes sur deux monuments inédits de l'ancien empire.' In *Ann. Serv.* 42 (1943), 107–25.
6. Helck, W. *Untersuchungen zu den Beamtentiteln des ägyptischen alten Reiches* (*Ägyptol. Forsch.* 18). Glückstadt–Hamburg–New York, 1954.
7. Junker, H. *Gîza* (*Bericht über die von der Akademie der Wissenschaften in Wien...unternommenen Grabungen auf dem Friedhof des alten Reiches bei den Pyramiden von Gîza*, vols. I–XII). Vienna and Leipzig, 1929–55.
8. Kees, H. 'Archaisches ⳛ = 𓀻 ⳛ 𓀾 "Erzieher"?' In *Z.Ä.S.* 82 (1957), 58–62.
9. Kees, H. *Kulturgeschichte des alten Orients, Ägypten* (*Handbuch der Altertumswissenschaft*). Munich, 1923.
10. Moret, A. *Du caractère religieux de la royauté pharaonique.* Paris, 1902.
11. Pirenne, J. *Histoire des institutions et du droit privé de l'ancienne Égypte*, vol. I, *Des origines à la fin de la IVe Dynastie.* Brussels, 1932.
12. Quibell, J. E. 'Stone Vessels from the Step Pyramid.' In *Ann. Serv.* 34 (1934), 70–5.

13. Smith, S. 'The Structure of the Past. Ancient Egypt: Expansion and Decline.' In *The Geographical Magazine*, July 1943, pp. 126–37.
14. Vikentiev, V. 'Études d'epigraphie protodynastique.' In *Ann. Serv.* 55 (1948), 25–9.

VI. FOREIGN RELATIONS

1. Arkell, A. J. *A History of the Sudan from the Earliest Times to 1821*. Ed. 2. London, 1961.
2. Bénédite, G. 'The Carnarvon Ivory.' In *J.E.A.* 5 (1918), 1–15, 225–41.
3. von Bissing, F. W. *Ägyptische und mesopotamische Siegelzylinder des III. Jahrtausends vor Christus* (Nachr. Göttingen, 1943, Nr. 12). Göttingen, 1943.
4. Bonnet, H. *Ein frühgeschichtliches Gräberfeld bei Abusir*. Leipzig, 1928.
5. Borchardt, L. *Das Grabdenkmal des Königs Sa₃ḥu-Reʿ*. 2 vols. Leipzig, 1910, 1913.
6. Burton-Brown, T. *Studies in Third Millennium History*. London, 1946.
7. Derry, D. E. 'The Dynastic Race in Egypt.' In *J.E.A.* 42 (1956), 80–5.
8. Dunand, M. *Fouilles de Byblos*. 2 vols. Paris, 1939–58.
9. Engelbach, R. 'An Essay on the Advent of the Dynastic Race in Egypt and its Consequences.' In *Ann. Serv.* 42 (1943), 193–221.
10. Falkenstein, A. *Archaische Texte aus Uruk. Ausgrabungen der deutschen Forschungsgemeinschaft in Uruk-Warka*, vol. 2. Berlin, 1936.
11. Firth, C. M. *The Archaeological Survey of Nubia* (Report for 1908–9). 2 vols. Cairo, 1912.
12. Frankfort, H. *The Birth of Civilization in the Near East*. London, 1951.
13. Frankfort, H. *Cylinder Seals*. London, 1939.
14. Frankfort, H. 'Egypt and Syria in the First Intermediate Period.' In *J.E.A.* 12, pp. 80–99.
15. Frankfort, H. 'The Origin of Monumental Architecture in Egypt.' In *A.J.S.L.* 58 (1941), 329–58.
16. Frankfort, H. *Studies in Early Pottery of the Near East*, 1 (*Royal Anthropological Institute, Occasional Papers, no. 6*). London, 1924.
17. Garstang, J. 'Jericho: City and Necropolis (Report for Sixth and Concluding Season, 1936).' In *Ann. Arch. Anthr.* 23 (1936), 67–100.
18. Garstang, J. and J. B. E. *The Story of Jericho*. London, 1948.
19. Griffith, F. Ll. 'Oxford Excavations in Nubia.' In *Ann. Arch. Anthr.* 8 (1921), 1–18.
20. Hölscher, W. *Libyer und Ägypter: Beiträge zur Ethnologie und Geschichte libyscher Völkerschaften nach den altägyptischen Quellen* (*Ägyptol. Forsch.* 4). Glückstadt–Hamburg–New York, 1937.
21. Jéquier, G. *Le monument funéraire de Pepi II*. 3 vols. (*Service des Antiquités de l'Égypte: Fouilles à Saqqarah*.) Cairo, 1936–40.
22. Junker, H. *Bericht über die Grabungen der Akademie der Wissenschaften in Wien auf den Friedhöfen von El-Kubanieh-Süd, Winter 1910–1911* (*Denkschriften. Akademie der Wissenschaften in Wien. Phil.-Hist. Kl.*, Band 62, Abh. 3). Vienna, 1919.
23. Kantor, H. J. 'The Final Phase of Predynastic Culture, Gerzean or Semainean(?).' In *J.N.E.S.* 3 (1944), 110–36.
24. Kantor, H. J. 'Further Evidence for Early Mesopotamian Relations with Egypt.' In *J.N.E.S.* 11 (1952), 239–250.
25. Keimer, L. 'Sur deux représentations égyptiennes du Gerenuk (*Lithocranius Walleri*).' In *Ann. Serv.* 41 (1942), 161–81.

26. Marquet-Krause, J. 'La deuxième campagne de fouilles à Ay (1934).' In *Syria*, 16 (1935), 325–45.
27. Montet, P. *Byblos et l'Égypte*. 2 vols. Paris, 1928–9.
28. Petrie, W. M. F. 'The Earliest Inscriptions.' In *Anc. Egypt*, 1914, pp. 61–77.
29. Petrie, W. M. F. 'More of the Earliest Inscriptions.' In *Anc. Egypt*, 1915, pp. 78–83.
30. Porada, E. *Corpus of Ancient Near Eastern Seals in North American Collections*, 1 (The Bollingen Series, 14). Washington, D.C., 1948.
31. Randall-Maciver, D. *The Earliest Inhabitants of Abydos—A Craniological Study*. Oxford, 1901.
32. Reisner, G. A. *The Archaeological Survey of Nubia (Report for 1907–8)*. 2 vols. Cairo, 1910.
33. Säve-Söderbergh, T. *Ägypten und Nubien: Ein Beitrag zur Geschichte altägyptischer Aussenpolitik*. Lund, 1941.
34. Scharff, A. *Archäologische Beiträge zur Frage der Entstehung der Hieroglyphenschrift (Sitzungsb. München, 1942, Heft 3)*. Munich, 1942.
35. Scharff, A. 'Neues zur Frage der ältesten ägyptisch-babylonischen Kulturbeziehungen.' In *Z.Ä.S.* 71 (1935), 89–106.
36. Schott, E. *Fünfter vorläufiger Bericht über die von der Notgemeinschaft der deutschen Wissenschaft in Uruk unternommenen Ausgrabungen*. Berlin, 1934.
37. Smith, G. E. *The Ancient Egyptians and the Origin of Civilization*. London, 1923.
38 Smith, G. E. and Jones, F. W. *The Archaeological Survey of Nubia* (Report for 1907–8). Vol. II, *Report on the Human Remains*. Cairo, 1910.
39. Starkey, J. L. 'Excavations at Tel el-Duweir 1934–35.' In *P.E.F.* 1935, 198–207.
40. Steindorff, G. 'Nubien, die Nubier und die sogenannten Trogodyten.' In *Studies Presented to F. Ll. Griffith*, 358–68. London, 1932.
41. Yadin, Y. 'The Earliest Record of Egypt's Military Penetration in Asia.' In *I.E.J.* 5, no. 1 (1955), 1–16.
42. Yeivin, S. 'Early Contacts between Canaan and Egypt.' In *I.E.J.* 10, no. 4 (1960), 193–203.

VII. RELIGION AND FUNERARY BELIEFS

1. Blackman, A. M. 'Some Remarks on a Clay Sealing found in the Tomb of Hemaka.' In *An. Or.* 7 (1938), 2–9.
2. Breasted, J. H. *Development of Religion and Thought in Ancient Egypt*. London, 1912.
3. Breasted, J. H. 'The Philosophy of a Memphite Priest.' In *Z.Ä.S.* 39 (1901), 39–54.
4. Černý, J. *Ancient Egyptian Religion*. London, 1952.
5. de Buck, A. *De egyptische voorstellingen betreffende den oerheuvel*. Leiden, 1922.
6. Derry, D. E. 'Mummification.' In *Ann. Serv.* 41 (1942), 240–65.
7. Emery, W. B. *A Funerary Repast in an Egyptian Tomb of the Archaic Period*. Leiden, 1962.
8. Erman, A. 'Ein Denkmal memphitischer Theologie.' In *Sitzungsb. Berlin*, 1911, pp. 924–45.
9. Erman, A. *Die Religion der Ägypter, ihr Werden und Vergehen in vier Jahrtausenden*. Berlin and Leipzig, 1934.
10. Gardiner, A. H. 'An Archaic Funerary Stele.' In *J.E.A.* 4 (1917), 256–60.

11. Griffiths, J. G. *The Conflict of Horus and Seth*. Liverpool, 1960.
12. Junker, H. *Die Geisteshaltung der Ägypter in der Frühzeit (Sitzungsb. Wien*, 237. Band 1. Abh.). Vienna, 1961.
13. Junker, H. *Die Götterlehre von Memphis (Abh. Berlin*, 1939, Nr. 23). Berlin, 1940.
14. Kaplony, P. 'Gottespalast und Götterfestungen in der ägyptischen Frühzeit.' In *Z.Ä.S.* 88 (1962), 5–16.
15. Kaplony, P. 'Zwei neue Götterfestungen der ägyptischen Frühzeit.' In *Z.D.M.G.* 111 (= N.F. 36, 1961), 379–80.
16. Kees, H. *Der Götterglaube im alten Ägypten*. Leipzig, 1941.
17. Kees, H. *Horus und Seth als Götterpaar (MVAG [E.V.]* 1923, 1 and 1924, 1). 2 parts. Leipzig, 1923, 1924.
18. Kees, H. 'Die Opfertanzdarstellung auf einem Siegel des Königs Usaphais.' In *Nachr. Göttingen*, N.F. 3 (1938), 21–30.
19. Kees, H. *Totenglauben und Jenseitsvorstellungen der alten Ägypter*. Ed. 2. Berlin, 1956.
20. Mercer, S. A. B. *Horus, Royal God of Egypt*. Grafton, Mass., 1942.
21. Mercer, S. A. B. *The Pyramid Texts in Translation and Commentary*. 4 vols. New York, London, Toronto, 1952.
22. Ricke, H. 'Der hohe Sand in Heliopolis.' In *Z.Ä.S.* 71 (1935), 107–11.
23. Saad, Z. Y. *Ceiling Stelae in Second Dynasty Tombs from the Excavations at Helwan (Ann. Serv. Supplément.* Cahier no. 21). Cairo, 1957.
24. Sandman Holmberg, M. *The God Ptah*. Lund, 1946.
25. Scharff, A. 'Eine archaische Grabplatte des Berliner Museums.' In *Studies Presented to F. Ll. Griffith* (E.E.S. London, 1932), 346–57.
26. Scharff, A. *Die Ausbreitung des Osiriskultes in der Frühzeit und während des Alten Reiches (Sitzungsb. München*, 1947, Heft 4). Munich, 1948.
27. Scharff, A. *Das Grab als Wohnhaus in der ägyptischen Frühzeit (Sitzungsb. München*, 1944–46, Heft 6). Munich, 1947.
28. Schott, S. *Mythe und Mythebildung im alten Ägypten (Unters.* 15). Leipzig, 1945.
29. Sethe, K. *Die altägyptischen Pyramidentexte*. 4 vols. Leipzig, 1908–22.
30. Sethe, K. *Dramatische Texte zu altaegyptischen Mysterienspielen (Unters.* 10). Leipzig, 1928.
31. Sethe, K. *Übersetzung und Kommentar zu den altägyptischen Pyramidentexten.* 4 vols. Glückstadt, 1935–9.
32. Stock, H. 'Das Ostdelta Ägyptens in seiner entscheidenden Rolle für die politische und religiöse Entwicklung des Alten Reiches.' In *We. Or.*, Heft 3 (1948), 135–45.
33. Vandier, J. *La religion égyptienne* ('Mana': *Introduction à l'histoire des religions*, 1. *Les anciennes religions orientales*). Ed. 2. Paris, 1949.

VIII. ARCHITECTURE, SCULPTURE AND THE SMALL ARTS

1. Aldred, C. *Old Kingdom Art in Ancient Egypt*. London, 1949.
2. Ayrton, E. R., Currelly, C. T. and Weigall, A. E. P. *Abydos III* (E.E.F. Special Extra Publication). London, 1904.
3. Badawy, A. *A History of Egyptian Architecture*, 1. Giza, 1954.
4. Balcz, H. 'Die altägyptische Wandgliederung.' In *Mitt. deutsch. Inst. Kairo*, 1 (1930), 38–92.
5. Barsanti, A. 'Fouilles autour de la pyramide d'Ounas.' In *Ann. Serv.* 3 (1902), 182–4.

6. Baumgartel, E. J. 'The Three Colossi from Koptos and their Mesopotamian Counterparts.' In *Ann. Serv.* 48 (1948), 533–59.

7. Borchardt, L. *Statuen und Statuetten von Königen und Privatleuten* (*C.C.G.*), vol. I. Berlin, 1911.

8. Daressy, G. 'Un édifice archaïque à Nezlet Batran.' In *Ann. Serv.* 6 (1905), 99–106.

9. Edwards, I. E. S. *The Pyramids of Egypt* (Penguin Books). Ed. 2. Harmondsworth, Middlesex, 1961.

10. Edwards, I. E. S. 'Some Early Dynastic Contributions to Egyptian Architecture.' In *J.E.A.* 35 (1949), 123–8.

11. Fischer, H. G. 'An Egyptian Royal Stela of the Second Dynasty.' In *Art. A.* 24 (1961), 45–56.

12. Glanville, S. R. K. 'An Archaic Statuette from Abydos.' In *J.E.A.* 17 (1931), 65–6.

13. Hall, H. R. *A General Introductory Guide to the Egyptian Collections in the British Museum*. London, 1930.

14. Haman, R. *Ägyptische Kunst*. Berlin, 1947.

15. Harris, J. R. *Lexicographical Studies in Ancient Egyptian Minerals* (*Deutsche Akademie der Wissenschaften zu Berlin, Institut für Orientforschung, Veröffentlichung Nr. 54*). Berlin, 1961.

16. Hassan, S. 'Excavations at Saqqara, 1937–8.' In *Ann. Serv.* 38 (1938), 503–21.

17. Hayes, W. C. *The Scepter of Egypt*. 2 vols. New York, 1953, 1959.

18. Jéquier, G. *Deux pyramides du moyen empire* (*Service des Antiquités de l'Égypte: Fouilles à Saqqarah*). Cairo, 1933.

19. Kemp, B. 'Excavations at Hierakonpolis Fort, 1905: A Preliminary Note.' In *J.E.A.* 49 (1963), 24–8.

20. Klasens, A. 'The Excavations of the Leiden Museum of Antiquities at Abu-Roash.' In *Oudheidkundige Mededelingen*, pp. 38–42 (1957–61).

21. Lange, K. and Hirmer, M. *Egypt: Architecture, Sculpture and Painting in Three Thousand Years*. London, 1956.

22. Lauer, J.-P. *Études complémentaires sur les monuments du roi Zoser à Saqqarah*, 1er Fasc. (*Ann. Serv. Supplément*. Cahier no. 9.)

23. Lauer, J.-P. 'Évolution de la tombe royale égyptienne jusqu'à la Pyramide à degrés.' In *Mitt. deutsch. Inst. Kairo*, 15 (1957), 148–65.

24. Lauer, J.-P. *Histoire monumentale des pyramides d'Égypte*, vol. I (*Inst. fr. Caire, Bibliothèque d'Étude*, 39). Cairo, 1962.

25. Mace, A. C. *The Early Dynastic Cemeteries of Naga ed-Dêr*, Part II (*University of California Publications: Egyptian Archaeology*, vol. III). Leipzig, 1909.

26. Macramallah, R. *Un cimetière archaïque de la classe moyenne du peuple à Saqqarah*. Cairo, 1940.

27. Maspero, G. 'Note sur les objets recueillis sous la pyramide d'Ounas.' In *Ann. Serv.* 3 (1902), 185–90.

28. Montet, P. 'Tombeaux de la Ire et de la IVe dynasties à Abou Roach.' In *Kêmi*, 7, 11–69 and 8, 157–227.

29. Morgan, J. de *Recherches sur les origines de l'Égypte*. 2 vols. Paris, 1896–7.

30. Müller, H. W. 'Ein neues Fragment einer reliefsgeschmückten Schminkpalette aus Abydos.' In *Z.Ä.S.* 84 (1959), 68–70.

31. Murray, M. A. 'An Early Sed-Festival.' In *Anc. Egypt*, 1932, pp. 70–2.

32. Needler, W. 'A Flint Knife of King Djer.' In *J.E.A.* 42 (1956), 41–4.

33. Petrie, W. M. F. *Abydos. Parts I–II* (E.E.F. 22nd and 24th Memoirs). London, 1902–3.

34. Petrie, W. M. F. *Corpus of Proto-Dynastic Pottery* (B.S.A. Egypt, Vol. 66 B). London, 1953.
35. Petrie, W. M. F. *Funeral Furniture and Stone Vases* (B.S.A. Egypt, and E.R.A. 43rd Year, 1937). London, 1937.
36. Petrie, W. M. F. *Gizeh and Rifeh* (B.S.A. Egypt, and E.R.A. 13th Year, 1907). London, 1907.
37. Petrie W. M. F. *Tarkhan II* (B.S.A. Egypt, and E.R.A. 19th Year, 1913). London, 1914.
38. Petrie, W. M. F. *Tools and Weapons* (B.S.A Egypt, and E.R.A. 22nd Year, 1916). London, 1917.
39. Petrie W. M. F., Wainwright, G. A. and Gardiner, A. H. *Tarkhan I and Memphis V* (B.S.A. Egypt, and E.R.A. 18th Year, 1912). London, 1913.
40. Quibell, J. E. *Archaic Objects* (*C.C.G.* nos. 11001–12000, 14001–14754). Cairo, 1905.
41. Quibell, J. E. *El-Kab* (E.R.A., 1897). London, 1898.
42. Quibell, J. E. *Excavations at Saqqara* (1912–14): *Archaic Mastabas.* Cairo, 1923.
43. Quibell, J. E. *Excavations at Saqqara* (1911–12): *The Tomb of Hesy.* Cairo, 1913.
44. Ranke, H. *Alter und Herkunft der ägyptischen Löwenjagd-Palette* (*Sitzungb. Heidelberg,* 1924–5, 5 Abhandlung). Heidelberg, 1925.
45. Ranke, H. 'Eine Bemerkung zur "Narmer"-Palette.' In *Studia Orientalia* of *Societas Orientalis Fennica,* 1 (1925), 167–75.
46. Reisner, G. A. *The Development of the Egyptian Tomb down to the Accession of Cheops.* Cambridge, Mass., 1936.
47. Reisner, G. A. *The Early Dynastic Cemeteries of Naga-ed-Dêr,* Part 1 (*University of California Publications: Egyptian Archaeology,* vol. II). Leipzig, 1908.
48. Ricke, H. *Bemerkungen zur ägyptischen Baukunst des Alten Reichs,* I and II, (*Beitr. z. äg. Bauforsch. u. Altertumskunde,* 4 and 5). 2 parts. Zurich and Cairo, 1944, 1950.
49. Ross, E. D. *The Art of Egypt through the Ages.* New York, 1931.
50. Saad, Z. Y. *Royal Excavations at Saqqara and Helwan* (1941–1945) (*Ann. Serv. Supplément.* Cahier no. 3). Cairo, 1947.
51. Saad, Z. Y. *Royal Excavations at Helwan* (1945–1947) (*Ann. Serv. Supplément.* Cahier no. 14). Cairo, 1951.
52. Schäfer, H. *Von ägyptischer Kunst.* Ed. 3. Leipzig, 1930.
53. Scharff, A. *Die Altertümer der Vor- und Frühzeit Ägyptens* (*Staatliche Museen zu Berlin: Mitteilungen aus der ägyptischen Sammlung,* Band IV, 1 and Band V). Berlin, 1931 and 1929.
54. Schweitzer, U. *Löwe und Sphinx im alten Ägypten* (*Ägyptol. Forsch.* 15). Glückstadt–Hamburg, 1948.
55. Simpson, W. K. 'A Statuette of King Nyneter.' In *J.E.A.* 42 (1956), 45–9.
56. Smith, E. B. *Egyptian Architecture as Cultural Expression.* New York and London, 1938.
57. Smith, W. S. *A History of Egyptian Sculpture and Painting in the Old Kingdom.* Ed. 2. London, 1949.
58. Smith, W. S. *The Art and Architecture of Ancient Egypt* (*The Pelican History of Art,* Z 14). Harmondsworth, 1958.
59. Vandier, J. *Manuel d'archéologie égyptienne:* Vol. I, *Les époques de formation.* Paris, 1952.

A. ADDENDA

1. Baumgartel, E. J. 'Scorpion and Rosette and the Fragment of the Large Hierakonpolis Mace Head'. In *Z.Ä.S.* 93 (1966), 9–13.
2. de Cenival, J. L. 'Un nouveau fragment de la pierre de Palerme.' In *Bull. Soc. fr. égyptol.* 44 (December 1965), 13–17.
3. Derchain, P. 'Ménès, le roi "Quelqu'un".' In *Rev. d'égyptol.* 18 (1966), 31–6.
4. Helck, W. *Die Beziehungen Ägyptens zu Vorderasien im 3. und 2. Jahrtausend v. Chr. (Ägyptol. Abh.* 5). Wiesbaden, 1962.
5. Kaiser, W. 'Einige Bemerkungen zur ägyptischen Frühzeit'—Part III, 'Die Reichseinigung.' In *Z.Ä.S.* 91 (1964), 86–125.
6. Kaplony, P. 'Bemerkungen zu einigen Steingefässen mit archaischen Königsnamen.' In *Mitt. deutsch. Inst. Kairo,* 20 (1965), 1–46.
7. Kaplony, P. 'Eine Schminkpalette von König Skorpion aus Abu 'Umâri.' In *Or.* 34 (1965), 132–67.
8. Kaplony, P. *Kleine Beiträge zu den Inschriften der ägyptischen Frühzeit (Ägyptol. Abh.* 15). Wiesbaden, 1966.
9. Kemp, B. J. 'Abydos and the Royal Tombs of the First Dynasty.' In *J.E.A.* 52 (1966), 13–22.
10. Kemp, B. J. 'The Egyptian 1st Dynasty Cemetery.' In *Antiq.* 41 (1967), 22–32.
11. Klasens, A. 'A Stela of the Second Dynasty in the Leiden Museum of Antiquities.' In *Oudeheidkundige Mededelingen,* 46 (1965), 1–9.
12. Lacau, P. et Lauer, J.-Ph. *La pyramide à degrés,* tome v, *Inscriptions à l'encre sur les vases (Inst. fr. Caire),* 1965.
13. Lauer, J.-P. 'A propos de la stèle de l'Horus Raneb.' In *Or.* 35 (1966), 21–7.
14. Lauer, J.-P. 'Quelques remarques sur la 1re dynastie.' In *Bull. Inst. fr. Caire,* 64 (1966), 169–84.
15. Smith, W. S. 'Two Archaic Egyptian Sculptures.' In *Bull M.F.A.* 65 (1967), 70–84.

CHAPTER XII

G. GENERAL

1. Amiet, P. *La Glyptique mésopotamienne archaïque.* Paris, 1961.
2. Contenau, G. *Manuel d'Archéologie orientale,* I–IV. Paris, 1927–47.
3. Frankfort, H. *The Art and Architecture of the Ancient Orient.* Harmondsworth, 1954.
4. Frankfort, H. *Cylinder Seals.* London, 1939.
5. Parrot, A. *Archéologie mésopotamienne,* I, II. Paris, 1946, 1953.
6. Parrot, A. *Sumer.* London, 1960.
7. Perkins, A. L. *The Comparative Archeology of Early Mesopotamia (S.A.O.C.* no. 25). Chicago, 1949.
8. Strommenger, E. and Hirmer, M. *The Art of Mesopotamia.* London, 1964.

I. SOURCES AND GENERAL CHARACTER OF THE PERIOD

1. Biggs, R. D. 'The Abū Salābīkh Tablets.' In *J.C.S.* 20 (1966), 74 ff.
2. Genouillac, H. *Fouilles de Telloh I: Époques Présargoniques.* Paris, 1934.
3. Delougaz, P. 'A Short Investigation of the Temples at Al-'Ubaid.' In *Iraq,* 5 (1938), 1 ff.
4. Falkenstein, A. *Archaische Texte aus Uruk.* Berlin, 1936.

5. Frankfort, H. *Progress of the Work of the Oriental Institute in Iraq, 1934/35* (*O.I.C.* no. 20). Chicago, 1936.
6. Hall, H. R. and Woolley, C. L. *Al-'Ubaid* (*U.E.* 1). London and Philadelphia, 1927.
7. Heinrich, E. *Fara*. Berlin, 1931.
8. Langdon, S. *Excavations at Kish*, 1. Paris, 1924.
9. Lloyd, S. 'Uruk Pottery.' In *Sumer*, 4 (1948), 39 ff.
10. Mackay, E. *Report on Excavations at Jemdet Nasr, Iraq*. Chicago, 1931.
11. Moorey, P. R. S. 'A Reconsideration of the Excavations at Tell Ingharra (East Kish), 1923–33.' In *Iraq*, 28 (1966), 29 ff.
12. Parrot, A. *Tello: vingt campagnes de fouilles*. Paris, 1948.
13. Schmidt, E. F. 'Excavations at Fara, 1931.' In *M.J.* 22 (Philadelphia, 1931), 192 ff.
14. Sollberger, E. *Royal Inscriptions*, Part II (*U.E.T.* VIII). London, 1965.
15. Watelin, L. C. *Excavations at Kish*, III, IV. Paris, 1925–30.

II. THE EARLIER PHASE (URUK 4)

1. Delougaz, P. *Pottery from the Diyala Region* (*O.I.P.* 63). Chicago, 1952.
2. Delougaz, P. and Lloyd, S. *Pre-Sargonid Temples in the Diyala Region* (*O.I.P.* 58). Chicago, 1942.
3. Jordan, J., Lenzen, H. J. and others. 'Vorläufige Berichte über die...in Uruk-Warka...Ausgrabungen.' I–XI in *Abh. Berlin, phil.-inst. Klasse* (1930–40); nos. XII–XXII in *Abh. D.O.G.* (1950–66).
4. Legrain, L. *Archaic Seal Impressions* (*U.E.* III). London and Philadelphia, 1936.
5. Lenzen, H. J. 'Die Tempel der Schicht Archaisch IV in Uruk.' In *Z.A.* 49 (1950), 1 ff.
6. Lloyd, S. 'The Oldest City of Sumeria: Establishing the Origins of Eridu.' In *Ill. Ldn News*, 31 May 1947, 303 ff.
7. Lloyd, S. and Safar, F. 'Eridu, a Preliminary Communication on the first season's excavations.' In *Sumer*, 3 (1947), 84 ff.
8. Lloyd, S. and Safar, F. 'Tell 'Uqair, Excavations by the Iraq Government Directorate of Antiquities in 1940 and 1941.' In *J.N.E.S.* 2 (1943), 131 ff.
9. Mallowan, M. E. L. 'A Cylinder Seal in the Uruk–Jamdat Nasr Style.' In *Baghdader Mitteilungen*, Band 3 (1964), 65 ff.
10. Mallowan, M. E. L. *Early Mesopotamia and Iran*. London, 1965.

III. THE LATER PHASE (JAMDAT NAṢR)

1. Buchanan, Briggs. *Catalogue of the Ancient Near Eastern Seals in the Ashmolean Museum: I. Cylinder Seals*. Oxford, 1966.
2. Childe, V. G. 'The First Waggons and Carts—from the Tigris to the Severn.' In *P.P.S.* 17 (1951), 177 ff.
3. Dyson, R. H. 'A Note on Queen Shub-ad's "onagers".' In *Iraq*, 22 (1960), 102 ff.
4. Falkenstein, A. *Die Inschriften Gudeas von Lagaš: Einleitung*. Rome, 1966.
5. Falkenstein, A. 'Zu den Tontafeln aus Tărtăria.' In *Germania*, 43 (1965), 269 ff.
6. Frankfort, H. *More Sculpture from the Diyala Region* (*O.I.P.* 60). Chicago, 1943.
7. Ghirshman, R. *Tchoga Zanbil* (*Dur-Untash*), vol. 1, *La Ziggurrat* (*Mém. D. Iran*, XXXIX). Paris, 1966.

8. Heinrich, E. *Bauwerke in der altsumerischen Bildkunst.* Wiesbaden, 1957.
9. Hilzheimer, M. *Animal Remains from Tell Asmar* (*S.A.O.C.* 20). Chicago, 1941.
10. Jacobsen, T. 'Early Political Development in Mesopotamia.' In *Z.A.* 52 (1957), 91 ff.
11. Jacobsen, T. 'Primitive Democracy in Ancient Mesopotamia.' In *J.N.E.S.* 2 (1943), 159 ff.
12. Lambert, M. Review of A. Salonen, *Hippologica accadica.* In *R.A.* 51 (1957), 211 ff.
13. Landsberger, B. 'Mezopotamya'da Medeniyetin Doğuşu'. In *Ankara Universitesi, Dil ve Tarih-Coğrafya Fakültesi Dergisi*, II, no. 3 (1944), 419 ff.
14. Lenzen, H. *Die Entwicklung der Zikkurrat von ihren Anfängen bis zur Zeit der III Dynastie von Ur.* Leipzig, 1941.
15. Lloyd, S. 'Iraq Government Soundings at Sinjar.' In *Iraq*, 7 (1940), 13 ff.
16. Mackay, E. and Mackay, D. *Early Indus Civilizations.* 2nd ed. London, 1948.
17. Malamat, A. 'Kingship and Council in Israel and Sumer: A Parallel.' In *J.N.E.S.* 22 (1963), 247 ff.
18. Mallowan, M. E. L. 'The Excavations at Tall Chagar Bazar, and an Archaeological Survey of the Ḫabur Region: second campaign.' In *Iraq*, 4 (1937), 91 ff.
19. Parrot, A. *Ziggurrats et Tour de Babel.* Paris, 1949.
20. Salonen, A. 'Das Rad der Altmesopotamischen Wagen.' In *C.R. Rencontr. Assyriol. Internat.* 2, 59 ff. Paris, 1951.
21. Salonen, A. *Hippologica accadica.* Helsinki, 1956.
22. Schmidt, E. F. *Excavations at Tepe Hissar Damghan.* Philadelphia, 1937.
23. Van Buren, E. D. 'Places of Sacrifice (Opferstätten).' In *Iraq*, 14 (1952), 76 ff.
24. Vlassa, N. 'Chronology of the Neolithic in Transylvania, in the light of the Tǎrtǎria Settlement's stratigraphy.' In *Dacia*, n.s. 7 (1963), 485 ff.
25. Woolley, C. L. *The Early Periods* (*U.E.* iv). London and Philadelphia, 1955.
26. Woolley, C. J. *The Ziggurat and its Surroundings* (*U.E.* v). London and Philadelphia, 1939.
27. Zeuner, F. E. *A History of Domesticated Animals.* London, 1963.

CHAPTER XIII

G. GENERAL

1. Amiet, P. *La Glyptique mésopotamienne archaïque.* Paris, 1961.
2. Barton, G. A. *The Royal Inscriptions of Sumer and Akkad.* New Haven, 1929.
3. Christian, V. *Altertumskunde des Zweistromlandes*, i. Leipzig, 1940.
4. Contenau, G. *Manuel d'archéologie orientale*, i–iv. Paris, 1927–47.
5. Deimel, A. *Šumerische Tempelwirtschaft zur Zeit Urukaginas und seiner Vorgänger* (*An. Or.* 2). Rome, 1931.
6. Ebeling, E., Meissner, B. and Weidner, E. F. (eds.). *Reallexikon der Assyriologie*, i–iii. Berlin and Leipzig, 1932.
7. Falkenstein, A. 'La cité-temple sumérienne.' In *Cahiers d'Histoire mondiale*, i (1954), 784 ff.
8. Frankfort, H. *Cylinder Seals.* London, 1939.
9. Frankfort, H. and H. A. (eds.). *The Intellectual Adventure of Ancient Man.* Chicago, 1946.

10. Gelb, I. J. *Old Akkadian Writing and Grammar.* Ed. 2. Chicago, 1961.
11. Gelb, I. J. *Glossary of Old Akkadian.* Chicago, 1957.
12. Hallo, W. W. *Early Mesopotamian Royal Titles.* New Haven, 1957.
13. Jacobsen, T. *The Sumerian King-list (Assyriological Studies,* no. 11). Chicago, 1939.
14. Kramer, S. N. *Sumerian Mythology.* Philadelphia, 1944.
15. Kramer, S. N. *From the Tablets of Sumer.* Indian Hills, Colorado, 1956.
16. Le Strange, G. *The Lands of the Eastern Caliphate.* Cambridge, 1905.
17. Moortgat, A. *Vorderasiatische Rollsiegel.* Berlin, 1940.
18. Parrot, A. *Archéologie mésopotamienne,* i. Paris, 1946.
19. Parrot, A. *Tello; synthèse de vingt campagnes.* Paris, 1948.
20. Parrot, A. *Mari: documentation photographique.* Neuchâtel and Paris, 1953.
21. Parrot, A. *Glyptique mésopotamienne.* Paris, 1954.
22. Parrot, A. *Sumer.* London, 1960.
23. Porada, E. and Buchanan, B. *Corpus of Ancient Near-Eastern Seals in North American Collections,* i. Washington, 1948.
24. Pritchard, J. B. (ed.). *Ancient Near-Eastern Texts relating to the Old Testament.* Ed. 2. Princeton, 1955.
25. Sarzec, E. de and Heuzey, L. *Découvertes en Chaldée.* Paris, 1884–1912.
26. Soden, W. von. 'Zweisprachigkeit in der geistigen Kultur Babyloniens.' In *Öster. Akad. Wiss., phil.-hist. Kl., Sitzungsb.,* 235 Band, 1 Abh. (1960).
27. Sollberger, E. (ed.). 'Aspects du contact suméro-akkadien'. In *Genava,* n.s. 8 (1960), 241 ff.
28. Thureau-Dangin, F. *Die sumerischen und akkadischen Königsinschriften.* Leipzig, 1907.

I. THE SECOND AND THIRD EARLY DYNASTIC PERIODS

1. Borowski, E. *Cylindres et cachets orientaux conservés dans les collections suisses,* i. Ascona, 1947.
2. Burrows, E. *Archaic Texts (U.E.T.* ii). London, 1935.
3. David, A. 'Remarques sur l'origine de l'écriture sumérienne.' In *Symb. F. Hrozný,* pars quarta, 48 ff. Praha, 1950.
4. Deimel, A. *Die Inschriften von Fara,* i–iii. Leipzig, 1922–4.
5. Delougaz, P. and Lloyd, S. *Pre-Sargonic Temples in the Diyala Region (O.I.P.* lviii). Chicago, 1942.
6. Falkenstein, A. *Archaische Texte aus Uruk.* Berlin, 1936.
7. Frankfort, H. *Archaeology and the Sumerian Problem (S.A.O.C.* 4). Chicago, 1932.
8. Frankfort, H. *Tell Asmar and Khafaje (O.I.C.* 13). Chicago, 1932.
9. Frankfort, H. *Progress of the Work of the Oriental Institute in Iraq, 1934/35 (O.I.C.* 20). Chicago, 1936.
10. Frankfort, H. *Stratified Cylinder-seals from the Diyala Region (O.I.P.* lxxii). Chicago, 1955.
11. Frankfort, H. and Jacobsen, T. *Oriental Institute Discoveries in Iraq, 1933/34 (O.I.C.* 19). Chicago, 1935.
12. Ghirshman, R. *Fouilles de Sialk,* i, ii. Paris, 1938–9.
13. Herzfeld, E. *Archäologische Mitteilungen aus Iran,* no. 5. Berlin, 1933.
14. Landsberger, B. 'Mezopotamya'da Medeniyetin Doğuşu.' In *Ankara Universitesi, Dil ve Tarih-Coğrafya Fakültesi Dergisi,* ii, no. 3 (German summary, 431 ff.). Ankara, 1944.

15. Langdon, S. *Pictographic Inscriptions from Jemdet Nasr* (*O.E.C.T.* VII). Oxford, 1928.
16. Mecquenem, R. de. *Épigraphie proto-élamite* (*Mem. D.P.* XXXI). Paris, 1949.
17. Moortgat, A. *Frühe Bildkunst in Sumer* (*M.V.A.G.* XL, no. 3). Berlin, 1940.
18. Oates, J. 'Ur and Eridu; the Prehistory.' In *Iraq*, 22 (1960), 32 ff.
19. Offner, G. 'Les grandes écoles de glyptique à l'époque archaïque.' In *R.A.* 41 (1947), 111 ff.
20. *Rencontre assyriologique internationale, Compte-rendu de la seconde.* Paris, 1951.
21. Speiser, E. A. *Mesopotamian Origins.* Philadelphia, 1930.
22. Speiser, E. A. 'The Beginnings of Civilization in Mesopotamia.' In *J.A.O.S.* 59 (1939), supplement IV, 17 ff.
23. Speiser, E. A. 'The Sumerian Problem Reviewed.' In *H.U.C.A.* 23 (1950–1), 339 ff.
24. Stephens, F. J. in Hackman, G. G. *Sumerian and Akkadian Administrative Texts* (*B.I.N.* VIII), 3 f. New Haven, 1958.
25. Wheeler, M. *The Indus Civilization. The Cambridge History of India*, supplementary volume. Cambridge, 1953.
26. Wheeler, M. *Civilizations of the Indian Valley and beyond.* London, 1966.

II. EXTENT AND CONSTITUENTS OF THE EARLY DYNASTIC CIVILIZATION

1. Andrae, W. *Die archaischen Ischtar-Tempel in Assur.* Leipzig, 1922.
2. Gadd, C. J. 'The Spirit of Living Sacrifices in Tombs.' In *Iraq*, 22 (1960), 51 ff.
3. Jacobsen, T. 'The Assumed Conflict between Sumerians and Semites in Early Babylonian History.' In *J.A.O.S.* 59 (1939), 485 ff.
4. Langdon, S. H. 'Sumerian Origins and Racial Characteristics.' In *Archaeologia*, 70 (1920), 145 ff.
5. Le Breton, L. 'The Early Periods at Susa; Mesopotamian Relations.' In *Iraq*, 29 (1957), 79 ff.
6. Lees, G. M. and Falcon, N. L. 'The Geographical History of the Mesopotamian Plains.' In *Geographical Journal*, 118 (1952), 24 ff.
7. Meissner, B. 'Sumerier und Semiten in Babylonien.' In *Arch.f. Or.* (1928–9), 1 ff.
8. Roux, G. 'Recently Discovered Ancient Sites in the Hammar Lake District.' In *Sumer*, 16 (1960), 20 ff.
9. Voûte, C. 'A Prehistoric Find near Razzaza (Karbala Liwa).' In *Sumer*, 13 (1957), 135 ff.

III. IDEAS AND INSTITUTIONS

1. Andersen, F. I. 'The Early Sumerian City-state in recent Soviet Historiography.' In *Abr-Nahrain*, 1 (1959–60), 56 ff.
2. Diakonoff, I. M. *Vozniknovenie despotičeskogo gosudarstva v drevnem Dvurečije.* (Full German summary and comments by J. Klíma in *Arch. Orient.* 25 (1957), 660 ff.)
3. Edzard, D. O. 'Enmebaragesi von Kiš.' In *Z.A.* 53 (1959), 9 ff.
4. Gadd, C. J. *Ideas of Divine Rule in the Ancient East.* London, 1948.
5. Heidel, A. *The Babylonian Genesis.* Ed. 2. Chicago, 1951.
6. Jacobsen, T. 'Primitive Democracy in Ancient Mesopotamia.' In *J.N.E.S.* 2 (1943), 159 ff.

7. Jacobsen, T. 'Early Political Development in Mesopotamia.' In *Z.A.* 52 (1957), 91 ff.
8. Labat, R. 'Les origines et la formation de la Terre dans le poème babylonien de la Création.' In *An. Biblica*, 12 (1959), 205 ff.
9. Safar, Fuad. 'The Identification of Dudu.' In *Sumer*, v (1949), 133 ff.
10. Schnabel, P. *Berossos und die babylonisch-hellenistische Literatur.* Leipzig–Berlin, 1923.
11. Speiser, E. A. 'Authority and Law in Mesopotamia.' In *J.A.O.S.* Supplement 17 (1954), 8 ff.
12. Speiser, E. A. 'Ancient Mesopotamia.' In R. C. Dentan (ed.), *The Idea of History in the Ancient Near East.* New Haven, 1955.

IV. HISTORY IN CONTEMPORARY RECORD AND LATER TRADITION

1. Albright, W. F. 'The Anatolian Goddess Kubaba.' In *Arch. f. Or.* 5 (1928–9), 229 ff.
2. Barton, G. A. *Sumerian Business and Administrative Documents from the Earliest Times to the Dynasty of Agade (P.B.S.* ix). Philadelphia, 1915.
3. Basmachi, Faraj. 'The Stele of Ur-Nanshe in the Iraq Museum.' In *Sumer*, 16 (1960), 45 ff.
4. Böhl, F. M. Th. 'Das Menschenopfer bei den alten Sumerern.' In *Z.A.* 39 (1930), 83 ff.
5. Buchanan, Briggs, 'The Date of the "2nd Dynasty" graves in the Royal Cemetery of Ur.' In *J.A.O.S.* 74 (1954), 147 ff.
6. Buren, E. D. van. 'Akkadian Sidelights on a Fragmentary Epic.' In *Or.* 1950, 159 ff.
7. Clemen, C. *Lukians Schrift über die syrische Göttin (Alte Or.* no. 37, Heft 3/4). Leipzig, 1938.
8. Cornelius, F. 'Zur sumerischen Geschichte.' In *Arch. f. Or.* 19 (1959–60), 132 ff.
9. Cornwall, P. B. 'Bahrain–Tilmun.' In *Bull. A.S.O.R.* no. 103 (1946), 3 ff.
10. Deimel, A. *Šumerische Grammatik.* Rome, 1924.
11. Delougaz, P. 'A Short Investigation of the Temple at al-'Ubaid.' In *Iraq*, 5 (1938), 1 ff.
12. Diakonoff, I. M. 'The Gilgamesh Epic.' Review article in *Bi. Or.* 18 (1961), 61 ff.
13. Edzard, D. O. *Die 'zweite Zwischenzeit' Babyloniens.* Wiesbaden, 1957.
14. Gadd, C. J. and Legrain, L. *Royal Inscriptions* (U.E.T. 1). London and Philadelphia, 1928.
15. Garelli, P. (ed.) *Gilgameš et sa légende.* Paris, 1960.
16. Gelb, I. J. *Hurrians and Subarians.* Chicago, 1944.
17. Goetze, A. 'Historical Allusions in Old-Babylonian Omen-Texts.' In *J.C.S.* 1 (1947), 253 ff.
18. Gordon, E. I. 'Mesilim and Mesannepadda—are they identical?' In *Bull. A.S.O.R.* no. 132 (1953), 27 ff.
19. Güterbock, H. G. 'Die historische Tradition und ihre literarische Gestaltung bei Babyloniern und Hethitern bis 1200.' In *Z.A.* 42 (1934), 1 ff.
20. Hall, H. R. and Woolley, C. L. *Al-'Ubaid* (Ur Excavations, 1). London and Philadelphia, 1927.
21. Jacobsen, T. 'La géographie et les voies de communication du pays de Sumer.' In *R.A.* 52 (1958), 127 ff.
22. Jacobsen, T. 'The Waters of Ur.' In *Iraq*, 22 (1960), 175 ff.

23. Jestin, R. R. 'Le poème d'En-me-er-kar.' In *Rev. hist. rel.* 151 (1957), 145 ff.
24. Jordan, J., Lenzen, H. and others. 'Vorläufige Berichte über die...in Uruk-Warka...Ausgrabungen', I–XVI: nos. I–XI in *Abh. Berlin, Phil.-hist. Klasse*, 1930–40; nos. XII–XVI in *A.D.O.G.* nos. I–5 (1956–60).
25. Kramer, S. N. *Enki and Ninhursag. Bull. A.S.O.R.* Supplementary Study, no. 1. Philadelphia, 1945.
26. Kramer, S. N. 'Gilgamesh and Agga.' In *A.J.A.* 53 (1949), 1 ff.
27. Kramer, S. N. *Enmerkar and the Lord of Aratta.* Philadelphia, 1952.
28. Kramer, S. N. 'Dilmun, the Land of the Living.' In *Bull. A.S.O.R.* no. 96 (1944), 18 ff.
29. Kraus, F. R. 'Zur Liste der älteren Könige von Babylonien.' In *Z.A.* 50 (1952), 29 ff.
30. Kraus, F. R. 'Provinzen des neusumerischen Reiches von Ur III.' In *Z.A.* 51 (1955), 64 ff.
31. Lambert, M. 'Les dieux-vivants à l'aube des temps historiques.' In *Sumer*, 5 (1949), 8 ff.
32. Lambert, M. 'La période présargonique.' In *Sumer*, 8 (1952), 57 ff.
33. Lambert, M. 'Le jeu d'Enmerkar.' In *Syria*, 32 (1935), 212 ff.
34. Lambert, M. 'L'intronisation de Lugalanda.' In *R.A.* 50 (1956), 85.
35. Lambert, M. 'Une histoire du conflit entre Lagash et Umma.' In *R.A.* 50 (1956), 141 ff.
36. Legrain, L. *Business Documents of the Third Dynasty of Ur* (U.E.T. III). London and Philadelphia, 1947.
37. Libby, W. F. *Radio-carbon Dating.* Ed. 2. Chicago, 1955.
38. Nougayrol, J. 'Textes hépatoscopiques d'époque ancienne.' In *R.A.* 40 (1945–6), 56 ff.
39. Parrot, A. 'Les fouilles de Mari, première campagne.' In *Syria*, 16 (1935), 1 ff.
40. Parrot, A. 'Les fouilles de Mari, huitième campagne.' In *Syria*, 30 (1953), 196 ff.
41. Parrot, A. *Mission archéologique de Mari*, I–II. Paris, 1956–9.
42. Poebel, A. *Historical and Grammatical Texts* (*P.B.S.* v). Philadelphia, 1914.
43. Rowton, M. B. 'The Date of the Sumerian King-list.' In *J.N.E.S.* 19 (1960), 156 ff.
44. Schneider, N. *Die Zeitbestimmungen der Wirtschaftsurkunden von Ur III.* Rome, 1936.
45. Smith, S. 'A Babylonian Fertility-cult.' In *J.R.A.S.* 1928, 849 ff.
46. Smith, S. 'Notes on the Gutian Period.' In *J.R.A.S.* 1932, 295 ff.
47. Soden, W. von. 'Assyriologische Miszellen: 7. Der Anfang des Etana-Mythus.' In *W.Z.K.M.* 55 (1959), 59 ff.
48. Sollberger, E. *Le système verbal dans les inscriptions 'royales' présargoniques de Lagaš.* Geneva, 1952.
49. Sollberger, E. *Corpus des inscriptions 'royales' présargoniques de Lagaš.* Geneva, 1956.
50. Sollberger, E. 'La frontière de Šara.' In *Or.* 1959, 336 ff.
51. Sollberger, E. 'Notes on the early inscriptions from Ur and el-'Obēd.' In *Iraq*, 22 (1960), 69 ff.
52. Stephens, F. J. 'Notes on Some Economic Texts of the Time of Urukagina: 1. Who was Urukagina's Predecessor?' In *R.A.* 49 (1955), 129 ff.
53. Thureau-Dangin, F. 'Une incursion élamite en territoire sumérien.' In *R.A.* 6 (1904–7), 139 ff.
54. Thureau-Dangin, F. 'Une tablette en or provenant d'Umma.' In *R.A.* 34 (1937), 177 ff.

55. Thureau-Dangin, F. 'Il, roi d'Umma.' In *R.A.* 38 (1941), 90.
56. Ungnad, A. *Subartu*. Berlin and Leipzig, 1936.
57. Ungnad, A. 'Datenlisten.' In *R.L.A.* 2 (1938), 131 ff.
58. Watelin, L. C. *Excavations at Kish*, III, IV. Paris, 1925–30.
59. Weidner, E. F. 'Historisches Material in der babylonischen Omina-Literatur.' In *M.A.O.G.* 4 (1928), 226 ff.
60. Woolley, C. L. 'Excavations at Ur.' Preliminary accounts, in *A.J.* 3 (1923)–14 (1934).
61. Woolley, C. L. *The Royal Cemetery* (Ur Excavations, II). London and Philadelphia, 1934.
62. Woolley, C. L. *The Early Periods* (Ur Excavations, IV). London and Philadelphia. 1956.

V. ARMIES AND WARFARE

1. Burrows, E. 'The Constellation of the Wagon, and Recent Archaeology.' In *Miscellanea Orientalia dedicata Antonio Deimel*. (*An. Or.* 12, 1935), 34 ff.
2. Dyson, R. H. 'A Note on Queen Shub-ad's "onagers".' In *Iraq*, 22 (1960) 102 ff.
3. FitzGerald, G. M. 'Palestine in the Roman Period, 63 B.C.–A.D. 324.' In *P.E.Q.* 1956, 38 ff.
4. Gadd, C. J. 'Babylonian Chess?' In *Iraq*, 8 (1946), 66 ff.
5. Groenewegen-Frankfort, H. A. *Arrest and Movement*. London, 1951.
6. Hilzheimer, M. *Animal Remains from Tell Asmar* (*S.A.O.C.* 20). Chicago, 1941.
7. Langdon, S. H. *Excavations at Kish*, I. Paris, 1924.
8. Marshall, Sir John. *Mohenjo-Daro and the Indus Civilization*. London, 1931.
9. Parrot, A. 'Un "chef de guerre" mésopotamien.' In *Mon. Piot*, 38 (1941), 7 ff.
10. Perkins, A. L. 'Narration in Babylonian Art.' In *A.J.A.* 61 (1957), 54 ff.
11. Perry, W. J. 'War and Civilization.' In *Bull. Ryl. Libr.* 4 (1918), 411 ff.
12. Salonen, A. *Die Landfahrzeuge des alten Mesopotamien*. Helsinki, 1951.
13. Salonen, A. *Hippologica accadica*. Helsinki, 1956.
14. Yadin, Yigael. 'Hyksos Fortifications and the Battering-ram.' In *Bull. A.S.O.R.* 137 (1955), 23 ff.

VI. FOUNDATIONS OF POWER; HUSBANDRY, TRADES, ARTS

1. Bilgiç, E. 'Asurca vesikalara göre Etilerden önce.' In *Sumeroloji Araştırmaları*. Istanbul, 1941.
2. Buren, E. D. Van 'Fish-offerings in Ancient Mesopotamia.' In *Iraq*, 10 (1948), 101 ff.
3. Delougaz, P. *Plano-convex Bricks and the Methods of their Employment* (*S.A.O.C.* 7, 1). Chicago, 1933.
4. Delougaz, P. *Pottery from the Diyala Region* (*O.I.P.* 63). Chicago, 1952.
5. Diakonoff, I. M. 'Sale of Land in Pre-Sargonic Sumer.' In *Papers presented by the Soviet Delegation at the XXIII International Congress of Orientalists*. Moscow, 1954.
6. Forbes, R. J. 'Gold in the Ancient Near East.' In *J.E.O.L.* 6 (1939), 237 ff.
7. Forbes, R. J. *Metallurgy in Antiquity*. Leiden, 1950.
8. Frankfort, H. *Sculpture of the Third Millennium B.C. from Tell Asmar and Khafājah* (*O.I.P.* 44). Chicago, 1939.

9. Frankfort, H. *More Sculpture from the Diyala Region* (*O.I.P.* 60). Chicago, 1943.
10. Garelli, P. *Histoire générale du travail, livre deuxième: L'Asie occidentale ancienne*. Paris, 1960.
11. Gettens, R. J. 'Lapis-lazuli and Ultramarine in Ancient Times.' In *Alumni* (Brussels), 19 (1949–50), 342 ff.
12. Koschaker, P. 'Zur staatlichen Wirtschaftsverwaltung in altbabylonischer Zeit.' In *Z.A.* 47 (1942), 135 ff.
13. Kraus, F. R. 'Altmesopotamische Tonnägel mit Keilinschriften.' In *Halil Edhem hâtira kitabı*, 71 ff.
14. Lambert, M. 'La naissance de la bureaucratie.' In *Rev. hist.* 224 (1960), 1 ff.
15. Lambert, M. 'Textes commerciaux de Lagash.' Parts I and II in *R.A.* 47 (1953), 57 ff., 105 ff., part III in *Arch. Orient.* 23 (1955), 557 ff.
16. Lewy, H. 'Origin and Development of the Sexagesimal System.' In *J.A.O.S.* 69 (1949), 1 ff.
17. Matouš, L. 'Zu den Ausdrücken für "Zugaben" in den vorsargonischen Grundstückkaufurkunden.' In *Arch. Orient.* 22 (1954), 434 ff.
18. Piggott, S. (ed.). *The Dawn of Civilization*. London, 1961.
19. Pohl, A. 'Zu einer Klausel altsumerischer Rechtsurkunden.' In *Symb.... P. Koschaker*, 61 ff.
20. Rosengarten, Y. *Le concept sumérien de consommation dans la vie économique et religieuse*. Paris, 1960.
21. Tyumenev, A. I. *Gosudarstvennoe khozyaistvo drevnego Shumera*. Moscow–Leningrad, 1956. Summaries: (in French) by Achsa Belkind in *R.A.* 52 (1958), 95 ff.; (in German) by J. Klíma in *Bi. Or.* 15 (1958), 29 ff.
22. Wachtsmuth, F. 'Zur Altersbestimmung der vorgeschichtlichen Kulturen des Zweistromlandes.' In *Arch. f. Or.* 13 (1939–41), 194 ff.

VII. RELIGION AND CULT-PRACTICES

1. Frankfort, H. 'Gods and Myths on Sargonid Seals.' In *Iraq*, 1 (1934), 2 ff.
2. Labat, R. *Le Caractère religieux de la royauté assyro-babylonienne*. Paris, 1939.
3. Rosengarten, Y. 'La notion sumérienne de souveraineté divine.' In *Rev. hist. rel.* 156 (1959), 129 ff.

VIII. SOCIETY AND SOCIAL PROBLEMS

1. Diakonoff, I. M. 'Some Remarks on the "Reforms" of Urukagina.' In *R.A.* 52 (1958), 1 ff.
2. Kramer, S. N. and Bernhardt, I. *Sumerische literarische Texte aus Nippur*, 1 (*T.u.M.* n.F. III). Berlin, 1961.
3. Lambert, M. 'Les "réformes" d'Urukagina.' In *R.A.* 50 (1956), 169 ff.

A. ADDENDA

1. Adams, R. McC. *Land behind Baghdad*. Chicago and London, 1965.
2. Barrelet, M.-Th. 'Une "construction énigmatique" à Tello.' In *Iraq*, 29 (1965), 100 ff.
3. Biggs, R. D. 'The Abū Ṣalābīkh Tablets: A Preliminary Survey.' In *J.C.S.* 20 [1966], 73 ff.
4. Biggs, R. D. 'Semitic Names in the Fara Period.' In *Or.* n.s. 36 (1967), 55 ff.

5. Biggs, R. D. 'Le lapis-lazuli dans les textes sumériens archaïques.' In *R.A.* 60 (1967), 175 ff.
6. van Dijk, J. 'Die Inschriftenfunde.' In *U.V.B.* 18 (1963), 39 ff.
7. van Dijk, J. 'Einige Bemerkungen zu sumerischen religionsgeschichtlichen Problemen.' In *O.L.Z.* 1967, 229 ff.
8. Dossin, G. 'Les découvertes épigraphiques de la XVe campagne de fouilles à Mari.' In *C.-R. Ac. Inscr. B.-L.* 1965, 400 ff.
9. Falkenstein, A. 'Zu den Tontafeln aus Tărtăria.' In *Germania*, 43 (1965), 269 ff.
10. Falkenstein, A. *Die Inschriften Gudeas von Lagaš: I. Einleitung (An. Or.* 30). Rome, 1966.
11. Finkelstein, J. J. 'The Antediluvian Kings.' In *J.C.S.* 17 (1963), 39 ff.
12. Gadd, C. J. 'Some contributions to the Gilgamesh Epic.' In *Iraq*, 28 (1966), 105 ff.
13. Gelb, I. J. 'The ancient Mesopotamian ration-system.' In *J.N.E.S.* 24 (1965), 230 ff.
14. Gelb, I. J. On the Tartaria tablets, in *Nestor*, 1966, p. 488.
15. Hansen, D. F. 'New votive plaques from Nippur.' In *J.N.E.S.* 22 (1963), 145 ff.
16. Hood, M. S. F. 'The Tartaria tablets.' In *Antiq.* 41 (1967), 99 ff.
17. János, Makkay. 'Die in Tărtăria (Alsótatárlaka) gefundenen piktographischen Tafeln und die jüngere Steinzeit Südosteuropas.' In Különnyomat a Móra Ferenc Múzeum évkönyve 1966–1967 évi kötetéböl. Szeged, 1967.
18. Kramer, S. N. *The Sumerians.* Chicago, 1963.
19. Lambert, M. 'La vie économique de Shuruppak.' In *Sumer*, 9 (1953), 193 ff.
20. Lambert, M. 'L'occupation de Girsu par Urlumma, roi d'Umma.' In *R.A.* 59 (1965), 81 ff.
21. Landsberger, B. 'Excurs I: Meluḫḫa.' In *We. Or.* 3 (1966), 261 ff.
22. Malamat, A. 'Kingship and Council in Israel and Sumer.' In *J.N.E.S.* 22 (1963), 247 ff.
23. Mallowan, M. E. L. 'A cylinder-seal in the Uruk—Jamdat Naṣr style.' In *Baghdader Mitteil.* 3 (1964), 65 ff.
24. Mallowan, M. E. L. 'Noah's Flood reconsidered.' In *Iraq* 26 (1964), 62 ff.
25. Mallowan, M. E. L. 'Tell Chuera in Nordost-Syrien.' In *Iraq* 28 (1966), 89 ff.
26. Matouš, L. 'Zur neueren Literatur über das Gilgameš-Epos.' In *Bi. Or.* 21 (1964, 3 ff.
27. Moorey, P. R. S. 'Some aspects of incised drawing and mosaic in the Early Dynastic period.' In *Iraq*, 29 (1967), 97 ff.
28. Nagel, W. *Der mesopotamische Streitwagen und seine Entwicklung im ost-mediterranen Bereich.* Berlin, 1966.
29. Neustupný, Evžen. 'The Tartaria Tablets: a chronological issue.' In *Antiq.* 42 (1968), 32 ff.
30. Nissen, H. J. *Zur Datierung des Königsfriedhofes von Ur.* Bonn, 1966.
31. Renfrew, C. On the Tartaria Tablets, in *Nestor*, 1966, p. 469.
32. Römer, W. H. Ph. 'Studien zu altbabylonischen hymnisch-epischen Texten (3).' In *We. Or.* 4 (1967), 12 ff.
33. Rosengarten, Y. *Répertoire commenté des signes présargoniques sumériens de Lagaš.* Paris, 1967.
34. Seux, M.-J. 'Les titres royaux šar kiššati et šar kibrāt arba'i.' In *R.A.* 59 (1965), 1 ff.
35. Sollberger, E. 'The Tummal Inscription.' In *J.C.S.* 16 (1962), 40 ff.

36. Sollberger, E. 'Geierstele (historisch).' In *R.L.A.* 3 (1964), 194 f.
37. Sollberger, E. *Royal Inscriptions*, Part II (*U.E.T.* VIII). London and Philadelphia, 1965.
38. Spycket, A. *Les Statues de culte dans les textes mésopotamiens des origines à la Ire. dynastie de Babylone*. Paris, 1968.
39. Vaiman, A. A. 'Preliminary report on the decipherment of Proto-Sumerian writing.' In *Peredneasiatskiy Sbornik*, II, 3 ff. (English summary, 161 ff.) Moscow, 1966.
40. Vlassa, N. 'Chronology of the Neolithic in Transylvania, in the light of the Tărtăria settlement's stratigraphy.' In *Dacia* n.s., 7 (1963), 485 ff.

CHAPTER XIV

G. GENERAL

1. Abu-Baker, Abdel-Moneim. *Excavations at Giza 1949–1950*. Cairo, 1953.
2. Anthes, R. *Die Felsinschriften von Hatnub* (*Unters*. 9). Berlin, 1928.
3. Borchardt, L. *Die Annalen und die zeitliche Festlegung des Alten Reiches der ägyptischen Geschichte*. Berlin, 1917.
4. Breasted, J. H. *Ancient Records of Egypt*, I. Chicago, 1906.
5. Daressy, G. 'La pierre de Palerme et la chronologie de l'Ancien Empire.' In *Bull. Inst. fr. Caire*, 12 (1916), 161–214.
6. Drioton É. and Vandier, J. *Les peuples de l'Orient méditerranéen*. II. *L'Égypte* ('*Clio*' I). Ed. 3. Paris, 1952. Chs. V, VI.
7. Dunand, M. *Fouilles de Byblos, 1926–1932*, vol. I (Paris, 1937, 1939); *1933–1938*, vol. II (Paris, 1950, 1954).
8. Edwards, I. E. S. *The Pyramids of Egypt*. Ed. 2. Harmondsworth, 1961.
9. Farina, G. *Il papiro dei re restaurato*. Rome, 1938.
10. Frankfort, H., Frankfort, H. A., Wilson, J. A. and Jacobsen, T. *Before Philosophy*. Harmondsworth, 1949. Original ed.: *The Intellectual Adventure of Ancient Man*. Chicago, 1946.
11. Gardiner, A. H. 'Regnal Years and Civil Calendar in Pharaonic Egypt.' In *J.E.A.* 31 (1945), 11 ff.
12. Gardiner, A. H., Peet, T. E. and Černý, J. *The Inscriptions of Sinai*, parts I, II. Ed. 2. London, 1952, 1955.
13. Gauthier, H. *Le livre des rois d'Égypte*, I. Cairo, 1907.
14. Gauthier, H. 'Quelques additions au "Livre des rois d'Égypte" (Ancien et Moyen Empire)'. In *Rec. trav.* 40 (1923), 177 ff.
15. Gauthier, H. 'Quatre nouveaux fragments de la pierre de Palerme.' In Maspero, G. *Le Musée Égyptien*, III (Cairo, 1915), 29–53.
16. Hassan, S. *Excavations at Giza*, I–VIII (Seasons 1929–37). Oxford and Cairo, 1932–53.
17. Helck, W. *Untersuchungen zu Manetho und den ägyptischen Königslisten* (*Unters*. 18). Berlin, 1956.
18. Helck, W. *Untersuchungen zu den Beamtentiteln des ägyptischen Alten Reiches* (*Ägyptol. Forsch*. 18). Glückstadt, 1954.
19. Junker, H. *Giza*, I–XII. Vienna and Leipzig, 1929–55.
20. Kantor, H. in Ehrich, R. W. *Relative Chronologies in Old World Archaeology*. Chicago, 1954, pp. 1–27.
21. Kees, H. *Aegypten. Kulturgeschichte des Alten Orients*, I. Munich, 1933.
22. Kees, H. *Götterglaube*. Leipzig, 1941.

23. Lepsius, C. R. *Denkmaeler aus Aegypten und Aethiopien.* Berlin, 1849–59. Text, Leipzig, 1897–1913 (especially vol. 1). *Ergänzungsband*, Leipzig, 1913.
24. Manetho, English translation by W. G. Waddell. The Loeb Classical Library, Cambridge Mass. and London, 1948.
25. Mariette, A. *Les Mastabas de l'Ancien Empire.* Paris, 1889.
26. Meyer, E. *Geschichte des Altertums,* 1. Stuttgart, 1926.
27. Meyer, E. *Die ältere Chronologie Babyloniens, Assyriens und Ägyptens; Nachtrag zum ersten Bande der Geschichte des Altertums.* Stuttgart, 1931.
28. Montet, P. *Byblos et l'Égypte.* Paris, 1928.
29. Montet, P. *Géographie de l'Égypte ancienne.* Première partie. Paris, 1957.
30. Morgan, J. de. *Carte de la nécropole memphite.* Cairo, 1897.
31. Murray, M. A. *Index of Names and Titles of the Old Kingdom.* London, 1908.
32. Naville, E. 'La pierre de Palerme.' In *Rec. trav.* 25 (1903) 64–81.
33. Nelson, H. 'Fragments of Egyptian Old Kingdom Stone Vessels from Byblos.' In *Berytus,* 1 (1934), 19–22.
34. Pendlebury, J. D. S. *The Archaeology of Crete.* London, 1939. Pp. 74–5, 89–90.
35. Petrie, W. M. F. *Researches in Sinai.* London, 1906.
36. Porter, B. and Moss, R. L. B. *Topographical Bibliography of Ancient Hieroglyphic Texts, Reliefs and Paintings,* I–VII. Oxford, 1927–51.
37. Reisner, G. A. *The Development of the Egyptian Tomb.* Cambridge, Mass., 1936.
38. Reisner, G. A. 'A Scribe's Tablet found by the Hearst Expedition at Giza.' In *Z.Ä.S.* 48 (1910), 113.
39. Schäfer, H. *Ein Bruchstuck altägyptischer Annalen.* Berlin, 1902.
40. Sethe, K. *Die Entwicklung der Jahresdatierung bei den alten Aegyptern (Unters.* 3). Leipzig, 1905. Pp. 60–100.
41. Sethe, K. *Urkunden des ägyptischen Altertums,* 1. *Urkunden des Alten Reiches.* Leipzig, 1932.
42. Wilson, J. A. *The Culture of Ancient Egypt.* Chicago, 1956. Original ed.: *The Burden of Egypt.* Chicago, 1951.
43. Vandier, J. *Manuel d'Archéologie égyptienne,* I–III. Paris, 1952–8.
44. Vandier, J. *La Religion égyptienne.* Ed. 2. Paris, 1949.
45. Vercoutter, J. *L'Égypte et le monde égéen préhellénique (Inst. fr. Caire, Bibliothèque d'étude,* 22). Cairo, 1956.
46. Vercoutter, J. *Essai sur les relations entre Égyptiens et Préhellènes.* Paris, 1954.

I. THE THIRD DYNASTY

1. Arkell, A. J. 'Stone Bowls of Kha'ba (Third Dynasty).' In *J.E.A.* 42 (1956), 116.
2. Barguet, P. *La stèle de la famine, à Séhel (Inst. fr. Caire, Bibliothèque d'étude,* 24). Cairo, 1953.
3. Barsanti, A. 'Fouilles de Zaouiét el-Aryân.' In *Ann. Serv.* 7 (1906), 257–86; 8 (1907), 201–10; 12 (1912), 57–63.
4. Barsanti, A. 'Ouverture de la pyramide de Zaouiét el-Aryân.' In *Ann. Serv.* 2 (1901), 92–4.
5. Borchardt, L. *Altägyptische Festungen.* Leipzig, 1909. (P. 41, n. 4, for Huni Inscription.)
6. Borchardt, L. 'König Huni (?).' In *Z.Ä.S.* 46 (1909), 12–13.
7. Erman, A. 'Geschichtliche Inschriften aus dem Berliner Museum.' In *Z.Ä.S.* 38 (1900), 114–23.

8. Firth, C. M. and Quibell, J. E. *The Step Pyramid*. Cairo, 1935.
9. Garstang, J., with a chapter by Sethe, K. *Mahâsna and Bêt Khallâf* (E.R.A.). London, 1903.
10. Gauthier, H. 'Un nouveau nom royal.' In *Bull. Inst. fr. Caire*, 5 (1906), 41–2.
11. Goedicke, H. 'The Pharaoh Ny-Śwtḥ.' In *Z.Ä.S.* 81 (1956), 18–24.
12. Goedicke, H. 'The King Ḥwdf?.' In *J.E.A.* 42 (1956), 50–3.
13. Goneim, M. Z. *Excavations at Saqqara, Horus Sekhem-khet, The Unfinished Step Pyramid at Saqqara*, 1. Cairo, 1957.
14. Gunn, B. 'Inscriptions from the Step Pyramid Site.' In *Ann. Serv.* 26 (1926), 177 ff.
15. Helck, W. 'Das Kleidertäfelchen aus der Pyramide des Śḥm-ḥ.t.' In *W.Z.K.M.* 54 (1957), 91–111.
16. Junker, H. 'Die Grabungen der Universität Kairo auf dem Pyramidenfeld von Giza.' In *Mitt. deutsch. Inst. Kairo*, 3 (1932), 139–40.
17. Lauer, J.-P. *La Pyramide à degrés*, I–IV. Cairo, 1936–59.
18. Lauer, J.-P. 'L'Apport historique des récentes découvertes du Service des Antiquités dans la Nécropole Memphite.' In *C.-R. Ac. Inscr. B.-L.* (1954), 368–79.
19. Lauer, J.-P. 'Les Pyramides à degrés.' In *Rev. arch.* 47 (1956), 1–19.
20. Lichtheim, M. 'Songs of the Harper.' In *J.N.E.S.* 4 (1945), 178 ff.
21. Murray, M. A. *Saqqara Mastabas*, 1 (E.R.A.). London, 1905.
22. Petrie, W. M. F. *Abydos*, I–III (E.E.F. 22nd, 24th and Special Memoirs). London, 1903–4.
23. Petrie, W. M. F. *The Royal Tombs of the First Dynasty* (E.E.F. 18th Memoir). London, 1900.
24. Petrie, W. M. F. *The Royal Tombs of the Earliest Dynasties* (E.E.F. 21st Memoir) and vol. extra plates. London, 1901.
25. Quibell, J. E. *The Tomb of Hesy*. Cairo, 1913.
26. Quibell, J. E. *Archaic Mastabas*. Cairo, 1923.
27. Quibell, J. E. *Hierakonpolis*, I, II. London, 1901, 1902.
28. Reisner, G. A. 'The Work of the Harvard University-Museum of Fine Arts Expedition.' In *Bull. M.F.A.* 9 (1911), 54–9.
29. Ricke, H. *Bemerkungen zur ägyptischen Baukunst des Alten Reiches*, 1 (*Beitr. z. äg. Bauforsch. u. Altertumskunde*, 4). Zurich, 1944.
30. Sethe, K. *Dodekaschoinos das Zwölfmeilenland an der Grenze von Aegypten und Nubien* (*Unters.* 2, iii). Leipzig, 1901.
31. Sethe, K. *Imhotep der Asklepios der Ägypter* (*Unters.* 2, iv). Leipzig, 1902.
32. Smith, W. S. 'The Origin of some Unidentified Old Kingdom Reliefs.' In *A.J.A.* 46 (1942), 518–20.
33. Weill, R. 'Les IIe et IIIe dynasties égyptiennes.' In *Ann. Mus. Guimet*, 25. Paris, 1908.
34. Weill, R. 'Monuments nouveaux des premières dynasties.' In *Sphinx*, 15 (1911–12), 9–26.

II. THE FOURTH DYNASTY

1. Barsanti, A. 'Rapport sur la fouille de Dahchour.' In *Ann. Serv.* 3 (1902), 198–208.
2. Borchardt, L. *Die Entstehung der Pyramide*. Berlin, 1928.
3. Borchardt, L. 'Ein Königserlass aus Dahschur.' In *Z.Ä.S.* 42 (1905), 1–11.
4. Borchardt, L. 'Die Stammutter der 5ten Dynastie.' In *Ann. Serv.* 38 (1938), 209 ff.

5. Chassinat, É. 'A propos d'une tête en grès rouge du roi Didoufrî.' In *Mon. Piot*. 25 (1921–2), 53–75.
6. Daressy, G. 'La Stèle de la fille de Chéops.' In *Rec. trav.* 30 (1908), 1–10.
7. Daressy, G. 'La tombe de la mère de Chéfren.' In *Ann. Serv.* 10 (1910), 41–9.
8. Drioton, É. 'Une Liste de Rois de la IVe Dynastie dans l'Ouâdi Hammâmât.' In *Bull. Soc. fr. d'Égyptol.* 16 (1954), 41–9.
9. Engelbach, R. 'The Quarries of the Western Nubian Desert.' In *Ann. Serv.* 33 (1933), 65–80.
10. Engelbach, R. 'The Quarries of the Western Nubian Desert and the Ancient Road to Tushka.' In *Ann. Serv.* 38 (1938), 369–90.
11. Fakhry, A. *The Bent Pyramid of Dahshur*. Cairo, 1954. (Extracts from *Ann. Serv.* 51 (1951), 510–21; 52 (1954), 563–623.)
12. Gauthier, H. 'Le Roi Zadfré successeur immédiat de Khoufou-Kheops.' In *Ann. Serv.* 25 (1925), 178–80.
13. Gilbert, P. 'La date du Temple de Kasr-el-Saga.' In *Chron. d'Ég.* 37 (1944), 31–4.
14. Goedicke, H. 'Ein Verehrer des Weisen Ddfḥr.' In *Ann. Serv.* 55 (1958), 35–55.
15. Grdseloff, B. 'Deux inscriptions juridiques de l'Ancien Empire.' In *Ann. Serv.* 42 (1943), 25–70.
16. Grdseloff, B. 'Notes sur deux monuments inédits de l'Ancien Empire.' In *Ann. Serv.* 42 (1943), 107–25.
17. Hassan, S. *Excavations at Giza*, iv. Cairo, 1943.
18. Helck, W. 'Bemerkungen zu den Pyramidenstädten im Alten Reich.' In *Mitt. deutsch. Inst. Kairo*, 15 (1957), 91–111.
19. Helck, W. 'Zur Entstehung des Westfriedhofs an der Cheops-Pyramide.' In *Z.Ä.S.* 81 (1956), 62–5.
20. Hölscher, U. *Das Grabdenkmal des Königs Chephren*. Leipzig, 1912.
21. Jéquier, G. *L'architecture et la décoration dans l'ancienne Égypte*, i. Paris, 1920.
22. Junker, H. 'Pḥrnfr.' In *Z.Ä.S.* 75 (1939), 63 ff.
23. Junker, H. 'Die Grabungen der Universität Kairo auf dem Pyramidenfeld von Giza.' In *Mitt. deutsch. Inst. Kairo*, 3 (1932), 139 ff.
24. Lauer, J.-P. 'Le Temple funéraire de Khéops à la grande pyramide de Guizeh.' In *Ann. Serv.* 46 (1947), 245–59.
25. Lauer, J.-P. 'Note Complémentaire.' In *Ann. Serv.* 49 (1949), 111 ff.
26. Maspero, G. 'Trois années de fouilles.' In *Mém. Miss. fr. Caire*, 1 (Cairo, 1884), 189 ff.
27. Maspero, G. *Études de mythologie et archéologie égyptiennes*, vi. Paris, 1912.
28. Le Maystre, C. 'Les dates des pyramides de Sneferou.' In *Bull. Inst. fr. Caire*, 35 (1935), 89 ff.
29. Menghin, O. and Bittel, K. 'Kasr el Sagha.' In *Mitt. deutsch. Inst. Kairo*, 5 (1934), 1–10.
30. Morgan, J. de. *Fouilles à Dahchour*, i–ii. Vienna, 1895, 1903.
31. Murray, G. W. 'A Note on the Sadd el-Kafara: The Ancient Dam in the Wadi Garawi.' In *Bull. Inst. d'Ég.* 28 (1947), 33–46.
32. Murray, M. A. *Saqqarah Mastabas*, i (E.R.A.). London, 1905.
33. Petrie, W. M. F. *Medum*. London, 1892.
34. Petrie, W. M. F., Wainwright, G. A. and Mackay, A. *Meydum and Memphis*, iii (E.R.A. and B.S.A. Egypt). London, 1910.
35. Petrie, W. M. F. *The Labyrinth, Gerzeh and Mazghuneh* (B.S.A. Egypt). London, 1912.

36. Reisner, G. A. *Mycerinus*. Cambridge, Mass., 1931.
37. Reisner, G. A. 'The Tomb of Meresankh, a Great Grand-daughter of Queen Hetep-heres I and Sneferuw.' In *Bull. M.F.A.* 25 (1927), 64–79.
38. Reisner, G. A. *A History of the Giza Necropolis*, I. Cambridge, Mass., 1942.
39. Reisner, G. A., and Smith, W. S. *A History of the Giza Necropolis*. II. *The Tomb of Hetep-heres*. Cambridge, Mass., 1955.
40. Ricke, H. and Schott, S. *Bemerkungen zur ägyptischen Baukunst des Alten Reiches*, II (*Beitr. z. äg. Bauforsch. u. Altertumskunde*, 5). Cairo, 1950.
41. Rougé, J. de. *Inscriptions hiéroglyphiques copiées en Égypte*. Paris, 1877.
42. Rowe, A. 'The Eckley B. Coxe Jr. Excavations at Meydum 1929–1930.' In *M.J.* 22 (1931), 5–46.
43. Smith, W. S. 'Inscriptional Evidence for the History of the Fourth Dynasty.' In *J.N.E.S.* 11 (1952), 113–28.

III. THE FIFTH DYNASTY

1. Abdel Salam Mohamed Hussein, 'Fouilles sur la chaussée d'Ounas 1941–1943.' In *Ann. Serv.* 43 (1943), 439–48.
2. Bissing, F. W. von. *Das Re-Heiligtum des Königs Ne-Woser-Re (Rathures)*: vol. I, Borchardt, L., *Der Bau* (Berlin, 1905); vol. II, Bissing, F. W. von and Kees, H., *Die kleine Festdarstellung* (Leipzig, 1923); vol. III, Kees, H., *Die grosse Festdarstellung* (Leipzig, 1928).
3. Bissing, F. W. von and Kees, H. *Untersuchungen zu den Reliefs aus dem Re-Heiligtum des Rathures* (*Abh. München*, 32, i). Munich, 1922.
4. Bissing, F. W. von. 'Le Chambre des trois saisons.' In *Ann. Serv.* 53 (1956), 319–38.
5. Bisson de la Roque, F. *Tod* (*Flles Inst. fr. Caire*, 17). Cairo, 1937.
6. Borchardt, L. *Das Grabdenkmal des Königs Ne-user-Reʿ*. Leipzig, 1907.
7. Borchardt, L. *Das Grabdenkmal des Königs Nefer-ìr-keȝ-Reʿ*. Leipzig, 1909.
8. Borchardt, L. *Das Grabdenkmal des Königs Saȝhu-Reʿ*, 2 vols. Leipzig, 1910–13.
9. Borchardt, L. 'Ein Rechnungsbuch des königlichen Hofes aus dem alten Reiche.' In *Aegyptiaca, Festschrift für Georg Ebers*. Leipzig, 1897. Pp. 8–15.
10. Borchardt, L. *Allerhand Kleinigkeiten*. Leipzig, 1933. Pp. 43 ff.
11. Davies, N. de G. *The Rock Tombs of Sheikh Said*. London, 1901.
12. Drioton, É. 'Une représentation de la famine sur un bas-relief égyptien de la Ve dynastie.' In *Bull. Inst. d'Ég.* 25 (1943), 45–54.
13. Evans, A. E. 'Further Discoveries of Cretan and Aegean Script.' In *J.H.S.* 17 (1897), 349.
14. Firth, C. M. 'Excavations of the Department of Antiquities at Saqqarah (October 1928–March, 1929).' In *Ann. Serv.* 29 (1929), 64–70.
15. Fischer, H. G. 'The Easternmost Nomes of the Delta.' In *J.N.E.S.* 18 (1959), 129–42.
16. Fraser, G. 'The Early Tombs at Tehneh.' In *Ann. Serv.* 3 (1902), 67–76.
17. Hassan, Selim. 'Excavations at Saqqara 1937–1938.' In *Ann. Serv.* 38 (1938), 503–14.
18. Hassan, Selim. *Archiv für Aegyptische Archaeologie*, I. Vienna, 1938. Pp. 175–83.
19. Hassan, Selim. 'The Causeway of Wnis at Saqqara.' In *Z.Ä.S.* 80 (1955), 136–9.
20. Kaiser, W. 'Zu den Sonnenheiligtümern der 5. Dynastie.' In *Mitt. deutsch. Inst. Kairo*, 14 (1956), 104–16.

21. Kees, H. 'Zu den Gaulisten im Sonnenheiligtum Neuserrê.' In *Z.Ä.S.* 81 (1956), 33–40.
22. Lauer, J.-P. 'Le Temple Haut de la Pyramide du Roi Ouserkaf.' In *Ann. Serv.* 53 (1956), 119–33.
23. Mackay, E., Harding, L. and Petrie, F. *Bahrein and Hemamieh*. London, 1929.
24. Petrie, W. M. F. *Deshasheh* (E.E.F. 15th Memoir). London, 1898.
25. Saad, Z. Y. 'A Preliminary Report on the Excavations at Saqqara, 1939–1940.' In *Ann. Serv.* 40 (1940), 675–93.
26. Schäfer, H. *Priestergräber . . . vom Totentempel des Ne-user-rê*. Leipzig, 1908.
27. Sethe, K. 'Ein ägyptisches Denkmal des Alten Reiches von der Insel Kythera.' In *Z.Ä.S.* 53 (1917), 55–8.
28. Smith, W. S. 'The Judge Goes Fishing.' In *Bull. M.F.A.* 56 (1958), 56–61.
29. Stock, H. 'Das Sonnenheiligtum des Königs Userkaf.' In *Z.Ä.S.* 80 (1955), 140–4.
30. Vandier, J. *Bulletin, Musées de France*, 15 (1950), 29.

IV. THE SIXTH DYNASTY

1. Arkell, A. J. *A History of the Sudan to A.D. 1821*. London, 1955.
2. Blackman, A. M. *The Rock Tombs of Meir*, I, IV, V (E.E.F. and E.E.S. Arch. Survey, 22nd, 25th and 28th Memoirs). London, 1914, 1924, 1953.
3. Borchardt, L. *Denkmäler des Alten Reiches. C.C.G.* Berlin, 1937.
4. Clédat, J. 'Deux Monuments nouveaux de Tell El-Maskhoutah.' In *Rec. trav.* 32 (1910), 40–2.
5. Davies, N. de G. *The Rock Tombs of Deir el Gebrawi* (E.E.F. Arch. Survey, 11th and 12th Memoirs). London, 1902.
6. Drioton, É. 'Notes diverses, 2. Une Corégence de Pepy Ier et de Mérenrê (?).' In *Ann. Serv.* 44 (1945), 55–6.
7. Gardiner, A. H. 'Was the Vizier Dja'u one of Six Brothers?' In *Z.Ä.S.* 79 (1954), 95–6.
8. Habachi, L. *Tell Basta* (*Ann. Serv. Supplément. Cahier* no. 22). Cairo, 1957.
9. Jéquier, G. *Le monument funéraire de Pepi II*, I–III. Cairo, 1936–40.
10. Jéquier, G. *Les pyramides des reines Neit et Apouit*. Cairo, 1933.
11. Jéquier, G. *La pyramide d'Oudjebten*. Cairo, 1928.
12. Kees, H. 'Beiträge zur Geschichte des Vezirats im Alten Reich. Die Chronologie der Vezire unter Phiops II.' In *Nachr. Göttingen*, N.F. 4, ii (1940), 39–54.
13. Morgan, J. de. *Catalogue des Monuments et Inscriptions de L'Égypte antique*. Vienna, 1894.
14. Nelson, H. H. 'Fragments of Egyptian Old Kingdom Stone Vessels from Byblos.' In *Berytus*, I (1934), 19–22.
15. Quibell, J. E. *Excavations at Saqqarah, 1907–1908*. Cairo, 1909.
16. Reisner, G. A. *Excavations at Kerma* (Harvard African Studies, vol. V, 29–33; vol. VI, 506–10). Cambridge, Mass., 1923.
17. Säve-Söderbergh, T. *Aegypten und Nubien*. Lund and Copenhagen, 1941.
18. Smith, G. E. 'The Antiquity of Mummification.' In *Cairo Scientific Journal*, 2 (1908), 204–5.
19. Smith, G. E. and Dawson, W. R. *Egyptian Mummies*. London, 1924.

V. THE SEVENTH AND EIGHTH DYNASTIES

1. Albright, W. F. Review of H. Stock, *Die Erste Zwischenzeit Ägyptens.* In *Bull. A.S.O.R.* 119 (1950), 29.
2. Dunham, D. *Naga-ed-Dêr Stelae of the First Intermediate Period.* London, 1937.
3. Fischer, H. G. *Denderah in the Old Kingdom and its Aftermath.* Doctoral Dissertation, University of Pennsylvania, 1955.
4. Hayes, W. C. 'Royal Decrees from the Temple of Min at Coptos.' In *J.E.A.* 32 (1946), 3–23.
5. Jéquier, G. *La Pyramide d'Aba.* Cairo, 1935.
6. Kees, H. 'Beiträge zur altägyptischen Provinzialverwaltung und der Geschichte des Feudalismus.' In *Nachr. Göttingen* (1932), 85 ff.
7. Kees, H. *Studien zur aegyptischen Provinzialkunst.* Leipzig, 1921.
8. Newberry, P. E. 'A Sixth Dynasty Tomb at Thebes.' In *Ann. Serv.* 4 (1903), 97–100.
9. Newberry, P. E. 'Queen Nitocris of the Sixth Dynasty.' In *J.E.A.* 29 (1943), 51–4.
10. Peck, C. N. *Some Decorated Tombs of the First Intermediate Period at Naga-ed-Der.* Doctoral Dissertation, Brown University; 1959.
11. Petrie, W. M. F. *Dendereh 1898* (E.E.F. 17th Memoir) and vol. extra plates. London, 1900.
12. Quibell, J. E. *Excavations at Saqqara 1905–1906.* Cairo, 1907.
13. Scharff, A. 'Der historische Abschnitt der Lehre für König Merikare.' In *Sitzungsb. München,* 8 (1936).
14. Sethe, K. Review of R. Weill, *Décrets royaux.* In *G.G.A.* 174 (1912), 705–25.
15. Stock, H. *Die Erste Zwischenzeit Ägyptens* (*Studia Aegyptiaca,* 11, *An. Or.* 31). Rome, 1949.
16. Vandier, J. *Mo'alla.* Cairo, 1950.
17. Weill, R. *Les décrets royaux de l'ancien empire égyptien.* Paris, 1912.
18. Winlock, H. E. *The Rise and Fall of the Middle Kingdom in Thebes.* New York, 1947.
19. Wreszinski, W. *Bericht über die photographische Expedition von Kairo bis Wadi Halfa.* Halle, 1927.

VI. LITERATURE AND ART

1. Aldred, C. *Old Kingdom Art in Ancient Egypt.* London, 1949
2. Badawy, A. *A History of Egyptian Architecture,* 1. Giza, 1954.
3. Brunner-Traut, E. 'Die Weisheitslehre des Djedef-Hor.' In *Z.Ä.S.* 76 (1940), 3 ff.
4. Davies, Nina M. and Gardiner, A. H. *Ancient Egyptian Paintings.* Chicago, 1936.
5. Erman, A. *Die Märchen des Papyrus Westcar.* Berlin, 1890.
6. Erman, A. *The Literature of the Ancient Egyptians.* English translation by A. M. Blackman. London, 1927.
7. Gardiner, A. H. 'An Administrative Letter of Protest.' In *J.E.A.* 13 (1927), 75–8.
8. Gardiner, A. H. 'The Instruction Addressed to Kagemni and his Brethren.' In *J.E.A.* 32 (1946), 71–4.
9. Garnot, J. S. F. 'Quelques aspects du parallélisme dans les textes des pyramides.' In *Rev. hist. rel.* 123 (1941), 5–26.

10. Goedicke, H. 'Das Verhältnis zwischen königlichen und privaten Darstellungen im Alten Reich.' In *Mitt. deutsch. Inst. Kairo*, 15 (1957), 57–67.
11. Gunn, B. *The Instruction of Ptah-hotep and the Instruction of Keʾgemni.* London, 1918.
12. Hayes, W. C. *The Scepter of Egypt*, 1. New York, 1953. Chs. III–IX.
13. Junker, J. 'Der Maler ʾIrj.' In *Anzeiger der Österreichischen Akademie der Wissenschaften. Phil. hist. Klasse*, 3 (1956), 59–79.
14. Leclant, J. 'Fouilles et travaux en Égypte, *1955–1957*.' In *Or.* 27 (1958), 87–8, pl. VII.
15. Möller, G. *Hieratische Paläographie*, 1. Leipzig, 1927. Pp. 9–10.
16. Möller, G. *Hieratische Papyrus aus den königlichen Museen zu Berlin*, III. Leipzig, 1906.
17. Posener, G. *Littérature et politique dans l'Égypte de la XIIe Dynastie.* Paris, 1956.
18. Pritchard, J. B. (ed.). *A.N.E.T.* Princeton, 1950.
19. Schäfer, H. 'Eine Statue des Chnumwidders aus der Zeit des Cheops (*Ḥw.f Ḥnmw*).' In *O.L.Z.* 29 (1926), 723.
20. Sethe, K. *Die altägyptischen Pyramidentexte.* 4 vols. Leipzig, 1908–22.
21. Sethe, K. *Übersetzung und Kommentar zu den altägyptischen Pyramidentexten*, I–IV. Glückstadt, 1935–9.
22. Shoukry, M. Anwar. *Die Privatgrabstatue im Alten Reich* (*Ann. Serv.*, Supplément, Cahier no. 15). Cairo, 1951.
23. Smith, W. S. *A History of Egyptian Sculpture and Painting in the Old Kingdom.* Oxford, 1946. Ed. 2, 1949.
24. Smith, W. S. *The Art and Architecture of Ancient Egypt.* Harmondsworth, 1958. Revised printing, 1965; chs. IV–VIII.
25. Smith, W. S. *Ancient Egypt as Represented in the Museum of Fine Arts.* Boston, 1942, 1946, 1952, 4th revised ed. 1960. Chs. I, II and chronological table, pp. 193–202.
26. Smith, W. S. 'Old Kingdom Sculpture.' In *A.J.A.* 45 (1941), 514–28.
27. Smith, W. S. 'Fragments of a Statuette of Chephren.' In *W.Z.K.M.* 54 (1957), 186–90.
28. Smither, P. C. 'An Old Kingdom Letter Concerning the Crimes of Count Sabni.' In *J.E.A.* 28 (1942), 16–19.
29. Wolf, W. *Die Kunst Aegyptens, Gestalt und Geschichte.* Stuttgart, 1957. 'Das Alte Reich' 105–295.
30. Wreszinski, W., Grapow. H. and Schäfer, H. *Atlas zur altaegyptischen Kulturgeschichte*, part III. Leipzig, 1938.

A. ADDENDA

1. Lacau, P. and Lauer, J.-Ph. *La pyramide à degrés*, vol. 5. Cairo, 1965.
2. Posener-Kriéger, P. and de Cenival, J. L. *Hieratic Papyri in the British Museum*, Fifth Series: *The Abu Sir Papyri.* London, 1968.

CHAPTER XV

I. CLASSIFICATION OF THE MATERIAL

1. Albright, W. F. 'The Excavations of Tell Beit Mirsim, I. The Pottery of the First Three Seasons.' In *Ann. A.S.O.R.* 12 (1932), 1 ff.
2. Albright, W. F. 'The Excavation of Tell Beit Mirsim. IA. The Bronze Age Pottery of the Fourth Campaign.' In *Ann. A.S.O.R.* 13 (1933), 55 ff.

3. Albright, W. F. 'The Excavations of Tell Beit Mirsim. II. The Bronze Age.' In *Ann. A.S.O.R.* 17 (1938), 12 f.
4. Albright, W. F. 'Early Bronze Pottery from Bâb ed-Dra' in Moab.' In *Bull. A.S.O.R.* 95 (1944), 3 ff.
5. Bliss, F. J. *A Mound of Many Cities or Tell el Hesy Excavated.* London, 1894.
6. Engberg, R. M. and Shipton, G. H. *Notes on the Chalcolithic and Early Bronze Age Pottery of Megiddo (S.A.O.C.* 10). Chicago, 1934.
7. Fitzgerald, G. M. 'Excavations at Beth-Shan.' In *P.E.F.Q.S.* (1934), 123 ff.
8. Fitzgerald, G. M. 'The Earliest Pottery of Beth-Shan.' In *M.J.* 24 (1935), 5–22.
9. Garstang, J. 'Jericho, City and Necropolis.' In *Ann. Arch. Anthr.* 19 (1932), 8 ff., 19 ff., 38 ff.
10. Garstang, J. 'Jericho, City and Necropolis.' In *Ann. Arch. Anthr.* 22 (1935), 143 ff.
11. Garstang, J. 'Jericho, City and Necropolis.' In *Ann. Arch. Anthr.* 23 (1936), 73 ff., 91 ff.
12. Guy, P. L. O. *Megiddo Tombs (O.I.P.* 33). Chicago, 1938.
13. Iliffe, J. H. 'Pottery from Ras el 'Aïn'.' In *Q.D.A.P.* 5 (1935), 113 ff.
14. Kaplan, J. 'An Early Bronze Tomb at Tel-Aviv.' In *Bull. I.E.S.* 16 (1951–52), 22 ff.
15. Kenyon, K. M. 'Excavations at Jericho.' In *P.E.Q.* 84 (1952), 62 ff.; 85 (1953), 88 ff.; 86 (1954), 55 ff.; 87 (1955), 114 f.; 88 (1956), 77; 92 (1960), 103 f.
16. Kenyon, K. M. 'Some Notes on the Early and Middle Bronze Age Strata of Megiddo.' In *Eretz-Israel*, 5 (1958), 51* ff.
17. Kenyon, K. M. *Excavations at Jericho.* I. *The Tombs excavated in 1952–54.* London, 1960.
18. Loud, G. *Megiddo.* II. *Seasons of 1935–39 (O.I.P.* 62). Chicago, 1948.
19. Macalister, R. A. S. *The Excavations of Gezer*, I–III. London, 1912.
20. McCown, C. C. *Tell en-Naṣbeh.* I. *Archaeological and Historical Results.* Berkeley and New Haven, 1947.
21. Maisler, B. and Stekelis, M. 'The Excavations at Beth Yerah (Khirbet Kerak).' In *I.E.J.* 2 (1952), 165 ff., 218 ff.
22. Maisler, B. 'An Early Bronze Age Tomb at Kinnereth.' In *Bull. I.E.S.* 10 (1942–43), 1–9.
23. Marquet-Krause, J. *Les Fouilles de 'Ay (et-Tell) (Bibliothèque Archéologique et Historique*, 45). Paris, 1949.
24. Ory, J. 'Excavations at Rās el 'Aïn.' In *Q.D.A.P.* 6 (1938), 99 ff.
25. Rowe, A. 'The 1934 Excavations at Gezer.' In *P.E.F.Q.S.* 1935, 19 ff.
26. Sellin, E. and Watzinger, C. *Jericho. Die Ergebnisse der Ausgrabungen.* Leipzig, 1913.
27. Shipton, G. M. *Notes on the Megiddo Pottery of Strata VI–XX (S.A.O.C.* 17). Chicago, 1939.
28. Sukenik (Yadin), Y. 'On the Technique of Khirbet Kerak Ware.' In *Bull. A.S.O.R.* 106 (1947), 9 ff.
29. Tadmor, M. and Prausnitz, M. 'Excavations at Rosh Hanniqra.' In *'Atiqot*, 2 (1959), 72 ff.
30. Tufnell, O. *Lachish IV. The Bronze Age.* Oxford, 1958.
31. Vaux, R. de. 'Les fouilles de Tell el-Fâr'ah.' In *Rev. bibl.* 54 (1947), 403 ff.; 55 (1948), 548 ff.; 58 (1951), 394 ff.; 62 (1955), 553 ff.; 64 (1957), 557 ff.; 68 (1961), 576 ff.; 69 (1962), 212 ff., 252.

32. Wampler, J. C. *Tell en-Naṣbeh*. II. *The Pottery*. Berkeley and New Haven, 1947.
33. Wright, G. E. *The Pottery of Palestine from the Earliest Times to the end of the Early Bronze Age*. New Haven, 1937.

II. THE FORTIFIED CITIES

See bibliography for §1.

III. ARCHITECTURE: DWELLINGS

See bibliography for §1 and:

1. Dunand, M. In *Bull. M.B.* 4 (1940), 69 ff.
2. Yeivin, S. 'The Masonry of the Early Bronze Age People.' In *P.E.F.Q.S.* 1934, 189 ff.

IV. SANCTUARIES

See bibliography for §1

V. BURIALS

See bibliography for §1, and:

1. Woolley, L. *Ur Excavations*. II. *The Royal Cemetery*. London, 1934.

VI. MATERIAL CONDITIONS: INDUSTRY AND COMMERCE

1. Borchardt, L. *Das Grabdenkmal des Königs Saʒḥu-reʿ*, II. Leipzig, 1913.
2. Crowfoot, J. 'Notes on the Flint Implements of Jericho, 1936.' In *Ann. Arch. Anthr.* 24 (1937), 35 ff.
3. Dunand, M. *Byblia Grammata*. Beyrouth, 1945.
4. Engberg, R. M. and Shipton, G. M. 'Another Sumerian Seal Impression from Megiddo.' In *P.E.F.Q.S.* 1934, 90 ff.
5. Hestrin, R. and Tadmor, M. 'A Hoard of Tools and Weapons from Kfar Monash.' In *I.E.J.* 13 (1963), 265 ff.
6. Kenyon, K. M. 'A Crescentic Axehead from Jericho and a group of Weapons from Tell el Hesi.' In *Eleventh Annual Report of the Institute of Archaeology, University of London*, 1955, 1 ff.
7. Petrie, Fl. *The Royal Tombs of the First Dynasty*, I. London, 1900.
8. Prausnitz, M. W. 'Earliest Palestine Seal Impressions.' In *I.E.J.* 5 (1955), 190 ff.
9. Tzori, N. 'A Cylinder Seal Impression from Mount Gilboa.' In *P.E.Q.* 87 (1955), 89 f.

VII. FOREIGN RELATIONS: CHRONOLOGY

1. Amiran, R. 'Connections between Anatolia and Palestine in the Early Bronze Age.' In *I.E.J.* 2 (1952), 89 ff.
2. Braidwood, R. J. *Mounds in the Plain of Antioch* (*O.I.P.* 48). Chicago, 1937.
3. Braidwood, R. J. and Braidwood, L. S. *Excavations in the Plain of Antioch*. I. *The earlier assemblages, Phases A–J* (*O.I.P.* 61). Chicago, 1960.
4. Dunand, M. *Fouilles de Byblos*. I. Paris, 1936.
5. Ehrich, A. M. H. *Early Pottery of the Jebeleh Region*. Philadelphia, 1939.
6. Frankfort, H. *Oriental Institute Discoveries in Iraq 1933–34* (*O.I.P.* 19). Chicago, 1935.

7. Frankfort, H. *More Sculpture from the Diyala Region* (*O.I.P.* 60). Chicago, 1943.
8. Free, J. 'The fifth Season at Dothan.' In *Bull. A.S.O.R.* 152 (1958), 10 ff.
9. Guigues, P. L. 'Lébéa, Kafer Ḡarra, Qrayé.' In *Bull. M.B.* 1 (1937), 35 ff.
10. Hood, S. 'Excavations at Tabara el Akrad.' In *A. St.* 1 (1951), 113 ff.
11. Ingholt, H. *Rapport préliminaire sur sept campagnes de fouilles à Hama en Syrie*. Copenhagen, 1940.
12. Parr, P. J. 'Palestine and Anatolia: A Further Note.' In *Fourteenth Annual Report of the Institute of Archaeology*, University of London, 1958.
13. Petrie, Fl. *The Royal Tombs of the Earliest Dynasties*, II. London, 1901.
14. Petrie, Fl. *Abydos*, I. London, 1902.
15. Petrie, Fl. *Corpus of Prehistoric Pottery and Palettes*. London, 1921.
16. Reisner, G. A. *Mycerinus*. Cambridge, U.S.A., 1931.
17. Rowe, A. *A Catalogue of Egyptian Scarabs...in the Palestine Archaeological Museum*. Cairo, 1936.
18. Schaeffer, Cl. F. A. *Stratigraphie comparée et chronologie de l'Asie Occidentale*. Oxford, 1948.
19. Scharff, A. *Das urgeschichtliche Gräberfeld von Abusir-el-Meleq. Die Archäologischen Ergebnisse*. Leipzig, 1926.
20. Scharff, A. *Grundzüge der ägyptischen Vorgeschichte*. Leipzig, 1927.

VIII. OUTLINE OF HISTORY

1. Breasted, J. H. *Ancient Records of Egypt*. 1. Chicago, 1906.
2. Chiera, E. *Sumerian Religious Texts*. Upland, Pa., 1924.
3. Gardiner, A. H. *The Admonitions of an Egyptian Sage*. Leipzig, 1909.
4. Gardiner, A. H. 'Pap. Petersburg 1116A.' In *J.E.A.* 1 (1914), 29 ff.
5. Petrie, Fl. *Deshasheh*. London, 1898.
6. Quibell, J. E. *Hierakonpolis*, 1. London, 1900.
7. *Reallexikon der Assyriologie*, I–III. Berlin and Leipzig, 1932–.
8. Yadin, Y. 'The Earliest Record of Egypt's Military Penetration into Asia.' In *I.E.J.* 5 (1955), 1 ff.
9. Yeivin, S. 'Early Contacts between Canaan and Egypt.' In *I.E.J.* 10 (1960), 193 ff.
10. Yeivin, S. 'Further Evidence of Narmer at "Gath".' In *Or. Antiq.* 2 (1963), 205 ff.

A. ADDENDA

1. Aharoni, Y. and Amiran, R. 'Excavations at Tell Arad.' In *I.E.J.* 14 (1964), 131 ff., 280 ff.; 15 (1965), 251 ff.; *Rev. bibl.* 74 (1967), 68 ff.
2. Amiran, R. 'A Preliminary Note on the Synchronisms between the Early Bronze Strata of Arad and the First Dynasty.' In *Bull. A.S.O.R.* 179 (1965), 30 ff.
3. Amiran, R. 'Yanik Tepe, Shengavit and the Khirbet Kerak Ware.' In *A. St.* 15 (1965), 165 ff.
4. Callaway, J. A. 'The 1964 'Ai (Et-Tell) Excavations.' In *Bull. A.S.O.R.* 178 (1965), 13 ff.
5. Lapp, P. 'The Cemetery at Bab edh-Dhra'.' In *Archaeology*, 19 (1966), 104 ff.
6. Lapp, P. 'Bâb edh-Dhrâ', Jordan.' In *Rev. bibl.* 73 (1966), 556 ff.
7. Saller, S. 'Bâb edh-Dhra', Jordan.' In *Studii Biblici Franciscani Liber Annuus*, 15 (1964–5), 137 ff.

CHAPTER XVI

I. BABYLONIA: ARCHAEOLOGICAL DEVELOPMENT

1. Buchanan, B. *Catalogue of Ancient Near Eastern Seals in the Ashmolean Museum, Oxford,* I. Oxford, 1966.
2. Buren, E. D. van. Review of H. Frankfort, *Stratified Cylinder Seals from the Diyala Region* (*O.I.P.* 72). In *Arch. f. Or.* 17 (1956), 380 ff.
3. Contenau, G. *Manuel d'archéologie orientale,* I–IV. Paris, 1927–47.
4. Edzard, D. O. 'Enmebaragesi von Kiš.' In *Z.A.* 53 (1959), 9 ff.
5. Frankfort, H. *Cylinder Seals.* London, 1939.
6. Frankfort, H. *The Art and Architecture of the Ancient Orient.* Harmondsworth, 1954.
7. Gadd, C. J. *History and Monuments of Ur.* London, 1929.
8. Hrozný, B. *Ancient History of Western Asia, India and Crete.* Prague, 1951.
9. Jordan, J., Lenzen, H. and others. 'Vorläufige Berichte über die...in Uruk-Warka...Ausgrabungen' (*U.V.B.*), beginning in *Abh. Berlin, Phil.-hist. Klasse,* 1930.
10. Kramer, S. N. *Enmerkar and the Lord of Aratta.* Philadelphia, 1952.
11. Kramer, S. N. *From the Tablets of Sumer.* Colorado, 1956.
12. Kramer, S. N. *Sumerian Mythology.* Philadelphia, 1944.
13. Lloyd, S. *The Art of the Ancient Near East.* London, 1961.
14. Mallowan, M. E. L. *Early Mesopotamia and Iran.* London, 1965.
15. Parrot, A. *Archéologie mésopotamienne,* I, II. Paris, 1946, 1953.
16. Parrot, A. *Sumer.* London, 1960.
17. Roux, G. *Ancient Iraq.* London, 1964.
18. Saggs, H. W. F. *The Greatness that was Babylon.* London, 1962.
19. Smith, S. *Early History of Assyria to 1000 B.C.* London, 1928.
20. Spycket, A. *Les statues de culte dans les textes mésopotamiens des origines à la Ire. dynastie de Babylone.* Paris, 1968.
21. Strommenger, E. *The Art of Mesopotamia.* London, 1964.

II. THE DIYĀLĀ VALLEY

1. Agrawal, D. P. 'Harappa Culture: new evidence for a shorter chronology.' In *Science* 143 (1964), 950 ff.
2. Agrawal, D. P. 'Banas Culture and the Aryans.' In *Current Science,* 35 (1966), 114 ff.
3. Agrawal, D. P. and Kusumgar, S. In *Current Science,* 34 (1965), 42 ff.
4. Andrae, W. *Die Archaischen Ischtar-Tempel in Assur.* Leipzig, 1922.
5. Delougaz, P. *Pottery from the Diyala Region* (*O.I.P.* 63). Chicago, 1952.
6. Delougaz, P. *The Temple Oval at Khafajah* (*O.I.P.* 53). Chicago, 1940.
7. Delougaz, P. and Lloyd, S. *Pre-Sargonid Temples in the Diyala Region* (*O.I.P.* 58). Chicago, 1942.
8. Field, H. 'Steatite Vases from Kish.' In *Antiq.* VII (1933), 84 ff.
9. Frankfort, H. *More Sculpture from the Diyala Region* (*O.I.P.* 60). Chicago, 1943.
10. Frankfort, H. *Sculpture of the Third Millennium B.C. from Tell Asmar and Khafajah* (*O.I.P.* 44). Chicago, 1939.
11. Frankfort, H. *Iraq Excavations of the Oriental Institute 1932/33. Third Preliminary Report of the Iraq Expedition* (*O.I.C.* 17). Chicago, 1934.
12. Frankfort, H. *Stratified Cylinder Seals from the Diyala Region* (*O.I.P.* 72). Chicago, 1955.

13. Frankfort, H. and Jacobsen, T. *Oriental Institute Discoveries in Iraq, 1933/34. Fourth Preliminary Report of the Iraq Expedition* (*O.I.C.* 19). Chicago, 1935.
14. Frankfort, H., Lloyd, S. and Jacobsen, T. *The Gimilsin Temple and the Palace of the Rulers at Tell Asmar* (*O.I.P.* 43). Chicago, 1940.
15. Lal, B. B. 'A Picture Emerges: an assessment of the Carbon 14 datings of the proto-historic cultures of the Indo-Pakistan sub-continent.' In *Ancient India*, 18, 19 (1963), 208 ff.
16. Mackay, E. *Further Excavations at Mohenjo Daro*. 2 vols. Delhi, 1937.
17. Thureau-Dangin, F. *Die sumerischen und akkadischen Königsinschriften*. Leipzig, 1907.
18. Thureau-Dangin, F. *Rituels Accadiens*. Paris, 1921.

III. THE PRINCIPAL BABYLONIAN SITES

1. Abu al-Suf, B. 'A Study of Uruk pottery, its origins and distribution.' Doctoral thesis submitted to the University of Cambridge (1966).
2. Banks, E. J. *Bismya or the Lost City of Adab*. New York, 1912.
3. Barrelet, M.-Th. 'Une "Construction Enigmatique" à Tello.' In *Iraq*, 27 (1965), 100 ff.
4. Biggs, R. D. 'The Abū Ṣalābīkh Tablets: A Preliminary Survey.' In *J.C.S.* xx (1966), 73 ff.
5. Buren, E. D. van. 'Places of sacrifice (Opferstätten).' In *Iraq*, 14 (1962), 76 ff.
6. De Genouillac, H. and others. *Fouilles de Telloh, I, Époques Présargoniques*. Paris, 1934.
7. De Genouillac, H. *Premières Recherches Archéologiques à Kich*, I and II. Paris, 1924–5.
8. De Vaumas, E. 'L'écoulement des eaux en Mésopotamie et la provenance des eaux de Tello.' In *Iraq*, 27 (1965), 81 ff.
9. Deimel, A. *Schultexte aus Fara* (*W.V.D.O.G.* 43). Leipzig, 1923.
10. Deimel, A. *Šumerische Tempelwirtschaft zur Zeit Urukaginas und seiner Vorgänger* (*An. Or.* 2). Rome, 1931.
11. Deimel, A. *Wirtschaftstexte aus Fara* (*W.V.D.O.G.* 45). Leipzig, 1924.
12. Delougaz, P. 'A Short Investigation of the Temple at Al-'Ubaid.' In *Iraq*, 5 (1938), 1 ff.
13. Ehrich, R. W. (ed.). *Chronologies in Old World Archaeology*. Chicago, 1965.
14. Emery, W. B. *Archaic Egypt*. London, 1961.
15. Haines, R. C. 'Further excavations at the Temple of Inanna...at Nippur...' In *Ill. Ldn News*, 6 Sept. 1958, 386 ff.
16. Hall, H. R. and Woolley, C. L. *Al-'Ubaid* (*U.E.* 1). London and Philadelphia, 1927.
17. Hansen, D. P. 'New votive plaques from Nippur.' In *J.N.E.S.* 22 (1963), 145 ff.
18. Heinrich, E. *Fara*. Berlin, 1931.
19. Jacobsen, T. 'La Géographie et les Voies de Communication du Pays de Sumer.' In *R.A.* 52 (1958), 127 ff.
20. Jacobsen, T. 'Summary of Report by the Diyala Basin Archaeological Project, 1 June 1957 to 1 June 1958.' In *Sumer*, 14 (1958), 79 ff.
21. Jacobsen, T. 'The Waters of Ur.' In *Iraq*, 22 (1960), 174 ff.
22. Kramer, S. N. 'The Death of Gilgamesh.' In *Bull. A.S.O.R.* 94 (1944), 2 ff.
23. Le Breton, L. 'The Early Periods at Susa: Mesopotamian Relations.' In *Iraq*, 19 (1957), 79 ff.
24. Mackay, E. *A Sumerian Palace and the 'A' Cemetery at Kish, Mesopotamia*. Chicago, 1929.

25. Madhlum, T. A. 'The Excavations at Tell al-Wilayah.' In *Sumer*, 16 (1960), 62 ff. (Arabic section).
26. Mallowan, M. E. L. 'A Cylinder Seal in the Uruk–Jamdat Nasr style.' In *Baghdader Mitteilungen*, 3 (1964), 65 ff.
27. Mallowan, M. E. L. 'Noah's Flood Reconsidered.' In *Iraq*, 26 (1964), 62 ff.
28. Moorey, P. R. S. 'A Reconsideration of the Excavations on Tell Ingharra (East Kish), 1923–33.' In *Iraq*, 28 (1966), 18 ff.
29. Parrot, A. *Tello: Vingt Campagnes de Fouilles (1871–1933)*. Paris, 1948.
30. Raikes, R. L. 'The Physical Evidence for Noah's Flood.' In *Iraq*, 28 (1966), 52 ff.
31. Rashid, S. A. 'Die Ausgrabung von Tell el-Wilayah und die Bedeutung ihrer Rollsiegel.' In *Sumer*, 19 (1963), 82 ff.
32. Safar, F. 'Eridu. A Preliminary Report on the Third Season's Excavations, 1948–9.' In *Sumer*, 6 (1950), 27 ff.
33. Sarzec, E. de et Heuzey, L. *Découvertes en Chaldée*. Paris, 1884–1912.
34. Watelin, L. Ch. *Excavations at Kish*, IV. Paris, 1934.
35. Woolley, C. L. *The Royal Cemetery* (*U.E.* II). London and Philadelphia, 1934.
36. Woolley, C. L. *The Early Periods* (*U.E.* IV). London and Philadelphia, 1956.
37. Woolley, C. L. *The Ziggurat and its Surroundings* (*U.E.* v). London and Philadelphia, 1939.
38. Woolley, C. L. 'Excavations at Ur.' Preliminary reports in *A.J.* 3 (1923) to 14 (1934).

IV. ASSYRIA AND MESOPOTAMIA

1. Andrae, W. *Das wiedererstandene Assur*. Leipzig, 1938.
2. Dossin, G. 'XVe Campagne de Fouilles de Mari.' In *C.-R. Ac. Inscr. B.-L.* 1965. Paris, 1966.
3. Gadd, C. J. 'Tablets from Chagar Bazar, 1936.' In *Iraq*, 4 (1937), 178 ff.
4. Jacobsen, T. *The Sumerian King List*. Chicago, 1939.
5. Mallowan, M. E. L. 'Excavations at Brak and Chagar Bazar.' In *Iraq*, 9 (1947), 1 ff.
6. Mallowan, M. E. L. 'The Excavations at Tall Chagar Bazar, and an Archaeological Survey of the Ḫabur Region, 1934–5.' In *Iraq*, 3 (1936), 1 ff.
7. Mallowan, M. E. L. 'The Excavations at Tall Chagar Bazar and an Archaeological Survey of the Ḫabur Region. Second Campaign, 1936.' In *Iraq*, 4 (1937), 91 ff.
8. Mallowan, M. E. L. 'The Mechanics of Ancient Trade in Western Asia.' In *Iran*, III (1965), 1 ff.
9. Mallowan, M. E. L. 'Ninevite 5.' In *Vorderasiatische Archäologie, Studien und Aufsätze, Festschrift Moortgat*, 142 ff. Berlin, 1964.
10. Moortgat, A. *Archäologische Forschungen der Max Freiherr von Oppenheim—Stiftung im Nördlichen Mesopotamien* (1956). Köln und Opladen, 1959.
11. Moortgat, A. *Tell Chuēra in Nordost-Syrien*:
   Vorläufiger Bericht über die Grabung 1958. Köln und Opladen, 1960.
   Vorläufiger Bericht über die zweite Grabungskampagne 1959. Wiesbaden, 1960.
   Vorläufiger Bericht über die dritte Grabungskampagne 1960. Köln und Opladen, 1962.
   Vorläufiger Bericht über die vierte Grabungskampagne 1963. Köln und Opladen, 1965.
   Vorläufiger Bericht über die fünfte Grabungskampagne 1964. Wiesbaden, 1967.
12. Parrot, A. 'Les Fouilles de Mari; première campagne.' In *Syria*, 16 (1935), 1 ff.

13. Parrot, A. 'Les fouilles de Mari, quatorzième campagne (printemps 1964).' In *Syria*, 42 (1965), 1 ff.
14. Parrot, A. *Mission archéologique de Mari, I. Le Temple d'Ishtar*. Paris, 1965.
15. Parrot, A. 'XIVᵉ Campagne de fouilles de Mari.' In *C.-R. Ac. Inscr. B.-L.* 1964.
16. Speiser, E. A. *Excavations at Tepe Gawra*, i. Philadelphia, 1935.
17. Speiser, E. A. 'The pottery from Tell Billa.' In *M.J.* (Philadelphia), 23 (1933), 249 ff.
18. Speiser, E. A. 'Ethnic Movements in the Near East in the Second Millennium B.C.' In *Ann. A.S.O.R.* 13 (1931–32). New Haven, 1933.
19. Starr, R. F. S. *Nuzi*, i and ii. Cambridge (Mass.), 1939.
20. Thompson, R. C. and Hamilton, R. W. 'The British Museum Excavations on the Temple of Ishtar at Nineveh, 1930–1931.' In *Ann. Arch. Anthr.* 19 (1932), 55 ff.
21. Thompson, R. C. and Mallowan, M. E. L. 'The British Museum Excavations at Nineveh, 1931–1932.' In *Ann. Arch. Anthr.* 20 (1933), 71 ff.
22. Woolley, C. L. 'Hittite Burial Customs.' In *Ann. Arch. Anthr.* 6 (1914), 87 ff.

CHAPTER XVII

G. GENERAL

1. Albright, W. F. *The Archaeology of Palestine*. Harmondsworth, 1956.
2. Albright, W. F. 'The Present State of Syro-Palestinian Archaeology.' In *The Haverford Symposium on Archaeology and the Bible*. New Haven, 1939.
3. Albright, W. F. 'The Role of the Canaanites in the History of Civilization.' In *The Bible and the Ancient Near East: Essays in honor of William Foxwell Albright*, 328 ff. London, 1961.
4. Breasted, J. H. *Ancient Records of Egypt*. 5 vols. Chicago, 1906–7.
5. Dussaud, R. *La pénétration des Arabes en Syrie avant l'Islam*. Paris, 1955.
6. Dussaud, R. *Topographie historique de la Syrie antique et médiévale*. Paris, 1927.
7. Ebert, M. (ed.). *Reallexikon der Vorgeschichte*. Berlin, 1924–32.
8. Ehrich, R. W. *Relative Chronologies in Old World Archaeology*. Chicago, 1954.
9. Fisher, W. B. *The Middle East*. London, 1948.
10. Frankfort, Henri. *The Art and Architecture of the Ancient Orient*. Pelican History of Art. Harmondsworth, 1954.
11. Grant, Christina. *The Syrian Desert*. London, 1937.
12. Hitti, P. *Lebanon in History*. London, 1957.
13. Hommel, F. *Ethnologie und Geographie des alten Orients*. In W. Otto, *Handbuch der Altertumswissenschaft*, iii, 1, 1. Munich, 1926.
14. Kenyon, K. M. *Archaeology in the Holy Land*. London, 1960.
15. Moscati, S. *The Semites in Ancient History*. Cardiff, 1959.
16. Olmstead, A. T. *History of Palestine and Syria*. New York, 1931.
17. Pritchard, J. B. (ed.). *Ancient Near Eastern Texts relating to the Old Testament*. Ed. 2, Princeton, 1955.
18. Schaeffer, C. F. A. *Stratigraphie comparée et chronologie de l'Asie occidentale*. London, 1948.

I. THE BACKGROUND

1. Alt, A. *Völker und Staaten Syriens im frühen Altertum* (*Alte Or.* no. 34, Heft 4). Leipzig, 1936.
2. Bauer, Th. *Die Ostkanaanäer*. Leipzig, 1926.

3. Dhorme, E. 'Les Amorrhéens (à propos d'un livre récent).' In *Rev. bibl.* 37 (1928), 63 ff., 161 ff.; 39 (1930), 161 ff., 40 (1931), 161 ff.

4. Dillemann, L. *Haute Mésopotamie orientale et pays adjacents. Contribution à la géographie historique de la région, du Ve S. avant l'ère chrétienne au VIe S. de cette ère (Inst. fr. d'arch. de Beyrouth: Bibliothèque arch. et hist.* 72). Paris, 1962.

5. Driver, G. R. *Semitic Writing: From Pictograph to Alphabet (The Schweich Lectures of the British Academy,* 1944). London, 1949.

6. Dunand, M. *De l'Amanus au Sinaï: Sites et Monuments.* Beyrouth, 1953.

7. Edzard, D. O. *Die 'Zweite Zwischenzeit' Babyloniens.* Wiesbaden, 1957.

8. Frankfort, H. *Cylinder Seals.* London, 1939.

9. Gelb, I. J. 'The early history of the West Semitic Peoples.' In *J.C.S.* 15 (1961), 27 ff.

10. Gibson, John C. L. 'Observations on some important ethnic terms in the Pentateuch.' In *J.N.E.S.* 20 (1961), 217 ff.

11. Honigmann, E. *Historische Topographie von Nordsyrien im Altertum.* Leipzig, 1923.

12. Landsberger, B. 'Die Fauna des alten Mesopotamien, nach der 14. Tafel der Serie ḪAR.RA–ḫubullu.' In *Abh. Leipzig,* 1934.

13. Leemans, W. F. 'The Contribution of the Nomads to the Babylonian Population.' In *J.E.S.H.O.* 1 (1957), 138 ff.

14. Lewy, J. 'Zur Amoriterfrage.' In *Z.A.* 38 (1929), 243 ff.

15. Littmann, E. 'Unsemitische Ortsnamen in Nordsyrien.' In *Anatolian Studies presented to William Hepburn Buckler,* ed. W. M. Calder and Josef Keil, 151 ff. Manchester, 1939.

16. Mattern, J. 'A travers les villes mortes de la Syrie.' *Mélanges de l'Université Saint-Joseph, Beyrouth,* tome 17, fasc. 1. Beyrouth, 1953.

17. Moscati, S. *Ancient Semitic Civilisations.* London, 1957.

18. Moscati, S. *I Predecessori d'Israele: Studi sulle più antiche genti semitici in Siria e Palestina.* Rome, 1956.

19. O'Callaghan, R. T. *Aram Naharaim. A contribution to the History of Upper Mesopotamia in the Second Millennium B.C. (An. Or.* 26). Rome, 1948.

20. Parrot, A. (ed.). *Studia Mariana.* Leyden, 1950.

21. Speiser, E. A. 'Ethnic Movements in the Near East in the Second Millennium B.C.' In *Ann. A.S.O.R.* 13 (1933), 13 ff.

22. Tchalenko, Georges. *Villages antiques de la Syrie du nord,* I–III (*Inst. fr. de l'arch. de Beyrouth, Bibliothèque arch. et hist.* 50). Beyrouth, 1953–8.

23. Tocci, F. M. *La Siria nell'età di Mari (Università di Roma, Centro di Studi Semitici, Studi Semitici,* 3). Rome, 1960.

24. Vidal de la Blache, P. and Gallois, L. *Géographie universelle. 8. Asie Occidentale.* Paris, 1929.

II. SYRIA AT THE TIME OF THE KINGS OF AGADE

1. Albright, W. F. 'New light on the history of Western Asia in the Second Millennium B.C.' In *Bull. A.S.O.R.* 78 (1940), 23 ff.

2. Barton, G. A. *The Royal Inscriptions of Sumer and Akkad.* New Haven, 1929.

3. *C.A.D. The Assyrian Dictionary.* Chicago-Glückstadt, 1956.

4. *C.T. Cuneiform Texts from Babylonian tablets etc. in the British Museum.* London, 1896.

5. Dossin, G. 'Une lettre de Zimri-Lim à Iarim-Lim.' In *Proc. 23rd Internat. Congr. Orient.* Cambridge, 1954. London, undated.

6. Falkner, M. 'Studien zur Geographie des alten Mesopotamien.' In *Arch. f. Or.* 18 (1957–8), 1 ff.
7. Gadd, C. J. and Legrain, L. *U.E.T.* 1. *Royal Inscriptions. London,* 1928.
8. Gelb, I. J. *Hurrians and Subarians.* Chicago, 1944.
9. Gelb, I. J. *Old Akkadian Writing and Grammar.* Ed. 2. Chicago, 1961.
10. Gelb, I. J. 'Studies in the Topography of Western Asia.' In *A.J.S.L.* 55 (1938), 65 ff.
11. Genouillac, H. de. 'Inscriptions diverses.' In *R.A.* 10 (1913), 101 ff.
12. Güterbock, H. 'Die historische Tradition und ihre literarische Gestaltung bei Babyloniern und Hethitern bis 1200.' In *Z.A.* 42 (1934), 1 ff.
13. Hirsch, H. 'Die Inschriften der Könige von Agade.' In *Arch. f. Or.* 20 (1963), 1 ff.
14. Jacobsen, T. *The Sumerian King-list (Assyriological Studies, no.* 11). Chicago, 1939.
15. Knudtzon, J. A. *Die El-Amarna Tafeln.* Leipzig, 1915.
16. Kupper, J. R. *Les Nomades en Mésopotamie au temps des rois de Mari.* Liège-Paris, 1957.
17. Kupper, J. R. 'Uršu.' In *R.A.* 43 (1949), 79 ff.
18. Moscati, S. *Le antiche divinità semitiche.* Rome, 1958.
19. Parrot, A. 'Les fouilles de Mari: huitième campagne.' In *Syria,* 30 (1953), 196 ff.
20. Parrot, A. 'Les fouilles de Mari: neuvième campagne.' In *Syria,* 31 (1954), 151 ff.
21. Parrot, A. 'Les fouilles de Mari: dixième campagne.' In *Syria* 32 (1955), 185 ff.
22. Poebel, A. *Historical Texts (P.B.S.* v). Philadelphia, 1964.
23. *Reallexikon der Assyriologie.* Berlin and Leipzig, 1932–.
24. Rutten, M. 'Trente-deux modèles de foies en argile inscrits, provenant de Tell-Hariri (Mari).' In *R.A.* 35 (1938), 36 ff.
25. Smith, S. *The Statue of Idri-mi.* London, 1949.
26. Thureau-Dangin, F. *Die sumerischen und akkadischen Königsinschriften.* Leipzig, 1907.
27. Thureau-Dangin, F. 'Inscriptions diverses sur des statuettes de Ma'eri.' In *R.A.* 31 (1934), 137 ff.
28. Weidner, E. F. 'Das Reich Sargons von Akkad.' In *Arch. f. Or.* 16 (1952–3), 1 ff.
29. Weidner, E. F. *Der Zug Sargons von Akkad nach Kleinasien (Bo. Stu.* 6). Leipzig, 1922.

III. CITIES OF THE EUPHRATES AND THE KHABUR

1. Gadd, C. J. 'Tablets from Chagar Bazar and Tall Brak.' In *Iraq,* 7 (1940), 22 ff.
2. Lloyd, Seton. 'Some Ancient Sites in the Sinjar District.' In *Iraq,* 5 (1938), 123 ff.
3. Mallowan, M. E. L. 'Excavations in the Balikh Valley, 1938.' In *Iraq,* 8 (1946), 111 ff.
4. Mallowan, M. E. L. 'The Excavations at Tall Chagar Bazar, and an Archaeological Survey of the Habur Region, 1934–5.' In *Iraq,* 3 (1936), 1 ff.
5. Mallowan, M. E. L. 'The Excavations at Tall Chagar Bazar and an Archaeological Survey of the Habur Region, Second Campaign, 1936.' In *Iraq,* 4 (1937), 91 ff.

6. Mallowan, M. E. L. 'Excavations at Brak and Chagar Bazar.' In *Iraq*, 9 (1947), 1 ff.
7. Mallowan, M. E. L. *Twenty-five Years of Mesopotamian Discovery*. London, 1956.
8. Moortgat, A. *Tell Chuēra in Nordost Syrien. Vorläufiger Bericht über die Grabung 1958 (Wissenschaftliche Abhandlungen der Arbeitsgemeinschaft für Forschung des Landes Nordrhein-Westfalen.* Bd. 14). Köln und Opladen, 1960.
9. Moortgat, A. *Tell Chuēra in Nordost Syrien. Vorläufiger Bericht über die Grabung 1960 (Ibid.* Bd. 24). 1962.
10. Parrot, A. *Archéologie mésopotamienne*, I, II. Paris, 1946, 1953.
11. Parrot, A. 'Les fouilles de Mari: douzième campagne (automne 1961).' In *Syria*, 39 (1962), 151 ff.
12. Parrot, A. 'Les fouilles de Mari: treizième campagne (printemps 1963).' In *Syria*, 41 (1964), 3 ff.
13. Parrot, A. *Mari: Documentation photographique de la mission archéologique de Mari*. Neuchâtel et Paris, 1953.
14. Parrot, A. *Mission archéologique de Mari*. I. *Le Temple d'Ishtar*. Paris, 1956.
15. Speiser, E. A. *Excavations at Tepe Gawra*. I. Philadelphia, 1935.
16. von Oppenheim, Max. *Der Tell Halaf*. London and New York, 1933.
17. Yadin, Y. *The Art of Warfare in Biblical Lands in the Light of Archaeological Discovery*. London, 1963.

IV. CITIES OF THE PLAIN AND THE COAST

1. Amiet, Pierre. 'La glyptique syrienne archaïque. Notes sur la diffusion de la civilisation mésopotamienne en Syrie du Nord.' In *Syria*, 40 (1963), 57 ff.
2. Amiran, Ruth. 'Connections between Anatolia and Palestine in the Early Bronze Age.' In *I.E.J.* 2 (1952), 89 ff.
3. Anati, E. *Palestine before the Hebrews*. London, 1961.
4. Braidwood, Robert J. and Braidwood, Linda S. *Excavations in the Plain of Antioch.* I. *The Earlier Assemblages, Phases A–J* (*O.I.P.*61). Chicago, 1960.
5. Braidwood, Robert. 'Report on two sondages on the coast of Syria, south of Tartous.' In *Syria*, 21 (1940), 183 ff.
6. Du Mesnil du Buisson, Comte. *Le site archéologique de Mishrifé-Qatna*. Paris, 1935.
7. Du Mesnil du Buisson, Comte. 'Sourān et Tell Maṣin.' In *Berytus*, 2 (1935), 121 ff.
8. Ehrich, A. M. H. *Early Pottery of the Jebeleh Region* (*Mem. of the American Philosophical Society* 13). Philadelphia, 1939.
9. Fugmann, E. *Hama. Fouilles et Recherches de la Fondation Carlsberg 1931–1938. L'architecture des périodes préhellénistiques* (*Nationalmuseets Skrifter, Større beretninger* 4). Copenhagen, 1958.
10. Hallo, W. W. 'The Road to Emar.' In *J.C.S.* 18 (1964), 57 ff.
11. Goetze, A. 'Remarks on the Old Babylonian Itinerary.' In *J.C.S.* 18 (1964), 114 ff.
12. Hood, Sinclair. 'Excavations at Tabara el Akrad, 1948–49.' In *A.S.* 1 (1951), 113 ff.
13. Ingholt, H. *Rapport préliminaire sur sept campagnes de fouilles à Hama en Syrie (1932–1938). Archaeol. Kunsthist. Medd. Dan. Vid. Selsk.* 3, no. 1. Copenhagen, 1940.
14. Leemans, W. F. *Foreign Trade in the Old Babylonian Period*. Leiden, 1960.

15. Lewy, J. 'Studies in the Historic Geography of the Ancient Near East.' In *Or.* 21 (1952), 1 ff., 265 ff., 393 ff.
16. Mallowan, M. E. L. 'The Amq Plain.' In *Antiquity*, 37 (1963), 185 ff.
17. Mallowan, M. E. L. 'The Syrian City of Til-Barsip.' In *Antiquity*, 11 (1939), 338 f.
18. Matthiae, P. 'Le Sculture in Pietra.' In *Missione Archeologica Italiana in Siria: Rapporto preliminare della campagna 1965 (Tell Mardikh)*, 103 ff. Rome, 1966.
19. Maxwell-Hyslop, R. 'Western Asiatic Shaft-hole axes.' In *Iraq*, 11 (1949), 90 ff.
20. Maxwell-Hyslop, R., Taylor, J. du Plat, Seton-Williams, M. V. and Waechter, J. d'A. 'An archaeological Survey of the Plain of Jabbul, 1939.' In *P.E.Q.* 1942–3, 8 ff.
21. Schaeffer, C. F. A. 'Les fondements pré- et protohistoriques de Syrie du néolithique précéramique au bronze ancien.' In *Syria*, 38 (1961), 7 ff., 221 ff.
22. Schaeffer, C. F. A. *Ugaritica.* 4 vols. Paris, 1939–61.
23. Seton-Williams, M. V. 'Preliminary Report on the Excavations at Tell Rifa'at.' In *Iraq*, 23 (1961), 68 ff.
24. Sollberger, E. 'Bylos sous les rois d'Ur'. In *Arch. f. Or.* 19 (1959–60), 120 ff.
25. Thureau-Dangin, F. and Dunand, M. *Til-Barsib*, 2 vols., text and pls. Paris, 1936.
26. van Liere, W. J. and Lauffray, J. 'Nouvelle prospection archéologique dans la Haute Jézireh Syrienne.' In *Ann. Arch. de Syrie*, 4–5 (1954–5), 129 ff.
27. Woolley, Sir Leonard. *The Beginnings of Civilisation (History of Mankind: Cultural and Scientific Development*, vol. 1, part 2). London, 1963.
28. Woolley, C. L. and others. *Carchemish. Report on the Excavations at Jerablus on behalf of the British Museum*, 3 vols. London, 1921–52.
29. Woolley, C. L. *A Forgotten Kingdom*. Harmondsworth, 1950.
30. Woolley, C. L. 'Hittite Burial Customs.' In *Ann. Arch. Anthr.* 6 (1914), 87 ff.

V. BYBLOS AND THE LAND OF NEGAU

1. Albright, W. F. 'The Eighteenth Century Princes of Byblos and the Chronology of the Middle Bronze'. In *Bull. A.S.O.R.* 176 (1964), 38 ff.
2. Brunton, G. and Caton-Thompson, G. *The Badarian Civilisation and predynastic remains near Badari* (B.S.A. Egypt and E.R.A. 30th Year, 1924). London, 1928.
3. Dunand, M. *Byblia Grammata. Documents et Recherches sur le développement de l'écriture en Phénicie.* Beyrout, 1945.
4. Dunand, M. *Fouilles de Byblos.* 2 vols. Paris, 1939, 1954–8.
5. Dunand, M. 'Rapport préliminaire sur les fouilles de Byblos en 1949.' In *Bull. M.B.* 9 (1949–50), 65 ff.
6. Erman, A. *Die Literatur der Aegypter.* Leipzig, 1923.
7. Gressmann, H. 'Die Reliquien der kuhköpfigen Göttin in Byblos.' In *Stud. und Forschungen zur Menschen- und Völkerkunde*, 14 (1917), 250 ff.
8. Helck, W. *Die Beziehungen Ägyptens zu Vorderasien im 3. und 2. Jahrtausend v. Chr. (Äg. Abh.* 5). Wiesbaden, 1962.
9. Herrmann, S. 'Isis in Byblos.' In *Z.Ä.S.* 82 (1957), 48 ff.
10. Hopfner, T. *Fontes historiae religionis aegyptiacae (Fontes historiae religionis ex auctoribus graecis et latinis collecti*, fasc. 2, 1–4). Bonn, 1922–4.
11. Junker, H. *Bericht über die Grabungen auf dem Friedhof des Alten Reiches bei den Pyramiden von Giza.* Vol. 8, *Der Ostabschnitt des Westfriedhofes*. 2. Teil. *Denkeschr. der deutschen Akademie d. Wiss. in Wien*, phil.-hist. Kl. 73, 1. Vienna, 1947.

12. Lefebvre, G. *Le Mythe Osirien*. Études égyptologiques, 3, 4.
13. Loret, V. 'Quelques notes sur l'arbre *âch*.' In *Ann. Serv.* 16 (1916), 33 ff.
14. Lucas, A. *Ancient Egyptian Materials and Industries*, ed. 4 (revised by J. R. Harris). London, 1962.
15. Lucian *De Dea Syria*. (Translated by L. A. Strong, with notes by J. R. Harris.) London, 1962.
16. Mackay, Dorothy. *A Guide to the Archaeological Collections in the University Museum (American University of Beirut)*. Beirut, 1951.
17. Montet, Pierre. *Byblos et l'Egypte. Quatre Campagnes de Fouilles à Gebeil, 1921-1922—1923-1924*. Paris, 1928.
18. Montet, Pierre. 'Notes et documents pour servir á l'histoire des relations entre l'ancienne Égypte et la Syrie.' In *Kêmi*, 1 (1928), 19 ff., 83 ff.
19. Montet, Pierre. 'Le roi Sahurê et la princesse lointaine.' In *Mélanges Syriens offerts à M. René Dussaud*, vol. 1, 191 ff. Paris, 1939.
20. Nelson, H. H. 'Fragments of Egyptian Old Kingdom Stone Vases from Byblos.' In *Berytus*, 1 (1934), 19 ff.
21. Olmstead, A. T. *History of Assyria*. New York and London, 1923.
22. Petrie, W. M. F. *Prehistoric Egypt* (B.S.A. Egypt and E.R.A. 23rd year, 1917). London, 1920.
23. Porter, B. and Moss, R. L. B. *Top. Bibl.* vii. *Nubia, the Deserts and Outside Egypt*. Oxford, 1951.
24. Rowe, A. *A Catalogue of Egyptian Scarabs, Scaraboids, Seals and Amulets in the Palestine Archaeological Museum*. Cairo, 1936.
25. Säve-Söderbergh, T. *The Navy of the Eighteenth Egyptian Dynasty*. Uppsala and Leipzig, 1946.
26. Schäfer, H. 'Djed-Pfeiler, Lebenszeichen, Osiris, Isis.' In *Studies presented to F. Ll. Griffith*, 424 ff. London, 1936.
27. Schaeffer, C. F. A. 'La contribution de la Syrie ancienne à l'invention du bronze.' In *J.E.A.* 31 (1945), 92 ff.
28. Sethe, K. 'Zur ältesten Geschichte des ägyptischen Seeverkehrs mit Byblos und dem Lebanongebiet.' In *Z.Ä.S.* 45 (1908), 7 ff.
29. Sethe, K. *Urkunden des Alten Reichs*. Leipzig, 1903-33.
30. Sethe, K. *Urkunden der* 18. *Dynastie*. Leipzig, 1906-9.
31. Singer, C., Holmyard, E. J. and Hall, A. R. *A History of Technology*, vol. 1. Oxford, 1955.
32. Smith, Sidney. *Early History of Assyria to 1000 B.C.* London, 1928.
33. Wainwright, G. A. 'The occurrence of tin and copper at Byblos.' In *J.E.A.* 20 (1934), 29 ff.
34. Ward, W. A. 'Relations between Egypt and the Eastern Mediterranean from Prehistoric Times to the end of the Middle Kingdom.' In *J.E.S.H.O.* 6 (1963), 1 ff.

VI. EGYPTIANS IN SINAI AND PALESTINE

1. Albright, W. F. 'The Egyptian Empire in Asia in the twenty-first century B.C.' In *J.P.O.S.* 8 (1928), 229 ff.
2. Albright, W. F. 'Palestine in the earliest historical period.' In *J.P.O.S.* 15 (1933-5), 193 ff.
3. Albright, W. F. *The Vocalization of the Egyptian Syllabic Orthography (A.O.S. 5)*. New Haven, 1934.
4. Ball, John. *The Geography and Geology of West-Central Sinai*. Cairo, 1961.
5. Barrois, A. 'Aux mines du Sinai.' In *Rev. bibl.* 39 (1930), 578 ff.

6. Borchardt, L. *Das Grabdenkmal des Königs Saʒhu-Reʿ.*) 2 vols. (*Ausgrabungen der deutschen Orient-Gesellschaft in Abusir 1902–15.*) Leipzig, 1910–13.

7. Boreux, Ch. *Études de nautique égyptienne: l'art de la navigation en Égypte jusqu'à la fin de l'ancien empire* (*Mém. Inst. fr. Caire*, 50). Cairo, 1925.

8. Bourdon, Claude. *Anciens canaux, anciens sites et ports de Suez* (*Mém. de la Soc. roy. de Géogr. de l'Égypte*, tom. 7). Cairo, 1925.

9. Clère, J. J. 'Sur un nom du Wâdi Maghâra (Sinai).' In *J.E.A.* 24 (1938), 125 f.

10. Drioton, E. and Vandier, J. *L'Égypte* (*Clio: Introduction aux études historiques*), 1. Paris, 1952.

11. Emery, W. B. *Archaic Egypt.* Harmondsworth, 1961.

12. Emery, W. B. *Great Tombs of the First Dynasty*, vols. 1–3. Cairo and London, 1949–58.

13. Emery, W. B. *The Tomb of Hor-Aha.* Cairo, 1939.

14. Fischer, H. G. 'A scribe of the army in a Saqqara mastaba of the early fifth dynasty.' In. *J.N.E.S.* 18 (1959), 233 ff.

15. Forbes, R. J. *Studies in Ancient Technology*, vol. 9: *Metallurgy in Antiquity.* London, 1964.

16. Frankfort, H. 'Egypt and Syria in the First Intermediate Period.' In *J.E.A.* 12 (1926), 80 ff.

17. Frankfort, H. *Studies in early pottery of the Near East.* 1. *Mesopotamia, Syria and Egypt in their earliest interrelations* (*Royal Anthrop. Inst. Occasional Papers*, no. 6). London, 1924.

18. Gardiner, A. H. *Egypt of the Pharaohs.* Oxford, 1961.

19. Gardiner, A. H. 'The Military Road between Egypt and Palestine.' In *J.E.A.* 6 (1920), 99 ff.

20. Gardiner, A. H., Peet, T. E. and Černý, J. *The Inscriptions of Sinai.* Ed. 2, 2 vols., Oxford, 1952, 1955.

21. Goedicke, H. 'A Cylinder Seal of a Ruler of Byblos of the Third Millennium.' In *Mitt. deutsch. Inst. Kairo*, 19 (1963), 1 ff. and pl. 1.

22. Helck, W. 'Herkunft und Deutung einiger Züge des frühägyptischen Königs.' In *Anthropos*, 49 (1954), 961 ff.

23. Hassan, Selim. 'The Causeway of *Wnis* at Saqqara.' In *Z.Ä.S.* 80 (1955), 136 ff.

24. Hassan, Selim. 'Fouilles à Saqqarah 1937–1938.' In *Arch. f. Aeg. Arch.* 1 (1938), 175 ff.

25. Kantor, H. J. 'The early relations of Egypt with Asia.' In *J.N.E.S.* 1 (1942), 174 ff.

26. Kees, H. *Ancient Egypt: A Cultural Topography.* Ed. T. G. H. James. London, 1961.

27. Lucas, A. 'Copper in Ancient Egypt.' In *J.E.A.* 13 (1927), 162 ff.

28. Marquet-Krause, Juliet. *Les fouilles de ʿAy (et-Tell), 1933–1935.* Paris, 1949.

29. Mohammad Zaki Nour, Mohammad Salah Osman and Ahmad Youssof Moustafa. *The Cheops Boats*, part 1. Cairo, 1960.

30. Montet, Pierre. *Le Drame d'Avaris. Essai sur la pénétration des Sémites en Égypte.* Paris, 1941.

31. Montet, Pierre. 'Le Pays de Negaou, près de Byblos, et son dieu.' In *Syria*, 4 (1923), 181 ff.

32. Morgan, Jacques de. *Recherches sur l'origine de l'Égypte.* 2 vols. Paris, 1896–7.

33. Petrie, W. M. F. *Deshasheh*, 1897 (E.E.F. 15th Memoir). London, 1898.

34. Petrie, W. M. F. *Researches in Sinai.* London, 1906.

35. Petrie, W. M. F. *The Royal Tombs of the First Dynasty at Abydos*, 2 vols. (E.E.F. Memoirs, 18–21). London 1900, 1901.
36. Quibell, J. B. and Hayter, A. G. K. *Teti Pyramid, North Side. Excavations at Saqqara, Service des Antiquités de l'Égypte.* Cairo, 1927.
37. Smith, W. Stevenson. *A History of Egyptian Sculpture and Painting in the Old Kingdom.* Oxford, 1946.
38. Vandier, J. *Manuel d'archéologie égyptienne*, 5 vols. Paris, 1952–69.
39. Weill, R. *La presqu'île du Sinai: étude de géographie et d'histoire (Bibliothèque de l'École des Hautes Études*, 171). Paris, 1908.
40. Wilson, J. M. *The Burden of Egypt.* Chicago, 1951.
41. Yadin, Y. 'The Earliest Record of Egypt's Military Penetration in Asia.' In *I.E.J.* 5, no. 1 (1955), 1 ff.
42. Yeivin, S. 'Early Contacts between Canaan and Egypt.' In *I.E.J.* 10, no. 4 (1960), 193 ff.

A. ADDENDA

1. Davico, A., Squarciapino, M. F., Liverani, M. *etc. Missione archeologica italiana in Siria. Rapporto preliminare della campagna 1966 (Tell Mardikh). (Centro di Studi Semitici* 9.) Rome, 1967.
2. Hestrin, R. and Tadmor, M. 'A Hoard of Tools and Weapons from Kfar Monash.' In *I.E.J.* 13 (1963), 265 ff.
3. Klengel, H. 'Der Libanon und seine Zedern in der Geschichte des Alten Vorderen Orients.' In *Altertum*, 13 (1967), 67 ff.
4. Matthiae, P. 'Mission archéologique de l'Université de Rome à Tell Mardikh.' In *A.A.S.* 15 (1965), 83 ff.
5. Moortgat, A. *Tell Chuēra in Nordost Syrien. Vorläufige Bericht über die vierte Grabungskampagne 1963.* Köln und Opladen, 1965.
6. Moortgat, A. *Tell Chuēra in Nordost Syrien. Vorläufiger Bericht über die fünfte Grabungskampagne 1964.* Wiesbaden, 1967.
7. Moortgat-Correns, U. 'Ein Rollsiegel aus Arsameia.' In *Z.A.* 57 (1965), 6 ff.
8. Parrot, A. 'Les fouilles de Mari: quatorzième campagne (Printemps 1964).' In *Syria* 42 (1965), 1 ff.
9. Parrot, A. 'Les fouilles de Mari: quinzième campagne (Printemps 1966).' In *Syria* 42 (1965), 197 ff.
10. Parrot, A. 'Les fouilles de Mari: seizième campagne (Printemps 1967).' In *Syria* 44 (1967), 1 ff.
11. Parrot, A. *Mission archéologique de Mari, III. Les Temples d'Ishtarat et de Ninni-zaza.* Paris, 1967.
12. Rowton, M. B. 'The Woodlands of Ancient Western Asia.' In *J.N.E.S.* 26 (1967), 261 ff.
13. Sasson, J. M. 'Circumcision in the Ancient Near East.' In *J. Bibl. Lit.* 85 (1966), 473 ff.
14. Tadmor, M. 'Contacts between the 'Amuq and Syria-Palestine.' In *I.E.J.* 14 (1965), 258 ff.
15. Yeivin, S. 'Additional Notes on the Early Relations between Canaan and Egypt.' In *J.N.E.S.* 27 (1968), 37 ff.

CHAPTER XVIII

I. END OF THE LATE CHALCOLITHIC PERIOD

1. Bernabò Brea, L. 'Greater than Troy and Older: Poliochni in Lemnos.' In *Ill. Ldn. News*, 18 April 1959.
2. French, D. H. 'Late Chalcolithic Pottery in North-West Turkey and the Aegean.' In *A.St.* 11 (1961), 99–141.
3. Garstang, J. *Prehistoric Mersin.* Oxford, 1953.
4. Koşay, H. Z. and Akok, M. *Büyük Güllücek Kazı.* Ankara, 1957.
5. Koşay, H. Z. and Akok, M. 'The Pottery of Alaca Höyük.' In *A.J.A.* 51 (1947), 152 ff.
6. Koşay, H. Z. and Sperling, J. *Troad'da dört yerleşme yeri.* Istanbul, 1936.
7. Mellaart, J. 'Preliminary Report on a Survey of Pre-classical Remains in Southern Turkey.' In *A.St.* 4 (1954), 175–240.
8. Mellaart, J. 'Excavations at Beycesultan, 1957. Pottery from the Lower Levels at Beycesultan.' In *A.St.* 8 (1958), 113–25.
9. Mellaart, J. 'Archaeological Survey of the Konya Plain.' Short note in *A.St.* 9 (1959), 31–3.
10. Mellaart, J. 'Excavations at Beycesultan, 1958. II. The Chalcolithic Sounding.' In *A.St.* 9 (1959), 38–47.
11. Mellaart, J. 'Anatolia and the Balkans.' In *Antiq.* 34 (1960), 270–8.
12. Mellink, M. In H. Goldman, *Excavations at Gözlü Kule, Tarsus,* II. Princeton, 1956.
13. Mikov, V. 'The Prehistoric Mound of Karanovo.' In *Archaeology,* 12 (1959), 88–97.
14. Özgüç, T. 'Das prähistorische Haus beim Felsrelief von Fraktin.' In *Anatolia,* I (1956), 65 ff.
15. Temizer, R. Report on Yazır Hüyük in *V Türk Tarih Kongresi.* Ankara, 1960, 156–64.

II. THE EARLY BRONZE AGE

1. Bittel, K. *Kleinasiatische Studien.* Istanbul, 1942.
2. Forbes, R. J. *Metallurgy in Antiquity.* Leiden, 1950.
3. Mellaart, J. 'Anatolian Chronology of the Early and Middle Bronze Age.' In *A.St.* 7 (1957), 55–88.

III. THE EARLY BRONZE AGE I PERIOD

1. Akurgal, E. 'Yortankultur-Siedlung in Ovabayindir bei Balikesir.' In *Anatolia,* 3 (1958), 156 ff.
2. Bittel, K. 'Ein Gräberfeld der Yortan-Kultur bei Babaköy.' In *Arch. f. Or.* 13 (1939), 1 ff.
3. Bittel, K. and Otto, H. *Demirci Hüyük.* Berlin, 1939.
4. Blegen, C. W., Caskey, J. L., Rawson, M. and Sperling, J. *Troy.* I. *The First and Second Settlements.* Princeton, 1950.
5. Boardman, J. 'The Island of Chios.' In *Archaeology,* 8 (1955), 245 ff.
6. Bernabò Brea, L. 'Recenti scavi a Poliochni nell'isola di Lemnos.' In *Bollettino d'Arte,* 42 (1957), 193–217, with earlier bibliography.
7. Burney, C. A. 'Northern Anatolia before Classical Times.' In *A.St.* 6 (1956), 179–203.

8. Childe, V. G. 'Anatolia and Thrace.' In *A.St.* 6 (1956), 45–8.
9. Demangel, R. *Le tumulus dit de Protésilas.* Paris, 1926 (Karaağaçtepe).
10. Driehaus, J. 'Prähistorische Siedlungsfunde in der unteren Kaikosebene und an dem Golfe von Çandarlı.' In *Istanbuler Mitteilungen,* 7 (1957), 76–101.
11. Forsdyke, E. J. *Prehistoric Aegean pottery. British Museum Catalogue,* i, i. London, 1925.
12. Hood, M. S. F. 'British Excavations—Chios.' In *Archaeology in Greece* (*J.H.S.* supplement), 1955, 20.
13. Koşay, H. Z. *Pazarlı Hafriyatı raporu.* Ankara, 1941.
14. Lamb, W. *Excavations at Thermi in Lesbos.* Cambridge, 1936.
15. Lloyd, Seton and Mellaart, J. 'Beycesultan Excavations. Fourth Preliminary Report.' In *A.St.* 8 (1958), 93–125.
16. Mellaart, J. 'Beycesultan Excavations. Fourth Preliminary Report. Pottery from the Lower Levels of Beycesultan.' In *A.St.* 8 (1958), 113–25.
17. Mikov, V. 'Fouilles du site préhistorique près de Mikhalitch.' In *Razkopki i Proučvaniye (Fouilles et Recherches),* i (1948).
18. Müller, V. *Frühe Plastik in Griechenland und Vorderasien.* Augsburg, 1929.
19. von der Osten, H. H. *Alishar Hüyük,* i. Chicago (O.I.P. xxviii), 1937.
20. Özgüç, T. *Die Bestättungsgebräuche im vorgeschichtlichen Anatolien.* Ankara, 1948.
21. Özgüç, T. *Excavations at Horoztepe.* Ankara, 1958.
22. Rubensohn, O. 'Die prähistorischen und frühgeschichtlichen Funde auf dem Burghügel von Paros.' In *Athenische Mitteilungen,* 42 (1917), 1 ff.
23. Schachermeyr, F. *Die Ältesten Kulturen Griechenlands.* Stuttgart, 1956.
24. Schliemann, H. (and Calvert, F.). *Ilios.* London, 1880.
25. Seton-Williams, M. V. 'Cilician Survey.' In *A.St.* 4 (1954), 121–74.
26. Stewart, J., in Lamb, W. 'Excavations at Kusura. The Cemetery.' In *Archaeologia,* 86 (1937), 54 ff.
27. Stronach, D. B. 'The Development and Diffusion of Metal Types in Early Bronze Age Anatolia.' In *A.St.* 7 (1957), 89–126.
28. Temizer, R. 'Kayapınar Höyüğü buluntuları.' In *Belleten,* 18 (1954), 317 ff.
29. Woodward, A. M. and Ormerod, H. A. 'A Journey in South-Western Asia Minor.' In *B.S.A.* 16 (1909–10), 76 ff.

IV. THE EARLY BRONZE AGE 2 PERIOD

1. Arik, R. O. *Les fouilles d'Alaca Höyük.* Ankara, 1937.
2. Braidwood, R. J. and L. S. *Excavations in the Plain of Antioch,* i. Chicago (*O.I.P.* lxi), 1960.
3. Bernabò Brea, L. 'A Bronze Age House at Poliokhni in Lemnos.' In *P.P.S.* 22 (1955—Childe volume), 144 ff.
4. Bernabò Brea, L. 'Recenti scavi a Poliochni nell'isola di Lemnos.' In *Bollettino d'Arte,* 42 (1957), 193–217.
5. Brown, T. Burton. *Excavations in Azarbaijan,* 1948. London, 1951.
6. Burney, C. A. 'Eastern Anatolia in the Chalcolithic and Early Bronze Age.' In *A.St.* 8 (1958), 157–210.
7. Childe, V. G. *The Dawn of European Civilisation.* Ed. 6. London, 1957.
8. Field, H. 'Contributions to the Anthropology of the Soviet Union. Résumé of B. A. Kuftin, *Urarskii Kolumbarii,* in *Vestnik Gos. Muz. Gruzi,* xiii b. Tbilisi, 1943. In *Smithsonian Miscellanies,* 1948.
9. Gimbutas, M. *The Prehistory of Eastern Europe.* Cambridge (Mass.), 1956.

10. Hood, M. S. F. 'Excavations at Tabara el Akrad, 1948–49.' In *A.St.* (1951), 113–47.
11. Kansu, Ş. A. *Etiyokuşu hafriyatı raporu.* Ankara, 1940.
12. Kökten, K. I., Özgüç, N. and Özgüç, T. 'Samsun Kazıları.' In *Belleten*, 9 (1945), 361 ff.
13. Körte, A. 'Ein altphrygischer Tumulus bei Bos-öjük.' In *Athenische Mitteilungen*, 24 (1899), 1 ff.
14. Koşay, H. Z. 'Ahlatlıbel Hafriyatı.' In *T.T.A.E.D.* 2 (1934), 3 ff.
15. Koşay, H. Z. *Ausgrabungen von Alaca Höyük.* Ankara, 1944.
16. Koşay, H. Z. *Les fouilles d'Alaca Höyük*, 1937–39. Ankara, 1951.
17. Koşay, H. Z. and Turfan, K. 'Erzerum-Karaz Kazısı raporu.' In *Belleten*, 23, (1959), 349–413.
18. Kuftin, B. A. *Arkheologischeskie raskopki 1947 goda v Tsalkinskom raione.* Tiflis, 1948.
19. Lamb, W. 'Excavations at Kusura.' In *Archaeologia*, 87 (1938), 217 ff.
20. Lamb, W. 'The Culture of Northeastern Anatolia and its Neighbours.' In *A.St.* 4 (1954), 21–32.
21. Lloyd, Seton and Gökçe, N. 'Excavations at Polatlı.' In *A.St.* 1 (1951), 21–6.
22. Lloyd, Seton and Mellaart, J. 'Beycesultan Excavations. Fourth Preliminary Report.' In *A.St.* 8 (1958), 93–125.
23. Luschan, F. von. *Die Kleinfunde von Sendschirli.* Berlin, 1943.
24. Mellaart, J. 'The End of the Early Bronze Age in Anatolia and the Aegean.' In *A.J.A.* 62 (1958), 1–31.
25. Mellaart, J. 'Notes on the Architectural Remains of Troy I and II.' In *A.St.* 9 (1959), 131–62.
26. Mellaart, J. 'The Royal Treasure of Dorak.' In *Ill. Ldn News*, 28 Nov. 1959.
27. Özgüç, T. 'Samsun hafriyatının 1941–42 yılı necticeleri.' In *III. Türk Tarih Krongresi.* Ankara, 1948.
28. Perrot, G. and Chipiez, C. *History of Art in Phrygia, Lydia, Caria and Lycia.* London, 1892.
29. Schachermeyr, F. 'Prähistorische Kulturen Griechenlands.' In *P.W.* (Sonderdruck).
30. Schliemann, H. *Ilios.* London, 1880.
31. Schmidt, H. *Schliemanns Sammlung Trojanischer Altertümer.* Berlin, 1902.
32. Tezcan, B. 'Nallıhan-Beypazarı çevresinden getirtilen kaplar hakkında.' In *Belleten*, 20 (1956), 343 ff., with earlier references.

VI. THE CATASTROPHE AT THE END OF THE EARLY BRONZE AGE 2 PERIOD

1. Albright, W. F. 'Dunand's New Byblos Volume: A Lycian at the Byblian Court.' In *Bull. A.S.O.R.* 155 (1959), 31 ff.
2. Laroche, E. 'Comparaison du Louvite et du Lycien.' In *Bulletin de la Société de Linguistique*, 53 (1958), 159–97.
3. Mellaart, J. 'Archaeological Survey of the Konya Plain.' A short note in *A.St.* 9 (1959), 31–3.
4. Palmer, L. R. 'Luvian and Linear A.' In *Trans. Phil. Soc.* (1958), 75–100.

VII. TROY I
VIII. TROY II } See Bibliography to ch. xxiv (*a*), sect. vii.

CHAPTER XIX

G. GENERAL

1. Andrae, W. *Die archaischen Ischtar-Tempel in Assur* (*W.V.D.O.G.* 39). Leipzig, 1922.
2. Andrae, W. *Das wiedererstandene Assur*. Leipzig, 1938.
3. Barton, G. A. *The Royal Inscriptions of Sumer and Akkad*. New Haven, 1929.
4. Bernhardt, I. and Kramer, S. N. 'Sumerische literarische Texte in der Hilprecht-Sammlung.' In *Wissens. Zeitschr. der. . . Universität Jena*, Jahrg. 5 (1955–6), 753 ff.
5. *C.A.D. The Assyrian Dictionary*. Chicago, 1956– .
6. Cameron, G. G. *History of Early Iran*. Chicago, 1936.
7. Christian, V. *Altertumskunde des Zweistromlandes*. Leipzig, 1938.
8. Contenau, G. *Manuel d'archéologie orientale*, I–IV. Paris, 1927–47.
9. Contenau, G. *La divination chez les Assyriens et les Babyloniens*. Paris, 1940.
10. Ebeling, E., Meissner, B. and Weidner, E. F. (eds.). *Reallexikon der Assyriologie*, I, II. Berlin and Leipzig, 1932, 1938.
11. Edmonds, C. J. *Kurds, Turks, and Arabs*. London, 1957.
12. Forbes, R. J. *Metallurgy in Antiquity*. Leiden, 1950.
13. Gadd, C. J. *Ideas of Divine Rule in the Ancient East*. London, 1948.
14. Gadd, C. J. and Legrain, L. *Royal Inscriptions* (*U.E.T.* I). London and Philadelphia, 1928.
15. Gelb, I. J. *Hurrians and Subarians* (*S.A.O.C.* 22). Chicago, 1944.
16. Gelb, I. J. *Glossary of Old Akkadian*. Chicago, 1957.
17. Gelb, I. J. *Old Akkadian Writing and Grammar*. Ed. 2. Chicago, 1961.
18. Jacobsen, T. *The Sumerian King-list* (*Assyriological Studies*, no. 11). Chicago, 1939.
19. Jastrow, M. *Die Religion Babyloniens und Assyriens*. Giessen, 1905–12.
20. King, L. W. *Chronicles concerning Early Babylonian Kings*. London, 1907.
21. King, L. W. *A History of Sumer and Akkad*. London, 1910.
22. Kramer, S. N. *From the Tablets of Sumer*. Indian Hills, Colorado, 1956.
23. Legrain, L. *Historical Fragments* (*P.B.S.* 13). Philadelphia, 1922.
24. Legrain, L. *Royal Inscriptions and Fragments from Nippur and Babylon* (*P.B.S.* 15). Philadelphia, 1926.
25. Legrain, L. 'The Inscriptions of the Kings of Agade'. In *M.J.* 14 (1923), 203 ff.
26. Le Strange, G. *The Lands of the Eastern Caliphate*. Cambridge, 1905.
27. Meer, P. van der. *De Agadeperiode, haar geschiedenis en cultuur*. Leiden, 1947.
28. Meissner, B. *Babylonien und Assyrien*, I, II. Heidelberg, 1920, 1925.
29. *Mém. D.P. Délégation en Perse: Mémoires*. Paris, 1900– .
30. Mercer, S. A. B. *Sumero-Babylonian Year-formulae*. London, 1946.
31. Parrot, A. *Sumer*. London, 1960.
32. Poebel, A. *Historical and Grammatical Texts* (*P.B.S.* 4, 5). Philadelphia, 1914.
33. Pritchard, J. B. (ed.). *Ancient Near-Eastern Texts relating to the Old Testament*. Ed. 2. Princeton, 1955.
34. Singer, C., Holmyard, E. J. and Hall, A. R. *A History of Technology*, I. Oxford, 1954.
35. Smith, S. *Early History of Assyria*. London, 1928.
36. Soden, W. von. *Akkadisches Handwörterbuch*. Wiesbaden, 1959– .

37. Speiser, E. A. *Mesopotamian Origins*. Philadelphia, 1930.
38. Speiser, E. A. 'Some Factors in the Collapse of Akkad.' In *J.A.O.S.* 72 (1952), 97 ff.
39. Thureau-Dangin, F. *Die sumerischen und akkadischen Königsinschriften*. Leipzig, 1907.
40. Ungnad, A. *Subartu*. Berlin and Leipzig, 1936.
41. Ungnad, A. 'Datenlisten.' In *R.L.A.* 2 (1938), 131 ff.
42. Woolley, C. L. *The Royal Cemetery* (Ur Excavations, II). London and Philadelphia, 1934.

I. THE REIGN OF SARGON

1. Albright, W. F. 'The Epic of the King of Battle.' In *J.S.O.R.* 7 (1923), 1 ff.
2. Albright, W. F. 'A Babylonian Geographical Treatise on Sargon of Akkad's Empire.' In *J.A.O.S.* 45 (1925), 193 ff.
3. Albright, W. F. 'The Nebuchadnezzar and Neriglissar Chronicles.' In *Bull. A.S.O.R.* 143 (1956), 28 ff.
4. Basmachi, Faraj. 'An Akkadian Stele.' In *Sumer*, 10 (1954), 116 ff.
5. Bilgiç, E. 'Die Ortsnamen der "kappadokischen" Urkunden im Rahmen der alten Sprachen Kleinasiens.' In *Arch. f. Or.* 15 (1945–51), 1 ff.
6. Dhorme, E. 'La tablette de Sargon l'Ancien.' In *Rev. bibl.* 33 (1924), 20 ff.
7. Dossin, G. 'Les archives économiques du Palais de Mari.' In *Syria*, 21 (1939), 97 ff.
8. Dossin, G. 'L'inscription de fondation de Iaḫdun-Lim, roi de Mari.' In *Syria*, 32 (1955), 1 ff.
9. Ebeling, E., Meissner, B. and Weidner, E. F. *Die Inschriften der altassyrischen Könige*. Leipzig, 1926.
10. Falkenstein, A. Review of Meek, T. J., *Old Akkadian, Sumerian, and Cappadocian Tablets from Nuzi*. In *Z.D.M.G.* 90 (1936), 711 ff.
11. Falkner, M. 'Studien zur Geographie des alten Mesopotamien.' In *Arch. f. Or.* 18 (1957–8), 1 ff.
12. Feigin, S. I. 'Ḫum-Ḫum.' In *An. Or.* 12 (1935), 82 ff.
13. Forbes, R. J. 'Silver and Lead in Antiquity.' In *J.E.O.L.* 7 (1943), 489 ff.
14. Gadd, C. J. 'Une donnée chronologique.' In *Rencontre assyriologique internationale*, 2 (1951), 70 f.
15. Garstang, J. and Gurney, O. R. *The Geography of the Hittite Empire*. London, 1959.
16. Genouillac, H. de. *Textes religieux sumériens du Louvre* (*T.C.L.* 15, 16). Paris, 1930.
17. Goetze, A. 'Historical Allusions in Old Babylonian Omen-texts.' In *J.C.S.* 1 (1947), 253 ff.
18. Goetze, A. 'An Old Babylonian Itinerary.' In *J.C.S.* 7 (1953), 51 ff.
19. Goetze, A. 'Ḫulibar of Duddul.' In *J.N.E.S.* 12 (1953), 114 ff.
20. Güterbock, H. G. 'Die historische Tradition und ihre literarische Gestaltung bei Babyloniern und Hethitern bis 1200.' Erster Teil in *Z.A.* 42 (1934), 1 ff., zweiter Teil in *Z.A.* 44 (1938), 45 ff.
21. Jacobsen, T. 'Early Political Development in Mesopotamia.' In *Z.A.* 52 (1957), 91 ff.
22. Kupper, J.-R. *Les Nomades en Mésopotamie au temps des rois de Mari*. Paris, 1957.
23. Læssøe, Jørgen. 'Akkadian *annakum*: "Tin" or "Lead"?' In *Acta Or.* 24 (1959), 83 ff.

24. Landsberger, B. 'Über die Völker Vorderasiens im dritten Jahrtausend.' In
    Z.A. 35 (1924), 213 ff.
25. Lewy, J. 'Tabor, Tibar, Atabyros.' In H.U.C.A. 23 (1950–1), 357 ff.
26. Limet, H. Le travail du métal au pays de Sumer. Paris, 1960.
27. Luckenbill, D. D. Ancient Records: Assyria. Chicago, 1926.
28. Mallowan, M. E. L. 'The Bronze Head of the Agade Period from Nineveh.'
    In Iraq, 3 (1936), 104 ff.
29. Nassouhi, Essad. 'La stèle de Sargon l'Ancien.' In R.A. 21 (1924), 65 ff.
30. Nougayrol, J. 'Note sur la place des "présages historiques" dans l'extispicine
    babylonienne.' In École Pratique des Hautes Études, Annuaire 1944–5, 1 ff.
31. Nougayrol, J. 'Un chef-d'œuvre inédit de la littérature babylonienne.' In R.A.
    45 (1951), 169 ff.
32. Poebel, A. 'The Assyrian king-list from Khorsabad.' In J.N.E.S. 1 (1942),
    247 ff., 460 ff.
33. Pohl, A. Vorsargonische und sargonische Wirtschaftstexte (T. u. M. 5.) Leipzig,
    1935.
34. Rutten, M. 'Trente-deux modèles de foies...de Tell-Hariri (Mari).' In
    R.A. 35 (1938), 36 ff.
35. Scheil, V. 'Nouveaux renseignements sur Šarrukin.' In R.A. 13 (1916),
    175 ff.
36. Scheil, V. 'Dynasties élamites d'Awan et de Simaš.' In R.A. 28 (1931), 1 ff.
37. Smith, S. 'The Face of Humbaba.' In Ann. Arch. Anthr. 11 (1924), 107 ff.
38. Smith, S. 'Uršu and Ḫaššum.' In A.St. 6 (1956), 35 ff.
39. Sollberger, E. (ed.) 'Aspects du contact suméro-akkadien.' In Genava, n.s. 8
    (1960), 241 ff.
40. Thompson, R. C. A Dictionary of Assyrian Botany. London, 1949.
41. Thureau-Dangin, F. 'Numération et métrologie sumériennes.' In R.A. 18
    (1921), 123 ff.
42. Thureau-Dangin, F. 'Humbaba.' In R.A. 22 (1925), 23 ff.
43. Thureau-Dangin, F. 'Iaḫdunlim, roi de Ḫana.' In R.A. 33 (1936), 49 ff.
44. Unger, E. Sargon II von Assyrien, der Sohn Tiglatpilesers III. Istanbul, 1933.
45. Wainwright, G. A. 'Early Tin in the Aegean.' In Antiq. 18 (1944), 57 ff.
46. Weidner, E. F. Der Zug Sargons von Akkad nach Kleinasien (Bo. Stu. 6).
    Leipzig, 1922.
47. Weidner, E. F. 'Historisches Material in der babylonischen Omina-Literatur.'
    In M.A.O.G. 4 (1928), 226 ff.
48. Weidner, E. F. 'Das Reich Sargons von Akkad.' In Arch. f. Or. 16 (1952–3),
    1 ff.

II. THE SUCCESSORS OF SARGON

1. Dales, G. F. 'Harappan Outposts on the Makran Coast.' In Antiq. 36 (1962),
   86 ff.
2. Falkenstein, A. 'Enḫedu'anna, die Tochter Sargons von Akkade.' In R.A. 52
   (1958), 129 f.
3. Gelb, I. J. 'The Early History of the West Semitic Peoples.' In J.C.S. 15
   (1961), 27 ff.
4. Gershevitch, I. 'Sissoo at Susa.' In Bull. S.O.A.S. 19 (1957), 317 ff.
5. Jacobsen, T. 'The Assumed Conflict between Sumerians and Semites in Early
   Babylonian History.' In J.A.O.S. 59 (1939), 485 ff.
6. Jacobsen, T. 'The Waters of Ur.' In Iraq, 22 (1960), 174 ff.
7. King, L. W. 'The Cruciform Monument of Manishtusu.' In R.A. 9 (1912),
   91 ff.

8. König, F. W. 'Anshan.' In *R.L.A.* 1 (1932), 111 ff.
9. Kramer, S. N. 'Dilmun, the Land of the Living.' In *Bull. A.S.O.R.* 96 (1944), 18 ff.
10. Leemans, W. F. *Foreign Trade in the Old Babylonian Period.* Leiden, 1960.
11. Leemans, W. F. 'The Trade Relations of Babylonia and the Question of Relations with Egypt in the Old Babylonian Period.' In *Journ. of Econ. and Social Hist. of the Orient*, 3 (1960), 21 ff.
12. Mallowan, M. E. L. 'Excavations at Brak and Chagar Bazar.' In *Iraq*, 9 (1947), 1 ff.
13. Oppenheim, A. L. 'The Seafaring Merchants of Ur.' In *J.A.O.S.* 74 (1954), 6 ff.
14. Piggott, Stuart. *Prehistoric India.* Harmondsworth, 1950.
15. Poebel, A. *Miscellaneous Studies (Assyriological Studies*, no. 14). Chicago, 1947.
16. Scheil, V. 'Inscription de Maništusu.' In *R.A.* 7 (1910), 103 ff.
17. Stein, A. *An Archaeological Tour in Gedrosia* (Mem. of Arch. Survey of India, 43). Calcutta, 1931.
18. Thureau-Dangin, F. 'Notes assyriologiques: 1. La tablette S. 3.' In *R.A.* 7 (1910), 179 ff.
19. Wheeler, M. *The Indus Civilization. The Cambridge History of India*, supplementary volume. Cambridge, 1953.
20. Woolley, C. L. *The Early Periods* (Ur Excavations, 4). London and Philadelphia, 1956.

III. THE REIGN OF NARAM-SIN

1. Bottéro, J. and Finet, A. *Archives royales de Mari XV: Répertoire analytique des tomes I à V.* Paris, 1954.
2. Forrer, E. 'Assyrien.' In *R.L.A.* 1 (1932), 228 ff.
3. Gurney, O. R. 'The Sultantepe Tablets, IV: The Cuthaean Legend of Naram-Sin.' In *A.St.* 5 (1955), 93 ff.
4. Güterbock, H. G. 'Bruchstück eines altbabylonischen Naram-Sin-Epos.' In *Arch. f. Or.* 13 (1939–41), 46 ff.
5. Hallo, W. W. *Early Mesopotamian Royal Titles.* New Haven, 1957.
6. Herzfeld, E. *Am Tor von Asien.* Berlin, 1920.
7. Herzfeld, E. 'Reisebericht.' In *Z.D.M.G.* 80 (1926), 228 f.
8. Læssøe, J. 'The Shemshāra Tablets.' In *Arkæol. Kunsthist. Medd. Dan. Vid. Selsk.* 4 (1959), 5 ff.
9. Landsberger, B. 'Ḫabiru und Lulaḫḫu.' In *K.F.* 1 (1930), 321 ff.
10. Lewy, J. 'Ḫatta, Ḫattu, Ḫatti, Ḫattuša and "Old Assyrian" Ḫattum.' In *Arch. Orient.* 18 (1950), 366 ff.
11. Naab, J. P. and Unger, E. *Die Entdeckung der Stele des Naram-Sin in Pir-Hüseyin.* Istanbul, 1934.
12. Noth, M. 'Zum Ursprung der phönikischen Küstenstädte.' In *W.O.* 1 (1947), 21 ff.
13. Speiser, E. A. *Southern Kurdistan in the Annals of Ashurnasirpal and To-day (Ann. A.S.O.R.* 8, 1926–7). New Haven, 1928.
14. Ungnad, A. 'Der Akkader Naram-Sin und der Ägypter Mani.' In *Arch. f. Or.* 14 (1941–4), 199 ff.
15. Wiseman, D. J. *The Alalakh Tablets.* London, 1953.

IV. THE STATE OF BABYLONIA UNDER THE DYNASTY OF AGADE

1. Barnett, R. D. 'Early Shipping in the Near East.' In *Antiq.* 32 (1958), 220 ff.
2. Diakonoff, I. M. 'Sale of Land in Pre-Sargonic Sumer.' In *Papers presented by the Soviet Delegation at the XXIII International Congress of Orientalists.* Moscow, 1954.
3. Falkenstein, A. *Die neusumerischen Gerichtsurkunden,* I–III. Munich, 1956, 1957.
4. Frankfort, H. *Cylinder Seals.* London, 1939.
5. Gadd, C. J. 'Seals of Ancient Indian Style Found at Ur.' In *Proc. Brit. Acad.* 18 (1932), 191 ff.
6. Gelb, I. J. *Sargonic Texts from the Diyala Region.* Chicago, 1952.
7. Gelb, I. J. 'Old Akkadian Inscriptions in Chicago Natural History Museum.' In *Fieldiana: Anthropology,* 44 (1955), 161 ff.
8. Goetze, A. *The Laws of Eshnunna (Ann. A.S.O.R.* 31, 1951–2). New Haven, 1956.
9. Hackman, G. G. and Stephens, F. *Sumerian and Akkadian Administrative Texts (B.I.N. 8).* New Haven, 1958.
10. Ḥaurānī, G. F. *Arab Seafaring in the Indian Ocean, in Ancient and Medieval Times (Princeton Oriental Studies,* 13). Princeton, 1951.
11. Kraus, F. R. 'Provinzen des neusumerischen Reiches von Ur.' In *Z.A.* 51 (1955), 45 ff.
12. Poebel, A. 'The City Aktab.' In *J.A.O.S.* 57 (1937), 359 ff.
13. Porada, E. and Buchanan, B. *Corpus of Ancient Near-Eastern Seals in North American Collections,* I. Washington, 1948.
14. Wilson, A. T. *The Persian Gulf.* Oxford, 1928.

V. THE LAST KINGS OF AGADE AND THE GUTIAN SUPREMACY

1. Falkenstein, A. and Soden, W. von. *Sumerische und akkadische Hymnen und Gebete.* Zürich–Stuttgart, 1953.
2. Kinnier Wilson, J. V. 'Lugal ud melambi nirgal: New Texts and Fragments.' In *Z.A.* 54 (1961), 71 ff.
3. Kramer, S. N. 'Ur-Nammu Law Code.' In *Or.* n.s. 23 (1954), 40 ff.
4. Lambert, M. and Tournay, J.-R. 'La statue B de Gudéa.' In *R.A.* 45 (1951), 49 ff.
5. Lambert, M. and Tournay, J.-R. 'Les statues D, G, E, et H de Gudéa.' In *R.A.* 46 (1952), 75 ff.
6. Levy, Selim J. 'A New King of the Akkadian Dynasty.' In *Arch. f. Or.* 10 (1935–6), 281.
7. Parrot, A. *Tello; synthèse de vingt campagnes.* Paris, 1948.
8. Sarzec, E. de, and Heuzey, L. *Découvertes en Chaldée.* Paris 1884–1912.
9. Smith, S. 'Notes on the Gutian Period.' In *J.R.A.S.* 1932, 295 ff.
10. Sollberger, E. 'Sur la chronologie des rois d'Ur et quelques problèmes connexes.' In *Arch. f. Or.* 17 (1954–6), 10 ff.
11. Strommenger, Eva. 'Das Menschenbild in der altmesopotamischen Rundplastik von Mesilim bis Hammurpi.' In *Baghdader Mitteilungen,* 1 (1960), 1 ff.
12. Szlechter, E. 'Le code d'Ur-Nammu.' In *R.A.* 49 (1955), 169 ff.
13. Weidner, E. F. Review of W. Andrae, *Das wiedererstandene Assur.* In *Arch. f. Or.* 13 (1939–41), 157 ff.
14. Weidner, E. F. 'Zum babylonischen Prodigienbuch.' In *Arch. f. Or.* 16 (1952–53), 262.

VI. THE EXPULSION OF THE GUTIANS

1. Gadd, C. J. 'Clay Cones of Utu-ḥegal, King of Erech.' In *J.R.A.S.* 1926, 684 ff.
2. Kraus, F. R. 'Zur Liste der älteren Könige von Babylonien.' In *Z.A.* 50 (1952), 29 ff.
3. Schaumberger, J. 'Astronomische Untersuchung der "historischen" Mondfinsternisse in Enûma Anu Enlil.' In *Arch. f. Or.* 17 (1954–6), 89 ff.
4. Stephens, F. J. *Votive and Historical Texts from Babylonia and Assyria* (*Y.O.S.* 9). New Haven, 1937.
5. Thureau-Dangin, F. 'La fin de la domination gutienne.' In *R.A.* 9 (1912), 111 ff.
6. Thureau-Dangin, F. 'Notes assyriologiques: XXIII. Un double de l'inscription d'Utu-ḥegal.' In *R.A.* 10 (1913), 98 ff.
7. Virolleaud, C. *L'astrologie chaldéenne.* Paris, 1905–12.
8. Weidner, E. F. 'Die astrologische Serie Enûma Anu Enlil' (Fortsetzung). In *Arch. f. Or.* 17 (1954–6), 71 ff.

A. ADDENDA

1. Adams, R. McC. *Land behind Baghdad.* Chicago and London, 1965.
2. Biggs, R. D. 'Semitic names in the Fara Period.' In *Or.* n.s. 36 (1967), 55 ff.
3. Biggs, R. D. 'Le lapis-lazuli dans les textes sumériens archaïques.' In *R.A.* 60 (1966), 175 f.
4. Boehmer, R. M. *Die Entwicklung der Glyptik während der Akkad-Zeit.* Berlin, 1965.
5. Boehmer, R. M. 'Zur Datierung des Epirmupi.' In *Z.A.* 58 (1967), 302 ff.
6. Buccellati, G. *The Amorites of the Ur III period.* Naples, 1966.
7. Buchanan, Briggs. 'A dated "Persian Gulf" seal and its implications.' In *Studies in Honor of B. Landsberger* (*A.S.* 16). Chicago, 1965.
8. Buchanan, Briggs. 'A dated seal impression connecting Babylonia and ancient India.' In *Archaeology*, 20 (1967), 104 ff.
9. Donald, T. 'Old Akkadian tablets in the Liverpool Museum.' In *M.C.S.* 9 Part One.
10. Dossin, G. 'Les découvertes épigraphiques de la XV campagne de fouilles à Mari.' In *C.-R. Ac. Inscr. B.-L.* 1965, 400 ff.
11. Dossin, G. 'Un "panthéon" d'Ur III à Mari.' In *R.A.* 61 (1967), 97 ff.
12. Edmonds, C. J. 'Some ancient monuments on the Iraqi–Persian border.' In *Iraq* 28 (1966), 159 ff.
13. Falkenstein, A. 'Zu den Tontafeln aus Tărtăria.' In *Germania* 43 (1965), 269 ff.
14. Falkenstein, A. 'Fluch über Akkade.' In *Z.A.* 57 (1965), 43 ff.
15. Falkenstein, A. *Die Inschriften Gudeas von Lagaš,* 1, Einleitung (*An. Or.* 30). Rome, 1966.
16. Finkelstein, J. J. 'The genealogy of the Ḥammurapi Dynasty.' In *J.C.S.* 20 (1966), 95 ff.
17. Garelli, P. *Les Assyriens en Cappadoce.* Paris, 1963.
18. Gelb, I. J. 'The Philadelphia Onion-Archive.' In *Studies...B. Landsberger* (*A.S.* 16), 57 ff.
19. Goetze, A. 'Remarks on the Old Babylonian Itinerary.' In *J.C.S.* 18 (1964), 114 ff.

20. Güterbock, H. G. 'Sargon of Akkad mentioned by Ḫattušili I of Hatti.' In *J.C.S.* 18 (1964), 1 ff.
21. Hallo, W. W. 'Beginning and end of the Sumerian king list in the Nippur recension.' In *J.C.S.* 17 (1963), 52 ff.
22. Hartmann, H. *Die Musik der sumerischen Kultur.* Frankfurt-am-Main, 1960.
23. Herrmann, Georgina. 'Lapis-lazuli: the early phases of its trade.' In *Iraq* 30 (1968), 21 ff.
24. Hinz, W. 'Elams Vertrag mit Narām-Sîn.' In *Z.A.* 58 (1967), 66 ff.
25. Hirsch, H. 'Die Inschriften der Könige von Agade.' In *Arch. f. Or.* 20 (1963), 1 ff.
26. Kramer, S. N. and Bernhardt, I. *Sumerische Literarische Texte aus Nippur,* Band ii. Berlin, 1967.
27. Kraus, F. R. 'Kazallu und andere nordbabylonische Kleinstaaten vor der Zeit des Ḫammurabi.' In *Arch. f. Or.* 16 (1952–3), 319 ff.
28. Labat, R. *Annuaire du Collège de France: Résumé des Cours de 1961–1962,* 279 ff.
29. Landsberger, B. 'Tin and Lead; the adventures of two vocables.' In *J.N.E.S.* 24 (1965), 285 ff.
30. Landsberger, B. 'Excurs I: Meluḫḫa.' In *We. Or.* 3 (1966), 261 ff.
31. Malamat, A. 'Campaigns to the Mediterranean by Iaḫdunlim and other early Mesopotamian rulers.' In *Studies in Honor of B. Landsberger (A.S.* 16), 365 ff.
32. Oppenheim, A. L. *Letters from Mesopotamia.* Chicago, 1967.
33. Renger, J. 'Untersuchungen zum Priestertum in der altbabylonischen Zeit.' In *Z.A.* 58 (1967), 110 ff.
34. Römer, W. H. Ph. 'Studien zu altbabylonischen hymnisch-epischen Texten (3).' In *We. Or.* 4 (1967), 12 ff.
35. Sauren, H. 'Der Feldzug Utuḫengals gegen Tirigan und das Siedlungsgebiet der Gutäer.' In *R.A.* 61 (1967), 75 ff.
36. Seux, M.-J. 'Les titres royaux *šar kiššati* et *šar kibrāt arbaʾi.*' In *R.A.* 59 (1965), 1 ff.
37. Sollberger, E. *Royal Inscriptions,* Part ii (*U.E.T.* viii). London and Philadelphia, 1965.
38. Sollberger, E. *Texts from Cuneiform Sources,* i. *The Business and Administrative Correspondence under the Kings of Ur.* New York, 1966.
39. Spycket, A. *Les statues de culte dans les textes mésopotamiens des origines à la Ire. dynastie de Babylone.* Paris, 1968.
40. Strommenger, E. and Hirmer, M. *Fünf Jahrtausende Mesopotamien.* Munich, 1962.
41. Wheeler, M. *Civilizations of the Indus Valley and beyond.* London, 1966.

CHAPTER XX

I. THE HERACLEOPOLITAN KINGDOM

1. Anthes, R. *Die Felseninschriften von Hatnub* (*Unters.* 9). Leipzig, 1928.
2. Brunner, H. *Die Texte aus den Gräbern der Herakleopolitenzeit von Siut* (*Ägyptol. Forsch.* 5). Glückstadt–Hamburg–New York, 1937.
3. Clère, J. J. 'Histoire des XIe et XIIe Dynasties égyptiennes.' In *Cah. H.M.* 1 (1954), 643–68.
4. Clère, J. J. and Vandier, J. *Textes de la Première Période Intermédiaire et de la XIème Dynastie* (*Bibl. Aeg.* 10). Brussels, 1948.

5. Faulkner, R. O. 'The Rebellion in the Hare Nome.' In *J.E.A.* 30 (1944), 61–3.
6. Gardiner, A. H. 'The Eloquent Peasant.' In *J.E.A.* 9 (1923), 5–25.
7. Gardiner, A. H. *The Royal Canon of Turin.* Oxford, 1959.
8. Golénischeff, W. (ed.). *Les papyrus hiératiques nos. 1115, 1116 A et 1116 B de l'Ermitage Impérial à St-Pétersbourg.* [St Petersburg], 1913.
9. Griffith, F. Ll. *The Inscriptions of Siût and Dêr Rîfeh.* London, 1889.
10. Hayes, W. C. *The Scepter of Egypt.* 2 parts. New York, 1953, 1959.
11. Kamal, A. 'Un monument nouveau du pharaon Khatouî.' In *Ann. Serv.* 10 (1910), 185–6.
12. Kees, H. 'Aus den Notjahren der Thebais.' In *Or.* 21 (1952), 86–97.
13. Newberry, P. E. 'King ☉▽ᶙ¦ of the Story of the Eloquent Peasant.' In *Z.Ä.S.* 50 (1912), 123.
14. Petrie, W. M. F. *Hyksos and Israelite Cities (B.S.A. Egypt, and E.R.A.* 12th Year, 1906). London, 1906.
15. Petrie, W. M. F. *A History of Egypt from the Earliest Kings to the XVIth Dynasty.* Ed. 11. London, 1924.
16. Polotsky, H. J. Review of H. Brunner, *Die Texte aus den Gräbern der Herakleopolitenzeit von Siut.* In *O.L.Z.* 42 (1939), 155–60.
17. Posener, G. Review of H. Stock, *Die Erste Zwischenzeit Aegyptens.* In *Bi. Or.* 8 (1951), 165–72.
18. Sayce, A. H. 'Letter from Egypt.' In *The Academy (A Weekly Review of Literature, Science, and Art),* 41 (1892), 332–3.
19. Scharff, A. *Der historische Abschnitt der Lehre für König Merikarê (Sitzungsb. München,* 1936, Heft 8). Munich, 1936.
20. Vandier, J. *Mo'alla. La tombe d'Ankhtifi et la tombe de Sébekhotep (Inst. fr. Caire, Bibliothèque d'Étude,* 18). Cairo, 1950.
21. Vogelsang, F. *Kommentar zu den Klagen des Bauern (Unters.* 6). Leipzig, 1913.
22. Vogelsang, F. and Gardiner, A. H. *Die Klagen des Bauern (Hierat. Pap. Berlin,* IV, 1). Leipzig, 1908.
23. Wilson, J. A. 'Egyptian Texts'. In *A.N.E.T.* Princeton, 1950.
24. Winlock, H. E. *The Rise and Fall of the Middle Kingdom in Thebes.* New York, 1947.

II. THE NOMARCHS OF MIDDLE EGYPT

1. Breasted, J. H. *Ancient Records of Egypt. Historical Documents.* Vol. 1: *The First to the Seventeenth Dynasties.* Chicago, 1906.
2. Brunner, H. *Die Anlagen der ägyptischen Felsgräber bis zum mittleren Reich (Ägyptol. Forsch.* 3). Glückstadt–Hamburg–New York, 1936.
3. Davies, N. de G. *The Rock Tombs of Sheikh Saïd (Archaeological Survey of Egypt,* 10th Memoir). London, 1901.
4. Davies, N. de G. *The Rock Tombs of Deir el Gebrawi.* 2 parts (*Archaeological Survey of Egypt,* 11th and 12th Memoirs). London, 1902.
5. Gardiner, A. H. *Ancient Egyptian Onomastica.* 3 vols. Oxford, 1947.
6. Kees, H. *Beiträge zur altägyptischen Provinzialverwaltung und der Geschichte des Feudalismus (Nachr. Göttingen).* 2 parts. Berlin, 1932 and 1933.
7. Newberry, P. E. 'The Inscribed Tombs of Ekhmîm.' In *Ann. Arch. Anthr.* 4 (1911), 99–120.
8. Newberry, P. E. and others. *Beni Hasan.* 4 parts (*Archaeological Survey of Egypt,* 1st, 2nd, 5th and 7th Memoirs). London, 1893–1900.

9. Newberry, P. E. and Griffith, F. Ll. *El Bersheh* (*Archaeological Survey of Egypt*, 3rd and 4th Memoirs). London, [1895].

10. Porter, B. and Moss R. L. B. *Lower and Middle Egypt* and *Upper Egypt* (*Top. Bibl.* 4 and 5). Oxford, 1934, 1937.

III. THEBES AND THE 'HEAD OF THE SOUTH'

1. Allen, T. G. 'The Story of an Egyptian Politician.' In *A.J.S.L.* 38 (1921), 55–62.
2. Daressy, G. 'Inscriptions tentyrites.' In *Ann. Serv.* 18 (1919), 183–9.
3. Dunham, D. *Naga-ed-Dêr Stelae of the First Intermediate Period* (Museum of Fine Arts). Boston, 1937.
4. Fischer, H. G. 'Four Provincial Administrators at the Memphite Cemeteries.' In *J.A.O.S.* 74 (1954), 26–34.
5. Fischer, H. G. *Dendereh in the Old Kingdom and its Aftermath* (Dissertation for the degree of Doctor of Philosophy at the University of Pennsylvania). University Microfilms, Ann Arbor (Mich.), 1955. (Re-published as *Dendera in the Third Millennium B.C.* Glückstadt, 1969.)
6. Fischer, H. G. 'Notes, Mainly Palaeographical, on the Mo'alla Inscriptions and Some Contemporaneous Texts.' In *W.Z.K.M.* 57 (1961), 59–77.
7. Gardiner, A. H. 'A Stela of the Earlier Intermediate Period.' In *J.E.A.* 8 (1922), 191–2.
8. Gardiner, A. H. *Egyptian Grammar, being an Introduction to the Study of Hieroglyphs*. Ed. 3. London, 1957.
9. Gardiner, A. H. 'The Reading of the Geographical Term 𓊖𓏤 .' In *J.E.A.* 43 (1957), 6–9.
10. Goedicke, H. 'The Inscription of *Dmỉ*.' In *J.N.E.S.* 19 (1960), 288–91.
11. Hayes, W. C. 'Royal Decrees from the Temple of Min at Coptus.' In *J.E.A.* 32 (1946), 3–23.
12. Hayes, W. C. *A Papyrus of the Late Middle Kingdom in the Brooklyn Museum* [Papyrus Brooklyn 35.1446]. Brooklyn, 1955.
13. Helck, W. *Zur Verwaltung des mittleren und neuen Reichs* (*Probleme der Ägyptologie*, 3). Leiden–Cologne, 1958.
14. Kees, H. 'Thebai (Ägypten).' In *P.W.*, neue Bearbeitung begonnen von G. Wissowa: Zweite Reihe [R–Z], v, cols. 1553–82. Stuttgart, 1934.
15. Kees, H. *Der Götterglaube im alten Ägypten*. Ed. 2. Berlin, 1956.
16. Otto, E. *Topographie des thebanischen Gaues* (*Unters.* 16). Berlin, 1952.
17. Peck, C. N. *Some Decorated Tombs of the First Intermediate Period at Naga ed-Dêr* (Thesis submitted in partial fulfilment of the requirements for the Degree of Doctor of Philosophy in the Department of Egyptology at Brown University). University Microfilms, Ann Arbor (Mich.), 1958.
18. Petrie, W. M. F. *Dendereh 1898* (*E.E.F.* 17th Memoir). London, 1900.
19. Polotsky, J. *Zu den Inschriften der 11. Dynastie* (*Unters.* 11). Leipzig, 1929.
20. Polotsky, J. 'The Stela of Ḥeka-yeb.' In *J.E.A.* 16 (1930), 194–9, pl. 29.
21. Porter, B. and Moss, R. L. B. *The Theban Necropolis* (*Top. Bibl.* 1). Oxford, 1927.
22. Prisse d'Avennes, A. *Monuments égyptiens: bas-reliefs, inscriptions, etc.,* .... Paris, 1847.
23. Säve-Söderbergh, T. *Ägypten und Nubien. Ein Beitrag zur Geschichte alt-ägyptischer Aussenpolitik*. Lund, 1941.
24. Schiaparelli, E. *Museo archeologico di Firenze: Antichità egizie*. Rome, 1887.

25. Sethe, K. *Amun und die acht Urgötter von Hermopolis: Eine Untersuchung über Ursprung und Wesen des ägyptischen Götterkönigs* (*Abh. Berlin*, 1929, Nr. 4). Berlin, 1929.
26. Spiegelberg, W. and Pörtner, B. *Aegyptische Grabsteine und Denksteine aus süddeutschen Sammlungen.* I. *Karlsruhe, Mülhausen, Strassburg, Stuttgart.* Strassburg, 1902.
27. Steindorff, G. and Wolf, W. *Die thebanische Gräberwelt* (*Leipziger ägyptol. St.* 4). Glückstadt and Hamburg, 1936.
28. The Toledo Museum of Art: *Museum News*, no. 129, October, 1951.
29. Vandier, J. *La famine dans l'Égypte ancienne* (*Inst. fr.: Recherches d'archéologie, de philologie et d'histoire,* 7). Cairo, 1936.
30. Vandier, J. 'La stèle 20.001 du Musée du Caire.' In *Mél. Maspero,* 1, 137–45.
31. Vandier, J. *La religion égyptienne* ('*Mana*': *Introduction à l'histoire des religions,* 1. *Les anciennes religions orientales*). Ed. 2. Paris, 1949.
32. Winlock, H. E. 'The Theban Necropolis in the Middle Kingdom.' In *A.J.S.L.* 32 (1915), 1–37.

IV. THE EARLY KINGS OF THE ELEVENTH DYNASTY

1. Blackman, A. M. 'The Stela of Thethi, Brit. Mus. No. 614.' In *J.E.A.* 17 (1931), 55–61.
2. Gardiner, A. [H.] 'The First King Menthotpe of the Eleventh Dynasty.' In *Mitt. deutsch. Inst. Kairo,* 14 (1956), 42–51.
3. Habachi, L. 'Hekaib, the Deified Governor of Elephantine.' In *Archaeology,* 9, no. 1 (spring 1956), 8–15.
4. Habachi, L. 'God's Fathers and the Role they Played in the History of the First Intermediate Period.' In *Ann. Serv.* 55 (1958), 167–90.
5. Habachi, L. 'Aswan and the Famous Men who Made it.' In *Egypt Travel Magazine,* no. 56 (April 1959), 6–11.
6. Lange, H. O. and Schäfer, H. *Grab- und Denksteine des mittleren Reiches im Museum von Kairo* (*C.C.G.* nos. 20001–780). 4 vols. Berlin, 1902–25.
7. de Morgan, J. and others. *Catalogue des monuments et inscriptions de l'Égypte antique,* 1ère série, I. *De la frontière de Nubie à Kom Ombos.* Vienna, 1894.
8. Newberry, P. E. 'On the Parentage of the Intef Kings of the Eleventh Dynasty.' In *Z.Ä.S.* 72 (1936), 118–20.
9. Petrie, W. M. F. *Qurneh* (*British School of Archaeology in Egypt and Egyptian Research Account,* 15th Year). London, 1909.
10. Vandier, J. 'Un nouvel Antef de la XIe Dynastie.' In *Bull. Inst. fr. Caire,* 36 (1936), 101–16.
11. Vandier, J. 'L'ordre de succession des derniers rois de la XIe Dynastie.' In *An. Or.* 17 (1938), 36–47.
12. Vandier, J. 'Une inscription historique de la Première Période Intermédiaire' (Turin Suppl. 1310). In *Mél. Polotsky,* 9–16. Jerusalem, 1964.

V. REUNION OF EGYPT UNDER NEBHEPETRE MENTUHOTPE

1. von Bissing, F. W. *Denkmäler ägyptischer Sculptur.* 3 vols. Munich, 1911–14.
2. von Bissing, F. W. *Vom Wadi Es S'aba Rigâle bei Gebel Silsile* (*Sitzungsb. München,* 1913, 10. *Abhandlung*). Munich, 1913.
3. Bisson de la Roque, F. *Tôd* (*1934 à 1936*) (*Flles. Inst. fr.* 17). Cairo, 1937.
4. Cassirer, M. 'An Egyptian Funerary Stele with a Rare Title.' In *Ann. Serv.* 52 (1954), 41–4.

5. Clère, J. J. 'Une nouvelle forme du nom d'Horus de Neb-ḥepet-Re' Mentou-ḥotep II.' In *J.N.E.S.* 9 (1950), 37–9.
6. Couyat, J. and Montet, P. *Les inscriptions hiéroglyphiques du Ouâdi Ham-mâmât (Mém. Inst. fr. 34).* Cairo, 1912.
7. Daressy, G. 'Chapelle de Mentouhotep III a Dendérah.' In *Ann. Serv.* 17 (1917), 226–36, pls. 1–3.
8. Evers, H. G. *Staat aus dem Stein. Denkmäler, Geschichte und Bedeutung der ägyptischen Plastik während des mittleren Reichs.* 2 vols. Munich, 1929.
9. Fischer, H. G. 'Eleventh Dynasty Relief Fragments from Deir el Bahri.' In *Yale University Art Gallery Bulletin,* 24 (1958), no. 2, 28–38.
10. *Fouilles d'El Kab, exécutées par la Fondation Égyptologique Reine Élisabeth. Documents.* 2 vols. Brussels, 1940.
11. Hayes, W. C. 'Career of the Great Steward Ḥenenu under Nebḥepetrē, Mentuḥotpe.' In *J.E.A.* 35 (1949), 43–9.
12. Lepsius, C. R. *Denkmaeler aus Aegypten und Aethiopien.* 6 parts. Berlin, 1849–59.
13. Lutz, H. F. *Egyptian Tomb Steles and Offering Stones of the Museum of Anthropology and Ethnology of the University of California (University of California Publications. Egyptian Archaeology,* vol. IV). Leipzig, 1927.
14. Mond, R. and Myers, O. H. *Temples of Armant, a preliminary survey.* 2 vols. London, 1940.
15. Naville, E. *The XIth Dynasty Temple at Deir el-Bahari (E.E.F.* 28th, 30th, and 32nd Memoirs). London, 1907–13.
16. Newberry, P. E. 'Extracts from my Notebooks. VII.' In *P.S.B.A.* 25 (1903), 357–62.
17. Petrie, W. M. F. *A Season in Egypt, 1887.* London, 1888.
18. Petrie, W. M. F. *Abydos. Part II. 1903 (E.E.F.* 24th Memoir). London, 1903.
19. Posener, G. 'À propos des graffiti d'Abisko.' In *Arch. Orient.* 20 (1952), 163–6.
20. Riefstahl, E. 'Two Hairdressers of the Eleventh Dynasty.' In *J.N.E.S.* 15 (1956), 10–17.
21. Roeder, G. *Debod bis Bab Kalabsche (Service des Antiquités de l'Égypte: Les temples immergés de la Nubie).* 3 vols. Cairo, 1911, 1912.
22. Säve-Söderbergh, T. Review of H. E. Winlock, *The Rise and Fall of the Middle Kingdom in Thebes.* In *Bi. Or.* 6 (1949), 85–90.
23. Stock, H. *Die erste Zwischenzeit Aegyptens (St. Aeg. 2 = An. Or. 31).* Rome, 1949.
24. Vandier, J. 'L'ordre de succession des derniers rois de la XIe Dynastie' (*St. Aeg.* 1 = *An. Or.* 17). Rome, 1938, 36–47.
25. Winlock, H. E. *The Slain Soldiers of Neb-ḥepet-Rēꜥ Mentu-ḥotpe (Pub. M.M.A.E.E.* 16). New York, 1945.

VI. REORGANIZATION AND RECOVERY

1. Anthes, R. 'Eine Polizeistreife des mittleren Reiches in die westliche Oase.' In *Z.Ä.S.* 65 (1930), 108–14, pl. 7.
2. Fischer, H. G. 'An Example of Memphite Influence in an Egyptian Stela of the Eleventh Dynasty.' In *Art. A.* 22 (1959), 240–52.
3. Gardiner, A. H. 'The Tomb of a much-travelled Theban Official.' In *J.E.A.* 4 (1917), 28–38, pls. 6–9.
4. Gardiner, A. H., Peet, T. and Černý, J. *The Inscriptions of Sinai.* 2 parts. London (E.E.S.), 1952, 1955.

5. Helck, H.-W. 'Zur Reichseinigung der 11. Dynastie.' In *Z.Ä.S.* 80 (1955), 75–6.
6. Petrie, W. M. F. *Researches in Sinai.* New York, 1906.
7. Porter, B. and Moss, R. L. B. *Theban Temples (Top. Bibl.* 2). Oxford, 1929.

VII. FOREIGN POLICY: PROGRESS TOWARDS THE RECONQUEST OF NUBIA

1. Drioton, É. and Vandier, J. *L'Égypte ('Clio': Introduction aux études historiques. Les peuples de l'orient méditerranéen*, 2). Ed. 3. Paris, 1952.
2. Posener, G. '⟨hieroglyphs⟩, et ⟨hieroglyphs⟩.' In *Z.Ä.S.* 83 (1958), 38–43.
3. Posener, G. 'Pour une localisation du pays Koush au Moyen Empire.' In *Kush*, 6 (1958), 39–68.
4. Sethe, K. *Urkunden des alten Reichs (Urk.* I). Ed. 2. Leipzig, 1932–3.

VIII. EGYPT UNDER KING MENTUHOTPE III: THE HEKANAKHTE PAPERS

1. Clédat, J. 'Un nouveau monument du roi Sankherâ.' In *Rec. trav.* 31 (1909), 64–5.
2. Hölscher, U. *The Excavation of Medinet Habu* 2. *The Temples of the Eighteenth Dynasty (O.I.P.* 41). Chicago, 1939.
3. James, T. G. H. *The Hekanakhte Papers and other Early Middle Kingdom Documents (The Metropolitan Museum of Art Egyptian Expedition).* New York and Oxford, 1961.
4. Petrie, W. M. F. *Tanis (E.E.F.* 2nd and 5th Memoirs). 2 parts. London, 1885, 1888.
5. Schweinfurth, G. 'Ein neuentdeckter Tempel in Theben.' In *Z.Ä.S.* 41 (1904), 22–5.
6. Winlock, H. E. *Excavations at Deir el Baḥri 1911–1931.* New York, 1942.
7. Winlock, H. E. *Models of Daily Life in Ancient Egypt from the Tomb of Meket-Rēʿ at Thebes (Pub. M.M.A.E.E.* 18). Cambridge (Mass.), 1955.

IX. RESUMPTION OF THE RED SEA TRAFFIC AND REOPENING OF THE WĀDI HAMMĀMĀT

1. Goyon, G. 'Le papyrus de Turin dit "des mines d'or" et le Wadi Hammamat.' In *Ann. Serv.* 49 (1949), 337–92.
2. Goyon, G. *Nouvelles inscriptions rupestres du Wadi Hammamat.* Paris, 1957.
3. Helck, W. Review of G. Goyon, *Nouvelles inscriptions rupestres....* In *O.L.Z.* 54 (1959), cols. 17–21.
4. Lucas, A. *Ancient Egyptian Materials and Industries.* Ed. 3. London, 1948.
5. Posener, G. 'Le canal du Nil à la Mer Rouge avant les Ptolémées.' In *Chron. d'Ég.* 13 (1938), 259–73.
6. Säve-Söderbergh, T. *The Navy of the Eighteenth Egyptian Dynasty (Uppsala Universitets Årsskrift* 1946: 6). Uppsala, 1946.
7. Simpson, W. K. 'Historical and Lexical Notes on the New Series of Hammamat Inscriptions.' In *J.N.E.S.* 18 (1959), 20–37.

X. THE END OF THE ELEVENTH DYNASTY: MENTUHOTPE IV AND THE VIZIER AMMENEMES

1. Albright, W. F. 'Northwest-Semitic Names in a List of Egyptian Slaves from the Eighteenth Century B.C.' In *J.A.O.S.* 74 (1955), 222–33.
2. Erichsen, W. *Papyrus Harris I: Hieroglyphische Transkription (Bibl. Aeg. 5).* Brussels, 1933.
3. Erman, A. *The Literature of the Ancient Egyptians* (translated into English by Aylward M. Blackman). London, 1927.
4. Fakhry, A. *The Inscriptions of the Amethyst Quarries at Wadi el Hudi (Service des Antiquités de l'Égypte: The Egyptian Deserts).* Cairo, 1952.
5. Gardiner, A. H. 'New Literary Works from Ancient Egypt. II. Pap. Petersburg 1116B recto.' In *J.E.A.* 1 (1914), 100–6.
6. Goedicke, H. 'King Ḥwdf?.' In *J.E.A.* 42 (1956), 50–3.
7. Helck, W. 'Zur Geschichte der 19. und 20. Dynastie.' In *Z.D.M.G.* 105 (1955), 27–52.
8. Helck, W. *Untersuchungen zu Manetho und den ägyptischen Königslisten (Unters. 18).* Berlin, 1956.
9. Lansing, A. 'The Egyptian Expedition. Excavations at Lisht.' In *Bull. M.M.A.* 28 (1933), November, sect. 2, 4–26.
10. Posener, G. *Princes et pays d'Asie et de Nubie: Textes hiératiques sur des figurines d'envoûtement du Moyen Empire.* Brussels, 1940.
11. Posener, G. *Littérature et politique dans l'Égypte de la XIIe Dynastie.* Paris, 1956.
12. Pritchard, J. B. (ed.). *Ancient Near Eastern Texts relating to the Old Testament.* Princeton, 1950 (= *A.N.E.T.*).
13. Ranke, H. *Die ägyptischen Personennamen.* 2 vols. Glückstadt and Hamburg, 1935, [1952].
14. Sethe K. *Urkunden der 18. Dynastie (Urk. iv).* 4 parts. Leipzig, 1906–9.
15. Vandier, J. 'Réflexions sur l'histoire de la XIIe Dynastie.' In *Rev. hist.* 1958, 16–31.
16. Winlock, H. E. 'Neb-ḥepet-Rēʿ Mentu-ḥotpe of the Eleventh Dynasty.' In *J.E.A.* 26 (1940), 116–19.
17. Yoyotte, J. 'Égypte ancienne.' In *Histoire universelle*, 1 (Paris, 1956), 103–283.

XI. THE FOUNDING OF THE TWELFTH DYNASTY: AMMENEMES I AND THE ADMINISTRATION

1. Adam, S. 'Recent Discoveries in the Eastern Delta (Dec. 1950–May 1955).' In *Ann. Serv.* 55 (1958), 301–24. See also 56 (1959), 208–18.
2. Benson, M. and Gourlay, J. *The Temple of Mut in Asher*.... The inscriptions and translations by Percy E. Newberry. London, 1899.
3. Blackman, A. M. *Middle-Egyptian Stories.* Part 1 (*Bibl. Aeg.* 2). Brussels, 1932.
4. Blackman, A. M. 'Some Notes on the Story of Sinuhe and other Egyptian Texts.' In *J.E.A.* 22 (1936), 35–44.
5. de Buck, A. 'The Instruction of Amenemmes.' In *Mél. Maspero*, 1 (*Mém. Inst. fr. Caire*, 66), 847–52.
6. de Buck, A. 'La composition littéraire des enseignements d'Amenemhat.' In *Muséon*, 59 (1946), 183–200.
7. Clère, J. J. 'Sur un Passage de la Stèle Louvre C1.' In *J.E.A.* 24 (1938), 242.

8. Engelbach, R. 'The Quarries of the Western Nubian Desert. A Preliminary Report.' In *Ann. Serv.* 33 (1933), 65–74.
9. Erman, A. *Die Religion der Ägypter, ihr Werden und Vergehen in vier Jahrtausenden.* Berlin and Leipzig, 1934.
10. Faulkner, R. O. 'Egyptian Military Organization.' In *J.E.A.* 39 (1953), 32–47.
11. Gardiner, A. H. *Notes on the Story of Sinuhe.* Paris, 1916.
12. Gardiner, A. H. 'The Accession Day of Sesostris I.' In *J.E.A.* 32 (1946), 100.
13. Gauthier, H. *Le livre des rois d'Égypte,* I. *Des origines à la fin de la XIIe Dynastie (Mém. Inst. fr. Caire,* 17). Cairo, 1907.
14. Gauthier, H. 'Une nouvelle statue d'Amenemḥêt Ier.' In *Mél. Maspero,* I *(Mém. Inst. fr. Caire,* 66), 43–53.
15. Goedicke, H. 'The Route of Sinuhe's Flight.' In *J.E.A.* 43 (1957), 77–85.
16. Habachi, L. 'Khatâ'na-Qantîr: Importance.' In *Ann. Serv.* 52 (1954), 443–562.
17. Mace, A. C. 'Excavations at Lisht.' In *Bull. M.M.A.* 17 (1922), December, part 2, 3–18.
18. Mariette, A. *Monuments divers recueillis en Égypte et en Nubie par A. Mariette-Pacha* (text by G. Maspero). Paris, 1872–89.
19. Mariette, A. *Karnak. Étude topographique et archéologique....* 2 vols. Paris, 1875.
20. Mariette, A. *Catalogue général des monuments d'Abydos découverts pendant les fouilles de cette ville.* Paris, 1880.
21. Müller, H. W. *Die Felsengräber von Elephantine (Ägyptol. Forsch.* 9). Glückstadt, 1940.
22. Parker, R. A. *The Calendars of Ancient Egypt (S.A.O.C.* 26). Chicago, 1950.
23. Porter, B. and Moss, R. L. B. *Upper Egypt: Chief Temples (Top. Bibl.* 6). Oxford, 1939.
24. Reisner, G. A. *Excavations at Kerma (Harvard African Studies,* v, vi). Cambridge (Mass.), 1923.
25. Reisner, G. A. 'Ancient Egyptian Forts at Semna and Uronarti.' In *Bull. M.F.A.* 27 (1929), 64–75.
26. Sethe, K. *Historische-biographische Urkunden des mittleren Reiches (Urk.* vii, i). Leipzig, 1935.
27. Simpson, W. K. 'The Single-dated Monuments of Sesostris I: An Aspect of the Institution of Coregency in the Twelfth Dynasty.' In *J.N.E.S.* 15 (1956), 214–19.
28. Steckeweh, H. *Die Fürstengräber von Qaw (Veröffentlichungen der Ernst von Sieglin-Expedition,* 6). Leipzig, 1936.
29. Vandier, J. *Manuel d'archéologie égyptienne.* 5 vols. Paris, 1952–69.

XII. EXPANSION UNDER SESOSTRIS I AND HIS SUCCESSORS

1. Allen, T. G. 'A Middle Kingdom Egyptian Contact with Asia Minor.' In *A.J.S.L.* 43 (1927), 294–6.
2. Balcz, H. and Bittel, K. 'Grabungsbericht Hermopolis 1932.' In *Mitt. deutsch. Inst. Kairo,* 3 (1932), 9–45.
3. von Bissing, F. W. 'Grundsteinbeigaben Sesostris' I. aus dem Tempel von Dendere?' In *Z.Ä.S.* 68 (1932), 68–9.
4. Bisson de la Roque, R. *Trésor de Tôd (C.C.G.* nos. 70501–754). Cairo, 1950.
5. Bisson de la Roque, R., Contenau, G. and Chapouthier, F. *Le trésor de Tôd (Documents de Flles. Inst. fr. Caire,* 11). Cairo, 1953.

6. Boeser, P. A. A. *Beschreibung der aegyptischen Sammlung des niederländischen Reichmuseums der Altertümer in Leiden*, vols. 2, 3. The Hague, 1909, 1910.

7. Borchardt, L. 'Der zweite Papyrusfund von Kahun und die zeitliche Festlegung der mittleren Reiches der ägyptischen Geschichte.' In *Z.Ä.S.* 37 (1899), 89–103.

8. Breasted, J. H. *A History of Egypt from the Earliest Times to the Persian Conquest.* Ed. 2. London, 1927.

9. de Buck, A. 'The Building Inscription of the Berlin Leather Roll.' In *An. Or.* 17 (1938), 48–57.

10. de Buck, A. 'A Note on Sinuhe B, 71–72.' In *J.E.A.* 25 (1939), 100.

11. Capart, J. 'L'Égyptienne d'Adana.' In *Bulletin de la Classe des Lettres,* etc., *Académie Royale de Belgique,* 7 novembre 1921, 543–7.

12. Černý, J. 'Semites in Egyptian Mining Expeditions to Sinai.' In *Arch. Orient.* 7 (1935), 384–9.

13. Černý, J. 'Graffiti at the Wādi el-'Allāḳi.' In *J.E.A.* 33 (1947), 52–7.

14. Chevrier, H. 'Rapport sur les travaux de Karnak (1938–1939).' In *Ann. Serv.* 39 (1939), 553–70; (1948–9), *ibid.* 49 (1949), 241–67.

15. Dunham, D. and Janssen, J. M. A. *Second Cataract Forts, I: Semna-Kumma.* Boston, 1960.

16. Edwards, I. E. S. *The Pyramids of Egypt (Penguin Books).* Ed. 2. West Drayton, Middlesex, 1961.

17. Emery, W. B. 'The Work of an Egyptian Master Castle-architect of 3900 Years ago revealed in New Excavations at Buhen in the Sudan.' In *Ill. Ldn. News,* vol. 232, no. 6211 (21 June 1958), 1048–51.

18. Emery, W. B. 'A Masterpiece of Egyptian Military Architecture of 3900 Years ago: the Great Castle of Buhen in the Sudan.' *Ibid.* vol. 235, no. 6267 (12 Sept. 1959), 232–3, 249–51.

19. Erman, A. and Grapow, H. *Wörterbuch der aegyptischen Sprache.* 6 vols. Leipzig, 1926–50.

20. Gayet, A. J. *Stèles de la XIIe Dynastie, Musée du Louvre (École des Hautes Études. Bibliothèque: Sciences philologiques et historiques,* fasc. 68). Paris, 1889.

21. Goyon, G. 'Trouvaille à Tanis de fragments appartenant à la statue de Sanousrit Ier, No. 634 du Musée du Caire.' In *Ann. Serv.* 37 (1937), 81–4.

22. Grdseloff, B. 'Un nouveau graffito de Hatnoub.' In *Ann. Serv.* 51 (1951), 143–6.

23. Griffith, F. Ll. *Hieratic Papyri from Kahun and Gurob.* 2 vols. London, 1898.

24. Habachi, L. 'A Group of Unpublished Old and Middle Kingdom Graffiti on Elephantine.' In *W.Z.K.M.* 54 (1957), 55–71.

25. Hayes, W. C. 'Notes on the Government of Egypt in the Late Middle Kingdom.' In *J.N.E.S.* 12 (1953), 31–9.

26. *Hieroglyphic Texts from Egyptian Stelae, etc., in the British Museum* (edited by E. A. W. Budge, H. R. Hall, and others). 9 parts. London, 1911–70.

27. Jéquier, G. *Le monument funéraire de Pepi II (Service des Antiquités de l'Égypte: Fouilles à Saqqarah).* 3 vols. Cairo, 1936–40.

28. Kantor, H. J. *The Aegean and the Orient in the Second Millennium B.C. (Monographs on Archaeology and Fine Arts sponsored by the Archaeological Institute of America and the College Art Association of America,* 4). Bloomington (Indiana), 1947.

29. Kees, H. *Das alte Ägypten, eine kleine Landeskunde.* Ed. 2. Berlin, 1958.

30. Kees, H. 'Die weisse Kapelle Sesostris' I. in Karnak und das Sedfest.' In *Mitt. deutsch. Inst. Kairo,* 16 (1958), 194–213.

31. Lacau, P. and Chevrier, H. *Une chapelle de Sésostris Ier à Karnak* (*Service des Antiquités de l'Égypte*). Cairo, 1956.
32. Lange, K. *Sesostris: Ein ägyptischer König in Mythos, Geschichte und Kunst.* Munich, 1954.
33. Lansing, A. 'The Museum's Excavations at Lisht.' In *Bull. M.M.A.* 19 (1924), December, part 2, 33–43.
34. Lansing, A. and Hayes, W. C. 'The Egyptian Expedition: The Excavations at Lisht.' *Ibid.* 28 (1933), November, sect. 2, 4–38; 29 (1934), November, sect. 2, 4–40.
35. Montet, P. 'Un Égyptien, roi de Byblos, sous la XIIe Dynastie.' In *Syria*, 8 (1927), 85–92.
36. Pendlebury, J. D. S. *Aegyptiaca. A Catalogue of Egyptian Objects in the Aegean Area.* Cambridge, 1930.
37. Porter, B. and Moss, R. L. B. *Nubia, the Deserts, and Outside Egypt* (*Top. Bibl.* 7). Oxford, 1951.
38. Posener, G. 'Les Asiatiques en Égypte sous les XIIe et XIIIe Dynasties.' In *Syria*, 34 (1957), 145–63.
39. Ricke, H. 'Ein Inventartafel aus Heliopolis im Turiner Museum.' In *Z.Ä.S.* 71 (1935), 111–33.
40. Roeder, G. (ed.). *Hermopolis 1929–1939* (*Pelizaeus-Museum zu Hildesheim — Wissenschaftliche Veröffentlichung*, 4). Hildesheim, 1959.
41. Rowe, A. 'Three New Stelae from the South-eastern Desert.' In *Ann. Serv.* 39, (1939), 187–94, pls. 25–6.
42. Säve-Söderbergh, T. 'A Buhen Stela from the Second Intermediate Period (Kharṭūm No. 18).' In *J.E.A.* 35 (1949), 50–8.
43. Schaeffer, C. F.-A. *Ugaritica* I = *Mission de Ras Shamra* III (*Inst. fr. Beyrouth, Bibliothèque archéologique et historique*, 31). Paris, 1939.
44. Schäfer, H. 'Ein Zug nach der grossen Oase unter Sesostris I.' In *Z.Ä.S.* 42 (1905), 124–8.
45. Scharff, A. 'Briefe aus Illahun.' In *Z.Ä.S.* 59 (1924), 20–51 (see also 51–5).
46. Sethe, K. *Sesostris* (*Unters.* II, 1). Leipzig, 1900.
47. Seyrig, H. 'Antiquités syriennes: 59. Note sur le trésor de Tôd.' In *Syria*, 31 (1954), 218–24.
48. Simpson, W. K. 'A Hatnub Stela of the Early Twelfth Dynasty.' In *Mitt. deutsch. Inst. Kairo*, 16 (1958), 298–309.
49. Steindorff, G. *Aniba* (*Service des Antiquités de l'Égypte: Mission archéologique de Nubie*, 1929–1934). 2 vols. Glückstadt–Hamburg–New York, 1935, 1937.
50. Stern, L. 'Urkunde über den Bau des Sonnentempels zu On.' In *Z.Ä.S.* 12 (1874), 85–96, pls. 1–2.
51. Vandier, J. 'À propos d'un dépôt de provenance asiatique trouvé à Tôd.' In *Syria*, 18 (1937), 174–82, pls. 28–9.
52. Vercoutter, J. *L'Égypte et le monde égéen préhellénique* (*Inst. fr. Caire, Bibliothèque d'Étude*, 22). Cairo, 1956.
53. Vercoutter, J. 'Upper Egyptian Settlers in Middle Kingdom Nubia.' In *Kush*, 5 (1957), 61–9.
54. Weigall, A. E. P. 'A Report on Some Objects recently found in Sebakh and other Diggings.' In *Ann. Serv.* 8 (1907), 39–50.
55. Williams, C. R. *Gold and Silver Jewelry and Related Objects* (*The New York Historical Society: Catalogue of Egyptian Antiquities*, nos. 1–160). New York, 1924.
56. Wilson, J. A. 'The Egyptian Middle Kingdom at Megiddo.' In *A.J.S.L.* 58 (1941), 225–36.

XIII. THE ADMINISTRATIVE REFORMS AND FOREIGN CAMPAIGNS
OF SESOSTRIS III; THE EXECRATION TEXTS

1. *Aegyptische Inschriften aus den Königlichen Museen zu Berlin*, 1. Leipzig, 1901, 1913.

2. Blackman, A. M. 'A Reference to Sesostris III's Syrian Campaign.' In *J.E.A.* 2 (1915), 13–14.

3. Borchardt, L. *Altägyptische Festungen an der zweiten Nilschnelle (Veröffentlichungen der Ernst von Seiglin-Expedition*, 3). Leipzig, 1923.

4. Clarke, S. 'Ancient Egyptian Frontier Fortresses.' In *J.E.A.* 3 (1916), 155–79, pls. 24–32.

5. Edgerton, W. F. 'Egyptian Phonetic Writing, from its Invention to the Close of the Nineteenth Dynasty.' In *J.A.O.S.* 60 (1940), 473–506.

6. Gardiner, A. H. 'An Ancient List of the Fortresses of Nubia.' In *J.E.A.* 3 (1916), 184–92.

7. Janssen, J. M. A. 'La stèle de Mentouemhat trouvée à Semna.' In *Arch. Orient.* 20 (1952), 442–5.

8. Janssen, J. M. A. 'The Stela (Khartoum Museum No. 3) from Uronarti.' In *J.N.E.S.* 12 (1953), 51–5.

9. Junker, H. *Gîza VIII (Bericht über die von der Akademie der Wissenschaften in Wien...unternommenen Grabungen auf dem Friedhof des alten Reiches bei Pyramiden von Gîza*, vol. VIII). Vienna, 1947.

10. Kees, H. 'Zu einigen Fachausdrücken der altägyptischen Provinzialverwaltung.' In *Z.Ä.S.* 70 (1934), 83–91.

11. Peet, T. E. *The Stela of Sebek-khu, the Earliest Record of an Egyptian Campaign in Asia (The Manchester Museum, Museum Handbooks*, Publication no. 75). Manchester, 1914.

12. Porter, B. and Moss, R. L. B. *Memphis (Top. Bibl.* 3). Oxford, 1931.

13. Posener, G. 'Nouveaux textes hiératiques de proscription.' In *Mél. Dussaud* (1938), 313–17.

14. Posener, G. 'Nouvelles listes de proscription (Ächtungstexte) datant du moyen empire.' In *Chron. d'Ég.* 14 (1939), 39–46.

15. Posener, G. 'Les empreintes magiques de Gizeh et les morts dangereux.' In *Mitt. deutsch. Inst. Kairo*, 16 (1958), 252–70.

16. Reisner, G. A. 'Excavations at Semna and Uronarti by the Harvard–Boston Expedition.' In *Sudan Notes and Records*, 12 (1929), 143–61.

17. Robichon, C. and Varille, A. 'Médamoud. Fouilles du Musée du Louvre, 1938.' In *Chron. d'Ég.* 14 (1939), 83–7 (also 265–7).

18. Sethe, K. *Aegyptische Lesestücke zum Gebrauch im akademischen Unterricht. Texte des mittleren Reiches.* Leipzig, 1924.

19. Sethe, K. *Die Ächtung feindlicher Fürsten, Völker und Dinge auf altägyptischen Tongefässscherben des mittleren Reiches...(Abh. Berlin*, 1926, Nr. 5). Berlin, 1926.

20. Simpson, W. K. 'Sobkemḥēt, a Vizier of Sesostris III.' In *J.E.A.* 43 (1957), 26–9.

21. Smith, W. S. *The Art and Architecture of Ancient Egypt (The Pelican History of Art*, Z 14). Harmondsworth, 1958.

22. Smither, P. 'The Semneh Despatches.' In *J.E.A.* 31 (1945), 3–10, pls. 2–7.

23. Spiegel, J. 'Zum Osiriskult von Abydos im mittleren Reich.' In *We. Or.* 2 (1959), 397–403.

24. Wheeler, N. F. 'Harvard–Boston Expedition in the Sudan, 1930–1931.' In *Bull. M.F.A.* 29 (1931), 66–70.

XIV. ECONOMIC MEASURES UNDER AMMENEMES III

1. Ball, J. *Contributions to the Geography of Egypt* (*Ministry of Finance, Egypt: Survey of Egypt*). Cairo, 1939.
2. Ball, J. *Egypt in the Classical Geographers* (*Ministry of Finance, Egypt: Survey of Egypt*). Cairo, 1942.
3. Borchardt, L. 'Ein ägyptischer Grab auf der Sinaihalbinsel.' In *Z.Ä.S.* 35 (1897), 112–15.
4. Brown, R. H. *The Fayûm and Lake Moeris*. London, 1893.
5. Caton-Thompson, G. and Gardner, E. W. *The Desert Fayum* (*Royal Anthropological Institute*). 2 vols. London, 1934.
6. Gardiner, A. H. *The Wilbour Papyrus* (*The Brooklyn Museum*). 4 vols. Oxford, 1941–52.
7. Gardiner, A. H. and Bell, H. I. 'The Name of Lake Moeris.' In *J.E.A.* 29 (1943), 37–50.
8. Gauthier, H. *Dictionnaire des noms géographiques contenus dans les textes hiéroglyphiques* (*La Société royale de géographie d'Égypte*). 7 vols. Cairo, 1925–31.
9. Habachi, L. 'Une "vaste salle" d'Amenemhat III à Kiman-Farès (Fayoum).' In *Ann. Serv.* 37 (1937), 85–95.
10. Habachi, L. 'The Monument of Biyahmū.' In *Ann. Serv.* 40 (1941), 721–32.
11. Kees, H. *Tanis: Ein kritischer Überblick zur Geschichte der Stadt* (*Nachr. Göttingen*, 1944). Göttingen, 1944.
12. Mercer, S. A. B. *The Pyramid Texts in Translation and Commentary*. 4 vols. New York–London–Toronto, 1952.
13. Meyer, E. *Geschichte des Altertums*, vol. 1, part 2. Ed. 5. Stuttgart and Berlin, 1926.
14. Montet, P. *Tanis, douze années de fouilles dans une capitale oubliée du delta égyptien* (*Bibliothèque historique*). Paris, 1942.
15. de Morgan, J. *Fouilles à Dahchour, Mars–Juin 1894* and *Fouilles à Dahchour en 1894–1895*. 2 vols. Vienna, 1895 and 1903.
16. Sandford, K. S. and Arkell, W. J. *Paleolithic Man and the Nile–Faiyum Divide* (*O.I.P.* 10). Chicago, 1929.
17. Sethe, K. *Die altaegyptischen Pyramidentexte*. 4 vols. Leipzig, 1908–22.
18. Sethe, K. *Übersetzung und Kommentar zu den altägyptischen Pyramidentexten*. 4 vols. Glückstadt, 1935–9.

XV. ART AND ARCHITECTURE

1. Aldred, C. *Middle Kingdom Art in Egypt, 2300–1590 B.C.* London, 1950.
2. Badawy, A. *Le dessin architectural chez les anciens Égyptiens* (*Service des Antiquités de l'Égypte*). Cairo, 1948.
3. Boreux, C. 'À propos d'un linteau réprésentant Sésostris III trouvé à Médamoud.' In *Mon. Piot*, 32 (1932), 1–20.
4. Bothmer, B. V. 'Block Statues of the Middle Kingdom.' In *Brooklyn Museum Bulletin*, 21 (1959–60), and 22 (1960–1).
5. Breasted, J. H., Jr. *Egyptian Servant Statues* (*The Bollingen Series*, 13). Washington, 1948.
6. Brunton, G. *Lahun I, the Treasure* (*British School of Archaeology in Egypt and Egyptian Research Account*, 20th year, 1914). London, 1920.
7. Dunham, D. and Smith, W. S. 'A Middle Kingdom painted Coffin from Deir El Bersheh.' In *Studi in memoria di Ippolito Rosellini*, 1 (Pisa, 1949), 263–8.

8. Engelbach, R. 'The So-called Hyksos Monuments.' In *Ann. Serv.* 28 (1928), 13–28, pls. 1–4.
9. Farina, G. *La pittura egiziana.* Milan, 1929.
10. Farina, G. 'La prima pittura di negro.' In *Rassegna di Studi etiopici,* 3 (1934), 139–47.
11. Firchow, O. *Studien zu den Pyramidenanlagen der 12. Dynastie (Dissertation zur Erlangung des Doktorgrades der philosophischen Fakultät der Georg-August-Universität zu Göttingen).* Gottingen, 1942.
12. Fischer, H. G. 'An Example of Memphite Influence in an Egyptian Stela of the Eleventh Dynasty.' In *Art A.* 22 (1959), 240–52.
13. Gautier, J. and Jéquier, G. *Mémoire sur les fouilles de Licht (Mém. Inst. fr. 6).* Cairo, 1902.
14. M[ace], A. C. 'The Egyptian Expedition. III. The Pyramid of Amenemhat.' In *Bull. M.M.A.* 3 (1908), 184–8.
15. Maspero, G. 'Note sur le pyramidion d'Amenemhaît à Dahchour.' In *Ann. Serv.* 3 (1902), 206–8.
16. Müller, H. W. 'Die Totendenksteine des mittleren Reiches, ihre Genesis, ihre Darstellungen und ihre Komposition.' In *Mitt. deutsch. Inst. Kairo,* 4 (1933), 165–206.
17. Pflüger, K. 'The Private Funerary Stelae of the Middle Kingdom and their Importance for the Study of Ancient Egyptian History.' In *J.A.O.S.* 67 (1947), 127–35.
18. Robichon, C. and Varille, A. *Description sommaire du temple primitif de Médamoud (Publications de l'Inst. fr.* 11). Cairo, 1940.
19. Senk, H. 'Fragen und Ergebnisse zur Formgeschichte des ägyptischen Würfelhockers.' In *Z.Ä.S.* 79 (1954), 149–56.
20. Smith, W. S. *A History of Egyptian Sculpture and Painting in the Old Kingdom.* Ed. 2. Boston, 1949.
21. Smith, W. S. 'Paintings of the Egyptian Middle Kingdom at Bersheh.' In *A.J.A.* 55 (1951), 321–32, pls. 18–21.
22. Vernier, É. *Bijoux et orfèvreries (C.C.G.* nos. 52001–3855). 2 vols. Cairo, 1927.
23. Winlock, H. E. *The Treasure of el Lāhūn (The Metropolitan Museum of Art, Department of Egyptian Art,* vol. iv). New York, 1934.
24. Wolf, W. *Die Kunst Aegyptens: Gestalt und Geschichte.* Stuttgart, 1957.

XVI. RELIGION AND FUNERARY BELIEFS

1. Allen, T. G. *Occurrences of Pyramid Texts, with Cross Indexes of these and other Egyptian Mortuary Texts (S.A.O.C.* 27). Chicago, 1950.
2. Allen, T. G. 'Additions to the Egyptian Book of the Dead.' In *J.N.E.S.* 11 (1952), 177–86.
3. Bisson de la Roque, F. 'Notes sur le dieu Montou.' In *Bull. Inst. fr. Caire,* 40 (1941), 1–49.
4. Bonnet, H. *Reallexikon der ägyptischen Religionsgeschichte.* Berlin, 1952.
5. Breasted, J. H. *Development of Religion and Thought in Ancient Egypt (Lectures delivered on the Morse Foundation at Union Theological Seminary).* New York, 1912.
6. Breasted, J. H. *The Oriental Institute (The University of Chicago Survey,* vol. 12). Chicago, 1933.
7. Brunner, H., Grapow, H., Kees, H., Morenz, S., Otto, E., Schott, S. and Spiegel, J. *Ägyptologie,* sect. 2: *Literatur (Handbuch der Orientalistik,* edited by B. Spuler, I). Leiden, 1952.

8. de Buck, A. *The Egyptian Coffin Texts I–VI* (*O.I.P.* vols. 34, 49, 64, 67, 73, 81). Chicago, 1935–56.

9. de Buck, A. 'The Earliest Version of Book of the Dead 78.' In *J.E.A.* 35 (1949), 87–97.

10. Davies, Nina de G. and Gardiner, A. H. *The Tomb of Amenemhēt* (no. 82) (*E.E.F. The Theban Tomb Series*, 1st Memoir). London, 1915.

11. Donadoni, S. 'Testi geroglifici di Madinet Madi.' In *Orientalia*, 16 (1947), 333–52, 506–24.

12. Gardiner, A. H. *Egyptian Grammar, being an Introduction to the Study of Hieroglyphs.* Ed. 3. London, 1957.

13. Grapow, H. 'Zweiwegebuch und Totenbuch.' In *Z.Ä.S.* 46 (1909), 77–81.

14. Hayes, W. C. *The Burial Chamber of the Treasurer Sobk-mosě from er Rizeiḳat* (*The Metropolitan Museum of Art, Papers*, no. 9). New York, 1939.

15. Kees, H. 'Der Name des Suchosheiligtum von Illahun.' In *Z.Ä.S.* 59 (1924), 154–6.

16. Kees, H. 'Göttinger Totenbuchstudien. Ein Mythus vom Königtum des Osiris in Herakleopolis aus dem Totenbuch Kap. 175.' In *Z.Ä.S.* 65 (1930), 65–83.

17. Kees, H. 'Suchos.' In *P.W.*, neue Bearbeitung begonnen von G. Wissowa, Zweite Reihe [R–Z], Band IV, cols. 540–60.

18. Kees, H. 'Zu den Krokodil- und Nilpferdkulten im Nordwestdelta Aegyptens.' In *Studi in memoria di Ippolito Rosellini*, 2 (Pisa, 1949), 141–52.

19. Kees, H. 'Göttinger Totenbuchstudien: Die älteste Fassung der Einleitung des Totenbuchkapitels 99.' In *Miscellanea Academica Berolinensia* (Berlin, 1950), 77–96.

20. Kees, H. *Totenglauben und Jenseitsvorstellungen der alten Ägypter.* Ed. 2. Berlin, 1956.

21. Kuentz, C. 'Quelques monuments du culte de Sobk.' In *Bull. Inst. fr. Caire*, 28 (1928), 113–72.

22. Legrain, G. 'Notes sur le dieu Montou.' In *Bull. Inst. fr. Caire*, 12 (1912), 75–124

23. Lepsius, R. *Aelteste Texte des Todtenbuchs nach Sarkophagen des altaegyptischen Reichs im Berliner Museum.* Berlin, 1867.

24. Mond, R. and Myers, O. H. *The Bucheum* (*E.E.S.* 41st Memoir). 3 vols. London, 1934.

25. Moret, A. 'L'accession de la plèbe égyptienne aux droits religieux et politiques sous le Moyen Empire.' In *Rec. Champ.* 331–60, 1922.

26. Otto, E. *Beiträge zur Geschichte der Stierkult in Aegypten* (*Unters.* 13). Leipzig, 1938.

27. Roeder, G. 'Sobk.' In W. H. Roscher, *Ausführliches Lexikon der griechischen und römischen Mythologie* (Leipzig, 1909–15), IV, cols. 1093–120.

28. Schack-Schackenburg, H. *Das Buch von den zwei Wegen des seligen Toten* (*Zweiwegebuch*). *Texte aus der Pyramidenzeit nach einem im Berliner Museum bewahrten Sargboden des Mittleren Reiches.* Part 1. Leipzig, 1903.

29. Schäfer, H. *Die Mysterien des Osiris in Abydos unter König Sesostris III...* (*Unters.* IV, 2). Leipzig, 1904.

30. Sethe, K. *Urgeschichte und älteste Religion der Ägypter* (*Abh. für die Kunde des Morgenlandes*, XVIII, 4). Leipzig, 1930.

31. Sethe, K. *Die Totenliteratur der alten Ägypter* (*Sitzungsb. Berlin*, 1931, 18).

32. Speleers, L. *Textes des cercueils du Moyen Empire égyptien.* Brussels, 1947.

33. Vogliano, A. 'Rapporto preliminare della IVa campagna di scavo a Madînet Mâdi (R. Università di Milano).' In *Ann. Serv.* 38 (1938), 533–49.

34. Yoyotte, J. 'Le Soukhos de la Maréotide et d'autres cultes régionaux de dieu-crocodile d'après les cylindres du Moyen Empire.' In *Bull. Inst. fr. Caire*, 56 (1957), 81–95.

XVII. LITERATURE

1. Anthes, R. *Lebensregeln und Lebensweisheit der alten Ägypter* (*Alt. Or.* 32, 2). Leipzig, 1933.
2. Barns, J. W. B. *Five Ramesseum Papyri*. Oxford, 1956.
3. von Bissing, F. W. *Altägyptische Lebensweisheit, eingeleitet und übertragen* (*Die Bibliothek der alten Welt: Der alte Orient*). Zürich, 1955.
4. Blackman, A. M. Review of Kurt Sethe, *Dramatische Texte zu altaegyptischen Mysterienspielen*, I. In *J.E.A.* 16 (1930), 263–6.
5. Breasted, J. H. *The Edwin Smith Surgical Papyrus* (*O.I.P.* vols. III–IV). Chicago, 1930.
6. Brunner, H. *Die Lehre des Cheti, Sohnes des Duauf* (*Ägyptol. Forsch.* 13). Glückstadt, 1944.
7. Caminos, R. A. *Literary Fragments in the Hieratic Script* (The Griffith Institute). Oxford, 1956.
8. Chace, A. B., Manning, H. P. and Bull, L. *The Rhind Mathematical Papyrus. British Museum 10057 and 10058*. 2 vols. Oberlin, 1927, 1929.
9. Daressy, G. 'Calculs égyptiens du Moyen-Empire.' In *Rec. trav.* 28 (1906), 62–72.
10. Drioton, É. 'Le monothéisme de l'ancienne Égypte.' In *Cahiers d'histoire égyptienne*, January 1949, 151–68.
11. Drioton, É. *Pages d'égyptologie*. Cairo, 1957.
12. Ebers, G. *Papyros Ebers. Das hermetische Buch über die Arzeneimittel der alten Ägypter in hieratischer Schrift*. 2 vols. Leipzig, 1875.
13. Erman, A. *Die Märchen des Papyrus Westcar* (*Königliche Museen zu Berlin. Mitt. aus den orientalischen Sammlungen*, 5–6). Berlin, 1890.
14. Erman, A. *Die Sprache des Papyrus Westcar. Eine Vorarbeit zur Grammatik der älteren aegyptischen Sprache* (*Abh. Göttingen*, 36). Göttingen, 1890.
15. Faulkner, R. O. 'Ptaḥḥotpe and the Disputants.' In *Ägyptol. Studien Hermann Grapow zum 70. Geburtstag gewidmet* (Berlin, 1955), 81–4.
16. Faulkner, R. O. 'The Man who was Tired of Life.' In *J.E.A.* 42 (1956), 21–40.
17. Gardiner, A. H. *The Admonitions of an Egyptian Sage from a Hieratic Papyrus in Leiden* (*Pap. Leiden 344* recto). Leipzig, 1909.
18. Gardiner, A. H. *The Library of A. Chester Beatty. The Chester Beatty Papyri, No. 1: Description of a Hieratic Papyrus with a Mythological Story, Love-songs, and other Miscellaneous Texts*. London, 1931.
19. Gardiner, A. H. *Hieratic Papyri in the British Museum*, 3rd series: *Chester Beatty Gift*. 2 vols. London, 1935.
20. Gardiner, A. H. *The Ramesseum Papyri*. Oxford, 1955.
21. Gaster, T. H. *Thespis. Ritual, Myth and Drama in the Ancient Near East*. New York, 1950.
22. Gilbert, P. 'Les chants du harpiste.' In *Chron. d'Ég.* 15 (1940), 38–44.
23. Gilbert, P. *La poésie égyptienne*. Ed. 2. Brussels, 1949.
24. Gillain, O. *La science égyptienne. L'arithmétique au Moyen Empire* (*Fondation Égyptologique Reine Élisabeth*). Brussels, 1927.
25. Glanville, S. R. K. 'The Mathematical Leather Roll in the British Museum.' In *J.E.A.* 13 (1927), 232–9, pls. 58–62.

26. Grapow, H. *Sprachliche und schriftliche Formung ägyptischer Texte (Leipziger ägyptol. St.* 7). Glückstadt, 1936.
27. Grapow, H. 'Beiträge zur Untersuchung des Stils ägyptischer Lieder.' In *Z.Ä.S.* 79 (1954), 17–27.
28. Grapow, H. 'Beschreibung und Kollation des Papyrus Ebers.' In *Z.Ä.S.* 84 (1959), 38–54.
29. Grapow, H. and others. *Grundriss der Medizin der alten Ägypter.* 5 vols. Berlin, 1954–8.
30. Hermann, A. *Die ägyptische Königsnovelle (Leipziger ägyptol. St.* 10). Glückstadt, 1938.
31. Hermann, S. *Untersuchungen zur Überlieferungsgestalt mittelägyptischer Literaturwerke (Deutsch. Akad. Berlin, Inst. f. Or. Veröffentlichung,* Nr. 33). Berlin, 1957.
32. Hermann, S. 'Zum Verständnis der "Klagen des Bauern" als Rechtsforderungen.' In *Z.Ä.S.* 82 (1957), 55–7.
33. Junker, H. *Die Götterlehre von Memphis (Abh. Berlin,* 1939, Nr. 23). Berlin, 1940.
34. Kuentz, C. 'Deux versions d'un panégyrique royal.' In *Studies presented to F. Ll. Griffith (E.E.S.* London, 1932), 97–110.
35. Lanczkowski, G. 'Das Königtum im Mittleren Reich.' In *The Sacral Kingship [la regalità sacra] (Studies in the History of Religions,* IV) (Leiden, 1959), 269–80.
36. Lichtheim, M. 'The Songs of the Harpers.' In *J.N.E.S.* 4 (1945), 178–212.
37. Maystre, C. 'Le Livre de la Vache du Ciel dans les tombeaux de la Vallée des Rois.' In *Bull. Inst. fr. Caire,* 40 (1941), 53–115.
38. Myers, O. H. 'Zeberged.' In *J.E.A.* 34 (1948), 119–20.
39. Neugebauer, O. *Die Grundlagen der ägyptischen Bruchrechnung.* Berlin, 1926.
40. Neugebauer, O. 'Zur ägyptischen Bruchrechnung.' In *Z.Ä.S.* 64 (1929), 44–8.
41. Neugebauer, O. and others. *(Quellen und Studien zur Geschichte der Mathematik,* Abt. B, Bd. 1). Berlin, 1931.
42. Peet, T. E. *The Rhind Mathematical Papyrus. British Museum 10057 and 10058. Introduction, Transcription, Translation and Commentary.* London, 1923.
43. Peet, T. E. *A Comparative Study of the Literatures of Egypt, Palestine, and Mesopotamia (British Academy: Schweich Lectures,* 1929). London, 1931.
44. Peet, T. E. 'A Problem in Egyptian Geometry.' In *J.E.A.* 17 (1931), 100–6.
45. Piankoff, A. *The Shrines of Tut-ankh-Amon (Bollingen Series,* XL, 2). New York, 1955.
46. Posener, G. 'Les richesses inconnues de la littérature égyptienne' (*Recherches littéraires,* 1). In *Rev. d'Égyptol.* 6 (1949), 27–48.
47. Reisner, G. A. *The Hearst Medical Papyrus (University of California: Egyptian Archaeology,* 1). Leipzig, 1905.
48. Rusch, A. 'Dramatische Texte aus dem alten Ägypten.' In *O.L.Z.* 32 (1929), cols. 145–56.
49. Rusch, A. Review of K. Sethe, *Der Dramatische Ramesseumpapyrus.* In *O.L.Z.* 33 (1930), cols. 342–55.
50. Schack-Schackenburg, H. 'Der Berliner Papyrus 6619.' In *Z.Ä.S.* 38 (1900), 135–40.
51. Sethe, K. *Von Zahlen und Zahlworten bei den alten Ägyptern (Schriften der Wissenschaftlichen Gesellschaft Strassburg,* part 25). Strassburg, 1916.
52. Sethe, K. *Dramatische Texte zu altaegyptischen Mysterienspielen (Unters.* 10). Leipzig, 1928.

53. Simpson, W. K. 'Allusions to *The Shipwrecked Sailor* and *The Eloquent Peasant* in a Ramesside Text.' In *J.A.O.S.* 78 (1958), 50–1.

54. Spiegel, J. *Die Erzählung vom Streite des Horus und Seth in Pap. Beatty I als Literaturwerk (Leipziger ägyptol. St.* 9). Glückstadt, 1937.

55. Spiegel, J. *Soziale und weltanschauliche Reformbewegungen im alten Ägypten.* Heidelberg, 1950.

56. Steindorff, G. 'Das Lied an's Grab, ein Sänger und ein Bildhauer des mittleren Reiches.' In *Z.Ä.S.* 32 (1894), 123–6.

57. Stricker, B. H. 'De Indeeling der Egyptische Taalgeschiednis.' In *Oudheidkundige Mededeelingen,* 25 (1944), 12–51.

58. Struve, W. W. *Mathematischer Papyrus des Staatlichen Museums der Schönen Künste in Moskau (Quellen und Studien zur Geschichte der Mathematik,* Abt. A, Bd. 1). Berlin, 1930.

59. Thausing, G. 'Betrachtungen zum "Lebensmüden".' In *Mitt. deutsch. Inst. Kairo,* 15 (1957), 264–7.

60. Thomas, W. R. 'Moscow Mathematical Papyrus, No. 14.' In *J.E.A.* 17 (1931), 50–2.

61. Vergote, J. 'Une nouvelle interprétation de deux passages du Naufragé.' In *Mitt. deutsch. Inst. Kairo,* 15 (1957), 275–87.

62. Vikentiev, V. 'À propos d'un extrait de la stèle d'Emheb.' In *Bulletin of the Faculty of Arts* (Fouad I University, Cairo), 9 (1947), 113–29.

63. Volten, A. *Zwei altägyptische politische Schriften: Die Lehre für König Merikarê (Pap. Carlsberg VI) und die Lehre des Königs Amenemhet (An. Aeg.* 4). Copenhagen, 1945.

64. Vycichl, W. 'Notes on the Story of the Shipwrecked Sailor.' In *Kush,* 5 (1957), 70–2.

65. Wainwright, G. A. 'Zeberged: The Shipwrecked Sailor's Island.' In *J.E.A.* 32 (1946), 31–8 (see also *ibid.* 34 [1948], 119).

66. van de Walle, B. *La transmission des textes littéraires égyptiens (Édition de la Fondation Égyptologique Reine Élisabeth).* Brussels, 1948.

67. Wilson, J. A. *The Burden of Egypt. An Interpretation of Ancient Egyptian Culture.* Chicago, 1951.

68. Wreszinski, W. *Der grosse medizinische Papyrus des Berliner Museums.* Leipzig, 1909.

69. Žába, Z. *Les Maximes de Ptahhotep (Éditions de l'Académie Tchécoslovaque des Sciences).* Prague, 1956.

A. ADDENDA

1. von Beckerath, J. 'Die Dynastie der Herakleopoliten (9./10. Dynastie).' In *Z.Ä.S.* 93 (1966), 13–20.

2. Fischer, H. G. 'The Nubian Mercenaries of Gebelein during the First Intermediate Period.' In *Kush,* 9 (1961), 44–80.

3. Fischer, H. G. 'Further Remarks on the Gebelein Stelae.' In *Kush,* 10 (1962), 333–4.

4. Fischer, H. G. *Inscriptions from the Coptite Nome, Dynasties VI–XI (An. Or.* 40). Rome, 1964.

5. Goedicke, H. 'Zur Chronologie der sogenannten "Ersten Zwischenzeit".' In *Z.D.M.G.* 112 (1962), 239–54.

6. Habachi, L. 'King Nebhepetre Menthuhotp: His Monuments, Place in History, Deification and Unusual Representations in the Form of Gods.' In *Mitt. deutsch. Inst. Kairo,* 19 (1963), 16–52.

7. Hintze, F. 'Das Kerma-Problem.' In Z.Ä.S. 91 (1964), 79–86.
8. Schenkel, W. *Frühmittelägyptische Studien (Bonner Orientalistische Studien, Neue Serie,* 13). Bonn, 1962.
9. Schenkel, W. *Memphis–Herakleopolis–Theben, die epigraphischen Zeugnisse der 7.–11. Dynastie Ägyptens (Ägyptol. Abh.* 12). Wiesbaden, 1965.
10. Terrace, E. L. B. *Egyptian Paintings of the Middle Kingdom.* London, 1968.

CHAPTER XXI

I. SYRIA AND PALESTINE IN THE HERACLEOPOLITAN PERIOD AND THE ELEVENTH DYNASTY

1. Albright, W. F. 'Dunand's New Byblos Volume: a Lycian at the Byblian Court.' In *Bull. A.S.O.R.* 155 (1959), 31–4.
2. Anthes, R. *Die Felseninschriften von Hatnub (Unters.* 9). Leipzig, 1928.
3. von Bissing, F. W. *Denkmäler ägyptischer Sculptur.* 3 vols. Munich, 1911–14.
4. Borchardt, L. *Das Grabdenkmal des Königs Ne-user-Reʿ (Deutsche Orient-Gesellschaft. Wissenschaftliche Veröffentlichungen,* 7). Leipzig, 1907.
5. Borchardt, L. *Das Grabdenkmal des Königs Saẖu-Reʿ.* 2 vols. *(Deutsche Orient-Gesellschaft. Wissenschaftliche Veröffentlichungen,* 14, 26.) Leipzig, 1910, 1913.
6. Breasted, J. H. *Ancient Records of Egypt. Historical Documents.* Vol. 1: *The First to the Seventeenth Dynasties.* Chicago, 1906.
7. British Museum, *Hieroglyphic Texts from Egyptian Stelae, etc. in The British Museum* (edited by P. D. Scott-Moncrieff, H. R. Hall, I. E. S. Edwards). 8 parts. London, 1911–39.
8. Clère, J. J. and Vandier, J. *Textes de la Première Période Intermédiaire et de la XIème Dynastie (Bibl. Aeg.* 10). Brussels, 1948.
9. Davie, M. R. *La guerre dans les sociétés primitives. Son rôle et son évolution (Bibliothèque scientifique).* Paris, 1931.
10. Drioton, E. 'Le désert du Sinaï couvert par une forêt impénétrable?' In *Rev. d'égyptol.* 12 (1960), 90–1.
11. Ember, A. 'Partial Assimilation in Old Egyptian.' In *Oriental Studies Published in Commemoration of the Fortieth Anniversary of Paul Haupt* (Baltimore, 1926), 300–12.
12. Erman, A. *The Literature of the Ancient Egyptians,* translated into English by A. M. Blackman. London, 1927.
13. Erman, A. and Grapow, H. *Wörterbuch der aegyptischen Sprache.* 6 vols. Leipzig, Berlin, 1926–50.
14. Fakhry, A. *The Inscriptions of the Amethyst Quarries at Wadi el Hudi (Service des Antiquités de l'Égypte: The Egyptian Deserts).* Cairo, 1952.
15. Faulkner, R. O. 'The Rebellion in the Hare Nome.' In *J.E.A.* 30 (1944), 61–3.
16. Frankfort, H. 'Egypt and Syria in the First Intermediate Period.' In *J.E.A.* 12 (1926), 80–99.
17. Gardiner, A. H. *The Admonitions of an Egyptian Sage from a Hieratic Papyrus in Leiden (Pap. Leiden* 344 recto). Leipzig, 1909.
18. Gardiner, A. H. 'New Literary Works from Ancient Egypt.' In *J.E.A.* 1 (1914), 20–36, 100–6.
19. Gardiner, A. H. 'The Tomb of a Much-travelled Theban Official.' In *J.E.A.* 4 (1917), 28–38, pls. 6–9.

20. Gardiner, A. H. 'Piankhi's Instructions to his Army.' In *J.E.A.* 21 (1935), 219–23.
21. Gardiner, A. H., Peet, T. E. and Černý, J. *The Inscriptions of Sinai.* 2 parts. London (E.E.S.), 1952, 1955.
22. Gauthier, H. *Dictionnaire des noms géographiques contenus dans les textes hiéroglyphiques* (*La Société royale de géographie d'Égypte*). 7 vols. Cairo, 1925–31.
23. Golénischeff, W. (ed.). *Les papyrus hiératiques nos. 1115, 1116 A et 1116 B de l'Ermitage Impérial à St-Pétersbourg.* [St Petersburg], 1913.
24. Gunn, B. and Gardiner, A. H. 'New Renderings of Egyptian Texts. II. The Expulsion of the Hyksos.' In *J.E.A.* 5 (1918), 36–56.
25. Hayes, W. C. 'Career of the Great Steward Henenu under Nebḥepetrē, Mentuḥotpe.' In *J.E.A.* 35 (1949), 43–9.
26. Hayes, W. C. *A Papyrus of the Late Middle Kingdom in the Brooklyn Museum* (Papyrus Brooklyn 35.1446). Brooklyn, 1955.
27. Jéquier, G. *Le monument funéraire de Pepi II* (*Service des Antiquités de l'Égypte: Fouilles à Saqqarah*). 3 vols. Cairo, 1936–40.
28. Kantor, H. J. 'The Chronology of Egypt and its Correlation with that of Other Parts of the Near East in the Periods before the Late Bronze Age.' In Ehrich, *Relative Chronologies in Old World Archeology* (Chicago, 1954), 1–27.
29. Montet, P. *Le drame d'Avaris. Essai sur la pénétration des Sémites en Égypte.* Paris, 1940.
30. Montet, P. *La vie quotidienne en Égypte au temps des Ramsès.* Paris, 1946.
31. Moscati, S. *I predecessori d'Israele. Studi sulle più antiche genti semitiche in Siria e Palestina* (*Università di Roma. Studi orientali pubblicati a cura della Scuola orientale.* Vol. IV). Rome, 1956.
32. Müller, W. M. *Asien und Europa nach altägyptischen Denkmälern.* Leipzig, 1893.
33. Naville, E. *The XIth Dynasty Temple at Deir el-Bahari* (*E.E.F.* 28th, 30th, and 32nd Memoirs). London, 1907–13.
34. Newberry, P. E. and others. *Beni Hasan.* 4 parts (*Archaeological Survey of Egypt*, 1st, 2nd, 5th and 7th Memoirs). London, 1893–1900.
35. Petrie, W. M. F. *Deshasheh* (*E.E.F.* 15th Memoir). London, 1898.
36. Petrie, W. M. F. *A History of Egypt from the Earliest Kings to the XVIth Dynasty.* Ed. 10. London, 1917.
37. Petrie, W. M. F. *Buttons and Design Scarabs* (*British School of Archaeology in Egypt and Egyptian Research Account*, 24th Year, 1918). London, 1925.
38. Pinches, T. G. and Newberry, P. E. 'A Cylinder-Seal Inscribed in Hieroglyphic and Cuneiform in the Collection of the Earl of Carnarvon.' In *J.E.A.* 7 (1921), 196–9, pl. 32.
39. Porter, B. and Moss, R. L. B. *Topographical Bibliography of Ancient Egyptian Hieroglyphic Texts, Reliefs, and Paintings.* 7 vols. Oxford, 1927–60.
40. Posener, G. 'Trois passages de l'Enseignement à Mérikarê.' In *Rev. d'égyptol.* 7 (1950), 176–80.
41. Posener, G. *Littérature et politique dans l'Égypte de la XIIe dynastie* (*Bibliothèque de l'École des Hautes Études*, fasc. 307). Paris, 1956.
42. Pritchard, J. B. *The Ancient Near East in Pictures Relating to the Old Testament.* Princeton, 1954 (=*A.N.E.T.*).
43. Quibell, J. E. and Hayter, A. G. K. *Teti Pyramid, North Side* (*Service des Antiquités de l'Égypte: Excavations at Saqqara*). Cairo, 1927.
44. Roeder, G. *Debod bis Bab Kalabsche* (*Service des Antiquités de l'Égypte: Les temples immergés de la Nubie*). 3 vols. Cairo, 1911, 1912.

45. Säve-Söderbergh, T. *Ägypten und Nubien. Ein Beitrag zur Geschichte alt-ägyptischer Aussenpolitik.* Lund, 1941.
46. Scharff, A. 'Über einige fremdartige Darstellungen auf Siegelbildern aus dem späten Alten Reich und der ersten Zwischenzeit.' In *Z.Ä.S.* 67 (1931), 95–102.
47. Scharff, A. *Der historische Abschnitt der Lehre für König Merikarê (Sitzungsb. München, 1936, Heft 8).* Munich, 1936.
48. Schenkel, W. *Frühmittelägyptische Studien (Bonner Orientalistische Studien, N.S., Band 13).* Bonn, 1962.
49. Selim Hassan. 'The Causeway of *Wnis* at Sakkara.' In *Z.Ä.S.* 80 (1955), 136–9.
50. Sethe, K. *Die Ächtung feindlicher Fürsten, Völker und Dinge auf altägyptischen Tongefässscherben des mittleren Reiches . . . (Abh. Berlin, 1926, Nr. 5).* Berlin, 1926.
51. Sethe, K. *Historisch-biographische Urkunden des mittleren Reiches (Urk. VII, 1).* Leipzig, 1935.
52. Stock, H. *Die erste Zwischenzeit Aegyptens (St. Aeg. 2 =An. Or. 31).* Rome, 1949.
53. Ungnad, A. 'Der Akkader Narâm-Sin und der Ägypter Mani.' In *Arch.f. Or.* 14 (1941–4), 199–201.
54. Vercoutter, J. *L'Égypte et le monde égéen préhellénique (Inst. fr. Caire, Biblio-thèque d'Étude, 22).* Cairo, 1956.
55. Volten, A. *Zwei altägyptische politische Schriften: Die Lehre für König Merikarê (Pap. Carlsberg VI) und die Lehre des Königs Amenemhet (An. Aeg. 4).* Copenhagen, 1945.
56. Ward, W. A. 'Egypt and the East Mediterranean in the Early Second Millennium B.C.' In *Or.* 30 (1961), 22–45, 129–55.
57. Weigall, A. *A History of the Pharaohs.* 2 vols. London, 1925, 1927.
58. Wilson, J. A. 'Egyptian Texts.' In Pritchard, J. B. (ed.), *Ancient Near Eastern Texts relating to the Old Testament.* Princeton, 1950 (=*A.N.E.T.*).
59. Wreszinski, W. *Atlas zur altägyptischen Kulturgeschichte.* Part II. Leipzig, 1935.
60. Yeivin, S. 'Topographic and Ethnic Notes.' In '*Atiqot (Journal of the Israel Dept. of Antiquities*), 2 (1959), 155–64.

II. SYRIA AND PALESTINE DURING THE TWELFTH DYNASTY

1. Albright, W. F. 'The Egyptian Empire in Asia in the Twenty-First Century B.C.' In *J.P.O.S.* 8 (1928), 223–56.
2. Albright, W. F. 'Palestine in the Earliest Historical Period.' In *J.P.O.S.* 15 (1935), 193–234.
3. Albright, W. F. 'The Land of Damascus between 1850 and 1750 B.C.' In *Bull. A.S.O.R.* 83 (1941), 30–6.
4. Albright, W. F. 'Northwest-Semitic Names in a List of Egyptian Slaves from the Eighteenth Century B.C.' In *J.A.O.S.* 74 (1954), 222–33.
5. Alt, A. 'Die asiatischen Gefahrzonen in den Ächtungstexten der 11. Dynastie.' In *Z.Ä.S.* 63 (1928), 39–45.
6. Alt, A. 'Herren und Herrensitze Palästinas im Anfang des zweiten Jahrtausends v. Chr. Vorläufige Bemerkungen zu den neuen Ächtungstexten.' In *Z.D.P.V.* 64 (1941), 21–39.
7. Alt, A. *Die Herkunft der Hyksos in neuer Sicht (Berichte Leipzig, 101, 6).* Berlin, 1954.

8. Barnett, R. D. *A Catalogue of the Nimrud Ivories with other examples of Ancient Near Eastern Ivories in the British Museum.* London, 1957.

9. Bisson de la Roque, F. *Médamoud (Flles. Inst. fr. Caire,* 4, 1). Cairo, 1927.

10. Bisson de la Roque, F. *Tôd (1934 à 1936) (Flles. Inst. fr. Caire,* 17). Cairo, 1937.

11. Bisson de la Roque, F. *Trésor de Tôd (C.C.G.* nos. 70501–754). Cairo, 1950.

12. Bisson de la Roque, F., Contenau, G. and Chapouthier, F. *Le trésor de Tôd (Documents de Flles. Inst. fr. Caire,* 11). Cairo, 1953.

13. Blackman, A. M. *The Rock Tombs of Meir.* 6 Parts (*E.E.F.* and *E.E.S. Arch. Survey,* 22nd–25th, 28th and 29th Memoirs). London, 1914–53.

14. Blackman, A. M. 'A Reference to Sesostris III's Syrian Campaign.' In *J.E.A.* 2 (1915), 13–14.

15. Blackman, A. M. *Middle-Egyptian Stories (Bibl. Aeg.* 2). Brussels, 1932.

16. Brunner, H. *Die Lehre des Cheti, Sohnes des Duauf (Ägyptol. Forsch.* 13). Glückstadt, 1944.

17. Černý, J. 'Semites in Egyptian Mining Expeditions to Sinai.' In *Arch. Orient.* 7 (1935), 384–9.

18. Chéhab, M. 'Un trésor d'orfèvrerie syro-égyptien.' In *Bull. du Musée de Beyrouth* 1 (1937), 7–21.

19. Davies, N. M. and Gardiner, A. H. *Ancient Egyptian Paintings.* 2 vols. Chicago, 1936.

20. Dessenne, A. *Le sphinx, étude iconographique.* 1. *Des origines à la fin du second millénaire (Bibliothèque des Écoles françaises d'Athènes et de Rome,* fasc. 186). Paris, 1957.

21. Dunand, M. *Fouilles de Byblos,* t. 1–11 (*République libanaise. Direction de l'Instruction publique et des Beaux-Arts. Études et documents d'archéologie,* 1 and 3). 5 vols. Paris, 1937–58.

22. Dussaud, R. 'Nouveaux renseignements sur la Palestine et la Syrie vers 2000 avant notre ère.' In *Syria,* 8 (1927), 216–33.

23. Fischer, H. G. 'A Scribe of the Army in a Saqqara Mastaba of the Early Fifth Dynasty.' In *J.N.E.S.* 18 (1959), 233–72, pls. 4–11.

24. Griffith, F. L. 'Fragments of old Egyptian Stories.' In *P.S.B.A.* 14 (1892), 451–72.

25. Hayes, W. C. *The Scepter of Egypt.* 2 parts. New York, 1953, 1959.

26. Helck, W. 'Die ägyptische Verwaltung in den syrischen Besitzungen.' In *M.D.O.G.* 92 (1960), 1–13.

27. Helck, W. *Die Beziehungen Ägyptens zu Vorderasien im 3. und 2. Jahrtausend v. Chr. (Äg. Abh.* 5). Wiesbaden, 1962.

28. Junker, H. *Gîza VIII (Denkschr. Wien,* 73, 1). Vienna, 1947.

29. Kantor, H. J. *The Aegean and the Orient in the Second Millennium B.C. (Monographs on Archaeology and Fine Arts sponsored by the Archaeological Institute of America and the College Art Association of America,* 4). Bloomington (Indiana), 1947.

30. Kitchen, K. A. 'An Unusual Stela from Abydos.' In *J.E.A.* 47 (1961), 10–18, pls. 2–3.

31. Landsberger, B. 'Assyrische Königsliste und "Dunkles Zeitalter".' In *J.C.S.* 8 (1954), 31–45, 47–73, 106–33.

32. Lange, H. O. and Schäfer, H. *Grab- und Denksteine des mittleren Reiches im Museum von Kairo (C.C.G.* nos. 20001–780). 4 vols. Berlin, 1902–25.

33. Lefebvre, G. *Romans et contes égyptiens de l'époque pharaonique.* Paris, 1949.

34. Loud, G. *Megiddo II. Seasons of 1935–39 (O.I.P.* 62). 2 parts. Chicago, 1948.

35. Lucas, A. *Ancient Egyptian Materials and Industries.* Ed. 3. London, 1948.

36. Macalister, R. A. S. *The Excavation of Gezer,* 1902–5 and 1907–9. 3 vols. London, 1912.

37. Maisler, B. 'Palestine at the Time of the Middle Kingdom in Egypt.' In *Rev. hist. juive en Égypte,* 1 (1947), 33–68.

38. Malamat, A. 'Hazor "the Head of All those Kingdoms".' In *J. Bibl. Lit.* 79 (1960), 12–19.

39. Meyer, E. *Geschichte des Altertums,* vol. 1, part 2. Ed. 3. Stuttgart and Berlin, 1913.

40. Montet, P. *Byblos et l'Égypte, quatre campagnes de fouilles à Gebeil, 1921–1922–1923–1924* (*Haut-Commissariat de la République française en Syrie et au Liban. Service des antiquités et des beaux-arts. Bibliothèque archéologique et historique,* tome 11). 2 parts. Paris, 1928, 1929.

41. Montet, P. 'Notes et documents pour servir à l'histoire des relations entre l'ancienne Égypte et la Syrie.' In *Kêmi,* 1 (1928), 19–28, 83–93.

42. Montet, P. 'Notes et documents pour servir à l'histoire des relations entre l'Égypte et la Syrie.' In *Kêmi,* 16 (1962), 76–96.

43. de Morgan, J. *Fouilles à Dahchour, mars–juin 1894.* Vienna, 1895.

44. Moscati, S. 'Un avorio di Ugarit e l'iconografia egiziana del nemico vinto.' In *Or. antiq.* 1 (1962), 3–7, pl. 1.

45. Munn-Rankin, J. M. 'Diplomacy in Western Asia in the Early Second Millennium B.C.' In *Iraq,* 18 (1956), 68–110.

46. Newberry, P. E. and others. *El Bersheh.* 2 parts (*Archaeological Survey of Egypt,* 3rd and 4th Memoirs). London, 1894–5.

47. Nielsen, E. 'The Burial of Foreign Gods.' In *Studia Theologica,* 8 (1955), 103–22.

48. Olmstead, A. T. *History of Palestine and Syria.* New York, 1931.

49. Peet, T. E. *The Stela of Sebek-Khu, the Earliest Record of an Egyptian Campaign in Asia* (*The Manchester Museum, Museum Handbooks,* Publication 75). Manchester, 1914.

50. Petrie, W. M. F. *Ancient Gaza: Tell El Ajjūl* (*Publications of the Egyptian Research Account and British School of Archaeology in Egypt,* nos. 53–6). 4 parts. London, 1931–4.

51. Posener, G. *Princes et pays d'Asie et de Nubie: Textes hiératiques sur des figurines d'envoûtement du Moyen Empire.* Brussels, 1940.

52. Posener, G. 'Les richesses inconnues de la littérature égyptienne' (*Recherches littéraires,* 1). In *Rev. d'égyptol.* 6 (1951), 27–48.

53. Posener, G. 'Les Asiatiques en Égypte sous les XIIe et XIIIe dynasties.' In *Syria,* 34 (1957), 145–63.

54. Posener, G. 'Les empreintes magiques de Gizeh et les morts dangereux.' In *Mitt. deutsch. Inst. Kairo,* 16 (1958), 252–70, pls. 26–7.

55. Rowe, A. *A Catalogue of Egyptian Scarabs, Scaraboids, Seals and Amulets in the Palestine Archaeological Museum* (*Government of Palestine, Department of Antiquities*). Cairo, 1936.

56. Rowe, A. 'Three New Stelae from the South-Eastern Desert.' In *Ann. Serv.* 39 (1939), 187–94, pls. 25–6.

57. Schaeffer, C. F. A. *Ugaritica II* (*Mission de Ras Shamra,* v). Paris, 1949.

58. Schaeffer, C. F. A. 'Reprise des recherches archéologiques à Ras Shamra–Ugarit.' In *Syria,* 28 (1951), 1–21.

59. Schweitzer, U. *Löwe und Sphinx im alten Ägypten* (*Ägyptol. Forsch.* 15). Glückstadt, 1948.

60. Sethe, K. *Aegyptische Lesestücke zum Gebrauch im akademischen Unterricht. Texte des mittleren Reiches.* Leipzig, 1924.
61. Sethe, K. and Helck, W. *Urkunden der 18. Dynastie (Urk.* iv). Heft 1–22. Leipzig–Berlin, 1906–58.
62. Seyrig, H. 'Antiquités syriennes : 59. Note sur le trésor de Tôd.' In *Syria,* 31 (1954), 218–24.
63. Simpson, W. K. 'Papyrus Lythgoe : A Fragment of a Literary Text of the Middle Kingdom from El-Lisht.' In *J.E.A.* 46 (1960), 65–70, pls. 15–15A.
64. Smith, S. 'Babylonian Cylinder Seals from Egypt.' In *J.E.A.* 8 (1922), 207–10, pl. 23.
65. Smith, S. *Alalakh and Chronology.* London, 1940.
66. Smith, W. S. *The Art and Architecture of Ancient Egypt (The Pelican History of Art).* Great Britain, 1958.
67. Smither, P. 'The Semneh Despatches.' In *J.E.A.* 31 (1945), 3–10, pls. 2–7.
68. Steindorff, G. 'Skarabäen mit Namen von Privatpersonen der Zeit des mittleren und neuen Reichs aus der Sammlung S.M. des Königs Fuâd I.' In *Ann. Serv.* 36 (1936), 161–86, pls. 1–5.
69. Vandier, J. 'A propos d'un dépôt de provenance asiatique trouvé à Tôd.' In *Syria,* 18 (1937), 174–82, pls. 28–9.
70. Vernier, É. *Bijoux et orfèvreries (C.C.G.* nos. 52001–3855). 2 vols. Cairo, 1927.
71. Vincent, L.-H. 'Les pays bibliques et l'Égypte à la fin de la XIIe dynastie égyptienne.' In *Vivre et Penser (=Rev. bibl.),* 2 (1942), 187–212.
72. Wilson, J. A. 'The Egyptian Middle Kingdom at Megiddo." In *A.J.S.L.* 58 (1941), 225–36, pls. 1–3.
73. Wilson, J. A. *The Burden of Egypt.* Chicago, 1951.
74. Woolley, L. *Alalakh* (Reports of the Research Committee of the Society of Antiquaries of London, 18). Oxford, 1955.

III. EGYPTIAN SOURCES

1. Albright, W. F. *The Vocalization of the Egyptian Syllabic Orthography (American Oriental Series,* 5). New Haven, 1934.
2. Albright, W. F. *From the Stone Age to Christianity.* Baltimore, 1940.
3. Albright, W. F. 'New Egyptian Data on Palestine in Patriarchal Age.' In *Bull. A.S.O.R.* 81 (1941), 16–21.
4. Albright, W. F. 'An Indirect Synchronism between Egypt and Mesopotamia, cir. 1730 b.c.' In *Bull. A.S.O.R.* 99 (1945), 9–18.
5. Albright, W. F. *The Archaeology of Palestine* (Pelican Books, A199). Harmondsworth, 1949.
6. Albright, W. F. 'Some Important Recent Discoveries : Alphabetic Origins and the Idrimi Statue.' In *Bull. A.S.O.R.* 118 (1950), 11–20.
7. Alt, A. 'Ein Reich von Lydda.' In *Z.D.P.V.* 47 (1924), 169–85.
8. Alt, A. 'Amurru in den Ächtungstexten der 11. Dynastie ?' In *Z.A.W.* 46 (1928), 77–8.
9. Alt, A. 'Die älteste Schilderung Palästinas im Lichte neuer Funde.' In *P.J.B.* 37 (1941), 19–49.
10. Barns, J. W. B. *The Ashmolean Ostracon of Sinuhe.* Oxford, 1952.
11. Bonnet, H. *Die Waffen der Völker des alten Orients.* Leipzig, 1926.
12. Breasted, J. H. 'The Ras Shamra Statue of Sesostris-Onekh.' In *Syria,* 16 (1935), 318–20.

13. Celada, B. 'Nuevos documentos para la primitiva historia de Palestiña, Nubia y Libia.' In *Sefarad*, 3 (1943), 429–55.
14. Clère, J. J. 'Sinouhé en Syrie.' In *Mélanges Syriens offerts à M. R. Dussaud* (1939), 829–40.
15. Dussaud, R. 'Nouveaux textes égyptiens d'exécration contre les peuples syriens.' In *Syria*, 21 (1940), 170–82.
16. Fischer, H. G. 'The Inspector of the *Šḥ* of Horus, *Nby*.' In *Or*. 30 (1961), 170–5, pl. 25.
17. Galling, K. 'Archäologisch-historische Ergebnisse einer Reise in Syrien und Liban im Spätherbst 1952.' In *Z.D.P.V.* 69 (1953), 88–93.
18. Gardiner, A. H. *Ancient Egyptian Onomastica*. 3 vols. Oxford, 1947.
19. Goetze, A. 'Remarks on some Names occurring in the Execration Texts.' In *Bull. A.S.O.R.* 151 (1958), 28–33.
20. Harrelson, W. 'Shechem, the "Navel of the Land". I. Shechem in extra-biblical References.' In *Bi. Ar.* 20 (1957), 2–10.
21. Hrozný, B. 'Die Länder Churri und Mitanni und die ältesten Inder.' In *Arch. Orient.* 1 (1929), 91–110.
22. Kuentz, Ch. *La bataille de Qadech* (*Mém. Inst. fr. Caire*, 55). Cairo, 1928–34.
23. Kuschke, A. 'Beiträge zur Siedlungsgeschichte der Biḳāʿ.' In *Z.D.P.V.* 74 (1958), 81–120.
24. Lévy, I. 'Lotanu–Loṭan.' In *Sphinx*, 9 (1906), 70–86.
25. Maisler, B. 'Canaan on the Threshold of the Age of the Patriarchs.' In *Eretz-Israel*, 3 (1954), 18–32.
26. Malamat, A. 'Campaigns of Amenhotep II and Thutmose IV to Canaan.' In *Studies in the Bible. Scripta hierosolymitana*, 8 (1961), 218–31.
27. Maspero, G. 'Notes sur quelques points de Grammaire et d'Histoire, §xxxv.' In *Z.Ä.S.* 21 (1883), 65–7.
28. Maxwell-Hyslop, R. 'Western Asiatic Shaft-hole Axes.' In *Iraq*, 11 (1949), 90–125 and pls. 34–9.
29. Möller, G. *Hieratische Papyrus aus den königlichen Museen zu Berlin*, II. Leipzig, 1905.
30. Montet, P. 'Note sur les inscriptions de Sanousrit-Ankh.' In *Syria*, 15 (1934), 131–3.
31. Montet, P. 'A propos de la statuette de Sanousrit-Ankh.' In *Syria*, 17 (1936), 202–3.
32. Moran, W. L. 'Mari Notes on the Execration Texts.' In *Or.* 26 (1957), 339–45.
33. Müller, W. M. *Egyptological Researches. Results of a Journey in 1904*. Washington, 1906.
34. Newberry, P. E. 'Miscellanea.' In *J.E.A.* 14 (1928), 109–11.
35. Newberry, P. E. 'A Statue and a Scarab.' In *J.E.A.* 19 (1933), 53–4, pl. 10.
36. Noth, M. 'Die syrisch-palästinische Bevölkerung des zweiten Jahrtausends v. Chr. im Lichte neuer Quellen.' In *Z.D.P.V.* 65 (1942), 9–67.
37. Sauneron, S. 'Deux mentions d'Houroun.' In *Rev. d'égyptol.* 7 (1950), 121–6.
38. Scharff, A. 'Briefe aus Illahun.' In *Z.Ä.S.* 59 (1924), 20–51, pls. 1–12.
39. Spiegelberg, W. 'Der Siegeshymnus des Merneptah auf der Flinders Petrie-Stele.' In *Z.Ä.S.* 34 (1896), 1–25, pl. 1.
40. Wolf, W. *Die Bewaffnung des altägyptischen Heeres*. Leipzig, 1926.
41. Wreszinski, W. *Ägyptische Inschriften aus dem K. K. Hofmuseum in Wien*. Leipzig, 1906.
42. Yeivin, S. 'The Extent of Egyptian Domination in Hither Asia under the Middle Kingdom.' In *Eretz-Israel*, 4 (1956), 37–40.

IV. SYRIA DURING THE THIRD DYNASTY OF UR

1. Albright, W. F. 'The Land of Damascus between 1850 and 1750 B.C.' In *Bull. A.S.O.R.* 83 (1941), 30 ff.
2. Barton, G. A. *The Royal Inscriptions of Sumer and Akkad.* New Haven, 1929.
3. Bilgiç, E. 'Die Ortsnamen der "kappadokischen" Urkunden im Rahmen der alten Sprachen Anatoliens.' In *Arch. f. Or.* 15 (1945–51), 1 ff.
4. Boson, G. *Tavolette cuneiformi sumere degli Archivi di Drehem e di Djoha.* Milano, 1936.
5. *C.A.D. The Assyrian Dictionary.* Chicago–Glückstadt, 1956– .
6. Çığ, M., Kızılyay, H. and Salonen, A. *Die Puzriš-Dagan-Texte der Istanbuler archäologischen Museen,* Teil I. Helsinki, 1954.
7. Clay, A. T. *Babylonian Records in the Library of J. Pierpont Morgan,* part IV. New Haven, 1923.
8. Clay, A. T. *Miscellaneous Inscriptions in the Yale Babylonian Collection.* New Haven, 1915.
9. Contenau, G. *Umma sous la Dynastie d'Ur.* Paris, 1916.
10. Deimel, A. *Wirtschaftstexte aus Fara.* Leipzig, 1924.
11. Dhorme, E. 'Tablettes de Dréhem à Jérusalem.' In *R.A.* 9 (1912), 39 f.
12. Dossin, G. 'Inscriptions de fondation provenant de Mari.' In *Syria,* 21 (1940), 152 ff.
13. Dossin, G. 'Kengen, pays de Canaan.' In *Riv. stud. or.* 32 (1957), 35 f.
14. Dossin, G. 'Note sur "Apil-kîn šakkanakku de Mari".' In *Syria,* 25 (1946–8), 322.
15. Dunand, M. *Fouilles de Byblos.* Paris, 1926–32 and 1933–8.
16. Ebeling, E., Meissner, B. and Weidner, E. F. (eds.). *Reallexikon der Assyriologie,* I, II. Berlin and Leipzig, 1932, 1938.
17. Edzard, D. O. 'Sumerer und Semiten in der frühen Geschichte Mesopotamiens.' In *Genava,* n.s. 8 (1960), 241 ff.
18. Edzard, D. O. *Die 'zweite Zwischenzeit' Babyloniens.* Wiesbaden, 1957.
19. Falkenstein, A. 'Ibbī-Sîn—Išbī-Erra.' In *Z.A.* 49 (1949), 59 ff.
20. Falkenstein, A. Review of J. R. Kupper, *Les Nomades en Mésopotamie.* . . . In *Z.A.* 53 (1959), 280 ff.
21. Falkner, M. 'Studien zur Geographie des alten Mesopotamien.' In *Arch. f. Or.* 18 (1957–8), 1 ff.
22. Frank, C. *Strassburger Keilschrifttexte in sumerischer und babylonischer Sprache.* Berlin–Leipzig, 1928.
23. Gelb, I. J. 'Studies in Topography of Western Asia.' In *A.J.S.L.* 55 (1938), 65 ff.
24. Gelb, I. J. *Glossary of Old Akkadian.* Chicago, 1957.
25. Gelb, I. J. *Hurrians and Subarians.* Chicago, 1944.
26. Gelb, I. J. 'New Light on Hurrians and Subarians.' In *Studi Orientalistici in onore di Giorgio Levi della Vida,* I, 378 ff. Rome, 1956.
27. Gelb, I. J. 'The Early History of the West Semitic Peoples.' In *J.C.S.* 15 (1961), 27 ff.
28. Genouillac, H. de. *Tablettes de Dréhem.* Paris, 1911.
29. Genouillac, H. de. *La Trouvaille de Dréhem.* Paris, 1911.
30. Goetze, A. 'An Old-Babylonian Itinerary.' In *J.C.S.* 7 (1953), 51 ff.
31. Goetze, A. 'Ḫulibar of Duddul.' In *J.N.E.S.* 12 (1953), 114 ff.
32. Goetze, A. 'Four Ur-Dynasty Tablets Mentioning Foreigners.' In *J.C.S.* 7 (1953), 103 ff.
33. Hrouda, B. 'Waššukanni, Urkiš, Šubat-Enlil.' In *M.D.O.G.* 90 (1958), 22 ff.

34. *Inventaire des Tablettes de Tello.* Paris, 1910–21.
35. Jacobsen, T. 'Early Political Development in Mesopotamia.' In *Z.A.* 52 (1957), 91 ff.
36. Jacobsen, T. 'The Reign of Ibbī-Suen.' In *J.C.S.* 7 (1953), 36 ff.
37. Jestin, R. *Tablettes sumériennes de Šuruppak.* Paris, 1937.
38. Kupper, J.-R. 'Uršu.' In *R.A.* 43 (1949), 79 ff.
39. Kupper, J.-R. *Les Nomades en Mésopotamie au temps des rois de Mari.* Liège–Paris, 1957.
40. Kupper, J.-R. *L'iconographie du dieu Amurru.* Brussels, 1961.
41. Landsberger, B. *Materialien zum sumerischen Lexikon,* III. Rome, 1955.
42. Landsberger, B. 'Über die Völker Vorderasiens im dritten Jahrtausend.' In *Z.A.* 35 (1923), 213 ff.
43. Legrain, L. *Le temps des rois d'Ur.* Paris, 1912.
44. Lewy, J. 'Amurritica.' In *H.U.C.A.* 32 (1961), 31 ff.
45. Lewy, J. *Tablettes cappadociennes,* III/2. Paris, 1936.
46. Luckenbill, D. D. *Inscriptions from Adab* (*O.I.P.* 14). Chicago, 1930.
47. Nesbit, W. M. *Sumerian Records from Drehem.* New York, 1914.
48. Oppenheim, A. L. *Catalogue of the Cuneiform Tablets of the Wilberforce Eames Collection.* New Haven, 1948.
49. *Recueil E. Dhorme.* Paris, 1951.
50. Scheil, V. *Textes élamites-sémitiques,* série 5. (*Mém. D.P.* 14.) Paris, 1913.
51. Soden, W. von. 'Unregelmässige Verben im Akkadischen.' In *Z.A.* 50 (1952), 163 ff.
52. Sollberger, E. 'Byblos sous les rois d'Ur.' In *Arch.f. Or.* 19 (1959–60), 120 ff.
53. Sollberger, E. 'Sur la chronologie des rois d'Ur.' In *Arch.f. Or.* 17 (1954–6), 10 ff.
54. Thureau-Dangin, F. *Die sumerischen und akkadischen Königsinschriften.* Leipzig, 1907.
55. Unger, E. 'Tempelweihinschrift des Gimil-Sin. . . .' In *Z.A.* 29 (1914–15), 179 ff.

V. ARCHAEOLOGICAL EVIDENCE FROM PALESTINE

1. Albright, W. F. 'The Excavation of Tell Beit Mirsim I.' In *Ann. A.S.O.R.* 12, and 'The Excavation of Tell Beit Mirsim IA.' In *Ann. A.S.O.R.* 13, 55 ff. New Haven, 1932, 1933.
2. Kenyon, K. M. *Archaeology in the Holy Land.* London, 1960.
3. Petrie, W. M. F. *Ancient Gaza,* II. London, 1932.

VI. PALESTINE: THE SITES

1. FitzGerald, G. M. 'The Earliest Pottery of Beth-shan.' In *M.J.* 24 (1935), 5 ff.
2. Glueck, N. 'Explorations in Eastern Palestine, I–III.' In *Ann. A.S.O.R.* 14, 15, 18–19. Philadelphia and New Haven, 1934, 1935–9.
3. Glueck, N. *Rivers in the Desert.* New York, 1959.
4. Guy, P. L. O. and Engberg, R. M. *Megiddo Tombs* (*O.I.P.* 33). Chicago, 1938.
5. Harding, G. L. 'Four Tomb Groups from Transjordan.' In *Ann. P.E.F.* 6. London, 1953.
6. Kenyon, K. M. *Digging up Jericho.* London, 1957.
7. Kenyon, K. M. *Excavations at Jericho,* I, II. London, 1960, 1965.

8. Kenyon, K. M. 'Excavations at Jericho 1954.' In *P.E.Q.* 1954, 45 ff.
9. Kenyon, K. M. 'Excavations at Jericho 1955.' In *P.E.Q.* 1955, 108 ff.
10. Kenyon, K. M. 'Excavations at Jericho 1956.' In *P.E.Q.* 1956, 67 ff.
11. Kenyon, K. M. 'Tombs of the Intermediate Early Bronze Age at Tell Ajjul.' In *Ann. D.A.J.* 3 (1956), 41 ff.
12. Kenyon, K. M. 'Some Notes on the Early and Middle Bronze Age Strata of Megiddo.' In *Eretz-Israel*, 5 (1958), 51* ff.
13. Loud, G. *Megiddo II: Seasons of 1935–1939* (*O.I.P.* 62). Chicago, 1948.
14. Tufnell, O. *Lachish IV: The Bronze Age*. Oxford, 1958.

VII. SYRIA: THE SITES

1. Childe, V. G. *New Light on the Most Ancient East*. London, 1934.
2. Dunand, M. *Fouilles de Byblos*, I, II. Paris, 1939, 1954.
3. Dunand, M. 'Fouilles de Byblos' (interim reports). In *Syria*, 8 (1927), 9 (1928), 10 (1929).
4. Dunand, M. 'Byblos au temps du Bronze Ancien et de la Conquête Amorite.' In *Rev. bibl.* 59 (1952), 82 ff.
5. Mallowan, M. E. L. 'Excavations at Brak and Chagar Bazar.' In *Iraq*, 9 (1947), 1 ff.
6. Mesnil du Buisson, Comte du Excavations at Mishrifé-Qatna and its neighbourhood (interim reports). In *Syria*, 7 (1926), 8 (1927), 9 (1928), 11 (1930).
7. Mesnil du Buisson, Comte du. *Le site archéologique de Mishrifé-Qatna*. Paris, 1935.
8. Montet, P. *Byblos et l'Égypte*. Paris, 1928.
9. Schaeffer, C. F. A. *Stratigraphie comparée et chronologie de l'Asie occidentale*. Oxford, 1948.
10. Schaeffer, C. F. A. *Ugaritica*, I. Paris, 1934.
11. Schaeffer, C. F. A. *Ugaritica*, II. Paris, 1949.
12. Sellin, E., and Watzinger, C. *Jericho*. (*W.V.D.O.G.* 22). Leipzig, 1913.

A. ADDENDA

1. Albright, W. F. 'The Eighteenth-Century Princes of Byblos and the Chronology of Middle-Bronze.' In *Bull. A.S.O.R.* 176 (1964), 38–46.
2. Albright, W. F. 'Further Light on the History of Middle-Bronze Byblos.' In *Bull. A.S.O.R.* 179 (1965), 38–43.
3. Albright, W. F. *The Proto-Sinaitic Inscriptions and their Decipherment* (*Harvard Theol. Studies*, XXII). Cambridge, 1966.
4. Arnold, D. and Settgast, J. 'Erster Vorbericht über die vom Deutschen Archäologischen Institut Kairo im Asasif unternommenen Arbeiten.' In *Mitt. deutsch. Inst. Kairo*, 20 (1965), 47–61, pls. 11–20.
5. von Beckerath, J. *Untersuchungen zur politischen Geschichte der zweiten Zwischenzeit in Ägypten* (*Ägyptol. Forsch.* 23). Glückstadt, 1965.
6. Faulkner, R. O. 'The Admonitions of an Egyptian Sage.' In *J.E.A.* 51 (1965), 53–62.
7. Giveon, R. 'An Egyptian Statuette from the Ayn Hashofet Region.' In *Yediot*, 27 (1964), 293–6, pl. 14.
8. Giveon, R. 'Royal Seals of the XIIth Dynasty.' In *Rev. d'égyptol.* 19 (1967).
9. Laroche, E. *Les hiéroglyphes hittites*, part 1, *L'écriture*. Paris, 1960.

10. Montet, P. 'Notes et documents pour servir à l'histoire des relations entre l'Égypte et la Syrie.' In *Kêmi*, 17 (1964), 61–8.
11. Posener, G. 'Les textes d'envoûtement de Mirgissa.' In *Syria*, 43 (1966), 277–87.
12. Schaeffer, C. F. A. *Ugaritica IV* (*Mission de Ras Shamra*, xv). Paris, 1962.
13. Van Seters, J. *The Hyksos. A new Investigation*. New Haven, 1966.

CHAPTER XXII

G. GENERAL

1. Andrae, W. *Die archaischen Ischtar-Tempel in Assur* (*W.V.D.O.G.* 39). Leipzig, 1922.
2. Andrae, W. *Das wiedererstandene Assur*. Leipzig, 1938.
3. *C.A.D. The Assyrian Dictionary*. Chicago, 1956– .
4. *C.T. Cuneiform Texts . . . in the British Museum*. London, 1896– .
5. Ebeling, E., Meissner, B. and Weidner, E. F. (eds.). *Reallexikon der Assyriologie*, i–iii. Berlin and Leipzig, 1932– .
6. Edmonds, C. J. *Kurds, Turks, and Arabs*. London, 1957.
7. Edzard, D. O. *Die 'zweite Zwischenzeit' Babyloniens*. Wiesbaden, 1957.
8. Falkenstein, A. und Soden, W. von. *Sumerische und akkadische Hymnen und Gebete*. Zürich–Stuttgart, 1953.
9. Fish, T. 'Chronological List of Ur III Economic Texts from Lagash.' In *M.C.S.* 5 (1955), 33 ff.
10. Fish, T. 'Chronological List of Ur III Economic Texts from Umma.' In *M.C.S.* 5 (1955), 61 ff.
11. Fish, T. 'Chronological List of Ur III Economic Texts from Drehem.' In *M.C.S.* 5 (1955), 92 ff.
12. Frank, C. *Kultlieder aus dem Ischtar-Tammuz Kreis*. Leipzig, 1939.
13. Frankfort, H. *Cylinder Seals*. London, 1939.
14. Frankfort, H. *The Art and Architecture of the Ancient Orient*. Harmondsworth, 1954.
15. Gadd, C. J. and Legrain, L. *Royal Inscriptions* (*U.E.T.* 1). London and Philadelphia, 1928.
16. Garelli, P. (ed.). *Gilgameš et sa légende*. Paris, 1960.
17. Gelb, I. J. *Glossary of Old Akkadian*. Chicago, 1957.
18. Gelb, I. J. *Old Akkadian Writing and Grammar*. Ed. 2. Chicago, 1961.
19. Jacobsen, T. *The Sumerian King-list* (*Assyriological Studies*, no. 11). Chicago, 1939.
20. Jordan, J., Lenzen, H. and others. 'Vorläufige Berichte über die . . . in Uruk-Warka . . . Ausgrabungen', i–xi. In *Abh. Berlin*, 1930–40, and in *Abh. D.O.G.* Berlin, 1956– .
21. King, L. W. *History of Babylon*. London, 1915.
22. Kramer, S. N. *The Sumerians: Their History, Culture, and Character*. Chicago, 1963.
23. Legrain, L. *Business Documents of the Third Dynasty of Ur* (*U.E.T.* iii). London and Philadelphia, 1947.
24. Mercer, S. A. B. *Sumero-Babylonian Year-formulae*. London, 1946.
25. North, R. 'Status of the Warka Excavation.' In *Or. n.s.* 26 (1957), 185 ff.
26. Nougayrol, J. 'Note sur la place des "présages historiques" dans l'extispicine babylonienne.' In *École Pratique des Hautes Études*, annuaire 1944–5, 1 ff.

27. Oppenheim, A. L. 'The Seafaring Merchants of Ur.' In *J.A.O.S.* 74 (1954), 6ff.
28. Parrot, A. *Archéologie mésopotamienne*, I, II. Paris, 1946, 1953.
29. Pritchard, J. B. (ed.). *Ancient Near-Eastern Texts relating to the Old Testament*. Ed. 2. Princeton, 1955.
30. Rutten, M. 'Trente-deux modèles de foies . . . de Tell-Hariri (Mari).' In *R.A.* 35 (1938), 36 ff.
31. Schmidtke, E. *Der Aufbau der babylonischen Chronologie.* Münster, 1952.
32. Smith, S. *Early History of Assyria.* London, 1928.
33. Thureau-Dangin, F. *Die sumerischen und akkadischen Königsinschriften.* Leipzig, 1907.
34. Weidner, E. F. 'Historisches Material in der babylonischen Omina-Literatur.' In *M.A.O.G.* 4 (1928), 226 ff.
35. Woolley, C. L. 'Excavations at Ur of the Chaldees.' Preliminary Reports in *A.J.* 3 (1923)–14 (1934).

I. THE THIRD DYNASTY OF UR

1. Awad, Gurgis. 'Bibliography relating to Excavations in Iraq.' In *Sumer*, 8 (1952), 90 ff.
2. Aynard, J.-M. 'Les clous d'argile du Musée du Louvre.' In *R.A.* 54 (1960), 11 ff.
3. Barnett, R. D. 'Xenophon and the Wall of Media.' In *J.H.S.* 83 (1963), 1 ff.
4. Castellino, G. 'Ur-Nammu; Three Religious Texts.' In (i) *Z.A.* 52 (1957), 1 ff., (ii) *Z.A.* 53 (1959), 106 ff.
5. Civil, M. 'Un nouveau synchronisme Mari–IIIe Dynastie d'Ur.' In *R.A.* 56 (1962), 213.
6. Crawford, V. E. *Sumerian Economic Texts from the First Dynasty of Isin* (*B.I.N.* IX). New Haven, 1954.
7. Dijk, J. J. A. van. 'Textes divers du Musée de Baghdad, III.' In *Sumer*, 15 (1959), 5 ff.
8. Dijk, J. J. A. van. Review of H. Schmökel, *Geschichte des alten Vorderasiens.* In *Z.A.* 55 (1963), 273 ff.
9. Dossin, G. 'Inscriptions de fondation provenant de Mari.' In *Syria*, 21 (1940), 152 ff.
10. Ebeling, E., Meissner, B. und Weidner, E. F. *Die Inschriften der altassyrischen Könige.* Leipzig, 1926.
11. Edzard, D. O. 'Neue Inschriften zur Geschichte von Ur III unter Šūsuen.' In *Arch. f. Or.* 19 (1959–60), 1 ff.
12. Falkenstein, A. 'Ein sumerischer "Gottesbrief".' In *Z.A.* 44 (1938), 1 ff.
13. Falkenstein, A. 'Der "Sohn des Tafelhauses".' In *We. Or.* 1 (1947–52), 172 ff.
14. Falkenstein, A. 'Die Ibbīsîn Klage.' In *We. Or.* 1 (1947–52), 377 ff.
15. Falkenstein, A. 'Ibbīsîn–Išbi'erra.' In *Z.A.* 49 (1950), 59 ff.
16. Falkenstein, A. 'Sumerische religiöse Texte: 3. Ein Šulgi-Lied.' In *Z.A.* 50 (1952), 61 ff.
17. Falkenstein, A. 'Ein Lied auf Šulgi.' In *Iraq*, 22 (1960), 139 ff.
18. Gadd, C. J. 'Clay Cones of Utu-ḫegal, King of Erech.' In *J.R.A.S.* 1926, 684 ff.
19. Gadd, C. J. 'The Second Lamentation for Ur.' In *Hebrew and Semitic Studies presented to Godfrey Rolles Driver* (Oxford, 1962), 59 ff.
20. Garelli, P. *Les Assyriens en Cappadoce.* Paris, 1963.

21. Goetze, A. 'Historical Allusions in Old-Babylonian Omen-Texts.' In *J.C.S.* 1 (1947), 253 ff.
22. Goetze, A. 'Ḫulibar of Duddul.' In *J.N.E.S.* 12 (1953), 114 ff.
23. Goetze, A. 'Four Ur Dynasty Tablets.' In *J.C.S.* 7 (1953), 103 ff.
24. Goetze, A. 'The Chronology of Šulgi again.' In *Iraq*, 22 (1960), 151 ff.
25. Goetze, A. 'Šakkanakkus of the Ur III Empire.' In *J.C.S.* 17 (1963), 1 ff.
26. Goetze, A. Review of T. B. Jones, and J. W. Snyder, *Sumerian Economic Texts from the Third Ur Dynasty*. In *J.C.S.* 17 (1963), 33 ff.
27. Guterbock, H. G. 'Die historische Tradition und ihre literarische Gestaltung bei Babyloniern und Hethitern bis 1200.' Erster Teil in *Z.A.* 42 (1934), 1 ff.; zweiter Teil in *Z.A.* 44 (1938), 45 ff.
28. Hallo, W. W. 'Zāriqum.' In *J.N.E.S.* 15 (1956), 220 ff.
29. Hallo, W. W. *Early Mesopotamian Royal Titles*. New Haven, 1957.
30. Hallo, W. W. 'The Royal Inscriptions of Ur : a Typology.' In *H.U.C.A.* 33 (1962), 1 ff.
31. Jacobsen, T. 'The Reign of Ibbī-Suen.' In *J.C.S.* 7 (1953), 36 ff.
32. Jacobsen, T. 'The Waters of Ur.' In *Iraq*, 22 (1960), 174 ff.
33. Jestin, R. 'Textes économiques de Mari (IIIe dynastie d'Ur).' In *R.A.* 46 (1952), 185 ff.
34. Jones, T. B. and Snyder, J. W. *Sumerian Economic Texts from the Third Ur Dynasty*. Minneapolis, 1961.
35. Keiser, C. E. *Patesis of the Ur Dynasty* (*Y.O.S.* IV, 2). New Haven, 1919.
36. King, L. W. *Chronicles concerning Old Babylonian Kings*. London, 1907.
37. Kramer, S. N. *Lamentation over the Destruction of Ur* (*Assyriological Studies*, 12). Chicago, 1940.
38. Kramer, S. N. 'The Death of Gilgamesh.' In *Bull. A.S.O.R.* 94 (1944), 2 ff.
39. Kramer, S. N. 'Ur-Nammu Law-code.' In *Or.* n.s. 23 (1954), 40 ff.
40. Kraus, F. R. 'Altmesopotamische Tonnaegel mit Keilinschriften.' In *Halil Edhem hâtıra kitabı*, Cilt I, 71 ff. Ankara, 1947.
41. Kraus, F. R. 'Zur Chronologie der Könige Ur-Nammu und Sulgi.' In *Or.* n.s. 20 (1951), 385 ff.
42. Kraus, F. R. 'Provinzen des neusumerischen Reiches von Ur.' In *Z.A.* 51 (1955), 45 ff.
43. Kraus, F. R. 'Altbabylonische Quellensammlungen zur altmesopotamische Geschichte.' In *Arch. f. Or.* 20 (1963), 153 ff.
44. Kupper, J.-R. 'Un gouvernement provincial dans le royaume de Mari.' In *R.A.* 41 (1947), 149 ff.
45. Langdon, S. H. *Die neubabylonischen Königsinschriften*. Leipzig, 1912.
46. Langdon, S. H. 'Three New Hymns in the Cults of Deified Kings.' In *P.S.B.A.* 40 (1918), 30 ff., 45 ff.
47. Legrain, L. 'Quelques tablettes d'Ur.' In *R.A.* 30 (1933), 117 ff.
48. Limet, H. *Le travail du métal au pays de Sumer au temps de la IIIe Dynastie d'Ur*. Paris, 1960.
49. Lloyd, Seton and Safar, Fuad. 'Excavations at Eridu : Preliminary Reports.' In *Sumer*, 3 (1947), 4 (1948), 6 (1950).
50. Mallowan, M. E. L. 'Excavations at Brak and Chagar Bazar.' In *Iraq*, 9 (1947).
51. Oppenheim, A. L. '"Siege-documents" from Nippur.' In *Iraq*, 17 (1955), 69 ff.
52. Schaumberger, J. 'Die Mondfinsternisse der Dritten Dynastie von Ur.' In *Z.A.* 49 (1950), 50 ff.

53. Schaumberger, J. 'Astronomische Untersuchung der "historischen" Mond-finsternisse in Enûma Anu Enlil.' In *Arch. f. Or.* 17 (1954–6), 89 ff.
54. Schneider, N. *Die Zeitbestimmungen der Wirtschaftsurkunden von Ur III* (*An. Or.* 13). Rome, 1936.
55. Sjöberg, Åke W. 'Ein syllabisch geschriebener Urnammu-Text.' In *Or. Suecana*, 10 (1961), 3 ff.
56. Sollberger, E. 'New Lists of the Kings of Ur and Isin.' In *J.C.S.* 8 (1954), 135 ff.
57. Sollberger, E. 'Sur la chronologie des rois d'Ur et quelques problèmes connexes.' In *Arch. f. Or.* 17 (1954–6), 10 ff.
58. Sollberger, E. 'Byblos sous les rois d'Ur.' In *Arch. f. Or.* 19 (1959–60), 120 ff.
59. Sollberger, E. 'The Tummal Inscription.' In *J.C.S.* 16 (1962), 40 ff.
60. Stephens, F. J. *Votive and Historical Texts from Babylonia and Assyria* (*Y.O.S.* IX). New Haven, 1937.
61. Szlechter, E. 'Le code d'Ur-Nammu.' In *R.A.* 49 (1955), 169 ff.
62. Thureau-Dangin, F. 'Inscriptions votives de Mari.' In *R.A.* 34 (1937), 172 ff.
63. Unger, E. *Babylon, die heilige Stadt.* Berlin and Leipzig, 1931.
64. Woolley, C. L. *The Ziggurat and its Surroundings* (*U.E.* v). London and Philadelphia, 1939.

II. THE KING AND HIS OFFICERS

1. Çığ, M., Kızılyay, H. and Falkenstein, A. 'Neue Rechts- und Gerichtsur-kunden der Ur III-Zeit.' In *Z.A.* 53 (1959), 51 ff.
2. Driver, G. R. and Miles, J. C. *The Babylonian Laws*, 1. Oxford, 1952.
3. Falkenstein, A. *Die neusumerischen Gerichtsurkunden*, i–iii. Munich, 1956, 1957.
4. Fish, T. 'The Cult of Dungi during the Third Dynasty of Ur.' In *Bull. Ryl. Libr.* 11 (1927), 322 ff.
5. Fish, T. 'The Contemporary Cult of Kings of the Third Dynasty of Ur.' In *Bull. Ryl. Libr.* 12 (1928), 75 ff.
6. Fish, T. 'Some Aspects of Kingship in the Sumerian City and Kingdom of Ur.' In *Bull. Ryl. Libr.* 34 (1951), 37 ff.
7. Frankfort, H., Lloyd, Seton and Jacobsen, T. *The Gimilsin Temple and the Palace of the Rulers at Tell Asmar* (*O.I.P.* xliii). Chicago, 1940.
8. Gadd, C. J. *Ideas of Divine Rule in the Ancient East.* London, 1948.
9. Jones, T. B. 'Bookkeeping in Ancient Sumer.' In *Archaeology*, 9 (1956), 16 ff.
10. Kraus, F. R. 'Le rôle des Temples depuis la troisième Dynastie d'Ur jusqu'à la première Dynastie de Babylone.' In *Cahiers d'Histoire mondiale*, 1 (1954), 518 ff.
11. Kraus, F. R. *Ein Edikt des Königs Ammi-ṣaduqa von Babylon.* Leiden, 1958.
12. Kraus, F. R. 'Di-til-la, sumerische Prozess-protokolle und Verwandtes aus der Zeit der III Dynastie von Ur.' In *Bi. Or.* 15 (1958), 70 ff.
13. Lambert, M. 'La naissance de la bureaucratie.' In *Rev. hist.* 224 (1960), 1 ff.
14. Lambert, M. 'Le premier triomphe de la bureaucratie.' In *Rev. Hist.* 225 (1961), 21 ff.
15. Lambert, M. 'Les finances de Lagash sous la IIIe dynastie d'Ur.' In *R.A.* 56 (1962), 147 ff.
16. Landsberger, B. *Die Serie ana ittišu* (*M.S.L.* 1). Rome, 1937.
17. Langdon, S. H. 'The Sumerian Law-code compared with the Code of Hammurabi.' In *J.R.A.S.* 1920, 489 ff.

18. Matouš, L. 'Purchase of Landed Property in Ur by Balmunamḫe.' In *Charisteria Orientalia* (Ioanni Rypka...volumen sacrum), 179 ff.
19. Schneider, N. 'Die *arad-zu-, dumu-ni-,* und *in-na-ba* Siegel von Ur III.' In *Or.* n.s. 5 (1936), 109 ff.
20. Schneider, N. 'Ein deifizierter Patesi zur Zeit der 3. Dynastie von Ur.' In *Or.* n.s. 9 (1940), 17 ff.
21. Schneider, N. 'Der *dub-sar* als Verwaltungsbeamter im Reiche von Sumer und Akkad zur Zeit der 3. Dynastie von Ur.' In *Or.* n.s. 15 (1946), 64 ff.
22. Schneider, N. 'Die *ensi*-Siegel der Vertragsurkunden der Dynastie von Ur III.' In *Or.* n.s. 15 (1946), 416 ff.
23. Schneider, N. 'Der *sangu* als Verwaltungsbehörde und Opfergabenspender im Reiche der dritten Dynastie von Ur.' In *J.C.S.* 1 (1947), 122 ff.
24. Schneider, N. 'Göttertempel im Ur III-Reich.' In *Or.* n.s. 19 (1950), 257 ff.

III. ECONOMY AND WEALTH

1. Curtis, J. B. and Hallo, W. W. 'Money and Merchants in Ur III.' In *H.U.C.A.* 30 (1959), 103 ff.
2. Dávid, A. 'La balance d'inventaire d'un dépôt de laine....' In *Acta Orientalia Acad. Sc. Hungaricae*, 2 (1952), 165 ff.
3. David, M. *Die Adoption im altbabylonischen Recht.* Leipzig, 1927.
4. Fish, T. 'Food of the Gods in Ancient Sumer.' In *Bull. Ryl. Libr.* 27 (1942–3), 308 ff.
5. Fish, T. 'More *gá-dub-ba* texts.' In *M.C.S.* 1 (1951), 20 ff.
6. Fish, T. 'The Smith at Lagash.' In *M.C.S.* 1 (1951), 46 ff.
7. Fish, T. 'New *kuš*-texts.' In *M.C.S.* 1 (1951), 50 ff.
8. Fish, T. 'Texts from Umma about Reeds.' In *M.C.S.* 3 (1953), 42 ff.
9. Fish, T. 'Seasonal Labour according to *guruš* Texts from Umma.' In *M.C.S.* 4 (1954), 1 ff.
10. Fish, T. 'Umma Texts concerning кuš.' In *M.S.6.* 6 (1956), 1 ff.
11. Fish, T. 'Lagash Texts concerning кuš.' In *M.C.S.* 6 (1956), 55 ff.
12. Fish, T. 'Drehem Texts concerning кuš.' In *M.C.S.* 6 (1956), 85 ff.
13. Goetze, A. 'Umma Texts concerning Reed Mats.' In *J.C.S.* 2 (1948), 165 ff.
14. Goetze, A. 'A Drehem Text dealing with Leather Objects.' In *J.C.S.* 9 (1955), 19 ff.
15. Hallo, W. W. 'Contributions to Neo-Sumerian.' In *H.U.C.A.* 29 (1958), 69 ff.
16. Lambert, M. Review of T. B. Jones, and J. W. Snyder, *Sumerian Economic Texts from the Third Ur Dynasty.* In *R.A.* 56 (1962), 217 ff.
17. Oppenheim, A. L. *Catalogue of the Cuneiform Tablets of the Wilberforce Eames Collection in the New York Public Library: Tablets of the Time of the Third Dynasty of Ur.* New Haven, 1948.
18. Salonen, A. *Die Wasserfahrzeuge in Babylonien.* Helsinki, 1939.
19. Schneider, N. 'Die Lohnbücher der Mühle von Sagdana.' In *Arch. f. Or.* 3 (1926), 121 f.
20. Schneider, N. 'Der Viehbestand des é-gal in Lagaš.' In *Arch. f. Or.* 4 (1927), 206 ff.
21. Schneider, N. 'Die Urkundenbehälter (*pisan-dub-ba*) von Ur III und ihre archivalische Systematik.' In *Actes du XXe Congrés international des Orientalistes* (Louvain, 1940), 111 ff.
22. Sjöberg, Åke. *Der Mondgott Nanna-Suen in der sumerischen Überlieferung.* I. Teil: Texte. Uppsala, 1960.

IV. FOREIGNERS FROM THE EAST

1. Finkelstein, J. J. 'Subartu and Subarians.' In *J.C.S.* 9 (1955), 1 ff.
2. Gelb, I. J. *Hurrians and Subarians (S.A.O.C.* 22). Chicago, 1944.
3. Gelb, I. J. 'New Light on Hurrians and Subarians.' In *Studi orientalistici in onore di Giorgio Levi della Vida,* 1 (Rome, 1956), 378 ff.
4. Hrouda, B. 'Waššukanni, Urkiš, Šubat-Enlil.' In *M.D.O.G.* 90 (1958), 22 ff.
5. Jean, C.-F. 'L'Élam sous la Dynastie d'Ur.' In *R.A.* 19 (1922), 1 ff.
6. Læssøe, J. 'The Shemshara Tablets.' In *Arkaeol. Kunsthist. Medd. Dan. Vid. Selsk.* 4, no. 3 (1959).
7. Læssøe, J. 'The Second Shemshara Archive.' In *Sumer,* 16 (1960), 12 ff.
8. Parrot, A. and Nougayrol, J. 'Un document de fondation hurrite.' In *R.A.* 42 (1948), 1 ff.
9. Speiser, E. A. 'Hurrians and Subarians.' In *J.A.O.S.* 68 (1948), 1 ff.
10. Thureau-Dangin, F. 'Tablette de Samarra.' In *R.A.* 9 (1912), 1 ff.
11. Ungnad, A. *Subartu.* Berlin and Leipzig, 1936.
12. Weidner, E. F. 'Simurrum und Zaban.' In *Arch. f. Or.* 15 (1945–51), 75 ff.

V. THE AMORITE INVASION

1. Bauer, T. *Die Ostkanaanäer.* Leipzig, 1926.
2. Gelb, I. J. 'The Early History of the West Semitic Peoples.' In *J.C.S.* 15 (1961), 27 ff.
3. Kupper, J.-R. *Les Nomades en Mesopotamie au temps des rois de Mari.* Paris, 1957.
4. Kupper, J.-R. 'L'Iconographie du dieu Amurru.' In *Mém. de l'Acad. roy. de Belgique,* Classe des Lettres, 55, 1 (1961).
5. Landsberger. B. 'Über die Völker Vorderasiens im dritten Jahrtausend.' In *Z.A.* 35 (1924), 213 ff.

VI. CHANGES IN ART

1. Contenau, G. *Manuel d'Archéologie orientale,* i–iv. Paris, 1927–47.
2. Gadd, C. J. 'Early Sumerian Sculpture.' In *B.M. Quart.* 1 (1926), 38 ff.
3. Lewy, H. 'The Babylonian Background of the Kay-Kâûs Legend.' In *An. Or.* 17 (1949), 28 ff.
4. Nassouhi, E. 'Statue d'un dieu de Mari.' In *Arch. f. Or.* 3 (1926), 109 ff.
5. Parrot, A. *Tello: vingt campagnes de fouilles.* Paris, 1948.
6. Parrot, A. *Mari: documentation photographique.* Neuchâtel and Paris, 1953.
7. Pritchard, J. B. *The Ancient Near East in Pictures.* Princeton, 1954.
8. Salonen, A. *Die Möbel des alten Mesopotamien.* Helsinki, 1963.
9. Strommenger, E. 'Das Menschenbild in der altmesopotamischen Rundplastik von Mesilim bis Hammurapi.' In *Baghdader Mitteilungen,* 1 (1960), 1 ff.
10. Van Buren, E. D. *Foundation Figurines and Offerings.* Berlin, 1931.
11. Wiseman, D. J. *The Vassal-treaties of Esarhaddon.* [*Iraq,* 20 (1958), part 1.]
12. Woolley, C. L. *Excavations at Ur: a Record of Twelve Years' Work.* London, 1954.

VII. SUCCESSORS OF THE UR DYNASTY

1. Falkenstein, A. 'Zu den Inschriftfunden der Grabung in Uruk-Warka 1960–1961.' In *Baghdader Mitteilungen,* 2 (1963), 1 ff.
2. Figulla, H. H. 'Accounts concerning Allocation of Provisions for Offerings in the Ningal-temple at Ur.' In *Iraq,* 15 (1953), 171 ff.

3. Finkelstein, J. J. 'Ammiṣaduqa's Edict and the Babylonian "law-codes".' In *J.C.S.* 15 (1961), 91 ff.
4. Gadd, C. J. 'En-an-e-du.' In *Iraq*, 13 (1951), 27 ff.
5. Goetze, A. 'Mesopotamian Laws and the Historian.' In *J.A.O.S.* 69 (1949), 115 ff.
6. Goetze, A. 'Sin-idinnam of Larsa.' In *J.C.S.* 4 (1950), 83 ff.
7. Goetze, A. *The Laws of Eshnunna* (*Ann. A.S.O.R.* xxxi). New Haven, 1956.
8. Hallo, W. W. 'Royal Inscriptions of the Early Old Babylonian Period: a Bibliography.' In *Bi. Or.* 18 (1961), 4 ff.
9. Hallo, W. W. 'Royal hymns and Mesopotamian Unity.' In *J.C.S.* 17 (1963), 112 ff.
10. Kraus, F. R. 'Nippur und Isin nach altbabylonischen Rechtsurkunden.' [*J.C.S.* 3 (1951).]
11. Kraus, F. R. 'Zur Liste der älteren Könige von Babylonien.' In *Z.A.* 50 (1952), 29 ff.
12. Matouš, L. Zur Chronologie der Geschichte von Larsa bis zum Einfall der Elamiter.' In *Arch. Orient.* 20 (1952), 288 ff.
13. San Nicolò, M. 'Rechtsgeschichtliches zum Gesetz des Bilalama von Ešnunna.' In *Or.* n.s. 18 (1949), 258 ff.
14. Steele, F. R. 'The Code of Lipit-Ishtar.' In *A.J.A.* 52 (1948), 425 ff.
15. Thureau-Dangin, F. 'Ašduni-erim roi de Kis.' In *R.A.* 8 (1911), 65 ff.
16. Thureau-Dangin, F. 'La chronologie de la Dynastie de Larsa.' In *R.A.* 15 (1918), 1 ff.

VIII. INTERVENTION FROM ABROAD

1. Albright, W. F. 'A Third Revision of the Early Chronology of Western Asia.' In *Bull. A.S.O.R.* 88 (1942), 28 ff.
2. Böhl, F. M. Th. 'Die Tochter des Königs Nabonid.' In *Symbolae . . . Paulo Koschaker dedicatae* (Leiden, 1939), 151 ff.
3. Cameron, G. G. *History of Early Iran.* Chicago, 1936.
4. Thureau-Dangin, F. 'Une inscription de Kudur-Mabuk.' In *R.A.* 9 (1912), 121 ff.
5. Weidner, E. F. 'Ilušumas Zug nach Babylonien.' In *Z.A.* 43 (1936), 114 ff.

A. ADDENDA

1. Buccellati, G. *The Amorites of the Ur III Period.* Naples, 1966.
2. Civil, M. 'New Sumerian law-fragments.' In *Studies in Honor of Benno Landsberger (A.S.* 16), 1 ff.
3. Dijk, J. van. 'Une insurrection générale au pays de Larša avant l'avènement de Nūradad.' In *J.C.S.* 19 (1965), 1 ff.
4. Dossin, G. 'Un "panthéon" d'Ur III à Mari.' In *R.A.* 61 (1967), 97 ff.
5. Fadhil Ali. 'Two collections of Sumerian letters.' In *Arch. Orient.* 35 (1965), 529 ff.
6. Falkenstein, A. 'Eine Inschrift Waradsîns aus Babylon.' In *Baghdader Mitteil.* 3 (1964), 25 ff.
7. Falkenstein, A. 'Fluch über Akkade.' In *Z.A.* 57 (1965), 43 ff.
8. Finkelstein, J. J. 'Some new *misharum* material and its implications.' In *Studies. . . Landsberger,* 233 ff.
9. Finkelstein, J. J. 'Sex offenses in Sumerian Laws.' In *J.A.O.S.* 86 (1966), 355 ff.

10. Finkelstein, J. J. 'The genealogy of the Ḫammurapi Dynasty.' In *J.C.S.* 20 (1966), 95 ff.

11. Gadd, C. J. and Kramer, S. N. *Literary and religious texts*, I, II (*U.E.T.* VI). London and Philadelphia, 1963, 1966.

12. Gelb, I. J. 'The Philadelphia Onion-archive.' In *Studies...Landsberger*, 57 ff.

13. Gurney, O. R. and Kramer, S. N. 'Two fragments of Sumerian laws.' In *Studies...Landsberger*, 13 ff.

14. Huffmon, H. B. *Amorite personal names in the Mari texts.* Baltimore, 1965.

15. Kilmer, A. D. 'The strings of musical instruments; their names, numbers, and significance.' In *Studies...Landsberger*, 261 ff.

16. Klíma, J. 'Au sujet de nouveaux textes législatifs de la Babylonie ancienne.' In *Arch. Orient.* 35 (1967), 121 ff.

17. Korošec, V. *Novi fragmenti Sumerskega Prava iz Ura* (German summary, 21 ff.). Ljubljana, 1966.

18. Kramer, S. N. 'Literary texts, Part II.' In *Iraq* 25 (1963), 171 ff.

19. Kramer, S. N. and Bernhardt, I. *Sumerische literarische Texte aus Nippur,* Band II. Berlin, 1967.

20. Kraus, F. R. 'Ein Edikt des Königs Samsu-iluna von Babylon.' In *Studies... Landsberger*, 225 ff.

21. Læssøe, J. 'IM. 62100: a letter from Tell Shemshāra.' In *Studies...Landsberger*, 189 ff.

22. Læssøe, J. *Det første Assyriske Imperium et Aspekt.* Copenhagen, 1966.

23. Le Strange, G. *The Lands of the Eastern Caliphate.* Cambridge, 1905.

24. Lewy, J. 'Amurritica.' In *H.U.C.A.* 32 (1961), 31 ff.

25. Liere, W. J. van. 'Urkiš, centre religieux hurrite, retrouvé dans la Haute Jezireh syrienne.' In *A.A.S.* 7 (1957), 91 ff.

26. Munn-Rankin, J. M. 'Diplomacy in Western Asia in the early second millennium, B.C.' In *Iraq* 18 (1956), 68 ff.

27. Parrot, A. *Mission archéologique de Mari*, II, 3: *Le Palais, documents et monuments.* Paris, 1959.

28. Renger, J. 'Untersuchungen zum Priestertum in der altbabylonischen Zeit.' In *Z.A.* 58 (1967), 110 ff.

29. Römer, W. H. Ph. 'Studien zu altbabylonischen hymnisch-epischen Texte (3).' In *We. Or.* 4 (1967), 12 ff.

30. Sauren, H. 'Der Feldzug Utuḫengals gegen Tirigan und das Siedlungsgebiet der Gutäer.' In *R.A.* 61 (1967), 75 ff.

31. Sollberger, E. 'Remarks on Ibbi-Sin's Reign.' In *J.C.S.* 7 (1953), 48 f

32. Sollberger, E. *Royal Inscriptions*, II (*U.E.T.* VIII). London and Philadelphia 1965.

33. Sollberger, E. *Texts from Cuneiform Sources*, I: *The Business and Administrative Correspondence under the Kings of Ur.* New York, 1966.

34. Spycket, A. *Les statues de culte dans les textes mésopotamiens des origines à la première dynastie de Babylone.* Paris, 1968.

35. Strommenger, E. and Hirmer, M. *Fünf Jahrtausende Mesopotamien.* Munich, 1962.

36. Thomas, D. Winton (ed.). *Archaeology and Old Testament Study.* Oxford, 1967.

CHAPTER XXIII

G. GENERAL

1. Billerbeck, A. *Susa. Eine Studie zur alten Geschichte Westasiens.* Leipzig, 1893.
2. Cameron, G. G. *History of Early Iran.* Chicago, 1936.
3. Dhorme, E. 'Elam.' In *Supplément au Dictionnaire de la Bible,* II (Paris, 1934), 920 ff.
4. Eickstedt, E. von. *Türken, Kurden und Iraner seit dem Altertum.* Stuttgart, 1961.
5. Ghirshman, R. *L'Iran des origines à l'Islam.* Paris, 1951.
6. Herzfeld, E. *Archaeological History of Iran.* London, 1935.
7. Herzfeld, E. *Iran in the Ancient East.* London, 1941.
8. Huart, C. and Delaporte, L. *L'Iran antique—Élam et Perse et la civilisation iranienne.* Paris, 1943.
9. König, F. W. *Geschichte Elams.* Leipzig, 1931.
10. Mayer, R. *Elam als politischer und kultureller Faktor in der Geschichte des alten Orients.* Regensburg, 1955 (Privatdruck).
11. Mayer, R. 'Die Bedeutung Elams in der Geschichte des alten Orients.' In *Saeculum,* 7 (1956), 198 ff.
12. *Mém. D.P.* = *Mémoires de la Délégation en Perse,* vols. I–XIII, Paris, 1900–12; *Mémoires de la Mission archéologique de Susiane,* vol. XIV, Paris, 1913; *Mémoires de la Mission archéologique de Perse,* vols. XV–XXVIII, Paris, 1914–39; *Mémoires de la Mission archéologique en Iran,* vols. XXIX–XXXIII, Paris, 1943–53; vol. XXXVI, Paris, 1954; vol. XXXIV, Paris, 1961.
13. Osten, H. H. von der. *Die Welt der Perser.* Stuttgart, 1956.
14. Soden, Wolfram von. 'Sumer, Babylon und Hethiter bis zur Mitte des zweiten Jahrtausends v. Chr.' In *Propyläen-Weltgeschichte* (Berlin, 1961), 525 ff.
15. Speiser, E. A. *Mesopotamian Origins.* Philadelphia/London, 1930.
16. Vanden Berghe, L. *Archéologie de l'Irān ancien.* Leiden, 1959.

I. THE ELAMITE KINGS OF AWAN

1. Albright, W. F. 'A Babylonian Geographical Treatise on Sargon of Akkad's Empire.' In *J.A.O.S.* 45 (1925), 193 ff.
2. Barton, G. A. *The Royal Inscriptions of Sumer and Akkad.* New Haven, 1929.
3. Edmonds, C. J. 'Two Ancient Monuments in Southern Kurdistan.' In *G.J.* 65 (1925), 63 f.
4. Edzard, E. O. 'Enmebaragesi von Kiš.' In *Z.A.* 53 (1959), 9 ff.
5. Gelb, I. J. 'The Date of the Cruciform Monument of Maništušu.' In *J.N.E.S.* 8 (1949), 346 ff.
6. Gelb, I. J. *Old Akkadian Writing and Grammar.* Ed. 2. Chicago, 1961.
7. Goetze, A. 'Historical Allusions in Old Babylonian Omen Texts.' In *J.C.S.* 1 (1947), 253 ff.
8. Goetze, A. 'Ḫulibar of Duddul.' In *J.N.E.S.* 12 (1953), 114 ff.
9. Güterbock, H.-G. 'Die historische Tradition und ihre literarische Gestaltung bei Babyloniern und Hethitern bis 1200.' In *Z.A.* 42 (1943), 1 ff.
10. Hallo, W. W. *Early Mesopotamian Royal Titles: A Philologic and Historical Analysis.* New Haven, 1957.
11. Hinz, W. 'Zur Entzifferung der elamischen Strichschrift.' In *Iranica Antiqua,* 2 (1962), 1 ff.

12. Hüsing, G. *Die einheimischen Quellen zur Geschichte Elams. I. Teil: Altelamische Texte.* Leipzig, 1916.
13. Jacobsen, Th. *The Sumerian King List.* Chicago, 1939.
14. König, F. W. *Corpus Inscriptionum Elamicarum*, 1. *Die altelamischen Texte. Tafeln.* Hanover [1923].
15. Leemans, W. F. 'Trade Relations of Babylonia.' In *J.E.S.H.O.* 3 (1960), 21 ff.
16. Meer, P. van der. 'De Agadeperiode—haar geschiedenis en cultuur.' In *Kernmomenten der antieke beschaving en haar moderne beleving* (Leiden, 1947), 179 ff.
17. Poebel, A. 'The Name of Elam in Sumerian, Akkadian, and Hebrew.' In *A.J.S.L.* 48 (1931–2), 20 ff.
18. Poebel, A. *Historical Texts* (*P.B.S.* 4, no. 1). Philadelphia, 1914.
19. Scheil, V. 'Documents et arguments.' In *R.A.* 26 (1929), 1 ff.
20. Scheil, V. 'Dynasties élamites d'Awan et de Simaš.' In *R.A.* 28 (1931), 1 ff.
21. Smith, S. 'Notes on the Gutian Period.' In *J.R.A.S.* (1932), 295 ff.
22. Sollberger, E. *Corpus des inscriptions 'royales' présargoniques de Lagaš.* Geneva, 1956.
23. Ungnad, A. 'Der Akkader Narâm-Sin und der Ägypter Mani.' In *Arch.f. Or.* 14 (1942), 199 ff.
24. Weidner, E. F. 'Historisches Material in der babylonischen Omina-Literatur.' In *Festschrift Meissner* (Leipzig, 1928/9), 226.
25. Weidner, E. 'Das Reich Sargons von Akkad.' In *Arch.f. Or.* 16 (1952–3), 1 ff.

II. THE ELAMITE KINGS OF SIMASHKI

1. D'yakonov, I. M. *Istoriya Midii* (History of Media). Moscow/Leningrad, 1956.
2. Edzard, D. O. *Die 'Zweite Zwischenzeit' Babyloniens.* Wiesbaden, 1957.
3. Edzard, D. O. 'Neue Inschriften zur Geschichte von Ur III unter Šusuen.' In *Arch.f. Or.* 19 (1959–60), 1 ff.
4. Falkenstein, A. 'Ibbīsîn–Išbi'erra.' In *Z.A.* 49 (1950), 59 ff.
5. Falkenstein, A. 'Die Ibbīsîn-Klage'. In *We. Or.* 1 (1947–52), 377 ff.
6. Fish, T. 'Towards a Study of Lagash "Mission" or "Messenger" Texts.' In *M.C.S.* 4, 4, 78 ff. and 5, 1, 1 ff.
7. Gadd, C. J. and Legrain, L. *Ur Excavations. Texts* 1: *Royal Inscriptions.* London, 1928.
8. Hallo, W. W. 'Zāriqum.' In *J.N.E.S.* 15 (1956), 220 ff.
9. Herzfeld, E. *Am Tor von Asien.* Berlin, 1920
10. Jacobsen, Th. *Cuneiform Texts in the National Museum.* Copenhagen/Leiden, 1939.
11. Jacobsen, Th. 'The Reign of Ibbī-Suen.' In *J.C.S.* 7 (1953), 36 ff.
12. Jean, Ch.-F. 'L'Élam sous la Dynastie d'Ur.' In *R.A.* 19 (1922), 1 ff.
13. Jones, T. B. and Snyder, J. W. *Sumerian Economic Texts from the Third Ur Dynasty.* Minneapolis, 1961.
14. Keiser, C. E. *Selected Temple Documents of the Ur Dynasty* (Yale Oriental Series. Babylonian Texts, IV). New Haven/London/Oxford, 1919.
15. Kramer, S. N. *Lamentation over the Destruction of Ur.* Chicago, 1940. Important review by Th. Jacobsen in *A.J.S.L.* 58 (1941), 219 ff.
16. Matouš, L. 'Zur Chronologie der Geschichte von Larsa bis zum Einfall der Elamiter.' In *Arch. Orient.* 20 (1952), 288 ff.
17. Poebel, A. 'Sumerische Untersuchungen IV.' In *Z.A.* 39 (1930), 129 ff.

18. Scheil, V. 'Diplomatica.' In *Hilprecht Anniversary Volume* (Leipzig/London/ Paris/Chicago, 1909), 152 ff.
19. Sollberger, E. 'Sur la chronologie des rois d'Ur et quelques problèmes connexes.' In *Arch. f. Or.* 17 (1954–6), 10 ff.
20. Thureau-Dangin, F. *Die sumerischen und akkadischen Königsinschriften.* Leipzig, 1907.
21. Ungnad, A. 'Datenlisten.' In *R.L.A.* 2 (1938), 131 ff.
22. Virolleaud, Ch. 'Quelques textes cunéiformes inédits.' In *Z.A.* 19 (1905–6), 377 ff.

III. RELIGION IN ANCIENT ELAM

1. Bork, F. 'Zur Religion der alten Elamier.' In *Z.M.R.W.* 48 (1933), 161 ff.
2. Edzard, D. O. 'Die Mythologie der Sumerer und Akkader.' In *Wörterbuch der Mythologie, Teil I: Vorderer Orient* (Stuttgart, 1961), 1 ff.
3. Frank, C. 'Elamische Götter.' In *Z.A.* 28 (1914), 323 ff.
4. Friedrich, J. 'Altpersisches und Elamisches.' In *Or.* n.s. 18 (1949), 1 ff.
5. Gelderen, C. van. 'Elamietische Goden en Koningen.' In *Stemmen des Tijds,* 13 (1924).
6. Genouillac, H. de 'Les dieux de l'Élam.' In *Rec. trav.* 27 (1905), 94 ff.
7. Hinz, W. 'Elamisches.' In *Arch. Orient.* 18 (1950), 282 ff.
8. Hinz, W. 'Elamisch *is-ma-lu.*' In *Or* n.s. 19 (1950), 408 ff.
9. Hinz, W. 'Die elamischen Inschriften des Hanne.' In *Volume in Honour of S. H. Taqizadeh* (London, 1962), 105 ff.
10. Hinz, W. 'Elamisch *husa.*' In *Or.* n.s. 31 (1962), 34 ff.
11. Hüsing, G. 'Die Götter Elams.' In *O.L.Z.* 9 (1905), 385 ff.
12. Hüsing, G. 'Der elamische Gott Memnon.' In *M.V.Ae.G.* 21 (1916), 35 ff.
13. Jensen, P. 'Elamitische Eigennamen.' In *W.Z.K.M.* 6 (1892), 47 ff., 209 ff.
14. König, F. W. 'Zur Frage ^{d}GAL = ^{nap}Hutran.' In *Arch. f. Or.* 2 (1924–5), 130 ff.
15. König, F. W. 'Pinikir.' In *Arch. f. Or.* 5 (1928–9), 101 ff.
16. Koschaker, P. 'Göttliches und weltliches Recht nach den Urkunden aus Susa.' In *Or.* n.s. 4 (1935), 38 ff.
17. Labat, R. 'La mort du roi d'Élam Humban-Haltaš I.' In *Arch. Orient.* 17 (1949), 1 ff.
18. Lambert, M. 'Épigraphie élamite.' In *R.A.* 49 (1955), 42 ff., 149 ff.
19. Langdon, S. *Babylonian Menologies and the Semitic Calendars.* London, 1935.
20. Le Breton, L. 'The Early Periods at Susa, Mesopotamian Relations.' In *Iraq,* 19 (1957), 79 ff.
21. Meier, G. 'Die zweite Tafel der Serie *bīt mēseri.*' In *Arch. f. Or.* 14 (1942), 139 ff.
22. Pézard, M. *Mission à Bender-Bouchir. Documents archéologiques et épigraphiques.* = *Mém. D.P.* 15 (1914), 1 ff.
23. Poebel, A. 'The Acropolis of Susa in the Elamite Inscriptions.' In *A.J.S.L.* 49 (1932–3), 125 ff.
24. Rutten, M. 'Les dieux de Tchogha Zembil.' In *Mém. D.P.* 32 (1953), 10 ff.
25. Scheil, V. 'Textes funéraires.' In *R.A.* 13 (1916), 165 ff.
26. Scheil, V. 'Passim.' In *R.A.* 22 (1925), 141 ff.
27. Schmidt, E. F. *Persepolis.* Volume II, Chicago, 1957. (Plates 27 and 28 = Elamite Bronze Plaque.)
28. Weissbach, F. H. 'Neue Beiträge zur Kunde der susischen Inschriften.' In *Abh. Leipzig,* 14, 7 (1894), 731 ff.

IV. CIVILIZATION OF ANCIENT ELAM

1. Amiet, P. 'Glyptique susienne archaïque.' In *R.A.* 51 (1957), 121 ff.
2. Amiet, P. 'Représentations antiques de constructions susiennes.' In *R.A.* 53 (1959), 39 ff.
3. Belaiew, N. T. 'Métrologie élamite.' In *Mém. D.P.* 25 (1934), 134 ff., 19 plates.
4. Bork, F. 'Die elamische Klammer.' In *Arch. f. Or.* (1933–4), 292 ff.
5. Cameron, G. G. *Persepolis Treasury Tablets.* Chicago, 1948.
6. Christian, V. 'Elam (ethnologisch).' In *R.L.A.* 2 (1938), 338 ff.
7. Debevoise, N. C. 'The Rock Reliefs of Ancient Iran.' In *J.N.E.S.* 1 (1942), 76 ff.
8. Falkenstein, A. *Archaische Texte aus Uruk.* Berlin/Leipzig, 1936.
9. Falkenstein, A. 'Die Keilschrift.' In *Handbuch der Orientalistik*, Erste Abt., Zweiter Band, Lieferung 1 (Leiden, 1959), 6 ff.
10. Frankfort, H. *Cylinder Seals. A Documentary Essay on the Art and Religion of the Ancient Near East.* London, 1939.
11. Ghirshman, R. *Fouilles de Sialk.* Vol. 1, Paris, 1938.
12. Hertz, A. *Die Kultur um den Persischen Golf und ihre Ausbreitung (Klio*, Beiheft 20). Leipzig, 1930.
13. Hinz, W. 'Zu den Persepolis-Täfelchen.' In *Z.D.M.G.* 110 (1961), 236 ff.
14. Hinz, W. 'Elamica.' In *Or.* n.s. 32 (1963), 1 ff.
15. Labat, R. 'Structure de la langue élamite.' In *Conférences de l'Institut de linguistique de l'Université de Paris*, 9 (1950–1), 23 ff.
16. Landsberger, B. 'Jahreszeiten im Sumerisch-Akkadischen.' In *J.N.E.S.* 8 (1949), 248 ff.
17. Legrain, L. 'Empreintes de cachets élamites.' In *Mém. D.P.* 16 (1921), 1 ff., 23 plates.
18. McCown, D. E. 'The Material Culture of Early Iran.' In *J.N.E.S.* 1 (1942), 424 ff.
19. Mecquenem, R. de. 'Épigraphie proto-élamite.' In *Mém. D.P.* 31 (1949), 5 ff.
20. Mecquenem, R. de. 'Notes protoélamites.' In *R.A.* 50 (1956), 200 ff.
21. Rutten, M. 'Glyptique susienne—empreintes et cylindres.' In *R.A.* 44 (1950), 161 ff., 6 plates.
22. Scheil, V. 'Textes de comptabilité proto-élamites.' In *Mém. D.P.* 26 (1935), i–xiv, 65 plates.
23. Toscanne, P. 'Études sur le serpent figure et symbole dans l'antiquité élamite.' In *Mém. D.P.* 12 (1911), 153 ff.
24. Toscanne, P. 'Notes sur quelques figurations d'animaux en Chaldée-Susiane.' In *R.A.* 9 (1912), 13 ff.

A. ADDENDA

1. Amiet, P. 'Il y a 5000 ans les Élamites inventaient l'écriture.' In *Archaeologia*, 12 (1966), 16 ff.
2. Amiet, P. *Elam.* Auvers-sur-Oise, 1966.
3. Boehmer, R. M. 'Datierte Glyptik der Akkade-Zeit.' In *Festschrift A. Moortgat.* Berlin, 1964, 42 ff.
4. Boehmer, R. M. 'Die Datierung des Puzur/Kutik-Inšušinak und einige sich daraus ergebende Konsequenzen.' In *Or.* n.s. 35 (1966), 345 ff.
5. Boehmer, R. M. 'Zur Datierung des Epirmupi.' In *Z.A.* 58 (1967), 302 ff.

6. Brice, W. C. 'The Writing System of the Proto-Elamite Account Tablets of Susa.' In *Bull. Ryl. Libr.* 45 (1962), 15 ff.

7. Ghirshman, R. 'Suse au début du IIe millénaire avant notre ère et un sanctuaire iranien dans les monts des Zagros.' In *C. R. Ac. Inscr. B.-L.*, juillet-décembre 1965 (1966), 375 ff.

8. Hinz, W. *Das Reich Elam.* Stuttgart, 1964.

9. Hinz, W. 'The Elamite God d.*GAL*.' In *J.N.E.S.* 24 (1965), 351 ff.

10. Hinz, W. 'Elams Vertrag mit Narām-Sîn von Akkade.' In *Z.A.* 58 (1967), 66 ff.

11. Hirsch, H. 'Die Inschriften der Könige von Agade.' In *Arch. f. Or.* 10 (1963), 1 ff.

12. König, F. W. *Die elamischen Königsinschriften* (*Arch. f. Or. Beiheft* 16). Graz, 1965.

13. Meriggi, P. 'L'Elamico.' In *Accademia Naz. dei Lincei*, Quaderno 76 (1966), 559 ff.

14. Reich, J. J. 'The Horse-Head Ideogram in the Proto-Elamite Script and Minoan B.' In *Kadmos*, 2 (1963), 151 f.

15. Reiner, Erica, 'The Earliest Elamite Inscription?' In *J.N.E.S.* 24 (1965), 337 ff.

16. Strommenger, Eva. 'Statueninschriften und ihr Datierungswert.' In *Z.A.* 53 (1959), 27 ff.

17. Strommenger, Eva. 'Das Menschenbild in der altmesopotamischen Rundplastik von Mesilim bis Hammurapi.' In *Baghdader Mitteilungen* 1, (1960), 1 ff.

CHAPTER XXIV(a)

I. INTRODUCTORY

1. Burney, C. A. 'Northern Anatolia before Classical Times.' In *A. St.* 6 (1956), 179 ff.

2. Driehaus, J. 'Prähistorische Siedlungsfunde in der unteren Kaikosebene und an dem Golfe von Çandarlı.' In *Istanbuler Mitt.* 7 (1957), 76 ff.

3. Goldman, H. *Excavations at Gözlü Kule, Tarsus*, II. Princeton, 1956.

4. Lloyd, Seton and Mellaart, J. *Beycesultan*, I. London, 1962.

5. Mellaart, J. 'The End of the Early Bronze Age in Anatolia and the Aegean.' In *A.J.A.* 62 (1958), 9 ff.

6. Milojčič, V. *Samos*, I: *Die prähistorische Siedlung unter dem Heraion.* Bonn, 1961.

II. WESTERN ANATOLIA AFTER THE LUWIAN INVASION

1. Blegen, C. W., Caskey, J. L. and Rawson, M. *Troy, II: the Third, Fourth, and Fifth Settlements.* Princeton, 1951.

2. Lloyd, Seton. 'Anatolia.' In Piggott, Stewart (ed.), *The Dawn of Civilization.* London, 1961.

3. Mellaart, J. 'Anatolian Chronology of the Early and Middle Bronze Age.' In *A. St.* 7 (1957), 55 ff.

4. Mellaart, J. 'Notes on the Architectural Remains of Troy I and II.' In *A. St.* 9 (1959), 131 ff.

5. Özgüç, T. 'Kültepe: summary of archaeological work in Turkey in 1956.' In *A. St.* 7 (1957), 19 f.

III. CENTRAL ANATOLIA

1. Goetze, A. *Kleinasien*. Ed. 2. Munich, 1957.
2. Koşay, H. Z. and Akok, M. 'Amasya Mahmutlar köyü definesi.' In *Belleten*, 14 (1950), 481 ff.
3. Osten, H. H. von der. *The Alishar Hüyük*, 1. (*O.I.P.* 28.) Chicago, 1940.
4. Özgüc, N. 'Marble Idols and Statuettes from the Excavations at Kültepe.' In *Belleten*, 21 (1957), 71 ff.
5. Özgüc, T. *Excavations at Horoztepe*. Ankara, 1958.
6. Özgüc, T. 'Kültepe: Summary of Archaeological Work in Turkey in 1957.' In *A. St.* 8 (1958), 25 f.

IV. EASTERN CULTURES

1. Burney, C. A. 'Eastern Anatolia in the Chalcolithic and Early Bronze Ages.' In *A. St.* 8 (1958), 157 ff.
2. Burney, C. A. 'Excavations at Yanik Tepe, North-west Iran.' In *Iraq*, 24 (1962), 134 ff.
3. Chaput, E. *Phrygie*, 1. Paris, 1941.
4. Koşay, H. Z. and Turfan, K. 'Erzurum-Karaz kazısı raporu.' In *Belleten*, 23 (1959), 349 ff.
5. Markovine, V. I. 'Concernant les origines de la civilisation archéologique du Nord Caucasien' (in Russian). In *Sov. Arkh.* 1959, no. 1.
6. *Oriental Silver Atlas*. Ed. by the Imperial Archaeological Commission on its 50th anniversary. St Petersburg, 1909.
7. Özgüc, T. and N. *Karahöyük hafriyatı raporu 1947*. Ankara, 1949.
8. Özgüc, T. 'Die Grabung von Maltepe bei Sivas.' In *Belleten*, 11 (1947), 657 ff.
9. Schaeffer, C. F. A. and Weidner, E. 'Arslantepe.' In *Arch. f. Or.* 16 (1952–3), 151 f.

V. A PONTIC CULTURE

1. Childe, V. G. 'The Axes from Maikop and Caucasian Metallurgy.' In *Ann. Arch. Anthr.* 23 (1936), 113 ff.
2. Hančar, F. *Urgeschichte Kaukasiens*. Wien, 1937.
3. Kökten, K. I. and Özgüc, T. 'Tekeköy kazısı.' In *Belleten*, 9 (1945), 382 ff.
4. Schaeffer, C. F. A. *Stratigraphie comparée et chronologie de l'Asie Occidentale* (*IIIe et IIe millénaires*). Oxford, 1948.
5. Stronach, D. B. 'The Development and Diffusion of Metal Types in Early Bronze Age Anatolia.' In *A. St.* 7 (1957), 89 ff.
6. Temizer, R. 'Kayapınar Höyügü buluntuları.' In *Belleten*, 18 (1954), 317 ff.

VI. TRANSITION TO THE MIDDLE BRONZE AGE

1. Alp, S. 'Karahüyük.' In *A.J.A.* 60 (1956), 373 f.
2. Alp, S. 'Karahöyük.' In *A. St.* 9 (1959), 30 f.
3. Arik, R. O. 'Le Hüyük de Karaoğlan.' In *Belleten*, 3 (1939), 43 ff.
4. Arik, R. O. 'Karaoğlan Höyüğü Bakır Çağı mimarliğindaki özellikler.' In *III Turk Tarih Kongresi*. Ankara, 1948.
5. Beran, Th. 'Boğazköy: Summary of Archaeological Research in Turkey in 1961.' In *A. St.* 12 (1962), 22 ff.
6. Bittel, K. Review of Blegen, C. W. and others, *Troy, III*. In *Gnomon*, 28 (1956), 241 ff.

7. Blegen, C. W., Caskey, J. L. and Rawson, M. *Troy, III: the Sixth Settlement.* Princeton, 1953.
8. Caskey, J. L. 'The Early Helladic Period in the Argolid.' In *Hesperia,* 29 (1960), 285 ff.
9. Güterbock, H. G. 'Kanes and Nesa.' In *Eretz Israel,* 5 (1958), 46 ff.
10. Lloyd, Seton and Gökçe, N. 'Excavations at Polatlı.' In *A. St.* 1 (1951), 21 ff.
11. Lloyd, Seton. 'Excavations at Beycesultan, 1957.' In *A. St.* 8 (1958), 93 ff.
12. Lloyd, Seton. 'Excavations at Beycesultan, 1958.' In *A. St.* 9 (1959), 35 ff.
13. Lloyd, Seton. 'Excavations at Beycesultan, 1959.' In *A. St.* 10 (1960), 31 ff.
14. Mellaart, J. 'Some Prehistoric Sites in North-western Anatolia.' In *Istanbuler Mitt.* 6 (1955), 52 ff.
15. Mellaart, J. 'Second Millennium Pottery from the Konya Plain and Neighbourhood.' In *Belleten,* 22 (1958), 311 ff.
16. Mellink, M. J. *A Hittite Cemetery at Gordion.* Philadelphia, 1956.
17. Özgüç, T. *Kültepe-Kaniş.* Ankara, 1959.

VII. TROY I–V

1. Blegen, C. W., Boulter, C. G., Caskey, J. L., Rawson, M. and Sperling, J. *Troy: Excavations Conducted by the University of Cincinnati, 1932–8* 4 vols. Princeton, 1950–8.
2. Dörpfeld, W. *Bericht über die im Jahre 1893 in Troja veranstalteten Ausgrabungen.* Leipzig, 1894.
3. Dörpfeld, W. *Troja un Ilion.* Athens, 1902.
4. Leaf, W. *Troy. A Study in Homeric Geography.* London, 1912.
5. Leaf, W. *Strabo on the Troad.* Cambridge, 1923.
6. Leake, W. M. *Journal of a Tour in Asia Minor.* London, 1824.
7. Lechevalier, J. F. *Voyage de la Troade.* Paris, 1802.
8. Maclaren, C. *Dissertation on the Topography of the Plain of Troy.* Edinburgh, 1822.
9. Matz, F. *Kreta, Mykene, Troja, die minoische und die homerische Welt.* Ed. 2. Stuttgart, 1956.
10. Meyer, E. *Briefe von Heinrich Schliemann,* 1936.
11. Meyer, E. *Heinrich Schliemanns Briefwechsel,* I (1953), II (1958).
12. Page, D. L. *History and the Homeric Iliad.* California University Press, 1959.
13. Schachermeyr, F. *Die ältesten Kulturen Griechenlands.* Stuttgart, 1955.
14. Schachermeyr, F. *Prähistorische Kulturen Griechenlands* (Pauly–Wissowa–Kroll, Bd. 22). Stuttgart, 1954.
15. Schliemann, H. *Ithaka, der Peloponnes und Troja.* Leipzig, 1869.
16. Schliemann, H. *Troy and its Remains.* London, 1875.
17. Schliemann, H. *Ilios, the City and Country of the Trojans.* London, 1880.
18. Schliemann, H. *Troja: Results of the Latest Researches and Discoveries on the Site of Homer's Troy.* London, 1884.
19. Schliemann, H. *Bericht über die Ausgrabungen in Troja im Jahre 1890.* Leipzig, 1891.
20. Schmidt, H. *Heinrich Schliemann's Sammlung Trojanischer Altertümer.* Berlin, 1902.
21. Schuchhardt, C. *Schliemann's Excavations* (English trans. E. Sellers). London, 1892.

CHAPTER XXIV(*b*)

VIII. HISTORY

1. *A.R.M.T. Archives Royales de Mari*, texts in transliteration and translation, vols. I–IX. Paris, 1950–60.
2. Balkan, K. 'Observations on the chronological problems of the kārum Kaniš.' In *Türk Tarih Kurumu Yayınlarından*, ser. VII, no. 28, 41 ff. Ankara, 1955.
3. Balkan, K. 'Letter of King Anum-Hirbi of Mama to King Warshama of Kanish.' In *Türk Tarih Kurumu Yayınlarından*, ser. VII, no. 31A. Ankara, 1957.
4. Eisser, G. und Lewy, J. *Die altassyrischen Rechtsurkunden vom Kültepe*, 1. und 2. Teil, *M.V.Ae.G.* 33 (1930); 3. und 4. Teil, *M.V.Ae.G.* 35, Heft 3 (1935).
5. Finkelstein, J. J. 'The so-called "Old-Babylonian Kutha Legend".' In *J.C.S.* 11 (1957), 83 ff.
6. Gelb, I. J. *Inscriptions from Alishar and Vicinity* (*O.I.P.* 27). Chicago, 1935.
7. Güterbock, H. G. 'Sargon of Akkad mentioned by Ḫattušili of Ḫatti.' In *J.C.S.* 18 (1964), 1 ff.
8. *Inscriptions cunéiformes du Kültépé.* 1 (by B. Hrozný); II (by L. and M. Matouš). Prague, 1952 and 1962.
9. *Keilschrifttexte aus Assur historischen Inhalts.* 1 (by L. Messerschmidt); II (by O. Schroeder). Leipzig, 1911 and 1922.
10. Landsberger, B. und Balkan, K. 'Die Inschrift des assyrischen Königs Irişum, gefunden in Kültepe, 1948.' In *Belleten*, 14 (1950), 219 ff.
11. Lewy, H. 'The kingdom of Ḫana at the time of the Mari texts.' In *Proc. 23 Congress of Orientalists*, 127 f. Cambridge, 1954.
12. Lewy, H. 'The historical background of the correspondence of Baḫdi-Lim.' In *Or.* n.s. 25 (1956), 324 ff.
13. Lewy, H. 'Šubat-Šamaš and Tuttul.' In *Or.* n.s. 27 (1958), 1 ff.
14. Lewy, H. 'The synchronism Assyria–Ešnunna–Babylon.' In *We. Or.* 2 (1954–9), 438 ff.
15. Lewy, H. 'Notes on the political organization of Asia Minor at the time of the Old Assyrian Texts.' In *Or.* n.s. 33 (1964), 181 ff.
16. Lewy, J. 'Die Keilschriftquellen zur Geschichte Anatoliens.' In *Nachr. d. Giessener Hochschulgesellschaft*, 6 (1925), 35 ff.
17. Lewy, J. 'Old Assyrian documents from Asia Minor,' 1 and II. In *Arch. hist. dr. or.*, 1 (1937), 91 ff. and 2 (1938), 111 ff.
18. Lewy, J. 'Apropos of a recent study in Old Assyrian chronology.' In *Or.* n.s. 26 (1957), 12 ff.
19. Lewy, J. 'Some aspects of commercial life in Assyria and Asia Minor in the nineteenth pre-Christian century.' In *J.A.O.S.* 78 (1958), 89 ff.
20. Lewy, J. 'The Biblical institution of Dᵉror in the light of Akkadian documents.' In *Eretz-Israel*, 5 (1958), 21 ff.
21. Matouš, L. Review of no. 2, above. In *O.L.Z.* 53 (1958), cols. 342 ff.
22. Özgüç, N. 'Vorbericht über die Siegel und Siegelabdrücke.' In *Belleten*, 17 (1953), 123 ff.
23. Parrot, A. (ed.). *Studia Mariana*. Leiden, 1950.
24. Thureau-Dangin, F. 'La date des tablettes cappadociennes.' In *R.A.* 8 (1911), 142 ff.
25. Weidner, E. F. 'Ilušumas Zug nach Babylonien.' In *Z.A.* 43 (1936), 114 ff.

IX. PEOPLES AND GOVERNMENT

1. Bilgiç, E. 'Die Ortsnamen der "kappadokischen" Urkunden im Rahmen der alten Sprachen Anatoliens.' In *Arch. f. Or.* 15 (1945–51), 1ff.
2. Chiera, E. *Joint Expedition with the Iraq Museum at Nuzi.* Vol. 1. *Inheritance Texts.* Paris, 1927.
3. Clay, A. T. *Letters and Transactions from Cappadocia; Babylonian Inscriptions in the Collection of James B. Nies*, vol. IV. New Haven, 1927.
4. Contenau, G. *Tablettes Cappadociennes; Textes cunéiformes du Louvre*, IV. Paris, 1920.
5. Cornelius, F. 'Neue Aufschlüsse zur hethitischen Geographie.' In *Or.* n.s. 32 (1963), 233 ff.
6. Cornelius, F. 'Zur hethitischen Landeskunde.' In *Bi. Or.* 21 (1964), 11 ff.
7. Dhorme, E. *Recueil Édouard Dhorme.* Paris, 1951.
8. Garelli, P. *Les Assyriens en Cappadoce.* Paris, 1963.
9. Goetze, A. 'The linguistic continuity of Anatolia as shown by its proper names.' In *J.C.S.* 8 (1954), 74 ff.
10. Goetze, A. 'Suffixes in "Kanishite" proper names.' In *R.H.A.* 18 (1960), 45 ff.
11. Hirsch, H. *Untersuchungen zur altassyrischen Religion (Arch. f. Or.* Beiheft 13/14). Graz, 1961.
12. Hirsch, H. 'Die Inschriften der Könige von Agade.' In *Arch. f. Or.* 20 (1963), 1 ff.
13. Hrozný, B. 'Assyriens et Hittites en Asie Mineure vers 2000 av. J.C.' In *Arch. Orient.* 4 (1932), 112 ff.
14. Landsberger, B. *Assyrische Handelskolonien in Kleinasien aus dem dritten Jahrtausend (Der Alte Or.* 24, 4). Leipzig, 1925.
15. Lewy, H. 'Neša.' In *J.C.S.* 17 (1963), 103 f.
16. Lewy, J. *Studien zu den altassyrischen Texten aus Kappadokien.* Berlin, 1922.
17. Lewy, J. *Die Altassyrischen Texte vom Kültepe bei Kaisarīje; Keilschrifttexte in den Antiken-Museen zu Stambul.* Konstantinopel, 1926.
18. Lewy, J. 'Les textes paléo-assyriens et l'Ancien Testament.' In *Rev. hist. rel.* 110 (1934), 29 ff.
19. Lewy, J. *Tablettes Cappadociennes; Textes cunéiformes du Louvre*, XIX, XX, XXI. Paris, 1935–7.
20. Lewy, J. 'The old West Semitic Sun-God Ḥammu.' In *H.U.C.A.* 18 (1943–4), 429 ff.
21. Lewy, J. 'Tabor, Tibar, Atabyros.' In *H.U.C.A.* 23 (1950–1), 357 ff.
22. Lewy, J. 'On some institutions of the Old Assyrian empire.' In *H.U.C.A.* 27 (1956), 1 ff.
23. Lewy, J. 'Amurritica.' In *H.U.C.A.* 32 (1961), 31 ff.
24. Lewy, J. 'Old Assyrian evidence concerning Kuššara and its location.' In *H.U.C.A.* 33 (1962), 45 ff.
25. Otten, H. 'Pirva—der Gott auf dem Pferde.' In *Jahrb. für kleinasiatische Forschung*, 2 (1953), 62 ff.
26. Smith, S. *Cuneiform Texts from Cappadocian Tablets in the British Museum*, I–IV, V (with D. J. Wiseman). London, 1921–56.
27. Stephens, F. J. *Old Assyrian Letters and Business Documents; Babylonian Inscriptions in the Collection of James B. Nies*, vol. VI. New Haven, 1944.
28. Stephens, F. J. 'The Cappadocian Tablets in the University of Pennsylvania Museum.' In *J.S.O.R.* 11 (1927), 101 ff.

X. THE ARTICLES OF TRADE

1. Grothe, H. *Meine Vorderasienexpedition 1906 und 1907*. Leipzig, 1911.
2. Lewy, H. 'The ass-load, the sack, and other measures of capacity.' In *Riv. stud. or.* 39 (1964), 181 ff.
3. Lewy, J. 'The Old Assyrian surface measure *šubtum*.' In *An. Biblica*, 12 (1959), 216 ff.
4. Tylecote, R. F. *Metallurgy in Archaeology*. London, 1962.

CHAPTER XXV

G. GENERAL

1. Andrae, W. *Das wiedererstandene Assur*. Leipzig, 1938.
2. Borger, R. *Einleitung in die assyrischen Königsinschriften. Handbuch der Orientalistik*. Ergänzungsband 5. Leiden, 1961.
3. Budge, E. A. W. and King, L. W. *Annals of the Kings of Assyria*. London, 1902.
4. Ebeling, E., Meissner, B. and Weidner, E. F. *Die Inschriften der altassyrischen Könige* (*A.O.B.* 1). Leipzig, 1926.
5. Eisser, G. and Lewy, J. *Die altassyrischen Rechtsurkunden vom Kültepe. M.V.A.G.* 33 (1930); 35, Heft 3 (1935).
6. Forrer, E. 'Assyrien.' In *R.L.A.* 1 (1932), 228 ff.
7. Garelli, P. *Les Assyriens en Cappadoce*. Paris, 1963.
8. King, L. W. *Chronicles Concerning early Babylonian Kings*, 2 (*Studies in Eastern History*, 3). London, 1907.
9. Layard, A. H. *Populärer Bericht über die Ausgrabungen zu Niniveh*. Leipzig, 1852.
10. Luckenbill, D. D. *Ancient Records of Assyria and Babylonia*, 1, 11. Chicago, 1926, 1927.
11. Poebel, A. 'The Assyrian King List from Khorsabad.' In *J.N.E.S.* 1 (1942), 247 ff., 460 ff.; 2 (1943), 56 ff.
12. Soden, W. v. *Grundriss der akkadischen Grammatik* (*An. Or.* 33). Roma, 1952.
13. Soden, W. v. *Akkadisches Handwörterbuch*. Wiesbaden, 1959.
14. Thompson, R. C. *The Reports of the Magicians and Astrologers of Nineveh and Babylon in the British Museum*, 2 vols. London, 1900.
15. Thompson, R. C. and Hutchinson, R. W. *A Century of Exploration at Nineveh*. London, 1929.
16. Thureau-Dangin, F. *Die sumerischen und akkadischen Königsinschriften*. Leipzig, 1907.

I. THE PRE-SARGONIC PERIOD

1. Delaporte, L. *Catalogue des cylindres orientaux*, 11. Paris, 1923.
2. Ebeling, E. 'Kultische Texte aus Assur.' In *Or.* n.s. 22 (1953), 25 ff.
3. Frankena, R. 'New Materials for the *Tākultu* Ritual: Additions and Corrections.' In *Bi. Or.* 18 (1961), 199 ff.
4. Gadd, C. J. 'Inscribed Barrel Cylinder of Marduk-apla-iddina II.' In *Iraq*, 15 (1953), 123 ff.
5. Gelb, I. J., Purves, P. M. and MacRae, A. A. *Nuzi Personal Names* (*O.I.P.* 57). Chicago, 1943.

6. Haller, A. and Andrae, W. *Die Heiligtümer des Gottes Assur und der Sin-Šamaš-Tempel in Assur* (*W.V.D.O.G.* 67). Berlin, 1955.
7. Herzfeld, E. *Geschichte der Stadt Samarra. Die Ausgrabungen von Samarra*, 6. Hamburg, 1948.
8. Jean, Ch.-F. *Contrats de Larsa* (*T.C.L.* 11). Paris, 1926.
9. Lacheman, E. R. *Miscellaneous Texts from Nuzi*, part II (*Harvard Semitic Series*, 14). Cambridge, Mass., 1950.
10. Langdon, S. *Die neubabylonischen Königsinschriften* (*V.A.B.* 4). Leipzig, 1912.
11. Lewy, H. 'The Babylonian Background of the Kay Kâûs Legend.' In *Arch. Orient.* 17 (1949), 28 ff.
12. Lewy, H. 'The historical background of the correspondence of Baḫdi-Lim.' In *Or.* n.s. 25 (1956), 324 ff.
13. Lewy, H. 'The synchronism Assyria-Ešnunna-Babylon.' In *We. Or.* 2(1954–9), 438 ff.
14. Lewy, J. 'The late Assyro-Babylonian Cult of the Moon and its Culmination at the Time of Nabonidus.' In *H.U.C.A.* 19 (1946), 405 ff.
15. Lewy, J. 'Old Assyrian *subrum.*' Communication made at the meeting of the *A.O.S.* at Washington, D.C., on 26 March 1963.
16. Mallowan, M. E. L. 'The Prehistoric Sondage of Nineveh, 1931–1932.' In *Ann. Arch. Anthr.* 20 (1933), 127 ff.
17. Mallowan, M. E. L. and Cruikshank, Rose J. 'Prehistoric Assyria. The Excavations at Tall Arpachiyah 1933.' In *Iraq*, 2 (1935), 1 ff.
18. Messerschmidt, L. 'Die Inschrift der Stele Nabuna'id's, Königs von Babylon.' In *M.V.A.G.* 1 (1896), 1 ff.
19. Nougayrol, J. and Laroche, E. 'Le bilingue accado-hourrite.' In *Le palais royal d'Ugarit*, III = *Mission de Ras Shamra*, VI, 3 (1955), 309 ff.
20. Nougayrol, J. 'Documents du Habur, 2: Le sceau de Daguna.' In *Syria*, 37 (1960), 209 ff.
21. Parrot, A. and Nougayrol, J. 'Un document de fondation hurrite.' In *R.A.* 42 (1948), 1 ff.
22. Pfeiffer, R. H. and Lacheman, E. R. *Miscellaneous Texts from Nuzi*, part I (*Harvard Semitic Series*, 13). Cambridge, Mass., 1942.
23. Scheil, V. 'La déesse Nina et ses poissons.' In *R.A.* 15 (1918), 127 ff.
24. Speiser, E. A. *Excavations at Tepe Gawra*. Philadelphia, 1935.
25. Speiser, E. A. 'Hurrians and Subarians.' In *J.A.O.S.* 68 (1948), 1 ff.
26. Speiser, E. A. 'Nuzi or Nuzu.' In *J.A.O.S.* 75 (1955), 52 ff.
27. Thompson, R. C. 'The Buildings on Quyunjiq, the larger Mound of Nineveh.' In *Iraq*, 1 (1934), 95 ff.

II. THE SARGONIC PERIOD

1. Andrae, W. *Die archaischen Ischtar-Tempel in Assur* (*W.V.D.O.G.* 39). Leipzig, 1922
2. Falkenstein, A. *Literarische Keilschrifttexte aus Uruk*. Berlin, 1931.
3. Feigin, S. I. 'ḪUM-ḪUM'. In *An. Or.* 12 (1935), 82 ff.
4. Finkelstein, J. J. 'The so-called "Old Babylonian Kutha Legend".' In *J.C.S.* 11 (1957), 83 ff.
5. Gadd, C. J. and Legrain, L. *Royal Inscriptions* (*U.E.T.* 1). London and Philadelphia, 1928.
6. Gurney, O. R. 'The Sultantepe Tablets.' In *A. St.* 5(1955), 93 ff.
7. *Keilschrifttexte aus Assur historischen Inhalts*, I (by L. Messerschmidt); II (by O. Schroeder). Leipzig, 1911 and 1922.

8. King, L. W. *C.T.* 34. London, 1914.
9. Landsberger, B. 'Assyrische Königsliste und "Dunkles Zeitalter".' In *J.C.S.* 8 (1954), 31 ff.; 47 ff.; 106 ff.
10. Lewy, H. 'Points of comparison between Zoroastrianism and the moon-cult of Ḥarrân.' In *A Locust's Leg; Studies in honour of S.H. Taqizadeh* (London, 1962), 139 ff.
11. Loud, G. *Khorsabad*, part 1 (*O.I.P.* 38). Chicago, 1936.
12. Luckenbill, D. D. *The Annals of Sennacherib* (*O.I.P.* 2). Chicago, 1924.
13. Mallowan, M. E. L. 'Excavations at Brak and Chagar Bazar.' In *Iraq*, 9 (1947), 1 ff.
14. Meek, Th. J. *Old Akkadian, Sumerian, and Cappadocian Texts from Nuzi* (*Harvard Semitic Series*, 10). Cambridge, Mass., 1935.
15. Meissner, B. 'Eine unerkannte Inschrift Naram-Sin's.' In *O.L.Z.* 18 (1915), 173 f.
16. Poebel, A. *Historical Texts* (*P.B.S.* 4, 1). Philadelphia, 1914.
17. Poebel, A. *Historical and Grammatical Texts* (*P.B.S.* 5). Philadelphia, 1914.
18. Preusser, C. *Die Wohnhäuser in Assur* (*W.V.D.O.G.* 64). Berlin, 1954.
19. Thompson, G. Caton *The Tombs and Moon Temple at Hureidha* (*Hadhramaut*). Oxford, 1944.
20. Thompson, R. C. and Hamilton, R. W. 'The British Museum Excavations on the Temple of Ishtar at Nineveh, 1930–31.' In *Ann. Arch. Anthr.* 19 (1932), pp. 55 ff. and plates 46 ff.
21. Thureau-Dangin, F. *Une relation de la huitième campagne de Sargon.* Paris, 1912.
22. Weidner, E. F. 'Die Annalen des Königs Aššurbêlkala von Assyrien.' In *Arch. f. Or.* 6 (1930–1), 75 ff.
23. Weidner, E. F. Review of G, 15. In *Arch. f. Or.* 7 (1931–2), 278 ff.
24. Weidner, E. 'Bemerkungen zur Königsliste aus Chorsābād.' In *Arch. f. Or.* 15 (1945–51), 85 ff.

III. KING-LIST AND CHRONOLOGY

1. Andrae, W. *Die Stelenreihen in Assur* (*W.V.D.O.G.* 24). Leipzig, 1913.
2. Andrae, W. 'Die jüngeren Ischtar-Tempel in Assur.' In *M.D.O.G.* 73 (1935), 1 ff.
3. *A.R.M.T. Archives Royales de Mari*; texts in transliteration and translation, vols. I–IX. Paris, 1950–60.
4. Borger, R. *Die Inschriften Asarhaddons, Königs von Assyrien* (*Arch. f. Or.* Beiheft 9). Graz, 1956.
5. Fine, H. A. *Studies in Middle-Assyrian Chronology and Religion.* Cincinnati, 1955.
6. Forrer, E. *Die Provinzeinteilung des assyrischen Reiches.* Leipzig, 1920.
7. Gelb, I. J. 'Two Assyrian King Lists.' In *J.N.E.S.* 13 (1954), 209 ff.
8. Hallo, W. W. 'Zāriqum.' In *J.N.E.S.* 15 (1956), 220 ff.
9. Huffmon, H. B. *Amorite Personal Names in the Mari Texts.* Baltimore, 1965.
10. Kohler, J. and Ungnad, A. *Assyrische Rechtsurkunden.* Leipzig, 1913.
11. Lewy, H. 'On Some Problems of Kassite and Assyrian Chronology.' In *Ann. Inst. phil. hist. or.* 13 (1953), 241 ff.
12. Lewy, H. 'Miscellanea Nuziana, I.' In *Or.* n.s. 28 (1959), 1 ff.
13. Lewy, J. 'Le nom du père de Šamši-Adad Iᵉʳ.' In *R.A.* 31 (1934), 170.
14. Lewy, J. 'Apropos of a recent study in Old Assyrian Chronology.' In *Or.* n.s. 26 (1957), 12 ff.
15. Meissner, B. 'Assyriologische Studien, v.' In *M.V.A.G.* 15 (1910), 476 ff.

16. Michel, E. 'Die Assur-Texte Salmanassars III.' In *We. Or.* 1 (1947–52), 5 ff., 57 ff., 205 ff., 255 ff., 385 ff., 454 ff.; *We. Or.* 2 (1954–9), 27 ff., 137 ff.; 221 ff.
17. Nassouhi, Essad. 'Grande liste des rois d'Assyrie.' In *Arch. f. Or.* 4 (1927), 1 ff.
18. Piepkorn, A. C. *Historical Prism Inscriptions of Ashurbanipal (Assyrological Studies,* 5). Chicago, 1933.
19. Schroeder, O. *Keilschrifttexte aus Assur verschiedenen Inhalts.* Leipzig, 1920.
20. Streck, M. *Assurbanipal und die letzten assyrischen Könige bis zum Untergange Niniveh's (V.A.B.* 7), 2. Leipzig, 1916.
21. Thompson, R. C. *The Prisms of Esarhaddon and Ashurbanipal found at Nineveh, 1927–8.* London, 1931.
22. Unger, E. 'Harrân.' In *Reallexikon der Vorgeschichte,* 5 (Berlin, 1926), 127 f.
23. Ungnad, A. 'Eponymen'. In *R.L.A.* 2 (1938), 412 ff.
24. Weidner, E. F. 'Die Könige von Assyrien.' In *M.V.A.G.* 26, 2 (Leipzig, 1921), 1 ff.
25. Weidner, E. F. 'Die grosse Königsliste aus Assur.' In *Arch. f. Or.* 3 (1926), 66 ff.
26. Weidner, E. F. Review of G, 1. In *Arch. f. Or.* 13 (1931–41), 157 ff.
27. Weidner, E. F. 'Die assyrischen Eponymen.' In *Arch. f. Or.* 13 (1931–41), 308 ff.
28. Weidner, E. *Die Inschriften Tukulti-Ninurtas I. und seiner Nachfolger (Arch. f. Or.* Beiheft 12). Graz, 1959.

IV. THE OLD ASSYRIAN PERIOD

1. Balkan, K. 'Observations on the chronological problems of the kārum Kaniš.' In *Türk Tarih Kurumu Yayınlarından,* ser. VII, no. 28, Ankara, 1955.
2. Brown, Th. B. 'Anatolian relations with the Aegean before 2400 B.C.' In *Ann. Arch. Anthr.* 20 (1933), 43 ff.
3. Cornelius, F. 'Chronology. Eine Erwiderung.' In *J.C.S.* 12 (1958), 101 ff.
4. Dossin, G. 'L'inscription de fondation de Iaḫdun-Lim, roi de Mari.' In *Syria,* 32 (1955), 1 ff.
5. Eisser, G. and Lewy, J. *Die altassyrischen Rechtsurkunden vom Kültepe.* 1. und 2. Teil, *M.V.A.G.* 33 (1930); 3. und 4. Teil, *M.V.A.G.* 35, Heft 3 (1935).
6. Frankfort, H., Lloyd, S. and Jacobsen, T. *The Gimilsin Temple and the Palace of the Rulers at Tell Asmar (O.I.P.* 43). Chicago, 1940.
7. Garelli, P. *Les Assyriens en Cappadoce.* Paris, 1963.
8. Hirsch, H. *Untersuchungen zur altassyrischen Religion (Arch. f. Or.* Beiheft 13/14). Graz, 1961.
9. Jacobsen, T. *The Sumerian King List (Assyriological Studies,* 11). Chicago, 1939.
10. Johns, C. H. W. 'The Mananâ-Japium Dynasty of Kish.' In *P.S.B.A.* 32 (1910), 279 ff.; 33 (1911), 98 ff.
11. Lacheman, E. R. *The Administrative Archives (Harvard Semitic Series,* 15). Cambridge, Mass. 1955.
12. Landsberger, B. and Balkan, K. 'Die Inschrift des assyrischen Königs Irišum, gefunden in Kültepe, 1948.' In *Belleten,* 14 (1950), 219 ff.
13. Langdon, S. 'Tablets from Kiš.' In *P.S.B.A.* 33 (1911), pp. 185 ff. and plates 30 ff.; pp. 232 ff. and plates 42 ff.
14. Legrain, L. 'Restauration de la stèle d'Ur-Nammu.' In *R.A.* 30 (1933), 111 ff.

15. Lewy, H. 'The Titennûtu Texts from Nuzi.' In *Or.* n.s. 10 (1941), 313 ff.
16. Lewy, H. 'Marginal notes on a recent volume of Babylonian Mathematical texts.' In *J.A.O.S.* 67 (1947), 305 ff.
17. Lewy, H. 'The historical background of the correspondence of Baḫdi-Lim.' In *Or.* n.s. 25 (1956), 324 ff.
18. Lewy, H. 'Notes on the political organization of Asia Minor at the time of the Old Assyrian texts.' In *Or.* n.s. 33 (1964), 181 ff.
19. Lewy, J. 'Notes on pre-Ḫurrian texts from Nuzi.' In *J.A.O.S.* 58 (1938), 450 ff.
20. Lewy, J. 'On some institutions of the Old Assyrian empire.' In *H.U.C.A.* 27 (1956), 1 ff.
21. Reiner, E. 'The Year Dates of Sumu-Jamūtbāl.' In *J.C.S.* 15 (1961), 121 ff.
22. Rutten, M. 'Un lot de tablettes de Mananâ.' In *R.A.* 52 (1958), 208 ff.; 53 (1959), 77 ff.; 54 (1960), 19 ff.
23. Simmons, S. D. 'Early Old Babylonian Tablets from Ḫarmal and Elsewhere.' In *J.C.S.* 13 (1959), 71 ff. 2. In 14 (1960), 75 ff.
24. Soden, W. v. 'Eine altassyrische Beschwörung gegen die Dämonin Lamaštum.' In *Or.* n.s. 25 (1956), 141 ff.
25. Thureau-Dangin, F. 'Ašduni-erim roi de Kiš.' In *R.A.* 8 (1911), 65 ff.
26. Thureau-Dangin, F. 'Wardum.' In *Arch. Orient.* 1 (1929), 271 f.
27. Ungnad, A. *Altbabylonische Privaturkunden* (*V.A.S.* 8). Leipzig, 1909.
28. Ungnad, A. 'Datenlisten.' In *R.L.A.* 2 (1938), 131 ff.
29. Weidner, E. F. 'Ilušuma's Zug nach Babylonien.' In *Z.A.* 43 (1936), 114 ff.

V. THE RELIGION

1. Balkan, K. 'Ein kurzer Bericht über die neuen Tafeln aus Kültepe.' In *Proceedings of the Twenty-second Congress of Orientalists*, 2, 18 ff. Leiden, 1957.
2. Contenau, G. *Tablettes cappadociennes* (*T.C.L.* iv). Paris, 1920.
3. *Inscriptions cunéiformes du Kültépé* i (by Hrozný); ii (by L. and M. Matouš). Prague, 1952 and 1962.
4. Lewy, H. 'Istar-ṣâd and the Bow-Star.' In *Studies in Honor of Benno Landsberger on his Seventy-fifth Birthday*. Chicago, 1965, 273 ff.
5. Lewy, J. 'Die Keilschriftquellen zur Geschichte Anatoliens.' In *Nachr. d. Giessener Hochschulgesellschaft*, 6 (1925), 35 ff.
6. Lewy, J. 'Studies in Old Assyrian Grammar and Lexicography; 4. *mazlugum*, *šuggariā'um, a šalâšîšu mazlugû*, and *a šalâšîšu šugarriā'û*.' In *Or.* n.s. 19 (1950), 15 ff.
7. Lewy, J. 'Amurritica.' In *H.U.C.A.* 32 (1961), 31 ff.
8. Matouš, L. *Preliminary Publication of Old Assyrian Letters and Documents.* No date.
9. Otten, H. *Keilschrifttexte aus Boghazköi*, 9. Berlin, 1957.

VI. THE CALENDAR

1. Labat, R. *Le poème babylonien de la création.* Paris, 1935.
2. Landsberger, B. *Der kultische Kalender der Babylonier und Assyrer* (*L.S.S.* 6, 1/2). Leipzig, 1915.
3. Landsberger, B. and Kinnier Wilson, J. V. 'The Fifth Tablet of Enuma Eliš.' In *J.N.E.S.* 20 (1961), 154 ff.

4. Lewy, H. 'Le calendier Perse.' In *Or.* n.s. 10 (1941), 1 ff.
5. Lewy, H. *Calendar*, subsection VI: *Babylonian and Assyrian Calendars.* In *Encyclopaedia Britannica*, vol. 4 (1964), 622 f.
6. Lewy, J. 'The Assyrian Calendar.' In *Arch. Orient.* 11 (1939), 35 ff.

CHAPTER XXVI(*a*)

G. GENERAL

1. Åberg, N. *Bronzezeitliche und früheisenzeitliche Chronologie.* IV, *Griechland.* Stockholm, 1933.
2. Blegen, C. W. 'Preclassical Greece—A Survey.' In *B.S.A.* 46 (1951), 16–24.
3. Blegen, C. W. 'The Roof of the Mycenaean Megaron.' In *A.J.A.* 49 (1945), 33–44.
4. Bossert, H. Th. *The Art of Ancient Crete.* London, 1937.
5. Childe, V. G. *The Dawn of European Civilization* (6th ed.). London, 1957.
6. Dinsmoor, W. B. 'Notes on Megaron Roofs.' In *A.J.A.* 46 (1942), 370–2.
7. Ehrich, R. W. (ed.). *Relative Chronologies in Old World Archaeology.* Chicago, 1954.
8. Evans, J. D. 'Bossed Bone Plaques of the Second Millennium.' In *Antiquity*, 30 (1956), 80–93.
9. Evans, J. D. 'The "Dolmens" of Malta and the Origins of the Tarxien Cemetry Culture.' In *P.P.S.* n.s. 22 (1956), 85–101.
10. Fimmen, D. *Die kretisch-mykenische Kultur* (2nd ed.). Berlin, 1924.
11. Frankfort, H. *Studies in Early Pottery of the Near East.* II, *Asia, Europe and the Aegean, and their Earliest Interrelations* (Royal Anthropological Institute. Occasional Papers, no. 8). London, 1927.
12. Fuchs, S. *Die griechischen Fundgruppen der frühen Bronzezeit.* Berlin, 1937.
13. Haley, J. B. and Blegen, C. W. 'The Coming of the Greeks.' In *A.J.A.* 32 (1928), 141–54.
14. Harland, J. P. 'The Peloponnesos in the Bronze Age.' In *Harv. Stud. Class. Phil.* 34 (1923), 1–62.
15. Higgins, R. A. *Greek and Roman Jewellery.* London, 1961.
16. Holland, L. B. 'Primitive Aegean Roofs.' In *A.J.A.* 24 (1920), 323–31.
17. Kohler, E. L. and Ralph, E. K. 'C–14 Dates for Sites in the Mediterranean Area.' In *A.J.A.* 65 (1961), 357–67.
18. Marinatos, S. and Hirmer. M. *Crete and Mycenae.* London, 1960.
19. Matz, F. 'Die Ägais.' In *Handbuch der Archäologie*, 11 (Munich, 1954), 179–309.
20. Matz, F. *Kreta, Mykene, Troja* (2nd ed.). Stuttgart, 1956.
21. Milojčić, V. 'Die Askoskanne und einige andere ägäischbalkanische Gefäss-formen.' In *Mitt. des d. arch. Inst.* 3 (1950), 107–18.
22. Müller, V. 'The Beginnings of Monumental Sculpture in Greece.' In *Metr. Mus. Studies*, 5 (1934–6), 157–67; bibliography, 167–9.
23. Myres, J. L. *Who Were the Greeks?* (University of California, Sather Classical Lectures VI), Berkeley, 1930.
24. Pendlebury, J. C. S. *Aegyptiaca, a Catalogue of Egyptian Objects in the Aegean Area.* Cambridge, 1930.
25. Pendlebury, J. D. S. 'Egypt and the Aegean.' In *Studies presented to D. M. Robinson*, 1 (St Louis, 1951), 184–97.
26. Schachermeyr, F. *Die ältesten Kulturen Griechlands.* Stuttgart, 1955.

27. Schachermeyr, F. 'Forschungsbericht über die Ausgrabungen und Neufunde zur ägäischen Frühzeit 1957–1960.' In *Arch. Anz.* 1962, 105–382.
28. Schachermeyr, F. 'Prähistorische Kulturen Griechenlands.' In *P.W.* 22, 2, cols. 1351–1548.
29. Smith, E. B. 'The Megaron and its Roof.' In *A.J.A.* 46 (1943), 99–118.
30. Vercoutter, J. *Essai sur les relations entre Égyptiens et Préhellènes.* Paris, 1954.
31. Wace, A. J. B. 'The History of Greece in the Third and Second Milleniums B.C.' In *Historia*, 2 (1953/4), 74–94.
32. Wace, A. J. B. 'The Prehistoric Exploration of the Greek Mainland.' In *B.C.H.* 70 (1946), 628–38.
33. Wace, A. J. B. and Blegen, C. W. 'The Pre-Mycenaean Pottery of the Mainland.' In *B.S.A.* 22 (1916–18), 179–89.
34. Weinberg, S. S. 'Aegean Chronology: Neolithic Period and Early Bronze Age.' In *A.J.A.* 51 (1947), 165–82. See also G, 7, 86–107.

II. NORTH-EASTERN GREECE

1. Heurtley, W. A. *Prehistoric Macedonia.* Cambridge, 1939.
2. Hope Simpson, R. and Lazenby, J. F. 'The Kingdom of Peleus and Achilles.' In *Antiquity*, 33 (1959), 102–5.
3. Lazarides, D. Notice of excavations at Kikili Tash, 1961. In *Ergon*, 1961, 82–98; *B.C.H.* 86 (1962), 912–33.
4. Milojčić, V. 'Ausgrabungen in Thessalien.' In *Neue deutsche Ausgrabungen im Mittelmeergebiet und im vorderen Orient* (Boehringer, E., ed.; Deutsches Archäologisches Institut.) Berlin, 1959, 225–36.
5. Milojčić, V. 'Hauptergebnisse der deutschen Ausgrabungen in Thessalien 1935–1958.' In *Jahrb, des röm.-germ. Zentral museum in Mainz*, 6 (1959), 1–56.
6. Rey, L. *Observations sur les premiers habitats de la Macédoine recueillies par le Service Archéologique de l'Armée d'Orient.* Paris, 1921. (*B.C.H.* 41–3, 1917–19.)
7. Tsountas, C. Αἱ προϊστορικαὶ ἀκροπόλες Διμηνίου καὶ Σέσκλου. Athens, 1908.
8. Wace, A. J. B. and Thompson, M. S. *Prehistoric Thessaly.* Cambridge, 1912.

III. CENTRAL GREECE; THE EASTERN SHORES

1. Angel, J. L. 'Early Helladic Skulls from Aghios Kosmas.' In §III, 22 (*infra*), 169–79, with additional bibliography, 179.
2. Blegen, C. W. 'Athens and the Early Age of Greece.' In *Athenian Studies presented to William Scott Ferguson* (*Harv. Stud. Class. Phil.*, suppl. 1) (Cambridge, Mass., 1940), 1–9.
3. Blegen, C. W. 'Gonia.' In *Metr. Mus. studies*, 3 (1930–1), 55–80.
4. Blegen, C. W. 'Hyria.' In *Commemorative Studies in Honor of Theodore Leslie Shear* (*Hesperia*, suppl. 8, 1949), 39–42.
5. Blegen, C. W. *Korakou, a Prehistoric Settlement near Corinth.* Boston and New York, 1921.
6. Blegen, C. W. *Zygouries, a Prehistoric Settlement in the Valley of Cleonae.* Cambridge, Mass., 1928.
7. Caskey, J. L. and E. G. 'The Earliest Settlements at Eutresis. Supplementary Excavations, 1958.' In *Hesperia*, 29 (1960), 126–67.

8. Caskey, J. L. 'The Early Helladic Period in the Argolid.' In *Hesperia*, 29 (1960), 285–303.

9. Caskey, J. L. Preliminary reports on excavations at Lerna. In *Hesperia*, 23 (1954), 3–30; 24 (1955), 25–49; 25 (1956), 147–73; 26 (1957), 142–62; 27 (1958), 125–144; 28 (1959), 202–7.

10. Dor, L., Jannoray, L. and van Effenterre, H. and M. *Kirrha, étude de préhistoire phocidienne*. Paris, 1960.

11. Frödin, O. and Persson, A. *Asine, Results of the Swedish Excavations, 1922–1930*. Stockholm, 1938.

12. Gebauer, K. 'Forschungen in der Argolis.' In *Arch. Anz.* 1939, 268–94.

13. Goldman, H. *Excavations at Eutresis in Boeotia*. Cambridge, Mass., 1931.

14. Heath, M. C. 'Early Helladic Clay Sealings from the House of the Tiles at Lerna.' In *Hesperia*, 27 (1958), 81–121. See also Sakellariou-Xenaki, A. in Κρητικὰ Χρονικά, 15/16 (1961/2), I, 79–87.

15. Heermance, T. W. and Lord, G. D. 'Pre-Mycenaean Graves in Corinth.' In *A.J.A.* 2nd ser. 1 (1897), 313–32.

16. Hopf, M. 'Pflanzenfunde aus Lerna/Argolis.' In *Der Züchter*, 31 (1961), 239–47. (Preliminary report.)

17. Keramopoullous, A. D. Αἱ βιομηχανίαι καὶ ἐμπόριον τοῦ Κάδμου. In *Arch. Eph.* 1930, 29–58.

18. Keramopoullos, A. D. Θηβαϊκά. In *Arch. Delt.* 3 (1917), 1–503; particularly 1–5.

19. Kunze, E. *Orchomenos*, III, *Die Keramik der frühen Bronzezeit (Abh. der bayer. Akad. der Wiss.*, phil.-hist. Abt., n.F. 8). Munich, 1934.

20. Lerat, L. *Les Locriens de l'ouest*. Paris, 1952. Particularly 1, 159–62.

21. Müller, K. *Tiryns, die Ergebnisse der Ausgrabungen des Instituts*, III, *Die Architektur der Burg und des Palastes*. Augsburg, 1930. IV, *Die Urfirniskeramik*. Munich, 1938.

22. Mylonas, G. E. *Aghios Kosmas, An Early Bronze Age Settlement and Cemetery in Attica*. Princeton, 1959.

23. Mylonas, G. E. Προϊστορικὴ Ἐλευσίς. Athens, 1932.

24. Papavasileiou, G. Περὶ τῶν ἐν Εὐβοίᾳ ἀρχαίων τάφων. Athens, 1910.

25. Segall, B. *Museum Benakti. Katalog der Goldschmiede-Arbeiten*. Athens, 1938.

26. Shear, T. L. 'The Campaign of 1938' (excavations in the Athenian Agora). In *Hesperia*, 8 (1939), 201–46.

27. Soteriadis, G. 'Fouilles préhistoriques en Phocide,' In *R.E.G.* 25 (1912), 253–99.

28. Theochares, D. R. Ἀνασκαφὴ ἐν Παλαιᾷ Κοκκινιᾷ Πειραιῶς. In *Praktika Arch. Et.* 1951, 93–116.

29. Theochares, D. R. Ἀνασκαφὴ ἐν Ἀραφῆνι. In *Praktika Arch. Et.* 1951, 77–92; 1952, 129–51; 1953, 105–18; 1954, 104–22; 1955, 109–17.

30. Theochares, D. R. Ἀσκηταριό. In *Arch. Eph.* 1953–4, vol. 3 (1961), 59–76.

31. Theochares, D. R. Ἐκ τῆς προϊστορίας τῆς Εὐβοίας καὶ τῆς Σκύρου. In Ἀρχεῖον Εὐβοϊκῶν Μελετῶν, 8 (1959), 279–328.

32. Weinberg, S. S. 'Remains from Prehistoric Corinth.' In *Hesperia*, 6 (1937), 487–524.

33. Welter, G. *Aigina*, Berlin, 1938.

34. Yeroulanos, I. M. Ἀρχαιολογικὰ εὑρήματα Τραχώνων. Α. Οἱ ὀψιανοὶ τῆς Συλλογῆς Τραχώνων. In *Arch. Eph.* 1956, 73–105.

IV. THE CENTRAL PELOPONNESE AND THE WESTERN COASTS

1. Benton, S. 'Excavations in Ithaka, III; The Cave at Polis, II.' In *B.S.A.* 39 (1938–9), 1–51.
2. Benton, S. 'Hagios Nikolaos near Astakos in Akarnania.' In B.S.A. 42 (1947), 156–83.
3. Benton, S. 'The Ionian Islands.' In *B.S.A.* 32 (1932–1), 213–46.
4. Bulle, H. 'Ausgrabungen bei Aphiona auf Korfu.' In *Ath. Mitt.* 59 (1934), 147–96.
5. Childe, V. G. 'A Gold Vase of Early Helladic Type.' In *J.H.S.* 44 (1924), 163–5.
6. Dörpfeld, W. *Alt-Ithaka.* Munich, 1927.
7. Dörpfeld, W. *Alt-Olympia.* Berlin, 1935.
8. Evangelides, D. Ἠπειρωτικαὶ ἔρευναι, I. Ἡ ἀνασκαφὴ τῆς Δωδώνης, 1935. In Ἠπειρωτικὰ Χρονικά, 10 (1935), 192–212.
9. Heurtley, W. A. 'Excavations in Ithaca, II. The early Helladic settlement at Pelikata.' In *B.S.A.* 35 (1934–5), 1–44.
10. Holmberg, E. J. *The Swedish Excavations at Asea in Arcadia.* Lund, 1944.
11. Hope Simpson, R. 'Identifying a Mycenaean State.' In *B.S.A.* 52 (1957), 231–59.
12. Marinatos, S. Notice of excavations in the region of Pylus. In *Ergon*, 1954, 41–3.
13. Mastrokostas, E. 'The Wall of the Dymaeans.' In *Archaeology*, 15 (1962), 133–4; *Ergon*, 1962, 171–5.
14. McDonald, W. and Hope Simpson, R. 'Prehistoric Habitation in Southwestern Peloponnese.' In *A.J.A.* 65 (1961), 221–60.
15. Petrocheilou, A. Notice of excavations in the cave of Alepotrypa in Mani. In *B.C.H.* 86 (1962), 724.
16. Sperling, J. 'Exploration in Elis, 1939.' In *A.J.A.* 46 (1942), 77–89.
17. Taylour, Lord William. Notices of excavations at Ayios Stephanos in Laconia. In *B.C.H.* 84 (1960), 692–3; *Archaeological Reports*, 1959–60; 9, 1960–1, 32.
18. Valmin, M. N. *The Swedish Messenia Expedition.* Skrifter Utgivna av Kungl. Humanistiska Vetenskapssamfundet i Lund, XXVI. Lund, 1938.
19. Waterhouse, H. 'Prehistoric Laconia: A Note.' In *B.S.A.* 51 (1956), 168–71.
20. Waterhouse, H. and Hope Simpson, R. 'Prehistoric Laconia: Parts I, II.' In *B.S.A.* 55 (1960), 67–107; 56 (1961), 114–75.

V. THE ISLANDS OF THE AEGEAN

1. Akurgal, E. 'Bayrakli kazısı: ön rapore.' In *Ankara Universitesi Dilve Tarih-Cografya Fakültesi Dergisi*, 8 (1950), 1–97.
2. Atkinson, T. D. *et al. Excavations at Phylakopi in Melos (Soc. Prom. Hell. Stud., Suppl. Paper no.* 4). London, 1904.
3. Bernabò Brea, L. 'A Bronze Age House at Poliokhni (Lemnos).' In *P.P.S.* 21 (1955, volume in honour of V. G. Childe), 144–55.
4. Bernabò Brea, L. Notice of excavations at Poliochni in Lemnos. In *Boll. d'Arte*, 37 (1952), 339–48.
5. Bernabò Brea, L. 'Recenti scavi a Poliochni nell'isola di Lemnos (Relazione preliminare).' In *Boll. d'Arte*, 42 (1957), 193–217.
6. Blegen, C. W. *et al. Troy. Excavations conducted by the University of Cincinnati, 1932–1938*, I, II. Princeton, 1950, 1951.

7. Bossert, E.-M. 'Die gestempelten Verzierungen auf fruhbronzezeitlichen Gefässen der Ägäis.' In *Jahrb. des. d. arch. Inst.* 75 (1960), 1–16.

8. Bossert, E.-M. 'Zur Datierung der Gräber von Arkesine auf Amorgos.' In *Festschrift für Peter Goessler*, Tübinger Beiträge zur Vor- und Frühgeschichte (Stuttgart, 1954), 23–34.

9. v. Bothmer, D. *Ancient Art from New York Private Collections.* New York, 1961.

10. Caskey, J. L. 'Chalandriani in Syros.' In Sandler, L. F. (ed.), *Essays in memory of Karl Lehmann.* New York, 1964.

11. Dawkins, R. M. and Droop, J. P. 'The Excavations at Phylakopi in Melos.' In *B.S.A.* 17 (1910–11), 1–22.

12. Dümmler, F. 'Mittheilungen von den griechischen Inseln.' In *Ath. Mitt.* 11 (1886), 15–46.

13. Edgar, C. C. 'Prehistoric Tombs at Pelos.' In *B.S.A.* 3 (1896–7), 35–51.

14. Gallet de Santerre, H. *Délos primitive et archaïque.* Paris, 1958.

15. Hansen, H. D. 'Prehistoric Skyros.' In *Studies presented to D. M. Robinson*, 1 (St Louis, 1951), 54–63.

16. Heidenreich, R. 'Vorgeschichtliches in der Stadt Samos. Die Funde.' In *Ath. Mitt.* 60/1 (1935/6), 125–83.

17. Hogarth, D. G. 'Aegean Sepulchral Figurines.' In *Essays presented to Sir Arthur Evans* (Oxford, 1927), 55–62.

18. Hood, M. S. F. Notices of excavations at Emporio in Chios. In *J.H.S.* 73 (1953), 124; 74 (1954), 162–3; *Archaeological Reports*, 1954, 20.

19. Lamb, W. *Excavations at Thermi in Lesbos.* Cambridge, 1936.

20. Levi, D. 'Le due prime campagne di scavo a Iasos (1960–1961).' In *Ann. della R. Scuola archeol. di Atene*, 39–40 (1961–1962), 505–71 (La necropoli preistorica, 555–71).

21. Lloyd, S. 'The Early Settlement of Anatolia.' In *The Dawn of Civilization* (London, 1961), 161–94.

22. Milojčić, V. *Samos.* 1, *Die prähistorische Siedlung unter dem Heraion. Grabung 1953 und 1955.* Bonn, 1961.

23. Plassart, A. *Les sanctuaires et les cultes du Mont Cynthe (Expl. archéologique de Délos*, XI). Paris, 1928.

24. Rubensohn, O. 'Delische Kultstätten.' In *Arch. Anz.* 1931, 360–86.

25. Rubensohn, O. 'Die prähistorischen und frühgeschichtlichen Funde auf dem Burghügel von Paros.' In *Ath. Mitt.* 42 (1917), 1–98.

26. Schmidt, H. *Heinrich Schliemann's Sammlung trojanischer Altertümer.* Berlin, 1902.

27. Scholes, K. 'The Cyclades in the Later Bronze Age: a Synopsis.' In *B.S.A.* 51 (1956), 9–40.

28. Tsountas, C. Κυκλαδικά, I, II. In *Arch. Eph.* 1898, 137–212; 1899, 73–134.

29. Varoucha, E. Κυκλαδικοὶ τάφοι τῆς Πάρου. In *Arch. Eph.* 1925–6, 98–114.

30. Wolters, P. 'Marmorkopf aus Amorgos.' In *Ath. Mitt.* 16 (1891), 46–58.

31. Zervos, C. *L'art des Cyclades du début à la fin de l'âge du bronze, 2500–1100 avant notre ère.* Paris, 1957.

32. Zschietzschmann, W. 'Kykladenpfannen.' In *Arch. Anz.* 1935, 652–68.

VI. CRETE

1. École française d'Athènes. *Fouilles exécutées à Mallia*: Palais (1925–6), Paris 1936; Nécropoles (1921–33), Paris 1945; Maisons (1921–48), Paris 1953; Maisons (1948–54), Paris 1959. (*Études crétoises*, IV, VII, IX, XI.)

2. Evans, A. J. *The Palace of Minos at Knossos*, I–IV. London, 1921–35.
3. Grace, V. R. 'A Cypriote Tomb and Minoan Evidence for its Date.' In *A.J.A.* 44 (1940), 10–52.
4. Hall, E. H. 'Early Painted Pottery from Gournia, Crete.' In *Trans. Dept. of Archaeol., Univ. of Pennsylvania*, I (1905).
5. Hawes, H. B. *Gournia*. Philadelphia, 1908.
6. Hutchinson, R. W. *Prehistoric Crete*. Harmondsworth, 1962.
7. Karo, G. 'Kreta in vorgriechischer und griechisch-römischer Zeit.' In *P.W.* 11, 2, cols. 1743–1801.
8. Kenna, V. E. G. *Cretan Seals, with a Catalogue of the Minoan Gems in the Ashmolean Museum*. Oxford, 1960.
9. Levi, D. 'L'archivio di cretule a Festos.' In *Ann. della R. Scuola archeol. di Atene*, 35–6 (1957–8), 7–192.
10. Levi, D. 'One of the Richest Finds of Minoan Treasures in Crete.' In *Ill. Ldn News*, 19 Jan. 1952, 106–8.
11. Levi, D. 'Per una nuova classificazione della civiltà Minoica.' In *La Parola del Passato*, 15 (1960), 81–121.
12. Mylonas, G. E. 'Athens and Minoan Crete.' In *Athenian Studies Presented to William Scott Ferguson (Harv. Stud. Class. Phil.* suppl. 1). Cambridge, Mass. 1940, 11–36.
13. Pendlebury, J. D. S. *The Archaeology of Crete*. London, 1939.
14. Platon, N. 'La chronologie minoenne.' In §VI, 21 (*infra*), 509–12.
15. Seager, R. B. 'Excavations at Vasiliki, 1904.' In *Trans. Dept. of Archaeol., Univ. of Pennsylvania*, I (1905), 207–20.
16. Seager, R. B. 'Report of Excavations at Vasiliki, Crete, in 1906.' In *Trans. Free Museum of Science and Art, Univ. of Pennsylvania*, 2 (1907), 111–32.
17. Seager, R. B. *Explorations in the Island of Mochlos*. Boston and New York, 1912.
18. Xanthoudides, S. Μέγας πρωτομινωϊκὸς τάφος Πύργου. In *Arch. Delt.* 4 (1918), 136–70.
19. Xanthoudides, S. *The Vaulted Tombs of Mesara*. London, 1924.
20. Xenaki-Sakellariou, A. *Les cachets minoens de la collection Giamalakis (École française d'Athènes, Études crétoises*, X). Paris, 1958.
21. Zervos, C. *L'art de la Crète néolithique et minoenne*. Paris, 1956.

A. ADDENDA

1. Bernabò-Brea, L. *Poliochni, città preistorica nell'isola di Lemnos*. Rome, 1964.
2. Caskey, J. L. 'Preliminary reports on excavations in Ceos.' In *Hesperia*, 31 (1962), 263–83; 33 (1964), 314–35; 35 (1966), 363–76.
3. Caskey, J. L. 'Houses of the Fourth Settlement at Lerna.' In *Charisterion eis Anastasion K. Orlandon*, 3, 144–52. Athens, 1966.
4. Ehrich, R. W. (ed.). *Chronologies in Old World Archaeology*. Chicago, 1965.
5. Fischer-Bossert, E.-M. 'Kastri auf Syros.' In *Arch. Delt.* 22 (1967), 53–76.
6. McDonald, W. and Hope Simpson, R. 'Further Exploration in south-western Peloponnese.' In *A.J.A.* 68 (1964), 229–45.
7. Mellaart, J. 'The End of the Early Bronze Age in Anatolia and the Aegean.' In *A.J.A.* 62 (1958), 9–33.
8. Milojčić, V., Boessneck, J. and Hopf, M. *Die deutschen Ausgrabungen auf der Argissa-Magula in Thessalien*, 1: *Das präkeramische Neolithikum sowie die Tier- und Pflanzreste*. Bonn, 1966.
9. Mylonas, G. E. 'Eleusis in the Bronze Age.' In *A.J.A.* 36 (1932), 104–17.

10. Popham, M. R. and Sackett, L. H. (eds.). *Excavations at Lefkandi, Euboea, 1964–66.* London, 1968.
11. Renfrew, C. 'Cycladic Metallurgy and the Aegean Bronze Age.' In *A.J.A.* 71 (1967), 1–20.
12. Sackett, L. H. and others. 'Prehistoric Euboea.' In *B.S.A.* 61 (1966), 33–112.
13. Vermeule, E. *Greece in the Bronze Age.* Chicago, 1964.

CHAPTER XXVI(*b*)

G. GENERAL

1. Catling, H. W. 'Patterns of settlement in Bronze Age Cyprus.' In *Op. Anth.* 4 (1963), 129–69.
2. Dikaios, P. *A Guide to the Cyprus Museum*, 3rd ed. Nicosia, 1961.
3. Karageorghis, V. *Treasures in the Cyprus Museum.* Nicosia, 1962.
4. Wideson, R. *Cyprus in Pictures.* London, 1955.

VIII. THE IDENTITY OF THE EARLIEST BRONZE AGE SETTLERS

1. Bossert, H. *Alt-Syrien.* Tübingen, 1951.
2. Dikaios, P. 'Les cultes préhistoriques dans l'île de Chypre.' In *Syria*, 13 (1932), 345–54.
3. Dikaios, P. 'The Excavations at Vounous-Bellapais in Cyprus, 1931–32.' In *Archaeologia*, 88 (1938), 1–174.
4. Dikaios, P. 'The Stone Age.' In *The Swedish Cyprus Expedition IV*, part Ia (Lund, 1962), 1–204.
5. Dussaud, R. 'Culte funéraire et culte chthonien à Chypre à l'âge du bronze.' In *Syria*, 13 (1932), 223–6.
6. Gjerstad, E. *Studies on Prehistoric Cyprus.* Uppsala, 1926.
7. Grace, V. 'A Cypriote Tomb and Minoan Evidence for its Date.' In *A.J.A.* 44 (1940), 10–52.
8. Karageorghis, V. 'Finds from Early Cypriot Cemeteries.' In *R.D.A.C.* 1940–8 (Nicosia, 1958), 115–52.
9. Myres, J. L. 'Excavations in Cyprus in 1894.' In *J.H.S.* 17 (1897), 134–73.
10. Schaeffer, C. F. A. *Stratigraphie Comparée et Chronologie de l'Asie Occidentale.* Oxford, 1948.
11. Schaeffer, C. F. A. 'Chronologie et origine de la civilisation du Bronze Ancien de Chypre.' In *R.A.* 33 (1949), 129–49.
12. Stewart, J. R. 'Decorated Tomb Façades, Cyprus.' In *Antiquity*, 13 (1939), 461–3.
13. Stewart, J. R. 'Toggle pins in Cyprus.' In *Antiquity*, 14 (1940), 204–9.
14. Stewart, E. and Stewart, J. R. *Vounous, 1937–8.* Lund, 1950.
15. Stewart, J. R. 'The Early Cypriote Bronze Age.' In *The Swedish Cyprus Expedition*, IV, part Ia (Lund, 1962), 205–401.
16. Weinberg, S. S. 'Exploring the Early Bronze Age in Cyprus.' In *Archaeology*, IX (1956), 112–21.
17. Wright, G. E. 'The Syro-palestinian Jar from Vounous, Cyprus.' In *P.E.Q.* (1940), pp. 154–7.

CHAPTER XXVII

G. GENERAL

1. Bosch-Gimpera, P. *Les indo-européens: problèmes archéologiques.* Paris, 1961. (Translation of *El problema indoeuropeo.* Mexico City, 1960.)
2. Childe, V. G. *The Aryans.* London, 1926.
3. Crossland, R. A. 'Indo-European origins: the linguistic evidence.' In *Past and Present*, 12 (1957), 16–45; 13 (1958), 88.
4. Devoto, G. *Origini indeuropee.* Florence, 1961.
5. Gimbutas, M. 'The Indo-Europeans: archaeological problems.' In *American Anthropologist*, 65 (1963), 815 ff.
6. Hencken, H. 'Indo-European languages and archaeology.' In *American Anthropologist*, 57 (1955); also *American Anthropological Association Memoir* 84.
7. Krahe, H. *Sprache und Vorzeit.* Heidelberg, 1954.
8. Thieme, P. *Die Heimat der indogermanischen Gemeinsprache. Abhandlungen der geistes- und sozialwissenschaftlichen Klasse*, 11. *Akademie der Wissenschaften und der Literatur in Mainz.* Wiesbaden, 1953.

I. LINGUISTIC COMPARISON

1. Benveniste, E. 'Noms d'animaux en indo-européen.' In *Bull. de la Soc. de Linguistique de Paris*, 45 (1949), 74 ff.
2. Collinder, B. *Fenno-Ugric Vocabulary.* Stockholm, 1955.
3. Couvreur, W. Review of: A. Cuny, *Invitation à l'étude comparative des langues i.-e. et chamito-sémitiques.* In *Bi. Or.* 3 (1946), 77 ff.
4. Jacobsohn, H. *Arier und Ugrofinnen.* Göttingen, 1922.
5. Kammenhuber, A. 'Zur Stellung des Hethitisch-Luvischen innerhalb der indogermanischen Gemeinsprache.' In *Z. f. vergleich. Sprachforschung*, 77 (1961), 31 ff.
6. Krahe, H. *Sprachverwandtschaft im alten Europa.* Heidelberg, 1931.
7. Kronasser, H. 'Zur Verwandtschaft zwischen Finnisch-Ugrisch und Indogermanisch.' In *Frühgeschichte und Sprachwissenschaft*, 1 (ed. von Brandenstein) (Vienna, 1948), 162 ff.
8. Lees, R. B. 'The basis of glottochronology.' In *Language*, 29 (1953), 113 ff.
9. Meillet, A. 'Essai de chronologie des langues indo-européennes.' In *Bull. de la Soc. de Linguistique de Paris*, 32 (1931), 1 ff.
10. Meillet, A. *Introduction à l'étude comparative des langues indo-européennes*, 8th ed. Paris, 1937 (reprinted by University of Alabama, 1965).
11. Pedersen, H. 'Le groupement des dialectes indo-européens.' In *Kgl. Dan. Vid. Selsk., histo.-fil. Medd.* 11. Copenhagen, 1925.
12. Pedersen, H. *Linguistic Science in the Nineteenth Century.* Cambridge, Mass., 1931.
13. Polomé, E. 'Considérations sur la valeur des données lexicostatistiques.' In *Communications et Rapports du 1er Congrès International de Dialectologie Générale* (Louvain, 1964), 29 ff.
14. Porzig, W. *Die Gliederung des indogermanischen Sprachgebiets.* Heidelberg, 1954.
15. Swadesh, M. 'Towards greater accuracy in lexicostatistic dating.' In *International Journal of American Linguistics*, 21 (1955), 121 ff.
16. Vendryes, J. 'Les correspondances de vocabulaire entre l'indo-iranien et l'italo-celtique.' In *Mémoires de la Soc. de Linguistique de Paris*, 20 (1918), 265 ff.

II. ANATOLIA

1. Bilgiç, E. 'Die Ortsnamen der "kappadokischen" Urkunden in Rahmen der alten Sprachen Anatoliens.' In *Arch. f. Orient.* 15 (1951), 1ff.
2. Bilgiç, E. 'Die einheimischen Appellativa der kappadokischen Texte und ihre Bedeutung für die anatolischen Sprachen.' In *Ankara Universitesi Dil ve Tarih-Coğrafya Fakultesi Yayınları*, no. 96. Ankara, 1954.
3. Bittel, K. *Grundzüge der Vor- und Frühgeschichte Kleinasiens*, 2nd ed. Tübingen, 1950.
4. Bittel, K., Herre, W., Otten, H., Rohrs, M. and Schaeuble, J. *Die hethitischen Grabfunde von Osmankayası. Wissenschaftliche Veröffentlichungen der Deutschen Orient-Gesellschaft*, 71 (1958), Berlin.
5. Blegen, C. W. *Troy and the Trojans*. London, 1963.
6. Bossert, H. T. *Asia*. Istanbul, 1946.
7. Bossert, H. T. *Ein hethitisches Königssiegel*. Istanbul, 1944.
8. Diakonov, I. M. and G. V. Tsereteli. *Peredneaziatskiy Sbornik: Voprosy Khettologii i Khurritologii*. Moscow, 1961.
9. Forrer, E. 'Die Inschriften und Sprachen des Hatti-Reiches.' In *Z.D.M.G.* 76 (1922), 174 ff.
10. Friedrich, J. *Hethitisch und 'Kleinasiatische' Sprachen*. Berlin, 1931.
11. Friedrich, J. *Hethitisches Elementarbuch*, I (2nd ed.), II (1st ed.). Heidelberg, 1960, 1946.
12. Friedrich, J. *Die hethitischen Gesetze*. Leiden, 1959.
13. Gamkrelidze, T. V. 'The Akkado-Hittite syllabary and the problem of the origin of the Hittite script.' In *Arch. Orient.* 29 (1961), 406 ff.
14. Gamkrelidze, T. V. '"Anatolian languages" and the problem of Indo-European migration into Asia Minor.' In *Preliminary Reports of the VIIth International Congress of Anthropological and Ethnological Sciences*. Moscow, 1964.
15. Goetze, A. 'The theophorous elements of the Anatolian proper names from Cappadocia.' In *Language*, 29 (1953), 263 ff.
16. Goetze, A. 'The cultures of early Anatolia.' In *Proc. Amer. Philos. Soc.* 97 (1953), 214 ff.
17. Goetze, A. 'The linguistic continuity of Anatolia as shown by its proper names.' In *J.C.S.* 8 (1954), 74 ff.
18. Goetze, A. 'Some groups of ancient Anatolian proper names.' In *Language*, 30 (1954), 349 ff.
19. Goetze, A. *Kleinasien*, 2nd ed. Munich, 1957.
20. Goetze, A. 'Suffixes in "Kanishite" proper names.' In *R.H.A.* 66 (1960), 45 ff.
21. Gurney, O. R. 'Mita of Pahhuwa.' In *Liverpool Annals of Arch. and Anthr.* 28 (1948), 32 ff.
22. Gurney, O. R. *The Hittites*, 2nd ed. London, 1954.
23. Gusmani, R. *Lydisches Wörterbuch*. Heidelberg, 1964.
24. Güterbock, H. G. 'Toward a definition of the term Hittite.' In *Oriens*, 10 (1957), 233 ff.
25. Güterbock, H. G. 'A view of Hittite literature.' In *J.A.O.S.* 84 (1964), 107 ff.
26. Hauschild, R. *Die indogermanischen Völker und Sprachen Kleinasiens*. Berlin, 1964.
27. Jokl, N. 'Phryger.' In M. Ebert, *Reallexikon der Vorgeschichte*, 10 (1928), 141 ff.
28. Kammenhuber, A. 'Die hethitische Geschichtsschreibung'. In *Saeculum*, 9 (1958), 136 ff.

29. Kammenhuber, A. 'Zur hethitisch-luvischen Sprachgruppe.' In *Z. f. vergleich. Sprachforschung*, 76 (1960), 1 ff.
30. Kammenhuber, A. *Hippologia Hethitica*. Wiesbaden, 1961.
31. Kronasser, H. *Vergleichende Laut- und Formenlehre des Hethitischen*. Heidelberg, 1956.
32. Landsberger, B. 'Assyrische Konigsliste und "dunkles Zeitalter"'; vi: Exkurs 1.' In *J.C.S.* 8 (1954), 47 ff., 120 ff.
33. Laroche, E. 'Études "proto-hittites".' In *R.A.* 41 (1948), 187 ff.
34. Laroche, E. *Recueil d'onomastique hittite*. Paris, 1952.
35. Laroche, E. 'Comparaison du louvite et du lycien.' In *Bull. de la Soc. de Linguistique de Paris*, 53 (1958), 159 ff., and 55 (1960), 155 ff.
36. Laroche, E. *Dictionnaire de la langue louvite*. Paris, 1959.
37. Laroche, E. *Les hiéroglyphes hittites, 1: l'écriture*. Paris, 1960.
38. Meriggi, P. 'Der Indogermanismus des Lykischen.' In H. Arntz, *Germanen und Indogermanen: Festschrift H. Hirt*, ii. Heidelberg, 1936, 257 ff.
39. Meriggi, P. 'Der indogermanische Charakter des Lydischen.' *Ibid.* 283 ff.
40. Otten, H. 'Zum Palaischen.' In *Z.A.* 48 (1944), 119 ff.
41. Otten, H. 'Zu den Anfangen des hethitischen Geschichte'. In *M.D.O.G.* 83 (1951), 33 ff.
42. Otten, H. *Zur grammatikalischen und lexikalischen Bestimmung des Luvischen*. Berlin, 1953.
43. Otten, H. 'Vorläufiger Bericht über die Ausgrabungen in Boğazköy im Jahre 1952: Die inschriftlichen Funde.' In *M.D.O.G.* 86 (1953), 59 ff.
44. Otten, H. *Hethitische Totenrituale*. Berlin, 1958.
45. Pedersen, H. 'Lykisch und Hittitisch.' *Kgl. Dan. Vid. Selsk., hist.-fil. Medd.* 30. Copenhagen, 1945.
46. Sommer, F. *Hethiter und Hethitisch*. Stuttgart, 1947.
47. Sommer, F. and Falkenstein, A. *Die hethitisch-akkadische Bilingue des Hattušili* I. Munich, 1938.
48. Sturtevant, E. H. and Bechtel, G. *Hittite Chrestomathy*. Baltimore, 1935.
49. Sturtevant, E. H. and Hahn, E. A. *A Comparative Grammar of the Hittite Language*, 1. New Haven, 1951.
50. Tritsch, F. J. 'Lycian, Luwian and Hittite.' In *Arch. Orient.* 18 (*Symbolae B. Hrozný* III), 1950, 494 ff.
51. Walser, G. and others. 'Neuere Hethiterforschung': *Historia, Einzelschrift* 7, 1964.
52. Weidner, E. F. *Politische Dokumente aus Kleinasien*, 1 (*Bo. Stu.* 8, ed. O. Weber). Leipzig, 1923.

III. IRAN, MESOPOTAMIA AND INDIA

1. Balkan, K. *Kassitenstudien*, 1: *Die Sprache der Kassiten*. New Haven, Connecticut, 1954.
2. Brandenstein, W. von. 'Die alten Inder in Vorderasien und die Chronologie des Rigweda.' In *Frühgeschichte und Sprachwissenschaft*, 1 (ed. von Brandenstein) (Vienna, 1948), 134 ff.
3. Ghirshman, R. *Iran*. London, 1954.
4. Gordon, D. H. 'The chronology of the third cultural period at Tepe Hissar.' In *Iraq*, 13 (1951), 40 ff.
5. Gordon, D. H. *The Prehistoric Background of Indian Culture*, 2nd ed. Bombay, 1960.
6. Hauschild, R. *Über die frühesten Arier im alten Orient*. Berlin, 1962.

7. Keith, A. B. 'The age of the Rigveda.' In *Cambridge History of India*, 1 (ed. E. J. Rapson), 1922.
8. Mellink, M. J. *Dark Ages and Nomads: Studies in Iranian and Anatolian Archaeology* (*Publ. of the Netherlands Hist. and Arch. Inst. in Istanbul*, 18). Istanbul, 1964.
9. Meyer, E. 'Die ältesten datierten Zeugnisse der iranischen Sprache und der zoroastrichen Religion.' In *Z. f. vergleich. Sprachforschung*, 42 (1909), 1 ff.
10. O'Callaghan, R. T. and Dumont, P. E. *Aram Naharaim: a Contribution to the History of Upper Mesopotamia in the Second Millennium B.C.* Rome, 1948.
11. Piggott, S. *Prehistoric India*. London, 1950.
12. Pritchard, J. B. and others. *Ancient Near Eastern Texts to illustrate the Old Testament*. Princeton, 1950.
13. Schmökel, H. 'Die Kassiten.' In B. Spuler, *Handbuch der Orientalistik*, II, 3 (Leiden, 1957), 171 ff.
14. Thieme, P. 'The "Aryan" gods of the Mitanni treaties.' In *J.A.O.S.* 80 (1960), 301 ff.

IV. GREECE, THE AEGEAN REGION AND THE BALKANS

1. Childe, V. G. 'Anatolia and Thrace.' In *A. St.* 6 (1956), 45 ff.
2. Crossland, R. A. 'The supposed Anatolian origin of the place-name formants in -ss- and -tt-.' In *Atti del VII Congr. Int. di Scienze Onomastiche*, 1 (Florence, 1961), 375 f.
3. Georgiev, V. *Vorgriechische Sprachwissenschaft* I, II. Sofia, 1941, 1945.
4. Georgiev, V. *Contribution à l'étude de la toponymie grecque*. Sofia, 1948.
5. Georgiev, V. 'La toponymie ancienne de la péninsule balkanique et la thèse méditerranéenne.' In *Linguistique balkanique*, 3 (1961), 5 ff.
6. Haley, J. B. and Blegen, C. W. 'The coming of the Greeks.' In *A.J.A.* 32 (1928), 141 ff.
7. Houwink ten Cate, P. H. J. *The Luwian Population Groups of Lycia and Cilicia Aspera during the Hellenistic Period*. Leiden, 1961.
8. Jokl, N. 'Thraker.' In Ebert, M. *Reallexikon der Vorgeschichte*, 13 (1929), 277 ff.
9. Lejeune, M. 'Linguistique préhellénique.' In *Rev. ét. anc.* 49 (1947), 25 ff.
10. Mellaart, J. 'The end of the Early Bronze Age in Anatolia and the Aegean.' In *A.J.A.* 62 (1958), 9 ff.
11. Mylonas, G. E. 'The Luvian invasions of Greece.' In *Hesperia*, 31 (1962), 284 ff.
12. Neumann, G. *Untersuchungen zum Weiterleben hethitischen und luwischen Sprachgutes in hellenistischer und römischer Zeit*. Wiesbaden, 1961.
13. Palmer, L. R. 'Luvian and Linear A.' In *Trans. Philol. Soc.* 1958, 75 ff.
14. Rodden, R. J. 'Recent discoveries from prehistoric Macedonia.' In *Balkan Studies*, 5 (1964), 109 ff.

V. OTHER REGIONS

1. Bailey, H. W. 'Recent work in "Tokharian".' In *Trans. Philol. Soc.* 1947, 126 ff.
2. Berciu, D. 'Quelques données préliminaires concernant la civilisation de Cernavoda.' In *Slovenská Archeológia*, 12 (1964), 269 ff.
3. Böhm J. and others. *L'Europe à la fin de l'âge de la pierre*. Prague, 1961.
4. Brjussow, A. J. *Geschichte der neolithischen Stämme im europäischen Teil des UdSSR*. Berlin, 1957.
5. Childe, V. G. *Prehistoric Migrations in Europe*. Oslo, 1950.

6. Childe, V. G. *The Dawn of European Civilization*, 6th ed. London, 1957.
7. Gimbutas, M. 'Culture change in Europe at the start of the second millennium B.C.' In *Selected Papers of the Vth Int. Congr. of Anthropological and Ethnological Sciences* (Philadelphia, 1956), 540 ff.
8. Gimbutas, M. *The Prehistory of Eastern Europe*. Cambridge, Mass., 1956.
9. Häusler, A. 'Ockergrabkultur und Schnurkeramik.' In *Jahresschrift für mitteldeutsche Vorgeschichte*, 47 (1963), 157 ff.
10. Hawkes, C. F. C. *The Prehistoric Foundations of Europe to the Mycenaean Age.* London, 1940.
11. Kilian, L. 'Schnurkeramik und Ockergrabkultur.' In *Suomen Muinaismuistoyhdistyksen Aikakauskirja/Finska Fornminnesföreningens Tidskrift*, 59 (1958), 3 ff.
12. Köszegi, F. 'Contribution à la question de l'origine des tombes à ocre en Hongrie.' In *Archaeologiai Ertesitö*, 89 (1962), 15 ff.
13. Krause, W. 'Tocharisch.' In B. Spuler, *Handbuch der Orientalistik*, iv, 3. Leiden, 1955.
14. Lane, G. S. 'The present state of Tocharian studies.' In *Proc. of the VIIIth Int. Congr. of Linguists* (Oslo, 1958), 252 ff.
15. Neustupný, E. and Neustupný, J. N. *Czechoslovakia before the Slavs*. London, 1961.
16. Palmer, L. R. *The Latin Language*. London, 1954.
17. Pulgram, E. *The Tongues of Italy*. Cambridge, Mass., 1958.
18. Struve, K. W. *Die Einzelgrabkultur in Schleswig-Holstein und ihre kontinentalen Beziehungen*. Neumünster, 1955.
19. Van der Waals, J. D. *Prehistoric Disc Wheels in the Netherlands*. Groningen, 1964.

VI. INDO-EUROPEAN SOCIETY AND CIVILIZATION

1. Falkenstein, A. 'Sumerische religiöse Texte: 2. Ein Šulgi-Lied.' In *Z.A.* 50 (N.F. 1b, 1946), 61 ff.
2. Ivanov, V. V. 'Sotsial'naya organizatsiya indoevropeyskikh plemen po lingvisticheskim dannym.' In *Vestnik Istorii Mirovoy Kul'tury*, 21 (1957), 43 ff.
3. Palmer, L. R. 'Mycenaean Greek texts from Pylos.' In *Trans. Philol. Soc.* (1954), 18 ff.
4. Powell, T. G. E. 'Some implications of chariotry.' In *Culture and environment: Essays in Honour of Sir Cyril Fox* (ed. I. L. Foster and L. Alcock) (London, 1963), 153 ff.
5. Salonen, A. *Die Landfahrzeuge des alten Mesopotamien*. Helsinki, 1951.
6. Salonen, A. *Hippologica Accadica*. Helsinki, 1955.

A. ADDENDA

1. Bosch-Gimpera, P. 'El neolítico y la discusión del problema indoeuropeo.' In *Anales de Antropología*, 3 (Mexico City, 1966), 119 ff.
2. Friedrich, P. 'Proto-Indo-European kinship.' In *Ethnology*, 5 (1966), 1 ff.
3. Georgiev, V. I. *Introduzione alla storia delle lingue indeuropee*. Rome, 1966. (Section 'G'.)
4. Kammenhuber, A. *Die Arier im Vorderen Orient*. Heidelberg, 1968. (Section III.)
5. Mayrhofer, M. *Die Indo-Arier im alten Vorderasien* (Wiesbaden, 1966).
6. Scherer, A. 'Indogermanische Altertumskunde (seit 1956).' In *Kratylos*, 10 (1965), 1 ff.

CHRONOLOGICAL TABLES

(A) EGYPT

B.C.

Before 12000   Lower and Middle Palaeolithic Periods
Upper Palaeolithic i
(Nomadic food-gatherers)

c. 12000   Upper Palaeolithic ii
(Camps of fisherfolk in the Kom Ombo Basin)

c. 8000   Final Palaeolithic or Mesolithic Period
(Introduction of bow and arrow)

c. 4500   Neolithic-Cuprolithic Period
(Tāsa-Badāri and Naqāda i Cultures)

c. 3500   Naqāda ii, Faiyūm B and Ma'ādi Cultures

KINGS FROM THE FIRST TO THE TWELFTH DYNASTIES
EARLY DYNASTIC PERIOD

First Dynasty: c. 3100–2890 B.C.

Horus Name	Personal Name	Years of Reign
Narmer	Men (Menes)	
Aha	Iti (Athothis)	
Djer	Iti (Athothis)	47
Djet	Iterty	
Den	Khasty	55–60
Anedjib	Merpebia (Miebis)	7
Semerkhet	Irynetjer	8
Qaa	Qaa	25

Second Dynasty: c. 2890–2686 B.C.

Horus Name	Personal Name	Years of Reign
Hetepsekhemwy	Hetep	
Reneb	Nubnefer	
Nynetjer	Nynetjer	45–47
	Weneg (Wadjnes)	19
	Sened (Sethenes)	
Peribsen*	Peribsen	
	Aka (?)	
	Neferkasokar (?)	8
Khasekhem	('lacuna' in lists)	21 (?)
Khasekhemwy†	Khasekhemwy	17

    * Seth name.   † Horus and Seth name.

OLD KINGDOM

Third Dynasty: c. 2686–2613 B.C.

Horus Name	Personal Name	Years of Reign
Sanakhte	Nebka	19
Netjerykhet	Djoser	19
Sekhemkhet	Djoser Teti	6
Khaba	('lacuna' in lists)	6
......	Huni (Nysuteh?)	24

Fourth Dynasty: c. 2613–2498 B.C.

Sneferu	24 years	Baufre(?)		
Cheops	23	Mycerinus	28(?)	
Redjedef	8	Shepseskaf	4	
Chephren	25(?)	Dedefptah? ('Thamphthis')	2	

Fifth Dynasty: c. 2494–2345 B.C.

Userkaf	7 years	Nyuserre	[3]1
Sahure	14	Menkauhor Akauhor	8
Neferirkare Kakai	10	Djedkare Isesi	39
Shepseskare Isi	7	Unas	30
Neferefre	7(?)		

Sixth Dynasty: c. 2345–2181 B.C.

Teti	12 years	Neferkare Phiops II	94(?)
Userkare	1(?)	Merenre Antyemsaf II	1
Meryre Phio(p)s I	49	Netjerykare	
Merenre Antyemsaf I (9)	14	Menkare (?) Nitocris	2(?)

FIRST INTERMEDIATE PERIOD

Seventh Dynasty: c. 2181–2173 B.C.

Neferkare, 'the Younger'	Neferkamin
Neferkare Neby	Nykare
Djedkare Shemay	Neferkare Tereru
Neferkare Khendu	Neferkahor
Meryenhor	

Eighth Dynasty: 2173–2160 B.C.

Wadjkare Pepysonbe (Horus Kha-[bau?])	4 +x years
Neferkamin Anu	2 years 1 month
Kakare Ibi	4 years 2 months
Neferkare	2 years 1 month
Neferkauhor Kapuibi (Horus Netjerybau)	1 year ½ month
Neferirkare (Horus Demedjibtowy)	

Ninth Dynasty: c. 2160–2130 B.C.

Meryibre Achthoes I	......	......
......	Mery-...	......
Neferkare	Shed-...	......
Nebkaure Achthoes II	H-....	User(?)...
Setut		

Tenth Dynasty: c. 2130–2040 B.C.

Meryhathor(?)	Merykare
Neferkare	...... *x* months
Wahkare Achthoes III	

MIDDLE KINGDOM

Eleventh Dynasty: c. 2133–1991 B.C.

Horus Name	Throne and Personal Names	Date B.C.
Tep(y)a	Mentuhotpe(-a) I ⎫	2133–2118
Sehertowy	Inyotef I ⎭	
Wahankh	Inyotef II	2117–2069
Nakhtnebtepnefer	Inyotef III	2068–2061
Sankhibtowy ⎫		
Netjeryhedjet ⎬	Nebhepetre Mentuhotpe II	2060–2010
Smatowy ⎭		
Sankhtowyef	Sankhkare Mentuhotpe III	2009–1998
Nebtowy	Nebtowyre Mentuhotpe IV ⎫	1997–1991
	The God's Father Sesostris ⎭	

Twelfth Dynasty: 1991–1786 B.C.

	B.C.
Sehetepibre Ammenemes I	1991–1962
Kheperkare Sesostris I (10)	1971–1928
Nubkaure Ammenemes II (2)	1929–1895
Khakheperre Sesostris II (3)	1897–1878
Khakaure Sesostris III	1878–1843
Nymare Ammenemes III	1842–1797
Makherure Ammenemes IV	1798–1790
Sobkkare Sobkneferu	1789–1786

(Figures in brackets indicate the lengths of co-regencies.)

(B) WESTERN ASIA

PREHISTORY

B.C.

c. 10000–4300	See Table 6 in *C.A.H.* i³, Part 1, p. 253.
4300–3500	'Ubaid Period (Eridu, Qal'at Ḥajji Muḥammad and 'Ubaid pottery)
3500–3100	Uruk Period (Uruk 12–5 levels)

PROTOHISTORIC PERIOD

3100–2700	Uruk 4, Jamdat Naṣr (= Uruk 3) and Early Dynastic I (First written documents in Uruk 4*b*)

SYNCHRONISTIC LISTS OF KINGS

(See following pages)

DATE	SOUTH			NORTH
	LAGASH	UR	URUK	KISH
2700				Enmebaragisi
			Gilgamesh (// Agga) Urlugal I (son) (30)	Agga (son) (// Gilgamesh)
			Utulkalamma (son) (15) La-ba-'-[š]um (9)	
2600	Enkhegal Lugalshagengur (// Mesilim)	Meskalamdug Akalamdug	En-nun-dàra-an-na (8) MES(?)-HÉ (36 ?)	
		Mesannipada A'annipada (son) Meskiagnunna (brother)	Melamanna (6) Lugal-ki-tùn (?) (36?)	
2550				Su₈-[…]
	Ur-Nanshe	Ananne (= A'annipada?)		Dadasig
	Akurgal (son)			
				Mamagalla
		Meskiag-Nanna (son) (36?)		
	Eannatum (son) (// Galbum?) (// Zuzu)	Elulu (25)	En-PIRIG(?)-du-an-na Ur-lugal II Ar-ga-an-de-a (7) Enshakushanna	Galbum (son) (// Eannatum?)
	Enannatum I (brother)	Balulu (36?)		TÚG-e Mennunna
2450	Entemena (son) (// Lugalkinishedudu) Enannatum II (son) Enetarzi Lugalanda (7) 2384–2378	Second Dynasty of Ur, 4 kings, names lost	Lugalkinishedudu Lugalkisalsi (son) Lugal-TAR (perhaps identical with Lugaltarsi, titular king of Kish)	I-bí-[Ištar] (?)⎫ perhaps En-bi-Ištar ⎭ same king Lugalmu Ku-Baba (// Puzur-Nirakh) Puzur-Sin (son) (25) Ur-Zababa
	Urukagina (8?) 2378–2371			
2370			Lugalzaggisi of Umma (25) (c. 2371–2347)	Simudar (30?) Uṣi-watar (7?)
		Kaku (// Rimush)		Ishtar-muti (11?)
				Ishme-Shamash (11?)
				Nannia (7?)
2230	Lugalushumgal	Elili II	Urnigin	
	Puzur-Mama *Some or all of the following:* Ur-Utu, Ur-Mama, Lu-Baba, Lugula, Kakug		Urgigir (son) (Lugalmelam?) (son?) Kuda	
	Ur-Baba (14+x)		Puzur-ili	
	Gudea (16+x) (son-in-law of Ur-Baba)		Urutu	
2120	Ur-Ningirsu (5+x) (son) Ugme (2+x) (son) Urgar (son-in-law of Ur-Baba)	*Third Dynasty of Ur:*	Utu-khegal (8) 2120–2114 (after defeat of Gutium)	
	Nammakhni (son-in-law of Ur-Baba) (// Ur-Nammu)	Ur-Nammu (18) 2113–2096) Shulgi (48) 2095–2048 Amar-Sin (9) 2047–2039 Shu-Sin (9) 2038–2030 (// Girnamme)		
2000		Ibbi-Sin (24) 2029–2006		

North			ELAMITE COUNTRIES: I. AWAN II. SIMASHKI	DATE
I. AKSHAK, II. AKKAD	MARI	VARIA		
		Early titular kings of Kish: (before *c.* 2600) Lugal-e-[x]-gal, king of X (perhaps X = Uruk)		2700
		Urzaged, king of Ki-dingir		
		Mesilim (// Lugalshagengur)		2600
		Kings of Khamazi and of Adab, probably titular kings of Kish:	I. *Awan:* A dynasty of 3 kings, names lost	2550
	Ilum-Pû (*or* Ilshu) (30 ?)	Khatanish of Khamazi		
	5 other kings, names damaged, total 136 (?) years	Lugalannemundu of Adab		
	5 pre-Sargonic kings known from inscriptions (order unknown):	Lugaltarsi of Kish (*see* Lugal-TAR of Uruk)		
	Lamgi-Mari	*Kings of Umma in the later pre-Sargonic period:*		
I. *Akshak:*	Ikun-Shamash			
Zuzu (// Eannatum)	Iblul-Il	Ush (or Gish)	Peli	
	Ikun-Shamagan	Enakalli (son ?)	Tata	
Unzi (30 ?)	Shalim	(// Eannatum)	Ukkutakhash	
		Urlumma (son)		
Undalulu (12)		(// Entemena)	Khishur	
Ur-ur (6)		Il (nephew)		2450
		(// Entemena)	Shushuntarana	
Puzur-Nirakh (20)		Gishakkidu (son)	Napilkhush	
(// Ku-Baba)		Bubu		
Ishu-Il (24)				
Shu-Sin (7) (son)		Lugalzaggisi (son)	Kukku-siwe-temti	
		(// Urukagina)		2370
II. *Akkad:*			Lukh-ishshan (// Sargon)	
Sargon (56) 2371–2316			Khishep-ratep (// Sargon)	
(// Lukh-ishshan and Khishepratep)				
Rimush (9) 2315–2307			Khelu	
(// Kaku)				
Manishtusu (15)			Epir-mupi	
2306–2292			Khita	
Naram-Sin (37)		*Dynasty of Gutium,*	Puzur (*or* Kutik)-In-	
2291–2255		21 kings, including:	Shushinak	
Shar-kali-sharrī (25)		Sarlagab (// Shar-kali-		
2254–2230 (// Sarlagab)		sharri)		
Anarchy (3) 2229–2227				2230
Dudu (21) 2226–2206				
Shu-Durul (15) 2205– 2191				
		Iarlaganda (// Nammakhni of Umma)		
			Tazitta I	
			Eparti I	
			Tazitta II	
		Si'um (// Lugalannatum of Umma)		
		Tirigan (// Utu-khegal)		2120
		Assyria:	II. *Simashki:*	
	Apil-kin (// Ur-Nammu)			
	Iddin-Ilum	Zariqum (vassal of Amar-Sin)		
	Ishma-Dagan			
	Ishtup-Ilum } (order unknown)			
	Ilum-ishar		Girnamme (// Shu-Sin)	
	Niwar-Mer			
			Lu...-luhhan	2000

DATE	LARSA	ISIN	BABYLON	ESHNUNNA	ELAMITE COUNTRIES II. SIMASHKI III. ANSHAN & SUSA	
2030	Ibbi-Sin (see preceding table) reigns over gradually contracting territory				*II. Simashki:*	
	Naplanum (21) 2025–2005	Ishbi-Erra (33) 2017–1985		Ilshu-ilia Nur-akhum	(Khutran-temti?) Kindattu	
	Emiṣum (28) 2004–1977	Shu-ilishu (10) 1984–1975		Kirikiri	Indattu I	
	Samium (35) 1976–1942	Iddin-Dagan (21) 1974–1954		Bilalama (son) (// Tan-Rakhuratir of Elam) Ishar-ramashshu	Tan-Rukhuratir (son) (// Bilalama of Eshnunna)	
1940	Zabaia (9) 1941–1933	Ishme-Dagan (19) 1953–1935		Uṣur-awassu Azuzum	Eparti II	
	Gungunum (27) 1932–1906	Lipit-Ishtar (11) 1934–1924		Ur-Ninmar	Indattu II Indattu III	historicity doubtful,
	Abisare (11) 1905–1895	Ur-Ninurta (28) 1923–1896		Ur-Ningizzidda Ip(p)iq-Adad I (son of Ur-Ninmar)	Indattu IV	perhaps a period of domination by Larsa
1895	Sumuel (29) 1894–1866	Bur-Sin (21) 1895–1875	Sumuabum (14) 1894–1881	Sharria Belakum (son)		
		Lipit-Enlil (5) 1874–1870	Sumulael (36) 1880–1845	Warassa		
	Nur-Adad (16) 1865–1850	Erra-imitti (8) 1869–1862		Ibalpiel I	*III. Anshan & Susa:*	
1860		Enlil-bani (24) 1861–1838		Ip(p)iq-Adad II (son)	Eparti III	
	Sin-iddinam (7) 1849–1843		Sabium (14) 1844–1831			
	Sin-eribam (2) 1842–1841					
	Sin-iqisham (5) 1840–1836	Zambia (3) 1837–1835				
	Ṣilli-Adad (1) 1835					
1830	Warad-Sin (12) 1834–1823	Iter-pisha (4) 1834–1831		Naram-Sin (son) (probably same as king of Assyria)	Shilkhakha (son) Attakhushu (nephew)	
		Ur-dukuga (3) 1830–1828	Apil-Sin (18) 1830–1813			
	Rim-Sin I (60) 1822–1763	Sin-magir (11) 1827–1817			Shirukdukh I	
		Damiq-ilishu (23) 1816–1794	Sin-muballiṭ (20) 1812–1793	Dadusha (brother)	Shimut-wartash	
1750			Hammurabi (43) 1792–1750	Ibalpiel II (son) c. 1784– ? Ṣilli-sin	Siwe-palar-khuppak	

ASSYRIA	MARI	ALEPPO	KHATTI	DATE
(Sulili ?)				2030
Kikkia				
Akkia	Iṣi-Dagan			
	Tura-Dagan (son ?)	'governors' of Mari, exact date uncertain		
Puzur-Ashur I	Puzur-Ishtar (son) N. (son)			
Shallim-ahhe (son)				
				1940
Ilushuma (son)				
Erishum I (40 ?) (son) c. 1906–1867				
				1895
Ikunum (son) c. 1866 ?				
				1860
Sargon I (son)				
Puzur-Ashur II (son)				
Naram-Sin (probably same as king of Eshnunna)	Iagitlim Iakhdunlim (son)			1830
Erishum (son ?) ?–1814			Pitkhana	
Shamshi-Adad I (33) 1813–1781	Iasmakh-Adad (son of Shamshi-Adad I)			
Ishme-Dagan I (40 ?) (son) 1780–1741	Zimrilim (son of Iakhdunlim)	Iarimlim I	Anitta (son)	
Mut-Ashkur (son)		Hammurabi I (son ?)		1750

(C) CRETE, THE AEGEAN ISLANDS AND MAINLAND GREECE

B.C.	CRETE	AEGEAN ISLANDS	MAINLAND GREECE
Before			
6000	Level X at Cnossus		Aceramic Neolithic
6000			Early Neolithic: (pre-Sesklo cultures in Thessaly)
5000			Middle Neolithic A: (Sesklo)
4500	Early Neolithic Level IX at Cnossus	Neolithic	Middle Neolithic B
4000	Middle Neolithic		
3500	Late Neolithic	Early Cycladic begins	
?3000	Early Minoan I begins		
		Pelos group of tombs	Late Neolithic of South Greece: Dimini culture in south Thessaly. (Fortified site with megaron cf. Troy I)
		Syra group of tombs: (bird-pins have parallels in Troy I)	Early Helladic begins: (early E.H. pottery has parallels in Troy I)
?2500	Early Minoan II begins: (stone vases imitating Egyptian work of Dyns. IV–VI)		Lerna and other sites destroyed at end of E.H. II
?2200	Early Minoan III begins: (seals comparable with Egyptian scarabs of Dyns. VII–X)		?First Indo-European invaders of Greece Grey Minyan pottery appears
?1900	Middle Minoan I begins: Beginning of palaces at Cnossus, Mallia, Phaestus	Middle Cycladic	Middle Helladic

B.C.	CRETE	AEGEAN ISLANDS	MAINLAND GREECE
1800	Middle Minoan II begins: (at Cnossus)	(Second city of Phylakopi in Melos importing both grey Minyan and	
	'Hieroglyphic' Minoan script	M.M.II pottery)	
	Destruction (?hostile) of Cnossus, Phaestus, Mallia, Pseira, Mochlos, Gournia, Palaikastro		
1700	Middle Minoan III begins		

INDEX TO MAPS

The Arabic definite article (Al-, El-, etc.) has been disregarded as an element in the alphabetical arrangement of place-names. For example, Al-'Ubaid is to be found under 'U'·

Abādīya, 4
Abgīg, 2
Abisko, 5
Abu Rawāsh, 2
Abu Simbel, 5
Abusīr, 2
Abusīr el-Malaq, 2
Abydos, 1, 4
Açana (Alalakh), 8
Acarnania, 12
Achaea, 12
Adab, 6
Adonis, R., 8
Aegina, 12
Afqa, 8
Afyonkarahisar, 10
El-Agamīyīn, 2
Aghirda, 14, 15
Ahlatlibel, 10
'Ai, 7
Akaki, 14
Akanthou, 14, 15
Akhisar, 9
Akhmīm (Panopolis), 3
Akhyritou, 15
Aksaray, 10
Akshak (?), 6
Alaca, 9, 10
Alalakh (Açana), 8
Alambra, 15
Alaminos, 14, 15
Alashiya, 16
Aleppo, 8
Alexandria, 1, 2
Alişar, 9, 10
Alīshtar, 6
Altın Köprü, 6
Altıntaş, 10
Amada, 5
Amanus Mts., 8
Amāra West, 5
El-Amarna, 3
Ambelikou, 14, 15
Amorgos, 12
El-Amra, 4
'Amūq, 8
Analiondas, 14
Anayia, 14
Androlikou, 14

Andros, 12
Anība, 5
Ankara, 9
Anoyira, 14, 15
Anshan, 11
Antaeopolis (Qāw el-Kebīr), 3
Antinoopolis, 3
Antioch, 8
Aphendrika, 14
Aphroditopolis (Atfīh), 2
Aphroditopolis (Kōm Ishqāw), 3
Apostolos Andreas, 14
Araq, 11
Aras, R., 16
Arcadia, 12
Argissa, 12
Argo, 5
Argolis, 12
El-Arīsh, 1
Armant (Hermonthis), 4
Armenochori, 14
Arpad (Tell Rifa'at), 8
Arpera, 15
Arslantepe, 10
Arzawa, 16
Asea, 12
Asfūn el-Matā'na, 4
El-Ashmūnein (Hermopolis), 1, 3
Ashur, 8
Asine, 12
Askitario, 12
Astacus, 12
Aswān, 1, 4
Asyūt, 1, 3
Atbara, R., 5
Atfīh (Aphroditopolis), 2
Athalassa, 15
Athens, 12
Athribis, 2
Attica, 12
Ayia Irini, 12
Ayia Marina, 12, 14, 15
Ayii Anargyri, 14
Ayioryitika, 12
Ayios Epiktitos, 14, 15
Ayios Iakovos, 14
Ayios Konon, 14
Ayios Kosmas, 12
Ayios Nikolaos, 14

[1005]

Ayios Sozomenos, 15
Ayios Stephanos, 12
Ayios Thomas, 14
Ayios Yeoryios, 14

Bāb ed-Drāʿ, 7
Babylon, 6
El-Badāri, 3
Bad-tibira, 6
Baghdad, 6
Bahr Yūsef, 2, 3
Bahrīya Oasis, 1
El-Balābīsh, 4
Balansūra (Nefrusy), 3
Balāṭa, 7
Balıkesir, 9
Balīkh, R., 8
El-Ballās, 4
Bandibāl (Tepe Bandibāl), 6
Baʿqūbā, 6
Bardawīl, L., 1
Barrāmīya, 1
Basar (Jebel el-Bishrī), 8
Bashimi (Bāsht), 11
Bāsht (Bashimi), 11
Bayburt, 16
Behbehan (Hidali), 11
Beirut, 8
Beit Khallāf, 4
Beit el-Wāli, 5
Bellapais, 14, 15
Beni Hasan, 3
Berenice, 1
Beth-shan, 7
Beth-Shemesh, 7
Bethel, 7
Beycesultan, 9, 10, 16
Bey Keuy, 15
Bīga, 4
Birket Qārūn, 2
Bir Nakhlai, 5
Biyahmu, 2
Blue Nile, R., 5
Boeotia, 12
Boğazkale (Boğazköy)/Khattusha, 16
Boğazköy (Boğazkale)/Khattusha, 16
Bozüyük, 10
Bubastis, 2
Buhen, 5
Bulgar Maden, 10
Burdur, 10
Bushire (Liyan), 11
Busiris, 2
Buto, 2
Byblos (Jubeil), 8, 16

Cairo, 1, 2
Canopus, 2

Cape Andreas, 14
Cape Greco, 14
Carchemish (Jerablūs), 8
Ceos, 12
Cephallenia, 12
Cernavoda, 16
Chagar Bazar, 8
Chalandriani, 12
Chalcidice, 12
Chamchamal, 6
Chanhu Daro, 16
Chios, 12
Çiğle, 9
Cirrha, 12
Cnossus, 13, 16
Corcyra, 12
Corinth, 12
Corum, 10
Crocodilopolis (Kīmān Fāris), 2
Cucuţeni, 16
Cusae, 3
Cynopolis, 3
Cythera, 12

Dahshūr, 2
Dākhla Oasis, 1
Ed-Dakka, 5
Damanhūr, 2
Damietta, 2
Danube, R., 16
Darāw, 4
Deir el-Bahri, 4
Deir el-Bersha, 3
Deir el-Gabrāwi, 3
Deir Rīfa, 3
Deir ez-Zōr, 8
Delfan, 6
Demirci Hüyük, 9, 10
Dendera, 4
Deraheib, 5
Ed-Derr, 5
Dhali, 14
Dhemenagaki, 12
Dhenia, 14, 15
Dhikomo, 14, 15
Dhiorios, 14
Ed-Dibābīya, 4
Dikili Tash, 12
Dimini, 12
Diorite Quarries, 5
Diospolis Parva (Hū), 4
Dirā Abu n-Naga, 4
Dishāsha, 3
Diyārbakr, 8
Dizful, 11
Djeret (Tōd), 4
Dnieper, R., 16
Dodona, 12

Don, R., 16
Donetz, R., 16
Dorak, 10
Dramesi, 12
Dündartepe, 10
Dunqul Oasis, 1
Dyme, 12

Edfu, 1, 4
Edremit, 9
Edwa, 2
Elaphonisi, 12
Elbe, R., 16
Elea, 14
Elephantine, 4
Eliophotes, 14
Elis, 12
Elkāb, 1, 4
Elmalı, 9
Elmalı Plain, 9
Emporio, 9
Epano Englianos, 16
Epirus, 12
Episkopi, 15
Erbaa, 9
Eridu, 6
Erimi, 14, 15
Erivan, 10
Erzurum, 10
Eshnunna (Tell Asmar), 6
Eskişehir, 9
Esna, 4
Etiyokuşu, 10
Euboea, 12
Euphrates, R., 6, 8, 9, 10
Eutresis, 12
Evdimou, 15
Eylenja, 15

Fahliyān, 11
El-Faiyūm, 1, 2
Fallūjah, 6
Farāfra Oasis, 1
Faras, 5
Fifth Cataract, 1, 5
Fırat, R., 16
First Cataract, 1
Fourth Cataract, 1, 5

Galales, 14
Gammai, 5
Gaza, 1
Gebel el-Ahmar, 2
Gebel el-Araq, 4
Gebel Barkal (Napata), 5
Gebelein, 4
Gebel es-Silsila (East and West), 4
Gebel et-Tārif, 4

Gerf Husein, 5
Gezer, 7
Ghurāb, 2
Girga, 4
Girsu (Tello), 6
El-Girza, 2
Giza, 2
Gonia, 12
Gordion, 10
Greater Zab, R., 8

Hacılar, 10
Ḥajji Muḥammad (Qal'at Ḥajji Muḥam-
    mad), 6
Halys, R., 9, 10
Hama (Hamath), 8
Hamadān, 6
Hamath (Hama), 8
El-Hammāmīya, 3
Hamra Dom, 4
El-Haraga, 2
Harappā, 16
Harrān, 8
Harsīn, 6
Ḥawāra, 2
Heliopolis (El-Matarīya), 1, 2
Helvaciköy, 9
Helwān, 2
Heracleopolis Magna (Ihnāsiya el-Medīna),
    1, 2
Heraea, 12
Heraeum, 12
Heraion, 10
Hermonthis (Armant), 4
Hermopolis (El-Ashmūnein), 1, 3
Het-Nub, 3
El-Hība, 3
El-Hibbeh (Lagash), 6
Hidali (Behbehan), 11
Hierakonpolis, 4
Hipponus, 3
Hisarlık–Troy, 16
Homs, 8
Horoztepe, 10
Hū (Diospolis Parva), 4

Iasus, 12
Ihnāsiya el-Medīna (Heracleopolis Magna),
    1, 2
Ikkur, 5
Ilam, 11
Indus, R., 16
Inia, 14
Iran, 16
Ishchali, 6
Ismāīliya, 2
Ithaca, 12
Iznik, L., 9, 10

Jabbul, L., 8
Jackovice (Jackowica), 16
Jackowica (Jackovice), 16
Ja'farābād (Tepe Ja'farābād), 6
Jamdat Naṣr, 6
Jankovici (Jankoviči), 16
Jankoviči (Jankovici), 16
Jarmo, 6
Jaui (Tepe Jaui), 6
Jebel 'Abd el-'Azīz, 8
Jebel Anṣāriyyah, 8
Jebel el-Aqra' (Mons Casius), 8
Jebel el-Bishrī (Basar), 8
Jebeleh, 8
Jebel Sinjār, 8
Jebelet el-Beidha, 8
Jerablūs (Carchemish), 8
Jericho, 7
Jerusalem, 7
Jhukar, 16
Jubeil (Byblos), 8

El-Kāb (Elkāb), 1, 4
Kābul, R., 16
Kafr Ammār, 2
Kaki Thalassa, 12
Kalābsha, 5
Kalavassos, 14, 15
Kalinin (Königsberg), 16
Kalopsidha, 15
Kambia, 15
Kambyli, 14
Karabayir, 10
Kara Hassan, 8
Karavas, 14
Karmi, 14, 15
Karnak, 4
Karoy, 5
Karpasha, 14
Kāshān, 11
Kataliondas, 14
Kato Moni, 14
Katydata, 15
Kavalla, 12
Kawa, 5
Kayseri, 10
Kazakstān, 16
Kedhares, 14, 15
Kephala, 12
Kerma, 5
Keumurju, 14
Kfar Monash, 7
Khabur, R., 6, 8
Khafājī (Tutub), 6
Kharcha, 14
Khārga Oasis, 1
Khartūm, 5
Khatā'na, 2

Khatti, 16
Khawālid, 3
Khirbet Karak, 7
Khirokitia, 14
Khlorakas, 14
Khrysiliou, 14, 15
Khukhnur, 11
Khūrramābād, 11
Kifrī, 6
Kiliya, 9
Kīmān Fāris (Crocodilopolis), 2
Kirkuk, 6
Kirmānshāh, 6
Kish, 6
Kissonerga, 14, 15
Kiti, 14
Kızıl Irmak, R., 16
Klavdia, 15
Knovíz, 16
Kokkina, 14
Kōm el-Ahmar Sawāris, 3
Kōm el-Aqārib, 2
Komi Kebir, 15
Kōm Ishqāw (Aphroditopolis), 3
Kōm Ombo, 4
Königsberg (Kalinin), 16
Konosso, 4
Konya, 9, 10
Kophinou, 14
Koptos, 4
Kormakiti, 14, 15
Kornos, 14
Korosko, 5
Koufovounos, 14
Kouklia, 14
Krini, 14, 15
Kritsana, 12
Ktima, 14
El-Kūbānīya, 4
Kudish Ṣaghīr, 6
Kültepe, 10, 16
Kumma, 5
Kūrangān, 11
Kurkur Oasis, 1
Kurram, R., 16
Kush, 5
Kusura, 10
Kütahya, 16
Kutha (Tell Ibrāhīm), 6
Kyra, 14, 15
Kyrenia, 14
Kythrea, 14, 15

Laconia, 12
Lagash (El-Hibbeh), 6
El-Lāhūn, 2
Lapithos, 14, 15
Larissa, 12

Larnaka, 14, 15
Larsa, 6
Latakia, 8
Latzi, 14
Leben, 13
Lefka, 15
Lemnos, 12
Lengyel, 16
Lerna, 12, 16
Lesbos, 12
Lesser Zab, R., 6, 8
Letopolis, 2
Leucas, 12
Lianokladhi, 12
Limassol, 15
Linou, 15
El-Lisht, 2
Livadhia, 15
Liveras, 14
Liyan (Bushire), 11
Loutra Tis Aphroditis, 14
Loutros, 14
Lukka, 16
Luristān, 11
Luxor (Thebes), 1, 4
Lythrankomi, 14
Lythrodondas, 15

El-Ma'ādi, 2
Macedonia, 12
El-Madāmūd (Madu), 4
Madu (El-Madāmūd), 4
Maghāgha, 3
El-Maharraqa, 2
El-Mahāsna, 4
Maidūm, 2
Makrān (Mekrān), 11
Mālamīr/Izeh, 11
Malthi, 12
El-Ma'marīya (Mohamerīya), 4
Mandali, 6
Manfalūt, 3
Manika, 12
Manisa, 9
Mardin, 8
Margi, 14, 15
Mari, 14, 15
Mari (Tell Ḥarīrī), 6, 8
Mariupol, 16
El-Markhā, 1
Maroni, 14, 15
El-Ma'sara, 2
El-Matarīya (Heliopolis), 2
Matarrah, 6
Mathiati, 14
El-Matmar, 3
Mazghūna, 2
Meander, R., 9, 10

Medīnet el-Faiyūm, 2
Medīnet Habu, 4
Medīnet Ma'ādi, 2
Medja, 5
Megiddo, 7
Meir, 3
Mekrān (Makrān), 11
Meladhia, 14
Melos, 12
Memphis (Mīt Rahīna), 1, 2
Mendes, 2
Meniko, 14
Mereijeb, 6
Merimda Beni Salāma, 2
Meroe, 5
Mesakhorio, 14
Meskineh, 8
Messara, 13
Messenia, 12
Methone, 12
El-Mi'alla, 4
Mikhalits, 9, 10
Minia, 3
Mirgissa, 5
Mishrifeh (Qatna), 8
Mīt Rahīna (Memphis), 1, 2
Mochlos, 13
Mohamerīya (El-Ma'marīya), 4
Mohenjo Daro, 16
Moni, 14, 15
Mons Casius (Jebel el-Aqra'), 8
Morphou, 15
Mosul, 8
Murat, R., 16
El-Mustagidda, 3
Mycenae, 12, 16
Myconos, 12
Myrtou, 14

Naga ed-Deir, 4
Napata (Gebel Barkal), 5
Naqāda (Ombos), 4
Naucratis, 2
Naxos, 12
Nazlat- esh-Shurafa, 3
Nebesha, 2
Nefrusy (Balansūra), 3
Nemea, 12
Neokhorio, 14
Nicosia, 14, 15
Nidri, 12
Nile, R., 1, 2, 3, 4, 5
Nina (Zerghūl), 6
Nippur, 6
Nisibis, 8
Nisi Tou Ayiou Yeoryiou, 14
Nubia, 1, 5
Nuzi, 6

Oder, R., 16
Olympia, 12
Ombos (Naqāda), 4
Omodhos, 14
Orchomenus, 12
Orga, 14
Orontes, R., 8
Ovabayindir, 9
Oxyrhynchus, 3

Panopolis (Akhmīm), 3
Paramali, 14
Paroikia, 12
Paros, 12
Pazarlí, 9
Pelikata, 12
Pelusium, 2
Pera, 15
Peristerona, 14
Persepolis, 11
Persian Gulf, 11
Petra Tou Limniti, 14
Phaestus, 13
Pheia, 12
Philia, 14, 15
Philousa, 14
Phlamoudhi, 14
Phlius, 12
Phocis, 12
Phrenaros, 14
Phthiotic Thebes, 12
Phylakopi, 12
Pileri, 15
Pithom, 2
Platani, 14
Platymatis, 14
Polatlı, 10
Polemidhia, 15
Poliochni, 9, 10
Polis, 14, 15
Politiko, 15
Port Said, 2
Potamia, 15
Propontis, 12
Psematismenos, 15
Pyla, 14, 15
Pyrgos, 12
Pyrgos, 13
Pyrgos, 14, 15

Qal'at Ḥajji Muḥammad, 6
Qal'at er-Rus, 8
El-Qantara, 2
Qantīr, 2
Qaṣr Ibrīm, 5
Qaṣr-i Shīrīn, 6
Qatna (Mishrifeh), 8
El-Qatta, 2

Qāw el-Kebīr (Antaeopolis), 3
Qūbān, 5
El-Qurna (Sheikh Abd el-Qurna), 4
El-Quseir, 1

Rakhmani, 12
Raphina, 12
Rapiqum, 8
Ras el-'Ain, 7
Ras el-'Amiya, 6
Ras Shamra (Ugarit), 8
Ravi, R., 16
Red Sea, 1, 2
Reijibeh, 6
Rhine, R., 16
Rhodes, 12
Er-Ridīsīya, 4
Er-Rizeiqāt, 4
Rizokarpaso, 14, 15
Rosetta, 2
Rōsh Hanniqra, 7
Ruad, 8

Saft el-Hinna, 2
Sā el-Hagar (Sais), 1, 2
Sai, 5
Sais (Sā el-Hagar), 2
Sakha (Xois), 2
Sāmarrā, 6
Samos, 12
Samothrace, 12
Sangarius, R., 9, 10
Sān el-Hagar (Tanis, Zoan), 2
Saqqara, 2
Sarāb (Tepe Sarāb), 6
Sawu, 1
Sayāla, 5
Scyros, 12
Sebennytos, 2
Sebīl, 4
Es-Sebūa, 5
Second Cataract, 1, 5
Sedeinga, 5
Seiga, 5
Seila, 2
Selīma Oasis, 1
Semna East and West, 5
Serābīt el-Khādim, 1
Serra, 5
Sesebi, 5
Sha, 14
Esh-Shallāl, 4
Shatt er-Rigāl, 4
Sheikh Abd el-Qurna (El-Qurna), 4
Sheikh Farag, 4
Sheikh Sa'īd, 3
Sherikhum, 11
Shīrāz, 11

Shuruppak, 6
Es-Sibā'īya, 4
Sidmant, 2
Siheil, 4
Sinai, 1
Siphnos, 12
Sippar, 6
Sisklipos, 14, 15
Sīwa Oasis, 1
Sixth Cataract, 5
Skarinou, 14
Skouriotissa, 15
Smyrna, 12
Sotira, 14, 15
Souskiou, 14
Speos Artemidos, 3
Starčevo, 16
Suez, 2
Suez, Gulf of, 1
Sulaimaniyyah, 6
Sulb, 5
Sultandağ, 10
Susa, 6, 11
Sutlej, R., 16
Swat, R., 16
Syros, 12

Tabara el-Akrād, 8
Tabbat el-Hammām, 8
Tanis (Zoan, Sān el-Hagar), 1, 2
Tanta, 2
Tarkhān, 2
Tarsus, 8, 10
Tavşanlı, 9, 10, 16
Teheran, 11
Tel Avīv, 7
Tell Abu Seifa (Tjel), 2
Tell Aḥmar (Til Barsib), 8
Tell el-'Ajjūl, 7
Tell 'Arad, 7
Tell Asmar (Eshnunna), 6
Tell Beit-Mirsim, 7
Tell Brak, 8
Tell ed-Duweir, 7
Tell el-Fār'ah, 7
Tell Gat, 7
Tell Halaf, 8
Tell Ḥarīrī (Mari), 8
Tell el-Ḥesi, 7
Tell el-Ḥuṣn, 7
Tell Ibrāhīm (Kutha), 6
Tell Judaidah, 8
Tell Khuaira, 8
Tell Maṣin, 8
Tell en-Naṣbeh, 7
Tello (Girsu), 6
Tell er-Ratāba, 2
Tell Rifa'at (Arpad), 8

Tell es-Sawwān, 6
Tell Simiriyān, 8
Tell 'Uqair, 6
Tell el-Yahūdīya, 2
Tenos, 12
Tepe Bandibāl, 6
Tepe Gawra, 8
Tepe Giyān, 6, 16
Tepe Gūrān, 6
Tepe Hisar, 16
Tepe Ja'farābād (Ja'farābād), 6
Tepe Jaui, 6
Tepe Mussian, 6
Tepe Sabz, 6
Tepe Sarāb (Sarāb), 6
Tepe Sialk, 16
Terra, 14
Thasos, 12
Thebes, 12
Thebes (Luxor), 1, 4
Theletra, 14
Thera, 12
Thermi, 9, 12
Thermia, 14
Thessaly, 12
Third Cataract, 1, 5
This, 4
Thrace, 12, 16
Tigris, R., 6, 8, 9, 10
Tihna, 3
Til Barsib (Tell Aḥmar), 8
Tiryns, 12
Tjel (Tell Abu Seifa), 2
Tōd (Djeret), 4
Tokat, 9
Tomās, 5
Tōshka, 5
Toumba, 14
Trimitousha, 14
Tripoli, 8
Tripolye, 16
Troad, 12
Troulli, 14
Troy, 9, 10, 12
Trypimeni, 15
Tsani Magula, 12
Tūkh, 4
Tumbos, 5
Tura, 2
Tuttul, 6, 8
Tutub (Khafājī), 6
Tyre, 8

Al-'Ubaid, 6
Ugarit (Ras Shamra), 8
Umbarakāb, 5
Umma, 6
Umm Nabardi, 5

Umm Qareiyāt, 5
'Uqair (Tell 'Uqair), 6
Ur, 6
Uronarti, 5
Urshu, 8
Uruk (Warka), 6
Uşak, 10
Uzbekistān, 16

Vān, L., 10, 11
Vardarophtsa, 12
Vasilia, 14, 15
Vasiliki, 13
Vavilas, 14
Velatice, 16
Vinča, 16
Vistula, R., 16
Volga, R., 16
Volo, 12

Wādi Abbād, 1
Wādi el-Allāqi, 5
Wādi Babā, 1
Wādi Gabgaba, 5
Wādi el-Gāsūs, 1
Wādi Halfa, 1, 5
Wādi Hammāmāt, 1, 4
Wādi el-Hūdi, 5
Wādi Maghāra, 1

Wādi Miāh, 1
Wādi en-Natrūn, 1, 2
Wādi el-Qash, 1
Wādi Qena, 4
Wādi Tummilāt, 2
Warka (Uruk), 6
Wawat, 5
Weser, R., 16
White Nile, R., 5

Xylomandra, 14

Yeri, 15
Yeroskipos, 14
Yialia, 15
Yialousa, 15
Yortan, 9, 10

Zacynthos, 12
Zāwiyet el-Aryān, 2
Zāwiyet el-Maiyitīn, 3
Zeberged Is., 1
Zerelia, 12
Zerghūl (Nina), 6
Zoan (Tanis, Sān el-Hagar), 2
Zygouries, 12

Xois, 2

GENERAL INDEX

The Arabic definite article (Al-, El-, etc.) has been disregarded as an element in the alphabetical arrangement of place-names. For example, Al-'Ubaid is to be found under 'U'.

Apart from the above, the order of main headings is strictly alphabetical by letters, e.g. Karacaahmet, Kara-Dağ, Kara Hasan, Karahüyük.

Bold figures indicate main references; italic figures indicate maps, plans, line-drawings, tables, etc.

A'annipada of Ur, 112, 245, 287, 288
Aba (god), 437, 667
Abalgamash, King of Barakhshe (Warakhshe), 436, 649
Abarnium, in Cappadocia (?), 560
Abattum, on the Euphrates, 333
'Abbasiyah, in Northern Mesopotamia, 303
Abgīg, in the Faiyūm (Map 2 (48)), 4, 501
Abieshu' of Babylon, 120
Abisarē of Larsa, 628, 637
Abisha, Bedawin chieftain, 504
Abishemu, Prince of Byblos, 408
Abisko, near Aswān, 480, 487
Abraham, 744
Abu Kamāl, on the Euphrates, 291, 426
Abu Rawāsh, near Cairo (Map 2 (25)), 4, 19, 56, 58, 157, 173, 174, 178, 207
Abu Shahrain, *see* Eridu
Abu Simbel, in Lower Nubia (Map 5 (20)), 48, 167, 183, 486
Abusīr, in Egypt (Map 2 (31)), 4, 178, 179, 182, 185, 207, 350; papyri, 178, 186
Abusīr el-Malaq, in the Faiyūm (Map 2 (52)), 4, 232 and n. 5
Abu Zenīma, 355
Abydos, in Upper Egypt (Maps 1 and 4), 2, 12, 24, 40, 58, 59, 68, 70, 147, 149, 150, 152, 190, 191, 192, 198, 199, 286, 357, 466, 481, 489, 498, 504, 513, 515, 521, 543 n. 7, 544; king-list, 11, 14, 23–31 *passim*, 35, 157, 175, 190, 196, 197, 198, 354; clay-seal impression from, 14; ivory dockets from, 27; cemetery (necropolis) at, 17–22, 23–35 *passim*, 56, 58, 59, 64–5, 66, 69, 198, 202; vase, 356; and Thebes, 478; as a national shrine, 521
Açana (Alalakh, q.v.), in Syria (Map 8 (3)), 316, 320, 337, 547
Acem Hüyük, in Anatolia, 722
Achaea, in Greece (Map (12)), 788–9
Achshaph, in Palestine, 555
Achthoes I of Heracleopolis (*see also* Meryibre Achthoes I), 464

Achthoes (I), Nomarch of Asyūt, 468–9
Achthoes II (Nebkaure) of Egypt, 465
Achthoes (II), Nomarch of Asyūt, 467, 469
Achthoes III (Wahkare) of Egypt, 237, 466–7, 472, 533–5 *passim*
Achthoes, Chancellor of Egypt, 480–3 *passim*, 487
Achthoes, leader of mining expeditions into Sinai, 484 *bis*
Achthoes, Nomarch of Oryx nome, 471
Achthoes, a scribe, 498
Achthoes, son of Djefi, 474, 477
Adab (Bismaya), in Babylonia (Map 6 (20)), 97, 115, 132, 289
Adad (Mesopotamian god), 564, 667, 718, 767
Adamdun, in Susiana, 611, 658
Adana, in Asia Minor, 504
Ader, in Transjordan, 214
'Adhaim river, in Babylonia, 602
Adonis (Syrian god), 348, 349
Adonis river, in Lebanon (Map 8), 181, 316, 347, 348–9
adornment (personal), articles of, *see* jewellery
Adriatic ware, 791
Aegean islands (Map 12, *see also under their names*), 383, 384, 414, **793–9**
Aegean sea and coasts (Map 12), 370, 383, 411, 682, 701, 702, 771, 781, 782
Aegean world and culture, 180–1, 416, 503, 790
Aegina, Greek island (Map 12), 781, 782, 783
'Affūleh, in Palestine, 213, 337
Afghanistān, 240, 285, 392
Agade (Akkad), in Mesopotamia (*see also* Sargon), 113, 114, 236, 246, 257, 265, 297, 308, 321, 331, 332; dynasty and period of (*see also next below*), 115, 132, 237, 239, 254, 255, 289, 299, 300, 307, 308, 311, 313, 314, 322, 323, 331, 420, 432, 439, 443, 446, 456, 458, 559, 562 n. 11, 563, 565, 600, 624, 650, 707, 739; at its most prosperous, 433;

imports stone, 438; downfall of, 456; patron goddess of, 738

Agade dynasty and Gutian invasion, **417–63**, 654; Sargon's reign, **417–34** (*see also* Sargon); his successors, **434–40**; Naram-Sin's reign, **440–5**; state of Babylonia, **446–53**; last Agade kings and Gutian invasion and supremacy, **454–61**; expulsion of Gutians, **461–3**

Agade, kings of, 321–8 *passim*, 432, 458, 564, 596, 600, 604, 607, 608, 619; and Sumerians, 447–8; internal policies of, 448–9

Agade, rise and fall of (poem on), 433

Agade tablets (cuneiform), 450–1

El-Agamīyīn, in the Faiyūm (Map 2 (44)), 4, 511

Agga of Kish, 110, 111, 272

Aghirda, in Cyprus (Maps 14 (44) and 15 (14)), *810*, *814*, 816

agriculture (*see also* irrigation): in Babylonia, 126–7; in Palestine, 229

agricultural products traded in Anatolia, 726

Ahanakhte, Nomarch of Hare nome, 470

Aha of Egypt, 11–14, 17, 18, 19, 22–3, 23, 36, 50, 59

Ahhiyawa, kingdom of, in Anatolia, 410

Ahlatlibel, in Northern Anatolia (Map 10), 368, *385*, 386, 387, 393, 398, 407, 695, 697

'Ai (Et-Tell), in Palestine (Map 7), 208, *209*, 211–19 *passim*, 227, 230, 231, 235, 236, 356, 575; Palace of, 218, 220, 221

Aiapir (Mālamīr, q.v.), province of Anshan, 663, 674

Aka (Neferkare) of Egypt, 35

Akalamdug of Babylonia, 138, 244, 283

Akauhor (Menkauhor, Menkhau) of Egypt, 185–6

Ak Daǧ, in Anatolia, 430

Akhet (a season), 204 and n. 2, 205

Akhetaa (priest) of Egypt, 148, 158, 160

Akhethotep of Egypt, 175

Akhisar, in N.W. Anatolia (Map 9), *373*, 394; plain and region, 372, 701, 702

Akhisar–Manisa culture and region, in N.W. Anatolia (Map 9), 372, *373*, 379, 380, 384, 396

Akhmīm, in Middle Egypt (Map 3), *8*, 468, 471, 472, 483, 512

Akhyritou, in Cyprus (Map 15 (42)), *814*, 816

Akkad (*see also* Agade *and* Sumer), 78, 79, 91, 100, 297, 431, 672; immunity of, 638; 'a likeness of Babylon' near, 737; dynasty of, 739

Akkadian: empire, 609, 707, 735–6; ideology (imperialism), 735–7; kings of Babylonia, internal policies (*see also* Agade, kings of), 448–9; language and script, 72, 98, 100, 111, 445, 565, 650, 718, 735 (Old Akkadian, 450); names, 297, 431, 625, 735

Akkadians, 72, 297, 332, 335, 434, 446, 455, 708; cult objects of, 332; invasion of Babylonia, 419, 735; in Elam, 666; and Assyria, 735; and Babylonia, 735

Aksaray region of Central Anatolia (Map 10), *385*, 397, 696

Akshak, in Babylonia (Map 6), 117, 255, 289, 455

Akurgal of Lagash, 117

alabaster, 67, 78–9, 82, 86, 158, 187, 190, 312, 345, 357, 437, 445, 505, 688, 802; quarries, *see* Het-nub

Alaca (Alaca Hüyük), in Central Anatolia (Maps 9 and 10), 368, 369, 370, *373*, *385*, 392, 395, 401, 695; metalwork, 370, 377, 392, 395, 690–1; pottery, 367, 382, 383, 398, 399, 400, 686, 689; building levels, 369; cemetery, 388, 390; royal tombs, 369, 377, 386, 390–2, 686; houses, 386; town/city site, 386; costume, and metal vessels, 394–5; female jewellery, 394; trade with the West, 395

Ala Daǧ, in Anatolia, 430

Alalakh (Açana, q.v.), in Syria (Map 8 (3)), *316*, 320, 547, 550, 558

Alambra, in Cyprus (Map 15), *814*, 816, 817, 821

Aleppo (Khalap, Khalpu), in Syria (Map 8), *316*, 333, 334, 335, 442, 550, 561; pines, 347; Museum, 546

Alexander the Great, 610

Alexandria, in Lower Egypt (Map 2), 4, 501

Alişar, in Central Anatolia (Maps 9 and 10), 90, 368, 369, 371, *373*, *385*, 709, 713, 714; levels, 369; stone weapons, 378; pottery, 382, 399, 683, 687; houses, 386; weapons, 691; town site, 386; citadel, 688

Alişar cultures and periods: I*a*, 369, 399; I*b*, 369, 399, 400

altars (podia), 76, 222, 223, 257–62 *passim*, 268, 278, 280, 282, 292, 308, 332, 375, 388–9, 498

Altın-Köprü, in Babylonia (Map 6 (1)), 432, 655

A.MAL (Akkadian god), 437 n. 1

Amanus mountains (Map 8), *316*, 324–9 *passim*, 335, 371, 397, 425, 559, 682

El-Amarna (Map 3(18)) letters, *8*, 324, 327, 426 *bis*, 540, 541

Amar-Sin (Bur-Sin) of Ur, 301, 602, **607–8**, 609, 610, 612, **656**, 746; zikkurrat of, 75

Ambelikou, in Cyprus (Maps 14 and 15(3)), *810*, *814*, 821

amber, 386, 392

Amen-Re, *see* Amon-Re

amethysts of Nubia, 500

Ammenemes I (Amenemhet, 'Ameny', Sehetepibre,Wehem-Meswet) of Egypt (*see also* Ammenemes, Vizier), 471 n. 1, *493–5 passim*, **495–9**, 502, 505, 514–19 *passim*, 537, 541, 544; and co-regent Sesostris (his son), 497–9; and the succession, 497; his end, 498–9; his pyramid, 516

Ammenemes II (Nubkaure) of Egypt, 502–3, 504 *bis*, 509, 518, 535, 540, 542, 543, 546; his daughter's sphinx, 546

Ammenemes III (Nymare) of Egypt, 505, 506 n. 1, 507, **509–12**, 517, 518, 538, 545, 545–6, 589, 590, 591; co-regency suggested, 509 n. 4; his pyramid and its complex, 511–12, 513; portraits of, 514; expedition to Sinai, 539

Ammenemes IV of Egypt, 517, 545, 546, 590, 591

Ammenemes, Governor of Oryx nome, 503

Ammenemes, Vizier (*see also* Ammenemes I), 492–5 *passim*, 495; his *coup d'état*, 495

Ammenon (Enmengalanna) of Babylonia, 102

Ammisaduqa of Babylonia, 634

Amnan-Iakhrur (bedawin tribe), 636

Amon-Re (Amen-Re), Egyptian composite deity, 501, 520; temple of, 498

Amor, land of, 556

Amorgos, Aegean island (Map 12), 797, 798

'Amorite wall', 615

Amorites, 127, 234, 237, 321, 434, 446, 455, 535, 558, 563, 594, 610, 612, 614–15, 615, 641, 717, 719–21, 824; invasion of Babylonia, **625–8**, 658; their kingdoms in Babylonia, 631, 632, 637 (*see also* Babylon, First Dynasty); dynasty, 738; kingship titles of, 755

Amosis I of Egypt, 22, 479

Amu (Asiatics, q.v.), 360, 534, 535, 538, 540

'Amuda, near Nisibis, q.v., 565 n. 5

Amun of Luxor (Theban god), 472, 473, 478, 479, 480, 496, 498, 502, 517–20 *passim (see also* Amon-Re)

'Amūq, the (plain of Antioch, q.v.), in Syria (Map 8), *316*, 335, 336, 338, 340, 342, 364; pottery, 363, 364, 382, 397, 399, 401

Amurru, 327, 425, 556 n. 7, 562 and n. 8, 603, 641; the god, 626, 630; 'Mountains of...', 559; town of, 562 (*see also* Tidnum); ethnic group (*amurrū*), 562–6, 592, 594, 615; 'kings', 564; language of, 564; land of, 564 n. 4; 'wall of...', 597, 609; 'father of...', 640

amurru (*martu*), ethnic group, 562–6, 592, 594, 625

Amurrum (West Semitic god), 720, 721, 768

Amurrum (town), near Ashur, q.v., 721

Anaku ('tin country'), 429

Anam of Uruk, 636, 637

Anat (a goddess), 558 *bis*

Anatolia (*general*), (Maps 9 and 10), 42, 90, 133, 228, 231, 312, 328, 335, 337, 340,' 341, *373*, *385*, 441, 585, 781; material cultures of, 370–1; immigrants, 841–5 (*see also* Indo-European immigrants); houses in, 374–5; coast-trade, 381; migrations within, 384–6; overseas trade, 386, 794; political organization (E.B. 2), 386; royal wealth and power in, 386; Luwian (?) invasion of, 407–10; Thracian invasion of (*c.* 1200 B.C.), 410; Egyptian iconographic symbols in, 550; and Assyrians, 717; Indo-European languages in, 830–7; Hittites in, 830–7

Anatolia (*geographical divisions*) (Maps 9 and 10), *373*, *385*; Central, 366–9 *passim*, 382, 387–8, 390, 393, 398–401 *passim*, 416, 681, 682, 683, **685–8**, 691–703 *passim*; Eastern, 397, 399, **688–90**; North-Western, 369, 378–80, 381–4 *passim*, 388–93 *passim*, 396, 407, 408–10, 775; Pontic, q.v., 367–400 *passim*, 682, **690–1**; Southern, 368, 381–2, 407, 408, 409; South-Western, 368, 380–1, 383, 384, 388, 397, 398, 407, 409, 681; Western, 368, 369, 374–6 *passim*, 381, 388, 395–401 *passim*, 407, 408, **683–5**

Anatolia (*c.* 4000–2300 B.C.), **363–416**:
End of late Chalcolithic period, **363–7**: Cilicia, 363–5; Konya plain, q.v., 365–6; West, North-West and Central Anatolia, 366–7

Early Bronze Age, **368–403**: introduction, 368–9; origins, 369–71; *1 Period* (Map 9), **371–83**, *373*; north-western group, 371–8; pottery, 372–4, 378–83; 2 *Period* (Map 10), **383–403**, *385*; introduction, 383–6; architecture, 387–90; burial customs, 390–2; metalwork, 392–4; costume, and metal vessels, 394–5; pottery, 395–403

Chronology, **403–5**, *404*; catastrophe, 383–4, 392, **406–10**, 808, 813, 820; Troy, q.v., 411–16, *412*

Anatolia (*c.* 2300–1750 B.C.), **681–706**: introductory, **681–3**; Western, after the Luwian (?) invasion, **683–5**; Central, **685–8**; Eastern cultures, **688–90**; a Pontic culture, **690–1**; transition to M.B.A., **691–704**; Troy III, IV and V, **704–6**

Anatolia in the Old Assyrian Period, **707–28**: history, **707–15**; peoples, **715–21**; government and administration, **721–3**; articles of trade, **723–7**

Anatolian sites, Early and Middle Bronze Age levels at, *693*

'anchor-hooks', terra-cotta, 774, 776, 780

Andjeti (local god of Busiris), 54, 202

Anedjib of Egypt, 15, 18, 19, 26, 27–8, 29, 36, 46, 52, 62, 161

Aníba, fortress of, in Nubia (Map 5(14)), *48*, 503

animal friezes and mosaics, 77–8

Anitta, Hittite king, 714, 715

Ankara, in Central Anatolia (Map 9), 371, *373*, 382, 383, 387; plain and region, 387, 388, 504, 695, 699

Ankara-Eskişehir region of Anatolia (Maps 9 and 10), *373*, *385*, 397–9

Ankara-Polatlı region of Anatolia (Maps 9 and 10), 398

Ankhhaf, Prince and Vizier of Egypt, 166, 171, 174, 206

Ankhka, 'Count' (Egyptian royal official), 26, 39

Ankhkhau (Merenre, q.v.) of Egypt, 192

Ankhmare of Egypt, 162, 163

Ankhtify of El-Mi'alla, 200, 465, 474–5, 490

Anna (Amorite god), 720

Annals of Tiglath-Pileser I, 741

Annubanini of Lullubi, 444, 664

Anoyira, in Cyprus (Maps 14(84) and 15(45)), *810*, 813, *814*

Anshan (Anzan, Persis), in Elam (Map 11), 431, 433, 438 *bis* and n. 4, 439 and n. 4, 440, 459, 607, 612, 616, 633, *646*, 647, 654 *bis*, 655, 658 *bis*, 661; 'Key to ...' (Khukhnur, q.v.), 647

Antaeopolis (Qāw el-Kebir), in Middle Egypt (Map 3(30)), 8, 472, 506 n. 1, 517

Antelope Nose (Mount Carmel promontory?), in Palestine, 192, 236, 361

Anten temples, in Mesopotamia, 310

Antilebanon mountain range, 338

Antilebanon (Sirion) region, 555

Antinoopolis, in Middle Egypt (Map 3 (14)), 8, 54

Antioch, plain of, in Syria (Map 8), 90, 230, *316*, 335, 337, 350, 682

Antiparos, Aegean island, 797

Antitaurus mountains, 367

Antyemsaf (Merenre, q.v.) of Egypt, 192

Anu (Mesopotamian god), 101, 102, 103, 558, 643, 766; zikkurrat of, at Uruk, 81

Anu-Adad temple at Ashur, 741

Anubis (Egyptian jackal-god), 22, 53, 202

Anum-muttabil, Governor or Viceroy of Dēr, 633, 661

Anunitum (goddess), 667, 673

Anzan (Anshan, q.v.), 431

Anzanzan (Subartu(m), q.v.), 431

Aphroditopolis (Atfih), in Egypt (Map 2(43)), 1, *4*

Aphroditopolis (Kōm Ishqāw), in Egypt (Map 3 (31)), 8, 467, 477; nome of, 467, 477, 483

Apis (Egyptian bull-god), 53

Apishal, in Syria (?), 326 n. 5, 429, 442, 560, 564 n. 7

Apkallat (Aplakkat) canal, 610, 614

Apolyont, Lake, in Anatolia, 390

Apsu, in Babylonia, 100

'Aqarquf, in Mesopotamia, 611

Aqqi (a labourer), 418

Arabia (the Nejd), 285, 440

Arabian peninsula, 736

Arad-kubi, 668

Aramaeans, 446

Aratta, in Babylonia, 111, 131, 240, 244, 276

Arbela, in Assyria, 743

Arbit, in Khabur valley, 306

Arcadia, in Greece (Map 12), 788–9

architecture, domestic: Aegean islands, 793–9 *passim*; Anatolia, 366, 374–5, 387–9, 685; Babylonia, 273; Crete, 799–804 *passim*; Cyprus, 808–23 *passim*; Egypt, 518; Greece, 771–9 *passim*, 804–7 *passim*; Palestine, 218–21, 568; Syria, 336; Troy, see Troy

architecture, monumental and public: Aegean islands, 793–9 *passim*; Anatolia, 363, **387–90**, 699–700; Babylonia, 81–5, 240–1; Crete, 799–804 *passim*; Cyprus, 808–23 *passim*, Egypt, see Egyptian architecture; Greece, 771–9 *passim*, 804–7 *passim*; Imhotep's

(Egypt), 155; Mesopotamia, 43, 240–1, 246–96 *passim*, 298–9, **308–12**; Palestine, **218–23**; Syria, **308–12**, 329, 331; Troy, 411–16 *passim*, 704–6 *passim* (*see also* Troy)

architecture of Elamite temples, 670–1

Argissa, in Greece (Map 12 (9)), 776

Argive plain, in the Peloponnese, 787

Argo island, in the Sudan (Map 5 (38)), *48*, 500

Argolid, the, in Greece, 774, 783–9 *passim*, 795, 805, 806, 807

Argolis, in Greece (Map 12), 786–8

Argos, in the Peloponnese, 784

El-'Arīsh (Raphia, Rhinocolura, Wenet (?)), in Sinai (Map 1), 2, 352, 356

Armant (Hermonthis, q.v.), in Upper Egypt (Map 4 (24)), 12, 200, 513, 519

Armanum, in Syria, 325–7 *passim*, 426, 433, 441, 442, 561

Armenia, 739

'Armenoids' (dynastic race of Egypt), 40

armour, *see* weapons

Arpachiyah, near Nineveh, 730

Arrapkha (Kirkuk, q.v.), 298, 443, 752, 753; lands of, 433

Arsinoe-Crocodilopolis, 22, 511

Arslantepe, near Malatya (q.v.), in Eastern Anatolia (Map 10), 367, 368, *385*, 401, 689

Arts, the: of Aegean islands, 793–9 *passim*; of Anatolia, 378–83, 392, 395–403 *passim*; of Babylonia, 77–80, 134–6, 450–1, 628–31; of Crete, 799–804 *passim*; of Cyprus, 808–23 *passim*; of Egypt, *see* Egyptian arts; of Elam, 673–7, 679–80; of Greece, 771–9 *passim*, 804–7 *passim*; of Mesopotamia, 42–3, 45; of Sumer, 134–6; of Syria, 341–51 *passim*; of Troy, 415–16

Asag (a demon), 125

Asea, in the Peloponnese, 789

Ash (Egyptian anthropomorphic god), 52 n. 2, 54

Asharid, *ensi* of Kazallu, 436

Ashduni-arim of Kish, 637–8

'ashērāh (sacred pole), 221

Ashkhara (Ishkhara, Mesopotamian goddess), 667

El-Ashmunein (Hermopolis, q.v.) (Map 3 (15)), 8

Ashnakkum (Chagar Bazar, q.v.), 330, 331

Ashur (Assyrian god), 638, 718, 720, 745, 754, 763–8 *passim*

Ashur, ('The City'), in Northern Mesopotamia (Map 8 (28)), 98, 117, 252, 255, 259, 262, 269, **298–301**, *316*, 333, 431,

452, 602, 604, 629, 638, 656, 708, 709, 721, 724, 726, 728, 730, 734 *bis*, 737, 739, 741, 745, 746, 752, 758–61 *passim*, 764–5; Subarians in, 300–1; Gutians in, 457–8; 'royal city' of, 729; an important administrative centre, 734; Old Palace at, 734; temple at, *see* Ashur temple; 'Semitic' city of, 745; gods of, 764–7

Ashurbanipal of Assyria, 450, 662, 670, 736, 741

Ashur-bel-kala's Annals, 739

Ashur-daiiān of Qabra, Eponym, 742

Ashur-dan of Assyria, 741

Ashur-mutakkil of Qabra, Eponym, 742

Ashurnasirpal I of Assyria, 332

Ashur sanctuaries in Asia Minor, 764–5

Ashur temple at Ashur, 744, 745; building and reconstruction of, 744–52 *passim*, 754, 755

Ashur-uballiṭ I of Assyria, 745, 753, 770

Asia Minor (*see also* Anatolia), 427, 429, 430, 443, 504

Asiatic: livestock in Egypt, 542–3, 549; overlordship of Egypt, 512; products in Egypt, 543–4; political and social organization, 554–6

Asiatics ('Sand-dwellers', *see also* Amu), 27, 68, 226, 236, 351, 352, 467, 480, 482, 487, 491, 494, 497, 508, 539, 592; bearded, 189; of Sinai, 191, 192, 485; Egyptian expeditions against (Palestine and Syria), 192, 360–2; in Egypt, 237, 352, 466, 532–7, 541–2; as slaves in Egypt, 357; as domestic servants etc. in Egypt, 504, 541; Achthoes III's comments on, 534; described, 536; represented on Egyptian monuments of the Twelfth Dynasty, 550–3; in Story of Sinuhe, 553–4; in Execration Texts, 554–5

Asine, in the Peloponnese (Map 12 (37)), 785, 787; isthmus south of, 783

Askalon (Askelon), in Palestine, 509, 555

Askitario, in Greece (Map 12 (28)), 782

askos, 'duck-vase', 684

asphalt, 601

asses: 'black', 725, 727; Damascus, 725; in Assyrian caravans, 724–6 *passim*; use of, by Asiatics, 552–3, 554

Assyria (*general*), 117, 241, 297, 298, 302, 307, 333, 370, 431, 609, 636, 638, 683; Sumerian culture and civilization in, 301; prehistoric, 303; Naram-Sin in, 431, 443, 762; Gutians in, 457; its power established, 602; Ilushuma's incursion into Sumer and Akkad, 638–9; and Shamshi-Adad, q.v., 639; early population of, 730–1; Naram-Sin and Babylonia, 762

Assyria and Mesopotamia, **291–314**: Mari, **291–7**; Kirkuk district, **297–8**; Ashur, **298–301**; Nineveh, **301–3**; Ninevite pottery on other sites, **303–4**; Northern Syria, **304–14**; Chagar Bazar, **304–6**; Tell Brak, **306–8**; Tell Khuaira, **308–14**

Assyria (c. 2600–1816 B.C.), **729–70**: pre-Sargonic period, **729–33**; Sargonic period, **733–40**; king-list and chronology, **740–52**; Old Assyrian period, **752–62**; religion of, **763–9**; the calendar, 728, **769–70**

Assyrian business-community in Asia Minor, 427, 442, 561, 707–9, 710, 712, 717–21, 723, 752; marital customs, 717–18; their wives, and their god, 764–5

Assyrian: calendar, 728, 769–70; chronology and astrology, 740–52; deities, 718; farmer-militia, 723; imperial administration and government, **715–23**; kingdom and territory in Asia Minor, 707–28

Assyrian kings, 601; and Sargon's title, 419; campaigns of, 444; their titles, 754–5

Assyrian: language, 718–19, 753; merchants, 752–4 (*see also* Assyrian business-community); names, 735, 736; religion, **763–9**; royal residences (religious principle involved in), 737–8; sculptures, 121; 'settlements' in Anatolia, 723 and n.4; wealth (sources of), 754; weights and measures, 727–8

Assyrians, 111, 124, 448; in Anatolia, 696, 707–28 *passim*; and Indo-Europeans and Hurrians, 717; inherit Akkadian imperialism, 736–7; and Sargon and Naram-Sin, 737

Astacus, in Southern Greece (Map 12(8)), 791

Astarte (Syrian goddess), 348, 349

Aswān, in Upper Egypt (Maps 1 and 4), 2, 12, 66, 167, 177, 187, 188, 193, 194, 195, 200, 351, 464, 484, 487, 493, 497, 501, 506; (red) granite quarries at, 467, 484, 500, 510; tomb chapels of nomarchs at, 516

Asyūt, in Middle Egypt (Maps 1 and 3), 2, 8, 11, 53, 464, 466, 467, 468–70, 482, 496, 512; nomarchs of, 468–70, 482

Atfîh (Aphroditopolis, q.v.), in Lower Egypt (Map 2(43)), 1, 4

Athens (Map 12(25)), 430; the Agora at, 781; Benaki Museum, 781

Athosis of Egypt, 15, 23

Attica, in Greece (Map 12), 781–3, 785, 806

Atum-Re (Egyptian sun-god), 202

augurers ('seers' or diviners), Sumerian, 423 (*see also* omens)

Awak, in Elam, 656

Awal, in Elam, 445, 638

Awan, city of, in Susiana, 432, 436, 444, 647, 648, 658, 660

Awan, kingdom and land of, 455, 611, 650–1, 654, 657; Elamite kings of, **644–54**, 662; last king of, 670

Awibre Hor, of Egypt, 512

Axius river, in Greece, 775

Ayia Analepsis, near Methone in the Peloponnese, 791

Ayia Marina, in Greece (Map 12(19)), 780

Ayia Paraskevi, in Cyprus, 813, 817

Ayio Gala, in Anatolia, 367

Ayioryitika (Hageorgitika), in the Peloponnese (Map 12(39)), 788

Ayios Kosmas, in Attica (Map 12(26)), 781, 782 *bis*, 796, 798

Ayios Sozomenos, in Cyprus (Map 15 (33)), *814*, 816

Azarbayjān, in Persia, 403, 689

Azov, Sea of, 400

Azupiranu, village on the Euphrates, 418

Ba'al (god), 558; temple of, at Ras Shamra, 545

Ba'alat (goddess), 558; temple of, at Byblos, 589

Ba'al-Kronos (a god), 343

Baba (a goddess), 126, 128, 142

Babaköy, in Anatolia, 376

Bāb ed-Drā, in Transjordan (Map 7), *209*, 210, 214, 224, 225

Babylon (city) (Map 6), 89, 97, 101, 259, 279, 419, 764; First Dynasty of, 565 *bis*, 594, 630, 637–8, 639, 642, 643, 758; 'likenesses of' (built elsewhere), 737

Babylonia (*general*) (Map 6): early population of, 730–1; invaded by Lullubi, 739; and Assyria, 756–7, 761–2

Babylonia, archaeological development in, **238–46**; principal sites, **272–90**: Eridu, 276; Kish, 272–5; Lagash, 288–9; Nippur, 278–80; Shuruppak, 277; Al-'Ubaid, 287–8; Ur, 280–7; Uruk, 289; others, 289; conclusions, 290

Babylonia, cities of, **93–144**: second and third Early Dynastic periods, 93–6; Early Dynastic civilization, 96–100; ideas and institutions, 100–5; history, recorded and traditional, 105–20;

armies and warfare, 121–4; foundations of power: husbandry, trades and arts, 124–36; foreign trade, 131–3, 445; religion and cult-practices, 137–9; society and social problems, 139–42; transition to empire, 143–4

Babylonia, last pre-dynastic period in, 71–92: sources and general character of, 71–4; earlier phase (Uruk 4), 74–81; later phase (Jamdat Naṣr), 81–92; *for continuation, see* Mesopotamia

Babylonia under Agade kings, 446–53: the 'golden age', 447; re-distribution of land, 448–50; economic and social conditions, 450–5

Babylonia (*c.* 2120–1800 B.C.), 595–643: the Third Dynasty of Ur, q.v., 595–617; the king and his officers, 617–20; economy and wealth, 620–3; foreigners from the East, 624–5; Amorite invasion, 625–8; change in art, 628–31; successors of the Ur Dynasty, 631–8; intervention from abroad, 638–43

Babylonian: 'city-rulers', 755; king-lists, 103, 106–7, 109–16 *passim*, 121, 144 (animal names in, 109); kings, generally *not* imperialistic, 736; nationalism, 737; solidarity, 106; weights and measures, 727–8 *passim*

Babylonians, later: and Assyrian conquerors, 448; and 'world-power', 448

Badakhshān, in E. Afghanistān, 132, 240, 285, 350, 392, 452

Badere, near Svilengrad in Turkish Thrace, 396

Badrah (Dēr, q.v.), N.-E. of Babylon, 738

Bad-tibira, in Babylonia (Map 6 (23)), 101

Baghdad (Map 6), 98, 610

Bahr Yūsef (Map 2), 510

Bahran II, Sassanian king (A.D. 276–93), 674

Bakare of Egypt, 173, 175

Bakhtyari mountains, 647, 653, 657

Balāṭa (Shechem, q.v.), in Palestine (Map 7), 209, 547

baldaquins, 391

Balıkesir plain, in N.-W. Anatolia (Map 9), 372, 373, 376, 684, 701, 702

Balīkh river (Map 8), 308, 316, 318, 324 n. 1, 327, 561, 707

Balīkh valley, 324, 325, 332, 333, 560

Balkan peninsula (*geographical*), 407; Southern, 366; Eastern, 367, 371

Balkans, the (countries), 408, 409; E.B.A. in, 371

El-Ballās, in Upper Egypt (Map 4 (14)), 12, 481, 486, 513

Baltic Sea and region, 392

Baltil(a), city of, in Assyria, 731–2, 766

Baluchistān, 295, 453

bāmāh (high-place), 223

'Bandkeramik' (linear pottery), 799, 869

Banetjeren (Banetjeru, Binōthris) of Egypt, 31

bank ('brow') of the Euphrates, 325, 326

bankers, Assyrian, 759

Baqet III, Nomarch of Oryx, 471

Bara-irnum, Princess, 119 n. 6

Barakhshe (Warakhshe, q.v., Markhashe) in Mesopotamia, 332, 432, 433, 436, 437, 444 n. 7, 600, 648

barcasses, 292, 293, 296

Barnamtarra (wife of Lugalanda, q.v.), 120

Basar (Basallu, Jebel el-Bishrī, q.v.), 325, 327, 455, 559, 562, 626

Bashimi (Bāsht), city in Elam (Map 11), 633, 646, 661

Bastet (Egyptian cat-headed goddess), 54

Battlefield Palette (Egyptian, proto-dynastic), 41 n. 8

Baufre, Prince, of Egypt, 172

Baunetjer (Biēnechēs, Ubienthēs) of Egypt, 29, 30

Baurdjeded, Isesi's Chancellor, 187

Bayraklı, in Anatolia, 372, 381, 398; desertion of, 383

bears, 183, 350

Bebi, Vizier, 483

Bebty (Beby) of Egypt, 35

Bedjapu of Egypt, 30

Bedjau (Bōchos, Boēthos) of Egypt, 30, 150

Bedjmes (Egyptian ship-builder), 160

Behdet, in Egypt, 51

'Beholder of Horus' (royal title), 152

'Beholder of Horus and Seth' (royal title), 36, 152, 179

Beilan pass, in Syria, 328, 337

Beirut, in Lebanon (Map 8), 316, 546

Beisān (Beth-shan, q.v.), 547

Beit Jibrīn, in Palestine, 218

Beit Khallāf, in Upper Egypt (Map 4 (4)), 12, 150, 151, 157, 198

Beit Mirsim, *see* Tell Beit Mirsim

Bellapais, in Cyprus (Maps 14 (49) and 15), 809, 810, 814

Ben (Buhen?), 487 and n. 1

Benben stone, 180

Beni Hasan, in Middle Egypt (Map 3 (12)), 8, 468, 471, 472, 483, 496, 504, 512, 515, 541; tomb chapels of nomarchs at, 516

Bent (South Stone) Pyramid (of Sneferu) at Dahshūr, 154, 156, 158, 162, 163, 164, 167; valley temple of, 155, 162; priest of, 163

Bereketlı-Maden, in the Taurus (Anatolia), 370, 696
Berenice (Red Sea port) (Map 1), 2, 25
Berossus (priest–historian), 102, 107, 109
El-Bersha, see Deir el-Bersha
Besh, 33, 47
Beshru, in Babylonia, 607
Beşiktepe, in Anatolia, 374
Bethel, in Palestine (Map 7), 209, 210, 214, 236
Bethlehem (Bēth-lekhem, Efrath), 720, 766
Beth-shan (Beisān), in Palestine (Map 7), 208, 209, 211–14 passim, 217, 219, 220, 236, 337, 547
Beth Shemesh, in Palestine (Map 7), 209, 210, 214, 236
Beth Yeraḥ (Khirbet Karak, q.v.), in Palestine (Map 7), 209, 210
Betrest, Queen, 36
Beycesultan, in W. Anatolia (Maps 9 and 10), 373, 385; phases, 366 (see also levels below); Late Chalcolithic period at, 366, 367; pottery, 367, 380, 381, 396, 398, 684, 685, 692–701 passim; culture, 368, 396; houses, 366, 375, 386, 388, 390; burning of, 377, 383, 384, 407; twin temples at, 388–9; child and infant burials at, 376–7; weapons, 377; stone objects, 378; figurines, 378; pottery, 380; city site, 386; metal vessels, 395
Beycesultan levels: XIII, 386, 388, 397, 407; XIV, 386, 388, 397; XV, 386, 388, 389, 394, 397; XVI, 386, 388, 389; XVIIa, 383, 384; XVIIb, 377, 378, 389
Beyşehir, Lake, 386
bibliography, 877–993
Bicheris (a king of Egypt?), 172–6 passim
Bihistān, sculpture of Darius at, 608
Bilalama, Governor of Eshnunna, 660, 661
Bin-kali-sharri, son of Naram-Sin, 455
Biqā' valley, and region, 234, 337, 338, 555
bird-vase, Yortan, 379, 398
bird-vessels, 395
Birket-Qārūn (site of Lake Moeris, q.v.), in the Faiyūm (Map 2), 4, 22, 510
Bismaya (Adab, q.v.), 289
Bīt Agusi (Aramaean state), 335
Bitum-rabium, in Babylonia, 607
Biyahmu, in the Faiyūm (Map 2 (45)), 4, 511
Black Planet, the (Saturn), 737, 738
Black Sea (Euxine), and its coasts, 383, 392, 393, 400; seafaring and trade on, 400
'Blau Monuments', 88–9
'boat-pit', Egyptian, 61
boats, see ships

Boeotia, in Greece (Map 12), 777, 778–80, 781, 783, 786, 788, 805
Boğazköy, in Anatolia, 682, 686, 694–7 passim, 707, 709 bis
book-keeping and accounts in Babylonia, 600
Book of the Dead, 27, 171, 202, 522
Book of the Two Ways, 523
Bor, plain of, in Anatolia, 696
'bowmen', 351
bows and arrows, 3, 6, 122, 123–4, 189, 374, 393, 552
bow symbol, Egyptian, 3, 6
Bozköy-Hüyücek, in Anatolia, desertion of, 383
Bozüyük, in N.-W. Anatolia (Map 10), 366, 385, 395, 398, 701
brachycephalics in Anatolian graves, 375, 386
Brak, see Tell Brak
bricks, plano-convex, 112, 241, 244, 246 bis, 249, 265, 266, 273, 275 n. 2, 276–81 passim, 287–9 passim, 307, 330
Bridges, Robert (poet laureate), quoted, 285
'brocade-pattern' on cylinders, 134, 239, 261, 273, 290, 301
bronze, 227–8, 306, 341, 344, 350, 377, 392, 394, 415, 452, 543, 567–8, 609, 612, 657, 771–9 passim, 793–823 passim
Bronze Ages, see Early, Middle and Late Bronze Ages
Bubastis, in the Delta (Map 2 (14)), 4, 54, 191, 494, 495, 498
Buchis (Egyptian bull-god), 519
'Bückelkeramik' ('knobbed' ware), 857
Buhen, near Second Cataract, in Nubia (Map 5 (24)), 48, 499, 507
Bulgar Maden, in the Taurus (Anatolia): silver mines, 370, 397, 696; lead mines, 430
bullae (clay seals, impressed), 89, 306
Bunefer, Queen, 177
burial (funerary) customs and rites: Aegean, 793–9 passim; Anatolian, 366, 375–7, 386, 387–8, 390–2, 401, 403; Babylonian, 82–3, 88, 137–9; Cretan, 799–804 passim; Cypriot, 808–23 passim; Egyptian, 18, 54–9, 59–60, 158, 168, 173, 177, 520–3; Elamite, 680; Grecian, 771–9 passim, 804–7 passim; Indo-European, 824–59 passim; Mesopotamian, 282–7; Palestinian, 223–5, 568, 570–5 (Jericho); Syrian, 334, 344
burials of children, 344, 366, 375–6, 376–7
Bursa-Iznik region of Anatolia, 699, 701
Bur-Sin (Amar-Sin, q.v.), 607
Bushire, see Liyan

Busiris, in the Delta (Map 2 (6)), *4*, 54, 202, 520, 521

Buto, in the Delta (Map 2 (1)), 1, *4*, 54

Büyük Güllücek, forest hamlet in Anatolia, 367, 399

Byblite cylinder, 532 n. 4

Byblos (city and port, Gebal, Jubeil Kupna) in the Lebanon (Map 8 (12)), 90, 156, 167, 181, 183, 187, 189, 190, 194, 200, 219, 227, 230, 233, 235, 237, 319, 324, 325, 337, **343–51** *passim*, 408, 426, 501, 509, 512, 523, 546 *bis*, 547, 548, 555 *bis*, 560, **586–90**, 592, 593 *bis*, 604; wares, 320; relations with Egypt, 45–6, 344, **345–51**, 361–2, 504, 545, 548, 550; and Sumer, 351 n. 5; Egyptians in, 549; Egyptian influence in, 550; political unit, 555

'Byblos-boats' ('Byblos-farers', Byblites, ocean-going craft), 348, 351, 358, 491

Caesarea (Kayseri, q.v.), in Cappadocia, 427

Caicus valley, in N.-W. Anatolia, 372, 379, 383, 409, 682, 700, 702

Cairo Annals, 16, 23, 27, 28, 30, 36, 53, 148, 162, 167

calendars (*see also* date-formulae): Assyrian, 728, 769–70; Elamite, 678

Callidromus mountains, in Greece, 777

Calycadnus river, in Anatolia, 365

Calycadnus valley, in Anatolia, 364, 381, 696

Calymnos, Aegean island, 684

camels, 343

Canaan, 234, 236, 329

Canaanite (Semitic dialect), 564–5

Canaanites, 234, 243, 360

Canaanite town or city, capture of a, 226, 235

Çanakkale, in Anatolia, 378

canals: as political boundaries, 125, 599; for irrigation (q.v.) and transportation, 125, 140, 193; Apkallat, 610, 614; Me-Enlil, 614; Esh-Shallāl (Nile), 506–7; near Sidari, 653; Tigris–Euphrates link, 119, 125; Ur-Nammu's, 599–600

Cappadocia, 324 n. 9, 326, 427, 560, 685, 708, 717; merchants of, 427, 442, 561 (*see also* Assyrian business-community); Assyrian traders in (and towns they occupied, *named*), 561, 712, 721; date-formulae from, 728

Cappadocian: names, 716; period, 368; texts, 681; ware (painted), 682, 686–8, 694–5, 697, 841, 844–5

caravans, trade, Assyrian, 723–7; routes of, 726–7

Carchemish (Jerablūs), in Syria (Map 8 (16)), *316*, 328, 333–4, 426, 561, 691

Caria, in Anatolia, 682

Carmel, Mount, 192, 236, 361

carnelian, 132

cartouches, Egyptian, 157, 158, 159, 162, 172, 177, 183 n. 6, 184, 192, 196, 345, 492, 501, 545 *bis*

carts (*see also* chariots), 873

Çatal Hüyük, in Konya plain (Anatolia), 90, 381; West, 365, 398

Cataracts of River Nile (Maps 1 and 5), *2*, *48*; First, 193, 464, 480, 484, 497, 500, 501, 506, 520; Second, 488, 497, 499, 503, 507, 518; Third, 499, 500, 506, 512, 549

cattle-counts in Egypt, 161

cattle imported into Egypt, 542–3, 549

cattle, Palestinian, 361

Caucasia and the Caucasus, 337, 430, 452, 585, 689, 691

Caves, Valley of (Wādi Maghāra, q.v.), 353

'Cedar Forest' (*see also* Forest of Cedars), 324 n. 7, 424, 425, 431

'Cedar Mountain', 442

cedar-oil, 46

cedar wood, 167, 183, 325, 329, 559

Central Anatolian culture and pottery, 400

Ceos, Aegean island (Map 12), 797

Cephallenia, Greek island (Map 12), 791

Cephissus river, in Central Greece, 777, 806

ceramics, *see* pottery

Cerastes-Mountain nome (province) of Egypt, 192, 472

Chagar Bazar (Ashnakkum?), in Syria (Map 8 (22)), 89, 292, 296, 302, 304, **304–6**, 307, 313, *316*, 330–1, 712

Chairēs of Egypt, 35

Chalandriani, on Syros (Map 12 (51)), 783, 796–7, 797, 798, 806

Chalcidice, in Greece (Map 12), 774, 775

Chalcis, in Euboea, 684, 781

Chalcolithic Age: in Cyprus, 808, 812, 813, 816, 820; in Greece, 771

Chalcolithic periods and cultures in Anatolia: Early, 364, 381; Middle, 365; Late, 363–7, 369, 371, 375, 380–4 *passim*, 399, 401; Final, 364

Chalcolithic remains at Byblos, 343, 344

Chaldaea (Babylonia, q.v.), 102

'Champs des offrandes', at Byblos, 589

chariots (war-wagons), 91, 118–23 *passim*, 136, 138–9, 269, 274, 343, 844, 873, 874

Chedorlaomer (Kutir-Lakamar), 666 n. 4

Chenerēs of Egypt, 35

Cheops (Khufu, Medjedu) of Egypt, 147, 148, 158, 159, 161, 165–75 *passim*, 181,

206, 207, 345, 353; his pyramid at Giza, 145, 168, 169, 172, 173, 174, 180; his pyramid-temple, 154–5; his chief queen, 170; his family, 178; his funerary-boat, 347, 348; his diorite quarries, 497, 500

Chephren (Khafre) of Egypt, 150, 161, 166–81 passim, 206; his reign, 174; his family cemetery, 174–5, 182; his pyramid-temple at Giza, 154, 155, 180; his valley-temple, 207

Chersonese, the Thracian, 372

Chinese pottery, 395

Chios, Aegean island (Map 12), 366, 372, 374, 414, 794, 805

Choga-Zanbil (Dūr-Untash), 85, 663

chronological tables: Aegean islands, 1002–3; Crete, 1002–3; Egypt, 994–6; Greece mainland, 1002–3; Old Babylonian period (to 1750 B.C.), 998–9; Sumerian period, 1000–1; Western Asia, 997

Çiğle, in W. Anatolia (Map 9), 373, 378

Cilicia (see also Mersin), 363–5, 368, 559, 682, 692; Late Chalcolithic period in, 363–4; pottery, 363–4, 365, 694, 696; Early Bronze Age in, 364; Western, 365; houses, 388, 389; and potter's wheel, 395

Cilician Gates, 365, 696

Cilician plain (Maps 9 (5) and 10 (5)), 373, 385; E.B.A. on, 369, 370, 381–2, 397; prehistory of, 364–5; on trade route, 370; pottery, 363–4, 381–2

Cilician ware, 363–4

Cincinnati, University of, 411

circumcision, 342

cire-perdue (lost-wax) process, 239, 245, 258, 268, 272, 341, 392

Cirrha, below Delphi in Greece (Map 12 (18)), 780

Cithaeron, in Central Greece, 777

cities, development of, in Babylonia, 92

Cities of plain and coast (Syrian), 333–43

'City of the Dead' at Giza (planned by Cheops), 169

city-states: in Mesopotamia, 71–2, 92, 103–4 (rivalries of, 104, 110); in Palestine, 555; in Syria, 327, 555

Civilization in ancient Elam (see also Elam), 673–80

Cleonae, valley of, in the Peloponnese, 785, 787

cloisonné work, 392

clothing, see costume

Cnossus, in Crete (Map 13 (61)), 773, 800, 802

'Codes' of laws in Mesopotamia, 635

Coffin Texts, 202, 522

Cogamus valley, in Anatolia, 384

Çokyatan, in Central Anatolia, 397

Colchis, in Anatolia, 401

Colias, Cape (of classical Greece), 781

commerce and industry, Palestinian, 225–30

commerce, external, see trade

communications (mails etc.), Assyrian, 726, 739

cone-mosaics, 75–8 passim, 84, 86

Copais, Lake, in Central Greece, 777

Copper Age (see also Early Bronze Age), 368, 369, 567, 575, 771, 776

copper as currency, 726, 754

copper: in Aegean islands, 771; in Anatolia, 368, 370, 377, 392, 394, 708, 722, 723, 724–5; Asiatic, 355; in Assyria, 757, 758; in Babylonia, 82, 452, 609, 612; in Crete, 771, 801, 802; in Cyprus, 819, 820–1; in Egypt, 24, 47, 58, 69, 147, 151, 355–6, 500, 533; in Greece, 771; in Mesopotamia, 254, 268, 269, 272, 305, 306, 640, 657; in Palestine, 228, 567–8; in Sinai, 355, 539; in Syria, 337, 344, 345, 347, 350; at Troy, 413, 415; state monopolies of, 708–9; as money, 726, 754

copper trading in Anatolia, 726

coppersmiths, 69, 341

'Corded ware', 871

Corfu, Greek island, 792

Corinth, in Greece (Map 12 (30)), 781, 785, 788

Corinth, Gulf of, 777, 788, 791 bis

Corinthia, in Greece, 783, 786–8

Coronation Drama, 528

costume and headdress, 116; Anatolian, 394; of Asiatics, 226, 536, 551; Babylonian, 277, 282, 286, 629; Egyptian, 481, 482; Mesopotamian, 300; pharaonic, 481; Syrian, 328, 342

court officials, Egyptian, 37–8

Creation, Epic of, 766, 769 bis

creation myths, 100–2

cremation (see also burial customs), 224, 311, 843–4, 852, 855

Crete (general) (Map 13), 181, 429–30, 504, 544, 773, 798; Minoan, 696 (see also next below); trade with Greece, 787

Crete (Kaptara, Kaptura, Kaphtor) (Map 13), 799–804, 805; E.B.A. sites in, 773; introduction, 799–800; Early Minoan: I, 800–1; II, 801–2; III, 802–4; chronological summary, 804–7 passim

Crisean plain, in Central Greece, 777

Crocodilopolis (Kīmān Fāris, Shedet), in the Faiyūm (Map 2(46)), 4, 22, 511 bis, 517, 520
'cruciform monument', 438 nn. 1 and 3, 439
cultures, some classifications of, 872
cult-wagon, of Mesopotamia, 251–2
cuneiform script and tablets, 72, 80, 90, 95, 279–80, 319, 320, 321, 332, 450–1, 544, 677–8
cupellation processes (for separating silver from copper and lead ores), 724–5
currencies: copper, 726, 754; gold, 726, 754; silver, 726
Cusae, in Middle Egypt (Map 3(21)), 8, 194, 496
Cyclades, the (Map 12), 379, 414, 416, 682, 684, 777, 778, 779, 781, 793–9, 805, 806; trade with Greece, 787; described, 793–4
Cycladic: culture and cultural areas, 416, 772, 774, 781, 782, **793–9**, 802, 803, 806; decoration on pottery, 778, 800
cylinder-seals, 42–3, 60, 79–80, 87–8, 89, 90, 93, 124 n. 1, 134–5, 181, 231, 238, 239, 245, 277, 293, 301, 319–20, 336, 337, 343, 345, 356, 451, 452, 453, 503, 544, 590, 630–1, 670, 674, 696, 711–12
Cypriot cultural periods: early, middle and late, 808–23 passim
Cyprus (general) (Maps 14 and 15), 803, 810, 814; Philia phase of E.B.A. in, 407 (see also Philia culture); Sargon II in, 425; and Anatolian disaster, 808, 813, 819–20; trade with Aegean islands and Crete, 822
Cyprus, Early Bronze Age in, **808–23**; Neolithic sites, 810–11; E.B.A. sites, 814–15
Cythera (Kithira), Greek island (Map 12), 180, 790

Dadusha of Eshnunna, 635, 762
Dagan (Amorite god), 321–31 passim, 424, 564, 707; -names, 564 n. 6
Dagan-abu of Tuttul, 564 n. 6
Dagi, father of Djefi, 474
Dagi, Vizier, 481, 483
Dahshūr in Lower Egypt (Map 2(35)), 4, 20, 154–68 passim, 177, 504, 509–16 passim, 538; North Stone Pyramid, 161–4 passim, 161 n. 1; South Stone Pyramid, 154, 156, 158, 162–4 passim; Decree of Phiops I, 186, 191, 192
Dai-Salkhupa, son of Akuta, of Anshan, 657
Dākhla Oasis, in Egypt (Map 1), 2, 482

Damascus, city and region, 229, 541, 555, 561
Damiq-ilishu of Isin, 642, 643
Darband-i Gawr gorge, in N. Mesopotamia, 443
Darband-i Ramkan, in N. Mesopotamia, 601
Dardanelles, the, 407, 411, 413, 414
Darius of Persia, 608
date-formulae: of Assyria, 728; of Cappadocia, 728; of Ur, 596, 597 bis, 600, 603; see also calendars
Dead Sea, 224
'decade' (Assyrian town-governing body), 723
Dedefptah of Egypt, 175
Deir el-Baḥri, in Upper Egypt (Map 4 (19)), 12, 21, 481, 482, 513, 514, 515, 536
Deir el-Bersha, in Middle Egypt (Map 3 (16)), 8, 470, 512, 515, 516, 522–3, 542, 546
Deir el-Gabrāwi, in Middle Egypt (Map 3 (22)), 8, 192, 198, 471, 474, 483
Deir Rīfa, in Middle Egypt (Map 3(23)), 8, 472, 516
deities: Asian, 558; Egyptian lesser, 54; for others, see under their names
Delphi, in Greece, 780
Delta, the (of the Nile), in Lower Egypt (Maps 1 and 2), 1, 2, 4, 6, 7, 10, 16, 22, 23, 39–45 passim, 51, 52 n. 2, 53, 60, 170, 191, 202, 351, 352, 465, 466, 482, 489, 493, 497, 520; 'foreigners' in, 201, 237, 466, 494, 532–3; conditions in (late Eleventh Dynasty), 494
Deluge, the (great flood in S. Mesopotamia), 97, 102, 106–13 passim, **243–4**, 444; date of, 109; see also floods
Demedjibtowy of Egypt, 198
demigods, Egyptian, 1, 3
Demirci Hüyük, in N.-W. Anatolia (Maps 9 and 10), 373, 385; culture, 368, 372, 382, 398; fortification of, 386; pottery, 397–8, 398; desertion of, 407
demonology, 763
De Morgan (archaeologist), 19
Den, King of Egypt, 18, 19, 25–8 passim, 39, 46, 50, 62, 64, 66, 69, 152, 352; his name, 26 n. 2
Dendera, in Upper Egypt (Map 4(13)), 12, 199, 474–81 passim, 488, 498, 512, 513, 'Mistress of...', 493
Denizli river, in Anatolia, 699; basin of, 384
Dep, in the Delta, 1
depas amphikypellon, 395, 416, 683, 699, 780, 796
depas-cups, 395, 396, 684

depas-forms, 398, 684
Dēr (Badrah), in Elam, 132, 436, 632, 633, 638, 738, 739, 756, 757 bis; dynasty of, 757
Derbisīye, 314
Develi plain, in Anatolia, 686
Dhemenagaki mountain ridge, on Melos (Map 12(55)), 793
Dhenia village, in Cyprus (Maps 14(65) and 15(29)), 809, 810, 814, 817
Dhikomo, in Cyprus (Maps 14(50) and 15(15)), 810, 814, 816
Dhimini, in Thessaly, 775–6; period, 797
Didanu (Dedan), nomadic chieftain, 744
Dikili Tash, near Philippi in Greece (Map 12(2)), 774
Dilmun island (Baḥrain, in Persian Gulf), 738
Diodorus, 15, 22
Diospolite nome, in Egypt, 474
Diqdiqqah, near Ur, 599–600
Dirā Abu'n-Naga, 473, 476
Dishāsha, in Middle Egypt (Map 3(1)), 8, 189, 235; relief, 215, 358–60, 359
Dispute of a Man, Weary of Life, 524, 527–8
Dit(a)nu(m) (Tidnum, q.v.), 562 and n. 8, 563 n. 1
diviners (augurers or 'seers'), Sumerian, 423
Diyālā river, 83, 238, 302, 305, 624, 641; district and region, 238, 241, 269, 274, 290 and n., 295, 298, 312; heads (female), 299
Diyālā valley, 238, 239, 241, 244, 246–72, 280, 296, 298, 302; Sin temples, q.v., at Khafājī, 246–57; Nintu temple, q.v., and others, in, 257–72
Diyārbakr, in Anatolia, 332
Dizful, near Susa in Elam (Map 11), 646, 647, 648
Dja (Medīnet el-Ma'ādi, q.v.), 520
Djadja of Egypt, 35
Djadjaemankh (a magician), 168
Djari, Overseer of Interpreters (Egyptian), 477
Djati, land of, 487
Djau, Vizier, 191–8 passim
Djed Sneferu in Egypt, 164
Djedi (a magician), 164, 172
Djedkare (Isesi, q.v.), 186, 187, 188, 354
Djedkhau (Isesi, q.v.), 186
Djefaihapi, Nomarch of Asyūt, 500, 549
Djefi, Nomarch of Koptos, 474 and n. 2
Djemi of Gebelein (Theban general), 474 and n. 3
Djer (Iti, q.v., Khent) of Egypt, 14, 18, 19, 23, 24, 25, 36, 46, 50, 58, 59, 64, 65, 69, 147 n. 4, 152, 354, 357; and the 'Smiting of Asia', 357

Djeret (Tōd, q.v.), village in Upper Egypt (Map 4(25)), 12, 472, 519
Djet of Egypt, 18, 19, 24 and n. 6, 25, 26, 64, 65
Djoser of Egypt, 34, 35, 37, 59, 65, 66, 70, 145–56 passim, 160, 167, 169, 171, 206, 207, 353; his step pyramid, see Step Pyramids; his temple, 154
Djosernub of Egypt, 150
Dodona, in north-west Greece (Map 12(5)), 791
dolichocephalics in Anatolian graves, 386, 392
Dorak, in N.-W. Anatolia (Map 10), 133, 181 n. 1, 351, 385, 390–5 passim; metalwork at, 370, 392, 394; royal tombs, 386, 390–3, 394, 396; female jewellery, 394; metal vessels, 394, 395
Dörpfeld, Wilhelm, 411, 415, 704, 792
Dothan, in Palestine, 232
Dramesi village, near Aulis in Central Greece (Map 12(24)), 780
dream-visions, 755, 768
Drehem, near Nippur, 560, 622
Duare of Egypt, 162–3
Dubrum (town) in Mesopotamia, 462
Duddul, see Tuttul
Dudu (a high-priest), 105, 131, 137
Dumuzi (Tammuz, a god), 111
Dumuzi, King, 111
'Dumuzi the Shepherd' (a king), 111
Dündartepe, in Pontic Anatolia (Map 10), 368, 385, 400
Dūr-Sin, city of, in Mesopotamia, 448
Dūr-Untash (Choga-Zanbil), in Elam, 85
dwarf, a dancing, 187, 195
Dynastic Race of Egypt ('Armenoids'), 40

Ea (Enki, q.v., a god), 101, 604, 667, 763
E-anna precinct, at Uruk, 73, 77, 83, 84, 289
Eannatum of Lagash, 104 n. 1, 117–19, 120–5 passim, 131, 245, 246, 255, 270, 288, 296, 308, 448, 563 n. 1
Early Bronze Age in Aegean islands, 793–9
Early Bronze Age in Anatolia, 682–5 passim; armoury, 374; levels, 693; E.B.1, 368, 369, 371–83, 383, 384, 389, 396, 398, 401, 402, 408, 409; E.B.2, 368, 369, 375, 377, 378, 381, 382, 383–403, 408, 681; E.B.3, [368, 369, 371, 389, 395, 399, 400, 408, 409, 410, 681, 685
Early Bronze Age: in Crete, 773, 799–804; in Cyprus, 808–23; in Greece, 771–99, 804–7; in Macedonia, 383
Early Bronze Age in Palestine, 567–8, 568–83 passim; phases I–IV, 211–14

Early Bronze Age in Syria, 583–92 *passim*
East Anatolian cultures, 401–3
'Eastern Defûfa' (fort at Kerma, in the Sudan), 518
Ebers medical papyrus, 23, 27
Ebikh-il (an official), 116, 295
eclipse of the moon at Ur, 615
eclipse of the sun in Assyria, 750
Edfu, in Upper Egypt (Maps 1 and 4), *2, 12, 24, 33, 145, 194, 465, 474*
Edjo (Egyptian cobra-goddess), 1
Edremit (Köylüce), in N.-W. Anatolia (Map 9), *373, 377, 381, 383*; plain of, 384, 682
Edwa, in the Faiyûm (Map 2 (49)), *4, 511*
Efrath (Bethlehem, q.v.), 720
Egigi, oracular priest of Narundi, 650, 672
Egypt (*general; see also* Egyptian, Egyptians *and* Lower, Middle *and* Upper Egypt) (Maps 1, 2, 3 and 4), *2, 4, 8, 12, 71, 90, 96, 159, 333, 350, 545*; government and administration of, 159–60, 170; the royal succession, 166, 173, 174; wealth of, 169, 195; external military activities, 357–62; tribal incursions, 485; temple building, 498; 'feudal lords' of, 505; rise of a middle class, 506
Egypt: the Early Dynastic Period, 1–70; early monarchy and unification, 1–15; foundation of Memphis, q.v., 15–17, 36; coronation ceremonies, 16, 36; cemeteries of Abydos, q.v., and Saqqara, q.v., 17–22; the successors of Menes, q.v., 22–35; royalty, royal officials and the State, 35–40; immigration, 40–1; foreign relations, 40–51 (*see also* Egypt, foreign relations (*below*)); religion, deities and funerary beliefs, 51–9 (*see also* Egyptian religion); architecture, 59–66, 70 (*see also* Egyptian architecture); sculpture, 42, 66–8 (*see also* Egyptian sculpture); small arts, 68–70 (*see also* Egyptian arts)
Egypt: the Old Kingdom, 145–207; Third Dynasty, 145–60; Fourth Dynasty, 160–79; Fifth Dynasty, 179–89; Sixth Dynasty, 189–97; literature and art, 200–7 (*see also* Egyptian arts, kingdoms *and* literature)
Egypt: the First Intermediate Period (decadence), 197–200, 233, 237, 445, 464–8, 508 n. 2, 512, 518, 519, 532–7, 591, 803
Egypt: the Middle Kingdom, 464–531; Heracleopolitan (q.v.) kingdom, 464–

8, 471, 481, 486, 521–3 *passim*; nomarchs of, 468–72; Thebes, q.v., and the 'Head of the South', 472–5; Eleventh Dynasty, early kings of, 476–9; reunion of Egypt, 479–81; reorganization and recovery, 481–5; foreign policy and reconquest of Nubia, 485–8; Mentuhotpe III, 488–90; Red Sea and Wadi Hammâmât, 491–2; end of Eleventh Dynasty, Mentuhotpe IV, q.v., and Vizier Ammenemes, q.v., 492–5; Twelfth Dynasty, Ammenemes I, q.v., 495–9; Sesostris I, q.v., and his successors (expansion), 499–505; Sesostris III, q.v. (reforms and foreign campaigns), the 'Execration Texts', 505–9; Ammenemes III, q.v. (Economic measures), 509–12; art and architecture, 512–18 (*see also* Egyptian arts *and* Egyptian architecture); religion and funerary rites, 518–23 (*see also* Egyptian religion); literature, 523–31 (*see also* Egyptian literature)
Egypt, foreign relations of: general (and immigration), 40–1; with the Aegean world, 180–1; Byblos, 344, 345–51, 361–2, 504, 545, 548; Libya, 47; Mesopotamia (Southern), 41–5; Nubia, 50–1, 485–8, 506–7, 509; Palestine, 46, 192, 231–3, 235–6, 237, 356–62, 501, 508, 537–50; Sinai, 46–7, 50, 351–6, 539–40; the Sudan, 549; Syria, 45–6, 232–3, 336, 345–51, 498, 501, 508, 532, 537–50; Western Asia, 501, 503, 504, 508, 509
Egyptian: architecture, 59–66, 70, 145–79 *passim*, 205–6, 484, 515–18 (domestic, 518); arts, 26, 53, 66–70, 203–7, 484, 489, 512–15
Egyptian dynasties: First, 1, 6–15, 22–30 *passim*, 39–45 *passim*, 50–5 *passim*, 58–70 *passim*, 146, 148, 151, 152, 161, 197, 199, 226, 231, 232, 233, 346, 352, 355, 357, 445; Second, 17, 20, 29, 30–5, 38, 51, 52 n. 2, 56, 59–69 *passim*, 146, 148, 150, 154, 156, 161, 167, 232; Third, 20, 21, 23 n., 29, 34, 39, 40, 50, 62, 145–60, 167, 201–7 *passim*, 232, 346, 353; Fourth, 20, 30, 39, 40, 149, 152, 154–60 *passim*, 160–79, 189, 206, 207, 232, 346, 353, 357, 584, 594; Fifth, 30, 31, 37, 39, 54, 70, 133, 147, 148, 156, 161, 162, 167, 169, 173, 175, 178, 179, 179–89, 195, 198, 201, 202–7 *passim*, 229, 353, 354, 357, 391, 445; Sixth, 16, 23, 31, 54, 69, 156, 161, 183 n. 6, 188, 189, 189–97, 197–203 *passim*, 206,

346, 351, 353, 357, 445, 473, 475, 485–6, 492, 515, 519; Seventh, 197–200, 475; Eighth, 194, 197–200, 470, 473, 475; Ninth, 197, 200, 465–6, 470, 475; Tenth, 408, 466, 470, 473, 475, 591; Eleventh, 21, 468, 476–9, 473, 475, 489, 492–6 passim, 513, 514, 515, 519, 521, 522, 591, 592; Twelfth, 320, 408, 471, 472, 473, 485, 488, 489, 492, 493, 495, 495–512, 514, 517, 519, 520, 521, 540, 542, 544–7 passim, 550, 558, 591, 592; Thirteenth, 502, 504, 520, 542, 558; Eighteenth, 24, 145, 193, 473, 479; Nineteenth, 15, 22, 29, 147; Twenty-first, 171

Egyptian: 'empire', 537–50; iconographic symbols and themes, 550; imports of cattle and slaves, 542–3, 549

Egyptian kingdoms: the Old (see also Egypt: the Old Kingdom), 11, 30, 34, 37, 45, 47, 56, 57, 70, 133, 145–207, 200–1, 202, 351, 356, 357, 358, 479, 491, 496, 502, 508 n. 2, 511, 512, 516–20 passim, 520, 521, 548, 589, 591; the Middle (see also Egypt: the Middle Kingdom), 46, 70, 159, 168, 200, 202, 355–61 passim, 464–531, 540–7 passim, 550, 553, 555, 556, 590; the New, 23, 30, 35, 352, 355, 360, 479, 492, 502, 518, 522, 542, 554, 555; Northern, see Lower Egypt; Southern, see Upper Egypt; the 'Two Lands', 11, 15, 16, 36–9 passim, 44–5, 51, 156, 468

Egyptian literature, 168–9, 200–4, 466, 499, 523–31: drama, 528–9; instructional works, 523, 524, 526–7; legal and business documents, 531; mathematical treatises, 529–30; onomasticon, 531; philosophical and contemplative works, 523, 524, 527–8; poetry, 528; prophecy, 523; stories, 523, 524, 525–6; technical literature, 529–31

Egyptian: middle class, rise of, 506; objects in Syria and Palestine, 544–8, 590–1, 594; public works, 169; religion and funerary beliefs, 51–9, 518–23; sculpture and statuary, 19, 42, 66–8, 70, 174, 206–7, 505, 511; sources, 550–8; traditions, 92

Egyptians, deceased, pilgrimages of, 521

Egyptians in Syria and Palestine, 351–62, 544–5

E-khulkhul (temple), in Harran, 741

'El (generic term for 'god'), 558

Elam (Map 11), 42, 89, 110, 117, 132, 332, 432, 433, 434, 438, 444, 448, 454, 455, 459, 460, 563 n. 3, 600, 607, 613, 614, 616, 633, 646, 649, 660, 661; principal

sites in, 646; Rimush and, 436–7, 649–50; Eparti kings of, 641; Elamite names for, 644; history of, 645–54; and Mesopotamia, 645–7; treaty with Naram-Sin, 650–2; and Lagash, 654; Pax Sumerica in, 656; Ibbi-Sin and, 658; its brief independence, 659; civilization of, 645, 673–80; federal structure of, 645, 648, 664; religion in, 662–73; invaded by Lullubi, 739

Elamite: calendar, 678; cities (Shu-Sin's governors of), 609; dynasties, 640; king-list, 649, 650, 654

Elamite kings: of Awan, 644–54, 665; of Simashki, 654–62, 665

Elamite: language, 445, 644, 650–1, 678; measures, numeration and fractions, 676; names, 640; pantheon, 662–70; royal succession, 649, 660, 667; sacrifices, ritual, 671–2

Elamite scripts: 'proto-Elamite', 89, 95, 652, 675–6; 'linear', 675, 676–7

Elamite: temples, 670–3; traditions, 659; worship, 674

Elamites, 98, 111, 120, 254, 433, 437, 438, 444, 603, 612, 613, 615, 616, 645, 654; and Ur, 616, 625, 628, 631; ethnological definition of, 644; political unity through federation, 645, 648, 664

Elaphonisi, Greek islet (Map 12), 790

Elbistan, in Eastern Anatolia: plain of, 688, 726; town/city of, 726

Elburz region and sites, in Northern Iran, 307, 331

electrum (metal), 283, 392, 395

Elephantine Island, in the Nile near Aswan in Upper Egypt (Map 4 (42)), 12, 23, 159, 188, 193, 194, 200, 201, 473–80 passim, 487, 489, 495, 496 bis, 518

Eleutheros valley, in Phoenicia, 541

Elili of Ur, 114

Elis, in the Peloponnese (Map 12 (41)), 788, 791

Elkāb, see El-Kāb (under 'K')

Elmalı plain, in S.-W. Anatolia (Map 9), 373, 378, 380, 398

Elulu of Gutium, 113, 457

Emar, near modern Meskeneh in Syria, 333

Emery, W. B., 17

Emporio, on Chios (Map 9), 366, 368, 372, 373, 379, 380, 383, 398

Emutbal, in Mesopotamia, 640, 641

en, meaning of (see also ensi), 105

Enakalli, father of Urlumma, 119

E-nam-zu temple (Adab), 115

Enanedu (priestess of moon-god at Ur), 641

Enannatum I of Lagash, 119, 120
Enbi-Ishtar of Kish, 114
Enentarzi (priest and city-governor) of Lagash, 120, 137, 276
E-Ninmar (a city of Lagash), 422
E-ninnu temple (Lagash), 85, 289, 459, 460
Enkheduanna (priestess of moon-god at Ur), 435; her lament, 435
Enkhegal of Lagash, 116, 131
Enki (Ea, q.v., a god), 101, 281, 609, 643, 667, 671
Enkidu (a Sumerian hero), 424
Enlil (a god), 101, 103, 143, 144, 289, 295, 421, 433, 437, 438, 456, 462, 599, 609, 615, 643, 650, 657, 667, 732, 734, 738, 766–7
Enlil-bani of Isin, 632
Enlil-bani (a merchant), 710
Enmebaragisi, King, 94 n. 1, 103, 107, 108, 110, 244, 272, 645
Enmengalanna (Ammenon, legendary king of Babylonia), 102
Enmerkar of Uruk, 95 n. 3, 110–11, 131, 137, 240, 244, 276, 626
Enannatum (priestess of moon-god at Ur), 634
Ennigi, in Mesopotamia, 462
Enshakushanna of Uruk, 114
ensi (Sumerian city-governor), 103–4, 104, 121, 126, 128, 137, 143, 351 n. 5, 420, 422, 432, 436, 447, 449, 560, 604, 609, 618, 619
Entemena of Lagash, 105, 114, 119–20, 121, 125 and n. 2, 137, 265, 276, 288
Eparti of Anshan and Susa, 661, 662
Epidauria, in the Peloponnese, 787
Epir-mupi, *ensi* of Susa and *later* Governor-General or Regent (*sukkal*) of Elam, 445, 650
Episkopi, in Cyprus (Map 15 (48)), *814*, 816
eponym (Assyrian official, *līmum*), 742–3, 770
equus caballus (*see also* horses), 775
Erbaa, in Central Anatolia (Map 9), *373*, 383
Erçis, on Lake Vān in E. Anatolia, 403
Erdiwy-Khnum, Steward, 477, 478
Ergani Maden copper mine, in Asia Minor, 758
Eridu (Abu Shahrain), in Babylonia (Map 6), 72, 75, 77, 96, 97, 101, 102, 103, 107, 247, 287, 604, 633, 730; Palace, 241 and n. 2, 262, 274, 276, 296; principal sites at, 276; *apsu* at, 608
Erishum I (Irishum) of Assyria, 708, 708–9, 710, 748 *bis*, 753, 754, 755; his scribes, 753; his reign, 758–60; and 'free enterprise', *759*

Erishum II of Assyria, 749 *bis*, 762
Erra (a god), 667
Erra-imitti of Isin, 632
E-sagil(a) (a temple), 419, 604
Esarhaddon of Assyria, 736 *bis*, 744
Esdraelon, plain of, in Palestine (*see also* Jezreel), 213, 581
Eshnunna (Tell Asmar, q.v.), in Babylonia (Map 6 (12)), 92, 97, 135, 457, 607, 609, 614, 617, 628, 629, 632, 635, 636, 660, 732, 761, 762; laws of, 635
Eshpum, *ensi* of Susa and Viceroy of Awan, 437, 650, 672 *bis*
Eskişehir, in W. Anatolia (Map 9), *373*, 398, 689
Eskişehir–Ankara region of Anatolia (Maps 9 (3) and 10 (3)), *373*, *385*, 397–9
Eskişehir plain, in Anatolia (*see* Eskişehir on Map 9), 368, 372, *373*, 397–9, 382, 694, 698, 703
Etana, King, 110
Ethiopia (Abyssinia), 439
Etiyokuşu, in W. Anatolia, 388, 695, 697
Euboea, Greek island (Map 12), 684, 777, 780–1, 805
Euphrates river (Maps 6 and 8), 89, 96, 97, 98, 116, 119, 125, 143, 241, 245, 288, 318, 322, 323, 328, 418, 419, 421, 426, 431, 442, 446, 455, 561, 603, 609, 610, 614, 628, 639, 641; lower, 330; middle, 291, 597, 603; upper, 291, 603, 631
Euphrates plain or valley, 71, 73, 92, 313, 626; cities of, **328–33** *passim*; trade route, 333, 336; Sargon in, 424–5
Euphrates–Tigris plain, 73, 89, 92, 306, 310
Euripus, the, in Greece, 780–1
Eusebius, 22
Eutresis, in Boeotia (Central Greece), 774, 778–80, 783, 795, 805
Evans, Sir Arthur, 799–800, 802
'Execration Texts', 320, 338, 508–9, 541, 548–9, 554–5, 556 n. 7, 557 and nn. 4 and 10, 593
'Eye-Temples' at Tell Brak, 247, 307, 329–30

Fahliyān, in Anshan (Map 11), *646*, 673
Faiyūm, the, in Egypt (Maps 1 and 2), 2, 4, 33, 54, 169, 189, 464, 482, 501, 505, 514, 517, 520; land reclamation and flood control in, 505, 509, 510–12
falcon (hieroglyph), 7
Fallūjah (Pallukat?), near Baghdad (Map 6), 98, 610, 611
famines: in Egypt, 169, 189, 468–9, 475, 479, 490; at Ur, 616
Farāh (Shuruppak, q.v.), in Babylonia, 72,

243, 273, 289, 563; tablets, 94 and n. 1, 277 and n. 6; principal sites at, 277
Fedar (Phaedrus) river, in Syria, 344
federation: in Elam, 645, 648, 664; in Warakhshe, 648
Fegu (an Egyptian warrior), 474 and n. 2
'Fender of Tidnum' (Muriq Tidnim), 609–11, 612
Fenkhu (inhabitants of Negau), 347
Fertile Crescent, the, 236, 556, 558, 593, 766, 769
festivals, agricultural (loan), Assyrian, 728
figurines (divine, human and animal), 57, 68, 86–7, 92, 258, 259, 300, 341–2, 371, 378, 381, 391, 394, 413, 590, 688, 718, 798, 802
financing of merchandise exchange between Assyria and Asia Minor, 759
Firaktin, in Anatolia, 367
fisheries, Babylonian, 127
floods in Mesopotamia (see also Deluge), 243–4, 273, 297, 423, 444, 615, 631; Noah's (?), 273
'Followers of Horus', 3, 11
'Following of Horus' (royal tour of inspection), 11, 38, 161
food storage in Anatolia, 375
'Forest of Cedars', 322, 324 and n. 7, 326, 424
'Fortress before the Mountain', 611, 615
fortresses and fortifications (see also siege warfare), in Anatolia, 374, 386, 387, 413, 415; in Egypt, 507, 518; in Palestine, 214–18, 358; in Syria, 334; slits for archery, 374; Ahlatlibel, 386; Troy, 386, 413, 415; Shu-Sin's 'wall', 609–11
'free enterprise' in Assyria, 759
funerary customs and rites, see burial
funerary figures, 57

Gababa (people) from Mukish, 565
galena (ore of lead, q.v.), 430, 724, 725
Gallipoli peninsula, 414
G[an]-su(d) of Mari, 297
Gasur (Nuzi, q.v.), 99, 297, 431, 450, 734
Gawra (see also Tepe Gawra): levels IX and XIa, 364
Gaza, in Palestine (Map 1), 2, 218, 356
Gebel el-Araq, in Upper Egypt (Map 4 (9)), 12, 42, 44, 68
Gebelein, in Upper Egypt (Map 4 (27)), 12, 200, 475, 476, 480, 481, 486, 512, 535
Gebel Sidmant, in the Faiyūm (Map 2 (56)), 4, 511
Gebel es-Silsila, East and West, in Upper Egypt (Map 4 (37)), 1, 12, 23, 50, 60, 478, 484

Gelenbe plain, in Anatolia, 372
Geöy Tepe (Geöytepe), in E. Anatolia, 302 n. 3, 368, 403
Gerf Husein, in Nubia (Map 5 (4)), 48, 497
Germayir, in Khabur valley, 300, 306, 313
Gezer, in Palestine (Map 7), 209, 210, 211, 212, 224, 226, 228, 544, 546
Ghāb gorge, in Syria, 338
El-Gharrāf (Shaṭṭ el-Ḥazy), 116, 120, 288
Ghassūl, in Palestine, 226
Ghassūl-Beersheba civilization and culture, 212, 233
Gilead, in Palestine, 541
Gilgamesh epic, 109, 111, 112, 243, 324 n. 8
Gilgamesh of Uruk, 42, 94 n. 1, 110, 111–12, 137, 138, 144, 244, 266, 268, 286, 424, 606, 636
Gilgamos, 111
Gimil-Sin, see Shu-Sin
giraffes, 41 and n. 8, 188
Girga, in Upper Egypt (Map 4 (5)), 12, 198
Girnamme of Simashki, 657, 659
Girsu, in Babylonia (Map 6), 116
Gish (or Ush) of Umma, 119
Giza, near Cairo in Lower Egypt (Map 2 (26)), 4, 19, 30, 58, 145, 150, 156, 165, 166, 168, 177, 179, 183, 187, 207, 346; the Great Sphinx at, 154, 174; mastabas at, 155, 166, 170, 172, 173, 175, 206; Great Pyramid (Cheops's) at, 145, 168, 169, 172, 173, 174, 180, 204; pyramids at, 169, 171, 174, 179; necropolis at, 169–70, 174–5, 180, 182; the Second Pyramid at, 174–5; the Third Pyramid at, 176–7, 179, 197; the 'Unfinished Pyramid' at, 178; 'writing board', 205; portrait heads (limestone), 206
Giza (province), in Egypt, 15
glyptic (engraving on seals and precious stones), see seals
gods and men in Sumer, 137, 460
'God's Land' (the Lebanon), 346
'gods of our fathers', 768–9
Gölbaşı, Lake, and plain, in Anatolia, 387
gold: in Aegean islands, 793–9 passim; in Anatolia, 370, 377, 392, 394, 395, 726; in Assyria (at Nuzi), 735; in Babylonia, 80, 82, 132, 136; in Crete, 799–804 passim; in Cyprus, 808–23 passim; in Egypt, 38, 69, 168, 169, 194, 207, 484, 487, 499, 500, 543; in Greece, 771–9 passim, 804–7 passim; in Mesopotamia, 244, 269, 612, 650, 657, 726, 754; in Nubia, 132, 487; in Palestine, 226, 545; in Syria, 330, 350, 427, 545, 559; at Troy, 415; as money, 726, 754

Gonia, near Corinth (Greece) (Map 12 (31)), 783
Gordion, in N. Anatolia (Map 10), *385*, 698
Goreg Shema To-mehu (Mentuhotpe II, q.v.), 486
Goshen, Land of, in Egypt, 352
Grai Resh, in Jebel Sinjār, in Mesopotamia, 84, 88, 364
granaries: in Anatolia, 387; in Egypt, 38, 59, 230, 468, 517; in Elam, 679; in Mesopotamia, 266; in Palestine, 229–30
'Grand-Regent' (*sukkal-maḫ*) at Ur, 656; in Elam, 662
graves, *see* burial customs
Greece (Map 12), 383, 408, 410, 414, 682, 700–3 *passim*, **771–9**, **804–7**; geographical divisions of, 772; North-East, **773–7**; Central, and the Eastern shores, **777–88**; Central Peloponnese and the Western coasts, **788–93**; the Aegean islands, **793–9**; chronological summary, **804–7**; Indo-European immigrants, **845–50**; Indo-European languages in, 839
Greece, Crete and the Aegean islands, the Bronze Age in, **771–807**; definition of the inquiry, 771–2; *for details, see* Crete *and* Greece
Greek: islands, *see* Aegean islands; language, 700, 839, 845, 850
Greeks, 1, 410
gryphons in Elamite and Egyptian art, 675
Gudea of Lagash, 85, 121, 129, 132, 140–1, 270, 425, 426, 439 n. 4, 459–61, 559, 560, 562, 564, 601, 629, 654, 671 n. 1, 673, 755
Gumelniţa culture of Eastern Bulgaria, 366, 395
Gungunum of Larsa, 633–4, 661, 672
Gunilakha, in Elam, 648
Gutians, the (*later* Qutu), 434, 444, 447, 454, 460, 563, 599, 602–3, 616, 653, 654; invasion of Babylon, 456–7, 824; supremacy of, 457–8, 559, 602, 618, 654; expulsion of, **461–3**, 595, 597, 602, 627, 824
Gutium (Gutu), land of, 433, 444, 454–7 *passim*, 651, 653; invaded by Lullubi, 739
gypsum, head modelled in, 80

Ḥabbaniyah, Lake, in Mesopotamia, 611
Hacılar, in S.-W. Anatolia (Map 10), 367, 381, *385*, 387, 394
Hadad (Adad?, Semitic god of storm), 321, 558, 564

Hageorgitika (Ayioryitika), in the Peloponnese (Map 12 (39)), 788
Hagy (a governor), 199
Haifa, 228
hair styles, *see* costume and headdress
Halaf imports into Anatolia, 365
Halaf influences in Cilicia, 363, 364, 365
Haliacmon river, in Greece, 774
Halkavun, in Central Anatolia, 383
Halys people and region, in Anatolia, 686, 687
Halys river, in Central Anatolia (Maps 9 and 10), *373*, 383, *385*, 399, 686, 698
Hama (Hamath), in Syria (Map 8), 231, *316*, 337–43 *passim*
Hamitic peoples, 50
El-Ḥammām (Tabbat el-Ḥammām), in N. Syria (Map 8 (8)), 307 n. 4, *316*, 340
El-Hammāmīya, in Middle Egypt (Map 3 (29)), *8*, 182
Hammurabi of Babylon, 88, 90, 636 *bis*, 639, 643, 661, 741; Age of, 643; Code of, 323, 461, 620, 635 *bis*; his empire, 662
Ḥanay Tepe, in Anatolia, 375, 376; figurines, 378
Har (mountain-god), 558
El-Haraga, in the Faiyūm (Map 2 (55)), *4*, 504
Harakhte (Egyptian god), 481
Harappā, in Indus valley, 132, 453, 852
Harappā people, 439 n. 4
Hare nome, in Egypt: Nomarchs, 470–1, 470 n. 7, 483, 505
Harkhuf (a nomarch), 193, 194, 195
harpoon (ensign), 7
harpooners, 33
Harran, in Syria (Map 8 (18)), 312, *316*, 736, 738, 741
haruspical superstition, 423, 456
Hathor (Egyptian goddess), 180, 181, 207, 349, 353, 354, 474, 481, 484, 493, 510, 539; temples of, 498, 510
Hathorneferhetepes of Egypt, 158
Hatiu-a (Libyans), 47
Hattic people, 686
'Hau-nebu' (Haunebut, Asiatics of remote littorals, quoted in Pyramid Texts), 181, 504
Haurān (Palestinian god), 558
Ḥaurān, the, in Syria, 229
Hawāra, in the Faiyūm (Map 2 (51)), *4*, 516
Hazor, in Palestine, 333, 555, 736
headdress, *see* costume
'Head of the South' (southern Upper Egypt), 473
hearths, elaboration and decoration of (in Anatolian culture), 402

34

Hebron, in Palestine, 218

Hebrus, the, in Thrace, 774

Heb Sed (Egyptian jubilee festival), 21, 185, 186, 204, 481, 501, 517

Heb Sed court (Djoser's), 59

Hecataeus, 15

Hedjhekenu, Queen, 175

Hedj-wawesh, Prince, of Libya, 485

Hefat (El-Mi'alla, q.v.), 475

Hekanakhte, and his letters and papers, 489–90, 491

Hekayeb, of Elephantine, 195–6, 478

Hekayeb, of Gebelein, 475

Heliopolis, in Lower Egypt (Maps 1 and 2 (23)), 30, 32, 53, 152, 153, 170, 179, 180, 187, 190, 352–3, 501, 517; High-Priest of, 40, 54; priests of, 202, 518; solar doctrine of, 203; theologians of, 521

Helladic: cultural areas (H), 772–8 *passim*, 805, 806, 807; culture and influences, 414, 416, 684, 700, 702, 704; invaders, 410, 703

Hellas and the Hellenes, 106

helmets, 393–4

Helvaciköy-Hüyücek, in W. Anatolia (Map 9), *373*, 381, 383

Helwān, near Cairo (Map 2 (34)), *4*, 56, 66, 161

Hemaka (Den's Chancellor), 26–7, 62, 69

Hemetre, Princess, 175

Hemiunu, Prince and Vizier, 166, 206

Henenu, Chief Steward, 481, 483 *bis*, 489; his expedition to Red Sea and Wādi Hammāmāt, 491–2

Henqu (Kheteti), a nomarch, 471–2

Henuni (a courtier), 478

Henutsen (minor wife of Cheops), 165, 171

Heracleopolis, in Middle Egypt (Maps 1 and 2 (58)), 2, *4*, 26, 198, 199, 200, 408, 465, 466, 470; fall of, 471, 481; and Thebes, 475, 479; nome of, 483

Heracleopolitan: armies, 482; pharaohs, 464–79 *passim*, 521

Heraea, in Central Peloponnese (Map 12 (44)), 788

Heraeum, on Samos (Map 12 (59)), 396, 682, 683, 685, 694, 795

Heraion, on Samos (Map 10), 381, *385*

Herishef (Arsaphes), 408

Hermionid, the, in the Peloponnese, 787

Hermonthis (Armant, q.v.), in Upper Egypt (Map 4 (24)), *12*, 472, 473, 475, 481, 518, 519

Hermopolis (El-Ashumunein, Khmunu), in Middle Egypt (Maps 1 and 3 (15)), 2, 8, 171, 469–72 *passim*, 482, 505, 519

Hermopolite nome, in Egypt, 467, 546

Hermus valley (in Anatolia) route to the Aegean, 370, 384

Herneith, Queen, 19, 24, 36, 66, 67

Herodotus, 11, 15, 16, 168, 169, 179, 259, 511

Hesyre (an official of Djoser), 153–4, 158, 206

Hetepheres I, Queen, 158, 164, 165, 168, 171, 178, 183; her burial and re-burial, 168

Hetepheres II, Queen, 170–5 *passim*

Hetephernebty, Queen or Princess, 152, 153

Hetepsekhemwy (Hetep) of Egypt, 30, 65

Hetep-Sesostris, in the Faiyūm, 505

Het-nub, in Middle Egypt (Map 3 (19)), 8, 470; alabaster quarries, 190, 191, 192, 195, 466, 470, 480, 484, 500, 505; graffito at, 470

El-Hibbeh, in Babylonia (Map 6), 116

Hierakonpolis, in Upper Egypt (Map 4 (34)), 1, 3, 6, *12*, 21, 32, 34, 42, 50, 59, 66, 68, 69, 70, 146, 154, 156, 207; mace-heads at, 3–6, 10; slate palettes at, 6, 7, 10; ivory cylinder from, 7; King of, 11; copper statue-group, 192

Hierapolis, in Syria, 115

hieroglyphic signs and script, 3, 7, 37–8, 43, 45; principles of, 43–4; Egyptian and Sumerian, 43–4, 90; beauty and meaning of, 203; in Negau, 319; in Anatolia, 408; at Byblos, 545; Hittite, 830, 832

'high-places' (*bāmāh*), 223

Ḥillah, in Assyria, 732

Hirkaköy, in Anatolia, 398

Hirmās river, in Syria, 739

Hisar, *see* Tepe Hisar

Hisarlik, in Anatolia (*see also* Troy), 90, 411–14

history: beginnings of, 93; dependent on writing, 80

Hīt (Tuttul, q.v.), 322, 424, 425, 426, 431, 610

Hittite: empire (in Anatolia), destruction of, 856–7; 'Old Kingdom', 683, 700; wars, 694, 845

Hittites, 311–12, 332, 407, 426, 427, 428, 626, 702, 703, 709, 716; in Anatolia, 830–7, 835–7

Homer, 411

Homs, in Syria (Map 8), *316*, 338, 585

Hordedef, a prince of Egypt, 145, 164, 171, 172

Horhotpe, Treasurer, 481

Horoztepe, in Pontic Anatolia (Map 10), 383, *385*, 388, 391, 393, 400, 686, 689, 690, 691

horses, 775, 844, 873–4

Horus (Egyptian falcon-god), 1, 3, 7, 27, 31, 32, 35, 51–2, 51 n. 2, 169, 481, 521; 'Beholder of...', 152; 'Followers of...', 3, 11; 'Following of...', 11, 38, 116; myth of, 33; and resurrection, 202

Horus names (of Egyptian kings), 11–15, 183 n. 6

Horus the Elder (Egyptian god), 511, 520

'House of the Tiles', at Lerna in the Argolid (Greece), 784, 785 bis, 787

houses, see architecture, domestic

'Hudjefa' (?), 35, 149

human sacrifice: in Babylon, 138, 285–7 passim; in Egypt, 58, 59, 185

'Humbaba, face of', 424

Huni of Egypt, 149, 150, 156–66 passim, 171, 201

Hureidah, in Arabia, 736

Hurrian personal and place names, 320, 716–17, 731, 749

Hurrians, of Northern (Upper) Syria, 101 n. 9, 310, 320, 565, 566, 603, 624–5, 682, 716, 717, 730, 733, 749, 752, 767

El-Ḥuṣn, village in Palestine, 583

'Hyksos' rulers of Egypt, 33, 148, 360, 458, 512, 514

hypogeum at Til Barsib, in Syria, 334

Hyria, Homeric, 780

Iakhdunlim of Mari, 425

Iakhzirel of Kazallu, 637

Iamkhad, royal family of (Aleppo), 550

Iamutbal (Amorite tribe and state), 641, 757, 758

Iaprum, in Babylonia, 607

Iarim(m)uta, see Iarmuti

Iarmuti (Iarim(m)uta), in the 'Upper Country', 322–7 passim, 339, 424, 426

Iashilim (a god), 564 nn. 7 and 9

Iashilim, ensi of Tuttul, 560

Iasmakh-Adad of Mari, 712, 713, 732

Iawium of Kish, 756, 757

Ibalpiel II of Eshnunna, 635

Ibbi-Sin of Ur, 109, 455, 456, 562, 563, 597, 607, 611–17, 626, 658–9, 711, 756; foreign policy, 611–12, 614–15, 616, 658; campaigns, 613, 658; home affairs, 612; captured by Elamites, 613, 616, 617, 657, 658, 659; and Ishbi-Erra, q.v., 612–14; and Puzur-Shulgi (letters), 614–15; and Amorites and Elamites, 614–15, 625; his ape, 615; and fall of Ur, 615–17, 658–9; his death, 617

Ibdati, ensi of Byblos, 560

Ibi (Kakare Ibi, q.v.) of Egypt, 197

Ibi (a governor), 192, 194, 198; and his sons, 198

Ibiq-Adad II of Eshnunna, 762

Ibis symbol (Egyptian), 11

Ibla, in Syria, 322–7 passim, 424, 426, 441, 559, 561, 564 n. 6, 565, 604; mountain of, 426

Iblul-il, King of Mari, 323

Ibrāhīm (Adonis) river, in Syria, 344

Ibzeikh, in Babylonia, 436 n. 2

Idattu I, of Simashki, 660; see also Indattu-In-Shushinak

Ideni of Abydos, Prince, 478

ideograms, 451, 719

Idi, son of Shemay, 198

Idi-Narum (a miller), 116

Igdir region of East Anatolia, 403

Iha I and II, of the Hare nome, 470

Ihi (son of goddess Hathor), 207

Ihnāsya el-Medīna, in Egypt, 464

Ihy, Nomarch of Thebes, 199, 200, 473; his wife, 199

Ikunum of Assyria, 709–10, 711, 761

Iku-Shamagan of Mari, 116, 323

Iku-Shamash of Mari, 323

Il, a prince of Umma, 119, 137

Ilam, in Persia (Map 11), 646, 649

Ilaprat (West Semitic god), 720, 766, 768

Ili-Dagan of Ibla, 564 n. 6

Ilushum(m)a of Assyria, 638, 639, 708, 738–9, 744, 747–8, 753, 754; and Babylonia, 756–8; his copper, 757–8; and Manana dynasty, 758

Imbros, Aegean island, 372

Imhotep (architect), 65, 66, 145, 146, 150, 155, 160, 171, 172, 360

Imi (mother of Mentuhotpe IV), 492

immigrants from the North (Map 16) (see also Indo-European immigrants in Anatolia), 824–76; the problem, 824–9; Indo-European languages, q.v., 830–40; archaeological evidence for, 840–59; dates, and region of origin, 859–73; their impact on indigenous cultures, 873–6

immortality (after-life), beliefs in: Cypriot, 819; Egyptian, 54, 55, 202, 520–2; Elamite, 680; see also burial customs

imperialism, Akkadian and Assyrian, 735–7; Egyptian, 537–50

Impy of Egypt, 187

Inanna (Ishtar, Ninegal, Pinikir, Kiri-risha, a goddess), 77, 78, 79, 87, 101, 117, 279, 433, 442, 462, 660; temples, 83, 242 n. 2, 278–9; zikkurrat (temple tower) of, 599

Indasu, Governor of Zabshali, 608, 657

Indattu-In-Shushinak (Idattu I) of Simashki, 660–1; his titles, 660 bis

Indattu II of Simashki and Elam, 633, 661

Indattu-napir of Simashki, 661 and n. 6
Indattu-temti of Simashki, 661
India, 132, 240, 254, 286, 295; Indo-European immigration into, 850–3
Indo-European immigrants in Anatolia (see also Immigrants from the North), 371, 386, 407–10 passim, 681–3 passim, 703, 716, 717, 841–5
Indo-European languages (Map 16), 824–30, 830–40, 859–68 passim; in Anatolia, 830–7; in Greece, 839; in Northern Mesopotamia, 837–9; in Syria, 837–9; in other areas, 839–40
Indo-European migrations, dates and region of origin (Map 16), 859–73; linguistic evidence, 859–68; archaeological evidence, 868–73
Indus river, 439
Indus valley, 96, 239, 240, 254, 295, 453, 851–2
industry and commerce: Babylonian, 127; Palestinian, 225–30 passim; see also Assyrian business community
Inegöl plain, in Anatolia, 694, 701
infantry, Babylonian, 123
Ini, king of Egypt, see Nyuserre
inlay: Egyptian, 69; Mesopotamian, 78, 87, 136
Inoqer (a nomarch), 474
In-Shushinak (chief god of Susa), 651–60 passim, 665–9 passim, 671, 675
Instruction for King Merykare, 466, 466–7, 467, 495, 523, 526–7, 533
Instruction of King Ammenemes I, 498–9, 523, 526–7
Instruction of Ptahhotpe, 201
insulae (blocks of houses), 387
Intef Cemetery (Theban necropolis), 476
intercalary months, 770
Intermediate (E.B.A./M.B.A.) Age: in Palestine, 567–8, 568–83 passim; in Syria, 583–92 passim
Inti of Egypt, 226, 235, 358, 359
Intkaes, Princess, 152, 153
Inyotef I (Sehertowy) of Egypt, 476
Inyotef II (Wahankh) of Egypt, 467, 475, 476, 477
Inyotef III, the Great (Nakhtnebtepnefer) of Egypt, 476, 477, 478
Inyotefnakhte, Chief Sculptor, 484
Inyotef of Heracleopolis, 483
Inyotef, Prince and Count, Nomarch of Thebes, 200, 473–6 passim
In(yotef), Qakare (Senefertowyef), King of Nubia, 486
Inyotef, son of Ka (a courtier), 478
Ionian Sea, 791
Ipi, Vizier, 481, 483, 489, 490

Iput, Queen, 190 bis, 191, 196, 197
Ipuwer, 200, 237 n. 2, 592; lamentations and prophecies of, 200–1, 237, 347, 532, 533
Iran (Persia, q.v.), 227, 240, 254, 286, 300, 302, 303, 307, 331, 401, 409, 653, 666, 674; Eastern, 644; South-West (Elam, q.v.), 644; Indo-European immigrants into, 850–3
Iraq (see also Mesopotamia), 72, 289, 303; Northern, 363, 655; Southern (Lower, alluvial), 81, 93, 97, 101
Iraqi/Kurdish mountain territory, 655
Irbil, in Mesopotamia, 298, 303, 432, 655
Irmaat (Userkaf, q.v.) of Egypt, 180
Ir-mu (Ir-Nanna, 'high commissioner' of Ur), 605, 609
Ir-Nanna, see Ir-mu
iron: in Anatolia, 370, 392; in Mesopotamia, 305–6; in Syria, 305–6, 341
irrigation: in Egypt, 6, 169; in Mesopotamia, 125, 127, 290 and n. 2; in Syria, 318
Ishchali, in Babylonia (Map 6 (14)), 88
Isesi (Djedkare, Djedkhau) of Egypt, 167, 181, 185–8 passim, 190, 201, 207, 355; his pyramid, 188, 191
Isesiankh, Prince, 188
Isesikha, High-Priest of Heliopolis, 190
Isetibtowy (Nyuserre, q.v.), 185
Isfahān, in Elam (ancient capital of Iran (Persia)), 647, 658
Ishbi-Erra of Isin, 562, 612–14, 616, 617, 627, 631, 643, 658, 659–60; his usurpation, 613, 614; his reign, 631–2; and his daughter, 659
Ishkhara (Ashkhara, a Mesopotamian goddess), 667
Ishme-Dagan of Isin, 634 bis, 708, 746, 749
Ishme-karab (Elamite goddess), 666, 667
Ishtar (a goddess, see also Inanna), 294, 298, 638, 663, 667, 718, 731, 767, 769; and Sargon, 418, 423, 433, 738; temples of, 73, 98, 117, 246, 252, 259, 262, 291, 293, 294, 300, 301, 328, 431, 457, 733, 734 bis, 739, 740, 741, 746, 757, 758
Ishtarat temples, 296
Ishtar-Inanna temple, at Uruk, 73
Ishtar-sād (the star Sirius), 718, 767
Ishum (a god), 667
Isi (Hemre) of Egypt, 471–2
Isi (Sekhemkhau, Shepseskare, q.v.) of Egypt, 184
Isin, in S. Babylonia, 114, 613, 614, 617, 631, 635, 642–3; dynasty of, 106, 107 n. 1, 628, 630–7 passim, 639, 642, 660
Isis (Egyptian goddess), 171, 348
Isparta plain, in Anatolia, 395

Israelites (biblical), sons of Jacob,745, 755
Issus, Gulf of (Map 12(60)), 430
Ita, King of Egypt, 24
Ithaca, Greek island (Map 12), 791, 792–3
Iti, king of Egypt (*see also* Djer), 14, 23
Iti, Treasurer of Gebelein, 200, 475, 476
Itj-towy: city of (El-Lisht), 496, 499, 501; House of, 482 n. 3
Itju, Governor of Lower Egypt, 483
'Iuntiu of Nubia', the, 507, 508
Iunu (On, Heliopolis, q.v.), 519
Iuny (Armant), 519
ivory, 7, 29, 42, 51, 68, 70, 193, 231, 295, 300, 350, 352, 392, 439, 590; carvings (Egyptian), 68–9, 70; magic wand, 550
Iyebkhentre (Goregtowyef), King of Nubia, 486
Iynefert, Vizier, 188
Izin-Dagan of Ibla, 564 n. 6
Izmir (Smyrna)| (Map 12(58)), 372, 684, 700, 805
Izmit, Gulf of, 371
Iznik, Lake, in N.-W. Anatolia (Maps 9 and 10), *373, 385,* 698, 701, 702

Jaffa river, in Palestine, 210
Jaghjagha river, in Syria, 329
Jamdat Naṣr, in Babylonia (Map 6(19)), 72–3, 73, 93, 94, 227, 231, 345
Jamdat Naṣr period (Uruk 3), 42, 44, 73 and n. 4, 74–8 *passim*, **81–92**, 94, 95, 124, 238, 239, 241, 246–51 *passim*, 263, 266 n. 3, 268, 281, 288, 290, 291, 297, 301, 302, 303, 307, 329, 330, 336, 338, 675, 730
Jazīrah-ibn-'Umar, in Anatolia, 727
Jazīrah, the, in Syria, 315–18
Jebel 'Abd el-'Aziz, in Syria, 318
Jebel Anṣāriyyah, in Syria (Map 8), *316,* 339
Jebel Aqra' (Mons Casius), in Syria (Map 8), *316,* 339
Jebel el-Bishrī (Basar), in Syria (Map 8), *316,* 325, 327, 455
Jebeleh, in Syria (Map 8), *316,* 337
Jebelet el-Beidha, in Syria (Map 8(21)), 312, *316,* 332–3
Jebel Sinjār, in N. Mesopotamia (Map 8), 84, 303, 304, 307, *316,* 318, 333, 726
Jerablūs (Carchemish, q.v.), on Turkish/ Syrian border (Map 8(16)), *316,* 333
Jericho (Map 7), 208, 209, 210–36 *passim,* 320, 547
Jerusalem (Map 7), 209, 211, 231, 509, 738 *bis*; first mention in history, 555
jewellery, and precious and semi-precious stones: in Aegean islands, 793–9 *passim*; in Anatolia, 377–8, 394; in

Crete, 799–804 *passim*; in Cyprus, 808–23 *passim*; in Egypt, 18, 23, 69, 168, 354, 356, 504, 515; in Elam, 680; in Greece, 771–9 *passim*, 803–7 *passim*; in Mesopotamia, 269–70, 285, 305,313, 439, 452; in Palestine, 226, 590; in Syria, 328–51 *passim*, 583–92 *passim*
Jezreel, plain of, in Palestine (*see also* Esdraelon), 543
Jordan (state), *see* Transjordan
Jordan river, 235, 538, 583
Jordan valley, 218, 229, 234, 357
Joseph, son of Jacob (Israel), 542
Jubeil (Byblos, q.v.), in the Lebanon (Map 8 (12)), *316,* 343, 347
Jūkhā (mound), in Babylonia (*see also* Umma), 118

Ka (pre-dynastic king of Upper Egypt, *see also* Scorpion), 3, 11
Ka, father of Inyotef, 478
El-Kāb (Elkāb, Nekheb), in Upper Egypt (Maps 1 and 4(33)), 1, *2, 12,* 33, 34, 54, 480, 506 n. 1
Kabīr-Kuh, in Susiana, 658
Kabta (a god), 667
Kagemni, Vizier, 159, 172, 190, 201
Kai-Aper (Egyptian royal official), 358
Kaiechōs (Kakau) of Egypt, 30
Kaiemhesit of Egypt, 358
Kakai (Neferirkare, q.v.), of Egypt, 181, 183
Kakare Ibi of Egypt, 197–8
Kakau (Kaiechōs) of Egypt, 30
Kaku of Ur, 113, 435, 459; and Rimush, 436
Kalakh (biblical town), in Upper Mesopotamia, 729
Kalam Dynasty, of Mesopotamia, 244, 245
Kalavassos, in Cyprus (Maps 14 and 15), 810, 814, 816
Kalecik (Çorum), in Pontic Anatolia, 400
Kaledoroğu, in Pontic Anatolia, 400
Kalkhu, in Assyria, 729
Kalopsidha, in Cyprus (Map 15(41)), *814,* 816
Kamares ware (Minoan), 504
Kanefer, Prince and Vizier, 166
Kanesh (Kanish, Kültepe, q.v.), in Anatolia (Map 10), *385,* 427, 703, 713, 716–21 *passim*, 726–8 *passim*, 755 and n. 2, 763–5 *passim*
Kangal, west of Euphrates, 401
Kaptara (Kaptura, Kaphtor, Crete, q.v.), 429–30
Karaağaçtepe, in N.-W. Anatolia, 379, 384
Karabayir, in S.-W. Anatolia (Map 10), *385,* 393

Karaburun peninsula, near Izmir in Anatolia, 372, 383
Karacaahmet, near Afyon in Central Anatolia, 395
Kara-Dağ, near Sulaimaniyyah in Iraq, 443
Kara Hassan, in Syria (Map 8(15)), *316*, 334
Karahüyük-Konya, in Anatolia, 696 *bis*, 698
Karakhar (unlocated), 601, 609, 624, 631, 655
Karaman, in Anatolia, 365, 697; ware, 697
Karaoğlan, in Central Anatolia, 368, 387, 388, 398, 695, 697, 698
Karasu valley, in Anatolia, 397
Karaz, near Erzurum, in E. Anatolia, 368, 401, 402, 691
Karkhah river, in Elam, 657
Karnak, near Luxor in Upper Egypt (Map 4(21)), *12*, 472, 473, 495, 498, 501, 514, 517, 519, 520; Table of Ancestors, 476, 492
Karpass peninsula, in Cyprus, 816
kārum (Assyrian governing and judicial body), 721–3
Kāshān, in Iran (Map 11), *646*, 676
Kassite period at Ur, 596
kaunakes (sheepskin cloaks), 328
Kawab, Crown Prince of Egypt, 165–74 *passim*
Kay, leader of Western Desert patrol, 482
Kay, son of Neheri, 467–71 *passim*, 471 n. 1
Kayapinar, in Pontic Anatolia, 383
Kaykhet (Mycerinus, q.v.), 176
Kayseri (Caesarea), in Central Anatolia (Map 10), *385*, 427; region, 367, 399
Kazallu, in N. Babylonia, 428, 436, 613, 617, 637, 640, 756, 757; governor of, 614
Kenkenēs of Egypt, 24
Kephala, on Ceos (Map 12(49)), 797
Kerbschnitt (triangular design on pottery), 799
Kerma, in N. Sudan (Map 5(37)), *48*, 156, 194, 512, 518, 549; fortified trading post at, 497
Keros, Aegean island, 798
Kesrwan district (of Lebanon), 344
Kfar Monash, in Palestine (Map 7), *209*, 228, 232, 348 n. 1
Khaba, King of Egypt, 150, 156, 158
Khabausokar of Egypt, 158, 160
Khabur-Jaghjagha valley, 304
Khabur river (Maps 6 and 8), 308, *316*, 318, 323, 328, 329, 331, 437, 557, 597, 625; Upper, 296, 726, 730
Khabur valley (and region), 300, 306, 307,

314, 328–32 *passim*, 336, 560; cities of, **328–33** *passim*
Khaduwa (a royal official), 714–15
Khafājī (Tutub), in Babylonia (Map 6 (13)), 72, 74, 78, 83–8 *passim*, 108, 110, 135, 238, 241, 244, 246, 255 n. 5, 274, 278, 292, 295, 298, 314 n., 330; Sin temples (q.v.) at, **246–57**; Temple oval at, 257, **270–2**, *271*, 287
Khafre (Chephren, q.v.), 169
Khahhum, country of, 559, 560
Khaitaw (a god), 349
Khamazi, in Babylonia: dynasty, 114; land of, 607, 614; town, 609
Khamerernebty I, Queen, 175
Khamerernebty II, Queen, 175, 176, 177
Khanians (nomadic tribe), 744
Khanni, a prince of Elam, 663–4, 674
Kharāna, on the Euphrates ('gateway to Asia Minor'), 758
El-Khārga, Great Oasis of (Map 1), 2, 500
Kharsi, in N. Mesopotamia, 602, 655
Khasekhem, King of Egypt, 32–4, 47, 50, 52, 67, 68, 146
Khasekhemwy, King of Egypt, 34–5, 35, 45, 65–9 *passim*, 146, 147, 151–4 *passim*, 161, 167, 181, 345; his tomb, 18, 20, 59
'Kha Sneferu', 162–3
Khatā'na, in the Eastern Delta, 489, 498
Khattian Central Anatolia, 703
Khattian pottery, 686
Khattina (Unqi), kingdom of, 335
Khelu of Awan, 650
Khent (*see also* Djer), 23
Khentekhtay-wer, Captain of the Gate, 504
Khentetenka, Queen, 173, 174
Khenthap, Queen, 36
Khenti (a royal official), 200
Khentiamentiu (Abydos local jackal-god), 22, 199, 202
Khentiamentiu-Osiris, temple of, 198
Khentkaues I, Queen, 176–9 *passim*
Khentkaues II, Queen, 179
Khenuka of Egypt, 181–2
Khenut, Queen, 188
Kheper (Redjedef, q.v.) of Egypt, 173
Kherty (Egyptian ram-god), 54
Khidadida, Governor of Gunilakha, 648
Khirbet Karak (Beth Yerah), in Palestine (Map 7), *209*, 210–17 *passim*, 227, 229, 230, 236, 337; cemetery, 224; culture, 401, 402
Khirbet Karak wares, 213, 227, 231, 235, 337–8, 340, 341, 397, 399, 402
Khirbet Qumrān, in Palestine, 227
Khishep-ratep (-rashir?) I, of Elam and Awan, 432 and n. 4, 649, 650 *bis*

Khishep-ratep II, 649 *bis*
Khita of Elam and Awan, 444, 651–2, 653; his treaty with Naram-Sin, 444, 650–2, 662–3 (*see also* Khita treaty)
Khita treaty (with Naram-Sin, *c*. 2280 B.C.), 444, 650–2, 662–9 *passim*
Khmunu (El-Ashmunein, Hermopolis, q.v.), 470
Khnum (Egyptian ram-god), 54, 520
Khnumhotpe I, Nomarch of Beni Hasan, 496–7, 504
Khnumhotpe, Treasurer, 504
Khnumenty, Vizier, 186
El-Khōkha (a hill), in Egypt, 472–3
Khons (Egyptian falcon-headed god), 520
Khosr river, 303
Khrysiliou village, in Cyprus (Map 15 (25)), 809, *814*
Khufu (Chiops, q.v.), 169
Khufukhaf, Prince, 165, 166, 171
Khuit, Queen, 190
Khukhnur (Qal'a-i Toll), in Anshan (Map 11), *646*, 647, 653, 658, 666
Khukhnuri, in Anshan, 607 *bis*, 612
Khumban (Elamite god), 664–7 *passim*, 673; his titles, 665
Khumurti, in Mesopotamia, 601
Khunere, Prince, 176
Khupsana, in Elam, 652
Khurāsān, in E. Persia, 392
Khurrama (Elbistan), in E. Anatolia, 726, 727
Khurramābād, in Luristān (Map 11), *646*, 653, 654, 657
Khurri (Hurrian), 556
Khusobk, Egyptian general, 508, 538, 543 and n. 2
Khutowyre Ugaf of Egypt, 512
Khutran (Elamite god), 665
Khutran-temti of Simashki (assumed destroyer of Ur), 659, 660
'Khuwaruwash, King of Amurri', 626
Kikku-siwe-temti of Elam and Awan, 649
kilim (grave-mat), 391
Kiliya, in Gallipoli (Map 9), *373*, 378
kilns, closed, 227
Kīmān Fāris (Crocodilopolis, q.v.), in the Faiyūm (Map 2 (46)), *4*, 511, 517
Kimash, in N. Mesopotamia, 601, 655
Kindattu of Simashki, 659, 660 *bis*
King of the Battle (Akkadian epic), 425–30 *passim*, 707
kingship and hierarchy, origins of (mythological), 102
kingship and priesthood relations in Babylonia, 104–5
Kinnereth, in Palestine, 210, 213, 224, 232

Kiririsha (Inanna, q.v., Elamite goddess), 663–6 *passim*, 671–3 *passim*
Kirkuk (Arrapkha, q.v.), in Iraq, 298, 303, 431, 432, 716; district, **297–8**
Kish, in Babylonia (Map 6 (18)), 72, 85, 87, 92, 97, 100, 104, 107, 109–17 *passim*, 120, 121, 140, 143, 144, 239, 243, 244, 251, 254, 286, 295, 313, 314 n., 323, 418, 420, 441, 447, 448, 606, 614, 617, 628, 637–8, 645, 756; principal sites, 272–5; Palace of, 241 and n. 2, 274 and n. 7, 275, 275 and n. 2, 278 and n. 3, 296; dynasty of, 419; Sargon at the Court of, 419; revolts at, 422, 441; defeat (fall) of, 420, 423, 433; omen of, and of Sargon, 423; Amorites at, 637; and Awan, 647
Kismar, in Elam, 638
'knobbed' ware (*Bückelkeramik*), 857
kohl (eye-paint), 541
Kombabos (an eunuch-priest), 115
Komotini, in the Balkans, 367
Konya plain, Southern plateau of Anatolia (Maps 9 (4) and 10 (4)), **365–6**, *373*, *385*, 681, 682; pottery, 363, 365, 367, 381–2, 396, 397, 407, 686, 694, 696; route to Cilicia, 364; and Cilician plain, 364–5; Late Chalcolithic period in, 365–6; immigration, 365–6, 409; silver mines, 370; culture, 386, 402; fortified towns in, 390; signs of conflagration and desertion, 407; Cyprus, 813
Köprüören plain, in Anatolia, 372, 701
Koptos (town), in Upper Egypt (Map 4 (15)), *12*, 194, 465, 472–4 *passim*, 498, 500, 519; Road (to Red Sea ports), 485, 491; temple of, 191, 198
Korosko, in Lower Nubia, 497
Kouris river, in Cyprus, 816
Koyunçik (Nineveh, q.v.), 729
Köylüce (Edremit, q.v.), 381
Kozağaci, in S.-W. Anatolia, 378, 381
Krini, in Cyprus (Maps 14 (42) and 15 (13)), *810*, *814*, 816
Kritsana, in N.-E. Greece (Map 12 (4)), 774–5
Kryoneri, in N.-W. Peloponnese, 791
Kubaba (Anatolian goddess), 115
Ku-Baba, Queen (of Kish), 115
Kudur-Mabuk, of Larsa, 640–2 *passim*, 757
Kukkuli of Assuwa, 408
Kukkuni (Lycian name), 408
Kukkunis of Wilusa, 408
Kukun, son of Lycian (Lukka-man), 408
Kula, in Anatolia, 372
Kullab, near Uruk, in Babylonia, 462

'Kulli culture', on Oman peninsula, 440 n. 2
Kültepe (Kanesh, q.v.), in Central Anatolia (Map 10), 367, 368, *385*, 386, 399, 427, 682–99 *passim*, 703, 708–16 *passim*, 723; 'palace', 685, 688; layout of, 694
Kumma (Semna East), near Second Cataract, in Nubia (Map 5(29)), *48*, 503, 507
kumrum (priest), 719
Kumtepe (Kum Tepe), in Anatolia, 366, 367, 371, 372, 374, 377, 413; sites: I*a*, 366, 367, 372, 374; I*b*, 366, 367, 372, 374, 379; I*c*, 377
Kūrangān relief, near Fahliyān in Elam, 673–4
Kurdish mountains, 733
Kurdistān, 303, 601, *655*
Kurds, the, 444
Kürigen Kaleh, near Ankara, 504
Kurishshak, of Elam, 647
Kurkur Oasis, in Upper Egypt, 488
Kush, land of, 499, 507
Kushar (craftsman-god), 558
Kushites, 508
Kusura, in S.-W. Anatolia (Map 10), 368, *385*, 394, 398, 407; (A), 376; (B), 386, 388, 396, 407
Kut, in S. Mesopotamia, 289
Kutik-In-Shushinak of Awan and Elam (*see also* Puzur-), 454, 652, 669, 670, 671, 677 *bis*; his titles, 652, 660; his campaigns, 652–3; his rise and reign, 653–4; and the goddess Narundi, 669; his stone-relief at Susa, 675
Kyra village, in Cyprus (Maps 14 and 15 (28)), 809, *810*, *814*
Kyrenia hills, in Cyprus (Map 14(47)), *810*, 813 *bis*, 816; pass in, 816

Laban, the moon, the 'White One', 736, 738
Labarnash (Labarsha), Hittite king, 713
Lachish (Tell ed-Duweir, q.v.), in Palestine, 210, 320, 547
Laconia, in the Peloponnese (Map 12), 789–90; Gulf of, 790
Lagash (El-Hibbeh), in Babylonia (Map 6), 72, 85, 97, 104, 105, 114–20 *passim*, 124, 126, 135, 138–44 *passim*, 245, 255, 265, 270, 276, 289, 290, 296, 422, 449, 458, 559, 563, 599, 600, 605, 609, 620, 622, 633, 763; king-list, 114–20; and Umma, 118–20, 125, 132, 143, 288, 420, 422, 595–6; military levy at, 121; society and land-holding in, 126–31; extent of the city, 130; external trade of, 130–1; principal sites at, 288–9; in

revolt, 435–6; prosperity in, 458–61; and Ur, 459, 595, 597; and Elam, 654; foreign mercenaries in, 656
Lagashites, 117, 118, 130
El-Lāhūn, in the Faiyūm (Map 2(54)), 4, 504, 505, 511–18 *passim*
Lakamar (Lakamal, Elamite goddess), 666 and n. 4
Lakhma (Lakhama, Lakhmu, Lakhamu, Assyrian god), 766
Lama (a goddess), 667
Lamgi-Mari, King of Mari, 116, 295, 323
Lamgium, son of Epir-mupi, q.v., 650
land and land-holding in Sumer, 126–7, 130–1
land reclamation in Egypt, 505
Langadus, Lake, in Macedonia, 396
Lankadhas river basin, in Greece, 773–4
Lapethus, in Cyprus, 803 (*see also* Lapithos)
lapis-lazuli, 68, 87, 132, 240, 269, 276, 281, 283, 292, 293, 297, 305, 312, 350, 386, 392, 427, 452, 503, 543
Lapithos, in Cyprus (Maps 14(37) and 15), *810*, *814*, 817, 821 (*see also* Lapethus)
lapwing symbol (Egyptian), 3, 6
Larak, in Mesopotamia, 97, 101, 289
Larissa, in Central Greece (Map 12(10)), 366, 776, 777
Larnaka bay, in Cyprus (Map 15(60)), *814*, 816
Larsa, in Babylonia (Map 6), 289, 420, 599, 628, 633, 636, 641–3 *passim*; water supply, 633; dynasty of, 127, 628–40 *passim*, 660, 661
Lasithi, in Crete, 803
Late Bronze Age: in Anatolia, 407; in Cyprus, 812, 822; in Greece, 790
latrines, 374
Laurium lead mine, 430
Layer Pyramid of Zāwiyet el-Aryān, q.v., 155, 156
lead (metal), 392, 394, 430, 657; sources of its ore (galena), 430, 754; traded, in Anatolia, 724–5, 726
Lebanon (country) (Map 8), *316*, 325, 344, 425; timber of, 46, 318, 325, 328, 346–7, 484, 532, 535 (*see also* cedar wood); and Syria, 315; ports of, 333; and Egypt, 361–2; moon-cult in, 736, 768
Lebanon mountain range (Map 8), *316*, 324–9 *passim*, 338, 339, 346, 349
Lebe'a, near Sidon in the Lebanon, 230
lecanomancy, 252
'Legend of Naram-Sin', 707, 739
'Legend of Sargon', 738–9
legionaries, foreign, in Sumerian garrisons, 656, 659

Lemnos, Aegean island (Map 12), 366, 372, 374, 778, 794; see also Poliochni

Lerna, in the Argolid (Greece) (Map 12 (38)), 684, 774, 777, 783, 784–6, 787, 792, 795, 796, 806 bis, 807

Lernaean spring, South of Argos in the Peloponnese, 784

Lesbos (Mytilene), Aegean island (Map 12), 372, 374, 778, 794; see also Thermi

Letopolis, in Egypt, 54

Leucas, Greek island (Map 12), 791, 792–3

Lianokladhi, in Greece (Map 12 (17)), 777

Libanugshabash, Governor of Warakhshe, 656, 657

'Library of the High Priest', in Syria, 340

Libya, in North Africa, west of Egypt, 7, 71, 498, 509; relations with Egypt, 47

Libyans, 24, 33, 47, 167, 171, 182, 352, 360, 471, 480, 482, 485; Tjehenu, 500, 509; Tjemehu, 498, 500, 509

Lim (a god), 558, 564

līmum, see eponym

linear pottery ('Bandkeramik'), 799, 869

lion (as symbol), 7

Lipari island (Italy), 791

Lipit-Ishtar of Sumer and Akkad, 634–5, 637; his laws, 635

Lisān, the, of Dead Sea, 224–5

El-Lisht village, in Lower Egypt (Map 2 (37)), 4, 464, 493–6 passim, 502 bis, 504, 514, 516, 525 n. 10, 538

literature: of Egypt, see Egyptian literature; of Lagash, 461

'lituus-end', 391

Liyan (Bushire), Elamite port on Persian Gulf (Map 11), 646, 663, 664

Locris, in Central Greece, 777, 780

lost-wax process, see cire-perdue process

Lōtān, in Sinai, 557

Lower (Northern) Egypt (Map 2), 1–7 passim, 4, 21, 23, 26, 27, 32, 36, 38, 39, 43, 45, 51–5 passim, 477, 482, 506; crown of, 353; governors of, 483

'Lower Sea', the (Persian Gulf, q.v.), 322, 421, 440, 460, 597, 736

lugal (Sumerian king or ruler), 103–4, 618–19

Lugalanda of Lagash, 120

Lugalannimundu of Adab, 115

Lugalbanda of Uruk, 94 n. 1, 100, 111, 446, 606, 626

Lugal-da-lu, King, 115

Lugalkinishedudu, King, 114

Lugalshagengur of Lagash, 116

Lugalushumgal, ensi of Lagash, 458

Lugalushumgal, ensi of Zabalam, 436

Lugalzaggisi of Uruk, 104, 114, 124, 143–4, 246, 289, 308, 321, 323 n. 8, 331, 333,

436 n. 1, 447, 448, 449; his reign and career, 420; his 'empire', 420–1; his end, 421, 422

Lukh-ishshan of Elam and Awan, 432 and n. 4, 647, 649

Lukka lands, and men, 408, 410

Lullu (Lullubi): the people, 443 and n. 7, 444, 655, 664; their campaigns, 739–40

Lullubi (Lullubum), land of, 433, 443 and n. 7, 444, 601

Lu...luhhan of Simashki, 658, 659

lumber, see timber

Lummatur (a prince of Lagash), 131

Luristān, in Persia (Map 11), 653, 646, 654, 657

Lurs, the, 444

Luwian language, 849

Luwians, the, 407–10, 703, 716; in Anatolia, 832, 835–7

Luxor, in Upper Egypt (Map 4), 12, 180, 472, 519; see also Thebes

Lycia, in Anatolia, 378, 408, 409; Central, 682

Lydda (Lud), in Palestine, 557

Lydia, in Anatolia, 372

Maatkha, Princess, 176

Macedonia (Map 12), 383, 396, 773–5, 792

mace-heads and maces, 6, 7, 10, 42, 53, 67, 265, 268, 288, 343, 344, 459, 734

Macestus valley, in Anatolia, 372

Maclaren, Charles, 411

El-Madāmūd (Madu), village near Karnak in Upper Egypt (Map 4 (22)), 472, 509, 514, 515, 517, 519, 544

Madenşehir ('mine city'), in Anatolia, 722

Madqa, 601

Madu, see El-Madāmūd

Maeander river, in S.-W. Anatolia (Maps 9 and 10), 373, 385; route to the Aegean, 370

Mafdet (Egyptian feline goddess), 54

Magan, port on Gulf of Oman, 439 and n. 3, 441, 445, 448, 453, 454, 600

Magan, Sea of, 614

magic: divine, mimetic and symbolic, 56, 57, 58, 202, 353, 522, 548, 662, 665, 668

magical wand, ivory (at Megiddo), 550

El-Maharraqa village, in Lower Egypt (Map 2 (38)), 4, 496

Mahesa, King's Herald (Egyptian), 483–4

Mahmutlar, in Pontic Anatolia, 400, 686, 690, 691

Maidūm, in Lower Egypt (Map 2 (42)), 4, 189, 206

Maidūm Pyramid, 156, 159, 161 and n. 1, 162–4 passim

Maidūm temple and chapels (Fourth Dynasty), 154; tombs, 165, 166
Maikop, in the Kuban, 689, 691; royal tomb at, 689
Makrān, on Gulf of Oman (Map 11), 439, 453, 646
Mālamīr (Aiapir, q.v.), province of Anshan, 658, 663, 666
Mālamīr/Izeh, in Elam (Map 11), 646, 647 and n. 8
Malatya (Arslantepe site), in Anatolia, 367, 401, 688, 689
Malatya-Elâziğ region of Eastern Anatolia, 403
Malea, Cape, in Greece, 790
Malgium, on Babylonia/Elam border, 633
Maltepe, in Anatolia, 364, 395, 689, 694
Malthi, in Messenia (Greece) (Map 12 (46)), 790-1
Mama, in Eastern Anatolia, 717, 725-6
Manana of Kish, 756; dynasty, 756-7
Manetho of Sebennytos (Ptolemaic historian), 1, 3, 11, 15, 17, 20-31 passim, 35, 65, 146, 172-9 passim, 194, 195, 197, 464
Manika, in Euboea (Map 12 (23)), 798; promontory, 781
Manisa plain, in Western Anatolia (Map 9), 372, 373, 701, 702
Manishtusu of Agade, 431, 434, 437, 448, 650, 669, 672, 734, 740, 741 bis; his reign, 437-40; his silver-mine, 438, 440 n. 2; his death, 440; his land-purchases, 448-9
Manishtusu's obelisk, 422, 424, 448-9, 650
Manium (or Mannu) of Magan, 445
'Man of Ur', see Ur-Nammu
Mantar, in Syria, 337
Manzat (Manzit, a goddess), 669, 669-70
'Map of the World', Babylonian, 426, 427
Marad, Babylonian city, 448, 637
marble, 797-8, 803
Mardaman, Elamite state, 444
Marduk (Babylonian god), 418, 419, 434, 454, 461, 604, 732, 764
Marduk-apal-iddina II of Babylon, 733
Margi, in Cyprus (Maps 14 (73) and 15 (38)), 810, 814, 816
Mari (Mera, Tell el-Ḥarīrī), in N. Mesopotamia (Maps 6 and 8 (24)), 97-8, 98, 100, 113, 117, 121, 123, 136, 245, 246, 279, 291-7, 307, 312, 313, 316, 319-25 passim, 325 n. 4, 328-9, 328 n. 4, 333, 338, 340, 342, 424, 425, 426, 432, 441, 448, 558, 560, 564 and nn. 6 and 7, 566, 597, 603 bis, 612 bis, 616, 628, 629 bis, 636, 712-13; dynasty of, 115-16; Palace of Zimrilim at, 241;

276, 329; temples of, 331-2; letters and archives, 338, 444, 540, 555; divination at, 423
Mariette, Auguste, 170, 188
Maritsa-Ergene plain, in Anatolia, 371
Maritsa river, in Anatolia, 372
Mariupol, in Pontic Anatolia, 400
El-Markhā', port in Sinai, on Gulf of Suez (Map 1), 2, 355
Markhashe (Barakhshe, q.v.), in Mesopotamia, 432, 444 and n. 7, 600, 607, 624
Marmara, Sea of (Propontis) (Map 12), 133, 372, 395, 410, 684, 701
Martu (a god), 667
martu region and ethnic group (see also amurru), 321, 625
maṣṣēbāh (cult symbol), 222, 329
mastabas (Egyptian tombs, see also Abydos, Giza and Saqqara), 17-21 passim, 27, 42, 43, 45, 55-9 passim, 60-4, 65, 67, 70, 155, 158, 177; at Naqāda, 42, 43, 45; trench-graves, 59, 60-1; monumental, 62-4; meaning of, 155
Mastabat Faraʿūn, in Egypt, 177
El-Matarīya (Heliopolis, q.v.) (Map 2 (23)), 4, 518
Medes, 644, 645
Media, 744
Medīnet el-Faiyūm, in the Faiyūm (Map 2 (47)), 4, 511
Medīnet el-Maʿādi (Dja), in the Faiyūm (Map 2 (57)), 4, 511, 517, 520
Mediterranean Sea and coasts (the 'Upper Sea', q.v.), 321, 322, 323, 326, 333, 392, 421, 426, 501; ships of, 348; ports of, 484; coasting voyages on, 788
Medjay peoples, of Nubian deserts, 488, 508
Medjedu (Cheops, q.v.), 169
Me-Enlil canal, in Babylonia, 614
Megalopolis, in the Peloponnese, 789
Meganisi, Greek island, 791
megaron (type of building), 366, 374, 375, 387, 413, 415
Megegi (an official of Egypt), 478
Megiddo, in Palestine (Map 7), 208, 209, 211-28 passim, 232, 236, 337, 350, 503, 542-50 passim, 543 n. 4, 567, 568, 578-83, 585, 593; tomb at (plan and section), 580; pottery types from tomb at, 582
Mehy (Unas's Vizier and son of Inti), 186, 187
Meir, in Middle Egypt (Map 3 (20)), 8, 194, 195, 464, 472, 515, 542; see also Cusae
Meketre, Chancellor (of Egypt), 489, 518
Me-kubi, daughter of Bilalama, q.v., 660, 661

Melos, Greek island (Map 12), 780, 782, 788, 791, 793–5 *passim*, 797
Meluhha, city of (location doubtful), 132 n. 2, 439–40, 439 nn. 2 and 4, 453, 454, 600
Memeshura (people), 565
Memphis (Mīt Rahīna), near Cairo (Maps 1 and 2 (32)), 2, 4, 20, 21, 22, 28, 38, 52, 159, 170, 178, 186, 197–201 *passim*, 473, 491, 496, 498, 510, 514, 521; foundation of, 15–17, 36; gods and priests of, 53, 518; High-Priest of, 184; royal cemeteries at, 198, 466; Royal House of, 200, 464, 465; as artistic centre, 512–15 *passim*
Memphite Drama, 528–9
Menat-Khufu, Counts of, 496
Menderes Su (Scamander), in Anatolia, 413
Menes, first King of United Egypt, 11, 14, 15, 16, 23, 28, 36, 37, 39, 53, 54, 242, 445, 479; his successors, 22–35, 37, 39, 197; and Crocodilopolis, 22
menhirs, 312
Menka (a vizier), 37, 160
Menkare of Egypt, 196
Menkauhor (Akauhor, Menkhau), 185–6
Menkaure (Mycerinus, q.v.), 169
Menkhau (Mankauhor, Akauhor), 185–6
Mentjiu, 351, 354, 508
Mentuemhat, Egyptian Treasurer and General, 538
Mentuhotpe I (Tepya) of Thebes, 476, 519
Mentuhotpe II (Nebheptre Sankhibtowy) of Egypt, 21, 467, 468, 470–1, 478, 486, 495 *bis*, 513, 515, 519, 521, 535–6, 557 n. 3; his reign, **478–88**; his elaborate titulary, 479–80; his reorganization and recovery (of Egypt), 481–5; his foreign policy, 485–8; his death, 488
Mentuhotpe III (Sankhkare, Sankhtowyef) of Egypt, 481, 483, 486, 492, 495 *bis*, 519; his reign, **488–92**; his tomb, 489
Mentuhotpe IV (Nebtowy, Nebtowyre) of Egypt, **492–5** *passim*, 519
Mentuhotpe, Vizier, 538
Mēr *or* Wēr (a god), 564
mercenaries, Elamite, in Ur, 656, 659
merchandise, Assyrian/Anatolian, 723–7; *see also* trade
Merenre I (Antyemsaf, Ankhkhau) of Egypt, 34, 181, 188 *bis*, 191–8 *passim*; his pyramid, 188; his canals, 506
Merenre (Antyemsaf II), 196
Merer (a nomarch), 474
Mereruka, of Egypt, 205, 206
Meresankh I, Queen, 159, 164–5, 171
Meresankh III, Queen, 165, 171–6 *passim*
Meresankh, Queen (wife of Isesi), 188

Merisu, son of Hekanakhte, 489, 490
Meritites, Crown Princess and Queen, 165, 166, 170–4 *passim*
Mer(it)neith, Queen, 18, 19, 25–6, 28, 36, 53, 58, 64, 67
Merka (Egyptian high official), 20
Merodach-Baladan (721–710 B.C.), 733
Merpe(bia) (Anedjib, q.v.), 27
Mersin, in S. Anatolia, 368; destruction of, 363; re-fortified, 363; pottery, 363–4, 365, 374, 381, 398, 694; imports from Konya plain, 364
Mersin levels: XII, 363–4, 365, 381, 398; XIII, 363–4, 365; XIV, 363–4, 365; XV, 363–4, 365; XVI, 363, 365, 374
Meru of Egypt, Treasurer, Chancellor and Governor, 481, 483
Mery, Treasurer, 502
Meryhathor of Egypt, 466, 470
Meryib of Egypt, 346
Meryibre Achthoes I of Egypt, 464, 465
Merykare, Prince and King (of Egypt), 237, 464, 467–8, 470; 'Instruction for...', 466–7 *passim*; attends installation of a nomarch, 467, 469
Meryre (Phiops I, q.v.), 191
Meryreankhnes, Queens (two), 191, 192, 196
Meryremerptahankh (Nekhebu), of Egypt, 186, 187, 191
Mery-Teti, Count (of Egypt), 483, 487
Merytowy (Phiops I, q.v.), 191
Mesannipada of Ur, 108, 112, 113, 138, 245, 246, 283, 287, 296, 297; dynasty of, 288, 294
Mesaoria, the, in Cyprus, 816
mēšarum, see righteousness
Mesilim (a 'King of Kish'), 104 n. 1, 116, 118, 119, 272, 595; his period, 272 n. 5, 313
Meskalamdug, Prince and King, 124, 136, 138, 244, 245, 283–4
Meskeneh (Meskineh), in N. Mesopotamia (Map 8), 316, 333
Meskiagnunna, King, 113
Meskigala, *ensi* of Adab, 436
Mesopotamia (*now* Iraq, q.v., Maps 6 and 8, *see also* Babylonia) (*general*), 71, 316, 370; ships of, 42; art of, 42–3, 45; architecture of, 43, 240–1, 246–93 *passim*, 298–9, 308–12; relations with Palestine, 231, 236; and Syria, 559–66; Amorites and, 237; and Sind, 439; Egyptian iconographic symbols in, 550; reunited as an empire, 559, 560; ancient and modern external problems of, 603; and Elam, 645–7, 653
Mesopotamia, Early Dynastic period in,

238-314 (*for previous period, see* Babylonia); E.D. I, II and III, 238-314 *passim*; archaeological developments in Babylonia, **238-46**; the Diyālā valley, q.v., **246-72**; principal Babylonian sites, **272-90**; Assyria, q.v., **291-314**

Mesopotamia, Northern (Upper) (Map 8), 71, *316*, 437, 636; pottery, 292, 301-4; Sargon and, 448; immigrants in, 625; Indo-European languages in, 837-9

Mesopotamia, Southern, 72, 73, 77; relations with Egypt, 41-5; and Persia, 71

Mesopotamian: 'colonies' in Anatolia and Syria, 560-1; culture and influence, 74, 87, 89-90, 92

Messara, the, in Crete, 800-3 *passim*

Messenia, in the Peloponnese (Map 12), 790-1, 793

Messenian plain, 790

metallic ware, 227-8, 231, 341, 380, 381, 397; in Anatolia, 381, 391, **394-5**

metals and metallurgy, 71, 91, 92, 239, 304, 305, 313, 341, 344-5, 370, 591, 594, 708-9; in Anatolia, 370, 392, 400, 724-5, 726-7; in Greece, Crete and the Aegean islands, 771; in Syria and Palestine, 591, 594

metals, Assyrian, traded, 723, 724-7

metalwork and metal-workers, 136, 212, 239-40, 305-6, 307, 313; Anatolian, 362, 370, 377-8, 386, **392-4**, 690-1, 699; at Ur, 370

Metjen ('Overseer of Inspectors'), 152, 159, 163, 170

El-Mi'alla (Hefat), in Upper Egypt (Map 4 (29)), *12*, 200, 465, 474, 475, 490, 512

Middle Bronze Age: in Aegean islands, 794; in Anatolia, 384, 408, 681-3 *passim*, *693* (transition to, **691-704**); in Crete, 800, 801, 803; in Cyprus, 809, 818, 822; in Greece, 777, 786, 790-2, 799; in Palestine, **567-8**; in Syria, **583-92** *passim*

Middle Egypt (Map 3), *8*, 46, 51, 506, 512

Midian, 554, 555

Migir-Dagan of Mari, 325 n. 4

migrations (and other movements of peoples, *see also* Asiatics in Egypt *and* immigrants from the North), 236, 556, 558, 562-6, **583-94** *passim*, 624-5, 625-8, 636, 788, 804-7 *passim*, 808-16, 819-20, **824-9, 840-76**

Mikhalits, in Thrace (Maps 9 and 10), 371, *373*, 379, 380, *385*, 396

military activities and forces: in Babylonia, 121-4; in Egypt, 38, 167, 169, 469; in Mesopotamia, 322-7 *passim*, 420-34, 456-7, 461-3; in Palestine, 357-61; in Syria, 324-7

military prognostication (by omens), 423

Minkhaf, Prince and Vizier, 171, 174

Minoan cultural areas (M), 772, 790, 799, 800-7 *passim*

Minoan cultures, *see* Crete

Min of Akhmīm and Koptos (Egyptian god), 11, 53, 472, 481, 519; temple of, 498

El-Minya, in Egypt, 181

'Minyan' pottery and culture, 410, 682, 684, 685, 700, 701, 702, 777, 786, 792, 845-8, 850

Mirabella, Gulf of, in Crete, 800

Mishrifeh (Mishrifé, Mesherfa, Qatna), in Syria (Map 8 (10)), *316*, 338, 503, 546 *bis*

Mochlos, in Crete (Map 13 (65)), *773*, 790, 801, 802

Moeris, Lake in the Faiyūm (Map 2), *4*, 22, 510

Mohenjo Daro, in Indus valley, 254, 439, 453, 852

Molfetta, in Apulia (Italy), 792

money (gold and silver) conveyed from Anatolia to Assyria, 726

Mons Casius (Jebel Aqra'), 339

'Montet Jar', 590-1

Mont of Hermonthis (Egyptian falcon-god), 472, 473, 477, 479, 481, 503, 509, 515, 517-20 *passim*

Mont-Re (Egyptian composite god), 519

moon, cult of the, 736-8

Moon-god: of Assyria, 718, 738, 767-8; of Elam, 668; of Ur, *see* Moon-god of Ur

Moon-god of Ur, 435, 442, 459, 615, 622, 656, 755; Ur-Nammu's tower, 599; eclipse of moon at Ur, 615; his temple at Ur, 628-9; high-priestesses of, 634, 641

Morphou village and bay, in Cyprus (Map 15 (27)), 809, 813, *814*

Moses and the Israelites, 352

Mosul, in Northern Mesopotamia (Map 8), 302, *316*, 609, 729; *liwa*, 303

'mother goddesses', 663-4

'Mother of Pots' (Umm el-Qaāb), 24

'Mountain of Cedars', 324 and n. 7, 325, 326, 335, 559

'Mountains of Amurru', 559

'Mountains of Silver', 322, 324, 424, 425-6

Mozan, in Khabur valley, 313

Mukish, in Syria, 561, 565

mummification in Egypt, 56-7, 347, 349

Muriq-Tidnim ('Fender of Tidnum'), 609-11, 612

musical instruments, 553; Shulgi's 606; Elamite, 671
Mut-Ashkur of Assyria, 749, 750
Mutiabal, in Mesopotamia, 640
Mut of Ishru (Egyptian vulture-goddess), 498, 520
Mycenaean culture (Map 12(35)), 787, 791
Mycerinus (Kaykhet, Menkaure) of Egypt, 169, 172–8 passim, 181, 206, 345; his pyramid temple, 30, 156, 180, 195, 196
Mysian lakes, in Anatolia, 372
mythology, Babylonian (Sumerian), 100–3
Mytilene, see Lesbos

Nabi Yūnis (Nineveh), 729
Nablus, in Palestine, 210, 236
Nabonidus of Babylonia, 448, 599, 641, 732, 736 bis, 737, 741
Nabu (a god), 667
Naga ed-Deir, in Upper Egypt (Map 4 (2)), 12, 69, 156, 190, 198, 474, 483, 512; Thinite cemetery at, 199
Nagsh-i Rustam, near Persepolis in Iran, 674
Nahal Mishmar, in Palestine, 228
Nahcevan, in Transcaucasia, 401
'Nahcevan lugs' on Anatolian pottery, 402–3, 689
Nahhunte (Elamite sun-god and god of law and of trade), 651, 667–8, 671
Nāhiya, in Egypt, Coptic convent at, 173
Nahr el-'Āṣi (River Orontes, q.v.), in Syria (Map 8), 316, 338
Nahr el-Kebīr, in Syria, 339
'naked goddess', the, 664
names adopted by kings of the ancient world, 419–20
Nammakhni of Lagash, 459, 597
Nanna (Sumerian moon-god), 667, 756, 757
Nanna-gugal, canal between Lagash and Ur, 599
Nanshe (goddess of Lagash), 130, 140–1, 595, 731, 763
Napir (Elamite god), 651, 668–9
Naplanum (first king of Larsa dynasty), 628, 632, 659
Naqāda (Ombos), in Upper Egypt (Map 4 (17)), 12, 19, 32, 52 and n. 2, 90, 474 and n. 2, 520; ivory label from, 11; architecture, 42, 43, 45
Naram-Sin of Assyria, 741, 761–2
Naram-Sin of Eshnunna, 635, 741, 762
Naram-Sin of Kish and Agade, 144, 297, 308, 321, 324, 325, 331, 332, 339, 420, 425–31 passim, 448, 456, 601, 619, 624, 626, 635, 650, 667, 711, 733–4, 734,

737, 741; his campaigns and inscriptions, 325–7; his daughters, 331; and omens, 423; his reign, 440–5, 454, 458; his titles, 440–1, 442, 448; his last year, and death, 454; his treaty with Khita of Elam, 444, 650–2, 662–3 (see also Khita treaty); 'Legend of...', 707; the 'empire builder', 736; meaning of his name, 737; his realm invaded, 739; and Northern Mesopotamia, 739; his palace at Tell Brak, 739–40
Narmer, King of Egypt, 6–7, 10, 11, 14, 18, 19, 32, 37, 41, 42, 45, 46, 47, 52, 53, 67, 68, 235, 356; Horus name of, 14, 15, 22; his mace-heads, 42, 67; his slate palette, 67, 215, 235
Narundi (Elamite goddess), 650, 651, 669, 671
Naṣiriyyah district, in Mesopotamia, 289
Naxos, Aegean island (Map 12), 372, 797, 798
Nebemakhet, Prince, 175
Nebet, Queen, 188
Nebhepetre Mentuhotpe, see Mentuhotpe II
Nebka, King of Egypt, 147, 148, 150, 157, 158
Nebkare, King of Egypt, 148 n. 3, 149, 150, 156, 157; his unfinished pyramid, 157, 158
Nebkaure Achthoes of Egypt (Achthoes II), 465
Nebkhau (Sahure, q.v.) of Egypt, 182
Neb-ma'at (Sneferu, q.v.) of Egypt, 162, 360
Nebsoyet, near Thebes, 489, 490
Nebtowyre Mentuhotpe, see Mentuhotpe IV
Nebuchadrezzar II of Babylonia, 448, 737
Nebwy Hetepimef of Egypt, 34; see also Khasekhemwy
Nedjemankh of Egypt, 152, 160
Nefer (Egyptian treasury official), 170
Nefercherēs, King of Egypt, 35
Neferefre (Neferkhare, Neferkhau) of Egypt, 182, 183, 184–5
Neferhetepes, Princess, 173, 178
Neferirkare (Kakai) of Egypt, 150, 159, 178, 179, 181–5 passim, 186. 204, 207; his temple, 201, 204
Neferka of Egypt, 157
Neferkare (Aka), King of Egypt, 35
Neferkare (Phiops II, q.v.), 194
Neferkare, King of Egypt (Seventh Dynasty), 196, 197
Neferkare, King of Egypt (Ninth Dynasty), 464, 465, 474
Neferkare, King of Egypt (successor of Meryhathor), 466

Neferkasokar, King of Egypt, 35
Neferkauhor, King of Egypt, 198
Neferkhare (Neferefre, q.v.), 184–5
Neferkhau (Neferefre, q.v.), 185
Nefermaat, Prince and Vizier, 166, 171, 174
Nefersahor (Phiops I, q.v.), 191
Neferseshemptah of Egypt, 190
Nefert, mother of Ammenemes I, 495
Nefert (wife of Rehotpe), 206
Neferthanebty, Queen, 179
Nefertkau, Princess, 171, 174
Neferty, lector-priest of Bubastis, 494, 495 *bis*, 497, 527, 537
Neferu, Queen, 476–7, 478
Neferu III, Queen, 478, 481
Neferukayet, Queen, 477
Negau, land of, 347–51 *passim*, 361–2
Negeb (Negev), the, of Southern Palestine, 210, 218, 236, 351, 583
Neheri, Vizier and Nomarch of Hermopolis, 467, 469, 470
'Nehesyu', the, 508
Neith (Egyptian goddess), 23, 25, 53, 69
Neith, Queen, 196, 197
Neithotpe, Queen, 19, 36, 53
Nejd, the (Arabia), 285, 440
Nekaure, Prince, 174, 175
Nekhbet (Egyptian vulture-goddess), 1, 32, 54, 480
Nekheb, *see* El-Kāb
Nekhebu (Meryremerptahankh) of Egypt, 186, 187, 191
Nekhen (Hierakonpolis), 1, 51; kings of, 3; souls of, 3; pre-dynastic king of, 11; 'Keeper of...', 39
Nemea valley, in Southern Greece (Map 12 (33)), 787
Neolithic period and sites, 336, 343, 370, 383, 413, 773–8 *passim*, 783, 784, 789, 791–3 *passim*, 797, 804–5; in Cyprus, 810
Nergal (Mesopotamian god), 325, 667, 671
Neser (Egyptian fish-god), 54
Nesumont, Egyptian 'Commander of Soldiers', 497–8
Netjeraperef, Prince, 163
Netjerkhau (Phiops II, q.v.), 194
Netjerpunesut (Egyptian official), 176
Netjeryhedjet, *see* Mentuhotpe II
Netjerykare, King of Egypt, 196
Netjerykhet (Djoser, q.v.), 145–6, 150, 151, 152
Niarzina (a goddess), 669
Nicosia, in Cyprus (Maps 14 (66) and 15), 810, 813, *814*, 817
Nidri plain, on Leucas (Map 12 (6)), 792
Niǧde area of Anatolia, 397

Nile Delta, *see* Delta
Nile river (Maps 1–5), 1, *2*, *4*, 6, 8, *12*, 15, *48*, 96, 169, 198, 200, 202, 464, 467, 472, 474, 496, 499, 512, 520, 806; barges or boats, 348, 351; floods, and water-supply, regulated, 496, 505; canal at Esh-Shallāl, 506–7
Nile valley (Map 1), *2*, 23, 25, 40, 44, 336, 345, 351, 478, 493; immigrants into, 40–1, 44–5, 592; and Red Sea ports, 491–2
Nina (Zerghūl), in Sumer, 130, 140, 730, 731, 763
Ninbanda (wife of Mesannipada), 283
Ninegal (Inanna, a goddess), 667, 671
Nineveh (Ninua), in Upper Mesopotamia, 89, 98, **301–3**, 303–7 *passim*, 314, 432, 726, 729–34 *passim*, 738–41 *passim*, 763; Assyrian royal library at, 423; Ishtar temple at, 733, 734
Ninevite pottery, 298, **301–4**
Ningal (consort of the moon-god), 656, 667, 737
Ningirsu (god of Lagash), 118, 119, 137, 140–3 *passim*, 276, 459, 461, 559, 595, 654
Ninkarrak (a goddess), 667, 670
Ninkhursag (a goddess), 112, 287, 296
Ninmu (a goddess), 279
Ninni-Zaza, temple of, 296, 329
Ninshubur (a god), 667
Ninsun (a goddess), 606
Nintu (a goddess), 115
Nintu temple (and others) in the Diyālā valley, **257–72**; plans, *258*, *261*, *263*, *265*, *267*; isometric projection, *271*
Ninurta (Shulmānu, Mesopotamian god), 125, 667, 738
Nippur, in Babylonia (Map 6), 97, 101, 110, 111, 132, 144, 238, 242 and n. 2, 417, 420, 421, 436, 437, 438, 440, 456, 598, 599, 600, 607, 608, 613, 614, 617, 622, 638, 641, 649, 657, 733; Tummal at, *see* Tummal; principal sites, 278–80; defences of, 611
Nisaba (a goddess), 143
Nīshāpūr, in Khurāsān (E. Persia), 392
Nisibis, in N. Mesopotamia (Map 8), *316*, 329, 565, 727
Niṣir, Mount, in Mesopotamia, 444
Nitocris, Queen (?), 179, 196, 197
Niwar-Mēr of Mari, 564 n. 7
Noah's ark, 444
nomarchs (governors of Egyptian nomes (provinces)), 194, 199, 201
nomarchs of the Middle Kingdom in Egypt, **468–72**, 482–3, 496, 505–6; 'feudal' dues of, to pharaohs, 496

North Stone Pyramid at Dahshūr, 161–4 passim, 161 n. 1
North-West Anatolian culture, 406–10
Nubia (Maps 1 and 5), 2, 33, 48, 71, 132 and n. 2, 159, 167, 190, 191, 439, 474, 475, 481, 483, 503, 543; relations with Egypt, 50–1, 485–8, 506–7, 509, 538; Lower, 187, 497 bis, 499, 518; gold in, 132, 484, 488, 503; reconquest of (by Egypt), 485–8; amethysts from, 500; turquoise in, 503
Nubian desert, diorite quarries in, 497, 500, 510
Nubians, 23, 32, 167, 188, 192, 193 bis, 195, 352, 360, 467, 469, 471, 480, 482, 485, 487, 488, 542; in Execration Texts, 508
Nubnefer, King of Egypt, 30
Numushda (a god), 756
Nur-Adad of Larsa, 633
Nur-daggal (Nur-Dagan) of Purushkhanda, 426, 427, 707
Nuzi (Nuza, Nuzue, Gasur, q.v., Yorgan Tepe), in Babylonia (Map 6), 99, 297, 716, 730, 731, 734 bis, 735, 752, 753; people of, 739
Nykaankh (Egyptian court official), 181
Nymaathap, Queen, 35, 36, 146, 151–3 passim, 151 n. 1, 178
Nynetjer, King of Egypt, 20, 30, 30–1, 65
Nyuserre (Ini, Isetibtowy) of Egypt, 148, 176, 180–5 passim, 189, 354; temple of, 204; valley temple of, 205

'Oannes and his Brethren, Story of' (Babylonian myth), 102–3
Oases, Egyptian (Map 1), 2, 201, 482, 483, 487, 488, 500; see also Faiyūm, the
obsidian, in Greece and the Aegean islands, 774, 790, 791, 793
Oeta, Mount, in Central Greece, 777
'Old Akkadian': Empire, 729; language, 450, 735; period, in Assyria, 739
Old Akkadians and Old Assyrians, 735
Oman: state in Arabia, 132, 286; Gulf of, 439; peninsula, 440 n. 2
'Ombite, The' (Seth, q.v.), 31
Ombos (Naqāda, q.v.), in Upper Egypt (Map 4(17)), 12, 32, 52 and n. 2, 520
omens, interpretation of, 422–4, 437, 456–7, 462, 493, 612, 615–16, 616
onagers (wild asses), 122 and n. 3, 269, 343
'On-of-Mont' (Hermonthis, q.v.), 519
onomastica, Egyptian, 205
Onuris (Egyptian god), 199
Opferstätten, 83 and n., 280, 286
Ophel, in Palestine, 211, 215
oracular priests, Elamite, 672–3

Orchomenus, in Central Greece (Map 12 (20)), 777, 778, 780
Öresun Hüyük, in Central Anatolia, 397
ornaments, personal, see jewellery
Orontes river (Nahr el-'Āṣi), in Syria (Map 8), 316, 320, 328, 335, 338, 339, 564 n. 4
Orontes valley, 337, 338
Oryx nome and nomarchs, in Egypt, 471, 483, 496, 503, 505
Osiris, 'Lord of Abydos' (Egyptian herogod), 22, 24, 54, 199, 202, 481, 498, 515, 517, 520, 521, 544; cult of, 203; death of (legend), 348–9
Ottoman court, 395
Ovabayindir, in N.-W. Anatolia (Map 9), 373, 375, 377, 378, 379, 386, 398; cemetery, 390, 391, 393
Ovgos valley, in Cyprus, 809, 812, 813, 816

'Painted Temple', the, at Tell 'Uqair, 76
painters and painting: Babylonian, 77; Egyptian, 206, 512–18 passim
palaces, royal, in Babylonia: earliest, 241; Early Dynastic, 274, 275, 275, 276
palaces, royal, in Egypt, 36
Palaeans, in Anatolia, 703
'Palatial' periods, in Crete, 799–800, 804
Palermo Stone, 1, 16, 22, 23, 27, 30, 31, 34, 37, 38, 50, 53, 66, 69, 147, 159, 165, 167, 180, 183–4, 207, 346, 357
Palestine (general), 90, 192; principal sites, 209, 567, 568–83
Palestine, Early Bronze Age in, 208–37; classification of material, 208–14; principal sites (Map 7), 209; fortified cities of, 214–18, 358; architecture, 218–23 (dwellings, 218–21; sanctuaries, 221–3); burials in, 223–5; crops, industry and commerce, 225–30; foreign relations of, 230–3 (see also Palestine, foreign relations); chronology, 233; historical outline, 233–7
Palestine, Middle Bronze Age in, 209; principal sites (Map 7), 209; Khirbet-Karak culture in, 399, 401; Egyptian settlers in, 501; the 'Mentju' of, 508; moon-cult in, 736
Palestine (c. 2160–1780 B.C.), 532–83; in the Heracleopolitan period and Eleventh Dynasty, 532–7; during the Twelfth Dynasty, 537–50; Egyptian sources, 550–8; social and political organization, 554–6; archaeological evidence from, 567–8; sites in, 568–83 (see also Palestine (general))
Palestine, foreign relations, 230–3; Egypt,

46, 192, 231–3, 235–6, 237, **356–62**, 501, 508, **537–50**; Mesopotamia, 231, 236; Syria, 230, 231, 233
palettes, slate, decorated: 'Battlefield', 41 n. 8; Egyptian, 6–7, 10, 14, 15, 41, 42, 46, 47, 53, 67
Pallakottas (Apkallat) canal, in Mesopotamia, 610, 614
Pallukat (Fallūjah (?), q.v.), 610
Palmyra (Tadmor), in Syria, 561
Pangaeum, Mount, in Thrace, 774
Panopolite nome, in Egypt, 471
Paphlagonia, in Anatolia, 682
papyrus symbol (Egyptian), 7
parallelism in Egyptian literature, 203
Parashi, land of, 433
Parnassus, Mount, in Central Greece, 777
Parnon, Mount, in Laconia (Greece), 789
Paroikia, on Paros (Map 12 (52)), 795
Paros, Aegean island (Map 12), 372, 780, 795, 797
Parti (Elamite goddess), 664
pastoralism in East Anatolian cultures, 401
Patras, on Gulf of Corinth (Greece), 791
Pazarli, in Central Anatolia (Map 9), *373*, 383
Pazaryeri, in Anatolia, 366
Pe (Egyptian sanctuary), 1, 51; souls of, 3; pre-dynastic kings of, 3, 11; Keeper of, 39
'peaceful co-existence' in Egypt, 467
Pediaios river, in Cyprus, 816
Pehernefer (official of Queen Meresankh), 159, 170
Peli, first king of Elamite dynasty in Awan, 647, 649
Pelikata, in Ithaca (Map 12 (7)), 792
Peloponnese, the, 777, 779; Central, 788–93; coastal region of, 791; North-Eastern, 778, 783; North-Western, 791–2
Peloponnesian pottery, 780
Pelos, on Melos (Map 12), 794, 797; culture, 797; wares, 795, 801
'Peoples of the Sea', 856, 857
Pepiankh of Egypt, 195
Pepiankhnes, Queen, 196
Per (Persenti), Queen, 175
Perhaa, near Nebsoyet, q.v., 490
Peribsen (Sekhemib?), of Egypt, 18, 20, 31–2, 33–4, 35, 39, 52, 65, 357
Persen (an Egyptian), 178
Persenti (Per), Queen, 175
Persepolis, in Iran (Map 11), *646*, 673, 674
Persia (*general*) (*see also* Iran), 133; and Mesopotamia, 71, 88, 89, 96; Western (Map 6), *facing* 112
Persia (Iran, q.v.) (*c.* 2400–1800 B.C.), **644–80**; Elamite kings of Awan,

644–54; and of Simashki, **654–62**; religion in ancient Elam, **662–73**; civilization of ancient Elam, **673–80**
Persian Gulf ('Lower Sea') (Map 11), 96, 117, 132, 133, 285, 313, 322, 421, 422, 433, 441, 444, 448, 453, 454, *646*, 663
Persians, 33, 644, 645
Per-Uadjit ('House of Edjo'), in Egypt, 1
Petrie, (Sir) William Flinders, 17, 567, 575–6
Phaestus, in Crete (Map 13 (63)), *773*, 800 *bis*
phalanx, 118, 123
phallus-sheaths, Egyptian, 47
pharaohs (of Egypt), universal domination by, 548
Philae, in Upper Egypt, 497
Philia culture and sites in Cyprus, 809–13, 816, 817, 818, 821, 822; and the Anatolian disaster, 813
Philia village, in Cyprus (Maps 14 and 15), 809, *810*, *814*, 817
Philippi, in Macedonia, 774
Phiops I (Nefersahor, Meryre, Merytowy) of Egypt, 16, 34, 69, 162, 181, 186–93 *passim*, 194, 196, 206, 226, 345, 361; his Dahshūr decree, 186, 191, 192; his pyramid, 188, 191, 193; his two queens, 191
Phiops II (Neferkare, Netjerkhau) of Egypt, 181, 185, 187, 191–3 *passim*, 194–6, 197, 198, 201, 206, 207, 237, 345, 361, 465, 519, 589, 592; his pyramid, 200; his temple, 206, 515, 516; and Byblos, 361
Phlius valley, in the Peloponnese, 787
Phocian plain, in Central Greece, 780
Phocis, in Central Greece (Map 12), 777, 780, 786
Phoenicia (Syria, q.v.), 315, 339, 341, 541, 561
Phoenicians, 343
Phrourion, the, at Paroikia on Paros, 795
Phthiotic Thebes, in Greece (Map 12 (15)), 776, 777
Phthiotis region, in Greece, 776
Phylakopi, on Melos (Map 12 (54)), 788, 794, 794–5, 803
pictographs, 94, 95, 675–6
'Pillar Hall', at Uruk, 75, 76, 77
Pines, Valley of, in Syria, 349
Pinikir (Pinenkir, Inanna, q.v., a goddess), 651, 663, 664, 667, 672, 673
Pisidia, in Anatolia, 409, 682
pithoi, burial, 376
place-names: significance of, 520; variants of, 730–3
Pleiades, the (star-cluster in Taurus), 769

Plutarch, 348
podia, see altars
Polatlı, in Northern Anatolia (Map 10), 368, 382, *385*, 388, 393, 398, 695, 697, 698, 703; burning of, 407
Poliochni, on Lemnos (Maps 9 and 10), *373, 374, 385*, 395, 414, 682; huts, 366; culture, 368; pottery, 372, 692; houses, 374, 375, 387; weapons, 377; metalwork, 377–8; site of town or city, 386, 387; architecture, 387, 685; fortress, 387, 414; burning of, 407; levels: I, 366, 372, 374; II, 374; IV, 377, 383; V, 384, 386, 387, 388, 394, 407
Politiko (site of ancient Tamassus), in Cyprus (Map 15(36)), *814*, 816, 821
Pontic culture, a, **690–1**
Pontic (steppe) region of Anatolia (Maps 9 (7) and 10(7)), 367–71 *passim, 373*, 382, *385*, 392–3, 399–400, 409, 689; culture, 371, 392, 400, 690–1
Pontic region of South-East and Central Europe (suggested 'homeland' of Indo-European migrants), 868–73 *passim*
'*Porteurs de Torques*' (Schaeffer), 340, 585
potter's wheel, 91, 156, 227, 336, 340, 345, 378, 395, 396, 414, 416; slow, 340, 345
pottery (*general*), 74, 81, 239, 363–7, 397, 576; wheel-turned, 91, 156, 301–4, 364, 367, 382, 395, 397, 694–5, 699, 775; shapes derived from metal vessels, 377, 382, 684; types of: from Jericho, *573*; from Megiddo, *582*
Pottery (periods): Late Chalcolithic, 363–7 *passim*; E.B.1, 365, 372–4, **378–83**; E.B.2, 384, **395–403**
pottery (provenances): Aegean, 793–9 *passim*; Anatolian, 363–7, 372–4, 378–83, 391, 395–403, 683–705; Asiatic (in Egypt), 350; Babylonian, 134; Chinese, 394; Cretan, 504, 799–804 *passim*; Cypriot, 808–23 *passim*; Egyptian, 46, 156, 232, 356–7; Grecian, 771–9 *passim*, 804–7 *passim*; Mesopotamian, 239, 292, 298, 301–4, 306, 307, 313–14; Minoan (Cretan), 504; Minyan, 410 (*see also* Minyan pottery and culture); Ninevite, 301–4, 314; Palestinian, 212–13, 227, 230–5 *passim*, 337, 356–7, 568–83 *passim*; Syrian, 331, 336–8, 339–41, 350, 584–92 *passim*; Trojan, *see* Troy
precious stones, *see* jewellery
priestesses: Assyrian, 718; Elamite, 673
priests, Elamite, 672–3

Prisse Papyrus, the, 159
'Procession Around the Wall' (Egyptian), 16, 36
Prophecy of Neferty of Bubastis, The, 494, 495, 497, 523, 537
Propontis, the (Sea of Marmara, q.v.), 133
prosperity in the ancient world, zenith of, 133
'Proto-literate' period in Mesopotamia, 73 and n. 4, 74–92 *passim*, 336, 364
provincial administration and officials, Egyptian, 39, 187
Ptah (Egyptian god), 15, 22, 52–3, 170, 178; High-Priest of, 176; temple of, 498
Ptahhotpe, Vizier, 201
Ptahshepses, High-Priest, 176, 184
Ptolemies, the, of Egypt, 3, 24, 33, 144
Pu-Abi, Queen, *see* Shub-ad
Pulur, in Anatolia, 401
Punt, on Somali coast, 183, 187, 190, 194, 196, 348, 355, 485, 491, 504
Purushkhaddum, city in Anatolia, 721, 722, 725, 739, 740; *see next entry*
Purushkhanda(r) (Parshukhanda), city in Anatolia, 324 and n. 9, 326, 426, 427, 429, 442, 454
Pūshu-kēn, Assyrian merchant, 710, 717, 764
'Puzrish-Dagan, House of', near Nippur, 622
Puzur-Ashur I, 747
Puzur-Ashur II, 711
Puzur-Ashur dynasty, 737, 740, 745–6, 747, 754, 762; titles of, 754–5
Puzur(Kutik)-In-Shushinak, Governor-General of Elam, 445, 454, 455, 652
Puzur-Marduk, a military commander of Ur, 615
Puzur-Nirakh of Akshak, 115
Puzur-Numushda, a governor of Kazallu, 614
Puzur-Shulgi, a governor of Kazallu, 614
Pyla, in Cyprus (Maps 14(78) and 15 (41)), *810, 814*, 816
Pylus, in Greece, 791
pyramids (*see also* Bent Pyramid, Dahshūr, Giza, Maidūm *and* Saqqara): small (for queens), 169, 170; and their temples (Fifth Dynasty), 182; and resurrection, 202; of kings of Twelfth Dynasty, 516
Pyramid Temple of Chephren, at Giza, 154, 155, 180
Pyramid Texts (of Fifth and Sixth Egyptian Dynasties), 31, 54, 57, 181, 187, 188, 197, 201, 202, 521, 522 *bis*; lack of synthesis in, 203, 519

Pyrgos, in Crete (Map 13 (62)), *773*, 801, 803

Pyrgos, on Paros (Map 12 (53)), 795

Qaa, King of Egypt, 18, 19, 28–9, 58, 59, 60, 62, 64, 66, 68, 226, 357

Qabra, a fortress-city, 742

Qadesh, in Syria, 327

Qal'a-i Toll, near Mālamīr in Persia, 647, 666

Qal'at er-Rus, in Syria (Map 8 (6)), 231, *316*, 337

Qal'at Shergāt (site of Ashur, q.v.), 729

El-Qantara, in Lower Egypt (Map 2 (11)), *4*, 356

Qar (a nomarch), 194

Qatna (Mishrifé, Mishrifeh, Mesherfa), near Homs in Syria (Map 8 (10)), *316*, 333, 338, 546 *bis*, 548, 581, 585–6, 588

El-Qatta, in the Delta (Map 2 (21)), *4*, 60

Qāw el-Kebīr (Antaeopolis), in Middle Egypt (Map 3 (30)), *8*, 472, 506 n. 1, 517

Qūbān, in Lower Nubia (Map 5 (6)), *48*, 499, 500, 503

El-Qurna, in Upper Egypt (Map 4 (20)), *12*, 472

El-Quseir (port on West coast of Red Sea) (Map 1), *2*, 355

Qutu (*formerly* Gutians, q.v.), 444

radio-carbon dating, 242–3, 403

Rakhmani, in Greece (Map 12 (11)), 776

Ramesses II of Egypt, 502

Rania, in Kurdistān, 601; plain, 303

Raphia (El-'Arīsh, q.v., Wenet (?), q.v.), in Sinai (Map 1), *2*, 352

Raphina, in Greece (Map 12 (27)), 782

Rapiqum, in N. Mesopotamia (Map 8 (26)), *316*, 333, 603, 642, 762

Raqqah, in Syria, 561

Ras el-'Ain, in Palestine (Map 7), *209*, 210, 213, 214, 232, 236, 308, 332

Ras Shamra (Ugarit, q.v.), in Syria (Phoenicia) (Map 8 (5)), *316*, 337, 339, 340, 341, 501, 503, 545–50 *passim*, 585–8 *passim*, 592, 593, 821

Ratoisis, King of Egypt (?), 175

Re-Atum (Egyptian god), temple of, 501

'red-gritty ware' (Cilician pottery), 381, 397

Redjedef (Kheper) of Egypt, 147, 150, 158, 161, 167, 171–8 *passim*, 206, 207; his pyramid and temple, 157, 207

Red Sea (Maps 1 and 2), *2*, *4*, 44, 90, 195, 348, 353, 355; traffic, 491–2; ports, 485, 492; coast, 493, 504

Rehotpe of Egypt, 206

Rehuy, Nomarch of Thebes, 473

rein-rings of Babylonian chariots, 122, 123, 136, 334

Rekhetre, Queen, 175

religion: Anatolian, 371; Assyrian, 763–9; Babylonian, 137–9; Egyptian, **51–9**, 202, **518–23**; Elamite (ancient), 662–73; Indo-European, 875–6

Reneb, King of Egypt, 20, 30, 54, 65

Renefer, Crown-Prince of Egypt, 179

Renenutet (Egyptian cobra-goddess, consort of Sobk), 511, 517

Re of Heliopolis (Egyptian sun-god, *see also* Seth-Re), 31, 170, 179, 180, 202, 204, 479, 519, 521; priest of, 179; Sons of, 179–80; temples of, 180, 518; sun-barque of, 202; of the Foreign Land, 349

repoussé work, 392, 395

Reputneb, Queen, 185

Resaina, on Khabur river, 557

resins, 46, 347, 350, 532, 559

resurrection, belief in, *see* immortality

Retenu (*included* Sinai, Palestine *and* Syria), 508, 539, 542, 557 and nn. 2 and 4; Upper, *described*, 553

Rewer (a priest), 184

Riemchen (sun-dried bricks), 76, 81, 281, 289

Riemchengebäude (buildings of sun-dried bricks), 74, 82, 83, 287

'righteousness' (*mēšarum*), in Sumer and Akkad, 634–5

Rim-Sin of Larsa, 636 *bis*, 640–3

Rimush of Agade (son of Sargon), 113, 332, 434, 447, 455, 734, 741; his reign and campaigns, 434–7, 649–50; his death, 437, 457

Rish-Adad of Apishal, 326 n. 5, 442, 564 n. 7

Rish-Adad of Armanum, 326, 441–2

rivets and riveting, 392

Er-Rizeiqāt (Sumenu), in Upper Egypt (Map 4 (26)), *12*, 520

Rizokarpaso, in Cyprus (Maps 14 (61) and 15 (24)), *810*, *814*, 816

Romania, 90, 94

Rōsh Hanniqra (Tell et-Taba'iq), in Palestine (Map 7), *209*, 210, 212, 213, 214, 217

Rukhuratir (Elamite god), 666

Rundbauten, 778

rushlights, copper, from Kish, 87

sabitum (a musical instrument), 671

Sabium of Babylon, 636

Sabni of Egypt, 195

Sabun, Mount, in Persia, 658

Sacred Marriage, the, 259, 272
sacrifices, ritual, Elamite, 671–2
'Saffron Town' (Azupiranu), on the Euphrates, 418
saff tombs, 515
Saft el-Hinna, in the Delta (Map 2 (15)), 4, 54
Sahure (Nebkhau) of Egypt, 133, 150, 167, 176, 178, 179, 181 and n. 1, 182–3, 183, 185, 189, 195, 204, 233, 351, 391; his pyramid, 156; his mortuary temple, 205, 350, 357
Sai island, in Nubia (Map 5 (32)), 48, 500
Sais (Sā el-Hagar), in the Delta (Map 2 (4)), 4, 23, 26, 53
Saïte times, in Egypt, 522
Sakcagözü, in Anatolia, 363
šakkana ('commander' of Sumerian towns and districts), 560, 609, 618
Salcuţa, in Thrace, 366
Salt Lake (Tuz Gölü), in Central Anatolia, 371, 399, 427, 696
Samaria, famine in (biblical), 616
Sāmarrā, in Mesopotamia (Map 6), 98, 730
Samos, Aegean island (*see also* Heraeum *and* Heraion) (Map 12), 414, 682, 683, 684, 794, 801, 805
Samothrace, Aegean island (Map 12), 794
Samsuiluna of Babylon, 635, 643
Sanakhte, King of Egypt, 146–7, 150–3 *passim*, 157, 158, 167, 353
Sanam-Simut, *ensi* or Viceroy of Elam, 432, 647
sanctuaries: in Palestine, 221–3; in Syria, 323
sanctuary (open-air), terracotta model of (at *Vounous*, in Cyprus), 817, 819
'Sand-dwellers', *see* Asiatics
Sangarius river, in N.-W. Anatolia (Maps 9 and 10), 367, 373, 385, 698; basin, 382
Sankh, Egyptian 'Commander of Soldiers', 493
Sankhkare Mentuhotpe, *see* Mentuhotpe III
Saqqara, near Cairo in Lower Egypt (Map 2 (33)), 4, 177, 178, 179, 182, 185, 189, 205, 207, 286, 355, 358, 508, 515, 516; king-list, 27–31 *passim*, 35, 149, 157, 159, 170, 175, 184, 346; cemeteries, 15, 16, 17–22, 24, 25, 55, 56, 158, 172, 188, 242 n. 2; step pyramids at, *see* Step Pyramids; mastabas, 55–70; *passim*, 147, 188; trench-graves, 59; cavernous tombs, 65; side-chapel, 150; Sekhemkhet's pyramid and tomb, 151, 155; chapel of Metjen, 151, 159; Ti's tomb, 185; Unas's pyramid, 187, 188, 190, 193; Isesi's pyramid, 188, 191; Phiops I's pyramid, 188, 191; Merenre's pyramid, 188; Teti's pyramid, 190, 193; relief (siege scene) at, 360; figurines, 555, 556

Saqqara: North, 17; South, 16, 20
sarcophagi, royal, 158, 168, 177, 187, 193; stone blocks for, 493
Sargon of Agade, 113, 114, 144, 236, 246, 257, 265, 296, 297, 321, 331, 332, 436–44 *passim*, 448, 449, 454, 463, 559, 560, 604, 625, 647, 648–9, 667, 707, 737, 741; his 'mysterious' origins, 417–19; his conquests, 322–7 *passim*, 420–34, 738; his reign, **417–34**; his new city, 419, 447; and Lugalzaggisi and Uruk, 421, 422; and Ur, 421; and Lagash, 421; and E-Ninmar, 422; and Persian Gulf, 422; events of his reign, **422–34**; and omens, 423; his successors, **434–40**; his policies, 447; his 'world empire', 448, 736, 738; and Elam, 647, 648–9; his Legend, 738–9; *see* Sharrumkin
Sargon I of Assyria, *see* Sharrum-kēn
Sargon II (the Younger) of Assyria, 425, 733, 737, 739, 761
Sargonic periods, 112; kings, 432
Sargonids, 649
Sariyer, in W. Anatolia (Map 10), 385, 398
Sataran (a god), 667
Satire on the Trades, 524, 526, 540
Satis (Egyptian goddess), 478, 480
Satuni of Lullubi, 443
Sawu, in Wādi el-Gāsūs (Red Sea coast) (Map 1), 2, 504
Scamander (Menderes Su), in Anatolia, 413
scarabs (Egyptian beetle symbols), 547 and n. 8, 590, 591
'scarlet ware', 239, 261, 263, 266 and n. 3, 292, 298
Sceptre, nome of the, 472
Schliemann, Heinrich, 411, 415, 416, 704
'scored ware', 381
'Scorpion' (pre-dynastic king of Upper Egypt, *see also* Ka), 3, 6, 10, 11, 45, 53; his mace-head, 42, 67
scorpion (hieroglyph), 3, 7, 52
sculpture (*see also* statuary): Babylonian, 135–6, 240, 628–30; Egyptian, *see* Egyptian sculpture and statuary; Elamite temple, 670–1, 672; Grecian, 771–93 *passim*, 804–7 *passim*; Mesopotamian, 249, 252, 259, 279, 299; Sumerian, 460–1; Syrian, 329
'Sealand' of Elam (*see also* Sherikhum), 663, 664, 666
seals: button, 533, 590; clay (bullae), 89, 306; cylinder, *see* cylinder-seals; Egyp-

tian, found in Palestine and Syria, 547; Elamite, 675, 679; flat, 227; Indian, 453; stamp, 336, 344, 696; various, 14, 79, 88, 146, 273, 590, 719
seasons, the, portrayed (Egyptian), 204–5
Sebekheres (Shepseskaf, q.v.) of Egypt, 175
Sed-festivals (Egyptian jubilees), 11, 21, 27, 28, 29, 185, 186, 191, 195, 345, 489, 502, 517
'Sedjes', 149
'seers' (augurers or diviners), Sumerian, 423
Sehertowy, see Inyotef I
Seheteptowy (Teti, q.v.) of Egypt, 189
Sekhemib (Peribsen?, q.v.) of Egypt, 31, 32
Sekhemkare, Prince, 175, 176
Sekhemkhet, King of Egypt, 150, 151, 155, 158, 167, 353
Sekhen (Ka?, q.v.), 3
Sekmem (Shechem?, q.v.), in Palestine, 508
Seljūk Turks, 409
Semerkhet (Semsem, Semempsēs) of Egypt, 18, 19, 28, 29, 36, 54, 58, 64, 147 n. 4, 151; his hieroglyph, 28
Semites, 41, 99, 109, 234, 320, 321, 342, 435, 446, 455, 564–6 passim, 656, 733, 824; in Anatolia, 717–18, 719–21; and moon-cult, 736; and honesty in (credit) business, 766
Semites, Western, 564–6, 602, 625–6, 707, 719–21, 766, 768–9
Semitic: languages, 72, 99, 100, 109, 301, 321, 450–1, 557 n. 2, 558, 564–5, 627; names (personal and place-), 100 and n. 2, 297, 320–1, 419, 449, 545, 558, 564, 566, 627, 636, 731, 732; peoples, see Semites; prophecy, 738
Semitic (West) immigration into Mesopotamia, 602, 746; Amorites, 625–8, 658
Semna East, border fortress, near Second Cataract (Map 5(28)), 48, 497, 507
Senbi, Chief Treasurer of Twelfth Dynasty, 547
Sened (Sethenēs), King of Egypt, 20, 31; his successors, 35
Senedjemib Inti (Isesi's Vizier), 186, 187, 191
Seneferka (Sekanefer, Neferseka) of Egypt, 29
Seniiker, 'Chancellor of the God', 199 n. 7, 200
Sennefer of Egypt, 347
Senwosretankh, Vizier, 503
Serābīt el-Khādim, in Sinai (Map 1), 2, 151, 355, 356, 485, 498, 501, 510, 539 bis
Serakhis valley, in Cyprus, 813
serpent-worship in Elam, 662, 672, 674–5
Seshat (Egyptian goddess), 54, 182
Seshatseshemnefer, Vizier, 188

Seshseshet, Queen, 190
Sesklo, in Greece, 797
Sesōchris, King of Egypt, 35
Sesostris I of Egypt, 471 n. 1, 473, 495, 497–9 passim, 504, 517, 518, 537–43 passim, 543 n. 7, 557, 592, 594; his reign, 499–502; statues of, 514; his festival pavilion, 514; his pyramid temple, 515, 516
Sesostris II of Egypt, 503–5, 512, 541, 542; his pyramid, 505, 512; his new town, 518
Sesostris III (Khakaure) of Egypt, 22, 471, 502, 505–9, 517, 538, 541–4 passim, 546, 555, 592; his pyramid, 509; co-regency suggested, 509 n. 4; portrait of 514; statues of, 514
Sesostris, father of Ammenemes I, 495
Sesostrisankh, Vizier, 546, 549
Seth (Egyptian god), 27, 31, 32, 33, 51, 52 and n. 2, 53, 54; Beholder of Horus and..., 36, 152
Sethenēs, see Sened
Sethos I of Egypt, 22
Seth-Re (Egyptian god, see also Re), 32, 54
'Setjet', 'Setjety' (Asia, Asiatic), 23, 357
Setka (a priest), 200
Shabako, King of Egypt, 53
Shahrazūr valley, in Mesopotamia, 443
Shala (a goddess), 667
Esh-Shallāl, on the Nile in Upper Egypt (Map 4(45)), 12; new canal at, 506–7
Shallim-akhum of Assyria, 754, 755, 756
Shalmaneser I (Shulmānu-ashared) of Assyria, 738, 744, 770
Shalmaneser II of Assyria, 741
Shalmaneser III of Assyria, 747
Shamash (Akkadian sun-god), 296, 558, 667, 718, 764; his temple, 741
Shamshi-Adad I of Assyria, 425, 431, 639, 712, 713, 717, 732–40 passim, 748, 762; his ancestors, 746; his expedition to Babylonia, 762; his usurpation, 762
Shara (god of Umma), 119
Shar-kali-sharri, of Agade, 321, 327, 454, 562, 609, 626, 627, 652; his reign, 454–7, 458; and campaigns, 454–7; and Gutium, 455
Sharlak of Gutium, 455
Sharon, plain of, in Palestine (the coastal plain), 231, 356
Sharrish-takal (minister and oracular priest) of Agade, 652
Sharrum-bani, Governor of Awak, 656
Sharrum-bani (a Sumerian official), 610, 615
Sharrum-kēn (Sargon I of Assyria), 710–11, 741, 761–2; his 'Ashur' seal, 767–8

Sharrumkin, 432; *see* Sargon of Agade
Shasha (wife of Urukagina of Lagash), 120
Shashert, in Nubia, 33
Shashrum (Shusharra, Shemshāra), on the Lesser Zab river in Mesopotamia, 601, 602, 607, 624
Shaṭrah, in Babylonia, 288
Shaṭṭ el-Ḥayy (el-Gharrāf), in Mesopotamia, 116, 120, 288
Shatt er-Rigāl, in Upper Egypt (Map 4 (36)), *12*, 478, 479, 480, 487
Shechem (Balāṭa, Sekmem?), in Palestine (Map 7), *209*, 509, 538 *bis*, 543, 547, 555
Shedet (town), in the Faiyūm (Crocodilopolis, q.v.), 511 *bis*, 520
Shedyetsha, in Egypt, 470–1; 'Day of . . .', 471
Sheikh Abd el-Qurna, in Upper Egypt (Map 4 (20)), *12*, 472
Sheikh Farag, in Upper Egypt (Map 4 (1)), *12*, 474
Sheikh Saʿīd, in Middle Egypt (Map 3 (17)), *8*, 182, 470
Shemay (a vizier and nomarch), 194, 198
Shemshara (Shusharra, Shashrum, q.v.), in Mesopotamia, 602
Shemu (Egyptian season), 204 and n. 2, 205
Shensi, near Mosul in N. Mesopotamia, 303
Shepseskaf, King of Egypt, 161, 172, 175–8 *passim*, 184
Shepseskare, King of Egypt, 184
Shepsesre (a vizier), 187 *bis*
Shepsesykhet (Shepseskaf, q.v.), 177
Sherikhum, land of (*see also* 'Sealand' of Elam), 438 *bis*, 439, 440, 648
Shery (Egyptian priest), 20, 31
Shiashum (a goddess), 669, 670
shields, *see* weapons
Shilkhakha of Anshan and Susa, 640, 662
Shilkhak-In-Shushinak of Elam, 659, 660, 663, 670
Shimut (Simut, Elamite god), 669, 670, 672
Shinakhūtum (town), in Asia Minor, 722
Shinpi-khish-khuk of Elam, 652
ships (and boats), 42, 58, 188, 196, 201, 277, 343, 348, 350–1, 392, 440, 484, 485, 487, 491, 496; of Magan, Meluhha and Tilmun brought (by Sargon) to Agade, 422
'Shrine of Ili-tabba', 462
shrines, *see* temples
Shub-ad (Pu-Abi), Queen, 100 n. 3, 244, 254, 269, 284, 300, 314
Shubar, Shubartu, *see* Subar
Shubaru, *see* Subarians

Shubat-Enlil, in N. Mesopotamia, 707, 737, 738, 739
Shu-Durul of Gutium, 457
Shulgi of Ur, 279, 441, 600–7, 617, 618; foreign policy, 600; fiscal control, 600–1; his wars and foreign conquests, 601–3, 609; his rule in Elam, 654–7; his Tummal at Nippur, 604; and Eridu and Marduk, 604, 608; his letters, 605; his hymns, 605–6; his record journey, 606; his instrumental prowess, 606; his death and burial, 607
Shulmānu (Ninurta, q.v.), 738
Shulmānu-ashared (Shalmaneser) I, 738, 744, 770
Shuruppak (Fārah, q.v.), in Babylonia (Map 6 (21)), 72, 93, 94, 97, 101, 107, 109, 131 n. 3, 244, 290, 445
Shu-Sin (Gimil-Sin) of Ur, 562 *bis*, 563, 597, **608–11**, 612, 625, 626, 627, **656–8**; his defensive 'wall', 603, 609–10, 612; his governors and commissioners, 609; and 'a new danger' (Tidnum), 609–10; and Anshan, 657; his campaigns, 657
Shutruk-Nahhunte of Elam, 668
Sialk, near Kāshān in N.-W. Persia, 89, 227, 302
Siashum (a goddess), 651
Sidgau, Governor or Viceroy of Warakhshe (Barakhshe), 436, 648, 649 *bis*
Sidmant, in the Faiyūm (Map 2 (56)), *4*, 511
Sidon, in Lebanon, 230, 320, 561
siege warfare, 124 and n. 4, 189, 358–60, 359, 471, 481, 535
Siheil island, in Upper Egypt (Map 4 (43)), *12*, 145
Sile, fortress of (Tell Abu Seifa, Tjel), near El-Qantara in Lower Egypt (Map 2 (12)), *4*, 356
Silifke, in Calycadnus valley, Anatolia, 364
Ṣilli-Adad of Larsa, 640
silver, *132*, 269, 288, 305, 377, 394, 395, 543, 612, 724–5, 771–823 *passim*; mines, 370, 438, 440 n. 2, 696, 699, 754; as money, 613, 616, 725, 726, 754
silver mountains, *see* Mountains of Silver
Simanum (a city), 607, 608, 624
Simashki, in Elam, 603, 612, 633, 653, 654, 657, 658, 660; Elamite kings of, **654–62**
Simav, in Anatolia, 372
Simti-Shilkhak (father of Kudur-Mabuk), 640
Simurrum, near Altın Köprü on Lower Zab river (N. Mesopotamia), 432, 601, 603, 611, 624, 631, 655

Sin (Assyrian moon-god), 667, 718, 736–7, 757, 768
Sinai (Map 1), 2, 23, 24, 27, 132, 151, 183, 185, 191, 194, 226, 498; *described*, 352–3; relations with Egypt, 46–7, 50, 351–6 *passim*, 485, 539–40; mines (copper and turquoise) in, 151, 183, 195, 235, 352, 354, 355, 392, 484 *bis*, 509–10, 532, 535, 539, 543, 553; rock-carvings and inscriptions in, 167, 183, 353–4, 509–10, 540, 553, 554, 557 nn. 4 and 10, 558; Egyptians in, **351–6**, 549; Egyptian names for bedawin of, 351; Egyptian expeditions to, 352–5, 484
Sind, province of India, 439
Sin-iddinam of Larsa, 633, 642
Sin-kashid of Uruk, 636
Sin-muballiṭ of Babylon, 636 *bis*, 639, 642
Sin Temples at Khafājī, 83 n. 2, 238, 241–2, 244, 246, **246–57** (plans of, *248, 250, 253, 256*), 274, 275, 278, 292, 295, 330
Sinuhe (a royal official, *see also* Story of Sinuhe), 499, 500, 525 n. 10, 544, 552, 553, 554
Sippar, in Babylonia (Map 6), 97, 98, 101, 438, 628, 636, 637, 741, 764
Sirenpowet (I), Nomarch of Elephantine, 500
Sirion (Antilebanon) region, 555
Sirius (dog-star), 718, 767, 769
Sitnebsekhtu, letter of, 490
Sit-Sneferu (an Egyptian nurse), 504
Sivrihisar, in Anatolia, 367
slavery: in Agade, 650; in Babylonia, 608, 624, 625, 627, 634, 733; in Egypt, 357, 361, 543, 549
slits (in walls) for archery, 374
Smyrna (Izmir), in Anatolia (Map 12 (58)), 372, 684, 700, 805
Sneferu (Neb-ma'at) of Egypt, 148, 152, 155–71 *passim*, 174, 181, 186, 206, 207, 353, 356, 360–1, 494, 504; two pyramids of, 20, 191 (*see also* Bent Pyramid *and* North Stone Pyramid); and a third (?), 164; and Hetepheres, 164–5; his policy, 166–7; his palace, 168, 346
Sneferukhaf of Egypt, 171
Sobk of Hes (Egyptian god), 520
Sobk (Suchos) of Shedet (Egyptian crocodile-god), 'Lord of Sumenu', 54, 511, 517; his consort (Renenutet), 511; his temple, 511; his 'guest' (Horus the Elder), 511
Sobk-Re (Egyptian composite god), 520
social problems, Babylonian, 139–42
Sokar (Egyptian falcon-god), 53
Somaliland (*see also* Punt), 183

Sopd (Egyptian god), 54, 504, 539
Sotira, in Cyprus (Maps 14 and 15 (47)), *810, 813, 814*
South Stone (Bent) Pyramid at Dahshūr, 154, 156, 158, 162, 163, 164
Spain, 430
spear and sword, development of (from dagger), 393
'spectacle idols', 329
Spercheus valley, in Greece, 777
Sphinx, the Great (at Giza), 154, 174
sphinxes, Egyptian, in Syria, 545–6
Spirits of the Dead (Egyptian), 1, 3
'Standard of Ur', *see* Ur
'Standards' in Babylonian tombs, 138, 139
Star (a god), 558
statuary (*see also* sculpture *and* statuettes): Babylonian, 135, 240; Egyptian, *see* Egyptian sculpture and statuary; in Elamite temples, 670–1, 672; Greek marble, 797–8; Mesopotamian, 240, 254–5, 259, 264, 282, 299–300, 312; Sumerian, 328
statuettes (*see also* statuary), 30, 80, 86, 115, 207, 258, 268, 269, 276, 282, 345, 502–6 *passim*, 513, 514, 549, 650, 670, 798
stelae: in Anatolia, 388, 413; Assyrian (of eponyms), 742–3; in Babylon, 80, 282, 628; in Egypt, 18–21 *passim*, 30, 55, 56, 67, 118, 170, 177, 197, 199, 474 nn. 2 and 3, 477, 478, 482, 483, 497, 502, 504, 506, 512, 515, 521, 540; in Mesopotamia, 312; at Ras Shamra, 550; at Susa (Sargon's), 443, 649; in Syria, 332, 333; at Troy, 413; Naram-Sin's, 443; of General Nesumont, 537
Stele of Victory, 451–2
Stele of the Vultures, 118, 121, 123, 245, 288
Stele of Warka, 124
Step Mastaba at Saqqara, 62
Step Pyramids at Saqqara: Djoser's, 19, 20, 29, 31, 59, 60, 66, 70, 145, 146, 149, 150, 155, 156, 160, 180, 187 (appearance of, 153, 154); Sekhemket's, 148, 155–6; complex of, 151, 153
Stibos, near Lake Langadas in Macedonia, 396
stone-carvers and stone-carving, 377, 378
Stone-Cone Temple (Uruk), 76
stone figures and figurines: Anatolian, 378; Egyptian, 68
stone, hewn, as building material, 65–6; *see also* mastabas
stone-quarrying in Egypt, 167–8
stones (precious and semi-precious) used in ornaments, 392; *see also* jewellery
stone vessels: Anatolian, 381, 394; Egyptian, 67

Story of Sinuhe, 499, 523, 525, 526, 538 *bis*, 540–5 *passim*, 557 and nn. 3 and 4
Subar (Subartu, Subir, qq.v.), 117, 605
Subarian slaves in Babylonia, 733
Subarians (*Su*-people), 609, 612, 616 *bis*, 625, 657, 658, 769
Subartu(m), land of, in N. Mesopotamia (*see also* Subar), 323, 430–1, 442, 616, 638, 707
Subir (Subar, Subartu, qq.v.), 605, 732
Suchos (Sobk, q.v., Egyptian| crocodile-god), 520
Sudan, the, 71, 156, 194, 488, 507, 549; Northern, 23
Suez: town, 353; isthmus of, 44, 491, 544
sukkal (regent), 650
sukkal-maḥ (grand-regent), 656, 662
Sulaimaniyyah, in Mesopotamia (Map 6(6)), 443, 444, 601
Sulili of Assyria, 746 *bis*
Sumenu (Er-Rizeiqāt), in Upper Egypt (Map 4(26)), *12*, 520
Sumer (*see also* Sumer and Akkad), 72, 89, 90, 91, 107, 116, 117, 143, 336, 342, 595, 627; princes of, 278; gods of, 321; and Lebanon coast, 351 n. 5; Ur-Zababa rules the cities of, 420; Lugalzaggisi rules over, 421; Rimush and, 434–6; 'cities of', 434, 435, 447; Western invaders of, 446–7; city revolts in, 447
Sumer and Akkad (*see also* Sumer), 89, 307, 447; invaded, 454; influence in Syria, 559, 561; and in Anatolia, 561; first king of (Ur-Nammu, q.v.), 599 (*see also* Third Dynasty of Ur); devastated, 617; cities of, and Ur, 617; divided, 631–8; after division, 638–9
Sumerian: architecture, 75–85; cities and homeland, 420, 422, 434, 435, 445; communities, 91–2; culture and influence, 291–314 *passim*, 329, 432, 446, 447, 636, 665, 674; deities (*listed*), 328 n. 4; economy, 91, 126–30; king-list, 417, 418, 420, 421, 434, 435, 440, 456, 458, 461, 462, 463, 631, 645 *bis*, 647, 742; language, 72, 81, 94–8 *passim*, 109, 306 (*see also* cuneiform script); legends and traditions, 92, 108, 111–12, 458; pantheon, 328 and n. 4; patriotism, 463; problem, 94–6; scribes, 618
Sumerian script, 89, 90–1, 675–6; earliest, 94–6; and hieroglyphs, 43–4, 90; Sargon and, 419
Sumerian: sculpture and statuary, 98, 460–1; 'seers', 423; traditions, *see* Sumerian legends *above*

Sumerians, 42–5, *passim* 72, 94–5, 321, 824; and Semites, 99–100, 321, 435, 446; in Ashur, 300–1; and Agade dynasty, 446–53 *passim*; 'a rebellious people', 448; and Assyria, 730
Sumero-Akkadian pantheon, 667
Sumuabum, founder of First Dynasty of Babylon, 637, 638, 756–7
Sumuel of Larsa, 628, 637
Sumulael of Babylon, 757
Sungasur gorge, in N. Mesopotamia, 601
Sun-gods: of Assyria, 718, 767–8; of Egypt, 53, 54, 179, 202 (*see also* Re); of Sumer, 437, 438, 606, 633; of Susa, 666
Sun-temples, 180, 184, 185, 186, 189, 204, 640
Su-people (Subarians), 609, 612, 616 *bis*, 625, 657, 658, 769
Susa, capital of Elam (Maps 6 and 11), 89, 96, 98, 227, 254, 274, 286, 330, 431, 432, 436, 437, 438, 444–5, 450, 609, 611, 613, 646, 647–75 *passim*; occupied, 658
Susian king-list, 657, 659, 660, 661
Susiana, 603, 644, 647, 653–64 *passim*; and Sumerians, 654; daily life in, 679–80; burials in, 680
Susians, 645, 654, 657
Sutu nomads, 642
synchronisms and synchronization, 405
Syria (*basic details*): *defined*, 315; boundaries of, 315; zones of, 315–18; map of, *316*; climate and fauna of, 318; history and peoples of, 318–21
Syria (*general*) (Map 8), 42, 44, 115, 133, 229, 230, 241, 247, 302, 304, 314, *316*, 370, 409; material civilization of, 340–3; Sargon in, 424, 425, 426, 448; Naram-Sin in, 442; Egyptian settlers in, 501; Indo-European languages in, 837–9; physical and political geography of, 559–62, 565–6; demography and ethnography of, 562–6
Syria (*geographical divisions*): Northern, 71, 90, 230, 231, **304–14**, 321, 331, 341–5 *passim*, 594; North-Eastern, 303, 306, 331; Eastern, 303; Southern, 230, 233, 540
Syria before 2200 B.C., **315–62**; background, **315–21**; period of kings of Agade, **321–8**; cities of Euphrates and Khabur, **328–33**; cities of plain and coast, **333–43**; Byblos and the land of Negau, **343–51**; Egyptians in Sinai and Palestine, **351–62**
Syria (and Palestine), c. 2160–1780 B.C., **532–94**; in the Heracleopolitan period

and the Eleventh Dynasty, **532–7**;
during the Twelfth Dynasty, **537–50**;
Egyptian sources, **550–8**; social and
political organization, **554–6**; Syria
during the Third Dynasty of Ur,
559–66; archaeological evidence from
Palestine, **567–8**; Palestine sites, q.v.,
568–83; Syrian sites, **583–94**
Syria, foreign relations of: Egypt, 45–6,
232–3, 501, 508, 532, **537–50**;
Palestine, 230–1; Mesopotamia, 559–66
Syrian: bottles, 336, 350; mountain bears,
183; sites, **583–94**
Syros, Aegean island (Map 12), 783, 796,
806; culture, 796

Tabara el-Akrād, in Syria (Map 8 (4)), 231,
316, 337
Tabrīz in Azarbayjān (Persia), 286
Tadmor (Palmyra), in Syria, 561
Tale (Story) of the Eloquent Peasant, 465,
523, 525, 525–6
Tales of King Cheops and the Magicians, 523,
525
Talkhatum, in N. Mesopotamia *or* Syria,
442
Talmu-Sharri of Turukku and Assyria,
749, 750
Tammuz (Dumuzi, a god), 111, 462
Tammuz-Marduk (a god), 349
Tanis, in the Delta (Maps 1 and 2 (7)), 2, 4,
498, 514
Tan-rukhuratir, Governor of Susa, 660,
661
Tappa-darakh (an enemy of Shulgi), 603
Tar...dunni, King of the Lullu, 444
Tarkhān, in Lower Egypt (Map 2 (40)), 4,
19, 66
Tarsus, in Anatolia (Map 8 (1)), *316*, 389,
685; pottery, 363, 364, 365, 692, 694;
culture, 364, 368; houses, 386, 389;
town site (fortified), 386, 389–90;
burning of, 407
Taurus mountains, in Anatolia, 324, 325,
335, 370, 426, 448; silver mines in,
370, 426
Tavşanlı-Iznik area and culture, in Anatolia (Map 9), 372, *373*, 379, 380, 398,
410
Tavşanlı-Kütahya region, in Anatolia
(Map 9), *373*, 694, 695, 699
Tavşanlı plain, in N.-W. Anatolia (Maps 9
and 10), 372, *373*, 379, *385*, 395, 698,
701
Tazehkand, near Tabrīz in Persia, 401
'tea-pots', Anatolian, 690, 695
Tefibi, Nomarch of Asyūt, 466, 469, 470
Tekkeköy, on the Black Sea coast, 393

Tel Aviv, in Palestine (Map 7), *209*, 228
Teleilat Ghassūl, in Palestine, 320
Tel Gat (Tell esh-Sheikh el-'Areini, q.v.),
in Palestine (Map 7), *209*, 215, 218
Et-Tell ('Ai, q.v.), in Palestine (Map 7),
208, *209*
Tell Abu Seifa (Sile, Tjel), near El-
Qantara, in Lower Egypt (Map 2 (12)),
4, 356
Tell Abyad, in N. Syria, 308
Tell Afis (Khazrek, Hatarikka?), in Syria,
335
Tell Agrab, in Babylonia, 72, 87; Shara
temple at, **266–70**, *267*
Tell Ahmad el-Hatu, near Kopri in Meso-
potamia, 298
Tell Aḥmar (Til Barsib, q.v.), in Syria
(Map 8 (17)), *316*, 333
Tell Ailun, on Syrian/Turkish frontier,
314
Tell el-'Ajjūl, near Gaza in Palestine
(Map 7), *209*, 218, 546, 547, 575–6,
577, 585
Tell 'Arad, in the Negev, Palestine
(Map 7), *209*, 210, 213, 215, 217
Tell Arbit, in Syria, 331
Tell 'As, in Palestine, 581, 586, 588
Tell Asmar (Eshnunna, q.v.), in Babylonia
(Map 6 (12)), 72, 91, 138, 302 n. 6,
302; Abu temple at, 255, **260–2**, *261*;
single-shrine temple at, **264–6**, *265*;
square temple at, 231, **262–4**, *263*;
Akkadian palace at, 305
Tell Beit Mirsim, in Palestine (Map 7), *209*,
210, 214, 218, 236, 567, 576, 577
Tell Billa, in Mesopotamia, 302, 303
Tell el-Biya' (Tuttul?, q.v.), 324 n. 1
Tell Brak, in Syria (Map 8 (23)), 89, 241,
247, 269, 288, 291, 293, 296, **306–8**,
312, 313, *316*, 318, 319, 329, 330, 332,
338, 342, 437, 443, 586, 597; 'Eye
Temples' at, 247, 307, 329–30;
Naram-Sin's palace at, 332, 443, 734,
739–40
Tell Chagar Bazar, in Syria, 341
Tell ed-Duweir (Lachish), in Palestine
(Map 7), *209*, 210, 213, 218, 225, 226,
228, 547, 576–7
Tell el-Fār'ah, near Nablus in Palestine
(Map 7), *209*, 210–22 *passim*, 227, 228,
236, 575
Tell Gath, 356
Tell Ḥalaf, in Syria (Map 8 (19)), 308, *316*,
332, 730
Tell el-Harīrī (Mari, q.v.), in N. Mesopo-
tamia (Map 8 (24)), *316*, 328
Tell el-Ḥesi, in Palestine (Map 7), *209*, 210,
213, 218, 228

Tell el-Ḥuṣn, in Transjordan (Map 7), *209*, 583
Tell Inghara, in Babylonia, 273
Tell Jemma, 547
Tell Jidleh, in Syria, 332
Tell Judaidah, in Syria (Map 8 (2)), 90, 230, 231, *316*, 336, 341, 342
Tell Jūkhā, *see* Umma
Tell Khuaira, in N.-E. Syria (Map 8 (20)), 98, 297, 307, *316*, **308–14**, 332; 'North Temple' at, *309*, 310, 332; stone building at, *311*
Tell Mardikh, in Syria, 335
Tell Maṣin, near Hama in Syria (Map 8 (7)), *316*, 339
Tell en-Naṣbeh, in Palestine (Map 7), *209*, 210, 211, 575
Tello, in Babylonia (Map 6), 72, 116, 130, 288, 296, 652
Tell er-Ratāba, in Lower Egypt (Map 2 (16)), *4*, 465
Tell Rifa'at (Arpad), in Syria (Map 8 (13)), *316*, 334–5
Tell esh-Shaikh, in Anatolia, 363, 364
Tell esh-Sheikh el-'Areini (Tel Gat, q.v.), in Palestine (Map 7), *209*, 215, 217, 235
Tell Simiriyān, in Syria (Map 8 (9)), *316*, 340
Tell Sukas, in Alawite country, 231
Tell et-Taba'iq (Rōsh Hanniqra, q.v.), in Palestine (Map 7), *209*, 210
Tell Ta'yīnāt, in Syria, 336
Tell Tuqān, in Syria, 335
Tell 'Uqair, in Babylonia (Map 6 (15)), 72, 76, 364
Tell el-Wilayah, in Babylonia, 289
Tell Zaydān, in N. Mesopotamia, 561
Tem (Atum?), Queen, 481
Tēmā, in Arabia, 736
Temple of (the) Ba'alat, at Babylon, 589
Temple of Ishkur, 462
Temple of the Obelisks, at Byblos, 589
temple oval at Khafaji, 257, **270–2**, *271*, 287
temples, Babylonian, *described*: Abu temple (Tell Asmar), **260–2**, *261*; Mintu temple (Khafājī), **257–60**, *258*; Shara (Tell Agrab), **266–70**, *267*; single-shrine temple (Tell Asmar), **264–6**, *265*; Sin temples, *see* Sin Temples; square temple (Tell Asmar), **262–4**, *263*; temple oval (Khafājī), 257, **270–2**, *271*, 287
temples, Elamite, **670–3**
temples and shrines, Anatolian, 388–9
temples and shrines, Babylonian, 73, 75–7, 81–5, 241; and agriculture and

fisheries (Lagash), 126–7; economics of (Lagash), 127–30
temples and shrines, Egyptian, 59–60, 62–3; mortuary, 59–60; pyramid, 65 (*see under names of kings*); Syrian, 331–2
temples: horn-, 670, 671; 'male' and 'female', 389
Tenedos, Aegean island, 372
'tent-dwellers', Assyrian royal, 744–5
Tepecik, in Pontic Anatolia, 378, 383
Tepe Gawra, near Nineveh (Map 8 (27)), 98, 108, 303, 304, 310, *316*, 342, 730; pottery, 363, 364
Tepe Hisar, in Persia, near Caspian Sea, 89, 302
Tepya Mentuhotpe, *see* Mentuhotpe I
Terqa, on the Euphrates, 561
Teti (Seheteptowy) of Egypt, 14, 23, 150, 156, 181, 186, 189–91, 191–3 *passim*; his pyramid, 190, 193
textiles, 226; Assyrian manufactured and traded, 723–6 *passim*, 752
Thamphthis (a king of Egypt?), 172, 175, 176
Tharthar river, in N. Mesopotamia, 726
Thasos, Aegean island, 794
'theatres' (assembly halls), 387
Thebaid, the (nome of Thebes, q.v.), 496
Theban artists, 514
Theban revolution (2133 B.C.), 466–8, 470–5 *passim*
Thebans in Egyptian government offices, 483–4
Thebes (Luxor, Wāset, Wēse, Diospolis), in Upper Egypt (Maps 1 and 4), *2*, *12*, 22, 180, 199, 200, 465, 467, 474, 477, 479, 481, 487–98 *passim*, 508, 512, 515, 519; cemetery (necropolis) of, 472, 476; 'Head of the South', **472–5**; Nebhepetre's tomb-temple at, 481; central government at, 482
Thebes, Phthiotic, in Greece (Map 12 (15)), 776, 777
theophorous names, 25, 558, 663, 666–70 *passim*, 719–20, 738, 766, 767, 768
Thera, Aegean island (Map 12), 798
Thermi, on Lesbos (Map 12 (57)), 368, 372, 414, 682; fortifications, 374, 384; houses, 375; metalwork, 377, 378; weapons, 377, 378; marble bowls, 378; figurines, 378; pottery, 379, 380; desertion of, 383; levels, 357, 377, 378, 414
Thessalonica (Salonika), in Macedonia, 773
Thessaly, in Greece (Map 12), 383, 775–7, 784
Thinite nome, in Egypt, 467, 474, 475, 477, 483

Third Dynasty of Ur (*see also* Babylonia *c.* 2120–1800 B.C.), 559–66 *passim*, 592, 594, **595–617**, 654, 655, 658, 711, 746 *bis*, 756; Ur-Nammu, q.v., **595–600**; Shulgi, q.v., **600–7**; Shu-Sin, q.v., **608–11**; Ibbi-Sin, q.v., **611–17**; business documents of, 601, 617

This (city), near Abydos in Upper Egypt (Map 4(3)), *12*, 17, 21, 198, 199, 464, 466, 473, 474, 477, 479; 'rebellion' of, 467

Thoth (Egyptian ibis-god), 53, 171, 353, 354, 470, 489

Thrace, in Greece (Map 12), 366, 773–5

Thrace, Turkish, 371, 380, 384, 396

Thracian invasion of Anatolia, 384, 410

Thracian–Troy I culture, 371

'throwstick-people', 351

Thucydides, 16

Thuthotpe, Nomarch of Hermopolis, 503, 505, 542; his statuette, 543, 546, 549

Thutnakhte I, II, III and IV, Nomarchs of the Harenome, 470; V, 471

Tiberias, Lake (Sea of Galilee), in Palestine, 210, 229

Tidan/Ditan (Dit(a)num, *see also* Tidnum), in N. Mesopotamia, 559 and n. 2

Tidnum *or* Dit(a)num (town), in N. Mesopotamia, 562; *see also* Tidan

Tidnum (western tribes of Babylonia), 609–10, 617

Tieszkewicz seals, 696

Tiflis, in Transcaucasia, 401

Tigani, in Samos, 367, 374

Tiglath-Pileser I of Assyria, 420, 739, 741, 767, 770; his Annals, 741

Tigris plain or valley, 71, 73, 92, 98, 304, 752; trade route, 333

Tigris river (Maps 6 and 8), 96, 98, 116, 119, 125, 143, 288, 298, 303, *316*, 332, 421, 434, 598, 602, 603, 610, 614, 624, 625, 628, 632, 638, 639, 641, 739, 752; upper reaches of, 291; and Assyria, 729; course-changes of, 730

Tihna, in Middle Egypt (Map 3(8)), *8*, 181–2

Til Barsib (Tell Aḥmar, q.v.), in Syria (Map 8(17)), *316*, 333, 334, 691

Tilla (Assyrian god), 732

Tilmun (land beyond Persian Gulf), 117, 131, 132, 422, 453, 454, 631

timber (lumber, mostly conifer): for Egyptian tombs, 346–8; for Gudea of Lagash, 460, 559; for Sippar, 438; from Amanus mountains, 559; from the Lebanon and Syria, 46, 318, 325, 328, 346–8, 350, 362, 466, 484, 501,

532; from Meluhha, 439; from Tilmun, 422

tin, 344, 350, 392, 430, 452, 609; trade in, 724–5

'Tin (or Lead) Country', 429, 430

'tinkers', 591

Tirigan of Gutium, 462, 654

Tiryns, in Argolis (Greece) (Map 12(36)), 684, 785, 787; Mycenaean palace at, 787

Tisari (Tisatal) of Urkish, 565, 731

Tjamerery (an Egyptian governor), 199

Tjehemau (a Nubian mercenary), 487

Tjehenu-land (Libya, q.v.), 7, 47

Tjel, *see* Sile

Tjetji (an Egyptian chancellor), 477

Tlas (a king of Egypt?), 31

Tōd (Djeret) village, in Upper Egypt (Map 4(25)), *12*, 180, 472, 476, 481, 503, 513, 517, 519, 540, 543

Tokat, in Central Anatolia (Map 9), *373*, 383

Tomās, in Nubia (Map 5(12)), *48*, 187, 190, 191

tombs: Egyptian, 54–6, 64–5 (*see also* Abydos, Egypt, mastabas, pyramids *and* Saqqara); at Jericho, **570–5**, *571*; at Megiddo, **579–81**, *580*

tools, 228–9, 276, 377, 691, 738, 739, 771–823 *passim*; copper tools as currency, 726

Tōshka, in Nubian desert (Map 5(19)), *48*; diorite quarries near, 497, 500, 510

town planning, 344

trade, external: of Anatolia, 715–21, 723–7; of Assyria, 715–21, 723–7, 752–4; of Babylonia, 131–3, 285–6, 452–3; of Egypt, 40–51 *passim*, 183, 189, 193–4, 195–6, 484, 501, 504; of Mesopotamia, 240, 254; of Palestine, 225–30; of Syria, 333, 501

Transcaucasia, 402

Transjordan (*now* Jordan), 210, 214, 235, 236, 583

Trialeti, in E. Anatolia, 689, 691

'triangle' ware, 853 n. 2

Tripolis, in the Peloponnese, 789

Troad, the (Map 12), 372, 384, 395, 411, 413, 414, 416, 682, 700, 702, 703, 774, 801; 'face-lids' and 'face-urns' of, 395

Troödos mountains, in Cyprus, 813, 816, 820

Troy, in N.-W. Anatolia (Maps 9 and 12 (56)), 90, 133, 368–410 *passim*, *373*, **411–16**, *412*, 682, 805, 806; cultures, 370–83 *passim*, 392 (*see also* Troy, cultures and levels); destroyed, 383–4, 386, 393, 406–16; weapons, 378, 393;

marble bowls, 378; pottery, 379, 384, 395, 396, 398, 414, 415–16, 681–7, 692, 697–706 *passim*; houses, 380, 388, 390, 704–6 *passim*; treasures, 386; fortress of, 386, 387; *megaron*, 387; metalwork, 392; metal vessels, 394, 395; and the catastrophe at end of E.B.2, 406–16 *passim*; burning of Troy II, 407; immigrants, 407–10; discoveries at Hisarlik, 411–16; plan of, *412*; first and second settlers at, 413–14, 415–16

Troy cultures and levels: I, 368–84 *passim*, 396, 403, 407–15 *passim*, 683; II, 368, 369, 380, 383–97 *passim*, 403–16 *passim*, 775, 776, 796; III, 368, 369, 395, 396, 407, 413, 682–5 *passim*, **704**, 775, 776, 796; IV, 368, 369, 396, 413, 682–5 *passim*, **704–5**, 776; V, 368, 369, 376, 384, 396, 413, 682, **705–6**; VI, 376, 384, 410, 413, 698, 844; VII, 413

Tserna river, in Macedonia, 774

Tukin-khatta-migrisha (daughter of Ibbi-Sin), 611, 658

Tukrish (Urukish), land of, 433, 624, 639

Tukulti-Ninurta I of Assyria, 738, 739, 747, 751, 752

Tulūl eth-Thalāthat, in N. Mesopotamia, 303

Tummal, the (sanctuary in Nippur), 111, 112, 113, 244, 599, 604

tumuli at Trialeti, in E. Anatolia, 689

Tura, near Cairo (Map 2 (29)), *4*; cemetery, 6; limestone quarries, 66, 187, 201, 510

Turin Canon, 1 n, 1–3, 11, 14, 28, 29, 30, 35, 147, 148 and n. 3, 149, 157, 159, 160, 162, 165, 172–7 *passim*, 180–8 *passim*, 195–7 *passim*, 465, 466, 478, 492

Turkey, 304, 314, 337, 546

Turkomans, 409

Turks, Seljūk, 409

turquoise, 23, 24, 47, 69, 151, 167, 353, 354, 386, 392, 501, 503, 509, 539, 543; mines, *see* Sinai; Mistress of Turquoise, 354, 510; Terraces of the Turquoise, 354, 358

Turquoise Land, 183

Turukku, Hurrian tribe of, 749

Tuthmosis III of Egypt, 347, 543 n. 4

Tuttul (Duddul, Hīt), in N. Mesopotamia (Maps 6 and 8 (25)), *316*, 322–5 *passim*, 324 n. 1, 334 n. 9, 424–6 *passim*, 431, 560, 564 nn. 6 and 7, 603, 609, 707; a second, 560

Tutub (Khafājī, q.v.), in Babylonia (Map 6 (13)), 110, 244, 246

Tuz Khurmatli, in Mesopotamia, 602

'Two Brothers, The' (a romance), 349

'Two Ladies' (Egyptian royal title), 14

Tyre, in Lebanon (Map 8), *316*, 320

Uadjit (Egyptian cobra-goddess), 1, 54

Al-'Ubaid, near Ur (Map 6(26)), 72, 78, 86, 112, 136, 245, 287 and n. 4, 288, 298, 310; principal sites, 287–8; and Anatolia, 364, 365; culture and influence, 364, 365; period, 73 and n. 4, 75, 76, 107, 108, 290 and n., 288 n. 1, 364, 730

'Ubaid ware, 74, 363–4, 367; post-'Ubaid ware, 364

Ubar-Tutu, King, 109

Uchoreus (a king of Thebes?), 15

Udjebten, Queen, 195, 196

Uenephēs of Egypt, 24

Ugarit (Ras Shamra, q.v.), in Syria (Map 8 (5)), *316*, 320–1, 339, 501, 548, 558, 584

Ukraine, the, in Russia: figurines from, at Dündartepe in Anatolia, 400

Ulisum, near Tyre in Lebanon, 325, 326, 327, 442

Ullaza (same as Ulisum?), 327, 555

Uluköy, in Anatolia, 398

'Umanu, a mountain of Menua', 559

Umbarakāb, in Lower Nubia, 486

Umma (Tell Jūkhā), in Babylonia (Map 6 (22)), 104, 116, 118 and n. 2, 121, 124, 137, 143, 420, 422, 445, 449; and Lagash, 118–20, 125, 132, 143, 288, 420, 422, 595–6; in revolt, 435–6, 436

Umman Manda (barbarous people), 454

Umm el-Qaāb ('Mother of Pots'), 24

Unas (Wadjtowy), King of Egypt, 20, 65, 156, 169, 181, 186, 188, 189, 190, 193, 202, 345, 360; his pyramid, 187, 188, 190, 193, 350; his causeway, 205

Unasankh (an Egyptian governor), 188, 199

Ungapi, Viceroy of Zakhari, 649 *bis*

Uni (an Egyptian royal official and judge), 192, 193, 194, 198, 203, 226, 236, 237; his expeditions against the Asiatics, 360–1

Unqi (Khattina), kingdom of, 335

Untash-napirisha, King, 663

'Upper Country', the (N. and N.-W. parts of ancient Mesopotamia), 322, 323, 325, 559, 560, 562

Upper (Southern) Egypt (Map 4), 1, 3, 6, 7, *12*, 16, 21, 23, 26, 27, 32, 36, 38–47 *passim*, 51, 52 and n. 2, 54, 163, 187, 192, 194, 195, 198, 202, 473, 477, 480, 493, 495, 506, 512, 513, 515, 519, 520; crown of, 353; nomes of, 473; governors of, 483

'Upper Sea', the (Mediterranean Sea, q.v.), 321, 322, 331, 421, 429, 460, 560, 597, 736

'Uqair, in Babylonia, 77, 78, 84, 89, 247; painted temple at, 330

Ur (city, *see also* Third Dynasty of Ur) (Map 6), 72, 77, 85, 88, 93, 97, 100 and n. 2, 107, 108, 112, 117, 120, 122 n. 3, 124, 132, 133, 136, 138, 224, 238, 243, 245–9 *passim*, 274, 280 and n. 2, 288, 289, 290, 294, 295, 300, 301, 313, 325, 420, 421, 441, 598, 633, 638, 642, 645, 730; royal cemetery and tombs, 100 n. 3, 108, 123, 137–9, 245 and n. 2, 249–54 *passim*, 255 n. 5, 259, 264, 269–80 *passim*, 284, 285, 292, 293, 306, 314, 452; 'Royal Standard of...', 121–3 *passim*, 136, 138, 139, 283, 295, 328; principal sites at, 280–7; external trade of, 285–6; moon-god at, 331; metal-work, 370; 'king' of, 435; revolt and disaster at, 435; and Lagash, 459, 595, 597; neo-Sumerian kings of, 560; kings of, 602; collapse and destruction of, 602, 613, **615–17**, 658–9; defences of, 611; Elamites and, 612; Ishbi-Erra and, 614; transferred from Isin to Larsa, 633–4

Urartu, in Armenia, 305, 739

Ur-Baba of Lagash, 85, 270, 458, 459; his daughters, 459

Urbilum (Arba'ilu, Arbela, Irbil, q.v.), in Mesopotamia, 601, 607, 609, 624, 655

Ur-gar of Lagash, 459

'Uringiriaz of the Upper Sea' (a mysterious mountain), 559

Ur-kisal (*sanga*-priest), 255

Urkish, in Upper Syria, 565 and n. 5, 624, 731

Ur-Lugalbanda (a scribe), 711

Urlumma of Umma, 119 and n. 6, 137

Urmia, Lake, in N.-W. Iran, 401

Ur-Nammu (first king of Third Dynasty of Ur), 104 n. 1, 289, 459, 559–60, **595–600**, 604, 654, 755; his Laws, 598; his tower to moon-god, 599; his canals, 599–600; his stele, 628–9

Ur-Nanshe, King of Lagash, 116–17, 120, 131, 138–9, 141, 255, 288, 422, 459; his dynasty, 245

Ur-Nanshe ('the great singer'), 116

Ur-Ningirsu of Lagash, 460

Ur-Ningizzida of Eshnunna, 636

Ur-Ninmar of Eshnunna, 636

Uronarti, in Nubia (Map 5(27)), 48; fortifications at, 507

Urs(h)u, in Syria (Map 8(14)), *316*, 324 and n. 1, 426, 559 and n. 6, 561

Urua, in Elam, 117, 131, 609

Uruaz (?), 132

Uruk (Warka, q.v.), in Babylonia (Map 6), 41, 72–114 *passim*, 131, 132, 143, 144, 244, 262, 266, 291, 321, 364, 420, 421, 447, 461–3, 595, 596, 597, 599, 636, 637, 642 *bis*, 731; principal sites, 289; defeat of, 433; Amorites at, 637; *periods in Mesopotamia*: Uruk 5–4, 73 and n. 4, 74–8 *passim*, 83, 84, 111, 124 n. 1, 288 n. 1, 330, 344, 364, 365; Uruk 4, **74–81**, 82, 278

Urukagina, *ensi*, later King of Lagash, 105, 120, 121, 125, 128, 131, 140–2, 140 n. 1, 143, 246, 289, 449, 619–20, 634; his reforms, 141–2

Ur-Zababa of Kish, 418–20 *passim*, 606

Usatova, near Odessa on the Black Sea coast, 392

User of Egypt, 'Overseer of Prophets', 474

Userib (Khafre, Chephren, q.v.), 174

Userkaf (Irmaat) of Egypt, 150, 173, 176–83 *passim*, 204; his pyramid, 180, 190; his reign, 180; his temple, 205

Userkare of Egypt, 190, 191

Userkhau (Neferirkare, q.v.) of Egypt, 183

Ush (Gish), Governor of Umma, 119

Ushpia, tribal ancestor of Assyrians, 744–5

Uṣi-Malik (officer in Lagash), 563

'Uta-rapashtum, land of', 428

Utu-khegal of Uruk, 461–3, 595, 597, 599

Valley of Pines, 349

Vān, Lake, in E. Anatolia, 403

Vardarophtsa, in Macedonia (Map 12(1)), 775

vases: alabaster, 67, 78–9, 86, 187, 190; animal-shaped, 85–6

vases, stone, 28, 29; Babylonian, 86, 87, 240; Egyptian, 45, 53, 58, 67, 82, 154, 156, 167, 189, 190

Vasilia, in Cyprus (Maps 14 and 15), *810*, 813, *814*, 816–18 *passim*, 821

Vasiliki, in Crete (Map 13(66)), *773*, 801, 802, 803

Vedic literature of India, 851

Venus (the planet), 738, 767

Veselinovo-Karanovo II, in the Balkans, 367

Vinča, in the Danube valley, 366

vineyards in Egypt, royal, 38, 39

viziers, Egyptian, functions of, 159–60, 166, 168, 170, 187, 506

'Völkerwanderungen', *see* immigrants from the North *and* migrations

Volo (Volos), in Greece (Map 12(13)), 776

Vounous cemetery and tombs at Bellapais in Cyprus, 809, 812, 816–22 *passim*

Vrysis tou Barba, in Cyprus, 817

Wādi el-Allāqi, in Nubia, 500, 503
Wādi el-'Arīsh, south of Gaza (Map 1), 2, 352
Wādi Babā, in Sinai (Map 1), 2, 355
Wādi Dara, on Syrian/Turkish frontier, 304
Wādi el-Gāsūs, on west coast of Red Sea (Map 1), 2, 491, 493, 504 bis
Wādi Halfa, in Nubia (Maps 1 and 5(23)), 2, 24, 48, 50, 187, 507
Wādi Hammāmāt, in Upper Egypt (Map 1), 2, 44, 172, 186, 191, 480, 484; stone quarries, 491, 492, 498, 500, 510; inscriptions at, 491, 493, 494, 509 n. 4, 510
Wādi el-Hūdi, on west coast of Red Sea, 493, 500
Wādi Maghāra (Valley of Caves), in Sinai (Map 1), 2, 151, 167, 183, 185, 186, 191, 353, 355, 356, 510, 539
Wādi Miāh, in Upper Egypt (Map 1), 2, 24
Wādi Naṣb, in Syria, 355, 510
Wādi en-Natrūn, in Lower Egypt (Map 1), 2, 465, 498
Wādi el-Qash, near Thebes in Upper Egypt (Map 1), 2, 22
Wādi esh-Shallāl, in Sinai, 353
Wādi Tummilāt, in Egypt (Map 2), 4, 353, 465, 497, 537
Wadjnes (a king of Egypt?), 31
Wadjtowy (Unas, q.v.) of Egypt, 188
Wahankh Inyotef of Thebes (see also Inyotef II), 467, 475, 477–8
Wahka II, Nomarch of Antaeopolis, 506 n. 1
Wahkare Achthoes III of Egypt, 237, 466–7, 470
Wall(s), the, see White Wall(s)
'Walls of the Ruler', 497, 501
Warad-Sin of Larsa, 640, 641, 642
Warakhshe (Barakhshe, q.v., Markhashe), in Mesopotamia, 432, 600, 633, 649–50, 655–7 passim, 661; federalism in, 648
Wârets (departments of Egyptian government), 506
warfare: in Egypt, 167; in Mesopotamia, 121–4; see also military activities
Warka (Uruk, q.v.), in Babylonia (Map 6), 72, 73, 74, 238, 281, 287, 290 and n.; period, 73
Washptah, Vizier, 184
Wasta, in Egypt, 15
'Wawat' (Lower Nubia, see also Nubia), 487; fortresses of, 503
Wawatis, 508
'Ways of Horus', 356, 358
weapons (and armour): Aegean, 793–9

passim, Anatolian, 377, 378, 388, 391, 392, 393, 690–1; of Asiatics, 552; Babylonian, 82, 122, 123–4, 136; Cretan, 799–804 passim; Cypriot, 808–23 passim; Egyptian, 469; Grecian, 771–93 passim, 804–7 passim; Mesopotamian, 244; Palestinian, 228, 568–83 passim, 592; Sumerian, 343; Syrian, 342, 343, 583–91 passim, 592; at Troy II, 415; of copper (state monopolies), 708–9
Weather-god of Ennigi, 462
weights and measures: Assyrian and Babylonian, 727–8; Elamite, 676
'Weltkammer', in the temple of Neferirkare, 204
Weneg (Egyptian god), 31
Weneg (Wadjnes, Wet-las, Tlas), King of Egypt, 31
Wenet (Raphia?, q.v.), 358
Wepwawet (Egyptian wolf-god), 11, 53, 469
West Anatolian E.B.2 culture, 369
Westcar Papyrus, 164, 168 bis, 172, 179 bis
'Westerners' (amurru or martu) in Mesopotamia, 562 n. 11, 563–6
Western Semites, see Semites
'Western Wall' of Babylonia, 626
West-Semitic deities, 719–20
West-Semitic dialects and names, 627–8, 719, 720
Wet-las (a king of Egypt?), 31
wheel, invention of the, 91
'White Temple', the (Uruk), 81–2, 84
'White Wall(s)', 16; processions around the, 16, 36
wool in Anatolia, 726
Woolley, Sir Leonard, 280, 281, 285, 286, writing, invention and use of (see also cuneiform and hieroglyphic scripts), 43–4, 80–1, 90–1, 93–6, 95 n. 3, 108, 133, 319, 320
Wubartum- (Ubartum-) settlements (Assyrian), in Asia Minor, 723 and n. 4

Yah, Queen, 478
Yalias river, in Cyprus, 816
Yarimjah, near Mosul, 302
Yazilikaya, in Anatolia, 393
Yazir, in Anatolia, 367
Yelten, in S.-W. Anatolia, 393
Yerakh (Semitic moon-god), 321
Yeşilirmak, river in Anatolia, 383
'Yoke-Star' (Jupiter), 615, 616
Yorgan Tepe (Nuzi, q.v.), 297
Yortan, in N.-W. Anatolia (Maps 9 and 10), 372, 373, 375–7, 384, 385, 390, 395, 684; pottery, 379, 380; burial customs,

375–7; stone weapons, 378; cemetery, 386

Yushenshen village, near Thebes, 474

Zababa (a god), 756
Zaban, on Lesser Zab river, 672
Zab rivers and valleys (Maps 6 and 8), 303, 601, 754; Lesser, 444, 601 *bis*, 672, 730, 742; Greater, 724, 729
Zabshali (Zapzali), an Eastern land, 608 *bis*, 611, 657, 658; prince of, 658
Zagros mountains (*see also Su*-people), 454, 647, 657, 658
Zakhara: land of, 436, 455, 649; 'prince' of, 649
Zalpa, in Anatolia, 713
Zariqum, Governor of Ashur and Susa, 602, 655, 656
Zāwiyet el-Aryān, near Cairo (Map 2 (28)), 149, 150, 155–8 *passim*; limestone and granite blocks at, 156–7; open excavation at, 158
Zāwiyet el-Maiyitīn, in Middle Egypt (Map 3 (10)), *8*, 182
Zaziya, King of Hurrian tribe, 749

Zerelia, in Greece (Map 12 (16)), 776
Zerghūl (*see also* Nina) (Map 6), 130, 140
Zidanum (Sidon?), in Phoenicia, 561
zikkurrats (staged or stepped towers): origins of, 84, 235 n. 1; earliest, 84–5, 273; Ur-Nammu's, 280–1; in Chogha-Zanbil, 663; of Susa, 670
Zimrilim, of Khana and Mari, 712; Palace of, 296
Zina, Governor of Khukhnur, 647
Zincirli, in Karasu valley (Anatolia), 397
Zinuba, Viceroy of Elam, 650
Ziringu, Governor of Zabshali, 608, 657
Zit (Elamite god), 667
Ziusudra, King, 109, 244, 277
zoological parks (royal) in the Near East, 350
Zoroaster (*c*. 630–533 B.C.), and Zoro-astrianism, 644, 876
Zuhab, near Sar-i pul, in Mesopotamia, 444
Zuzu, King of Akshak, 117
Zygouries, in the Peloponnese (Map 12 (34)), 694, 785, 787 *bis*; burning at, 785